Sedative, hypnotic, or anxiolytic
   dependence
   abuse
Polysubstance dependence
Psychoactive substance dependence NOS
Psychoactive substance abuse NOS

## SCHIZOPHRENIA

Schizophrenia
   catatonic
   disorganized
   paranoid
   undifferentiated
   residual

## DELUSIONAL (PARANOID) DISORDER

Delusional (paranoid) disorder
   erotomanic
   grandiose
   jealous
   persecutory
   somatic
   unspecified

## PSYCHOTIC DISORDERS NOT ELSEWHERE CLASSIFIED

Brief reactive psychosis
Schizophreniform disorder
   without good prognostic features
   with good prognostic features
Schizoaffective disorder
   bipolar type or depressive type
Induced psychotic disorder
Psychotic disorder NOS (atypical psychosis)

## MOOD DISORDERS

**Bipolar Disorders**
Bipolar disorder
   mixed
   manic
   depressed
Cyclothymia
Bipolar disorder NOS

**Depressive Disorders**
Major depression
   single episode
   recurrent
Dysthymia (or depressive neurosis)
   primary or secondary type
   early or late onset
Depressive disorder NOS

## ANXIETY DISORDERS (or Anxiety and Phobic Neuroses)

Panic disorder
   with agoraphobia
   without agoraphobia
Agoraphobia without history of panic disorder
Social phobia
   generalized type
Simple phobia
Obsessive compulsive disorder (or obsessive compulsive neurosis)
Post-traumatic stress disorder
   delayed onset
Generalized anxiety disorder
Anxiety disorder NOS

## SOMATOFORM DISORDERS

Body dysmorphic disorder
Conversion disorder (or hysterical neurosis, conversion type)
   single episode or recurrent
Hypochondriasis (or hypochondriacal neurosis)

Somatization disorder
Somatoform pain disorder
Undifferentiated somatoform disorder
Somatoform disorder NOS

## DISSOCIATIVE DISORDERS (or Hysterical Neuroses, Dissociative Type)

Multiple personality disorder
Psychogenic fugue
Psychogenic amnesia
Depersonalization disorder (or depersonalization neurosis)
Dissociative disorder NOS

## SEXUAL DISORDERS

**Paraphilias**
Exhibitionism
Fetishism
Frotteurism
Pedophilia
Sexual masochism
Sexual sadism
Transvestic fetishism
Voyeurism
Paraphilia NOS

**Sexual Dysfunctions**
   lifelong or acquired
   generalized or situational
Sexual desire disorders
   hypoactive sexual desire disorder
   sexual aversion disorder
Sexual arousal disorders
   female sexual arousal disorder
   male erectile disorder
Orgasm disorders
   inhibited female orgasm
   inhibited male orgasm
   premature ejaculation
Sexual pain disorders
   dyspareunia
   vaginismus
Sexual dysfunction NOS

**Other Sexual Disorders**
   sexual disorder NOS

## SLEEP DISORDERS

**Dyssomnias**
Insomnia disorder
   related to another mental disorder (nonorganic)
   related to known organic factor
Primary insomnia
Hypersomnia disorder
   related to another mental disorder (nonorganic)
   related to a known organic factor
Primary hypersomnia
Sleep-wake schedule disorder
   advanced or delayed phase
   frequently changing type
Other dyssomnias
   dyssomnia NOS

**Parasomnias**
Dream anxiety disorder (nightmare disorder)
Sleep terror disorder
Sleepwalking disorder
Parasomnia NOS

## FACTITIOUS DISORDER

Factitious disorder
   with physical symptoms
   with psychological symptoms
Factitious disorder NOS

## IMPULSE CONTROL DISORDERS NOT ELSEWHERE CLASSIFIED

Intermittent explosive disorder
Kleptomania
Pathological gambling
Pyromania
Trichotillomania
Impulse control disorder NOS

## ADJUSTMENT DISORDER

Adjustment disorder
   with anxious mood
   with depressed mood
   with disturbance of conduct
   with mixed disturbance of emotions and conduct
   with mixed emotional features
   with physical complaints
   with withdrawal
   with work (or academic) inhibition
Adjustment disorder NOS

## PSYCHOLOGICAL FACTORS AFFECTING PHYSICAL CONDITION

Psychological factors affecting physical condition

## PERSONALITY DISORDERS (AXIS II)

**Cluster A**
Paranoid
Schizoid
Schizotypal

**Cluster B**
Antisocial
Borderline
Histrionic
Narcissistic

**Cluster C**
Avoidant
Dependent
Obsessive compulsive
Passive aggressive
Personality disorder NOS

## CONDITIONS NOT ATTRIBUTABLE TO A MENTAL DISORDER THAT ARE A FOCUS OF ATTENTION OR TREATMENT

Academic problem
Adult antisocial behavior
Borderline intellectual functioning (Axis II)
Childhood or adolescent antisocial behavior
Malingering
Marital problem
Noncompliance with medical treatment
Occupational problem
Parent-child problem
Other interpersonal problem
Other specified family circumstances
Phase of life problem or other life circumstance problem
Uncomplicated bereavement

## ADDITIONAL CLASSIFICATIONS

Unspecified mental disorder (nonpsychotic)
No diagnosis or condition on Axis I
Diagnosis or condition deferred on Axis I
No diagnosis or condition on Axis II
Diagnosis or condition deferred on Axis II

# ABNORMAL PSYCHOLOGY

# ABNORMAL PSYCHOLOGY

Ronald J. Comer

Princeton University

W. H. FREEMAN AND COMPANY
NEW YORK

*To*
*Herman and Claire Comer,*
*my models of strength,*
*with great love and appreciation*

Library of Congress Cataloging-in-Publication Data

Comer, Ronald J.
    Abnormal psychology / Ronald J. Comer.
       p.    cm.
    Includes bibliographical references and index.
    ISBN 0-7167-2057-4
    1. Psychology, Pathological.    I. Title.
  RC454.C634   1992
  616.89 — dc20                       91-37855
                                    CIP

Printed in the United States of America

1  2  3  4  5  6  7  8  9  0    RRD    9  9  8  7  6  5  4  3  2

# CONTENTS IN BRIEF

# CONTENTS

Preface     xv

## CHAPTER 1
## Abnormal Psychology: Past and Present     1

## CHAPTER 2
## Models of Psychological Abnormality     29

**CHAPTER 3**
**Research in Abnormal Psychology    67**

**CHAPTER 4**
**Clinical Assessment, Interpretation, and Diagnosis    91**

**CHAPTER 5**
**Treatments for Abnormal Psychological Functioning    131**

**CHAPTER 6
Anxiety
Disorders   177**

**CHAPTER 7
Treatments
for Anxiety
Disorders   223**

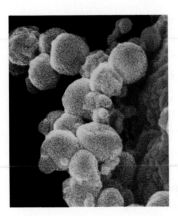

## CHAPTER 11
## Psychological Factors and Physical Disorders    363

## CHAPTER 12
## Eating Disorders    397

## CHAPTER 13
## Substance Use Disorders    427

**CHAPTER 17**
**Personality**
**Disorders    545**

*By Theodore Millon*
*Harvard Medical School*
*and University of Miami*
*and*
*George S. Everly, Jr.*
*The Johns Hopkins Health*
*System and Loyola College*

**CHAPTER 18**
**Dissociative**
**Disorders    573**

**CHAPTER 19**
**Problems of Childhood**
**and Adolescence    593**

## CHAPTER 20
## Problems of Aging    631

*By Dolores Gallagher-Thompson*
*Stanford University and Palo Alto Veterans Affairs Medical*
*Center*
*and*
*Larry Wolford Thompson*
*Stanford University and Palo Alto Veterans Affairs Medical*
*Center*

## CHAPTER 21
## Law, Society, and the Mental Health Profession    661

# PREFACE

Ten years ago, Linda Chaput walked into my office at Princeton University. It was an entrance that was to change my professional life. As an editor at W. H. Freeman and Company, Linda had been reading and assessing the various textbooks in abnormal psychology and had formed a number of ideas for presenting the subject more effectively. I had been analyzing the same texts during my years of teaching, clinical practice, and research, and I too was full of opinions about how abnormal psychology should be presented. During a lively discussion, Linda and I discovered that our specific thoughts on the subject were remarkably similar. In fact, by the time she departed two hours later, we had outlined the principles that should underlie the "ideal" abnormal psychology textbook, and we had, in effect, a deal. All that was left was for me to write the book.

End of Act I. When the curtain rises again, it is ten years later. Linda is president of W. H. Freeman and Company. I am still teaching at Princeton. And, oh yes, that small detail, "The *BOOK*," as my family and I have come to call it, has now been completed. I am older, humbler, and more fatigued than the person who started this undertaking a decade ago. But most of all, I am very pleased and appreciative. After so many years of researching and writing, a textbook has emerged that succeeds, I believe, in all the ways Linda and I had originally hoped and intended. I have tried to make it both comprehensive and balanced, coherent and concise, scientifically accurate and humane.

## FEATURES

At the risk of seeming shamefully immodest, let me describe what I believe is special about this book.

- *This book captures all facets of abnormal psychology.* Abnormal psychology is a science and a profession within which numerous theoretical perspectives hold court, research studies abound, hundreds of disorders have been identified, and methods of assessment and treatment are legion. I have tried to present *all* these aspects of abnormal psychology accurately and equally (rather than attend to only some of them or to some more than others), to highlight the most relevant points of each, and to incorporate them into a logical, unified picture that students can easily understand. In addition, I have tried to capture some of the field's rich history by including a carefully selected mix of both classic and recent material. And although the clinical discussions are organized largely around the current diagnostic system, DSM-III-R, they also refer to classification systems of the past, and even to DSM-IV, the upcoming classification system.

- *The major psychological, biological, and sociocultural models are presented in a balanced and integrated way.* This is not predominantly a psychodynamic or behavioral or biological or any other type of textbook. It is a book about *all* these models, drawing insight from all of them and showing how they coexist in the field, how they differ, and how they interrelate. If students are to understand abnormal psychology, they must learn about each of the major models in the field today—its assertions, contributions, strengths, and shortcomings—and the collective influence of these models on the study and practice of abnormal psychology. In fact, I believe that scientists and practitioners from all the different theoretical and treatment perspectives will appreciate the attention and respect given to their positions.

- *Complete discussions of treatment are presented throughout the book.* Rather than taking the traditional approach of placing treatment chapters at the end of the book, preceded by a series of necessarily incomplete "sneak previews" along the way, I have presented a general chapter on treatment early in the book (Chapter 5) as well as separate chapters on "Treatments for Anxiety Disorders" (Chapter 7), "Treatments for Mood Disorders" (Chapter 9), and "Treatments for Schizophrenia" (Chapter 16). In addition, each of the other psychopathology chapters contains a full discussion of treatment approaches to that problem. This presentation reflects the specificity of treatment that is now characteristic of the field and complements the way in which many professors prefer to discuss treatment in class.

- *Numerous case studies bring clinical, theoretical, and treatment considerations to life.* In writing the text I have worked hard to find case studies and other case materials that would provide vivid descriptions of the different pathologies, the many possible contributing causes, and the various approaches to treatment.

- *The book is designed to be adaptable to different courses and teaching preferences.* Each chapter is essentially self-contained, with cross-referencing to other parts of the book whenever that might be useful. Thus, while the first four chapters cover introductory topics and build on one another, Chapters 5 through 21 may be read in whatever order makes sense to a professor. For example, professors who prefer to cover treatments collectively at the end of the course can postpone the four treatment chapters without creating any problems for their students. Chapters can also be skipped or made optional without affecting a student's grasp of basic concepts.

•   *The text raises broad contextual issues.* For example, it examines questions about cross-cultural and gender differences in diagnosis and treatment; political and economic influences on the clinical field; the impact of the individual needs of therapists and scientists; and the interaction of the field with a public fascinated by psychological notions and practices.

•   *The text devotes full chapters to subjects that are receiving increasing research and clinical attention and that are of special interest to college-age readers, without stinting topics that are traditionally covered.* Complete chapters are devoted to such problems as *eating disorders, suicide,* and *dissociative disorders*—topics heretofore given limited coverage in abnormal psychology textbooks.

•   *The book is written with a single voice, in clear and straightforward language.* Given the variety and complexity of topics that must be covered in an abnormal psychology textbook, it is all the more important to present them in a coherent and integrated way. This, I believe, is the primary advantage of having a single author. On the other hand, just as students in a classroom may value and profit from guest lecturers, whose personal involvement and expertise add greatly to the course, so I hope will my student readers benefit from the three chapters I chose to have written by guest authors, all major figures in their respective areas of expertise:

Chapter 14, "Sexual Disorders"

Joseph LoPiccolo
University of Missouri-Columbia

Chapter 17, "Personality Disorders"

Theodore Millon
Harvard Medical School
and University of Miami

George S. Everly, Jr.
The Johns Hopkins Health System
and Loyola College

Chapter 20, "Problems of Aging"

Dolores Gallagher-Thompson
Stanford University
and Palo Alto Veterans Affairs Medical Center

Larry Wolford Thompson
Stanford University
and Palo Alto Veterans Affairs Medical Center

Like the other writings of these contributors, their chapters in this text are absolutely superb. Moreover, they worked closely with me in developing the chapters to make sure they are well integrated with the rest of the book, fulfill its goals, and answer the needs of the introductory reader.

•   *The book is designed to affect and motivate students.* Abnormal psychology is, after all, a moving and exciting subject that should strike all sorts of chords in readers. I have tried to write with humanity, to communicate my excitement, enthusiasm, and sense of discovery about the subject, and to incorporate my years of experience in teaching, practice, and research. Moreover, in choosing the case excerpts, special boxed discussions, authentic photographs, and telling illustrations and tables my goal has been to move as well as to enlighten, for it is always important to bear in mind that the subject is people— often people in great pain.

•   *The book provides "tools" for thinking critically about abnormal psychology.* I have tried to help readers grasp the *logic* underlying research and assessment; the *connections* between a model's principles and the studies, assessment tools, and treatment approaches used by its proponents; and the *weaknesses and strengths* of various studies and interventions. Moreover, each chapter ends with a "State of the Field" section that provides a sense of perspective about where the clinical field is today, where it came from, and where it seems to be going. Ideally, readers will acquire not only an extensive body of information from this text but also an ability to assess and question it, process it effectively, and remember it accurately.

## SUPPLEMENTS

The textbook itself is enhanced by a series of highly effective supplemental materials.

•   An *Instructor's Manual,* by Janet A. Simons of Central Iowa Psychological Services and Ronald J. Comer, provides detailed outlines of each chapter, lists of principal learning objectives, and exciting and novel ideas for varying lectures and launching class discussions.

•   A *Student Study Guide,* by Norris Vestre of Arizona State University, reexamines the content of each chapter by means of chapter summaries, lists of key names and terms, special elucidations of important ideas, numerous sample test questions (both multiple-choice and short-answer, with all answers provided), and suggestions for additional reading.

•   A comprehensive set of **Test Questions,** written by me and several of my colleagues, offers approximately 2,000 multiple-choice, true-false, and short-answer test questions, all graded as to difficulty, identified as "applied" or "factual," and keyed to specific pages in the textbook.

- A **Computerized Test Bank,** identical to the printed *Test Questions,* is available in both IBM and Macintosh formats.

- **Video recordings** of the complete thirteen-part telecourse, *The World of Abnormal Psychology,* produced by the Annenberg/CPB Collection, examines the complex factors underlying abnormal psychology, demonstrates the various approaches to treatment, and elucidates current directions in research.

## ACKNOWLEDGMENTS

I am enormously grateful to the many people who have contributed to the writing and production of this textbook. A simple thank you fails to do justice to the importance of their work and to the quality of their performance. Their efforts have meant much more to me than I can possibly express.

I begin with the guest writers, who contributed three important chapters to the book. Joseph LoPiccolo, Theodore Millon, George Everly, Dolores Gallagher-Thompson, and Larry Thompson have brought expertise and consummate skill to their presentations, and the results are simply wonderful.

In addition, Dr. Steven Winshel wrote many of the boxed discussions that appear throughout the book. Steve invested the boxes with great insight, vitality, and humor and made sure that they complemented the text discussions. He also prepared the chapter summaries and the book's glossary. I greatly appreciate Steve's enthusiasm, his extraordinary work ethic, and the warm friendship that he extended throughout the undertaking.

There are also a number of very talented colleagues and individuals who wrote early drafts of various sections of the book. They include Bob Croyle, Lisa Fisher, Allison Fishman Gartner, Dan Gilbert, Nimali Jayasinghe, Aimee McCullough, Rona Milch, Tracy Munn, Betsy Preston, Fred Rhodewalt, Lauren Siegler, Susan Stein, and Gita Wilder. I also greatly appreciate the conscientiousness and hard work of the many research assistants who helped with the book, including Linda Chamberlain, Meath Bowen, Jeff Gossett, Robin Bennett, Terry Caton, Rob Falk, Millet Israeli, Karen McQuillen, Mary Parker, Lisa Tanners, Sue Varga, and Alicia Williams.

Throughout the past ten years, I have also received valuable feedback and ideas from a number of outstanding academicians and clinicians, who have reviewed portions of the manuscript and who have commented on the state of its clarity, accuracy, and completeness. The final product is in large part due to their collective knowledge and insight and to their willingness to share these with me. They are:

Kent G. Bailey
Virginia Commonwealth University

Allan Berman
University of Rhode Island

Douglas Bernstein
University of Illinois

Kirk R. Blankstein
University of Toronto in Mississauga

Victor B. Cline
University of Utah

Morris N. Eagle
York University

Alan Fridlund
University of California, Santa Barbara

Stan Friedman
Southwest Texas State University

Bernard Kleinman
University of Missouri, Kansas City

Alan G. Krasnoff
University of Missouri, St. Louis

Robert D. Langston
University of Texas, Austin

Harvey R. Lerner
Kaiser-Permanente Medical Group

Michael P. Levine
Kenyon College

Robert J. McCaffrey
State University of New York, Albany

Jeffery Scott Mio
Washington State University

Paul A. Payne
University of Cincinnati

David V. Perkins
Ball State University

Norman Poppel
Middlesex County College

Max W. Rardin
University of Wyoming, Laramie

Leslie A. Rescorla
Bryn Mawr College

Vic Ryan
University of Colorado, Boulder

A. A. Sappington
University of Alabama, Birmingham

Roberta S. Sherman
Bloomington Center for Counseling and
Human Development

David E. Silber
The George Washington University

Janet A. Simons
Central Iowa Psychological Services

Jay R. Skidmore
Utah State University

Thomas A. Tutko
San Jose State University

Norris D. Vestre
Arizona State University

Joseph L. White
University of California, Irvine

Amy C. Willis
Washington D.C. Veterans Administration
Medical Center

Often overlooked by others, though certainly not by an author, are the individuals who help prepare the manuscript, doing everything from typing to photocopying to mailing to hand-holding. I was particularly blessed in this regard and fervently thank Arlene Kerch and Arlene Kronewitter for their outstanding work, cheerful dispositions, tireless efforts, understanding, and repeated willingness to put my endeavor above their personal schedules. Similarly, I am grateful to Elaine Bacsik, Ashley Blackwell, Daphne Flowers, Linda Holmak, Marion Kowalewski, Theresa Mizenko, Bernie Muccilli, and Barbara Pallotti for their many efforts over the years.

And, then, of course, there are the people at W. H. Freeman and Company. I am indebted to Linda Chaput, the president of the company, for standing by the book for so long and making sure that it became what we first envisioned. She placed the confidence and resources of the company behind me and always put a standard of excellence before all other considerations. As special as Linda has been to me, the list of talented and caring people at W. H. Freeman only begins with her.

I have worked with three editors over the years, each of whom performed remarkably, showed superb editorial skills, and became a close and valued friend. Jonathan Cobb worked with me during the early years of the book and taught me how to transform ideas, ambitions, and teaching insights into an authoritative, clear, and engaging textbook. Nancy White, the editor during the middle years, provided special dimensions of support and gentleness, which, along with her many editorial contributions, brought me and the book into position for the stretch run. Moira Lerner has been the editor during the past several years and has helped bring the book to

fruition. Virtually every sentence in the book has her mark. She is truly a magician in her work, a person of whom I am in awe. Moreover, she is as delightful a person as I have ever known. I will not miss the phone bills of our coast to coast relationship, but I will certainly miss our daily discussions. I wish every author a Moira Lerner for an editor.

Three other persons at Freeman have also made very special contributions that I would like to mention. During the past year, Philip McCaffrey, the project editor, has worked tirelessly and unselfishly to shepherd this book through the process of production. I greatly admire and appreciate his total dedication, his gentle and caring manner, and his extraordinary contribution to both the content and the form of the book. Travis Amos, the book's photo researcher, has worked with great taste, diligence, and enthusiasm to bring the subject matter of abnormal psychology to life. His endless searches for the perfect photograph or painting and his uncompromising commitment to excellence have greatly enriched this book. I also wish to thank Megan Higgins, the art director. Her impressive talent and unceasing efforts to create a compelling and enriching design have led to as handsome an appearance as I can imagine. Even a cursory glance through the pages of the book attests to this accomplishment.

In addition, I would like to thank Mary Shuford, managing editor; Barbara Salazar, copy editor; Bernice Soltysik, indexer; Mary Louise Byrd, proofreader; Nancy Giraldo Walker, rights and permissions manager; Susan Stetzer, production coordinator; Mara Kasler, illustration coordinator; Maura Fadden Rosenthal, page makeup designer; and Jodi Creditor, all-around great worker. Some former members of the company also left their mark on this book: Neil Patterson, past president; Linda Davis, past vice president; and Elisa Adams, past director of development. Obviously, I've enjoyed and profited from my association with this gifted group of professionals.

Finally, I must take some space to acknowledge those who have provided me with an educational, professional, and personal climate in which I could accomplish this task. I thank my graduate teachers at Clark University—particularly, Bob Baker, Roger Bibace, Len Cirillo, Jim Laird, and Mort Weiner—and my undergraduate teachers at the University of Pennsylvania—particularly Jane Piliavin—all of whose wisdom, theoretical skills, and research know-how fill the pages of this book. I also greatly appreciate my stimulating and engaging colleagues at Princeton University, particularly Joel Cooper, John Darley, and Ron Kinchla, who have been so considerate and supportive since I first started teaching at Princeton almost twenty years ago. Similarly, I thank Dr. Carl Meier of Somerset Medical Center and Drs. Frank Snope and Joe Lieberman of the Robert Wood Johnson Medical School, who have taught me so much about family dynamics and the relationship between the mind and the body.

In closing, I cannot imagine completing a project of this magnitude in the absence of a loving and supportive family, and I am truly grateful to mine. I have already thanked my father and mother in the book's dedication. Their love has been an enduring and motivating presence in my life. I also greatly appreciate my wonderful and loving parents-in-law, Hadaso and David Slotkin. Similarly, I thank my always-terrific sons, Jon and Greg, who fill my life with pride and laughter and joy and love. Most of all I thank and express my love to my magnificent wife Marlene, who has approached this undertaking of mine in the same manner as other messes I have gotten into — with love, concern, and support, grace and humor, and an occasional "I told you so." She is, quite simply, the best.

*Ronald J. Comer*
*Princeton University*
*November 1991*

The Blue Devils

# TOPIC OVERVIEW

# CHAPTER 1

# ABNORMAL PSYCHOLOGY: PAST AND PRESENT

**M**ental dysfunctioning crosses all boundaries—cultural, economic, emotional, and intellectual. It affects the famous and the obscure, the rich and the poor, the upright and the perverse. Politicians, actors, writers, and other public icons of the present and the past have struggled with mental dysfunctioning (see Box 1-1). It can bring great suffering, but it can also be the source of inspiration and energy.

Because they are so ubiquitous and so personal, mental problems capture the interest of us all. Hundreds of novels, plays, films, and television programs have explored what many people see as the dark side of human nature, and self-help books flood the market to offer advice on how to overcome such problems as compulsive overeating, sexual dysfunctioning, and so-called addictive relationships. Psychologists and psychiatrists are popular guests on both television and radio, and some even have their own shows and encourage troubled people to call or to appear for instant advice.

The field devoted to the scientific study of the abnormal behavior we find so fascinating is usually called *abnormal psychology.* As in the other sciences, workers in this field, called clinical scientists, gather information systematically so that they may describe, predict, explain, and exert some control over the phenomena they study. The knowledge that they acquire is then used by a wide variety of mental health, or clinical, practitioners to detect, assess, and treat abnormal patterns of functioning.

Although their general goals are similar to those of other scientific disciplines, clinical investigators and practitioners confront problems that make their work especially difficult. One of the most troubling problems is that psychological abnormality is extremely hard to define.

## DEFINING PSYCHOLOGICAL ABNORMALITY

*Miriam cries herself to sleep every night. She is certain* that the future holds nothing but misery. Indeed, this is the only thing she does feel certain about. "I'm going to die and my daughters are going to die. We're doomed. The world is ugly. I detest every moment of this life." She has great trouble sleeping. She is afraid to close her eyes, afraid that she will never wake up, and what will happen to her daughters then? When she does drift off to sleep, her dreams are nightmares filled with blood, dismembered bodies, thunder, decay, death, destruction.

One morning Miriam has trouble getting out of bed. The thought of facing another day overwhelms her. Again she wishes she were dead, and she wishes her daughters were dead. "We'd all be better off." She feels paralyzed by her depression and anxiety, too tired to move and too afraid to leave her house. She decides once again to stay home and to keep her daughters with her. She makes sure that all shades are drawn and that every conceivable entrance to the house is secured. She is afraid of the world and afraid of life. Every day is the same, filled with depression, fear, immobility, and withdrawal. Every day is a nightmare.

═══════════════ BOX 1-1 ═══════════════

# Famous Sufferers of Mental Disorders

**M**any well-known figures in history have suffered from mental disorders. Clinicians often speculate about the nature of their problems on the basis of written accounts of these people's behavior. In more recent years a number of public figures have chosen to reveal their struggles with mental dysfunctioning. Here are some of the well-known people who have suffered from mental disorders.

### DISORDERS OF FEAR OR ANXIETY

John Keats
*poet*

Howard Hughes
*inventor, entrepreneur*

Jim Piersall
*baseball player*

Jim Backus
*actor*

Emily Dickinson
*poet*

Carolyn Wyeth
*artist*

Victoria
*Queen of England*

Mary Baker Eddy
*founder of Christian Science*

### DISORDERS OF DEPRESSION

Arthur Schopenhauer
*philosopher*

Frédéric Chopin
*composer*

John Stuart Mill
*philosopher, economist*

Graham Greene
*author*

Thomas Wolfe
*author*

F. Scott Fitzgerald
*author*

Buzz Aldrin
*astronaut*

Dylan Thomas
*poet*

Sylvia Plath
*poet*

Honoré de Balzac
*author*

Louisa May Alcott
*author*

Samuel Johnson
*lexicographer, author*

Clara Barton
*philanthropist, founder of Red Cross*

Marilyn Monroe
*actress*

Mike Wallace
*television journalist*

William Styron
*novelist*

Art Buchwald
*political satirist*

### DISORDERS OF DEPRESSION ALTERNATING WITH MANIA

Saul
*King of Israel (11th century B.C.)*

*During the past year Brad has been hearing mysterious* voices that tell him to quit his job, leave his family, and prepare for the coming invasion. These voices have brought tremendous confusion and emotional turmoil to Brad's life. He believes that they come from beings in distant parts of the universe who are somehow wired to him. Although it gives him a sense of purpose and specialness to be the chosen target of their communications, they also make him tense and anxious. He dreads the coming invasion. When he refuses an order, the voices insult and threaten him and turn his days into a waking nightmare.

Brad has put himself on a sparse diet to avoid the possibility that his enemies may be contaminating his food. He has found a quiet apartment far from his old haunts where he has laid in a good stock of arms and ammunition. His family members and friends have tried to reach out to Brad, to understand his problems, and to dissuade him from his disturbing activities. Every day, however, he retreats further into his world of mysterious voices and imagined dangers.

Miriam and Brad are the kinds of people we think of when abnormal behavior is mentioned. Most of us would probably label their emotions, thoughts, and behavior *psychologically abnormal,* or, alternatively, as *psychopathological, maladjusted, emotionally disturbed,* or *mentally ill.*

But *are* Miriam and Brad psychologically abnormal, and if so, why? What is it about their thoughts, emotions, and behavior that might lead us to this conclusion? Many definitions of abnormal mental functioning have been proposed over the years, but none of them has won universal acceptance. Still, most of the definitions do have common features: deviance, distress, dysfunction, danger. Psychologically abnormal patterns of functioning, then, are those that, in a given context, are *deviant —* that is, different, extreme, unusual, perhaps even bizarre; *distressful,* or unpleasant and upsetting to the individual; *dysfunctional,* or disruptive to the person's ability to conduct daily activities in a constructive

---

Thomas Eagleton
*U.S. senator*

Abraham Lincoln
*U.S. president*

Virginia Woolf
*author*

Theodore Roosevelt
*U.S. president*

Robert Lowell
*poet*

Winston Churchill
*British prime minister*

Freddie Prinze
*comedian*

Ernest Hemingway
*author*

Patty Duke
*actress*

George Frederick Handel
*composer*

Robert Schumann
*composer*

James Joyce
*author*

### DISORDERS INVOLVING A LOSS OF REALITY

Jean-Jacques Rousseau
*philosopher*

Vincent Van Gogh
*artist*

Vaslav Nijinsky
*dancer*

Sirhan Sirhan
*assassin*

John Hinckley
*would-be assassin*

David Berkowitz
*serial killer*

George III
*King of England*

Mark Vonnegut
*author*

### DISORDERS OF DEPENDENCE ON ALCOHOL AND OTHER SUBSTANCES

Cambyses
*King of Persia (6th century B.C.)*

Samuel Taylor Coleridge
*poet*

Francois Rabelais
*author*

Elvis Presley
*singer*

Samuel Butler
*poet*

Dick Van Dyke
*actor*

Robert Burns
*poet*

John Belushi
*comedian*

Lord Byron
*poet*

John Barrymore
*actor*

Judy Garland
*singer*

Edgar Allan Poe
*author, poet*

Truman Capote
*author*

Thomas De Quincey
*author*

Jim Morrison
*musician*

Betty Ford
*U.S. first lady*

Jason Robards
*actor*

### OTHER DISORDERS

Karen Carpenter
*singer: Eating disorder*

Woody Guthrie
*singer and songwriter: Huntington's chorea*

Renée Richards
*tennis player: Transsexualism*

Al Capone
*gangster: General paresis, syphilis*

Rita Hayworth
*actress: Alzheimer's disease*

Audiences are fascinated by movie characters who behave abnormally, such as the unstable Alex Forrest in *Fatal Attraction*. She relentlessly pursues a married man with whom she has had a brief relationship, eventually becoming deeply depressed, suicidal, and dangerous.

manner; and possibly ***dangerous.*** This definition provides a useful starting point from which to explore the phenomena of psychological abnormality, although, as we shall see, it has significant limitations.

## Deviance

Abnormal mental functioning is functioning that is deviant, but deviant from what? Before any functioning can be said to be deviant, there must be a standard of appropriate and normal functioning against which behavior can be measured. Miriam's behavior, thoughts, and emotions are different from those that are considered normal in our place and time. We do not expect normal people to cry themselves to sleep every night, to wish themselves dead, or to endure paralyzing depression and anxiety. Similarly, Brad's obedience to voices that no one else can hear contradicts our expectation that normal people perceive only the material world accessible to everyone's five senses.

In short, abnormal behavior, thoughts, and emotions are those that violate a society's ideas about proper functioning. Each society establishes ***norms*** — explicit and implicit rules for appropriate conduct. Behavior that violates legal norms is called criminal. Behavior, thoughts, and emotions that violate norms of psychological func-

tioning are called abnormal. Typically, the norms of psychological functioning focus on conduct that is common in a society, such as our society's expectations that people will remember important events in their lives. Sometimes, however, a society may value certain psychological deviations, such as superior intelligence and extreme selflessness, and may include these forms of functioning within its norms.

This focus on social values as a yardstick for measuring deviance suggests that judgments of abnormality vary from society to society. A society's norms emerge from its particular *culture* — its history, values, institutions, habits, skills, technology, and arts. Thus a society whose culture places great value on competition and assertiveness may accept aggressive behavior, whereas one that highly values courtesy, cooperation, and gentleness may consider aggressive behavior unacceptable and even abnormal. A society's values may also change over time, causing its views of what is psychologically abnormal to change as well. In Western society, for example, a woman's participation in the business or professional world was considered inappropriate and strange a hundred years ago, but today the same behavior is valued.

Judgments of abnormality depend on specific circumstances as well as on psychological norms. The description of Miriam, for example, might lead us to conclude that she is functioning abnormally. Certainly her unhappiness is more intense and pervasive than that of most of the people we encounter every day. Before you conclude that this woman is abnormal, however, consider that Miriam lives in Lebanon, a country pulled apart by years of combat. The happiness she once knew with her family

Along the Niger River, men of the Wodaabe tribe don elaborate makeup and costumes to attract women. In Western society, the same behavior would violate behavioral norms and probably be judged abnormal.

vanished when her husband and son were killed. Miriam used to tell herself that the fighting had to end soon, but as year follows year with only temporary respites, she has stopped expecting anything except more of the same.

In this light, Miriam's reactions do not seem inappropriate. If anything is abnormal here, it is her situation. Sometimes overwhelming or unusual situations elicit reactions that appear abnormal out of context but are understandable in the surroundings in which they occur. Many things in our world elicit intense reactions—large-scale catastrophes and disasters, rape, child abuse, war, terminal illness, chronic pain. Is there an "appropriate" way to react to such things? Should we ever call reactions to them abnormal?

As we shall see in Chapter 4, today's leading diagnostic system holds that some people's reactions to traumatic events are indeed excessive, and assigns such cases to the category of post-traumatic stress disorder. Many theorists deny the merits of this category, however, arguing that there can be no such thing as an excessive reaction to brutality or catastrophe.

## Distress

Even functioning that is considered unusual and inappropriate in a given context does not necessarily qualify as abnormal. According to many clinical theorists, one's behavior, ideas, or emotions usually have to cause one distress before they can be labeled abnormal. Consider the Ice Breakers, a group of people in Michigan who go swimming in lakes throughout the state every weekend from November through February. The colder the weather, the better they like it. One man, a member of the group for seventeen years, says he loves the challenge. Man against the elements. Mind versus body. A 37-year-old lawyer believes that the weekend shock is good for her health. "It cleanses me," she says. "It perks me up and gives me strength for the week ahead." Another avid Ice Breaker likes the special feelings the group brings to him. "When we get together, we know we've shared something special, something no one else understands. I can't even tell most of the people I know that I'm an Ice Breaker. They wouldn't want anything to do with me. A few people think I'm a space cadet."

Certainly these people are different from most of us, but they are enjoying themselves. Far from experiencing distress, they feel invigorated and challenged. The absence of internal distress must cause us to hesitate before we conclude that these people are functioning abnormally.

Should we conclude, then, that feelings of distress must *always* be present before a person's functioning can

be considered abnormal? Not necessarily. Some people who function abnormally may maintain a relatively positive frame of mind. Consider once again Brad, the young man who hears mysterious voices. Brad does experience severe distress over the coming invasion and the changes he feels forced to make in the way he lives. But what if he felt no such anxiety? What if he greatly enjoyed listening to the voices, felt honored to be chosen, and looked forward to the formidable task of saving the world? Shouldn't we still consider his functioning abnormal? As we shall discover in Chapter 8, people who are described as manic often feel just wonderful, yet still are diagnosed as psychologically disturbed. Indeed, in many cases it is their euphoria and disproportionate sense of well-being that help make them candidates for this diagnosis.

## Dysfunction

Abnormal behavior tends to interfere with daily functioning. It so upsets, distracts, or confuses its victims that they cannot care for themselves properly, participate in ordinary social relationships, or work effectively. Brad, for example, has quit his job, left his family, and prepared to withdraw from the productive and meaningful life he once led to an empty and isolated existence in a distant apartment.

In Val d'Isère, France, these students bury themselves in snow up to their necks. Far from experiencing distress, they are engaging in a Japanese practice designed to open their hearts and enlarge their spirits, so diagnosticians are unlikely to judge them to be abnormal.

Here again one's culture plays a role in the definition of abnormality. Our society holds that it is important to carry out daily activities in an effective, self-enhancing manner. Thus Brad's behavior is likely to be regarded as abnormal and undesirable, whereas that of the Ice Breakers, who continue to perform well at their jobs and maintain appropriate family and social relationships, would probably be considered unusual but not a sign of psychological abnormality.

Of course, dysfunction alone does not necessarily indicate psychological abnormality. Some people in our society (Gandhi, Dick Gregory, or Cesar Chavez, for example) fast or in other ways deprive themselves of things their bodies need in order to protest social injustice. Far from being called abnormal, they are viewed by many as caring, sacrificing, even heroic.

## Danger

Perhaps the ultimate in psychological dysfunctioning is behavior that becomes dangerous to oneself or others. A pattern of functioning that is marked by carelessness, poor judgment, hostility, or misinterpretation can jeopardize one's own well-being and that of many other people. Brad, for example, seems to be endangering himself by his diet and others by his stockpile of arms and ammunition.

Although danger to oneself or others is usually cited as a criterion of abnormal psychological functioning, research suggests that it is more often the exception than the rule. Despite popular misconceptions, most people struggling with anxiety, depression, and even bizarre behavioral patterns pose no immediate danger to themselves or to anyone else.

## Difficulties in Defining Psychological Abnormality

Efforts to define psychological abnormality typically raise as many questions as they answer. The major difficulty is that the very concept of abnormality is relative, dependent on the norms and values of the society in question. Ultimately a society *selects* the general criteria for defining abnormality and then *interprets* them in order to judge the normality or abnormality of each particular case.

One clinical theorist, Thomas Szasz (1987, 1961), places such emphasis on society's role that he finds the whole concept of mental illness to be invalid (see Box 1-2). According to Szasz, the deviations that society calls abnormal are simply "problems in living," not signs of something inherently wrong within the person. Socie-

ties, he is convinced, invent the concept of mental illness to justify their efforts to control or change people whose unusual patterns of functioning threaten the social order. In extreme cases the category even serves to justify the removal of those individuals from society. Although most theorists do not share Szasz's extreme view, they agree that the concept of abnormal psychological functioning is elusive, embedded as it is in the values and institutions of a society.

Even if we assume that psychological abnormality is a valid concept and that such abnormalities are unhealthy, a society may have difficulty agreeing on a definition and applying it consistently. If a certain behavior — consumption of alcohol among college students, say — is common in a society, the society may fail to recognize that the behavior is often a symptom of deviance, a source of distress, highly dysfunctional, and dangerous. Thousands of college students throughout the United States are so dependent on alcohol that it interferes greatly with their personal and academic functioning, causes them significant discomfort, places their health in jeopardy, and often endangers them and the people around them. Yet their problem often goes unnoticed, certainly undiagnosed, by college administrators, other students, and health professionals. Alcohol consumption is so much a part of the college subculture that it is easy to overlook drinking behavior that has become abnormal.

Conversely, a society may have trouble distinguishing an abnormality that requires intervention from an eccentric individuality that others have no right to interfere with. From time to time, we see or hear about people who behave in ways we consider strange — a woman who keeps a dozen cats in her apartment or a man who lives alone and rarely talks to anyone. The behavior of these people is deviant and may well be distressful and dysfunctional, yet such propensities are thought of by most professionals as eccentric rather than abnormal. When does an unusual pattern of functioning cross the line from eccentricity to psychological abnormality? When is it deviant, distressful, and dysfunctional enough to be considered abnormal? Such questions may be impossible to answer.

Problematic as they are, it is important to keep these questions in mind. While we may agree that abnormal patterns of functioning are those that are deviant, distressful, dysfunctional, and sometimes dangerous in a given context, we should always be aware of the ambiguity and subjectivity of this definition. We should also be aware that few of the current categories of abnormality are as clear-cut as they may seem to be. Most of them continue to be debated within the clinical community (APA, 1987).

## BOX 1-2

# Is Mental Illness a Myth?

Some clinicians and philosophers, most notably Thomas Szasz, question whether the label "mentally ill" is appropriate under any circumstances. They believe that behavior deemed abnormal is actually a rational, or at least understandable, response to a specific set of circumstances, and that one need only be privy to the circumstances to see that the behavior makes sense. Mental illness is therefore a label that serves no good purpose.

Proponents of this view argue that labeling is a convenient way for society to deal with a perceived threat to our emotional and physical well-being, as well as our sense of self. When we identify the people who disturb us as deviant and decide that *they* are the ones who are disturbed, we can relegate them to mental hospitals and clinics and treat them differently from people like us. The pervasive prejudice against the mentally ill helps protect us from our fears. This discrimination is difficult to control because we have no clear, accepted criteria for identifying mental illness. According to Szasz, "looking for evidence of illness is like searching for evidence of heresy: Once the investigator gets into the proper frame of mind, anything may seem to him to be a symptom of mental illness" (Szasz, 1961).

A relevant and poignant case is that of Kate Millet. The author of *Sexual Politics* and other highly regarded feminist books, Kate Millet has spent her life challenging male cultural icons

Thomas Szasz

and defining the issues of the women's movement. She has also waged an ongoing battle with the clinical community. She has been hospitalized several times and labeled manic-depressive, and feels that she has been stigmatized by her experiences with the mental health profession. Millet admits to having had unusual experiences in her life but rejects the label that has been attached to her. She was hospitalized at the behest of her family, who believed that her activist lifestyle and behavior they regarded as erratic indicated that she had lost touch with reality. In *The Loony-Bin Trip* Millet describes her nightmarish experiences in mental hospitals in the United States and Ireland. Madness, she tells us, is manufactured when clinical treatment in-

tervenes. It is a form of social control—a way of maintaining control over an individual's mind. Like Szasz, she believes mental illness is a myth that is detrimental to the well-being of those who are required to wear the label. She has suffered for years under this burden, and the goal of her book is to break the cycle of using clinical treatment to rid society of people who disturb its comfort and then pointing to the effects of that treatment as proof that the treatment is needed. Phyllis Chesler, a feminist psychologist and author, disagrees with this view in its extreme form, but says that Millet may be a "true literary eccentric who fights for the right of the individual against the might of the state."

Perhaps the wisest approach is to acknowledge that clinical labeling can be abused and misused, both intentionally and through ignorance, but that it plays an important part in the evolution of our understanding of abnormal behavior. Clinical diagnosis has allowed practitioners and researchers to help many troubled people at the same time that it has furthered our understanding of the roots of mental disorders. Until such advances in knowledge have succeeded in ridding our society of the biases and stigmas attached to mental dysfunctioning, however, it is important that people such as Thomas Szasz and Kate Millet continue to raise their questions, reminding us of the clinical field's potential to harm as well as to help the people it touches.

## PAST VIEWS AND TREATMENTS

The current facts and figures on psychological abnormality are almost numbing. It is estimated that more

than 25 percent of the people in the United States display serious mental disturbances and are in need of clinical treatment. It is estimated that approximately seven of every hundred people have a significant anxiety disorder, five suffer from profound depression, five display

For twenty years Litto Damonte has nailed countless hubcaps and other objects to every available surface at his ranch in Northern California. Initially considered strange, his behavior has come to be appreciated, and many people now recognize him as an artist.

a personality disorder (inflexible and maladaptive personality traits that cause significant impairment or distress), one is schizophrenic (loses touch with reality for an extended period of time), one experiences the brain deterioration of Alzheimer's disease, and seven abuse alcohol or other drugs. Add to these figures at least 200,000 suicide attempts, 300,000 rapes, and 300,000 cases of child abuse each year, and it becomes apparent that abnormal psychological functioning is a major, indeed pervasive, problem in our society (Regier et al., 1988; APA, 1987; Myers et al., 1984; Dohrenwend & Dohrenwend, 1982; Dohrenwend et al., 1980). Beyond these disturbances, most people have difficulty coping at various points in their lives and experience high levels of tension, demoralization, or other forms of psychological discomfort. At such times, they too experience at least some of the distress caused by broad psychological disorders.

Given such numbers, it is tempting to conclude that something about today's world fosters emotional maladjustment. Some observers have suggested that the rapid changes and technical advancements of our world create enormous pressure and emotional turmoil — that recent improvements in the fields of science, communication, and business bring with them such problems as the threat of nuclear warfare, economic instability, and job insecurity. Some have also argued that our world lacks key elements that used to help people bear life's pressures. The family, for instance, is no longer the reliable haven it was once assumed to be: divorce has become more common (see Figure 1-1) and adult children now move farther away from their families. A continuing decline in religious, community, and other support systems forces people to face a changing, sometimes frightening, world on their own.

Although such recent developments probably do contribute to psychological dysfunctioning, they are hardly its primary cause. Every society, past and present, has contended with psychological abnormality. Some disorders, such as schizophrenia, occur at the same rate in all societies. Others, such as anxiety disorders and depression, fluctuate from society to society, partly as a reflection of societal differences, yet remain common in all societies. Relatively few psychological disorders are unique to specific societies, caused and defined by the particular pressures those societies engender. In short, abnormal psychological functioning, rampant though it may be, is hardly unique to today's world.

Perhaps the proper place to begin our examination of abnormal behavior and treatment is in the past. If we look back, we may better understand such issues as the nature of psychological abnormality, which of its features remain constant in human societies and which vary from place to place and from time to time, how each society has struggled to understand and treat it, and how present ideas and treatments can often be traced to the past (see Box 1-3). A look backward may also prepare us to appreciate the significance of recent developments and breakthroughs in the field, as well as the journey that lies ahead.

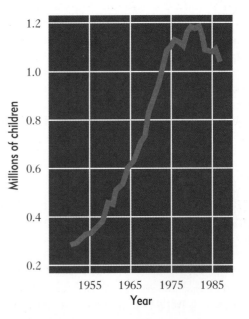

FIGURE 1-1 Number of American children under 18 years of age affected by divorce. Divorce increases stress for millions of children while leaving them with fewer personal resources. *(U.S. Census Bureau, National Center for Health Statistics.)*

## Ancient Views and Treatments

Knowledge of prehistoric societies is difficult to acquire. It is based on inferences made from archaeological discoveries. Historians observe the unearthed bones, artwork, artifacts, and other remnants of ancient societies, and then draw inferences about those societies' customs, beliefs, and daily life. Such conclusions are at best tentative and always subject to revision in the face of new discoveries.

Thus our knowledge of how ancient societies viewed and treated mentally disturbed people is limited. Historians have concluded that prehistoric societies probably viewed abnormal behavior as the work of evil spirits. They believe that people in these early societies explained the phenomena around and within them as resulting from the actions of magical, sometimes sinister, beings who shaped and controlled the world. In particular, these early people viewed the human body and mind as sites of battle between external forces, and they viewed behavior, both normal and abnormal, as the outcome of battles between good and evil spirits, positive forces and demons, or good and bad gods. Often abnormal behavior was interpreted as a victory by evil spirits, and the cure for such behavior was to force the spirits to leave the person's body.

This supernatural view of abnormality may have begun as far back as the Stone Age, a half-million years ago. Some skulls from that period recovered by archaeologists in Europe and South America show evidence of an operation called *trephination,* in which a stone instrument, or *trephine,* was used to cut away a circular section of the skull. Some historians have surmised that this operation was performed as a treatment for severe abnormal behavior—either "hallucinatory" experiences, in which people saw or heard things not actually present, or "melancholic" reactions, characterized by extreme sadness and immobility—and that the purpose of opening the skull was to release the evil spirits that were supposedly causing the problem (Selling, 1940).

In recent years other historians have raised doubts about this interpretation of trephination, suggesting that the procedure may have been used to remove bone splinters or blood clots caused by stone weapons during tribal warfare (Maher & Maher, 1985). Whether or not Stone Age people actually believed that evil spirits caused abnormal behavior, archaeological findings from later societies clearly indicate that ancient people did eventually account for such behavior by reference to demonic possession. The early writings of the Egyptians, Chinese, and Hebrews, for example, attribute psychological deviance to the influences of evil spirits or

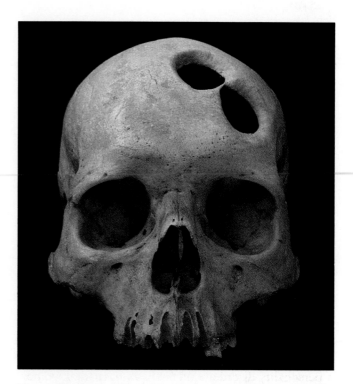

The skulls of some Stone Age people show evidence of trephination, possibly for the purpose of releasing evil spirits and thus remedying abnormal psychological functioning. Signs of bone regrowth around the two holes in this skull suggest that this patient survived two trephinations.

demons. This view of abnormality is frequently expressed in the Bible, which describes how an evil spirit of the Lord affected King Saul and how David feigned madness in order to convince his enemies that he was inhabited by divine forces.

People of these early societies practiced *exorcism* as a common treatment for abnormality. The idea was to coax the evil spirits to leave or to make the person's body an uncomfortable place for the spirits to live. A shaman, or priest, might recite prayers, plead with the evil spirits, insult them, perform magic, make loud noises, or have the person drink noxious solutions. If these techniques failed, a more extreme form of exorcism, such as whipping or starvation, was employed.

## Greek and Roman Views and Treatments

In the years when the Greek and Roman civilizations flourished (from 500 B.C. to A.D. 500), philosophers and physicians described a number of mental disorders. Heading the list were *melancholia,* a condition marked by unshakable sadness; *mania,* a state of euphoria and

Exorcism, one of the earliest forms of treatment for mental disorders, was revived during the Middle Ages. In this detail from the fifteenth-century painting *St. Catherine Exorcising a Possessed Woman,* the devil flees after being cast out of the woman's head by the saint.

frenzied activity; *dementia,* a general intellectual decline; *hysteria,* a physical ailment that has no apparent physical cause; *delusions,* blatantly false beliefs; and *hallucinations,* the experience of imagined sights or sounds as if they were real. Although demonological views concerning mental and physical illness were still widespread, philosophers and physicians began to offer alternative explanations during this period.

Hippocrates (460 – 377 B.C.), often called the father of modern medicine because of his teaching that illnesses had natural causes rather than metaphysical ones, saw abnormal behavior as a disease caused by internal medical problems rather than by conflicts between gods or spirits. Specifically, he believed that brain pathology was the culprit, and that it resulted — like all other forms of disease, in his view — from an imbalance of four fluids, or *humors,* that flowed through the body: *yellow bile, black bile, blood,* and *phlegm.* An excess of yellow bile, for example, caused mania; an excess of black bile was the source of melancholia.

---

=== BOX 1-3 ===

# The Ship of Fools

**G**eorge Washington threw a silver dollar across the Potomac River. Or so we are told. Historians (and anyone who has seen the Potomac River) realize that this cannot be a historical account of a real event; it is apocryphal, a tale intended to convey certain characteristics of the man and the times. Such stories abound in the literature of all fields, from history to astronomy and botany and, yes, even abnormal psychology. Though the stories serve a purpose, it is the nature of scientists to wish to separate fact from fiction. In recent years, one set of investigators discovered that one of the most widely accepted accounts from the history of abnormal psychology was actually a puff of smoke.

In 1967 the French historian Michel Foucault published a book containing accounts of the early treatment of mentally ill persons. He wrote of "ships of fools" that carried insane people from port to port during the Middle Ages, sometimes simply drifting at sea. Many later texts on abnormal psychology included similar accounts. For years the story of the ship of fools was widely used to illustrate

how society segregated and mistreated the mentally ill. The ships were seen as precursors of the mental hospitals of the nineteenth and twentieth centuries.

Then a decade ago psychologists Winifred and Brendan Maher (1982) searched the records of the period that is reported to have spawned the ship of fools. The Mahers did find scattered accounts of individuals who exhibited bizarre behavior and were shipped off to be unloaded somewhere else, but such isolated incidents do not constitute compelling evidence that there ever was a ship of fools. These investigators worked long and hard to find logs, diaries, or other kinds of documentation. They wrote to Foucault and to the libraries that were purported to

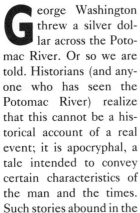

Imbalances of the four humors were believed to affect personality and cause mental disorders. In these depictions of two of the humors, *(left)* yellow bile drives a choleric husband to beat his wife; *(right)* black bile renders a man melancholic and sends him to bed.

have relevant holdings. No evidence was found. How, then, had the notion of a ship of fools emerged and proliferated?

Like all rumors, this one started as a good story and became embellished in the telling. Foucault apparently relied heavily on a book published in 1494 by Sebastian Brant titled *Das Narrenschiff* (The Ship of Fools), a volume of allegorical poems illustrated by woodcuts. Of the 112 poems and woodcuts, 4 depict medieval ships carrying people wearing the traditional clothing of the court jester. Brant's book addressed only moral and ethical issues of the times. It was not intended as a depiction of the mentally ill, yet his woodcuts set Foucault to thinking.

When the Mahers contacted the director of a Danish museum with holdings relevant to the period, their inquiry was respectfully treated as an April Fool's Day joke: "You know as well as we that Sebastian Brant's didactic-satirical poem 'Das Narrenschiff' (1494) — and all its imitations — is just a literary fiction without base in reality." The letter also described a practice that originated in Nuremburg in 1350: during the Shrovetide cele-

brations a procession of jugglers, dancers, clowns, and soldiers wended its antic way through the streets while costumed revelers danced and made merry. Since 1475 this procession had included a ship — a real one — that was hoisted on wheels and carted down the street; it represented hell, which the revelers dared to mock only during these three days before the start of Lent (when presumably they would repent). The museum director concluded that Brant must have known of this procession and based his woodcuts on it.

Because Brant's title and woodcuts meshed with historians' notions about the medieval world's perceptions of mental illness, Foucault interpreted them as describing an actual practice of shipping off boatloads of "fools." Subsequent writers apparently parroted Foucault unquestioningly and even gave the impression that the existence of ships of fools was a well-known fact, not something they had read about in a single source. It is not unusual for researchers and writers to cite secondary sources. Imagine Scientist Jones, who writes a paper in which she includes historical informa-

tion on the topic she is researching. Scientist Kalawi performs a follow-up study in which he discusses Jones's findings and includes the history he has read in Jones's paper. Author Chin writes a textbook and cites Jones's research, which he knows only from having read Kalawi's paper. Then Author Winshel reads Chin and cites Jones. Because Winshel does not go to the original source — Jones herself — he has no idea whether or not the information is well founded or has been embellished or reformulated in later citations.

This all too common practice can lead to the dissemination of misinformation and the creation of powerful myths that can influence our perceptions of a field. The result may be a blurring of the vision needed to conduct unbiased, rigorous studies that will advance our knowledge of the field. Perhaps the only benefit to be derived from the dissemination of apocryphal stories is the opportunity it provides for careful researchers to hone their investigative skills in debunking the myths — and to force transgressors to admit having been taken for a ride on a ship of fools.

To treat these patterns of psychological dysfunctioning, Hippocrates sought to correct the underlying physical pathology. He believed, for instance, that the excess of black bile underlying melancholia could be reduced by a quiet life, a vegetable diet, temperance, exercise, celibacy, and even bleeding. Such explanations and treatments represented a major departure from the demonological views that had dominated people's thinking until then.

Hippocrates' focus on internal causes for abnormal behavior was later shared and in some cases extended by the great Greek philosophers Plato (427–347 B.C.) and Aristotle (384–322 B.C.) and by influential Greek physicians. The physician Aretaeus (A.D. 50–130), for example, suggested that emotional problems could also cause abnormal behavior. The physician Galen (A.D. 130–200) systematically distinguished emotional causes (such as financial worries and loss of love) from medical ones (such as head injuries and alcohol abuse).

Roman physicians adopted such theories when Rome gained power over the ancient world.

These theories led Greek and Roman physicians to treat mental illnesses with a mixture of medical and psychological techniques. Before resorting to such severe methods as bleeding patients or restraining them with mechanical devices, many Greek physicians first prescribed a warm and supportive atmosphere, music, massage, exercise, and baths. Roman physicians were even more emphatic about the need to soothe and comfort patients who had mental disorders.

## Europe in the Middle Ages: Demonology Returns

That demonological views were dismissed by noted physicians and scholars during the Greco-Roman period was

---

= BOX 1-4 =

# The Moon and the Mind

As time passes, every society undergoes changes that redefine both the range of behavior considered normal and the explanations for behavior that deviates from that norm. The belief in demonic possession as a cause of abnormal behavior has been replaced by the assumption that biological, psychological, and sociocultural explanations can be found; yet some ancient theories still have a hold on us today. One is the persistent belief that the phases of the moon have a direct effect on personality and behavior.

> It is the very error of the moon;
> She comes more near the earth than she was wont,
> And makes men mad.

When Shakespeare put these words into the mouth of Othello, he was expressing the thoughts of people of

Moonstruck maidens dance in the town square in this eighteenth-century French engraving.

centuries past and centuries to come. Primitive societies believed that the moon had magical, mystical powers and that its changes portended events of many kinds. The moon had the power to impregnate women, to make plants grow, and to drive people crazy. Later societies also accepted the power of the moon to affect behavior, and they applied the terms "lunatic" and "lunacy" to the person and the behavior to capture their moonlike, or lunar, qualities. Today many respected institutions and individuals actively support the idea that behavior is affected by the phases of the moon. The belief that bizarre behavior increases when the moon is full is so prevalent that a successful lunar newsletter services a number of hospitals and law enforcement officials, warning them to be wary on nights of a full moon (Gardner, 1984).

Anecdotal evidence abounds: New York City police officers note more violent and bizarre crimes during the full moon, and hospitals claim to experience an increase in births. One has linked the full moon to the onset of ulcers and heart attacks. A Wall

not enough to shake many people's belief in demons. Such views and practices never disappeared entirely, and with the decline of Rome they enjoyed a strong resurgence (see Box 1-4).

After the Roman Empire fell, a growing distrust of science spread throughout Europe. In the years from A.D. 500 to 1350, the period known as the Middle Ages, the power of the clergy increased greatly. The church rejected secular studies and scientific forms of investigation, and it controlled all education. Religious beliefs — themselves highly superstitious and demonological at this time — came to dominate all aspects of life. Planetary phenomena, world events, and personal experience and conduct were all interpreted in religious terms, often as a conflict between good and evil, a battle between God and the devil. Deviant behavior of all kinds was seen as evidence of an association with Satan. Although some scientists and physicians still argued for medical explanations and treatments for mental dys-

functioning, their views carried little weight in this atmosphere of rigid religious doctrine.

The Middle Ages were centuries of great stress and anxiety, times of war, urban uprisings, and plagues. Social institutions were in constant flux. People blamed the devil for these hard times and feared him intensely; specifically, they feared being possessed by the devil. The incidence of abnormal behavior apparently increased dramatically during this stressful period. Melancholia, guilt, and anxiety were common problems. In addition, there were outbreaks of so-called *mass madness* in which large numbers of people apparently shared the same delusions and hallucinations. Two prevalent forms were tarantism and lycanthropy.

*Tarantism* (also known as *St. Vitus's dance*) was a mania that occurred throughout Europe between A.D. 900 and 1800. Groups of people would suddenly start to jump around, dance, and go into convulsions (Siegrist, 1943). They might bang into walls or roll on the ground.

---

Street broker has for years used the schedule of the full moon as a guide in giving investment advice — successfully (Gardner, 1984).

Scientists, who generally rely on explanations other than the inherent mystical prowess of the moon, have advanced many theories to make sense of a lunar effect on human behavior. Some say that since the moon causes the tides of the oceans, it is reasonable to expect that it has a similar effect on the bodily fluids of human beings (whose composition is more than 80 percent water). The increase in births might therefore be explained by the force of the moon on the expectant mother's amniotic fluid. Similar tidal and gravitational effects have been posited to explain the increase in bizarre behavior in people who may already be viewed as unbalanced. Aside from the abundant anecdotal evidence, a study of clams by the biologist Frank Brown is often cited to show the ubiquitous power of the moon over the behavior of creatures of the earth (Gardner, 1984). Brown reports moving a group of clams gathered in Connecticut to a laboratory in the landlocked city of Evanston, Illi-

nois. At first the clams opened up to receive food during the times of high tide in Connecticut, as they had done all of their lives. After two weeks, however, the clams adopted an eating pattern that followed what would have been the schedule of high tides in Evanston — if Evanston had actually had any tides.

This evidence may seem to be compelling, but any hypothesis devised to explain the alleged effects of the moon is only a tentative assumption; none has been substantiated. Some researchers, less moonstruck, have performed rigorous statistical analyses of the actual numbers of births, crimes, and incidents of bizarre behavior that occur during the full moon. They have found no evidence supporting the influence of the moon on any of a variety of scales of human behavior. In view of this lack of support for the popular lunacy theory, some scientists have suggested that we drop the entire question. Other researchers, undissuaded, claim that the lack of statistical evidence is not the problem — the problem has been the researchers' failure to look at the right variables, to use the appropriate mea-

sures, or to look at enough days both before and after the actual full moon. It has been suggested, for example, that studies of mental hospital admissions should take a lag time into account because the moon-induced behavior may not be identified or the individuals may not be processed until a week or more after the full moon (Cyr & Kalpin, 1988).

Most clinicians remain convinced that moon-induced abnormality is a myth, yet some people do exhibit strange behavior during the full moon, or report strange sensations or increased sexual desire. The simplest explanation for these phenomena is most likely the most accurate. Personal belief, superstition, and bias can be powerful motivators of behavior. For people who already exhibit abnormal behavior, or for people who are searching for an excuse or a cue to break with society's behavioral norms, the historical belief in the power of the moon provides a convenient outlet. One waives personal responsibility by attributing one's behavior to the moon. The cause of lunacy may lie far less in the heavens than in our minds.

Peasant women are overcome by St. Vitus's dance in this engraving, based on a fifteenth-century painting by Pieter Brueghel.

great weakness, they believed). These milder forms of exorcism were sometimes supplemented by torture in the form of starvation, whipping, scalding, or stretching—a procedure calculated to drive the devil out of the afflicted person's body.

As the Middle Ages drew to a close, demonology and its methods began to lose favor. Cities throughout Europe grew larger, and municipal authorities gained more power and increasingly took over the secular activities of the church. Among other responsibilities, they began to administer hospitals and direct the care of ill people, including the mentally ill. Medical views of psychological abnormality started to gain prominence once again. In the British lunacy trials of the late thirteenth century, for example, a natural cause such as a "blow to the head" or "fear of one's father" was likely to be cited as responsible for the behavior that had brought these people to trial to determine their sanity (Neugebauer, 1979, 1978). During these same years, many of the mentally ill were treated in medical hospitals, under municipal authority, rather than by the clergy. The Trinity Hospital in England, for example, was established to treat "madness" along with other kinds of illness, and to keep the mad "safe until they are restored to reason" (Allderidge, 1979, p. 322).

## The Renaissance and the Rise of Asylums

Demonological views of abnormality continued to decline in popularity during the first half of the period of flourishing cultural and scientific activity known as the Renaissance (approximately 1400–1700). During these years the German physician Johann Weyer (1515–1588) apparently became the first medical practitioner to specialize in mental illness. Weyer rejected the demonological explanations of abnormality. Although some of his colleagues scoffed at his view that the mind was as susceptible to sickness as the body, his work represents the age's renewed commitment to science and skeptical thinking, and Weyer is now considered the founder of modern psychopathology.

Care for many of the mentally ill continued to improve in this atmosphere. In England many mental patients were kept at home, and their families were given extra funds by the local parish. Across Europe a number of religious shrines became consecrated to the humane and loving treatment of the mentally ill. Perhaps the best-known such shrine was at Gheel in Belgium. Beginning in the fifteenth century, people with mental problems ranging from melancholia to hallucinations came from

Some dressed oddly, others tore off their clothing. All were convinced that they had been bitten and possessed by a wolf spider, now called a tarantula, and they sought to cure their disorder by performing a folk dance called a "tarantella." The dance was thought to have originated in the town of Taranto in southern Italy; thus the name tarantism.

People with *lycanthropy* thought they were possessed by wolves or other animals. They acted wolflike and might imagine that fur was growing all over their bodies. Stories of lycanthropes, more popularly known as *werewolves,* have been passed down to us and continue to capture the imagination of moviemakers and their audiences.

Many earlier demonological treatments for psychological abnormality reemerged in the Middle Ages. Once again the key to a cure was to rid the person's body of the devil that possessed it, and techniques of exorcism were revived. Clergymen, who generally were in charge of treating the mentally disturbed during this period, would plead, chant, or pray to the devil or evil spirits. They might also administer holy water or bitter-tasting solutions, and if these techniques did not work, they might try to insult the devil and attack his pride (Satan's

Belief in demonological possession persisted into the Renaissance. A great fear of witchcraft, for example, swept Europe during the fifteenth and sixteenth centuries. Tens of thousands of people, most of them women, were thought to have made a pact with the devil for the power to visit storm, flood, pestilence, sexual impotence, crop failure, and other kinds of harm upon their enemies. Although "the typical accused witch was . . . an impoverished woman with a sharp tongue and a bad temper" (Schoeneman, 1984), a few appear to have had mental disorders that caused them to act strangely (Zilboorg & Henry, 1941). In this illustration from a book by the French demonologist Pierre de Lancré, Satan takes the form of a five-horned goat *(upper right)* and presides over a witches' Sabbath.

teries into **asylums,** institutions to which mentally ill people could be sent. These institutions apparently began with the best of intentions—to provide care for the mentally ill. Once the asylums started to overflow with patients, however, they abandoned such goals and eventually became virtual prisons in which patients were held in filthy and degrading conditions and treated with unspeakable cruelty.

The first asylum was founded in Muslim Spain in the early fifteenth century, but the idea did not gain full momentum until the next century. In 1547 the Bethlehem Hospital in London was given to the city by Henry VIII for the exclusive purpose of confining the mentally ill. Here patients, restrained in chains, cried out their despair for all to hear. The hospital actually became a popular tourist attraction; people were eager to pay to look at the howling and gibbering inmates. The hospital's name, pronounced "Bedlam" by the local people, has become synonymous with a chaotic uproar. Asylums later founded in Mexico, France, Russia, the United States, and Austria offered similar forms of "care." In the Lunatics' Tower in Vienna, for example, mental patients were kept in narrow hallways by the outer walls, so that tourists outside could look up and see them. In La Bicêtre in Paris, patients were shackled to the walls of cold, dark, dirty cells with iron collars and given spoiled food that could be sold nowhere else (Selling, 1940).

The inability of municipal authorities to address the needs of large numbers of mental patients was not the

all over the world to visit this shrine (actually established centuries earlier) for psychic healing. Local residents welcomed them into their homes, and many pilgrims stayed on to form the world's first "colony" of mental patients. This colony set the stage for many of today's community mental health and foster care programs, and Gheel continues to demonstrate that the mentally ill can respond to loving care and respectful treatment (Aring, 1975, 1974). Many patients still live in foster homes there until they recover, interacting with and accepted by the town's other residents.

Unfortunately, the improvements in the care for the mentally ill began to fade by the mid–sixteenth century. Municipal authorities eventually discovered that only a small percentage of the severely mentally ill could be accommodated in private homes and community residences, and that medical hospitals were too few and too small. They began to convert some hospitals and monas-

London's Bethlehem Hospital, or Bedlam, was typical of insane asylums from the sixteenth to the nineteenth centuries. In his eighteenth-century work from *A Rake's Progress,* William Hogarth depicted the asylum as a chaotic place where ladies and gentlemen of fashion came to marvel at the strange behavior of the inmates.

only reason for the poor quality of care in asylums. A lingering fear of the mentally ill was also responsible. Even the best-intentioned theoreticians and caregivers really knew very little about mental illness, and large segments of the population still equated abnormal behavior with possession by mysterious and dangerous forces. The authorities addressed their concerns by restraining and confining mental patients.

The medical theories and cures developed during this period were often misguided and unintentionally cruel. In the eighteenth century no less a figure than Benjamin Rush (1745–1813), often called the father of American psychiatry, treated some mental patients by drawing blood from their bodies, a technique used to treat many bodily illnesses during that period. This treatment was meant to lower an excessively high level of blood in the brain, which Rush believed was causing the patient's abnormal behavior (Farina, 1976). Thus, suspicion, ignorance, and erroneous medical theory conspired to keep asylums a shameful form of care until the late eighteenth century.

## The Nineteenth Century: Reform and Moral Treatment

As 1800 approached, the treatment of mentally ill people began to change for the better once again. Historians usually point to the Parisian asylum of La Bicêtre (for male patients) as the initial site of asylum reform. In 1793, during the French Revolution, Philippe Pinel (1745–1826) was named the chief physician there. In-

fluenced by the humane work of Jean-Baptiste Pussin, the hospital's superintendent of incurable patients, Pinel began a series of reforms. He argued that the patients were sick people whose mental illnesses should be treated with support and kindness rather than with chains and beatings. He would not allow patients to be abused and tortured. He unchained them and gave them the liberty of the hospital grounds, replaced the dark dungeons with sunny, well-ventilated rooms, and offered patients support and advice. Pinel described his philosophy this way:

> I viewed the scene that was opened to me with the eyes of common sense and unprejudiced observation. . . . I then discovered that insanity was curable in many instances, by mildness of treatment and attention to the state of the mind exclusively, and when coercion was indispensable, that it might be very effectually applied without corporal indignity. . . . I saw, with wonder, the resources of nature when left to herself, or skillfully assisted in her efforts. . . . Attention to these principles alone will, frequently, not only lay the foundation of, but complete a cure: while neglect of them may exasperate each succeeding paroxysm, till, at length, the disease becomes established . . . and incurable. The successful application of moral regimen exclusively, gives great weight to the supposition that, in a majority of instances, there is no organic lesion of the brain.
>
> *(Pinel [1806] 1962, pp. 5, 108–109)*

Pinel's new approach did indeed prove remarkably successful. Many patients who had been locked away in darkness for decades were now enjoying fresh air and sunlight and being treated with dignity. Some improved

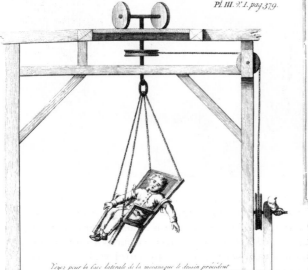

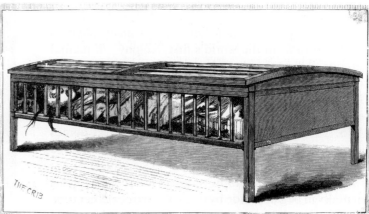

Outrageous devices and techniques continued in use even during the reforms of the nineteenth century. Many depressed patients were spun in a rotating chair to elevate their mood, and violent patients were often placed in the "crib," a precursor to the straitjacket.

Philippe Pinel supervised the unchaining of the insane at La Bicêtre asylum in Paris in 1793. His successful reforms helped usher in a worldwide movement of humanitarian "moral treatment" for the mentally ill.

significantly over a short period of time and were released. Pinel and Pussin were later commissioned to reform yet another Parisian mental hospital, La Salpetrière (for female patients), and had excellent results there as well. Jean Esquirol (1772–1840), Pinel's student and successor, followed his teacher's lead and went on to help establish ten new mental hospitals that operated by the same principles.

During this period an English Quaker named William Tuke (1732–1819) was bringing similar reforms to northern England. In 1796 he founded the York Retreat, a rural estate where about thirty mental patients were lodged as guests in quiet country houses and treated with a combination of rest, talk, prayer, and manual work. He believed that this form of treatment would have better results than mechanical restraints or medical interventions based on unsupported notions about the human brain (see Figure 1-2).

**The Spread of Moral Treatment** The methodologies espoused by Pinel and Tuke, called *moral treatment* by their contemporaries because of their emphasis on moral guidance and on humane and respectful intervention, caught on throughout Europe and the United States. Increasingly mental patients were perceived as potentially productive human beings whose mental functioning had broken down under overwhelming personal stresses. These unfortunate (rather than possessed) people were considered deserving of individualized care that included discussions of their problems, constructive activities, work, companionship, and quiet.

The person most responsible for the early spread of moral treatment in the United States was Benjamin Rush. As we have seen, Rush's earlier medical views were sometimes naive and harsh by today's standards, but he fully embraced the concept of moral treatment when he learned about it. As an eminent physician at Pennsylvania Hospital, he limited his practice and study to mental illness, and he developed numerous humane approaches to treatment. One of his innovations was to require the hospital to hire intelligent and sensitive attendants to work closely with patients, reading and talking to them and taking them on regular walks. He also suggested that it would be of therapeutic value for doctors to give small gifts to their patients now and then.

Rush was a most influential physician. He wrote the first American treatise on mental illness, *Medical Inquiries and Observations upon the Diseases of the Mind*, published in 1812, and organized the first American course in psychiatry. It was a Boston schoolteacher named Dorothea Dix (1802–1887), however, who was largely responsible for the passage of new laws that mandated more humane care for the mentally ill. In 1841 Dix had

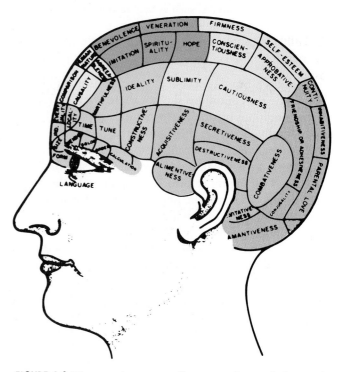

**FIGURE 1-2** Nineteenth-century efforts to understand abnormal behavior in less demonological terms were not always scientifically sound. One hypothesis was called *phrenology.* Franz Joseph Gall (1758–1828) and his followers held that the brain consisted of discernible portions, each responsible for some aspect of personality. Phrenologists tried to assess personality by feeling bumps and indentations on a person's head.

Benjamin Rush, considered the father of American psychiatry, embraced and helped spread the concept of moral treatment during the early nineteenth century. Some of his earlier treatment techniques, however, such as the "restraint chair," reflected contemporary medical thought.

gone to teach Sunday school at a local prison and been shocked by the conditions she saw there. Her interest in prison conditions broadened to include the plight of poor and mentally ill people throughout the country. A powerful campaigner, Dix went from state legislature to state legislature speaking of the horrors she had observed and calling for reform. In an address to the Massachusetts legislature, she proclaimed that the mentally ill were being "confined within this Commonwealth, in cages, closets, cellars, stalls, pens; chained, naked, beaten with rods, and lashed into obedience" (Deutsch, 1949, p. 165). She told the Congress of the United States that mentally ill people across the country were still being "bound with galling chains, bowed beneath fetters and heavy iron balls attached to drag chains, lacerated with ropes, scourged with rods and terrified beneath storms of execration and cruel blows" (Zilboorg & Henry, 1941, pp. 583–584).

Dix's campaign, which spanned the decades from 1841 until 1881, led to new laws and the appropriation of funds to improve the treatment of the mentally ill. Each state was made responsible for developing effective public mental hospitals. Dix personally helped establish thirty-two of these state hospitals, all intended to offer moral treatment (Bickman & Dokecki, 1989). Similar government-funded hospitals for the mentally ill were established throughout Europe and run by humanitarian principles.

For years the moral treatment movement improved the care of the mentally ill. By the 1850s, a number of mental hospitals throughout Europe and America reported that most of their patients were recovering and being released (Bockoven, 1963). At Worcester State Hospital in Massachusetts, for example, almost 60 percent of long-term mental patients and more than 70 percent of short-term mental patients recovered enough to be discharged. Unfortunately, social changes at the end of the nineteenth century eventually altered this promising situation for the worse.

**The Decline of Moral Treatment** As we have observed, the treatment of abnormality has followed a crooked path. Over and over again, relative progress has been followed by serious decline. Viewed in this context, the decline of moral treatment in the late nineteenth century is disappointing but not surprising.

Several factors contributed to this decline (Bockoven, 1963). One was the reckless speed with which the moral

From 1841 to 1881 the Boston schoolteacher Dorothea Dix tirelessly campaigned for more humane forms of treatment in mental hospitals throughout the United States. Her efforts led to new laws providing for the establishment of public mental hospitals, supported and administered by the states.

treatment movement had advanced. As mental hospitals multiplied, severe money and staffing shortages developed. In the United States, for example, legislatures could not allocate sufficient funds to run the state hospitals properly, so too few professionals were hired, and recovery rates declined. Fewer and fewer patients left the hospitals each year, and admissions continued unabated; overcrowding became a major problem. Under these conditions it was impossible to provide the individual care and genuine concern that were the cornerstones of moral treatment.

The basic assumptions of moral treatment also contributed to its downfall. The major one was that patients would begin to function normally if they were treated with dignity and if their physical needs were met. For some patients this was indeed the case. Others, however, needed more effective treatments than any that had yet been developed. Many of these people remained hospitalized till they died.

A further reason for the decline of moral treatment was the emergence of a new wave of prejudice against the mentally ill. As more and more patients disappeared into the large, distant mental hospitals, the public once again came to view them as strange and dangerous and were less open-handed when it came to making donations or allocating government funds. Moreover, by the end of the nineteenth century, many of the patients entering public mental hospitals in the United States were impoverished foreign immigrants, and as such were already the objects of considerable prejudice. The public had little interest in helping people from other countries; even the hospital personnel were less conscientious and caring in treating them.

By the early years of the twentieth century, the moral treatment movement had ground to a halt in both the United States and Europe. Public mental hospitals provided minimal custodial care and medical interventions that did not work and became more overcrowded and less effective every year. Long-term hospitalization became the norm once again.

This state of affairs was powerfully described in 1908 by Clifford Beers (1876–1943) in *A Mind That Found Itself*, an autobiographical account of his severe mental disturbance and of the "treatment" he received in three mental institutions. Beers revealed that he and other patients were repeatedly restrained, beaten, choked, and spat on in these places, all in the name of treatment. His moving account aroused both public and professional sympathy, and he went on to found the National Committee for Mental Hygiene, dedicated to educating the public about mental illness and the need for proper treatment. Unfortunately, although Beers's work brought considerable attention to the terrible conditions in public mental hospitals, these institutions were not to improve significantly for forty more years.

**The Somatogenic Perspective** Another significant trend that began in the late nineteenth century was a dramatic resurgence of the *somatogenic perspective,* the view that abnormal psychological functioning has physical causes. This perspective had at least a 2,300-year history — remember Hippocrates' view that abnormal behavior resulted from brain pathology and an imbalance of humors, or bodily fluids — but it had never before been so widely accepted as it was at this time.

Two factors were responsible for this development. One was the work of Emil Kraepelin (1856–1926), a German researcher who was interested in the relation between abnormal psychological functioning and such physical factors as fatigue, and who had measured the effects of various drugs on abnormal behavior. In 1883 Kraepelin published an influential textbook, which he revised seven times over the next forty years, expounding the view that physical factors are responsible for mental illness. In addition, as we shall see in Chapter 4, he constructed the first system for classifying abnormal behavior. He identified various *syndromes,* or clusters of

Overcrowding and limited funding led to the formation of back wards in state hospitals across the United States during the early twentieth century. In a throwback to the asylums of earlier times, many patients languished in these wards for years, without therapy or hope of recovery.

symptoms, listed their organic causes, and discussed their expected course.

The rise of the somatogenic perspective was also spurred by a series of biological and anatomical discoveries that increased the precision of medical practice and paved the way for further advances. One of the most important discoveries was that general paresis was caused by an organic disease, syphilis. *General paresis* is an irreversible, progressive disorder with both physical and mental symptoms, including paralysis and delusions of grandeur. The organic basis of the disorder had been suspected as early as the mid–nineteenth century, but concrete evidence did not emerge until decades later.

In 1897 Richard von Krafft-Ebing (1840–1902), a German neurologist, established a direct link between general paresis and syphilis. He inoculated paretic patients with matter from syphilis sores and found that none of the patients developed symptoms of syphilis. Their immunity could have been caused only by an earlier case of syphilis, and since all paretic patients were immune to syphilis, Krafft-Ebing theorized that it was the cause of their general paresis. Finally, in 1905, Fritz Schaudinn (1871–1906), a German zoologist, discov-

ered that the microorganism *Treponema pallida* was responsible for syphilis, which in turn was responsible for general paresis.

The work of Kraepelin and the discoveries in regard to general paresis led many researchers and practitioners to suspect that organic factors were responsible for many mental illnesses, perhaps all of them. These theories and the possibility of quick and effective medical solutions for mental illnesses were especially welcomed by those who worked in mental hospitals, where patient populations were now growing at an alarming rate.

Despite the general optimism, the biological approach yielded largely disappointing results throughout the first half of the twentieth century. True, many medical treatments were developed and applied to hospitalized mental patients during that time, but most of the techniques — extraction of teeth, tonsillectomy, hydrotherapy (alternating hot and cold baths to soothe excited patients), insulin coma shock (a "therapeutic" convulsion induced by lowering a patient's blood sugar level with insulin), and lobotomy (a surgical severing of certain nerve fibers in the brain) — proved ineffectual. Not until the middle of the century, when a number of effective medications were finally discovered, did the somatogenic perspective truly begin to pay off for mentally ill patients (Klerman, 1986, 1981).

**The Psychogenic Perspective**   Yet another important trend to unfold in the late nineteenth century was the emergence of the *psychogenic perspective,* the view that the chief causes of abnormal functioning are psychological. This perspective, too, has a long history. The Roman scholar Cicero (106–43 B.C.) held that psychological disturbances could cause bodily ailments, and the Greek physician Galen believed that many mental disorders were caused by fear, disappointment in love, and other psychological events. However, the psychogenic perspective did not achieve a significant following until the late nineteenth century, when studies of the technique of hypnotism demonstrated the potential of this line of inquiry.

*Hypnotism* is the inducing of a trancelike mental state in which a person becomes extremely suggestible. Its use as a means of treating psychological disorders actually dates back to 1778. In that year an Austrian physician named Friedrich Anton Mesmer (1734–1815) established a clinic in Paris where he employed an unusual treatment for patients with *hysterical disorders,* mysterious bodily ailments that had no apparent physical basis. Mesmer's patients sat in a darkened room filled with music. In the center of the room, a tub held bottles of chemicals from which iron rods protruded. Suddenly Mesmer appeared in a flamboyant costume, withdrew the rods, and touched them to the troubled area of each patient's body. Surprisingly, a number of patients did seem to be helped by this treatment. Their pain, numbness, or paralysis disappeared.

As we shall observe in Chapter 11, Mesmer's treatment, called *mesmerism,* was so controversial that eventually he was banished from Paris. But few could deny that at least some patients did indeed improve after being mesmerized. Several scientists believed that Mesmer was inducing a trancelike state in his patients, and that this state caused their symptoms to disappear. In later years the technique was developed further and relabeled *neurohypnotism,* later shortened to *hypnotism* (from *hypnos,* the Greek word for sleep).

It was not until years after Mesmer died, however, that many researchers had the courage to investigate hypnotism and its effects on hysterical disorders. In the late nineteenth century two competing views emerged among these researchers. That a technique that enhanced the power of suggestion could alleviate hysterical ailments indicated to one group of scientists that hysterical disorders must be caused by the power of suggestion — that is, by the mind — in the first place. Another group of scientists believed that hysterical disorders had subtle physiological causes. Jean Charcot (1825–1893), an eminent Parisian neurologist, argued that hysterical disorders were the result of degeneration in portions of the brain.

The experiments of two physicians practicing in the city of Nancy in France finally seemed to settle the matter. Hippolyte-Marie Bernheim (1840–1919) and Ambroise-Auguste Liébault (1823–1904) showed that hysterical disorders could actually be induced in otherwise normal subjects while they were under the influence of hypnosis. That is, they could make normal people experience deafness, paralysis, blindness, or numbness by means of hypnotic suggestion — and they could remove these artificially induced symptoms by the same means. In short, they established that a mental process — hypnotic suggestion — could both cause and cure a physical dysfunction. Most leading scientists, including Charcot, finally embraced the idea that hysterical disorders were largely psychological in origin.

Among those who studied the effects of hypnotism on hysterical disorders was a Viennese doctor named Josef Breuer (1842–1925). He discovered that his hypnotized patients sometimes awoke free of hysterical symptoms after speaking freely about past traumas under hypnosis. During the 1890s Breuer was joined in his work by another Viennese physician, Sigmund Freud (1856–1939). As we shall see in greater detail in Chapter 2, Freud's work eventually led him to develop the theory of psychoanalysis, which holds that many forms of abnormal and normal psychological functioning are psychogenic. He believed that conflict between powerful psychological processes operating at an unconscious

Friedrich Anton Mesmer works with hysterical patients in his Parisian clinic. Mesmer stands at the back in this painting, on the right. He believed that hysterical ailments were caused by an improper distribution of magnetic fluid in the body and that touching an ailing part of the body with an iron rod would help correct this problem. Patients in the clinic try to correct their imbalanced fluid distributions by touching each other with rods while they await Mesmer's expert touch.

The nineteenth century's leading neurologist, Jean Charcot, gives a clinical lecture on hypnotism and hysterical disorders in Paris. Initially Charcot did not believe that the two were related, but research later convinced him that hysterical symptoms could indeed be induced by hypnotic suggestion and that hysterical disorders were ordinarily caused by psychological processes.

level is the source of much abnormal psychological functioning. Freud also developed the technique of psychoanalysis, a form of discussion in which psychotherapists help troubled people acquire insight into their psychological conflicts. Such insight, he believed, would help the patients overcome their psychological problems.

To many, Freud's psychogenic perspective seemed the antithesis of the increasingly influential somatogenic view of mental illness. Thus, his ideas were initially

Sigmund Freud, student of Jean Charcot and colleague of Josef Breuer, came to believe that abnormal behavior is usually caused by psychological factors. His psychoanalytic theory and treatment changed the clinical field at the turn of the century, and his work continues to have a profound influence on it today.

criticized and rejected. Freud persevered in his writings, studies, and practice, however, and by the early twentieth century psychoanalytic theory and treatment were widely accepted throughout the Western world. Indeed, it would be difficult to name another school of thought that has had greater influence on Western culture.

Freud and his followers applied the psychoanalytic treatment approach primarily to patients with relatively modest mental disorders, problems of anxiety or depression that did not require hospitalization. These patients visited psychoanalytic therapists in their offices for sessions of approximately an hour and then went about their daily activities — a format of treatment now known as *outpatient therapy.*

The psychoanalytic approach had little effect on the treatment of severely disturbed patients in mental hospitals. This type of therapy requires levels of clarity, insight, and verbal skill beyond the capabilities of most such patients. Moreover, psychoanalysis often takes years to be effective, and the overcrowded and understaffed public mental hospitals could not accommodate such a leisurely pace.

## CURRENT TRENDS

The past forty years have brought significant changes in the understanding and treatment of abnormal functioning. There are more theories and types of treatment, more research studies, more information, and, perhaps for these reasons, more disagreements about abnormal functioning today than at any time in the past. In some ways the study and treatment of mental disorders have come a long way, but in other respects, clinical scientists and practitioners are still struggling to make a difference. The current era of abnormal psychology can be said to have begun in the 1950s.

### New Treatments for the Severely Disturbed

In the 1950s researchers discovered a number of new *psychotropic medications* — drugs that primarily affect the brain and alleviate many symptoms of mental dysfunctioning. They included the first *antipsychotic drugs,* to correct grossly confused and distorted thinking; *antidepressant drugs,* to lift the mood of severely depressed people; and *antianxiety drugs,* to reduce tension and anxiety.

With the discovery and application of these drugs, many severely disturbed patients in mental hospitals—the same patients who had languished there for years—began to show signs of significant improvement. Hospital administrators, encouraged by the effectiveness of the drugs and pressured by a growing public outcry over the high cost of care and the terrible conditions in public mental hospitals, began to discharge patients almost immediately.

Since the discovery of these medications, the mental health field in the United States and Europe has followed a policy of *deinstitutionalization,* and hundreds of thousands of patients have been released from public mental hospitals. On any given day in 1955, close to 600,000 people were confined in public mental institutions across the United States. Today the daily patient population in the same hospitals is under 125,000 (see Figure 1-3).

In short, outpatient care has now become the primary mode of treatment for people with severe psychological disturbances as well as for those with more moderate problems. When severely impaired people do require institutionalization, the current practice is to provide them with short-term hospitalization and then return them to the community. Ideally, they are then provided with outpatient psychotherapy and medication monitoring in community mental health centers. Other community programs such as supervised residences (halfway houses) and vocational rehabilitation centers may also be available.

This recent emphasis on community care for people with severe psychological disturbances, called the *community mental health approach,* will be discussed further in Chapters 5 and 16. Although the approach has been very helpful for many patients, unfortunately too few community facilities and programs are available to address the needs of severely disturbed people in the United States. As a result, hundreds of thousands fail to make lasting recoveries, and are shuffled back and forth between the mental hospital and the community. After they are released from the hospital, they receive at best minimal care and often wind up living in decrepit rooming houses or on the streets. Their plight is truly a national disgrace.

## New Treatment Settings for Less Severe Psychological Problems

The treatment picture for people with less severe psychological disturbances has been more positive since the 1950s. Outpatient care has continued to be the preferred mode of treatment for these people, and the number and types of facilities that offer such care have expanded to meet the need.

Before the 1950s, almost all outpatient care took the form of *private psychotherapy,* an arrangement by which an individual directly paid a psychotherapist for counseling services. This tended to be an expensive form of treatment, available almost exclusively to the affluent. Since the 1950s, however, many medical health insurance plans have expanded coverage to include private psychotherapy, so that this service is now more widely available to people with more modest incomes. In addition, outpatient therapy has become increasingly available in a variety of relatively inexpensive settings—community mental health centers, crisis intervention centers, family service centers, and other social service agencies. The new settings have spurred a dramatic increase in the number of persons seeking outpatient care for psychological problems.

The growth in the use of outpatient services by both severely disturbed and less disturbed persons is seen in Figure 1-4. In 1955 approximately 23 percent of people treated for psychological disturbances were treated as outpatients. Today that figure is about 74 percent.

Another change in outpatient care since the 1950s has been the development of specialized programs that focus exclusively on one kind of psychological problem.

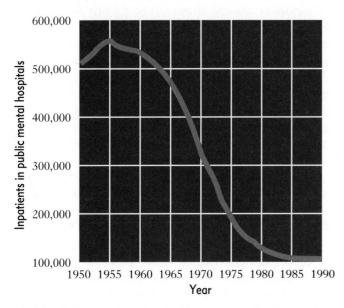

**FIGURE 1-3** The number of patients now hospitalized in public mental hospitals in the United States is a small fraction of the number hospitalized in 1955. *(Adapted from Torrey, 1988.)*

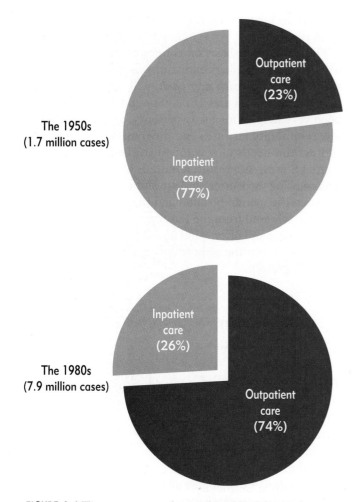

**The 1950s**
**(1.7 million cases)**

**The 1980s**
**(7.9 million cases)**

**FIGURE 1-4** The percentage of mental health patients who are treated on an outpatient basis has grown steadily since the 1950s. "Inpatient care" refers to treatment in state, county, and private mental hospitals, general hospitals, and Veterans Administration hospitals. "Outpatient care" refers to treatment by community mental health agencies, private therapists, day care centers, and specialists in social and vocational rehabilitation. *(Adapted from Witkin et al.; NIMH, 1983.)*

We now have suicide prevention centers, drug abuse programs, eating disorder programs, phobia clinics, and sexual dysfunction programs. Practitioners in these programs acquire the kind of expertise that can come only by concentrating one's efforts in a single area.

## Today's Practitioners

Today a variety of professionals offer help to people with psychological problems—both those who warrant a clinical diagnosis and others who simply want to learn how to cope with the stresses in their lives. This, too,

Therapy for people with mild or moderate psychological disturbances is widely available today in individual, group, or family therapy formats. It can be obtained privately or in less expensive government-subsidized mental health centers and agencies.

represents a change from the situation of several decades ago. Before the 1950s psychotherapy was the exclusive province of *psychiatrists,* physicians who had completed three to four additional years of training after medical school (a residency) in the treatment of abnormal mental functioning. After World War II, however, the demand for mental health services expanded more rapidly than the ranks of psychiatrists, so other professional groups stepped in to fill the gap.

Prominent among those other groups are *clinical psychologists*—professionals who earn a doctorate in clinical psychology by completing four years of graduate training in abnormal functioning and its treatment and also complete a one-year internship at a mental hospital or mental health agency. Before their professional responsibilities expanded into the area of treatment, clinical psychologists were principally assessors and researchers of abnormal functioning. Some of them still specialize in those activities.

Other important groups that provide psychotherapy and related services are *counseling psychologists, educational psychologists, psychiatric nurses*, and—the largest group—*psychiatric social workers* (see Figure 1-5). Each of these specialties requires completion of its own graduate training program. Theoretically, each specialty conducts therapy in a distinctive way, but in reality there is considerable overlap in the ways practitioners of the various specialties work. Indeed, the individual differences within a given professional group are sometimes much greater than the general differences between groups.

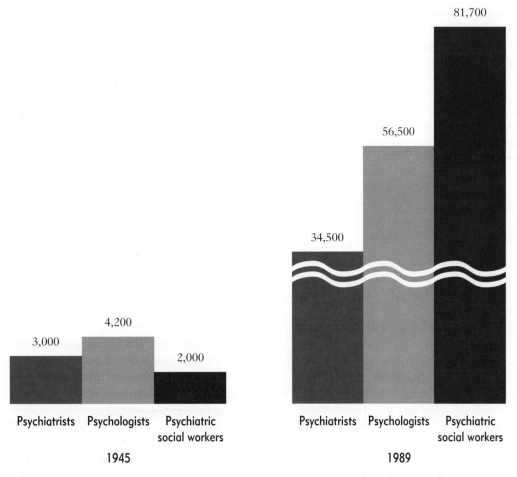

**FIGURE 1-5** The number of trained mental health professionals in the United States has multiplied more than fourteen times since World War II, while the total population has yet to double. Today a therapist is more likely to be a psychiatric social worker than a psychiatrist or psychologist. *(Adapted from Dial et al., 1990; Knesper & Pagnucco, 1987; AMA, 1986.)*

## Emerging Perspectives

One of the most significant developments in the understanding and treatment of abnormal psychological functioning has been the emergence of numerous, often competing theoretical perspectives. Before the 1950s, the *psychodynamic* perspective, with its emphasis on unconscious conflicts as the cause of psychopathology, was dominant. Then the discovery of effective psychotropic drugs in the 1950s brought new stature to somatogenic views of abnormality. The development of various *biological* theories of abnormality has opened promising avenues of biological research that continue to be explored today.

As we shall see in Chapter 2, other influential perspectives have also emerged since the 1950s, including the *behavioral, cognitive, humanistic-existential,* and *sociocultural* schools of thought, which explain and treat abnormality in very different ways. At present no single perspective dominates the clinical field as the psychodynamic perspective once did. All these theories have influenced the current understanding and treatment of abnormal functioning.

## The Emphasis on Research

One final important development in the study and treatment of mental disorders since World War II has been a heightened appreciation of the need for systematic research. As numerous theories and forms of treatment have been proposed, researchers have tried to single out the concepts that best explain and predict abnormal behavior, to determine which treatments are most effective, and to discover whether they should be modified and, if so, how.

Today well-trained clinical researchers are conducting studies in academic institutions, laboratories, mental hospitals, mental health centers, and other clinical settings throughout the world. Their work has already yielded important discoveries and changed many of our ideas about abnormal psychological functioning. Just as important, it repeatedly demonstrates that properly conducted research is essential for continued progress in the study and practice of abnormal psychology.

## ORGANIZATION OF THE TEXT

The study and treatment of abnormal psychological functioning are exciting and confusing in equal measure. New ideas, discoveries, and refinements are continually being introduced, and the proliferating theories and treatment approaches can be difficult to evaluate and compare.

How, then, should we proceed in our examination of the various kinds of psychological abnormality? To begin with, we need to appreciate the basic perspectives and tools that today's scientists and practitioners find most useful. This is the task we turn to in the next several chapters: Chapter 2 examines the major views in the clinical field, showing how today's professionals conceptualize abnormal psychological functioning; Chapter 3 looks at the way abnormal functioning is studied — the research tools and strategies used to test the various theories and treatments; Chapter 4 explores how the various patterns of abnormality are assessed and diagnosed; and Chapter 5 examines the many forms of treatment currently employed by clinical practitioners.

Later chapters examine the major kinds of psychological abnormality and the leading treatments for them. In the final chapter we shall see how the science of abnormal psychology and its professionals address current issues and interact with legal, social, and other institutions in today's society.

## SUMMARY

The field devoted to the scientific study of abnormal behavior is called **abnormal psychology.** Its goals are to understand and to treat abnormal patterns of functioning.

Abnormal patterns of psychological functioning are generally considered to be those that are **deviant, distressful, dysfunctional,** and **dangerous.** Behavior must be considered in the context in which it occurs, however; behavior considered deviant in one set of circumstances may be the norm in another. The very concept of abnormality is relative, dependent on the norms and values of the society in question.

Mental illness has a history as long as that of humankind. A look at some of this history can provide clues to the nature of psychological abnormality by revealing the features of abnormality that remain constant in human beings, the ways past societies have understood and treated psychological dysfunctioning, the ancient roots of many current ideas and treatments, and the significance of recent developments in the field.

Historians have concluded that prehistoric societies probably viewed abnormal behavior as the work of evil spirits. There is evidence that Stone Age cultures used **trephining,** a primitive form of brain surgery, to treat mental illness. People of early societies also sought to drive out evil spirits by *exorcism.*

Physicians of the Greek and Roman empires describe such conditions as *melancholia, mania, dementia, hysteria, delusions,* and *hallucinations,* all of which correspond to conditions recognized today. Hippocrates, considered the father of modern medicine, believed that abnormal behavior was due to an imbalance of the four bodily fluids: *black bile, yellow bile, blood,* and *phlegm.* Treatment consisted of correcting the underlying physical pathology through diet and lifestyle.

In the Middle Ages, Europeans resurrected the demonological explanation of abnormal behavior. The combination of great strife in the Western world and the preeminence of the clergy during this period contributed to the popular view that mental illness was the work of the devil. These same factors may have led to an increase in the incidence of mental illness, including outbreaks of **mass madness** in such forms as *tarantism* and *lycanthropy.* As the Middle Ages drew to a close, demonology and its harsh treatment methods began to lose favor. Medical views of psychological abnormality started to grow in prominence, and many mentally ill people were treated in hospitals instead of by the clergy.

Care of the mentally ill continued to improve during the Renaissance. A number of religious shrines became consecrated to the humane treatment of the mentally ill and set the stage for today's community mental health and foster care programs. This enlightened approach was short-lived, however, and by the middle of the sixteenth century the mentally ill were being warehoused in **asylums.**

Care of the mentally ill started to improve again in the nineteenth century, initially at La Bicêtre asylum in Paris. There Philippe Pinel treated inmates as people suffering from an illness that required support and kindness. Similar reforms were brought to England by William Tuke. This *moral treatment* methodology was adopted in the United States by Benjamin Rush, who wrote the first American treatise on mental illness. In the mid- and late nineteenth century in Massachusetts, Dorothea Dix spearheaded a movement to ensure the mentally ill of legal rights and protection and to establish *state hospitals* for their care.

Unfortunately, moral treatment was costly, and as hospitals grew it became impossible to provide the individual care and genuine concern that were its cornerstones. Besides, some psychological disorders did not yield to moral treatment. As a result, the system disintegrated and mental hospitals reverted to warehouses where the inmates received minimal care.

The late nineteenth century saw the return of the *somatogenic perspective,* the view that abnormal psychological functioning is rooted in physical causes. This change was brought about by two factors: (1) the work of the German medical researcher Emil Kraepelin and (2) anatomical and biological discoveries that increased the precision of medical practice, particularly the finding that *general paresis* was caused by the organic disease syphilis. These discoveries led numerous researchers and practitioners to suspect that organic factors were responsible for many mental illnesses.

The same period saw the emergence of the *psychogenic perspective,* the view that the chief causes of abnormal functioning are psychological. One of the key developments at this time was Jean Charcot's use of *hypnotism* to treat patients with hysterical disorders. Later work by the physicians Bernheim and Liébault showed that hysterical disorders could be induced under hypnosis, suggesting that a physical disorder could have a purely psychological basis. The related finding by the Viennese doctor Josef Breuer that patients sometimes awoke free of hysterical symptoms after speaking candidly about past traumas during hypnosis served as one of the bases for the future work of another well-known Viennese doctor, Sigmund Freud. Freud's *psychoanalytic* approach differed dramatically from the influential somatogenic view of mental illness, but eventually it gained wide acceptance and influenced future generations of researchers and practitioners.

The past forty years have brought significant changes in the understanding and treatment of abnormal functioning. In the 1950s, researchers discovered a number of new *psychotropic drugs,* drugs that affected perceptions and emotions. *Antipsychotic drugs, antidepressant drugs,* and *antianxiety drugs* helped many severely disturbed patients who had languished in mental hospitals for years. Their success led to a policy of *deinstitutionalization,* under which hundreds of thousands of patients were released from public mental hospitals. One result of this movement was a focus on outpatient treatment as the primary approach for helping the mentally ill. The wider availability of outpatient care and private therapy has led to a dramatic increase in treatment for patients suffering less severe psychological disturbances.

Today a variety of professionals — *psychiatrists, clinical psychologists, psychiatric social workers, counseling psychologists, educational psychologists,* and *psychiatric nurses* — offer help to people with psychological problems. Each specialty requires completion of its own graduate training.

Over the past forty years numerous theoretical perspectives have emerged, including the *psychodynamic, behavioral, cognitive, humanistic-existential,* and *sociocultural* schools of thought. Each explains and treats abnormality in a distinctive way. At the same time, there has been a heightened appreciation of the need for systematic research in the clinical field.

# TOPIC OVERVIEW

# CHAPTER 2

# MODELS OF
# PSYCHOLOGICAL
# ABNORMALITY

hilip Berman, a 25-year-old single unemployed former copy editor for a large
publishing house, . . . had been hospitalized after a suicide attempt in which he
deeply gashed his wrist with a razor blade. He
described [to the therapist] how he had sat on the
bathroom floor and watched the blood drip into
the bathtub for some time before he telephoned
his father at work for help. He and his father went
to the hospital emergency room to have the gash
stitched, but he convinced himself and the hospital physician that he did not need hospitalization.
The next day when his father suggested he
needed help, he knocked his dinner to the floor
and angrily stormed to his room. When he was

calm again, he allowed his father to take him back
to the hospital.

The immediate precipitant for his suicide attempt was that he had run into one of his former
girlfriends with her new boyfriend. The patient
stated that they had a drink together, but all the
while he was with them he could not help thinking that "they were dying to run off and jump in
bed." He experienced jealous rage, got up from
the table, and walked out of the restaurant. He
began to think about how he could "pay her
back."

Mr. Berman had felt frequently depressed for
brief periods during the previous several years.
He was especially critical of himself for his lim-

ited social life and his inability to have managed to have sexual intercourse with a woman even once in his life. As he related this to the therapist, he lifted his eyes from the floor and with a sarcastic smirk said, "I'm a 25-year-old virgin. Go ahead, you can laugh now." He has had several girlfriends to date, whom he described as very attractive, but who he said had lost interest in him. On further questioning, however, it became apparent that Mr. Berman soon became very critical of them and demanded that they always meet his every need, often to their own detriment. The women then found the relationship very unrewarding and would soon find someone else.

During the past two years Mr. Berman had seen three psychiatrists briefly, one of whom had given him a drug, the name of which he could not remember, but that had precipitated some sort of unusual reaction for which he had to stay in a hospital overnight. Another gave him three treatments with electroconvulsive therapy (ECT) because he complained that he was suicidal. These had no effect on his mood but, according to him, caused significant memory loss. He saw the third psychiatrist for three months, but while in treatment he quit his job and could no longer afford the therapy. When asked why he quit, he said, "The bastards were going to fire me anyway." When asked whether he realized he would have to drop out of therapy when he quit his job, he said, "What makes you think I give a damn what happens to therapy?" Concerning his hospitalization, the patient said that "It was a dump," that the staff refused to listen to what he had to say or to respond to his needs, and that they, in fact, treated all the patients "sadistically." The referring doctor corroborated that Mr. Berman was a difficult patient who demanded that he be treated as special, and yet was hostile to most staff members throughout his stay. After one angry exchange with an aide, he left the hospital without leave, and subsequently signed out against medical advice.

Mr. Berman is one of two children of a middle-class family. His father is 55 years old and employed in a managerial position for an insurance company. He perceives his father as weak and ineffectual, completely dominated by the patient's overbearing and cruel mother. He states that he hates his mother with "a passion I can barely control." He claims that his mother used to call him names like "pervert" and "sissy" when he was growing up, and that in an argument she once "kicked me in the balls." Together, he sees his parents as rich, powerful, and selfish, and, in turn, thinks that they see him as lazy, irresponsible, and a behavior problem. When his parents called the therapist to discuss their son's treatment, they stated that his problem began with the birth of his younger brother, Arnold, when Philip was 10 years old. After Arnold's birth Philip apparently became an "ornery" child who cursed a lot and was difficult to discipline. Philip recalls this period only vaguely. He reports that his mother once was hospitalized for depression, but that now "she doesn't believe in psychiatry."

Mr. Berman had graduated from college with average grades. Since graduating he had worked at three different publishing houses, but at none of them for more than one year. He always found some justification for quitting. He usually sat around his house doing very little for two or three months after quitting a job, until his parents prodded him into getting a new one. He described innumerable interactions in his life with teachers, friends, and employers in which he felt offended or unfairly treated, . . . and frequent arguments that left him feeling bitter . . . and spent most of his time alone, "bored." He was unable to commit himself to any person, he held no strong convictions, and he felt no allegiance to any group.

The patient appeared as a very thin, bearded, and bespectacled young man with pale skin who maintained little eye contact with the therapist and who had an air of angry bitterness about him. Although he complained of depression, he denied other symptoms of the depressive syndrome. He seemed preoccupied with his rage at his parents, and seemed particularly invested in conveying a despicable image of himself. When treatment was discussed with Mr. Berman, the therapist recommended frequent contacts, two or three per week, feeling that Mr. Berman's potential for self-injury, if not suicide, was rather high. The judgment was based not so much on the severity of Mr. Berman's depression as on his apparent impulsivity, frequent rages, childish disregard for the consequences of his actions, and his pattern of trying to get other people to suffer by inflicting injury on himself. Mr. Berman willingly agreed to the frequent sessions, but not because of eagerness to get help. "Let's make it five sessions a week," he said. "It's about time my parents paid for all that they've done to me."

*(Spitzer et al., 1983, pp. 59–61)*

Philip is clearly a troubled person, but how did he come to be that way? How do we explain his many problems? In confronting this question, we must acknowledge its complexity. First, we must appreciate the wide range of complaints we are trying to understand: Philip's depression and anger, his social failures, his lack of employment, his distrust of those around him, and the problems within his family. All point to less than optimal psychological functioning, and each problem can be the source of others. Second, we must sort through all kinds of potential primary causes, internal and external, biological and interpersonal, past and present, and decide which, if any, is the key to the rest: which is having the biggest impact on Philip's behavior. Such are the challenges facing every investigator of abnormal psychology, whether in research or clinical practice, and the answers have been many and varied, some based on philosophical assumptions, others on principles of science, some resting mostly on subjective experience, others on quantitative empirical evidence.

Although we may not recognize it, we are all probably using implicit theoretical frameworks of our own as we attempt to explain Philip's conduct. Over the course of our lives, each of us has developed a perspective that helps us make sense of the things other people say and do. Such a perspective helps us to explain other people's behavior to our own satisfaction. In science, such perspectives are known as *paradigms* or *models.* Each is an explicit set of basic assumptions that gives structure to an area under study and sets forth guidelines for its investigation (Kuhn, 1962). The paradigm or model influences what the investigators observe, what questions they ask, what information they consider legitimate, and how they interpret this information. To understand how a clinical scientist explains and treats a specific pattern of abnormal functioning, such as Philip's pattern of symptoms, we must appreciate the model that shapes his or her view of abnormal functioning.

Until recent times the models used by clinical scientists were usually monolithic and culturally determined; that is, a single model was paramount in a particular place and at a particular time, couched in the metaphors of the prevalent world view. Recall the demonological model used to explain abnormal functioning during the Middle Ages. Practitioners of that period constructed a model of mental abnormality that borrowed heavily from their society's preoccupation with religion, superstition, and warfare. Each person was viewed as a battleground where the devil challenged God. Abnormal behavior signaled the devil's victory.

Medieval practitioners would have seen the devil's guiding hand in Philip Berman's efforts to commit suicide, and they would have pointed to demonological possession as the ultimate explanation for Philip's feelings of depression, rage, jealousy, and hatred. Actually, some might have disagreed on the immediate cause of Philip's abnormal behavior, arguing that he was possessed not by the devil but by a tarantula or a wolf, but they would not have doubted that some form of possession was involved. Similarly, while medieval practitioners might have employed any of a variety of treatments to help Philip overcome his difficulties, from prayers to bitter drinks to whippings, all such treatments would have had the common purpose of driving a foreign spirit from his body. Anyone brazen enough to offer an explanation or treatment outside of the accepted demonological model would have been harshly criticized for failure to appreciate the fundamental issues at stake.

Whereas one model was dominant during the Middle Ages, a variety of models are being employed to explain and treat abnormal functioning today. This state of affairs has resulted from shifts in values and beliefs over the past half century and from improvements in the quality and quantity of clinical research. At one end of the spectrum is the *biological model,* which cites organic processes as the key to human behavior. At the other end is the *sociocultural model,* which scrutinizes the effect of society and culture on individual behavior. In between are four models that focus on more psychological and personal dimensions of human functioning: the *psychodynamic model,* which looks at people's unconscious internal conflicts; the *behavioral model,* which emphasizes ingrained behavior and the ways in which it is learned; the *cognitive model,* which concentrates on the process and content of the thinking that underlies behavior; and the *humanistic-existential model,* which stresses the role of values and choices in determining human individuality and fulfillment.

Rooted as they are in different assumptions and concepts, the models are sometimes in conflict, and proponents of one perspective often scoff at the "naive" interpretations, investigations, and treatment efforts of the rest. At the same time, none of the models is complete in itself; each focuses primarily on one aspect of human functioning, and none is capable of explaining the entire spectrum of abnormality.

# THE BIOLOGICAL MODEL

Philip Berman is a biological being. His thoughts and feelings are the results of complex biochemical and bioelectrical processes throughout his brain and body. Biological theorists believe that a full understanding of his psychological functioning, including any psychological abnormality, must include an understanding of the biological basis of his thoughts, emotions, and behavior. Not surprisingly, they believe that once this understanding is attained, the most effective interventions for problems such as Philip's will be biological ones.

## Origins of the Biological Model

As we saw in Chapter 1, the roots of the biological model of abnormal psychology stretch back thousands of years. A variety of factors combined to enhance its status during the late nineteenth century: the dissemination of Kraepelin's somatogenic theory; research that linked the mental illness called general paresis to an organic illness, syphilis; and several breakthroughs in medical technology. The model's influence has continued to grow throughout the twentieth century and has been especially strong since the 1950s, when researchers learned to refine or synthesize several kinds of effective *psychotropic drugs,* drugs that have their dominant effect on thought processes and in some cases alleviate symptoms of mental dysfunctioning. Antianxiety, antidepressant, antipsychotic, and other psychotropic medications have changed the treatment picture for mentally disturbed persons and are now used frequently, either as an adjunct to other forms of therapy or as the dominant form of treatment for psychological dysfunction.

## Biological Explanations of Abnormal Behavior

Adopting a medical perspective, biological theorists view abnormal behavior as an illness brought about by malfunctioning parts of the organism. Specifically, they point to a malfunctioning brain as the primary cause of abnormal behavior (Rosen, 1991; Rosenzweig & Leiman, 1989; Snyder, 1986). The brain comprises billions of nerve cells, called *neurons,* and thousands of billions of support cells, called *glia.* Within the brain large groups of neurons form anatomically distinct areas, or *brain regions.* These regions may be conceptualized as continents, countries, and states. At the bottom of the brain is the "continent" known as the *hindbrain,* which is in turn composed of countrylike regions called the *medulla, pons,* and *cerebellum* (see Figure 2-1). In the middle of the brain is the "continent" called the *midbrain.* And at the top is the "continent" called the *fore-*

*brain,* which is composed of countrylike regions called the *cerebrum* (the two cerebral hemispheres), the *thalamus,* and the *hypothalamus,* each in turn made up of statelike regions. The cerebrum, for instance, consists of the *cortex* (see Figure 2-2), *corpus callosum, basal ganglia, hippocampus,* and *amygdala.* The neurons in each of these brain regions control important functions. For example, the hippocampus helps regulate emotions, the cerebellum helps coordinate movement, and the hypothalamus helps regulate hunger.

Biological theorists believe that just as lung and kidney disorders result from problems in the cells of those organs, mental disorders are linked to problems in brain-cell functioning. The problems may be *anatomical* (the size or shape of certain brain regions may be abnormal) or *biochemical* (the chemicals that enable neurons to operate may not work properly). Such difficulties may be the result of various factors, such as excessive stress, inherited metabolic disorders, infections, allergies, tumors, inadequate blood supply, and physical trauma (Haroutunian, 1991; Murphy & Deutsch, 1991).

Using a variety of neurological tests, clinicians have discovered unambiguous connections between a number of mental disorders and specific problems in the

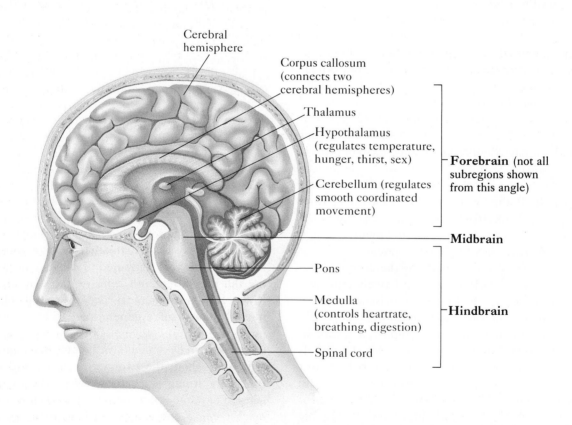

**FIGURE 2-1** Many of the regions of the human brain can be seen in a side view of the brain sliced down the center. Each region, composed of numerous neurons, is responsible for certain functions.

brain. For example, Huntington's chorea, a degenerative disease marked by violent emotional outbursts, delusions (that is, false and absurd beliefs that are firmly held), suicidal thinking, and involuntary body movements, has been traced to a loss of neurons in the brain area called the basal ganglia. Mental disorders that have such clear physical causes are called *organic mental disorders* (this group of mental disorders is discussed in Chapters 19 and 20).

Clinicians have traditionally distinguished organic mental disorders from *functional mental disorders,* abnormal behavior patterns without clear links to physical abnormalities in the brain. Proponents of the biological model, however, hold that many so-called functional disorders, including anxiety disorders, depression, and schizophrenia (examined in Chapters 6, 8, and 15, respectively), are also related to physical dysfunctions in the brain. They have taken this position mainly as a result of insights gained from the study of the psychotropic medications (Snyder, 1989, 1986). By studying where these drugs go and what they do in the brain, biological researchers have learned much about the mental disorders they alleviate (Hollister & Csernansky, 1990). They have learned, for example, that mental disorders are often related to subtle dysfunctioning in the transmission of brain messages from neuron to neuron.

Information spreads throughout the brain in the form of electrical impulses that travel from one neuron to one

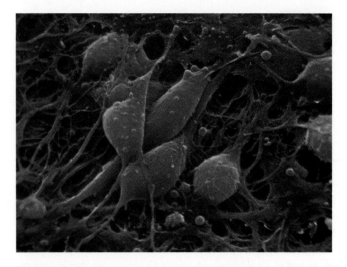

State-of-the-art electron microscopes and color-enhancement techniques produce remarkable close-up photographs of neurons and highlight the complex network of cell bodies, axons, and dendrites that make up the brain.

or more other neurons. An impulse is received by a neuron's *dendrites,* extensions (or antennae) located at one end of the neuron; travels down the neuron's *axon,* a long fiber; and is transmitted to other neurons through the *nerve endings* at the axon's terminus (see Figure 2-3). An important question is how messages get from the nerve endings of one neuron to the dendrites of another neuron. After all, the neurons do not actually touch each other. A tiny space, called the *synapse,* separates one neuron from the next, and the message must somehow move across that space. When an electrical impulse reaches a neuron's ending, apparently the nerve ending is stimulated to release a chemical, called a *neurotransmitter,* that travels across the synaptic space to receptors on the dendrites of the adjacent neurons (see Figure 2-4). The neurotransmitter in turn leads the receiving neurons either to generate another electrical impulse ("firing" or "triggering") or to cease firing, depending on the neurotransmitter involved. Obviously, neurotransmitters play a key role in moving information through the brain (Kanof, 1991).

Researchers have learned that there are various kinds of neurotransmitters in the brain, and that each neuron uses only one kind. Neurological studies indicate that abnormalities in the activity of different neurotransmitters can cause different mental disorders (Iversen, 1989). Anxiety disorders, for example, have been linked to insufficient activity of the neurotransmitter gamma aminobutyric acid, or *GABA* (Murphy & Handelsman, 1991; Costa, 1986, 1983; Braestrup et al., 1982), schizophrenia to excessive activity of the neu-

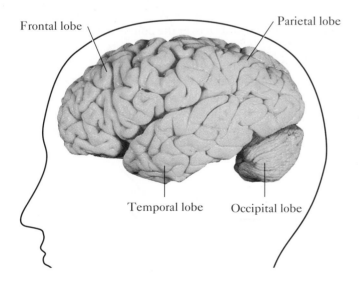

**FIGURE 2-2** Researchers have estimated that the *cortex*, the gray outer layer of the cerebrum, contains at least 70 percent of all the neurons in the central nervous system and is responsible for the highest levels of cognitive and perceptual analysis, including reasoning, speaking, reading, hearing, and seeing. Anatomists separate the cortex of each hemisphere into four regions called *lobes.*

Frontal lobe

Parietal lobe

Temporal lobe

Occipital lobe

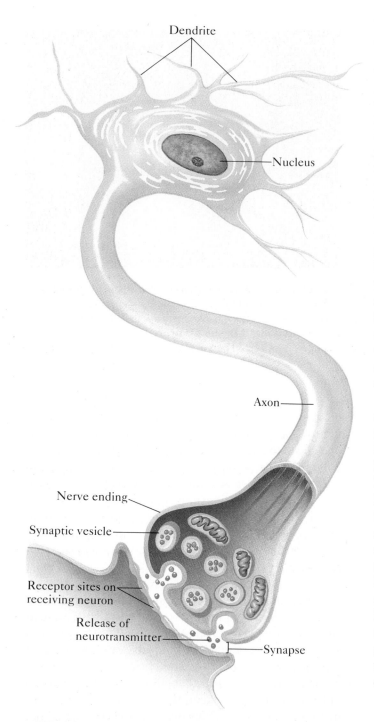

Dendrite

Nucleus

Axon

Nerve ending

Synaptic vesicle

Receptor sites on receiving neuron

Release of neurotransmitter

Synapse

**FIGURE 2-3** A typical neuron. A message travels down the neuron's axon to the nerve ending, where neurotransmitters carry the message across the synaptic space to a receiving neuron. *(Adapted from Bloom et al., 1985, p. 35.)*

rotransmitter *dopamine* (Davis & Greenwald, 1991; Snyder, 1986, 1981; Angrist et al., 1974), and depression to low activity of the neurotransmitters *norepinephrine* and *serotonin* (Siever, Davis, & Gorman, 1991; Schildkraut, 1965). Indeed, biological theorists would

probably point to deficient norepinephrine and serotonin activity to account for Philip Berman's pattern of depression and rage.

Biological researchers also have examined the frequencies with which mental disorders occur among biological relatives. In *family-pedigree studies,* researchers look to see how many members of a given family have a particular disorder. If the disorder occurs with greater frequency in the family than in the general population, perhaps some family members are inheriting a genetic predisposition to the disorder. Several such studies have traced unusually high rates of depression, for example, through several generations (Bloom, Lazerson, & Hofstadter, 1985). In *risk studies,* researchers survey the biological relatives of a patient who has been diagnosed with a specific psychological abnormality to see how many and which of them have the same disorder Sameroff & Seifer, 1990). Many of these studies have similarly demonstrated that the risk of developing severe depression increases directly with the closeness of one's biological relationship to someone with that disorder (Gottesman, 1991; Gottesman & Shields, 1976).

Given their orientation, practitioners of the biological school look for certain kinds of clues when they search for the cause of a particular person's abnormal behavior. Does the family have a history of that behavior, and hence a possible genetic predisposition to it? (Philip Berman's case history mentions that his mother was once hospitalized for depression.) Does the disorder seem to be related to a past illness or accident, or to follow its own course, irrespective of situational changes? (Philip's depressed feelings were described as periodic; they seemed to come and go over the course of several years.) Is the behavior exacerbated by events that could be construed as having a physiological effect? (Philip was having a drink when he flew into a jealous rage at the restaurant.) Once these practitioners have pinpointed particular areas of presumed organic dysfunctioning, they are in a better position to choose a course of biological treatment.

## Assessing the Biological Model

Today the biological model enjoys considerable prestige in the clinical field, and investigations into the biological underpinnings of abnormal functioning are proliferating. The new medications that are constantly being developed have themselves become important research tools. Most major new psychotropic drugs are discovered through a serendipitous chain of events, but once researchers know that a particular drug alleviates a particular mental disorder, they start investigating the drug's biochemical action in the body in the hope of discovering clues to possible biological causes of the disorder (Iversen, 1989).

The biological model of abnormal functioning has many virtues. First, it serves to remind us that psychological processes, however complex and subtle, have biological causes worthy of examination and study. Sec-

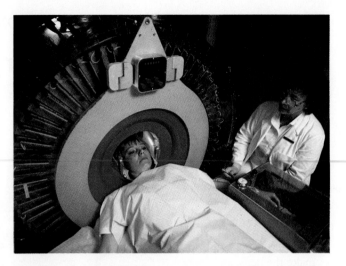

Elaborate biological tests such as positron emission tomography (PET) are often administered to help detect abnormalities that may be causing psychological problems. A PET scan produces moving pictures of metabolic activity at sites throughout the brain, thus revealing problems in *functioning* as opposed to *anatomy*.

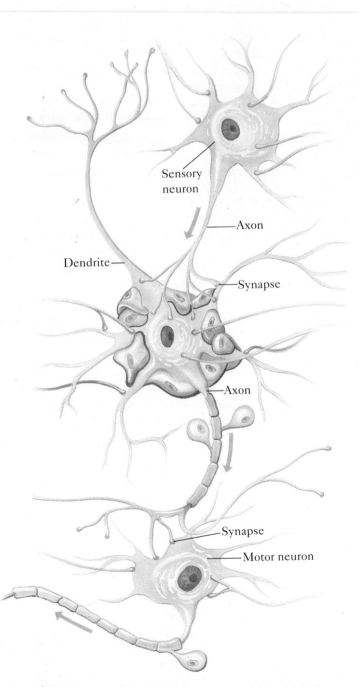

**FIGURE 2-4** A neural circuit. A large neuron with multiple dendrites receives a synaptic contact from another neuron *(top)* and sends the message to a third neuron *(bottom)*. *(Adapted from Bloom et al., 1985, p. 31.)*

ond, thanks to sophisticated procedures developed over centuries of experimentation, research into the biological aspects of abnormal functioning often progresses rapidly, producing valuable new information in a relatively short time. Finally, biological treatments have often been known to afford significant help and relief for abnormal functioning after other interventions have failed. This kind of effectiveness is most welcome in a world where psychological disturbances are so prevalent and often so resistant to change.

At the same time, the biological model has characteristic limitations and problems. Some of its proponents seem to expect that all human behavior can be explained in biological terms and treated with biological methods. This narrow view can limit rather than enhance our understanding of abnormal functioning. Although biological processes certainly do affect our behavior, thoughts, and emotions, they are just as certainly affected by our behavior, thoughts, and emotions. When we perceive the negative events in our lives to be beyond our control, for example, the activity of norepinephrine or serotonin in our brains usually drops off, thus intensifying a depressive reaction. Our mental life is an interplay of biological and nonbiological factors, and it is important to explore that interplay rather than to focus exclusively on biological variables.

A second problem is that the evidence for biological explanations is often incomplete or inconclusive. Many neurological studies, for example, must be conducted on

## BOX 2-1

# Whose Memory Is It, Anyway?

**M**y earliest memory . . . my earliest memory . . . I know—I was in the kitchen, and some cookies were in the oven. Alice had gone off to make the beds, and I was waiting for her to finish so I could have some milk and warm cookies. They smelled so good, I can almost smell them now. I must have been 3 or 4 years old, and my parents had told me not to touch the hot stove, but I guess I didn't think that meant the oven, too. So I went over and looked through the glass oven door, and saw that one of the cookies looked like it was ready. I opened the door, reached down, and tried to take one off of the hot tray. It was so hot that when I touched it, I pulled my hand back so fast that I hit the top of the inside of the oven, and that's when I really hurt myself. The next thing I know, Alice is running into the room and going to the refrigerator for butter for the burn, and at the same time Marcia and Greg get home from school and my parents walk in and . . . Wait a minute, this isn't my family, these are the Bradys! This isn't my memory—it's an old *Brady Bunch* episode!

We are all notoriously bad at recalling very early experiences in our lives. Most early childhood memories are fragmented images or brief scenes, rarely the comprehensive, detailed recollections that we have of events during our later childhood and adult years. Interestingly, our early memories are usually of trauma or trivia rather than such major events as birth, our first step, or our first words. Memories seem to begin to be recorded and retrievable from about the fourth year. For events that occurred before that, we all seem to suffer some sort of amnesia.

Take a minute right now to think of your earliest memory. It is most likely of a single event that you have accepted over the years as a firsthand recollection of your childhood. Maybe it was the time your parents brought you home a special toy, or the time your brother pushed you out of the treehouse, or something as trivial as

---

animals in whom apparent symptoms of depression, anxiety, or some other abnormality have been induced by drugs, surgery, or behavioral manipulation. Researchers can never be certain that these animals are experiencing the human disorder under investigation and therefore cannot be certain that the biological insights derived from such studies are relevant. Similarly, the human genetic and genealogical studies often cited in support of biological explanations are open to alternative interpretations. Evidence that close relatives are more likely to develop certain disorders than more distant relatives may simply mean that close relatives are more likely to have the same harmful "psychological" experiences. Perhaps a given pair of siblings under study have been traumatized by the loss of the same loved one, or have together been exposed to an extraordinarily frightening situation as children. Indeed, the first of the psychological models that we shall examine, the psycho-

dynamic model, places primary emphasis on the psychological effects of early childhood experiences.

## THE PSYCHODYNAMIC MODEL

We have seen how the biological theorists view Philip Berman: as a biological being. He is also a *psychological* being, interpreting, creating, feeling, initiating, and interacting. Several currently influential models of abnormal behavior focus on these and other psychological dimensions of human functioning. The oldest and most famous is the psychodynamic model.

Like biological theorists, psychodynamic theorists adopt a medical perspective and view abnormal behavior as an illness brought about by malfunctioning parts of

your favorite plaid dress. The strength of the memory convinces you that it is real, and it has the *feel* of remembering, but there is a strong possibility that you have reconstructed the event from descriptions and information given by parents and family.

As time passes, memories fade. One study found that subjects had very good memory for events in the past year; their ability to locate in time events that occurred from two to six years earlier declined 6 percent, and it continued to decline as events receded in the past (Linton, 1979). This finding does not fully explain, though, the almost complete lack of memories of the events of our earliest years. In this respect we should distinguish between the events themselves and the things we learned from them (Cutts & Ceci, 1989; Neisser, 1978). Certainly we do not forget how to walk, or the words that we learned to speak and understand during our earliest years. Childhood amnesia applies only to autobiographical memory, perhaps because it is not until the early school years that our lives have an organized structure. Without the kind of knowledge about the world that allows us to classify and organize our experiences, they are just a string of unrelated happenings. Structure gives us hooks on which to hang our memo-

ries, so that we can recall them later.

First memories may actually be the key to our present sense of self and are therefore of central importance to psychotherapies that are based on dialogue and discussion (Cutts & Ceci, 1989). Freud believed that our early memories open the secret chambers of our lives. Alfred Adler (1927) insisted that the content of the earliest memory is related to one's self-style and is therefore molded to meet one's sense of self (Adcock & Ross, 1983). He contended that these memories are critical to the diagnostic process whether they are real or not, because they reveal people's attitudes toward themselves, others, and life in general. Research has shown that people reconstruct autobiographical events in accord with their self-theories about how they are most likely to act (Barclay, 1981). People will give plausible, consistent accounts of their intentions and actions during very early experiences, but these accounts reflect their *present* beliefs about their personalities and themselves. Clinicians today continue to turn to a client's earliest memories as a way to learn more about their views of themselves and the world around them.

Even children experience childhood amnesia. A "childhood early memory scoring system" has been de-

vised to help identify and diagnose childhood psychopathologies (Last & Bruhn, 1985). Appropriately, it is less interested in accuracy than in the type and qualities of the memories.

Back to the "memory" that opened this discussion—how might this apparent mixup be explained? One possibility is that our society's heavy reliance on television has made the tube a surrogate for real life, taking it beyond entertainment and confusing our sense of actual versus vicarious experience.

A second explanation is that the scene represents a self-view consistent with that of the person claiming the memory. Perhaps he sees himself as having been an adventurous child with a loving family (and maid) who lived an ideal life in a model suburb; at the same time, the trauma of the remembered event and his disobedience could be cues to a therapist about aspects of his personality that require further exploration. In either case, early childhood memories, whether real or constructed, are fertile ground for the therapist who wants to understand and diagnose the client seeking help. Of course, there is always the possibility that somewhere, in a split-level house with six bikes in the driveway, a man named Brady who had three boys of his own . . .

the organism. But psychodynamic theorists point to psychological rather than to organic parts as the primary culprit. They believe that a person's behavior, whether normal or abnormal, is determined to a large extent by underlying psychological forces of which the person is unaware. These forces are considered *dynamic*—that is, they interact with one another; and their interaction in turn gives shape to an individual's behavior, thoughts, and emotions.

Psychodynamic theorists would view Philip Berman as a person in conflict, a person whose underlying needs and motives are in a state of disharmony. They would want to explore his past because, in their view, people's psychological conflicts are related to their early relationships with their parents and to traumatic experiences during their formative years (see Box 2-1). Thus Philip's hatred for his mother, his recollections of her as cruel and overbearing, the weakness and ineffectuality of his fa-

ther, and the birth of a younger brother when Philip was 10 may all be relevant issues.

## Origins of the Psychodynamic Model

The psychodynamic model was first formulated by the Viennese neurologist Sigmund Freud (1856–1939) at the turn of the century. As we saw in Chapter 1, Freud became so interested in the use of hypnosis to treat hysterical illnesses—mysterious physical ailments with no apparent medical cause—that in 1885 he went to Paris to study hypnosis under the famous neurologist Jean Charcot. After returning to Vienna, he worked with Josef Breuer (1842–1925), a physician who had been conducting experiments on hypnosis and hysteria.

In a famous case, Breuer had treated a woman he called "Anna O.," whose extensive hysterical symptoms included paralysis of the legs and right arm, deafness, and disorganized speech. Breuer placed the woman under hypnosis, expecting that suggestions made to her in that state would help rid her of her hysterical symptoms. While she was under hypnosis, however, she began to talk about traumatic past events and to express deeply felt emotions. This venting of repressed memories seemed to enhance the effectiveness of the treatment. Anna O. referred to it as her "talking cure"; Breuer called it the "cathartic method" (borrowing the term from the Greek *katharsis,* purgation).

Breuer and his new colleague collaborated on a number of case studies in the 1890s and together published an important paper and book on this treatment technique *(Studies in Hysteria).* They proposed that hysterical illnesses were caused by psychological conflicts, principally sexual in origin, of which the patient was not consciously aware, and that these conflicts would exert less negative influence after they had been brought into consciousness by hypnosis and the cathartic method.

Over the course of the next several decades, Freud developed and expanded these ideas into a general theory of *psychoanalysis.* He proposed that "unconscious" conflicts account not just for hysterical illnesses but for all forms of normal and abnormal psychological functioning. Freud also formulated a corresponding method of treatment (which we shall explore in Chapter 5). He came to believe that hypnosis was not necessary to cure psychopathologies and developed instead a conversational approach in which patients would explore their unconscious with a psychoanalyst and come to terms with the conflicts they discovered there.

In 1909 Freud came to the United States to present a series of lectures at Clark University in Worcester, Massachusetts. These "Introductory Lectures on Psychoanalysis" brought his theory to the attention of the American psychological community. Over the next few years, Freud and several of his colleagues in the Vienna Psychoanalytic Society—including Carl Gustav Jung (1875–1961) and Alfred Adler (1870–1937)—became the most influential clinical theorists in the Western world. Freud's twenty-four volumes on psychoanalytic theory and treatment are still widely studied today.

## Freudian Explanations of Normal and Abnormal Functioning

As Freud studied the lives and problems of his patients, he came to believe that three central forces shape or "constitute" the personality—instinctual needs, rational thinking, and moral standards. All these forces, he believed, operate at the *unconscious* level, unavailable to

There are no verbal accidents, according to Freud. Apparent "slips of the tongue" actually reflect unconscious feelings or wishes seeking expression.

immediate, cognizant awareness; and he believed them to be dynamic, or interactive, components whose jostling for expression molds the person's behavior, feelings, and thoughts. Freud called these three forces the id, ego, and superego.

**The Id**    Freud used the term "id" to denote the instinctual needs, drives, and impulses. He believed that people are motivated primarily by the id, which he described as "a cauldron of seething excitement" (Freud, 1933, pp. 103–104).

The id operates in accordance with the *pleasure principle;* that is, it always seeks gratification. One source of id gratification is direct, or *reflex,* activity, as when an infant seeks and receives milk from the mother's breast to satisfy its hunger. Another source, *primary process thinking,* consists of activation of a memory or image of the desired object. When a hungry child's mother is not available, for example, the child may imagine her breast. Such imaginings are at least partially satisfying because the id cannot distinguish between objective and subjective realities. Gratification of id instincts by primary process thinking is called *wish fulfillment.*

Freud also believed that all id instincts tend to be sexual, noting that from the very earliest stages of development a child's gratification has sexual dimensions, as much of its pleasure is derived from nursing, defecating, and masturbating. Freud created the concept of *libido* to represent the sexual energy that fuels not only the id but the other forces of personality as well.

**The Ego** During our early years we come to recognize that our environment will not meet every instinctual need. Our mother, for example, is not always available to provide nurturance at our bidding; and later she may punish us for doing in our pants what she wants us to do in the toilet. Indeed, we may become anxious when we experience many of our instinctual needs. Thus a part of the id becomes differentiated into a separate force called the ego. Like the id, the ego unconsciously seeks gratification, but it does so in accordance with the *reality principle,* the knowledge we acquire through experience and from the people around us that it can be dangerous or unacceptable to express our id impulses outright. The ego, employing reason and deliberation, guides us to recognize when we can and cannot express those impulses without negative consequences. The ego's mode of operation, called *secondary process,* is to assess new situations, weigh in past experiences, anticipate consequences, and plan how best to obtain gratification.

The ego develops basic strategies, called *ego defense mechanisms,* to control unacceptable id impulses and avoid or reduce the anxiety they arouse. The most basic defense mechanism, *repression,* prevents unacceptable impulses from ever reaching consciousness. Another defense mechanism is *displacement.* If it is dangerous for us to express an id impulse (sexual desire, say) toward one person, the ego may channel the impulse toward another, safer person. This defense also takes place at an unconscious level. There are many other ego defense mechanisms, and each of us tends to favor some over others.

**The Superego** The superego grows from the ego, just as the ego grows out of the id. As we learn from our parents that many of our id impulses are unacceptable, we unconsciously incorporate, or *introject,* our parents' values. We identify with our parents and judge ourselves by their standards. When we uphold their values, we feel good; when we go against them, we feel guilty.

The superego has two components, the conscience and the ego ideal. The *conscience* is always reminding us that certain behavior, feelings, or thoughts are good or bad, right or wrong. The *ego ideal* is a composite image of the values we have acquired, the kind of person we believe we should strive to become. Parents are usually the chief source of this ideal when children are young, but as children grow older they may come to identify with other people, too; then those people's values become incorporated in the ego ideal.

According to Freud, these three parts of the personality are often in conflict, so that we often seem impelled to act, think, and feel in contradictory ways. A healthy personality is one in which an effective working relationship, a stable and acceptable compromise, has been established among the three forces. If the id, ego, and superego are in excessive conflict, the person's behavior may show signs of dysfunction. Freudians would therefore view Philip Berman as someone whose personality forces have a poor working relationship. His rational, constructive ego is unable to control his id impulses, which lead him repeatedly to act in impulsive and often dangerous ways—suicide gestures, jealous rages, job resignations, outbursts of temper, frequent arguments. At the same time, his superego seems to be poorly formulated and largely ineffective. Having had weak and ineffectual parental models, Philip never incorporated an effective set of values, a positive ego ideal that might have helped to channel and guide his id impulses.

**Developmental Stages** Freud proposed that the forces of personality are called to action throughout one's development, beginning in early infancy. At each developmental stage the child is confronted with events and pressures that challenge and perhaps threaten his or her habitual way of doing things. Such clashes require adjustments in the id, ego, and superego. If the adjustments are successful, they foster personal growth.

New environmental demands are always unpleasant for growing children, and some can be so traumatic that instead of promoting a child's development, they tend to stifle it. Under certain pressures, the id, ego, and superego may not mature properly or interact effectively, and the child becomes *fixated,* or entrapped, at an early stage of development. Then all subsequent development suffers, and the child may well be headed for abnormal functioning in the future. Because parents provide the primary environmental input during the early years of life, they are often seen as the cause of this improper development.

Freud (1905) distinguished most stages of normal development by the body area, or *erogenous zone,* that he considered representative of the child's sexual drives and conflicts at that time. He called these phases the oral, anal, phallic, latency, and genital stages.

*Oral Stage* The earliest developmental stage, embracing the first 18 months of life, is called the *oral stage* because the infant's main libidinal gratification comes from feeding and from the body parts involved in it—the mouth, lips, and tongue. To be held and fed at the mother's breast or from a bottle with a nipple is very pleasant and relaxing. The sucking and biting associated with drinking enable the child to gratify the oral drives.

At the beginning of the oral stage, the child is totally narcissistic—focused solely on its own needs, with no

Freud believed people may become excessively dependent on others if their oral needs are not adequately met during the first year of life. They may seek to gratify their lingering oral needs for years by such forms of oral expression as thumb sucking.

recognition of an outside world. Gradually, however, the child comes to perceive the mother and other people as *objects* rather than as extensions of itself and begins to appreciate them as separate sources of sustenance, gratification, and protection. A maturing child is increasingly able to identify, need, want, and love such objects. The most significant threat to children during the oral stage is the possibility that the mother who feeds and comforts them will disappear — that is, the risk of *object loss.* Recognition of this possibility makes the child anxious and triggers ego defense mechanisms into action to reduce the anxiety.

If, however, mothers consistently fail to gratify the oral needs of their children, the defense mechanisms they have developed will not be sufficient to reduce their anxiety. These children may become fixated at the oral stage, unable to grow beyond their oral needs, to develop a genuine sense of independence and self-confidence, and to establish appropriate object relations. They may be particularly prone to develop certain forms of abnor-

mal functioning, and their personalities and behavior may display an "oral character" throughout their lives.

According to Freud, people with oral characters have difficulties with issues such as independence and dependence, patience and impatience, giving and taking, and optimism and pessimism (Fisher & Greenberg, 1977). Some display extreme dependence, helplessness, and passivity. Others energetically resist their lingering oral needs, on the surface at least, and display extreme independence or cynicism, and still others strive to gratify their needs with such oral activities as thumb sucking, pencil chewing, constant talking, or overindulgence in eating, smoking, and drinking.

*Anal Stage*  During the second 18 months of life, the *anal stage,* the child's focus of pleasure shifts to the anus. Libidinal gratification comes from retaining and passing feces. The child becomes very interested in this bodily function and in smelling, touching, and playing with feces. Indeed, to the child they are valuable possessions.

Parents, of course, view feces quite differently and try to toilet train the child during this period. They try to teach the child to give up this possession and to do so in a prescribed place and in a hygienic manner. Parents who use disapproval and withdrawal of love as tools in this endeavor may inadvertently cause the child to feel great shame and to lose self-esteem.

If parental toilet-training techniques are too severe, an anal fixation may result, and the child may develop into an adult with an "anal character" and be prone to various kinds of psychological abnormalities. Anal people may be stubborn, contrary, stingy, or overcontrolling, qualities that originally helped them assert their anal wishes against their harsh and demanding parents. Some behave in a so-called passive-aggressive manner, expressing their anger in "retentive" ways — by habitually withholding enthusiasm, for example, and arriving late for appointments or forgetting them altogether. Others repress their anal desire to be messy and rebellious and instead, using the defense mechanism of *reaction formation,* develop opposite personality traits: they become orderly, meticulous, punctual, and hateful of waste — a style referred to as obsessive-compulsive.

*Phallic Stage*  During the *phallic stage,* between the third and fourth years, the focus of sexual pleasure shifts to the genitals — the penis for boys and the clitoris for girls. Boys become attracted to their mother as a fully separate object, a sexual object, and see their father as a rival they would like to push aside. This pattern of desires is called the *Oedipus complex,* after Oedipus, a character in a Greek tragedy who unknowingly kills his father and marries his mother.

At the same time, boys fear retaliation and punishment from their father for their forbidden sexual and aggressive impulses. According to Freud, most boys fantasize that their punishment will take the form of injury to their genitals. Specifically, they fear castration. To eliminate this fear, they repress their sexual desire for their mother and *identify* with their father. That is, they aspire to be like him in behavior, values, and sexual orientation.

The phallic conflict for girls is somewhat different. During this stage, girls become aware that they do not have a penis—an organ that, according to Freud, they value and desire. They develop a sexual attraction for their father, rooted in the fantasy that by seducing him they can have a penis. Later they even fantasize having his baby, which, according to Freud, unconsciously represents a penis. This pattern of desires in girls is called the *Electra complex,* after Electra, a character in another Greek tragedy who conspired to kill her mother to avenge her father's death. Girls, like boys, fear their phallic impulses. They fear that their wishes will cause their mother to stop loving them or to hurt them. Thus they too repress their desires and come to identify with their mother. The primary yearning for a penis attributed to girls during the phallic stage—*penis envy*—has become one of the most controversial concepts in Freudian theory.

It is important that children resolve the Oedipus and Electra conflicts by coming to identify with the parent of their own sex. If they are punished too harshly for sexual behavior during this stage, or if they are subtly encouraged to pursue their desire for the parent of the opposite sex, their sexual development may suffer. As Freud saw it, they might later develop a sexual orientation different from the norm, fear sexual intimacy, be overly seductive, or have other difficulties in romantic relationships.

When children identify with the parent of the same sex during the phallic stage, they particularly identify with that parent's moral standards. Thus it is during this stage that the superego is formulated. The superego can be a constructive or a destructive force. It may generate self-praise, self-affection, and high esteem; or it may call for self-condemnation, self-punishment, and reparation. Children who become fixated at the phallic stage may suffer pervasive feelings of guilt throughout their lives.

**Latency Stage** At 6 years of age children enter the *latency stage,* in which their sexual desires apparently subside and their libidinal energy is devoted to developing new interests, activities, and skills. They seek friends of the same sex, express dislike for the opposite sex, and are embarrassed by sexual displays. The broader process of socialization, of learning one's roles in family and society, takes place at this time.

**Genital Stage** At approximately the age of 12, with the onset of puberty and adolescence, the child's sexual

The psychoanalytic notion of the Electra complex holds that 4-year-old girls repress threatening desires for their fathers and identify with their mothers, trying to emulate them by dressing, acting, and talking as their mothers do. The behavioral notion of modeling also holds that children often imitate others, but behaviorists do not limit models to parents and do not see imitation as a defensive strategy.

urges emerge once again. Now, in what is termed the *genital stage,* sexual pleasure begins to be found in heterosexual relationships. Initially, adolescents are not fully capable of the genuine affection and caring for others that are required in such relationships. They still have many of the narcissistic qualities of earlier stages of development and have yet to outgrow the earlier conflicts. During the genital stage, however, they make more mature efforts in these areas, and in the normal course of events learn to participate fully in affectionate and altruistic relationships.

The genital stage establishes the foundation for effective adult functioning. Adolescents learn to cope with their major psychosexual conflicts and solidify their sexual roles and social identity. At the same time, they invest a lot of energy in the development of vocational interests and abilities. In psychodynamic terms, they have **sublimated,** or rechanneled, their narcissistic impulses into endeavors that are both socially acceptable and personally gratifying. The genital stage ends when sexual, social, and vocational maturity is achieved.

## Other Psychodynamic Explanations

Personal and professional differences between Freud and his colleagues led to a split in the Vienna Psychoanalytic Society early in this century. Carl Jung, Alfred Adler, and others left to develop new theories, many of which perpetuated Freud's basic belief that all human functioning is shaped by dynamic (interacting) psychological forces, though they departed from his model in other respects. Accordingly, all such theories, including Freud's psychoanalytic theory, are referred to as *psychodynamic* (see Box 2-2).

## Assessing the Psychodynamic Model

Freud and his many followers have had a most significant impact on the ways abnormal functioning is understood and treated (Joseph, 1991). Their theories of personality and abnormality are eloquent and comprehensive. Largely because of their groundwork, a wide range of theorists today look for answers and explanations outside the confines of biological processes, focusing instead on less tangible concepts — underlying conflicts, learned habits, cognitive processes, human values. In addition, the techniques of psychotherapy developed by Freud and his followers have demonstrated the potential of psychological treatments and have led to the development of many more such approaches.

Psychodynamic theorists have also helped us to understand that abnormal functioning may be rooted in the same processes that underlie normal functioning (Brenner, 1989). Psychological conflict, for example, is a universal experience; it leads to abnormal functioning, the psychodynamic theorists say, only if the conflict becomes excessive. This notion argues for a humane and respectful attitude toward people deemed to be mentally ill.

At the same time, the psychodynamic model has shortcomings and limitations. First, its concepts can be difficult to define and to research (Erdelyi, 1985). Because processes such as id drives, ego defenses, and fixation are abstract entities and supposedly operate at an unconscious level, it is often impossible to determine if they are occurring. Not surprisingly, then, psychodynamic explanations have received little research support and psychodynamic theorists have been forced to rely largely on individual case studies to support their theories. And though case studies are useful in many ways, they do not provide compelling evidence in support of theoretical explanations.

Another problem is that psychodynamic explanations often fail to establish clear guidelines for predicting abnormality (Edelson, 1985). It is a widely accepted psychodynamic principle, for example, that oral fixation is caused by either insufficient or excessive gratification of needs during the first year of life, yet psychodynamic theorists rarely specify how much or what kind of gratification is in fact insufficient or excessive. Without such guidelines, we cannot effectively predict who is likely to become orally fixated.

Partly in response to these problems, other psychological models have emerged over the past several decades — the behavioral, cognitive, and humanistic-existential models. Although these newer explanations and corresponding treatments often differ significantly from the psychodynamic perspective, they all have roots in the psychodynamic model (see Box 2-3). Because so many of the people who developed these models were trained in the psychodynamic tradition, certain psychodynamiclike notions have often been retained in the new models (Garfield & Bergin, 1986). Moreover, it is important to recognize that despite the significant growth of alternative psychological models, the psychodynamic perspective continues to be one of the most widely applied models in the clinical field today (Smith, 1982).

## THE BEHAVIORAL MODEL

Like psychodynamic theorists, behavioral theorists hold a deterministic view of human functioning: they believe that our actions are largely determined by our experiences in life. The psychological dimensions on which behavioral theorists focus, however, are quite different from those the psychodynamic theorists favor. They concentrate on specific *behaviors,* the responses that an organism makes to the stimuli in its environment, and on the *principles of learning,* the processes by which behaviors change in response to the environment. In the behavioral view, people are the sum total of their learned behaviors — both external (going to work, say) and internal (having a feeling or thought).

Many learned behaviors are constructive and adaptive, helping people to cope with daily challenges and to lead happy, productive lives. However, abnormal and undesirable behaviors also can be learned. According to the behavioral model, these behaviors are acquired by the same principles of learning as adaptive behaviors. Thus behavioral theorists reject the medical illness perspective adopted by biological and psychodynamic theorists.

Behaviorists who tried to explain Philip Berman's problems would concentrate on his inappropriate behaviors and on the principles of learning by which those behaviors have been acquired. They might view him as a man who has received improper training in life. He has learned behaviors that alienate and antagonize others, behaviors that repeatedly work against him. He does not know how to engage other people, express his emotions constructively, or enjoy himself.

## Origins of the Behavioral Model

The behavioral model was the first clinical perspective to be developed in psychological laboratories. Whereas the biological model grew from medical and biological research and the psychodynamic model had its origins in neurological research and in the clinical work of physicians, the behavioral model was conceived in laboratories run by psychologists who were conducting experiments on *conditioning,* simple forms of learning in which scientists manipulate stimuli and rewards and observe how the responses of experimental subjects are affected.

Since the turn of the century, conditioning has been one of experimental psychology's chief areas of study. The work of eminent conditioning theorists such as Ivan Pavlov (1849–1936), John Watson (1878–1958), Edward Thorndike (1874–1949), Edwin Guthrie (1886–1959), B. F. Skinner (1904–1990), and Neal Miller (b. 1909) has elucidated three principles of conditioning: *classical* (or *respondent*) *conditioning,* operant (or *instrumental*) *conditioning,* and *modeling.*

Efforts to modify abnormal behaviors by means of conditioning were made as early as the 1920s (Jones, 1924). Not until decades later, however, were these principles applied in clinical practice. During the 1950s, many clinicians were growing disenchanted with what they viewed as the vagueness, slowness, and imprecision of the psychodynamic model. Looking for an alternative approach, some of them began to apply the principles of conditioning to the study and treatment of psychological problems (Wolpe, 1987). These efforts gave rise to the behavioral model of psychopathology.

## Classical Conditioning and Explanations of Abnormal Behavior

*Classical conditioning* is a process of learning by *temporal association.* Theoretically, two events that repeatedly occur close together in time become fused in a person's mind, and before long the person responds in the same way to both events. If one event elicits a response of joy, the other brings joy as well; if one event brings feelings of relief, so does the other.

The early animal studies of Ivan Pavlov (1849–1936), the Russian physiologist who first demonstrated classical conditioning, illustrate this process. Pavlov placed a bowl of meat powder before a dog, eliciting the innate response that all dogs have to meat: they start to salivate (see Figure 2-5). Next Pavlov inserted an additional step: just before presenting the dog with meat powder, he sounded a metronome. After several such

**FIGURE 2-5** In Ivan Pavlov's experimental device, the dog's salivation was collected in a tube as it was secreted, and the amount was recorded on a revolving cylinder called a kymograph. The experimenter observed the dog through a one-way glass window.

The initial interest of Pavlov, a physiologist, was the digestive system, and he used surgery and other techniques to study it. Pavlov accidentally discovered classical conditioning, the learning process by which an organism comes to respond to one stimulus just as it automatically responds to another stimulus, after the two stimuli have repeatedly been paired.

BOX 2-2

# Freud's Followers: Alternative Psychodynamic Views

The perspectives of the post-Freudian theorists differ from the classical Freudian approach in three primary ways: the post-Freudians (1) emphasize ego rather than id functions, (2) stress the psychosocial over the psychosexual factors influencing behavior, and (3) consider the critical period of development to extend beyond the first few years of childhood.

### THE NEO-FREUDIANS

*Carl Gustav Jung* (1875–1965) rejected Freud's emphasis on sexual drives. Freud erred, he believed, in seeing the libido as simply the repository of sexual energy; for Jung it was a broader and more spiritual force, just as the unconscious had creative functions that Freud failed to recognize. Jung believed that each of us inherits a collective unconscious, a set of archetypes (symbols or innate ideas) that provide a foundation for our creative endeavors. These symbols are shared by all humankind and represent the human experience over time. Jung also differed from Freud in the focus and methodologies of his therapy. He saw therapy as a way to integrate opposing tendencies in the personality, particularly the masculine and feminine traits found in each of us. Jung's goal of spiritual and psychological growth paved the way for the humanistic therapies that emerged later.

Alfred Adler

*Alfred Adler* (1870–1937) agreed that Freud overemphasized the role of sexual drives, but for him the primary force that motivates human beings was the drive to dominate others. Adler proposed that every person is born with a sense of inferiority, which he termed the *inferiority complex*. We spend our lives compensating for this sense of inferiority by trying to gain power over others. Adler believed that our struggle to gain power is not antisocial but actually ties us to society in an important and useful way. In his view, psychological functioning depends more on social relationships than on past developmental events. In our struggle to overcome our inferiority complex, we interact with others and develop meaningful, nonselfish relationships. This process enhances our ego strength and permits us to interact with others in positive, mutually beneficial ways. Adler's greater emphasis on the ego set the stage for ego psychology, another psychodynamic perspective.

### EGO PSYCHOLOGISTS

Ego psychologists believe that the ego is a more independent and powerful force than Freud recognized. Rather than growing from the id and serving primarily to redirect id impulses, they contend, the ego grows independently of the id and has autonomous, "conflict-free" functions in addition to its id-related responsibilities. The ego guides memory and perception and strives for mastery and competence independent of the id. Both the conflict-free and conflict-resolving activities of the ego must be considered if psychological functioning is to be explained properly.

Erik Erikson

*Erik Erikson* (b. 1902), for example, believes that a person develops an integrated, unique sense of self, called the *ego identity*, that is a product of psychosocial rather than psychosexual development. He also believes that people change throughout their lives, and he developed a series of psychosocial stages that describe the events that occur at each stage of development. Each stage presents a crisis that challenges the ego. Successful resolution of the crisis brings the person closer to ego identity; failure to resolve the crisis hampers this process

Carl Jung

and may lead to psychological problems. Unlike Freud, Erikson does not conclude that failure at any one stage guarantees a complete arrest in development. The ego is strong enough to overcome many problems. Erikson's eight stages and their primary conflicts are infancy (0 to 1 year of age; trust vs. mistrust), early childhood (1 to 3 years; autonomy vs. shame), play age (3 to 6 years; initiative vs. guilt), school age (7 to 11 years; industry vs. inferiority); adolescence (12 to 20 years; identity vs. identity confusion), young adulthood (20 to 30 years; intimacy vs. isolation), adulthood (30 to 65 years; generativity vs. stagnation), and mature age (65 and older; integrity vs. despair).

## INTERPERSONAL RELATIONSHIP THEORIES

Several psychodynamic theorists center their theories on interpersonal relationships, somewhat in the tradition of Adler. *Harry Stack Sullivan* (1892–1949), a well-known American psychiatrist, believed that emotional problems are generally caused by a fear of human relationships, and that such fears develop out of our earliest interactions with our parents. If parents reject their children, the children develop severe anxieties. They either withdraw from others or develop strongly self-protective behavior. In either case, their fear prevents them from forming close relationships with other people. In therapy, Sullivan focused on interpersonal relationships as the root of most problems, and

Harry Stack Sullivan

he took whatever approach seemed necessary to meet the client's need. He was the first psychodynamic therapist to achieve significant success in the treatment of psychosis.

Both *Karen Horney* (1885–1952) and *Erich Fromm* (1900–1980) proposed that during childhood we develop *basic orientations,* or dispositions, toward other people, which then influence our behavior and interactions as adults. Horney believed that negligent or overprotective parents may induce a "basic anxiety" in a child, so

Karen Horney

that other people are generally seen as hostile. This orientation leads to a strategy for dealing with people based on helplessness, hostility, and isolation. Fromm also viewed social influences, including the earliest interaction with one's parents, as the major determinant of personality. He believed that a person becomes more isolated over time and that the strategies for overcoming isolation determine his or her psychological health.

## SELF THEORY

A recent movement in psychodynamic theory has focused on the role of the *self*—the unified personality that defines one's sense of identity—rather than on the various components of personality, such as the id, ego, and superego. According to the theory of self psychology developed by *Heinz Kohut* (1913–1981), the way a child's personality develops depends on the

Heinz Kohut

support the child receives from the parents. The self has three aspects. The *core self* arises within six months of birth. It consists of the child's dawning awareness that he or she is physically separate from others. This most basic sense of self includes the sense that one may control one's own actions but not the actions of others, the sense that one does not lose one's identity as time passes, and the awareness of one's emotional experiences. The *subjective self* develops during the next two to three months and involves the understanding that other people have experiences and feelings that can be shared. This awareness serves as the basis for human interaction and the building of empathic relationships. Finally, the *verbal self* arises around the fifteenth to eighteenth month and is based on the use of language. The child sees him- or herself as a repository of information that can be communicated through language. Because these three forms of the self are not entirely self-supporting or stable, Kohut proposed that people who encourage the process of unifying these selves are critically important—*self objects.* (An object such as a dog or teddy bear may serve the same purpose.) The development of a self allows us to understand our own experiences and develop systems of values, while a poorly developed self can lead to psychological disorders. The role of therapy, according to self theorists, is to help the client accept and express needs unfulfilled in childhood and so arrive at a unified sense of self.

pairings of metronome tone and presentation of meat powder, Pavlov observed that the dog began to salivate as soon as it heard the metronome. The dog had learned to salivate in response to a sound.

In the vocabulary of classical conditioning, the meat in this demonstration is an *unconditioned stimulus* (US); it elicits the *unconditioned response* (UR) of salivation (that is, a natural response the dog is born with). The sound of the metronome is a *conditioned stimulus* (CS), a previously neutral stimulus that comes to be associated with meat in the dog's mind. As such, it too elicits a salivation response. When the salivation response is elicited by the conditioned stimulus rather than by the unconditioned stimulus, it is called a *conditioned response* (CR).

**Before conditioning**
CS: Tone ⟶ No response
US: Meat ⟶ UR: Salivation

**After conditioning**
CS: Tone ⟶ CR: Salivation
US: Meat ⟶ UR: Salivation

If, after conditioning, the conditioned stimulus is repeatedly presented alone, without being paired with the unconditioned stimulus, it will eventually stop eliciting the conditioned response. When Pavlov stopped pairing the metronome tone and meat powder, for example, the dog salivated less and less in response to the tone. The conditioned response was undergoing *extinction* (see Figure 2-6).

According to behaviorists, many human behaviors are acquired through classical conditioning. The amorous feelings a young man experiences when he smells his girlfriend's perfume, say, may represent a conditioned response. Initially this perfume may have had no emotional effect on him, but because the fragrance was

---

BOX 2-3

# Today's Theorists Evaluate Freud

There is no question that Sigmund Freud's is the best-known name in the clinical field. His theories still pervade popular literature and public consciousness. In 1989, on the fiftieth anniversary of Freud's death, a number of prominent psychologists were asked by the editors of the magazine *Psychology Today* to comment on his contributions and his reputation among today's practitioners. Some of the responses are excerpted here.

**James Hillman,** Jungian analyst and author of *The Myth of Analysis* and *A Blue Fire*

Freud's primary emphasis was on the sexual genital life as crucial to life, the human animal, as an organic-driven creature. Nobody likes that anymore. Freud said that sexual genital life can never be satisfied instinctually. So you're driven and at the same time you cannot be satisfied. That part of Freudian theory hasn't been taken to its fullest consequences. It really locates the human being very deeply in

the body and in animal nature. It ties us to the animal world.

**Stephen M. Sonnenberg,** psychoanalyst and chair of the Committee on Public Information of the American Psychoanalytic Association

What we can still learn from Freud is what we could always learn from

Freud—that most mental activity goes on outside of conscious awareness, that much of the mental pain and anguish that people experience is the result of conflict that is not conscious, and that there is resistance to recognizing that there is unconscious process.

**Alice Miller,** psychologist and author of *For Your Own Good* and *Thou Shalt Not Be Aware*

Do I owe anything to Sigmund Freud, psychoanalyst? Today, I would say: twenty years of blindness toward the reality of child abuse as well as toward the most important facts of my life. In 1896, Sigmund Freud discovered the truth about the repression of childhood traumas and its effects on the adult. Unable to bear his truth, he finally decided to deny his own discovery. One year later, in 1897, he developed the psychoanalytic theory which actually conceals the reality of child abuse and supports the tradition of blaming the child and protecting the parents.

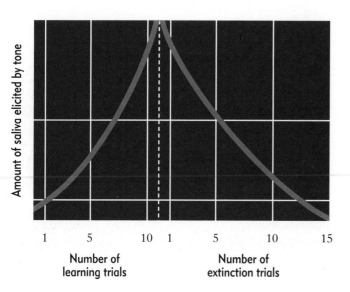

**FIGURE 2-6** Classical conditioning. During learning trials, a stimulus such as a loud tone is repeatedly paired with another stimulus such as meat. The dog learns to salivate in response to the tone, just as it naturally salivates whenever it sees meat. During extinction trials, the tone is no longer paired with the meat, and salivation in response to the tone eventually stops.

**Thomas Szasz,** psychiatrist and author of *The Myth of Mental Illness*

We can learn from what he talked about but did not practice—in fact, he systematically lied about it—which is the concept of the *absolutely confidential,* totally voluntary, uncoerced conversation with another person, who comes to see you and pays for the service. The conversation should always be paid for; this ensures that the person isn't coming to you for any other reason. But Freud betrayed this concept through his training analysis, through his child analysis and through his so-called analysis of his daughter, which was pure existential incest. Freud was like a pope who preached celibacy but didn't practice it.

**Jerome L. Singer,** professor of psychology and child study, Yale University

We all have much to learn about scientific integrity and commitment from Freud's willingness to study his own dreams, reexamine his theories and persist in a lifelong exploration that has stirred the imagination of thousands of thinkers of this century.

**Albert Ellis,** president of the Institute for Rational Emotive Therapy

We can constructively learn from Freud what he first said in 1895 and later, alas, forgot: that "emotional" disturbances are "ideogenic"—that is, importantly related to ideas. We can learn that most of us naturally and easily tend to severely defame our *self* (and not merely our *behavior*) when we act imperfectly, and thereby bring about needless "horror."

**Hans J. Eysenck,** professor emeritus at the University of London's Institute of Psychiatry

I think Freud has been a wholesale disaster for psychology and what we can learn from him is how not to do things.

In psychology as in other sciences one must provide proof for any assertion. Freud intentionally and deliberately refused to look at his cases in comparison with control cases. He never followed them up to see whether in actual fact what he claimed to have been successes were successful. We now know that in fact many of them were not.

**Phyllis Chesler,** psychologist and author of *Women and Madness* and *About Men*

Freud taught us—and this has not been accepted here because we're Americans—that life is tragic, that there are real limitations, that everything is a trade-off, that nobody can have a free lunch, that we're not getting out of this alive. He said that there is also Thanatos, a death instinct. And there is real death. Freud was a mournful meditator. He was not Dale Carnegie. He didn't say "Read this book and you're going to be happy and get everything you want." He wasn't saying that, and I don't think that we've picked up his humbling tragic message.

**Rollo May,** author of *Love and Will* and a founder of the existential movement in psychotherapy

Freud knew that the nineteenth century was finished, gone to pieces. The meaning of psychoanalysis gave men and women a new view of life. Freud brought us understanding of depth, death, also our moods, negation of ideas, our fatigue, our sickness. We can still learn from Freud—not mainly from the rules of psychoanalysis, but rather from how he pictured a whole new culture, a culture in which people would be more broadly understood and more broadly human because the unconscious was part of the experience of the twentieth century.

present during several romantic encounters, it too came to elicit an amorous response.

Abnormal behaviors can also be acquired by classical conditioning (Wilson, 1990). Consider the situation of a young boy who is repeatedly frightened by a neighbor's large German shepherd dog. Whenever the child walks past the neighbor's front yard, the dog barks loudly and lunges at him, stopped only by a rope tied to the porch. In this unfortunate situation, the boy's parents are not surprised to discover that he develops a fear of dogs. They are mystified, however, by another intense fear the child displays, a fear of sand. They cannot understand why he cries whenever they take him to the beach, refuses to take a single step off the beach blanket, and screams in fear if sand even touches his skin.

Where did this fear of sand come from? The answer is found in the principle of classical conditioning. It turns out that a big sandbox is set up in the neighbor's front yard for the fearsome dog to play in. Every time the dog barks and lunges at the boy, the sandbox is there too. After repeated associations of this kind, the child comes to fear sand as much as he fears the dog. In classical conditioning terms, an unconditioned stimulus — the loud and hostile dog — initially elicits an unconditioned response of fear; then, after repeated associations, a conditioned stimulus — sand — begins to elicit a similar, conditioned response of fear. Through this simple process of conditioning, the child develops a fear response that may persist throughout his life. The child may be so successful at avoiding sand that he never learns how harmless it is.

As we shall see in Chapter 14, behaviorists also suggest that sexual fetishes may be acquired through classical conditioning. Many people are sexually aroused by inanimate objects such as undergarments and sheer stockings, but some repeatedly use such objects as a preferred, or at least very intentional, method of achieving sexual excitement. When such an object, called a *fetish,* becomes the focus of sexual satisfaction, the person is exhibiting a disorder called fetishism. One study tried to show that this disorder could be created in the laboratory by classical conditioning procedures (Rachman & Hodgson, 1968). Male subjects were shown pictures of naked women (US), which induced in them a response of sexual arousal (UR). Then the nude pictures were paired with pictures of boots (CS), and the feelings of arousal continued to be elicited. Eventually, after numerous pairings, the pictures of the boots alone served to arouse the subjects (CR). In all but a handful of the men studied, these conditioned responses were extinguished soon after the experimenters stopped pairing the boot pictures with the pictures of naked women; however, the study suggests that in some cases classical conditioning may help fetishes to develop.

## Operant Conditioning Explanations of Abnormal Behavior

In *operant conditioning,* humans and animals learn to behave in certain ways because they receive *reinforcement* from their environment whenever they do so. This form of conditioning was first elucidated by the eminent psychologist Edward L. Thorndike (1874–1949), whose research led him to formulate the *law of effect* — the principle that responses that lead to satisfying consequences will be strengthened and are likely to be repeated, whereas responses that lead to unsatisfying consequences will be weakened and are unlikely to be repeated. Years later, researcher B. F. Skinner renamed this law the *principle of reinforcement* and asserted that it is the primary mechanism for explaining and controlling human behavior.

Using the principle of operant conditioning, experimenters have taught animal subjects a wide range of behaviors, from pulling levers and turning wheels to

Pet owners have discovered that they can teach animals a wide assortment of tricks through shaping — rewarding successive approximations of a desired behavior.

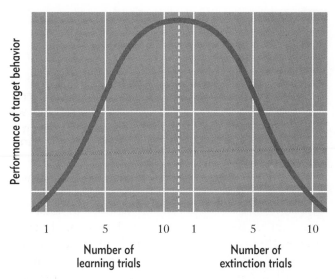

**FIGURE 2-7** Operant conditioning. During learning trials, a target behavior (such as lifting a paddle) is repeatedly rewarded, and the subject increasingly performs the target behavior. During extinction trials, the target behavior is no longer rewarded, and the subject steadily stops performing the target behavior.

B. F. Skinner, one of the most influential theorists and researchers of the twentieth century, helped develop the principle of reinforcement and applied it by training pigeons and other animals to perform a wide variety of behaviors. He believed that reinforcement accounts for most human behaviors, too.

navigating mazes and even playing Ping-Pong (Skinner, 1948). To teach complex behaviors, they typically employ *shaping*— a procedure in which successive approximations of the desired behavior are rewarded. In teaching a pigeon to play Ping-Pong, for example, the experimenter may initially reward the animal merely for picking up a paddle. Once this response is acquired, the experimenter may reward the pigeon only when it further carries the paddle in the direction of the ball, and so on until the animal actually learns to return serves (Figure 2-7).

Behaviorists believe that many human behaviors are learned by operant conditioning. Children acquire manners by receiving praise, attention, or treats for desirable behaviors and censure for undesirable ones. Adults work at their jobs because they are paid when they do and fired when they do not.

Behaviorists also claim that many abnormal behaviors develop as a result of reinforcement. Some people learn to abuse alcohol and drugs because initially such behaviors brought feelings of calm, comfort, or pleasure (Conger, 1951). Others exhibit bizarre, psychotic behaviors because they enjoy the attention they get when they do so. A number of studies have found that when the bizarre talk and other unusual behaviors of schizophrenic patients are consistently ignored by hospital personnel and appropriate behaviors are repeatedly rewarded with privileges, money, or attention, many patients begin to show marked changes for the better (Braginsky, Braginsky, & Ring, 1969; Ayllon & Michael, 1959).

Some of Philip Berman's maladaptive behaviors may have been acquired through operant conditioning. When he first became "ornery" at the age of 10, how did his parents react? Perhaps they unintentionally reinforced his rebellious behavior by giving him more attention; and rather than teaching him alternative ways to express his needs, perhaps they simply gave in and let him have his way. Making a related point about child rearing, one psychologist writes, "Parents may pick up a child who is whining. Whining is an aversive event for the parents which is terminated after they respond. . . . However, the child is . . . reinforced" (Kazdin, 1975, p. 31).

## Modeling Explanations of Abnormal Behaviors

*Modeling* is a form of learning in which individuals acquire responses through *observation* and *imitation* (Bandura, 1977, 1976, 1969) — that is, by observing others (the models) and repeating their behaviors. Behaviors are especially likely to be imitated when the models are themselves being rewarded for the behaviors or when the models are important to the observers.

Behaviorists believe that many everyday human behaviors are learned through modeling. Children may acquire language, facial gestures, tastes in food, and the like by imitating the words, gestures, and eating behaviors of their parents. Similarly, adults may acquire inter-

Modeling may account for some forms of abnormal behavior. A well-known study by Albert Bandura and his colleagues (1963) demonstrated that children learned to abuse a doll by observing an adult model hit it. Children who had not been exposed to the adult model did not mistreat the doll.

personal skills or vocational interests by imitating the behaviors and preferences of important people in their lives.

This form of conditioning, too, can lead to abnormality. A famous study showed that aggressive behaviors could be acquired through modeling (Bandura, Ross, & Ross, 1963). The experimenters had young children observe adult models acting aggressively toward a doll. Later, in the same setting, many of the children behaved in the same highly aggressive manner. Other children who had not observed the adult models behaved much less aggressively.

Similarly, children of poorly functioning people may themselves develop maladaptive reactions because of their exposure to inadequate parental models. Certainly the selfish and demanding behaviors displayed by Philip Berman's mother could have served as the model for his own self-centered and hypercritical style. Just as his mother was repeatedly critical of others, Philip was critical of every person with whom he developed a close relationship. Similarly, the severe depressive symptoms exhibited by his mother, which led her to be hospitalized, could have been a model for Philip's own depression and discontent.

## Assessing the Behavioral Model

The number of behavioral psychologists has grown steadily since the 1950s, and the behavioral model has become a powerful force in the clinical field (Franks, 1990; Smith, 1982). Various schools of behavioral thought have emerged over the years, and many treatment techniques have been developed.

Perhaps the most prominent reason that the behavioral model is so attractive is that behavioral explanations and treatments can be tested in the laboratory, whereas the psychodynamic theories generally cannot. The behaviorists' basic concepts—stimulus, response, and reinforcement—can be observed and measured. Even more important, the results of laboratory research have lent considerable support to the behavioral model (Wolpe, 1987). Experimenters have successfully used the principles of conditioning to create a number of clinical symptoms in laboratory subjects, thus suggesting that mental disorders may indeed develop in this way (Seligman, 1975).

Research has also, however, revealed weaknesses in the behavioral model. Although behavioral researchers have induced specific symptoms in subjects, they have not established that such symptoms are ordinarily acquired in this way. There is still no indisputable evidence that the mentally ill people in our society are largely victims of improper conditioning.

Another current problem is that behavioral explanations and treatments have not been adjusted to account for the research findings coming out of today's conditioning laboratories (Rescorla, 1988; Krasner, 1976). The stimulus-response and reinforcement principles that were once the cornerstone of this model have been challenged in conditioning experiments; some studies even reveal that animal and human subjects can acquire and maintain behaviors in ways that contradict the basic principles of conditioning. Yet most behaviorists have been largely unaffected by these developments and have continued to rely on the principles of conditioning set forth years ago.

Finally, some critics hold that the behavioral perspective is too simplistic, that its concepts and principles fail to capture the complexity of human behavior. They argue that behaviorists often overlook or minimize the human capacity to think critically. Many behaviorists have themselves been concerned about this issue and in the 1950s began an important movement that continues to the present day. A number of behaviorists felt that they should be looking at more than *overt behaviors*, such as aggressive actions or verbal statements. They recognized that human beings also engage in *cognitive behaviors,* such as private thoughts and beliefs, which were being largely ignored in behavioral theory and therapy. Accordingly, they developed *cognitive-behavioral* theories that took unseen cognitive behaviors into account (Kendall, 1990; Meichenbaum, 1986; Goldiamond, 1965).

Cognitive-behavioral theorists bridge the behavioral model and cognitive model, the perspective that we shall be turning to next. On the one hand, their explanations are firmly entrenched in behavioral principles. They believe, for example, that cognitive processes are acquired and maintained by classical conditioning, operant conditioning, and modeling. On the other hand, cognitive-behavioral theorists share with other kinds of cognitive theorists a belief that the ability to think is the most important aspect of both normal and abnormal human functioning. They hold that people's overt behaviors follow from their interpretations and thoughts, so it is their thoughts rather than their actions that must be examined most closely. Given this central concern with human thought, cognitive-behavioral theories and therapies are now often seen as adjuncts to the cognitive model.

# THE COGNITIVE MODEL

Philip Berman, like the rest of us, has *cognitive* abilities — special intellectual capacities to think, remember, and anticipate. These cognitive abilities serve him in all his activities and can help him accomplish a great deal in life. Yet they can also work against him. As he cognitively organizes and records his experiences, Philip may be developing false ideas or misinterpreting experiences in ways that lead to counterproductive decisions, maladaptive responses, and unnecessarily painful emotions.

According to the cognitive model, to understand human behavior, we must understand the content and process of human thought. What assumptions and attitudes color a person's perceptions? What thoughts run through that person's mind, and what conclusions do they lead to? When people display abnormal patterns of functioning, cognitive theorists assume that cognitive problems are to blame. Like the behaviorists, they reject a medical view of abnormal psychological functioning.

## Origins of the Cognitive Model

In the late 1950s, scientists in the field of social psychology — the branch of experimental psychology that studies the individual's interactions with the social environment — became interested in cognitive phenomena they called *attributions*. Social psychologists proposed that we regularly explain the things we see going on around us by attributing them to particular causes and that these causal attributions then influence the way we feel about ourselves and others (Heider, 1958, 1944). For example, a group of test subjects who were physically stimulated by the effects of a drug felt greater anger when they mistakenly attributed their arousal to a person nearby making irritating comments than when they attributed it to the effects of the drug (Schacter & Singer, 1962; Schacter & Wheeler, 1962). Other social psychology research during the late 1950s and early 1960s indicated that our causal attributions may also influence our ideas, decisions, expectations, and impressions, including our impressions of ourselves. If attributional cognitions play such a critical role in behavior and emotion, shouldn't they also be important in the development and treatment of abnormal behaviors and emotions?

While attributions were becoming the dominant focus in social psychology, the movement toward a more cognitively oriented behaviorism was gaining strength in

Aaron Beck proposes that many forms of abnormal behavior can be traced to cognitive factors, such as upsetting thoughts and illogical thinking. Originally trained as a psychoanalytic therapist, Beck came to reject that model and developed a cognitive approach in which therapists challenge clients' dysfunctional beliefs and ways of thinking. Cognitive therapy is especially effective in cases of depression.

some segments of the clinical community. These two developments set the stage for the emergence of the cognitive model of abnormal psychology. In the early 1960s two clinicians, Aaron Beck and Albert Ellis, proposed cognitive theories of abnormality (Beck, 1963; Ellis, 1962). Building on earlier work in this area (Kelley, 1955; Rotter, 1954), these theorists claimed that cognitive processes are at the center of behavior, thought, and emotions, and that we can best understand abnormal functioning by looking to the cognitive realm. A number of theorists and therapists soon incorporated the ideas and techniques of Beck and Ellis, refining and expanding the model and greatly influencing the clinical field as a whole (Beck, 1991, 1987, 1967; Ellis, 1987, 1984, 1962; Lazarus, 1987, 1971; Meichenbaum, 1986, 1977, 1969; Mahoney, 1974).

## Cognitive Explanations

To cognitive theorists, we are all artists who are both reproducing and creating our worlds in our minds as we try to understand the events going on around us. If we are effective artists, our cognitive representations tend to be accurate (agreed upon by others) and useful (adaptive). If we are ineffective artists, however, we may create a cognitive inner world that is alien to others and

painful and harmful to ourselves. Abnormal functioning can result from several kinds of cognitive problems: *maladaptive assumptions or attitudes, specific upsetting thoughts,* and *illogical thinking processes.*

**Maladaptive Assumptions** Albert Ellis (1987, 1984, 1962) proposes that each of us holds a unique set of assumptions about ourselves and our world that serve to guide us through life and determine our reactions to the various situations we encounter. Unfortunately, some people's assumptions are largely irrational, guiding them to act and react in ways that are inappropriate and that prejudice their chances of happiness and success. Ellis calls these *basic irrational assumptions.*

Some people, for example, irrationally assume that they are abject failures if they are not loved or approved of by virtually every person they know. Such people constantly seek approval and repeatedly feel rejected. All their interactions and interpretations are affected by this assumption, so that an otherwise successful presentation in the classroom or boardroom can make them sad or anxious because one listener seems bored, or an evening with friends can leave them dissatisfied because the friends do not offer enough compliments. The basic irrational assumption sets the stage for a life of tension and disappointment.

According to Ellis (1962), the most common irrational assumptions are these:

> The idea that it is a dire necessity for an adult human being to be loved or approved of by virtually every significant other person in his community.
>
> The idea that one should be thoroughly competent, adequate, and achieving in all possible respects if one is to consider oneself worthwhile.
>
> The idea that certain people are bad, wicked, or villainous and that they should be severely blamed and punished for their villainy.
>
> The idea that it is awful and catastrophic when things are not the way one would very much like them to be.
>
> The idea that human unhappiness is externally caused and that people have little or no ability to control their sorrows and disturbances.
>
> The idea that if something is or may be dangerous or fearsome one should be terribly concerned about it and should keep dwelling on the possibility of its occurring.
>
> The idea that it is easier to avoid than to face certain life difficulties and self responsibilities.
>
> The idea that one should be dependent on others and need someone stronger than oneself on whom to rely.

The idea that one's past history is an all-important determiner of one's present behavior and that because something once strongly affected one's life, it should indefinitely have a similar effect.

The idea that one should become quite upset over other people's problems and disturbances.

The idea that there is invariably a right, precise, and perfect solution to human problems and that it is catastrophic if this perfect solution is not found.

Philip Berman often seems to hold the basic irrational assumption that his past history has inexorably determined his present behavior, and that something that once affected his life will have the same effect indefinitely. Philip believes he was victimized by his parents and that he is now doomed by his oppressive past. He seems to approach all new experiences and relationships with expectations of failure and disaster.

**Specific Upsetting Thoughts**   Cognitive theorists believe that *specific upsetting thoughts* may also contribute to abnormal functioning. As we confront the myriad situations that arise in life, numerous thoughts come into our minds, some comforting, others upsetting. Beck has called these unbidden cognitions **automatic thoughts.** When a person's stream of automatic thoughts is overwhelmingly negative, Beck would expect that person to become depressed (Beck, 1991, 1987, 1976). Within a span of seconds, a depressed man may be assaulted by such automatic thoughts as "I should know how to do this. . . . I failed my wife. . . . The future is bleak. . . . I look ugly in this shirt." Philip Berman has made it clear what fleeting thoughts and images keep popping into his mind as he interacts with others: "My old girlfriend wants to jump into bed with her date. . . . I'm a 25-year-old virgin. . . . The therapist wants to laugh at me. . . . My boss wants to fire me. . . . My parents think I'm lazy and irresponsible." Certainly such automatic thoughts are contributing to his pervasive feelings of despondency.

Similarly, Donald Meichenbaum, a cognitive-behavioral theorist, suggests that people who suffer from anxiety have inadvertently learned to generate counterproductive **self-statements** (statements about oneself) during stressful situations and as a result react to any difficult situation with automatic fear and discomfort (Meichenbaum, 1986, 1969; Meichenbaum, Henshaw, & Himel, 1982). When Philip Berman met his old girlfriend and her date, his mind may have been flooded with such self-statements as "Oh, no, I can't stand this. . . . I look like a fool. . . . I'm getting sick. . . . Why do these things always happen to me?" These statements may have fueled his anxiety and rage and

prevented him from handling the encounter constructively.

**Illogical Thinking Processes**   Cognitive theorists also point to *illogical thinking processes* to explain abnormal functioning. Beck has found that certain people habitually think in illogical ways and keep drawing self-defeating and even pathological conclusions (Beck, 1991, 1987, 1969). As we shall observe in Chapter 8, Beck has identified a number of illogical thought processes characteristic of depression: *selective perception*, seeing only the negative features of an event; *magnification*, exaggerating the importance of undesirable events; and *overgeneralization*, drawing broad negative conclusions on the basis of a single insignificant event. One depressed student couldn't remember the date of Columbus's third voyage to America during a history class and, overgeneralizing, spent the rest of the day in despair over her invincible ignorance.

Whether they focus primarily on irrational assumptions, self-defeating thoughts, illogical thinking processes, or a combination of the three, cognitive theorists believe that the cognitive sphere is the key to abnormal functioning. Most abnormal behavior is caused not by illness but by incorrect and counterproductive thinking. If malfunctioning people can start to think differently, they can overcome their difficulties.

## Assessing the Cognitive Model

The cognitive model has had very broad appeal. In addition to the many behaviorists who have incorporated cognitive concepts into their theories about learning, a great many clinicians believe that thinking processes are much more than conditioned reactions. Cognitive theory, research, and treatment techniques have developed in so many interesting ways that the model is now viewed as distinct from the behavioral school that spawned it.

There are several reasons for this model's appeal. First, it focuses on the most singular of human processes, human thought. Just as our special cognitive abilities are responsible for so many human accomplishments, they may also be responsible for the special problems that characterize human functioning. Thus many theorists find themselves drawn to a model that views human thought as the primary contributor to normal or abnormal behavior.

Cognitive theories also lend themselves to testing. Researchers have found evidence that people often do exhibit the assumptions, specific thoughts, and thinking processes that supposedly contribute to abnormal functioning, and have shown that these cognitive phenomena are indeed operating in many cases of pathology (Kendall, 1990). When experimental subjects are manipulated into adopting unpleasant assumptions or thoughts, for example, they became more anxious and depressed (Rimm & Litvak, 1969; Velten, 1968). Similarly, many people with psychological disorders, particularly depressive, anxiety, and sexual disorders, have been found to display maladaptive assumptions, thoughts, or thinking processes (Shaw & Segal, 1988; Beck, Epstein, & Harrison, 1983; Beck, Laude, & Bohnert, 1974).

Yet the cognitive model, too, has its drawbacks (Beck, 1991). Although it is becoming clear that cognitive processes are involved in many forms of abnormality, their precise role has yet to be ascertained. The maladaptive cognitions seen in psychologically troubled people could well be a consequence rather than a cause of their difficulties. Certainly processes so central to human functioning must be highly vulnerable to disturbances of any kind.

Like the other models, the cognitive model has been criticized for the narrowness of its scope. Although cognition is a very special human dimension, it is still but one part of human functioning. Are human beings not more than their thoughts — indeed, more than the sum total of their fleeting thoughts, emotions, and behaviors? For those who believe that they are, explanations of human functioning must at least sometimes embrace broader issues, such as how people approach life, what they get from it, and how they deal with the question of life's meaning. This is the contention of the humanistic-existential perspective.

## THE HUMANISTIC-EXISTENTIAL MODEL

Philip Berman is more than his organic processes, psychological conflicts, learned behaviors, and cognitions. Being human, he also has the ability to confront complex and challenging philosophical issues such as self-awareness, values, meaning, and choice, and to incorporate them into his life. And according to humanistic and existential theorists, Philip's problems can be understood *only* in light of those issues. Humanistic and existential theorists are usually grouped together because of their common focus on the broader dimensions of human existence. At the same time, there are some important differences between them.

Humanists believe that all humans have a natural drive to "self-actualize" — to fulfill their potential for goodness and growth — but that some people drift away from this basic drive. Abraham Maslow suggested that self-actualized people, such as this volunteer who regularly cares for babies afflicted with AIDS, show concern for the welfare of humanity. They are also thought to be highly creative, spontaneous, independent, and humorous.

*Humanists,* the more optimistic of the two groups, believe that human beings are born with a natural inclination to be friendly, cooperative, and constructive, and are driven to *self-actualize* — that is, to fulfill this potential for goodness and growth (Rogers, 1987, 1959; Maslow, 1967). They will be able to do so, however, only if they can honestly appraise and accept their weaknesses as well as their strengths and establish a satisfying system of personal values to live by. If they habitually deceive themselves and create a distorted view of the things that happen to them, they are likely to suffer some degree of psychological dysfunction.

*Existentialists* agree that human beings must have an accurate awareness of themselves and live subjectively meaningful — they say "authentic" — lives in order to be mentally well adjusted. These theorists do not believe, however, that people are naturally inclined to live constructively. They believe that from birth we have total freedom, either to face up to our existence and give meaning to our lives or to shrink from that responsibility. Those who choose to "hide" from responsibility and choice will view themselves as helpless and weak and may live empty, inauthentic, and dysfunctional lives as a consequence. Thus neither humanists nor existentialists embrace a medical illness view of abnormal psychological functioning.

# Origins of the Humanistic-Existential Model

The humanistic and existential views of abnormality both date back to the 1940s. At that time Carl Rogers (1902–1987), often considered the pioneer of the humanistic perspective, began to develop ideas about psychotherapy that contrasted sharply with the influential psychodynamic principles of the day. He suggested that clients would do better in treatment if therapy were focused on their unique subjective perspective rather than on someone else's definition of objective reality. Rogers also proposed that clients would respond better if therapists were particularly warm, genuine, and understanding. He described this new therapeutic approach, called *client-centered therapy,* in an influential book published in the early 1950s.

Carl Rogers, one of the founders of the humanistic model, believed that therapists must be empathic, accepting, and genuine if clients are to be helped to trust other people, accept themselves, and overcome their psychological problems. His call for systematic research in the clinical field helped start a trend that still continues. Ironically, most humanistic theorists now consider empirical research an improper and inaccurate method of psychological investigation.

Rogers then went on to develop a theory of personality and abnormality based on the approach he took in his therapy. He concluded that if people respond to a therapist's warmth with greater honesty about themselves and with a reduction of symptoms, then the human personality must be rooted in more than the irrational instincts and conflicts emphasized in the psychodynamic model. This "humanistic" theory of personality, reminiscent of the theories of the French philosopher Jean-Jacques Rousseau (1712–1778) and the American psychologist and philosopher William James (1842–1910), emphasized a special, positive potential inherent in human beings. About the same time, other humanistic theories developed by Abraham Maslow (1908–1970) and Fritz Perls (1893–1970) also received widespread attention.

The existential view of personality and abnormality came into prominence during this same period. It derived from the ideas of such European existential philosophers as Søren Kierkegaard (1813–1855), Karl Jaspers (1883–1969), Edmund Husserl (1859–1938), Martin Heidegger (1889–1976), and Jean-Paul Sartre (1905–1980), all of whom held that human beings are constantly defining their existence through their actions and that the meaning of individual existence lies in such efforts at definition. In 1942 Ludwig Binswanger, a Swiss psychoanalyst, combined this existential principle with psychoanalytic therapy in an approach called *Daseinanalyse* ("existential analysis"). According to Binswanger, therapists could help their patients only by guiding them through the indispensable process of *being,* the process of developing in one's own unique ways through one's actions.

Other clinical theorists, including Medard Boss, Rollo May, and Viktor Frankl, espoused similar existential ideas throughout the 1950s. A book titled *Existence,* now considered a classic work on the clinical existential perspective, described all the major existential ideas and treatment approaches of the time and helped them gain widespread attention (May, Angel, & Ellenberger, 1958).

The humanistic and existential theories were extremely popular during the 1960s and 1970s, years of considerable soul-searching and social upheaval in Western society. People were worried that twentieth-century society had become too affluent and materialistic, that human values and concerns had been cast aside, and that feelings of alienation, purposelessness, and spiritual emptiness had become common in the face of rapid technological and bureaucratic growth. Humanistic theories, which reaffirmed the human spirit, and existential theories, which challenged people to take charge of their lives, addressed these growing concerns.

Although the humanistic-existential model lost some of its popularity in the 1980s, it continues to influence the treatment techniques of many clinicians.

## Humanistic Explanations of Abnormal Behavior

According to Carl Rogers (1987, 1981, 1967, 1961), the road to dysfunction begins in infancy. We all have a basic need to receive *positive regard* from the significant other people in our lives (primarily from our parents). Those who receive *unconditional* (nonjudgmental) *positive regard* early in life are likely to develop *unconditional self-regard.* That is, they come to recognize their worth as persons, even while recognizing that they are not perfect. They feel comfortable about themselves and are able to evaluate themselves in a clear-sighted way. Such people are in a good psychological position to actualize their inherently positive potential.

Unfortunately, some children are repeatedly made to feel that they are not worthy of positive regard. As a result, they acquire *conditions of worth,* standards that tell them they are lovable and acceptable only when they conform to the standards they have been exposed to, and they constantly judge themselves accordingly. Much of the time, they will feel that their thoughts, behavior, or emotions fall short of those standards, and will judge themselves as being unworthy as a result.

Such people are in a difficult psychological position. On the one hand, they have the basic universal need for positive self-regard. On the other hand, they are unable to like themselves unless they are always conforming to a highly critical set of standards. In order to maintain positive self-regard, these people have to look at themselves in a very selective fashion, denying or distorting thoughts and actions that do not measure up to their conditions of worth.

The constant self-deception makes it impossible for these people to self-actualize. They have a distorted view of themselves and their experiences, and so they do not know what they are genuinely feeling or needing, or what values and goals would be meaningful for them. Moreover, they spend so much energy trying to protect their self-image that little is left to devote to self-actualizing. Problems in functioning are then inevitable.

Thus humanistic clinicians might view Philip Berman as a man who has gone astray. Rather than striving to fulfill his positive human potential, he drifts from job to job, relationship to relationship, and outburst to out-

*"I suggest that in future you eat all your lunch."*

Far from "thanking" their parents, people who have been repeatedly judged and criticized as children may, according to Carl Rogers, become self-critical, self-deceiving, incapable of self-actualization, and troubled by psychological problems. *(Drawing by Edward Frascino; © 1991, The New Yorker Magazine, Inc.)*

burst. In every interaction he is defending himself, trying to interpret events in ways he can live with. He always considers his problems to be someone else's fault, and he keeps presenting himself as a strong person who cares little about what other folks may think. Yet his constant efforts at self-defense and self-enhancement are only partially successful. His basic negative self-image and his assumption that others will think badly of him keep breaking through. This problem would probably be ascribed to the way he was treated as a child. Rather than offering him unconditional positive regard, his mother apparently kept calling him a "pervert" and a "sissy," bullied him, and even abused him. Small wonder that Philip never learned to accept and value himself unconditionally.

## Existential Explanations of Abnormal Behavior

Like humanists, existentialists believe that psychological dysfunctioning is caused by self-deception; but existentialists are talking about a kind of self-deception in which people hide from life's responsibilities and fail to recognize that it is up to them to give meaning to their lives and that they have the capacity and freedom to do so. According to existentialists, people start to hide from personal responsibility and choice when they become engulfed in the constant change, confusion, and emotional strain of present-day society, as well as in the particular stresses of their immediate environment. Overwhelmed by these pressures, many people look to others for guidance and authority, and conform excessively to social standards. Others may build resentment toward society. Either way, they overlook their personal freedom of choice and avoid responsibility for their lives and decisions (May, 1987, 1983, 1981, 1967; Bugental, 1965). This abdication of responsibility and choice may offer a form of refuge, but at a cost. Such people are left with empty, inauthentic lives. Their prevailing emotions are anxiety, frustration, alienation, and depression.

Thus existentialists might view Philip Berman as a man who considers himself incompetent to resist the forces of society. He views his parents as "rich, powerful, and selfish," and he sees teachers, acquaintances, and employers as perpetrators of abuse and oppression. Overwhelmed, he fails to appreciate his choices in life and his capacity for finding meaning and direction. Quitting becomes a habit with him — he leaves job after job, ends every romantic relationship, flees difficult situations, and even tries suicide. For existentialists, Philip's problems are best summarized by the part of the case description that states, "He spent most of his time alone, 'bored.' He was unable to commit himself to any person, he held no strong convictions, and he felt no allegiance to any group."

## Assessing the Humanistic-Existential Model

The humanistic-existential model appeals to many people in and out of the clinical field for several reasons. First, the model focuses on broad human issues rather than on a single aspect of psychological functioning. In recognizing the special features and challenges of human existence, humanistic and existential theorists tap into a dimension of psychological life that is typically missing from the other models (Fuller, 1982). Moreover, the factors that they say are essential to effective

psychological functioning — self-acceptance, personal values, personal meaning, personal choice, and so on — are undeniably lacking in many people who are psychologically disturbed.

The optimistic tone of the humanistic-existential model is also an attraction. Humanistic and existential theorists offer great hope when they assert that despite the often overwhelming pressures of modern society, we can make our own choices, determine our own destiny, and accomplish much.

Still another attractive feature of the humanistic-existential model is its emphasis on health rather than illness (Cowen, 1991). Unlike proponents of some of the other models who see individuals as patients with psychological illnesses, humanists and existentialists view them simply as people whose special potential has yet to be fulfilled. And although they acknowledge the impact of past events on present behavior, they do not hold a deterministic view of behavior. They believe our behavior can be influenced by our innate goodness and potential, and by our willingness to take responsibility, more than by any factor in our past.

Although appealing in these ways, the humanistic-existential focus on abstract issues of human fulfillment also gives rise to a significant problem: these issues are resistant to research. In fact, with the notable exception of Rogers, who spent years empirically testing his psychotherapeutic methods, humanists and existentialists tend to reject the experimental approaches that now dominate the field. They believe that such methods cannot accurately examine their ideas, and they hold that today's researchers typically miss subtle, internal experiences by looking only at what they can define objectively. Humanists and existentialists have tried to establish the merits of their views by appealing to logic, introspection, and individual case histories. Although they are sincere and true to their principles in taking this position, the result is that the model has received limited empirical examination or support. Sherlock Holmes once observed, "It is a capital mistake to theorize before one has data. Insensibly one begins to twist facts to suit theories, instead of theories to suit facts." Many critics would argue that humanistic and existential theorists are particularly vulnerable to this danger.

A final problem is the model's heterogeneity. Theories and therapies called humanistic or existential are so numerous and so varied that it is almost misleading to lump them together into a single category. Still, this extremely varied group of theorists and practitioners does share a belief that human beings are self-determining and have an enormous potential for growth, and that self-exploration is the key to this growth.

# THE SOCIOCULTURAL MODEL

Philip Berman is also a social being. He is surrounded by people and by institutions, he is a member of a family and a society, and a participant in social and professional relationships. Thus external social forces are always operating upon Philip, setting rules and expectations that guide and at times pressure him, helping to shape his behavior, thoughts, and emotions as surely as any internal biological or psychological mechanism.

According to the sociocultural model of psychology, abnormal behavior is best understood in light of the social and cultural forces brought to bear on an individual. What are the norms and values of the society? What roles does the person play in the social environment? What kind of family structure is this person exposed to? And how do other people view and react to him or her?

## Origins of the Sociocultural Model

The sociocultural view of abnormality derives its basic assumptions from the fields of *sociology,* the study of human relationships and social groups, and *anthropology,* the study of human cultures and institutions. These fields first emerged as independent areas of study in the nineteenth century and have generated numerous theories touching on the subject of abnormal psychology.

Sociologists have proposed that societies themselves are capable of generating abnormal behavior in their members. Certain communities may be so disorganized that many of their members are forced to engage in odd behavior to adapt to the community's norms or standards (Anderson, 1923). Sociologists also claim that even stable societies may help produce and maintain abnormal behavior among some of their members by the common practice of identifying certain individuals as unusual, reacting to them in special ways, and expecting and encouraging them to take on the roles that the society assigns to abnormal people (Scheff, 1967; Becker, 1964, 1963).

In consonance with this sociological notion, anthropologists have found that some patterns of abnormality vary from society to society, from culture to culture (Malinowsky, 1972; Yap, 1951; Mead, 1949; Benedict, 1934). For example, the disorder of "windigo," an intense fear of being turned into a cannibal by a flesh-eating monster, was found only among Algonquin Indian hunters, and "koro," a fear that one's penis will withdraw into the abdomen, was found only in Southeast Asia. Each of these abnormal patterns seemed uniquely tied to the society's particular history and culture (see Box 2-4).

By the 1950s, these sociological and anthropological notions were beginning to have considerable influence on the study and treatment of abnormal psychology. Finally, a new clinical model — the sociocultural model — emerged, marked by three key events. One was the publication in 1958 of a major study, *Social Class and Mental Illness,* by August Hollingshead and Frederick Redlich, which linked various forms of mental illness to particular social classes. The study found that psychotic, aggressive, and rebellious behavior was much more common in the lower socioeconomic classes, whereas problems involving anxiety, depression, and inadequate coping skills were more common in the upper classes.

A second event marking the emergence of the sociocultural model was the development of family theory and therapy during the 1950s. After observing interactions between people with schizophrenia and their families, some theorists concluded that mentally disturbed individuals were often the products of a disturbed family structure and they developed an intervention technique in which *all* members of the family are treated, not just the individual identified as "the sick one" (Bowen, 1978, 1960; Satir, 1967, 1964; Lidz, 1965; Bell, 1961; Bateson, Jackson, Haley, & Weakland, 1956; Wynne, Ryckoff, Day, & Hirsch, 1958; Ackerman, 1956).

Finally, the emergence of the sociocultural model was marked by the influential work of Thomas Szasz (1987, 1961), the outspoken psychiatrist who in the 1950s launched an attack against the mental health system and challenged the very concept of mental illness. As we observed in Chapter 1, Szasz took the extreme position that mental illnesses are the creations of society. They are simply problems in living that come to be labeled as illnesses because other members of society feel confused and threatened by them. A prolific writer and speaker, Szasz has widely broadcast his arguments among clinical theorists, practitioners, and the public at large over the past three decades. His views have been influential in directing explanations of abnormality away from an exclusive focus on the individual and toward the possible involvement of society.

## Sociocultural Explanations of Abnormal Behavior

Because behavior is shaped by social forces, sociocultural theorists hold, we must examine the social context if we are to understand abnormal behavior in individual

---

## BOX 2-4

# Culture-Bound Abnormality

Red Bear sits up wild-eyed, his body drenched in sweat, every muscle tensed. The horror of the dream is still with him; he is choked with fear. Fighting waves of nausea, he stares at his young wife lying asleep on the far side of the wigwam, illuminated by the dying embers.

His troubles began several days before, when he came back from a hunting expedition empty-handed. Ashamed of his failure, he fell prey to a deep, lingering depression. Others in the village, noticing a change in Red Bear, watched him nervously, afraid that he was becoming bewitched by a windigo. Red Bear was also frightened. The signs of windigo were all there: depression, lack of appetite, nausea, sleeplessness and, now, the dream. Indeed, there could be no mistake.

He had dreamed of the windigo — the monster with a heart of ice — and the dream sealed his doom. Coldness gripped his own heart. The ice monster had entered his body and possessed him. He himself had become a windigo, and he could do nothing to avert his fate.

Suddenly, the form of Red Bear's sleeping wife begins to change. He no longer sees a woman, but a deer. His eyes flame. Silently, he draws his knife from under the blanket and moves stealthily toward the motionless figure. Saliva drips from the corners of his mouth, and a terrible hunger twists his intestines. A powerful desire to eat raw flesh consumes him.

With the body of the "deer" at his feet, Red Bear raises the knife high, preparing to strike. Unexpectedly, the deer screams and twists away. But the knife flashes down, again and again. Too late, Red Bear's kinsmen rush into the wigwam. With cries of outrage and horror, they drag him outside into the cold night air and swiftly kill him.

*(Lindholm & Lindholm, 1981, p. 52)*

Red Bear was suffering from *windigo,* a disorder once common among Algonquin Indian hunters who believed in a supernatural monster that ate human beings and also had the power to bewitch them and turn them into cannibals. Like Red Bear, a small number of afflicted hunters actually did kill and eat household members.

Windigo is one of the unusual mental disorders discovered around the world, each unique to a particular culture, each apparently growing from the particular pressures, history, institutions, and ideas of the culture (Lindholm & Lindholm, 1981; Kiev, 1972; Lehmann, 1967; Yap, 1951). Sociocultural theorists cite disorders such as windigo as evidence that societies often help to produce abnormal behavior in their members. The following are other exotic disorders that have been reported:

*Susto,* a disorder found among members of Indian tribes in Central and South America and non-Indian natives of the Andean highlands of Peru, Bolivia, and Colombia, is most likely to occur in infants and young children. The symptoms are extreme anxiety, excitability, and depression, along with loss of weight, weakness, and rapid heartbeat. The culture holds that this disorder is caused by contact with supernatural beings or with frightening strangers, or by bad air from cemeteries and other supposedly dangerous places. Treatment includes rubbing certain plants and animals against the skin.

*Amok,* a disorder found in Malaya, the Philippines, Java, and some parts of Africa, is more likely to occur in men than in women. Those who are afflicted jump around violently, yell loudly, grab weapons, such as knives, and attack any people and objects they encounter. This behavior is usually preceded by an earlier stage in which the victim withdraws socially and suffers some loss of contact with reality. The periods of violent behavior are followed by depression and by amnesia concerning the outburst. Within the culture, amok is thought to be caused by stress, severe shortage of sleep, alcohol consumption, and extreme heat.

*Koro* is a pattern of anxiety found in Southeast Asia in which a man suddenly becomes intensely fearful that his penis will withdraw into his abdomen and that he will die as a result. Cultural lore holds that the disorder is caused by an imbalance of "yin" and "yang," two natural forces believed to be the fundamental components of life. Accepted forms of treatment include having the individual keep a firm hold on his penis until the fear passes, often with the assistance of family members or friends, and clamping the penis to a wooden box.

*Latah* is a disorder found in Malaya, usually among uneducated middle-aged or elderly women. Certain circumstances (hearing the word "snake"; being tickled) trigger a fright reaction marked by repeating others' words and acts, using obscene words, and doing the opposite of what others ask.

---

cases. Their explanations focus on family structure and communication, societal stress, and societal labels and reactions.

**Family Structure and Communication**   According to *family systems theory,* the family is a *system* of interacting parts, the family members, who relate to one another in consistent ways and operate by implicit rules (Bowen, 1987, 1978; Minuchin, 1987; Whitaker, 1987). The parts interact in ways that enable the system to maintain itself and survive—a state known as ***homeostasis.*** Family systems theorists believe that the structure, rules, and communication patterns of some families actually force individual members to behave in a way that the society at large may define as abnormal. If these members were to behave normally, they would severely upset the family's homeostasis and actually increase their own and their family's turmoil.

Some family theorists have proposed, for example, that people with schizophrenia tend to come from families in which parents continually give *double-bind communications* to their children—simultaneous messages that are mutually contradictory (Bateson et al., 1956). A mother who tells her daughter, "I love you," while frowning and avoiding eye contact is sending a double-bind message. So are parents who keep asking for hugs and kisses yet seem to freeze whenever their children show affection. Children who are repeatedly subjected to such communications cannot win; nothing they do will earn their parents' approval. As a result, some may become overly suspicious of other people's actions and statements and may interpret the world around them in seemingly aberrant ways. In extreme cases, their suspicious style may warrant the diagnosis schizophrenia, paranoid type. Although terribly dysfunctional in many ways, this pattern does, according to family theorists, enable the individuals to survive in their double-bind families and to maintain some form of balance among family members. Their behavior may enable the parents to stay together and maintain their parental identities, for example, and may keep the children themselves dependent upon and tied to the family structure.

Philip Berman's angry and impulsive personal style can also be seen as the product of a disturbed family structure—a structure in which the mother regularly criticized and abused her son, calling him cruel names and physically attacking him, and the father exhibited a "weak and ineffectual" style that allowed the mother to dominate the family as a whole and Philip as an individual. A family theorist might argue that Philip's manner of responding to this family situation actually served an important function for the family. His "lazy, irresponsible, and ornery" behavior, for example, may have served to legitimize his mother's critical style. With Philip acting out the role of the misbehaving child, his parents may have had little need to question their own behavior, and the family may have continued to operate in a state of relative stability.

**Societal Stress**    The unique characteristics of a given society may create special problems that heighten the likelihood of abnormal functioning in its members. As we shall see in Chapter 3, researchers often conduct epidemiological studies to identify such societies. That is, they measure the *prevalence,* or total number of cases occurring in a population over a specific period of time; the *incidence,* or number of new cases that occur over a specific period of time; and the distribution of a specific psychological disorder in a particular population. Studies of this kind have found correlations between rates of abnormal functioning and such factors as widespread social change, social class membership, ethnic and national background, race and sex, and cultural institutions and values.

*Social Change*    When a society undergoes major change, the mental health of its members can be greatly affected. Societies undergoing rapid urbanization, for example, usually show a rise in mental disorders, although it is not known which features of urbanization—overcrowding, technological change, social isolation, migration, and so forth—are most to blame (Vazquez, Munoz, & Mandoz-Jauregui, 1982; Zimbardo, 1970). Similarly, a society in the throes of economic depression is likely to show

Social unrest and change, such as the changes now being experienced in Eastern Europe, may adversely affect the mental health of large numbers of people. Even if social change leads to reform and progress, it may produce significant pressures—increased migration, political instability, military suppression, and the like—that make many members of the society vulnerable to mental dysfunctioning.

a significant rise in rates of clinical depression and suicide (Brown, 1983; Dooley & Catalano, 1980), which may be explained in part by an increase in unemployment and the resulting loss of self-esteem and personal security (Roy, 1982; Stack, 1982).

***Social Class***  As we saw earlier, membership in a lower social class appears to increase vulnerability to certain patterns of abnormality. Studies have found that rates of psychological abnormality, especially severe psychological abnormality, are three times higher in the lower socioeconomic classes than in the higher ones (Eron & Peterson, 1982; Dohrenwend & Dohrenwend, 1982, 1977).

Perhaps the special pressures of lower-class life help explain this relationship. The higher rates of crime, unemployment, and overcrowding, the inferior medical care, and the limited educational opportunities that so often characterize lower-class life may place great stress upon members of these groups. Of course, other factors could also be to blame. People who suffer from significant mental disturbances may be less effective at work, earn less money, and as a result drift downward to settle in a lower socioeconomic class.

***Ethnic, Religious, and National Background***  Ethnic, religious, and national groups have distinctive traditions that may influence the kinds of abnormal functioning to which they are vulnerable. Alcoholism, for example, is more prevalent in groups that tolerate heavy drinking (Catholics, Irish, Western Europeans, Eastern Europeans) than in groups that frown on it (Jews, Protestants) (Barry, 1982).

***Racial and Sexual Prejudice***  Prejudice and discrimination may also contribute to certain forms of abnormal functioning. Women in Western society receive diagnoses of anxiety and depression disorders at least twice as often as men (APA, 1987; Dean & Ensel, 1983), and American Indians display unusually high alcoholism and suicide rates (Meketon, 1983; Peters, 1981). Although many factors may combine to produce these differences, racial and sexual prejudice and the limited opportunities that result from it may contribute to pathological patterns of tension, unhappiness, and escape.

***Cultural Institutions and Values***  Disorders such as windigo and koro are thought to grow out of the institutions and values of the cultures where they arise. So is *anorexia nervosa*, a disorder particularly prevalent among young women in Western society (Garner, Shafer, & Rosen,

Research indicates that people in the lower socioeconomic class have higher rates of psychological dysfunctioning than those in the middle and upper classes. Extraordinary economic pressures may contribute, especially among those who lose their homes, possessions, and dignity.

1991; Garner & Rosen, 1990). As we will see in Chapter 12, people with this disorder intentionally deprive themselves of food and lose dangerous amounts of weight. Many theorists believe that the current emphasis on thinness as the female aesthetic ideal in Western culture is largely responsible for anorexia nervosa's high, and apparently increasing, incidence there. Studies have found a growing preference for very thin female frames in North American and European magazines, movies, and advertisements over the past two decades, the same period of time in which the rates of anorexia nervosa have shown a significant rise (Garner et al., 1978).

**Societal Labels and Reactions**  Sociocultural theorists also believe that abnormal functioning is influenced greatly by the diagnostic *labels* given to troubled people and by the ways other people react to those labels (Szasz, 1987, 1964; Scheff, 1984; Rosenhan, 1973). The theorists hold that when people violate the norms of their society, the society categorizes them as deviant and assigns them labels such as "mentally ill."

According to these theorists, the initial label of mental illness may or may not be justified. Regardless, once the label is assigned, a vicious cycle is initiated that ensures the development of further abnormal behavior. The label of mental illness tends to stick to a person, condemning him or her to be viewed in stereotyped ways, reacted to as "crazy," and expected and subtly encouraged to be incapacitated. Gradually the person learns to accept and play the assigned role, functioning and behaving in an increasingly disturbed manner. Ultimately the label seems fully justified.

A famous and controversial study by clinical investigator David Rosenhan (1973) supports this position. Eight normal people presented themselves at various mental hospitals, complaining that they had been hearing voices say the words "empty," "hollow," and "thud." On the basis of this complaint alone, each "pseudopatient" was diagnosed as schizophrenic and admitted to the hospital. According to the researchers, the events of the following weeks highlighted several issues. First, it was hard to get rid of the label. The length of hospitalization ranged from seven to fifty-two days, even though the pseudopatients behaved normally as soon as they were admitted to the hospital. Second, the schizophrenic label kept influencing the way staff viewed and dealt with the pseudopatients. A pseudopatient who paced the corridor out of boredom was said to be "nervous." Third, pseudopatients reported that the staff's attitudes and reactions toward patients in general were often authoritarian, limited, and counterproductive. Overall, the pseudopatients came to feel powerless, depersonalized, and bored. Their treatment in the hospital seemed to undermine their mood.

## Assessing the Sociocultural Model

The sociocultural model has added an important dimension to the understanding of abnormal functioning. Today most clinicians take family structure and society into account in their efforts to understand individual cases of mental disorder, factors that were largely overlooked just thirty years ago. Moreover, practitioners are by and large more sensitive to the negative impact of clinical labels, addressing the issue during therapy and working to improve the use and accuracy of labels in diagnosis and assessment.

At the same time, the sociocultural model, like other models, leaves some questions unanswered and problems unresolved. To begin with, the research used to support this model is sometimes inaccurate. Epidemiological studies, for example, often base prevalence rates on hospital admissions or visits to counseling centers, and figures from those sources do not always reflect a disorder's incidence in the public at large (Cooke, 1989; Bromet, 1984).

A second problem is that the studies done to date have failed to support certain key predictions of the sociocultural model (Lindsay, 1982; Gove, 1982). Although some forms of abnormality are indeed associated with certain societies, as the model predicts, other forms, particularly the most severe ones, appear to be universal, with a similar incidence and similar symptoms in a wide range of settings. As we noted in Chapter 1, for example, schizophrenia occurs throughout the world: approximately 1 percent of people everywhere appear to exhibit this disorder's central symptoms of confusion, distorted ideas, and hallucinations; and every society considers these symptoms abnormal (World Health Organization, 1980, 1975; Strauss, 1979; Murphy, 1976).

Still another problem is that sociocultural research findings are often difficult to interpret. Studies that reveal a relationship between sociocultural factors and mental disorders may fail to establish that the former *cause* the latter. For example, a number of studies show a link between family conflict and schizophrenic disorders (Goldstein, 1990; Hirsch, 1979; Fontana, 1966). Although this finding may indicate that family dysfunction helps cause schizophrenia, it is equally possible that the schizophrenic behavior of a family member disrupts normal family functioning and creates conflicts.

Perhaps the most serious limitation of the sociocultural model is its inability to predict psychopathology in specific individuals. If, say, the current emphasis on thinness in women is a major reason for the growing incidence of anorexia nervosa in Western nations, why are only a small percentage of the women in these countries anorexic? Certainly, most women are exposed to the same standards of beauty. Are still other factors necessary for the disorder to develop? In response to such criticisms, most clinicians choose to view sociocultural explanations as going hand in hand with biological or psychological explanations. They believe that sociocultural variables may set a climate favorable to the development of certain mental disorders, but that biological or psychological conditions or both must also be present for the mental disorders to unfold.

# RELATIONSHIPS BETWEEN THE MODELS

The models we have just examined vary widely in the dimensions of behavior they focus on, the assumptions they employ, and the conclusions they reach. Each has proponents, many of whom not only hold their particular model to be the most enlightened but criticize the other models as foolish or misleading (Marmor, 1987). Yet none of the models has proved consistently superior to the rest. Each helps us appreciate a critical dimension of human functioning, and each has important strengths and serious limitations.

In fact, while today's models may differ from one another in significant ways, their conclusions are often compatible (Marmor, 1987). Certainly our understanding of a person's abnormal behavior is more complete if we appreciate the biological, psychological, *and* sociocultural aspects of his or her problem rather than one of those aspects to the exclusion of the rest. Even the various psychological models can sometimes be compatible. In cases of sexual dysfunction, for example, psychodynamic causes (such as internal conflicts in childhood), behavioral causes (such as learning incorrect sexual techniques), and cognitive causes (such as misconceptions about sex) often seem to combine to produce the problem.

The models also demonstrate compatibility when each emphasizes a different kind of causal factor. When theorists talk about a disorder's cause, they are referring either to *predisposing factors*, events that occur long before the appearance of the disorder and set the stage for later difficulties; to *precipitating factors*, events that actually trigger the disorder; or to *maintaining factors*, events that keep the disorder going over time. When each of several models focuses on a different kind of causal factor, their explanations may be far from contradictory. Clinicians are increasingly embracing *diathesis-stress* explanations of abnormal behavior—the view that a person must first have a biological, psychological, or sociocultural predisposition to a disorder and must then be subjected to an immediate form of psychological stress to develop and maintain certain forms of abnormality. If we explore a case of depression, for instance, we are likely to find a neurotransmitter dysfunction as a predisposing factor, a major loss as a precipitating factor, and errors in logic as a maintaining factor.

As different kinds of disorders are presented throughout this textbook, we will look at how the proponents of today's models explain each disorder, how each model's practitioners treat people with the disorder, and how well the explanations and treatment approaches are supported by research. We will observe both how the explanations and treatments differ *and* how they may build upon each other. These examinations require that we have some preliminary information about how clinical scientists and clinical practitioners conduct their work. Thus, Chapter 3 will describe the tasks of clinical scientists and the standards by which they conduct their research. Chapter 4 and Chapter 5 will examine the assessment, diagnostic, and treatment responsibilities of clinical practitioners.

## SUMMARY

Scientists use *paradigms* or *models* to understand abnormal behavior. Each paradigm or model is a set of basic assumptions that influences what questions are asked, what information is considered legitimate, and how that information is interpreted. Each model in use today highlights a different dimension of human behavior and explains abnormality with reference to that dimension. Although proponents of the biological, psychodynamic, behavioral, cognitive, humanistic-existential, and sociocultural models may heartily disagree with one another, each model emphasizes only one aspect of human functioning, and none is capable of explaining the entire spectrum of abnormality.

The *biological model* is based on the belief that (1) a full understanding of psychological functioning must include an understanding of the biological basis of thought, emotion, and behavior and that (2) the most effective treatment for psychological abnormality is biological. Support for this view has increased as researchers have learned to refine or synthesize *psychotropic drugs*, which are now frequently used to treat mentally disturbed people. Biological theorists believe that mental disorders are linked to either anatomical or biochemical problems in the brain. Researchers have found that abnormalities in the activity of different *neurotransmitters*—chemicals released into the *synapse* between two *neurons*—are often connected with different mental disorders. Biological researchers also look at the biological relatives of a patient to see if there is a heritable genetic predisposition toward the disorder.

Supporters of the *psychodynamic model* believe that a person's behavior, whether normal or abnormal, is determined to a large extent by underlying psychological forces of which the person is unaware. They focus on the past, because they consider psychological conflicts to be rooted in early parent-child relationships and traumatic experiences during the formative years. The psychodynamic model was formulated by Sigmund Freud, who developed a general theory of psychoanalysis based on the idea that unconscious conflicts account for all forms of normal and abnormal functioning. Freud envisioned three unconscious dynamic forces constituting the personality and interacting to mold thought, feeling, and behavior. The *id* represents a person's instinctual needs, drives, and impulses. It operates in accordance with the *pleasure principle,* always seeking gratification. The *ego,* which also seeks gratification, grows out of the id but operates in accordance with the *reality principle.* To control unacceptable id impulses, the ego develops basic *defense mechanisms.* The *superego,* which grows out of the ego, comprises the values and standards by which we judge ourselves. A healthy personality is one in which an effective working relationship has been established among the three forces. This relationship is worked out over the course of five developmental stages — *oral, anal, phallic, latency,* and *genital* — in which conflicts and sexual drives are addressed. Failure at any stage to reach a stable, acceptable compromise between the three forces can lead to dysfunction. Other psychodynamic theories that have developed also focus on the interaction of psychological forces.

Theorists who espouse the *behavioral model* concentrate on a person's behaviors, which are held to develop in accordance with the behavioral *principles of learning.* This approach grew out of psychological experiments on *conditioning.* Three types of conditioning account for all behavior, whether normal or dysfunctional. In *classical conditioning,* two events that repeatedly occur close together in time become fused in a person's mind, and the person eventually responds similarly to both. Abnormal behaviors, such as fear of a harmless object, may be explained as a result of classical conditioning if the harmless object has been paired with a fear-evoking object or event. In *operant conditioning,* behaviors that receive reinforcement are repeated. Behaviorists believe that both normal and abnormal human behaviors are learned because they receive reinforcement such as attention or praise. Finally, *modeling* is a form of learning in which people acquire responses through observation and imitation.

The *cognitive model* claims that we must understand the content and process of human thought to understand human behavior. When people display abnormal patterns of functioning, cognitive theorists assume that cognitive problems are to blame. Cognitive problems include *maladaptive assumptions,* or irrational attitudes about oneself and one's world; *specific upsetting thoughts* that are counterproductive; and *illogical thinking processes,* in which one overgeneralizes, magnifies, or selectively perceives events and information, so as to arrive at self-defeating and even pathological conclusions. According to cognitive theorists, most forms of abnormal behavior are caused not by illness but by incorrect and counterproductive thinking.

The *humanistic-existential model* focuses on the human ability to confront complex and challenging philosophical issues such as self-awareness, values, meaning, and choice, and to incorporate them into one's life. The two groups that constitute the humanistic-existential approach share this general focus but have very different views of the basic inclinations of the human spirit. The humanist, exemplified by the psychologist Carl Rogers, believes that people are driven to *self-actualize;* that is, to fulfill their potential for goodness and growth. When this drive is interfered with, abnormal behavior may result. The existentialist, in contrast, believes that all of us have total freedom either to face up to our existence and give meaning to our lives or to shrink from that responsibility. Abnormal behavior is seen as the result of a person's hiding from life's responsibilities. The differences between humanists and existentialists can be seen in the therapeutic approaches of the two groups. The humanistic *client-centered* therapy provides a warm and supportive atmosphere in which the special, positive potential inherent in each human being can be expressed. The existential approach to therapy is to guide the person through the process of developing in his or her own unique way.

In the *sociocultural model,* abnormal behavior is understood in the light of social and cultural forces brought to bear on the individual. Sociocultural theorists hold that a person's behavior is shaped by social forces, so we must examine the larger social context to understand abnormal behavior in individual cases. Their explanations focus on three areas. Some theorists focus on *family structure and communication;* they see the family as a system of interacting parts in which structure, rules, and patterns of communication may force family members to behave in abnormal ways. Those who focus on *societal stress* consider the unique characteristics of a given society that may create special problems for its members and heighten the likelihood of abnormal functioning.

Theorists who focus on *societal labels and reactions* hold that society categorizes certain people as "crazy" or "mentally ill," and that the label produces expectations that influence the way the person behaves and is treated. Thus a vicious cycle is created in which dysfunctional behavior is perpetuated.

The models vary widely in the dimensions of behavior they focus on, the assumptions they employ, and the conclusions they reach. Despite these differences, the models often provide compatible conclusions, suggesting that our understanding of a person's abnormal behavior is more complete if we appreciate the biological, psychological, and sociocultural aspects of his or her problem. Clinicians are increasingly embracing *diathesis-stress* explanations of abnormal behavior — the view that people must first have a biological, psychological, or sociocultural predisposition to a disorder and must then be subjected to an immediate form of psychological stress to develop and maintain certain forms of abnormality.

# TOPIC OVERVIEW

# CHAPTER 3

# RESEARCH IN ABNORMAL PSYCHOLOGY

Schizophrenia is a severe disorder that causes people to lose contact with reality. Its victims often display distorted and disorganized thought, perception, and emotions, bizarre behavior, and social withdrawal. As we shall see in Chapter 15, for the first half of this century most clinical theorists proposed that inappropriate parenting was the primary cause of this disorder. They believed that schizophrenic people were reared by *schizophrenogenic* (that is, "schizophrenia-causing") *mothers*—cold and domineering women who were impervious to the needs of their children. This widely held belief turned out to be wrong.

In the 1940s, clinical practitioners developed a surgical procedure that supposedly cured schizo-

phrenia. In this treatment procedure, called a *lobotomy,* a pointed instrument is inserted into the frontal lobe of the brain and rotated, destroying a considerable amount of brain tissue. Reports soon spread that lobotomized patients showed near-miraculous improvement, and clinical practitioners administered the procedure to tens of thousands of mental patients (Bivens, 1989). This impression, also, turned out to be wrong; far from curing schizophrenia, lobotomies caused irreversible brain damage that left many patients withdrawn, excessively subdued, and even stuporous.

These errors underscore the importance of research in abnormal psychology. Theories and treatment procedures that seem reasonable and effective in individual instances may prove incorrect when they are applied to large numbers of people or situations. Only by testing theories and techniques on large representative groups of subjects can their accuracy and utility be determined. It was only through such testing that the notion of schizophrenogenic mothers was finally challenged and the indiscriminate use of lobotomies stopped.

Clinical researchers subject the ideas of clinical theorists and the techniques of clinical practitioners to systematic testing. Research is the key to accuracy and progress in all fields of study, and it is particularly important in abnormal psychology, because inaccurate beliefs in this field can cause or prolong enormous human suffering. Until clinical researchers conducted relevant studies, for example, millions of parents, already heartbroken by their children's schizophrenic disorders, were additionally stigmatized when they were pointed to as the primary cause of the disorders; and countless schizophrenic people, already debilitated by their symptoms, were then made apathetic and spiritless by lobotomies.

Unfortunately, although the need for effective and rigorous studies is especially important in this field, the nature of its subject matter makes such research particularly difficult. Researchers must figure out ways to measure such elusive concepts as unconscious motives, private thoughts, mood change, and human potential, and must address such ethical issues as the rights of subjects, both human and animal.

These issues notwithstanding, research in abnormal psychology has taken giant steps forward, especially during the past 30 years. The training provided by graduate clinical programs has enabled thousands of researchers to conduct relevant and appropriate studies on clinical topics. In the past, many clinical researchers had only limited skills. The development of new and effective research tools and methods has also contributed to impressive growth in knowledge and insight.

## THE TASK OF CLINICAL RESEARCHERS

Clinical researchers, also called clinical scientists, try to discover universal "laws" or principles of abnormal psychological functioning. Like researchers in other fields, they try to use the *scientific method* in their work — that is, they systematically acquire and evaluate information through observation to gain an understanding of the phenomena they are studying. They search for general, or *nomothetic,* truths about the nature, causes, and treatments of abnormality ("nomothetic" is derived from the Greek *nomothetis,* "lawgiver") by observing and identifying the "average" behaviors and "typical" reactions of large numbers of people. They do not assess, diagnose, or treat individual clients; that is the job of clinical practitioners, who seek an *ideographic,* or individualistic, understanding of abnormal behavior. We shall explore their work in Chapters 4 and 5.

To formulate a nomothetic explanation of abnormal psychology, scientists in abnormal psychology, like scientists in all disciplines, attempt to *identify and explain relationships between variables.* Simply stated, a *variable* is any characteristic or event that can vary, whether from time to time, from place to place, or from person to person. Age, sex, and race are human variables. So are eye color, occupation, and social status. Clinical researchers are particularly interested in such variables as childhood traumas and other life experiences, moods, levels of social and occupational functioning, and responses to treatment techniques. They seek to determine whether two or more such variables change together and whether a change in one variable causes a change in another. For example, will the death of a parent cause a child to become depressed? If so, will a given therapy reduce that depression?

Such questions cannot be answered by logic alone. Reasoning is only as accurate as the information available to reason with, so numerous observations are needed to establish a factual basis on which to build a conclusion. Even then, reasoning may fail to serve the scientific enterprise. Although human beings are marvelously sophisticated and complex, they are prone to frequent errors in thinking (Kahneman, Slovic, & Tversky, 1982; Nisbett & Ross, 1980). Witness the false impressions we often form of others, and the many times we jump to wrong conclusions.

To minimize such errors and acquire valid information about abnormal behavior, clinical researchers depend primarily on three methods of investigation: the *case study*, the *correlational method*, and the *experimental method.* Each is best suited to certain circumstances and to answer certain questions. Collectively, they enable clinical scientists to formulate and test hypotheses, or hunches, that certain variables are related in certain ways, and to draw broad conclusions as to why. More properly, a *hypothesis* is a tentative explanation advanced to provide a basis for an investigation.

## THE CASE STUDY

A case study is a detailed and often interpretive description of one person. It describes the person's background, present circumstances, and symptoms. It may also describe the application and results of a particular treatment, and it may speculate about how the person's problems developed.

In Freud's (1909) famous case study of Little Hans, he discusses a 4-year-old boy who has developed a fear of horses. Freud gathered his material from detailed letters sent him by Hans's father, a physician who had attended lectures on psychoanalysis, and from Freud's own limited interviews with the child. Because of the great length of the study (140 pages in Freud's *Collected Papers*), only key excerpts will be reproduced here.

*O*ne day while Hans was in the street he was seized with an attack of morbid anxiety. . . . *[Hans's father writes:]*

My Dear Professor:

On January 7th he went to the Stadtpark with his nursemaid as usual. In the street he began to cry and asked to be taken home, saying that he wanted to "coax" with his Mummy. At home he was asked why he had refused to go any farther and had cried, but he would not say. Till the evening he was cheerful, as usual. But in the evening he grew visibly frightened; he cried and could not be separated from his mother. . . .

On January 8th my wife decided to go out with him herself, so as to see what was wrong with him. They went to Schönbrunn, where he always likes going. Again he began to cry, did not want to start, and was frightened. In the end he did go; but was visibly frightened in the street. On the way back from Schönbrunn he said to his mother, after much internal struggling: "I was afraid a horse would bite me." He had, in fact, become uneasy at Schönbrunn when he saw a horse. In the evening he seems to have had another attack similar to that of the previous evening, and to have wanted to be "coaxed" with. He was calmed down. He said, crying: "I know I shall have to go for a walk again tomorrow." And later: "The horse'll come into the room."

. . . A few days earlier the child had woken from an anxiety-dream to the effect that his mother had gone away, and that now he had no mother to coax with. . . . We can easily reconstruct what actually occurred in the unconscious. The child dreamed of exchanging endearments with his mother and of sleeping with her; but all the pleasure was transformed into anxiety. . . .

But the beginnings of this psychological situation go back further still.

The first reports of Hans date from a period when he was not quite three years old. At that time, by means of various remarks and questions, he was showing a quite peculiarly lively interest in that portion of body which he used to describe as his "widdler" [his word for penis]. . . .

When he was three and a half his mother found him with his hand to his penis. She threatened him in these words: "If

you do that, I shall send for Dr. A. to cut off your widdler. And then what'll you widdle with?"

*Hans:*   With my bottom.

He made this reply without having any sense of guilt as yet. But this was the occasion of his acquiring the "castration complex," the presence of which we are so often obliged to infer in analyzing neurotics, though they one and all struggle violently against recognizing it.

During the preceding summer [prior to his fear of horses] Hans had . . . been in a state of intensified sexual excitement, the object of which was his mother. The intensity of this excitement was shown by his two attempts at seducing his mother [the second of which occurred just before the outbreak of his anxiety].

My Dear Professor:

Hans, four and a quarter. This morning Hans was given his usual daily bath by his mother and afterwards dried and powdered. As his mother was powdering round his penis and taking care not to touch it, Hans said: "Why don't you put your finger there?"

*Mother:*   Because that'd be piggish.

*Hans:*   What's that? Piggish? Why?

*Mother:*   Because it's not proper.

*Hans [laughing]:*   But it's great fun.

. . . That afternoon the father and son visited me during my consulting hours. I already knew the queer little chap. . . . I do not know whether he remembered me, but he behaved irreproachably and like a perfectly reasonable member of human society. The consultation was a short one. His father opened it by remarking that, in spite of all the pieces of enlightenment we had given Hans, his fear of horses had not yet diminished. . . . Certain details which I now learnt — to the effect that he was particularly bothered by what horses wear in front of their eyes and by the black round their mouths — were certainly not to be explained from what we knew. But as I saw the two of them sitting in front of me and at the same time heard Hans's description of his anxiety-horses, a further piece of the solution shot through my mind, and a piece which I could well understand might escape his father. I asked Hans jokingly whether his horses wore eyeglasses, to which he replied that they did not. I then asked him whether his father wore eyeglasses, to which, against all the evidence, he once more said no. Finally I asked him whether by "the black round the mouth" he meant a moustache; and I then disclosed to him that he was afraid of his father, precisely because he was so fond of his mother. It must be, I told him, that he thought his father was angry with him on that account; but this was not so, his father was fond of him in spite of it, and he might admit everything to him without any fear. Long before he was in the world, I went on, I had known that a little Hans would come who would be so fond of his mother that he would be bound to feel afraid of his father because of it; and I had told his father this. "But why do you think I'm angry with you?'' his father interrupted me at this point; ''have I ever scolded you or hit you?'' Hans corrected him: ''Oh yes! You have hit me.'' ''That's not true. When was it, anyhow?'' ''This morning,'' answered the little boy; and his father recollected that Hans had quite unexpectedly butted his head into his stomach, so that he had given him as it were a reflex blow with his hand. It was remarkable that he had not brought this detail into connection with the neurosis; but he now recognized it as an expression of the little boy's hostile disposition towards him, and perhaps also as a manifestation of a need for getting punished for it.

By enlightening Hans on this subject I had cleared away his most powerful resistance against allowing his unconscious thoughts to be made conscious; for his father was himself acting as his physician. The worst of the attack was now over; there was a plentiful flow of material; the little patient summoned up courage to describe the details of his phobia, and soon began to take an active share in the conduct of the analysis.

. . . It was only then that we learnt what the objects and impressions were of which Hans was afraid. He was not only afraid of horses biting him—he was soon silent upon that point—but also of carts, of furniture-vans, and of buses [their common quality being, as presently became clear, that they were all heavily loaded], of horses that started moving, of horses that looked big and heavy, and of horses that drove quickly. The meaning of these specifications was explained by Hans himself: he was afraid of horses falling down, and consequently incorporated in his phobia everything that seemed likely to facilitate their falling down.

It was at this stage of the analysis that he recalled the event, insignificant in itself, which immediately preceded the outbreak of the illness and may no doubt be regarded as the exciting cause of the outbreak. He went for a walk with his mother, and saw a bus-horse fall down and kick about with its feet. This made a great impression on him. He was terrified, and thought the horse was dead; and from that time on he thought that all horses would fall down. His father pointed out to him that when he saw the horse fall down he must have thought of him, his father, and have wished that he might fall down in the same way and be dead. Hans did not dispute this interpretation; and a little while later he played a game consisting of biting his father, and so showed that he accepted the theory of his having identified his father with the horse he was afraid of. From that time forward his behavior to his father was unconstrained and fearless, and in fact a trifle overbearing.

It is especially interesting . . . to observe the way in which the transformation of Hans's libido into anxiety was projected on to the principal object of his phobia, on to horses. Horses interested him the most of all the large animals; playing at horses was his favorite game with the older children. I had a suspicion—and this was confirmed by Hans's father when I asked him—that the first person who had served Hans as a horse must have been his father. . . . When repression had set in and brought a revulsion of feeling along with it, horses, which had till then been associated with so much pleasure, were necessarily turned into objects of fear.

[Hans later reported] two concluding phantasies, with which his recovery was rounded off. One of them, that of the plumber giving him a new and, as his father guessed, a bigger widdler, was . . . a triumphant wish-phantasy, and with it he overcame his fear of castration.

'The plumber came; and first he took away my behind with a pair of pincers, and then gave me another, and then the same with my widdler. He said: ''Let me see your behind!'' and I had to turn round, and he took it away; and then he said: ''Let me see your widdler!'' ' . . .

*Father:*   He gave you a *bigger* widdler and a bigger behind.

*Hans:*   Yes.

*Father:*   Like Daddy's because you'd like to be Daddy.

*Hans:*   Yes, and I'd like to have a moustache like yours and hairs like yours.

His other phantasy, which confessed to the wish to be married to his mother and to have many children by her, did not merely exhaust the content of the unconscious complexes which had been stirred up by the sight of the falling horse and which had generated his anxiety. It also corrected that portion of those thoughts which was entirely unacceptable; for, instead of killing his father, it made him innocuous by promoting him to a marriage with Hans's grandmother. With this phantasy both the illness and the analysis came to an appropriate end.

## Value of the Case Study

Case studies are often written in the context of treatment. Faced with the task of helping someone, a clinician must first gather all relevant information and search through it for factors that may have brought about the person's problems. The clues provided by the case study may also have direct implications for the person's treatment. But case studies also play nomothetic roles that go far beyond the individual clinical case.

Case studies often serve as a source of ideas about behavior. They can "open the way for discoveries" (Bolgar, 1965) and "act as a breeding ground for hypotheses" (Shaughnessy & Zechmeister, 1985). Indeed, Freud's theory of psychoanalysis was based mainly on the cases he saw in private practice. He pored over his case studies to ferret out what he believed to be universal psychological processes and principles of development.

A case study may also provide tentative support for a theory (Kratochwill, Mott, & Dodson, 1984). Freud used the case study of Little Hans in precisely this way. He believed that this case supported the notion that boys experience an Oedipus complex, that this complex accounts for phobic fear, and that childhood sexuality plays an important role in personality development. Previously, Freud's arguments in support of these ideas had been drawn from analyses of adults who recalled childhood events. In Hans he had the opportunity to examine the proposed concepts during the actual course of a child's development.

Conversely, case studies may serve to challenge theoretical assumptions (Kratochwill et al., 1984). Psychoanalytic theorists claim, for example, that if overt symptoms are removed by behavioral rather than psychoanalytic techniques, new symptoms will emerge (a process called *symptom substitution*). A number of behavioral case studies, however, describe the removal of problem behaviors without the emergence of new ones later on, thus casting doubt on the psychoanalytic position (Mowrer & Mowrer, 1938).

Case studies also may serve as a source of ideas for new therapeutic techniques or as examples of unique applications of existing techniques. As we saw in Chapter 2, it was Breuer's famous study of Anna O. that first suggested that encouraging the patient to discuss his or her problems and the underlying psychological issues could in itself be therapeutic. Freud believed that the case study of Little Hans had once again demonstrated the therapeutic potential of a verbal approach.

Finally, case studies offer opportunities to study unusual problems that do not occur often enough to permit more general observations and comparisons. For years, for example, information about multiple personality disorders was based almost exclusively on case studies, such as the famous *Three Faces of Eve,* a clinical account of a woman who displayed three alternating personalities, each having a distinct set of memories, preferences, and personal habits (Thigpen & Cleckley, 1957).

## Limitations of the Case Study

Although case studies are useful in many ways, they have limitations. To begin with, they are reported by biased observers. Freud's psychoanalytic bias is apparent throughout the case study of Little Hans. He describes, for instance, an interaction between Hans and his mother as "the occasion of his acquiring the castration complex," and at another point he calls Hans's problem "the transformation of . . . libido into anxiety." Therapists are participants as well as observers, and they have a personal stake in the outcomes of their cases and the apparent success of their treatments. Their selection of material to include in case studies and their impressions of their clients' progress must be considered subjective and unsystematic, however well intended (Hersen & Barlow, 1976; Mischel, 1968; Bolgar, 1965).

A second problem is that therapists do not provide objective evidence that the problems they are studying have in fact been caused by the events that they *say* are responsible. After all, the events they single out as significant are only a fraction of those that may have played a part in creating the person's predicament. When an investigator can show that of a host of possible causes, only one satisfies all criteria and the others must be ruled out, the study is said to have internal accuracy, or ***internal validity*** (Shapiro, 1989; Cook & Campbell, 1979). Obviously, case studies are low on this dimension.

A famous case study of identical quadruplets called the Genain sisters illustrates this limitation. These persons of identical genetic makeup all developed schizophrenia, suggesting that this disorder may be genetically transmitted. Careful investigation also revealed, however, that the quadruplets were kept in the hospital for the first six weeks of their lives, were severely restricted in their interactions with others during childhood, and were brought up by a hostile and accusatory father — environmental factors that could also have contributed to their disorders. The case study could not confirm or clarify the relevance of the genetic or environmental factors.

Finally, case studies provide little basis for generalization. Even if we agree that Little Hans did develop a fearful reaction to horses because of Oedipal conflicts and fear of his father, how can we be confident that the phobias of other people are rooted in the same kinds of causes? Factors or treatment techniques that seem important in one case may be of no help at all in understanding or treating others. When the findings of an

One of the most celebrated case studies in abnormal psychology is a study of identical quadruplets, all of whom developed schizophrenic disorders in their 20s. At the National Institute of Mental Health (NIMH) in Washington, D.C., where these sisters underwent extensive study (Rosenthal, 1963), they were given the pseudonyms Nora, Iris, Myra, and Hester (after the initials NIMH) and the family name Genain (after the Greek words for "dire birth").

Some twenty-five years after the initial case study of the Genain sisters, the four women returned to NIMH for a follow-up study that used new technology to detect brain activity and structure (Buchsbaum & Haier, 1987). Marked variations in the sisters' levels of functioning corresponded to variations found in their brain activity and structure, suggesting that biological factors or interactions of biological and environmental factors may contribute to schizophrenia.

investigation can be generalized beyond the immediate study, the investigation is said to have external accuracy, or *external validity* (Shapiro, 1989; Sechrest, 1984; Cook & Campbell, 1979). Case studies are low on this dimension, too.

## THE CORRELATIONAL METHOD

The limitations of the case study are largely addressed by two other methods of investigation: the correlational method and the experimental method. They do not offer the many details that make case studies such interesting reading, but they do help investigators draw broad conclusions about the occurrence and characteristics of abnormality in the population at large. Three characteristics of these methods enable clinical investigators to gain nomothetic insights. (1) Researchers observe many individuals to collect enough information, or data, on which to base a conclusion. (2) They apply carefully prescribed procedures uniformly, so that other researchers can replicate their studies to see whether they consistently yield the same findings and implications. (3) The results of studies conducted by these methods can be analyzed by statistical tests that help indicate whether broad conclusions are justified. The correlational and experimental methods were used only occasionally to study abnormal functioning earlier in this century, but they are now the preferred methods of investigation.

*Correlation* is the degree to which events or characteristics vary in conjunction with each other. The *correlational method* is a research procedure used to determine this "co-relationship" between variables. Let us see how this method has been used to answer a question that has stimulated numerous clinical studies: Is there a correlation between the amount of life stress people experience and the degree of psychological disturbance they display (Paykel, 1982; Barrett, 1979; Brown, Harris, & Peto, 1973)? That is, as people repeatedly experience stressful events, are they increasingly likely to become psychologically disturbed?

To test this question, researchers must first find a way to measure the two variables (life stress and psychological disturbance). They can do so only if they translate the abstract variables they are investigating into discrete, observable entities or events, a process called *operationalization.* Life stress has been operationalized in some studies as the number of threatening events (such as a significant health problem or the loss of a job) that a person experiences during a certain period of time (Miller, Ingham, & Davidson, 1976; Brown, Sklair, Harris, & Birley, 1973), and degree of psychological disturbance has been operationalized as a score on a questionnaire that asks a person to express feelings of depression, anxiety, or the like in terms of a numerical scale (Ingham, 1965; Miller et al., 1976). One question on a depression questionnaire, for example, might ask how often one feels like crying; a question on an anxiety scale might ask how easily one is startled by minor noises.

Once the variables being examined are operationalized, researchers can measure them in a number of individuals and determine whether a general correlation between the variables does indeed exist. Those who are chosen for a study, individually called *subjects* and collectively called the *sample,* must be representative of the larger population about whom the researchers wish to make a statement. Otherwise the relationship found in the study might differ from the relationship that exists in the real-world area of interest. A study that found a correlation between life stress and psychological disturbance in a group of very young subjects, for example, might tell researchers little about what, if any, correlation exists among adults.

### The Direction of Correlation

Let us suppose that we conduct such a study. We collect life stress scores and depression scores for ten subjects and plot these scores on the graph shown in Figure 3-1. As you can see, the subject named Jim has a recent life stress score of 7 (seven threatening events over the past

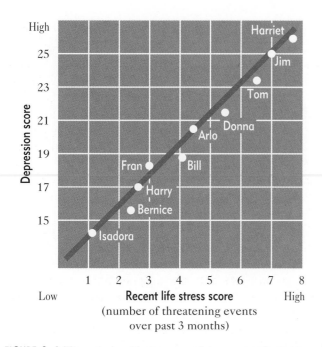

**FIGURE 3-1** The relationship between the amount of recent stress and feelings of depression shown by this hypothetical sample of ten subjects is a near-perfect *positive* correlation.

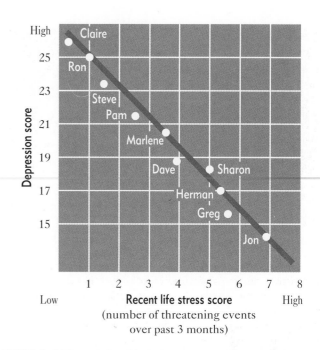

**FIGURE 3-2** The relationship between the amount of recent stress and feelings of depression shown by this hypothetical sample is a near-perfect *negative* correlation.

three months) and a depression score of 25; thus he is "located" at the point on the graph where these two scores meet. As you may also notice, it turns out that when the data points of all the individuals in this study are plotted, they fall along a roughly straight line that slopes upward. A straight line drawn so that each data point is as close to the line as possible is called the *line of best fit* — the one line that best fits all the data points.

The line of best fit in Figure 3-1 slopes upward to the right, indicating that the variables under examination are increasing or decreasing together. That is, the greater a particular individual's life stress score, the higher his or her score on the depression scale. Correlations of this kind are said to have a positive direction, and the correlation is referred to as a *positive correlation.* Most of the studies that have looked at the relationship between recent life stress and depression have indeed found a positive correlation between the two variables (Paykel, 1979; Miller et al., 1976; Brown et al., 1973; Paykel et al., 1969).

Correlations can have a negative rather than a positive direction. In a *negative correlation,* as the value of one variable increases, the value of the other variable decreases. If our subjects' scores had instead produced the downward-sloping graph shown in Figure 3-2, the correlation would have been negative and we would have said that depression decreases as life stress increases. Researchers have found, for example, a negative correlation between schizophrenia and socioeconomic status.

The lower one's socioeconomic status, the greater the probability of developing schizophrenia.

Finally, it is possible that two variables are *unrelated,* that there is no systematic relationship between them. As the measures of one variable increase, those of the other variable sometimes increase and sometimes decrease. If our subjects' scores had been uncorrelated in this way, the graph of their relationship would have looked like Figure 3-3. The line of best fit would have been a horizontal line with no slope. As we noted earlier, researchers have found such a lack of relationship between schizophrenia and the coldness of one's mother, despite past assumptions that these variables were positively correlated.

## The Magnitude of Correlation

In addition to knowing the direction of a correlation, researchers need to know its *magnitude,* or strength. That is, how closely do the two variables correspond? Does one always vary as a direct reflection of the other, or is their relationship less precise?

To appreciate this dimension of a correlation, look again at Figure 3-1. In this graph of a positive correlation, the data points all fall very close to the line of best fit. Such a configuration would enable researchers to predict with a high degree of confidence each person's score on one variable if they knew his or her score on the

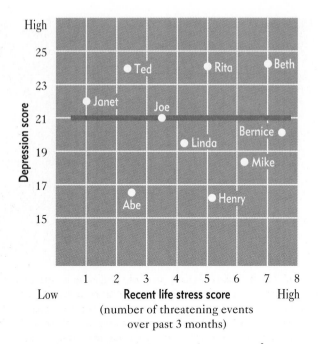

**FIGURE 3-3** The relationship between the amount of recent stress and feelings of depression shown by this hypothetical sample is a *near-zero* correlation.

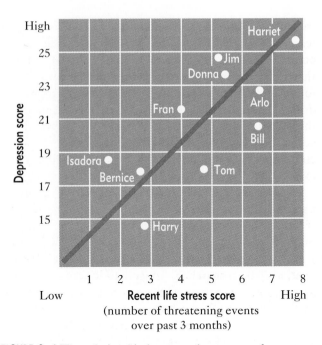

**FIGURE 3-4** The relationship between the amount of recent stress and feelings of depression shown by this hypothetical sample is a moderately *positive* correlation.

other. Figure 3-4, in contrast, shows a graph of a positive correlation in which the data points are loosely scattered around the upward-sloping line of best fit rather than hugging it closely. In this case, researchers cannot predict with as much accuracy a subject's score on one variable from the score on the other variable. Because the correlation in Figure 3-1 allows researchers to make more accurate predictions than the one in Figure 3-4, it is stronger, or greater in magnitude.

## The Correlation Coefficient

The direction and magnitude of a correlation can be calculated numerically and expressed by a statistical term called the *correlation coefficient,* symbolized by the letter *r* (technically, the Pearson product moment correlation coefficient, named after the man who devised it, Karl Pearson). The correlation coefficient can vary from + 1.00, which conveys a perfect positive correlation, down to − 1.00, which represents a perfect negative correlation between two variables. The sign of the coefficient (+ or −) signifies the direction of the correlation; the number represents its magnitude. An *r* of .00 reflects a *zero correlation,* or no relationship between variables. The closer *r* is to .00, the weaker, or lower in magnitude, the correlation. Thus correlations of + .75 and − .75 are of equal magnitude and equally strong, whereas a correlation of + .25 is weaker than either.

Because the behavior and reactions of every human being are subject to change and because many human responses can be measured only approximately, most correlations found in psychological research fall short of a perfect positive or negative correlation. One study of the correlation between recent life stress and depression had a sample of 68 adults and found a correlation of + .53 between the two variables (Miller et al., 1976). Although hardly perfect, a correlation of this magnitude with a sample of this size is considered large in psychological research.

## Statistical Analysis

Once scientists determine the correlation between variables for a particular group of subjects, they must decide whether it accurately reflects a real correlation in the general population from which the subjects are drawn. Even if they have been careful to choose a sample that is representative of the larger population, it is possible that the observed correlation occurred only by chance and that in actuality no such connection exists in the population of interest, or that a connection exists but with a different magnitude.

Scientists can never know for certain that the correlation they find is truly characteristic of the larger population, but they can test their conclusions to some extent by doing a *statistical analysis* of their data. In essence, they apply principles of probability to their findings to learn how likely it is that those particular findings have occurred by chance. If the statistical analysis suggests that chance is a likely reason for the correlation they found in the sample, the researchers have no basis for drawing broader conclusions from that correlation. But if the statistical analysis indicates that chance is unlikely to account for the relationship they found, they may conclude that their findings reflect a correlation that really exists in the general population.

By convention, psychology statisticians have defined a particular cutoff point to help them make this decision. If there is less than a 5 percent probability that a study's findings are due to chance, signified by the notation $p < .05$, those findings are said to be ***statistically significant,*** and the researcher may conclude that they reflect a situation that exists in the larger population. In one of the life stress studies described earlier, a statistical analysis did indicate a probability of less than 5 percent that the $+.53$ correlation found in the sample was due to chance (Miller et al., 1976). Therefore, the researchers concluded with some confidence that among adults in general, depression does tend to rise along with the amount of recent stress in a person's life. Certain dimensions of a correlational study are taken into consideration to determine whether the observed correlation is statistically significant, including the *size of the sample* (the number of subjects in the study) and the *magnitude of the correlation*. Of course, it is important to keep in mind that even when a study's results qualify as statistically significant, there is still as much as a 5 percent possibility that these results are due entirely to chance.

## Strengths and Limitations of the Correlational Method

The correlational method has certain advantages over the case study. When researchers quantify their variables, observe numerous individuals, and apply statistical analyses, they are in a better position to generalize their findings to people beyond the ones they have studied. That is, a correlational study exhibits more external validity than a case study. Researchers are also able to repeat correlational studies on new samples of subjects in order to support or clarify particular relationships, thus corroborating the results of a particular study.

On the other hand, correlational studies, like case studies, lack internal validity (Skinner, 1984). Although correlations give researchers predictive power by *describing* the relationship between two variables, they do not *explain* the relationship. Looking at the positive correlation found in many life stress studies, we might

Correlational studies of many pairs of twins have determined that a strong relationship exists between genetic factors and certain psychological disorders. These studies have typically compared the psychopathology concordance rate of pairs of identical twins (twins, like those pictured here, who have identical genes) with that of pairs of fraternal twins (twins whose genetic makeup is not identical). A *concordance* rate represents the likelihood that if one twin has a disorder, the other will develop it. Identical twins have higher concordance rates for some psychopathologies than fraternal twins do.

initially be tempted to conclude that increases in recent life stress *cause* people to feel more depressed. Actually, however, the two variables may be correlated for any one of three reasons:

1. *Variable A causes variable B.* Let us call amount of recent life stress variable *A* and depression variable *B*. It is possible that the two variables are positively correlated because *A* causes *B*. That is, increases in life stress cause people to feel sadder, particularly about the difficult situations they have been experiencing.

2. *Variable B causes variable A.* People who are depressed tend to become passive and to withdraw from their usual activities and social relationships (Gilbert, 1984; Lewinsohn et al., 1981; Beck, 1976, 1967; Lewinsohn, 1974). This depressive approach to life may cause them to mismanage their money, be less effective at work, and let social relationships deteriorate. That is, depression may tend to increase the number of stressful life situations.

3. *Variable C causes both A and B.* It is quite possible that an increase in both life stress and depression is caused by a third variable — poverty, for example. A limited income may cause people to experience more health crises, poorer living conditions,

extra job pressures, and other forms of life stress. At the same time, poverty may cause them to feel unhappy about their deprivations and limited opportunities. If this should be the case, the correlation between life stress and depression would simply be reflecting the effect of poverty on each of these variables.

That correlation says nothing about causation is not always a problem for clinicians. Sometimes it's enough to know the likelihood that two variables will occur together. Because clinicians are aware that suicide attempts increase as people become more depressed, for example (Beck, 1991, 1989, 1967), those who work with severely depressed clients can keep on the lookout for symptoms of suicidal thinking. It doesn't necessarily make a difference to them whether depression directly causes suicidal behaviors or whether a third variable, such as a sense of hopelessness, causes both depression and suicidal thoughts. As soon as the clinicians identify intense feelings of depression, they can stand ready to take suicide prevention measures (such as hospitalization).

Often, however, clinicians do want to know whether one variable causes another. Do parents' marital conflicts cause their children to be more anxious? Does job dissatisfaction lead to feelings of depression? Will a given therapeutic procedure help people to cope more effectively in life? Questions about causality call for the use of the experimental method.

## Special Forms of Correlational Research

Two kinds of correlational research are used widely by clinical researchers and warrant special consideration—epidemiological studies and longitudinal studies. *Epidemiological* studies are investigations that determine the incidence and prevalence of a disorder in a given population (Bromet, 1984). *Incidence* is the number of *new cases* of a disorder in the population that emerge within a particular time interval; *prevalence* is the *total number* of cases (that is, the sum of existing and newly emerging cases) of the disorder in the population at any given time. Epidemiological studies throughout the United States have indicated that women have a higher prevalence rate of anxiety disorders and depression than men, elderly people have a higher prevalence rate of suicide than younger people, and blacks have a higher prevalence rate of high blood pressure than whites. Findings of this sort help investigators identify groups at risk for particular disorders and often lead

them to suspect that something unique about the group is helping to cause the disorder. For example, declining health in elderly people may cause them to commit more suicides than younger people. Yet, as in other forms of correlational research, such suspicions cannot be clarified without use of the experimental method.

*Longitudinal studies* (also called *high risk* or *developmental studies*) are investigations in which the characteristics or behavior of the same subjects are observed on many different occasions over a long period of time. In one well-known longitudinal study (Griffith et al., 1980; Mednick, 1971), investigators observed the progress over the years of normally functioning children whose mothers were schizophrenic (that is, normal children who were considered to be at risk for schizophrenia). The researchers found, among other things, that the children of the mothers with the most severe cases of schizophrenia were more likely to develop a psychological disorder and to commit crimes at later points in their development. Because longitudinal studies ascertain the order of events, they provide stronger clues than conventional correlational studies about which events are causes and which are consequences. But they do not pinpoint causation. Are the psychological problems that certain high-risk children encounter later in their lives caused by a genetic factor inherited from their severely disturbed mothers, by their mothers' inadequate parenting, by the loss of their mothers to extended hospitalization, or by other factors? Again, experimental studies are necessary to answer these questions.

## THE EXPERIMENTAL METHOD

An *experiment* is a procedure in which a situation is manipulated and the effect of the manipulation is observed. The French playwright Molière created a character who was astonished to learn that he had been speaking prose all his life. Similarly, most of us perform experiments throughout our lives without knowing that we are behaving so scientifically.

Suppose that we go to a party on campus to celebrate the end of midterm exams. As we mix with people at the party, we begin to notice that many of them are becoming quiet and depressed. The more we talk, the more distraught they become. As the party deteriorates before our eyes, we decide we must do something, but before we can eliminate the problem, we need to know what's causing it. Our first hunch may be that something we're doing is responsible. Perhaps our incessant chatter about academic pressures is upsetting everyone. We decide to change the topic to skiing and the mountains of Colorado, and we watch for signs of depression in our next round of conversations. The problem seems to clear up; most people now smile and laugh as they converse with us. As a final check on our thinking, we could go back to talking about school with the next several people we meet. Their dark and hostile reaction would probably convince us that our academic focus of discussion has indeed been causing the problem.

In this scenario, we have performed an experiment. To test our *hypothesis* about the causal relationship between our discussions of academic matters and the depressed mood of the people around us, we have *manipulated* the variable that we suspect is the cause (the topic of discussion) and then *observed* the effect of that manipulation on the variable that we suspect is the effect (the mood of the people around us). In scientific experiments, the manipulated variable is called the **independent variable,** and the variable being observed is called the **dependent variable.**

## Confounds

The goal of an experiment is to isolate and identify the cause of a certain effect. If we cannot separate the true, or primary, cause from a host of other potential causes, then the experiment gives us very little information. It would not be very helpful, for instance, to find out that the depressed mood of others is caused *either* by our talk of school or by some other factor, such as the music at the party or midterm fatigue.

The major obstacles to isolating the true cause and thus carrying out an effective experiment are known as *confounds.* These are variables other than the independent variable that are also acting on the dependent variable. When there are confounds in an experiment, the experimenter cannot confidently attribute the results to the independent variable under investigation because it may actually be the confounding variables that are causing the observed changes.

One of the questions most frequently asked by clinical scientists is, "Does a particular therapy relieve the symptoms of a given disorder?" (Shapiro, 1989; Everitt, 1987; Luborsky & Spence, 1978; Bergin & Lambert, 1978; Smith & Glass, 1977). Because this question is about a causal relationship, it can be answered only by an experiment. Let us suppose that we have developed a new treatment called "buttermilk therapy" and that we have reason to believe it will alleviate anxiety in our clients. Our first thought might be to measure our clients' anxiety levels both before and after giving them a large glass of buttermilk and see whether their anxiety

levels decrease with this treatment. In so doing, we would be manipulating an independent variable (the presence or absence of buttermilk therapy) and observing its effect on a dependent variable (the clients' anxiety). But if we perform this experiment and observe a decrease in anxiety, what can we actually conclude?

Not much. Without realizing it, we have allowed our independent variable, buttermilk therapy, to change right along with the ever-present confound of time, and we cannot tell whether the decrease in our clients' anxiety is due to the independent variable that we manipulated or to the confound that we overlooked. That is, it is possible that the clients simply became less anxious during the hour they spent in the therapist's office, and that this simple passage of time was responsible for their decreased anxiety. Because we have not separated the effects of the independent variable from the effects of the confound, we do not know which one was the cause of the change in the dependent variable.

Other confounds also may have been present in this experiment. Situational variables such as the location of the therapy office (a quiet country setting) or a soothing color scheme in the office may have had an effect. Perhaps the subjects in this particular experiment were unusually motivated or had extraordinarily high expectations that the therapy would work, thus accounting for their improvement. Or perhaps the supportive tone of voice of the assistant who served the buttermilk actually made the subjects more relaxed. To minimize the influence of potential confounds, researchers incorporate three important features into their experiments — control groups, random assignment, and blind designs.

## The Control Group

A *control group* is a group of subjects who are not exposed to the independent variable under investigation. By comparing this group with the *experimental group,* the subjects who *are* exposed to the independent variable, an experimenter can better determine the effect of that variable. In our buttermilk therapy study, for example, we might divide our clients into two groups. The experimental group would come into the office and receive buttermilk therapy for an hour, and the control group would simply come into the office for an hour. Now time passes for both groups. The control group shows us the effect of the passage of time (and a host of other confounds present in the office) on anxiety, while the experimental group shows us the effect of both time (and those other confounds) *and* buttermilk therapy. If we were to find later that the anxiety levels of clients in the experimental group were lower than the anxiety levels of clients in the control group, we might conclude that buttermilk therapy was effective in reducing anxiety, above and beyond the effects of time and any other confounds. In short, our control group would have helped us rule out the possibility that something other than the independent variable was causing all of the observed changes in the dependent variable.

It is also important to make sure there are no systematic differences, besides therapy or no therapy, in the way the two groups are treated. This could become another kind of confound. If one of our groups were coming to the sessions at night and the other during the day, or if one were being greeted by a grumpy receptionist and the other by a friendly one, these differences rather than the buttermilk therapy could be responsible for the difference in their anxiety levels at the experiment's end. Experimenters must guard against this type of confound by trying to provide all subjects, both control and experimental, with experiences that are identical in every way except for the one critical item under investigation, the independent variable.

## Random Assignment

The way the members of the two groups are chosen is as important as the experimental protocol, for systematic differences that already exist in control and experimental subjects before the experiment may also confound the result. Let's suppose that in setting up our scheme for evaluating the effectiveness of buttermilk therapy, we allow the subjects themselves to choose the group they wish to join. It is likely that those who love buttermilk will choose the buttermilk group and those who detest it will choose the control group. This *self-selection* can result in quite a long list of differences between the control group and the experimental group. They will include not only differences in the therapy experiences of the two groups, but also every single systematic difference that exists between people who like buttermilk and those who do not. For example, people who like buttermilk may be healthier, stronger, older, more affectionate, and smarter than those who detest it. All these factors become confounded with the independent variable, so it cannot be known with certainty which is responsible for a decrease in anxiety in the experimental group.

To reduce the possibility that systematic differences already existing between subjects are somehow causing the differences observed between the groups, experimenters typically use **random assignment** (Shapiro & Shapiro, 1983). This selection procedure ensures that every subject in the experiment is as likely to be placed in one group as the other. Rather than allow subjects to

choose their own group in our buttermilk therapy experiment, we might randomly assign them to groups by flipping a coin or picking their names out of a hat. When experimenters randomly assign subjects to different groups, they have more reason to believe that any differences between the groups that arise during the experiment are indeed caused by the independent variable. (Box 3-1 shows what can happen when assignment is not random.) Of course, even if subjects were randomly assigned to the groups in our buttermilk therapy experiment, we might still end up with all the strongest, smartest, and most affectionate subjects accidentally grouped together, but the likelihood of that occurrence is greatly reduced.

## Blind Design

A final confound problem that must be addressed is the effect of bias, whether on the part of the subjects or of the people conducting the experiment (Lindsay & Powell, 1987). Subjects may bias an experiment's results by trying to please or help the experimenter. In the buttermilk therapy experiment, buttermilk subjects, knowing the purpose of the study and knowing which group they are in, might actually work harder to feel better to fulfill the experimenter's expectations. If so, **subject bias** rather than buttermilk therapy could be causing the anxiety reduction found in the experimental group.

Even if subjects do not wish to help an experimenter, their expectations about the outcome of a study may influence the way they respond. Numerous studies have indicated that just expecting a treatment to help them causes many people to improve, even if the treatment given is a phony substitute such as a sugar pill, called a **placebo** (Latin for "I shall please"). The improvement brought about by placebos is real and often substantial, even though the treatment itself is empty (see Box 3-2). One study compared the progress of anxious clients who were given placebos over a period of months with the progress of anxious clients who remained on a treatment waiting list during the same period of time, and found that many of those who took the pills and expected them to work improved significantly more than the people on the waiting list (Brill et al., 1964).

There is a straightforward way of preventing the potential effects of subject bias in an experiment: do not let subjects know which group they are in. In the buttermilk study, control subjects could be given a placebo, a buttermilk substitute that looks and tastes like buttermilk but has none of the ingredients of actual buttermilk. If the experimental (true buttermilk) subjects then improved more than the control (false buttermilk) subjects, we could more confidently conclude that but-

## BOX 3-1

# Artifacts: Stress and the Executive Monkey

An enormous quantity of scientific research is produced each year. Most of these studies can be thought of as brush strokes on a canvas—it takes many individual strokes before a recognizable image begins to emerge. Conclusions are generally built on accumulated evidence, and no single study is expected to prove a hypothesis independently. Every so often, however, a single experiment yields results so compelling that the thinking of an entire generation is affected.

But beware: an experiment that influences our view of the world may later prove to have serious flaws that have gone unnoticed. Even the best-intentioned and most painstaking researchers are only human. They do not always recognize every possible confound. Or they may have a good idea for an experiment but lack the specific technical skills needed to carry it out. Or in their eagerness to get results that support their theory, they may become a little sloppy in their procedures. Usually peer reviewers catch the mistake before the research is published; or if it is published, it does not become particularly influential and is lost in the crowd. If such an experiment passes peer review and is then seen as important, however, the consequences can be both embarrassing to the researcher and harmful to the discipline. Consider the "executive monkey study."

What happens if you take two monkeys, put them in separate wire cages, and then give them shocks every twenty seconds for six hours—shocks that *one* of the monkeys can terminate by pressing a lever? The psychologist J. V. Brady predicted that the monkeys who did *not* have a lever to press would develop ulcers because they had no control over the shocks (Brady et al., 1958). In his experiment ex-

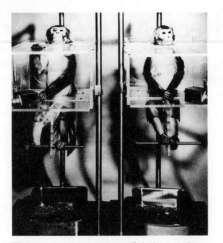

The executive monkey *(left)* learns that it can prevent shocks by pressing a lever with its hand. The control monkey *(right)* is given no control over the shocks and appears to lose interest in both the lever and its surroundings.

actly the opposite happened. In each of four pairs of monkeys, the "executive" monkey—the one who was able to stop the shocks—developed duodenal ulcers and died. The other monkey in each pair was not affected. This result ran counter to the theory of learned helplessness, which predicted that the monkeys without control would suffer a greater number of problems than those in control of the shocks. The research community and the public embraced the new finding, partly because it supported the intuitive notion that people with high-level positions in business, people who make important decisions every day, were prone to get ulcers. For thirteen years Brady's results exerted great influence on psychological views about the relationship between environment and stress.

To "replicate" an experiment is to repeat it exactly as it was done the first time and get the same results. The executive monkey study could not be replicated. Investigators who attempted and failed, including Brady himself, looked carefully at the original procedure used and finally found a glaring mistake. It turned out that Brady had failed to consider the importance of assigning his subjects at random to each of the conditions in the experiment. He had pretested all eight monkeys by giving them shocks. The first four monkeys to press the lever were assigned to the "executive" condition. A later study found that animals with a higher response rate (animals that would press the lever first in Brady's pretest) were more likely to develop ulcers (Weiss, 1977). It appeared that their higher emotionality was responsible for both the response rate and the ulcers. In later executive monkey studies in which there *was* random assignment, the animals without control over the shocks suffered more than those with control. Brady's finding had been an *artifact*—a product of his own activity, not the monkeys'.

Brady had made an honest mistake. His result was the opposite of his expectations and surprised him as much as anyone else. Unfortunately, it also was generally accepted and cited for more than a dozen years. Nevertheless, the erroneous experiment has proved to be valuable: it spurred an enormous amount of research that has ultimately led to a more accurate understanding of stress and how it relates to health. It also taught the scientific community a great lesson. Apart from the few researchers who intentionally alter data and results to gain status or influence, there will always be others who make inadvertent mistakes. The only way to minimize such mistakes is to train researchers as carefully as possible and review critically each study that is announced.

termilk was the cause of their improvement. This experimental strategy is called a **blind design** because subjects are blind as to which group they are in.

Even when subject bias is addressed, an experiment may still have the problem of **experimenter bias.** That is, an experimenter may have expectations that are subtly transmitted to subjects and affect the outcome of the experiment. In the buttermilk therapy experiment, for

---

= BOX 3-2 =

# The Placebo Effect: A Researcher's Best Friend?

A medical researcher wants to know if drug X can reduce migraine headache pain. She finds a sample of 300 patients who suffer from migraines and gives one-third of the group drug X, one-third of the group a bitter-tasting orange pill that is known to have no physiological effect on migraine headaches, and the remaining third no pill at all. Those who receive a pill are told that it is an experimental drug that is highly likely to reduce their pain. The researcher then finds that 85 percent of the subjects taking drug X, 40 percent in the fake-drug group, and 10 percent of the subjects in the no-drug control group report relief from headache pain. What can the researcher conclude? If you checked her experimental methodology and found that it followed all the rules, you would probably conclude that drug X is effective in treating migraine headache pain. You could also conclude that 10 percent of patients can be expected to recover over time without any treatment at all. And you would come to the somewhat troubling conclusion that the inert, chemically inactive orange pill is also very effective in reducing headache pain. For centuries physicians have known that patients suffering from many kinds of illness, from seasickness to angina, find relief from substances that have no known pharmacological effect. The *placebo* has emerged from the shadow of shamanism and mystery to become a rigorously studied phenomenon as well as a widely accepted treatment.

A startling discovery was made in 1975: the brain produces opiatelike substances known as **endorphins,** naturally occurring pain-relieving chemicals that fit into specific receptor sites in the brain. No one was quite sure why these chemicals were produced or what caused them to be released, but a partial answer came in the late 1970s. A group of doctors studying the use of placebos during dental surgery gave one set of patients an inert chemical and the other an inert chemical along with the drug *naloxone,* which is known to block the effects of endorphins. Both sets of patients believed they were receiving a pain-killing substance, but only the group who received the placebo alone reported a reduction in pain. The researchers concluded that placebos somehow caused a release of endorphins in the brain, an effect that was erased by the addition of naloxone. That is, taking a placebo can lead the body to release a powerful painkiller.

The placebo effect is often encountered during studies to test the efficacy of drugs for treating mental disorders, and it seems that the release of endorphins provides some relief for mental disorders, much as it does for physical disorders. Moreover, the placebo does not have to be a pill or any other physical substance. Almost any form of psychotherapy can have a placebo effect. Some researchers have even suggested that "the placebo effect is an important component" of many methods of psychotherapy (Shapiro & Morris, 1978).

This suggestion has been tested in experiments similar to the migraine study. Instead of migraines, the subjects are suffering from depression or some other psychological problem. Instead of a pill, one group of subjects receives real psychotherapy and a second group receives fake psychotherapy (a therapist spends time talking to the patient but does not follow any recognized therapeutic regimen). A third group receives no treatment of any kind. The results are the same as in the migraine study: strong improvement for the first group, significant improvement for the second group, and minimal improvement for the third—the classic placebo effect. Thus today's researchers often include a placebo group as a control group in their experiments. Real psychotherapy is considered to be effective, above and beyond its placebo effect, only when subjects given real psychotherapy improve more than subjects who receive placebo (fake) therapy.

What is it about psychotherapy that triggers the placebo effect? One element may be the unique and complex relationship that exists between healer and sufferer. The patient's confidence in the therapist's expertise and skill and in the methods being used are critical to successful treatment (O'Connell, 1983). Another element may be that psychotherapy involves ritualistic administration of a treatment. Specific interactions take place in a prescribed location according to definable rules of conduct. The basis for effective therapy is this mutual set of expectations (Fish, 1973). These factors have a powerful effect on the patient, and may trigger endorphin release or other processes that lead to relief.

example, the experimenter might use a more promising tone of voice when talking with buttermilk subjects than when talking with control subjects or be more thorough in answering their questions. This subtle difference in the experimenter's behavior might bring about greater improvement in the buttermilk subjects, confounding the effect of the buttermilk per se. This confound source is referred to as the **Rosenthal effect,** after the psychologist who first helped clarify the effects of experimenter bias (Rosenthal & Rubin, 1978; Rosenthal, 1966).

Experimenters can eliminate the potential effects of their own bias by contriving to be blind themselves. In the buttermilk study, an aide could prepare the buttermilk substitute, pour the buttermilk and the buttermilk substitute into coded bottles, and not tell the experimenter who administered the therapy which subjects were receiving true buttermilk and which were receiving false buttermilk. Only when the experiment was over and all the observations had been recorded would the experimenter learn which subjects actually received buttermilk and which ones received the substitute.

While subjects *or* the experimenter may be kept blind in an experiment, it is best that *both* be blind (a ***double-blind design***). In fact, most clinical experimenters now use double-blind designs to test the efficacy of antianxiety, antidepressant, and antipsychotic medications (Davis, 1980; Hollon & Beck, 1978; Claghorn, 1976; Morris & Beck, 1974). They typically compare the effect of a target drug with that of a placebo or some other drug, making sure that neither drug administrators nor patients know which patients are receiving which substance. Many experiments further have separate judges assess the patients' improvement and make sure that the judges, too, are blind to the group each patient is in — a *triple-blind design.*

## Statistical Analysis

The findings of experiments, like those of correlational studies, must be analyzed statistically. In any experiment, no matter how well designed, there is a possibility that the differences observed between the experimental and control groups have occurred simply by chance. The experimenter must apply a statistical analysis to the experimental data and determine how likely it is that the pattern of changes in the dependent variable is due to chance. If the likelihood is less than 5 percent ($p < .05$), the observed differences are considered to be statistically significant, and the experimenter may conclude with some confidence that they are due to the independent variable.

As with correlational studies, several dimensions of an experiment are taken into account in determining

whether a pattern of findings is statistically significant. These include the *size of the sample,* the number of subjects actually studied; the *extent of the difference* observed between the groups; the *central tendency* of each group's scores — that is, the average score, or *mean,* for each group of subjects; and the *variability* of each group's scores, or how widely the scores range within each group of subjects. The larger the sample, the greater the observed difference, and the lower the variability of scores within each group, the more likely it is that a pattern of findings will be ruled statistically significant. Yet even when experimenters statistically reject chance as the cause of an observed difference, they may be wrong. It is always at least remotely possible that a pattern of findings is due to nothing more than chance.

## Variations in Experimental Design

It is not easy to devise an experiment that is both well controlled and enlightening. The goal of manipulating a single variable without inadvertently manipulating others — that is, controlling *every possible* confound — is rarely attained in practice. Moreover, because psychological experiments must involve living things, there are numerous ethical and practical constraints on the kinds of manipulations that can be done. For these reasons clinical experimenters often settle for imperfect variations of optimal experimental designs to determine cause-and-effect relationships. The most common such variations are the quasi-experimental design, the natural experiment, the analogue experiment, and the single-subject experiment.

**Quasi-Experimental Design** *Quasi-experiments* are experiments in which investigators do not randomly assign subjects to control and experimental groups but instead make use of groups that already exist in the world at large (Owens, Slade, & Fielding, 1989; Campbell & Stanley, 1963). Because these groups already differ before the experiment, the investigator is technically "correlating" their existing difference with whatever manipulations are then carried out in the study, leading some researchers to refer to this research method as ***mixed design.*** Research into the problem of child abuse illustrates the use of a quasi-experimental design.

Clinical case studies have suggested that a history of child abuse may cause children to become depressed and withdrawn and to have a poor self-concept (Bender, 1976). To test this relationship most systematically, researchers would have to select a sample of small children and assign them randomly to either an experimental or a control group, with the experimental subjects receiving physical abuse throughout their childhood and the control subjects being raised without physical abuse. Clearly, such an experiment would be immoral.

Because they cannot inflict abuse on a randomly chosen group of children, experimenters instead compare children who already have a history of abuse with children who do not. Of course, this strategy violates the rule of random assignment and introduces a number of possible confounds into the study. Children who receive physical punishment, for example, usually come from poorer and larger families than children who are punished verbally (Goode, 1974). Any differences in mood or self-concept found between abused and nonabused children, then, might be due to differences in wealth or family size rather than to the abuse.

Some child-abuse researchers have addressed this problem by using the quasi-experimental design of **matched control groups.** In one such investigation, the experimenter matched experimental and control subjects who had a number of potentially confounding variables in common, including age, sex, race, birth order, number of children in the family, socioeconomic status, and type of neighborhood (Kinard, 1982). That is, for every abused child in the experimental group, she chose an unabused child of the same age, sex, race, and so on to be included in the control group. Thus, when the data showed that the children in the experimental group were significantly sadder and thought less of themselves than the children in the control group, the investigator was able to conclude with some confidence that abuse, and not one of those potential confounds, was causing the differences in mood and self-concept.

When scientists use random assignment, they are enlisting the laws of probability to help them eliminate any confounding differences between the experimental and control groups. When they use a matched control group, they are hoping that their deliberate and careful selection of subjects will have the same effect. Of course, those experimenters are eliminating only the confounds they are consciously matching for. Any important confounds they fail to consider will still remain and invalidate their findings. Clearly, then, although they are often necessary, quasi-experiments that use matched control groups are less dependable than experiments using random assignment (Owens et al., 1989).

**Natural Experiment** *Natural experiments* are those in which nature rather than an experimenter manipulates an independent variable, and the experimenter systematically observes the effects. This is the design that must be used for studying the psychological effects of unusual and unpredictable events, such as floods, earthquakes, plane crashes, and fires. Because the subjects in these studies are selected for the experimental group by an accident of fate rather than by conscious design, natural experiments are actually one kind of quasi-experiment.

On February 26, 1972, a dam gave way in the town of Buffalo Creek, West Virginia, releasing 132 million gallons of black slag, mud, and water into the valley below. The black swirling waters carried with them houses, trailers, cars, bridges, and human beings. The disaster killed 125 people, injured hundreds more, and left thousands homeless. A multimillion-dollar court settlement against those responsible for maintaining the dam later ruled that the flood had caused psychological impairment in many survivors. Accordingly, this tragedy has received considerable attention from investigators in psychology, including a comprehensive natural experiment conducted by Goldine Glesser and her colleagues (1981).

On the basis of clinical reports and studies of other disasters, the Glesser group formulated several expectations about the psychological effects that the flood might have on the survivors. For example, they expected the survivors to display pathological levels of anxiety, depression, and sleep disturbance as a result of the ordeal. These became the dependent variables of the experiment. Data collected from 381 survivors by means of extensive interviews, self-report checklists, surveys, and physical examinations administered approximately eighteen months after the flood confirmed the experimenters' expectations. The survivors scored significantly higher on anxiety and depression measures than did a control group of people who lived elsewhere. In fact, the anxiety and depression scores of the survivors were about the same as those of clients being treated for anxiety and depression at two mental health clinics in other parts of the country. Similarly, the survivors experienced more sleep disturbances (difficulty falling asleep or staying asleep and nightmares) than the control subjects did. The experimenters found the greatest psychological impairment among those survivors who had come closest to dying and among those who had lost family members and friends in the flood. Finally, the study found more severe psychological disturbances among older children than among preschool-age survivors.

Natural experiments suffer from the same limitation as other quasi-experiments. That is, confounds may be causing the observed effects. The researchers could not know, for example, whether the job pressures of Buffalo Creek residents had differed systematically from those of the control subjects, and so might have accounted for the differences in anxiety and depression scores and sleep disturbances.

Natural experiments also have other limitations. Because they rely on unexpected occurrences in nature, they cannot be repeated at will. Also, because each nat-

In 1972 a flash flood destroyed much of Buffalo Creek, West Virginia, injuring or killing hundreds of people and leaving thousands homeless. Natural experiments conducted in the aftermath found, as predicted, that survivors of the flood were significantly more anxious and depressed than people living elsewhere. This finding suggests that catastrophes typically cause lingering feelings of anxiety and depression among survivors.

ural event is unique in some ways, broad generalizations drawn from a single study could be incorrect. Nevertheless, findings obtained repeatedly over the years in hundreds of natural experiments have enabled clinical scientists to identify a pattern of anxiety-related symptoms that many people display in the wake of catastrophes. We shall be discussing these *post-traumatic stress disorders* in Chapter 6.

**Analogue Experiment**    There is one way in which investigators can freely manipulate independent variables while avoiding many of the ethical and practical limitations of clinical research. They can conduct *analogue experiments.* Experimenters who use this strategy induce laboratory subjects to behave in ways they believe to be like real-life abnormal behavior. They then conduct experiments on this laboratory-created, analogous form of abnormality in the hope of shedding light on the real-life counterpart.

Experimenters usually use animals as subjects in analogue studies. Animal subjects are easier to gather and manipulate than human subjects, and they present fewer ethical problems. While the needs and rights of animal subjects must also be considered, most experimenters are willing to subject animals to more manipulation and discomfort than human subjects (see Box 3-3). They feel that the insights gained from such experimentation outweigh the discomfort of the animals. In addition, experimenters can, and often do, use human subjects in analogue experiments.

As we shall see in Chapter 8, analogue studies have been used with great success by Martin Seligman

(1975) to investigate the causes of human depression. Seligman has theorized that people become depressed when they believe they no longer have any control over the good and bad things that happen in their lives and that life's pleasures, such as job satisfaction, love relationships, and monetary rewards, are really random events beyond their control. According to Seligman, while other factors may contribute to depression, this perception of helplessness is the primary cause.

Seligman's strategy for investigating his hypothesis experimentally has been to gather a group of subjects, attempt to change their perceptions of control (manipulate the independent variable), and see whether their moods change accordingly (observe the dependent variable). His subjects have often been dogs, and he has subjected them to random shocks — unpleasant events over which they have absolutely no control. The noxious stimuli are started and stopped at random intervals irrespective of anything the dogs try to do. Seligman has found that the dogs typically react to this loss of control with symptoms suspiciously similar to human depression. In contrast to the control subjects in his studies, who are allowed to escape or avoid shocks and do so with vigor and with no change in their overall behavior patterns, the experimental subjects become exceedingly passive, socially and sexually withdrawn, and slow moving, their demeanor resembling the sadness and pessimism of depression. They stop trying to avoid the shocks and just seem to give up. In short, under laboratory conditions Seligman has created a pattern of behavior — he calls it *learned helplessness* — that he believes to be an analogue of human depression.

Seligman and other researchers have conducted hundreds of experiments on the laboratory phenomenon of learned helplessness in an effort to improve their understanding of depression. They have manipulated all kinds of independent variables (shocks, loud noises, failure experiences, and so on) to determine which kinds of loss of control lead to learned helplessness and, by implication, to depression (Seligman, 1975). They have manipulated the early life experiences of experimental subjects to determine which kinds of experiences help immunize subjects against learned helplessness and, again by analogy, against depression (Hannom, Rosellini, & Seligman, 1975; Seligman & Maier, 1967). And they have studied whether certain interventions reverse learned helplessness and so might help reverse depression (Seligman, Rosellini, & Kozak, 1975; Seligman, Maier, & Geer, 1968).

Seligman and his colleagues have conducted similar analogue studies on human subjects. Typically, their laboratory human subjects are randomly exposed to unpleasant and unavoidable stimuli such as loud noises or failures on cognitive tasks. Given such losses of control,

BOX 3-3

# Ethical Issues in Research

There is no question that research is necessary if we are to understand and treat mental disorders or that this is a worthy goal—in fact, an essential one. The design of meaningful research, however, is fraught with ethical pitfalls. Should people be given experimental treatments that could be harmful? Is it right to withhold treatment from one group of patients to compare them with another group receiving a new therapy? When does the benefit to many outweigh the suffering of a few? These are but some of the questions facing researchers, patients, and society. To produce dependable results, an experiment must be conducted according to the scientific method. When this method conflicts with standards of ethical treatment of people and animals, society—not researchers alone—must decide the answer.

Obtaining informed consent from patients recruited to participate in an experiment is perhaps the most fundamental ethical safeguard in clinical human research. Informed consent "emphasizes societal respect for individual free choice and rational decision making as intrinsic to human dignity" (Annas, Glantz, & Katz, 1977). A dilemma arises when one must obtain consent from people who suffer from disorders that may affect their judgment. Does a mental disorder such as schizophrenia or depression render people unable to make this decision for themselves?

Some researchers argue that when a therapy is not considered harmful, it is not an abrogation of patients' rights to involve them in studies in which they receive treatment, whether or not they are able to make an informed decision to participate. Yet there is evidence that any therapy can have at least some harmful consequences (Mays & Franks, 1985).

Perhaps it should be said that there is *no* evidence of widespread, systematic abuse of patients with psychological disorders for research purposes. There are, however, isolated, highly publicized instances of misconduct, as when the U.S. military gave the hallucinogenic drug mescaline to a patient without his consent (Lubasch, 1982). Such instances highlight the ethical necessity for obtaining consent. Regulations that now govern the conduct of experimenters were written by the U.S. Department of Health and Human Services and include guidelines for making sure that potential human subjects are well informed on eight basic issues:

1. That they are participating in an experiment and what procedures will be used

2. Any potential or foreseeable risks

3. Any benefits to themselves or others

4. Any alternative procedures available to the patient

5. Whether or not their participation and performance are confidential

6. Whether or not they will receive any compensation if they are harmed during the experiment

7. Whom they may contact to ask questions about the experiment

8. That their participation is voluntary and that there is no penalty if they refuse to participate

While these are eminently reasonable guidelines for informing potential subjects, there are no accompanying guidelines for establishing whether or not a person is competent to understand these issues and make a truly informed decision. As a result, in some circumstances the regulations permit some of these requirements to be altered or waived—a questionable and ill-defined practice.

Today, due largely to government regulations, university, medical school, and other research facilities establish committees to oversee the well-being of research subjects. But even a consensus among well-educated, concerned, ethical individuals does not answer the underlying question: How does one weigh the suspension of individual rights against the potential benefit to others? This has become such a difficult and important issue that universities now train ethicists, who confer with philosophers, psychologists, physicians, civil rights experts, and people from all sectors of society in an effort to develop acceptable guidelines. Though the system is not perfect, it reflects the value our society places on maintaining a balance between scientific advances and individual, including animal, liberty.

Another ethical issue that is currently receiving much attention centers on the rights of animal subjects. For years, medical and psychological researchers have operated under the assumption that animal experiments are an ethically acceptable alternative to experimenting on humans, and they have gathered insights about human abnormal behavior by doing such things as shocking animals, separating them from their parents, starving them, surgically altering their brains, and even killing, or *sacrificing,* them to perform an autopsy. In recent years animal rights activists have protested that these research undertakings are often cruel, and they have questioned whether the pain inflicted upon research animals is always justified.

The debate over this issue has become heated. At one extreme, some animal rights activists describe medical and psychological researchers as insensitive monsters; at the other, some researchers claim animal rights activists are more interested in animals than in the human beings whose medical and mental health may be enhanced by animal research. Somewhere in the middle lies a serious and difficult ethical problem that must be addressed.

On the one hand, human health and functioning is a worthy goal that seems to justify at least some forms of animal experimentation, especially when no other forms of research are able to provide insights and solutions.

On the other hand, animals are also living creatures whose comfort and lives cannot simply be dismissed as irrelevant.

In response to this issue, the U.S. Congress passed the Animal Welfare Act in 1966 and in 1989 the U.S. Department of Agriculture developed numerous regulations governing the use and care of research animals. The regulations seek to define when animal sacrifice is acceptable in research, to limit the number of surgical operations that can be performed on a single animal, to control the sale of animals for research, to ensure the psychological well-being of animals, to enlarge the cage space of research animals, and to ensure that the animals receive a proper amount of exercise.

These measures are steps in the right direction, but hardly a final solution. Many animal researchers feel that the growing number of restrictions severely limit the scope of their investigations and in turn hinder potential gains for human beings. Animal rights activists argue that the government regulations do not yet adequately protect the rights and needs of animal subjects. They point out, for example, that the regulations cover research on some animals (dogs, cats, primates, guinea pigs, hamsters, and rabbits) more than others (birds, rats, mice, and farm animals). Clearly, this controversy has yet to be resolved, highlighting once again the significant ethical dilemmas that clinical researchers face.

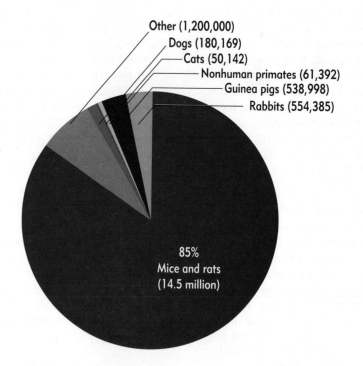

Other (1,200,000)
Dogs (180,169)
Cats (50,142)
Nonhuman primates (61,392)
Guinea pigs (538,998)
Rabbits (554,385)

85%
Mice and rats
(14.5 million)

At least 17 million animals are used in research each year. Approximately 85 percent are rats and mice. *(Office of Technology Assessment; U.S. Department of Agriculture; National Research Council.)*

these subjects also display symptoms of learned helplessness, including temporary passivity, pessimism about their effectiveness at future tasks, and sadness (Miller & Seligman, 1975; Hiroto, 1974).

It is important to recognize that Seligman's analogue experiments are enlightening only to the extent that the laboratory-induced condition of learned helplessness is indeed analogous to human depression. If it turns out that this laboratory phenomenon is only superficially similar to depression, then the clinical inferences drawn from such experiments may be wrong and misleading. This, in fact, is the major limitation of all analogue research. Although such studies enable scientists to control and manipulate variables more easily, researchers can never be certain that the phenomena they see in the laboratory are the same as the psychological disorders they are investigating. For this reason, researchers such as Seligman usually conduct many variations of an analogue study in hopes of demonstrating consistent parallels between the laboratory analogue and the real-life phenomenon. The more parallels they demonstrate, the more compelling their analogue findings are.

**Single-Subject Experiment**   As our discussion of the experimental method has suggested, experiments are usually done on groups of subjects rather than on one lone individual. By using representative groups of subjects, experimenters can be relatively confident that their findings are more than chance occurrences and represent general trends in larger populations. Sometimes, however, scientists do not have the luxury of experimenting on numerous subjects. For example, they may be investigating a disorder so rare that few subjects are available. Experimentation is still possible in such cases in the form of *single-subject,* or *single-case, experimental designs* (Morley, 1989).

In these kinds of designs, the single subject is observed and measured before the manipulation of an independent variable, an observation period known as the *baseline period.* Baseline data reveal what a subject's behavior is like without any manipulations or interventions, thus establishing a standard with which later changes may be compared. The experimenter next introduces the independent variable and observes the subject's behavior once again. Any changes in behavior are attributed to the effects of the independent variable. The most commonly used single-subject experimental designs are the ABAB and multiple-baseline designs.

**ABAB Design**   In an *ABAB,* or *reversal, design,* a subject's reactions are measured and compared not only during a baseline period (A) and after the introduction of the independent variable (B) but once again after the

"What it comes down to is you have to find out what reaction they're looking for, and you give them that reaction."

Animals' brains and bodies are different from humans', however, and so are their perspectives, perceptions, and experiences. Thus abnormal-like behavior produced in analogue experiments may differ in important ways from the human abnormality under investigation, and the conclusions about abnormality drawn from such studies may be incorrect.

independent variable has been removed (A) and yet again after it has been reintroduced (B). If the subject's responses change back and forth systematically with changes in the independent variable, the experimenter may conclude that the independent variable is causing the shifting responses. Essentially, in an ABAB design a subject is compared with him- or herself under different conditions rather than with other control subjects. Subjects therefore serve as their own controls.

Clinicians are likely to resort to an ABAB design when they wish to determine the effectiveness of a particular form of therapy on a client but are unable to obtain other clients with similar problems for a properly controlled experiment. One therapist used this design to determine whether a behavioral reinforcement treatment program was helping to reduce a retarded teenage boy's habit of talking out loud and disrupting his special education class (Dietz, 1977). The reinforcement program consisted of rewarding the boy with extra teacher time whenever he managed to go 55 minutes without talking out loud in class more than three times. First, the student's level of talking was measured during a baseline period and was found to consist of frequent verbal disruptions. Next the boy was given a series of teacher reinforcement sessions (the independent variable); as expected, his loud talk soon decreased dramatically.

Then the reinforcement treatment was stopped, and the student's loud talk was found to increase once again. Apparently the independent variable had indeed been the cause of the improvement.

To be more confident about this conclusion, the therapist reintroduced the teacher reinforcement treatment yet again and found that once again the subject's behavior improved. This reintroduction of the independent variable helped rule out the possibility that some confounding factor (such as the onset of magnificent spring weather or a present from a relative) had actually been causing the boy's improvement.

*Multiple-Baseline Design* A multiple-baseline design does not employ the reversals that are found in an ABAB design. Instead, the experimenter selects two or more behaviors displayed by a subject and observes the effect that the manipulation of an independent variable has on each of the behaviors (Morley, 1989; Barmann & Vitali, 1982; Barmann & Murray, 1981). Let us say that the teenage boy in the ABAB study exhibited two kinds of inappropriate behavior—the disruptive talk during class *and* making odd grimaces. In a multiple-baseline design, the experimenter would first collect baseline data on both the frequency of the boy's disruptive talk and the frequency of his facial grimaces during a 55-minute period. In the next phase of the experiment, the experimenter would reward the boy with extra teacher time whenever he cut down his verbalizations but not when he cut down his grimaces. The experimenter would then measure changes in the boy's verbal and grimacing behaviors, expecting the verbal interruptions to decrease in frequency but the grimacing to remain about the same as before, in accordance with the selective applications of reinforcement. In the final phase of the experiment, the experimenter would also reward the boy with extra teacher attention whenever he reduced his grimacing, expecting that this manipulation would now lead to a reduction in the frequency of grimacing, similar to the reduction in verbal interruptions. If the expected pattern of changes was found, it would be reasonable to conclude that the manipulation of the independent variable (teacher reinforcement), rather than some other factor, was responsible for the changes in the two behaviors. Had some extraneous factor such as an improvement in the weather or a gift from a relative been the cause of the boy's improvement, it would probably have caused improvements in both kinds of behavior in all phases of the study, not just in the final phase. In short, by choosing more than one behavioral baseline for observation, an experimenter can systematically eliminate confounding variables from his or her interpretations of the findings.

Obviously, single-subject experiments — both ABAB and multiple-baseline designs — are similar to individual case studies in their focus on one subject. In the single-subject experiment, however, the independent variable is systematically manipulated in such a way that the investigator can conclude with some confidence whether or not it is the cause of an observed effect. That is, the single-subject experiment has greater internal validity than the case study.

On the other hand, single-subject designs, like case studies, have only limited external validity. Because only one subject is studied, the experimenter cannot be sure that the subject's reaction to the independent variable is typical. Other subjects might react differently. In the single-subject designs described here, for example, there is no basis for concluding that other retarded adolescents with similar behavior problems would respond successfully to the same reinforcement programs.

# THE LIMITS OF CLINICAL INVESTIGATION

We began this chapter by observing that clinical scientists look for general laws that will help them to understand, prevent, and treat psychological disorders. A variety of circumstances impede their progress, however. We have already noted some of them. The most problematic are summarized below.

1. *Clinical subjects have needs and rights that investigators are obliged to respect.* Clinical scientists must respect the human and civil rights of their human subjects. Thus they may not instruct parents to abuse their children to determine the psychological effects of child abuse or induce catastrophic events or life crises to examine people's psychological reactions to such events. These kinds of ethical considerations set significant limitations on the kinds of investigations that clinical scientists can conduct.

2. *The origins of human functioning are very complex.* Because human behavior generally results from multiple factors working together, it is most difficult to pinpoint precise or principal causes of given behaviors. Moreover, as our discussion of the experimental method suggested, even in well-controlled studies unsuspected factors may be operating on and influencing a person's thoughts, feelings, and actions. Given the many factors that can influence human functioning, it has actually been easier to unravel the complexities of energy

and matter than to understand phenomena such as human sadness, stress, and anxiety.

3. *Human beings are changeable.* The moods, behaviors, and thoughts of human subjects fluctuate. Is the person clinical scientists are studying today truly the same as the one they were investigating yesterday? Does the person feel the same, perceive problems in the same way, or even *have* the same problems? Variability in a single person, let alone the normal variations from person to person, limits the kinds of conclusions researchers can draw about abnormal functioning.

4. *Human self-awareness may influence the results of clinical investigations.* When human subjects know they are being studied, they may behave in ways that differ from their usual patterns. Not only may they bias a study by trying to respond in expected ways or to present themselves in a favorable light but the attention they receive from investigators may in itself affect their perceptions and feelings (usually it increases their optimism and improves their mood). It is an axiom of science that the very act of measuring an object distorts the object to some degree. Nowhere is this more true than in the study of human beings.

5. *Clinical investigators have a special link to their subjects.* Clinical scientists have themselves experienced mood changes, troubled thoughts, family problems, and other difficulties that may be similar to the clinical problems they are investigating. They may identify with the pain of their subjects or have personal opinions about the causes and implications of their problems. As we see in Freud's case study of Little Hans and in the Rosenthal effect found in many experiments, the relationship of the clinical investigator to the topic under study can bias the experimenter's attempts to understand abnormality.

These complicating factors amount to yet another reason that clinical scientists must use a variety of methods to study abnormality. Although each approach addresses some of the problems inherent in investigating human behavior, no one approach overcomes them all. Case studies allow investigators to consider a broader range of causes than other methods of investigation, but experiments help them pinpoint precise causal factors in ways that case studies cannot. Thus it is best to view each method of investigation as one of a battery of approaches that collectively may shed considerable light on abnormal human functioning.

When more than one of these methods has been used to investigate a certain disorder, it is important to ask whether all the results seem to point in the same direc-

tion. If they do, it is likely that clinical investigators are close to attaining a clear understanding of that disturbance or an effective treatment for it. Conversely, if the various methods seem to produce conflicting results, investigators must admit that their knowledge in that clinical area is still limited.

Before accepting one another's research findings as conclusive, however, or even as highly suggestive, clinical investigators are obligated to review the details of the studies and experiments with a very critical eye. If it is an experiment, for example, have the variables been properly controlled, was the choice of subjects representative, was the sample large enough to be meaningful, and have subject and experimenter bias been eliminated? Are the investigator's conclusions justified? How else might the results be interpreted? Only after research findings have been scrutinized in this way can they be considered to expand our knowledge of abnormality.

## SUMMARY

**T**he history of abnormal psychology shows that theories and treatment procedures may seem reasonable and effective in some cases but prove useless and even harmful in others. Only through research can the dangers be discovered and the benefits proved. The researchers who systematically test the ideas of clinical theorists and clinical practitioners are faced with the challenge of figuring out meaningful yet ethical ways to measure such elusive concepts as unconscious motives, private thoughts, mood change, and human potential.

Clinical researchers use the **scientific method** to uncover **nomothetic,** or general, principles of abnormal psychological functioning — its nature, its causes, and how it may be changed for the better. They attempt to identify and examine relationships between *variables* — characteristics or events that can vary — to determine whether two or more variables change together and whether change in one variable causes a change in another. Researchers depend primarily on three methods of investigation: the case study, the correlational method, and the experimental method.

**T**he *case study* is a detailed account of one person's life and psychological problems. It describes the person's background, present circumstances, and symptoms, as well as the results of any particular treatment. Although it focuses on a single person, the case study can serve as a source of ideas about behavior in others. It may provide tentative support for a theory or it may challenge theoretical assumptions. It may serve as a source of ideas for new therapeutic techniques. A case study may also offer an opportunity to study an unusual problem that does

"You want proof? I'll give you proof!"

Because clinical research is so complex and difficult to evaluate, it is inevitable that personal and professional bias will have at least some influence on the opinions of clinical investigators and practitioners.

not occur often enough to permit more general observations and comparisons.

Case studies have limitations. The observer may be biased and therefore may be selective about what is included in the report. They tend to have low *internal validity* because it is difficult to establish that the problems being reported were actually related to the specific variables that the researcher discussed, and not to any of the countless other variables that play a part in every person's life. Finally, they may have low *external validity:* it may be a mistake to apply what is learned from a case study to people whose problems appear to be similar.

The *correlational method* is a procedure for systematically observing the extent to which events or characteristics vary together. This method allows researchers to draw broad conclusions about abnormality in the population at large because they (1) make many observations of numerous individuals, (2) uniformly apply carefully prescribed procedures so that the studies can be replicated, and (3) analyze the results by statistical methods. These three conditions apply equally to the experimental method.

*Correlation* is the degree to which variables change in accordance with one another. To determine whether a general correlation does indeed exist, the variables must be measured in a large number of individual cases. The *direction* of the correlation is determined by plotting the data on a graph and drawing a *line of best fit*—the line that best fits all of the points. When two variables increase or decrease together, they are said to have a *posi-*

*tive correlation.* When the value of one variable goes up as the other goes down, the correlation is *negative.* If the variables have no systematic relationship, they are said to be *unrelated.* Both the direction and the magnitude of a correlation can be calculated numerically and expressed by the *correlation coefficient (r),* which can vary between +1.00, a perfect positive correlation, and −1.00, a perfect negative correlation. The sign (+ or −) signifies the direction; the number represents the magnitude.

When a correlation has been found, the scientist wants to know if it is truly characteristic of the larger population. To find out, he or she does a statistical analysis of the data. If the probability is no more than 5 in 100 that these results would occur by chance, then the findings are said to be *statistically significant.*

The primary drawback to the correlational method is that it allows researchers to describe only the relationship between variables; it does not help them explain the relationship. Just because we find a positive correlation between two variables, we cannot conclude decisively that variable A *caused* variable B. When it is important to understand the causal relationship between variables, researchers generally turn to the experimental method.

In the *experimental method,* researchers manipulate suspected causes to see whether expected effects will result. The variable that is manipulated is called the *independent variable* and the variable that is expected to change as a result is called the *dependent variable.*

*Confounds* are variables other than the independent variable that are also acting on the dependent variable. They can be major obstacles to efforts to isolate the true cause of an effect. If confounds exist, the researcher cannot be sure that the observed effect is caused by the independent variable and not by some other variable. To minimize the possible influence of confounds, researchers use *control groups, random assignment,* and *blind designs.*

The findings of experiments, like those of correlational studies, must be analyzed statistically. If the likelihood is no more than 5 percent that the differences between the control and experimental groups are due to chance, the results are considered statistically significant.

For ethical and practical reasons, it is difficult to formulate and carry out an ideal experiment in human psychology. Clinical experimenters must often settle for imperfect variations of the optimal experimental design, including the *quasi-experimental design,* the *natural experiment,* the *analogue experiment,* and the *single-subject experiment.* Two versions of the single-subject experiment are the *ABAB design* and the *multiple-baseline design.*

# TOPIC OVERVIEW

## CLINICAL ASSESSMENT

Clinical Interviews

Clinical Tests

Projective Tests

Self-report Inventories

Psychophysiological Tests

Neuropsychological Tests

Intelligence Tests

Clinical Observations

## CLINICAL INTERPRETATION AND JUDGMENT

## DIAGNOSIS

# CHAPTER 4

# CLINICAL ASSESSMENT, INTERPRETATION, AND DIAGNOSIS

Angela Savanti was 22 years old, lived at home with her mother, and was employed as a secretary in a large insurance company. She . . . had had passing periods of "the blues" before, but her present feelings of despondency were of much greater proportion. She was troubled by a severe depression and frequent crying spells, which had not lessened over the past two months. Angela found it hard to concentrate on her job, had great difficulty falling asleep at night, and had a poor appetite. . . . Her depression had begun after she and her boyfriend Jerry broke up two months previously.

*(Leon, 1984, p. 109)*

Eventually Angela Savanti made an appointment with a therapist at a local counseling center. The first step the clinician took toward helping Angela was to learn as much as possible about her disturbance. Who is she, what is her life like, and what precisely are her symptoms? This information was expected to throw light on the causes and the probable course of her present dysfunction and help the clinician decide what kinds of treatment strategies would be likely to help her. The treatment program could then be tailored to Angela's unique needs and to her particular pattern of abnormal functioning.

Whereas researchers in abnormal psychology seek primarily a nomothetic, or broad, understanding of abnormal functioning, clinical practitioners are interested in compiling *ideographic,* or individual, information about their clients. If practitioners are to help particular people overcome their problems, they must have the fullest possible understanding of those people and know the nature and origins of their problems. Although they also apply general information and principles in their work, they can determine the relevance of such information only after they have thoroughly examined the person who has come for treatment. This ideographic understanding of the client is arrived at through *assessment, interpretation,* and *diagnosis.*

# CLINICAL ASSESSMENT

*Assessment,* the collection of relevant information about a subject, goes on at every stage and in every realm of life, from grade school to college admissions to the job market, and from shopping for groceries to voting for president. College admissions officers, who have to predict which students will succeed in college, depend on academic records, recommendations, achievement test scores, interviews, and application forms to give them information about prospective students. Employers, who have to decide which applicants are most likely to be effective workers, collect information about them from résumés, interviews, letters of reference, and perhaps on-the-job observations.

Clinical assessment techniques are used not only to determine how and why a person is behaving abnormally and how that person might be helped but also to evaluate clients after they have been in treatment for a while, to see what progress they are making and whether the treatment ought to be modified. Clinicians may also assess clients at the completion of treatment to determine the overall effectiveness of the therapy.

Clinical assessment also plays an important role in research. When researchers want to determine the causes of certain disorders or the responsiveness of disorders to various kinds of treatment, they have to be sure that the subjects they select are representative of people with those disorders. Sometimes researchers rely on assessments that have already been conducted by clinicians; at other times they conduct their own assessments. The accuracy of the assessments has a direct bearing on the value of the research.

Clinicians' selection of specific assessment techniques and tools depends on their theoretical orientation. Psychodynamic clinicians, for example, use assessment methods that provide information about the components of a person's personality and any unconscious conflicts he or she may be experiencing (Butler & Satz, 1989). This kind of assessment, called a *personality assessment,* enables them to piece together a clinical picture in accordance with the principles and concepts of the psychodynamic model. Behavioral and many cognitive clinicians, in contrast, use assessment methods that provide detailed information about the specific dysfunctional behaviors and cognitions (Haynes, 1990; Kendall, 1990; Ciminero, 1986). The goal of this kind of assessment, called *behavioral assessment,* is to carry out a *functional analysis* of the person's behaviors—an analysis of how the behaviors are learned and reinforced. Hundreds of assessment techniques and tools have been developed from all theoretical perspectives, but most of them fall into three general categories: clinical interviews, tests, and observations.

## Clinical Interviews

Most of us feel instinctively that the best way to get to know people is to meet with them. In face-to-face interactions we can see other persons' reactions to our questions, observe as well as listen as they answer, watch them observing us, and generally get a sense of who they are. The clinical interview is a face-to-face encounter of this kind (Wiens, 1990). Research has repeatedly suggested that the way people say something can be as revealing as what they say (Korchin, 1976; Mehrabian, 1972). If a woman becomes markedly restless and avoids eye contact when she talks about men, the clinician may suspect that she feels some anxiety about heterosexual relationships. If a man says that the death of his mother saddened him but looks as happy as can be, the clinician may suspect that the man actually has conflicting emotions about this loss. Almost all practitioners use clinical interviews as part of the assessment process.

**Conducting the Interview**    The interview is often the first contact between client and clinician. Because the client is likely to feel uneasy, the clinician's first tasks are to establish rapport and gain the person's trust, respect, and confidence and to present a nonjudgmental and accepting attitude.

Harry Stack Sullivan, the renowned American psychiatrist, said that the interviewer's primary task is to "discover who the client is—that is, he must review what course of events the client has come through to be who he is, what he has in the way of background and experience" (Sullivan, 1954, pp. 17–18). Correspondingly, clinical interviewers usually seek detailed information about the person's current problems and feelings, current life situations and relationships, and personal history. They may also examine the person's expectations of therapy and motives for seeking it. The clinician working with Angela Savanti reported:

*Angela was dressed neatly when she appeared for her* first interview. She was attractive, but her eyes were puffy and ringed with dark circles. She answered questions and related information about her life history in a slow, flat tone of voice, which had an impersonal quality to it. She sat stiffly in her chair with her hands in her lap, and moved very little throughout the entire interview.

The client stated that the time period just before she and her boyfriend terminated their relationship had been one of extreme emotional turmoil. She was not sure whether she wanted to marry Jerry, and he began to demand that she decide either one way or the other. Mrs. Savanti did not seem to like Jerry and was very cold and aloof whenever he came to the house. Angela felt caught in the middle and unable to make a decision about her future. After several confrontations with Jerry over whether she would marry him or not, he told her he felt that she would never decide, so he was not going to see her anymore.

Angela stated that she was both relieved and upset that Jerry had forced the issue and essentially made the decision for her. She did not attempt to contact him, but became increasingly depressed. She had stayed home from work several times during the past month and had just sat around the house and cried.

Angela came from a working-class family of Italian origin. . . . Both sets of grandparents emigrated from Italy, and her parents were born in the United States. . . . Angela's mother and father separated when Angela was 11 years old. Mr. Savanti had moved to another city, and he had never sent money to support the family, nor had he been heard from since his departure. . . . After he left, Mrs. Savanti got a job in a factory, and she has worked there ever since. . . .

Angela stated that her childhood was a very unhappy period. Her father was seldom home, and when he was present, her parents fought constantly. Sometimes the arguments became quite severe and her father would throw things and shout. Mrs. Savanti usually became sullen and withdrawn after an argument, refused to speak to her husband, and became uncommunicative with her daughters. Angela remembered that many times as a child she was puzzled because it seemed that her mother was angry at her, too. Sometimes after an argument, Mrs. Savanti told her daughters that she had ruined her life by marrying their father. . . .

Angela recalled feeling very guilty when Mr. Savanti left. . . . She revealed that whenever she thought of her father, she always felt that she had been responsible in some way for his leaving the family. Angela had never communicated this feeling to anyone, and her mother rarely mentioned his name.

Angela described her mother as the "long-suffering type" who said that she had sacrificed her life to make her children happy, and the only thing she ever got in return was grief and unhappiness. Angela related that her mother rarely smiled or laughed and did not converse very much with the girls. . . . When Angela and [her sister] Doreen began dating, Mrs. Savanti . . . commented on how tired she was because she had waited up for them. She would make disparaging remarks about the boys they had been with and about men in general. . . .

Angela said that she liked her grandparents. . . . Her grandparents and mother were very religious, and it seemed that there were always religious overtones to any discussions with them. Angela reported that she was having a great many doubts about her religious faith and beliefs, and these doubts especially troubled her around the time she stopped seeing Jerry. . . .

Angela had met Jerry at a party two years earlier, when she was 20 and he was 23. She liked him from the first time they met, but she was very careful not to give any indication that she was attracted to him. . . . Angela described Jerry as talkative and friendly, and of similar ethnic background. She said that he too had difficulty expressing his feelings, and many times he resorted to kidding around as a means of avoiding emotional expression.

Jerry began to talk about getting married six months before they stopped dating. He said that he had a good job and he wanted to marry Angela. Angela, however, was very ambivalent about what she wanted to do. She enjoyed being with Jerry, but her mother's indifference toward him troubled her. Mrs. Savanti made numerous comments to the effect that all men are nice before they get married, but later their true nature comes out. . . .

Angela revealed that she had often been troubled with depressed moods. During high school, if she got a lower grade in a subject than she had expected, her initial response was one of anger, followed by depression. She began to think that she was not smart enough to get good grades, and she blamed herself for studying too little. Angela also became despondent when she got into an argument with her mother or felt that she was being taken advantage of at work. However, these periods of depression usually lasted only about a day, and passed when she became involved in some other activity.

The intensity and duration of the [mood change] that she experienced when she broke up with Jerry were much more severe. She was not sure why she was so depressed, but she began to feel it was an effort to walk around and go out to work. Talking with others became difficult, and many times her lips felt as if they were stiff, and she had to make an effort to move them in order to speak. Angela found it hard to concentrate, and she began to forget things she was supposed to do. It took her a long time to fall asleep at night, and when she finally did fall asleep, she sometimes woke up in the midst of a bad dream. She felt constantly tired, and loud noises, including conversation or the television, bothered her. She preferred to lie in bed rather than be with anyone, and she often cried when alone.

At the point where Angela's depressed state was seriously beginning to interfere with her job, she decided she had better see the company physician. She asked the doctor to prescribe something to help her sleep, so she would not be so tired and could concentrate better. The physician suggested that Angela receive some professional help with her problems and she was referred to a counseling center in the area.

*(Leon, 1984, pp. 110–115)*

Beyond gathering basic interview data of this kind, clinical interviewers give special attention to whatever topics they believe are important. Psychodynamic interviewers try to learn about the person's needs and fantasies, elicit relevant memories about past events and relationships, and observe the way the person molds the interview (Shea, 1990; Pope, 1983). Behavioral interviewers have an acronym, SORC, for the kinds of information they gather in order to do a functional analysis: relevant information about the *stimuli* that trigger the abnormal functioning, about the *organism* or person (such as a low self-opinion), about the precise nature of the abnormal *responses,* and about the *consequences* of those responses (Reyna, 1989; Lindsay & Powell, 1987; O'Leary & Wilson, 1975). Cognitive interviewers try to discover assumptions, interpretations, and cognitive coping skills that influence the way the person acts and feels (Kendall, 1990; Meichenbaum, 1976). Humanistic clinicians ask about the person's self-concept and try to learn about his or her unique perceptions (Aiken, 1985; Brown, 1972). And biological clinicians use the interview to help pinpoint signs of any biochemical or neurological dysfunction (Kallman & Feuerstein, 1986; Epstein, 1976).

**Interview Formats**   Interviews can be either structured or unstructured. In an ***unstructured interview,*** the clinician asks open-ended questions ("Would you tell me about yourself?"), follows interesting leads, and places few constraints on what the client can discuss. The lack of structure allows clinicians to focus on important topics that they could not anticipate before the interview. Also, it gives them a better appreciation of the issues that are important to the client.

In a ***structured interview,*** clinicians ask a series of prepared questions. Sometimes they use a published ***interview schedule***—a standard set of questions or topics designed for use in all interviews (Shea, 1988; Robins, Helzer, Croughan, & Ratcliff, 1981; Endicott & Spitzer, 1978). Structured formats enable clinicians to cover the same kinds of important issues in every interview and to compare the responses of one individual with those of others.

Most clinical interviews have both structured and unstructured portions, but clinicians favor one kind over the other (Leon, Bowden, & Faber, 1989; Graham &

"So, Mr. Fenton . . . Let's begin with your mother."

In a structured interview, clinicians gather information by asking a set of standard questions irrespective of the client's particular symptoms. Critics argue that excessive structure may lead to irrelevant questions and to the omission of important information.

Lilly, 1984; Bellack & Hersen, 1980). Unstructured interviews typically appeal to psychodynamic clinicians because they allow interviewers to search freely for underlying issues and conflicts. They are also popular among humanists because they allow clinicians to guide the conversation in any direction the client's ideas and experiences indicate (Pope, 1983). Structured formats, on the other hand, are more widely used by behavioral clinicians, who need to do a systematic review of many pieces of information to complete a functional analysis of a person's behaviors (Pope, 1983). Structured formats are equally popular among cognitive interviewers because they can point to certain characteristic attitudes or thinking processes, and among biological interviewers because they can help clinicians search systematically for indicators of biological dysfunctioning.

**Limitations of Clinical Interviews**   Despite the value of the clinical interview as a source of information about a client, there are limits to what it can accomplish. One problem is that the information gathered during an interview is to some extent preselected by the client. Though most people seek help voluntarily, many come to clinicians under duress, sent by a court, a parent, or a threatening spouse. In such cases the information the client provides may be self-serving. Even clients who come voluntarily may try to present themselves in the best light or feel reluctant to introduce embarrassing topics.

Another problem is that some clients are simply unable to provide accurate information in an interview. The very disturbance that brings them to the clinician may seriously distort their perceptions and reports of events in their lives. People who suffer from depression, for example, take an unduly pessimistic view of themselves, their environment, and their future (Beck, 1991, 1967). Thus a depressed man might describe himself as incompetent at his job, whereas his boss and co-workers consider him all but indispensable.

Yet another drawback is that interviewers may make subjective judgments that skew the information they gather. They usually rely too heavily on first impressions, for example, and give too much weight to unfavorable information about a client (Aiken, 1985; Meehl, 1960; Dailey, 1952). The interviewers' biases may also influence the way they interpret what a client says.

Finally, clients respond differently to different interviewers. Studies show that clients feel uncomfortable with clinicians who are cold and distant, and offer them less information than they do to clinicians who are warm and supportive (Eisenthal, Koopman, & Lazare, 1983; Jourard, 1974). A clinician's race, sex, age, and appearance may also influence the client's responses (Paurohit, Dowd, & Cottingham, 1982; Johnson, 1977; Griffith, 1977). One study found that adolescent girls admitted more misbehaviors to younger interviewers than to older ones, and when they talked to older interviewers they were more likely to claim that they always did what their parents told them to do (Erlich & Reisman, 1961).

In these circumstances, it is not surprising that different clinicians can obtain different answers and draw different conclusions even when they ask the same questions of the same person. Accordingly, some researchers believe that interviewing, a time-honored approach to assessment, should be discarded. This might be a reasonable suggestion if there were other, problem-free techniques to use instead. As we shall see, however, the two other kinds of clinical assessment methods also have serious limitations.

## Clinical Tests

Tests are devices for gathering information about a few aspects of a person's psychological functioning, from which broader information about that person can be inferred (Goldstein & Hersen, 1990; Aikens, 1985; Gra-

ham & Lilly, 1984). Clinicians use them to uncover subtle information that might not become apparent during an interview or observation and to determine how one person's functioning compares with that of others. More than 500 standard clinical tests are currently used throughout the United States.

The kinds of tests that clinicians use most frequently are as follows:

1. *Projective tests,* consisting of unstructured or ambiguous material to which people are asked to respond. The material is so vague that the responses are likely to reflect the person's psychological makeup.
2. *Self-report inventories,* consisting of lists of items that people are asked to evaluate as characteristic or uncharacteristic of them. In the process they are assumed to reveal their personalities, behavior patterns, emotions, or beliefs.
3. *Psychophysiological tests,* which measure such physical responses as heart rate and muscle tension as possible indicators of psychological problems.
4. *Neuropsychological tests,* which reveal possible neurological impairment.
5. *Intelligence tests,* which are designed to measure a person's intellectual ability.

**Characteristics of Tests** On the surface, it may appear relatively simple to design an effective test. Every month in magazines and newspapers we come across new tests that purport to reveal information about ourselves, our relationships, our sex lives, our stresses, our ability to succeed in business, and more. These tests can seem convincing, but they are often misleading. Most of them do not yield consistent or accurate information about our functioning or say anything meaningful about where we stand in comparison with others (Woody & Robertson, 1988). If a test is to be useful, it must be *standardized* and must be proved to have *reliability* and *validity* (see Box 4-1).

**Standardization** Suppose a person scores 40 on a test designed to measure aggressiveness. What does that number mean? Even if we know that scores on this test range from 0 to 50, we still don't know whether 40 is what most people score. It may be far above or below the average. If a test score is to be meaningful, we must be able to compare it with the scores other people receive on the same test. We can do so if the test has gone through the process of *standardization;* that is, it has been administered to a large group of subjects whose performance then serves as a common standard, or norm, against which any individual's score can be mea-

═══════════════ BOX 4-1 ═══════════════

# The Lie of the Land: Polygraphs and Integrity Tests

In movies, criminals being grilled by the police reveal their guilt by sweating, shaking, cursing, or twitching. When they are hooked up to a *polygraph* (a lie detector), their rapid heartbeat and tense muscles cause the needles to bounce all over the paper. Such images have been with us since World War I, when some clinicians developed the theory that detectable physiological changes occur in people who are being deceptive (Marston, 1917). The logic behind and operation of a lie detector test are rather straightforward. A subject's respiration level, perspiration level, and heart rate are recorded while he or she answers questions. The clinician observes these physiological responses while the subject answers yes to *control* questions that are known to be true, such as "Are your parents both alive?", and then compares them to the subject's physiological responses when answering *relevant* questions, such as "Did you commit this robbery?" If, as shown here, the subject's breathing, perspiration, and heart rate increase while responding to the relevant questions, he or she may be judged to be lying (Raskin, 1982). However, the danger, if not the tragedy, of relying on such tests is that there is no compelling evidence that they work.

It is crucial that a test be valid if it is to be used as a diagnostic tool. Yet polygraph tests have enjoyed widespread popularity for many years despite an almost total lack of evidence that they are valid. Only recently has this inconvenient fact reduced people's reliance on these tests and instigated responsible inquiries into their validity.

In 1984, when President Ronald Reagan sought to expand the use of the polygraph in key government of-

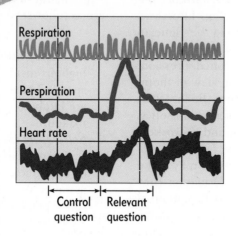

Control question    Relevant question

fices because classified information had been leaked, the American Civil Liberties Union opposed the policy on the grounds that it was an invasion of privacy and a suspension of civil rights. In response to the debate on the validity of these tests, more than in response to the civil rights issues raised by the ACLU, the government's Office of Technology Assessment reviewed all available literature on the polygraph and concluded that the test lacked validity *and* that the underlying theoretical assumption—that there is a unique physiological response associated with deception—was not necessarily true (Saxe, Dougherty, & Cross, 1985). As a result of this report, the House of Representatives voted to restrict the use of the polygraph in preemployment screening. Similarly, in 1986 the American Psychological Association concluded that polygraphs were inaccurate, and more fundamentally, that no physiological response pattern was associated with deception in the first place. As one team of reviewers concluded, "Modern lie detection is no more scientific than King Solomon's sword" (Kleinmuntz & Szucko, 1984, p. 774).

With the polygraph's popularity in decline, a rush began to develop a test that could replace it, especially as a screening tool for employment. Businesses and governments were losing billions of dollars to theft, low productivity, and other dishonest behavior. This need stimulated development of so-called *integrity tests,* personality tests that seek to measure whether the test takers are generally honest or dishonest and correspondingly whether they should be hired for a particular job. More than forty of these written tests are now in use, supposedly revealing other such broad characteristics as reliability, deviance, social conformity, wayward impulses, dependability, and hostility to rules. Despite what many of the test publishers claim, the effectiveness of most such tests is not supported by published studies. To establish the validity of integrity tests, the Office of Technology Assessment and the APA are now reviewing the literature. When the results become available, Congress will decide whether or not integrity tests may continue to be used in the hiring process (Adler, 1989). In the meantime, some states have banned them.

Lives can be changed dramatically when people are labeled, whether the label be "dishonest," "criminal," or "manic depressive." A psychophysiological or personality test may be as crucial to the well-being of the person being tested as a medical test, and those who administer one have an obligation to consider the consequences carefully, particularly before making any results public. Reliance on questionable devices such as polygraphs and integrity tests may violate civil rights as well as basic tenets of science and may needlessly jeopardize the welfare of the people being tested.

sured. The initial group of people who took the test is called the **standardization sample.**

A standardization sample must be representative of the larger population the test is intended for. If an aggressiveness test meant for the public at large were standardized on a group of Marines, for example, the norm might turn out to be much higher than it would be if the test were standardized on people from all walks of life. The Marines' scores would not provide normative information representative of most of the people who would be taking the test. Factors such as age, sex, and education level must also be considered in the selection of a standardization sample. In some cases, it may be useful to generate more than one set of norms. For example, given that women and men in our society may differ in expressions of aggressiveness, it might be a good idea for an aggressiveness test to have one norm for males and another for females. This strategy would allow clinicians to compare the test scores of male subjects with those of a male sample and the scores of female subjects with those of a female sample.

**Reliability** Reliability is a measure of the consistency of test results. A good test should always yield the same results in the same situation. A weigh scale, for example, is reliable if it measures the same weight every time we put the same object on it. If it were to read 10 pounds when we put a bag of sugar on it today and 12 pounds tomorrow, it would not be reliable. To make sure that a test yields the same results time and again, test designers must put it through specific kinds of trials. Generally speaking, a good test is one that demonstrates four kinds of reliability: test – retest reliability, alternate-form reliability, internal reliability, and interrater reliability.

A test has high **test – retest reliability** if it yields the same results when it is given again to the same people. If, for example, a woman's responses on a particular test indicate that she is a heavy drinker, the test should produce the same result when she takes it again a week later. A test dominated by time-specific questions ("Have you had a drink in the last hour?") may not be reliable, because the answers may be different the second time around. Questions that focus on more general drinking patterns ("How many drinks do you have per week?") may produce more reliable results. The scores subjects earn the first time they take a given test are correlated with their scores the second time they take it, and the resulting correlation coefficient (see p. 74) indicates the test – retest reliability. The higher the correlation, the greater the reliability.

One problem with the test – retest reliability measure is that the second time people take a test, they may try to give the same answers they gave the first time around, thus inflating the apparent reliability of the test. To avoid this problem, test designers may try to establish **alternate-form reliability** for a test. They devise an alternate test with the same kinds of items as the original test, give both forms of the test to trial subjects, and correlate their scores. A high correlation indicates alternate-form reliability.

A test has high **internal reliability** when different parts of it yield the same results. To check for this kind of consistency, researchers may use the **split-half** method: they compare responses on odd-numbered test items with responses on even-numbered items. If the test is internally reliable, scores on the two halves of the test will be highly correlated.

Finally, a test shows high **interrater** (or **interjudge**) **reliability** if different evaluators independently agree on the scoring of the test. True – false and multiple-choice tests yield consistent scores no matter who evaluates them, but other tests require the evaluator to make a judgment, and three evaluators may come up with three different scores. Consider a test that requires the subject to copy a picture, after which a judge rates the accuracy of the copy. Different judges may give different ratings to the same copy. A test's interrater reliability may be determined by the level of agreement when several evaluators score a single person's test performance.

**Validity** A test must also yield *accurate,* or **valid,** results. Suppose that a weigh scale reads 12 pounds every time a bag of sugar is put on it. The scale, then, may be considered reliable. But what if the sugar really weighs only 10 pounds? Although the scale is reliable because its readings are consistent, those readings are not valid. An instrument's validity is the accuracy with which it measures what it is supposed to be measuring.

Some tests appear to be valid because they seem to make sense. This sort of validity, called *face validity,* does not by itself establish a test's trustworthiness. A test for depression, for example, might include questions about how often an individual cries. Because it makes sense that depressed people would cry, these test questions would have face validity. It turns out, however, that many people cry a great deal for reasons other than depression and that extremely depressed people often fail to cry at all (Beck, 1987, 1967). Thus a test should not be used unless it has successfully been subjected to other, more exacting measures of validity.

*Predictive validity* is a test's ability to predict a person's future characteristics or behavior. Let us say that a test is designed to gather information about the habits of the parents of elementary school children, their personal characteristics, and their attitudes toward smoking, and on that basis to identify the children who will take up cigarette smoking in junior high school. We could establish its predictive validity by administering the test to a group of elementary school students, waiting until they were in junior high school, and then checking to see which children actually did become smokers.

In practice, it is often quite difficult to determine the predictive validity of a test because there is so much opportunity for complicating factors to arise in the interval between the time the test is administered and the time the predictions can be verified. Testers may lose track of some of the original subjects, or unexpected circumstances may alter the course of events. The elementary school students in the smoking test, for example, might be exposed to an intensive antismoking campaign.

*Concurrent validity* is the degree to which test scores agree with other available information. A test designed to measure students' anxiety, for example, should produce anxiety scores that agree with school counseling records and parents' reports.

A test displays high *content validity* if it assesses all important aspects of the behavior, skill, or quality it is designed to reveal. Consider *achievement tests,* designed to measure a student's ability in a particular school subject. A foreign-language achievement test would have low content validity if it tested only for vocabulary without paying attention to grammar, language usage, or comprehension.

Finally, tests should have high *construct validity;* that is, they should measure what they are intended to measure and not something else altogether (Cronbach & Meehl, 1955). We might ask, "Do achievement tests measure ability in given subject areas, or do they really measure something else?" Educators have noted that some students do very well and others very poorly on multiple-choice tests. Perhaps a high school student who does well on a chemistry achievement test is actually demonstrating skill at selecting multiple-choice answers rather than an exceptional knowledge of chemistry. In that case, the chemistry achievement test would be lacking in construct validity.

Before any test can be truly useful, it must meet the requirements of standardization, reliability, and validity. No matter how insightful or clever a test may be, clinicians cannot profitably use its results if they are uninterpretable, inconsistent, or inaccurate. Unfortunately, as we shall see, more than a few clinical tests fall short on these essential characteristics, suggesting that at least some clinical assessments miss their intended mark.

**Projective Tests**     Projective tests require subjects to give interpretive answers to questions about relatively vague stimuli such as inkblots or ambiguous pictures, or to follow open-ended instructions such as "Draw a person." The assumption behind these tests is that when clues and instructions are so vague, subjects must "project" aspects of their own personality into the task. As we shall observe in Chapter 6, psychodynamic theorists believe projection to be a common defense mechanism in which people project their own inner wishes onto others. Thus projective tests are used primarily by psychodynamic clinicians to help them assess the unconscious personality drives and conflicts that they believe to be at the root of abnormal functioning. Among the most widely used projective tests are the Rorschach test, the Thematic Apperception Test, sentence-completion tests, and drawings.

*Rorschach Test*     In 1911 Hermann Rorschach, a Swiss psychiatrist, experimented with the use of inkblots in psychiatric diagnosis. He made thousands of blots by dropping ink on paper, folding the paper in half, and then unfolding it to reveal a symmetrical but wholly accidental composition. Rorschach found that everyone saw images in these blots and that the perceived image corresponded in important ways with the psychological condition of the viewer. People diagnosed as schizophrenic, for example, tended to see images that differed radically from those that people with anxiety disorders saw.

Believing that inkblots might be a useful assessment tool, he selected ten and published them in 1921 with instructions for their use. This set of ten inkblots — five in black, white, and gray, and five in color — was called the Rorschach Psychodynamic Inkblot Test. Rorschach himself died just eight months later, at the age of 37, but his colleagues continued his work, and his inkblots have taken their place among the most widely used projective tests of this century.

Clinicians administer the Rorschach, as it is commonly called, by presenting one inkblot card at a time to subjects and asking them what they see, what the inkblot seems to be, or what it reminds them of. The subjects are encouraged to give more than one response. In the first phase of the test, called the *free association*, or *performance, phase,* the clinician records everything the subject says. Next the clinician conducts an *inquiry phase* to find out what influenced or determined the subject's responses. In an optional third phase, called *testing the limits,* the clinician may ask the subject whether he or she can see some of the images more commonly seen by other people. In the following exchange, a tense 32-

**FIGURE 4-1** Card VI of the Rorschach Test. When test subjects tell what they see in a Rorschach inkblot, testers are interested both in the thematic content of the response (the images they see) and in its style (the amount of detail in the answer, whether it incorporates differences in shading in the inkblot, and whether the subject sees movement in the inkblot). *(From Rorshach H., Psychodiagnostik; copyright Hans Huber, Bern. Reprinted by permission.)*

year-old woman who complains of feeling unworthy and lacking in confidence responds to the Rorschach inkblot reproduced in Figure 4-1. Her response is immediately followed by the clinician's inquiry.

Performance
*Subject:* Oh, dear! My goodness! O.K. Just this [upper] part is a bug. Something like an ant—one of the social group which is a worker, trying to pull something. I think this is some kind of food for the rest of the ants. It's a bee because it has wings, a worker bee bringing up something edible for the rest of the clan.

Inquiry
*Clinician:* Tell me about the bee.

*Subject:* Here is the bee, the mouth and the wings. I don't think bees eat leaves but it looks like a leaf or a piece of lettuce.

*Clinician:* What makes it look like a piece of lettuce?

*Subject:* Its shape and it has a vein up the middle. It is definitely a bee.

*(Klopfer & Davidson, 1962, p. 164)*

Clinicians evaluate a person's Rorschach responses on the basis of various criteria. In the early years, Rorschach testers paid greater attention to the themes, images, and fantasies evoked by the inkblots, called the ***thematic content.*** Subjects who saw numerous water images, for example, were often thought to be grappling with alcoholism, whereas those who saw bizarre images or saw themselves in the blots might be suffering from schizophrenia. Although thematic content is still of interest,

testers now pay more attention to the "style" of subjects' responses: Do the subjects view the design as a whole or see specific details? Do they focus on the blots or on the white spaces between them? Do they use or ignore the shadings and colors in several of the cards? Do they see human movement in the designs ("two witches fighting"), animal movement ("rams butting"), animals engaged in human actions ("birds talking"), or inanimate objects ("a house")? It is commonly thought that normal people typically perceive whole designs, but focus on details in at least one or two inkblots; that depressed people give few responses and do not mention color at all; and that impulsive persons respond intensely to color (Erdberg, 1990; Lerner & Lerner, 1988; Blatt & Berman, 1986; Exner, 1986, 1983, 1978, 1974).

The bug responses of the 32-year-old woman mentioned earlier were interpreted as revealing the following information:

Card VI has two major characteristics: It is the most strongly shaded card, and the one card in which the blot material offers a striking contrast between top and bottom portions. She reacts to both these challenges by interpreting the top part and establishing an interesting connection with the bottom part. She also uses the shading aspect clearly for the bottom part and implicitly for the top.

The bee may reflect the image she has of herself as a hard worker (a fact noted by her supervisor). In addition, the "bee bringing up something edible for the rest of the clan" suggests that she feels an overwhelming sense of responsibility toward others.

This card frequently evokes both masculine and feminine sexual associations, either in direct or symbolic form. Apparently [this woman] is not able to handle such material comfortably either overtly or in a more socialized manner, and so both sexual symbols are replaced by the oral symbolism of providing food.

*(Klopfer & Davidson, 1962, pp. 182–183)*

***Thematic Apperception Test*** The Thematic Apperception Test (TAT) is a pictorial projective test first developed by the psychologist Henry A. Murray at the Harvard Psychological Clinic in 1935 (Murray et al., 1938; Morgan & Murray, 1935). The most common version of this test, which Murray produced in 1943, consists of thirty black-and-white pictures, each depicting people in a somewhat unclear situation. Clinicians select the cards that they feel are most pertinent to the individual being tested. There is also a children's version of the test, known as the Children's Apperception Test, or CAT, which has pictures more evocative of the concerns of children (Bellak & Bellak, 1952).

Subjects who take the Thematic Apperception Test (TAT) are given pictures that show people in ambiguous situations and are asked to invent stories about them. Testers believe that the subjects identify with a character in each picture and thus reveal much about their own needs, feelings, and circumstances in their stories.

FIGURE 4-2 A picture used in the Thematic Apperception Test. One client who made up a story about this card seemed to be revealing resentment toward her mother, regret over the way she had treated her mother, and sadness over her relationship with her own children.

People who take the TAT are shown one picture at a time and asked to make up a dramatic story about each one, stating what is happening in the picture, what led up to it, what the characters are feeling and thinking, and what the outcome of the situation will be. An inquiry phase follows to clarify the responses.

Clinicians who use the TAT believe that people identify with one of the characters on each card. This character, called the *hero,* has certain *needs* and faces certain environmental demands, or *press.* In their stories, people are thought to be expressing their own circumstances, needs, pressures, emotions, and perceptions of reality and fantasy. For example, a female client seems to be identifying with the hero and revealing her own feelings in this story about the TAT picture shown in Figure 4-2:

*T*his is a woman who has been quite troubled by memories of a mother she was resentful toward. She has feelings of sorrow for the way she treated her mother, her memories of

her mother plague her. These feelings seem to be increasing as she grows older and sees her children treating her the same way that she treated her mother. She tries to convey this feeling to her own children, but does not succeed in changing their attitudes. She is living the past in her present, because this feeling of sorrow and guilt is reinforced by the way her children are treating her.

*(Aiken, 1985, p. 372)*

Clinicians evaluate TAT responses by looking not only at the content of the stories but also at the style in which the person responds to the cards in general. Slow or delayed responses, for example, are thought to indicate depression; overcautiousness and preoccupation with details are thought to suggest obsessive thoughts and indecisiveness (Aiken, 1985). Although quantitative scoring schemes have been developed for evaluating TAT responses, most clinicians rely on their own clinical experiences with the test to guide them in scoring and interpreting their clients' responses (Anastasi, 1982).

**Sentence-Completion Test**    The sentence-completion test, first developed more than sixty years ago (Payne, 1928), consists of a series of unfinished sentences that people are asked to complete. Various versions have been developed for different age groups. The following items are taken from a sentence-completion test for high school–age students:

I wish _____

I am best when _____

I suffer _____

My father _____

In the lower grades _____

People _____

My greatest worry is _____

*(The Psychological Corporation, 1950)*

The sentence-completion test can be taken without an examiner present. It is considered a good springboard for discussion and a quick and easy way to pinpoint topics to be explored.

**Drawings**    On the assumption that a drawing tells us something about its creator, clinicians often ask clients to draw human figures and talk about them. Evaluations of these drawings are based on the quality and shape of the drawing, solidity of the pencil line, location of the drawing on the paper, size of the figures, features of the figures, use of background, and comments made by the respondent during the drawing task.

The Draw-a-Person Test (DAP) is the most popular drawing test among clinicians (Machover, 1949). Subjects are first told to draw "a person"; that done, they are told to draw another person of the opposite sex. Evaluations of the drawings include such notions as that a disproportionately large or small head may reflect problems in intellectual functioning, social balance, or control of body impulses, while exaggerated eyes may indicate high levels of suspiciousness. Figure 4-3 is a DAP drawing produced by a depressed man. His clinical assessor evaluates this drawing in the following report:

He drew the large figure first; then when he saw that he could not complete the entire figure on the page, he drew the smaller figure. He momentarily paused, looked at both figures, said that the larger figure lacked a collar, picked up the pencil he had laid down, and drew the "collar" by slash-

**FIGURE 4-3** Drawing by a depressed man on the Draw-a-Person Test. *(From Hammer, 1981, p. 171.)*

ing the pencil across the throat of the drawn male. It was almost as if . . . the patient were committing suicide on paper.

*(Hammer, 1981, p. 170)*

**The Value of Projective Tests**    Until the 1950s, projective tests were likely to be relied on as the primary indicator of a client's personality. In recent years, however, clinicians have treated these instruments more as sources of "supplementary" insights about their clients (Lerner & Lerner, 1988; Anastasi, 1982). Similarly, clinical researchers have increasingly used projective tests in combination with more quantitative measures of psychopathology (Erdberg, 1990; Nash et al., 1988).

One reason for this shift is that practitioners and researchers who adopt the newly emerging models have found these kinds of tests less useful than have psychodynamic clinicians and investigators (Butler & Satz, 1989). Even more important, the tests have not typically demonstrated impressive levels of reliability and validity (Lanyon, 1984; Eysenck, 1959).

Reliability studies in which several clinicians have been asked to score the same person's projective test have usually found relatively low agreement (that is, low interrater reliability) among the clinicians' scores (Little

Drawing tests are commonly used to assess the functioning of children. Two popular tests are the *House-Tree-Person* test, in which subjects draw a house, tree, and person, and the *Kinetic Family Drawing* test, in which subjects draw a picture of all their household members engaged in some activity ("kinetic" means "active"). The drawings are thought to reflect the subjects' perceptions of themselves, their relatives, their home life, and their family relationships.

& Shneidman, 1959; Kostlan, 1954). Standardized procedures for administering and scoring projective tests do exist and might improve consistency if all practitioners used them, but none of these procedures has gained wide acceptance (Exner, 1986, 1983, 1978, 1974).

Similar research has challenged the projective tests' validity (Anastasi, 1982; Peterson, 1978). Various researchers have given clinicians the responses of clinical subjects to projective tests and asked them to describe the personalities and feelings that the responses revealed (Golden, 1964; Sines, 1959; Kostlan, 1954). The descriptions have then been compared with descriptions of the same subjects provided by their psychotherapists or gathered from extensive case histories. The conclusions drawn from projective tests have repeatedly proved inaccurate.

Given the weak reliability and validity of projective tests and the absence of appropriate normative data with which to assess subjects' responses, clinicians tend to fall back on their "general clinical experience" to interpret performance on projective tests (Anastasi, 1982). Thus their interpretations are sometimes subjective and biased.

**Self-report Inventories** An alternative approach to understanding individual clients is simply to ask them to assess themselves by filling out *self-report inventories.* One widely used class of self-report inventory is the *personality inventory,* which asks respondents a wide range of questions about their behavior, beliefs, and feelings. The typical personality inventory consists of a series of statements, and subjects are asked to indicate whether or not each statement applies to them. Clinicians then use the responses to draw broad conclusions about the person's psychological functioning. These inventories are designed to identify personality traits and underlying emotional needs and are therefore employed more by psychodynamic clinicians than by those of other orientations.

The first personality inventories were developed to screen recruits during World War I, when the army was looking for a fast way to identify and eliminate people with possible mental disturbances. One was the Woodworth Personal Data Sheet, which consisted of 116 yes-or-no questions about all kinds of possible psychological problems, from nightmares to phobias. This early instrument yielded a single score that was supposed to indicate the level at which a person was functioning. Clinicians no longer hold so simplistic a view of the personality and have since developed personality inventories that are more descriptive. They include the Minnesota Multiphasic Personality Inventory, the Edwards Personal Preference Schedule, and the Q-sort.

*Minnesota Multiphasic Personality Inventory* The Minnesota Multiphasic Personality Inventory (MMPI) is by far the most widely used personality inventory (Friedman, Webb, & Lewak, 1989; Levitt, 1989; Brown & McGuire, 1976). Two versions of this test are available — the original test, published in 1945 by the psychologists Starke Hathaway and J. C. McKinley, and the MMPI-2, a 1989 revision conducted under the supervision of a team of psychologists (Butcher & Pope, 1990; Butcher & Graham, 1988; Butcher, Dahlstrom, Graham, Tellegen, & Kaemmer, 1989). Currently the two versions are competing for the favor of clinicians (Adler, 1990).

The traditional MMPI consists of 550 self-statements — to be labeled "true," "false," or "cannot say" — about numerous areas of personal functioning, including the respondent's physical concerns; mood; morale; attitudes toward religion, sex, and social activities; and possible symptoms of psychological dysfunction, such as phobias and hallucinations.

The inventory was constructed by a method called *criterion keying.* Quantities of statements were gathered from already-existing scales of personal and social attitudes, from textbooks, from medical and neurologi-

Clinicians often view works of art as informal projective tests in which artists reveal their own conflicts and mental stability. The early twentieth-century artist Louis Wain painted these cat portraits at different points in his career. His portraits showed a steady disintegration, while he himself was developing symptoms of psychosis (loss of touch with reality) in his 50s.

cal case-taking procedures, and from psychiatric examination forms. The authors then asked 724 "normal" people (hospital visitors) and 800 hospitalized mental patients to indicate whether or not each statement was true for them. Only those statements that differentiated the hospitalized subjects from the normal subjects were incorporated into the inventory. For example, because most depressed patients answered true to the statement

"I often feel hopeless about the future," while most nondepressed subjects answered false, the statement was included in the MMPI. The advantage of this kind of test construction is that it is an empirical method rather than one that relies on common sense or clinical instincts. Rather than assuming that anxious, depressed, or schizophrenic people would respond in certain ways, the authors determined just how they do respond.

The items in the MMPI make up ten clinical scales:

1 or HS *(Hypochondriasis)* Thirty-three items derived from patients showing abnormal concern with bodily functions. For example, the item "I have chest pains several times a week" would be answered true.

2 or D *(Depression)* Sixty items derived from patients showing extreme pessimism, feelings of hopelessness, and slowing of thought and action. "I usually feel that life is interesting and worthwhile" would be answered false.

3 or Hy *(Conversion Hysteria)* Sixty items from patients using physical or mental symptoms as a way of unconsciously avoiding difficult conflicts and responsibilities. "My heart frequently pounds so hard I can feel it" would elicit a response of true.

4 or PD *(Psychopathic Deviate)* Fifty items from patients who show a repeated and flagrant disregard for social customs, an emotional shallowness and an inability to learn from punishing experiences. "My activities and interests are often criticized by others" would be answered true.

5 or Mf *(Masculinity-Femininity)* Sixty items differentiating between male and female respondents. "I like to arrange flowers" would indicate femininity if answered true.

6 or Pa *(Paranoia)* Forty items from patients showing abnormal suspiciousness and delusions of grandeur or persecution. "There are evil people trying to influence my mind" would receive a response of true.

7 or Pt *(Psychasthenia)* Forty-eight items based on patients showing obsessions, compulsions, abnormal fears, and guilt and indecisiveness. "I save nearly everything I buy, even after I have no use for it" would elicit a response of true.

8 or Sc *(Schizophrenia)* Seventy-eight items from patients showing bizarre or unusual thoughts or behavior, who are often withdrawn and experiencing delusions and hallucinations. "Things around me do not seem real" and "It makes me uncomfortable to have people close to me" would each be answered true.

9 or Ma *(Hypomania)* Forty-six items from patients characterized by emotional excitement, overactivity, and flight of ideas. "At times I feel very 'high' or very 'low' for no apparent reason" would be labeled true.

10 or Si *(Social Introversion)* Seventy items from persons showing shyness, little interest in people, and insecurity. "I have the time of my life at parties" would be answered false.

People who frequently respond in the affirmative to such items as "I certainly feel useless much of the time" and in the negative to such items as "I usually feel that life is worthwhile" would score relatively high on the depression scale. Similarly, if people repeatedly answer true to such statements as "I am easily embarrassed" and false to statements like "I do not mind meeting strangers," they receive a high score on the social introversion scale. Scores for each scale can range from 0 to 120. When people score above 70 on a particular scale, their functioning on the dimension measured by that scale is considered deviant.

Usually a person's scores on every scale in the MMPI are summarized graphically on an MMPI profile sheet. The pattern made when the scores are connected, called the person's "profile," is evaluated to determine that person's general personality style and underlying emotional needs (Friedman et al., 1989; Meehl & Dahlstrom, 1960; Meehl, 1951). To evaluate a client's profile, clinicians often use an *MMPI atlas,* a published compilation of the MMPI profiles and case histories of various kinds of patients (Graham, 1977; Hathaway & Meehl, 1951). By matching a client's profile to similar profiles in the atlas, a clinician can draw conclusions about that client's personality (Graham, 1987). It is also possible to send a client's MMPI responses to a professional interpretation service to be scored, profiled, and analyzed by computer (Butcher, 1981, 1979; Kleinmuntz, 1972; Eichman, 1972).

The profile approach to assessment is illustrated in the following evaluation of J. A. K., a depressed 27-year-old man whose MMPI profile is shown in Figure 4-4. Noting that J. A. K. scored 94 on the depression scale, above 70 on the psychasthenia, schizophrenia, social introversion, and hypochondriasis scales, and within normal range on the other scales, the clinician wrote the following report:

*J.* A. K. appears to be in a great deal of psychological discomfort. He feels anxious, depressed, and overwhelmed by his problems. . . . Most of the time he is likely to be rather unemotional and unexcitable and to have a slow personal tempo, but he may also experience episodes of unexplainable excitement and restlessness. He ruminates over his problems; he is very pessimistic about the possibility that things might get better; and he may have concluded that life is no longer worthwhile. He feels very guilty about perceived misdeeds, and he may harbor suicidal ideas, but he does not seem to be more likely than other depressed

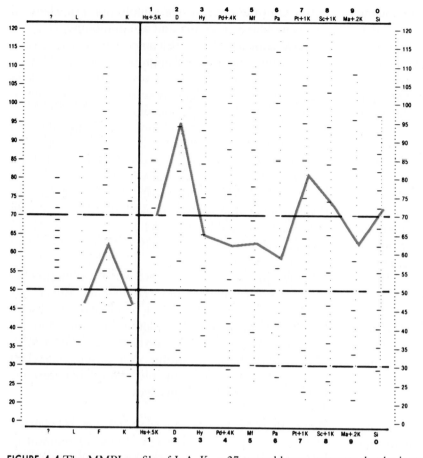

**FIGURE 4-4** The MMPI profile of J. A. K., a 27-year-old man, suggests that he is very depressed. He also appears to be anxious, prone to somatic complaints, indecisive, socially awkward, and suspicious of others. *(From Graham, 1977, p. 164.)*

patients to attempt suicide. He is likely to report somatic concerns. . . . J. A. K. is likely to have problems with concentration, attention, memory, and judgment. Decisions are especially difficult for him. He may have experienced periods during which he was unaware of what he was doing, and these episodes, coupled with obsessive and intruding thoughts, may lead him to fear that he is losing his mind.

J. A. K. has very strong unfulfilled dependency needs. He feels very inadequately prepared to handle problems and stresses on his own, and he is likely to turn to others for support and guidance. He has very strong needs for achievement, and he feels guilty when he falls short of his goals. . . .

J. A. K. views the world as a rather threatening and non-supportive place, and he feels that he is at the mercy of forces which are beyond his control. He has a very cynical, skeptical, and disbelieving attitude, and he feels mistreated and misunderstood by other people. . . . He anticipates problems before they occur, and he overreacts to stress.

J. A. K. has an extremely unfavorable self-concept. . . . J. A. K. is likely to have difficulty in establishing mature heterosexual relationships. He harbors doubts about his own masculinity and views women primarily as sources

of gratification for his strong dependency needs. . . . J. A. K.'s relationships with others tend to be very superficial and unrewarding. He needs other people and he has the capacity for developing deep emotional ties, but he is afraid of getting too involved with others because of fear of rejection and/or exploitation. He does not make friends easily, and other people see him as distant, aloof, and hard to get to know. . . .

Many of J. A. K.'s problems stem from his unrealistically high standards and goals for himself and his perceived failure to achieve them. Such attitudes often are produced by demanding and perfectionistic parents who are almost impossible to please. J. A. K.'s dependent, submissive style is directed at getting sympathy and support from other people. . . . His avoidance of deep emotional ties ensures that he will not be seriously hurt by other people. One suspects that his feelings of masculine inadequacy stem from a faulty identification with his father. His anger probably comes from perceived failures on the part of other people to fulfill his strong dependency needs and from their placing of demands on him that he feels he cannot meet.

*(Graham, 1977, pp. 178–180)*

***Response Sets and the MMPI*** Each person approaches a self-report inventory such as the MMPI with a particular ***response set,*** a tendency to respond in fixed ways. One response set might be ***acquiescence,*** describing people who tend to respond affirmatively to statements irrespective of their content ("yea-sayers"). Another might be *social desirability,* the response set of those who try to answer in ways that they believe are socially acceptable. Obviously, if people's answers are heavily influenced by their response set, their MMPI scores will be misleading. Thus three additional scales have been built into the MMPI to detect such influences.

The ***L scale,*** or lie scale, consists of fifteen items that test whether a person is trying to be viewed favorably. If people keep answering true to items such as "I smile at everyone I meet" and false to items like "I gossip a little at times," they will receive a high L score.

The ***F scale,*** or frequency scale, consists of sixty-four items that almost everyone responds to in the same way, such as "Everything tastes the same" (false) or "I enjoy children" (true). People who keep responding to these items in an unusual manner receive a high F score and are viewed as careless test takers, yea-sayers, or nay-sayers.

Finally, the ***K scale,*** or defensiveness scale, comprises thirty items that indicate whether people are protecting their image in their responses. If they keep answering true to unlikely items such as "I have very few quarrels with members of my family," and false to such items as "I feel bad when others criticize me," they will receive a high K score and be viewed as reluctant to admit problems. Clinicians also include these scale scores on the person's MMPI graphic profile (as in Figure 4-4) and use them to draw conclusions about the person's test-taking attitude. If the individual scores high on the L, F, or K scale, clinicians may alter their MMPI conclusions or deem the test results invalid.

***MMPI-2*** The new version of the MMPI tries to update and broaden the original while preserving those items and scoring techniques that so many clinicians are familiar with and find useful. The new inventory contains 567 items, many identical to those in the original, some rewritten to reflect contemporary language ("upset stomach," for instance, replaces "acid stomach"), and others that are totally new. In addition to the ten basic scales, which are the same as in the original, the MMPI-2 adds a number of new scales, to measure such things as a vulnerability to eating disorders, a tendency to abuse drugs, and poor functioning at work. The revised inventory was standardized using a large testing sample (2,600 subjects) whose composition reflected the demographics of the entire United States population

better than the original test sample did, especially on such variables as minority and age groupings.

Many clinicians have welcomed the MMPI-2 as a valuable improvement and appropriate update. Others, however, believe that the new test has significant flaws and may never be an adequate substitute for the original (Adler, 1990). One of the major complaints is that the sample for the new test was apparently more educated and more professional than the population at large. Another concern is that the large body of research that has been conducted on the original MMPI may not be applicable to the MMPI-2. Moreover, there are indications that a number of subjects who take both test versions get different scores on the two tests — showing a high level of depression on one version, say, yet a normal score on the other (Adler, 1990).

Some opposition is inevitable when a new product seeks to replace an older, more familiar one. But at least some of the concerns now being raised may be substantial. Researchers are now exploring the issue, and any decision to shelve one of the versions awaits the outcome of their work. In the meantime, at least some clinicians are using both versions of the test in order to determine the relative merits for themselves.

***Q-sort*** Because humanistic clinicians are particularly interested in people's subjective views of themselves and their experiences, they favor personality tests that reveal a person's self-concept. The Q-sort (Stephenson, 1953) is the most widely used self-concept instrument. Subjects are given a pile of cards, each containing a statement about personality or performance, and asked to sort them into nine piles ranging from "most descriptive of me" to "least descriptive of me." The cards contain such statements as "Behaves in a sympathetic or considerate manner," "Tends to be rebellious and nonconforming," and "Expresses hostile feelings directly." Because respondents are free to rearrange the piles as they proceed, they can produce a rather precise picture of how they view themselves. The Q-sort can also be used to obtain respondents' views of the way others see them (social self) or of the person they would like to be (ideal self). Some clinicians repeat the test during the course of therapy to measure changes in a client's self-perception.

***The Value of Personality Inventories*** The MMPI and other personality inventories have several advantages over projective tests. They are paper-and-pencil tests that do not take much time to administer, and they are objectively and easily scored. Most important, these inventories are usually standardized, so that one person's scores can be compared with many others'.

In addition, personality inventories usually display greater test–retest reliability than projective tests. People who take the MMPI a second time after an interval of less than two weeks receive approximately the same scores; various studies have found a reliability coefficient ranging from .70 to .85 (Graham, 1987, 1977). After an interval of a year or more, the test–retest reliability coefficient drops to approximately .40, but this is still an impressive correlation when we remember that anyone's psychological status is quite likely to change in the course of a year.

Personality inventories also appear to have greater validity than projective tests, so that clinicians can assess respondents' personal characteristics more accurately (Graham & Lilly, 1984; Little & Shneidman, 1959; Kostlan, 1954). To compare the two methods, investigators asked one group of test experts to predict what a number of people were like on the basis of their MMPI responses and another group of experts to make predictions about the same people on the basis of their responses to projective tests (Little & Shneidman, 1959). The evaluations were then compared with descriptions of the subjects derived from extensive case histories. The evaluations based on MMPI scores were found to be more accurate than those derived from projective tests.

All the same, personality inventories can hardly be considered *highly* valid test instruments. When clinicians use these tests alone, they have not consistently been able to judge a subject's personality accurately (Aikens, 1985). There are several reasons for this problem. First, respondents may compromise the accuracy of their inventory test scores by answering carelessly, defensively, or falsely. Although the safeguards built into some personality inventories alert clinicians to biases in responses, they usually do not eliminate these biases. Second, the profile-matching procedures that are used to evaluate scores on the MMPI and some other personality inventories are imprecise and bound to be wrong in some cases. A person might, for example, have an MMPI profile that is similar to that of depressed persons without actually being clinically depressed.

The validity of personality inventories is also limited by the very nature of what they are trying to measure. The qualities and traits these tests purport to measure are not physical entities whose existence and strength can be verified directly. How can we really know the character or depth of a person's emotions or needs when the only indications we have are the person's words and actions?

Despite these limitations, the MMPI and other personality inventories continue to be very popular assessment tools. Although they may not always help clinicians to identify specific disorders, research does suggest that they can be useful as gross screening devices, to help detect general dysfunctioning (Bellack & Hersen, 1980). Moreover, studies indicate that when personality inventories are used along with interviews or other assessment tools, they can help clinicians draw clearer pictures of people's characteristics and disorders (Levitt, 1989; Sines, 1959; Kostlan, 1954).

***Other Self-report Inventories*** Behavioral and cognitive clinicians also use self-report inventories in their assessments (Kendall, 1990, 1987; Adams, 1989). Yet unlike the broad personality inventories used by psychodynamic and humanistic clinicians, their paper-and-pencil inventories usually are designed to collect detailed information about one narrow area of functioning. Their purpose is to help clinicians complete a functional analysis of a client's disturbance so that they can set up an appropriate behavioral or cognitive therapy program. There are inventories to measure affect (emotion), social skills, cognitive processes, and reinforcements.

*Affective inventories* measure the severity of such emotions as anxiety, depression, and anger (Gotlib & Cane, 1989). The most widely used affective inventory is the Fear Survey Schedule, shown in Table 4-1, in which people rate how intensely they fear various objects and situations (Lang, 1985; Geer, 1965; Wolpe & Lang, 1964). *Social skill inventories* ask respondents to indicate how they would react in a variety of social situations. Clinicians use these inventories, such as the Assertive Behavior Survey Schedule in Table 4-2, to assess a person's social skills, deficits, and fears, and to determine the role these factors play in the person's disorder. *Cognition inventories* disclose the kinds of thoughts and assumptions that are typical of the client, as well as the frequency with which they come to mind (Kendall, 1990; Kendall, Howard, & Hays, 1989; Kendall & Hollon, 1989, 1981). These inventories are used to uncover the counterproductive thoughts and patterns of thinking that cognitive clinicians believe are at the root of abnormal functioning (see Table 4-3).

*Reinforcement inventories* require clients to report the nature, intensity, and frequency of various reinforcements in their lives. In the Reinforcement Survey Schedule, for example, respondents rate on a 5-point scale how much pleasure they receive from fifty-four different stimuli, such as eating particular foods, listening to various kinds of music, reading, playing sports, shopping, talking with people, and making love (Cautela & Kastenbaum, 1967). They also rate how much they would enjoy being in situations like the following:

TABLE 4-1

| PARTIAL FEAR SURVEY SCHEDULE | | | | | | | |
|---|---|---|---|---|---|---|---|
| Indicate how much fear you experience when confronted with the following: | | | | | | | |
| 1. Sharp objects | None | Very little | A little | Some | Much | Very much | Terror |
| 2. Being a passenger in a car | None | Very little | A little | Some | Much | Very much | Terror |
| 3. Dead bodies | None | Very little | A little | Some | Much | Very much | Terror |
| 4. Suffocating | None | Very little | A little | Some | Much | Very much | Terror |
| 5. Failing a test | None | Very little | A little | Some | Much | Very much | Terror |
| 6. Looking foolish | None | Very little | A little | Some | Much | Very much | Terror |
| 7. Being a passenger in an airplane | None | Very little | A little | Some | Much | Very much | Terror |
| 8. Worms | None | Very little | A little | Some | Much | Very much | Terror |
| 9. Arguing with parents | None | Very little | A little | Some | Much | Very much | Terror |
| 10. Rats and mice | None | Very little | A little | Some | Much | Very much | Terror |

*Source:* Geer, 1965.

You have just completed a difficult job. Your superior comes by and praises you highly for a "job well done." He also makes it clear that such good work is going to be rewarded very soon.

*(Cautela & Kastenbaum, 1967, p. 121)*

Behaviorists use the Reinforcement Survey Schedule as a source of clues to the objects and situations that may be reinforcing dysfunctional behaviors in their clients. It also tells them what kinds of rewards might be effective in a client's behavioral treatment program.

### The Value of Self-report Inventories

Like personality inventories, these less comprehensive self-report inventories collect information directly from the subjects themselves. This gives the inventories a strong face validity and a seeming efficiency, and as a consequence both the number of these tests and the number of clinicians using them have increased steadily in the past two decades.

At the same time, the other inventories have significant limitations (Kendall, 1990, 1987; Clark, 1988). First, unlike the personality inventories, they rarely contain response-set scales to help determine whether people are being careless or inaccurate in their accounts. Second, relatively few behavioral or cognitive self-report inventories have been subjected to rigorous standardization, reliability, and validity procedures. Surveys of clinicians suggest that self-report inventories are often improvised as the need for them arises, without being tested for accuracy and consistency (Reichalt, 1983; Wade, Baker, & Hartmann, 1979; Kasfer, 1972).

**Psychophysiological Tests**   More and more during the past decade clinicians have used tests that measure physiological responses (Kendall, 1990). The interest in psychophysiological measures began when a number of studies suggested that states of anxiety are regularly accompanied by physiological changes such as increases in heart rate, body temperature, blood pressure, electrical resistance in the skin (galvanic skin response), and muscle contraction (Boulougouris et al., 1977; May, 1977; Bloom & Trautt, 1977). Because measures of these psychophysiological changes were often more precise than interviews, projective tests, self-reports, and so on, behavioral and cognitive clinicians began to include them in their functional analyses of anxiety disorders (Cook et al., 1988; Lang, 1985). When related studies suggested that other disturbances, such as schizophrenia, were also accompanied by systematic physiological response patterns, the use of psychophysiological measures in clinical assessment increased even more (Zahn, 1977; Alexander, 1972).

Psychophysiological measurements are used widely in the assessment and treatment of sexual disorders (Hall, Proctor, & Nelson, 1988; Geer, 1976). A test instrument called the *vaginal plethysmograph,* for example, is used to measure sexual arousal in women. This instrument, a small tampon-shaped probe with a light at its end, is placed in a woman's vagina to measure the amount of light reflected by the vaginal wall (Sintchak & Geer, 1975). The reflected light increases when the wall arteries receive additional blood — that is, when the woman is sexually aroused. Studies find that this instru-

TABLE 4-2

## PARTIAL ASSERTIVE BEHAVIOR SURVEY SCHEDULE

What would you do in the following situations? Indicate by circling number 1, 2, or 3.

A. In a restaurant, you have ordered your favorite meal. When it comes, it is not cooked to your liking.
   1. You tell the waitress that it is not cooked to your taste or liking and have her take it back and [have it] cooked to your taste or liking.
   2. You complain that it is not cooked to your taste or liking, but you say you will eat it anyway.
   3. You say nothing.

B. You have been waiting in line to buy a ticket. Someone gets in front of you.
   1. You say it is your turn, and get in front of him.
   2. You say it is your turn, but you let the person go before you.
   3. You say nothing.

C. In a supermarket, you are waiting in line at the checkout counter. Someone gets in front of you.
   1. You say, "I'm sorry, but I was here first," and you take your turn.
   2. You say, "I'm sorry, but I was here first," but you let the person go ahead of you.
   3. You say nothing.

D. In a drugstore, the clerk has been waiting on someone for about five minutes. He finishes, and it is now your turn, but he starts to wait on someone else.
   1. You speak up to him and say it is your turn, and take your turn.
   2. You speak up to him and say it is your turn, but also say that you will let the other person go ahead of you.
   3. You say nothing.

*Source:* Cautela & Upper, 1976.

ment does detect a difference when female subjects are observing erotic films (Wincze & Lange, 1981; Heiman, 1977). A *penile plethysmograph,* sometimes called a strain gauge, is used to measure sexual arousal in men (Bancroft, Jones, & Pullan, 1966). Here a rubber tube filled with mercury is placed around the penis. As blood flows to the penis, the rubber tube is stretched and the diameter of the column of mercury changes, thus providing a measure of sexual arousal. Again, a difference is found when men are observing erotic material (Heiman, 1977; Rosen & Kopel, 1977).

Psychophysiological tests also have been used in the assessment of medical problems, such as headaches and hypertension (high blood pressure), that are thought to relate to a person's psychological state. As we shall see in Chapter 7, clinical researchers have discovered that the physiological components of these problems can sometimes be treated by *biofeedback,* a technique in which the client is given systematic information about key physiological responses as they occur and thus learns gradually to control them (Andrasik et al., 1984; Blanchard et al., 1982; Beatty & Haynes, 1980). For example, when tension-headache sufferers are given detailed feedback about the levels of tension in their head muscles, many can learn to relax those muscles at will, and the frequency of their headaches declines.

The measuring of physiological changes has become an integral part of the procedures used to assess many psychological disorders. Like other kinds of clinical tests, however, psychophysiological tests pose problems for clinicians. One is logistical. Most psychophysiological tests require expensive recording equipment that must be carefully maintained and expertly calibrated (Nelson, 1981; Bellack & Hersen, 1980).

A second problem is that psychophysiological measurements can be misleading because they are not always indicative of the person's usual state. The laboratory equipment itself—impressive, unusual, and sometimes frightening—may arouse a subject's nervous system and thus alter physiological readings.

Another problem is that physiological responses are often observed to change when they are measured repeatedly in a single session. Galvanic skin responses often decrease upon repeated testing (Montagu & Coles, 1966) and genital arousal responses may lessen because of fatigue (Abel, 1976).

Finally, psychophysiological measurements often pose an interpretation problem. Clients' psychophysiological responses are often inconsistent with their self-reports. Several studies have found, for example, that female subjects' subjective ratings of their sexual arousal failed to correlate closely with their plethysmograph readings, except for the fact that both the self-reports and the plethysmograph did indicate that erotic stimuli were more arousing than nonerotic stimuli (Van Dam et al., 1976). Which measure of sexual arousal, then, is a clinician to trust? On the one hand, self-reports of sexual arousal may be subject to error, but on the other hand, shouldn't a measure of sexual feelings include the person's own perception of sexual arousal?

**Neuropsychological Tests** As we observed in Chapter 2, some problems in personality or behavior are caused primarily by damage to the brain or alterations in brain activity, conditions referred to as *organic impairment, neurological damage,* or *organicity.* Head injury, brain tumors, brain malfunctions, blood-vessel diseases, degenerative diseases, alcoholism, and infections can all

TABLE 4-3

## PARTIAL THOUGHT-STOPPING SURVEY SCHEDULE

Check the appropriate box that indicates how often you have a particular thought.

| | Not at all | A little | A fair amount | Much | Very much |
|---|---|---|---|---|---|
| 1. I feel lonely | | | | | |
| 2. Life is hopeless | | | | | |
| 3. I feel stupid | | | | | |
| 4. I don't look attractive | | | | | |
| 5. People don't like me | | | | | |
| 6. I'd like to have a drink (alcohol) | | | | | |
| 7. I'd like to have something to eat | | | | | |
| 8. I'd like to have a smoke | | | | | |
| 9. I feel depressed | | | | | |
| 10. I am going to make a mistake | | | | | |
| 11. I am a failure | | | | | |
| 12. I would like to expose myself | | | | | |
| 13. The future looks hopeless | | | | | |
| 14. I feel guilty about something I have done | | | | | |
| 15. I am going crazy | | | | | |
| 16. I am going to panic | | | | | |

*Source:* Cautela & Upper, 1976.

cause organic impairment. If a psychological dysfunction is to be treated effectively, it is important to know whether it stems from some physiological abnormality in the brain.

Neurological problems can sometimes be detected through such procedures as brain surgery and biopsy; brain X rays; a *computerized axial tomogram (CAT scan),* for which X rays of the brain are taken at different angles; an *electroencephalogram (EEG),* which is a recording of electrical impulses in the brain gathered by wires attached to the scalp; a *positron emission tomogram (PET scan),* which is a computer-produced motion picture of rates of metabolism throughout the brain; and *nuclear magnetic resonance (NMR),* a complex procedure that uses the magnetic property of certain atoms in the brain to create a detailed picture of the brain's structure (see Box 4-2).

Subtle brain abnormalities, however, may escape these methods of detection. Clinicians have therefore developed less direct but sometimes more revealing neuropsychological tests that help identify neurological

Electrodes pasted to a patient's scalp detect electrical impulses from the brain. The impulses are then amplified and converted into ink tracings on a roll of graph paper to produce an electroencephalogram (EEG). The EEG is only a gross indicator of the activity of the brain. When diagnosticians observe abnormal brain-wave patterns on an EEG, they conclude that some part of the brain is functioning improperly, and they try to pinpoint the problem by using more specialized diagnostic tools.

problems by measuring a person's cognitive, perceptual, and motor skills (Levin et al., 1989). Because neurological damage is likely to affect visual perception, recent memory, and visual-motor coordination, neuropsychological tests usually focus on these areas of functioning.

The Bender Visual-Motor Gestalt Test (Bender, 1938), one of the most widely used neuropsychological tests, consists of nine cards, each displaying a simple design (see Figure 4-5). Test subjects look at the designs one at a time and copy each one on a piece of paper. Later they try to reproduce the designs from memory. By the age of 12, most people can remember and copy the designs accurately. Notable errors in the accuracy of the drawings are thought to reflect organic impairment.

Some clinicians interpret this test subjectively; others use one of several objective and standardized scoring systems that have been developed (Tolor & Brannigan, 1980; Hutt, 1977; Pascal & Suttell, 1951; Koppitz, 1975). Test–retest reliability has a correlation coefficient of .70 when the scoring systems are used. As for validity, clinicians are able to distinguish organically impaired from nonorganically impaired people on the basis of this test in approximately 75 percent of cases (Heaton, Baade, & Johnson, 1978; Pascal & Suttell, 1951). Because there is such a wide variety of organic impairments, however, no single neurological test can adequately test for them all, and no single test can consistently enable clinicians to distinguish one specific kind of neurological impairment from another (Goldstein, 1990; Smith, 1983; Lezak, 1976). This is the major limitation of the Bender Gestalt Test, and of any other neuropsychological test. At best it is a rough screening device for neurological impairment in general.

To achieve greater precision and accuracy in neurological assessment, clinicians frequently use a comprehensive group, or *battery,* of neuropsychological tests, each of which targets a specific neurological skill area (Goldstein, 1990). The Halstead-Reitan Neuropsychology Battery, a lengthy series of tests that measure sensorimotor, perceptual, and memory skills, and the shorter Luria-Nebraska Battery are widely used by today's clinicians (Reitan & Wolfson, 1985; Golden, 1978; Reitan, 1966; Halstead, 1947).

**Intelligence Tests** There is little agreement about the precise nature of intelligence, although most educators and clinicians agree in a general way with an early definition of intelligence as "the capacity to judge well, to reason well, and to comprehend well" (Binet & Simon, 1916, p. 192). Because intelligence is an inferred notion rather than a specific physical process or entity, it can be measured only indirectly. In 1905 the French psychologist Alfred Binet and his associate Theodore Simon pro-

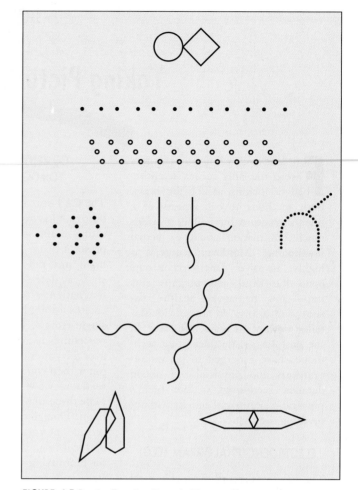

**FIGURE 4-5** In the Bender Gestalt Test, subjects copy each of nine designs on a piece of paper, then produce them again from memory. Sizable errors in the drawings may reflect organic brain dysfunctioning of some kind.

duced an intelligence test consisting of a series of tasks that require people to use various verbal and nonverbal skills. The test totals, adjusted in accordance with the test taker's age, furnish a general intelligence score for the person. Today the general score derived from intelligence tests is termed an *intelligence quotient,* or *IQ,* so called because it represents the ratio of a person's mental age to his or her chronological age, multiplied by 100.

Since Binet and Simon's first test, intelligence tests and studies of intelligence have been a major preoccupation of the educational and clinical fields. There are now more than eighty group tests of intelligence, thirty individual intelligence tests, and twenty tests of specific dimensions of intelligence, such as memory and reasoning skill. The intelligence tests most widely used today are the Wechsler Adult Intelligence Scale, the Wechsler Intelligence Scale for Children, and the Stanford-Binet Intelligence Scale. Information gathered from intelli-

## BOX 4-2

# Taking Pictures of the Brain

For many years X rays and surgery were the only means scientists had of looking at a living brain. Both methods reveal aspects of a brain's structure, but neither provides much information about its actual functioning. Moreover, surgery is highly "invasive" (the surgeon cuts open the skull and perhaps cuts into — and damages — healthy tissue), and X rays do not provide detailed views of the brain's structure. In the past several decades other techniques have emerged to permit researchers and physicians to obtain detailed recordings of the brain's physical makeup and activity without invading the tissue.

### ELECTROENCEPHALOGRAM (EEG)

The EEG is a record of the electrical activity of the brain obtained by placing electrodes on the scalp and recording and amplifying brain-wave impulses on a machine called an oscillograph. When the EEG reveals an abnormal brain-wave pattern, or *dysrythmia,* clinicians suspect the existence of brain abnormalities such as brain lesions, and they proceed to use other more precise and sophisticated techniques to ascertain the nature and scope of the problem.

### COMPUTERIZED AXIAL TOMOGRAPHY (CAT)

The CAT scan is a widely used procedure that has proved invaluable for locating brain structures. A machine passes a beam of X rays through the brain, and this beam is recorded by an X-ray detector on the other side of the patient's head. This procedure creates a thin, horizontal picture of a single cross section of the brain. The procedure is repeated many times over the patient's entire head. A computer then combines the many cross-sectional views to construct a complete three-dimensional picture of the brain. Though the CAT scan does not provide information about the activity of the brain, it is extremely useful for identifying the precise locations, sizes, and shapes of various structures. It reveals tumors, injuries, and anatomical abnormalities much more clearly than a conventional X ray, providing researchers and clinicians with important information about the correlation between a person's behavior and the physical characteristics of his or her brain. Diagnosticians have found that the scans of persons suffering from psychological disorders often deviate noticeably from the CAT scans of people who display no behav-

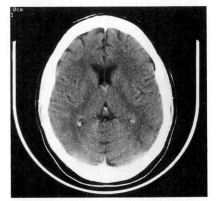

Computerized Axial Tomography (CAT). A CAT scan reveals detailed information about the location and amount of brain damage.

ioral abnormality, as we shall see in later chapters.

### POSITRON EMISSION TOMOGRAPHY (PET)

The development of PET has made it possible to watch the brain in action. A harmless radioactive isotope is injected into the patient's bloodstream and travels to the brain. The isotope emits subatomic particles, positrons, that collide with electrons to produce photons. The photons are detected

gence tests plays a large role in the diagnosis of mental retardation and can also be helpful in the diagnosis of other problems, such as neurological disorders.

Intelligence tests are among the most carefully constructed of all clinical tests. Large standardization samples have been selected for the major ones, so that clinicians can compare each person's scores with those of the general population. These tests have demonstrated high reliability. Within a test, people perform approximately the same on test items designed to tap the same ability, thus suggesting internal test consistency; and people who take the same IQ test years apart receive approximately the same scores (Lindemann & Matarazzo, 1990; Brown & Weiner, 1979; Willerman, 1979;

by a sensitive electronic device and recorded in a computer. The more physically active parts of the brain receive more of the isotope than the less active regions and produce a greater number of photons. The computer translates these data into a moving picture of the brain in which levels of blood flow and brain activity are represented by various colors. Here areas of orange and white in the scan on the left correspond to greater metabolic activity, and areas of blue and green correspond to less activity. Studies using PET scans have demonstrated some fascinating correlations between specific kinds of brain activity and specific psychological disorders. For example, PET scans of obsessive-compulsive patients show increased activity in the orbital gyrus and caudate nuclei structures and those of manic-depressive patients tend to show increased activity in the right temporal region during manic episodes.

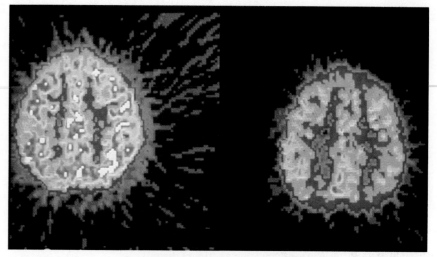

Positron Emission Tomography (PET)

## NUCLEAR MAGNETIC RESONANCE (NMR)

NMR, the most recent development in brain-imaging techniques, provides information on both the structure and the function of the brain and does not require any form of radiation. In this highly complex and elegant procedure a person lies on a machine that creates a magnetic field around his or her head, causing the hydrogen atoms in the brain to line up. When the magnet is turned off, the atoms return to their normal positions, emitting magnetic signals in the process. The signals are recorded, read by a computer, and translated into a detailed and accurate picture of the brain. In many cases NMR is so precise that the image it produces looks more like a photograph of the brain than a typical computer-produced image. NMR is believed to reflect the composition of cells and may be critical in detecting damaged areas of the brain containing different concentrations of hydrogen.

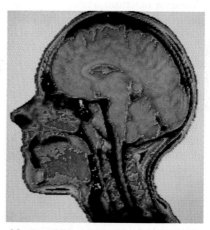

Nuclear Magnetic Resonance (NMR)

Weiner & Stewart, 1984). Finally, the major IQ tests appear to have relatively high validity. Studies that compare children's IQ scores with their performance in school, for example, have found validity correlations ranging from .40 to .75 (Anastasi, 1982; Matarazzo, 1972).

Although intelligence tests are impressive by these criteria, they have some significant shortcomings. Factors that have nothing to do with intelligence, such as low motivation and high anxiety, can influence a person's performance on these tests. In addition, IQ tests may contain culturally biased items or tasks that place people from one background at an advantage over those from another (Puente, 1990; Lampley & Rust, 1986; Kline-

The Wechsler Adult Intelligence Scale–Revised (WAIS-R) (1981) has 11 subtests. Six are verbal subtests: *Information* (factual questions), *Digit Span* (repeating a series of digits), *Vocabulary* (word definitions), *Arithmetic* (arithmetic story problems), *Comprehension* (questions about everyday living and social situations), and *Similarities* (determining how two objects or scenes resemble each other). Five are performance subtests: *Picture Completion* (determining what important feature is missing in a picture), *Picture Arrangement* (ordering a series of pictures so that they tell a story), *Block Design* (making particular designs with red and white blocks), *Object Assembly* (assembling simple jigsaw puzzles), and *Digit Symbol* (marking symbols that correspond to the numbers 1 through 9).

berg, 1963) (see Figure 4-6). Obviously, clinicians must be careful to watch for such factors when they use these tests to assess a person's mental functioning.

**Integrating Test Data**   Most clinical tests fall short on one or more of the three key criteria of standardization, reliability, and validity, so it is unwise to put too much faith in any one test. Clinicians usually administer a battery of tests to assess psychological functioning and use this collection of information primarily to clarify and supplement the information gathered in the clinical interview.

Let us return to Angela Savanti, the depressed young woman we met at the beginning of the chapter. We saw that Angela's clinician gathered a considerable amount of information about her during the interview—her symptoms, her unhappy childhood, her father's departure from home, her guilt over his departure, her mother's critical and controlling style, Angela's relationship and breakup with her boyfriend, and her tendency to blame herself for everything that went wrong. Angela's clinician collected additional data from a battery

of tests (TAT, MMPI, Q-sort, depression inventory, and an intelligence test) and composed the following test report:

*Angela cooperated during the psychological testing, and* attempted to do each task asked of her. However, she did not answer any question spontaneously, and it usually took her several seconds before she gave a response. . . .

The client scored in the average range of intelligence. The long reaction times to verbal stimuli and the slowness of her motor responses suggested an impairment in intellectual functioning. This slowness in verbal and motor behavior is consistent with the performance observed in persons who are depressed. The client's affect, as interpreted from the test material, was constricted and controlled. She appeared to react strongly to some of the events occurring around her, but she controlled her emotions so that other people were not aware of how she felt. . . .

A theme that emerged on several of the tests referred to a person who had an unrealistically high level of aspiration, who was extremely self-critical. As a result, this person labeled her accomplishments as poor or mediocre, no matter how hard she tried. She was constantly plagued with feelings of inadequacy, self-blame, and anger, because she could not live up to her high standards of performance.

Maternal figures were depicted as controlling and lacking in empathy and warmth. The client described a scene in which a woman was forcing her daughter to perform a chore that the mother did not want to do herself. The mother did not understand or care that the daughter was not willing to do the task, and the daughter eventually complied with the mother's wishes.

Male figures were described as nice, but not to be counted on. Part of the blame for this unreliability was placed with the woman with whom the man was interacting. The woman was assumed to have the ability to modify the man's behavior, so any blame for the man's failings had to be shared by the woman as well.

There were no indications of psychotic thought processes during the interviews or on the test material.

*(Leon, 1984, pp. 115–116)*

The test information serves several functions for Angela's clinician. First, it underscores several of the impressions gathered earlier during the clinical interview. It indicates, for example, that Angela is indeed depressed, carries lingering feelings of anger toward her mother, and views her father and other men as unreliable and likely to disappoint her. Second, the test information helps the clinician clarify certain points brought out in the interview and determine the scope of the client's problems. It indicates, for example, that Angela's depression is so pervasive that it even retards her verbal and motor behavior, and that her feelings of inadequacy, self-criticism, and anger are deeper and more

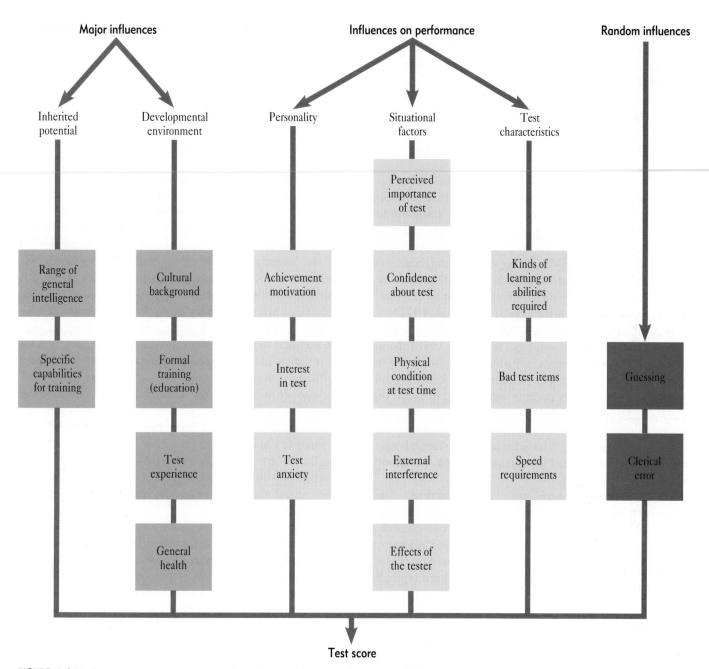

**FIGURE 4-6** Performance on *intelligence tests* is influenced by many factors in addition to inheritance and environmental learning. *(Adapted from Fischer & Lazerson, 1984, p. 481.)*

enduring than the interview itself may have conveyed. Finally, the test data reveal that Angela's intellectual functioning is average, that she is not psychotic, and that her aspirations are perhaps unrealistically high. With such information now in hand, the clinician is in a better position to understand Angela and her psychological problems.

## Clinical Observations

In addition to interviewing and testing people, clinicians may follow specific strategies for observing their behavior. One such technique is the ***naturalistic observation,*** also called an ***in vivo*** (literally, "in the living") ***observation,*** in which clinicians observe clients in their everyday environments. Another is the ***structured observation,*** in which clinicians monitor people in artificial settings created in their offices or laboratories. They may also have clients observe themselves, a technique called ***self-monitoring.*** These techniques are used most often by behavioral and cognitive clinicians as they search for vivid behaviors that will enable them to make a functional analysis of a person's disturbance.

**Naturalistic and Structured Observations** Most naturalistic clinical observations take place in homes, schools, institutions such as hospitals and prisons, and community settings such as restaurants, supermarkets, and apartment buildings. The observations have usually focused on parent–child, sibling–child, and teacher–child interactions; fearful, aggressive, or disruptive behavior; and self-injurious behavior (Barton & Osborne, 1978; Karoly & Rosenthal, 1977; Patterson, 1977).

Sometimes clinicians themselves are able to observe their clients in natural settings (Wellman, 1978). More often, however, they must rely on observations made by ***participant observers,*** key persons in the client's environment. In one study parents were asked to count the number of times their children displayed behavior problems (Christensen et al., 1980), and in another a mother kept track of how long it took for her son to finish household chores after he had been asked (Resick, Forehand, & McWhorter, 1976).

When naturalistic observation is impractical, clinicians may choose to observe some clients in a structured setting. Interactions between parents and their children, for example, may be observed in an office or laboratory on videotape or from behind a one-way mirror (Field, 1977; White, 1977). The parent and child are typically asked to play specific games or participate in certain tasks in a playroom while the observer looks on. Clinicians have used observation rooms also to monitor married couples engaging in a disagreement, speech-anxious people giving a speech, alcoholic people drinking, and fearful people approaching an object they find frightening (Floyd, O'Farrell, & Goldberg, 1987; Adams et al., 1978; Goldfried & Goldfried, 1977).

Obviously it is helpful for a clinician actually to watch the behavior, interactions, and situations that may be leading to a person's disturbances, but these methods have several disadvantages as well. For one thing, clinical observations are not always reliable (Foster & Cone, 1986). It is quite possible for various clinicians who observe the same person to focus on different aspects of behavior, evaluate the person differently, and draw different conclusions. Observations may become more consistent when the observers are carefully trained, the behavior under observation is clearly defined, and observer checklists are used (Alevison et al., 1978; Kent & Foster, 1977; Patterson, 1977).

Observers may make errors that also affect the validity of their observations, especially if they suffer from ***overload*** (Foster & Cone, 1986; Kazdin, 1977). So much is happening during an interaction that the observer may simply be unable to see or record all relevant behavior and events. Another problem is ***observer drift,*** a steady deterioration in accuracy as a result of fatigue or of a gradual inadvertent change in the criteria that an observer uses when judging behavior over a long period of time (O'Leary & Kent, 1973). Another possibility is ***observer bias*** — the observer's judgments are inappropriately influenced by information and expectations he or she already has about the client (Shuller & McNamara, 1980; Kent, O'Leary, Diament, & Dietz, 1974). Participant observers who are personally connected with the client are particularly prone to bias. A mother who observes her depressed teenage son, for example, may be inclined to minimize his pessimistic remarks, hoping that they are harmless adolescent complaints rather than indicators of severe depression.

Another factor that often limits the validity of clinical observations is the subject's ***reactivity*** — his or her behavior is affected by the very presence of the observer (Harris & Lahey, 1982; Tunnell, 1977; Roberts & Renzaglia, 1965). If schoolchildren are aware that someone special is watching them, for example, they may alter their usual classroom behavior, perhaps in the hope of impressing the observer.

Finally, clinical observations may lack ***cross-situational validity,*** also called ***external*** or ***ecological validity*** (Tunnell, 1977; Patterson, 1974). A child who behaves aggressively in school is not necessarily aggressive at home or with friends after school. Because behavior is often specific to particular situations, observations in one setting cannot always be applied to other settings (Simpson & Halpin, 1986). Problems of cross-situational validity are particularly likely in structured observations, since the office or laboratory may be quite different from the home, school, or community in which the disturbed functioning typically occurs (Reisinger & Ora, 1977; Edinburg, Karoly, & Gleser, 1970).

**Self-monitoring** Earlier we considered self-report inventories, assessment instruments in which subjects report their own behaviors, feelings, or cognitions. In a related procedure, self-monitoring, they observe themselves and carefully record designated behavior, feelings, or cognitions as they occur throughout the day (Bornstein, Hamilton, & Bornstein, 1986; Hollon & Kendall, 1981).

Subjects usually note the *frequency* of the responses they are recording. How frequently does a drug user have an urge for drugs (Thompson & Conrad, 1977) or a headache sufferer have a headache (Feuerstein & Adams, 1977)? Sometimes the subjects are instructed to keep a tally of the behavior on paper; or they may be asked to register their responses on a small counting machine they carry around with them.

Often self-monitoring subjects are also asked to observe and record the *circumstances* surrounding their responses. When self-monitoring is used to assess excessive smoking, for example, people are typically asked to record when and where they are smoking, who is present, what is happening, what they were thinking or feeling just before smoking, and what events followed the smoking. This information may reveal that a person smokes under particular conditions or certain kinds of stress (Conway, 1977; Dericco, Brigham, & Garlington, 1977).

Self-monitoring offers several advantages. First, it may be the only way to observe behavior that occurs relatively infrequently. When the problem is exhibitionism (exposing one's genitals in public), for instance, some clinicians have had the client keep a record of his or her exhibitionistic urges and actions (Maletsky, 1977, 1974). Second, self-monitoring is useful for observing behavior that occurs so frequently that any other comprehensive observation of it would be impossible. It has been employed to collect information about the nature and frequency of smoking, drinking, drug use, and feelings of anger and anxiety (Conway, 1977; Hay, Hay, & Nelson, 1977; Novaco, 1977). Third, self-monitoring is the only way covert cognitions can be observed and counted. In one study a woman who was having auditory hallucinations (hearing voices and sounds that were not really occurring around her) monitored the hallucinations for her clinician by raising a finger and keeping it raised throughout each such experience (Turner, Hersen, & Bellack, 1977).

Like all other clinical assessment procedures, however, self-monitoring has drawbacks. One is the question of its validity (Nelson, 1977; Nelson et al., 1977). Clients do not always receive proper instruction in this form of observation, nor are they always motivated to record their observations accurately (Mahoney, 1977). Furthermore, there is often a powerful reactivity effect when clients try to monitor themselves (Bornstein et al., 1986). It has been found, for example, that smokers smoke fewer cigarettes than usual when they are monitoring themselves (Kilmann, Wagner, & Satite, 1977), drug users take drugs less frequently (Hay et al., 1977), and teachers give more positive and fewer negative comments to their students (Nelson et al., 1977). Even a schizophrenic woman who was asked to record the frequency of her auditory hallucinations for three days re-

ported a sharp decrease in hallucinations, from 181 to 10 per day (Rutner & Bugle, 1969)! Indeed, these findings have persuaded many behavioral clinicians that self-monitoring, whatever its imperfections as an assessment technique, is a useful *treatment* technique, and they have incorporated it in their behavior modification programs (Watson & Tharpe, 1972).

## CLINICAL INTERPRETATION AND JUDGMENT

"The interviews have been completed; the Rorschach and TAT have been administered; the Incomplete Sentences Blank has been finished. Now, what does it all mean?" (Phares, 1979, p. 295). Before treating a client, a clinician must *interpret* the assessment data — that is, transform them into a clinical understanding of the person's problem and a diagnosis. By its very nature, interpretation requires one to make choices and distinctions. Perhaps the first distinction to be confronted is whether to use the data as samples, correlates, or signs (Sundberg, Tyler, & Taplin, 1973).

Clinicians use assessment information as a *sample* when they view a person's responses as typical of his or her everyday behavior. If Angela Savanti's slow verbal and motor responses during testing were viewed as an example of her way of responding at home and work, the clinician's reported observations of it would be considered a sample. Clinicians are using assessment data as *correlates* when they view the responses as predictors of the person's behavior, emotions, and thoughts in other areas of life. Angela's clinician, for example, might conclude from the self-blame and feelings of inadequacy revealed during testing that Angela was also pessimistic about the future and was thinking of suicide. Finally, clinicians are using assessment information as a *sign* when they take a person's responses as indicative of some underlying state, condition, or determinant. Angela's clinician might consider her TAT story about a controlling and cold mother an indication of unconscious resentment toward her mother or a repressed wish to disobey her.

Using the assessment data in these ways, clinicians generate hypotheses about the nature, causes, and course of a person's disturbed functioning. As assessment proceeds, the mounting data will seem to support some of these hypotheses and refute others. To a great extent, the principles and concepts embodied in each clinician's particular theoretical orientation help him or her decide which pieces of information should be considered samples, which correlates, and which signs.

It is not always clear exactly how clinicians go about testing their hypotheses. Clinicians themselves find it hard to step outside themselves and know what and how they are thinking and researchers have found it difficult to quantify and measure these covert cognitive processes. Some clinicians have invoked the notion of "clinical intuition" to explain the process of clinical interpretation. Clinicians are thought somehow to feel their way toward conclusions, aided by their clinical experiences and training, but without imposing on them a conscious systematic method. Although this view has a certain intuitive appeal, it hardly sheds light on the processes by which clinicians arrive at their conclusions (Peterson, 1968; Meehl, 1954).

In one useful line of research, investigators have tried to determine whether clinicians simply add and subtract assessment data when they formulate their conclusions or whether they combine the data in more complex ways (Wiggins, 1973). By and large, findings indicate that most clinicians use an *additive,* or *linear, model* when they interpret their data (Hammond & Summers, 1965). That is, they base their conclusions on how many assessment responses point in the same direction; as the number of concurring responses increases, the likelihood of a given conclusion increases as well.

Other lines of research have attempted to determine the kinds of logic most frequently used in clinical interpretation, the kinds of cues that have the greatest effect on clinicians, the amount of assessment data typically used, and the factors that bias clinical interpretations (Goldberg, 1968; Sarbin, Taft, & Bailey, 1960). Unfortunately, these efforts have revealed relatively little about the rules of logic used by clinicians. Apparently different clinicians proceed in different ways, and the success of their clinical interpretations varies (Slovic & Rorer, 1968; Kleinmuntz, 1967, 1963; Cline & Richards, 1961).

After they have collected and interpreted the assessment information, clinicians attempt to form a *clinical picture,* an integrated picture of the various factors causing and sustaining the person's disturbed functioning that enables the clinician to better select appropriate foci and methods for treatment (Sundberg et al., 1973). This picture, often written up formally as a report, is framed in the language and concepts of the clinician's theoretical orientation (Kaplan & Sadock, 1989). The clinician who worked with Angela Savanti held a cognitive-behavioral view of abnormality, so the clinical picture of Angela is constructed in terms of modeling and reinforcement principles and the proposition that Angela's expectations, assumptions, and interpretations are major components of her problem:

*A*ngela was rarely reinforced for any of her accomplishments at school, but she gained her mother's negative attention for what Mrs. Savanti judged to be poor performance at school or at home. Mrs. Savanti repeatedly told her daughter that she was incompetent, and any mishaps that happened to her were her own fault. . . . When Mr. Savanti deserted the family, Angela's first response was that somehow she was responsible. From her mother's past behavior, Angela had learned to expect that in some way she would be blamed. At the time that Angela broke up with her boyfriend, she did not blame Jerry for his behavior, but interpreted this event as a failing solely on her part. As a result, her level of self-esteem was lowered still more.

The type of marital relationship that Angela saw her mother and father model remained her concept of what married life is like. She generalized from her observations of her parents' discordant interactions to an expectation of the type of behavior that she and Jerry would ultimately engage in. Angela demanded that Jerry conform to her definition of acceptable interpersonal behavior, because of her belief that otherwise their marriage would not be a mutually reinforcing relationship. However, Angela set such high standards for Jerry's behavior that it was inevitable that she would be disappointed. . . .

Angela's uncertainties intensified when she was deprived of the major source of gratification she had, her relationship with Jerry. Despite the fact that she was overwhelmed with doubts about whether to marry him or not, she had gained a great deal of pleasure through being with Jerry. Whatever feelings she had been able to express, she had shared with him and no one else. Angela labeled Jerry's termination of their relationship as proof that she was not worthy of another person's interest. She viewed her present unhappiness as likely to continue, and she attributed it to some failing on her part. As a result, she became quite depressed.

*(Leon, 1983, pp. 123–125)*

With this report, Angela's clinician has largely accomplished the task of attaining an idiographic, or individual, understanding of the client. If clients are to be fully understood and effectively treated, however, the clinician has to determine not only what makes them unique but what they have in common with a specific group of other disturbed people. This is the purpose of diagnosis.

## DIAGNOSIS

Clinicians also use assessment information and interpretation processes to make a *diagnosis*—that is, to determine that a person's psychological problems constitute a particular disorder. Although clinicians can learn enough about a person from assessment information to develop ideas about the nature and causes of the person's problems, they need still other information to know the probable future course of the problem and what treatment strategies are likely to be helpful. It might also help them to know whether clinicians who treated similar cases found that less conspicuous symptoms were also involved in the problem and which factors were the most important to attend to.

When clinicians decide that a person's pattern of dysfunction constitutes a particular disorder, they are saying that the pattern is basically the same as one that has been displayed by many other people, has been observed and investigated in a variety of studies, and perhaps has responded to particular forms of treatment. If their diagnosis is correct, clinicians can fruitfully apply what is generally known about the disorder to the particular person they are trying to help. When, on the other hand, clinicians make an incorrect diagnosis, they may draw inaccurate conclusions about characteristics of the person and the course of the problem and may apply useless or even harmful treatment procedures (see Box 4-3).

## Classification Systems

The principle behind diagnosis is straightforward. When certain symptoms regularly occur together (a cluster of symptoms is called a *syndrome*) and follow a particular course, clinicians agree that those symptoms constitute a particular mental disorder. When people display this particular cluster and course of symptoms, diagnosticians assign them to that category. A comprehensive list of such categories, with a description of the symptoms characteristic of each and guidelines for assigning individuals to categories, is known as a *classification system.*

A classification system serves several important purposes (APA, 1987). First, as we have noted, it enables clinicians to *diagnose* a person's problem as a disorder. A diagnosis (from Greek for "a discrimination") in turn makes it possible for them to tap the general information that has already been gathered about that problem. A classification system also helps researchers to *study* abnormality and develop a body of knowledge about the causes of various patterns of abnormal functioning and ways to treat them. By using an agreed-upon classification system, clinical researchers can efficiently gather a representative sample of people with similar symptoms and investigate their problems. Finally, a classification system enables clinicians and researchers to *communicate* more easily. A clinician does not have to list every one of a client's symptoms in order to discuss that person with a colleague. Mention of the person's diagnostic category will suffice to give other clinicians a general picture of the kinds of difficulties the person is experiencing, which can then be enhanced by idiosyncratic details

Emil Kraepelin developed a system for classifying mental disorders on which today's classification systems are built.

about the individual's situation. Similarly, a researcher does not have to list all the symptoms shared by the subjects in his or her study before others can understand the kind of dysfunction under investigation.

As we saw in Chapter 1, Emil Kraepelin developed the first influential classification system for abnormal behavior in 1883. By collecting thousands of case studies of patients in mental hospitals, he was able to identify various syndromes, and to describe each syndrome's apparent cause and expected course (Zilboorg & Henry, 1941). The categories of disorders established by Kraepelin and the hierarchy in which he organized them have formed the foundation for the psychological part of the classification system now used by the World Health Organization, called the *International Classification of Diseases.* This system, which covers both medical and psychological disorders, is currently in its tenth revision, known as ICD-10.

Kraepelin's work has also been incorporated into the *Diagnostic and Statistical Manual of Mental Disorders,* a classification system developed by the American Psychiatric Association. Very similar to ICD-10, it too has been revised over time. The current edition, DSM-III-R, was published in 1987 and is by far the most widely used classification system in the United States today. All the descriptions of mental disorders presented throughout this book adhere to the categories and distinctions made in DSM-III-R.

Classification systems must be revised periodically to keep up with new knowledge and changing perspectives in the clinical field. As new insights and viewpoints emerge, new forms of classification are proposed to replace old ones. DSM has undergone major revisions in 1952 (DSM-I), 1968 (DSM-II), and 1980 (DSM-III), and a minor revision in 1987 (DSM-III-R). In a sense, then, a classification system actually freezes in time one

## BOX 4-3

# What Ailed Van Gogh?

Diagnosing mental disorders is a challenging and important task, and practitioners faced with a suffering patient are obliged to be as accurate and helpful as possible. Diagnosing the psychological problems of famous people who are no longer alive, though, is something of a parlor game. Old conclusions may change from time to time to conform to new theories and paradigms, as well as to incorporate newly discovered information about the person in question. A prime instance of such shifts is seen in the unfortunate case of Vincent Van Gogh.

Van Gogh led a turbulent and unhappy life. The legendary incident in which he cut off one of his ears, his voluntary commitment to a mental institution, and his ultimate suicide are the best-known pieces of evidence. But Van Gogh also wrote extensively about his pain and anguish, describing mental and physical torment and hallucinatory experiences. For years, his letters and the accounts of his friends and physicians led clinicians to diagnose Van Gogh as suffering from bipolar disorder, schizophrenia, or both. The available evidence seemed to support such a diagnosis. The picture changed in the mid-1980s, however, when the Harvard neurologist Shahram Khoshbin reviewed the many paintings and letters produced by Van Gogh in the months before his suicide. Khoshbin concluded that Van Gogh in

Vincent Van Gogh, a self-portrait.

fact suffered from Geschwind's syndrome, technically known as interictal personality disorder and believed to afflict people with epilepsy. Symptoms include excessive drawing (hypergraphia), hyperreligiosity, aggression, and other characteristics that Van Gogh is known to have exhibited. Khoshbin's conclusion, then, was that Vincent Van Gogh had epilepsy (Trotter, 1985).

The controversial issue was raised again more recently when the ear specialist I. Kaufman Arenberg of the

Swedish Medical Center in Colorado and his colleagues reevaluated Van Gogh's case. After reading almost eight hundred of Van Gogh's letters, they concluded that he suffered from Menière's syndrome, a disorder caused by an excessive buildup of fluid that exerts enormous pressure on the inner ear. Menière's syndrome may lead to nausea, vertigo, poor balance, pain, deafness, and buzzing or ringing. Some estimates put the number of sufferers in this country at 7 million. Arenberg suggested that Van Gogh suffered from an extreme form of this disorder and that he may have cut off his ear to reduce the pain. Many of Van Gogh's other problems and pains may have arisen from the severe secondary psychological problems that can accompany Menière's syndrome (Scott, 1990).

The study of abnormal psychology is a relatively young and fluid field, and many people suffering from a mental disorder receive more than one diagnosis during their search for help. New information about the person, new information about disorders, and other factors that can influence the views of clinicians may lead to different conclusions about the same case. Van Gogh has had the questionable honor of being posthumously diagnosed dozens of times. His case is worth bearing in mind in any discussion on assessment and diagnosis.

moment in the history of a constantly changing clinical field (Talbott & Spitzer, 1980). This is not to say, however, that there is universal agreement among clinicians whenever a new system or new categories are developed;

today's clinicians continually debate the merits of DSM-III-R, and their arguments have led the American Psychiatric Association to appoint a task force to revise it. DSM-IV is scheduled for publication in 1993.

# DSM-III-R

DSM-III-R lists more than two hundred mental disorders. Each entry describes the criteria for diagnosing the disorder, the essential clinical features of the disorder (features that are invariably present), and any associated features (features that are often but not invariably present), and gives information about onset, course, complications, predisposing factors, prevalence, sex ratio, and family patterns. The criteria in DSM-III-R, following the lead of DSM-III, are more detailed and objective than those of DSM-I and -II. DSM-III-R focuses entirely on verifiable symptoms, for example, and stipulates that a person's dysfunction must include certain specified symptoms if it is to qualify for a diagnosis. DSM-I and -II, in contrast, required diagnosticians to infer the underlying cause of a disorder in order to make a diagnosis. To make a diagnosis of **anxiety neurosis** according to DSM-II, for example, diagnosticians first had to conclude that a person was experiencing internal conflicts and defending against anxiety. In DSM-III-R such inferences are not required.

When clinicians use DSM-III-R to make a diagnosis, they must evaluate a client's condition on five separate *axes,* or areas of information. This requirement forces diagnosticians to review and use a broad range of information. First, clinicians must select an appropriate disorder from Axis I or Axis II or both, the axes that together list all categories of mental disorders. *Axis I* lists vivid disorders that cause significant impairment and that may emerge and end at various points in the life cycle. *Axis II* disorders are long-standing disorders that usually begin in childhood or adolescence and persist in a stable form into adult life. The Axis I disorders are organized into the following groups:

### Disorders of Infancy, Childhood, and Adolescence
Disorders in this group tend to emerge and often dissipate before adult life. They include *conduct disorders,* in which children persistently act aggressively and violate societal norms, rules, and the basic rights of others; *separation anxiety disorders,* in which children become excessively anxious over the possibility of being separated from their parents; and *anorexia nervosa,* in which people purposely lose dangerous amounts of weight because of their fear of becoming overweight.

### Organic Mental Disorders
These are disorders caused by known brain damage or disease. Many of them include such features as *delirium* (a clouded and confused state of consciousness), *dementia* (a deterioration in intellectual and cognitive functioning), memory impairment, recurrent hallucinations, and mood disturbances. Among the disorders in this group are *Alzheimer's disease* and *Huntington's chorea.*

### Psychoactive Substance Use Disorders
These disorders are brought about by regular use of substances that affect the central nervous system. With such regular use, persons may find their social and occupational functioning in disarray, need increasing amounts of the substance, and experience unpleasant symptoms when they stop taking it. Disorders in this group include *alcohol dependence, opioid dependence, amphetamine dependence, amphetamine abuse, cocaine abuse,* and *hallucinogen abuse.*

### Schizophrenia
In this group of disorders, functioning deteriorates until the patient loses contact with reality. Psychotic symptoms may include *delusions* (bizarre ideas with no basis in reality), *hallucinations* (perceptions of objects, sounds, or smells that are not actually present), *loose associations* (unconnected pieces of thought), and *flattened* or *inappropriate affect* (lack of emotion, or emotions that do not fit the situation).

### Delusional (Paranoid) Disorders
Persons with these disorders cling without reasonable cause to delusions that they are being persecuted or that loved ones are being unfaithful to them. Although such delusions greatly disturb the person's functioning, it is not as bizarre as the behavior displayed in schizophrenic disorders, nor is it accompanied by other psychotic symptoms.

### Mood Disorders
Disorders in this group are marked by severe disturbances of mood. People with mood disorders may feel extremely and inappropriately sad or elated for extended periods of time. These disorders include *major depression* and *bipolar disorder* (in which episodes of mania alternate with episodes of depression).

### Anxiety Disorders
Anxiety is the predominant disturbance in this group of disorders. People with anxiety disorders may experience broad feelings of anxiety *(generalized anxiety disorders)* or anxiety concerning a specific situation or object *(phobic disorders).*

### Somatoform Disorders
This group of disorders is marked by physical symptoms that apparently are caused by psychological rather than physiological factors. These disorders include *psychogenic pain disorders,* in which people experience severe pain; *conversion disorders,* in which there is a loss or change in physical functioning (for example, paralysis or

blindness); and *hypochondriasis,* in which people unrealistically interpret physical sensations as abnormal and become preoccupied with the belief that they have a serious illness.

**Dissociative Disorders**  People with these disorders experience a sudden change in consciousness, identity, or motor behavior that makes it difficult for them to carry on their normal functioning. Disorders in this group include *psychogenic amnesia,* in which people are unable to recall extensive pieces of important personal information; *psychogenic fugue,* in which people suddenly leave home, assume a new identity, and forget who they were before; and *multiple personality,* in which people display two or more distinct personalities, each with unique memories, behavior patterns, preferences, and social relationships.

**Sexual Disorders**  These disorders in sexual functioning, behavior, or preferences are caused in large part by psychological factors. They include *paraphilias,* in which people need unusual or bizarre imagery or acts to become sexually aroused (for example, *sexual sadism,* in which people must inflict suffering on their partners to achieve sexual excitement), and *psychosexual dysfunctions,* in which people are unable to complete the sexual response cycle (for example, *inhibited male orgasm* or *inhibited female orgasm,* once called impotence and frigidity).

**Sleep Disorders**  People with these disorders display chronic sleep problems (of more than a month's duration). The disorders may be *dyssomnias,* in which the primary disturbance is in the amount, quality, or timing of sleep (for example, *insomnia* or *hypersomnia*), or *parasomnias,* marked by the occurrence of abnormal events during sleep (for example, *sleep terror disorder* or *sleepwalking disorder*).

**Factitious Disorders**  People with these disorders intentionally produce or feign psychological or physical symptoms.

**Disorders of Impulse Control**  People with these disorders are chronically and progressively unable to resist impulses, drives, or temptations to perform certain acts that are harmful to them or to others. These disorders include *pathological gambling; kleptomania,* a recurrent failure to resist impulses to steal; *pyromania,* a recurrent failure to resist impulses to set fires; and *explosive disorders,* loss of control of aggressive impulses resulting in serious assault or destruction of property.

**Adjustment Disorder**  The primary feature of this disorder is a maladaptive reaction to a clear stressor such as divorce or business difficulties. The reaction may involve impairment in social or occupational functioning or symptoms beyond the normal, expected reaction to such a stressor.

**Psychological Factors Affecting Physical Condition**  These are physical disorders (such as headaches, asthma, ulcer, and angina pectoris) that are initiated or exacerbated by psychological factors. Such disorders are sometimes called *psychosomatic* or *psychophysiological.*

Axis II disorders are long-standing problems that are frequently overlooked in the presence of the disorders included in Axis I. DSM-III-R requires that they be considered. There are two major categories of Axis II disorders:

**Developmental Disorders**  The predominant symptom in this group of disorders is a disturbance in the acquisition of cognitive, language, motor, or social skills — a disturbance that tends to begin in childhood and persist into adult life. The disturbance may involve a general delay, as in *mental retardation;* a delay or failure to progress in a specific area of skill acquisition, as in *specific developmental disorders* (such as *dyslexia,* a *developmental reading disorder*); or multiple, qualitative distortions of normal development, as in the pervasive developmental disorder of *autism,* in which children are grossly unresponsive and uncommunicative to other people.

**Personality Disorders**  People with these disorders display enduring personality traits that are inflexible and maladaptive and cause significant social or occupational impairment or subjective distress. Some of the disorders in this group are *antisocial personality disorder,* in which people have a history of continuous and chronic antisocial behavior; *passive-aggressive personality disorder,* in which people indirectly resist demands for adequate performance in both occupational and social functioning; and *dependent personality disorder,* in which people passively allow others to assume responsibility for major areas of their life because of a lack of self-confidence or an inability to function independently.

Although people usually receive a diagnosis from *either* Axis I *or* Axis II, they may receive diagnoses from both axes. Angela Savanti received a diagnosis of *major depression,* an Axis I disorder (one of the mood disorders), because her pattern of dysfunction met these DSM-III-R criteria:

At least five of the following symptoms have been present during the same two-week period and represent a change from previous functioning:
1. Depressed mood most of the day, nearly every day
2. Markedly diminished interest or pleasure in all, or almost all, activities most of the day, nearly every day
3. Significant weight loss or weight gain when not dieting or decrease or increase in appetite nearly every day
4. Insomnia or hypersomnia nearly every day
5. Psychomotor agitation or retardation nearly every day
6. Fatigue or loss of energy nearly every day
7. Feelings of worthlessness or excessive or inappropriate guilt nearly every day
8. Diminished ability to think or concentrate, or indecisiveness, nearly every day
9. Recurrent thoughts of death (not just fear of dying), recurrent suicidal ideation without a specific plan, or a suicide attempt or a specific plan for committing suicide

*(APA, 1987, p. 222)*

Let us suppose that the diagnostician judged that Angela had also displayed a life history of chronic dependent behavior in that she had allowed others to assume responsibility for major areas of her life and had constantly subordinated her own needs to those of others. In this case, she would also have received an Axis II diagnosis of *dependent personality disorder.*

The remaining axes of DSM-III-R guide diagnosticians to recognize and report factors other than a client's symptoms that are potentially relevant to the understanding or management of the case. *Axis III* information is a listing of any physical ailments the person is currently suffering from (see Figure 4-7). *Axis IV* infor-

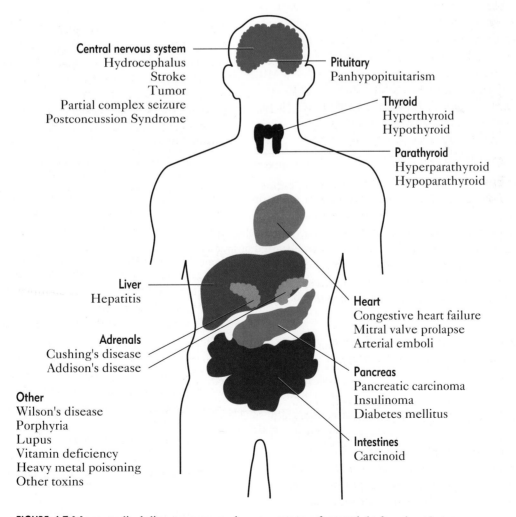

**FIGURE 4-7** Many medical diseases may produce symptoms of mental dysfunction. According to DSM-III-R, such medical causes must be ruled out before psychological symptoms can be diagnosed as a mental disorder. *(Adapted from Gold, 1987, p. 84.)*

mation is a rating of the severity of any psychosocial stresses the person is facing. And *Axis V* information is a rating of the person's psychological, social, and occupational functioning both currently and during the past year. If Angela Savanti had diabetes, for example, the clinician would include that under Axis III information. Because she recently went through the breakup of an engagement, the psychosocial stress in Angela's life would probably be considered "severe" on Axis IV and given a rating of 4 on DSM-III-R's six-point psychosocial stress scale (see Table 4-4). Because she seemed moderately impaired at the time of diagnosis but only minimally impaired six months prior, Angela's current level of functioning would probably be rated approximately 55 on Axis V, while her highest level of functioning during the past year would be about 90, in accordance with DSM-III-R's Global Assessment of Functioning Scale (see Table 4-5). The complete diagnosis for Angela Savanti would then be:

| Axis I: | Major depression |
|---|---|
| Axis II: | Dependent personality disorder |
| Axis III: | Diabetes |
| Axis IV: | Psychosocial stressors: termination of engagement<br>Severity: 4 — Severe |
| Axis V: | Current GAF: 55<br>Highest GAF past year: 90 |

Because several kinds of diagnostic information are used in DSM-III-R, each defined by a different "axis," it is known as a *multiaxial* system. The diagnoses arrived at under this classification system are expected to be more informative and more carefully considered than those derived from past systems.

TABLE 4-4

| SEVERITY OF PSYCHOSOCIAL STRESSORS SCALE: ADULTS | | | |
|---|---|---|---|
| | | **Examples of stressors** | |
| **Code** | **Term** | **Acute events** | **Enduring circumstances** |
| 1 | None | No acute events that may be relevant to the disorder | No enduring circumstances that may be relevant to the disorder |
| 2 | Mild | Broke up with boyfriend or girlfriend; started or graduated from school; child left home | Family arguments; job dissatisfaction; residence in high-crime neighborhood |
| 3 | Moderate | Marriage; marital separation; loss of job; retirement; miscarriage | Marital discord; serious financial problems; trouble with boss; being a single parent |
| 4 | Severe | Divorce; birth of first child | Unemployment; poverty |
| 5 | Extreme | Death of spouse; serious physical illness diagnosed; victim of rape | Serious chronic illness in self or child; ongoing physical or sexual abuse |
| 6 | Catastrophic | Death of child; suicide of spouse; devastating natural disaster | Captivity as hostage; concentration camp experience |
| 0 | Inadequate information, or no change in condition | | |

*Source;* APA, 1987, p. 11.

## Reliability and Validity in Classification

The value of a diagnostic classification system, like that of the various assessment methods, is judged by its reliability and validity. Here reliability means that different diagnosticians agree that a given pattern of observed behavior should be assigned to a given category. If different diagnosticians keep arriving at different diagnoses after observing the same behavior, then the classification system is not very reliable.

Past versions of the DSM have been only moderately reliable (Spitzer & Fleiss, 1974). In a study using DSM-I, for example, four clinicians independently interviewed and diagnosed 153 patients recently admitted to a mental hospital (Beck et al., 1962). Only 54 percent of these clinicians' diagnoses were in agreement. Some categories of classification brought greater agreement (were more reliable) than others, but none showed more

TABLE 4-5

## GLOBAL ASSESSMENT OF FUNCTIONING SCALE (GAF SCALE)

Consider psychological, social, and occupational functioning on a hypothetical continuum of mental health–illness. Do not include impairment in functioning because of physical (or environmental) limitations.

| Code | | Code | |
|---|---|---|---|
| 90 | **Absent or minimal symptoms** (e.g., mild anxiety before an exam), **good functioning in all areas, interested and involved in a wide range of activities, socially effective, generally satisfied with life, no more than everyday problems or concerns** (e.g., an occasional argument with family members). | 40 | **Some impairment in reality testing or communication** (e.g., speech is at times illogical, obscure, or irrelevant) **OR major impairment in several areas, such as work or school, family relations, judgment, thinking, or mood** (e.g., depressed man avoids friends, neglects family, and is unable to work; child frequently beats up younger children, is defiant at home, and is failing at school). |
| 81 | | 31 | |
| 80 | **If symptoms are present, they are transient and expectable reactions to psychosocial stressors** (e.g., difficulty concentrating after family argument); **no more than slight impairment in social, occupational, or school functioning** (e.g., temporarily falling behind in school work). | 30 | **Behavior is considerably influenced by delusions or hallucinations OR serious impairment in communication or judgment** (e.g., sometimes incoherent, acts grossly inappropriately, suicidal preoccupation) **OR inability to function in almost all areas** (e.g., stays in bed all day; no job, home, or friends). |
| 71 | | 21 | |
| 70 | **Some mild symptoms** (e.g., depressed mood and mild insomnia) **OR some difficulty in social, occupational, or school functioning** (e.g., occasional truancy, or theft within the household), **but generally functioning pretty well, has some meaningful interpersonal relationships.** | 20 | **Some danger of hurting self or others** (e.g., suicide attempts without clear expectation of death, frequently violent, manic excitement) **OR occasionally fails to maintain minimal personal hygiene** (e.g., smears feces) **OR gross impairment in communication** (e.g., largely incoherent or mute). |
| 61 | | 11 | |
| 60 | **Moderate symptoms** (e.g., flat affect and circumstantial speech, occasional panic attacks) **OR moderate difficulty in social, occupational, or school functioning** (e.g., few friends, conflicts with co-workers). | 10 | **Persistent danger of severely hurting self or others** (e.g., recurrent violence) **OR persistent inability to maintain minimal personal hygiene OR serious suicidal act with clear expectation of death.** |
| 51 | | 1 | |
| 50 | **Serious symptoms** (e.g., suicidal ideation, severe obsessional rituals, frequent shoplifting) **OR any serious impairment in social, occupational, or school functioning** (e.g., no friends, unable to keep a job). | | |
| 41 | | | |

*Source:* APA, 1987, p. 12.

than 63 percent agreement. Because all four clinicians were experienced diagnosticians, their failure to agree was attributed largely to deficiencies in the DSM-I classification system — vague descriptions of categories and categories determined more by theoretical biases than by specific symptoms.

The clearer and more objective criteria provided by DSM-III and DSM-III-R have yielded somewhat more reliable diagnoses than their predecessors (Akiskal, 1989; Eysenck, Wakefield, & Friedman, 1983; Mezzich, Coffman, & Goodpastor, 1982). Yet these systems also contain some vague, imprecisely defined categories, such as "depressive disorder not otherwise specified" and "anxiety disorder not otherwise specified." A few such categories have to be included because clients' symptoms do not always fit the more precisely specified primary categories. Unfortunately, although these vaguer categories bring needed flexibility to the classification system, they also bring a degree of imprecision and unreliability.

The validity of a classification system is the accuracy of the information that a diagnostic category provides about the people assigned to that category and about their symptoms. Categories are of most use to clinicians when they demonstrate predictive, etiological, and concurrent validity. A category has *predictive validity* when

it helps predict future symptoms or events. A common symptom of major depression, for example, is insomnia or hypersomnia. When clinicians give Angela Savanti a diagnosis of major depression, they expect her eventually to develop this symptom even though she may not manifest it now. Moreover, they expect her to respond to treatments that are effective for other depressed persons. The more often this category predicts such symptoms and treatment responsiveness accurately, the more predictive validity it has.

A category shows *etiological validity* when most cases assigned to it have similar histories and causes. DSM-III-R states, for example, that major depression is often precipitated by psychosocial stress in a person's life. Certainly, in Angela's case the stress of breaking up with her boyfriend seemed to trigger her pattern of depressive functioning. The more often cases of major depression are precipitated by stressful events of this kind, the more etiological validity the category has.

Finally, categories show *concurrent validity* when they give clinicians information about "associated" features of a disorder beyond the "essential" diagnostic symptoms. For example, DSM-III-R reports that people who manifest major depression often also become excessively concerned about their physical health. If Angela Savanti and most other people who receive this

As the list of mental disorders grows ever longer, some clinical observers believe that normal behavior is increasingly being viewed as the somewhat drab absence of abnormal functioning.

**NORMAL**

**DOMINANT SYMPTOMATOLOGY:** Characterized by unimpaired occupational, social, and sexual functioning for a period of one year or more. During this time individuals are free of neurotic or psychotic symptoms, i.e., anxiety, depression, hallucinations, or delusional thinking. Judgment is good, self-esteem high. Age onset: birth. More commonly diagnosed in the early twentieth century, this condition is rarely seen today.

diagnosis do indeed display this associated feature, the category is displaying a high degree of concurrent validity.

The developers of DSM-III and DSM-III-R have tried to improve upon the weak validity records of DSM-I and DSM-II by carefully reviewing the psychological literature to determine exactly what conclusions and expectations are appropriate for each category (APA, 1987; Talbot & Spitzer, 1980). Although the validity of DSM-III and DSM-III-R is stronger than that of DSM-I and -II, it is still limited — inevitably so, given the current state of knowledge in the field. Because the causes of almost all disorders are still being debated, the etiological validity of many categories is doubtful; because the associated features of some disorders have yet to be identified, the concurrent diagnostic validity of those categories is in question; and because the precise course of many disorders has yet to be determined, the predictive validity of those diagnoses is limited.

## Problems of Clinical Misinterpretation

Even with trustworthy assessment data and reliable and valid classification categories, clinicians will sometimes arrive at a wrong conclusion (Woody & Robertson, 1988). Numerous factors can adversely affect their thinking as they try to formulate a useful clinical picture and an appropriate diagnosis.

First, like all human beings, clinicians are flawed information processors whose judgments can be distorted by any number of personal biases — gender, age, race, and socioeconomic, to name just a few (DiNardo, 1975; Broverman et al., 1970). In addition, they often give too much weight to the data they encounter first and too little to data they acquire later (Meehl, 1960; Dailey, 1952). Finally, they may sometimes pay too much attention to certain sources of information, such as a parent's report about a child, and too little to others, such as the child's point of view (McCoy, 1976).

Second, clinicians may bring various misconceptions about methodology to the decision-making process. Many think that the more assessment techniques they use, the more accurate their interpretations will be — a belief that is not borne out by research (Kahneman & Tversky, 1973; Golden, 1964; Sines, 1959). Some also cling stubbornly to erroneous beliefs about the meaning of certain data. A classic study that investigated the interpretive processes used by thirty-two clinicians experienced in Rorschach testing revealed that the clinicians were inclined to diagnose male clients as homosexual whenever they made repeated references to human or animal anal images, feminine clothing, male or female genitalia, or similar themes in their Rorschach responses (Chapman & Chapman, 1967). Although research had repeatedly found no relationship between such Rorschach references and homosexuality, the clinicians adamantly clung to what the study's authors termed "illusory correlations" and continued to use them in making clinical judgments.

A third factor that can distort clinical interpretation is the clinicians' expectation that a person who consults them professionally must in fact have some disorder. Because they are looking for abnormal functioning, clinicians may overreact to any assessment data that suggest abnormality, a phenomenon that has been called the "reading-in syndrome" (Phares, 1979). The famous study by David Rosenhan (1973), discussed in Chapter 2, powerfully illustrates this problem. Eight normal people presented themselves at mental hospitals complaining that they had been hearing voices say the words "empty," "hollow," and "thud." On the basis of these complaints alone, hospital clinicians diagnosed these "pseudopatients" as schizophrenic and hospitalized them. Rosenhan was dismayed by how readily hospital clinicians made this diagnosis and how reluctant they were to change it. Although the pseudopatients dropped their symptoms immediately after being admitted to the hospital, the clinicians kept them hospitalized as long as fifty-two days. Apparently the setting in which these clinicians worked had primed them to expect and to diagnose certain kinds of mental disorders even when compelling clinical evidence was lacking.

A slightly earlier study also illustrated, in a different way, how greatly a diagnostic decision can be influenced by a clinician's expectations (Temerlin, 1970). Here trained clinical diagnosticians listened to a taped interview of a healthy man who presented himself as happy, successful, productive, warm, self-confident, and free of any psychological symptoms. Before listening to the interview, ninety-five of the diagnosticians were told by a highly respected clinician, "I know the man being interviewed today. He's a very interesting man because he looks neurotic but actually is quite psychotic." Another group of twenty diagnosticians heard the same clinician say that the man was quite healthy, and still another group of twenty-one clinicians heard no opinion at all from the respected clinician. After listening to the taped interview, all the diagnosticians were asked to diagnose the man. Ninety-two percent of the diagnosticians who had been led to expect a mental disturbance decided that the man on the tape had a significant mental disorder. A similar diagnosis was reached by 43 percent of those given no expectation at all, but by none of those who had expected that the man would be psychologically healthy!

Given such biases, misconceptions, and expectations, it is small wonder that investigations periodically uncover shocking errors in diagnosis, especially in hospitals. In one study a clinical team was asked to reevaluate the records of 131 randomly selected patients at a mental hospital in New York, conduct interviews with many of the patients, and arrive at a diagnosis for each patient (Lipton & Simon, 1985). The researchers then compared the team's diagnoses with the original ones. Although 89 of the patients had originally received a diagnosis of schizophrenia, only 16 received it upon reevaluation. And whereas 15 patients originally had been given a diagnosis of mood disorder, 50 received it now. Obviously, it is important for clinicians to be aware that diagnostic disagreements of this magnitude can occur.

## Dangers of Diagnosing and Labeling

Classification is intended to help clinicians understand, predict, and change abnormal behavior, but it can have some unfortunate and unintended consequences. As mentioned in the Chapter 2 discussion of the sociocultural model, some theorists believe that diagnostic labels may be self-fulfilling prophecies (Rosenhan, 1973; Szasz, 1970; Scheff, 1967). According to this notion, when a person is diagnosed as mentally disturbed, that label is often interpreted as a statement about the person's general behavior and potential. The person may therefore be viewed and treated in stereotyped ways, reacted to as sick or deficient, and expected to take on a sick role. In the Rosenhan (1973) study, for example, staff members spent limited time interacting with those labeled as patients, gave only brief responses to their questions, tended to be authoritarian in their dealings with the patients, and often made them feel invisible. In response to such attitudes and treatment, patients may increasingly consider themselves sick and deficient and eventually come to play the role that is expected of them. As the prophecy fulfills itself, the label "patient" seems justified.

Furthermore, there is a stigma attached to abnormality in our society, and as a result those labeled mentally ill may find it difficult to get a job, especially a position of responsibility, or to enter into social relationships. Indeed, they themselves may assume that they are incapable, irresponsible, or undesirable because of their emotional difficulties and may shy away from jobs or social interactions that they actually could handle perfectly well. This is the case despite massive, concerted efforts by various mental health organizations to educate the public.

Similarly, once people receive a clinical diagnosis, they may be viewed in light of it for a long time. Clinicians, friends, relatives, and the people themselves may all continue to apply the label long after the disorder has disappeared.

Because of these problems, some clinicians would like to do away with the clinical field's reliance on diagnosis. Others disagree. Although they too recognize the limitations and negative consequences of classifying and labeling, they believe that the best remedy is to work toward improving knowledge of the various disorders and the means of diagnosing them (Akiskal, 1989). They hold that classification and diagnosis can yield valuable information that helps greatly in understanding and treating people in distress. To throw the information away would be too drastic a measure; it would create more problems than it solves.

## SUMMARY

**C**linical practitioners are interested primarily in compiling *ideographic,* or individual, information about their clients. They seek a full understanding of the specific nature and origins of a client's problems through three steps: *assessment,* or the gathering of information about the person's problems; *interpretation,* or the piecing together of data to form a clinical picture of the person; and *diagnosis,* or the process of determining whether the person's dysfunction constitutes a particular psychological disorder.

**C**linical assessment is carried out before, during, and after treatment. The specific assessment techniques and tools that clinicians use often depend on their theoretical orientation. Most assessment methods fall into three general categories: clinical interviews, tests, and observations.

A *clinical interview* permits the practitioner to interact with a person and generally get a sense of who he or she is. The clinician tries to put the person at ease, displaying a nonjudgmental and accepting attitude while conducting either an *unstructured* or *structured interview.*

*Clinical tests* are devices that gather information about a few aspects of a person's psychological functioning from which broader information about that person can be inferred. They include *projective tests, self-report inventories, psychophysiological tests, neuropsychological tests,* and *intelligence tests.* To be useful a test must be *standardized, reliable,* and *valid.*

Because each type of test falls short on one or more of the key criteria of standardization, reliability, and validity, clinicians generally administer a battery of tests to assess psychological functioning. Even so, the results are usually used only to clarify and supplement the information gathered in the clinical interview.

The third method of clinical assessment is *clinical observation.* Two strategies for observing people's behavior are *naturalistic observation* and *structured observation.* The advantage of these methods is that they allow the clinician to watch actual behavior and interactions that may be leading to a person's disturbances. The disadvantages include weak reliability and validity. Practitioners also employ the related procedure of *self-monitoring:* subjects observe themselves and carefully record designated behavior, feelings, or cognitions as they occur throughout the day.

Clinicians must interpret the information they have collected to arrive at a diagnosis of the person's problem. They must decide whether the information represents a *sample* of the person's typical responses; *correlates* with predictable behaviors in other areas of the person's life; or is a *sign* of the underlying state or condition. The process of generating and testing a hypothesis about the nature, cause, and course of a person's disturbed functioning is complex and difficult. In general, it appears that clinicians use an *additive,* or *linear, model* when they interpret information about a client: they base their conclusions on the number of assessment responses that point in the same direction.

After collecting and interpreting the assessment information, clinicians form a *clinical picture,* which they often write as a *psychological report* framed by the language and premises of their own orientation.

The next step is to make a diagnosis, a determination that a person's psychological problems constitute a particular mental disorder. A *classification system* lists recognized disorders and describes the symptoms characteristic of each. The system developed by the American Psychiatric Association is the *Diagnostic and Statistical Manual of Mental Disorders.*

The most recent version of the manual, known as DSM-III-R, lists more than two hundred disorders. Clinicians who use it to make a diagnosis must evaluate a client's condition on five axes, or categories of information. The most recent versions of the DSM have proven to be somewhat more reliable and valid than earlier versions and other classification systems. Nevertheless, because the nature of almost all disorders are still being debated, the validity of DSM-III-R is not as high as clinicians hope for.

Even with trustworthy assessment data and reliable and valid classification categories, clinicians will not always arrive at the correct conclusion. Many factors can mar their judgment. They may be overly influenced by the initial data they receive about a person; they may bring misconceptions about methodology to the decision-making process; they may cling to erroneous beliefs; and they may have preconceptions about a person who is seeking help. In other words, clinicians are human and fall prey to the biases, misconceptions, and expectations that beset us all.

Some people think that diagnosing a patient does more harm than it does good, because the labeling process and the prejudices that labels arouse are damaging to the person being diagnosed. Nevertheless, most clinicians believe that classification and diagnosis yield valuable information that helps them understand and treat people in distress.

# TOPIC OVERVIEW

# CHAPTER 5

# TREATMENTS FOR ABNORMAL PSYCHOLOGICAL FUNCTIONING

*February:* He cannot leave the house; Bill knows that for a fact. Home is the only place where he feels safe — safe from humiliation, danger, even ruin. If he were to go to work, his co-workers would somehow reveal their contempt for him. A pointed remark, a quizzical look — that's all it would take for him to get the message. If he were to go shopping at the store, before long everyone would be staring at him. Surely others would see his dark mood and thoughts; he wouldn't be able to hide them. He dare not even go for a walk alone in the woods — his heart would probably start racing again, bringing him to his knees and leaving him breathless, incoherent, and unable to get home. No, he's much better off staying in his room, trying to get through another evening of this curse called life.

*July:* Bill's life revolves around his circle of friends: Bob and Jack, whom he knows from the office, where he was recently promoted to director of customer relations, and Frank and Tim, his weekend tennis partners. The gang meets for dinner every week at someone's house, and they chat about life, politics, and their jobs. Particularly special in Bill's life is Janice, with whom he has a promising relationship. They go to movies, restaurants, and shows together. She thinks Bill's just terrific, and Bill finds himself beaming whenever she's around. In fact, most people think Bill is terrific. They are eager to be with him and earn his respect, and Bill appreciates their admiration. He looks forward to work each day and his one-to-one dealings with customers. He is enjoying life and basking in the glow of his many activities and relationships.

Bill's thoughts, feelings, and behavior were so debilitating in February that they affected all aspects of his life. Most of his symptoms had disappeared by July, and he returned to his previous level of functioning. All sorts of factors may have contributed to Bill's improvement. Friends and family members may have offered support or advice. A new job or vacation may have lifted his spirits. Perhaps he changed his diet or started to exercise. Any or all of these things may have been useful to Bill, but they could not be considered *therapy.* That name is usually reserved for special, systematic processes for helping people overcome their psychological difficulties.

As defined by clinical theorist Jerome Frank, all forms of therapy have three essential features:

1. A sufferer who seeks relief from the healer.
2. A trained, socially sanctioned healer, whose healing powers are accepted by the sufferer and his social group or an important segment of it.
3. A circumscribed, more or less structured series of contacts between the healer and the sufferer, through which the healer, often with the aid of a group, tries to produce certain changes in the sufferer's emotional state, attitudes, and behavior. . . . (Frank, 1973, pp. 2–3)

The healing process may be exercised primarily by *psychotherapy*—in Frank's words, "by words, acts, and rituals in which sufferer, healer, and—if there is one—group participate jointly," or by *biological therapy,* consisting of "physical and chemical procedures."

Frank's straightforward definition of therapy belies the conflict and confusion that characterize the field of clinical treatment (Weiner & Borden, 1983; Reisman, 1971). Carl Rogers, whom we discussed in Chapter 2 as the pioneer of the humanistic model, was moved to write, "Therapists are not in agreement as to their goals or aims. . . . They are not in agreement as to what constitutes a successful outcome of their work. They cannot agree as to what constitutes a failure. It seems as though the field is completely chaotic and divided."

Clinicians even differ on such basic issues as what to call the person undergoing therapy. This person is called the *patient* by clinicians who view abnormality as an illness and therapy as a procedure that corrects the illness, and the *client* by clinicians who see abnormality as a maladaptive way of behaving or thinking and who see therapists as teachers of more functional behavior and thought. Because both terms are so common in the field, they will be used more or less interchangeably throughout this textbook.

On the other hand, there is general agreement in the clinical field that large numbers of people are in need of therapy of one kind or another and there is growing evidence that therapy is at least sometimes very helpful (O'Brien & Woody, 1989; Weissman et al., 1981; Smith, Glass, & Miller, 1980; Sloan et al., 1975).

## CLIENTS AND THERAPISTS

A nationwide survey of adults has suggested that 6 million people in this country receive therapy for psychological problems at any given time (Shapiro et al., 1984). This figure represents approximately one-fifth of the estimated 29 million adults in the United States who suffer from psychological problems (Myers et al., 1984). It has become increasingly common for children to be treated for psychological problems, too.

The number and variety of problems for which treatments are available have increased during this century. When Freud and his colleagues first began to conduct therapy, most of their patients suffered from anxiety or

The oldest of the modern adult therapy formats is individual, or one-to-one, therapy in which the therapist meets alone with a client, typically for weekly face-to-face sessions that last an hour. The frequency and length of sessions may vary, however, and orthodox psychoanalytic therapists have clients lie down instead of sit during therapy discussions.

depression. People with schizophrenia and other severe disorders were considered poor prospects for therapy, and treatment for them was confined to custodial care in institutions. The emergence of alternatives to psychodynamic therapies during the past several decades has helped change this situation. Anxiety and depression still dominate the therapy picture (approximately 50 percent of today's clients in the United States suffer from anxiety, depression, and personality disorders), but people with other kinds of disorders are also receiving therapy. Now people with schizophrenic disorders make up 10 percent of the clients in therapy, and people with substance abuse disorders make up 5 percent (Knesper, Pagnucco, & Wheeler, 1985). Moreover, large numbers of people with milder psychological problems, sometimes called "problems in living," are also in therapy. Surveys suggest that approximately 25 percent of clients enter therapy because of problems with marital, family, job, peer, school, or community relationships.

Other characteristics of clients have also changed over the years. Until the middle of this century, therapy was primarily a privilege of the wealthy, largely because of the high fees that outpatients were required to pay (Heller & Monahan, 1977; Hollingshead & Redlich, 1958). Today, with the expansion of medical insurance coverage and the emergence of publicly supported community mental health centers, people at all socioeconomic levels receive both outpatient and inpatient therapy (Simons, 1989; National Center for Health Services Research, 1988; Knesper et al., 1985). Women used to outnumber men in therapy by two to one, partly because they were less reluctant than men to seek help (Lichtenstein, 1980). Lately, however, our society's attitudes and sex-role expectations have been changing, and men are becoming increasingly willing to enter therapy. More than 40 percent of today's therapy patients are male (Knesper et al., 1985).

People enter therapy in various ways. Many decide on their own to consult a psychotherapist. Others may do so on the advice of a minister, physician, or other professional with whom they have discussed their difficulties. Still others (a minority) are *forced* into treatment. Parents, spouses, teachers, and employers may virtually order people to seek treatment if they are causing disruptions or are in obvious distress; or judges may formally deem people mentally ill and dangerous and commit them to a mental hospital for treatment.

The decision to seek therapy is rarely easy. Extensive studies indicate that most patients are aware of their problems well before they look for help (Strupp et al., 1969). Many wait more than two years after they first become aware that they have a problem. Generally speaking, therapy seems to hold few attractions for those who have no social network of "friends and supporters of psychotherapy"—people who have themselves been clients or who express confidence in psychotherapy as a solution to personal problems (Kadushin, 1969). During the 1970s the United Auto Workers negotiated a contract in which management agreed to pay the entire cost of both inpatient and outpatient mental health services for a million union members, yet after three years, only 1 percent of eligible workers had used the benefit (Brown, 1976). Apparently they and their referral agents (shop foremen, clergy, and the like) were unaware of the benefit, ignorant of what therapy could do for them, unlikely to think about personal problems in mental health terms, or worried about the stigma that mental problems might bring in their social set.

The length of time people spend in therapy varies with the nature of the problem and the approach the therapist takes. More than half of all clients visit their therapist 15 times or fewer (Knesper et al., 1985). At the other extreme, a small percentage continues in therapy for much of their lives.

When problems are not severe, longer-term treatment generally leads to more improvement than shorter-term treatment. An analysis of 2,400 patients with symptoms of anxiety and depression found that whereas 50 percent had improved significantly after 8 sessions of therapy, 75 percent had improved after 26 sessions (Howard et al., 1986). On the other hand, even long-term treatment generally has a limited effect on severe psychological problems. People with severe problems generally receive longer and more intense treatment than people with milder problems (Ware et al., 1984), but they are still more impaired at the end (Knesper et al., 1985).

As we observed in Chapter 1, a variety of professionals conduct therapy today, the greatest number being psychologists, psychiatrists, and psychiatric social workers. Whatever their profession, these therapists generally see the same kinds of patients (Knesper et al., 1985), that is, the majority of their cases are people with anxiety, depression, or relationship problems. At the same time, psychiatrists see a somewhat larger number of patients with schizophrenia and other severe disorders (16 percent of their cases) than do psychologists (5 percent) or social workers (7 percent). The providers of mental health services are concentrated in urban areas across the United States. In fact, there is a severe shortage of practitioners available to serve the needs of the 50 million people who live in the towns, villages, farms, and countryside of rural America (Human & Wasem, 1991; Murray & Keller, 1991).

Therapy takes place in all sorts of settings, from public institutions to schools to private offices. Most clients, even those who are severely disturbed, are treated as outpatients; they live in the community and make regular visits to the therapist's office or to a publicly supported mental health agency (Manderscheid & Witkin, 1983). Studies indicate that outpatients with higher incomes tend to be treated in private offices while those with lower incomes are treated through publicly supported community mental health centers (Knesper et al., 1985). Whatever the patients' psychological problems, therapy sessions in community mental health centers tend to be shorter, less frequent, and fewer than those offered by private therapists (Knesper et al., 1985).

Most of the people who receive inpatient treatment, either in privately funded institutions or in public institutions, such as state mental hospitals, have severe psychological problems. The private institutions usually offer better physical facilities, more trained staff members per patient, and more varied treatments. Personal wealth, more than any other factor, determines whether a patient is treated in a private or a public institution. In the 1980s the average annual income of patients who received treatment in private hospitals was approximately $18,000, whereas the average income of patients treated in public hospitals was under $8,000 a year (Knesper et al., 1985).

As we also saw briefly in Chapter 1, clinicians have become increasingly concerned about the negative effects of long-term institutionalization and have carried out a policy of deinstitutionalization during the past three decades. Whereas close to 600,000 patients were being cared for in public mental hospitals on any given day in 1955, fewer than 125,000 populate the same institutions today. Hospitalization now usually lasts weeks instead of months or years (Caton, 1982). When people develop severe mental disorders, therapists now try to treat them first as outpatients. If this strategy proves ineffective, the patient may be admitted to a hospital for a short period so that the condition can be monitored, diagnosed, and stabilized. As soon as hospitalization has served this purpose, the patient is returned to the community. In theory, this may be a reasonable treatment plan; but, as we observed in Chapter 1 and will see in more detail in Chapter 16, community treatment facilities have been so underfunded and understaffed over the years that they have not been able to meet the treatment needs of the majority of severely impaired people, and hundreds of thousands of people have been condemned to an endless cycle of hospital discharges and readmissions (see Box 5-1).

# SYSTEMS OF THERAPY

In the clinical field today there are approximately 250 different forms of therapy, each practiced by clinicians who believe that their chosen methodology is highly effective (Corsini, 1989; Herink, 1980). One way to start sorting out these many approaches is to distinguish therapy *systems* from therapy *formats*. A **system** of therapy is a set of principles and techniques employed in accordance with a particular theory of change. Carl Rogers's humanistic theory, for example, identifies self-awareness and self-actualization as fundamental to good mental health. Therapists who follow his "client-centered" system listen to and empathize with clients, expecting that such techniques will help the clients become aware of themselves and able to actualize their special human potential. A system of therapy may be applied in any of several **formats.** Rogers's client-centered therapy has been employed in individual, group, family, and marital therapy formats. In this section we shall discuss the clinical field's most influential therapy systems. In the next section, we shall examine the principal formats.

Each system of therapy approaches psychological treatment in its own way. In some systems therapists concentrate on helping clients gain insight into their problems, while in others they seek only to change the clients' behavior. In some systems therapists have a medical orientation and treat their clients as patients recovering from an illness; in others the therapists have an educational orientation and treat psychological problems as maladaptive patterns in need of corrective training. We shall be paying particular attention to whether a therapy system is global or specific. In **global therapies,** therapists try to help individuals recognize and change general features of their personality that the therapists believe are at the root of the problem. In **specific therapies,** therapists focus attention primarily on the symptoms; they address specific complaints without delving into broad personality issues.

## Global Therapies

Therapists who explain psychological problems by pointing to fundamental characteristics of a client's personality proceed in much the same way with every client, regardless of the particular symptoms. For this reason there is a considerable sameness in global treatments

========================= BOX 5-1 =========================

# Community Mental Health: A Movement Forward and Backward

In 1963 President John Kennedy called for a "bold new approach" to the treatment of mental illness —a community approach in which most people with psychological difficulties would receive mental health services from nearby publicly funded agencies. Soon after Kennedy's proclamation, Congress passed the Community Mental Health Act, launching the community mental health movement across the United States.

This movement has had both positive and negative consequences during the past three decades. On the one hand, it has increased the number of mental health services available to people with mild or moderate disturbances. On the other hand, it has inadvertently narrowed the treatment options available to those with severe mental disorders (see Chapter 16). Thus, some clinicians see the community movement as a major step forward for the field while others consider it a plan that has gone awry.

One aspect of the community movement that advocates and critics both seem to like is the principle of *prevention* that lies at its core. Since President Kennedy's proclamation, thousands of community workers have been hired for the purpose of preventing, or at least minimizing, mental disorders (Price, 1988). The principle of prevention has broadened the domain of the clinical field and has instilled in clinicians an active ("go-after-the-client") attitude that contrasts with the passive ("wait-for-the-client") posture of traditional therapy. Community workers have generally pursued three types of prevention — primary, secondary, and

Abuse hot-line operators in New York City receive calls from victims of abuse, or from their relatives or neighbors, and set in motion programs to help the victims and prevent further abuse.

tertiary (Okin & Borus, 1989; Albee, 1982; Caplan, 1964).

In *primary prevention,* community workers strive to improve community attitudes and policies with the goal of preventing mental disorders altogether. They may, for example, lobby for better community recreational programs or child-care facilities, consult with a local school board to help formulate a curriculum, or offer public workshops on stress reduction (Smith, 1983).

In *secondary prevention,* community workers try to identify and treat mental disorders at their earliest stages of development and thus prevent the disorders from reaching more serious levels. Workers may, for instance, consult with schoolteachers, ministers, or police to help them recognize the early signs of psychological

dysfunctioning and teach them how to involve persons in treatment (Zax & Cowen, 1976, 1969; Cowen, 1973; Bower, 1969). Similarly, communities may offer "hot lines" or "walk-in clinics" that encourage individuals to make early treatment contacts and receive immediate treatment before their psychological difficulties expand.

In *tertiary prevention,* workers seek to prevent moderate or severe mental disorders from becoming long-term problems by offering appropriate and effective treatment when it is needed. Community workers have earnestly provided tertiary care for millions of people with moderate psychological problems such as anxiety disorders by offering traditional therapy at community mental health centers across the country. They have generally failed, however, to provide the tertiary services needed for severely disturbed persons — *day centers* (or *day hospitals*), treatment facilities that provide daylong activities and treatment; *halfway houses,* residential group homes that have live-in staff offering support, guidance, and practical advice to residents; and *sheltered workshops,* protected and supervised workplaces that offer clients occupational training. These tertiary services are in woefully short supply in most communities, leaving hundreds of thousands of severely disturbed people without proper care and in a state of steady deterioration. The promise of prevention — whether primary, secondary, or tertiary — is a worthy and exciting one, but for many members of our society, it is a promise unfulfilled.

from client to client. This is not to say that global treatments are identical for all clients. On the contrary, each person's life, conflicts, problems, and family dynamics are unique, as are the person's therapy issues, reactions, defenses, and capacity for insight. Therapists must apply their techniques in ways that address this uniqueness. The primary global therapies are the *psychodynamic therapies* and the *humanistic-existential therapies.*

**Psychodynamic Therapies**     Adhering to the principles of the psychodynamic model, psychodynamic therapists contend that today's emotional disorder is the result of yesterday's emotional trauma. A variety of psychodynamic therapies are now being practiced, but all share the goals of helping clients to uncover past traumatic events and the inner conflicts that have resulted from them; to resolve, or settle, those conflicts; and to resume interrupted personal development (Arlow, 1989; Wolberg, 1987). Because awareness is the key to psychodynamic therapy, this system is considered an "insight therapy."

According to psychodynamic therapists, the process of gaining insight cannot be rushed or imposed. If therapists were simply to tell clients about their inner conflicts, the explanations would sound "off the wall" and the clients would not accept them. Thus therapists must subtly guide the therapeutic discussions so that the patients discover their underlying problems for themselves. To help them do so, psychodynamic therapists rely on such techniques as free association, therapist interpretation, catharsis, and working through.

**Free Association**     In psychodynamic therapies the patient is responsible for initiating and leading each discussion. The therapist tells the patient to describe any thought, feeling, or image that comes to mind, even if it seems unimportant or irrelevant (Brenner, 1989). This process is called *free association.* The therapist probes the patient's associations, expecting that they will eventually reveal unconscious events and unearth the dynamics underlying the individual's personality. Notice how free association helps the woman quoted below to discover threatening impulses and conflicts within her. She begins by describing a recent experience.

*Patient:*  So I started walking, and walking, and decided to go behind the museum and walk through Central Park. So I walked and went through a back field and felt very excited and wonderful. I saw a park bench next to a clump of bushes and sat down. There was a rustle behind me and I got frightened. I thought of men concealing themselves in the bushes. I thought of the sex perverts I read about in Central Park. I wondered if there was someone behind me exposing himself. The idea is repulsive, but exciting too. I think of father now and

feel excited. I think of an erect penis. This is connected with my father. There is something about this pushing in my mind. I don't know what it is, like on the border of my memory. *(Pause.)*

*Therapist:*  Mm-hmm. *(Pause.)* On the border of your memory?

*Patient:*  *(The patient breathes rapidly and seems to be under great tension.)* As a little girl, I slept with my father. I get a funny feeling. I get a funny feeling over my skin, tingly-like. It's a strange feeling, like a blindness, like not seeing something. My mind blurs and spreads over anything I look at. I've had this feeling off and on since I walked in the park. My mind seems to blank off like I can't think or absorb anything.

*(Wolberg, 1967, p. 662)*

**Therapist Interpretation**     Although psychodynamic therapists allow the patient to generate the discussion, they are privately trying to piece together a psychodynamic explanation of the person's disorder. They are listening carefully, looking for clues, and drawing tentative conclusions. They share their interpretations with the patient when they think the patient is ready to hear them. Otto Fenichel (1941), a highly respected psychodynamic theorist, once said that psychodynamic therapists should propose what is already apparent to the patient "and just a little bit more." The interpretation of three phenomena that occur during therapy is particularly important — *resistance, transference,* and *dreams.*

Patients demonstrate **resistance** when they encounter a block in their free associations or change the subject so as to avoid a potentially painful discussion. Having spent a lifetime using ego defense mechanisms to defend against their unconscious conflicts, people usually resist discussions that threaten to uncover those conflicts. Through the entire course of therapy, the therapist remains on the lookout for resistance, which is usually unconscious, and may point it out to the patient and interpret it. Consider again the woman who walked in Central Park. "My mind seems to blank off . . . ," she says. The therapist interprets the sensation as resistance, and helps her to move further along:

*Therapist:*  The blurring of your mind may be a way of pushing something out you don't want there. [Interpreting her symptoms as resistance.]

*Patient:*  I just thought of something. When father died, he was nude. I looked at him, but I couldn't see anything. I couldn't think clearly. I was brought up not to be aware of the difference between a man and a woman. I feared my father, and yet I loved him. I slept with him when I was very little, on Saturdays and Sundays. A wonderful sense of warmth and security. There was nothing warmer or more secure. A lot of pleasure. I tingle all over now. It was a wonderful holiday when I was allowed to sleep with

# THERAPY IS HELL

NUNNA YER BEESWAX.

Psychodynamic therapists believe that patients are reluctant to uncover painful conflicts or memories and so may unconsciously resist talking about them by losing track of what they were saying, changing the subject, cracking jokes, or simply refusing to talk.

father. I can't seem to remember anything now. There's a blur in my mind. I feel tense and afraid.

*Therapist:*   That blur contaminates your life. You are afraid of something or afraid of remembering something. [Focusing on her resistance.]

*Patient:*   Yes, yes, but I can't. How can I? How can I?

*Therapist:*   What comes to your mind?

*(Wolberg, 1967, p. 662)*

Psychodynamic therapists also believe that patients act and feel toward the therapist as they did toward important figures in their childhood, especially their parents and siblings. By interpreting this *transference* behavior, therapists may better understand how a patient unconsciously feels toward a parent or some other significant person in the patient's life. As the woman continues talking, the therapist helps her to explore some transference issues:

*Patient:*   I get so excited by what is happening here. I feel I'm being held back by needing to be nice. I'd like to blast loose sometimes, but I don't dare.

*Therapist:*   Because you fear my reaction?

*Patient:*   The worst thing would be that you wouldn't like me. You wouldn't speak to me friendly; you wouldn't smile; you'd feel you can't treat me and discharge me from treatment. But I know this isn't so, I know it.

*Therapist:*   Where do you think these attitudes come from?

*Patient:*   When I was nine years old, I read a lot about great men in history. I'd quote them and be dramatic. I'd want a sword at my side; I'd dress like an Indian. Mother would scold me. Don't frown, don't talk so much. Sit on your hands, over and over again. I did all kinds of things. I was a naughty child. She told me I'd be hurt. Then at fourteen I fell off a horse and broke my back. I had to be in bed. Mother then told me on the day I went riding not to, that I'd get hurt because the ground was frozen. I was a stubborn, self-willed child. Then I went against her will and suffered an accident that changed my life, a fractured back. Her attitude was, "I told you so." I was put in a cast and kept in bed for months.

*Therapist:*   You were punished, so to speak, by this accident.

*Patient:*   But I gained attention and love from mother for the first time. I felt so good. I'm ashamed to tell you this. Before I healed I opened the cast and tried to walk to make myself sick again so I could stay in bed longer.

*Therapist:*   How does that connect up with your impulse to be sick now and stay in bed so much?

*Patient:*   Oh . . . *(Pause)*

*Therapist:*   What do you think?

*Patient:*   Oh, my God, how infantile, how ungrown up. *(Pause)* It must be so. I want people to love me and be sorry for me. Oh, my God. How completely childish. . . . My mother must have ignored me when I was little, and I wanted so to be loved.

*Therapist:*   So that it may have been threatening to go back to being self-willed and unloved after you got out of the cast.

*Patient:*   It did. My life changed. I became meek and controlled. I couldn't get angry or stubborn afterward.

*Therapist:*   Perhaps if you go back to being stubborn with me, you would be returning to how you were before, that is, active, stubborn but unloved.

*Patient   (excitedly)* And, therefore, losing your love. I need you, but after all you aren't going to reject me. The pattern is so established now that the threat of the loss of love is too overwhelming with everybody, and I've got to keep myself from acting selfish or angry.

*(Wolberg, 1967, p. 662)*

Because the therapist's interpretations play such a major role in psychodynamic therapy, psychodynamic therapists must make every effort to listen and interpret without bias. This is easier said than done. Therapists are human beings with feelings, histories, and values that can subtly influence the way they listen to and interpret their patients' problems. Because unintentional *countertransference* of the therapist's personal issues onto the patient can undermine the therapeutic process, therapists must observe and analyze their own feelings as well as their patients'. This is one reason that during their training many psychodynamic therapists undergo therapy with a so-called training analyst.

Finally, many psychodynamic therapists try to help patients interpret their *dreams.* Freud (1924) called dreams the "royal road to the unconscious." He believed that repression and other defense mechanisms operate less completely during sleep. Thus a patient's dreams, correctly interpreted, can reveal the person's unconscious instincts, needs, and wishes (see Box 5-2).

Freud defined two kinds of dream content, manifest and latent. *Manifest content* is the consciously remembered dream, *latent content* its symbolic meaning. To interpret a dream, therapists must translate its manifest content into its latent content. Every dream is unique and has unique implications for the dreamer, but psychodynamic therapists believe that some types of manifest content are universal and have much the same meaning in everybody's dreams. For example, a house's basement, downstairs, upstairs, attic, and front porch are often identified as symbols of anatomical parts of the body (Lichtenstein, 1980).

**Catharsis** Insight must be an emotional as well as intellectual process. Psychodynamic therapists believe that patients must experience *catharsis,* a reliving of past repressed feelings, if they are to settle internal conflicts and overcome their problems. Only when catharsis accompanies intellectual insight is genuine progress achieved.

=== BOX 5-2 ===

# Dreams: A Meeting of Models

*The Nightmare* by Johann Einrich Füssli

All people dream; so do dogs, and maybe even fish. But what purpose do dreams serve? Some claim that dreams reveal the future; others see them as inner journeys or alternate realities. The Greek philosopher Plato saw dreams as reflections of inner turmoil and wish fulfillment,

. . . desires which are awake when the reasoning and taming and ruling power of the personality is asleep; the wild beast in our nature, gorged with meat and drink, starts up and walks about naked, and surfeits at his will; and there is no conceivable folly or crime, however shameless or unnatural—not excepting incest or parricide—of which such a nature may not be guilty. . . . In all of us, even in good men, there is such a latent wild beast nature, which peers out in sleep.

*(Phaedrus, c. 380 B.C.)*

Psychodynamic therapists consider dreams to be highly revealing. Rather like Plato, Freud (1900) contended that dreaming is a mechanism with which we express and attempt to fulfill the unsatisfied desires we spend our lives pursuing. His colleague Jung (1954) also believed them to be expressions of the unconscious psyche. Both claimed that patients would benefit from interpreting their dreams in therapy and understanding the underlying needs, aspirations, and conflicts symbolized in the dreams.

Despite their belief in the therapeutic importance of dreams, psychodynamic researchers have conducted relatively little empirical research on dreaming and have generated little evidence for the psychodynamic interpretations of

***Working Through and Resolving the Problem***    A single session of interpretation and catharsis will not change a person. For deep and lasting insight to be gained, the patient and therapist must examine the same issues over and over in the course of many sessions, each time with new and sharper clarity. This process is called ***working through.***

Working through a disorder can take a long time, so psychodynamic treatment is usually a long-term proposition. Many of Freud's patients came to him for therapy sessions every day for several years. In the 1930s, however, Franz Alexander (1936, 1930, 1929) proposed that weekly sessions might be sufficient for many people, and started a trend that has continued to the present day.

Psychodynamic treatment offered once a week—as most forms of it now are—is properly known as ***psychodynamic,*** or ***psychoanalytic, therapy.*** The term ***psychoanalysis,*** or simply ***analysis,*** is reserved for therapy given on a daily basis. Analysis is usually conducted by ***analysts,*** psychoanalytic therapists who receive several extra

Freud's office is dominated by the key tools of his therapy: a couch, a desk, and a writing pad. Freud had patients lie on the couch during therapy, while he sat behind them taking notes. He believed that this arrangement heightened concentration and facilitated the patient's free associations and recall of important memories or dream material.

dreams. Perhaps the most prolific and provocative research on dreams has actually come from biological investigators.

In 1977 J. Allan Hobson and Robert McCarley proposed their "activation-synthesis" model of dreams. They claimed that during ***REM sleep*** (the stage of sleep characterized by rapid eye movement, or REM), memories are elicited by random signals from the brain stem—in evolutionary terms, a very old region of the brain. The brain's cortex, the seat of higher cognitive functioning, attempts to make sense of this random bombardment of electrical activity. The result is a dream, often irrational or weird, but the best fit given the variety of signals received by the cortex (Begley, 1989). Hobson later revised the theory to include the idea that the resulting dream, far from being arbitrary, is influenced by the dreamer's drives, fears, and ambitions. Although this model is a far cry from the deep unconscious meaning attributed to dreams by psychoanalysts, it does support the contention that dreams

reflect the thoughts and emotions of the dreamer and may therefore provide insight into the person's psychology.

More recently the neuroscientist Jonathan Winson of Rockefeller University has contended that dreams are a "nightly record of a basic mammalian process: the means by which animals form strategies for survival and evaluate current experience in light of those strategies" (Winson, 1990). By recording electrical activity in the brains of sleeping and awake nonprimate mammals, Winson found that the brain waves measured when the animals were dreaming were similar to the brain waves measured while the animals engaged in survival activities. This finding coincided well with earlier research with cats in whom the portion of the brain that inhibited movement during dreaming had been destroyed. As they dreamed, these cats would act out scenes of attack and play. Thus Winson concluded that dreams are a means of *reprocessing* information necessary for an animal's survival. The information is "accessed

again and integrated with past experience to provide an ongoing strategy for behavior" (Winson, 1990). In essence, dreams rehash, reprocess, and reevaluate the day's activities, in preparation for the next day's fight for survival.

The theories of Hobson, McCarley, and Winson differ from psychodynamic theory in that they do not describe dreams as being laden with emotional significance that overflows into consciousness from a seething, bubbling unconscious. Their research does, however, support the underlying tenet that dreams provide insight into our ways of thinking and feeling about the world. Although the source of a dream may be random electrical brain activity, it is our cognizant, human self that interprets this information and organizes it into a form of narrative. Dreams are perhaps the Rorschach test of the unconscious: seemingly meaningless pictures take on significance when we bring our own biases and idiosyncrasies to the task of organizing and understanding their meaning.

years of training in a psychoanalytic training institute after earning their graduate degree in psychiatry, psychology, or social work.

***Short-Term Psychodynamic Therapies***  In recent years, several therapists have developed a much shorter version of psychodynamic therapy (Sifneos, 1987, 1984, 1980, 1979; Strupp & Binder, 1984; Luborsky, 1984; Davanloo, 1980; Malan, 1980, 1963). Their goal is to retain the basic concepts of psychodynamic theory, yet reduce the overall length of treatment by narrowing the goals and focus of therapy discussions and by more actively directing therapy discussions (Garske & Molteni, 1985).

In these short-term psychodynamic therapies, patients identify a single problem or issue—a ***dynamic focus***—early in therapy, such as difficulty getting along with certain persons or a marital problem. The therapist helps the patient maintain attention on this focus throughout treatment and helps him or her work only on psychodynamic issues, such as an unresolved Oedipal conflict, that relate to the focus. It is expected that resolution of this focus will generalize to other important life situations.

Typically, the short-term therapists pay particular attention to transference reactions. They help the patient relate patient-therapist interactions to current and past interpersonal relationships that may account for the present difficulties.

From the beginning, the therapist tells the patient that therapy will last for a fixed number of sessions, usually less than thirty. Theoretically, the time limit motivates the patient to explore his or her dynamic focus and to experiment with new behavior. The time limit also requires that the therapist sometimes be more anxiety-provoking or confrontational when making interpretations. People with high motivation, intelligence, and tolerance for anxiety and frustration are considered good candidates for these approaches; severely disturbed, suicidal, and drug-dependent patients are not. Freud himself tried short-term therapy with some of his patients and judged it to be relatively effective "provided that one hits the right time at which to employ it." Researchers have only recently begun to research the newer short-term psychodynamic approaches and have yet to determine their effectiveness (Strupp & Binder, 1984; Luborsky, 1984).

***Assessing Psychodynamic Therapies***  Freud and his many followers have had a most significant impact on the treatment of abnormal psychological functioning (Brenner, 1989; Garfield & Bergin, 1986). They were the first practitioners to demonstrate the value of systematically applying both theory and techniques to treatment. In addition, their systems of therapy were the first to underscore the potential of psychological, as opposed to biological, treatment and have served as a starting point for many other psychological treatments.

On the other hand, systematic research has generally failed to support the effectiveness of psychodynamic therapies. For the first half of the twentieth century, the value of these approaches was supported principally by the case studies of enthusiastic psychodynamic clinicians and by *uncontrolled* research studies. Controlled investigations have been conducted only since the 1950s, and only a minority of these have found psychodynamic therapies to be more effective than no treatment or than placebo treatments (Prochaska, 1984; Fisher & Greenberg, 1977).

Critics also argue that, with the exception of short-term psychodynamic therapies, these systems of treatment simply take too long and cost too much money and hence are impractical for millions of troubled people (Simons, 1981). Psychodynamic therapists respond that the necessary steps of free association, therapist interpretation, catharsis, and working through cannot usually be rushed if lasting change is to occur. Most believe that the quicker symptom reductions brought about by other approaches are superficial and likely to lead to ***symptom substitution,*** the replacement of old symptoms by new ones.

Given such limitations, it is understandable that psychodynamic therapies no longer dominate the clinical field as they did before the 1950s (see Figure 5-1). Still, between 14 and 19 percent of today's therapists identify themselves principally as psychodynamic therapists (Smith, 1982; Garfield & Kurtz, 1976). And, interestingly, many practitioners of other models report that when they seek help for their own problems, psychodynamic therapy is their choice (Norcross & Prochaska, 1984).

***Humanistic and Existential Therapies***  Believing that mental disorders are rooted in self-deceit, humanistic and existential therapists try to help clients look at themselves and their situations more accurately and acceptingly. They expect clients in turn to go much further toward actualizing their full potential as human beings. To achieve these goals they try to enter the client's ***phenomenological,*** or subjective, world. Unlike the psychodynamic therapists, humanistic and existential therapists usually emphasize present experiences rather than events in the client's past.

As we first observed in Chapter 2, humanistic and existential therapists differ mainly in their view of the human experience. Humanistic therapists believe that

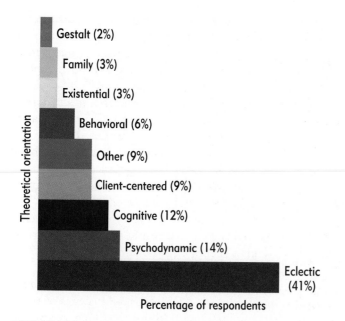

**FIGURE 5-1** Theoretical orientations of today's clinicians. Close to half of 415 clinical psychologists labeled themselves "eclectic" when they were surveyed. *(Smith, 1982.)*

people have a special inborn potential that they will automatically fulfill if only they can be helped to look at themselves accurately and acceptingly. Existential therapists, on the other hand, believe that human beings have absolute freedom to choose their own course in life, even a meaningless and empty one. Thus they try to help clients recognize their freedom, accept responsibility for their problems, and make more satisfying choices in their lives.

***Client-Centered Therapy*** In client-centered therapy, the humanistic treatment developed by Carl Rogers in the late 1940s, therapists try to create a supportive climate in which clients can look at themselves honestly and begin to accept what they discover themselves to be (Rogers & Sanford, 1989; Raskin & Rogers, 1989; Rogers, 1987, 1967, 1951). The therapist must display three important qualities throughout the therapy— unconditional positive regard for the client, accurate empathy, and genuineness.

Therapists show ***unconditional positive regard*** by conveying full and warm acceptance no matter what clients say, think, or feel (see Box 5-3). They show ***accurate empathy*** by accurately hearing what clients are saying and sensitively communicating it back to the clients. They neither interpret what clients are saying nor try to teach them; rather, they listen, and help their clients listen to themselves as well. Finally, therapists must convey ***genuineness,*** also referred to as ***congruence,*** to clients. Unless therapists' communications are honest

and sincere, clients may perceive them as mechanical and false. The following interaction shows the therapist using all these qualities to move the client toward greater self-awareness:

*Client:*   Yes, I know I shouldn't worry about it, but I do. Lots of things — money, people, clothes. In classes I feel that everyone's just waiting for a chance to jump on me. It's like they were breathing down my neck waiting for a chance to find something wrong. At school there were fellows like that waiting for me. I can't stand people laughing at me. I can't stand ridicule. That's why I'm afraid of kids. When I meet somebody I wonder what he's actually thinking of me. Then later on I wonder how I match up to what he's come to think of me.

*Therapist:*   You feel that you're pretty responsive to the opinions of other people.

*Client:*   Yes, but it's things that shouldn't worry me.

*Therapist:*   You feel that it's the sort of thing that shouldn't be upsetting, but they do get you pretty much worried anyway.

*Client:*   Just some of them. Most of those things do worry me because they're true. The ones I told you, that is. But there are lots of little things that aren't true. And time bothers me, too. That is, when I haven't anything to do. Things just seem to be piling up, piling up inside of me. When I haven't anything to do I roam around. I feel like — at home when I was at the theater and nobody would come in, I used to wear it off by socking the doors. It's a feeling that things were crowding up and they were going to burst.

*Therapist:*   You feel that it's a sort of oppression with some frustration and that things are just unmanageable.

*Client:*   In a way, but some things just seem illogical. I'm afraid I'm not very clear here but that's the way it comes.

*Therapist:*   That's all right. You say just what you think.
*(Snyder, 1947, pp. 21–24)*

In an atmosphere of unconditional positive regard, accurate empathy, and genuineness, clients can be expected increasingly to feel accepted by their therapist; they then may be able to look at themselves with honesty and acceptance — a process called ***experiencing.*** That is, they begin to value their own emotions, thoughts, and behaviors, and so are freed from the insecurities and doubts that prevented their self-actualization. The following excerpt shows that Mrs. Oak, a client of Rogers, is embarking on this process.

*[Rogers:]*   Your feeling at the present time is that you have been very much aware of all the cultural pressures — not always very much aware, but "there have been so many of those in my life — and now I'm going down more deeply into myself to find out what I really feel" and it seems very much at the present time as though that

somehow separates you a long ways from your culture, and that's a little frightening, but feels basically good. Is that—

*[Mrs. Oak:]*   Yeah. Well, I have the feeling now that it's okay, really. . . . Then there's something else—a feeling that's starting to grow; well, to be almost formed, as I say. This kind of conclusion, that I'm going to stop looking for something terribly wrong. . . . And now without any—without, I should say, any sense of apology or covering up, just sort of simple statement that I can't find what at this time appears to be bad.

*[Rogers:]*   Does this catch it? That as you've gone more and more deeply into yourself, and as you think about the kind of things that you've discovered and learned and so on, the conviction grows very, very strong that no matter how far you go, the things that you're going to find are not dire and awful. They have a very different character.

*[Mrs. Oak:]*   Yes, something like that.

*(Rogers, 1961)*

*"Why, you swine!"*

Criticizing a client's remarks, however subtly or carefully, is the worst thing a therapist can do, according to client-centered therapists. *(Drawing by Richter; © 1952, 1980 The New Yorker Magazine, Inc.)*

---

BOX 5-3

# Animals: A Source of Unconditional Positive Regard

For thousands of years humans have brought live animals into the home to serve every purpose from protector to herder to companion. In recent years pets have even been looked upon as facilitators in human relationships and in the process of achieving psychological and emotional relief. Has "man's best friend" been elevated to the role of therapist?

It is widely believed that animals can provide solace, comfort, and friendship to a person in need of emotional support. The undying loyalty of the pet dog can supersede all other human interactions in the eyes of a child who has been scolded for misbehaving or the elderly nursing home resident whose children no longer visit. Without judging, and without condition, our favorite pet provides love and companion-

ship. From the humanistic-existential perspective, these are qualities that help ensure a successful treatment outcome.

Physiological studies indicate that the presence of a dog can reduce heart rate and blood pressure in children—the same effect that was noted in children who were asked to read aloud from a book of poetry (Friedmann et al., 1983). Even survival rates in heart patients have been linked to ownership and interaction with a pet. Similar results have been suggested for elderly people who have little interaction with other human beings.

Studies have also indicated that animals can improve the emotions and behavior of persons with psychological problems. A technique called *pet-facilitated therapy* (Corson & Corson, 1978) has, for exam-

From the very beginning, Rogers (1987, 1951) and his followers believed strongly in the importance of researching client-centered therapy. Even though their phenomenological perspective presented some obvious impediments to objective research (how can one know for sure what is in another person's mind?), he believed that the effectiveness of client-centered therapy could be measured.

Early studies seemed to provide strong support for Rogers's approach. Repeatedly, people treated in client-centered therapy showed more improvement than controls who did not receive treatment (Cartwright, 1961; Cartwright & Vogel, 1960; Rogers & Dymond, 1954). But these early studies had major methodological flaws. Some of the control groups consisted of people who were well adjusted and may have had less need or room for improvement than people who sought client-centered therapy. Other control groups were made up of people who were troubled but had no in-

tention of seeking therapy, so they might have been less motivated to improve than the clients who elected therapy. In better-controlled studies, client-centered therapy has not fared so well. Although people who receive this therapy do seem to improve more than control subjects in some studies (DiLoreto, 1971; Truax, Wargo, & Silber, 1966), they show no such superiority in many others (Martin, 1972; Satz & Baraff, 1962).

All the same, Rogers's therapy has had a positive influence on clinical practice. It was the first major alternative to psychodynamic therapy, and as such it helped open up what had been a highly complacent field to new systems and formats. Second, Rogers helped open up the practice of psychotherapy to psychologists; it had previously been considered the province of psychiatrists. Third, Rogers's commitment to clinical research has strengthened the position of those who argue the importance of systematic research in the treatment domain

---

ple, been employed in helping emotionally disturbed children. A group of such children, all of whom had many problems in their relationships with peers and adults, participated in a program in which they lived and worked on a farm (Ross, 1983). Each child was given a special pet and was responsible for its care. After being involved in this program, the children showed improvements in their self-esteem and sense of control. Similar results have been reported in more formal therapeutic settings. Researchers reason that by making the situation feel less threatening, pets serve as a catalytic bridge between therapist and child, allowing the child to feel safe with the therapist. Moreover, the pet is an attractive addition to the session that most likely helps maintain the child's interest and attention.

One of the most exciting uses of pet therapy centers on the dramatic and heart-rending mental disorder of autism (see Chapter 19). The unusual set of behaviors in persons afflicted

with autism hinders their ability to form bonds and relationships with other people. Therapy with autistic people is typically slow and laborious as practitioners try to reduce disruptive behaviors and encourage the person to interact with others.

In one study, however, a dog was introduced into the treatment sessions of a number of autistic children (Redefer & Goodman, 1989). At first the children displayed typical autistic behaviors — hand posturing, making humming and clicking noises, jumping, continual spinning of objects, roaming. During a number of otherwise routine treatment sessions, the therapist interacted with the dog and encouraged the child to join in. By the end of the session, the children were showing significantly fewer autistic behaviors and a decrease in self-absorption. They also showed an increase in positive social behavior, such as joining the therapist in simple games, initiating activities themselves, reaching for hugs, and

imitating the therapist's actions.

The researchers conjectured that the presence of the dog and the interactions with it heightened the "affective and impulsive state of the children" so that they were better able to participate in and enjoy social interactions. The success of this experiment was not attributed solely to the dog's presence, however; it was the orchestration by the therapist of the interaction between the children and the dog that facilitated the improvement. Pets are not a magical solution, but they are a potentially important component in the treatment of autism.

Although evidence is scanty, both anecdotal and formal studies suggest that pets can and do influence our emotional and physical well-being. Particularly for people who are developing their sense of self or who suffer a psychological disorder that inhibits this development, pet therapy may prove instrumental. It is no wonder that pets occupy such an important and honored role in many societies.

(Rogers & Sanford, 1989; Sanford, 1987). The client-centered approach continues to be widely practiced today. Approximately 9 percent of surveyed therapists report that they employ it (Smith, 1982).

**Gestalt Therapy**   Gestalt therapy is a humanistic form of treatment developed in the 1950s by a charismatic clinician named Frederick (Fritz) Perls (1893–1970). Perls viewed life as a series of what he called *figure–ground relationships.* He believed that a healthy person's current needs can be perceived clearly in that person's life, just as any *figure* can be perceived against a distinct *ground* (background). When these needs are satisfied, they fade into the ground and are replaced by new needs, which stand out in their turn and are equally recognizable. Perls believed that mental disorders represent disruptions in these figure–ground relationships. People who are unaware of their needs or unwilling to accept or express them are avoiding their real inner selves. They lack self-awareness and self-acceptance, they fear the judgments of others, and their behavior becomes defensive. They act only to protect themselves from perceived threats and do little to actualize their potential.

Thus gestalt therapists, like client-centered therapists, try to move clients toward self-recognition and self-acceptance (Yontef & Simkin, 1989; Polster, 1987). But unlike client-centered therapists, they try to achieve this goal by frustrating and challenging clients. The numerous techniques they have developed for doing so are meant also to make the therapy process considerably shorter than it is in client-centered and psychodynamic therapy (Yontef & Simkin, 1989; Perls, 1973, 1971, 1969).

In the technique of *skillful frustration,* for example, gestalt therapists refuse to meet many of their clients' expectations and even their outright demands. Such frustration is meant to help clients see how they try to manipulate others into meeting their needs. Perls (1973) describes his use of skillful frustration with a male client:

> The first six weeks of therapy—more than half the available time—were spent in frustrating him in his desperate attempts to manipulate me into telling him what to do. He was by turn plaintive, aggressive, mute, despairing. He tried every trick in the book. He threw the time barrier up to me over and over again, trying to make me responsible for his lack of progress. If I had yielded to his demands, undoubtedly he would have sabotaged my efforts, exasperated me, and remained exactly where he was.
>
> *(p. 109)*

Unlike psychodynamic therapists, who guide clients toward events and emotions in their past, gestalt therapists make it a practice to keep clients in the *here and now.* Although problems may be rooted in past causes, the effects take place in the present. Clients have needs now, are camouflaging their needs now, and must observe them now. As clients talk about the events and people in their lives, the therapist may ask, "What are you feeling about that person now?" or "What are you doing now, as you speak?" Similarly, therapists will tell clients to "stay with" past feelings and events and observe how they are making them feel at present. When clients are forced to confront these things in the here and now, they are also confronting their inner selves.

Another way gestalt therapists try to promote self-awareness is by instructing clients to *role-play*—that is, to act out various roles assigned by the therapist. Clients may be told to be another person, an object, or even a part of the body. They are instructed to talk as the other would talk and to feel what the other would feel. Here Perls has a client named Glenn act out an interaction between two kinds of men—really two dimensions of himself:

*Fritz:*   I would like you to make up a dialogue. Two guys are having an encounter. One is called the Toughy, the other the Softy. Let them meet each other, get in touch with each other. Softy sits here; Toughy sits there. Or would you like the other way around? Let's put Toughy in there.

*Glenn:*   Yeah. He's the one you look down at. Sitting here now, I have no respect for you, particularly.

*Fritz:*   I guess they both are not willing to suffer each other.

*Glenn:*   Yeah. . . . You can't stand it . . . when I get all gooey. You think that it's better not to show anything. I'm not so sure you're tough at all. I think you're just kind of wooden. *(Sighs)*
    Yeah, but it's a lot better. I'm—I'm—I don't hurt nearly as much as you do. I push people around, and I kind of smile about it, now and then. Yeah. And you don't listen to what I say, 'cause when you're soft and feeling close to somebody, it's not going to come across. I keep telling you, you gotta play it cool, because if you start in really feeling in touch, people will go away. They'll withdraw. They won't have anything to do with you. Nobody wants somebody around holding onto them. . . .
    *(Sighs)* You are so lonely! I at least know I'm lonely. You think you're just alone. If I don't feel—if you don't let me feel *with* people, if you don't feel—let me feel so that I could reach out and touch—

*Fritz:*   "Reach out and touch." What is your right hand doing?

*Glenn:*  It's reaching out.

*Fritz:*  It's reaching out, yah.

*Glenn:*  *(Softly)* Wow.

*Fritz:*  Now change, change hands.

*Glenn:*  Yeah.

*Fritz:*  Say this again and reverse it.

*(Perls, 1969)*

Role playing can become intense, as clients are encouraged to be uninhibited in feeling and expressing emotions. Many cry out, scream, kick, or pound. Through this experience they gradually come to ***own*** (accept) feelings that were previously unknown to them.

Perls also developed a list of ***rules*** to ensure that clients will look at themselves more closely. For example, clients may not ask "why" questions. If they ask, "Why do you do that?" therapists make them change the question into a statement, such as "I hate it when you do that." Another rule is that clients must use "I" language rather than "it" language. They must say, "I am frightened," rather than "The situation is frightening."

Finally, gestalt therapists conduct ***exercises and games*** with clients. In the ***exaggeration game,*** clients must repeatedly exaggerate some gesture or verbal behavior—perhaps a phrase that they use regularly. This "game" is intended to help clients recognize the depth of their feelings, the meaning of particular behavior, and the effect of their behavior on others. Perls employs this strategy with a client named Jane:

*Fritz:*  Now talk to your Top Dog! Stop nagging.

*Jane:*  *(Loud, pained)* Leave me alone.

*Fritz:*  Yah, again.

*Jane:*  Leave me alone.

*Fritz:*  Again.

*Jane:*  *(Screaming it and crying)* Leave me alone!

*Fritz:*  Again.

*Jane:*  *(She screams it, a real blast)* Leave me alone! I don't have to do what you say! *(Still crying)* I don't have to be that good! . . . I don't have to be in this chair! I don't have to. You make me. You make me come here! *(Screams)* Aarhhh! You make me pick my face *(Crying)*, that's what you do. *(Screams and cries)* Aarhhh! I'd like to kill you.

*Fritz:*  Say this again.

*Jane:*  I'd like to kill you.

Clients in gestalt therapy are guided to express their needs and feelings in their full intensity, through role playing, banging on pillows, and other exercises. These techniques are expected to enable clients to "own" needs and feelings they previously were unaware they had, overcome fears of being judged, and stop behaving defensively. In the typical gestalt therapy group, members help each other to "get in touch" with their needs and feelings.

*Fritz:*  Again.

*Jane:*  I'd like to kill you.

*(Perls, 1969, p. 293)*

Approximately 2 percent of clinicians describe themselves as gestalt therapists (Smith, 1982). Because they believe that subjective experiences and self-awareness defy objective measurement, controlled research has rarely been conducted on the gestalt approach (Yontef & Simkin, 1989; Adesso et al., 1974). We have seen that this is not an unusual position among humanistic and existential theorists. Indeed, Rogers's strong belief in the merits of research stands as an exception to the rule.

***Existential Therapy***  Existential therapists encourage clients to accept responsibility for their lives (and for their problems), to recognize their freedom to choose a different course, and to choose to live an ***authentic life,*** one full of meaning and values (May & Yalom, 1989; May, 1987).

Like humanistic therapists, existential therapists emphasize the individual's phenomenological world (van den Berg, 1974, 1971) and the here and now (Havens, 1974; May, 1969). For the most part, however, these therapists care more about the goals of therapy than the use of specific therapeutic techniques, and their methods and the length of treatment vary greatly from practitioner to practitioner (May & Yalom, 1989; May, 1987, 1961, 1958).

While imprisoned in Nazi concentration camps from 1942 to 1945, psychotherapist Viktor Frankl observed that the victims who found some spiritual meaning in their suffering were able to resist despair and to survive. He later developed *logotherapy* (from the Greek, *logos,* for word or thought), an existential therapy which helps clients assign values and spiritual meaning to their existence through loving other people and confronting their own suffering. Frankl himself displays the positive atti-tute toward life and the sense of exploration that he espouses.

Existential therapists place great emphasis on the re-lationship between therapist and client (Frankl, 1975, 1962). The therapist and client must be open to each other, work hard together, and try to share, learn, and grow. The therapist's authenticity serves as a model for the client as they examine the meaning of existence and scrutinize the therapy encounter itself. This joint un-dertaking is not always pleasant, but the achievement of personal authenticity and growth depends on it. Here an existential therapist pushes hard for a patient to accept responsibility for her choices both in therapy and in life:

*Patient:*  I don't know why I keep coming here. All I do is tell you the same thing over and over. I'm not getting anywhere. [Patient complaining that therapist isn't curing her; maintenance of self-as-therapist's-object.]

*Doctor:*  I'm getting tired of hearing the same thing over and over, too. [Doctor refusing to take responsibility for the progress of therapy and refusing to fulfill patient's expectations that he cure her; refusal of patient-as-therapist's-object.]

*Patient:*  Maybe I'll stop coming. [Patient threatening therapist; fighting to maintain role as therapist's object.]

*Doctor:*  It's certainly your choice. [Therapist refusing to be intimidated; forcing patient-as-subject.]

*Patient:*  What do you think I should do? [Attempt to se-duce therapist into role of subject who objectifies patient.]

*Doctor:*  What do you want to do? [Forcing again.]

*Patient:*  I want to get better. [Plea for therapist to cure her.]

*Doctor:*  I don't blame you. [Refusing role of subject curer and supporting desire on part of patient-as-subject.]

*Patient:*  If you think I should stay, ok, I will. [Refusing role of subject-who-decides.]

*Doctor:*  You want me to tell you to stay? [Confrontation with patient's evasion of the decision and calling attention to how patient is construing the therapy.]

*Patient:*  You know what's best; you're the doctor. [Pa-tient's confirmation of her construing therapy.]

*Doctor:*  Do I act like a doctor?

*(Keen, 1970, p. 200)*

Existential therapists do not believe that experimental methods can adequately test the effectiveness of their treatment interventions (May & Yalom, 1989). They believe that research that reduces patients to test mea-sures or scale scores serves only to dehumanize them. Not surprisingly, then, virtually no controlled research has been conducted on the effectiveness of existential therapy (Prochaska, 1984). About 3 percent of all ther-apists use an approach that is primarily existential (Smith, 1982; Garfield & Kurtz, 1976).

## Specific Therapies

Specific therapies treat clients in accordance with their symptoms. Therapists who use these approaches believe that the best way to help people is to deal with their concrete problems directly and quickly. Unlike practi-tioners of the global therapies, these therapists vary their treatment techniques as necessary to treat each particu-lar problem, though they do adhere to a basic set of principles about abnormality and treatment (Reyna, 1989). The major specific therapies are the *behavioral, cognitive,* and *biological therapies.*

**Behavioral Therapies**  Behaviorists contend that the symptoms of a mental disorder are learned behaviors acquired through the same conditioning processes that produce normal behaviors (Wilson, 1989; Reyna, 1989;

Wolpe, 1987). The goal of behavioral therapy is to identify the client's specific problem-causing behaviors and manipulate and replace them with more appropriate ones. A client's early life history is focused on only to the extent that it provides clues about current reinforcers (Kanfer & Phillips, 1970). Similarly, relatively little attention is paid to subjective experiences and dreams. The therapist's attitude toward the client is that of teacher rather than healer. Behavioral techniques fall into three categories: classical conditioning, operant conditioning, and modeling.

***Classical Conditioning Techniques*** Classical conditioning treatments are intended to change clients' dysfunctional reactions to stimuli (Wilson, 1990, 1989; Rescorla, 1988). ***Systematic desensitization,*** for example, is a process of teaching phobic clients to react calmly instead of with intense fear to the objects or situations they dread (Wolpe, 1987, 1982, 1981, 1976, 1958). It is a step-by-step procedure that begins with teaching them the skill of deep muscle relaxation over the course of several sessions. Next, the clients construct a ***fear hierarchy,*** a list of feared objects or situations, starting with those that are minimally feared and ending with the ones that are most fearsome. The following hierarchy was developed by a man who was afraid of criticism, especially about his mental stability:

1. Friend on the street: "Hi, how are you?"
2. Friend on the street: "How are you feeling these days?"
3. Sister: "You've got to be careful so they don't put you in the hospital."
4. Wife: "You shouldn't drink beer while you are taking medicine."
5. Mother: "What's the matter, don't you feel good?"
6. Wife: "It's just you yourself, it's all in your head."
7. Service station attendant: "What are you shaking for?"
8. Neighbor borrows rake: "Is there something wrong with your leg? Your knees are shaking."
9. Friend on the job: "Is your blood pressure okay?"
10. Service station attendant: "You are pretty shaky, are you crazy or something?"

*(Marquis & Morgan, 1969, p. 28)*

Desensitization therapists next have clients either imagine or physically confront each item on the hierarchy while they are in a state of deep relaxation. Clients begin by pairing a relaxation response with the least-feared item on the list, and they move up to the next fear-arousing item only after they have mastered complete relaxation on the first item. Step by step they move up the hierarchy until at last they can relax in the presence of all the events that had previously aroused great

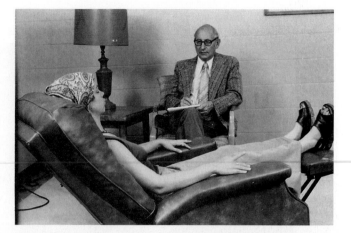

Joseph Wolpe, the psychiatrist who developed the behavioral treatment of systematic desensitization, first teaches a client to relax her mind and body, then guides her to confront feared objects or situations, real or imagined, while she remains relaxed. Systematic desensitization is one of several behavioral exposure techniques that have helped people with phobias.

fear in them. Here a behavioral therapist carefully teaches a client how to pair relaxation responses with scenes from his fear hierarchy:

Fine. Soon I shall ask you to imagine a scene. After you hear the description of the situation, please imagine it as vividly as you can, through your own eyes, as if you were actually there. Try to include all the details in the scene. While you're visualizing the situation, you may continue feeling as relaxed as you are now. If so, that's good. After 5, 10, or 15 seconds, I'll ask you to stop imagining the scene and return to your pleasant image and to just relax. But if you begin to feel even the slightest increase in anxiety or tension, please signal this to me by raising your left forefinger. When you do this, I'll step in and ask you to stop imagining the situation and then will help you get relaxed once more. It's important that you indicate tension to me in this way, as we want to maximize your being exposed to fearful situations without feeling anxious. OK? Do you have any questions? . . . Fine, we'll have ample opportunity afterwards to discuss things in full.

*(Goldfried & Davison, 1977, pp. 124–125)*

As we shall see in Chapter 7, research has repeatedly found systematic desensitization and other classical conditioning techniques to reduce phobic reactions more effectively than placebo treatments or no treatment at all (Wilson, 1990; Rachman & Wilson, 1980; Paul, 1966). These approaches have also been helpful in treating insomnia and other anxiety-related disorders (Steinmark & Borkovec, 1974), speech disorders (Walton & Mather, 1963), and asthma attacks (Moore, 1965).

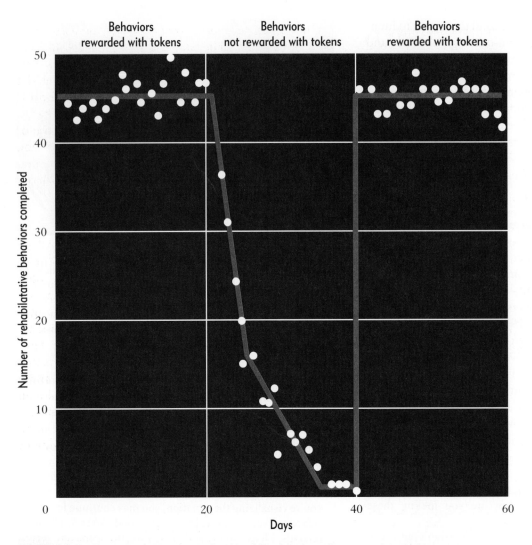

**FIGURE 5-2** A token economy program for 44 schizophrenic patients on a hospital ward. When rehabilitative behaviors, such as making one's bed, were rewarded with tokens for twenty days, patients performed them at a high rate. When rewards were stopped, the patients likewise stopped performing the behaviors. They later returned to a high rate of performance when token rewards were reinstituted. *(Adapted from Ayllon & Azrin, 1965.)*

In a diametrically opposite use of classical conditioning known as ***aversion therapy,*** therapists help clients to *acquire anxiety responses* to stimuli that the clients have been finding too attractive. This approach has been used with people who want to stop excessive smoking, for example (Whitman, 1972). In repeated sessions the clients may be given an electric shock, a nausea-producing drug, or some other noxious stimulus whenever they reach for a cigarette. After numerous pairings of this kind, the clients are expected to develop an unpleasant emotional reaction to cigarettes.

Aversion therapy has also been applied to help eliminate such undesirable behavior as self-mutilation in autistic children (Lovaas & Simmons, 1969), sexual deviance (McConaghy, 1972), and alcoholism (Cannon et al., 1981; Wallerstein, 1957). In the following case, aversion therapy was used successfully with a man who felt repeated urges to make obscene phone calls.

*He was a married, 32-year-old police officer who made* up to 20 obscene telephone calls a week to young women in his community. During the calls he would masturbate. He would continue masturbating to orgasm if the woman hung up before he reached orgasm. He ultimately was arrested because he telephoned a woman he knew. She recognized his voice and alerted the sheriff's office. After the details of his behavior surfaced, he lost his job but was permitted to seek psychiatric help in lieu of criminal charges being filed against him. Because he experienced considerable guilt and shame after he made the calls, the following procedure was felt to have a reasonable probability of success. Therapy consisted of the client making an obscene call to a female listener in another office who was instructed to listen and answer questions in a passive but noncomplying manner. Two young, attractive women listeners were part of the treatment; they were instructed not to hang up first. After each telephone contact, the client and listener shared their feelings. This evoked a great deal of anxiety, shame, and embarrassment on the part of the client. The therapist also was present at each of the meetings. Under these circumstances the client experienced the telephone calls as extremely unpleasant. These feelings apparently generalized to the client's real-life situation. For nine months after the brief three-week treatment, the client reported no strong urges to make an obscene call and the authorities in the community were not notified of any such calls.

*(Adapted from Boudewyns, Tanna, & Fleischman, 1975, pp. 704–707)*

**Operant Conditioning Techniques**   In operant conditioning treatments, therapists consistently provide rewards for appropriate behavior and withhold rewards for inappropriate behavior. This technique has been employed frequently, and often successfully, with people experiencing psychosis (Gomes-Schwartz, 1979; Paul & Lentz, 1977; Ayllon & Azrin, 1965; Lindsley, 1954). When these patients talk coherently and behave normally, they are rewarded with food, privileges, attention, or something else they value. Conversely, they receive no rewards when they speak bizarrely or display other psychotic behaviors.

In addition, parents, teachers, and therapists have successfully used operant conditioning techniques to change problem behaviors in children (such as repeated tantrums) and to teach skills to mentally retarded individuals (Franks, 1984; Ross, 1981). Rewards in these cases have included social rewards, meals, television watching, and recreation time.

As we shall see in Chapter 16, operant conditioning techniques typically work best in institutions or schools, where a person's behavior can be reinforced systematically throughout the day. Often a whole ward or classroom is converted into an operant conditioning arena (see Figure 5-2). Such programs are referred to as *token economy* programs because in many of them desirable behavior is reinforced with tokens that can later be exchanged for food, privileges, or other rewards (Ayllon & Azrin, 1968).

One token economy program was applied in a classroom where children were behaving disruptively and doing poorly at their studies (Ayllon & Roberts, 1974). The children earned tokens whenever they did well on daily reading tests or successfully performed other targeted behaviors. They could then exchange their tokens for a reward, such as extra recess time or seeing a movie (see Table 5-1). Under this system, reading accuracy increased from 40 to 85 percent, and the proportion of time spent in disruptive behavior decreased from 50 percent to 5 percent.

**Modeling Techniques**   Modeling therapy was first developed by the pioneering social learning theorist Albert Bandura (1977, 1969). The basic design is for therapists to demonstrate appropriate behaviors for clients, who, through a process of imitation and rehearsal, then acquire the ability to perform the behaviors in their own lives. In some cases, therapists model new emotional responses for clients. For example, therapists have calmly handled snakes to show snake-phobic clients that it is possible to be relaxed in the presence of these animals (Bandura, 1977, 1971). After several modeling sessions, clients themselves are encouraged to interact with the snakes. As we shall see in Chapter 7, the modeling of emotion can be quite effective in the treatment

TABLE 5-1

| TOKEN ECONOMY PROGRAM IN A FIFTH-GRADE READING CLASS | Number of Tokens |
|---|---|
| *Earnings* | |
| 80% correct on workbook assignments | 2 |
| 100% correct on workbook assignments | 5 |
| *Exchange value* | |
| Access to game room (per 15 minutes) | 2 |
| Extra recess time (10 minutes) | 2 |
| Review grades in teacher's book | 5 |
| Reduce detention (per 10 minutes) | 10 |
| Change cafeteria table | 15 |
| Have the lowest test grade removed | 20 |
| See a movie | 6 |
| Have a good work letter sent to parents | 15 |

*Source:* Ayllon & Roberts, 1974.

Mentally retarded clients at the Brooklyn Development Center earn tokens for completing designated behaviors and later exchange them for various rewards. Token economy programs have been instituted in a variety of settings other than mental hospitals—nursing homes, rehabilitation centers, schools, businesses—with the rewards adjusted appropriately. Office employees, for example, may be motivated to perform well by the offer of such rewards as extra breaktime, a job promotion, a computer terminal, a reserved parking space, and a voice in policy decisions (Potter, 1980).

of phobic disorders (Rosenthal & Bandura, 1978; Bandura, Adams, & Beyer, 1977; Rachman, 1976).

Behavioral therapists have also used modeling in combination with other techniques to help people acquire or improve their social skills and assertiveness. In an approach called *social skills training,* for example, therapists point out the social deficits of clients and then role-play social situations with the clients. In some enactments the therapist may take the role of the client and demonstrate appropriate social behaviors; in others, the client may try out and rehearse the behaviors, always receiving feedback from the therapist. Ultimately the client practices the behaviors in real-life situations. In the following role-playing session the client is a male college student who has difficulty making dates:

*Client:*   By the way *(Pause)* I don't suppose you want to go out Saturday night?

*Therapist:*   Up to actually asking for the date you were very good. However, if I were the girl, I think I might have been a bit offended when you said, "By the way." It's like your asking her out is pretty casual. Also, the way you phrased the question, you were kind of suggesting to her that she doesn't want to go out with you. Pretend for the moment I'm you. Now, how does this sound: "There is a movie at the Varsity Theater this Saturday that I want to see. If you don't have other plans, I'd very much like to take you."

*Client:*   That sounded good. Like you were sure of yourself and liked the girl, too.

*Therapist:*   Why don't you try it.

*Client:*   You know that movie at the Varsity? Well, I'd like to go, and I'd like to take you Saturday, if you don't have anything better to do.

*Therapist:*   Well, that certainly was better. Your tone of voice was especially good. But the last line, "if you don't have anything better to do," sounds like you don't think you have too much to offer. Why not run through it one more time.

*Client:*   I'd like to see the show at the Varsity, Saturday, and, if you haven't made other plans, I'd like to take you.

*Therapist:*   Much better. Excellent, in fact. You were confident, forceful, and sincere.

*(Rimm & Masters, 1979, p. 74)*

Using a combined strategy of modeling, rehearsal, feedback, and practice, therapists have successfully taught social and assertion skills to shy, passive, or socially isolated people, as well as to people who have a pattern of bursting out in rage or violence after building up resentment over perceived social slights (Bellack, Hersen, & Turner, 1976; Curran & Gilbert, 1975; Foy, Eisler, & Pinkston, 1975). As we shall note in later chapters, the approach has also been used to improve the social skills of people who are depressed, alcoholic, obese, or anxious (Wells, Hersen, Bellack, & Himmelhoch, 1977).

***Assessing Behavioral Therapies***   Behavioral interventions are among the most widely used and researched treatment approaches in the clinical field (Kendall, 1990). Approximately 6 percent of surveyed therapists report that their approach is primarily behavioral, and another 10 percent say that they combine behavioral and cognitive approaches (Smith, 1982). One reason for the popularity of behavioral therapies is that they are more amenable to research than the psychodynamic or humanistic approaches. The removal of symptoms—the criterion of progress in behavioral therapy—is easier to observe and measure than conflict resolution or self-actualization—the psychodynamic and humanistic criteria of improvement.

Moreover, behavioral approaches have been effective for numerous problems seen in clinical practice, including specific fears, social deficits, and mental retardation (Bierman & Furman, 1984; Aitken & Benson, 1983; Rachman & Wilson, 1980; Kazdin, 1979). Their effectiveness is all the more impressive in view of the relatively short duration and low overall cost of these therapies.

At the same time, behavioral therapies have certain limitations. First, the improvements they bring about do not always extend to the person's real life and do not necessarily maintain themselves without further behavioral interventions (Edelstein, 1989; Stokes & Osnes, 1989; Jacobson, 1989). Second, as we shall observe in later chapters, behavioral therapies do not appear to be particularly effective with psychological disorders that are broad or vaguely defined. Problems involving generalized anxiety, for example, are unlikely to be alleviated by step-by-step, behavior-by-behavior approaches (O'Leary & Wilson, 1987).

Third, some people have raised ethical questions about the behavioral approaches (Kipnis, 1987). It troubles them, for example, that token economy programs and other operant conditioning techniques are imposed on many clients without their permission. Similarly, they are concerned about the pain and discomfort that may be inflicted on clients in aversion therapy. While acknowledging these to be substantive issues, most behaviorists believe that when behavioral interventions are properly conducted, they proceed in a responsible manner that safeguards the client's rights and dignity.

**Cognitive Therapies**   Working from the premise that abnormal functioning is caused by counterproductive assumptions and thoughts, cognitive therapists try to help people recognize and change their faulty thinking processes. Because different forms of abnormality involve different kinds of cognitive dysfunctioning, a number of cognitive strategies have been developed.

**Ellis's Rational-Emotive Therapy**   In line with his belief that irrational assumptions give rise to abnormal functioning, Albert Ellis has developed an approach called *rational-emotive therapy* (Ellis, 1989, 1987, 1976, 1962). Therapists help clients to discover the irrational assumptions that govern their emotional responses and to change those assumptions into constructive ways of viewing themselves and the world.

In his own practice, Ellis is a direct and active therapist who tries to persuade clients that the rational-emotive perspective explains their difficulties. He points out their irrational assumptions in a blunt, confrontational, and often humorous way, and then he models the use of

alternative assumptions. After criticizing a man's perfectionistic standards, for example, he might say, "So what if you did a lousy job on your project? It's important to realize that one lousy project simply means one lousy project, and no more than that!" Ellis also gives clients homework assignments requiring them to observe their assumptions (Ellis also calls them "hypotheses") as they operate in everyday life and to think of ways to test the assumptions' rationality. He also has clients rehearse new assumptions during therapy and apply them in real-life situations.

*Therapist:* I'll explain in a minute. But first, the point is for you to decide exactly what hypothesis or nutty idea you want to work on for at least ten minutes a day. And, in your case, it would be the idea, again, that it's terrible for you to get rejected by a woman you find attractive. You would take this idea, and ask yourself several basic questions, in order to challenge and dispute it.

*Client:* What kind of questions?

*Therapist:* Usually, four basic questions—though they have all kinds of variations. The first one is, "What am I telling myself?" or, "What silly idea do I want to challenge?" And the answer, in your case, is, "It's terrible if a woman whom I find attractive rejects me." The second question is, "Is this, my hypothesis, true?" And the answer is—?

*Client:* Uh, well, uh. No, it isn't.

*Therapist:* Fine. If you had said it was true, the third question would have been, "Where is the evidence for its being true?" But since you said it isn't true, the third question is, "Where is the evidence that it's not true?" Well—?

*Client:* Well, uh, it's not true because, as we said before, it may be very inconvenient if an attractive woman rejects me, but it's not more, uh, than that. It's only damned inconvenient!

*(Ellis, 1976, pp. 29–30)*

Ellis has cited numerous studies in support of rational-emotive therapy (Ellis, 1989, 1973). Most of these studies have been conducted on people with experimentally induced anxieties or with nonclinical problems such as a mild fear of snakes (Kendall, 1990; Prochaska, 1984; Kendall & Kriss, 1983), but in the modest number of studies that have been done on actual clinical subjects, rational-emotive therapy has performed well. As we shall observe in Chapter 7, anxious clients in particular who are treated with this therapy improve more than anxious clients who receive no treatment or placebo treatments (Emmelkamp et al., 1988; Warren et al., 1988; Lipsky et al., 1980; DiLoreto, 1971).

**Beck's Cognitive Therapy**   Aaron Beck has independently developed a system of therapy that is similar to Ellis's rational-emotive therapy. Called simply *cognitive therapy,* this approach has been widely used in cases of depression (Beck, 1991, 1987, 1976, 1967). Cognitive therapists help clients to recognize the negative thoughts, biased interpretations, and errors in logic that pervade their thinking and, according to Beck, cause them to feel depressed. The therapists also guide clients to question and challenge their dysfunctional thoughts, try out new interpretations, and ultimately apply alternative ways of thinking in their daily lives. As we shall see in Chapter 9, depressed people who are treated with Beck's approach improve significantly more than those who receive no treatment or those treated with other systems of psychotherapy and about the same as those who receive biological treatments (APA, 1986; Hollon & Beck, 1986; Kovacs et al., 1981; Rush et al., 1977). Here a cognitive therapist guides a depressed 26-year-old graduate student to see the relationship between the way she interprets her experiences and the way she feels and to begin questioning the accuracy of her interpretations:

*Patient:*   I agree with the descriptions of me but I guess I don't agree that the way I think makes me depressed.

*Therapist:*   How do you understand it?

*Patient:*   I get depressed when things go wrong. Like when I fail a test.

*Therapist:*   How can failing a test make you depressed?

*Patient:*   Well, if I fail I'll never get into law school.

*Therapist:*   So failing the test means a lot to you. But if failing a test could drive people into clinical depression, wouldn't you expect everyone who failed the test to have a depression? . . . Did everyone who failed get depressed enough to require treatment?

*Patient:*   No, but it depends on how important the test was to the person.

*Therapist:*   Right, and who decides the importance?

*Patient:*   I do.

*Therapist:*   And so, what we have to examine is your way of viewing the test (or the way that you think about the

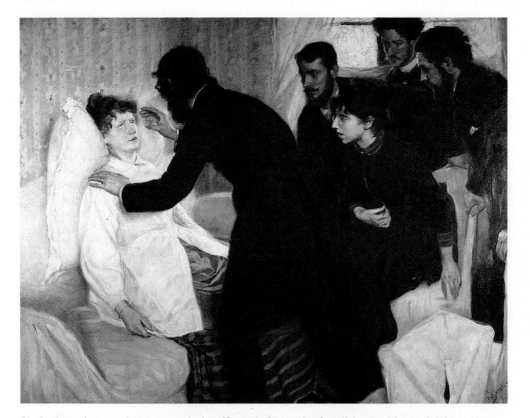

In the late-nineteenth-century painting *Hypnotic Séance* the Swedish practitioner Axel Munthe hypnotizes a hysterical patient while his students look on. At that time hypnosis was the exclusive property of psychodynamic therapists, but it is now used by practitioners of all orientations. Many cognitive and behavioral therapists find it a valuable adjunct to treatment. Hypnotism is also an important tool for clinical researchers and has itself become the subject of research investigations.

test) and how it affects your chances of getting into law school. Do you agree?

*Patient:*  Right.

*Therapist:*  Do you agree that the way you interpret the results of the test will affect you? You might feel depressed, you might have trouble sleeping, not feel like eating, and you might even wonder if you should drop out of the course.

*Patient:*  I have been thinking that I wasn't going to make it. Yes, I agree.

*Therapist:*  Now what did failing mean?

*Patient:*  *(Tearful)* That I couldn't get into law school.

*Therapist:*  And what does that mean to you?

*Patient:*  That I'm just not smart enough.

*Therapist:*  Anything else?

*Patient:*  That I can never be happy.

*Therapist:*  And how do these *thoughts* make you feel?

*Patient:*  Very unhappy.

*Therapist:*  So it is the meaning of failing a test that makes you very unhappy. In fact, believing that you can never be happy is a powerful factor in producing unhappiness. So, you get yourself into a trap — by definition, failure to get into law school equals "I can never be happy."

*(Beck, Rush, Shaw, & Emery, 1979, pp. 145–146)*

**Cognitive-Behavioral Therapies**  Cognitive-behavioral therapies treat cognitions as responses that can be altered by systematic reward or punishment, or, alternatively, as skills that can be modified by systematic training. The psychologist Donald Meichenbaum (1986, 1977, 1975) has developed a cognitive-behavioral technique called **self-instruction training** to help people solve problems and cope with stress more effectively. Using a step-by-step procedure, therapists teach clients how to make helpful statements to themselves — **self-statements** — and how to apply them in difficult circumstances. The therapists begin by explaining and modeling effective self-statements; they then have clients practice and apply the statements in stressful situations.

Using this procedure, Meichenbaum has taught anxious clients to make the following kinds of self-statements as they try to cope with anxiety-arousing situations:

Just think about what you can do about it. That's better than getting anxious.

Just "psych" yourself up — you can meet this challenge.

One step at a time: you can handle the situation.

Relax; you're in control. Take a slow deep breath.

Don't try to eliminate fear totally; just keep it manageable.

*(Meichenbaum, 1974)*

In comparison with no-treatment and placebo control groups, Meichenbaum's self-instruction training has been found helpful for people with impulsive disorders (Kendall & Braswell, 1985), social anxiety (Emmelkamp et al., 1985; Elder et al., 1981), test anxiety (Kaplan, McCordick, & Twitchell, 1979), pain (Jay et al., 1987), and problems with anger (Novaco, 1976, 1975). On the other hand, it is not clear whether the cognitive problem-solving skills that are learned by this technique are retained for an extended period of time (Schlichter & Horan, 1981).

**Assessing Cognitive Therapies**  The number of clinicians who employ cognitive approaches has been growing rapidly. Approximately 12 percent of therapists surveyed currently identify their orientation as cognitive (Smith, 1982). There are two major reasons for this growth in popularity. First, the cognitive perspective has proved attractive to clinicians of various orientations (Alford & Norcross, 1991). It shares with the psychodynamic model the belief that clients' insights, interpretations, and judgments can be a key to improvement; and, consistent with behaviorism, cognitive therapies often attempt to break thought processes down into discrete parts, change them through systematic instruction, and measure the changes with precision. Understandably, then, many psychodynamic and behavioral therapists have been comfortable including cognitive techniques in their therapies or changing to a cognitive or cognitive-behavioral approach altogether.

Another reason for the popularity of the cognitive therapies is their impressive performance thus far in research. As we shall see, cognitive therapy has proved to be very effective for treating depression and moderately effective for anxiety problems (Beck, 1991), and cognitive-behavioral approaches have been helpful in cases of sexual dysfunction (Anderson, 1983; Fox & Emery, 1981).

On the other hand, a period of more probing evaluation and criticism, even from cognitive practitioners and researchers, probably lies ahead for the cognitive therapies. When a new therapy system is still on the rise, it may hold a certain charm for many clinicians who are willing to try the techniques and give them the benefit of the doubt. It is reasonable to expect, however, that the initial enthusiasm will be modified somewhat as time and experience inevitably expose the system's limitations. The psychodynamic, humanistic, and behavioral approaches each enjoyed a similar period of admiration and even glory, and each later had to face serious ques-

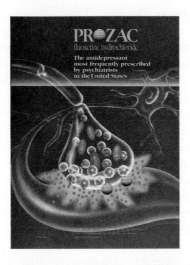

Psychotropic drugs now help millions of people to overcome psychological dysfunctioning. Unfortunately, a clinician's choices about which drugs to prescribe may be influenced not only by research literature but by a pharmaceutical company's promotional campaigns. Enticing ads for drugs fill the journals read by psychiatrists and other physicians.

tions and criticisms from proponents and opponents alike.

Is it enough to alter the cognitive features of a case of psychological dysfunctioning? Can such specific kinds of thought changes make a general and lasting difference in the way a person feels and behaves? These and related questions will probably receive more attention and analysis in the coming years.

**Biological Therapies**    Biological therapists use physical and chemical methods to help people overcome their psychological problems. The three principal kinds of biological interventions used today are *drug therapy, electroconvulsive therapy,* and *psychosurgery.* Drug therapy is by far the most common approach, whereas psychosurgery is relatively infrequent.

***Drug Therapy***    In the 1950s researchers discovered several kinds of effective **psychotropic drugs,** drugs that act primarily on the brain and often help to alleviate the symptoms of mental disorders. These drugs have radically changed the prognosis for a number of mental disorders and are now used widely, either as an adjunct or as the dominant form of therapy. In addition, as we saw in Chapter 2, the psychotropic drugs that have proved effective are leading scientists to a better understanding of the mental disorders that they alleviate (Iversen, 1989).

Unfortunately, the psychotropic drug revolution has also been accompanied by significant problems. Some of the drugs have serious side effects that must be weighed against the good the drugs can do (Wolfe et al., 1988). Often, when clinicians and patients alike become seduced by the possibility of rapid change, the drugs are overused. Finally, while drugs are effective in many cases, they do not help everyone. Four major groups of psychotropic drugs are used in therapy: antianxiety, antidepressant, antibipolar, and antipsychotic drugs (see Figure 5-3).

***Antianxiety drugs,*** also called **minor tranquilizers** or **anxiolytics** (from "anxiety" and the Greek *lytikos,* "able to loosen or dissolve"), reduce tension and anxiety. The pharmacologist Frank Berger discovered the first antianxiety drug, **meprobamate** (trade name Miltown), in the late 1940s while he was trying to develop an effective antibiotic medication to fight infections. In 1957 Lowell Randall observed that another group of drugs, **benzodiazepines,** also had an antianxiety effect, and these soon became the most popular group of antianxiety drugs (Pardes, 1989). By the late 1970s over 8,000 tons of benzodiazepines were being consumed in the United States each year; they had become the most widely prescribed drugs in the country (Hollister, 1980). Three widely prescribed benzodiazepines are *diazepam* (trade name Valium), *alprazolam* (Xanax), and *chlordiazepoxide* (Librium).

Research clearly indicates that these drugs help reduce anxiety (Woods & Charney, 1988; Noyes et al., 1984). They have been overused and even misused, however, and, as we shall see in Chapter 7, they can induce physical dependency if they are taken in high dosages over an extended period of time (Murphy, Owen, & Taylor, 1984; Winokur et al., 1980). Thus the drugs alone do not provide a long-term solution for most cases of anxiety.

*Antidepressant drugs* help lift the spirits of people who are depressed (Richelson, 1989). As Chapter 9 will reveal, a drug called *iproniazid* was developed in the early 1950s as a potential cure for tuberculosis. Research soon showed that it did not effectively combat that disease, but unexpectedly it did alleviate the feelings of depression felt by many of the tubercular patients (Loomes et al., 1957). Iproniazid and similar drugs, collectively called **MAO inhibitors** because they inhibit the action of the enzyme *monoamine oxidase (MAO)*, were soon marketed as antidepressant medications. Just a few years later, Roland Kuhn (1958), a psychiatrist, experimented with the drug *imipramine* while searching for a medication to treat schizophrenia. Although ineffective as a treatment for schizophrenia, imipramine and similar drugs, collectively called **tricyclics** because they each have three rings in their molecular structure, were also found to be effective in relieving depression (Davis, Klerman, & Schildkraut, 1967).

Today both of these groups of drugs are widely used in the treatment of depression (Murphy, 1989). Common MAO inhibitors include *phenelzine* (trade name Nardil) and *tranylcypromine* (Parnate). In addition to imipramine (Tofranil), some common tricyclics are *amitriptyline* (Elavil), *nortriptyline* (Aventyl), and *doxepin* (Sinequan). In the 1980s a third group of antidepressants was discovered. These new drugs, chemically different from MAO inhibitors and tricyclics, are sometimes referred to as "second-generation" antidepressants and include *fluoxetine hydrochloride* (trade name Prozac).

Tricyclics and second-generation antidepressants are prescribed much more often than MAO inhibitors (Richelson, 1989). The tricyclics have an average success rate of 65 percent in cases of depression, compared to a rate of 50 percent for MAO inhibitors (Dista, 1989; Wechsler, Grosser, & Greenblatt, 1967). In addition, tricyclics and second-generation antidepressants do not have the serious side effects of MAO inhibitors. The latter can cause dangerously high blood pressure, liver damage, and even death if they are mixed with foods containing the chemical *tyramine,* which is found in such everyday foods as cheese, chocolate, red wine, beer, chicken liver, and yogurt (Blackwell et al., 1967).

An antianxiety drug

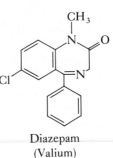

Diazepam
(Valium)

An antidepressant drug

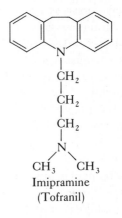

Imipramine
(Tofranil)

An antipsychotic drug

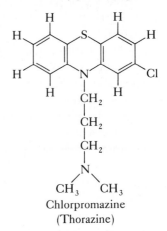

Chlorpromazine
(Thorazine)

**FIGURE 5-3** Chemical structures of important psychotropic drugs.

Today antidepressant drugs are prescribed in thousands of cases of depression, often in combination with psychotherapy. Research suggests that cognitive therapy is the only form of psychotherapy able to equal the effectiveness of this biological treatment (Beck, 1991; APA, 1986; Hollon & Beck, 1986). On the other hand, a combination of antidepressant drugs and cognitive therapy is often more effective than either treatment alone (Hollon et al., 1985; Weissman et al., 1981).

*Antibipolar drugs* help stabilize the moods of persons with a bipolar mood disorder, a disorder marked by mood swings from mania to depression. As we shall see in greater detail in Chapter 9, the most effective antibipolar drug is *lithium,* a metallic element that occurs in nature as a mineral salt (Jefferson & Greist, 1989). Lithium was discovered in 1817, but it was not until 1949 that an Australian psychiatrist named John Cade discovered its effectiveness as a psychotropic drug. Controlled research throughout the 1950s and 1960s confirmed that this drug can both reduce and prevent the manic and depressive episodes of bipolar mood disorders (Bunney, Goodwin, Davis, & Fawcett, 1968; Fiere, Platman, & Plutchic, 1968; Schou, Stromgren, & Voldby, 1954), and in 1970 the U.S. Food and Drug Administration approved lithium for use in their treatment.

Research indicates that lithium is helpful to approximately 70 to 80 percent of people with bipolar disorders, which until Cade's discovery had been unresponsive to all forms of biological and psychological therapy (Pardes, 1989; Depue, 1979). The dosage of lithium must be carefully monitored, however (Jefferson & Greist, 1989). Too high a concentration may dangerously alter the body's sodium level and even threaten the patient's life. Administered properly, however, this and related drugs represent a true medical miracle for people who previously would have spent their lives on an emotional roller coaster.

*Antipsychotic drugs,* also called *neuroleptic drugs* because they have side effects similar to the symptoms of neurological diseases, alleviate the confusion, hallucinations, and delusions of psychosis, a loss of contact with reality (Snyder, 1989). In the 1950s a French surgeon named Henri Laborit discovered that *phenothiazines,* a group of antihistamine drugs prescribed for allergic reactions, also had a calming effect on surgical patients. Soon the psychiatrists Jean Delay and Pierre Deniker (1952) found that the same drugs reduced the psychotic symptoms of patients with schizophrenic disorders. Since then, phenothiazines and several related groups of drugs have become the treatment of choice for schizophrenic disorders. Common phenothiazines are *chlorpromazine* (trade name Thorazine), *thioridazine* (Mellaril), *mesoridazine* (Serentil), and *fluphenazine*

(Prolixin). Other antipsychotic drugs that have been developed include *haloperidol* (Haldol) and *thiothixene* (Navane).

Research has repeatedly shown that antipsychotic drugs are more effective than any other single form of treatment for schizophrenic disorders (Davis, Barter, & Kane, 1989; May, Tuma, & Dixon, 1981; Davis, 1975; May, 1968). For many patients with schizophrenia the drugs alone are not sufficient treatment, but when drug therapy is combined with appropriate community programs and adjunct psychotherapy, many of these patients, too, can return to a reasonably normal life. Unfortunately, some patients fail to improve even when drugs are combined with psychotherapy and community care.

A major problem is that antipsychotic drugs may also cause serious undesired effects in many patients. The most troubling are *extrapyramidal effects,* movement disorders such as severe shaking, bizarre-looking contractions of the face and body, and extreme restlessness, which are believed to result from the drugs' effect on the extrapyramidal areas of the brain, areas just beneath the cortex. Some extrapyramidal effects appear soon after the antipsychotic drugs are taken; these can be remedied by adding other drugs or by discontinuing the antipsychotic drugs. However, there is a cluster of extrapyramidal effects, called *tardive dyskinesia* (meaning "late appearing movement disorder"), that emerges in some patients after they have taken antipsychotic drugs for a few years. Tardive dyskinesia is not always reversible even when patients are taken off antipsychotic drugs.

Despite these significant drawbacks, antipsychotic drugs continue to be widely used in cases of schizophrenia. The reason is simple: they often bring improvement and even recovery to patients who would otherwise be doomed to a life of hopeless confinement.

**Electroconvulsive Therapy** Another form of biological treatment used widely today, primarily on depressed patients, is *electroconvulsive therapy (ECT),* a technique first developed in the 1930s by two Italian physicians, Ugo Cerletti and Lucio Bini. One or two electrodes are attached to a patient's forehead and an electrical current of 50 to 150 watts is briefly passed through the brain. The current causes a brain seizure, or convulsion, that lasts up to a few minutes. After an average of seven to nine ECT sessions, spaced two or three days apart, many patients feel considerably less depressed (Fink, 1989). ECT helps approximately 72 percent of depressed subjects to improve, whereas placebo treatments help only 23 percent (Wechsler et al., 1967). Accordingly, the procedure is used on tens of thousands of depressed persons annually.

ECT has aroused concern in clinicians and the public

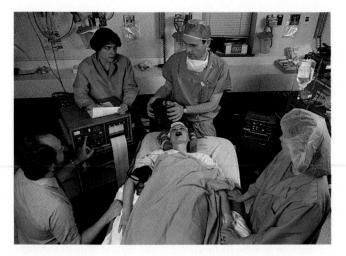

Patients who receive electroconvulsive therapy experience a brain seizure as an electric current passes through electrodes attached to their heads. They are given anesthetics and muscle relaxants so that they will sleep through the procedure and will not flail about during the seizure. Many patients who suffer from severe depression experience a significant rise in mood after a series of such treatments.

since its inception. First, it can be frightening, offensive, and sometimes dangerous. Second, it has a dark history: it has been used to punish and control patients in mental hospitals, especially during the 1940s and 1950s. Third, it can have troubling side effects, such as confusion and memory loss for events that occurred before and immediately after treatment, although these effects usually subside within several weeks.

In recent years, changes have been introduced into the ECT procedure to address these concerns. Patients are now given short-acting anesthetics before they receive ECT to help them sleep through the procedure and muscle relaxants to help prevent injury during the seizures. Many clinicians have come to favor *unilateral ECT,* in which only one electrode is used and the electrical current passes through only one side of the brain. This form of ECT is apparently safer than the traditional *bilateral ECT,* causes less confusion and memory loss, yet is no less effective (Squire & Slater, 1978; d'Elia, 1974; Lancaster, Steinert, & Frost, 1958).

ECT is administered less often today than it was in the past. With the growing success of antidepressant medications and of cognitive therapy, fewer depressed patients now need this extreme form of treatment. Moreover, today's licensing agencies and courts regulate and monitor the use of ECT more carefully than they used to do. Nevertheless, ECT is still applied when people have a suicidal or otherwise severe depressive episode that is unresponsive to other forms of treatment (Weiner, 1989; Fink, 1979). In a survey of 3,000 randomly selected psychiatrists, 86 percent stated that ECT is an appropriate form of treatment, though only 22 percent of them actually had used it (APA, 1983; Tapia, 1983).

***Psychosurgery*** Brain surgery as a treatment for mental disorders is thought to have roots as far back as trephining, the apparent prehistoric practice of chipping a hole in the skull of a person who behaved strangely. Modern forms of psychosurgery are derived from a technique first developed in the late 1930s by a Portuguese neuropsychiatrist, Antonio de Egas Moniz. In this procedure, known as a *lobotomy,* a surgeon cut the connections between the cortex of the brain's frontal lobes and the lower centers of the brain. The frontal cortex was believed to exaggerate the emotional responses originating in the lower brain (in the thalamus and hypothalamus), so Moniz reasoned that cutting the connections between the frontal lobes and the lower areas would have a calming effect on patients.

Moniz applied this procedure to human beings after observing that a similar procedure seemed to quiet highly emotional and violent chimpanzees (Valenstein, 1973). During the 1940s and 1950s, lobotomies became one of the most common forms of treatment for severe mental disorders, particularly schizophrenia and depression, and may have been performed on as many as 50,000 persons (Bivens, 1989). The procedure was considered a medical breakthrough, and Moniz received the 1949 Nobel Prize in medicine for developing it.

Two kinds of lobotomies were applied during the 1940s and 1950s. Both were crude procedures that resulted in the destruction of much brain tissue beyond the

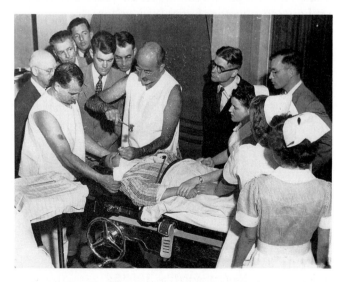

Neuropsychiatrist Walter Freeman performing a lobotomy in 1949. In this procedure he inserted a needle through an eye socket into the patient's brain and rotated it in an arc to sever the connections between the cortex of the frontal lobes and the lower centers of the brain.

intended separation of the frontal lobes from the lower brain centers. In one, the surgeon drilled a hole into one side of the person's head, inserted a blunt instrument, and rotated it in an arc, then repeated the procedure on the other side of the head, thus destroying a total of approximately 120 square centimeters of brain tissue (Shevitz, 1976). In the other kind of lobotomy, called the *transorbital* procedure, the surgeon inserted a needle into the brain by way of the eye socket and rotated it in an arc, again destroying about 120 square centimeters of brain tissue.

By the late 1950s it had become increasingly clear that lobotomies were not so effective as many psychosurgeons had been claiming. Lobotomy patients had only a slightly higher hospital discharge rate than control patients, and also had a higher readmission rate (Robbin, 1959, 1958). Even more disturbing, many lobotomized patients later suffered terrible and irreversible effects — seizures, extreme listlessness, stupor, and in some cases death (Barahal, 1958).

Given the ineffectiveness of lobotomies and the discovery of effective psychotropic drugs in the 1950s, this procedure declined in popularity during the 1960s. Although surgical procedures are still sometimes used to treat mental disorders, today's procedures are much more precise than the lobotomies of the past (Bivens, 1989). They enable surgeons to limit their destruction of brain tissue to 8 square centimeters. These procedures have fewer unwanted effects and are beneficial in some cases of severe depression, anxiety, and obsessive-compulsive disorders. Even so, they are considered experimental and are used infrequently, usually only after a severe disorder has continued for years without responding to any other form of treatment.

# FORMATS OF THERAPY

Therapists see a client either alone, in *individual therapy;* with other clients who share similar problems, in *group therapy;* or with family members, in *marital* and *family therapy.* Each of these formats is amenable to the techniques and principles of the therapist's particular theoretical orientation, whether it be psychodynamic, behavioral, or some other model. In addition, there are strategies that have been developed for use in specific formats.

## Individual Therapy

Individual therapy is the oldest of the modern therapy formats. The therapist sees the client alone for sessions that may last from fifteen minutes to two hours, depending on such factors as the client's problem, the therapist's orientation, and the cost of the therapy. In addition, the therapist may use adjunct treatment techniques such as biofeedback training or computer analysis that will affect the length of the session (see Box 5-4). Although patients usually meet with the therapist once a week, some are scheduled more often (as in orthodox psychoanalysis) and some less (as in some drug therapies).

## Group Therapy

At the turn of the century, a physician in Boston named Joseph Pratt brought tuberculosis patients together in groups to teach them about their illness and encourage them to provide emotional support for each other. This appears to have been the first clinical application of *group therapy* (Rosenbaum & Berger, 1974). American and British clinicians continued to experiment with group processes over the next fifty years, but it was not until after World War II that group therapy became a popular format for treating people with psychological problems. At that time, a growing demand for psychological services forced therapists throughout the United States and Europe to look for alternatives to individual therapy. Many who tried the group format found it to be efficient, time-saving, and relatively inexpensive. Some of them claimed that group therapy was often as helpful as individual therapy (Levine, 1979).

Thousands of therapists now specialize in group therapy, and countless others conduct therapy groups as one aspect of their practice (Goulding, 1987; Lubin, 1983). Typically, group members meet together with a therapist and discuss the problems or concerns of one or more of the members. The therapist usually follows the principles of his or her preferred model in conducting the group (Upper & Ross, 1980; Rogers, 1970; Perls, 1969; Lazarus, 1968). Groups are often created with particular client populations in mind; for example, there are groups for people with alcoholism, for those who are physically handicapped, and for people who are divorced, abused, or bereaved (Lynn & Frauman, 1985). The group format is sometimes used also for purposes that are educational rather than therapeutic, such as for "consciousness raising," religious inspiration, and "encounter" experiences (see Box 5-5).

Based on his own work and on a number of group investigations (Corder et al., 1981; Freedman & Hurley, 1980), group therapy theorist Irvin Yalom (1985) suggests that successful forms of group therapy share certain "curative" features:

1. *Guidance:* they usually provide information and advice for members.

BOX 5-4

# Computer Therapy: The Doctor Is In . . . Beep . . . Is In . . . Beep . . . Is In . . .

For years researchers and practitioners of clinical psychology have kept a watchful eye on advances in *artificial intelligence,* the attempt to simulate the cognitive functioning of the human brain in a computer. Their interest is both practical and progressive. Computers are already being put to practical uses in the assessment and diagnosis of psychological disorders, and some researchers predict that the computers can become useful and effective therapeutic tools as well.

Computers are powerful holders and sorters of information. They were created to liberate people from time-consuming repetitive tasks, and much of psychological assessment and diagnosis fits that description well. Many clinicians now use computer programs to help them gather clients' histories, assess self-report inventories, and even make preliminary diagnoses. Such uses of computer programs can save time and make psychological testing widely available.

Therapy would seem to be an entirely different matter. Most of us expect therapists to be responsive, empathetic, and insightful. Nevertheless, numerous attempts have been made to develop a computer program that can provide effective therapy. One of the earliest and best known is the ELIZA program (Weizenbaum, 1966), designed to simulate the experience of a client-centered therapy session. The patient types in a response to a question, and the computer selects the next question on the basis of key words that appear in the response. Sometimes the computer simply restates the patient's response, the way a client-centered therapist might choose to do (Servan-Schreiber, 1986). ELIZA's chief limitation, like that of all computer therapy programs, is that human language is extraordinarily complex and no one yet has created a software program capable of understanding it. As a result, the computer's responses tend to be simple and imitative (Murphy & Pardeck, 1986). Nevertheless, people who interact with ELIZA and other computer therapists have frequently attributed insight and reasoning ability to the computer and many even seem to experience a kind of personal relationship with the computer program (Zarr, 1984).

PLATO DCS (Wagman, 1980), another computer counseling system, helps people articulate their problems in "if–then" statements, a basic technique used by cognitive therapists (Binik, Servan-Schreiber, Freiwald, & Hall, 1988). One study on phobias found that this computer therapy was in fact as effective as a therapist using the same questioning approach (Ghost & Marks, 1987). Similar results were also documented with depressed patients (Selmi, 1983).

If computer-facilitated therapies are by necessity simple, why do they work for some clients? A number of researchers have suggested that people may find it easier to reveal sensitive personal information to a computer than to a live therapist (Griest, 1977). The computer offers them the freedom to express thoughts and emotions without being judged by another person (Lawrence, 1986). The computer therapist is never tired, angry, or bored (Colby, 1979). It does not use facial expressions, gestures, or harrumphing noises that, perhaps unintentionally, indicate surprise, approval, or dismay. It is always available — potentially to greater numbers of people — and it is less costly. These are all attractive attributes in a therapist.

Computers may never substitute fully for the intuition and judgment of a trained therapist. Yet, as researchers and practitioners learn more about the nature of mental disorders and as artificial intelligence researchers create more complex and humanlike computer programs, computer therapies may at least find a place as adjuncts to other forms of therapy. In a world where technology permeates all aspects of our lives, we probably should not be surprised to see computer technology finding a place among techniques for the treatment of psychological disorders.

2. *Identification:* they provide models of appropriate behavior.

3. *Group cohesiveness:* they offer an atmosphere of solidarity in which members can learn to take risks and accept criticism.

4. *Universality:* members discover that other people have similar problems.

5. *Altruism:* members develop self-worth by helping others.

6. *Catharsis:* members develop more understanding of themselves and of others and learn to express their feelings.

7. *Skill building:* members acquire or improve social skills.

══════ BOX 5-5 ══════

# Encounter Groups: A Social Phenomenon

Encounter groups, or *sensitivity groups,* began in the 1940s with Carl Rogers's development of humanistic therapy groups, and expanded in popularity in the 1960s with Fritz Perls's gestalt group work at the Esalen Institute in Big Sur, California (Rogers, 1970; Murphy, 1967). These are small nontherapy groups in which a leader guides members through intensive experiences so that they may develop greater self-awareness and, consequently, greater skill in human relationships.

Encounter groups vary greatly, but all share the humanistic goals of personal growth and change, fulfillment of one's potential, and enrichment of one's perceptions of oneself and one's world (Korchin, 1976; Stoller, 1970). To achieve these goals, leaders establish a highly charged atmosphere in which members are encouraged to drop all defenses and express their genuine emotions over the course of several group sessions. The focus is on the here and now, and nonverbal forms of expression are emphasized.

Techniques and exercises have been devised to help participants develop trust and expose their feelings (Schutz, 1967). Group members may be instructed to walk around for a while with their eyes closed ("blind mill") or to lift a particular member over their heads and pass the person around. More controversial are nude encounter groups; nudity is thought to help lower the participants' defenses (Bindrim, 1968). Hugging is permitted in such groups, but sexual expression is forbidden.

A popular variation of the encounter group is the extended one-session encounter, or *group marathon* (Stoller, 1968; Bach, 1966). In this event, ten to fifteen participants remain together for twenty-four to forty-eight hours straight, with little or no sleep, searching and sharing their emotions, receiving feedback, and building relationships. Some clinicians believe that the intensity, isolation from the outer world, and fatigue experienced during these marathons combine to produce "a release of emotion seldom seen in any other setting" (Schwartz & Schwartz, 1969). However, research has not shown that marathons are superior to the more standard series of shorter encounter group sessions (Kilmann & Sotile, 1976).

Rogers (1970) believed that encounter groups pass through typical phases over the course of their meetings. In the early phases, the members "mill around," feeling uncomfortable and indecisive after the leader states that he or she will not take responsibility for directing the group. They also show "resistance to personal expression and exploration" by trying to maintain their "public" facades before the group rather than reveal their "private" selves. Gradually, according to Rogers, they let their defenses down and begin to discuss their true feelings. This is what one participant said after another group member had made a comment about his strength:

Perhaps I'm not aware of or experiencing it that way, as strength. *[Pause]* I think, when I was talking with, I think it was the first day, I was talking to you, Tom, when in the course of that, I expressed the *genuine surprise* I had, the first time I realized that I could *frighten* someone — It really, it was a discovery that I had to just kind of look at and feel and get to know, you know, it was such a *new* experience for me. I was so used to the feeling of being frightened by *others* that it had never occurred to me that anyone could be — I guess it *never had* — that anyone could be frightened of *me.* And I guess maybe it

has something to do with how I feel about myself.

*(Rogers, 1970, pp. 22–22)*

Rogers says that in later phases of the encounter group, members develop the ability to express their immediate feelings about others in the group and to respond empathically to one another's hurt and pain. As a result, the participants attain greater self-acceptance and begin a process of change.

In still later phases of the encounter, the participants start to be more demanding of and confrontational with one another. They demand that each person reveal his or her true self ("the cracking of facades"). Members and leader give each other honest and sometimes extremely negative feedback. Rogers believes that this experience leads to closer and more meaningful communication. The following remarks were recorded during this stage of an encounter:

*(Loud sigh)* Well, I don't have *any* respect for you, Alice. None! *(Pause)* There's about a hundred things going through my mind I want to say to you, and *by God* I hope I get through 'em all! First of all, if you wanted us to respect you, then why couldn't you respect *John's* feelings last night? *Why have you been on him today?* H'mm? Last night — *couldn't you — couldn't you* accept — *couldn't you* comprehend in any way at all that — that *he felt* his unworthiness in the service of God? *Couldn't you accept this* or did you have to dig into it today to find something *else* there? H'mm? I personally don't think John has any problems that are *any* of *your damn business!* . . . Any real woman that I know wouldn't have acted as you have this week, and particularly what you said this afternoon. That was so *crass!!* It just made me want to puke, right there!!! And — I'm just *shaking* I'm so mad at you — I don't think you've been real once this

week! . . . I'm so infuriated that *I want to come over and beat the hell out of you!! I want to slap you across the mouth so hard and* — oh, and you're so, you're many years above me — and I respect age, and I respect people who are older than me, *but I don't respect you, Alice. At all! (A startled pause.)*

(Rogers, 1970, pp. 33–34)

Rogers claims that in the final phases of the encounter group, members achieve the "basic encounter" — extremely personal and honest communications and a new habit of expressing positive feelings and achieving closeness. By this point it is not unusual for members to have developed relationships with one another outside of the group sessions. By the last sessions, the participants are displaying positive behavior changes, both verbal and nonverbal (in tone of voice, for example), that, theoretically, they will also begin to display outside of the group.

In 78 out of 100 controlled studies of encounter groups, participants showed at least a few positive changes by the end of the last meeting, including a better self-concept and improved communication skills (Smith, 1975). On the other hand, it is not clear that those positive behavior changes were transferred to life outside of the group or continued to operate there for any extended period of time (Lieberman, Yalom, & Miles, 1973). Moreover, at least some of the groups have produced "encounter group casualties" — people who show "serious psychological harm six to eight months after the group experience" (Lieberman et al., 1983). Such casualties appear to be related to the intensity of the group sessions, the limited qualifica-

tions of some encounter group leaders, and the absence of general standards to regulate the way the groups are conducted (Lubin & Eddy, 1970).

Encounter groups are geared principally to people who are functioning normally. Yet it appears that many participants think of these groups as a form of therapy. A survey of over 400 prospective participants in encounter groups found that 81 percent of them had previously received or were currently receiving psychotherapy (Lieberman & Gardner, 1976).

The popularity of encounter groups in the United States throughout the 1960s and 1970s was a marked social phenomenon. During that period of social unrest and self-scrutiny, astounding numbers of people joined encounter groups in search of new directions and renewed hope (Kilmann & Sotile, 1976; Smith, 1975). Rogers (1968) proclaimed, "The encounter group is perhaps the most significant social invention of the century — the demand for it is utterly beyond belief. It is one of the most rapidly growing social phenomena in the United States. It has permeated industry, is coming into education, and is reaching many professionals in the helping fields." Although it lost some of its popularity in the 1980s, it continues

to be a commonly used group format. It is estimated that over 5 million Americans have participated in these groups. Most were well-educated upper- or middle-class professionals (Block, 1982).

Encounter groups are often confused with *T-groups,* which also began in the 1940s, after the death of Kurt Lewin in 1946. Several colleagues of this renowned social psychologist and researcher on group behavior sought to apply and extend his work by establishing the National Training Laboratories (NTL), an organization founded to educate people about group processes and to train them in working more effectively in groups. The training was conducted in *basic skills training groups,* also known as *sensitivity training groups* or simply *T-groups* — small groups in which a "trainer," or leader, would help participants to observe and think about their own interactions and, as a result, to develop greater insight and skill in human communications and relationships. T-groups are similar to encounter groups in intensity but are concerned primarily with educating people.

T-groups, like encounter groups, are not intended to provide therapy (Benne, 1964). The participants in T-groups are, after all, not seeking help for psychological disorders, but simply wish to develop greater understanding of group processes and greater skill at group interactions. These groups have been very popular since their inception, and they remain in wide use today, particularly in educational and industrial settings. Many of the groups are sponsored by employers who believe that the training will improve their employees' work performance.

These features are also at work in two specialized kinds of group therapy — *psychodrama* and *self-help groups.*

**Psychodrama**   In the 1920s Jacob Moreno, a Viennese psychiatrist and the first person to use the term "group psychotherapy," developed the therapy known as *psychodrama,* in which group members act out dramatic roles as if they were participating in an improvised play. The atmosphere of structured fantasy is expected to make the participants feel secure enough to express their feelings and thoughts, explore new behavior and attitudes, and empathize with the feelings and perspectives of others. Often the group members act on a stage and even in front of an audience.

Various role-playing techniques are used in psychodrama. In the *auxiliary ego technique,* also called *mirroring,* one group member portrays another, thus showing the latter how he or she appears to others. In *role reversal,* two group members play each other. In the technique of *magic shop,* participants temporarily exchange one of their undesirable personal characteristics for a quality that they desire. All these activities are guided by the therapist, or "director," who also provides feedback about each participant's performance. The audience, too, may give useful feedback.

Although relatively few therapists limit their groups' activities to psychodrama alone, many have incorporated its techniques and principles into their practice. As we saw earlier, many behavioral and humanistic therapists now use role playing to teach assertiveness and social skills and to facilitate interactions among members of their groups (Wood et al., 1981). Similarly, psychodrama's emphasis on spontaneity and empathy has permeated most group therapies (Lubin, 1983).

**Self-help Groups**   *Self-help groups* (or *mutual help groups*) are made up of people who have similar problems and come together to help and support one another without the direct leadership of a professional clinician. These groups have become increasingly popular over the last two decades, and today there are about 500,000 such groups attended by 15 million people in the United States alone, addressing a wide assortment of issues, including alcoholism and other forms of drug abuse, compulsive gambling, bereavement, overeating, phobias, child abuse, medical illnesses, rape victimization, unemployment, and divorce.

Self-help groups are popular for several reasons. Some of the participants are searching for inexpensive and interesting alternatives to traditional kinds of treatment and find self-help groups in their travels, along with self-help books, coping tapes, radio therapy shows, and

other modern-day approaches to feeling better (see Box 5-6). Many participants, however, have simply lost confidence in the ability of clinicians and social institutions to help with their particular problems (Katz & Bender, 1976). Alcoholics Anonymous, the well-known network of self-help groups for people dependent on alcohol, was developed in 1934 in response to the general ineffectiveness of clinical treatments for alcoholism. Still others are drawn to self-help groups because they find them less threatening and less stigmatizing than therapy groups. Finally, the popularity of self-help groups may be related to the decline of the extended family and other traditional sources of emotional support in Western society (Bloch, 1982).

Self-help groups have some unique characteristics that probably contribute to their effectiveness (Rodolfa & Hungerford, 1982; Killilea, 1976). For example, they encourage more helping among members than other groups do. Often new members are assigned to veteran members who take a special interest in them and help integrate them into the group. In addition, self-help groups encourage members to exchange information more than other groups do. People who are newly bereaved, for example, can obtain specific information from their self-help group about funeral arrangements and business matters, as well as about what feelings to expect and how to cope with them.

Many clinicians consider these groups a form of therapy despite the absence of a therapist-leader. At the very least, therapists usually view the groups as compatible

"Freud once said that he had never seen a patient the germs of whose disease he could not find in himself" (Karon, 1988). Self-help groups go Freud one better: they hold that people with similar problems are in the best position to support and advise one another. Thousands of such groups around the world help people cope with a variety of problems.

## BOX 5-6

# Pop Therapy: New Direction or Misdirection?

**A**nswer true or false:

1. Therapy is too expensive—there must be a cheaper way.
2. No one would take advantage of my psychological distress to make a buck.
3. There's an easy solution to every psychological problem.

If you answered true to any of these questions, you may be a candidate for pop therapy—"treatment" that comes in such forms as self-help books, radio and television call-in shows, newspaper advice columns, and audio and video tapes. Many of these offerings promise to solve psychological or social problems more quickly, easily, or inexpensively than traditional treatment methods. But, in fact, the advice that should be followed by people selecting a traditional form of therapy is ten times more important for anyone seeking help from a pop therapy: *caveat emptor*—buyer beware.

Perhaps the most popular form of pop therapy is the self-help book, in which an "expert" shares tips, techniques, or philosophies to help readers function more effectively, cope better with their problems, or reduce psychological stress. Some of these authors are professionally trained and experienced clinicians; others, however, have little or no formal training.

Gerald Rosen, a member of the Task Force on Self-help Therapies for the American Psychological Association (APA), is a vocal and respected critic of treatments found in self-help books. Citing many examples of research on the effectiveness of various

"Dr. Ruth" Westheimer offers counseling and advice on sexual functioning to millions of radio listeners and TV viewers.

psychological treatments appearing on mass-market bookshelves, Rosen (1987) comes to three basic conclusions. First, most of the psychological techniques presented in such books do not work when they are self-administered. Second, most authors of self-help books fail to test their treatments adequately. Third, the claims made in the books and in their advertising *do not* tell the consumer what research demonstrates about the effectiveness of the technique and *are*, in fact, exaggerated. Despite these problems, more and more such books are being written and read. One survey has even found that a growing number of psychologists recommend self-help books to their clients, in the belief that such books can sometimes be useful and at least not harmful (Starker, 1988).

Another form of pop therapy that has caught the public's fancy in a big way is radio therapy. In Los Angeles, for example, thousands of people regularly tune their radios to the psychologist Toni Grant, and many of them are convinced of the importance of her words and claim that she improves their lives and the lives of untold others. No research shows whether callers to radio therapy programs receive meaningful help leading to long-term relief or are actually harmed by the experience. The arguments generally given in defense of the shows are that they are intended more as entertainment than as therapy, do probably furnish some minor relief from psychological distress, and provide a forum in which people can express their concerns. When the host of the talk show is a qualified and capable therapist, these claims may have merit. Yet many of today's radio advisers lack professional credentials. Moreover, a great many listeners mistakenly view such programs as an established form of therapy, just as they may view self-help books as tried and true forms of treatment.

Are all pop therapies to be spurned, then? Certainly not. In an age when conventional forms of therapy help only some of the millions who suffer from psychological problems, it is appropriate to develop unconventional and alternative forms of therapy. The key is to research them before putting them into general practice, so that there is a consensus among clinical scientists about how they can best be used—by whom and under what circumstances. Pop therapies would then be vehicles to bring new discoveries to the public rather than potential misdirection for people seeking psychological relief.

with traditional forms of therapy (Levy, 1979). They often urge clients to participate in self-help groups as part of a broader treatment program for problems such as alcoholism, eating disorders, and victimization.

**Assessing Group Therapy** Because groups vary so widely in type and conduct and in the characteristics of their leaders and members, and because group interactions can be complex, it has been difficult to assess their effectiveness (Sadock, 1989; Kaul & Bednar, 1986; Bednar & Moeschl, 1981). Moreover, many of the studies that have been done have not used proper research methodology (Sadock, 1989; Lubin, 1983; Dies, 1979). Thus only a modest number of conclusions can be drawn about this format of therapy.

Research does indicate that group therapy is of help to many clients, often as helpful as individual therapy (Kaul & Bednar, 1986; Colson & Horwitz, 1982; Coche & Dies, 1982; Bednar & Moeschl, 1981; Bednar & Kaul, 1979, 1978). It appears that receiving candid feedback is usually useful for group members as long as a balance is struck between positive and negative feedback. Some people have been harmed by group therapy, but such occurrences are not frequent. Apparently skilled group leaders are usually able to screen out those prospective members who need more individual attention or who would not be able to tolerate the demands of the group experience (Sadock, 1989).

# Family Therapy

Adhering to the sociocultural position that disturbances in social structure often cause disturbances in individual functioning, several clinicians in the 1950s developed *family therapy* — a format in which therapists meet with all members of a family, point out problematic behavior and interactions between the members, and help the whole family to change (Mueser & Glynn, 1990; Foley, 1989; Satir, 1988, 1964; Bell, 1961; Bowen, 1960; Ackerman, 1956). Most family therapists meet with family members as a group, but some choose to see them in separate sessions. Either way, the family is viewed as the unit under treatment. Here is a typical interaction between family members and therapist:

"I just don't understand. We have had a happy family all along until Tommy started acting up." Bob Davis was visibly exasperated. "You are supposed to be the family expert, Ms. Fargo, what do you think?"

"We have tried so hard to be good parents to both of the children," Bob glanced at his wife, "but Tommy just

doesn't respond anymore. I wish he was more like his little sister. She is so well behaved and is a joy to have around."

Tommy sat motionless in a chair gazing out the window. He was fourteen and a bit small for his age. He looked completely disinterested in the proceedings.

Sissy was eleven. She was sitting on the couch between her Mom and Dad with a smile on her face. Across from them sat Ms. Fargo, the family therapist.

Ms. Fargo spoke. "Could you be a little more specific about the changes you have seen in Tommy and when they came about?"

Mrs. Davis answered first. "Well, I guess it was about two years ago. Tommy started getting in fights at school. When we talked to him at home he said it was none of our business. He became moody and disobedient. He wouldn't do anything that we wanted him to. He began to act mean to his sister and even hit her."

"What about the fights at school?" Ms. Fargo asked.

This time it was Mr. Davis who spoke first. "Ginny was more worried about them than I was. I used to fight a lot when I was in school and I think it is normal. I had a lot of brothers and sisters in my family and I learned early that I had to fight for whatever I could; it's part of being a boy. But I was very respectful to my parents, especially my Dad. If I ever got out of line he would smack me one."

"Have you ever had to hit Tommy?" Ms. Fargo inquired softly.

"Sure, a couple of times, but it didn't seem to do any good."

All at once Tommy seemed to be paying attention, his eyes riveted on his father. "Yeah, he hit me a lot, for no reason at all!"

"Now, that's not true, Thomas." Mrs. Davis has a scolding expression on her face. "If you behaved yourself a little better you wouldn't get hit. Ms. Fargo, I can't say that I am in favor of the hitting, but I understand sometimes how frustrating it may be for Bob."

"You don't know how frustrating it is for me, honey." Bob seemed upset. "You don't have to work all day at the office and then come home to contend with all of this. Sometimes I feel like I don't even want to come home."

Ginny gave him a hard stare. "You think things at home are easy all day? I could use some support from you. You think all you have to do is earn the money and I will do everything else. Well, I am not about to do that anymore."

"As you can see, Ms. Fargo, Ginny and I do not see eye-to-eye on everything about raising the kids. I think she is afraid that she has failed Tommy in some way."

"I've failed?" Ginny's face was now getting red. "You are the one who is never around to provide a good example for the kids. They have a mother; what they need is a father."

"I think you can see, Ms. Fargo" (*Bob winked at the therapist*), "what I am up against here and why it is no fun to come home anymore."

There was a long tense silence.

"What about you, Sissy," Ms. Fargo looked at the little girl, "what do you think about what's happening at home?"

"I think Tommy is a bad boy. I wish he would stop hitting me. I liked him before when he was nice."

Tommy began to fidget and finally he got up from his chair and started to walk around the room.

"Sit down, son," Mr. Davis demanded in a firm voice.

Tommy ignored him.

"Sit down before I knock you down!"

Tommy reluctantly sat down in a chair in the far corner of the room.

Mrs. Davis began to cry. "I just don't know what to do anymore. Things just seem so hopeless. Why can't people be nice in this family anymore? I don't think I am asking too much, am I?"

Ms. Fargo spoke thoughtfully. "I get the feeling that people in this family would like things to be different. Bob, I can see how frustrating it must be for you to work so hard and not be able to relax when you get home. And, Ginny, your job is not easy either. You have a lot to do at home and Bob can't be there to help because he has to earn a living. And you kids sound like you would like some things to be different too. It must be hard for you, Tommy, to be catching so much flack these days. I think this also makes it hard for you to have fun at home too, Sissy."

She looked at each person briefly and was sure to make eye contact. "There seems to be a lot going on. What I would like to do is talk with you together and then see the parents for a while and then maybe you kids alone, to hear your sides of the story. I think we are going to need to understand a lot of things to see why this is happening. I can hear, Tommy, that it is hard for you to be living in this family right now and that it is hard for your parents to have you. Also, as you have gotten older, it may be that you have thought you should be treated a little differently by your folks. What I would like everyone to do is to think about how each of you, if you could, would change the other family members so that you would be happier in the family. I will want everyone to tell me that and I want you all to listen to what the others have to say."

*(Sheras & Worchel, 1979, pp. 108–110)*

Like group therapists, family therapists may ascribe to any of the major theoretical models (Gurman et al., 1986). Whatever their orientation, most also adhere to the principles of *family systems theory.* This sociocultural perspective states that each family has its own implicit rules, relationship structure, and communication patterns that shape the behavior of the individual members, including dysfunctional behavior (Rosenberg, 1983; Wynne, 1981). For one family member to change, the family system must be changed.

In one family systems approach, *structural family therapy,* therapists pay particular attention to the family power structure, the role each member plays, and the alliances between family members (Minuchin, 1987, 1974; Minuchin & Fishman, 1981). The goal of therapy is to build a new family structure in which a working balance, or *homeostasis,* is achieved without the need for any member to adopt a sick role. In the case of the Davis family, for example, Tommy's misbehavior was interpreted as a shift in roles that was upsetting the family's homeostasis, forcing other family members also to change their roles and expectations to establish an alternative form of homeostasis:

As Tommy grew into adolescence and desired to have more independence in his family, his role began to change. He did not want to be treated as "Mommy's little boy." He began to fight frequently at school so that she would have to see his role differently. Mrs. Davis, however, still saw Tommy as her little boy who was now acting like a "bad" boy instead of the model child she expected him to be. Since what she expected from Tommy and what she observed in him were not the same behaviors, she had to change her behavior to treat him differently in an attempt to change his behavior. This also produced a change in Mr. Davis' behavior. Everyone in the system was affected by the change that began with Tommy's desire for independence.

*(Sheras & Worchel, 1979, p. 121)*

In *conjoint family therapy* the therapist focuses primarily on communication in the family system, helping members recognize harmful patterns of communication, appreciate the impact of such patterns on other family members, and change the patterns (Satir, 1987, 1967; Satir & Baldwin, 1984). Here a therapist helps a mother, father, and son identify their communication difficulties:

*Therapist:* *(To husband)* I notice your brow is wrinkled, Ralph. Does that mean you are angry at this moment?

*Husband:* I did not know that my brow was wrinkled.

*Therapist:* Sometimes a person looks or sounds in a way of which he is not aware. As far as you can tell, what were you thinking and feeling just now?

*Husband:* I was thinking over what she [His wife] said.

*Therapist:* What thing that she said were you thinking about?

*Husband:* When she said that when she was talking so loud, she wished I would tell her.

*Therapist:* What were you thinking about that?

*Husband:* I never thought about telling her. I thought she would get mad.

*Therapist:* Ah, then maybe that wrinkle meant you were puzzled because your wife was hoping you would do something and you did not know she had this hope. Do you suppose that by your wrinkled brow you were signalling that you were puzzled?

*Husband:* Yeh, I guess so.

Influential family therapist Salvador Minuchin developed the *structural* approach to family therapy, which focuses on changing dysfunctional power distributions, relationships, alignments, and boundaries in families. Animated and direct, Minuchin straightforwardly points out to family members that their comments and behavior are inappropriate and counterproductive, and pushes them toward alternative structures and behavior.

Family therapy pioneer Virginia Satir (1916–1988), first recognized the importance of *communication* in families during a series of sessions with a 28-year-old woman and her mother. "I noticed the tilting of a head, or an arm moving, or a voice drop, and then I would see a reaction. It didn't seem to have anything to do with the words. The words could be 'I love you' but all the rest of it was something else" (Satir, 1987, p. 67).

*Therapist:* As far as you know, have you ever been in that same spot before, that is, where you were puzzled by something Alice said or did?

*Husband:* Hell, yes, lots of times.

*Therapist:* Have you ever told Alice you were puzzled when you were?

*Wife:* He never says anything.

*Therapist:* (*Smiling, to Alice*) Just a minute, Alice, let me hear what Ralph's idea is of what he does. Ralph, how do you think you have let Alice know when you are puzzled?

*Husband:* I think she knows.

*Therapist:* Well, let's see. Suppose you ask Alice if she knows.

*Husband:* This is silly.

*Therapist:* (*Smiling*) I suppose it might seem so in this situation, because Alice is right here and certainly has heard what your question is. She knows what it is. I have the suspicion, though, that neither you nor Alice are very sure about what the other expects, and I think you have

not developed ways to find out. Alice, let's go back to when I commented on Ralph's wrinkled brow. Did you happen to notice it, too?

*Wife:* (*Complaining*) Yes, he always looks like that.

*Therapist:* What kind of message did you get from that wrinkled brow?

*Wife:* He don't want to be here. He don't care. He never talks. Just looks at television or he isn't home.

*Therapist:* I'm curious. Do you mean that when Ralph has a wrinkled brow that you take this as Ralph's way of saying, "I don't love you, Alice. I don't care about you, Alice"?

*Wife:* (*Exasperated and tearfully*) I don't know.

*Therapist:* Well, maybe the two of you have not yet worked out crystal-clear ways of giving your love and value messages to each other. Everyone needs crystal-clear ways of giving their value messages. (*To son*) What do you know, Jim, about how you give your value messages to your parents?

*Son:* I don't know what you mean.

*Therapist:*   Well, how do you let your mother, for instance, know that you like her, when you are feeling that way. Everyone feels different ways at different times. When you are feeling glad your mother is around, how do you let her know?

*Son:*   I do what she tells me to do. Work and stuff.

*Therapist:*   I see, so when you do your work at home, you mean this for a message to your mother that you're glad she is around.

*Son:*   Not exactly.

*Therapist:*   You mean you are giving a different message then. Well, Alice, did you take this message from Jim to be a love message? *(To Jim)* What do you do to give your father a message that you like him?

*Son:*   *(After a pause)* I can't think of nothin'.

*Therapist:*   Let me put it another way. What do you know crystal-clear that you could do that would bring a smile to your father's face?

*Son:*   I could get better grades in school.

*Therapist:*   Let's check this out and see if you are perceiving clearly. Do you, Alice, get a love message from Jim when he works around the house?

*Wife:*   I s'pose — he doesn't do very much.

*Therapist:*   So from where you sit, Alice, you don't get many love messages from Jim. Tell me, Alice, does Jim have any other ways that he might not now be thinking about that he has that say to you that he is glad you are around?

*Wife:*   *(Softly)* The other day he told me I looked nice.

*Therapist:*   What about you, Ralph, does Jim perceive correctly that if he got better grades you would smile?

*Husband:*   I don't imagine I will be smiling for some time.

*Therapist:*   I hear that you don't think he is getting good grades, but would you smile if he did?

*Husband:*   Sure, hell, I would be glad.

*Therapist:*   As you think about it, how do you suppose you would show it?

*Wife:*   You never know if you ever please him.

*Therapist:*   We have already discovered that you and Ralph have not yet developed crystal-clear ways of showing value feelings toward one another. Maybe you, Alice, are now observing this between Jim and Ralph. What do you think, Ralph? Do you suppose it would be hard for Jim to find out when he has pleased you?

*(Satir, 1967, pp. 97–100)*

## Marital Therapy

In *marital therapy,* or *couples therapy,* the therapist works with two people who are in a long-term relationship, focusing again on the structure and communication patterns in their relationship. Often this format of therapy focuses on a husband and wife, but the couple need not be married or even living together. Couples therapy is usually used when a relationship is unsatisfying or in conflict (Gurman, 1985; Cookerly, 1980; Jacobson et al., 1984). Also, a couples approach may be employed rather than family therapy when a child's psychological problems are traced to problems between the parents (Turkewitz & O'Leary, 1977; Framo, 1975).

Although some degree of conflict is inevitable in any long-term relationship, there is growing evidence that many adults in our society experience serious marital

Although most couples who are seen together in marital therapy are in fact married, the approach is now available and helpful to unmarried heterosexual couples and gay couples as well. Thus this format of treatment is as often called "couples therapy" as "marital therapy." Regardless of the kind of couple in treatment, therapists usually emphasize the structure of the relationship and the couple's communication patterns.

discord (see Figure 5-4). The divorce rate in the United States increased almost 50 percent during the 1970s (Doherty & Jacobson, 1982). A total of 1,122,000 marriages (2.2 percent of all marriages) ended in divorce in 1978, compared to 708,000 (1.5 percent) in 1970, and this rate continued to climb in the 1980s.

Certain complaints are particularly common among the people who enter couples therapy. The most common complaints by women are of feeling unloved by

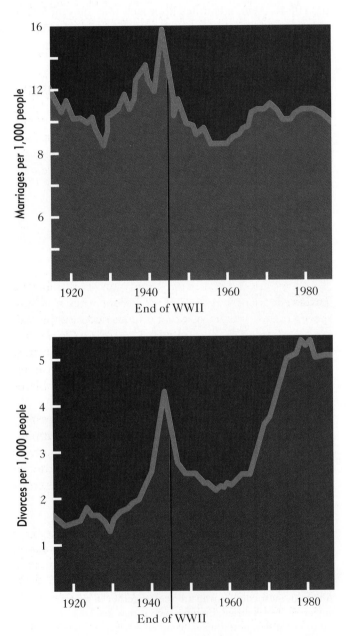

their spouses (66 percent), constantly belittled (33 percent), and repeatedly criticized (33 percent) (Kelly, 1982). Men complain of being neglected (53 percent) and unloved (37 percent) by their spouses and of sensing a long-standing incompatibility of one kind or another (39 percent). Approximately a third of both women and men also complain that they are sexually deprived and that their spouse is chronically angry or "bitchy."

Marital therapy, like family therapy, may be incorporated in any of the major therapy systems (Gurman et al., 1986). A version that has been employed increasingly, ***behavioral marital therapy,*** follows the behavioral perspective (Jacobson, 1989; Rappaport & Harrell, 1972; Stuart, 1969). Therapists who use this approach help spouses identify and change problem behaviors. The idea behind the approach is that spouses can help reinforce each other's positive behaviors and that they will enjoy their partner and their marriage more when the "rewards" of the relationship outnumber the "costs."

To replace detrimental marital behaviors with more productive ones, behavioral marital therapists often teach specific communication and problem-solving skills to spouses. Spouses may be instructed to follow such guidelines as these when they discuss their marital problems with each other:

1. Always begin with something positive when stating the problem.
2. Use specific behaviors to describe what is bothersome rather than derogatory labels or overgeneralizations.
3. Make connections between those specific behaviors and feelings that arise in response to them.
4. Admit one's own role in the development of the problem.
5. Be brief and maintain a current or future focus, that is, do not list all previous incidents of the problem, analyze causes, or ask "why" questions.

When deciding what action is in order to solve the problem, spouses are to:

6. Focus on solutions by brainstorming as many solutions as possible.
7. Focus on mutuality and compromise by considering solutions that involve change by both partners.
8. Offer to change something in one's own behavior.
9. Accept, for a beginning, a change less than the ideal solution.
10. Discuss the advantages and disadvantages of each suggestion before reaching agreement.
11. Prepare a final change agreement that is spelled out in clear, descriptive behavioral terms, that is recorded in writing, and that includes cues reminding each partner of changes she or he has agreed to make.

There are, in addition, the following general guidelines for problem solving:

**FIGURE 5-4** Although the rate of marriage has remained the same in the United States since 1920, the divorce rate has almost tripled. Eleven of every 1,000 people now get married each year, but 5 of every 1,000 get divorced. *(U.S. Census Bureau, National Center for Health Statistics.)*

12. Develop an agenda for each problem-solving discussion.
13. Discuss only one problem at a time, that is, be aware of sidetracking.
14. Do not make inferences; talk about only what you can observe.
15. Paraphrase what the partner has said and check out perceptions to what was said before responding to it.

*(Margolin, 1983, pp. 265–266; Jacobson & Margolin, 1979)*

To increase a couple's intimacy — that is, to solidify their relationship and bring them closer together — behavioral marital therapists may show them how to reestablish *core symbols* in their marriage — events, places, rituals, or objects that have special meaning for them (Stuart, 1975). The spouses may be told to reserve Friday nights for "dates" with each other, wear special clothes for each other, or regularly go to favorite places together. The therapist may also have the spouses designate specific times for performing considerate behaviors. In the technique of "caring days," for example, each spouse devotes a day to doing things the other has requested (Stuart, 1980). Similarly, in the "love days" technique, spouses must double the number of their pleasing actions on a designated day of the week (Weiss et al., 1973). And in an approach called "consideration," spouses are asked to show consideration at least once each day (Margolin & Weinstein, 1983).

The general goals of behavioral marital therapy are to help spouses develop more effective marital behaviors and derive more pleasure from their relationship. Research suggests that couples treated with this approach do indeed develop more effective interpersonal skills and feel greater satisfaction than those who receive no treatment at all (Baucom, 1982; Jacobson, 1978, 1977). One review of relevant studies computed that 64 percent of couples treated with this approach improved (Gurman & Kniskern, 1978).

## Assessing Family and Marital Therapy

As family and marital therapy have grown in popularity, more and more research has been conducted to evaluate their effectiveness. Overall, studies suggest that the approaches are indeed useful for certain problems and under certain circumstances. Reviews of methodologically sound studies (Gurman, Kniskern, & Pinsof, 1986; Todd & Stanton, 1983) reveal the following:

1. In comparison with other forms of treatment, family therapy is usually equal or superior in effectiveness at treating many kinds of problems. The overall improvement rate for cases seen in family therapy has been computed at 73 percent (Gurman & Kniskern, 1978).
2. The involvement of the father in family therapy substantially increases the likelihood of a successful outcome.
3. When the presenting complaint is a marital problem, the treatment outcome is significantly better if the spouses are seen together in therapy, as opposed to individual therapy for either spouse.
4. There is little comparative evidence that one marital or family therapy approach is superior to all others at treating a wide range of problems.
5. Short-term and time-limited marital and family therapy are as effective as longer-term therapy.
6. Many clinicians claim that *cotherapy,* a popular approach in which two therapists conduct the marital or family treatment, is a uniquely effective way of modeling appropriate forms of communication for families and couples; yet there is no empirical evidence that cotherapy is more effective than treatment conducted by a single therapist.

## IS TREATMENT EFFECTIVE?

Probably the most important question to ask about a particular treatment is whether it does what it is supposed to do — that is, whether it helps people cope with and overcome their psychological problems. On the surface, this may seem to be a simple question. In fact, it is one of the most difficult questions for clinical researchers to answer (Persons, 1991). Several problems must be addressed.

The first problem is how to define a "successful" treatment (Strupp, 1989). Consider the posttreatment statements of Louise and Helen, two women who have grappled with anorexia nervosa, the eating disorder in which people purposely lose excessive and dangerous amounts of weight:

Louise: *It's not just that I look normal again, but that I feel* normal. I'm no longer afraid of food, of gaining an ounce, or of being ugly. I no longer cut food for 15 minutes before eating it; and I don't have to chew each piece 12 times before swallowing. It's all so weird, I can hardly believe that I was caught up in it. But I was.

Most of all, I feel free now, free to be me, to run my own life and to meet my own needs. Oh, I love my parents and my sisters, I really do. But I don't have to be perfect and keep pleasing them in order to show my love or to win their love. I know that now. I have a lot of ground to make up, and I can hardly wait.

**H**elen: *I'm a lot better now. I weigh 105 pounds instead of* 90. I can eat salads, vegetables, and fish without worrying, although I still have problems with bread and potatoes, and sweets are just impossible. I still worry a lot about gaining too much weight; in fact, 105 feels pretty scary. But I weigh myself every day, so I don't think it will get out of hand. I've put my family through a lot and let them down. I'm really sorry about that. I guess they realize now what I've always known, that I'm a mess in many ways. Perhaps some day I'll win back their respect; I really hope so.

Both Louise and Helen have improved, but not to the same degree. Should a clinical researcher consider both of their recoveries successful, or just Louise's? Different researchers would answer this question differently. Some might even be reluctant to pronounce Helen recovered on her evaluation alone. A psychodynamic researcher, for example, might want to know whether she has satisfactorily resolved her underlying conflicts before making a judgment. Because definitions of success vary from study to study, it is not always appropriate to combine the results from different treatment studies and use them to draw general conclusions (Kazdin, 1986).

The second problem is how to measure improvement. Should researchers give equal weight to the reports of clients, friends, relatives, therapists, and teachers? Should they use rating scales, inventories, checklists, therapy insights, behavior observations, social adjustment scores, or some other measure? The various measures of improvement correlate only moderately with one another (Bloch, 1982). Louise's report that she has totally "overcome" her eating problems may be at odds with the reports of friends and relatives who see tension in her face or slowness in her movements whenever she is eating a meal with them. Given such differences, researchers cannot automatically combine findings from different studies to draw broad conclusions about the effectiveness of treatment.

Perhaps the biggest problem is the range and complexity of the treatments currently in use. Clients differ in their problems, personal styles, and motivation for therapy; therapists differ in skill, experience, orientation, and personality; and therapies differ in theory, format, and setting. Because a client's progress in therapy is influenced by all these factors and more, results from a particular study will not always apply to other clients and therapists.

Proper research procedures—use of control groups, random assignment, matched subjects, and the like—address some of these problems and allow clinicians to draw certain conclusions about various therapies. Even in studies that are well designed and well conducted, however, the enormous range and complexity of factors involved in treatment sets limits on the conclusions that can be reached (Kazdin, 1986).

Despite such difficulties, the job of evaluating therapies must be done and clinical researchers have plowed ahead with it (Powell & Lindsay, 1987). Thousands of studies have been conducted to test the effectiveness of various treatments, and numerous reviewers have tried to assess those studies and draw overall conclusions. The studies fall into three categories: (1) those that ask whether therapy in general is effective, (2) those that ask whether a particular therapy is generally effective, and (3) those that ask whether particular therapies are effective for particular problems.

## Is Therapy Generally Effective?

In 1952 conditioning theorist Hans J. Eysenck published a paper that raised serious questions about the general effectiveness of psychotherapy. After reviewing twenty-four studies, he concluded that 72 percent of control subjects who received no therapy managed to improve, whereas only 44 percent of subjects in psychoanalytic therapy and 66 percent of subjects in "eclectic" therapy—therapy that combines techniques from a variety of models—improved. In short, he suggested that therapy actually retards improvement. Over the next few decades Eysenck (1977, 1966, 1965, 1960) and Stanley Rachman (1973, 1971) conducted additional studies and reviews that again questioned the value of therapy, although their conclusions were somewhat less critical than Eysenck's had been in 1952.

Many therapists try to tap into a client's feelings by using art therapy or music therapy as an adjunct to treatment. Clients are expected to find, express, and work out relevant feelings through their art or music, and their creative accomplishments may also encourage feelings of confidence and self-respect.

Eysenck's research methods and interpretations have themselves been criticized in recent years, and most therapy researchers now disagree with his extreme conclusion. It has been pointed out, for example, that Eysenck's original criteria of improvement were stricter for treated subjects than for nontreated subjects (Bergen & Lambert, 1978). Nevertheless, Eysenck's claims have led to a number of careful investigations, most of which have suggested that therapy is often (though not always) more helpful than no treatment or than placebos (Lambert, Shapiro, & Bergin, 1986; Garfield & Bergin, 1986). A review that covered many kinds of therapies and mental disorders found therapy to be more effective than no therapy in 48 of 57 adequately controlled effectiveness studies (Meltzoff & Kornreich, 1970). A still broader review examined 375 controlled effectiveness studies, covering a total of almost 25,000 clients seen in a wide assortment of therapies (Smith, Glass, & Miller, 1980; Smith & Glass, 1977). The investigators combined the findings of these studies by standardizing their results, a statistical technique called a "meta-analysis." They rated the level of improvement in each treated person and in each untreated control subject and computed the average difference between those two groups. According to this meta-analysis, the average person who received treatment was better off than 75 percent of the untreated control subjects (see Figure 5-5). Still other meta-analyses have revealed a similar relationship between treatment and improvement (Howard et al., 1986).

A number of clinicians have also concerned themselves with an important related question: Can therapy be harmful? In his book *My Analysis with Freud* the psychoanalyst Abraham Kardiner (1977) wrote, "Freud was always infuriated whenever I would say to him that you could not do harm with psychoanalysis. He said: 'When you say that, you also say it cannot do any good. Because if you cannot do any harm, how can you do good?'" A number of studies conducted since the 1950s agree with Freud that some patients actually seem to worsen because of therapy (Grunebaum, 1985; Mays & Franks, 1985; Sachs, 1983; Truax, 1963). Similarly, a survey of 70 eminent clinicians and researchers showed a consensus that "deterioration effects" do occur in therapy (Hadley & Strupp, 1976).

The deterioration may take the form of a general worsening of symptoms or the development of new symptoms, including a sense of failure, guilt, low self-concept, or hopelessness over one's inability to profit from therapy (Lambert et al., 1986; Hadley & Strupp, 1976). These effects have been observed in a wide variety of client populations, therapy systems, formats, and settings. The frequency of client deterioration has varied from study to study (Smith et al., 1980; Hartley et al., 1977); but most studies on this issue find that between 5 and 10 percent of clients decline as a result of therapy. Thus, although many people do indeed seem to be helped by therapy in ways that would not otherwise be possible, at least some individuals in therapy would be better off having no treatment at all.

## Are Particular Therapies Effective?

Most of the studies that have considered the general effectiveness of therapy have lumped all therapies together and treated them all alike, a procedure that many researchers consider inappropriate. One critic suggested that such studies were operating under a *uniformity myth*—a false belief that all therapies are equivalent despite differences in the therapists' training, experience, theoretical orientation, and personalities (Kiesler, 1966).

An alternative approach has been to examine the effectiveness of particular therapies. Most such studies show each of the major systems and formats of therapy to be superior to no treatment or to placebo treatment. Psychodynamic therapies and client-centered therapy (the only humanistic approach to be studied empirically) have fared well occasionally in therapy outcome studies (Prochaska, 1984; Fisher & Greenberg, 1977; DiLoreto, 1971), while behavioral, cognitive, and biological therapies have frequently demonstrated considerable effectiveness (Franks et al., 1990; Rachman & Wilson, 1980; Beck, 1976; Wechsler et al., 1967).

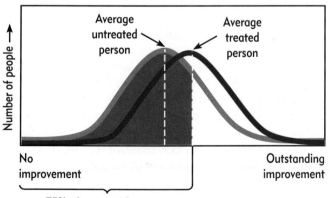

**FIGURE 5-5** Combining subjects and results from hundreds of studies, investigators have determined that the average person who receives psychotherapy experiences greater improvement than do 75 percent of all untreated people with similar problems. *(Adapted from Smith et al., 1980; Smith & Glass, 1977.)*

Many studies have also compared particular therapies with one another (Lambert et al., 1986). A well-known review of properly controlled comparative studies (Luborsky et al., 1975) failed to find that one form of therapy consistently stood out over others. Instead, client-centered and psychodynamic therapy were judged equally effective in four of five studies; behavior therapy was more effective than psychodynamic therapy in thirteen of nineteen studies; short-term therapy was just as effective as extended therapy in five of eight studies; and individual and group therapy were equally effective in nine of thirteen studies.

Another particularly well-done comparative study paints a similar picture (Sloan et al., 1975). The researchers assigned ninety-four clients with anxiety, depressive, and personality disorders to one of three treatment conditions: short-term psychodynamic therapy, behavior therapy, or a waiting-list control group. The subjects in all the conditions were matched on such variables as age, sex, and severity of symptoms. Six highly experienced therapists then provided treatment in weekly hour-long sessions. The researchers found that after four months, the clients who had been receiving either form of therapy, whether psychodynamic or behavioral, had improved to a similar degree, and significantly more than the control clients. Approximately 80 percent of the clients in each therapy group had improved but only 48 percent of the waiting-list clients. In a follow-up study eight months later, the waiting-list subjects had also improved significantly and had almost caught up to those in treatment, but by that time many of these control subjects had themselves become clients in therapy, a factor that probably contributed to their improvement.

This similar showing by different therapies, repeated across many studies, has suggested to some clinical theorists that the various therapies may share certain basic ingredients that in fact are the primary reasons that clients improve (Beitman et al., 1989; Powell & Lindsay, 1987; Frank, 1982, 1981, 1978, 1973; Bandura, 1981, 1977; Lichtenstein, 1980). These theorists have noted, for example, that successful therapies of all kinds provide clients with some individual attention, a credible rationale for their problems, the experience of mastery and success, and raised expectations for improvement. In addition, successful therapies typically establish a therapeutic alliance between clinician and client, with a basis in faith and trust (Strupp, 1989; Korhin & Sands, 1983).

The finding of similar overall success rates in various kinds of therapy has led to a *rapprochement movement,* an effort to delineate a set of "common therapeutic strategies" that characterize the work of all effective therapists (Marmor, 1987; Wachtel, 1987; Garfield &

The well-known therapist Arnold Lazarus argues that therapists must be "flexible, versatile, and technically eclectic" (1987, p. 166). In his *multimodal therapy,* the therapist focuses on all aspects of a client's problems and combines procedures drawn from various systems of therapy. Lazarus uses the acronym *BASIC I.D.* to identify the seven "pillars" of human temperament on which he focuses in assessing and treating a client: behavior, affect, sensation, imagery, cognition, interpersonal relationships, and drugs/biology.

Bergin, 1986; Norcross, 1986; Goldfried & Safran, 1986; Goldfried, 1980). One survey of highly esteemed and successful therapists of various orientations suggests that most provide feedback to patients, help patients focus on their own thoughts and behavior, pay attention to the way therapist and patient are interacting, and try to promote self-mastery in their patients. In short, effective therapists often seem to practice more similarly than they preach (Korchin & Sards, 1983). Given this growing appreciation of similarity among therapists, it is not at all surprising that 41 percent of recently surveyed therapists refused to identify themselves with one orientation and described themselves as eclectic (Lazarus, 1987; Smith, 1982) (see again Figure 5-1).

## Are Particular Therapies Effective for Particular Disorders?

People with different disorders may respond differently to different therapeutic systems, formats, and settings.

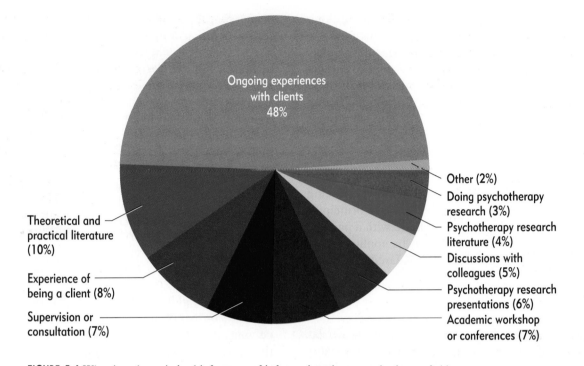

**FIGURE 5-6** What is a therapist's chief source of information about psychotherapy? Almost half of 245 psychologists who were surveyed reported that they learned more about therapy from their ongoing experience with clients than from any other source. Only 13 percent said that research presentations, literature, or activity was the most useful source of information for them. *(Adapted from Morrow-Bradley & Elliott, 1986.)*

As the influential clinical theorist Gordon Paul said some years back, the most appropriate question to ask regarding the effectiveness of therapy may be "*What* specific treatment, by *whom*, is most effective for *this* individual with *that* specific problem, and under *which* set of circumstances?" (Paul, 1967, p. 111).

This consideration has impelled a number of researchers to be as specific as possible in the design of therapy studies, investigating, for example, how effective particular therapies are at treating particular disorders (Kazdin, 1986; Beutler, 1983). These studies have often found sizable differences among the various therapies. Behavior therapies, for example, have emerged as the most effective of all therapies in the treatment of phobic disorders (Wilson, 1990; Emmelkamp & Kuipers, 1985; Wilson & O'Leary, 1980). Similarly, drug therapy is the single most effective treatment for schizophrenic disorders (May, Tuma, & Dixon, 1981; Hollon & Beck, 1978), cognitive-behavioral therapies have been very effective for sexual dysfunction (Heiman & LoPiccolo, 1983), and cognitive therapy and drug therapy have both proved highly successful in cases of depression (Beck, 1991, 1987; Gelenberg, 1989; APA, 1987; Kovacs et al., 1981; Rush et al., 1977). Studies of this kind have also revealed that some clinical problems respond better to combined therapy approaches than to any one therapy alone (Wilson, 1990). One example is the combined use of drug therapy and cognitive therapy to treat depression (Agras, 1987; Hollon et al., 1985; Weissman et al., 1981).

Specific information of this kind can help therapists and clients alike make better decisions about treatment (Wolberg, 1987; Lazarus, 1987), and it can provide researchers with a better understanding of therapy processes (see Figure 5-6) and ultimately of abnormal functioning. Thus the effectiveness of treatments is a question to which we shall keep returning as we examine the disorders they have been devised to treat.

## SUMMARY

*Therapy* is a systematic procedure for helping people overcome their psychological difficulties. All forms of therapy have three things in common: a sufferer seeking relief, a trained healer, and a series of contacts between healer and sufferer. At the same time, therapies vary in their goals, methods, and ways of measuring success.

They even disagree as to whether the person seeking therapy should be considered a client or a patient.

More than one-fifth of the adults in the United States are currently receiving therapy, for an array of disorders from anxiety disorders to schizophrenia. Most of these people are treated in a private office or mental health center; those with severe disorders are sometimes treated in mental hospitals.

Approximately 250 distinct forms of therapy are being practiced today. A *system* of therapy is a set of principles and techniques employed in accordance with a particular theory of change. The system may be applied in any of several *formats*—individual, group, family, and marital therapy.

Practitioners of *global therapies* try to help people recognize and change general features of their personality that the therapist believes are at the root of the problem. The primary global therapies are the psychodynamic and the humanistic-existential therapies.

*Psychodynamic therapies* help patients uncover past traumatic events and the inner conflicts that have resulted from those events. They are called "insight therapies" because awareness is considered to be the key to recovery. A number of techniques, such as *free association* and *therapist interpretations,* and psychological phenomena, such as *resistance, transference,* and *dreams,* help patients piece together explanations of their disorders. With growing insights and repeated experiences of *catharsis,* the patient joins with the therapist in the process of *working through* issues of significance. Although psychodynamic therapies remain popular and highly influential, there is little evidence that they are particularly effective for many disorders.

The other global therapies, the *humanistic-existential therapies,* help clients to look at themselves and their situations more accurately and acceptingly with the aim of actualizing their full potential as human beings. Humanistic and existential therapists emphasize the here and now.

Practitioners of *client-centered therapy* try to create a very supportive climate in which clients can look at themselves honestly and begin to accept what they discover themselves to be. The therapist conveys *unconditional positive regard* for the client, *accurate empathy,* and *genuineness.* Research has provided mixed support for the effectiveness of this humanistic approach.

*Gestalt therapists* view mental disorders as disruptions in the satisfaction of a person's current needs. The goal of this humanistic therapy is to move clients toward self-recognition and self-acceptance in light of those needs. Gestalt therapists challenge clients through the techniques of *skillful frustration, role playing, rules,* and *exercises and games.*

*Existential therapy* encourages clients to accept responsibility for their lives, to recognize their freedom to choose a different course, and to choose to live an authentic life. Like gestalt therapists, existential therapists focus on the here and now, and they place great emphasis on the relationship between patient and therapist. Like most of the humanistic theorists, existentialists question the merits of empirical research as a method for testing their system of therapy.

In contrast to global therapies, *specific therapies* focus primarily on symptoms and specific complaints, without delving into broad personality issues. The major specific therapies are the behavioral, cognitive, and biological therapies.

The goal of the *behavioral therapies* is to identify the client's problem-causing behaviors and replace them with more appropriate ones. Behavioral therapists use three categories of techniques: *classical conditioning, operant conditioning,* and *modeling.*

*Cognitive therapies* are based on the premise that abnormal functioning is caused by maladaptive assumptions and thoughts. Cognitive therapists try to help people recognize and change their faulty ideas and thinking processes. Among the most widely used cognitive therapies are *Ellis's rational-emotive therapy* and *Beck's cognitive therapy.*

*Biological therapies* comprise physical and chemical methods developed to help people overcome their psychological problems. The three principal kinds of biological interventions are *drug therapy, electroconvulsive therapy,* and *psychosurgery.*

*Individual therapy* is the most widely used therapy format. The therapist sees the client alone for some period of time, usually weekly. The format of *group therapy* became popular after World War II. Two specialized forms of group therapy are *psychodrama* and the *self-help group.* Research indicates that group therapy is of help to many clients. The candid feedback that group members experience is usually beneficial, and harm to group members is rare.

*Family therapy* is a format in which therapists meet with all members of a family, point out problematic behavior and interactions, and work on helping the whole family to change. Most family therapists adhere to the principles of *family systems theory,* which states that psychological disorders can be explained by examining family dysfunction rather than individual dysfunction, in particular, by examining the implicit rules, relationship structure, and communication patterns of a dysfunctional family. Similar to family therapy is **marital therapy** in which the therapist works with two people who share a long-term relationship. An increasing body of research on the effectiveness of various family and marital therapies suggests that they are useful for some problems and under some circumstances.

The critical question to be asked about these various treatments is whether or not they actually help people cope with and overcome their psychological problems. Three general conclusions have been reached. First, most recent findings indicate that people in therapy are usually better off than people with similar problems who receive no treatment. Second, the various therapies do not appear to differ dramatically in their *general* effectiveness. Third, certain therapies do appear to be more effective than others for certain disorders.

# TOPIC OVERVIEW

THE FEAR AND ANXIETY RESPONSE

PHOBIC DISORDERS

GENERALIZED ANXIETY DISORDERS

PANIC DISORDERS

OBSESSIVE COMPULSIVE DISORDERS

POST-TRAUMATIC STRESS DISORDERS

# CHAPTER 6

# ANXIETY DISORDERS

Think about a time when your breathing quickened, your muscles tensed, and your heart pounded with a sudden sense of dread. Was it when your car almost skidded off the road in the rain? When your professor announced a pop quiz? What about when the person you most cared about went out with someone else, or your boss suggested that your job performance ought to improve? Any time you confront what seems to be a serious threat to your well-being, you may react with the state of tension or alarm known as *fear* (Barlow, 1988; Marks, 1987; Lang, 1985; Izard, 1977). Sometimes, though, you cannot pinpoint a specific cause for alarm, but still you feel tense and edgy, as if something unpleasant were going to happen.

The ominous sense of being menaced by an unspecified threat is usually termed *anxiety,* and it has the same clinical features — the same acceleration of breathing, muscular tension, perspiration, and so forth — as fear (Barlow, 1988; Marks, 1987; Lang, 1985).

Although everyday experiences of fear and anxiety are not pleasant, they have an adaptive function: they prepare us for action — for "flight or fight" — when danger threatens. They may motivate us to drive more cautiously in a storm, keep up with our reading assignments, treat our date more sensitively, and work harder at our job. Unfortunately, some people suffer such continuous and disabling fear and anxiety that they cannot lead a normal life. Their discomfort is too severe, too frequent; it lasts too long; it is triggered too readily by what the sufferers themselves recognize as minimal, unspecified, or nonexistent threats. These people are said to have an anxiety disorder.

Anxiety disorders are the most common mental disorders in the United States. Between 8 and 10 percent of the adult population—between 13 and 16 million persons—currently suffer from one or another of the five anxiety disorders identified by DSM-III-R (Myers et al., 1984; Uhlenhuth et al., 1983; Weissman, Myers, & Harding, 1978); as many as 24 million people suffer from one of the disorders at some point in their lives (Ross, 1990). People with *phobic disorders* experience a persistent and irrational fear of a specific object, activity, or situation. People with *generalized anxiety disorders* experience general and persistent feelings of anxiety that are not associated with specific objects or situations. People with *panic disorders* have recurrent attacks of terror. Those with *obsessive compulsive disorders* are beset by recurrent and unwanted thoughts or the need to perform repetitive and ritualistic actions, and they experience intense anxiety whenever they try to suppress them. People with *post-traumatic stress disorders* are tormented by fear and related symptoms long after a traumatic event (military combat, rape, torture) has passed. Typically only one of these diagnoses is assigned, but studies suggest that most people with a primary diagnosis of one anxiety disorder warrant a secondary diagnosis of another as well (Barlow, 1985; see Figure 6-1).

Past editions of the DSM included anxiety disorders in Freud's category of the neuroses. A *neurosis,* according to Freud, was a disorder in which a person's ego defense mechanisms were incapable of preventing or reducing intense anxiety aroused by the person's unconscious conflicts. The resultant struggle with anxiety could take any of several malfunctional forms. In some neurotic disorders (phobic, anxiety, and obsessive compulsive neuroses), the person's anxiety was apparent. In others (hysterical, neurasthenic, depersonalization, depressive, and hypochondriacal neuroses) the anxiety was thought to be hidden and "controlled unconsciously and automatically by conversion, displacement, and various other psychological mechanisms" (DSM-II, p. 9).

Because DSM-III-R defines disorders by symptoms and without reference to possible causes, the category of neurosis has been dropped, and the neurotic disorders have been distributed among other categories. Those disorders of which anxiety is a central symptom are now simply called anxiety disorders. Several other of the so-called neurotic disorders, now defined as mood disorders, somatoform disorders, and dissociative disorders, are described in Chapters 8, 11, and 18, respectively.

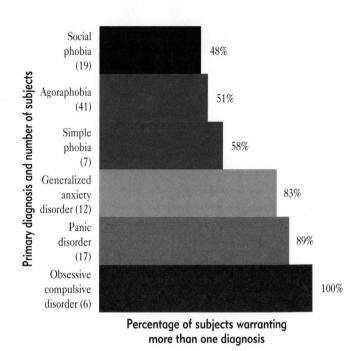

**FIGURE 6-1** Percentage of subjects who qualify for a diagnosis of a second anxiety disorder in addition to the primary one. An assessment of 102 anxious subjects revealed that 65 of them warranted more than one diagnosis. *(Adapted from Barlow, 1985.)*

## THE FEAR AND ANXIETY RESPONSE

Before we examine the various anxiety disorders, let us take a closer look at the changes we normally experience when we perceive a threat. Our response of fear and anxiety is actually a package of responses—physical, emotional, and cognitive.

Fear excites a number of physical responses in us. We perspire, our breathing quickens, our muscles tense, and our hearts beat faster. We may turn pale and develop goose bumps, our lips may tremble, and we may feel nauseated. If the situation is extremely threatening, we may feel horror, dread, and panic. Fear can interfere with our ability to concentrate and distort our view of the world. We may exaggerate the harm that actually threatens us or remember things incorrectly after the threat has passed.

These features of the fear and anxiety response are generated by the action of the body's *autonomic nervous system (ANS),* the extensive network of nerve fibers that connects the *central nervous system* (the brain and spinal cord) to all the other organs of the body (see Figure 6-2). The ANS helps regulate the *involuntary* activities

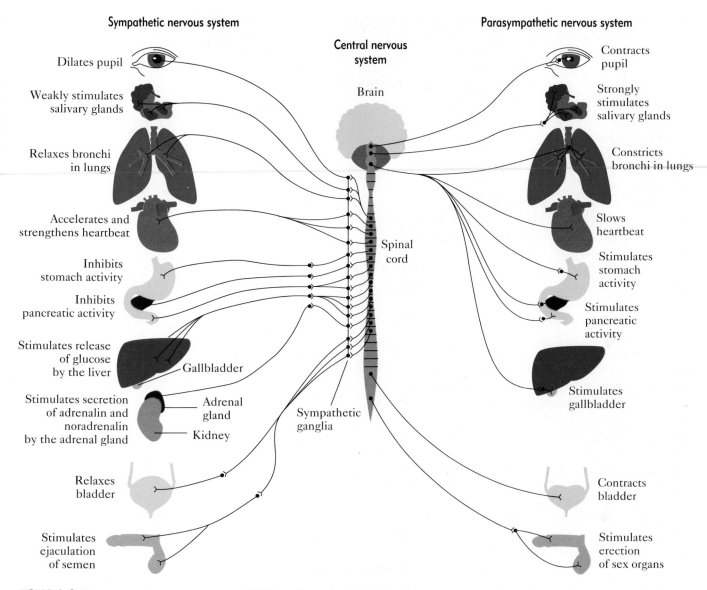

**FIGURE 6-2** The autonomic nervous system (ANS) regulates the involuntary functions of the body. Generally speaking, when stimulated, the sympathetic division of the ANS arouses the organs (it accelerates the heartbeat, for example); the parasympathetic division calms them (it slows the heartbeat, for example).

of these organs—breathing, heartbeat, blood pressure, perspiration, and the like.

When our brain interprets a situation as dangerous, it excites a special group of ANS fibers that quicken our heartbeat and produce the other changes that we experience as fear or anxiety. The ANS nerve fibers specifically responsible for these activities are referred to collectively as the **sympathetic nervous system** (in a sense, these nerve fibers are "sympathetic" to our emergency needs). The sympathetic nervous system is also called the fight-or-flight system, precisely because it prepares us for some kind of action in response to danger.

When a perceived danger passes, our functioning ordinarily returns to normal and our fear dissipates, thanks to the action of a second group of ANS nerve fibers, the **parasympathetic nervous system.** These fibers return our heartbeat and other body processes to normal.

These two parts of the ANS—the sympathetic and the parasympathetic nervous systems—thus work in complementary ways, each operating as a check on the other. Together they regulate our fear and anxiety reactions, as well as other responses to stress, and enable our body to maintain both the stability and the adaptability essential to life.

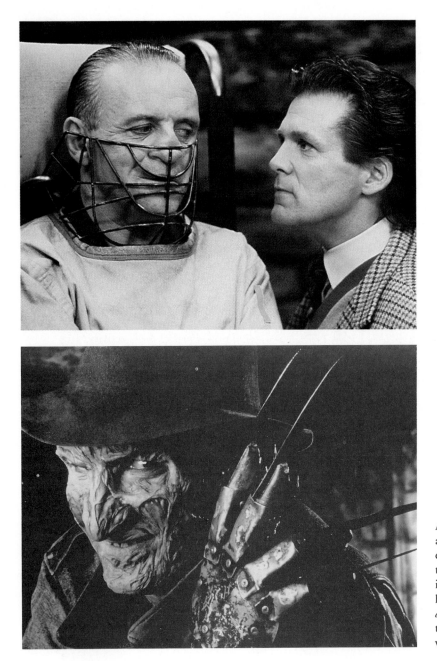

Although the experience of anxiety is usually perceived as unpleasant, most people enjoy the feeling when it occurs under controlled circumstances, such as when viewing a suspense or horror movie. Even here, however, viewers display differences in *situation anxiety.* Some are aroused by the sinister mind of Hannibal Lector, others by the violent acts of Freddy Krueger.

We all have our own patterns of autonomic nervous system functioning and our own ways of experiencing fear and anxiety. One person may respond to a threat by perspiring profusely and being gripped by a sense of dread; another may breathe faster and have difficulty concentrating, yet perspire very little. Similarly, we all have our own level of ongoing anxiety. Some people are always relaxed, while others almost always feel some tension, even when no threat is apparent. A person's general level of anxiety is sometimes called *trait anxiety,* because it seems to be a trait or characteristic that the person brings to each event in life (Spielberger,

1985, 1972, 1966). Some psychologists believe our trait anxiety reflects our early childhood experience — our feelings of safety or insecurity. But others have found that enduring differences in trait anxiety can be noted soon after birth (Marks, 1987; Fredrikson & Ohman, 1977; Thomas et al., 1963).

People also differ in their sense of which situations are threatening (Weiner, 1985; Stattin & Magnusson, 1980). Walking through a forest may be fearsome for one person but relaxing for another. Similarly, flying in an airplane may arouse terror in some people and boredom in others. Such variations are called differences in

Although most people are terrified by the very thought of hang gliding above the clouds, some are stimulated by the experience and others are calmed by it. Such individual reactions represent differences in situation, or state, anxiety.

*situation* or *state anxiety.* The fear and anxiety most of us have experienced, however, are quite different from the disproportionate, frequent, and enduring waves of tension and dread experienced by persons who suffer from an anxiety disorder.

# PHOBIC DISORDERS AND GENERALIZED ANXIETY DISORDERS

Phobic disorders, which involve excessive fears of specific objects or situations, and generalized anxiety disorders, which are marked by persistent and vague feelings of anxiety, are the two most common types of anxiety disorders. Although these disorders differ in character and impact, many theorists (sociological, psychodynamic, humanistic, and behavioral theorists, in particular) believe that they have similar roots.

## Phobic Disorders

Most of us are none too eager to visit the dentist (Chollar, 1989), but few of us have such dread of the drill as this woman:

*At the age of twelve, my eye teeth came through very* crooked and high up in the gum. I remember my mother dragging me along to the dentist and both of them standing behind me saying I would have to go into the hospital to have them out. . . . After that I would make up any excuse to get out of going. . . . I managed to bluff my way through school and it was such a relief when I actually left, as I knew no school dentist could come round wondering why I hadn't kept an appointment. Also, when I was at school we were always given a note asking us whether we would like to use the school dentist or the family one, and I always managed to forge my mother's signature stating the latter.

For the next ten years my life was unbearable. Looking back on it now, I honestly don't know how I didn't go off my head. I loved going out with boys, but most of them must have thought I was very shy or a miserable person: I could never laugh in public, only half-smile and bow my head. I could never relax, not even for a minute. Parties were unbearable, especially when someone told me a joke. And worst of all was the fact that I knew I would have to go to the dentist sometime in the future. As the years went by, my teeth got worse and I become more withdrawn. When I was twenty I did meet someone, and I knew if anyone would understand, it would be him, but I still could not bring myself to tell him, and on I went with my head bowed down and all the time thinking that I musn't open my mouth too much and knowing that I had to go the dentist in the end.

We became engaged on my twenty-first birthday, and a year later we got married. You can imagine my wedding day was unbearable for me. The wedding photos were a nightmare, with the photographers asking me to put my head up and smile, and the whole time I was in a cold sweat. Anyway, we moved to the south coast, my husband got a good job and I could stay at home and not talk to anyone, so therefore I didn't have to open my mouth at all. Then I became pregnant and of course I was petrified I would have a full medical check-up and would have to open my mouth. I told my husband that I had been to the doctor, but at seven months I was afraid that by not going I might endanger the baby, so eventually I went, and as luck would have it, nobody even bothered to look.

So my son was born and it was wonderful. While he was small my whole life changed. As a baby he didn't know what teeth were, and I could smile and laugh at him all day long. As I had never laughed, my face used to ache at the end of the day, but it was worth it. But all this time my phobia was growing; the teeth were getting worse and my son was getting older. Children are very honest, and I knew the time would come when I couldn't laugh with him any more, and this upset me more than anything. When he was two and a half we had our second child. And again laughing with her was wonderful, but I knew it couldn't last.

I had always wondered when my husband went to the dentist why he never mentioned that I never went, but I certainly wasn't going to. Every night I would lie in a cold sweat thinking about it, and as my son got older I knew I had to do something. Each night got worse; I couldn't sleep; I would wait until my husband was asleep and go downstairs and cry my eyes out. I honestly thought I was going mad. On one of my bad nights my husband came down, and I was in such a state that I managed to blurt the whole lot out. In the morning he got up and went to work, and . . . he came back at lunch time and said that he had had a long talk [with] the dentist and he understood how I felt and would see me the next day. That afternoon, and until 10:45 the next day, was unbearable. I was sick, I had diarrhea, I had a temperature and I certainly didn't sleep a wink. I took four tranquilizers that night and six the next morning, and in the end my husband had to practically carry me in. . . . Anyway, he told me I had left it so long that the roots were all twisted and that the front six teeth would have to come out. I still had about seven other fillings that needed doing, and I knew if I wanted the front ones done it would be no good not turning up for the other treatment. Each visit was a nightmare. Every time I went, my husband had to take hours off work, as if he hadn't been there I certainly wouldn't have turned up.

Eventually the dentist said that on the next visit he would take out the front six. My husband took the day off, and we went together. I had gas, and it was all over in a few seconds. I managed to get to the car and just sat there, and my husband handed me a present: a mirror. At first I was too afraid to look, but when I did I couldn't believe how radiant I looked. But I will never get over my phobia. In fact I am ashamed to admit I have not been back to the dentist since that last visit. I will walk half a mile out of my way rather than pass the door in case he sees me.

*(Melville, 1978, pp. 151–153)*

A phobia (from the Greek for "fear") is a persistent and unreasonable fear of a particular object, activity, or situation. People with a phobia become fearful if they even think about the dreaded object or situation, but they usually remain comfortable and functional as long as they avoid the object or thoughts about it. Like the woman who feared the dentist, people with phobias may continue to avoid their feared object or situation even after seemingly benign interactions with it. Most are well aware that their fears are excessive and unreasonable. Many have no idea how their fears started.

We all have our areas of special fear, and it is normal for some things to upset us more than other things. The objects and events we fear are often related to our stage in life. A survey of residents of a community in Burlington, Vermont, found that fears of crowds, death, injury, illness, and separation were more common among people in their 60s than in other age groups, whereas fears of snakes, heights, storms, enclosures, and social situations were much more prevalent among 20-year-olds (Agras, Sylvester, & Oliveau, 1969; see Figure 6-3).

How do these common fears differ from phobic disorders — that is, how does a "normal" fear of snakes differ from a snake phobia? DSM-III-R indicates that the fear experienced in a phobic disorder is more intense and persistent, and the desire to avoid the object or situation is more compelling. People with phobic disorders experience such distress that their fears often interfere dramatically with their personal, social, or occupational functioning.

Phobic disorders are common in our society. Random interviews of 9,000 people in the cities of St. Louis, New Haven, and Baltimore found phobia prevalence rates of 5.4 percent, 5.9 percent, and 13.4 percent, respectively (Myers et al., 1984). In all three cities phobic disorders were more than twice as common in women as in men.

Because some phobias share particular themes, DSM-II-R distinguishes three categories: agoraphobia, social phobias, and simple phobias. *Agoraphobia* (from the Greek for "fear of the marketplace") is a fear of public places, especially when one is alone. *Social phobias* are fears of some form of social evaluation and humiliation. All other phobias — the majority — are classified as simple phobias.

**Agoraphobia** The following reports describe the disorder of agoraphobia, a pervasive and complex phobia that makes people avoid public places or situations from which escape might be difficult should they develop symptoms that are incapacitating or embarrassing, such as dizziness or falling, loss of bladder or bowel control, vomiting, or chest pains. Between 2.7 and 5.8 percent of the people interviewed in St. Louis, New Haven, and

Baltimore reported having this problem, women twice as frequently as men (Myers et al., 1984). People typically develop agoraphobia in their 20s or 30s.

*For several months prior to her application for treatment* Veronica had been unable to leave her home. . . . "It is as if something dreadful would happen to me if I did not immediately go home." Even after she would return to the house, she would feel shaken inside and unable to speak to anyone or do anything for an hour or so. However, as long as she remained in her own home or garden, she was able to carry on her routine life without much problem. . . . Because of this agoraphobia, she had been unable to return to her position as a mathematics teacher in the local high school after the summer vacation.

. . . It was difficult for her to recall the first time . . . but it seemed to her that the first major experience was approximately a year before, when she and her mother had been Christmas shopping. They were standing in the middle of a crowded department store when she suddenly felt the impulse to flee. She left her mother without an explanation and drove home as fast as she could. Her mother was extremely angry, and she was unable to explain to her what had happened. She admitted that shopping with her mother was a trial, as her mother was a loud-voiced person who would badger store clerks and often "create a scene" if she did not get the immediate and complete service she demanded. Veronica said that she "just knew" that sooner or later her mother would embarrass her on this shopping tour. . . . After Christmas vacation she seemed to recover for a while and was at least able to return to her classroom duties without any ill effect. During the ensuing several months she had several similar experiences, usually when she was off duty; but by late spring these fears were just as likely to occur in the classroom. . . . In thinking further about the occurrence of her phobia, it seemed to Veronica that there was actually no particular stress which might account for her fear. Often it seemed to come over her when she was momentarily relaxed, although always when she was in public. For example, it might come over her while she was standing in the classroom watching her pupils during an examination, or, as in the initial experience, when she was standing in the middle of the ladies' dresses section of the store waiting for her mother to return from the restroom.

(*Goldstein & Palmer, 1975, pp. 163–164*)

*Barbara comes to the clinic because of fear of losing* her balance and either falling or fainting. (She has, in fact, never fallen or fainted.) The current difficulties began one year ago, shortly after she and her family moved away from her mother's neighborhood. Her husband went into his own business, which kept him away from home a lot. Before the move she could walk to her mother's and sister's houses. Now she lives so far from them that she knows they can't come over immediately if she needs them. At first she avoided going out of her new house, but she eventually

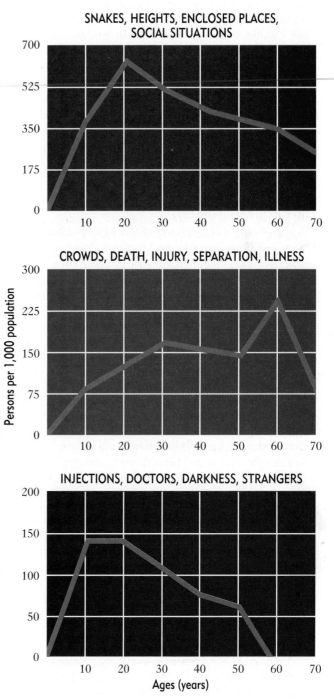

**FIGURE 6-3** Certain age groups are particularly likely to have certain fears. Close to 70 percent of all 20-year-olds surveyed in Burlington, Vermont—more than in any other age group—feared snakes and heights. On the other hand, 60-year-olds were more likely than persons of other ages to be afraid of crowds and of death, and 10-year-olds were more likely than others to fear injections and doctors. (*Adapted from Agras, Sylvester, & Oliveau, 1969, p. 153.*)

could go alone to small neighborhood stores and supermarkets if they were not crowded. . . .

The patient's present condition is a recurrence of symptoms she first experienced 12 years ago, immediately after her marriage. She began to fear losing her balance and falling. The more frightened she became, the more unsteady she felt. She became unable to go anywhere.

*(Spitzer et al., 1981, pp. 50–51)*

It is typical of people with agoraphobia to avoid entering crowded streets or stores, driving through tunnels or on bridges, traveling on public transportation, and using elevators (Table 6-1). If they venture out of the house at all, it is usually only in the company of close relatives or friends. Some people with agoraphobia further insist that family members or friends stay with them at home, but even at home and in the company of others they may continue to feel anxious.

In many cases the intensity of the agoraphobia fluctuates, as it did for Veronica and Barbara. In severe cases, people become virtual prisoners in their own homes. Their social life dwindles, and they cannot hold a job. Persons with agoraphobia may also become depressed, sometimes as a result of the severe limitations that their phobia places on their lives.

**Social Phobias**  Many people have qualms about talking or performing in front of others. The opera singer Maria Callas often shook with fear while waiting in the wings to perform, and Harold MacMillan, the former British prime minister, typically felt nauseous before question time in Parliament (Marks, 1987). Such normal social fears are inconvenient, but those who have them manage to function adequately, some at a very high level.

People with social phobias, on the other hand, have severe, persistent, and irrational fears of situations in which they may be exposed to scrutiny. A social phobia may be specific, such as a fear of talking or performing in public, eating in public, using a public bathroom, or writing in front of others, or it may be a broad fear of social situations, such as a general fear of functioning inadequately or inappropriately when others are watching. The distinguishing characteristic that sets social phobias off from normal social fears is the phobic person's inability to function in the feared situation.

Social phobias can be highly incapacitating. A person who is unable to speak in public may fail to perform important school or job responsibilities. One who cannot eat in public may reject dinner invitations and other social engagements. Since most of these people keep their fears secret, their social reluctance is often misinterpreted as snobbery, disinterest, or stubbornness. Consider this 28-year-old woman who was terrified that her hands would tremble in front of others:

*She therefore didn't like giving to or accepting from* strangers a drink or cup of tea or coffee. The first time this happened was when she was nineteen and was taken home by her boyfriend to meet his parents. Both this relationship and a succeeding one failed, and from then on she was conscious of her "phobia." She found her fears gradually spreading and affecting her work as a secretary. "At one time I found it difficult to take dictation and type it back if it

TABLE 6-1

| RANKING OF 20 WORST FEARS OF 76 AGORAPHOBICS "IF ENTIRELY ALONE IN THESE SITUATIONS" | | | |
|---|---|---|---|
| Rank | Fear | Rank | Fear |
| 1 | Feelings of panic | 11 | Being left alone |
| 2 | Fainting or collapsing | 12 | Going into crowded shops |
| 3 | Losing control | 13 | Standing in line |
| 4 | Causing a scene or public disturbance | 14 | Large open spaces |
| 5 | Going mad | 15 | Feeling anxious, nervous or agitated |
| 6 | Traveling by bus or train | 16 | Palpitations |
| 7 | Dying | 17 | Confusion; being unable to think clearly |
| 8 | Going far from home | 18 | Feeling that self and surroundings were strange or unreal |
| 9 | Having a heart attack | 19 | Trembling, shaking |
| 10 | Walking in busy streets | 20 | Weakness in the legs |

*Sources:* Marks, 1987, p. 332; Franklin, 1985.

George Tooker's painting *Subway* expresses the sense of threat, entrapment, and disorientation experienced by many people with agoraphobia when they enter public places.

was given to me just before I was due to leave the office, or if the work was needed urgently and my boss was waiting for it; I would panic and my fingers would just seize up. . . ." "I know everybody has some dread of something, but people accept somebody who has an aversion to mice or flies. If you don't like giving somebody a drink, though, they think you are antisocial and, if your hands shake, that you must either be 'on the bottle' or a complete wreck. It's strange, really, as I strike everybody as a confident person, but with certain people, regardless of whether they are 'ordinary' or 'impressive,' I become very self-conscious."

*(Melville, 1978, pp. 78–79)*

Social phobias are less common than agoraphobia. Between 1 and 2 percent of the population have this problem, again twice as many women as men (Myers et al., 1984). The disorder often begins in late childhood or early adolescence and may persist for many years, although its intensity may fluctuate over the years.

**Simple Phobias**   A *simple* or *specific phobia* is a persistent fear of an object or situation other than being in public places (agoraphobia) or in a socially humiliating situation (social phobia). The majority of phobic disorders fall into this category. Common simple phobias are intense fears of specific animals or insects, heights, closed

spaces, and thunderstorms. Many familiar and not-so-familiar simple phobias have been given names by clinicians (see Box 6-1). Here are a few firsthand descriptions (all in Melville, 1978):

*Spiders (arachnophobia) Seeing a spider makes me rigid* with fear, hot, trembling and dizzy. I have occasionally vomited and once fainted in order to escape from the situation. These symptoms last three or four days after seeing a spider. Realistic pictures can cause the same effect, especially if I inadvertently place my hand on one.

*(p. 44)*

*Birds (ornithophobia) When I'm in the house alone, I* always keep the windows and outside doors closed, even in hot weather. We live in an old house which has fireplaces in every room. I had the bedroom ones taken out and the chimneys blocked up. Downstairs we have gas fires, and I have had covers with small apertures made over these chimneys.

*(p. 124)*

*Flying (aerophobia) We got on board, and then there was* the take-off. There it was again, that horrible feeling as we gathered speed. It was creeping over me again, that old feeling of panic. I kept seeing everyone as puppets, all strapped to their seats with no control over their destinies, me included. Every time the plane did a variation of speed or route, my heart would leap and I would hurriedly ask what was happening. When the plane started to lose height, I was terrified that we were about to crash.

*(p. 59)*

*Thunderstorms (tonitrophobia) At the end of March each year, I start getting agitated because summer is coming and that means thunderstorms. I have been afraid since my early twenties, but the last three years have been the worst. I have such a heartbeat that for hours after a storm my whole left*

=== BOX 6-1 ===

# Phobias, Familiar and Not So Familiar

| | | | | | |
|---|---|---|---|---|---|
| Air | Aerophobia | Darkness | Achluophobia, nyctophobia | Foreigners | Zenophobia, xenophobia |
| Animals | Zoophobia | | | | |
| Bacteria | Bacteriophobia, microbiophobia | Dawn | Eosophobia | France and things French | Gallophobia |
| | | Daylight | Phengophobia | | |
| Beards | Pogonophobia | Death | Necrophobia, thanatophobia | Freedom | Eleutherophobia |
| Bees | Apiphobia, melissophobia | Demons, devils | Demonophobia | Fur | Doraphobia |
| Being afraid | Phobophobia | Depth | Bathophobia | Gaiety | Cherophobia |
| Being alone | Autophobia, monophobia, eremophobia | Dirt | Mysophobia, rhypophobia | Germany and things German | Germanophobia |
| | | Disease | Nosophobia, pathophobia | Germs | Spermophobia |
| Being beaten | Rhabdophobia | | | Ghosts | Phasmophobia |
| Being bound | Merinthophobia | Disorder | Ataxiophobia | Glass | Crystallophobia, hyalophobia |
| Being buried alive | Taphophobia | Dogs | Cynophobia | | |
| | | Dolls | Pediophobia | God | Theophobia |
| Being dirty | Automysophobia | Draft | Anemophobia | Grave | Taphophobia |
| Being scratched | Amychophobia | Dreams | Oneirophobia | Gravity | Barophobia |
| Being stared at | Scopophobia | Drugs | Pharmacophobia | Hair | Chaetophobia |
| Birds | Ornithophobia | Duration | Chronophobia | Heart disease | Cardiophobia |
| Blood | Hematophobia | Dust | Amathophobia | Heat | Thermophobia |
| Blushing | Ereuthophobia | Electricity | Electrophobia | Heaven | Ouranophobia |
| Books | Bibliophobia | Elevated places, heights | Acrophobia | Heights | Acrophobia |
| Cancer | Cancerophobia, carcinomato-phobia | | | Heredity | Patroiophobia |
| | | Empty rooms | Kenophobia | Home surroundings | Ecophobia, oikophobia |
| | | Enclosed space | Claustrophobia | | |
| Cats | Ailurophobia, gatophobia | England and things English | Anglophobia | Home | Domatophobia |
| | | | | Horses | Hippophobia |
| Chickens | Alektorophobia | Eyes | Ommatophobia | Human beings | Anthropophobia |
| Children | Pediophobia | Feces | Coprophobia | Ice, frost | Cryophobia |
| Choking | Pnigophobia | Failure | Kakorraphia-phobia | Illness | Nosemaphobia |
| Cholera | Cholerophobia | | | Imperfection | Atelophobia |
| Churches | Ecclesiaphobia | Fatigue | Ponophobia | Infection | Mysophobia, molysmophobia |
| Clouds | Nephophobia | Feathers | Pteronophobia | | |
| Cold | Psychrophobia, frigophobia | Fire | Pyrophobia | Infinity | Apeirophobia |
| | | Fish | Ichthyophobia | Inoculation, injections | Trypanophobia |
| Colors | Chromatophobia | Flood | Antlophobia | | |
| Corpse | Necrophobia | Flowers | Anthophobia | Insanity | Lyssophobia, maniaphobia |
| Crossing a bridge | Gephyrophobia | Flute | Aulophobia | | |
| | | Flying | Aerophobia | Insects | Entomophobia |
| Crowds | Ochlophobia | Fog | Homichlophobia | Itching | Acarophobia, scabiophobia |
| Crystals | Crystallophobia | Food | Sitophobia, cibophobia | | |
| Dampness | Hygrophobia | | | Jealousy | Zelophobia |

side is painful. Every time I promise myself that was the last time, I would rather kill myself than it happen again. I say I will stay in the room, but when it comes I am a jelly, reduced to nothing. I have a little cupboard and I go there, I press my eyes so hard I can't see for about an hour, and if I sit in the cupboard over an hour my husband has to straighten me up.

(p. 104)

*Closed spaces (claustrophobia) I can't bear being in a* room with the curtains drawn and the doors shut. As for

| | | | | | |
|---|---|---|---|---|---|
| Justice | Dikephobia | Pleasure | Hedonophobia | Speed | Tachophobia |
| Knees | Genuphobia | Points | Aichurophobia | Spiders | Arachnophobia |
| Lakes | Limnophobia | Poison | Toxiphobia | Spirits | Demonophobia |
| Leprosy | Leprophobia | Poverty | Peniaphobia | Stars | Siderophobia |
| Lice | Pediculophobia | Pregnancy | Maieusiophobia | Stillness | Eremophobia |
| Light | Photophobia, phengophobia | Punishment | Poinephobia | Stings | Cnidophobia |
| | | Rabies | Lyssophobia | Strangers | Xenophobia |
| Lightning | Astrapophobia, keraunophobia | Railways | Siderodromophobia | String | Linonophobia |
| | | | | Sun | Heliophobia |
| Machinery | Mechanophobia | Rain | Ombrophobia | Surgical operations | Ergasiophobia |
| Marriage | Gamophobia | Reptiles | Batrachophobia | | |
| Meat | Carnophobia | Ridicule | Katagelophobia | Swallowing | Phagophobia |
| Men | Androphobia | Rivers | Potamophobia | Syphilis | Syphilophobia |
| Metals | Metallophobia | Robbers | Harpaxophobia | Taste | Geumatophobia |
| Meteors | Meteotophobia | Ruin | Atephobia | Teeth | Odontophobia |
| Mice | Musophobia | Russia or things Russian | Russophobia | Thunder | Keraunophobia, tonitrophobia |
| Microbes | Bacilliphobia | | | | |
| Mind | Psychophobia | Rust | Iophobia | Touching or being touched | Haphephobia |
| Mirrors | Eisoptrophobia | Sacred things | Hierophobia | | |
| Missiles | Ballistophobia | Satan | Satanophobia | Travel | Hodophobia |
| Moisture | Hygrophobia | School | Scholionophobia, didaskaleinophobia | Trees | Dendrophobia |
| Money | Chrometophobia | | | Trembling | Tremophobia |
| Motion | Kinesophobia | | | Tuberculosis | Phthisiophobia, tuberculophobia |
| Nakedness | Gymnophobia | Sea | Thalassophobia | | |
| Names | Nomatophobia | Sex | Genophobia | Vehicles | Amaxophobia, ochophobia |
| Needles and pins | Belonophobia | Sexual intercourse | Coitophobia, cypridophobia | Venereal disease | Cypridophobia, venereophobia |
| New | Neophobia | Shadows | Sciophobia | | |
| Night | Nyctophobia | Sharp objects | Belonophobia | Vomiting | Emetophobia |
| Noise or loud talking | Phonophobia | Shock | Hormephobia | Walking | Basiphobia, batophobia |
| | | Skin | Dermatophobia | | |
| Novelty | Cainophobia, neophobia | Skin diseases | Dermatosiophobia | Wasps | Spheksophobia |
| | | Skin of animals | Doraphobia | Water | Hydrophobia |
| Odors | Osmophobia | Sleep · | Hypnophobia | Weakness | Asthenophobia |
| Odors (body) | Osphresiophobia | Slime | Blennophobia | Wind | Anemophobia |
| Open spaces | Agoraphobia, cenophobia, kenophobia | Smell | Olfactophobia | Women | Gynophobia |
| | | Smothering | Pnigerophobia | Words | Logophobia |
| | | Snakes | Ophidiophobia | Work | Ergasiophobia, ponophobia |
| Pain | Algophobia, odynephobia | Snow | Chionophobia | | |
| | | Society | Anthropophobia | Worms | Helminthophobia |
| Parasites | Parasitophobia, phthiriophobia | Solitude | Eremophobia | Wounds, injury | Traumatophobia |
| | | Sound | Akousticophobia | Writing | Graphophobia |
| Physical love | Erotophobia | Sourness | Acerophobia | | |
| Places | Topophobia | Speech | Lalophobia | | |

*(Melville, 1978, pp. 196–202)*

rooms with no windows, I would go raving mad if shut in one for five minutes. I can't stay down in large department stores with basement shopping for more than a few minutes; I have to go up to ground-floor level or I would pass out.

*(p. 139)*

The survey of residents in Burlington, Vermont, found that almost 7 percent of the sampled population had simple phobias, including phobias of illness and injuries (3.1 percent), storms (1.3 percent), animals (1.1 percent), death (0.5 percent), crowds (0.4 percent), and heights (0.4 percent) (Agras, 1969). The more recent tricity study found that 4.5 percent of St. Louis interviewees, 4.7 percent of New Haven interviewees, and 11.8 percent of Baltimore interviewees had simple phobias (Myers et al., 1984). Women with this disorder again outnumbered men by 2 to 1 — a gender difference that holds in studies extending across the United States and Europe (Weissman, 1988; Wittchen, 1987).

The impact of a simple phobia on a person's life depends on what arouses the fear. Some things are easier to avoid than others. People whose phobias center on dogs, insects, or water will repeatedly encounter the objects they dread. Their efforts to avoid them must be elaborate and impose great restrictions on their lives. People with snake phobias have a much easier time.

Simple phobias can develop at any time of life, although some, particularly animal phobias, tend to begin during childhood (Marks, 1987). These early-developing phobias often disappear on their own before adulthood. In one phase of the Vermont study the progress of children and adolescents with simple phobias was observed (Agras et al., 1969). Most improved to some degree over the course of five years, without any treatment at all, and 40 percent became totally free of symptoms. On the other hand, phobias that last into or begin during adulthood tend to hold on stubbornly and usually lessen only under treatment.

## Generalized Anxiety Disorders

*Bob Donaldson was a 22-year-old carpenter referred to the* psychiatric outpatient department of a community hospital. . . . During the initial interview Bob was visibly distressed. He appeared tense, worried, and frightened. He sat on the edge of his chair, tapping his foot and fidgeting with a pencil on the psychiatrist's desk. He sighed frequently, took deep breaths between sentences, and periodically exhaled audibly and changed his position as he attempted to relate his story:

*Bob:*   It's been an awful month. I can't seem to do anything. I don't know whether I'm coming or going. I'm afraid I'm going crazy or something.

*Doctor:*   What makes you think that?

*Bob:*   I can't concentrate. My boss tells me to do something and I start to do it, but before I've taken five steps I don't know what I started out to do. I get dizzy and I can feel my heart beating and everything looks like it's shimmering or far away from me or something — it's unbelievable.

*Doctor:*   What thoughts come to mind when you're feeling like this?

*Bob:*   I just think, "Oh, Christ, my heart is really beating, my head is swimming, my ears are ringing — I'm either going to die or go crazy."

*Doctor:*   What happens then?

*Bob:*   Well, it doesn't last more than a few seconds, I mean that intense feeling. I come back down to earth, but then I'm worrying what's the matter with me all the time, or checking my pulse to see how fast it's going, or feeling my palms to see if they're sweating.

*Doctor:*   Can others see what you're going through?

*Bob:*   You know, I doubt it. I hide it. I haven't been seeing my friends. You know, they say "Let's stop for a beer" or something after work and I give them some excuse — you know, like I have to do something around the house or with my car. I'm not with them when I'm with them anyway — I'm just sitting there worrying. My friend Pat said I was frowning all the time. So, anyway, I just go home and turn on the TV or pick up the sports page, but I can't really get into that either.

Bob went on to say that he had stopped playing softball because of fatigability and trouble concentrating. On several occasions during the past two weeks he was unable to go to work because he was "too nervous." Recently he felt especially easily distracted by roadside stimuli while driving and described a frightening sensation that the passing trees were falling over into his car.

*(Spitzer et al., 1983, pp. 11–12)*

Bob suffers from many of the symptoms of a generalized anxiety disorder, known in past diagnostic systems as *anxiety neurosis.* Like Bob, people with this disorder have chronic and persistent feelings of nervousness and agitation that are not clearly attached to a specific, identifiable threat. For this reason, their problem is often described as *free-floating anxiety.*

Like phobic disorders, generalized anxiety disorders are relatively common in our society. One survey of more than 3,000 people suggests that 6.4 percent of the general population have the symptoms (Uhlenhuth et al., 1983). Although the disorder may emerge at any age, it most commonly appears in the 20s and 30s. Women diagnosed with a generalized anxiety disorder, as with phobic disorders, outnumber men 2 to 1.

The DSM-III-R criteria for diagnosing a generalized anxiety disorder include at least six months of unrealistic or excessive anxiety about a variety of circumstances (APA, 1987). The anxiety is typically characterized by *muscular tension,* which causes the person to be shaky, jittery, jumpy, restless, or easily fatigued, and to feel tense, sore, or achy; *autonomic hyperactivity,* which results in perspiration, rapid breathing, palpitations, urinary frequency, diarrhea, dry mouth, a lump in the throat, or hot flashes or chills; and *vigilance and scanning,* which cause the individual to feel irritable, keyed up, on edge, or easily startled, and to have difficulty concentrating and falling or staying asleep (APA, 1987).

The majority of people with a generalized anxiety disorder also develop another anxiety disorder, such as a phobia, at some point in their life (Weissman, Myers, & Harding, 1978). Many experience mild depression as well (APA, 1987). Nevertheless, in contrast to those who suffer from agoraphobia or from a broad social phobia, most people with generalized anxiety are able to maintain adequate social relationships and occupational activities despite their discomfort. They may even achieve outstanding professional success—and feel anxious about it (see Box 6-2).

Pervasive anxiety is often difficult for friends and relatives to accept. It is unpleasant for them to see a loved one so anxious and tense, and a burden to be continually reassuring. Sometimes they accuse the anxious person of "wanting" to worry, "looking" for things to worry about, and being "happy" only when they worry. These characterizations are unfair and certainly foreign to the subjective experience of the sufferers themselves. People with a generalized anxiety disorder hardly feel happy. They feel that they are in a constant strug-

---

BOX 6-2

# I Hope They Don't Find Out . . .

In their struggles to become smart, successful, respected, and well liked, people are frequently beset by doubts and anxiety. Surprisingly, the same frightening feelings can also accompany the actual achievement of one's goals. Interviews with hundreds of successful men and women have shown that many of them suffer from what has come to be known as the *impostor phenomenon* — the deep, gnawing, anxious feeling that they do not deserve their success (Clance, 1987).

This anxiety is usually related to low self-esteem. The person recognizes his or her achievements, but attributes them not to competence and skill but to extreme hard work or the ability to flatter and manipulate others. People suffering from the impostor phenomenon simply deny that any real abilities of their own contributed to their achievements (Clance, 1985).

Some studies suggest that the impostor phenomenon may be more common in women than in men (Steinberg, 1986). Because women must fight the lingering belief that they are less fit than men personally, academically, and professionally, they are more susceptible to doubts about the true cause of their success. This finding is supported by the prevailing theories about the cause of the impostor phenomenon. One is that children who receive mixed signals about their achievements from parents, teachers, and friends may become confused. A child who is elected to a class office, for example, may be told by teachers and friends that she is smart, capable, and a good leader, but her parents may reinforce the idea that she won because she is pretty and popular. This judgment could lead the child to attribute future successes to factors other than skill and intelligence. Similarly, when a child does well in an area in which no other family member has any interest—music, say—the family's response may be to question and belittle the child's talent (Meer, 1985). When experiences of this sort are associated with other vulnerabilities, such as shyness and low self-esteem, they may lead to the impostor phenomenon.

"Impostors" may be motivated to accomplish a great deal in order to combat their feelings of inadequacy, but their anxiety never allows them to enjoy the fruits of their success. The impostor phenomenon is a painful cycle in which success leads to anxiety, which pushes the sufferer to greater achievements, which leads to more anxiety. Treatment typically focuses on instilling in these people a sense of competence and dispelling the myth that they are undeserving. A goal more difficult to attain would be to eliminate this form of societally induced stress by reevaluating our criteria for and obsession with success. In the meantime, clinicians will continue to try to reduce the effects of the impostor phenomenon.

gle, always threatened and defending themselves, and always trying to escape their pain.

# Explanations of Phobic and Generalized Anxiety Disorders

A variety of factors have been cited to explain the development of phobic and generalized anxiety disorders: the numerous stresses and changes of modern society; family pressures; personal conflicts, learning experiences, thoughts, and values; and predisposing biological processes. Supporters of the various models of psychopathology give different weights to different factors, and their explanations differ accordingly.

**Sociocultural Explanations**  According to sociocultural theorists, phobic and generalized anxiety disorders are more likely to develop in people who are confronted with situations and societal pressures that pose real danger. Studies have found that people in highly threatening environments are more likely to develop the general feelings of tension, anxiety, and fatigue, the exaggerated startle reactions, and the sleep disturbances that characterize generalized anxiety disorders, and the specific fears and avoidance behaviors that characterize phobic disorders (Melick, Logue, & Frederick, 1982; Kinston & Rosser, 1974).

Take the psychological impact of living near the Three Mile Island nuclear power plant in the aftermath of the March 1979 nuclear reactor accident (Bromet et al., 1982, 1980). In the months following the accident, mothers of preschool children living in the vicinity were found to display five times as many anxiety or depression disorders as mothers of comparable age and family structure living elsewhere. Although many of their disorders subsided during the following year, the Three Mile Island mothers continued to display elevated levels of anxiety or depression at a one-year follow-up.

Over the past several decades, a number of stressful changes have occurred in our society. Older workers have felt increasingly threatened by the introduction of computer technology, parents by the increased media attention to child abduction, and travelers by the heightened incidence of terrorism. In addition, there has been increased public concern about the dangers of nuclear energy. As sociocultural theorists might predict, these societal stresses have been accompanied by steady increases in the prevalence of phobic and generalized anxiety disorders throughout the United States. A 1975 survey of the general population indicated that 1.4 and 2.5 percent of the population suffered from phobic and

The stresses of living and working in a complex, highly technological society may also increase the prevalence of anxiety symptoms and disorders.

generalized anxiety disorders, respectively (Weissman et al., 1978). Those rates increased to 2.3 and 6.4 percent in a 1979 survey (Uhlenhuth et al., 1983); and a 1982 survey that examined phobic disorders but not generalized anxiety disorders indicated that between 5.4 and 13.4 percent of the population suffered from phobias (Myers et al., 1984).

Similarly, studies that have determined the rates in other societies (Japan, Britain, Poland, India, France, Italy, Chile, Israel, and Nigeria) suggest that the prevalence of anxiety symptoms often increases along with societal changes caused by war, political oppression, modernization, and related national events (Good & Kleinman, 1985; Inkeles, 1983; Lynn, 1982; Cattell & Scheier, 1961; Cattell & Warburton, 1961).

Nevertheless, although societal pressures may establish a climate in which phobic and generalized anxiety disorders are more likely to develop, sociocultural variables are not the only causes. After all, most people in war-torn, politically oppressed, or endangered societies do not develop anxiety disorders. Granted the broad influence of sociocultural factors, theorists still must explain why certain people develop these disorders and others do not. The psychodynamic, humanistic, behavioral, cognitive, and biological schools of thought have each tried to provide an explanation of this kind.

**Psychodynamic Explanations** Sigmund Freud (1933, 1917) formulated the initial psychodynamic explanations of phobic and generalized anxiety disorders. To begin with, he distinguished three kinds of anxiety: realistic, neurotic, and moral. We experience *realistic anxiety* when we confront genuine external dangers. This reaction is inborn, universal, and normal. We experience *neurotic anxiety* if we are repeatedly and excessively prevented, by our parents or by circumstances, from expressing our id impulses. We experience *moral anxiety* if we are punished or threatened for expressing our id impulses, come to perceive the id impulses themselves as threatening, and so become anxious whenever we feel those impulses.

As we saw in Chapter 2, Freud proposed that people try to control unacceptable impulses and accompanying neurotic and moral anxiety by employing ego defense mechanisms (see also Box 6-3). If these defenses perform unsatisfactorily, a person may develop an anxiety disorder. According to Freud, phobic disorders represent overreliance on certain defense mechanisms, whereas generalized anxiety disorders occur when defense mechanisms break down under stress.

In particular, Freud believed that phobic people make excessive use of the defense mechanisms of *repression* and *displacement* to control their underlying anxiety. Repeatedly they push their anxiety-producing impulses deeper into unconsciousness (repression) and transfer their fears to neutral objects or situations (displacement) that are easier to cope with and control. Although the new objects of fear are often related to the threatening impulses, the phobic person is not aware of the relationship.

Consider once again Freud's (1909) famous case of Little Hans, the child whose fear of horses was discussed in Chapter 3. Freud proposed that Hans became afraid of his own id impulses during his Oedipal stage (the third and fourth years of life). When he began to express sexual feelings toward his mother by handling his penis and asking his mother to place her finger on it, she threatened to cut off his penis and stressed that his desires were totally improper. This frightened Hans. He also became unconsciously afraid that his father would learn of his desires and castrate him. In short, Hans came to develop high levels of neurotic and moral anxiety. Rather than experience fear whenever he felt those id impulses and rather than fear his mother and father, Hans repressed the impulses and displaced his fears onto a neutral object — horses. According to Freud,

Hans chose horses because he had come to associate them with his father.

Freud saw generalized anxiety disorders, on the other hand, as a breakdown in a person's defenses. Defense mechanisms can become overwhelmed if one continually experiences extreme levels of anxiety, such as a child might experience when repeatedly and excessively punished for expressing id impulses. If, for example, a young boy is harshly spanked every time he cries for milk as an infant, messes his pants as a 2-year-old, and explores his genitals as a toddler, he may eventually come to believe that his various id impulses are extremely dangerous and may experience severe anxiety whenever he has such impulses. Ego defense mechanisms may also break down if they are weak or inadequate. Overprotected children, shielded by their parents from all frustrations and sources of anxiety, have little opportunity to develop effective defense mechanisms. Later, when they encounter the inevitable pressures of adult life, their defense mechanisms may be too weak to cope with the resulting anxieties.

To support the psychodynamic explanations of phobic and generalized anxiety disorders, researchers have tried to show that people do indeed employ repression and related defense mechanisms in the face of fear and anxiety (Eriksen & Kuethe, 1956; Zeller, 1950; Rosenzweig, 1938). In some studies of repression, experimenters have frightened subjects by presenting an apparent threat and have then measured how well the subjects remember the fear-arousing event. Consistent with psychodynamic expectations, researchers have found that subjects often forget many aspects of the upsetting events. In a famous study of this kind, Saul Rosenzweig (1943, 1933) arranged for subjects to fail half of the problems on an important test. He found that the subjects later remembered less about the problems they had answered incorrectly than about those they had answered successfully.

Still other psychodynamic researchers have tried to demonstrate that people with phobic and generalized anxiety disorders in particular use defense mechanisms excessively. Several evaluators have looked for evidence of repression in the transcripts of early therapy sessions with anxious patients. They have found that when patients with anxiety disorders are asked to discuss anxiety-arousing experiences, they do indeed often react defensively by quickly forgetting what they were just talking about, changing the direction of the discussion, or denying negative feelings (Horowitz et al., 1975; Luborsky, 1973).

Several findings are also consistent with the psychodynamic claim that extreme punishment for a child's early id impulses may lead to higher levels of anxiety at later points in life (Chiu, 1971; Whiting & Child, 1966; Whiting, 1963). An examination of different cultures in Kenya, India, Okinawa, Mexico, and the Philippines suggested a correlation between restrictive child-rearing practices and anxiety in adulthood (Whiting & Child, 1966). In cultures where children are regularly punished and threatened, adults seem to have more fears and anxieties. In addition, several studies have sup-

ported the psychodynamic position that extreme protectiveness by parents may also lead to heightened anxiety in their children (Jenkins, 1968; Eisenberg, 1958).

Although these studies are consistent with the psychodynamic explanations of phobic and generalized anxiety disorders, they have been criticized on several grounds. First, some scientists question whether certain studies show what they claim to show. When people are

---

BOX 6-3

# The Defense Never Rests

**S**igmund Freud claimed that the ego tries to defend itself from the anxiety arising out of the conflicts created by unacceptable desires. His daughter, Anna Freud (1895–1982), extended the concept of the ego defense mechanism beyond her father's reliance on repression as the key means for defense of the ego. Though repression is the cornerstone of the psychodynamic model of abnormality, it is but one of many methods by which the ego is thought to protect itself from anxiety. Some of these mechanisms are described below.

Anna Freud, the last of Sigmund Freud's six children, studied psychoanalysis with her father and then opened a practice next door to his. (In fact, they even shared a waiting room.) Her work on defense mechanisms, other ego activities, and child development eventually earned her a distinct identity and the respect of the clinical field.

ety-producing desires that would otherwise go unfulfilled.

*Example:* Pulling into the parking lot at school, a student finds the space he was about to enter suddenly filled by an aggressive, unpleasant person in an expensive sports car. Instead of confronting the offender, the student later fantasizes about getting out of his car and beating the other man to a pulp in front of admiring onlookers, who laud him for his courage and righteousness.

**Projection** is the attributing of one's own unacceptable motives or desires to others. Rather than admit to having an anxiety-producing impulse, such as anger toward another person, the individual represses the feelings and sees the other person as being the angry one.

*Example:* The disturbed executive who repressed his murderous desires may project his anger onto his employer and claim that it is actually the boss, not he, who is hostile.

**Rationalization,** one of the most common defense mechanisms, is the construction of a socially acceptable

---

**Repression** is the central focus of the psychoanalytic approach to therapy. All other defense mechanisms grow out of it. The person who engages in repression avoids anxiety by simply not allowing painful or dangerous thoughts to become conscious. Once thoughts have been repressed, other ego defense mechanisms may be employed to provide additional insulation.

*Example:* An executive's desire to run amok and kill his boss and colleagues at a board meeting is denied access to awareness.

**Denial** is an extreme sort of self-protection. A person who denies reality simply refuses to acknowledge the existence of an external source of anxiety.

*Example:* You have a final exam in abnormal psychology tomorrow and you are entirely unprepared, but you tell yourself that it's not actually an important exam and that there's no good reason not to go to see a movie tonight.

**Fantasy** is the use of imaginary events to satisfy unacceptable, anxi-

reluctant to talk about upsetting events early in therapy, they are not necessarily repressing those events. They may be consciously focusing on the positive aspects of their lives or be too embarrassed to share personal negative events until they develop trust in the therapist. Similarly, when studies show a relationship between parenting styles and individual anxiety, they are not necessarily establishing a causal relationship between these two variables. It could be that high levels of anxiety in children lead some parents to develop an overcontrolling or overprotective parenting style.

Second, even if people in these studies are exhibiting repression and if parenting styles do lead to anxiety, it does not necessarily follow that people with anxiety disorders are afraid of their id impulses or that ego defense mechanisms have broken down. Even proponents of the

reason for an action that actually reflects unworthy motives. Freud explained rationalization as an attempt to explain our behavior to ourselves and to others even though much of our behavior is motivated by unconscious drives that are irrational and infantile.
*Example:* A student explains away poor grades one semester to her concerned parents by citing the importance of the "total experience" of going to college and claiming that an overemphasis on grades would reduce the overall goal of a well-rounded education. This rationalization may hide an underlying fear of failure and lack of self-esteem.

**Reaction formation** is the adoption of behavior that is the exact opposite of impulses that one dare not express or even acknowledge.
*Example:* A man experiences homosexual feelings and responds by taking a strong antihomosexual stance in front of his colleagues.

**Displacement,** like projection, is a transferral of repressed desires and impulses. In this case one displaces one's hostility away from a dangerous object and onto a safer substitute.
*Example:* The student whose parking spot was taken may release his pent-up anger by going home and starting a fight with his girlfriend.

In **intellectualization (isolation)** one represses the emotional component of a reaction and resorts to a determinedly logical treatment of the problem at hand. Such an attitude is exemplified by Mr. Spock of the *Star Trek* television series, who believes that emotional responses interfere with the analysis of an event.
*Example:* A woman who has been raped gives a detached, methodical description of the effects that the ordeal is known to have on a victim.

**Undoing,** as the name suggests, is an attempt to atone for unacceptable desires or acts, frequently through ritualistic behavior.
*Example:* A woman who has murderous thoughts about her husband ceremoniously dusts and repositions their wedding photograph every time such thoughts occur to her.

**Regression** is a retreat from an anxiety-producing conflict to a developmental stage at which no one is expected to behave maturely and responsibly.
*Example:* A boy who is unable to cope with the anger he feels toward an unfeeling and rejecting mother reverts to infantile behavior, ceasing to take care of his basic needs and soiling his clothes, for instance.

**Identification** is the opposite of projection. Rather than attribute one's thoughts or feelings to someone else, one tries to increase one's sense of self-worth by taking on the values and feelings of the person who is causing the anxiety.
*Example:* In concentration camps during World War II, some prisoners adopted the behavior and attitudes of their oppressors, even to the point of harming other prisoners. By identifying with their captors, these prisoners were attempting to reduce their own fear.

**Overcompensation** is an attempt to cover up a personal weakness by focusing on another, more desirable trait.
*Example:* A very shy young woman overcompensates for her lack of social abilities and the problems that her awkwardness causes by spending many hours in the gym trying to perfect her physical condition.

**Sublimation** is the expression of sexual and aggressive energy in a way that is acceptable to society. This is a unique defense mechanism in that it can actually be quite constructive and beneficial to both the individual and the community. Freud saw love as sublimation at its best: it allows for the expression and gratification of sexual energy in a way that is socially acceptable.
*Example:* High achievers in our society—athletes, artists, surgeons, and other highly dedicated and skilled people—may be seen as reaching such high levels of accomplishment by directing other energies into their work.

psychodynamic perspective acknowledge that it is very difficult to develop research designs capable of testing the fundamental theoretical components of this model (Edelson, 1985; Fisher & Greenberg, 1978).

A final problem is that a number of research studies and clinical reports have actually contradicted the psychodynamic explanations (Heilbrun, 1980). In one, sixteen people with generalized anxiety disorders were interviewed to obtain development histories (Raskin et al., 1982). They reported relatively little of the excessive discipline or disturbed childhood environments that psychodynamic therapists might expect for people with this disorder.

**Humanistic and Existential Explanations**  Humanistic and existential theorists propose that phobic and generalized anxiety disorders, like other mental disorders, arise when people stop looking at themselves honestly and acceptingly, and instead deny and distort their true thoughts, emotions, and behavior. Their defensive lifestyles ultimately serve to make them extremely anxious and incapable of fulfilling their potential as human beings.

The humanistic position on why people develop phobic and generalized anxiety disorders is best illustrated by Carl Rogers's explanation. Rogers believes that certain people develop a defensive way of functioning when as children they fail to receive unconditional positive regard from significant others and in turn become overly critical of themselves. They develop harsh self-standards, called *conditions of worth,* which they try to meet by repeatedly distorting and denying their true experiences. Using such defensive techniques, individuals succeed only partially in feeling good about themselves; threatening self-judgments persist in breaking through and causing intense anxiety. This foundation of anxiety sets the stage for a phobic or generalized anxiety disorder or some other form of mental dysfunctioning.

Rogers and his colleagues have conducted a number of studies to test his explanation of abnormal functioning and have found some support for it (Chodorkoff, 1954). However, these investigations have usually grouped numerous kinds of mental disorders together and do not focus specifically on phobic and generalized anxiety disorders. Moreover, other humanistic theorists believe that traditional research methods cannot provide a fair test for humanistic explanations and have not even tried to test their ideas empirically. As a result, the humanistic explanations have received limited research verification.

Existentialists believe that phobic and generalized anxiety disorders grow out of *existential anxiety,* a universal human fear of the limits and responsibilities of one's existence (Tillich, 1952). We experience existential anxiety, they say, because as human beings we know that life is finite, and we fear that accidents, fate, and death await us. We also know that our actions and choices in life may have unexpected consequences, and we fear that we may hurt others unintentionally. Finally, we suspect that life in general has no purpose and that our own personal existence may ultimately lack meaning.

According to existentialists, people can confront their existential anxiety head on by taking responsibility for their actions, making decisions, making their lives meaningful, and appreciating their own uniqueness, or they can shrink from this confrontation. Caught up in the change, confusion, and strain of our highly organized, competitive, technical civilization, some people choose to lead "inauthentic lives": they deny their fears, overlook their freedom of choice, avoid taking responsibility for their lives, and conform excessively to the standards and guidelines imposed by society (May, 1967; Bugental, 1965). According to existentialists, such a lifestyle inevitably fails to reduce one's existential anxiety, and this anxiety continues to erupt in the form of anxiety disorders. Viktor Frankl explains phobias in this manner:

> The original total anxiety apparently seeks some concrete content, some objective representative of "death" and "life." . . . Often the very words in which patients describe their symptoms and complaints . . . can put us on the track of the real, the existential reason for the neurosis. Thus, a patient . . . expressed her anxiety as: "A feeling like hanging in the air." This was in fact an apt description of her whole spiritual situation.
>
> *(Frankl, 1965, p. 180)*

Like humanists, existentialists generally believe that traditional research methods are inadequate for examining the merits of their explanation. They argue that empirical investigations miss subtle, internal experiences by looking only at what can be observed and defined objectively. These theorists resort instead to logic, introspection, and individual case examples as evidence for their views on phobic and generalized anxiety disorders. As a result, little systematic research has been conducted on the existential viewpoint.

**Behavioral Explanations**  Behaviorists believe that people with phobic and generalized anxiety disorders learn, through conditioning, first to fear and later to avoid certain objects, situations, or events. In phobic disorders they learn to fear and avoid only a small number of objects or situations; in generalized anxiety disorders they acquire a broad range of such fears.

***Learning to Fear*** Behaviorists propose ***classical conditioning*** as a common way of acquiring fear reactions to objects or situations that are not inherently dangerous. Two events that occur close together in time become closely associated in a person's mind, and, as we saw in Chapter 2, the person then reacts similarly to each of them. If one event triggers a fear response, the other may also.

Approximately 70 years ago, a clinician described the case of a young woman who apparently acquired a phobic fear of running water through classical conditioning (Bagbey, 1922). As a child of 7 she went on a picnic with her mother and aunt, and ran off by herself into the woods after lunch. While she was climbing over some large rocks, her feet became deeply wedged between two of them, and the harder she tried to free herself, the more firmly trapped she became. No one heard her screams, and she became more and more terrified. In the terminology of behaviorists, the entrapment was eliciting a fear response.

Entrapment ⟶ Fear response

As she struggled to free her feet, the girl was also exposed to other stimuli. In particular, she heard a waterfall nearby. The sound of the running water became linked in her mind to her terrifying encounter with the rocks, and she developed a fear of running water as well.

Running water ⟶ Fear response

Eventually the aunt found the screaming child, freed her from the rocks, and gave her comfort and reassurance. However, significant psychological damage had occurred. From that day forward, the girl was terrified of running water. For years family members had to hold her down to bathe her. When she traveled on a train, friends had to cover the windows so that she would not have to look at any streams. The young woman had acquired a phobia through classical conditioning.

In conditioning terms, the entrapment was an ***unconditioned stimulus*** (US) that understandably elicited an ***unconditioned response*** (UR) of fear. The running water represented a ***conditioned stimulus*** (CS), a formerly neutral stimulus that became associated with entrapment in the child's mind and came to elicit a fear reaction. The newly acquired fear response was a ***conditioned response*** (CR).

CS: Running water ⟶ CR: Fear
US: Entrapment ⟶ UR: Fear

Another way of acquiring fear reactions is through ***modeling;*** that is, through observation and imitation (Bandura & Rosenthal, 1966). A person may observe that others are afraid of certain objects or events and develop fears of the same objects or events. Consider a

When people observe others (models) being afraid of or victimized by an object or situation, they themselves may develop a fear of the object. Alfred Hitchcock's film *The Birds* led to an increase in the incidence of ornithophobia (fear of birds) during the 1960s.

young boy whose mother is afraid of illnesses, doctors, and hospitals. She frequently expresses her fears over getting sick, visiting the doctor, and going to the hospital. After a while the boy himself may fear illnesses, doctors, and hospitals.

***Learning to Avoid*** Why should one fear-provoking experience develop into a long-term phobia? Shouldn't the trapped girl later have seen that running water would bring her no harm? Shouldn't the boy later see that illnesses are temporary and doctors and hospitals helpful? Behaviorists agree that fears will indeed undergo ***extinction*** if a person is repeatedly exposed to the feared object and sees that it brings no harm. After acquiring a fear response, however, people often try to avoid what they fear. Whenever they find themselves near a fearsome object, they quickly move away. They may also think ahead and take measures to ensure that such encounters will not occur. Remember that the girl had friends cover the windows on trains so that she could avoid looking at streams. Similarly, the boy may try to avoid visits to doctors, hospitals, and sick friends.

In the behavioral view, such ***avoidance behaviors*** develop through ***operant conditioning,*** the process by which we learn to behave in ways that are repeatedly rewarded. The girl and boy are repeatedly rewarded by a marked reduction in anxiety whenever they avoid the things they fear. Unfortunately, such avoidance also serves to preserve their fear responses (Miller, 1985,

1948; Mowrer, 1947, 1939). Phobic people do not get close to the dreaded objects often enough to learn that they are really quite harmless.

Behaviorists propose that specific learned fears will blossom into a generalized anxiety disorder when a person acquires a large number of them. This development is presumed to come about through *stimulus generalization:* responses to one stimulus are also elicited by similar stimuli. The fear of running water acquired by the girl in the rocks could have generalized to similar stimuli, such as milk being poured into a glass or even the sound of bubbly music. If a person experiences a series of upsetting events, if each event produces one or more feared stimuli, and if the person's reactions to each of these stimuli generalize to yet other stimuli, that person may build up a large number of fears and eventually develop a generalized anxiety disorder. According to behaviorists, then, the anxiety manifested in generalized anxiety disorders is broad but hardly free-floating.

***Evidence for the Behavioral Explanations***   A number of behavioral studies have indicated that fear reactions can indeed be acquired through conditioning. Some analogue experiments have found that laboratory animals can be taught to fear objects through classical conditioning (Miller, 1985, 1977, 1948; Mowrer, 1940, 1939). In these studies, experimenters typically place an animal in a shuttle box—a two-compartment box in which animals can jump over a barrier from one compartment to the other—and shock the animal through the floor after a few seconds. Initially, most animals react by running in circles, urinating, defecating, and crying out. After repeated trials, the animals show this reaction the moment they are placed in or even near the shuttle box, before the onset of shock. Because of its temporal association with shock, the box itself becomes a conditioned stimulus capable of eliciting conditioned fear responses.

These same studies have also demonstrated that animals can learn to avoid the shock of a shuttle box. While running around the box, most animals eventually cross the barrier into the other side of the box, which is safe from shock. In most cases, they discover that this is the road to safety, and henceforth jump over the barrier and escape to the safe side whenever they are shocked. Eventually the animals learn to avoid the threatening side altogether by going directly to the safe compartment before the current is even turned on. When experimenters use extremely traumatic stimuli (that is, higher levels of shock), fear and avoidance reactions are learned most rapidly—often in one trial—and are particularly hard to extinguish (Solomon, Kamin, & Wynne, 1953). In some experiments, animals have also learned to perform a task such as turning a wheel or pulling a lever to

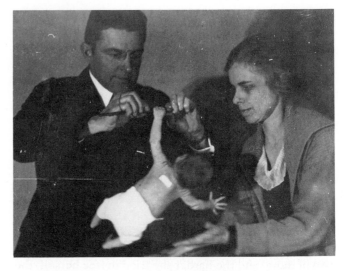

John B. Watson, pioneer of the American behaviorist movement, tests the grasping reflex of an infant. Watson never replicated the study in which he and his colleague Rosalie Rayner used classical conditioning to teach Little Albert to fear white rats. There is also some question as to whether the infant's fear reaction approached the strength of a phobia.

escape or avoid the dangerous side of a shuttle box. Their fear reaction seems to serve as a motive or drive that inspires them to acquire new behaviors.

Analogue studies with human beings have sometimes yielded similar results. In a famous report, J. B. Watson and R. Rayner (1920) described how they taught a baby boy called Little Albert to fear white rats. For weeks Albert was allowed to play with a white rat and appeared to enjoy doing so. One time when Albert reached for the rat, however, the experimenter struck a steel bar with a hammer, making a very loud noise that upset and frightened Albert. The next several times that Albert reached for the rat, the experimenter again made the loud noise. Albert acquired a fear and avoidance response to the rat. As Watson (1930) described it, "The instant the rat was shown, the baby began to cry . . . and began to crawl away so rapidly that he was caught with difficulty before he reached the edge of the mattress" (p. 161). According to some reports, Albert's fear of white rats also generalized to such objects as a rabbit, human hair, cotton, and even a Santa Claus mask.

Research has also supported the behavioral position that fears can be acquired through modeling. Albert Bandura and Theodore Rosenthal (1966) had human subjects observe a person apparently being shocked by electricity whenever a buzzer sounded. The victim was actually the experimenter's accomplice—in research terminology, a ***confederate***—who pretended to experience pain by twitching, writhing, and yelling whenever the buzzer went on. The unsuspecting subjects observed several such episodes, and before long they themselves underwent a fear reaction, indicated by an increase in their heart rate and in their galvanic skin response, whenever they heard the buzzer. When fear reactions are acquired through modeling in this way, the process is called *vicarious conditioning.* Clinical case reports of anxiety disorders sometimes paint a similar picture. During World War II, for example, cases were reported of combat airmen who became clinically anxious after observing other airmen display extreme anxiety (Grinker & Spiegel, 1945).

Similar modeling results have been obtained in a study of rhesus monkeys. Laboratory-reared adolescent monkeys, who had no fear of snakes, observed their wild-reared parents, who had a pronounced fear of snakes, behaving fearfully in the presence of real, toy, and model snakes. After six relatively short sessions of observation, the adolescent monkeys also demonstrated an intense fear of snakes (Mineka et al., 1984). In a follow-up study three months later, the adolescent monkeys continued to be afraid of snakes, real and simulated.

Although these studies support behaviorists' explanations of phobic and generalized anxiety disorders, other research has called those explanations into question (Marks, 1987). One study was unsuccessful in conditioning fear in fifteen infants as Watson and Rayner had done with Little Albert (Bregman, 1934). Indeed, Watson and Rayner themselves never reported a replication of their work and the study, as presented, has been challenged in recent years (Samelson, 1980; Harris, 1979). Similarly, several laboratory studies with adult subjects have attempted but failed to condition fear reactions (Hallam & Rachman, 1976; Bancroft, 1971; Marks & Gelder, 1967).

A number of clinical case reports also seem to contradict the behavioral position that phobic and generalized anxiety disorders result from specific conditioning incidents. Although specific events have been cited in some cases (Ost & Hugdahl, 1981), other cases suggest no such origin (Marks, 1987, 1983, 1977, 1969; Keuthen, 1980; Murray & Foote, 1979). In one investigation, only 25 percent of the phobic and generalized anxiety disorders of ninety-seven British airmen during peacetime could be traced to fearful incidents (Goorney & O'Connor, 1971). Similarly, although behaviorists propose that phobias are often acquired through modeling, people with phobic disorders do not usually have friends or relatives (models) with similar phobias (Marks, 1987; Marks & Herst, 1970). In summary, although researchers have found that these anxiety problems can be acquired by classical conditioning or modeling and retained by avoidance responses, they have not established that the disorders are ordinarily acquired in this way.

**A Behavioral-Biological Explanation** Some phobias are much more common than others. Phobic reactions to animals, heights, loud noises, illnesses, darkness, and water are relatively common, whereas phobic reactions to meat, grass, and houses are not (Marks, 1977, 1969). Behaviorists often account for this uneven distribution of fears by proposing that human beings, as a species, have a predisposition to develop certain fears (McNally, 1986; Marks, 1987, 1977, 1976; Ohman, 1986; Seligman & Hager, 1972; Seligman, 1971). This idea is referred to as *preparedness,* because human beings, theoretically, are "prepared" to acquire some phobias and not others. This point is clarified in the following case description:

> *A four-year-old girl was playing in the park. Thinking* that she saw a snake, she ran to her parents' car and jumped inside, slamming the door behind her. Unfortunately, the girl's hand was caught by the closing car door, the results of which were severe pain and several visits to the doctor. Before this, she may have been afraid of snakes, but not phobic. After this experience, a phobia developed, *not of cars or car doors, but of snakes.* The snake phobia persisted into adulthood, at which time she sought treatment from me.
>
> *(Marks, 1977, p. 192)*

Marks concludes, "Certain stimuli seem to act as magnets for phobias . . . as if human brains were preprogrammed to make these preferential connections easily" (p. 194).

Although Pavlov initially contended that "every imaginable phenomenon of the outer world . . . may be converted into a conditioned stimulus" (1928, p. 28), it may be that only certain stimuli — those that people are predisposed to fear — can be converted into conditioned fear stimuli. In one important test of this notion, investigators set out to condition fears in two groups of human subjects (Ohman, Erixon, & Lofberg, 1975). All subjects were shown slides of faces, houses, snakes, and spiders. One group received electric shocks whenever they observed the slides of faces and houses, while the other group was shocked during their observations of snakes and spiders. Using the subjects' galvanic skin responses as a measure of fear, the experimenters found that both groups initially learned to fear the intended objects after repeated shock pairings, but then they noted an interesting distinction: after a short shock-free period, the subjects who had learned to fear faces and houses stopped registering high GSRs in the presence of those objects; but subjects who had learned to fear snakes and spiders continued to show high GSRs in response to them for a long while. Their fears apparently continued even without the reinforcement of an accompanying shock. One interpretation of this finding is that animals and insects are stronger candidates for human phobias than faces or houses.

Researchers do not know whether such human fear predispositions are imposed biologically or culturally (McNally, 1986). Proponents of a biological predisposition argue that the fear propensities have been transmitted genetically through the evolutionary process (De Silva, Rachman, & Seligman, 1977). They suggest that the objects of common phobias represented real dangers to our ancestors and that the ancestors who more readily acquired a fear of animals, darkness, heights, and the like were more likely to survive long enough to reproduce. Proponents of a cultural predisposition argue that parents, friends, and experience teach us early in life that certain objects are legitimate sources of fear, and this training predisposes many people to acquire certain phobias (Carr, 1979). Research has supported each of these perspectives (McNally, 1986). As is so often the case in such circumstances, we may find that both biological and cultural factors are involved.

**Cognitive Explanations**    Cognitive explanations have focused on generalized anxiety disorders rather than on phobias. Some cognitive theorists believe that a generalized anxiety disorder can be caused by certain *maladaptive assumptions*. Others suggest that the people who develop such disorders are employing *faulty thinking processes.*

*Maladaptive Assumptions*    As we saw in Chapter 2, Albert Ellis believes that some people hold basic irrational assumptions that color their interpretations of events and lead to inappropriate emotional reactions (Ellis, 1984, 1977, 1962). According to Ellis, people with generalized anxiety disorders often hold the following assumptions:

> "It is a dire necessity for an adult human being to be loved or approved of by virtually every significant other person in his community."

> "It is awful and catastrophic when things are not the way one would very much like them to be."

> "If something is or may be dangerous or fearsome one should be terribly concerned about it and should keep dwelling on the possibility of its occurring."

When people with these basic assumptions are faced with a stressful event, such as an exam or a blind date, they are likely to interpret it as highly dangerous and threatening, to overreact, and to experience fear. As

they apply the assumptions to more and more life events, they may begin to develop a generalized anxiety disorder.

In a similar cognitive theory, Aaron Beck holds that people with a generalized anxiety disorder constantly hold unrealistic silent assumptions that imply that they are in imminent danger (Beck, 1991, 1976; Beck & Greenberg, 1988; Beck & Emery, 1985; Beck, Laude, & Bohnert, 1974):

> "Any strange situation should be regarded as dangerous."

> "A situation or a person is unsafe until proven to be safe."

> "It is always best to assume the worst."

> "My security and safety depend on anticipating and preparing myself at all times for any possible danger."

> "I cannot entrust my safety to someone else. I have to ensure my own security."

> "In unfamiliar situations, I must be wary and keep my mouth shut."

> "My survival depends on my always being competent and strong."

> "Strangers despise weakness."

> "If I am attacked, it will show that I appeared weak and socially inept."

> *(Beck & Emery, 1985, p. 63)*

Such silent assumptions lead people to experience narrow and persistent anxiety-provoking images and thoughts, called *automatic thoughts.* In a social situation they may have such automatic thoughts as "I'll make a fool of myself"; "I won't know what to say"; "People will laugh at me." When they work on important projects, they are plagued by thoughts of "What if I fail?"; "Other things might get in the way"; "I won't have enough time to do a good job"; "I'm falling behind."

Research has provided support for Ellis's and Beck's notion that maladaptive assumptions can induce anxiety. In several studies, nonanxious subjects who were manipulated into adopting negative views about themselves later developed signs of anxiety. For example, when normal college students were instructed to read to themselves such sentences as "My grades may not be good enough" and "I might flunk out of school," they temporarily responded with greater respiratory changes and emotional arousal than did control subjects who read neutral sentences (Rimm & Litvak, 1969).

Other studies have suggested that people who tend to worry and have negative thoughts and images typically experience such features of anxiety as general nervous tension, muscle tension, upset stomach, and a sinking and heavy feeling in the stomach (Borkovec, 1990, 1985; Borkovec et al., 1983). Such worriers also experience more thought intrusions and are more distracted than nonworriers when they try to concentrate on tasks.

Other experimenters have directly studied people with generalized anxiety disorders and have found that many do indeed hold dysfunctional assumptions (Himle et al., 1989; Mathews & MacLeod, 1986; Hibbert, 1984; Fox & Beck, 1983; Butler & Mathews, 1983). One study found that thirty-two subjects with generalized anxiety disorders held unrealistic notions of harm (Beck et al., 1974). Each subject reported upsetting assumptions, images, and automatic thoughts about at least one of the following danger areas: physical injury, illness, or death; mental illness; psychological impairment or loss of control; failure and inability to cope; and rejection, depreciation, and domination. Indeed, 70 percent of them had fears in three or more of these categories. Related studies have also found that people with generalized anxiety symptoms are more attentive to threatening cues than to other kinds of cues (MacLeod et al., 1986; Mathews & MacLeod, 1985).

Although these studies suggest that in the laboratory negative ideas can produce fear and that generalized anxiety disorders are often associated with negative assumptions, we must again recognize that cognitive researchers have not established that maladaptive assumptions are the actual cause of such disorders. It could be, for example, that once established, the higher level of anxiety experienced by people with these disorders predisposes them to view the world with fear and to develop negative ideas about themselves and their surroundings.

**Faulty Thinking Processes** Another cognitive perspective holds that people develop generalized anxiety disorders when they repeatedly employ faulty thinking processes, habitually interpreting harmless events as warning signals that danger is imminent. Cognitive theorists further believe that this type of thinking is likely to evolve in people who have repeatedly experienced unpredictable, painful, or negative events throughout their lives. To appreciate this explanation, we must first understand the relationship between unpredictability and fear.

**Unpredictability and Fear** Why do most people watching an Alfred Hitchcock movie experience so much tension and fear? It was Hitchcock's belief that audiences are *waiting* for something to happen. They know that a bomb blast, murder, or accident is going to occur, but they are not

sure when. He claimed it was the anticipation and lack of predictability that struck terror into the hearts of his fans.

Clinical investigators have found that Hitchcock understood fear quite well: studies have repeatedly demonstrated that the inability to predict a feared event brings about greater tension than an event that can be accurately predicted (Mineka, 1985). A series of studies compared the fear reactions of rats who were administered predictable electric shocks with those of rats given unpredictable shocks. A green light warned the former group that an electric shock was coming, but no such warning was given to the others. Rats given unpredictable shocks repeatedly manifested more signs of fear than those who received predictable shocks. The rats given unpredictable shocks spent less time exploring their cages (Badia & Culbertson, 1970), lost more weight (Pare, 1964; Brady, Thornton, & deFisher, 1962), and developed more severe ulcer problems (Price, 1972; Weiss, 1968). The results with human subjects tend to be similar. For example, human subjects show greater physiological arousal (that is, heightened galvanic skin responses) when they experience unpredictable shocks than when the shocks are delivered predictably (Price, 1972).

Similarly, subjects who have control over aversive events experience less fear in response to them than those who do not (Mineka & Hendersen, 1985; Weinberg & Levine, 1980). Human subjects who observed upsetting photographs showed lower galvanic skin responses when they believed they could turn off the photographs by pressing a button (Geer & Maisel, 1972); and human subjects taking important tests perspired less when they could at least control the order in which the tests were taken (Stotland & Blumenthal, 1964).

On the basis of such investigations, cognitive theorists have proposed that fear is generated by unpredictable negative events and is reduced by the presence of warning signals, such as a green light. Warning signals enable people to predict when danger is and is not imminent (Seligman, Maier, & Solomon, 1971; Seligman, 1968).

**Unpredictability and Generalized Anxiety Disorders** According to cognitive theorists, generalized anxiety disorders arise in people who have had too few warning signals in life. Whereas most people learn to feel safe and calm whenever warning signals are absent, those who experience few warning signals in life come to experience pervasive anxiety. They are like the viewer of an Alfred Hitchcock movie, always waiting for the boom to drop, never feeling confident that things are safe.

According to this perspective, people who have had few warning signals in life keep trying to identify warning signals to add predictability and calm to their lives. Because they are not experienced at specifying which events are legitimate signals, however, they wind up seeing warnings where none exists and generating broad anxiety. They are caught in an ever-widening circle of anxiety.

Consider two 3-year-olds at bedtime—a time many children seek to postpone. The parents of one toddler handle the issue with a set routine. They tell him that bedtime is approaching, read him a story, have a short talk in his bedroom, and finally say good night. The parents of the second toddler handle the situation differently: they go up to her at the last minute, take her directly to her bed, and quickly say good night. According to the cognitive view, the first couple are giving the child important warning signals each night: an announcement, a story, and bedtime conversation. The boy knows that in the absence of this bedtime routine he can relax; no one will be putting him to sleep. The second couple, however, are giving their child no warning signals. She does not know when to relax. Bedtime could be thrust upon her at any moment.

To reduce her fear, the second child may look for signals that warn her bedtime is coming, and she may incorrectly believe that she sees such signals in the expressions on her parents' faces, their tone of voice, the flush of a toilet, or other unconnected phenomena. In her search for predictability, she is creating mistaken warning signals, and each of these imagined signals generates more fear. If this child were to receive a sparsity of warning signals throughout her childhood, she might eventually develop a generalized anxiety disorder.

Although the research on unpredictability and anxiety is comprehensive, its application to the problem of generalized anxiety disorders remains tentative and largely theoretical. Researchers have yet to perform the difficult task of determining whether people with generalized anxiety disorders have as children experienced either fewer or qualitatively different warning signals than others.

**Biological Explanations**   Biological theorists have also focused chiefly on generalized anxiety disorders. Several important discoveries have led them to believe that these disorders are caused in part by biochemical dysfunctioning in the brain. The first of these discoveries was made in the 1950s, when researchers determined that *benzodiazepines,* the family of drugs that includes diazepam (Valium), alprazolam (Xanax), and chlordiazepoxide (Librium), provide relief from anxiety. No one understood, however, why they were effective.

It was not until the late 1970s that newly developed radioactive techniques enabled researchers to pinpoint the exact sites in the brain that are affected by benzodiazepines (Mohler & Okada, 1977; Braestrup et al., 1977; Squires & Braestrup, 1977). Apparently certain neurons receive the benzodiazepines, just as a lock receives a key. Particularly high concentrations of these neuroreceptors are located in the brain's limbic system and hypothalamus, brain areas known to be heavily involved in modulating emotional states (Costa, 1985; Hollister, 1982).

Investigators soon discovered that these same neuroreceptors ordinarily receive **gamma aminobutyric acid (GABA),** an important neurotransmitter in the brain (Costa et al., 1978, 1975; Haefely et al., 1975). As we saw in Chapter 2, neurotransmitters are chemicals that carry messages from one neuron to another neuron. GABA carries *inhibitory* messages: when GABA is received at a neuroreceptor, it causes the neuron to stop firing.

Researchers have gone on to study the possible role of GABA and GABA receptors in fear reactions (Snyder, 1986, 1981; Costa, 1985, 1983; Insel et al., 1984) and have pieced together the following scenario: in normal fear reactions, neurons throughout the brain fire more rapidly, trigger the firing of still more neurons, and create a general state of hyperexcitability throughout the brain and body; thus the increases in perspiration, breathing, and heartbeat. This state is experienced as fear or anxiety. After neuronal firing continues for a while, a feedback system is triggered and reduces the level of excitability. GABA-producing neurons throughout the brain release this neurotransmitter, which then binds to GABA receptors on receiving neurons and induces those neurons to stop firing. The state of excitability is thereby reduced, and the experience of fear or anxiety subsides.

Researchers believe that a problem in this feedback system can cause fear or anxiety to go unchecked. Some investigators have been able to generate and intensify fear or anxiety reactions in animals by reducing the capacity of GABA to bind to GABA receptors throughout the animals' brains (Costa, 1985; Haefely, 1985; Mohler et al., 1982; Braestrup et al., 1982). This finding suggests that people with a generalized anxiety disorder may have ongoing problems in their anxiety feedback system. Perhaps their brain supplies of GABA are too low, they have too few GABA receptors, or their GABA receptors do not readily bind the neurotransmitters.

If people with generalized anxiety disorders do have problems with their GABA feedback system, then corrections in the feedback system should reduce their chronically high levels of anxiety. This may be the reason that benzodiazepine drugs are so helpful to people

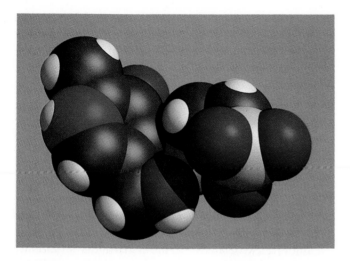

A computer-drawn molecule of gamma aminobutyric acid (GABA), the neurotransmitter that carries an inhibitory message to neuron receptors. Neurons that receive GABA stop firing, reducing the brain's state of excitability and the overall experience of anxiety.

with anxiety disorders. The benzodiazepines apparently go to GABA neuron receptors and enhance their ability to bind GABA (Costa & Guidotti, 1979).

Although promising, this explanation of generalized anxiety disorders has certain problems. One is that recent biological discoveries seem to complicate the picture. It has been found, for example, that GABA is only one of several body chemicals that can bind to the important GABA receptors (Bunney, 1981). Could these other chemicals, operating either alone or in conjunction with GABA, be critical factors in the brain's control of anxiety?

Another problem is that most of the research on the biological regulation of anxiety has been done on laboratory animals. When researchers generate fear responses in these animals, they are assuming that the animals are experiencing something that approximates human anxiety, but it is impossible to be certain. The animals may be experiencing a high level of arousal that is quite distinct from human anxiety.

Finally, biological theorists are faced with the problem of establishing a causal relationship. Although biological studies implicate physiological functioning in human anxiety disorders, they do not usually establish that the physiological events cause such disorders. The biological responses of chronically anxious adults may be the result rather than the cause of their anxiety disorders. Perhaps chronic anxiety eventually leads to poorer GABA reception.

Some researchers have tried to establish that biological dysfunctioning does actually precede the appearance of generalized anxiety disorders. Researchers have found, for example, that some infants become physically aroused very quickly while others remain placid in the face of the same degree of stimulation (Kagan, 1989; Thomas et al., 1963). It may be that these early differences reflect inborn arousal styles and that the easily aroused children are more likely to develop anxiety disorders later in life.

Some family pattern research is also consistent with the notion that generalized anxiety disorders are caused in part by a physiological predisposition. If biological tendencies toward generalized anxiety disorders are inherited, people who are biologically related should have more similar probabilities of developing this disorder. Concordance studies have indeed found that relatives of persons with a generalized anxiety disorder are more likely than nonrelatives to have the disorder too (Carey & Gottesman, 1981; Noyes et al., 1978). Approximately 15 percent of the relatives of people with generalized anxiety disorders themselves display a generalized anxiety disorder — proportionally many more than the 6 percent found in the general population. And the closer the relative (an identical twin, for example, as opposed to a fraternal twin or other sibling), the greater the likelihood that he or she will also have the anxiety disorder (Rosenthal, 1970; Slater & Shields, 1969). Similar data regarding phobic disorders are not available.

Of course, we must be careful in our interpretations of these studies. Although their findings are consistent with the view that biological abnormalities precede generalized anxiety disorders, they could also be suggesting that these disorders are caused by environmental experiences. Because relatives are likely to share aspects of the same environment, their shared disorders may be reflecting similarities in environment and upbringing rather than similarities in biological makeup. Indeed, the closer the relatives, the more similar their environmental experiences are likely to be. Because identical twins are more physically alike than fraternal twins, they may even experience more similarities in their upbringing.

Obviously, clinicians and researchers have generated many data and ideas about phobic and generalized anxiety disorders. At times, however, the sheer quantity of concepts and findings makes it difficult to grasp what is and what is not really known about the disorders. Moreover, each of the leading explanations has certain characteristic limitations. The psychodynamic and humanistic explanations have been difficult to research. Behavioral and cognitive researchers have been able to create anxiety symptoms in the laboratory by using the principles of their models but have failed to establish that anxiety disorders ordinarily develop in these ways. And biological researchers have yet to clarify the precise roles and importance of the biochemical correlates to these disorders. Given this state of affairs, it would be inaccurate to conclude that phobic and generalized anxiety disorders are well understood or that some explanations have a clear edge over others.

The same can be said of the remaining anxiety disorders — panic disorders, obsessive compulsive disorders, and post-traumatic stress disorders. Although clinicians and researchers now know more about them than they once did, an in-depth understanding remains elusive. As we shall see, obsessive compulsive and post-traumatic stress disorders have traditionally been even more difficult to explain than phobic and generalized anxiety disorders.

# PANIC DISORDERS

Sometimes an anxiety reaction accelerates into a smothering, nightmarish panic; one loses control of one's behavior, is practically unaware of what one is doing, and feels a sense of imminent doom. Anyone can react with panic if a situation is provocative enough. Usually such reactions occur when a threat is immense and comes on suddenly (see Box 6-4). Some people, however, experience *panic attacks* — discrete periods of panic that occur frequently, unpredictably, and without apparent provocation. Here two people describe their attacks:

*I was inside a very busy shopping precinct and all of* a sudden it happened: in a matter of seconds I was like a mad woman. It was like a nightmare, only I was awake; everything went black and sweat poured out of me — my body, my hands and even my hair got wet through. All the blood seemed to drain out of me; I went as white as a ghost. I felt as if I were going to collapse; it was as if I had no control over my limbs; my back and legs were very weak and I felt as though it were impossible to move. It was as if I had been taken over by some stronger force. I saw all the people looking at me — just faces, no bodies, all merged into one. My heart started pounding in my head and in my ears; I thought my heart was going to stop. I could see black and yellow lights. I could hear the voices of the people but from a long way off. I could not think of anything except the way I was feeling and that now I had to get out and run quickly or I would die. I must escape and get into the fresh air.

*(Hawkrigg, 1975)*

*When I experience an attack, I often feel dizzy and* off-balance. If the attack is particularly severe, I have difficulty concentrating and understanding things. Words, physical objects, and people may come to seem unreal, almost like in a dream. I sometimes don't know where I am or what I'm doing. The attacks are often followed by profound exhaustion. During parts of an attack, I sometimes experience involuntary thoughts and impulses — like having to walk a certain way. Shaking and trembling are common and I often feel hot afterwards. Much of the time I am sad and want to cry. Suicidal thoughts run through my mind and I have moments of feeling like I will soon kill myself. One of the most bizarre experiences during an attack is the feeling that I am two separate persons — one that thinks and one that acts. When I feel like this, it's like being in a bad dream — and I don't know what is real and I don't know if I am the thinking person or the acting one.

*(Nemiah, 1975)*

Panic attacks usually occur in harmless situations, come on suddenly, and last a matter of minutes. They typically include palpitations, tingling in the hands or feet, shortness of breath, sweating, hot and cold flashes, and trembling. These symptoms may be complemented by chest pains, choking sensations, faintness, dizziness, and a feeling of unreality. Small wonder that during an attack many people fear that they will die, go crazy, or lose control.

According to DSM-III-R, a diagnosis of **panic disorder** is warranted if a person's panic attacks include at least four of the symptoms mentioned above and if four attacks occur within a month or if one attack is followed by a month of persistent fear of another attack. Typically, however, people with panic disorders report far more than the required four symptoms. More than 85 percent of the panic patients in one study (Barlow, 1989) experienced palpitations, dizziness, sweating, difficult or painful breathing, fear of losing control, shaking, and hot or cold flashes. The panic disorder may disappear totally within months, but for most people it recurs several times or even becomes chronic (APA, 1987).

Between 0.7 and 3.0 percent of people in the United States suffer from panic disorders (Weissman, 1988; APA, 1987; Weissman et al., 1978; Uhlenhuth et al., 1983; Myers et al., 1984). The average age of onset is the late 20s. The disorder is equally common in men and women. In addition, many people experience panic attacks that are too mild or infrequent to be diagnosed as a panic disorder (Barlow, 1988). In one survey of 256 apparently normal young adults, 36 percent reported that they had had one or more panic attacks during the previous year (Norton et al., 1986). In another study of 173 students, 24 percent reported experiencing panic in the preceding week (Craske et al., 1986).

Past editions of the DSM linked panic disorders with generalized anxiety disorders in the category of "anxiety neurosis" because clinicians believed that panic attacks

## BOX 6-4

# Panic: Everyone Is Vulnerable

**M**ost people panic only in the face of a clear and overwhelming threat that unfolds at breakneck speed. Although people react to danger in a variety of ways (some even manage to think clearly and act constructively), panic is, unfortunately, quite common. The old vaudevillian Eddie Foy has described how a crowd reacted when fire broke out in a Chicago theater where he was performing:

As I ran around back of the rear drop, I could hear the murmur of excitement growing in the audience. Somebody had of course yelled "Fire!" — there is almost always a fool of that species in an audience; and there are always hundreds of people who go crazy the moment they hear the word. The crowd was beginning to surge toward the doors and already showing signs of a stampede. Those on the lower floor were not so badly frightened as those in the more dangerous balcony and gallery. Up there they were falling into panic.

I began shouting at the top of my voice, "Don't get excited. There's no danger. Take it easy!" And to Dillea, the orchestra leader, "Play, start an overture — anything! But play!" Some of his musicians were fleeing, but a few, and especially a fat little violinist, stuck nobly.

I stood perfectly still, hoping my apparent calm would have an equally calming effect on the crowd. Those on the lower floor heard me and seemed

Overflowing and uncontrollable crowds led to horror and panic when a wall collapsed at the European Cup soccer finals in Brussels in 1985. Thousands of persons were injured and thirty-eight were killed.

somewhat reassured. But up above, and especially in the gallery, they had gone mad. The horror in the auditorium was beyond all description. . . . As I left the stage the last of the ropes holding up the drops burned through, and with them the whole loft collapsed with a terrifying crash, bringing down tons of burning material. With that, all the lights in the house went out and another great balloon of flame leaped out into the auditorium. . . . The fire-escape ladders could not accommodate the crowd, and many fell or jumped to death on the pavement below. Some were not killed only because they landed on the cushion of bodies of those who had gone before.

But it was inside the house that the greatest loss of life occurred, especially on the stairways leading down from the second balcony. Here most of the dead were trampled or smothered, though many jumped or fell over the balustrade to the floor of the foyer.

In places on the stairways, particularly where a turn caused a jam, bodies were piled seven or eight feet deep. Firemen and police confronted a sickening task in disentangling them. An occasional living person was found in the heaps, but most of these were terribly injured. The heel prints on the dead faces mutely testified to the cruel fact that human animals stricken by terror are as mad and ruthless as stampeding cattle. Many bodies had the clothes torn from them, and some had the flesh trodden from their bones.

The fire department arrived quickly after the alarm and extinguished the flames in the auditorium so promptly that no more than the plush upholstery was burned off the seats. But when a fire chief thrust his head through a side exit and shouted, "Is anybody alive in here?" no one answered. The few who were not dead were insensible or dying. Within ten minutes from the beginning of the fire, bodies were being laid in rows on the sidewalks, and all the ambulances and dead-wagons in the city could not keep up with the ghastly harvest. Within twenty-four hours Chicago knew that at least 587 were dead and many more injured. Subsequent deaths among the injured brought the list up to 602.

*(From the book* Clowning through Life, *by Eddie Foy and Alvin F. Harlow. Copyright 1928 by E. P. Dutton & Co., Inc. Renewal © 1956 by Alvin F. Harlow. Reprinted by permission of the publishers.)*

emerge only within a larger pattern of general anxiety. DSM-III-R, however, views panic disorders as a separate disorder. Clinicians have concluded that the broad anxiety that often persists between panic attacks is generally the direct result of the panic attacks rather than part of a general pattern. That is, most people find a panic attack so terrifying that they become preoccupied with worry about the next one (Barlow, 1988; Munjack, 1984).

When they have to go somewhere, they wonder, "Will I have an attack while I'm driving?" As they get ready for a party, they worry that they will panic in front of the other people there. Many sufferers worry also that their symptoms indicate a significant medical problem, such as coronary heart disease (Hibbert, 1984).

Panic attacks are often accompanied by agoraphobia (fear of venturing into public places from which escape might be difficult), a pattern that DSM-III-R terms *panic disorder with agoraphobia.* In such cases, the agoraphobic pattern usually seems to emerge from the panic attacks (Barlow, 1988; Munjack, 1984; Klein, 1981). After initially experiencing unpredictable and recurrent panic attacks, people become fearful of having one someplace where help is unavailable or escape difficult. Anne Watson was one such person:

*Ms. Watson reported that until the onset of her current* problems two years ago, she had led a normal and happy life. At that time an uncle to whom she had been extremely close in her childhood died following a sudden unexpected heart attack. Though she had not seen her uncle frequently in recent years, Anne was considerably upset by his death. Nevertheless, after two or three months her mood returned to normal. Six months after his death she was returning home from work one evening when suddenly she felt that she couldn't catch her breath. Her heart began to pound, and she broke out into a cold sweat. Things began to seem unreal, her legs felt leaden, and she became sure she would die or faint before she reached home. She asked a passerby to help her get a taxi and went to a nearby hospital emergency room. The doctors there found her physical examination, blood count and chemistries, and electrocardiogram all completely normal. . . . By the time the examination was finished Anne had recovered completely and was able to leave the hospital and return home on her own. The incident had no effect on her daily life.

Four weeks later Ms. Watson had a second similar attack while preparing dinner at home. She made an appointment to see her family doctor, but again, all examinations were normal. She decided to put the episodes out of her mind and continue with her normal activities. Within the next several weeks, however, she had four attacks and noticed that she began to worry about when the next one would occur. . . .

She then found herself constantly thinking about her anxieties as attacks continued; she began to dread leaving the house alone for fear she would be stranded, helpless and alone, by an attack. She began to avoid going to movies, parties, and dinners with friends for fear she would have an attack and be embarrassed by her need to leave. When household chores necessitated driving, she waited until it was possible to take her children or a friend along for the ride. She also began walking the twenty blocks to her office to avoid the possibility of being trapped in a subway car between stops when an attack occurred.

*(Spitzer et al., 1983, pp. 7–8)*

Clinicians now believe that most cases of panic disorder may be accompanied by agoraphobia (APA, 1987). Surveys suggest that between 0.7 and 2.0 percent of the population manifest this kind of panic disorder at any given time (Weissman, 1988; Pollard & Henderson, 1988; Angst & Dobler-Mikola, 1983). Women who receive this diagnosis outnumber men 2 to 1. Like other panic disorders, this one typically begins during a person's late 20s. Cases of panic disorder without the symptoms of agoraphobia are simply designated *panic disorders without agoraphobia* in DSM-III-R. Cases of agoraphobia without panic origins are labeled *agoraphobia without history of panic disorder.*

Biological researchers have led the way in explaining panic disorders as a unique anxiety disorder with unique causes. Cognitive researchers have built upon the insights gathered from biological research.

## Biological Explanations

The biological explanation for panic disorders had its beginning in the 1960s with the surprising discovery that people with panic disorders were helped not by benzodiazepine drugs, the drugs so effective in treating other anxiety disorders, but by *antidepressant drugs,* drugs that are usually used to alleviate the symptoms of depression (Klein, 1964; Klein & Fink, 1962). Researchers thus reasoned that panic and anxiety may involve different biological processes and that panic disorders may have a different biological basis from other anxiety disorders (Redmond, 1985; Klein, 1964).

To understand the biology of panic disorders, researchers worked backward from their understanding of antidepressant drugs, just as they had worked backward from their knowledge of benzodiazepines to understand the biochemical underpinnings of generalized anxiety disorders. They knew that antidepressant drugs alter the activity of *norepinephrine,* a chemical that carries messages from neuron to neuron in the brain.

If antidepressant drugs alter norepinephrine activity in such a way as to eliminate panic attacks, researchers wondered, might it be that panic disorders are caused in the first place by abnormal norepinephrine activity? They have gathered evidence that norepinephrine activity may indeed be irregular in people who experience panic attacks (Gorman et al., 1989; Shear & Fyer, 1988). For example, when the *locus coeruleus*—a brain area rich in neurons that use norepinephrine (see Figure 6-4)—is electrically stimulated in monkeys, the monkeys display a paniclike reaction. Conversely, when this norepinephrine-rich brain area is surgically damaged, monkeys show virtually no reactions at all, even in the

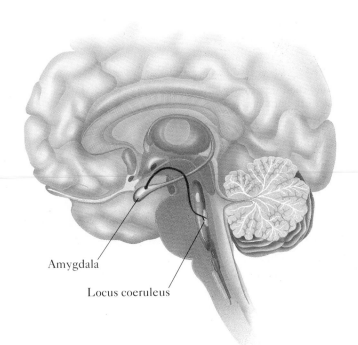

Amygdala

Locus coeruleus

**FIGURE 6-4** The locus coeruleus, a small area in the brain stem, sends its major messages to the amygdala, a structure in the brain's limbic system that is known to trigger emotional reactions. The neurons of the locus coeruleus use norepinephrine, a neurotransmitter implicated in panic disorders and in depression.

face of unmistakable danger. This finding suggests that panic reactions may be related to changes in norepinephrine activity in the locus coeruleus (Redmond, 1981, 1979, 1977; Redmond & Huang, 1979).

In another line of research, scientists have induced panic attacks in human beings by administering chemicals known to alter the activity of norepinephrine (Fyer et al., 1985; Liebowitz et al., 1985). When low doses of the chemical compound *yohimbine* were given to subjects who suffered from panic disorders, many of them immediately experienced a panic attack (Uhde et al., 1985). A placebo drug administered to the same subjects resulted in no such panic reactions. Another study successfully used yohimbine to induce panic symptoms even in people with no history of panic (Charney, Heninger, & Redmond, 1984, 1983). Such studies strongly implicate norepinephrine in the generation of panic attacks, because yohimbine alters norepinephrine functioning, particularly in the locus coeruleus, without having any effect at all on the operations of other neurotransmitters in the brain (Den Boer et al., 1990).

Still other drugs known to alter norepinephrine activity in the locus coeruleus have been tested and shown to *reduce* panic symptoms. One of them, a blood pressure medication named *clonidine,* was given intravenously to

eleven subjects suffering from panic disorder with agoraphobia, eighteen subjects suffering from anxiety mixed with depression, and nineteen subjects who were considered normal (Siever & Uhde, 1984; Uhde et al., 1984; Uhde et al., 1982). Clonidine reduced the symptoms of the subjects with panic disorders significantly more than a placebo did; it also reduced their general anxiety levels much more markedly.

Although these studies seem to point to abnormal norepinephrine activity in the locus coeruleus as a key cause of panic disorders (Gorman et al., 1989), the nature of this abnormal activity is still not fully understood. Nevertheless, whatever the precise biological abnormalities may be, they appear to be different from those that cause generalized anxiety disorders.

## Cognitive-Biological Explanations

A growing number of theorists believe that biological and cognitive factors combine to produce panic disorders (Barlow, 1989, 1988; Beck, 1988; Chambless, 1988; Shear, 1988; Rapee, 1988; Clark, 1988). They think that panic-prone people may be highly sensitive to certain physical sensations and misinterpret them as indicative of an imminent catastrophe. Rather than understanding the probable cause of their sensations as "something I ate" or "a fight with the boss," the panic-prone grow increasingly worried about losing control, fear the worst, lose all perspective, and rapidly deteriorate into panic. Expecting that their "dangerous" sensations may return at any time, they set themselves up for future misinterpretations and panic attacks.

Why might some people be prone to such misinterpretations? A variety of factors have been cited, including inadequate coping skills, lack of social support, and a childhood characterized by unpredictability and lack of control (Barlow, 1989, 1988). Whatever the precise causes, research suggests that panic-prone individuals become preoccupied with their bodily sensations and lose their ability to assess them in a logical and informed manner. In one study, panic patients responding to the self-report inventory shown in Table 6-2 reported much more difficulty "reasoning," "thinking objectively," and "focusing on the facts" in the face of bodily arousal than did patients with other kinds of anxiety disorders (Beck & Sokol-Kessler, 1986).

According to cognitive theorists, there are several kinds of sensations that such people tend to misinterpret. Some panic-prone individuals seem to "overbreathe" and hyperventilate in stressful situations. Apparently the abnormal breathing makes them think they are dying and so they panic (Turner et al., 1988; Gor-

TABLE 6-2

| COGNITIVE DYSFUNCTION INVENTORY, WITH SCORING KEY* | | | | |
|---|---|---|---|---|
| INSTRUCTIONS: Try to think back to your recent panic attacks and then determine how well each of the statements below seems to describe you at the time of the attack. | | | | |
| When I am having a panic attack . . . | | | | |
| | Not at all | Slightly | Moderately | Completely |
| 1. I have difficulty reasoning. | 0 | 1 | 2 | 3 |
| 2. I remain coolheaded. | 3 | 2 | 1 | 0 |
| 3. My mind goes blank. | 0 | 1 | 2 | 3 |
| 4. I can think clearly about what is happening to me. | 3 | 2 | 1 | 0 |
| 5. I can examine my fears realistically. | 3 | 2 | 1 | 0 |
| 6. I remember others' advice and apply it. | 3 | 2 | 1 | 0 |
| 7. All I can think of is how I feel. | 0 | 1 | 2 | 3 |
| 8. I am able to focus on the facts. | 3 | 2 | 1 | 0 |
| 9. I think of a variety of solutions. | 3 | 2 | 1 | 0 |
| 10. I imagine the worst. | 0 | 1 | 2 | 3 |
| 11. I can distract myself. | 3 | 2 | 1 | 0 |
| 12. My mind does not function normally. | 0 | 1 | 2 | 3 |
| 13. I am not able to think objectively about my symptoms. | 0 | 1 | 2 | 3 |
| 14. I picture frightening things that could happen to me. | 0 | 1 | 2 | 3 |
| 15. I am able to apply logic to my problem. | 3 | 2 | 1 | 0 |
| 16. I can't think straight. | 0 | 1 | 2 | 3 |

\* The more difficulty people have thinking clearly, the higher their total score.
Source: Beck, 1988, p. 100.

man et al., 1986; Liebowitz, 1985; Griez & Van Den Hout, 1983). Similarly, some people with panic disorders have *mitral valve prolapse (MVP),* a cardiac malfunction marked by periodic episodes of heart palpitations (Gorman et al., 1986, 1981; Grunhaus et al., 1981; Kantor et al., 1980). Stewart Agras (1985) found that 43 of 106 subjects with panic disorders also had mitral valve prolapse (40 percent), compared with 4 of 43 persons who did not have a panic disorder (9 percent). Some researchers have concluded that panic attacks may be misinterpreted MVP attacks. Of course, it is just as possible that repeated panic attacks come to cause valvular defects and MVP, or that both panic attacks and MVP are caused by yet another biological abnormality. Moreover, although mitral valve prolapse does share some important symptoms with panic attacks, the two disorders also differ on a number of symptoms (see Table 6-3).

The physical sensations that trigger misinterpretations in the panic-prone vary from individual to individual and include euphoric excitement, fullness in the abdomen, slowing of breathing, acute anger, and sudden tearing in one's eyes (Sokol-Kessler & Beck, 1987). One patient, on learning that her artwork had been accepted for exhibit at a gallery, became extremely excited, experienced "palpitations of the heart," misinterpreted them as a sign of a heart attack, and panicked. Another patient was told of a relative's death, felt tears spring to his eyes, feared he was about to cry uncontrollably, and began to panic.

This cognitive-biological explanation of panic disorders has only recently begun to capture the attention of panic theorists. As we have noted, research already suggests that the panic-prone may interpret bodily sensations in ways that are not at all common. How different and how important such misinterpretations are, and pre-cisely how they interact with biological factors, are questions that need to be answered in the coming years.

# OBSESSIVE COMPULSIVE DISORDERS

*Obsessions* are repetitive thoughts, ideas, impulses, or mental images that seem to invade a person's consciousness. *Compulsions* are repetitive and rigid activities that a person feels compelled to perform. Minor obsessions and compulsions are familiar to almost everyone. We may find ourselves preoccupied with thoughts about an upcoming concert, date, examination, or vacation; worry that we forgot to turn off the stove or lock the door; or be haunted for days by the same song, melody, or poem. Similarly, we may avoid stepping on cracks, turn away from black cats, follow a strict routine every morning, or arrange our closets in a carefully prescribed manner.

Minor obsessions and compulsions can play a helpful role in life. Distracting tunes or little rituals often calm us during times of stress. A man who repeatedly clicks his pen, hums a tune, or taps his fingers during a test may be releasing tension and thus improving his performance. Similarly, many people find it comforting to repeat religious or cultural rituals, such as touching a mezuzah, sprinkling holy water, or fingering rosary beads.

When obsessions and compulsions are extreme, unwelcome, persistent, and disabling, however, the pattern is diagnosed as a disorder (Solyom, Ledwidge, & Solyom, 1986). In these cases the repetitive thoughts and actions are intrusive and hard to dismiss, feel foreign to the victim, and are almost always unwanted and upsetting. According to DSM-III-R, a diagnosis of **obsessive compulsive disorder** is appropriate for people who suffer significant distress or impaired functioning because of such obsessions or compulsions. Obsessive compulsive disorders are classified as anxiety disorders because the victims experience intense anxiety if they try to resist their obsessions or compulsions. Consider the obsessive compulsive pattern displayed by Georgia, whose husband complained, "If neatness was an Olympic sport, Georgia would easily have been captain of the team."

*Y*ou remember that old joke about getting up in the middle of the night to go to the john and coming back to the bedroom to find your wife has made the bed? It's no joke. Sometimes I think she never sleeps. I got up one night at 4 A.M. and there she was doing the laundry downstairs. Look at your ash tray! I haven't seen one that dirty in years! I'll tell

TABLE 6-3

| RELATIVE FREQUENCY OF SYMPTOMS OF MITRAL VALVE PROLAPSE AND PANIC DISORDERS | | |
|---|---|---|
| Symptom | Mitral valve prolapse | Panic disorders |
| Fatigue | + | − |
| Dyspnea (difficulty breathing) | + | ++ |
| Palpitations | ++ | ++ |
| Chest pain | ++ | + |
| Syncope (faintness) | + | − |
| Choking | − | ++ |
| Dizziness | − | ++ |
| Derealization | − | ++ |
| Hot/cold flashes | − | ++ |
| Sweating | − | ++ |
| Fainting | − | ++ |
| Trembling | − | ++ |
| Fear of dying, going crazy, losing control | − | ++ |

+ *occasionally*
++ *often*
− *rarely*
*Source:* Hollander, Liebowitz, & Gorman, 1988, p. 455.

you what it makes me feel like. If I forget to leave my dirty shoes outside the back door she gives me a look like I had just crapped in the middle of an operating room. I stay out of the house a lot and I'm about half-stoned when I do have to be home. She even made us get rid of the dog because she said he was always filthy. When we used to have people over for supper she would jitterbug around everybody till they couldn't digest their food. I hated to call them up and ask them over because I could always hear them hem and haw and make up excuses not to come over. Even the kids are walking down the street nervous about getting dirt on them. I'm going out of my mind but you can't talk to her. She just blows up and spends twice as much time cleaning things. We have guys in to wash the walls so often I think the house is going to fall down from being scrubbed all the time. About a week ago I had it up to here and told her I couldn't take it any more. I think the only reason she came to see you was because I told her I was going to take off and live in a pig pen just for laughs.

Georgia's obsessive concern with cleanliness forced her to take as many as three showers a day, one in the morning, one before supper, and one before going to bed, and, on hot days, the number of showers would rise in direct proportion to the temperature. Her husband could not understand how she got dirty overnight, but Georgia always dismissed his objections by observing that "it isn't any skin off his nose if I take good care of myself" and that "he would be the first to holler if I turned sloppy." . . .

Georgia was aware, in part, of the effect she was having on her family and friends, but she also knew that when she tried to alter her behavior she got so nervous that she felt she was losing her mind. She was frightened by the possibility that "I'm headed for the funny-farm." As she said,

> I can't get to sleep unless I am sure everything in the house is in its proper place so that when I get up in the morning, the house is organized. I work like mad to set everything straight before I go to bed, but, when I get up in the morning, I can think of a thousand things that I ought to do. I know some of the things are ridiculous, but I feel better if I get them done, and I can't stand to know something needs doing and I haven't done it. I never told anybody but once I found just one dirty shirt and washed, dried, and ironed it that day. I felt stupid running a whole wash for one shirt but I couldn't bear to leave it undone. It would have bothered me all day just thinking about that one dirty shirt in the laundry basket.
>
> *(McNeail, 1967, pp. 26–28)*

Georgia's obsessive compulsive disorder consisted of both obsessions (her repeated concerns about becoming dirty or disordered) and compulsions (her repeated cleaning rituals). In fact, her obsessive worries seemed to generate and fuel her cleaning compulsions. In most but not all cases of this disorder, people display both obsessions and compulsions.

Between 1.3 and 2.0 percent of the population in the United States suffer from obsessive compulsive disorders (Myers et al., 1984). They are equally common in males and females and usually begin in adolescence or the early 20s, although some cases emerge during childhood (APA, 1987). As with Georgia, the disorder typically persists for many years, the symptoms and their severity fluctuating over time. Some people with an obsessive compulsive disorder are also depressed, and some are heavy drinkers of alcohol (APA, 1987).

## Obsessions

Obsessions feel both involuntary *(ego dystonic)* and foreign *(ego alien)* to the people who suffer from them, but attempts to ignore, resist, or dismiss them may arouse anxiety, and before long the thoughts come back more strongly than ever. Like Georgia, people with obsessions are quite aware that their cognitions are excessive and irrational, and many experience them as repugnant and torturous. Clinicians have found it useful to distinguish various kinds of obsessions, although a single person may have several kinds that overlap and complement one another (Akhtar et al., 1975; Buss, 1966).

Obsessions often take the form of *obsessive thoughts and wishes*. For example, a woman may have horrifying thoughts of killing, stabbing, injuring, mutilating, choking, or shooting her children. Consider Shirley, a 23-year-old woman:

> *During the preceding three months, she had been disturbed* by recurring thoughts that she might harm her two-year-old son, Saul, either by stabbing or choking him. She constantly had to check to reassure herself that Saul was still alive; otherwise she became unbearably anxious.
>
> *(Goldstein & Palmer, 1975, p. 155)*

Similarly, a man may keep wishing that his wife would die; a college student may repeatedly toy with the idea of crashing his car. These people do not believe that they actually want such things to happen, yet the wishes and fantasies keep forming in their minds.

Sometimes people experience *obsessive impulses* or urges to carry out certain acts — to jump in front of a truck, say; to yell out obscene words at work, in church, or at home; to kiss strangers passing by on the street. Shirley had such impulses, too:

> *If she read in the daily paper of the murder of a child,* she would become agitated, since this reinforced her fear that she too might act on her impulse. At one point, while

relating her fears, Shirley turned to the interviewer and asked, with desperation, whether this meant that she was going crazy.

*(Goldstein & Palmer, 1975, p. 155)*

*Obsessive images* may flood the mind, some of them quite graphic. One person may see fleeting images of his or her child bleeding from all parts of the body. Another may keep visualizing forbidden sexual scenes.

*Obsessive ideas* can make life difficult. Georgia, the woman with the cleaning obsession, had developed the idea that germs were lurking everywhere, threatening to contaminate her. People with such obsessions may believe that they will catch germs if they touch doorknobs, toilets, bannisters, unwashed clothing, car door handles, and the like.

A person may keep having *obsessive doubts* about the past or the future. Thinking back over his life, a man may wonder, "Did I do the right thing? Did I make the right decisions? If only I hadn't. . . . " He may also repeatedly question whether he is remembering the past correctly. Here a clinician describes a 20-year-old college junior who experienced obsessive doubts.

*He now spent hours each night "rehashing" the day's* events, especially interactions with friends and teachers, endlessly making "right" in his mind any and all regrets. He likened the process to playing a videotape of each event over and over again in his mind, asking himself if he had behaved properly and telling himself that he had done his best, or had said the right thing every step of the way. He would do this while sitting at his desk, supposedly studying; and it was not unusual for him to look at the clock after such a period of rumination and note that, to his surprise, two or three hours had elapsed.

*(Spitzer et al., 1981, pp. 20–21)*

Doubts about the future can be just as troubling. Whenever a person has to make a decision, for example, he or she may be overwhelmed with doubts: "What should I do? How will I know what's right? What if I do the wrong thing? How can I decide?"

Certain basic themes permeate the thoughts of 75 percent of the people troubled by obsessive thinking. A study carried out in New Delhi, India, examined the obsessions of eighty-two subjects and found that the most common theme, *dirt or contamination*, was present in 59 percent of the cases (Akhtar et al., 1975). Other common themes were *violence and aggression* (25 percent), *orderliness* (23 percent), *religion* (10 percent), and *sexuality* (5 percent). Contamination is the theme most commonly found in Western populations too, but here aggression, orderliness, and sexual obsessions are more prominent than in the New Delhi population (Stern & Cobb, 1978; Rachman & Hodgson, 1980, 1974).

## Compulsions

Although compulsive acts are technically under voluntary control, the people compelled to do them have little sense of choice in the matter. They believe something terrible, often unspecified, will happen if they don't act on their compulsion, all the time recognizing that their behavior is excessive and unreasonable. Most people with compulsions try to resist them at first but give in when anxiety overcomes them. Afterward, they usually feel less anxious for a short while. Aside from this release of tension, however, no pleasure is derived from the compulsive act itself (APA, 1987).

Some people develop the act into a *compulsive ritual,* a detailed and often elaborate manner of performing the compulsive act. They must go through the motions of the ritual in exactly the same way every time, according to certain carefully observed rules. Failure to complete it properly will generate further anxiety and often call for the ritual to be repeated from the beginning.

Like obsessions, compulsions take various forms and center on a variety of themes. A *cleaning compulsion* is very common. Like Georgia, people with these compulsions feel compelled to keep cleaning themselves, their clothing, their homes. The cleaning may follow ritualistic rules and be repeated dozens or hundreds of times a day. The requirements of the cleaning ritual may be so detailed, bizarre, and time-consuming that a normal life is virtually impossible:

*Ruth complained that her life was extremely restricted* because she was spending most of her time engaged in some type of behavior she felt driven to carry out. In addition, each ritual activity was becoming more involved and time consuming. At the time of the interview, she was washing her hands at least three or four times an hour, showering six or seven times a day, and thoroughly cleaning her apartment at least twice a day. . . .

Ruth stated that she felt frustrated and tired most of the time, due to the amount of effort involved in these rituals. She experienced a great deal of pain in her hands because the outer layer of skin was virtually rubbed off. Nonetheless, she felt compelled to thoroughly wash her hands and repeatedly clean her apartment each time she felt that she or her environment was contaminated in some way.

*(Leon, 1977, pp. 127–132)*

*Checking compulsions* cause people to check the same things over and over. Some people with checking compulsions believe their safety or that of others depends on the frequent checking of appliances and other belongings (door locks, gas taps, ashtrays, important papers), although such a connection is not always present. Another kind of checking compulsion consists of repeated

"Ronald is *extremely* compulsive."

checking of the accuracy of a story or the details of an event. Again, such behavior may be repeated dozens or even hundreds of times each day, far beyond any reasonable function.

A third common compulsion is displayed by people who repeatedly seek *symmetry, order,* or *balance* in their actions and surroundings. They must place certain items (such as clothing, books, or foods) in perfect order in accordance with strict rules. If they make the slightest error, they may have to start over again and build to a perfect placement. Again, this is more than simple orderliness.

*Ted is a 13-year-old referred to a Midwestern inpatient* psychiatric research ward because of "senseless rituals and attention to minutiae." He can spend 3 hours "centering the toilet paper roll on its holder or rearranging his bed and other objects in his room. When placing objects down, such as books or shoelaces after tying them, he picks them up and replaces them several times until they seem "straight." Although usually placid, he becomes abusive with family members who try to enter his room for fear they will move or break his objects. When he is at school, he worries that people may disturb his room. He sometimes has to be forced to interrupt his routine to attend meals. Last year he hid pieces of his clothing around the house because they

wouldn't lie straight in his drawers. Moreover, he often repeats to himself, "This is perfect; you are perfect."

*(Spitzer et al., 1983, p. 15)*

Touching, verbal, counting, and eating compulsions are also common. *Touching compulsions* cause people to feel they must touch or avoid touching certain items whenever they see them. *Verbal rituals* compel them to repeat expressions, phrases, or chants time and again. Some people conduct their verbal rituals internally; others feel the need to express them aloud. *Counting compulsions* cause people to count the things they see around them in the course of their daily activities. So-called *eating compulsions* — the compulsion to eat or to refrain from eating with no regard for hunger — are discussed in Chapter 12.

## Relationship between Obsessions and Compulsions

Although some people with an obsessive compulsive disorder experience obsessions only or compulsions only, approximately 70 percent experience both (Wilner et al., 1976). In fact, their compulsive acts often seem to be a reaction to their obsessive thoughts.

One investigation found that in 61 percent of the cases reviewed, a subject's compulsions seemed to represent a *yielding* to obsessive doubts, ideas, or urges (Akhtar et al., 1975). Remember how Shirley, the woman who obsessed about harming her young son, would yield to this obsession by repeatedly checking to see whether he was safe. Similarly, a man who keeps doubting that his house is secure may yield to that obsessive doubt by repeatedly checking locks and gas jets. Or a man who obsessively fears contamination may yield to that fear by performing cleaning rituals (see Box 6-5). In 6 percent of the cases reviewed, the compulsions seemed to serve to *control* obsessions. A man who is beset by obsessive sexual images and urges, say, may try to distract himself by repetitive verbal rituals. Here a teenager describes how she tried to control her obsessive fears of contamination by performing counting and verbal rituals:

*Patient:* If I heard the word, like, something that had to do with germs or disease, it would be considered something bad, and so I had things that would go through my mind that were sort of like "cross that out and it'll make it okay" to hear that word.

*Interviewer:* What sort of things?

*Patient:* Like numbers or words that seemed to be sort of like a protector.

*Interviewer:* What numbers and what words were they?

*Patient:*  It started out to be the number 3 and multiples of 3 and then words like "soap and water," something like that; and then the multiples of 3 got really high, and they'd end up to be 124 or something like that. It got real bad then. . . .

*(Spitzer et al., 1981, p. 137)*

Many people with obsessive compulsive disorders worry that they will act out their obsessions. A man with obsessive images of mutilated loved ones may worry that he is but a step away from committing murder; or a woman with obsessive urges to yell out in church may worry that she will one day give in to them and embarrass herself. Most of these concerns are unfounded. Although many obsessions lead to compulsive acts — particularly to cleaning and checking compulsions — they do not usually lead to acts of violence, immorality, or the like.

## Explanations of Obsessive Compulsive Disorders

Obsessive compulsive disorders are among the least understood of the mental disorders (Rachman & Hodgson, 1980). Although researchers are beginning to learn more about them, insights into the origins of these patterns remain limited. Psychodynamic, behavioral, and biological explanations have been proposed.

### The Psychodynamic View: Battle of the Id and Ego

Psychodynamic theorists believe that obsessive compulsive disorders, like other anxiety disorders, develop when children come to fear their own id impulses and use ego defense mechanisms to lessen the resulting anxiety. As we know, the interplay between id impulses and ego defense mechanisms is presumed to take place at an unconscious level. The ego is aware of the id impulses and knows that the impulses must not be allowed free expression, but its efforts to defend against the expression of the impulses or against the anxiety generated by the impulses are usually subtle and hidden. The distinguishing feature of obsessive compulsive disorders is that the battle between anxiety-provoking id impulses and anxiety-reducing defense mechanisms is played out very explicitly. The id impulses usually take the form of obsessive thoughts, and the ego defenses appear as counterthoughts or compulsive actions. This mechanism is at work when a woman keeps having images of family members horribly injured and counters those thoughts with repeated safety checks throughout the house, or when a man repeatedly has forbidden sexual thoughts and distances himself from them by constantly washing or meticulously avoiding sexual content in conversations.

Sigmund Freud believed that during the anal stage of development (about 2 years of age) some children experience intense rage and shame that fuel the id – ego battle and set the stage for obsessive compulsive functioning. During this period in their lives, children are deriving their psychosexual pleasure from their bowel movements while at the same time their parents are trying to toilet train them and teach them to delay their anal gratification. If parents are too premature or harsh in their toilet training, the children may experience rage and develop *aggressive id impulses,* antisocial impulses that repeatedly seek expression. They may soil their clothes all the more and become generally destructive, messy, or stubborn.

If parents then handle this aggressiveness by further pressuring and embarrassing the child, the child may also feel shameful, guilty, and dirty. The child's aggressive impulses will now be countered by a strong desire to control those impulses; the child who wants to soil will also have a competing desire to retain. This intense conflict between the id and ego may continue throughout life and eventually blossom into an obsessive compulsive disorder.

Not all psychodynamic theorists agree with Freud's toilet-training explanation of why some children develop aggressive id impulses. Some believe that the aggressive impulses simply reflect an unfulfilled need for self-expression, and others view them as efforts to overcome feelings of vulnerability or insecurity (Salzman, 1968; Erickson, 1963; Sullivan, 1953; Horney, 1937). But whatever their particular point of view, most psychodynamic theorists agree that people with an obsessive compulsive disorder have developed intense aggressive impulses as children, along with a competing need to control those impulses.

Psychodynamic theorists propose that three ego defense mechanisms are particularly common in obsessive compulsive disorders — isolation, undoing, and reaction formation. In *isolation,* people unconsciously isolate and disown undesirable and unwanted thoughts and experience them as foreign intrusions from unknown parts of the mind. In *undoing,* people perform acts that implicitly cancel out their undesirable impulses. People who wash their hands repeatedly or conduct elaborate symmetry rituals may be symbolically undoing their unacceptable id impulses. A *reaction formation* is a broad ego defense in which people take on lifestyles that directly oppose their unacceptable impulses. One person may live a life of compulsive kindness and total devotion to others to counteract unacceptably aggressive impulses. Another may lead a life of total celibacy to counteract obsessive sexual impulses.

=== BOX 6-5 ===

# Howard Hughes: A Study in Obsessive Compulsive Behavior

**H**oward Hughes was born on December 24, 1905, and died on April 5, 1976, aboard a private jet bound for a hospital in Houston, Texas. Hughes's career is legendary. After inheriting a company that made drill bits used in drilling for oil, he went on to become a successful movie producer and record-setting flyer, to build the world's largest flying boat, and to found an international airline, TWA.

Hughes's personal habits are also legendary. He vanished from view in 1951 and lived his last 25 years in isolation, dominated by obsessive fears of contamination and the compulsion to carry out bizarre cleaning rituals. James Phelan, an investigative reporter, wrote a biography of Hughes, gathering his information from Hughes's closest aides. As

When Howard Hughes was flying around the world setting records, starting an international airline, and running several businesses at once, no one suspected that he would one day become a near-helpless prisoner of phobias and an obsessive compulsive disorder.

the following excerpts show, Howard Hughes, one of the richest and most powerful men in the world, was at the

same time a sad figure helplessly imprisoned by his obsessive compulsive disorder:

*O*ne day at the Bel Air mansion Hughes observed that someone had dropped a bottle on a stairway, where it had broken and left shards of glass. . . . Hughes had a laser-beam attention that focused on small details, and an unreasoning terror of contamination. He was especially suspicious of floors.

Hughes delegated the broken-glass-on-the-stairway problem to his headquarters on Romaine Street. He described the problem and meticulously outlined the way he wanted it solved. The contaminated area was to be divided into inch-square segments with a ruler. He then wanted an employee to start at one side of this

---

**The Behavioral View: Anxiety Reduction** Concentrating on compulsions rather than obsessions, behaviorists have suggested that these repetitive behaviors develop through a process of operant conditioning. According to these theorists, people initially happen upon their compulsions quite randomly. In an anxiety-provoking situation, they happen to wash their hands, dress a certain way, or carry out a particular sequence of actions, and when the threat lifts, they link the improvement to those coincidental activities. They may believe that their actions brought them good luck or actually changed the situation, and may perform the same actions again the next time they find themselves in similar straits.

Repeated chance associations of this kind increase the likelihood that such people will associate certain acts

with a reduction of anxiety and continue to perform those acts to alleviate anxiety. Indeed, the acts may become their primary method of avoiding or reducing anxiety. Behaviorists have nothing to say, however, as to why some people go on to develop compulsions and others do not. Certainly everyone experiences some chance associations, yet relatively few become compulsive.

This behavioral view of compulsive behaviors is derived from B. F. Skinner's (1948) classic experiments on superstitious behavior in pigeons. He gave food to pigeons at regular time intervals, regardless of their actions. Although the feedings were based on time alone, each pigeon later acted as if some behavior were necessary to elicit the food. Each kept repeating an action that

checkerboard and brush off and wipe down each segment, a square inch at a time.

The project was assigned to Kay Glenn. He equipped himself with a ruler, hurried to the Bel Air mansion, and removed the broken glass the way Hughes had ordered it removed.

*Stewart* [a barber] *was admitted* by a man who introduced himself as John Holmes. Holmes gave Stewart detailed instructions. He was to scrub up, doctor-style, in the bathroom before beginning the hair cutting. Then he was to put on a pair of rubber surgical gloves. He was to have no foreign objects, such as pencils or pens, on his person. And, finally, he was not to speak to the man whose hair he would cut.

"You can make signs, but you are not to say a word to him," said Holmes. . . .

Finally Holmes said, "Okay, Mr. Hughes will see you now," and took him into the bedroom.

What he found stunned him.

"I'm a country boy," Stewart says, "and I expected that a billionaire would surround himself in luxury, with Rembrandt paintings on the walls and exquisite furniture.

"I found a skinny, bare-assed naked man sitting on an unmade three-quarter bed. His hair hung about a foot down his back. His beard was straggly and down to his chest. I tried not to act surprised, as if I was used to meeting naked billionaires sitting on unmade beds.

"I started to put my case with the barber tools on a chair. Hughes shouted, 'No, no! Not on the chair!' "

Hughes turned to Holmes and said, "Get some insulation for our friend to put his equipment on." Holmes got a roll of paper towels and laid out a layer on a nearby sideboard. The sideboard was already covered with a sheet, and so was the other furniture in the bedroom. . . .

Barbering Hughes took three hours. There was a series of special procedures, which Hughes outlined in detail. Stewart was to use one set of combs and scissors to cut his beard, but a different set to cut his hair. Before Stewart began, Hughes ordered a series of wide-mouthed jars filled with isopropyl alcohol. When Stewart used a comb he was to dip it into the alcohol before using it again, to "sterilize" it.

After using a comb a few times, he was to discard it and proceed with a new comb.

While Stewart was trimming his hair on either side of his head, Hughes carefully folded his ears down tight "so none of that hair will get in me."

Stewart trimmed his beard to a short, neat Vandyke and gave his hair a tapered cut well above the collar line.

When he finished, Hughes thanked him and Holmes escorted him out. A few days later an emissary came down to Huntington Park and gave Stewart an envelope. In it was $1000. . . .

*He would sit in his bathroom or on* his lounge chair and lave his hands and upper arms over and over with alcohol. Like Lady Macbeth's "damned spot," whatever he was trying to cleanse away would not wash out. He would wash and wash, the alcohol dripping down and turning his paper-towel "insulation" into a sodden pulp. When he gave up, the paper towels would be gathered up and a fresh paper carpet laid down. The towels were then run through a shredder.

*(Phelan, 1976, pp. 27–28, 44–46, 82)*

---

it happened to be performing just before the initial feeding. One pigeon kept turning counterclockwise; another kept running to a corner of the cage.

Experiments by Stanley Rachman and his associates are consistent with the operant explanation of compulsions. In one experiment twelve persons who had compulsive hand-washing rituals were placed in contact with objects that they considered contaminated (Hodgson & Rachman, 1972). As behaviorists would predict, the hand-washing rituals of these subjects seemed to lower their anxiety. Similarly, a study of persons with compulsive checking rituals found that subjects' anxiety levels dropped significantly after they completed their checking rituals (Roper, Rachman, & Hodgson, 1973). Of course, although such studies suggest that compulsions

may now be rewarded by a reduction in anxiety, they do not address the origins of the behaviors.

**The Biological View** Partly because obsessive compulsive disorders have been so difficult to explain, researchers have tried to identify hidden biological factors that may contribute to the disorder (Turner, Beidel, & Nathan, 1985). Two lines of biological research are beginning to look very promising. One points to abnormal activity of the neurotransmitter *serotonin* in obsessive compulsive people, the other to abnormal *glucose metabolism* in key regions of their brains.

*Serotonin,* like GABA and norepinephrine, is a brain chemical that carries messages from neuron to neuron.

It first became implicated in obsessive compulsive disorders when clinical researchers discovered unexpectedly that obsessive and compulsive symptoms were reduced by the antidepressant drug *clomipramine* (Goodman & McDougle, 1990; Ananth, 1989; Flament et al., 1985; Turner et al., 1985). Since clomipramine seems to alter serotonin activity while reducing obsessive and compulsive symptoms, some researchers conclude that the disorder is associated with abnormal serotonin activity (Zetin, 1990; Zohar et al., 1988; Flament et al., 1985). Biological researchers cannot agree on the precise nature of this abnormal serotonin activity. Some believe it to be excessive, others deficient (Zohar et al., 1988).

Another line of research appears to link obsessive compulsive disorders to heightened *glucose metabolism* in the *basal ganglia* of the brain, particularly in the structures called the *caudate nuclei* and the *orbital gyri*. These regions typically play a role in the brain's control of movement, learned behavior, and coping with repeated stimuli. It has been observed for many years that obsessive compulsive symptoms sometimes develop or subside after these brain areas are damaged by either accident or illness (McKeon, 1984; Barton, 1965; Grimshaw, 1964, Hillbom, 1960; Schilder, 1938). In one recent well-publicized case, an obsessive compulsive patient tried to commit suicide by shooting himself in the head. Although he survived the shot, he did considerable damage to the brain areas in question. Perhaps as a result of the injury, his obsessive and compulsive symptoms subsided.

Such cases have been taken more seriously in recent years in light of research with *positron emission tomography (PET scans)*. As we saw in Chapter 4, PET scans show the brain in action by tracking glucose (the brain's source of energy) and other natural compounds as they are being metabolized by the brain. PET scan studies have revealed that obsessive compulsive patients metabolize glucose in the caudate nuclei and the orbital gyri more rapidly than control subjects do (Baxter et al., 1990). Moreover, obsessive compulsive patients whose symptoms respond well to such medications as clomipramine subsequently show a lower rate of glucose metabolism in these brain areas than do patients who are unaffected by treatment.

Although these studies seem to be identifying important biological variables in obsessive compulsive disorders, they have not yet identified the precise role of the variables (Hollander, Liebowitz, & Gorman, 1988; Turner et al., 1985). The evidence suggests only that serotonin activity and glucose metabolism may be important correlates of the disorder, perhaps setting up some kind of biological predisposition for its development (Turner et al., 1985).

In general, then, obsessive compulsive disorders remain among the most elusive problems in abnormal psychology. None of the familiar concepts addresses the full range of clinical features found in these disorders; nor has research yet provided broad or compelling support for any of the explanations. The recent biological breakthroughs appear to offer the most promising clues for understanding the disorder, but even here the findings have been largely circumstantial and imprecise.

# POST-TRAUMATIC STRESS DISORDERS

*Mark remembers his first "firefight" and encountering the VC [Viet Cong] for the first time. He lost all bladder and bowel control—in a matter of a few minutes. In his own words,* "I was scared and literally shitless; I pissed all over myself, and shit all over myself too. Man, all hell broke loose. I tell you, I was so scared, I thought I would never make it out alive. I was convinced of that. Charlie had us pinned down and hitting the shit out of us for hours. We had to call in the napalm and the bombing." *During the first fight, Mark, an infantryman, experienced gruesome sights and strange sounds in battle. He witnessed headless bodies.* "One guy said to me, 'Hey, Mark, new greenhorn boy, you saw that head go flying off that gook's shoulder. Isn't that something?'" *Within 2 weeks Mark saw the head of a running comrade blown off his shoulders, the headless body moving for a few feet before falling to the ground. Mark, nauseous and vomiting for a long time, couldn't see himself surviving much longer:* "I couldn't get that sight out of my head; it just kept on coming back to me in my dreams, nightmares. Like clockwork, I'd see R's head flying, and his headless body falling to the ground. I knew the guy. He was very good to me when I first got to the unit. Nobody else seemed to give a damn about me; he broke me in. It's like I would see his head and body, you know, man, wow!" *Mark often found himself crying during his first weeks of combat.* "I wanted to go home. I was so lonely, helpless, and really scared. But I knew I could not go home until my year was up."

*(Brende & Parson, 1985, pp. 23–24)*

Mark's reaction to these combat experiences is normal and understandable. During or immediately after an unusual and traumatic situation, many people become highly anxious and depressed. For some, however, anxiety and depression persist long after the situation is over. These people may be suffering from a *post-traumatic stress disorder,* a distinct pattern of symptoms that arises in reaction to a psychologically traumatic event, generally one outside the range of normal human experience. The event usually presents a serious threat to the person's life or to a family member or friend. Unlike other anxiety disorders, which typically are triggered by objects or situations that most people would not find threatening, situations that cause post-traumatic stress disorders — combat, an earthquake, an airplane crash — would be traumatic for almost anyone.

The symptoms of a post-traumatic stress disorder typically include the following:

1. *Reexperiencing the traumatic event*  The person may have recurring recollections, dreams, or nightmares about the event. A few relive the event so vividly in their minds that they think they are back in the traumatic situation.
2. *Avoidance*  The person will usually avoid activities or situations that are reminiscent of the traumatic event. If such activities cannot be avoided, feelings of anxiety may intensify.
3. *Reduced responsiveness*  Reduced responsiveness to the external world, often called "psychic numbing" or "emotional anesthesia," often begins soon after the traumatic event. The person feels detached or estranged from other people or loses interest in activities enjoyed previously. The ability to experience such intimate emotions as tenderness and sexuality is often impaired.
4. *Increased arousal, anxiety, and guilt*  People with this disorder experience forms of increased arousal such as hyperalertness, an exaggerated startle response, and sleep disturbances (Glaubman et al., 1990) and may also have trouble concentrating or remembering things. They may feel extreme guilt because they have survived the traumatic event while others have not. Some also feel guilt over the things they had to do to survive.

We can see these symptoms in the reactions of Vietnam combat veterans years after they returned home:

*H*ank: *I woke up with my wife shaking me and my kids* standing at the door because they wondered what is wrong with their father, screaming like an idiot, running through the house chasing VC's and I couldn't get no help.

*B*ob: *As we left the fire base, there was a little village* right before we turned on the Highway 1, and there was a bunch of bodies just laying in the road, and they were kids and women. We had to drive right over them to get out, and I see that at nighttime. I see those kids and I see those women. I don't know.

*R*on: *It was like Dr. Jekyll and Mr. Hyde. I'd go on* self-destruct cycles you wouldn't believe, especially when I started drinking. My poor wife, she went through Hell. Vietnam started coming into my head. And she couldn't understand. She couldn't deal with it. . . . You get tired of being shot at again, over and over and over again. How many times do I gotta get blown up. I'm tired of seeing bullets hit me. I'm tired of seeing my friends get shot at. I'm tired. . . . I grew up and died right there [at the scene of battle]. And the last ten years have just been a space. I've just occupied space, just space. I've accomplished nothing. Nothing but occupied space.

(*"The War Within,"* 1985)

*L*ucas: *She also said that I wasn't the loving guy she used* to know and love, that something horrible must have happened to me over there to change me so completely. I told her I didn't know what she was talking about. She said that the look in my eyes was the look of a deeply terrorized person, with a long-distance stare, looking off into the beyond — not into the present with her at this time. She also mentioned that my frightened look and pallid complexion, my uptight way of sitting, talking, walking, you name it, my aloofness, and all that, made her too uncomfortable for us to continue our relationship. . . . Finally, as time went on, I realized that so many people couldn't be wrong about me. The change in me began to seem deep to me — deeper than I would ever have imagined to be the case. I myself was not fully aware of just how profound my transformation had been. I guess killing and hurting human beings have a way of catching up with you; just seeing so many guys die, some died in my arms; seeing guys die of snake bites; getting sick from malaria; feeling so tired and emotionally drained for so long, feeling so intensely angry and used; being terrorized myself so many times, so many close calls. I got hit three times with bullets. I guess that can change somebody, maybe most people.

(*Brende & Parson, 1985, pp. 46–47*)

A post-traumatic stress disorder can occur at any age, even in childhood, and can cause mild to severe impairment. The symptoms typically begin soon after the traumatic event, although some victims do not start to reexperience the trauma or suffer other symptoms until months or years afterward. When the disorder emerges more than six months after the trauma, it is said to have a *delayed onset* (APA, 1987).

## Post-traumatic Stress Disorders Caused by Combat

For years clinicians have recognized that soldiers often develop symptoms of severe anxiety and depression during combat (Oei, Lim, & Hennessy, 1990). The pat-

Soldiers often react to combat with severe anxiety or depression or both, reactions shown by these soldiers in Vietnam. These immediate responses to battle have at various times been called "shell shock" and "combat fatigue."

The addition of post-traumatic stress disorder as a category in DSM-III and DSM-III-R was largely a response to the symptoms observed in these many veterans.

Although it is not clear how many Vietnam veterans fit the criteria for this diagnosis, it is apparent that a great many suffer from the kinds of symptoms associated with post-traumatic stress disorders. One study of 1,168 Vietnam veterans found that more than a decade later 61 percent continued to think about the deaths they had seen during the war (Fisher, 1980). Other studies suggest that many veterans have continued to experience intrusive and repeated recollections of traumatic Vietnam experiences in the form of flashbacks, night terrors, nightmares, and persistent images and thoughts (Williams, 1983; Goodwin, 1980). Such recollections may be triggered by simple events that remind the veteran of conditions in Vietnam — a sudden downpour of summer rain or a rise in temperature to 80 degrees or more (Defazio, Rustin, & Diamond, 1975). They may also be triggered by combat scenes in novels, movies, or television shows. Indeed, in 1991 many veterans of World War II, the Korean War, and the Vietnam War reported new flashbacks, images, and nightmares on watching the graphic televised coverage of the war in the Persian Gulf.

tern of symptoms was called "nostalgia" during the American Civil War and was considered to be the result of extended absence from home (Bourne, 1970). The syndrome was called "shell shock" during World War I because it was thought to result from minute brain hemorrhages or concussions caused by explosions during battle. During World War II and the Korean War, it was referred to as "combat fatigue" (Figley, 1978). Not until after the Vietnam War, however, did clinicians come to recognize that a great many soldiers also experience serious psychological symptoms *after* combat.

In the first years after the Vietnam War, the psychological problems of combat veterans were generally overlooked, perhaps in part because of the nation's desire to put reminders of this unpopular war behind it. The initial belief was that less than 2 percent of Vietnam veterans had psychological problems, compared to 10 percent of World War II veterans (Figley, 1978). By the late 1970s, however, it had become apparent to staff members in veterans' hospitals throughout the United States that many Vietnam combat veterans were still experiencing war-related psychological problems that had been delayed in onset or previously ignored (Williams, 1983). Some signs of these disturbances were that one-quarter of the 1.5 million combat soldiers who returned from Vietnam had been arrested within two years of returning, and approximately 200,000 had become dependent on drugs. The divorce rate among Vietnam veterans was nearly double that of the general population, and their suicide rate was nearly 25 percent higher.

Unlike combat fatigue, the symptoms of post-traumatic stress disorder appear after combat (or after another traumatic event), often when the individual is safely back home. The emotion and pain displayed by tens of thousands of veterans at the unveiling of the Vietnam War Memorial in Washington, D.C., more than a decade after the war ended, served as a vivid reminder that the war and its psychological effects were far from over for many people.

## Post-traumatic Stress Disorders Caused by Other Traumas

Post-traumatic stress disorders may also follow natural and accidental disasters such as earthquakes, floods, tornados, fires, airplane crashes, and serious car accidents. In Chapter 3 we discussed the 1972 flood in Buffalo Creek, West Virginia, which killed 115 people, injured hundreds more, and destroyed the homes of thousands. Research found that 18 months after the flood, the survivors were more anxious and depressed and experienced more nightmares and other sleep disturbances than matched control subjects living elsewhere (Green et al., 1990; Glesser et al., 1981). The ones who had come closest to dying or who had lost family members showed the most psychological impairment. The lingering symptoms are powerfully seen in the comments of two survivors of the disaster:

*I listen to the news, and if there is a storm warning out,* why I don't go to bed that night. I sit up. I tell my wife, "Don't undress our little girls; just let them lay down like they are and go to bed and go to sleep and then if I see anything going to happen, I'll wake you in plenty of time to get you out of the house." I don't go to bed. I stay up.

My nerves is a problem. Every time it rains, every time it storms, I just can't take it. I walk the floor. I get so nervous I break out in a rash. I am taking shots for it now. . . .

What I went through on Buffalo Creek is the cause of my problem. The whole thing happens over to me even in my dreams, when I retire for the night. My dreams, I run from water all the time, all the time. The whole thing just happens over and over in my dreams. . . .

*I am neglecting my children. I just simply quit cooking. I* don't do no housework, I just won't do nothing. Can't sleep. Can't eat. Just want to take me a lot of pills and just go to bed and go to sleep and not wake up. I enjoyed my home and my family, but outside of them to me, everything else in life that I had any interest in is destroyed. I loved to cook. I loved to sew. I loved to keep house. I was all the time working in making improvements in my home. But now I just got to the point where it don't mean a thing in the world to me.

*(Erikson, 1976)*

Post-traumatic stress symptoms have been observed in many survivors of Nazi concentration camps years after their liberation (Eitinger, 1973, 1969, 1964; Warnes, 1973; Sigal et al., 1973). A study of 149 concentration camp survivors found that twenty years later 97 percent still experienced anxiety symptoms and feared that family members might be in danger when they were out of their sight; 71 percent had nightmares recalling their captivity, and dreamed that their children, born afterward, were now imprisoned with them; 80 percent felt guilty that they had survived while other family members and friends had not; and 92 percent blamed themselves for not saving their relatives and friends (Krystal, 1968).

Studies of more recent acts of inhumanity and torture reveal similar symptoms among survivors. One involved forty-four persons who had been subjected to beatings, electric shocks, near drownings, and burns in Latin American prisons in the 1970s. Years later, many of these people continued to experience high levels of anxiety and depression, and seventeen of them met the criteria for a diagnosis of post-traumatic stress disorder (Randall et al., 1985). A similar study of forty-one survivors of military torture found that for many of them such problems as nervousness, deep-seated fears, depression, insomnia, recurrent nightmares, and loss of concentration continued as long as six years after their ordeal (Allodi & Cowgill, 1982).

A common form of victimization in our society is sexual assault and rape. A Senate Judiciary Committee (1991) stated that more than 100,000 rapes are reported to police annually. Indeed, rape reports rose four times faster than the overall crime rate during the 1980s. And it is believed that these reports represent only a small portion of the actual number of such incidents (Freiberg, 1990). Many rape victims, both female and male, have been found to experience the symptoms of post-traumatic stress disorder (Steketee & Foa, 1986; Goyer & Eddleman, 1984; see Figure 6-5). One study found female rape victims to be more anxious, fearful, suspicious, and confused a year after their rape than a matched group of women who had not been raped (Kilpatrick et al., 1981). Another study of female rape victims found a common post-traumatic stress reaction pattern that the authors labeled the *rape trauma syndrome* (Burgess & Holmstrom, 1979, 1974). It included high anxiety and startle responses, depression, guilt and self-blame, reliving the sexual assault, and nightmares and other sleep disturbances. Four to six years after being raped, 25 percent of the women reported that they had still not recovered. Such symptoms are apparent in the following case description:

*Mary Billings is a 33-year-old divorced nurse, referred* to the Victim Clinic at Bedford Psychiatric Hospital for counseling by her supervisory head nurse. Mary had been raped two months ago. The assailant gained entry to her apartment while she was sleeping, and she awoke to find him on top of her. He was armed with a knife and threatened to kill her and her child (who was asleep in the next room) if she did not submit to his demands. He forced her to undress and repeatedly raped her vaginally over a period of

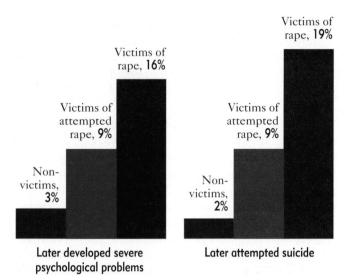

**FIGURE 6-5** Many rape victims develop symptoms of post-traumatic stress disorder. In one study, 19 percent of those surveyed by telephone revealed that they attempted suicide at some point after being raped, compared to 2 percent of nonvictims. *(Adapted from Kilpatrick et al., 1985.)*

1 hour. He then admonished her that if she told anyone or reported the incident to the police he would return and assault her child.

After he left, she called her boyfriend, who came to her apartment right away. He helped her contact the Sex Crimes Unit of the Police Department, which is currently investigating the case. He then took her to a local hospital for a physical examination and collection of evidence for the police (traces of sperm, pubic hair samples, fingernail scrapings). She was given antibiotics as prophylaxis against venereal disease. Mary then returned home with a girlfriend who spent the remainder of the night with her.

Over the next few weeks Mary continued to be afraid of being alone and had her girlfriend move in with her. She became preoccupied with thoughts of what had happened to her and the possibility that it could happen again. Mary was frightened that the rapist might return to her apartment and therefore had additional locks installed on both the door and the windows. She was so upset and had such difficulty concentrating that she decided she could not yet return to work. When she did return to work several weeks later, she was still clearly upset, and her supervisor suggested that she might be helped by counseling.

During the clinic interview, Mary was coherent and spoke quite rationally in a hushed voice. She reported recurrent and intrusive thoughts about the sexual assault, to the extent that her concentration was impaired and she had difficulty doing chores such as making meals for herself and her daughter. She felt she was not able to be effective at work, still felt afraid to leave her home, to answer her

phone, and had little interest in contacting friends or relatives.

The range of Mary's affect was constricted. She talked in the same tone of voice whether discussing the assault or less emotionally charged topics, such as her work history. She was easily startled by an unexpected noise. She also was unable to fall asleep because she kept thinking about the assault. She had no desire to eat, and when she did attempt it, she felt nauseated. Mary was repelled by the thought of sex and stated that she did not want to have sex for a long time, although she was willing to be held and comforted by her boyfriend.

*(Spitzer et al., 1983, pp. 20–21)*

## Explanations of Post-traumatic Stress Disorders

There is an obvious cause-and-effect relationship between an extraordinary trauma and an ensuing post-traumatic stress disorder. The stressful event alone, however, is not a complete explanation. Although everyone who experiences an unusual trauma is certainly affected by it, only some people develop the lingering symptoms of a post-traumatic stress disorder. Researchers do not yet understand why some people do and others do not develop this disorder, but they have called two factors to our attention: the survivor's personality and his or her social support systems.

It has been found that rape victims who had psychological problems before they were raped and those struggling with stressful life situations are at greater risk of developing lingering stress reactions (Sales, Baum, & Short, 1984). This finding is reminiscent of another: that many people respond to stress with a set of positive attitudes, collectively called *hardiness,* that enable them to carry on their lives with a sense of fortitude, control, and commitment (Kobasa et al., 1982, 1979; Kobasa, 1979).

It has also been found that people who are surrounded by strong support systems after a traumatic event are less likely to develop an extended disorder. Rape victims who feel loved, cared for, valued, and accepted by a group of friends or relatives are more likely to recover successfully from their sexual assault. Societal support appears to be just as important. When a rape victim is further devalued and traumatized by representatives or agencies of the criminal justice system, she is more likely to develop lingering symptoms (Sales et al., 1984).

Similarly, clinical reports suggest that weak social support systems have contributed to the development of post-traumatic stress disorders in some Vietnam veter-

Millions of people reacted to the San Francisco earthquake of 1989 with dread and panic, but some laid-back individuals seemed to thrive on all the excitement. Their "hardy" personality styles may have helped to protect them from the development of post-traumatic stress disorders.

ans (Figley & Leventman, 1980). This veteran's return home was, sadly, not at all unusual:

*N*ext morning my sisters went to school as usual, while my brother went to college. Everything seemed the same to them, real routine, you know. I didn't feel "routine." I felt out of it. I felt nervous, tense, jittery, even shaky. I wasn't able to fall asleep, so I got up at 10:00 A.M. I was home alone. So I walked down to the package store and bought me some liquor to help me out — you know, with the nervousness, and my anger about everything.

I had started drinking heavily in Vietnam after a battle at Khe Sanh. Alcohol usually worked for me. As I walked down the street, I was trying to avoid drawing attention to myself. I saw a good friend but I tried to hurry by so he wouldn't see me. I knew he might be glad to see me, but I didn't want him to see me, so I hurried by, hoping he or anyone else wouldn't see me pass by. I just wanted to get my bottle and make it back to my parents' crib [house] so I could get myself together quick.

In spite of all my efforts to avoid having anyone see me, a long-time friend saw me and really welcomed me home. It was really nice. Then, like out of nowhere, six guys showed up on the scene; I knew most of them. They wanted to know about the "good dope" in Vietnam. They didn't seem interested in me as a person. They had heard of the Thai red, the opium, and all that stuff. They asked me about the Vietnamese whores; and how many times I caught the clap [gonorrhea].

They also wanted to know what it was like having sex with Vietnamese women. One of them yelled out, "How many babies you've burned, man? How many young children don't have their fathers because of guys like you? Yeah, you killers, man; you heard me." Before I knew what had happened the cops were there. I had beaten four guys up severely; three had to be taken to the hospital. I seemed to have lost my head totally. I didn't want to hurt anybody. I had done a lot of killing in the 'Nam; I just wanted to be left alone, now. But I was really mad; I felt I had to defend myself against and kill the new "gooks" — the American gooks.

I was disappointed, so hurt, and bitter at myself for "going off" and losing control of myself. I was told later that I was attacked first; I don't remember. I came back to my room, and began really drinking. I just kept thinking to myself that the streets of Cholon, Saigon, Nha Trang, and other cities and villages in Vietnam were probably safer for me than back in the United States.

*(Brende & Parson, 1985, pp. 49–50)*

Although personality variables and social support may play an important role in a person's reactions to stress, it is important to keep in mind that the events that trigger post-traumatic stress disorders can sometimes be so extreme and traumatic that they override a positive personal and social context (Goldberg, 1990). A follow-up study of 253 Vietnam prisoners of war found that five years after their release 23 percent warranted a psychiatric diagnosis, though all had been effective Air Force officers and before their imprisonment had been evaluated as well adjusted (Ursano, Boydston, & Wheatley, 1981). It was the men who had been imprisoned longest and treated most harshly who had the highest percentage of such diagnoses. Personal and social variables notwithstanding, it is, as a survivor of trauma once said, "hard to be a survivor" (Kolff & Doan, 1985, p. 45).

# ANXIETY DISORDERS: THE STATE OF THE FIELD

The evidence that clinicians and researchers have gathered about anxiety disorders indicates that they are the most common mental disorders in the United States, that they are more prevalent among women than among men, and that they are likely to continue in the absence of treatment. Research has also determined that aside from the common denominator of anxiety, the various anxiety disorders differ in important ways. Panic disorders and generalized anxiety disorders, once lumped together under the label "anxiety neurosis," are now considered to be two distinct disorders, in recognition of their different features, courses, biological dimensions, and probable origins. Similarly, post-traumatic stress disorders have been set off from the other anxiety disorders because of their unique course, causes, and clinical features.

Some anxiety disorders are better understood than others. For years behavioral researchers have been gathering valuable insights into phobic disorders, and recently biological and cognitive researchers have made great strides toward explaining the once poorly understood panic disorders. Less impressive is the clinical field's inquiry into the nature of generalized anxiety disorders: only the biological correlates of this broad disorder seem to be unfolding clearly. Post-traumatic stress disorders, a newly identified syndrome, have yet to be fully investigated, and obsessive compulsive disorders continue to be relatively mysterious, despite some recent informative findings.

The various models of psychopathology all have something to say about anxiety disorders, but each is weakened by its model's characteristic limitations. The psychodynamic and humanistic explanations are very difficult to research. The behavioral and cognitive explanations often rely on laboratory studies in which researchers successfully create anxietylike symptoms but fail to establish that real-life anxiety disorders emerge in a similar manner. And biological explanations often fail to identify the precise nature, role, and importance of the biological variables linked to anxiety disorders.

Several important tasks lie ahead for those who theorize about and research anxiety disorders. They must demonstrate conclusively that the factors and variables they consider crucial are indeed important in the development or maintenance of anxiety disorders. They must clarify whether those factors are causal factors or factors that help maintain the disorder or both. Finally, they must discover the mechanisms by which the factors and variables emphasized in one model interact with the factors and variables emphasized in other models. Actually, there is already a growing trend in this direction. Composite biological-cognitive theories have been proposed to help explain panic disorders and obsessive compulsive disorders, and the behavioral-biological theory of preparedness has been used to help explain the development of phobic disorders. This trend toward combining viewpoints is most welcome. Such combinations may eventually yield complete and incisive explanations that allow clinicians to proclaim that at last they understand anxiety disorders.

# SUMMARY

*Fear* is a state of tension or alarm. *Anxiety* is a broader reaction that occurs when our sense of threat is more diffuse or vague. Everyday experiences of fear and anxiety are never pleasant, but they have an adaptive function: they prepare us to take action when danger threatens. People with anxiety disorders, however, experience ongoing fear and anxiety that disable them and prevent them from leading a normal life. Their experiences are severe, frequent, or long-lasting, and are triggered too readily by minimal, unspecified, or nonexistent threats. Anxiety disorders are collectively the most common mental disorders in the United States. DSM-III-R distinguishes five categories of disorder: *phobic disorder, generalized anxiety disorder, panic disorder, obsessive compulsive disorder,* and *post-traumatic stress disorder.*

The *fear* or *anxiety response* has physical, emotional, and cognitive components. Two parts of the autonomic nervous system, the *sympathetic* and the *parasympathetic* nervous systems, work in complementary ways to regulate fear and anxiety reactions.

A *phobia* is a persistent and unreasonable fear of a particular object, activity, or situation. There are three main categories of phobic disorders. *Agoraphobia* is a fear of being alone or of entering public places alone. *Social phobia* is a severe, persistent, and irrational fear of social situations in which one may be exposed to scrutiny. All other phobias — intense fear of animals, insects, heights, closed places, thunderstorms, or the like — are called *simple* or *specific phobias.*

People with *generalized anxiety disorder* feel persistent anxiety that is not clearly attached to any one object or situation. This anxiety is typically characterized by motor tension, autonomic hyperactivity, and vigilance and scanning.

A variety of factors may contribute to the development of phobic and generalized anxiety disorders. Proponents of the various models have focused on different factors and offered different explanations. Each of the leading explanations has limitations, and no single explanation has a clear edge over the others.

According to the *sociocultural* view, increases in societal dangers and pressures may establish a climate in which the anxiety disorders are more likely to develop.

Freud, the initial formulator of the *psychodynamic* view, said that phobic disorders result from excessive use of the defense mechanisms of *repression* and *displacement* to control underlying anxiety, whereas generalized anxiety disorders develop when defense mechanisms break down and function poorly.

Carl Rogers, the leading *humanistic* theorist, believes that people with phobic and generalized disorders first develop a defensive way of functioning when as children they fail to receive *unconditional positive regard* from significant others and so become overly critical of themselves.

*Existentialists* believe that phobic and generalized anxiety disorders result from the existential anxiety we experience because we know that life is finite and suspect it may have no meaning.

*Behaviorists* believe that phobic disorders are learned from the environment through *classical conditioning* and through *modeling.* They also believe that avoidance behaviors develop through *operant conditioning* and prevent extinction of a fear response. Behaviorists propose that specific learned fears produce a generalized anxiety disorder through *stimulus generalization.*

Some *cognitive* theorists believe that generalized anxiety disorders are caused by *maladaptive assumptions.* Others attribute the disorder to *faulty thinking processes.* The latter believe that generalized anxiety disorders occur in people who have received too few warning signals in advance of the negative events in their lives.

*Biological* theorists argue that generalized anxiety disorders result from a dysfunctioning of the autonomic nervous system and deficient activity of the neurotransmitter GABA. Concordance studies have lent some support to the notion that generalized anxiety disorders are caused in part by a physiological predisposition.

Anyone is capable of a panic reaction, but sufferers of *panic disorder* experience panic attacks frequently, unpredictably, and without apparent provocation. Because persons with panic disorders are often helped by antidepressant drugs, biological theorists believe that abnormal *norepinephrine* activity in the *locus coeruleus* is a key factor. The cognitive-biological position holds that panic-prone people become preoccupied with their bodily sensations and mental states and misinterpret them as indicative of imminent catastrophe.

People with an *obsessive compulsive disorder* experience intense anxiety if they try to resist their *obsessions* — repetitive and unwanted thoughts, ideas, impulses, or images that keep invading their consciousness — or *compulsions* — repetitive and rigid actions that they feel compelled to perform. The most common theme of obsessive thinking is contamination. Common forms of compulsions are cleaning; checking; symmetry, order, or balance; touching; verbal rituals; and counting.

Although some people with an obsessive compulsive disorder experience obsessions only or compulsions only, approximately 70 percent experience both. In many cases a person's compulsion is a yielding to obsessive doubts, ideas, or urges. In such cases, compulsions serve to control obsessions.

Obsessive compulsive disorders are among the least understood mental disorders. According to the *psychodynamic* view, obsessive compulsive disorders arise out of the battle between id impulses, which appear as obsessive thoughts, and ego defense mechanisms, which take the form of counterthoughts or compulsive actions. *Behaviorists* suggest that compulsive behaviors develop through chance associations and operant conditioning. *Biological* researchers have identified two biological factors that may contribute to this disorder: abnormal activity of the neurotransmitter *serotonin* and abnormal *glucose metabolism* in key regions of the brain.

People with *post-traumatic stress disorder* react with a distinct pattern of symptoms to some traumatic event, generally one that is outside the range of usual human experience and would be traumatic for almost anyone. The pattern of symptoms includes reexperiencing the traumatic event, avoidance of related events, reduced responsiveness and increased arousal, anxiety, and guilt. In most cases the symptoms begin soon after the trauma, but sometimes a longer period intervenes.

Post-traumatic stress disorder can emerge in response to combat conditions and is especially prominent among Vietnam veterans. It may also occur in the wake of natural disasters or after stress that is intentionally inflicted, for example, genocide or rape. In attempting to explain why some people develop post-traumatic stress disorder and others do not, researchers have focused on both personal variables and social support.

# TOPIC OVERVIEW

**GLOBAL THERAPIES**

Psychodynamic Therapies

Humanistic and Existential Therapies

**SPECIFIC THERAPIES**

Systematic Desensitization

Flooding and Implosive Therapy

Modeling

Social Skills Training

Cognitive Therapies

Stress Management Training

Paradoxical Intention

Exposure and Response Prevention

Drug Therapies

# CHAPTER 7

# TREATMENTS
# FOR ANXIETY
# DISORDERS

What does it mean to overcome an anxiety disorder? When should the treatment for such a disorder be deemed successful? Is it when symptoms are reduced, or must they be eliminated? Perhaps it is enough for the client to learn how to function in the face of anxiety. The answers depend partly on the perspective of the therapist and partly on the views and goals of the client. Here Fred describes his "triumph" over anxiety problems:

*Everything used to upset me. From big problems to the smallest of issues.* I would worry and worry, stay awake nights, and drive my wife up a wall. Therapy has helped to change all that. My wife says that I seem to be a different person. And I feel like a different person. I rarely get upset, certainly not over little things. Oh, sure, if there's an illness or accident, or a problem at work, I'll get concerned. But it doesn't get out of hand. I'm really enjoying my life again.

And Howard says:

*I'm feeling better since I first started treatment,* but it's a long way from perfect. I still have a lot of fears, worry a lot, blow things out of proportion. But I do have more of a handle on things now. At least I don't worry as often. I don't get scared in as many situations. I even have some evenings when I don't worry at all. It's a battle. I have to work at it. But, at least, I'm no longer anxious every second.

Although Fred and Howard are talking about different kinds of success, they both feel that they have made significant progress in their battles against anxiety. And in each case progress has been aided by a systematic treatment approach.

# GLOBAL THERAPIES: PSYCHODYNAMIC AND HUMANISTIC APPROACHES

The practitioner of a global therapy follows the same general procedure regardless of the client's particular disorder. Psychodynamic therapists try to help all their clients recognize and resolve the impact of past events. Using procedures such as free association and gently suggesting interpretations, they lead clients on a search for the deep-seated impulses, needs, and conflicts that underlie their emotions and behavior, expecting that the resulting insights will eventually foster recovery. Humanistic and existential therapists, on the other hand, try to help clients become more aware and accepting of their true thoughts and feelings, expecting that in this way they will learn to lead more authentic and fulfilling lives.

## Psychodynamic Therapies

Believing that people with anxiety disorders are in one way or another fearful of their id impulses and unable to control them successfully, psychodynamic therapists try to help clients uncover and understand these unconscious issues (dos Santos, 1985). In the following case, the therapist uses classic psychoanalytical techniques and interpretations to help a client overcome his generalized anxiety disorder. The client, a financially successful young man, was unable to enjoy his success, felt inferior to others, and had a very limited social life.

*In the course of analysis many facts were revealed that* explained his inability to enjoy his financial success, and his despair of having an intimate relationship with a respectable girl. Briefly stated these difficulties were all rooted in guilt arising from unresolved oedipal conflicts and incestuous feelings for his sisters. Material success and becoming the sole support of the family symbolized for him the childhood wish to replace and surpass his father. Hence when he accomplished his wholehearted desire to give his mother every comfort to compensate for her many years of hardship, he was faced with an acute conflict.

He had always retained his strong attachment to his mother, since she was the only understanding and mild person in his whole miserable environment. He also had very tender feelings for his two young sisters. Toward the male members of his family who had always abused him he felt hatred, rebellion, and a desire to excel them. . . .

[Over the course of treatment] he saw clearly how much his business was responsible for creating actual conflicts and neurotic difficulties because it was a stepping stone to realizing his competitive drives. Apart from the conscious reasons he also recognized the unconscious motivations for his ambitions to be an independent, successful businessman, the center of this being more powerful materially than brothers and father and to have power over them, make them dependent, if he could, on him. He became also more aware as analysis progressed why he gradually became tired of the business, lost his ambition, began to have anxieties that grew worse. By realizing his ambitions to be more successful than the older brothers and father, he also realized his childhood and puberty period ambitions, which then carried the oedipal desire and so were charged with a powerful sense of guilt. The adult success revived the early striving and brought forth the early repressed guilt feeling that accompanied these strivings, and this chaos created his desire to run away from it all, in the neurosis and illness. . . .

With this [insight] and working through of aggressiveness the patient began to achieve self-confidence in his business, social, and family relations. He became less afraid of his business associates and began to develop genuine feelings of affection for, or at least understanding of, various members of his family. He started meeting young people of college training and even putting up brave arguments against their opinions. At this period he bought a better car, which he had hitherto avoided doing, and he also began to interest himself in sports. He became ambitious to make up his lack of education, began to study, and went to the theater. Finally he decided to sell his business, to rest for a period.

*(Lorand, 1950, pp. 37–43)*

Controlled research has not consistently supported the effectiveness of psychodynamic approaches in cases of anxiety disorder (Prochaska, 1984). The bulk of evidence suggests that psychodynamic therapy is at best of modest help to people suffering from the broad symptoms of generalized anxiety disorders and of little help for those with other anxiety disorders, such as phobic and obsessive compulsive disorders (Berk & Efran, 1983; Salzman, 1980).

In fact, Freud himself said that psychodynamic techniques alone may be insufficient to cure phobic disorders. He wrote, "One can hardly ever master a phobia if one waits till the patient lets the analysis influence him to give it up. One succeeds only when one can induce them through the influence of analysis . . . to go about alone and to struggle with their anxiety while they make the attempt" (Freud, [1919] 1959, pp. 399–400).

Traditional psychodynamic therapy may actually add to the difficulties of patients with obsessive compulsive disorders (Salzman, 1980). It has been claimed that the psychodynamic focus on free association and interpretation inadvertently plays into the tendency of obsessive compulsive persons to ruminate and overinterpret (Noonan, 1971). Thus short-term psychodynamic therapies—more direct and action-based—have sometimes been used with these clients. In one technique, the therapist directly advises obsessive compulsive clients that their compulsions are defense mechanisms and urges them to stop acting compulsively (Salzman, 1985, 1980). Research has not yet clarified whether these newer approaches are indeed more effective than traditional psychodynamic therapies (Hirschfeld & Goodwin, 1988).

## Humanistic and Existential Therapies

Like psychodynamic therapists, humanistic and existential therapists treat all disorders more or less uniformly. Client-centered humanistic therapists try to show unconditional positive regard for their clients and to empathize with them, expecting that an atmosphere of genuine acceptance and caring will provide the security they need to recognize their true inner needs, thoughts, and emotions (Raskin & Rogers, 1989). The therapists' goal is to help clients "experience" themselves—that is, become completely trusting of their instincts and honest and comfortable with themselves. Their anxiety or other symptoms of psychological dysfunctioning will then subside. Carl Rogers describes how client-centered therapy helped Mrs. Oak overcome the anxiety and related symptoms that had been disrupting her life.

*Mrs. Oak was a housewife in her late thirties who was in a deeply discordant relationship with her husband and also much disturbed in her relationship with her adolescent daughter, who had recently been through a serious illness which had been diagnosed as psychosomatic. Mrs. Oak felt she must be to blame for this illness. She herself was a sensitive person, eager to be honest with herself and to search out the causes of her problems. She was a person with little formal education, though intelligent and widely read.*

*By the fifth interview any specific concentration on her problems had dropped out and the major focus of therapy had shifted to an experiencing of herself and her emotional reactions. She felt at times that she should be "working on*

*my problems" but that she felt drawn to this experiencing, that somehow she wanted to use the therapy hour for what she called her "vaguenesses." This was a good term, since she expressed herself in half-sentences, poetic analogies, and expressions which seemed more like fantasy. Her communications were often hard to follow or understand but obviously involved much deep feeling experienced in the immediate present.*

*She was unusually sensitive to the process she was experiencing in herself. To use some of her expressions, she was feeling pieces of a jigsaw puzzle, she was singing a song without words, she was creating a poem, she was learning a new way of experiencing herself which was like learning to read Braille. Therapy was an experiencing of herself, in all its aspects, in a safe relationship. At first it was her guilt and her concern over being responsible for the maladjustments of others. Then it was her hatred and bitterness toward life for having cheated and frustrated her in so many different areas, particularly the sexual, and then it was the experiencing of her own hurt, of the sorrow she felt for herself for having been so wounded. But along with these went the experiencing of self as having a capacity for wholeness, a self which was not possessively loving toward others but was "without hate," a self that cared about others. This last followed what was, for her, one of the deepest experiences in therapy . . . —the realization that the therapist cared, that it really mattered to him how therapy turned out for her, that he really valued her. She experienced the soundness of her basic directions. She gradually became aware of the fact that, though she had searched in every corner of herself, there was nothing fundamentally bad, but rather, at heart she was positive and sound. She realized that the values she deeply held were such as would set her at variance with her culture, but she accepted this calmly. . . .*

*One of the outstanding characteristics of the interviews was the minimal consideration of her outside behavior. Once an issue was settled in her, the behavioral consequences were mentioned only by chance. After she had "felt" her way through her relationship with her daughter, there was little mention of her behavior toward the daughter until much later when she casually mentioned that the relationship was much better. Likewise, in regard to a job. She had never worked outside the home, and the prospect terrified her, yet she thought it highly important if she were to feel independent of her husband. She finally settled the issue in her feelings to the extent that she said she thought now that she could look for or take a job. She never mentioned it again. Only through a chance outside source did the therapist learn that, at about the end of therapy, she chose an establishment in which she wished to work, applied for a position, ignored the turn-down which she received, and convinced the manager that he should give her a trial. She is still holding the position. It was the same in regard to her marriage. She decided that she could not continue in marriage but that she did not wish to break up the marriage in a battle or with resentment and hurt. Shortly after the conclusion of therapy she achieved this goal of a separation and divorce which was mutually agreed upon.*

When she left therapy, it was with the feeling that a process was going on in her which would continue to operate. She felt that the relationship with the therapist had been very meaningful and in a psychological sense would never stop, even though she walked out of the office for good. She felt ready, she thought, to cope with her life, though she realized it would not be easy.

*(Rogers, 1954, pp. 261–264)*

In spite of this and other optimistic case reports, research has failed to show that humanistic and existential approaches are generally effective treatments for anxiety disorders. Controlled studies of Rogers's client-centered approach suggest that this form of treatment is only sometimes more effective than providing placebo therapy or nothing at all (Martin, 1972; DiLoreto, 1971; Truax et al., 1966; Satz & Baraff, 1962). Moreover, there have been few such studies of other humanistic or existential approaches to treatment of anxiety disorders, largely because practitioners of these approaches believe that experimental methods cannot test the validity of their phenomenological focus, techniques, and goals (Prochaska, 1984; Adesso et al., 1974; Bornstein et al., 1974).

# SPECIFIC THERAPIES: BEHAVIORAL, COGNITIVE, AND BIOLOGICAL APPROACHES

Behavioral, cognitive, and biological therapists, in contrast to global therapists, practice specific therapies tailored to the idiosyncratic features of each disorder. Behaviorists have virtually ruled the clinical field in the treatment of phobic disorders, particularly of simple phobias. All three approaches, however, have made substantial contributions to treatment of the other anxiety disorders.

## Simple Phobias

The anxiety disorders that have had the longest record of successful treatment are the simple phobias. All the specific therapies have been used to treat these intense fears of specific objects, events, or situations, but behavioral therapists have consistently fared better than the others in head-to-head comparisons (Wilson, 1989; O'Leary & Wilson, 1987; Berk & Efran, 1983; Emmelkamp, 1982; Rachman & Wilson, 1980).

The major behavioral approaches to simple phobias are desensitization, flooding, and modeling. Collectively, these approaches are called *exposure-based treatments,* because in all of them clients are exposed to the dreaded object or situation (Foa & Kozak, 1985). The exposure may be vicarious or direct, brief or long, gradual or sudden.

**Systematic Desensitization**　Clients treated by *systematic desensitization,* a technique developed by Joseph Wolpe (1987, 1982, 1969, 1958), learn to relax while they are confronted with the objects or situations they fear. Since relaxation and fear are incompatible, the new relaxation response is thought to substitute for the previous fear response.

Wolpe began to develop this technique in 1944, when, as a military medical officer, he conducted classical conditioning experiments on cats. In the first phase of these experiments, he sounded a buzzer while hungry cats were eating. When he later sounded the buzzer at random times, the cats sought out food and ate it. Next he sounded a buzzer while the same cats were receiving electric shocks. Now the cats showed fear in response to the buzzer and would not eat while it sounded. Wolpe concluded that eating and fear were incompatible responses and that the stronger fear response had now substituted for the eating response. He had replaced the old bond (buzzer → eating) with a new bond (buzzer → fear).

Wolpe believed that this process of inhibition should work both ways. Just as he could stop an animal's eating response by teaching it a more powerful fear response, he should be able to stop its fear response. In fact, an earlier experiment by Mary Cover Jones (1924) supported this expectation. Jones had reported the case of a young boy who was afraid of rabbits. She helped the child to overcome this fear by giving him his favorite food while she moved a rabbit closer and closer. Soon the child could actually play with the rabbit.

Wolpe labeled this process *reciprocal inhibition,* a term then in use by physiologists (Sherrington, 1906), because he believed that he was dealing with a physiological incompatibility between the responses of eating and fear. He believed that the technique of reciprocal inhibition could be used to overcome phobias, and he searched for responses other than eating that might be incompatible with fear. He decided upon the relaxation response and developed a technique for teaching people to replace fear responses with relaxation responses, the technique now known as systematic desensitization. Systematic desensitization is taught in three phases: *relaxation training,* construction of a *fear hierarchy,* and

A person suffering from aerophobia once said, "I'm not afraid of flying—it's crashing and getting burned to a crisp I'm afraid of." Seeking to reduce the $1.5 billion a year lost to this phobia, the airline industry has offered desensitization programs for sufferers. USAir's Fearful Flyers Program begins with an instructor guiding would-be passengers in relaxation exercises.

*graded pairing* of feared objects and relaxation responses.

### Relaxation Training

Desensitization therapists first teach clients to release all the tension in their bodies on cue. Over the course of several sessions and homework assignments, clients learn to identify individual muscle groups, tense them, relax them, and ultimately relax the whole body. With continued practice, the clients are able to bring on a state of deep muscle relaxation at will.

In the case of Mrs. Schmidt, a woman with a "gross fear of rejection," Wolpe began with relaxation training. His instructions included the following points:

*Identifying and Tensing the Muscle Groups*

. . . Now, what I want you to do is, with your left hand, hold the arm of your chair quite tight. I want you to observe certain things that are a result of your holding this chair tight. First of all, there are certain sensations. To begin with, you have sensations . . . in your hand and you may have other sensations. With your right hand, point out to me all the places where you get any kind of feeling which seems to be a result of holding the chair tightly.

*(Wolpe, Counselor Recording and Tests)*

*Relaxing the Muscle Groups*

. . . I'm going to hold your *wrist* again and ask you to pull against it. When you pull, you will notice that the muscle becomes tight again. Then I will say to you, "Let go gradually." Now, when you let go, I want you to notice two things. The tight feeling will become less and I want you also to notice that the letting go is something that you do—

something active that you put in the muscle. Well, your forearm will eventually come down to rest on the arm of the chair and ordinarily that would seem to you as though that's the end of the matter. You have let go. But it will not really be quite the end, because some of the muscle fibers will still be contracted, so that when your forearm has come down to the chair I will say to you, "Keep on letting go. Go on doing that in the muscle, that activity which you were doing while it was coming down. . . . Try and make it go further and further.

*(Wolpe, Counselor Recording and Tests)*

### Construction of a Fear Hierarchy

During the early sessions of desensitization, therapists also help clients to make a list of their specific fears. The fears are then ranked in a hierarchy, ranging from situations that evoke only a trace of fear to those that the clients consider extremely frightening (see Table 7-1). Near the bottom of Mrs. Schmidt's hierarchy were slights by people she didn't know or care about; at the top were rejections by people who meant a great deal to her.

### Graded Pairings

Next the clients learn how to relax in the face of their fears. They are instructed to place themselves in a general state of relaxation. While they are in this state, the therapist has them confront the event at the bottom of their fear hierarchy. This may be an actual physical confrontation (for example, a person who fears heights may stand on a chair or climb a stepladder) — in which case the process is called *in vivo desensitization* — or the confrontation may be imagined, with the client creating an image of the frightening event while the therapist describes it — in which case the process is called *covert desensitization.*

The clients move through the entire list, pairing their relaxation responses with each feared item in the hierarchy. Because the first item is only mildly frightening, it is usually only a short while before they are able to relax totally when they confront it. Over the course of several sessions, clients move up the ladder of their fears until they reach and overcome the one that frightens them most of all. At this point they can relax in the face of all items on the hierarchy. Here Wolpe guides Mrs. Schmidt up her hierarchy of fears:

OK, now, you are quite nice and relaxed. Now, keep your eyes closed and I'm going to ask you to imagine some scenes. Now, you will imagine these scenes very clearly, and generally speaking they will not affect your state of relaxation. But if by any chance anything does affect your state of calm, you'll be able to signal that to me by raising your right forefinger about an inch. So now, I want you to imagine just that you're standing on a street corner and you're watching the traffic. Just a nice, pleasant, peaceful

TABLE 7-1

| FEAR HIERARCHIES |
| --- |
| **Fear of Examinations** |

• On the way to the university on the day of an examination.

• In the process of answering an examination paper.

• Before the unopened doors of the examination room.

• Awaiting the distribution of examination papers.

• The examination paper lies face down before her.

• The night before an examination.

• The day before an examination.

• Two days before an examination.

• Three days before an examination.

• Four days before an examination.

• Five days before an examination.

• A week before an examination.

• Two weeks before an examination.

• A month before an examination.

*(continued)*

*Source:* Wolpe, 1969, p. 117.

day, and you're watching the cars, and the taxis and trucks, and people all passing at this corner. OK, now, stop imagining this scene. Now, if the scene didn't worry you at all, do nothing. If that scene disturbed you, raise your finger now. *(No finger movement)* OK, that's fine, now just keep on relaxing.

Now, I want you to imagine that you're walking along the sidewalk and you see, walking toward you from the other side, Mrs. Benning. Now, as you pass Mrs. Benning, you see she is looking toward you and you get ready to greet her, and she just walks past as though she didn't recognize you. Now, stop imagining that. Now, if that, if imagining that disturbed you even a very small bit, I want you to raise your right index finger now. If it didn't worry you, don't do anything. *(No finger movement)*

Now, I want you to imagine again that you're walking on the sidewalk and you see, moving toward you, Selma and you get ready to greet her, and she seems to see you but she walks right on — she doesn't greet you. Now, stop imagining this. If you felt any disturbance at that. . . . *(Right forefinger rises)*

*(Wolpe, Counselor Recording and Tests)*

When a client is tense during a scene, as Mrs. Schmidt was during the last scene, the therapist stops and has the client focus exclusively on relaxing. Once the client is relaxed, they try the scene again until it can be imagined without arousing any fear. They do not move on to the next scene until each of the lower-ranked scenes has been mastered fully.

**Flooding and Implosive Therapy** Another behavioral treatment for phobic disorders is *flooding.* This technique was actually developed by a psychodynamic therapist, Thomas Stampfl (1975), who called it *implosive therapy.* Today "flooding" and "implosive therapy" are used almost interchangeably and the procedure is employed primarily by behaviorists. Flooding therapists believe that clients will stop fearing things when they are exposed to them repeatedly and made to see that they are actually quite harmless.

Flooding operates much like the extinction procedures that have been developed by conditioning researchers. In a famous extinction study, experimenters first gave dogs a series of intense electrical shocks always accompanied by the sound of a buzzer, thus conditioning the dogs to fear not only shock but the sound of the buzzer as well (Solomon, Kamin, & Wynne, 1953).

TABLE 7-1 *(continued)*

| **Fear of Flying** |
|---|
| • The plane has landed and stopped at the terminal. |
| • A trip has been planned, and I have decided "out loud" to travel by plane. |
| • I have called the travel agent and told him of my plans. |
| • It is the day before the trip, and I pack my suitcase, close it, and lock it. |
| • It is ten days before the trip, and I receive the tickets in the mail. |
| • It is the day of the flight, I am leaving home. |
| • I am driving to the airport for my flight. I am aware of every plane I see. |
| • I am entering the terminal. I am carrying my bags and tickets. |
| • I proceed to the airline desk and wait in line. |
| • I am in the lounge with many other people, some with bags also waiting for flights. |
| • I hear my flight number announced, and I proceed to the security checkpoint with my hand luggage. |
| • I walk down the ramp leading to the plane and enter the door of the plane. |
| • I am now inside the plane. I move in from the aisle and sit down in my assigned seat. |
| • I notice the seat-belt signs light up, so I fasten my seat belt and I notice the sound of the motors starting. |
| • Everyone is seated with their seat belts fastened, and the plane slowly moves away from the terminal. |
| • I notice the seat-belt signs are again lighted, and the pilot announces that we are preparing to land. |
| • I am looking out the window and suddenly the plane enters clouds and I cannot see out the window. |
| • The plane has stopped at the end of the runway and is sitting, waiting for instructions to take off. |
| • The plane is descending to the runway for a landing. I feel the speed and see the ground getting closer. |
| • The plane has taken off from the airport and banks as it changes direction. I am aware of the "tilt." |
| • The plane encounters turbulence. |
| • The plane starts down the runway, and the motors get louder as the plane increases speed and suddenly lifts off. |

*Source:* Martin & Pear, 1988, p. 380; Roscoe et al., 1980.

Later, the dogs were also taught that they could escape the stimulus they feared by jumping over a barrier and out of their box whenever the buzzer sounded. The dogs continued to display these acquired responses even when the experimenters later stopped the shocks. That is, their fear and avoidance responses persisted indefinitely because they never stayed in the box long enough to learn that the shocks had been stopped. The experimenters were able to extinguish these acquired responses only by forcibly restraining the dogs in their boxes until they finally saw that shocks were no longer accompanying the sound of the buzzer.

Therapists who use the technique of flooding believe that people with phobic disorders, like the dogs in this study, must be forced to confront what they fear so they will see that no real danger exists. These therapists use no relaxation training and no graduated approach. Flooding procedures, like desensitization, can be either

In the behavioral exposure technique of implosive therapy, or flooding, therapists have clients imagine or confront feared objects in their full intensity and often present the object in as frightening a way as possible. A person with a snake phobia might be shown a vivid picture of the animal's open mouth and sharp fangs or helped to imagine them in gruesome detail.

in vivo (Crow et al., 1972; Leitenberg & Callahan, 1973; Hand et al., 1974) or imaginal (Stampfl & Levis, 1967; Levis & Carrera, 1967). Some clinicians reserve the term "flooding" for the in vivo procedures and "implosive therapy" for imaginal ones.

When therapists guide clients in imagining the feared objects or situations, they often embellish and exaggerate the description so that the clients experience intense emotional arousal. In the case of a woman who had a phobic reaction to snakes, the therapist had her imagine the following scenes, among others:

> Close your eyes again. Picture the snake out in front of you, now make yourself pick it up. Reach down, pick it up, put it in your lap, feel it wiggling around in your lap, leave your hand on it, put your hand out and feel it wiggling around. Kind of explore its body with your fingers and hand. You don't like to do it, make yourself do it. Make yourself do it. Really grab onto the snake. Squeeze it a little bit, feel it. Feel it kind of start to wind around your hand. Let it. Leave your hand there, feel it touching your hand and winding around it, curling around your wrist.
>
> Okay, now put your finger out towards the snake and feel his head coming up. Its head is towards your finger and it is starting to bite at your finger. Let it, let it bite at your finger. Put your finger out, let it bite, let it bite at your finger, feel

its fangs go right down into your finger. Oooh, feel the pain going right up your arm and into your shoulder.

> Okay, feel him coiling around your hand again, touching you, slimy, now he is going up on your shoulder and he crawls there and he is sitting on your chest and he is looking you right in the eye. He is big and he is black and he is ugly and he's coiled up and he is ready to strike and he is looking at you. Picture his face, look at his eyes, look at those long sharp fangs. . . . He strikes out at you. *(Therapist slaps hand.)* Feel him bite at your face. Feel him bite at your face, let him bite; let him bite; just relax and let him bite; let him bite at your face, let him bite; let him bite at your face; feel his fangs go right into your cheeks; and the blood is coming out on your face now . . . feel it biting your eye and it is going to pull your eye right out and down on your cheek. It is kind of gnawing on it and eating it, eating at your eye. Your little eye is down on your cheek and it is gnawing and biting at your eye. Picture it. Now it is crawling into your eye socket and wiggling around in there, feel it wiggling and wiggling up in your head.

*(Hogan, 1968, pp. 423–431)*

Given the intensity of implosive therapy and the suddenness with which clients are exposed to the stimuli they fear, some clinicians hold that the procedure may do further damage to clients and should be considered only as a last resort. As we shall see shortly, however, when it is conducted by a properly trained therapist, implosive therapy is no more likely than other forms of treatment to cause harm and is more likely than most to help clients overcome their phobias.

**Modeling**   The behavioral technique of modeling, or *vicarious conditioning,* has also been used to treat simple phobias (Bandura, 1977, 1971; Bandura, Adams, & Beyer, 1977). In this procedure it is the therapist who confronts the feared object or situation while the fearful client observes. The therapist essentially acts as a model who demonstrates that the client's fear is groundless or highly exaggerated. It is expected that after several sessions clients will be able to approach the objects or situations with relative composure.

The most effective modeling technique is *participant modeling,* or *guided participation.* Here the therapist and client first construct a fear hierarchy, just as they would in desensitization. Then, while the client observes, the therapist experiences the least feared item in the hierarchy. Eventually the client is encouraged to join in. Using this technique, they move up the hierarchy until the client is able to confront the most feared object or situation on the list.

Here is a participant modeling procedure for the treatment of snake phobias:

In the behavioral exposure technique of participant modeling, a therapist treats a client with a snake phobia by first handling the snake himself and demonstrating its harmlessness, then encouraging the client to touch and handle the snake.

After these introductory interactions, the therapist may proceed to the major sequence of modeled interactions with the snake, which are as follows:

I. Gloved-hand procedure.
  1. Stroke the snake's midsection, then tail, then top of head.
  2. Raise the snake's midsection, then tail, then head.
  3. Grasp the snake gently but firmly a few inches from the head and about 6 inches from the tail, remove it from the cage (taking care not to approach the client or swing the snake obviously closer to him).
  4. Comfortably handle the snake, modeling how easy and comfortable the interaction process can be, how the model is in complete control, and so forth. This facet of the procedure should continue for several minutes . . . until external indications are that the client's anxiety level is rather low.
II. Bare-hand procedure.
  1–4. The above procedure should be repeated by the therapist/model using his bare hands.

. . . When these two modeling sequences have been successfully completed, the client may be asked if he is willing to approach the snake. . . . When the client agrees to approach the snake, the therapist should pick the snake up and hold it while he asks the client to don the gloves and briefly touch the snake's midsection. When the client successfully does so, reinforcement and support should be given; for example, "I'll bet that is the first time in your life you ever touched a snake. Good for you!"

The client may then be asked to stroke the midsection, then touch and stroke the tail, and finally touch and stroke the top of the head. Should the snake extend its tongue, the therapist might matter-of-factly note that it is harmless, merely a sensing device for sound waves.

When the gloved touching and stroking behaviors have been completed, the client should be asked to hold the snake in his gloved hands. He may be instructed to place his hand loosely about the midsection of the snake and hold it there until he feels fairly comfortable (the therapist continues to support the snake). If these actions appear to cause some anxiety (or, perhaps, excitement) in the client, it may be suggested that he take a deep breath to induce relaxation. When progress is apparent, praise should be given.

The procedure continues, with the client holding (in gloved hand) the snake's tail, then its head. Finally, he may be asked to support the entire snake. This progression is not rapid, of course; time is allowed at each step for the client to become comfortable and praise is given for progress. If at any point the client expresses anxiety, the therapist should immediately take the snake back (calmly) and offer reassurance before returning to the participation process.

*(Rimm & Masters, 1979, pp. 126–127)*

**Effectiveness of Behavioral Therapies**    Clinical researchers have repeatedly found that each of the behavioral approaches for simple phobias is indeed helpful. Moreover, in most cases once a phobia has been successfully treated by a behavioral method, new symptoms do not arise to replace it, as some psychodynamic theorists have predicted.

The first controlled experiment on desensitization measured the progress of two groups of subjects with snake phobias (Lang & Lazovik, 1963). One group received desensitization therapy; the control group received no therapy at all. After treatment, the desensitized subjects showed significantly less fear of snakes than the control subjects did. Even six months later, the desensitized subjects were less fearful of snakes. Overall, close to 75 percent of people with simple phobias improve in desensitization therapy (McNally, 1986; Kazdin & Wilcoxin, 1976).

Flooding, too, helps people overcome simple phobias. A single implosive therapy session was administered to twenty-one subjects who had an extreme fear of rats, during which the therapist had the subjects imagine scenes in which they touched rats, had their fingers nibbled by rats, were clawed by rats, and the like (Hogan & Kirchner, 1967). After this treatment, twenty of the subjects were able to open a rat's cage and fourteen could actually pick up the rat. A control group of twenty-two subjects were instructed to imagine irrelevant and neutral scenes while they relaxed. Only three of them could later open a rat's cage and seven refused even to enter the room!

Modeling has also proved to be an effective treatment for simple phobias. Albert Bandura and his colleagues (1969) used modeling to treat students who had snake phobias. One group of students went through a procedure consisting of live modeling and guided participation. A second group was treated by **symbolic modeling;** that is, they observed films of people who were safely and comfortably interacting with snakes. Each film in the sequence showed an increasingly threatening kind of interaction. Yet another group was treated with covert desensitization, while a control group received no treatment at all.

Ninety-two percent of the students treated with live modeling and guided participation overcame their fears of snakes. Many of the symbolic modeling and covert desensitization subjects also improved, but not nearly so much as the guided participation subjects. The untreated control subjects showed virtually no improvement.

At first glance, these findings seem to suggest that modeling may be superior to desensitization as a form of treatment, but other research has shown that this is not the case. The key factor leading to success with a behavioral approach appears to be actual in vivo contact by clients with the feared object or situation (Foa & Kozak, 1985). In vivo desensitization is more effective than covert desensitization, in vivo flooding more effective than imaginal flooding, and participant modeling more helpful than strictly observed modeling. Thus the apparent superiority of participant modeling over covert desensitization in Bandura's snake phobia study is probably just another case of real exposure outdoing imaginal exposure. When the exposure factor is kept constant, desensitization, flooding, and modeling appear to be equally effective treatments for simple phobias (O'Leary & Wilson, 1987; Foa & Kozak, 1985; Emmelkamp, 1982; Rachman, 1976).

Recognizing the similar efficacies of these approaches, many behavioral therapists now combine features of each, making sure they include the critical feature of in vivo exposure (Marks, 1987; McNally, 1986). One approach, called **prolonged exposure,** combines the gradualism of desensitization, the nonrelaxation of flooding, and the supportive modeling of guided participation (Watson, Gaind, & Marks, 1971). In a test of this approach, clients with long-standing simple phobias listened to tape recordings of the sounds of objects they feared before being presented with the objects themselves and urged to approach them as closely as possible and stay in contact with them until the fears lessened. The exposure sessions were tailored to each client's phobia. For example, 90 balloons were blown up and burst for a client who feared balloons; a client who feared birds was guided, through modeling, to touch and play with a pet budgerigar; and a client who feared water was encouraged to submerge her head in a bowl and eventually in a bath. The researchers reported that all clients treated with this approach were helped significantly in an average treatment time of five hours and continued to show those gains in follow-ups.

## Agoraphobia

For years clinicians made relatively little impact on agoraphobia, the phobic disorder in which people fear leaving their homes and entering public places. Yet approaches have since been developed that enable many such people to venture out of their homes with less anxiety. These new approaches do not typically help as many sufferers as do treatments for simple phobias, but they do bring considerable relief to many people.

Once again behaviorists have led the way by developing a variety of in vivo exposure approaches (Barlow & Waddel, 1985; Hallam, 1985; Foa & Kozak, 1985). Therapists typically help clients to venture farther and farther from their homes and to enter ouside places gradually, one step at a time. Sometimes the therapists use support, reasoning, and coaxing to get clients to confront the outside world (Emmelkamp, 1982). They also use more systematic exposure methods, such as the reinforcement technique described in the following case study:

*The first of our patients to take part in these experiments* was a young woman who, shortly after she married, found herself unable to leave home. Even walking a few yards from her front door terrified her and often led to panic; she felt she might faint, choke, or even die if she did not return home at once. This phobia could be traced back to her childhood. . . .

When the patient was eleven years old, her mother, who had for some time been complaining of a choking sensation, was suddenly hospitalized for thyroid surgery. Frightened by her mother's illness and imagining that her mother might die, she herself began to avoid eating solid foods, fearing that she might "choke to death." . . . The child's fear of choking, as we might expect, gradually dissipated when her mother returned from the hospital, but she remained afraid of being separated from her mother and never, for example, stayed overnight with friends.

It is not surprising, then, that this young woman found herself unable to function independently after leaving home to marry. Her inability to leave her new home was reinforced by an increasing dependence on her husband and by the solicitous overconcern of her mother, who was more and more frequently called in to stay with her. Her disability in a mobile society was enormous, and since she was cut off from her friends and from so much enjoyment in the outside world, depression added to her misery. Several years of psychotherapy brought her no relief, and she eventually became addicted to sleeping pills, which she discovered gave her enough courage to venture a little way alone. Eventually, she came to our laboratory for help.

To measure the patient's improvement, we laid out a mile-long course from the hospital to downtown, marked at about 25-yard intervals. Before beginning the experiment, we asked the patient to walk as far as she could along the course. Each time she balked at the front door of the hospital. Then the first phase of the experiment began: We held two sessions each day in which the patient was praised for staying out of the hospital for a longer and longer time. The reinforcement schedule was simple. If the patient stayed outside for 20 seconds on one trial and then on the next attempt stayed out for 30 seconds, she was praised enthusiastically. Now, however, the criterion for praise was raised — without the patient's knowledge — to 25 seconds. If she met the criterion she was again praised, and the time was increased again. If she did not stay out long enough, the therapist simply ignored her performance. To gain the therapist's attention, which she valued, she had to stay out longer each time.

This she did, until she was able to stay out for almost half an hour. But was she walking farther each time? Not at all. She was simply circling around in the front drive of the hospital, keeping the "safe place" in sight at all times. We therefore changed the reinforcement to reflect the distance walked. Now she began to walk farther and farther each time. Supported by this simple therapeutic procedure, the patient was progressively able to increase her self-confidence. The crucial question now became: What would happen if the reinforcement was stopped, if the therapist no longer praised the patient's progress?

Two things happened when praise was stopped. The patient at first walked farther, almost doubling her previous distance to reach a point within sight of downtown. Then, after a few sessions, she became increasingly less capable of walking alone, and her phobia completely returned. This phenomenon is well-known in reinforcement experiments as the "extinction burst." Animals pressing a lever for an occasional food reward will redouble their efforts temporarily if food is discontinued. . . . This reversal of progress demonstrated that improvement depended upon reinforcement, a conclusion that was strengthened when praise was begun once more, for soon the patient was able to walk downtown alone. Praise was then thinned out, but slowly, and the patient was encouraged to walk anywhere she pleased. Five years later, she was still perfectly well. We might assume that the benefits of being more independent maintained the gains and compensated for the loss of praise from the therapist.

*(Agras, 1985, pp. 77–80)*

Figure 7-1 demonstrates the steady progress of an agoraphobic client treated by this approach.

Exposure therapy often includes additional features, particularly support groups (Mavissakalian & Michelson, 1986, 1983; Hand et al., 1974) and home-based self-help programs (Cerney et al., 1988; Barlow et al.,

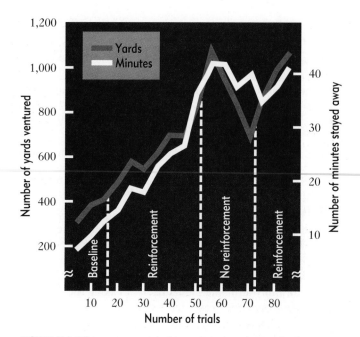

**FIGURE 7-1** When an agoraphobic patient was increasingly reinforced for walking out of and staying away from the front door of the hospital, she ventured increasingly farther and stayed away longer. When reinforcements were then stopped, she initially ventured even farther and stayed away even longer ("extinction burst"), but then steadily decreased the distance and time spent away from the hospital. When reinforcements were later reinstated, she again ventured farther and stayed away longer. *(Adapted from Agras et al., 1968.)*

1984; Emmelkamp, 1974), to motivate agoraphobic clients to work hard at their treatment. In the ***support group*** approach, a small number of people with agoraphobia go out together for exposure sessions that last for several hours. The group members support and encourage one another, and eventually coax one another to move away from the safety of the group and conduct exposure tasks on their own. In the ***home-based self-help programs,*** clinicians give clients and their families detailed instructions for carrying out exposure treatments themselves. Table 7-2 illustrates such instructions.

Between 60 and 70 percent of the agoraphobic clients who receive exposure-based treatment find it easier to enter public places, and the improvement persists four years or more (Craske, 1988; Cerny et al., 1988; Jansson et al., 1986, 1982). Unfortunately, these improvements tend to be partial rather than complete (Craske, 1988; Mathews, 1985; McPherson et al., 1980), and relapses may occur in as many as 50 percent of successfully treated clients, although these people readily recapture previous gains if they are treated again (Munby & Johnston, 1986). Those whose agoraphobic symptoms accompany a panic disorder seem to benefit less than

TABLE 7-2

| **SELF-HELP INSTRUCTIONS FOR THE CLIENT WITH AGORAPHOBIA** |
| --- |

When you are troubled by fear, the best treatment is to practice in those situations in which the fear occurs. When you practice *systematically* and *persistently,* you will experience a decrease of your fear. For those people who are fearful of going into the street alone the treatment procedure is as follows:

1. Each treatment session takes 90 minutes of your time. It is very important that you stick to these times. It is necessary to choose those times when you have nothing else to do and when you are at home alone. During treatment hours, you are therefore not allowed to receive any guests.

2. Since you will have to practice 90 minutes *in one session,* you *cannot* practice 60 minutes in the morning and then do the remainder in the afternoon. In that case, it is very likely your fear will increase rather than decrease. When you are tired of walking, you may, of course, rest for a few minutes.

3. Go into the street alone and start walking until you feel uncomfortable or tense. Then return to your home immediately. (Taking the dog and a bicycle with you is not permitted.)

4. Note the time that you are out on the street. Take a notebook in which you write down this period of time.

5. After this go outside again. Again, walk until you become tense or anxious. Then return to your home immediately, and, as before, write down the time that you have spent out on the street.

6. Continue practicing until 90 minutes have passed by.

7. Copy down the times you have scored during the last three practice sessions on the special form. Put this form in an envelope and send it to us that same day. We can then check how you are coming along. Postage is free.

8. It is very important to write down the times you have scored. In this way, you can see for yourself how much progress you have made. Research has shown that people who write down their times improve more than people who do not.

9. You are supposed to try to enlarge the distance you walk away from your home. Therefore, you are not allowed to walk in circles. You are not allowed to do any shopping or any talking to friends and acquaintances.

10. *Progress will not always continue at the same pace.* You should not let yourself be discouraged by this fact. Some people might notice rapid initial progress and later on a decrease. Usually this is only a temporary problem.

*Source:* Emmelkamp, 1982, pp. 299–300.

others from exposure-based therapy. We shall take a closer look at this group when we investigate treatments for panic disorders.

## Social Phobias

As with agoraphobia, it is only recently that clinicians have had any consistent success in treating social phobias — persistent fears of social situations where one might be scrutinized, feel embarrassed, and possibly make humiliating mistakes. This progress is due in large part to the growing recognition that social phobias have two distinct components that may feed each other: (1) people with these phobias may have incapacitating social fears, and (2) they may lack skill at initiating conversations, communicating their needs, or addressing the needs of others. Armed with this insight, clinicians now treat social phobias by either trying to reduce social fears, providing social skills training, or both, depending on the client (see Box 7-1).

**Reducing Social Fears** The behavioral approach of covert desensitization has frequently been employed to reduce social fears, but controlled studies suggest that it usually

## BOX 7-1

# Lights, Cameras, Anxiety: Treating Speech Anxiety

A fear of public speaking is only sometimes so severe and disabling as to be considered a social phobia. All the same, speaking before a group is something most people are afraid of. According to Michael Motley, professor of rhetoric and communications at the University of California, about 85 percent of the population feels uncomfortably anxious when speaking in public (Motley, 1988). Many very successful politicians, evangelists, and entertainers suffer extreme stage fright or speech anxiety. No less a public figure than Willard Scott, whose gift to gab with apparent ease entertains millions of viewers of the *Today Show* each morning, describes one of many instances of speech anxiety that he has experienced while on the air:

*I was on the air and the countdown* [was] normal . . . Stand by, 5, 4, 3, 2, 1, a strange feeling came over me, and I began to perspire, and I could find my breath laboring. I thought I was gonna pass out. . . . I'm a genuine, absolute, certified phobic. . . .

*(Later . . . with Bob Costas,*
*January 4, 1989)*

Motley offers public speaking courses to help people deal with this common form of anxiety. The thrust of his approach is to change people's attitudes toward public speaking and correct the myths they may have heard. He teaches his students to view speeches as communication rather than performance, to realize that audiences are really much more interested in hearing *what* they have to say than in criticizing *how* they are saying it. According to research, a speaker's nervousness is rarely noticed by the audience, even by those who are

trained to detect anxiety cues and told to look for them in a speaker.

In addition, Motley helps speakers to understand, anticipate, and recognize the physiological arousal that accompanies public speaking. Heart rate usually increases greatly just before a speech, rising from an average resting rate of 70 beats per minute to between 95 and 140. Once the speech begins, the heart rate jumps again to between 110 and 190 beats per minute. This second increase has taken many speakers by surprise, convincing them they were about to fall apart. Actually, it is only a temporary surge that tends to subside within thirty seconds, and the period can usually be made shorter yet if the speaker practices monitoring its rise and inevitable fall.

Finally, Motley offers the following tips for public speaking:

*Decide on your specific objectives first.* Before you think about anything else, know one or two major points you want to communicate. Then plan the best way to get them across.

*Put yourself in your audience's place.* Recognize how you and most of the audience differ in attitudes, interests and familiarity with what you are talking about. Then speak to them on their terms, in their language.

*Don't memorize, don't read.* Except for a few carefully chosen gems — memorable phrases or examples you know will work well — be as spontaneous as possible. Don't rehearse to the point that you find yourself saying things exactly the same way each time. Use brief notes to keep yourself organized.

*Speak to one person at a time.* Looking at and talking to individuals in

the audience helps keep you natural; it feels foolish orating at one person. Speak to that person as long as it is mutually comfortable, usually up to 15 seconds.

*Try not to think about your hands and facial expressions.* Instead, concentrate on what you want to get across and let your nonverbal communication take care of itself. Conscious attention to gestures leads to inhibition and awkwardness.

*Take it slow and easy.* People in an audience have a tremendous job of information-processing to do. They need your help. Slow down, pause and guide the audience through your talk by delineating major and minor points carefully. Remember that your objective is to help the audience understand what you are saying, not to present your information in record time.

*Speak the way you talk.* Speak as you do in casual conversation with someone you respect. Expecting perfection is unrealistic and only leads to tension. The audience is interested in your speech, not your speaking.

*Ask for advice and criticism.* For most people, careful organization and a conversational style add up to a good speech. A few speakers, however, have idiosyncrasies that distract an audience. Solicit frank criticism from someone you trust, focusing on what might have prevented you from accomplishing your objectives. Usually people can correct problems themselves once they are aware of them. If you don't feel you can, take a course in public speaking or see a speech consultant.

*(Motley, 1988, p. 49)*

has only a small and short-lived effect (Kanter & Gold-fried, 1979; Van Son, 1978; Trower et al., 1978). Recently behaviorists have started to apply in vivo exposure techniques instead (Marks, 1987, 1985). Here again the therapists guide, encourage, and persuade clients with social phobias to expose themselves to dreaded social situations and to remain until their fear subsides. Usually exposure is gradual, beginning with the situations they find least frightening and moving up the hierarchy from there. Some studies have indicated that in vivo exposure can be of considerable help in treating social phobias (Butler et al., 1984), but the effects of these interventions have yet to be explored comprehensively (O'Leary & Wilson, 1987; Foa & Kozak, 1985).

Group therapy often provides an ideal setting for these exposure treatments, enabling people to confront the social situations they fear head on in an atmosphere of support and concern. One woman who was afraid of blushing in front of people had to sit in front of other group members while wearing a slightly opened blouse until her fear dissipated (Emmelkamp, 1982). Similarly, a man who was afraid that his hands would tremble in the presence of others had to write on a blackboard in front of the group and serve tea to the other members.

Cognitive interventions have also been widely employed in the treatment of social fears. As we saw in Chapter 6, Albert Ellis (1989, 1976, 1967) believes that irrational assumptions are often at the root of these, and indeed other, mental disorders. Research suggests that several of the assumptions he cites are particularly likely to generate social fears; for example, "It is a dire necessity for an adult human being to be loved or approved of by virtually every significant other person in his community," or "Your general worth and self-acceptance depend upon the goodness of your performance and the degree that people approve of you" (Golden, 1981).

In Ellis's technique of *rational-emotive therapy* the practitioner's role is to point out the irrational assumptions held by clients with social phobias, offer alternative (more realistic) assumptions, and assign homework that gives clients practice at challenging old assumptions and applying new ones. As clients adopt new assumptions, their social fears are expected to lessen. The procedure is illustrated in the following discussion between Ellis and a client who fears that he will be rejected if he speaks up at gatherings. This discussion took place after the client had followed a homework assignment in which he was to observe his self-defeating thoughts and beliefs and force himself to say anything he had on his mind in social situations, no matter how stupid it might seem to him.

After two weeks of this assignment, the patient came into his next session of therapy and reported: "I did what you told me to do."

"Yes? And what happened?"

"Quite a lot! I found it much more difficult than I thought it would be to put what you said into effect. Really difficult!"

"But you did so, nevertheless?"

"Oh, yes. I kept doing, forcing myself to do so. Much more difficult than I expected, it was!"

"What was difficult, exactly?"

"First of all, seeing those sentences. The ones you said I was telling myself. I just couldn't see them at all at first. I seemed to be saying absolutely nothing to myself. But every time, just as you said, I found myself retreating from people, I said to myself: 'Now, even though you can't see it, there must be some sentences. What are they?' And I finally found them. And there were many of them! And they all seemed to say the same thing."

"What thing?"

"That I, uh, was going to be rejected."

"If you spoke up and participated with others, you mean?"

"Yes, if I related to them I was going to be rejected. And wouldn't that be perfectly awful if I was to be rejected. And there was no reason for me, uh, to take that, uh, sort of thing, and be rejected in that awful manner."

"So you might as well shut up and not take the risk?"

"Yes, so I might as well shut my trap and stay off in my corner, away from the others."

"So you did see it?"

"Oh, yes! I certainly saw it. Many times, during the week."

"And did you do the second part of the homework assignment?"

"The forcing myself to speak up and express myself?"

"Yes, that part."

"That was worse. That was really hard. Much harder than I thought it would be. But I did it."

"And — ?"

"Oh, not bad at all. I spoke up several times; more than I've ever done before. Some people were very surprised. Phyllis was very surprised, too. But I spoke up." . . .

"And how did you feel after expressing yourself like that?"

"Remarkable! I don't remember when I last felt this way. I felt, uh, just remarkable—good, that is. It was really something to feel! But it was so hard. I almost didn't make it. And a couple of other times during the week I had to force myself again. But I did. And I was glad!"

"So your homework assignments paid off?"

"They did; they really did."

Within the next few weeks, this patient, largely as a result of doing his homework assignments, became somewhat less inhibited socially and was able to express himself more freely than he had ever been able to do before. It is quite doubtful whether, without this kind of homework assignment, he would have made so much progress so quickly.

*(Ellis, 1966, pp. 202–203)*

It is apparent from cases such as this that Ellis, too, uses in vivo exposure in his therapy. He believes that this exposure is necessary to help clients change their assumptions: "Unless phobic individuals act against their irrational beliefs that they must not approach fearsome objects or situations . . . , can they ever really be said to have overcome such beliefs?" (Ellis, 1979, p. 162). Behaviorists might argue that exposure is playing a more direct and influential role in this cognitive treatment than Ellis acknowledges.

Numerous studies indicate that rational-emotive therapy and similar cognitive approaches help to reduce social fears (Emmelkamp et al., 1985; Butler et al., 1984; Gardner et al., 1980; Kanter & Goldfried, 1979; Wolfe & Fodor, 1977; Glass et al., 1976). Most of these studies focus on volunteers whose social fears are not severe enough to warrant a clinical diagnosis of social phobia (Arkowitz, 1977; Curran, 1977), but even the studies that do focus on people with full-blown cases of the disorder find this treatment helpful (Kanter & Goldfried, 1979). Ellis's therapy has been applied to other anxiety disorders, as well as to other categories of mental dysfunctioning, but nowhere does it perform better than as a treatment for social phobias.

At the same time, research also suggests that cognitive therapy rarely helps clients to overcome social phobias fully. Although it does reduce social fear, it does not consistently help people perform effectively in the social realm (Gardner et al., 1980). This is where social skills training has come to the forefront.

**Social Skills Training** *Social skills training* combines several behavioral techniques in an effort to help people acquire needed social skills. Therapists usually model appropriate social behaviors for clients and encourage the clients to try them out. Typically clients role-play with the therapists, rehearsing their new social behaviors until they become proficient. Throughout the process, therapists provide candid feedback and reinforce (praise) the clients for effective social performances.

Social skills training groups and assertiveness training groups often serve those functions (Landau & Paulson, 1977). Members try out and rehearse new social behavior with or in front of other group members. The group can provide a consensus on what is socially appropriate,

and social reinforcement from group members is often more powerful than reinforcement from a therapist alone.

Some practitioners have devised exercises to help group members develop the skills of social interaction (Rimm & Masters, 1979). One beginning exercise focuses on *greetings*, requiring that each member turn to a neighbor and say, "Hello, how are you?" The neighbor replies, "Fine, how are you?" This exchange is to be made with warmth, good eye contact, and a strong, assertive tone of voice. *Exchanging compliments* is an exercise designed to help group members who have difficulty giving and receiving compliments. One person turns to another and delivers a warm and emphatic compliment, such as "Gee, I really like the way you're wearing your hair today." The recipient is encouraged to respond with an acknowledgment, such as "Thank you, that makes me feel good," or "Thanks, I thought I'd try something different." An exercise called *small talk* has a member who is "it" designate two other members and give them a topic for light conversation ("Harry and Louise, discuss the weather"). As always, the therapist encourages and praises good eye contact, spontaneity, and warmth.

Studies have found that social skills training helps socially fearful people perform better in social situations (Hayes & Marshall, 1984; Frisch et al., 1982; Elder, Edelstein, & Fremouw, 1981; Gardner et al., 1980), but it appears that this form of treatment alone has only a limited effect on social phobias. Clients may become more adept socially as a result of treatment, but they often continue to experience uncomfortable levels of fear (Marks, 1987; Shaw, 1978; Falloon et al., 1977).

Thus, while cognitive therapy and social skills training are helpful in the treatment of social phobias, it appears that neither is consistently able to bring about a complete change. Studies directly comparing the two approaches usually find that each is helpful but that neither is superior to the other, and that they affect different aspects of social anxiety (Elder et al., 1981; Gardner et al., 1980; Alden et al., 1978; Fremouw, 1978). When the two approaches are combined, however, the results have been most encouraging (Derry & Stone, 1979; Linehan et al., 1979). One study compared the progress of four treatment groups: people who received social skills training, people who received social skills training combined with rational-emotive therapy, people in a consciousness-raising group, and control subjects on a waiting list (Wolfe & Fodor, 1977). The group that received the combined treatment showed significantly more improvement in both fear reduction and social performance than the other three groups.

# Generalized Anxiety Disorders

*Generalized anxiety disorders* — persistent vague feelings of anxiety — currently are the anxiety disorders least responsive to treatment. Psychodynamic and humanistic-existential therapies have been applied widely to these disorders, and have fared approximately as well as specific systems of therapy (Barlow & Beck, 1984), but neither global nor specific approaches have proved more than modestly helpful (O'Leary & Wilson, 1987; Mathews, 1985, 1984; Barlow & Beck, 1984; Barlow & Wolfe, 1981). Three kinds of specific therapies are commonly employed in cases of generalized anxiety disorder: cognitive therapies (see Box 7-2), stress management training, and antianxiety drugs.

**Cognitive Therapies** Ellis's (1989, 1984, 1962) rational-emotive therapy has frequently been applied in cases of generalized anxiety disorder. Rational-emotive therapists help clients pinpoint and change the assumptions that may be causing them to feel such all-encompassing anxiety; for example, "It is awful and catastrophic when things are not the way one would very much like them to be," and "There is invariably a right, precise, and perfect solution to human problems and it is catastrophic if this perfect solution is not found." Although controlled research has been limited (Prochaska, 1984), a few studies do suggest that rational-emotive therapy brings about modest reductions in anxiety in clients with generalized anxiety disorders (Lipsky, Kassinove, & Miller, 1980).

Aaron Beck has developed another cognitive treatment for generalized and other anxiety disorders that is similar to the rational-emotive approach (Beck, 1991; Beck & Emery, 1985, 1979). As we saw in Chapter 6, Beck believes that the underlying assumptions of people with generalized anxiety disorders are dominated by themes of imminent danger — such assumptions as "A situation is unsafe until it is proved to be safe" and "My security and safety depend on anticipating and preparing myself at all times for any possible danger." According to Beck, assumptions of this kind must be worked on if the people who hold them are to rid themselves of pervasive feelings of anxiety.

Beck centers therapy on altering the numerous anxiety-provoking images and thoughts, called *automatic thoughts,* that arise from the maladaptive assumptions of anxiety-prone persons and bombard their thinking in situation after situation ("What if I fail?" "Other things might get in the way." "I'm falling behind."). In a procedure that is somewhat more systematic than Ellis's approach, the therapist helps the client recognize his or her automatic thoughts, observe the faulty logic and assumptions underlying them, and test the validity of the thoughts. As clients increasingly recognize the inaccuracy of their automatic thoughts and underlying assumptions, they are expected to become less prone to see danger where there is none.

This cognitive treatment for generalized anxiety disorders is really an adaptation of Beck's influential and very effective treatment for depression (which is discussed in Chapter 9). Its application to generalized anxiety disorders is just beginning to be studied (Beck, 1991; Beck & Emery, 1985), but, given its distinguished background, it may indeed prove helpful in those cases as well (Durham & Turvey, 1987).

**Stress Management Training** Some clinicians believe that people with generalized anxiety disorders have simply never learned to manage anxiety in stressful situations. These therapists teach clients stress management skills that can be applied during stressful times to keep anxiety from building out of control (Marks, 1989; Lindsay et al., 1987). The most common forms of stress management training are self-instruction training, relaxation training, and biofeedback training (Lindsay et al., 1987).

*Self-instruction Training* Donald Meichenbaum has developed a cognitive-behavioral technique for coping with stress called *self-instruction training,* or *stress inoculation* (Meichenbaum & Cameron, 1983; Meichenbaum, 1977, 1975). It is based on the belief that during stressful situations, many people make statements to themselves (self-statements), similar to Beck's automatic thoughts, that heighten their anxiety and render them ineffective. In self-instruction training, therapists teach clients to rid themselves of these negative self-statements ("Oh, no, everything is going wrong") and replace them with coping self-statements ("One step at a time; I can handle the situation").

Clients are first taught coping self-statements that they can apply during four stages characteristic of a stressful situation (Meichenbaum, 1977). They begin by learning statements that help them prepare for stressful situations. For example, they may practice saying things to themselves that prepare them for the challenge of asking for a raise. Second, they learn self-statements that enable them to cope with stressful situations as they are occurring, the kind of self-statements that can help them when they are actually in the boss's office asking for a raise. Third, they learn self-statements that will help them through the very difficult moments when a situation seems to be going badly, such as when the boss glares back as they ask for more money. And finally, they learn to make reinforcing self-

## BOX 7-2

# What, Me Worry?

People with anxiety disorders worry, but they are hardly the only worriers. Most of us worry at times; in fact, many people without diagnosable conditions nevertheless feel as if they are worrying most or all the time. Thomas Borkovec and his colleagues (1990, 1985) have devoted themselves to the study and treatment of nonpathological yet troublesome worrying.

These researchers define worrying as a "chain of negative and relatively uncontrollable thoughts and images." They find that people worry in an attempt to cope with concerns and fears, particularly about the future; to solve certain problems; and to prepare themselves for possible problems. Many people feel that worrying is necessary, as if problems would not work out if they did not worry. Yet extreme worrying rarely serves a constructive purpose.

These researchers have also found that 15 percent of the population are chronic worriers, people who spend more than eight hours a day worrying. In contrast, 30 percent of the population worry less than an hour and a half each day and are classified as non-worriers.

How can worriers be helped? Borkovec and his colleagues believe that a specified period of time devoted to worrying each day helps cut down a person's overall amount of worrying. Their studies show that if this period of assigned worrying is either very short (less than ten minutes) or rather long (more than thirty minutes), overall worrying declines. A moderate period of assigned worrying (ten to twenty minutes), however, actually leads to an increase in worrying. On the basis of these and related findings, they have developed the following self-help treatment tips for worriers:

Whether you are a chronic or moderate worrier, or know someone who is, you may find useful a technique that provides some relief to those who feel they need it. . . .

Because one can worry at nearly any time and place, it becomes associated with many situations. So to reduce its frequency, a person ought to limit the conditions in which worrying happens. We have developed a self-control strategy involving five rules for doing this:

Observe your thinking during the day closely and learn to identify the early beginnings of worrying.

Establish a half-hour worry period, to take place at the same time and in the same place each day.

Postpone your worrying, as soon as you do catch yourself, until your worry period.

Replace the worrisome thoughts with focused attention on the task at hand or anything else in your immediate environment.

Use your daily worry period to think intensively about your current concerns.

The goal of these instructions is to isolate the worry process and to learn to associate it with only a limited set of circumstances. In two studies, we provided these instructions to groups of college students who were chronic worriers and asked them to follow the rules for four weeks while keeping track of how much time they spent worrying each day. They reported spending, on average, 35 percent less time than they had previously. Groups who simply monitored their daily worries without these instructions showed no change in time spent worrying.

*(Borkovec, 1985, pp. 62–63)*

statements after they have coped effectively. Here are a few examples of these four kinds of self-statements:

*Preparing for a Stressor*
What is it you have to do?

You can develop a plan to deal with it.

Just think about what you can do about it. That's better than getting anxious.

*Confronting and Handling a Stressor*
Just psych yourself up — you can meet this challenge.

This tenseness can be an ally: a cue to cope.

Relax: you're in control. Take a slow deep breath.

*Coping with the Feeling of Being Overwhelmed*
When fear comes, just pause.

Keep the focus on the present: what is it you have to do?

You should expect your fear to rise.

Don't try to eliminate fear totally: just keep it manageable.

*Reinforcing Self-statements*

It worked: you did it.

It wasn't as bad as you expected.

You made more out of your fear than it was worth.

Your damn ideas—that's the problem. When you control them, you control your fear.

Once clients are skilled at using self-statements, the next step is typically to subject them to stressful experiences in therapy and instruct them to apply what they have learned. The therapist may employ unpredictable electric shocks, imaging techniques, or stress-inducing films, or have the clients role-play unpleasant and embarrassing situations (Meichenbaum, 1977).

Self-instruction training has proved to be of modest help in cases of chronic and broad anxiety (Halcomb, 1986) and somewhat more helpful to people who suffer from test-taking anxiety or other mild forms of anxiety (Kirkland & Hollandsworth, 1980; Rimm & Masters, 1979; Meichenbaum, 1972). It has also been adapted with some success to help people behave less impul-

sively, control anger, and control pain (Novaco, 1977, 1976, 1975; Turk, 1976, 1975).

Given the limited effectiveness of self-instruction training in treating anxiety disorders, Meichenbaum (1972) himself has suggested that it should be used primarily to supplement other treatments. In fact, anxious people treated with a combination of self-instruction training and rational-emotive therapy have been seen to improve more than people treated by either approach alone (Glogower, Fremouw, & McCroskey, 1978).

**Relaxation Training**   The relaxation training used for generalized anxiety disorders is identical to that taught in desensitization therapy (p. 227). Over the course of several sessions clients learn how to relax their muscles. It is expected that they will then be able to relax at will during stressful situations, thus reducing or preventing anxiety.

Sometimes therapists actually create stressful situations during therapy sessions so that the clients can practice relaxing under stress (Suinn & Richardson, 1971). Suggestion, imagery, exercise, hyperventilation, and even short-acting drugs may be used for this purpose (Mathews, 1985). Such practice opportunities appear to enhance the effectiveness of relaxation training: anxious subjects treated in a program that combined relaxation training and induced-anxiety practice sessions were better able to reduce their general levels of anxiety than subjects treated with relaxation training alone or subjects given placebo treatment (Hutchings et al., 1980).

Research indicates that relaxation training is more effective than no treatment or placebo treatment in cases of generalized anxiety disorders (Barlow, 1989; Jannoun, Oppenheimer, & Gelder, 1982; Jannoun, McDowell, & Catalan, 1981; Borkovec & Sides, 1979). Again, however, the improvements it produces tend to be modest (Mathews, 1985, 1984), and other techniques that induce relaxation, such as meditation, often seem to be equally effective in reducing anxiety (Mathews, 1984).

**Biofeedback**   As we observed in Chapter 4, *biofeedback* is a behavioral-biological treatment technique in which people are connected to a monitoring device that gives them continuous information about a physiological activity (such as heart rate or muscle tension) in their body. By following the therapist's instructions and attending to the signals from the monitor, they gradually learn to control the activity (Blanchard & Epstein, 1978). With practice, a person can learn to control even seemingly involuntary physiological processes.

Biofeedback has been applied to a wide range of problems. Therapists have taught clients to control brain-

People who receive self-instruction training learn to make statements to themselves that reduce or eliminate the anxiety associated with upsetting events. The technique is most effective when it is combined with other anxiety-reduction techniques.

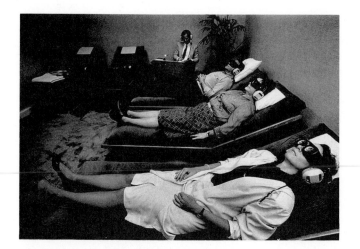

Many businesses now offer stress-reduction programs for employees to help reduce or prevent stress on the job. Using a machine called the Synchro-Energizer, this clinician leads employees through a "brain tune-up" that combines the principles of relaxation and biofeedback training.

wave activity to reduce brain seizures (Wyler et al., 1977), heart rate to reduce cardiac arrhythmias (Weiss & Engel, 1971), and blood pressure levels to reduce hypertension (Benson et al., 1981).

Biofeedback has also been used to reduce feelings of anxiety (Raskin et al., 1980; Canter, Kondo, & Knott, 1975; Townsend et al., 1975). The most widely applied technique uses a device called an *electromyograph (EMG)*, which provides feedback about the level of muscular tension in the body so that clients can learn to reduce it (and their anxiety) at will. Electrodes are attached to the client's muscles — usually the frontalis, or forehead, muscles — where they detect the minute electrical activity that accompanies muscle contraction (see Figure 7-2). The bioelectric potentials coming from the muscles are then amplified and converted into an easily interpreted image, such as lines on a screen, or into an audio tone whose pitch and volume vary along with changes in muscle tension. Thus clients "see" or "hear" when their muscles are becoming more or less tense. After repeated trial and error, they become skilled at voluntarily reducing muscle tension and, theoretically, at reducing tension and anxiety in everyday stressful situations.

Research indicates that EMG biofeedback training helps both normal and anxious subjects reduce their anxiety levels to a modest degree (Rice & Blanchard, 1982; Arnarson & Sheffield, 1980). Several direct comparisons have shown that EMG biofeedback training and relaxation training have similar effects on anxiety levels (Andrasik & Blanchard, 1983; Raskin, Bali, & Peeke,

1980; Schandler & Grings, 1976). The subjects given EMG feedback are better able than relaxation-trained subjects to reduce their EMG readings (Coursey, 1975; Canter et al., 1975), but the two techniques produce similar results on all other indicators of anxiety (Canter et al., 1975).

In efforts to reduce anxiety, biofeedback therapists have also used an *electroencephalograph (EEG),* which records electrical activity in the brain to teach clients to voluntarily produce *alpha waves.* Our brain-wave patterns — that is, the rhythmic electrical discharges in our brains — vary with our activities. Alpha waves occur when we are in a relaxed wakeful state. It has been suggested that biofeedback-induced increases in alpha-wave activity will lead to greater relaxation and be of help to anxious people (Hardt & Kamiya, 1978). Unfortunately, the production of alpha waves does not appear to promote relaxation consistently in either normal or highly anxious people. Thus this method appears to have only limited potential as a treatment for generalized anxiety disorders (Andrasik & Blanchard, 1983; Plotkin & Rice, 1981; Walsh, 1974).

Heart-rate feedback, which teaches clients voluntarily to slow their heartbeat, is yet another biofeedback technique that has been applied to generalized anxiety disorders (Schraeder & Rupert, 1983; Rupert & Holmes, 1978). Unfortunately, research suggests that this technique, too, is of limited help to anxious clients (Rice & Blanchard, 1982; Emmelkamp, 1982). Most subjects are able to slow their heart rate only slightly and are usually dismayed to learn how much easier it is to speed the rate up than to reduce it (Blanchard & Epstein,

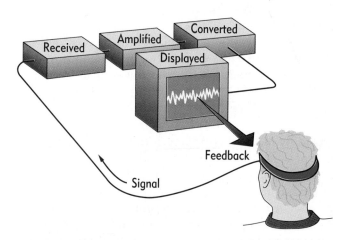

**FIGURE 7-2** This biofeedback system is recording tension in the forehead muscle of a headache sufferer. The system receives, amplifies, converts, and displays information about the tension, allowing the client to "observe" it and to try to reduce his tension responses.

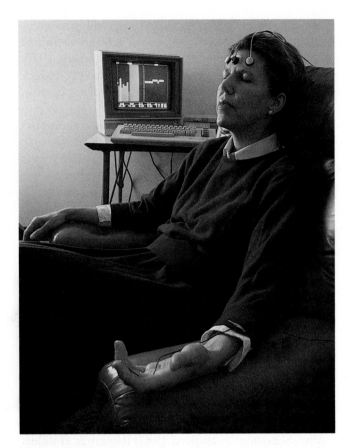

The muscular tension experienced by this client is detected by electrodes attached to her body and displayed on the nearby monitor. Electromyograph biofeedback training has proved modestly helpful in reducing anxiety.

1978). Moreover, even when anxious subjects do learn to slow their heart rate, the reduction is not consistently associated with a subjective feeling of lower anxiety (Nunes & Marks, 1976, 1975). Such findings have led George Engel (1974), a well-known theorist and researcher on the relationship between stress and physical functioning, to reflect, "If one taught an anxious patient to slow his heart, the end result could be an anxious patient whose heart beats slower" (p. 303).

In the 1960s and 1970s, biofeedback training was hailed by many as an approach that would change the face of clinical treatment. This early expectation has not been fulfilled. So far, biofeedback procedures have tended to be more cumbersome, less efficient, and less productive than mental health clinicians had envisioned (Blanchard & Epstein, 1978; Blanchard & Yung, 1973). The techniques have played an important adjunct role in the treatment of certain physical problems, including headaches, seizure disorders, and such neuromuscular disorders as cerebral palsy (Andrasik & Blanchard,

1983; Blanchard et al., 1982; Brudny et al., 1976), but they have played a limited role in the treatment of generalized anxiety disorders and other psychological problems.

**Drug Therapies**   It would be hard to find someone in our society who is not familiar with the words "tranquilizer" and "Valium." This familiarity reflects the enormous impact that antianxiety medications have had on our culture at large, not to mention the mental health profession. It is easy to forget that these medications have emerged only in the past thirty years.

Until the 1950s, *sedative-hypnotic drugs,* particularly *barbiturates,* were the major biological treatment for anxiety disorders (Hollister, 1986). These drugs created serious problems. They made people very drowsy, too high a dose could lead to death, and those who took barbiturates over an extended period could become physically dependent on them.

In the late 1940s, however, Frank Berger, a chemist who was trying to develop a more effective antibiotic, synthesized a compound called *meprobamate.* When he tested this drug on animals, he discovered that it was an excellent muscle relaxant. Subsequent testing showed that meprobamate also reduced anxiety both in animals and in humans (Berger, 1976, 1963). In the 1950s, meprobamate was released as a new kind of antianxiety medication under the brand name Miltown.

Meprobamate was less dangerous and less addictive than barbiturates, but it still caused drowsiness. Researchers therefore continued to search for more satisfactory antianxiety medications. In 1957 Lowell Randall tested a drug named *chlordiazepoxide,* a member of the family of drugs called *benzodiazepines* (see Table 7-3). This drug had actually been developed in the 1930s and put aside as seemingly useless, but Randall noticed that chlordiazepoxide tranquilized animals without making them extremely tired (Sternbach, 1979). Chlordiazepoxide was soon marketed under the brand name Librium. Several years later another benzodiazepine drug, *diazepam,* was developed and marketed under the brand name Valium (see Figure 7-3).

From the beginning, researchers confirmed that benzodiazepines reduced anxiety both in animals (Randall et al., 1960) and in humans (Rickels, 1978). Moreover, benzodiazepines often enhanced the effectiveness of other psychotherapeutic approaches (Noyes et al., 1984). The benzodiazepine drugs quickly became popular among health professionals. They not only reduced anxiety without making people exceptionally tired but were relatively nontoxic even in large dosages. Unlike barbiturates, they did not pose great danger to life, and

TABLE 7-3

| BENZODIAZEPINE DRUGS THAT REDUCE ANXIETY | | | |
|---|---|---|---|
| Class/generic name | Trade name | Usual daily dose (mg) | Absorption |
| Alprazolam | Xanax | 0.75–6.0 | Rapid |
| Chlordiazepoxide | Librium | 15–100 | Rapid |
| Clorazepate dipotassium | Tranxene | 15–60 | Very rapid |
| Clonazepam | Klonopin | 1–4 | Very rapid |
| Diazepam | Valium | 4–40 | Very rapid |
| Lorazepam | Ativan | 2–6 | Intermediate |
| Oxazepam | Serax | 30–120 | Slow |
| Flurazepam | Dalmane | 30 | Rapid |
| Triazolam | Halcion | 0.125–0.5 | Rapid |

*Source:* Silver & Yudofsky, 1988, pp. 807–809.

when taken alone, they did not slow the respiratory system. Doctors and patients alike looked at benzodiazepines as miracle drugs.

Only years later did researchers begin to understand the reasons for the effectiveness of benzodiazepines. As we saw in Chapter 6, in 1977 two separate research teams discovered that there are specific neuron sites in the brain that receive benzodiazepines (Mohler & Okada, 1977; Squires & Braestrup, 1977) and that these receptor sites are the same ones that ordinarily receive GABA (gamma-aminobutyric acid), a neurotransmitter that inhibits neuron firing, thus slowing physical arousal throughout the body and reducing anxiety (Snyder, 1986, 1981; Costa, 1988, 1983; Costa et al., 1978, 1975; Haefely et al., 1975). When benzodiazepines bind to these neuron receptor sites, they apparently enhance the ability of GABA to bind to them as well, and so improve GABA's ability to slow neuron firing and reduce bodily arousal (Snyder, 1981; Costa & Guidotti, 1979).

Antianxiety medications are prescribed for generalized anxiety disorders more than for other kinds of anxiety disorders. The drugs are not particularly helpful in cases of simple phobias (Klein, Rabkin, & Gorman, 1985; Berk & Efron, 1983), panic disorders, or obsessive compulsive disorders (Klein et al., 1985), but controlled studies reveal that they do sometimes reduce the symptoms of generalized anxiety disorder (Klein et al., 1985; Rickels et al., 1983; Aden & Thein, 1980).

Because they initially offered so much promise and appeared relatively safe, antianxiety medications became the most widely prescribed drugs in the United

States (Hollister, 1986, 1980). Lately, however, clinicians have begun to realize that this growth was excessive and potentially dangerous (Dubovsky, 1990; Rickels et al., 1987).

Several problems have emerged. First, it became clear that antianxiety drugs alone were not a long-term solu-

**FIGURE 7-3** A computer-drawn molecule of the antianxiety drug *diazepam*, known by the trade name Valium. Along with other benzodiazepines, this drug is more helpful in cases of generalized anxiety disorder than in alleviating simple phobias, pain disorders, or obsessive compulsive disorders.

tion for anxiety. When the medications were stopped, many clients' anxieties returned as strong as ever (Lindsay et al., 1987; Mathews, 1985; Marks, 1981). Second, although benzodiazepines are not addictive when they are taken for a short time and in a low dosage, it eventually became clear that people who take them in large dosages for an extended time can become physically dependent on them (Marks, 1988; Winokur et al., 1980). Third, although benzodiazepines are not toxic themselves, clinicians learned that they do *potentiate,* or multiply, the effects of other toxic drugs, such as alcohol. People on antianxiety drugs who drink even small amounts of alcohol can experience dangerous, sometimes fatal, respiratory slowdown. And finally, because these drugs act so quickly and are so easy to take, family physicians frequently prescribed them for patients who did not have serious anxiety disorders, unwisely exposing them to the drugs' addictive or potentiating effects (Woods, Katz, & Winger, 1988; Knesper et al., 1985). In fact, to this day family physicians prescribe more benzodiazepines than psychiatrists do.

In spite of these drawbacks, benzodiazepines continue to be widely used to help people who experience broad anxiety symptoms. The drugs often do provide temporary and modest relief for generalized anxiety disorders, but they cannot be relied on for significant and lasting improvements.

## Panic Disorders

Until recently clinicians were rarely successful in treating people who experienced sudden and unpredictable outbreaks of panic. Linked in the past with generalized anxiety disorders under the rubric of anxiety neurosis, panic disorders were usually treated with the same interventions; but while global therapies and stress management techniques were of modest help in treating generalized anxiety disorders, they brought almost no improvement at all in panic disorders (Sheehan, 1982). Even more telling was the fact that antianxiety drugs failed to reduce the frequency or intensity of panic attacks (Klein et al., 1985). These realizations led to the classification and study of panic disorders as a separate psychopathology and to the eventual development of highly effective biological and cognitive interventions.

**Drug Therapies** In 1962 clinical investigators Donald Klein and Max Fink discovered that panic attacks could be prevented or at least made less frequent by antidepressant drugs, the medications used primarily to lift the spirits of people suffering from depression. This unexpected finding was a clinical breakthrough. Since then,

studies have repeatedly confirmed that certain antidepressant drugs bring relief to many people with panic disorders (Fyer & Sandberg, 1988; Hollister, 1986; Uhde et al., 1984, 1982; Klein et al., 1980). Recently *alprazolam* (Xanax), a benzodiazepine drug whose action is somewhat different from that of the other benzodiazepine drugs, has also proved effective in the treatment of panic disorders (Taylor et al., 1990; Klerman, 1988; Ballenger et al., 1988). These drugs seem to be helpful whether or not the panic disorders are accompanied by depressive symptoms (Lesser, 1988).

As we saw in Chapter 6, researchers have come to believe that panic attacks may be related to abnormal activity of the neurotransmitter norepinephrine at certain neuron sites in the brain (Uhde et al., 1985; Redmond, 1985; Klein, 1964). It seems that the antidepressant drugs act to restore appropriate norepinephrine activity in people with a panic disorder, particularly in the locus coeruleus, a brain area filled with norepinephrine neurons, and, in so doing, help to reduce the symptoms of the disorder (Uhde et al., 1984, 1982).

Clinicians have also found antidepressant drugs and alprazolam to be helpful in many cases of panic disorder with agoraphobia, cases in which the client's outbreaks of panic are accompanied by a general fear of entering public places (Klerman, 1988; Lesser, 1988; Johnston, Troyer, & Whitsett, 1988; Barlow & Beck, 1984). Unlike panic-free agoraphobia, this kind of agoraphobia may actually be caused by the panic attacks themselves (Barlow, 1988; Zitrin et al., 1983, 1981). That is, after experiencing a number of spontaneous panic attacks, the person may begin to anticipate that he or she will have an attack in public and increasingly avoid going out. Antidepressant drugs and alprazolam help break this attack-anticipation-fear cycle, enabling many agoraphobic people to venture out into public places once again (Mavissakalian & Michelson, 1986; Noyes, Chaudry, & Domingo, 1986; Zitrin et al., 1983, 1981, 1978; Klein et al., 1980). As the drugs eliminate or reduce their panic attacks, clients become more confident that the attacks have ceased and less hesitant to approach the settings they have been avoiding.

At the same time, some studies suggest that an antidepressant drug or alprazolam alone is not always sufficient to relieve panic disorder with agoraphobia (Laraia et al., 1989; Gorman et al., 1989; Marks et al., 1983, 1982; Davis et al., 1981). In some of these studies, the prescribed dosage may have been too low to have an effect on the panic attacks (Fyer & Sandberg, 1988). Often, however, the problem seems to be that the client's anticipatory anxiety has become so severe that fear of public outings continues even after the panic attacks are eliminated or reduced by medication (Klein et al., 1987,

1983). For these clients, a combination of antidepressant drugs and behavioral exposure treatments may be more effective than either treatment alone (Mavissakalian, 1990; Noyes et al., 1986; Zitrin et al., 1983, 1980).

**Cognitive Therapy**   As we saw in Chapter 6, a growing number of theorists believe that panic attacks come on when people think that certain physical sensations (such as faintness, chest pains, or rapid heartbeat) indicate an imminent personal catastrophe (Barlow, 1989, 1988; Beck, 1988; Chambless, 1988). The misinterpretation itself causes further symptoms of panic and sets in motion a self-fulfilling prophecy. This view is the basis of the cognitive therapies for panic disorders (Barlow et al., 1990; Beck, 1988; Clark, 1988; Clark et al., 1986, 1985).

Aaron Beck (1988) tries to teach patients that their physical sensations are harmless, thus eliminating subsequent misinterpretations. Initially he briefs clients on the general nature of panic attacks, the actual causes of their bodily sensations, and their tendency to misinterpret them. People who experience sudden faintness before a panic attack may be taught that such sensations are often due to a faulty adjustment of their blood pressure mechanism to changes in posture; clients with chest pains are taught that the pain is due to tension in their intercostal muscles; and those who hyperventilate learn that this is typically a harmless reaction to stress. As the clients become convinced that such explanations are accurate interpretations of their physical sensations, they are able to remind themselves in real-life situations that the sensations are not signs of impending catastrophe, thus "shorting out" the panic sequence at an early point. Over the course of Beck's therapy, clients may also be taught to "distract" themselves from their sensations by, for example, starting conversations with other people when the sensations occur.

Beck also induces panic sequences in the therapy office so that clients can develop and apply their new insights and skills under watchful supervision. Patients whose attacks are ordinarily triggered by a rapid heart rate may be instructed to jump up and down for several minutes in the presence of the therapist or to run up a flight of stairs. They can then practice interpreting their heightened heart rate appropriately and distracting themselves from dwelling on their sensations.

Research indicates that this and similar cognitive treatments for panic disorders are often quite helpful (Barlow et al., 1990; Sokol-Kessler & Beck, 1987; Salkovskis et al., 1986; Clark et al., 1985). In one study thirteen clients with panic disorders received twelve weeks of Beck's cognitive treatment, while sixteen similar clients received eight weeks of general supportive therapy, consisting of a weekly monitoring of symptoms and brief support sessions (Sokol-Kessler & Beck, 1987). Those treated with cognitive intervention went from an average of five panic attacks per week to none over the course of treatment (see Figure 7-4). In contrast, those who received support treatment reduced their weekly panic attacks from an average of four to three.

## Obsessive Compulsive Disorders

Before the 1970s, few treatments seemed to be of much help in alleviating *obsessive compulsive disorders,* pathologies in which a person is plagued by repeated unwanted thoughts (obsessions), repeatedly feels compelled to carry out particular behaviors (compulsions), or both (Zetin, 1990; Black, 1974). Less than 60 percent of obsessive compulsive clients improved to any degree at all over the course of several years of treatment, regardless of the type they received, and even those improvements could not usually be attributed to the treatment itself (Goodwin et al., 1969; Kringlen, 1965; Grimshaw, 1964; Pollitt, 1960). One exception to

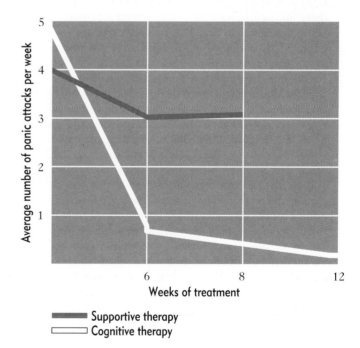

**FIGURE 7-4** When clients were treated with cognitive therapy for their panic disorders, the average frequency of their panic attacks declined from five per week to none. Those who received only support from their therapists went from an average of four panic attacks to three per week over the course of treatment. These findings suggest that cognitive therapy was much more effective in treating the disorder. *(Adapted from Beck, 1988, p. 108.)*

this gloomy picture was the technique of paradoxical intention, developed by Viktor Frankl.

**Paradoxical Intention** During the 1960s Viktor Frankl, an existential theorist whose ideas grew from his dehumanizing experiences of powerlessness and hopelessness in four Nazi concentration camps, developed a system of therapy called *logotherapy.* Here therapists sought to change clients' attitudes toward their existence, often using a technique called *paradoxical intention* to help them develop an attitude of control over their disorder. Therapists who use this technique employ direct and sometimes humorous confrontations to help clients embrace the very thoughts, fears, and behaviors that are causing them so much misery. Here is Frankl's (1972) description of paradoxical intention as applied to a 56-year-old obsessive compulsive lawyer:

*His neurosis began seventeen years ago, when he was* still in private practice. "All of a sudden, out of a clear blue sky, an awful obsession came into my mind that I had defrauded the government by underestimating my income tax by some three hundred dollars, even though I made it out as honestly as I knew how. I began to worry that it might be several hundred dollars more. Try as I might, I could not get these ideas out of my head." The patient imagined himself being prosecuted for fraud, going to jail, receiving newspaper publicity, and finally losing his job. He was hospitalized at a private sanitarium, receiving psychotherapy and twenty-five treatments with electro-convulsive therapy, without improvement. Meanwhile he had to give up his law practice and to take a job as a court clerk. Further obsessions developed. They shifted from day to day, and week to week. He developed the habit of checking and rechecking things, such as the wheels of his car and things he did at his office. He became obsessed about his insurance policies, fearing that perhaps one had expired or that one did not include the protection he wanted. It was at this time that he bought special insurance from Lloyds, because he feared he might make a mistake in court and be sued. He felt compelled to check and recheck everything, including his various insurance policies locked in a special steel box in a safe at home. The policies themselves were in envelopes secured by a number of strings. His fear of being sued was so great that off and on he had to go through the involved procedure of taking out his policies and making sure he was insured properly; and when he finally had put them back into the steel box in the safe, he wondered whether he had really checked everything. He had to repeat his process over and over until he finally "felt certain" that he was "safe." In court he became so completely incapacitated that he needed to be hospitalized. It was at this time that Dr. Gerz began treating him with paradoxical intention. He was in logotherapy for four months three times weekly, and was instructed to use the following "paradoxical intentions": "I

don't give a damn any more. Hell, who wants to be a perfectionist? I hope I get sued very soon, the sooner the better." Dr. Gerz instructed him to try "to get sued three times a day and get his money's worth from Lloyds of London!" He was told to wish that he would make many, many mistakes, really mess up his work, and show his secretaries that he was the greatest "mistake maker" in the world. No doubt, Dr. Gerz's complete lack of anxiety could be adopted by the patient, as a humourous situation was created and as Dr. Gerz kept telling the patient on each visit: "For heaven's sake, are you still around! I've been looking through the newspapers hoping to read about the big scandalous lawsuit." At these comments the patient would burst into laughter, and he finally adopted the attitude of: "To hell with everything. I don't care if I make mistakes; I don't give a damn what happens. Let 'em sue me." He would laugh and say: "My insurance companies will go bankrupt." About a year after therapy began, he said: "This formula has worked a miracle for me. Dr. Gerz has made a new person out of me in four months. I occasionally get a worry, but now I am able to cope with it. I know how to handle it."

(Frankl, 1972, pp. 245–247)

Like most other existential approaches, Frankl's technique was not subjected to controlled research, but his case studies caught the attention of many clinicians, particularly behaviorists, who saw exposure principles at work in paradoxical intention. Behaviorists went on to develop a treatment approach that has proved highly effective for those obsessive compulsive disorders in which compulsive acts are prominent. The approach combines prolonged in vivo exposure with response prevention, the blocking of compulsive behaviors.

**Exposure and Response Prevention** In the mid-1960s V. Meyer (1966) treated two patients with chronic obsessive compulsive disorders by instructing the hospital staff to supervise them around the clock and prevent them from performing their compulsive acts. The patients' compulsive behavior abated significantly, and the improvement was still apparent after fourteen months. Several years later Meyer and his associates (1974) tried the same approach on fifteen patients with moderate to severe obsessive compulsive disorders. With one exception, "every patient showed a marked diminution in compulsive behavior, sometimes amounting to a total cessation of the rituals. . . . 10 were either much improved or totally asymptomatic" (p. 251).

In the 1970s clinical researcher Stanley Rachman and his colleagues dropped the staff-supervision feature of this procedure and simply instructed clients to try to restrain themselves from performing compulsive acts (Rachman, 1985; Rachman et al., 1979; Rachman & Hogson, 1978; Marks & Rachman, 1978; Rachman,

Hogson, & Marks, 1971). Clients were repeatedly exposed to objects or situations that typically elicited anxiety, obsessive fears, and compulsive behaviors, but were instructed to refrain from performing any of the behaviors they might feel compelled to perform. Because clients found this very difficult to do, the therapists themselves first interacted with the objects without performing any compulsive actions and then encouraged the clients to do the same (a form of participant modeling). This exposure and response-prevention procedure is demonstrated in the following case description:

*The patient had developed some obsessional-compulsive* behaviour patterns during adolescence but did not seek psychological assistance until the age of twenty, when he was admitted to a psychiatric hospital suffering from a marked obsessional disorder. His request for treatment had been precipitated by dismissal from his job as a result of excessive washing rituals that interfered with his working capacity. At the time of his admission to the hospital, the washing rituals occupied the greater part of his day. . . . He experienced particular difficulties over elimination. For example, he had to undress before urinating or defecating. After elimination he had to wash intensively and frequently take showers or baths. . . . He also displayed extensive and elaborate avoidance behaviour (e.g., he never touched the floor, or grass, or door handles, etc.).

*Modelling*
In this phase of treatment the patient was asked to watch whilst the therapist touched the items in the avoidance test and then to attempt to touch them himself. This was a gradual process; for instance, the mud and the excrement were initially touched through a piece of paper. After watching the therapist touch the item, the patient was encouraged, but never forced, to imitate this approach behaviour. Inevitably, these sessions incorporated some period of response prevention.

After session fifteen the patient was touching the marmalade, ash and mud, during session twenty-one he touched the urine, and during session twenty-three he touched the smear of excrement. After session nineteen the patient began to report, for the first time, that he was noticing an improvement outside the experimental situation. During subsequent sessions he reported the following signs of improvement:

1. Showering once a week instead of twice a day.
2. Washing after urination was reduced from twenty minutes to six minutes.
3. Swimming for first time in five years. Previously he was put off by the thought of dirty water.
4. Played croquet and touched the dirty ball.
5. Stroked a cat.
6. Didn't worry when the sole of another patient's shoe touched him during his meal.
7. Sunbathing on the grass. Previously he worried about the possibility of dogs having messed on the grass.

*Response Prevention*
In each of the five sessions the patient spent half an hour touching the smear of excrement and then he was told not to wash his hands. The period of response prevention was progressively increased over the five sessions (one-quarter hour, three-quarters hour, two hours, three hours). Improvement outside the experimental situation was maintained over these five sessions.

*Treatment Phase*
During the next two months, the treatment procedure of "modelling and response prevention" was carried out in and around the ward. Each day between 10:00 A.M. and 12:00 noon the patient observed the therapist touching and handling dirty objects, participated himself, and was required to refrain from washing his hands or any part of his body or clothes. . . .

*Progress*
A subjective assessment of progress during the treatment was the patient's increased tolerance for dirt on his body or clothes. At the end of each session the patient reported a decrease in discomfort and anxiety, and over the treatment period as a whole, he reported that he found the modelling easier to perform. A more objective measure is the amount of time spent washing and . . . the number of times the patient washed. He meticulously kept a record of the times, and the record was converted into graph form [Figure 7-5]. A clear change in washing and toilet behaviour can be seen when the figures at the onset and at the end of treatment are compared.

The most marked and important decrease was the reduction of his washing frequency, from fifteen times a day to twice a day, as this reflects the total elimination of compulsive washing following chance contact with "dirty" or "contaminated" objects. At the end of the treatment the patient washed eighty-seven percent less frequently than before treatment, and spent seventy percent less time on this behaviour. Toilet times also decreased, partly because the patient spent less time washing his hands after going to the toilet — over the last month of treatment he never took longer than two to three minutes — and partly because he used less lavatory paper. The number of sheets was reduced from thirty to between eight and ten on each occasion.

*(Rachman, Hogson, & Marzillier, 1970, pp. 385–392)*

Some behavioral therapists believe that after several therapy sessions, clients can and should carry out self-help procedures in their own homes (Marks et al., 1986; Hoogduin, 1985). The following exposure and response-prevention homework assignments were given over the course of therapy to a woman with a cleaning compulsion:

1. Do not mop the floor of your bathroom for a week. After this, clean it within three minutes, using an ordinary mop. Use this mop for other chores as well without cleaning it.

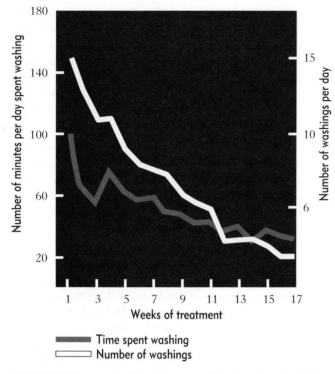

**FIGURE 7-5** When treated for his compulsive cleaning rituals by the behavioral technique of exposure and response prevention, a client showed a steady decline in the frequency of his daily washings and in the total amount of time he spent at them. Over the course of seventeen weeks of sessions, he went from washing himself fifteen times a day (1 hour and 21 minutes) to twice a day (31 minutes). *(Adapted from Rachman, Hogson, & Marzillier, 1970, p. 390.)*

2. Clean the window sill with a few broad sweeps within 20 seconds. The sill is cleaned in this way only once every other week.
3. Buy a fluffy mohair sweater and wear it for a week. When taking it off at night do not remove the bits of fluff. Do not clean your house for a week.
4. Dust the doormat in your livingroom. Do not clean the house for a week.
5. You, your husband, and children all have to keep shoes on. Do not clean the house for a week.
6. Do not have your children go upstairs naked, but let them undress in their bedroom. Do not clean the bedrooms for a week.
7. (The week after) Clean the playroom within ten minutes (only with the vacuum cleaner, no dusting).
8. Vacuum the house within 50 minutes (livingroom, kitchen, hall, and bedrooms) without doing things twice.
9. Drop a cookie on the contaminated floor, pick the cookie up and eat it.
10. Drop your knives and forks on the floor and use them for dinner.
11. Leave the sheets and blankets on the floor and then put them on the beds. Do not change these for a week.

*(Emmelkamp, 1982, pp. 299–300)*

Eventually therapists help such clients to determine a reasonable schedule and procedure for cleaning themselves and their houses and to institute more normal cleaning policies.

It has been found that between 60 and 85 percent of obsessive compulsive patients treated with this type of technique improve considerably (Perse, 1988; Kozak et al., 1988; Marks, 1987; Rachman, 1985; Foa et al., 1985, 1984, 1980; Salzman & Thaler, 1981; Emmelkamp et al., 1980). Improvements include a decrease in the frequency of compulsive acts and in consequent experiences of anxiety, a reduction in obsessive thinking, and better family, social, and work adjustments. Follow-up studies of up to four and one-half years indicate that such improvements continue (Marks, 1987; Emmelkamp & Rabbie, 1981; Boulougouris, 1977; Marks et al., 1975). On the other hand, relatively few of the clients in these studies lost all their symptoms, and as many as one-quarter of them apparently failed to improve at all (Rachman et al., 1979; Beech & Vaughan, 1978). Another limitation of this approach is that it does nothing to help people who have obsessions but no compulsions. After all, the way this intervention "reaches" obsessions is by blocking the resulting compulsive acts.

The effectiveness of the exposure and response-prevention technique suggests to many behaviorists that people with obsessive compulsive disorders are like the man in the old joke who keeps snapping his fingers to keep elephants away. When someone points out, "But there aren't any elephants around here," the man replies, "See?" One review concludes, "With hindsight, it is possible to see that the obsessional individual has been snapping his fingers, and unless he stops (response prevention) and takes a look around at the same time (exposure), he isn't going to learn much of value about elephants" (Berk & Efran, 1983, p. 546).

**Thought Stopping** A cognitive-behavioral technique called thought stopping has sometimes been used to treat people who have obsessions only (Leger, 1980, 1979; Wolpe, 1973, 1958). Here therapists teach clients to interrupt their obsessive thoughts, on the assumption that doing so will keep them from occurring so often.

Clients are first told to verbalize their obsessive thoughts. The therapist then interrupts each thought by loudly yelling, "Stop!" Somewhat startled, clients do indeed lose their train of obsessive rumination. Later the clients are instructed to yell out "Stop" themselves whenever they begin to experience an obsessive thought, and finally to say "Stop" to themselves silently whenever the thoughts emerge.

In most comparisons with control subjects who receive placebo treatment, people taught thought stopping fail to show a greater overall reduction in obsessive thinking or in levels of anxiety (Mark, 1981; Matthews & Shaw, 1977; Stern et al., 1973). In fact, evidence is growing that suppression of obsessive thoughts may only serve to intensify them (Pennebraker, 1990; Wegner, 1989). In one study on this issue, subjects were asked first to suppress a thought and then to think about it (Wegner, 1989). They experienced the thought *twice* as often under these circumstances as when they were not first asked to suppress it.

**Drug Therapies**  Ever since antianxiety drugs were discovered, clinicians have prescribed them in cases of obsessive compulsive disorders, but research has only occasionally indicated that the drugs have any effect on these stubborn conditions. At present antianxiety drugs are not considered to offer much promise for treating these disorders (Klein et al., 1985). On the other hand, as we have seen, certain antidepressant drugs have begun to emerge as a useful form of treatment for obsessive compulsive disorders (Goodman & McDougle, 1990; Perse, 1988). A number of studies have found that these drugs, particularly clomipramine, lead to a greater reduction in obsessive thinking and compulsive rituals than placebos do (Ananth, 1989; Flament et al., 1985; Ananth et al., 1981; Marks et al., 1981). In what some consider to be a breakthrough study, clomipramine was recently shown to be highly effective in treating people suffering from *trichotillomania,* an extremely painful and upsetting compulsion (believed to affect approximately 2 million women in the United States) in which people repeatedly pull at, and even yank out, their hair, eyelashes, and eyebrows (Swedo et al., 1989).

It is not clear why certain antidepressant drugs affect these disorders. Some theorists believe that the drugs have a direct chemical impact on obsessions (an "anti-obsessive" effect) much like the direct effects of certain antidepressant drugs on panic attacks (Goodman et al., 1990; Insel et al., 1983; Ananth et al., 1981; Asberg et al., 1980). Others believe that the drugs are helpful primarily for obsessive compulsive individuals who are also depressed, and act mainly on the depressive component of the disorder (Emmelkamp, 1982; Marks et al., 1981, 1980).

In a study that supported the anti-obsessive view, antidepressant drugs were given to obsessive compulsive subjects for six weeks. Symptoms were significantly reduced among those who had not been depressed as well as those who had been (Insel et al., 1983). In support of the depression view, however, another study found that

antidepressant drugs were effective in reducing rituals only among obsessive compulsive clients who were depressed as well (Marks et al., 1980).

Obviously, the treatment picture for obsessive compulsive disorders, like that for panic disorders, has improved over the past decade (Zetin, 1990). Once a very stubborn problem, unresponsive to all forms of treatment, these disorders now appear to be helped by such interventions as exposure and response-prevention and antidepressant drugs. Moreover, as we noted in Chapter 6, these treatment advances are beginning to shed light on the very origin and nature of these puzzling disorders.

## Post-traumatic Stress Disorders

The relatively recent identification of post-traumatic stress disorders as a specific psychopathological category has spurred the development of numerous treatment programs for the psychologically troubled survivors of unusual traumatic events (Jacobs et al., 1990). Although the specific features of these treatment programs vary from trauma to trauma, all the programs share certain basic goals: they try to help survivors reduce or overcome their lingering symptoms, gain perspective on their traumatic experiences, and return to constructive living (see Box 7-3). Treatment programs for Vietnam War veterans who suffer from this disorder illustrate how these issues may be addressed.

Therapists have used a combination of techniques to alleviate the post-traumatic symptoms of Vietnam veterans (Brodsky et al., 1990). Antianxiety drugs have helped to reduce the tension, hyperalertness, and exaggerated startle responses that many veterans experience (Kolb, Burris, & Griffiths, 1983). In addition, medications have sometimes been used to lessen nightmares, and antidepressant drugs to reduce depression (Goodwin, 1986).

Exposure-based techniques have also been employed. In one case, covert flooding along with relaxation training helped rid a 31-year-old veteran of his frightening combat flashbacks and nightmares (Fairbank & Keane, 1982). The therapist and client first singled out combat scenes that the veteran had been reexperiencing frequently. The therapist then helped the client to imagine one of these scenes in great detail and urged him to retain the image until his anxiety subsided. After each of these flooding exercises, the therapist switched to positive imagery and led the client through relaxation exercises. In response to this treatment, the man's flashbacks and nightmares diminished. Other studies have also suggested that both covert flooding and covert desensiti-

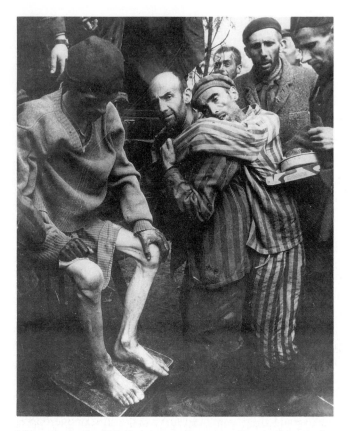

Many survivors of Nazi concentration camps faced a long road back to psychological health. Because knowledge of post-traumatic stress disorders was nonexistent until recent years, most survivors had to find their way back without professional help. The lingering emotional impact of their traumatic experiences was felt not only by them but often by their children and other close relatives.

zation can help to reduce the fears, nightmares, and flashbacks of war veterans (Keane & Kaloupek, 1982; Schinder, 1980; Kipper, 1977).

Although symptomatic relief of this kind is useful, most clinicians believe that veterans with post-traumatic stress disorders cannot fully recover until they also develop insight and perspective in regard to their combat experiences and the impact those experiences continue to have on them (Brende & Parson, 1985; Wilson, 1980; Figley, 1978; Horowitz, 1976). Sometimes clinicians help clients to bring out deep-seated feelings, accept what they have done and experienced, become less judgmental of themselves, and learn to trust others once again. In related work, the psychologist James Pennebaker (1990) has found that talking (or even writing) about suppressed traumatic experiences can help to reduce lingering anxiety and tension.

Most often, attempts at expressing feelings and devel-

oping insight are undertaken in group therapy, or "rap groups," in which Vietnam veterans meet to share experiences and give mutual emotional support. In an atmosphere of group trust and common experience, many individuals find it easier to recall events and confront feelings they have been trying to avoid for years. One of the major issues dealt with in rap groups is guilt — guilt about things the members may have done to survive or guilt about the very fact that they did survive while close friends died. Once the veterans are finally able to talk candidly about their combat experiences and guilt feelings, they may start to recover from them (Lifton, 1973). Many are eventually able to gauge their responsibility for past actions more accurately and experience a new sense of personal integrity.

Another important issue addressed in rap groups is the feeling of rage experienced by many veterans. Often these people are intensely angry that they had to fight for a questionable cause, face unbearable conditions and tensions in Vietnam, and deal with an accusing society upon their return. In the early stages of therapy these feelings are frequently taken out on the group leader or other members. As one team of therapists reported, "We sometimes had feelings akin to those of war prisoners being interrogated by their captors" (Frick & Bogart, 1982). Later the anger may take the form of grief: "Crying from anger may be something to welcome as a part of important growth in a group or individual" (Blank, 1979).

The use of rap groups began in 1971, when an organization called Vietnam Veterans Against the War decided that there was a pressing need for a forum in which veterans could discuss their experiences with other veterans and together heal their psychological wounds (Shapiro, 1978; Lifton, 1976). With the help of several prominent therapists, the organization set up some trial groups, whose effectiveness exceeded all expectations. Rap groups spread throughout the United States and were granted government funding in 1979. Today more than 150 small counseling centers (Veteran Outreach Centers) across the country, as well as numerous treatment programs in Veterans Administration hospitals, specialize in these problems (Brende & Parson, 1985). The high demand for services at such programs seems to increase still more during celebrations or anniversaries of wartime events and during new wars. In 1991, during the war in the Persian Gulf, there was an increased demand for services from veterans of the Vietnam War, Korean War, and World War II. In addition to rap groups, these agencies offer individual therapy, counseling for the spouses and children of troubled veterans, family therapy, and assistance in securing employment, education, and benefits (Blank, 1982).

Many people eventually overcome the effects of traumatic stress. During a reunion, these concentration camp survivors proudly display their tattooed camp identification numbers as symbols of their triumph over their psychological wounds.

Because most Veteran Outreach Centers have existed only a relatively short time, research into their effectiveness is just beginning. So far, clinical reports suggest that they offer an important, sometimes life-saving treatment opportunity that was previously unavailable. Julius's search for help upon his return from Vietnam was, unfortunately, an ordeal that many veterans have shared:

*When I got back from the 'Nam, I knew I needed psycho*-therapy or something like that. I just knew that if I didn't get help I was going to kill myself or somebody else. . . . I went to see this doctor; he barely looked at me. I felt he "saw me coming" and knew all about my sickness. I was the "sicky" to him. He just kept on asking me all that bullshit about how many children I had killed and was I guilty and depressed about it. He asked how it felt to kill people. He also kept on asking me about my brothers and sisters. But he never asked me about what my experiences were like in Vietnam. He never did. I saw him for treatment for about a month — about three visits, but I quit because we weren't

getting anywhere. . . . He just kept on giving me more and more medications. I could've set up my own pharmacy. I needed someone to talk to about my problems, my real problems, not some bullshit about my childhood. I needed someone who wanted to help. The clinic later referred me to another shrink. . . . I guess she thought she was being honest with me, by telling me that she was not a veteran, was not in Vietnam, and did not know what was wrong with me. She also told me that she had no experience working with Vietnam veterans, and that I should go to the Veterans Administration for help. . . .

Two years ago, I made another try to get some help at another agency close to where my mother lives. I was also told to go to the nearest VA. I was given some dope medicine, and I never came back. I kept getting angry and angrier; I felt I was being handed a line of shit by these doctors. I also became scared that there was something really wrong with me now. I just didn't want to go to the VA for help. . . . I blame the VA for my going to 'Nam anyway; I wanted no part of it.

It was only in the last 3 years when my wife made an

═══════════ BOX 7-3 ═══════════

# Preparing Victims for Rape's Aftermath

*Mary Koss and Mary Harvey*

Victims as well as significant others can benefit from some discussion of the usual symptomatic responses to rape, the psychological impact of rape, and the length of time required to feel recovered. Such information may prevent more serious problems from developing by making the expectations of involved others more realistic and by encouraging the victim to feel justified to seek help. The information that could be shared with victims and their families might be similar to the following comments. . . .

Rape is a trauma just like a major disaster such as a tornado or a bad car accident.

*Physical symptoms* Because of the shock that these events cause to your systems, some physical problems usually develop afterwards. You may experience symptoms you usually associate with extreme fear, such as pounding heart, shortness of breath, or dizziness. You may find your appetite or sleeping is changed as when you're worried about a major traumatic event like a court appearance or are under a lot of pressure at work.

You may notice problems with sex that you've rarely experienced before. Often this is a signal that you're not ready to resume your former activities so quickly. It's perfectly okay to substitute other forms of feeling close and [to avoid] intercourse until you feel ready.

Even though these physical symptoms are typical, they will still upset you. Seek a doctor's care but be sure to tell him or her of your recent rape so that they can treat you properly.

*Feelings* Nearly everyone experiences some psychological problems after a rape. Particularly upsetting are nightmares, flashbacks of the experience, and the feeling that you need to talk about your experience over and over again until everyone around you is fed up. These are normal psychological processes that operate after a major trauma. Their purpose is to gradually wear down the frightening impact of an experience. They will eventually help you put the experience behind you.

Even if you don't have any problems now, it's not unusual for some to crop up six months or a year from now. The problems that are most common are fears that you never had before or were never that pronounced, feeling bad about yourself and about life in general, conflicts in your intimate relationships, and problems getting back to your former enjoyment of sex.

You may find that the rape has affected your whole family. Don't be surprised if you develop negative feelings about someone that are stronger or different than you've ever had before. Try to talk your feelings over and be specific about what the other person can do to help you feel better. Family members may feel pretty impatient that it is taking you so long to get on top of things.

*Availability of services* You may find that although your enjoyment of life is less, you can live with your symptoms and cope. However, there may come a time when you feel that the toll is too great and you need relief. Or, you may notice that your important relationships are suffering or deteriorating. A number of people are available to help you at this point. I'm going to give you a sheet listing some of them so that you'll know who to call.

Besides counselors who could see you privately if you wanted, it is possible to become a member of a group made up of women who have been raped. It can often help to feel less crazy and alone if you know other people who share your experience and know what it's like.

*Length of recovery* It usually takes over a year to feel fully recovered from rape, to be able to think of your assault without crying, and to feel the same level of health you enjoyed previously. Going through a court process or anything else that reminds you of the assault may make you feel temporarily worse after you thought you were finally getting on top of things. It's not unusual for there to be ups and downs on the way to recovery.

If it's okay with you, I'd like to call you at home in a few days and see how you're doing. Then, or at a later time, I'd be glad to see you again or help you make an appointment with a counselor.

*(Koss & Harvey, 1987, pp. 109–110)*

---

important phone call to a local Veterans Outreach Center that I started feeling I had hope, that something could be done for me. I received the help that I have always needed. Finally, I found it easier to hold a job and take care of my family. My nightmares are not as frightening or as frequent as they used to be. Things are better now; I am learning to trust people and give more to my wife and children.

*(Brende & Parson, 1985, pp. 206–208)*

Rap groups for Vietnam veterans have helped many of their members overcome
the anxiety, depression, sleep disturbance, and flashbacks that linger for years after
the war.

# TREATMENTS FOR ANXIETY DISORDERS: THE STATE OF THE FIELD

Clearly the treatment picture for anxiety disorders has changed greatly over the past fifteen years. Many new approaches have been developed, and anxiety problems that once confounded therapists are now responding to clinical interventions. As we examine the various treatments for anxiety disorders, a number of important trends emerge:

1. Behavioral and drug therapies have dominated the treatment picture for anxiety disorders. Behavioral therapy is often effective in treating simple phobias, agoraphobia, and obsessive compulsive disorders, and indeed behavioral interventions are often viewed as the treatments of choice in these problem areas. Antianxiety drugs serve an important adjunct role in treating generalized anxiety disorders, and antidepressant drugs, surprisingly,

can have a major impact on panic disorders and obsessive compulsive disorders. Cognitive therapy, too, is fast becoming a major force in the treatment of anxiety disorders. Newly developed cognitive approaches have been extremely helpful to people with panic disorders, and social phobias often respond to rational-emotive therapy. Finally, global approaches such as psychodynamic and humanistic therapies have sometimes played helpful roles in cases of generalized anxiety disorder and post-traumatic stress disorder.

2. In view of these findings, clinicians now make greater efforts to match anxious clients to particular forms of treatment. They have also become more inclined to combine procedures from the various treatment models. Social phobias are now often treated with a combination of cognitive therapy and social skills training; panic disorders with agoraphobia are treated with a combination of exposure techniques and antidepressant drugs; clinicians often mix global therapies, relaxation training, and antianxiety drugs in treating generalized anxiety disorders and post-traumatic stress disorders; and antidepressant drugs are often used

to complement exposure and response-prevention treatments for obsessive compulsive disorders.

3. Research has guided clinicians to clarify and alter their treatment procedures for anxiety disorders. Over the past fifteen years behaviorists have become clearer about the importance of exposure in their various interventions and have placed this feature at the center of treatment; biological therapists have become more judicious in their use of antianxiety drugs in light of findings that these drugs can be addictive in high doses; and biological therapists have discovered that antidepressant drugs are more helpful than antianxiety drugs for some anxiety disorders, and have adjusted their medication decisions correspondingly.

For clinicians and for the millions of people who seek help for anxiety, the field's growing effectiveness is a most positive and momentous development.

## SUMMARY

**P**sychodynamic therapists believe that people with anxiety disorders are fearful of their id impulses and are unable to control and defend against them. They use global psychodynamic procedures such as free association to help clients uncover and resolve these unconscious issues. Research has not consistently supported the effectiveness of the psychodynamic approach in cases of anxiety disorder, nor have global humanistic and existential approaches proved to be effective treatments in such cases.

**T**he first anxiety disorders to be treated successfully were the simple phobias. They appear to respond to each of the specific therapies, but behavioral therapies have been much more successful than others. The three major behavioral approaches are all *exposure-based treatments:* desensitization, flooding, and modeling. *Desensitization* has three phases: *relaxation training,* construction of a *fear hierarchy,* and *graded pairing* of feared objects and relaxation responses. In *flooding,* or *implosive therapy,* clients are repeatedly exposed to feared objects or situations and made to see that they are actually harmless. The most effective modeling technique is *participant modeling,* or *guided participation,* in which clients observe and repeat the therapist's actions in the situations they fear.

**R**esearch has shown that the behavioral approaches to simple phobias are all helpful but that *in vivo exposure* is more effective than imaginal or observational exposure. Many behavioral therapists now combine features of all these methods, being sure to retain the critical feature of in vivo exposure.

Until recently, attempts at treating agoraphobia met with relatively little success. New approaches, however, have offered considerable relief to people with this disorder, particularly behavioral approaches. Therapists who use exposure approaches typically help clients to venture farther and farther from their homes and to participate in feared situations gradually, step by step. The therapist may use support, reasoning, and coaxing or reinforcement techniques. Sometimes support groups and home-based self-help programs include these techniques.

**C**linicians began to make progress in the treatment of social phobias when they recognized that social anxiety can have two distinct components: social fears and lack of specific social skills. Clinicians now design treatment according to the client's particular area of difficulty. Efforts to reduce social anxiety have included in vivo exposure techniques, group therapy, and various cognitive interventions. Social skills training combines a number of behavioral techniques, including modeling and role playing, in such formats as social skills training groups and assertiveness training groups. The best approach to treating social phobias may be a combination of cognitive therapy and social skills training.

**G**eneralized anxiety disorders are currently the anxiety disorders least responsive to treatment. Rational-emotive therapy is among the cognitive approaches that have been used in an attempt to change beliefs that may be at the root of generalized anxiety. Three forms of stress management training are also commonly employed: *self-instruction training, relaxation training,* and *biofeedback training.* Benzodiazepine drugs such as diazepam (Valium) help reduce anxiety by improving the ability of GABA to slow physical arousal throughout the body. However, these drugs can be addictive in high doses and are now prescribed less frequently than they were.

Like so many other kinds of anxiety disorders, panic disorders once defied treatment. Now some highly effective biological and cognitive interventions are available. Certain antidepressant drugs bring relief to many people with panic disorders, whether or not the disorders are accompanied by agoraphobia or depression.

Cognitive therapy teaches patients that their unusual physical sensations are actually harmless.

Until the 1970s few treatments seemed to help people with obsessive compulsive disorders. One exception was the technique of *paradoxical intention.* A more recent behavioral approach combines prolonged in vivo exposure with *response prevention,* the blocking of compulsive behaviors. Antianxiety drugs are not considered helpful for obsessive compulsive disorders, but antidepressant drugs have begun to emerge as a useful form of treatment for these disorders.

Numerous treatment programs have been developed for people with post-traumatic stress disorder. Techniques used for symptomatic relief include antianxiety drugs, sleeping medications, and exposure-based techniques. Most clinicians also use supportive and humanistic therapy, including group therapy, to help survivors with post-traumatic stress disorder develop insight and perspective in regard to the continuing impact of their traumatic experiences.

# TOPIC OVERVIEW

# CHAPTER 8

# MOOD DISORDERS

Most people's moods are transient. Their feelings of elation or sadness are understandable responses to daily events and change readily without affecting the overall tenor of their lives. In contrast, the moods of people with mood disorders tend to last a long time, color all their interactions with the world, and disrupt their normal functioning. Virtually all the actions of such people are dictated by their powerful moods.

Depression and mania are the dominating emotions in mood disorders. *Depression* is a low, sad state in which life seems bleak and its challenges overwhelming. *Mania,* the extreme opposite of depression, is a state of breathless euphoria, or at least frenzied energy, in which people have an exaggerated belief that the world is theirs for the taking. Most people with a mood disorder suffer exclusively from depression, a pattern often called *unipolar depression.* They have no history of mania and return to a normal or nearly normal mood state when their depression lifts. Others undergo periods of mania that alternate with periods of depression, a pattern called *bipolar disorder* or *manic-depressive disorder.* One might logically expect a third pattern of mood disorder, *unipolar mania,* in which people suffer exclusively from mania, but this pattern is so rare that there is some question as to whether it exists at all (APA, 1987; Krauthammer & Klerman, 1979).

Mood disorders have always captured people's interest, in part because so many prominent people have suffered from them. The Bible speaks of the severe depression of Nebuchadnezzar, Saul, and Moses. Queen Victoria of England and Abraham Lincoln seemed to experience recurring depressions. Similarly, depression and sometimes mania have plagued such artists as George Frideric Handel, Ernest Hemingway, Eugene O'Neill, Virginia Woolf, Robert Lowell, and Sylvia Plath (Goodwin & Jamison, 1986; Andreasen, 1980; Jamison, 1984).

The plight of these famous figures has been shared by millions. Approximately 16 percent of adults in the United States have experienced or will experience a mood disorder at some point in their lives (Weissman & Klerman, 1985). The economic consequences of these disorders (treatment, hospitalization, work loss, and so on) amount to billions of dollars each year (Gold, 1987;

Abraham Lincoln was one of many leaders who suffered from episodes of depression. In 1841 he wrote to a friend, "I am now the most miserable man living. If what I feel were equally distributed to the whole human family, there would be not one cheerful face on earth."

Secunda, 1973), while the human suffering they cause is incalculable.

# UNIPOLAR PATTERNS OF DEPRESSION

Because so much psychological terminology has entered the popular vernacular over the last thirty years, people more dejected and unhappy than usual often say they are "depressed." In most cases, what they are describing is a perfectly normal mood swing, a response perhaps to sad events, understandable fatigue, or unhappy thoughts. Unfortunately, this use of the term confuses a normal mood of dejection with a dysfunctional clinical syndrome of unipolar depression. The former is experienced by all of us, the latter by an unfortunate minority.

Normal dejection is seldom so severe as to alter daily functioning significantly, and it lifts within a reasonable period. Downturns in mood can even be beneficial. Some people spend such periods exploring themselves, their values, and their situations, and often emerge with a sense of greater strength, clarity, and resolve.

Clinical depression, on the other hand, is a serious psychological disturbance with no redeeming characteristics. The psychological pain experienced is severe and long-lasting and may intensify as the months and years go by. It is so debilitating that clinically depressed persons may reach a point where they are unable to carry out the simplest of life's activities; some, in fact, try to end their lives.

## The Prevalence of Unipolar Depression

Surveys suggest that approximately 6 percent of adults in the United States—currently 10 million people—are suffering from a unipolar pattern of depression (Regier et al., 1988; Myers et al., 1984; Weissman & Boyd, 1984). The prevalence rate is similar in many other countries, including England, Australia, Denmark, and Iceland, and has remained stable for several decades (Murphy et al., 1985). In fact, it is estimated that 15 percent of all adults in the world experience a severe episode of unipolar depression at some point in their lives (Weissman & Klerman, 1985).

In almost all industrialized countries, women are twice as likely as men to experience severe episodes of unipolar depression (see Box 8-1). Some 20 to 26 percent of women have a severe depressive episode at some time in their lives, compared with 8 to 12 percent of men

(Weissman & Klerman, 1985; Boyd & Weissman, 1981). This ratio holds in the United States, Europe, and Australia (Noll & Dubinsky, 1985; Bradshaw & Parker, 1983). Women are also more likely than men to experience episodes of *mild* unipolar depression, although not by so high a ratio. Among children, the prevalence rates of unipolar depression are similar for girls and boys. These prevalence rates are similar across all socioeconomic classes (Weissman & Boyd, 1984; Weissman & Myers, 1978).

Episodes of severe unipolar depression may begin at any age, but men in their 50s and women between 35 and 45 years old may be particularly vulnerable (Weissman & Boyd, 1984). Moreover, the incidence of depression among teenagers and young adults appears to be on the increase. Approximately 64 percent of severely depressed people recover within six months, many without treatment (Keller, 1988). At least 80 to 90 percent recover within five years. Having been depressed once, however, a person has an increased risk of becoming depressed again. Between 50 and 85 percent of those who recover from an episode of severe unipolar depression will have at least one subsequent episode in their lifetime (Keller, 1985).

## Clinical Picture of Depression

Some depressed people manage to function after a fashion, but their depression robs them of effectiveness and pleasure, as we see in the cases of Derek and Beatrice:

*D*erek has probably suffered from depression all of his adult life but was unaware of it for many years. Derek called himself a night person, claiming that he could not think clearly until after noon even though he was often awake by 4:00 A.M. He tried to schedule his work as editorial writer for a small town newspaper so that it was compatible with his depressed mood at the beginning of the day. Therefore, he scheduled meetings for the mornings; talking with people got him moving. He saved writing and decision making for later in the day.

Derek had always been a thoughtful person and was often preoccupied. His family and colleagues grew used to his apparent inattention and absentmindedness. He often failed to answer people when they spoke to him. Sometimes they were surprised to hear his slow, soft-spoken reply 20 or 30 seconds later. His wife tried to be patient when it took him 20 seconds to respond to "Do you want coffee or tea tonight?" Derek's private thoughts were rarely cheerful and self-confident. He felt that his marriage was a mere business partnership. He provided the money, and she provided a home and children. Derek and his wife rarely expressed affection for each other. Occasionally, he had images of his own violent death in a bicycle crash, in a plane crash, or in a murder by an unidentified assailant.

Derek felt that he was constantly on the edge of job failure. He was disappointed that his editorials had not attracted the attention of larger papers. He was certain that several of the younger people on the paper had better ideas and wrote more skillfully than he did. He scolded himself for a bad editorial that he had written ten years earlier. Although that particular piece had not been up to his usual standards, everyone else on the paper had forgotten it a week after it appeared. But ten years later, Derek was still ruminating over that one editorial. . . .

Derek attributed his inability to enjoy himself and his methodical, passionless marriage to his severe Anglo-Saxon Protestant upbringing. He had been taught that open expressions of affection were ill-mannered. He had never seen his own parents embrace in their fifty years of marriage. In his family, humility was valued more than self-confidence. He had been brought up to do the "right thing," not to enjoy himself. Raucous merrymaking was only for the irresponsible. Even a game of Go Fish had to be played in secret when he was a child.

Derek brushed off his morning confusion as a lack of quick intelligence. He had no way to know that it was a symptom of depression. He never realized that his death images might be suicidal thinking. People do not talk about such things. For all Derek knew, everyone had similar thoughts.

*(Lickey & Gordon, 1991, pp. 183–185)*

*F*or several years, Beatrice had been irritable, but then for a six-month period, her irritability bordered on the irrational. She screamed in anger or sobbed in despair at every dirty dish left on the coffee table or on the bedroom floor. Each day the need to plan the dinner menu provoked agonizing indecision. How could all the virtues or, more likely, vices of hamburgers be accurately compared to those of spaghetti? A glass of spilled milk was an occasion for panic. Beatrice would bolt from her chair and run from the dining room. Ten minutes later, she would realize that the spilled milk was insignificant. She had her whole family walking on eggs. She thought they would be better off if she were dead.

Beatrice could not cope with her job. As a branch manager of a large chain store, she had many decisions to make. Unable to make them herself, she would ask employees who were much less competent for advice, but then she could not decide whose advice to take. Each morning before going to work, she complained of nausea. In public, she was usually able to control her feelings of panic and felt a little better when she actually arrived at work and was away from the wary eyes of her family.

Beatrice's husband loved her, but he did not understand what was wrong. He thought that she would improve if he made her life easier by taking over more housework, cooking, and child care. His attempt to help only made Beatrice feel more guilty and worthless. She wanted to make a contribution to her family. She wanted to do the chores "like normal people" did but broke down crying at the smallest impediment to a perfect job. Because Beatrice's volatility put a stress on her marriage, the couple went to a psychiatrist for marriage counseling. The psychiatrist failed to diagnose Beatrice's depression. He provided marriage counseling that was designed for healthy people. Consequently, the counseling failed. Months passed, and Beatrice's problem became more serious. Some days she was too upset to go to work. She stopped seeing her friends. She spent most of her time at home either yelling or crying. Finally, Beatrice's husband called the psychiatrist and insisted that something was seriously wrong.

*(Lickey & Gordon, 1991, p. 181)*

As these case descriptions indicate, depression has many symptoms other than sadness, and the symptoms often reinforce one another. Chronic indecisiveness, for example, may lead to poor job performance, which in turn leads to a lower self-image, less self-confidence, and still more indecisiveness, as in Beatrice's case. The symptoms associated with depression span five areas of functioning: emotional, motivational, behavioral, cognitive, and somatic.

**Emotional Symptoms** Most people who are depressed feel intensely sad and dejected. They describe themselves as feeling "miserable," "empty," and "humiliated." They report getting little pleasure from anything, and they tend to lose their sense of humor. Some depressed people also experience anxiety, anger, or agitation (see Box 8-2). This sea of misery may find expression in frequent crying spells; those who do not actually cry often report that they feel like crying.

---

## BOX 8-1

# Depressing News for Women

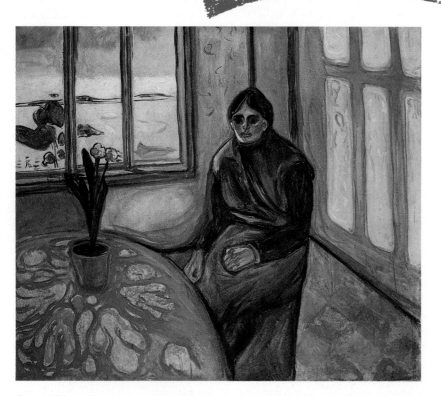

Edvard Munch's painting *Melancholy (Laura)* was inspired by his sister's bouts of severe depression.

**M**ore women than men are diagnosed with major unipolar depression. More women report being mildly depressed. The inescapable conclusion is that women appear to be at least twice as likely as men to suffer from unipolar depression (Klerman et al., 1989). Depressing news, indeed. This apparent gender difference has generated much theorizing and investigation. The psychologist Susan Nolen-Hoeksema (1987) has reviewed five possible explanations.

1. The ***artifact hypothesis:*** Women and men are *equally* prone to depression, but gender differences arise because studies fail to detect depression in men. One reason could be that men find it less socially acceptable to report feeling depressed or to seek treatment. Alternatively, depressed women may display emotional symptoms, such as sadness and crying, that are easily diagnosed, while depressed men may mask these symptoms. It has been suggested that depressed men turn to drink and are diagnosed as alcoholics. In fact the gender difference in

Many depressed people seem to lose their feelings of affection for friends and relatives. One woman said, "I envy everybody. I envy my own children. . . . I envy little girls who can play just like children" (Moriarty, 1967, p. 72). A depressed man said, "I feel I don't love anyone. I feel there are too many people demanding things of me — clinging to me" (Rowe, 1978, p. 49).

**Motivational Symptoms** Depressed people usually lose the desire to participate in their accustomed activities. They report a lack of drive, initiative, and spontaneity, and they may have to force themselves to go to work, converse with friends, eat meals, or have sex. Aaron Beck (1967) has described this state as a "paralysis of will." As one individual recalls, "I didn't want to do

anything — just wanted to stay put and be let alone. By nature I have initiative and I'm self-generating, but not then. Oh, I suppose that if a fire broke out, I'd have moved, but it usually took something of some magnitude to make me stir" (Kraines & Thetford, 1972, p. 20).

Suicide represents the ultimate escape from life's activities and pressures. Many depressed people become indifferent to life or wish to die; others wish that they could kill themselves, and some actually try. As we shall see in Chapter 10, many factors influence a suicidal person's actions, but depressed people are certainly at risk. It has been estimated that between 7 and 15 percent of people who suffer from depression commit suicide (Tsuang, 1978), compared with 1 percent of nondepressed people (U.S. Bureau of the Census, 1980).

---

alcoholism — men outnumber women two to one — is complementary to the gender difference in depression; moreover, many alcoholic persons show other symptoms of depression. Some researchers even go so far as to suggest that depression and alcoholism are similar genetically based disorders. As Nolen-Hoeksema notes, however, the artifact hypothesis lacks consistent research support.

2. The *X-linkage hypothesis:* Depression is caused by a dominant mutation on the X chromosome. Since women are genotypically XX, they run a greater risk of inheriting the gene than men, who are genotypically XY. The hypothesis is supported by the finding that depression is correlated with other X-chromosome abnormalities, such as color blindness. Family pedigree studies, however, have contradicted it. If depression were an X-chromosome disorder, a depressed father would always transmit it to his daughters but not to his sons; yet studies indicate that more father-son than father-daughter pairs are diagnosed with unipolar depression.

3. A *traditional psychoanalytic explanation:* At the Oedipal stage of

psychological development a girl realizes that she lacks a penis and believes herself to have been castrated by her mother; she feels both hostility toward her mother and a sense of her own inferiority. She also identifies with her mother. With this background, women's relationships with men are motivated by a desire to possess a phallus in symbolic form. They suffer low self-esteem as a result of their lifelong penis envy, are more vulnerable to loss, and in turn are more prone to develop depression. This model lacks empirical support and has been widely criticized as being chauvinistic.

4. A *sociocultural explanation:* The quality of women's roles in society makes them more vulnerable to depression. On the one hand, as the housewife role has become increasingly devalued and less rewarding, women in this role may become depressed because they have limited sources of gratification (Gove & Tudor, 1973). On the other hand, working wives may be prone to depression because they bear the double burden of housework and a job outside the home.

5. The *learned helplessness explanation* (see page 275): Women

are more vulnerable to depression because they are more likely to feel they have little control over their lives. A number of studies have shown that women are more prone to helplessness effects than men. One found that female college students who were exposed to a helplessness-inducing set of insoluble anagrams later performed other tasks much more poorly than their male counterparts (Le Unes, Nation, & Turley, 1980). Nolen-Hoeksema notes, however, that a stringent test of this explanation in depression remains to be carried out.

The artifact hypothesis implies that more effort should be made to identify and treat depression in men. The biological and psychoanalytic explanations say that therapeutic resources could be fruitfully focused on women themselves. The sociocultural and learned helplessness explanations suggest that it is society itself that requires "treatment," or restructuring. No explanation of gender differences in depression has gained unequivocal support. Certainly, if one is finally seen to be more persuasive than the others, it will have great influence on the way resources are allocated for the prevention and treatment of this debilitating disorder.

BOX 8-2

# Two Sides of the Same Coin?

Most clinicians view anxiety and depression as separate problems with different sets of symptoms, but others argue that the two diagnoses differ not in kind but in degree (Kendall & Watson, 1989). They contend that anxiety may grow so intense that it becomes depression. This notion is supported by the finding that many measures of depression and anxiety overlap — similarities are found both in the measures themselves and in the responses given by depressed or anxious patients (Dobson, 1985) — and clinicians often disagree as to whether a given subject is depressed or anxious or both (Deluty et al., 1986).

A contradiction is evident: either anxiety and depression are different points on the same scale or they are distinct disorders. If they are indeed different disorders, researchers and practitioners must learn to distinguish better one syndrome from the other. If they are the same disorder with different manifestations, the diagnostic system requires overhauling.

Some recent research suggests that depression and anxiety may actually have a common basis (Paul, 1988). Some of these studies focus on the theory that uncontrollable stress causes a feeling of helplessness, and hence that anxiety (in response to the stress) ordinarily precedes depression (the feeling of helplessness). In these studies, rats given a stress-reducing drug did not exhibit helplessness responses when they were exposed to uncontrollable stress: no anxiety, no ensuing depression. Another line of research has found that the drug alprazolam often is an effective treatment for *both* anxiety disorders and depression. In fact, it is listed as an antianxiety medication *and* an antidepressant drug.

Other research suggests that anxiety and depression are distinct entities that have certain symptoms in common, including unpleasant feelings and demoralization (Tellegen, 1985). Scales used to measure the *cognitive* components of anxiety and depression have shown significant differences between the two (Clark, Beck, & Steward, 1990). Depressed patients report more hopelessness, lower self-esteem, and more negative thoughts than anxious patients, who, for their part, report more feelings of danger.

Clinicians of all theoretical paradigms are interested in whether anxiety and depression are different facets of the same disorder or separate disorders that frequently occur together. Many believe that the future course of research into anxiety and depression and their treatments depends on the outcome of these investigations (Kendall & Watson, 1989).

---

Approximately half of all suicides are committed by people who are depressed (Whitlock, 1977).

**Behavioral Symptoms**  The activity of depressed people usually decreases dramatically. They do less and are less productive. They spend more time alone and may stay in bed for long periods. One man recalls, "I'd awaken early, but I'd just lie there — what was the use of getting up to a miserable day? I knew I had to go to the office, so finally I would get up. I'd dress on the installment plan and have several cups of coffee" (Kraines & Thetford, 1972, p. 21).

Depressed people may also move more slowly, with seeming reluctance and lack of energy. Even their speech may be slow, quiet, and monotonal, delivered with eyes cast down and back bent. In one study, mental hospital admission interviews were videotaped and then evaluated by a series of judges. The researchers found that depressed patients made less eye contact with their interviewers than did nondepressed patients and also turned down their mouths and hung their heads more (Waxer, 1974).

**Cognitive Symptoms**  Depressive disorders are also characterized by cognitive symptoms. First, depressed people hold decidedly negative views of themselves (Beer, 1988; Lorr & Wunderlich, 1988). They consider themselves inadequate, undesirable, inferior, and perhaps evil. Their opinions of their physical appearance are no kinder. They may view themselves as unattractive or even repulsive. Consider the self-judgments of a lawyer suffering from depression.

*He described himself as a "shell of a person" fit only* to be prosecuted for moral decay. A loud voice — "heh" — was ridiculing him. He was not a man. Had he not neglected

depressed people especially vulnerable to suicidal thinking. A successful businessman recalls, "Everything seemed black. The whole world was going to the devil, the country was going bankrupt, and my business was doomed to fail. . . . I was as pessimistic as hell—I was worse than that—I was almost hopeless about everything" (Kraines & Thetford, 1972, p. 20).

People with depression will frequently complain that their intellectual ability is deteriorating (Willner, 1984). They feel confused, unable to remember things, easily distracted by outside noises, and unable to solve even small problems. Time crawls for them, yet they feel that they cannot get anything done (Hawkins et al., 1988). Actually, these difficulties are often imagined rather than real. When researchers compared the performances of twenty-four depressed and twenty-four nondepressed undergraduates at tasks that required the subjects to respond to hypothetical social problems, the two groups performed comparably. The only difference

Some depressed persons mask their depression by smiling and looking happy most of the time. Movie star Marilyn Monroe was such an individual. Emotion researcher Paul Ekman and his colleagues (1988) claim that certain facial and behavioral clues distinguish genuine happiness from masked depression, but that "we learn to ignore them, not wanting the burden of knowing the truth."

his wife, both emotionally and sexually? Was he not cursed and ignored by God as a failure? All his benevolent acts were a cover for self-aggrandizement. . . . He had indulged himself in a life of pseudoservice. He should never have entered the legal profession . . . he was clearly an imposter, an empty, useless wretch who could no longer concentrate or make the simplest decisions, who paced his office late into the night, afraid to go home and face another restless, sleepless night.

*(Whybrow et al., 1984, pp. 3–4)*

Depressed people usually blame themselves for nearly every negative event, even things that have nothing to do with them, and they rarely credit themselves for positive achievements. Their guilt and self-criticism may seem harsh to everyone else, but they see it as perfectly appropriate. At the same time, they feel helpless to control or improve any of their daily encounters or circumstances.

Another cognitive symptom of depression is a negative view of the future. Depressed people are usually convinced that nothing will ever improve (Moore & Paolillo, 1984). They expect the worst and hence are likely to procrastinate. This sense of hopelessness also makes

William Styron, the Pulitzer Prize-winning author of *The Confessions of Nat Turner* and *Sophie's Choice*, describes the pessimism that characterized his own major depressive episode: "The pain is unrelenting, and what makes the condition intolerable is the foreknowledge that no remedy will come—not in a day, an hour, a month or a minute. It is hopelessness even more than pain that crushes the soul."

was that the depressed subjects predicted poorer performances for themselves and evaluated their performances less favorably than did the nondepressed subjects (Can & Gotlib, 1985).

On the other hand, research does seem to bear out the belief of many depressed people that they no longer remember things well. Several studies found that depressed subjects were less able than nondepressed subjects to remember events of the distant past (Weingartner & Silberman, 1984; Henry, Weingartner, & Murphy, 1973). Note, however, that this deficit may reflect motivational deficiencies rather than cognitive impairment per se. Studies suggest that depressed people often resist making the sustained effort required for long-term memory and related cognitive tasks (Tancer et al., 1990; Roy-Byrne et al., 1986).

**Somatic Symptoms** Depression is often accompanied by such physical ailments as headaches, indigestion, constipation, dizzy spells, unpleasant sensations in the chest, and generalized pain (see Figure 8-1). In fact, many depressions are initially diagnosed by family doctors who have been consulted because of these somatic problems (Stoudemire, 1985). Disturbances in appetite and sleep are particularly common, as are complaints of constant tiredness that is not relieved even when rest and sleep are increased (Ballenger, 1988; Gillen et al., 1984; Garvey et al., 1984; Harris, Young, & Hughes, 1984). As

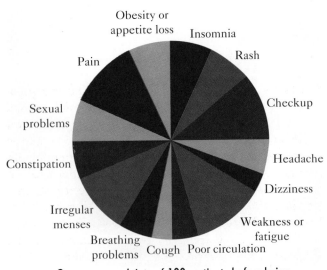

Common complaints of 100 patients before being diagnosed as depressed

**FIGURE 8-1** Depression is often detected when patients go to a physician complaining about one of the somatic symptoms that accompany depression. The most common complaints made by these patients are weakness, pain, and irregular menses. *(Adapted from Gold, 1987, p. 180.)*

one individual recalls, "I slept poorly, so I began taking sleeping pills. I was tired most of the time even though I did far less work than usual" (Kraines & Thetford, 1972, p. 20). Depressed people usually get less sleep overall than others and awaken more frequently during the night. At the other end of the spectrum, however, are the approximately 9 percent of depressed people who sleep excessively (Ballenger, 1988).

## Diagnosing Unipolar Patterns of Depression

Unipolar depression may occur in any of several patterns. Some clinicians believe that "unipolar depression" is really a catchall name for a variety of disorders, each of which has a distinct origin, prognosis, and responsiveness to treatment. Others believe that the patterns simply reflect different points on the continuum of a single disorder. While this debate currently goes unresolved, DSM-III-R distinguishes several patterns of unipolar depression.

People are said to be experiencing a *major depressive episode* if their depression is severely disabling, is characterized by at least five symptoms, and lasts for two weeks or more (see Figure 8-2). These people may receive a diagnosis of *major depression, single episode,* indicating that it is their first such episode, or *major depression, recurrent,* indicating a history of such episodes. Major depressive episodes are further described as *chronic* if they last more than two years, *seasonal* if they fluctuate with seasonal changes, or *melancholic* if the person is unaffected by pleasurable events, dominated by motor, sleep, and appetite disturbances, and very responsive to drug therapy.

People who display a less disabling depressed mood and fewer than five symptoms may receive a diagnosis of *dysthymia* (the term is Greek for "despondency"). To distinguish this milder form of depression from normal mood fluctuations, DSM-III-R also stipulates that the depressed mood must have persisted for at least two years (one year in children and adolescents). Periods of normal mood that may occasionally interrupt the mild depressed mood do not affect the diagnosis as long as these periods last only days or weeks.

The recovery rate among people with dysthymia is only 40 percent, compared to the previously noted recovery rate of 80 to 90 percent for people with a major depressive episode (Gonzales et al., 1985; Barrett, 1984). In a number of cases, dysthymia may lead to major depression, a sequence called *double depression* (Keller & Shapiro, 1982).

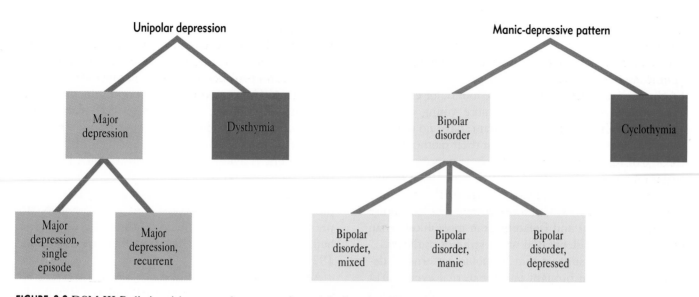

**FIGURE 8-2** DSM-III-R distinguishes several patterns of mood dysfunction. The major distinction is between unipolar and bipolar patterns. Other distinctions focus on the severity, recurrence, and precise nature of the current mood episode.

In past diagnostic systems, clinicians were required to distinguish *psychotic depression* from *neurotic depression* (Breslau & Meltzer, 1988; Klerman et al., 1987). "Psychotic depression" was reserved for those who seemed to lose contact with reality, experiencing **delusions** — bizarre ideas without foundation — or **hallucinations** — perceptions of things that are not actually present (Lehmann, 1985). A man with psychotic depression might imagine, for example, "I can't eat because my intestines are deteriorating and will soon stop working," or he might believe that he saw his dead wife. Those who remained in better contact with their surroundings would receive a diagnosis of neurotic depression.

During the 1950s and 1960s, clinicians viewed psychotic and neurotic depression as qualitatively different disorders, stemming from different causes and requiring different treatments, and researchers tried to substantiate this distinction (Foulds, 1960). Some suggested that people with psychotic depression had fewer daily mood variations, more severe symptoms, and more somatic symptoms than those with neurotic depression. As the 1960s drew to a close, however, a number of clinical theorists began to voice the opinion that the acceptance of this dichotomy was moving the study and treatment of unipolar depression in the wrong direction (Beck, 1967). These critics challenged the notion that psychotic and neurotic depression were qualitatively different, arguing that clinicians were quite arbitrary in their use of the categories. DSM-III-R has dropped the separate category of psychotic depression, but it does allow

diagnosticians to indicate the presence of psychotic features by adding the phrase "with psychotic features" to a classification of major depression. This distinction is not meant to imply any assumption about the cause, onset, or course of the disorder.

## Recent Life Events and Unipolar Depression

Clinicians have noted that episodes of unipolar depression often seem to be triggered by stressful events. Correspondingly, numerous studies by Eugene Paykel and his colleagues have found that depressed people as a group experience a greater number of stressful life events just before the onset of their disorder than do nondepressed people during the same period of time (Paykel, 1983, 1982; Bidzinska, 1984; Murphy, 1982; Vadher & Ndetei, 1981; Lloyd 1980; Paykel et al., 1969). This relationship holds in the United States, England, Italy, Kenya, and India (Paykel, 1983). Stresses begin to multiply up to a year before the onset of the depressive disorders but in most cases are greatest during the month before onset (Surtees, 1980; Brown et al., 1973; Paykel et al., 1969). Stressful life events also appear to precede schizophrenia, anxiety disorders, and other psychological disorders, but depressed people report significantly more such events than anybody else

(Paykel & Hollyman, 1984; Leff & Vaughn, 1980; Brown et al., 1973).

Researchers have tried to determine whether some people are more vulnerable to such stresses than others. Studies conducted in England have found, for example, that women who have three or more young children living at home, lack a close confidant, have no employment outside the home, or have lost their mother before the age of 11 are more likely to become depressed after experiencing stressful life events (Brown, 1985; Brown & Harris, 1978; Brown, Harris, & Peto, 1973; Prudo, Brown, & Harris, 1981). In short, people whose lives are generally stressful and isolated seem more likely than others to become depressed when stresses multiply.

These studies suggest that unipolar patterns of depression are often brought on by external events. Yet they also suggest that such patterns are not always a product of the environment. Only about 40 percent of the depressed subjects in the studies reported undesirable events before the onset of their depression. Although this figure is certainly higher than the approximately 10 percent of nondepressed subjects who reported undesirable events during the same period of time, it still means that 60 percent of the depressed subjects did not experience negative events before becoming depressed. Here are two people who did not:

*T*he onset was quite sudden. I went home and went to bed early. At five o'clock (I remember the time) I awoke into a different world. It was as though all had changed while I slept; that I awoke not into normal consciousness, but into a nightmare. I got up and dressed, came down, then broke into tears and told my wife that I couldn't face going to work. I didn't.

(Rowe, 1978, p. 269)

*I*t's quite obvious to me that there was something wrong with me inside — call it physical, chemical, or change of life. My personality was certainly O.K. before this depression hit me . . . and if there were things wrong with my personality, they certainly did not interfere with my intelligence, initiative, or mood. There was nothing unusual about my business — in fact, it was better — and my home situation was no different. There simply was no reason for me to have become depressed.

(Kraines & Thetford, 1972, p. 24)

Given such apparent differences in origin and onset, clinicians used to consider it important to distinguish reactive (exogenous) depression from endogenous depression (Mendels & Cochran, 1968). *Reactive depressions* supposedly followed clear-cut precipitating events, while *endogenous depressions* unfolded without apparent antecedents and were assumed to be caused by

internal factors (Young et al., 1986). But how does one know whether a depression is reactive or not? Even if stressful events have occurred before the onset of depression, clinicians cannot be certain that the depression is reactive. The events could be a minor factor only or even a pure coincidence (Paykel, 1982). Conversely, even when a depression seems to emerge in the absence of stressful events, clinicians cannot be sure that it is endogenous (Paykel, Rao, & Taylor, 1984). Perhaps a subtle stressor has escaped notice. Indeed, in one investigation, careful follow-up interviews of a group of people who had been categorized as endogenously depressed showed that for many of them the depression had in fact been preceded by stressful events (Leff et al., 1970).

Accordingly, today's clinicians usually concentrate on recognizing both the internal and the situational components of any given case of unipolar depression (Keller, 1988; Harlow et al., 1986; Lobel, 1984; Garvey et al., 1984). DSM-III-R, unlike earlier diagnostic systems, does not require diagnosticians to determine whether an individual's depression is externally or internally caused. All the same, some clinicians do believe that the melancholic depressive episodes described in DSM-III-R represent an endogenous form of depression (Hirschfeld & Goodwin, 1988).

## Explanations of Unipolar Patterns of Depression

The current leading explanations of unipolar depression fall into two major categories. Some focus on the *situational components* of the disorder, in an effort to understand why and how various stresses may lead to depression. Others concentrate on the possible role of *biological factors*. In line with the growing recognition that unipolar depression may involve both situational and biological causes, it is probably best to view each of these approaches as offering a partial rather than a comprehensive account of who develops unipolar depression and why.

**The Psychodynamic View** Sigmund Freud and his student Karl Abraham developed the initial psychoanalytic theory of depression (Freud, 1917; Abraham, 1916; Abraham, 1911). Their starting point was the similarity they noticed between clinical depression and the grief reactions of people who lose loved ones (see Box 8-3). Constant weeping, loss of appetite, difficulty sleeping, inability to find pleasure in life, and general withdrawal are common features of both mourning and depression

(Stroebe & Stroebe, 1987; Osterweis, Solomon, & Green, 1984).

According to Freud and Abraham, a series of unconscious processes are set in motion when a loved one dies or is lost in some other way. At first, unable to accept the loss, mourners regress to the oral stage of development, the period when infants are so dependent that they cannot distinguish themselves from their parents. By this regression the mourners fuse their own identity with that of the person they have lost, symbolically regaining the lost person in the process. In other words, they *introject* the loved one and then experience all their feelings toward the loved one as feelings about themselves.

For most mourners, this unconscious process is temporary and lasts only for the period of mourning. They soon begin to reestablish a separate identity and resume social relationships. For some, however, the grief reaction worsens. They feel empty, continue to avoid social relationships, and become more preoccupied with their own sense of loss. Introjected feelings of anger toward the loved one for departing, or perhaps over unresolved conflicts from the past, cause these people to experience self-hatred, which leads in turn to a negative mood, self-blame, and further withdrawal. In effect, these people become depressed.

Freud and Abraham believed that two kinds of people are particularly prone to introjection and depression in the face of loss: those whose parents failed to meet their nurturance needs during the oral stage of infancy and those whose parents gratified those needs excessively. Infants whose needs are inadequately met remain overly dependent on others throughout their lives, feel unworthy of love, and have low self-esteem. Those whose needs are excessively gratified find the oral stage so pleasant that they resist moving on to other stages in life. Given either of these backgrounds, a person is likely to experience a greater sense of loss when a loved one dies and greater anger toward the loved one for having departed.

Of course, many people become depressed without losing a loved one. To explain why, Freud invoked the concept of *imagined,* or *symbolic,* loss. A man who loses his job, for example, may unconsciously interpret the experience as the loss of his wife, believing that she will no longer want him if he is unsuccessful at work. A college student may experience failure in a calculus course as the loss of her parents, believing that they love her only when she excels academically.

Over the course of this century, some psychodynamic theorists have argued for changes in emphasis in Freud and Abraham's theory of depression (Coccaro, 1991). Several have deemphasized the notion of hostility turned inward (Cohen et al., 1954; Bibring, 1953;

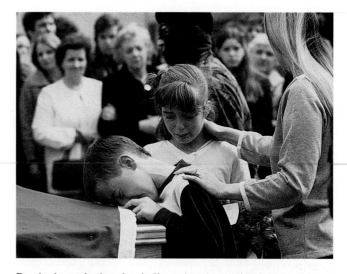

Psychodynamic theorists believe that depression is caused by the real or imagined loss of a loved one. Research has found that people who lose their parents as children have an increased likelihood of experiencing depression as adults.

Balint, 1952). Others have minimized the importance of oral fixation (Jacobson, 1971; Bibring, 1953). And some have argued that loss of self-esteem is the dominant issue in depression (Bibring, 1953). Nevertheless, Freud and Abraham's influence can still be seen in current psychodynamic evaluations of people with unipolar depression (Coccaro, 1991). The following clinical description of a depressed middle-aged woman is a case in point. Here we see early dependence, later dependence, loss of a loved one, symbolic loss, and introjection:

*Mrs. Marie Carls was in her middle fifties when she came* for the first interview. She appeared distinguished in her manner, with an almost aristocratic demeanor. . . . She had been born and had lived in Europe until a few years prior to the onset of treatment. . . .

All her complaints were somatic in nature. She tired easily, to the point of exhaustion. She knew she was melancholy, but she thought that it was because she did not feel well. She was very religious and had been brought up in an environment in which there was strict adherence to Catholicism. She went to confession very often.

A few sessions after the beginning of the treatment, she started to define her various complaints and general state of malaise as "an obscure force" which would take possession of her. She knew that this obscure force was a psychological experience. It was something which would come suddenly and make her depressed, tired, and often cause cramps in her stomach. . . .

The patient had always felt very attached to her mother. As a matter of fact, they used to call her "Stamp" because she stuck to her mother as a stamp to a letter. She always tried to placate her volcanic mother, to please her in every possible way. The mother, however, did not fulfill her maternal role very well. The patient remembered that when she started to menstruate at the age of thirteen, she did not know anything about it. She went to her mother, who explained, "It is a natural thing, but a dirty one." The subject of menstruation was never brought up again; it was taboo. . . .

When the man who became her husband (Julius) revealed his intention to marry her, she shared the unanimous opinion of her family that he was an excellent match. Although she was not enthusiastic about this man, she could find no fault in one who appeared so honest, reliable, a good provider, and a good Catholic. After marriage she continued her pattern of submission and compliance. Before her marriage she had difficulty in complying with a volcanic mother, and after her marriage she almost automatically assumed a submissive role. Actually, she described her husband as very considerate, egalitarian, and not domineering at all. His only fault was that he did not have a volcanic or

dynamic personality. He was too placid, too good, and rather boring. . . .

Several months after beginning treatment, the patient reported a dream. Ignatius and she had decided not to see each other again. She would have to leave him forever. I asked who Ignatius was, because I had not heard the name until then. The patient replied almost with surprise, "But the first time I came to see you, I told you that in the past I had had an infatuation." She then told me that when she was thirty years old, in the middle of the Second World War, she lived at the periphery of a city which was frequently bombed. Ignatius, a friend of the family, had had his home completely demolished by bombs. The patient and her husband invited Ignatius, who was single, to come and live with them. Ignatius and the patient soon discovered that they had an attraction for each other. They both tried to fight that feeling; but when Julius had to go to another city for a few days, the so-called infatuation became much more than that. There were a few physical contacts. . . . There was an intense spiritual affinity. Ignatius understood her: he

---

## BOX 8-3

# The Grieving Process

**E**ach year more than 8 million people in the United States experience the death of a member of their immediate family (Osterweis & Townsend, 1988). Many more lose a close friend or a more distant but still cherished relative. Such a loss is so painful that it can lead to depressed feelings and other psychological problems, a reaction so similar to clinical depression that Freud and Abraham based the psychoanalytic explanation of unipolar depression upon it. But mourning the loss of a loved one is a natural process, and there are normal mechanisms for coping with the stress. The bereavement process allows us eventually to come to grips with our loss and to continue on in our lives.

Unfortunately, there are many

A Bangladeshi woman cries out after learning that four of her relatives were killed by the devastating cyclone of April 30, 1991. Her reaction reflects the shock and disbelief that often initiate bereavement.

common misconceptions about the course of the normal grieving process, and some of these errant beliefs actu-

ally interfere with the process. The most common mistake people make is to believe that there is a set timetable for mourning. Friends and acquaintances often allow only a few weeks before they expect the mourner to begin a return to normal life. In fact, it sometimes takes many months before a person is ready to do so. If it does, the mourner's grief cannot be said to be pathological (Gelman, 1983). The amount of time needed varies from individual to individual, depending on such factors as the relationship of the mourner to the deceased, the age of the mourner, and, clearly, the personality of the mourner. Much suffering would be relieved if those who wanted to offer support did not impose their own

spoke her language, liked what she liked, and gave her the feeling of being alive. She remembered that before she married Julius, she had invented a slogan which she often emphatically repeated, "Long live life"; but only with Ignatius could she believe in that slogan again. Ignatius suggested that they elope, but she did not take him seriously. A few months later everybody had to leave the city. Ignatius and Marie promised to keep in touch, but both of them were full of hesitation because of Julius, a devoted husband to Marie and a devoted friend to Ignatius. Nothing was done to maintain contact. Two years later, approximately a year after the end of the war, Marie heard that Ignatius had married. She felt terribly alone and despondent. . . .

In a subsequent stage of therapy Marie concentrated on her marriage. . . . Her suffering had become more acute as she realized that old age was approaching and she had lost all her chances. Ignatius remained as the memory of lost opportunities. Yes, Ignatius had wanted her to go with him, but she wouldn't because she felt that her husband and God would never forgive her. Even that beautiful short relation-ship was spoiled by her feeling of guilt. Her life of compli-ance and obedience had not permitted her to reach her goal. An Ignatius existed in the world, but she had lost him for-ever. She had never loved her husband, and that was what was wrong with her marriage. . . .

For many years she had hoped she could make up for the loss of Ignatius, but now she could no longer do so. She could no longer scream, "Long live life!" She would rather think, "Down with life without Ignatius, a life which has lost its meaning."

When she became aware of these ideas, she felt even more depressed. She was complaining less and less about the obscure force, and more and more about her marriage. She felt that everything she had built in her life was false or based on a false premise. In a certain way her husband was not so compliant, permissive, and tolerant as she had seen him; but possessive because she had to live by his way of living, with all its placidity and the boredom. But this was impossible to do when she really did not love the man. . . .

---

timetable on the course of a person's grief.

Despite individual variations in duration, research has shown that mourners do typically share certain experiences (Osterweis & Townsend, 1988). The bereavement process often begins with **shock:** the survivor has **difficulty believing** that the person has died. The shock and disbelief are frequently followed by feelings of **separation** from the deceased, and these feelings sometimes lead to mis-perceptions and illusions, such as a belief that one sees the dead person in the street or dreams in which the person appears alive. Once the mourner fully accepts that the deceased is not coming back, **despair** may set in. De-pression, irritability, guilt, and anger are natural responses at this stage. So-cial relationships may also deteriorate as the mourner loses interest in the outside world and his or her customary activities. Some mourners further suf-fer medical problems.

Once the mourning process is com-plete it becomes possible to think of the deceased without being over-whelmed by feelings of despair and loss, although anniversaries and other special dates may cause flare-ups of mourning for many years to come. At this point, one is prepared to get on with one's life.

The normal grieving process is often disrupted, even prolonged, by society's treatment of the mourner. In addition to envisioning an unrealistic timetable for recovery, friends and relatives may have other expectations that will hinder rather than help. An-ticipating, for example, that the sur-viving spouse will feel like the odd person out, friends may be reluctant to invite the spouse to a social gather-ing. They may also visit the mourner less frequently at the very time the person most needs support. And when friends do visit, they may decide that the bereaved person is too upset to talk about the loss, depriving him or her of the relief that sometimes comes from talking.

As a result of such factors, many in the United States are surprisingly ill equipped to deal with loss of a loved one. Other cultures encourage the mourning process and may well be healthier for it. Some prescribe elab-orate ceremonies and periods of mourning. Researchers believe that rituals help survivors to cope with death and are an important part of the bereavement process (Gelman, 1985). This may be the reason the world's major religions offer detailed rituals to be performed upon the death of a family member. By helping survivors confront and accept their loss, rituals initiate the process of re-pair and healing.

Recently numerous self-help be-reavement groups have been devel-oped across the United States that allow mourners to gather with others in similar situations and discuss the emotional and practical problems they all face. These groups are often led by people who have completed a grieving process themselves and wish to offer insight and support to others. In the groups, the topic of death is not avoided, and no one promises—or demands—a speedy return to nor-mal. For many people, this can be the ideal environment for confront-ing and accepting their loss. It allows an important process to proceed as it should have been allowed to pro-ceed in the first place—without pressure, misinterpretation, or judg-ment.

A psychiatrist must agree that love is important, and a life without love is an impoverished life. But love means many things, just as there are many types of love. For Marie it meant only romantic love, all passion and flame, like the one she had imagined with Ignatius. Life without that type of love is not at all a life characterized by lovelessness, and by no means to be equated with death: but it was so for her. There are many strong and pleasant feelings that one can feel for family members, career, friends, humanity, cultural interests, and so on. They are different loves, but they count too. A life without the type of love she imagined with Ignatius can be a rich and rewarding life. . . .

*(Arieti & Bemporad, 1978, pp. 275–284)*

Studies by psychodynamic researchers have generally supported the psychodynamic notions that depression is often triggered by a major loss and that people who experience early losses and early dependent relationships are more vulnerable to losses later in life. In a famous study of 123 infants who were placed in a nursery after being separated from their mothers, René Spitz (1949, 1946, 1945) found that 19 of the infants became very weepy and sad upon separation, withdrew from their surroundings, ignored others, and lay passively in their cots. They moved slowly and sometimes had trouble sleeping. Many lost weight. Moreover, their development seemed to slow down. Later studies confirmed that maternal separations up to the age of six years often bring about a reaction of this kind, a pattern called ***anaclitic depression*** (Bowlby, 1980, 1977, 1973, 1969).

A remarkable series of experiments with monkeys conducted by Harry Harlow during the 1960s and 1970s also suggested a link between loss and depression. After first observing that infant monkeys whose mothers died often reacted in ways that suggested human anaclitic depression, Harlow and his colleagues proceeded to study separation and isolation in monkeys. In a typical study, the experimenters first raised an infant monkey in a laboratory playpen with its mother and then separated the two for a few weeks (Seay, Hansen, & Harlow, 1962). Harlow repeatedly found that the infant monkeys reacted first by protesting (crying out and jumping around) and then with apparent despair, expressed as a sharp decrease in vocalization, exploration, and play (Seay & Harlow, 1965; Harlow & Harlow, 1965; Seay et al., 1962). The longer the separation, the more severe the reaction (Suomi, 1976). Infant monkeys raised with and then separated from other young monkeys also showed protest-despair reactions of this kind (Suomi & Harlow, 1977, 1975; Suomi, Harlow, & Domek, 1970).

Other research has suggested that losses suffered early in life may also set the stage for depression during adulthood (Burbach & Bordvin, 1986). When a depression scale was administered to 1,250 medical patients during

In their experiments with monkeys, Harry Harlow and his colleagues found that infant monkeys reacted with apparent despair to separation from their mothers. Even monkeys raised with surrogate mothers — wire cylinders wrapped with foam rubber and covered with terry cloth — formed an attachment to them, and clung to them when anxious, and reacted with despair when separated from them.

visits to their family physicians, the patients whose fathers had died during their childhood earned higher depression scores (Barnes & Prosen, 1985). Likewise, several carefully controlled studies have found that more depressed adults than nondepressed adults have lost a parent before the age of 5 (Crook & Elliot, 1980), while related work has found that university students who emerge from childhood with a high degree of dependence tend to manifest higher levels of depression (Lopez et al., 1986).

In another line of psychodynamic research, investigators have studied dreams to determine whether depression involves hostility turned inward. The dreams reported by depressed subjects are compared with the dreams of nondepressed subjects by an evaluator who is trained in dream analysis but does not know which dreams belong to which subjects. The evaluator rates each dream for such factors as hostility and masochism (hostility toward oneself). Several studies have indicated that the dreams of depressed people do reflect higher levels of hostility and masochism than the dreams of nondepressed people (Hauri, 1976; Beck & Ward, 1961).

These various studies offer some support for the psychodynamic view of depression, but it is important to be aware of their limitations. First, although the findings indicate that losses sometimes precipitate depression, they do not establish that such losses are typically responsible for the disorder. In the studies of young children and young monkeys, for example, only some of the subjects who were separated from their mothers showed depressive reactions. The nineteen babies in the nursery study who suffered anaclitic depression represented only 15 percent of the separated infants. Altogether, it is estimated that only 5 to 10 percent of all people who experience major losses in life actually become depressed (Paykel, 1982).

Second, much of the supportive psychodynamic research focuses on depression among the very young. It may be that depression at this age is quite different from adult depression. Although the reactions of the infant monkeys in Harlow's research often paralleled the anaclitic depression seen in human children, they differed greatly from the depressive symptoms of human adolescents and adults (Suomi & Harlow, 1977). In fact, Harlow was able to generate depressive reactions in separated adolescent monkeys only by further isolating each monkey in an individual vertical chamber that hampered its physical activity. Clearly, such restraint goes far beyond the simple manipulation of separation and loss.

A third problem with the psychodynamic evidence is that many of the findings are inconsistent. While many studies find evidence of a relationship between childhood loss and later depression, a number of others do not (Owen, Lancee, & Freeman, 1986; Tennant, Bebbington, & Huffy, 1981), and while some studies indicate that depressed people may exhibit covert hostility toward others and themselves, others, again, do not (Klerman, 1984).

A final drawback to this research is that important components of the psychodynamic explanation of depression are nearly impossible to test. Because such processes as symbolic loss, fixation at the oral stage, and introjection are said to operate at an unconscious level, it is difficult for researchers to determine if and when they are occurring. In addition, some key psychodynamic notions are too vague to be used as the bases for significant predictions. The depression theory holds, for example, that oral fixation is caused by either insufficient or excessive need gratification during infancy, but how much gratification is enough and how much is excessive? Without some guidelines, clinical researchers cannot

test the theory by predicting who is likely to become orally fixated, experience symbolic losses, introject lost objects, and eventually become depressed.

**The Behavioral View** Peter Lewinsohn has developed a behavioral explanation of unipolar depression (Lewinsohn et al., 1984; Lewinsohn & Arconad, 1981; Lewinsohn, 1975, 1974; Lewinsohn, Weinstein, & Shaw, 1969). Building on the ideas of other behaviorists (Ferster, 1974, 1973, 1966; Costello, 1972), Lewinsohn suggests that for some people the rewards that ordinarily reinforce positive behaviors start to dwindle, and they respond by performing fewer and fewer positive behaviors and developing a depressed style of functioning.

Lewinsohn begins with the notion that each person has a *total rate of positive reinforcements,* defined as the number of daily rewards the person receives that effectively reinforce his or her positive behaviors. This rate is influenced by three factors: (1) *The number of events that are potentially reinforcing for the person* (One person may find the excitement of a football game reinforcing; another finds reward in the beauty of an art exhibit.); (2) *The number of reinforcing events that can be provided by the person's environment* (People who like to reward themselves with regular brisk walks through snowy woods will have little opportunity to do so unless they live in a cold climate.); and (3) *The number and kinds of skills possessed by the person* (People who value friendly relationships are more likely to experience them if they are skilled socially.).

According to Lewinsohn, a person's total rate of positive reinforcements may be reduced by significant changes in any of these factors. The rewards of campus life disappear for a young woman when she graduates from college and takes a job in the business world; an aging baseball player loses the reinforcements of high salary and crowd adulation when his athletic skills deteriorate. Some people manage to greet such changes with a sense of perspective and resolve to fill their lives with other forms of gratification. Others, however, become disheartened and perform fewer constructive behaviors. As their activity level drops, their positive reinforcements decrease even more, and the decline in reinforcements leads in turn to even fewer positive behaviors. In this manner, a person may spiral toward depression. A corollary to this theory states that a high rate of punishing experiences (say, a hostile work environment) may also lead to depression "by interfering with the person's engagement in and enjoyment of rewarding activities" (Lewinsohn & Arconad, 1981; see Figure 8-3).

To test his theory Lewinsohn has followed subjects into their homes and observed the reinforcements they

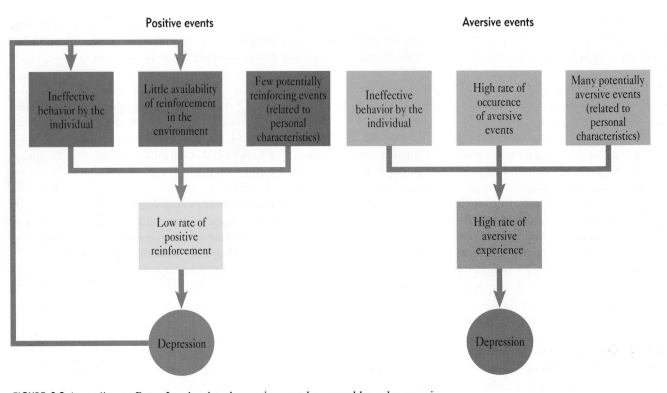

**FIGURE 8-3** According to Peter Lewinsohn, depression may be caused by a decrease in one's positive experiences or an increase in one's aversive experiences. The inactivity and low motivation of depressed people may lead to still fewer positive experiences in their lives. *(Adapted from Lewinsohn & Arconad, 1981.)*

receive there. In a series of studies he had research evaluators observe mealtime interactions in the families of depressed people and rate family members on positive verbal offerings and rewards (Libet & Lewinsohn, 1973; Lewinsohn & Shatter, 1971). Consistent with the behavioral theory, these evaluators repeatedly found that family members who were depressed received fewer verbal reinforcements than did the other people around them.

Lewinsohn has also found that a person's total rate of reinforcements is indeed related to the presence or absence of depression. Not only do depressed subjects report a lower rate of positive reinforcements, as measured on a "Pleasant Events Schedule," than nondepressed subjects over a thirty-day period, but when their reinforcement rate rises, the mood of these depressed subjects improves as well (Lewinsohn, Youngren, & Grosscup, 1979; Libet & Lewinsohn, 1973; Shaffer & Lewinsohn, 1971). Similarly, Lewinsohn (1975) has found that depressed people tend to experience more unpleasant events than others do in such categories as health, finances, social interactions, and job and academic achievement.

Lewinsohn believes that *social* reinforcements are par-

ticularly important (Lewinsohn et al., 1984; Lewinsohn & Amenson, 1978). He and his colleagues have found that depressed subjects tend to experience fewer positive social reinforcements than nondepressed subjects, and that as their mood improves, their rate of positive social reinforcements increases as well. Related studies have indicated that depressed patients tend to have fewer friends, less interpersonal support, and more unpleasant social interactions than other people (Coyne, 1985; Henderson et al., 1978). Although depressed persons may be the victims of social circumstances, it is also possible that they are partly responsible for the decreases in their social reinforcements. In one study phone callers reported feeling worse than usual after a short conversation with a depressed person (Coyne, 1976) and in another subjects became less verbal, less supportive, and less cheerful than usual when they interacted with someone who was mildly depressed (Gotlib & Robinson, 1982).

Lewinsohn has done an admirable job of compiling data to support his theory. However, his research, too, has significant limitations. In particular, it relies heavily on the self-reports of depressed and nondepressed subjects. As we saw in Chapter 4, such measures can be biased and inaccurate, and in the case of depressed individuals, they may be influenced heavily by a gloomy mood and negative outlook (Youngren & Lewinsohn, 1980).

It is also important to keep in mind that Lewinsohn's studies have been correlational and do not establish that decreases in reinforcing events are the initial causes of depression. A depressed mood in itself may lead to a decrease in activities and hence to fewer reinforcements. Causal relationships might be better established if it were somehow possible to measure a person's positive reinforcement rate just before the onset of the first episode of unipolar depression. According to Lewinsohn's theory, the rate should already be declining at that time. Another approach, one that obviously poses serious ethical problems, would be to deprive people of many of their usual positive reinforcements and see whether they become significantly depressed as a result.

**The Cognitive View** Aaron Beck's research and clinical observations have led him to believe that *negative thinking*, rather than underlying conflicts or fewer positive reinforcements, lies at the heart of unipolar depression (Beck, 1991, 1985, 1976, 1967). Other cognitive theorists (Albert Ellis, for one) have also pointed to maladaptive thinking as the key to depression, but Beck's theory is the one most often associated with the disorder. He argues that depressed people are so filled with negative thoughts about themselves, their situations, and the future that all aspects of their functioning are affected dramatically. According to Beck, *maladaptive attitudes*, a *cognitive triad, errors in thinking*, and *automatic thoughts* combine to produce this pervasive negativity.

*Maladaptive Attitudes* Beck believes that children's attitudes toward themselves and the world are based on their own experiences, their family relationships, and the judgments of the people around them. Unfortunately, some children develop negative attitudes, such as "My general worth is tied to every task I perform" and "If I fail, others will feel repelled by me." Many failures are inevitable in a full, active life, so such attitudes are inaccurate and self-defeating. The negative attitudes become templates, or schemas, against which the child evaluates every experience.

*The Cognitive Triad* The negative cognitive structure that develops in some persons during childhood may lie dormant for years, as long as life proceeds smoothly, without major disturbances or disappointments. But, at any time a traumatic situation — particularly one reminiscent of early failure or loss — can trigger an extended round of

pervasive negative thinking. According to Beck, the negative thinking takes three forms and is therefore termed the *cognitive triad:* the individuals repeatedly interpret (1) their experiences, (2) themselves, and (3) their futures in negative ways that lead them to feel depressed.

Experiences may be interpreted as burdens, obstacles, or traumas that repeatedly defeat, deprive, or disparage the person. The thinking of one depressed client proceeded in the following manner:

> *She made a terrible mistake in moving to this city,* she should never have taken the children from their father. . . . The climate is unbearable, she could slip and fall on those icy sidewalks at any time, and then what would happen to the children? The children don't love her, they treat her like dirt; other people's children have more time for their parents.
>
> *(Mendels, 1970, p. 3)*

At the same time, depressed people view themselves as deficient, undesirable, worthless, and inadequate:

> *I can't bear it. I can't stand the humiliating fact that* I'm the only woman in the world who can't take care of her family, take her place as a real wife and mother, and be respected in her community. When I speak to my young son Billy, I know I can't let him down, but I feel so ill-equipped to take care of him; that's what frightens me. I don't know what to do or where to turn; the whole thing is too overwhelming. . . . I must be a laughing stock. It's more than I can do to go out and meet people and have the fact pointed up to me so clearly.
>
> *(Fieve, 1975)*

Finally, the future regularly appears bleak to those who are depressed, sure to be a never-ending series of hardships, miseries, frustrations, and failures:

> *Joan lived her life in the constant expectation that the* outcome of every situation would be bad. If she went on a car journey with her husband she expected not to arrive safely. Numerous safe arrivals had not ameliorated her pessimism. "I think if I go over a bridge it will collapse. I think I should stay in bed all day if that's the things I always think. I always think that something bad is going to happen."
>
> *(Rowe, 1978)*

*Errors in Thinking* According to Beck, depressed people habitually employ errors of logic, forms of distorted thinking that help build and maintain the cognitive triad. Here are five of these common errors in logic:

*Arbitrary Inference* Depressed people often draw negative conclusions on the basis of little or even contrary evidence. For example, a man walking through the park passes a woman who is looking at nearby trees and flowers, and he concludes, "She's avoiding looking at me."

*Selective Abstraction*    Depressed people often focus on one negative detail of a situation while ignoring the larger context. For example, a nightclub comedienne performs for a very responsive audience who laugh and enthusiastically applaud all but one of her jokes. Focusing on that one joke, the performer concludes, "I didn't have it tonight."

*Overgeneralization*    Depressed people often draw a broad conclusion from a single, perhaps insignificant event. For example, a student in a history class is unable to remember the date of the signing of the Magna Carta and walks around the rest of the day convinced that he is stupid.

*Magnification and Minimization*    Depressed people often underestimate the significance of positive experiences or exaggerate that of negative ones (Wenzlaff & Grozier, 1988). A college student receives an A on a difficult English exam, for example, but concludes that the grade reflects the professor's generous mood rather than her own ability (minimization). Later in the week the same student catches a cold and must miss an English class. She is convinced that she will be unable to keep pace the rest of the semester and may fail the course because of this missed class (magnification).

*Personalization*    Depressed people often incorrectly view themselves as the cause of negative events. When Sunday's picnic is postponed by a sudden rainstorm, for example, a father blames himself for ruining his family's fun because he had selected that day for the picnic. Or a woman blames herself for her sister's divorce, believing that the infrequency

of her visits and her lack of sensitivity were somehow responsible.

*Automatic Thoughts*    Depressed people experience the cognitive triad in the form of *automatic thoughts,* hundreds of unpleasant thoughts that repeatedly remind them of their assumed inadequacy and the hopelessness of their situation. Beck labels these thoughts automatic because they seem to just happen, as if by reflex. In the course of only a few hours, depressed people may be visited by a long series of such thoughts. "I'm worthless. . . . I'll never amount to anything. . . . I let everyone down. . . . Everyone hates me. . . . My responsibilities are overwhelming. . . . I've failed as a parent. . . . I'm stupid. . . . Everything is difficult for me. . . . I've caused problems for my friends. . . . Things will never change." As one therapist describes a depressed client, "By the end of the day, she is worn out, she has lived a thousand painful accidents, participated in a thousand deaths, mourned a thousand mistakes" (Mendels, 1970).

*A Feedback System*    Beck believes that the emotional, motivational, behavioral, and somatic aspects of depression all follow from the cognitive processes described above. If people think they are unwanted by everyone else, they will feel the sadness of social outcasts. If they anticipate a future of misery, they will not be motivated to take on new projects. Once the cognitive processes generate additional symptoms of depression, Beck believes, the new symptoms act to confirm the original negative cognitions, thus creating a feedback system that reinforces the mistaken cognitions. That is, people who find themselves sad, crying, or without appetite may take this as further evidence that their lives are miserable. Similarly, people who are unmotivated to work may view their inactivity as proof that the future will indeed be bleak. In this way, the depressed person is soon caught in a vicious cycle.

Drawings by Charles Shultz. © 1956 United Feature Syndicate. Inc.

Charlie Brown's feelings of depression are caused by errors of logic, such as arbitrary inference.

***Investigating Beck's Theory*** Beck's cognitive view of unipolar depression has received considerable attention and support from researchers (Haaga et al., 1990). One study confirmed that depressed people tend to hold such maladaptive attitudes as "People will probably think less of me if I make a mistake" and "I must be a useful, productive, creative person, or life has no purpose." Moreover, the number of maladaptive attitudes correlated strongly with the degree of depression, suggesting that the more such attitudes one has, the more depressed one tends to be (Weissman & Beck, 1977).

Other research has supported Beck's notion that depressed people exhibit the cognitive triad (Shaw & Segal, 1988; Beck et al., 1987; Pietromonaco & Marcus, 1985). Depressed subjects recall unpleasant experiences more readily than positive ones, a tendency that reverses itself when the subjects' symptoms later improve (Lloyd & Fishman, 1975). Studies also indicate that depressed subjects rate themselves and their performances lower than nondepressed subjects do, even when they have performed just as well as nondepressed persons (Loeb, Beck, & Diggory, 1971). And in storytelling and projective assessment tests, depressed subjects usually select pessimistic statements such as "I expect my plans will fail" and "I feel like I'll never meet anyone who's interested in me" (Weintraub et al., 1974).

Beck's association of depression with errors in logic has also received research support (Wenzlaff & Grozier, 1988; Leitenberg, 1986; Cook & Peterson, 1986). In one study female subjects were asked to read paragraphs about women in difficult situations and then to answer multiple-choice questions about them. The multiple-choice options included examples of overgeneralization, arbitrary inference, selective abstraction, and magnification or minimization. The women who were depressed chose a significantly greater number of responses reflecting errors in logic than the nondepressed women did (Hammen & Krantz, 1976). Similarly, a study of 400 elementary school children found that depressed children scored significantly higher than nondepressed children on a scale called the "Children's Negative Cognitive Error Questionnaire" (Leitenberg, 1986).

Finally, research has supported Beck's claim that depressed people repeatedly experience negative automatic thoughts (Hollon et al., 1986; Dobson & Shaw, 1986). Hospitalized depressed patients scored significantly higher on an "Automatic Thought Questionnaire" than other kinds of patients did (Ross et al., 1986). Also, several studies have shown that nondepressed subjects who are manipulated into reading negative automaticlike statements about themselves become increasingly depressed (Hale & Stricklan, 1976; Stricklan, Hale, & Anderson, 1975).

This body of research clearly indicates that negative cognitions are associated with depressive functioning, but it fails to establish that cognitive dysfunctioning represents the cause and core of unipolar depression. The investigations leave open the possibility that a central mood problem leads to cognitive difficulties that take a further toll on mood, motivation, behavior, and physiology (Miranda & Persons, 1988; Lewinsohn et al., 1981). In fact, Beck's feedback model itself acknowledges that negative mood can have a significant impact on a person's cognitions.

Two studies have tried to establish that cognitive dysfunctioning does indeed precede the negative mood of depressed people, as Beck claims. One team of researchers followed the progress of fifteen severely depressed women and interviewed them after their depressive symptoms had markedly declined to determine whether they still held maladaptive attitudes. The researchers found that the women who continued to hold maladaptive attitudes were more likely to develop depressive symptoms again six months later. That is, their negative schemas remained in place even during periods of improved mood, apparently setting the stage for renewed depressive functioning at a later point (Rush et al., 1986).

The second study measured the cognitive functioning of a group of depressed middle-aged women to see whether it might predict the future course of their unipolar depressions. The women who initially displayed more automatic thoughts, lower self-esteem, and greater pessimism and hopelessness were found five months later to be significantly more depressed than the other subjects. Thus, in some cases at least, cognitive dysfunctioning seems to precede and predict the course and severity of depressive moods.

**A Cognitive-Behavioral View: Learned Helplessness** In this account of a young woman's depression, her feelings of helplessness emerge repeatedly:

*Mary was 25 years old and had just begun her senior* year in college. . . . Asked to recount how her life had been going recently, Mary began to weep. Sobbing, she said that for the last year or so she felt she was losing control of her life and that recent stresses (starting school again, friction with her boyfriend) had left her feeling worthless and frightened. Because of a gradual deterioration in her vision, she was now forced to wear glasses all day. "The glasses make me look terrible," she said, and "I don't look people in the eye much any more." Also, to her dismay, Mary had gained 20 pounds in the past year. She viewed herself as overweight and unattractive. At times she was convinced that with enough money to buy contact lenses and enough time to exercise she could cast off her depression; at other times she believed nothing would help. . . .

Mary saw her life deteriorating in other spheres, as well. She felt overwhelmed by schoolwork and, for the first time in her life, was on academic probation. Twice before in the past seven years feelings of inadequacy and pressure from part-time jobs (as a waitress, bartender, and salesclerk) had caused her to leave school. She felt certain that unless she could stop her current downward spiral she would do so again — this time permanently. She despaired of ever getting her degree.

In addition to her dissatisfaction with her appearance and her fears about her academic future, Mary complained of a lack of friends. Her social network consisted solely of her boyfriend, with whom she was living. Although there were times she experienced this relationship as almost unbearably frustrating, she felt helpless to change it and was pessimistic about its permanence. . . .

*(Spitzer et al., 1983, pp. 122–123)*

Mary feels that she is "losing control of her life." Often she believes that she can do nothing to change what she considers to be her unattractive appearance and excess weight. She "despairs of ever getting her degree" and feels helpless to change her frustrating relationship with her boyfriend. According to Martin Seligman, such feelings of helplessness are at the center of Mary's depression. Since the mid-1960s Seligman has been developing the learned helplessness theory of depression (Seligman et al., 1984; Seligman, 1975, 1974, 1973), which combines concepts from the behavioral and cognitive models and holds that people become depressed when (1) they think that they no longer have control over the reinforcements in their lives and (2) they believe that they themselves are responsible for this helpless state. In Seligman's view, all of the symptoms of depression grow from this perception of helplessness and self-blame.

Seligman's theory first began to take shape when he and his colleagues were conducting conditioning studies with laboratory dogs, trying to teach them to escape and then avoid shocks. They placed each dog in a ***shuttle box,*** a box partitioned by a barrier over which the animal could jump to reach the other side (see Figure 8-4). Then they dimmed the lights as a warning signal and seconds later administered shocks to the dog. The shocks continued until the dog learned to escape them by jumping over the barrier.

Some of the dogs in these studies had been allowed to rest the previous day (naive dogs); others had spent the previous day strapped into an apparatus called a hammock, in which they received a number of inescapable shocks at random intervals. What fascinated Seligman

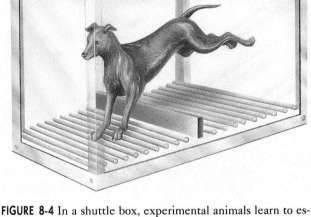

**FIGURE 8-4** In a shuttle box, experimental animals learn to escape shocks that are administered in one compartment by jumping to the other (safe) compartment of the box. They may also learn to avoid the shocks altogether by jumping to the safe compartment in response to a warning, such as the dimming of a light.

was how these two groups then differed in their reactions to the shocks in the shuttle box.

When placed in a shuttle box, an experimentally naive dog, at the onset of the first electric shock, runs frantically about until it accidentally scrambles over the barrier and escapes the shock. On the next trial, the dog, running frantically, crosses the barrier more quickly than on the preceding trial; within a few trials it becomes very efficient at escaping, and soon learns to avoid shock altogether. After about fifty trials the dog becomes nonchalant and stands in front of the barrier; at the onset of the signal for shock it leaps gracefully across and never gets shocked again.

A dog that had first been given inescapable shock showed a strikingly different pattern. This dog's first reactions to shock in the shuttle box were much the same as those of a naive dog: it ran around frantically for about thirty seconds. But then it stopped moving; to our surprise, it lay down and quietly whined. After one minute of this we turned the shock off; the dog had failed to cross the barrier and had not escaped from shock. On the next trial, the dog did it again; at first it struggled a bit, and then, after a few seconds, it seemed to give up and to accept the shock passively. On all succeeding trials, the dog failed to escape. This is the paradigmatic learned-helplessness finding.

*(Seligman, 1975, p. 22)*

Seligman concluded that the dogs who had previously received random inescapable shocks had learned that they had no control over aversive reinforcements (shocks) in their lives. That is, they had learned that they were helpless to do anything to change negative situations. Thus, even when these dogs were later placed in a new situation where they could in fact control their fate, they continued to believe that they had no control. They continued to act helpless and failed to learn to escape painful shock by jumping to the safe side of the shuttle box.

In subsequent experiments, Seligman and his colleagues demonstrated that such helplessness effects can be generated in various animal species and under a variety of conditions (Hiroto & Seligman, 1975). Believing that the effects of learned helplessness greatly resemble the symptoms of human depression, he proposed that humans in fact become depressed after developing the implicit belief that they have no control over reinforcements in their lives. Consequently, much of the helplessness research conducted during the past few decades has tried to demonstrate that helplessness in the laboratory is analogous to depression in the real world.

Laboratory studies of learned helplessness in humans have often produced reactions that mimic the passivity displayed in depression. In one helplessness study, nondepressed human subjects were pretreated in one of three ways: one group of subjects were exposed to a very loud noise that they could stop by pushing a button; a second group were also exposed to the loud noise but could do nothing to stop it; and a third group (naive subjects) heard no loud noise at all (Hiroto, 1974). All subjects were then placed in front of a finger shuttle box (a rectangular box with a handle on top) and subjected to a loud noise. Without the subjects' knowledge, the noise was now rigged to stop when the handle was moved from one side of the shuttle box to the other. Both the naive subjects and those who had previously had control over the loud noise quickly learned to move the handle and turn off the noise. The subjects who had been pretreated with unavoidable loud noise, however, failed to learn the simple task of moving the handle across the box. Most of them simply sat passively and accepted the abrasive sound. This reaction in nondepressed subjects is strikingly similar to the passivity of depressed people who make statements such as the following: "I ceased to wonder. I asked a member of my family where I was and having received an answer, accepted it. . . . The days dragged; there was no 'motive,' no drive of any kind. A dull acceptance settled upon me" (Hillyer, 1926).

Human and animal subjects who undergo helplessness training also display other reactions similar to depressive symptoms. When human subjects are given random aversive reinforcements, for example, they later score higher on a depression mood survey than do subjects who are allowed control over their reinforcements (Miller & Seligman, 1975; Gatchel, Paulus, & Maples, 1975); and just as depressed people often show reductions in overt aggressive behavior, helplessness-trained subjects withdraw more and compete less in laboratory games (Kurlander, Miller, & Seligman, 1974). Animals subjected to inescapable shock eat little and lose weight, and they lose interest in sexual and social activities— common symptoms of human depression (Linder, 1968). Finally, uncontrollable events result in lower activity of the brain neurotransmitter norepinephrine in rats, a depletion that has also been noted in the brains of people with unipolar depression, as we shall see (Hughes et al., 1984; Weiss, Stone, & Hariel, 1970; Weiss, Glazer, & Pohorecky, 1975).

***Perceived Lack of Control*** Since Seligman first formulated his theory, researchers have demonstrated that *actual* loss of control over reinforcements is not the critical feature in producing the learned helplessness response. It is necessary only that subjects *perceive* a loss of control. This point was emphasized in a study in which three groups of college students were subjected to a continuous loud noise (Glass & Singer, 1972). One group, who had no control over the noise, showed general increases in helpless behaviors— less persistence at a problem-solving task, higher levels of irritation, and poorer performance on a proofreading task. A second group, who could turn off the noise, were more persistent in the problem-solving task, less irritable, and better at proofreading. A third group had no actual control over the loud noise but were given to believe, falsely, that they could push a "panic button" to turn off the noise if they absolutely had to. These subjects performed like the second group, persisting in the problem-solving task, showing little irritation, and doing quite well on the proofreading assignment. The perception of control, even though illusory, was apparently enough to prevent a helplessness reaction.

On the basis of such findings, Seligman has argued that people will become depressed if they *believe* that they have lost control over the reinforcements in their lives. In support of this position, a recent review of close to 100 studies revealed that subjects who generally believe that their lives are largely under the control of external forces or chance tend to experience higher levels of depression (Benassi, Sweeney, & Dufour, 1988).

***Attributions and Helplessness*** An important question keeps arising with regard to Seligman's theory. If depressed people feel incapable of controlling the events in their lives, why do they persistently blame themselves for everything? Doesn't repeated self-blame reflect an overestimation of one's control over events rather than an underestimation? Actually, helpless feelings and self-blame can be quite compatible: people can blame their lack of control on the fact that they are inadequate, ineffective, or undesirable.

The clarification of this point has led to a major change in the helplessness theory during the past decade. According to the revised theory, when people perceive events to be beyond their control, they implicitly ask themselves why this is so (Abramson, Seligman, & Teasdale, 1978). If they attribute their present lack of control to some *internal* cause that is both *global* and *stable* ("*I* am inadequate at *everything* and I *always* will be"), they may well feel helpless and so experience unipolar depression; if they make other kinds of attributions, this reaction is unlikely (see Table 8-1).

The italics in the last sentence highlight the three important dimensions of these attributions: (1) the *internal–external* dimension (Does one see the cause as being located in oneself or elsewhere?), (2) the *global–specific* dimension (Does one believe the cause is relevant to many situations or just to this specific situation?), and (3) the *stable–unstable* dimension (Does one see the cause as enduring or short-lived?). Consider a college student whose girlfriend breaks up with him. If he attributes this loss of control over a key source of gratification to an internal cause that is both global and stable — "It's my fault [internal], I ruin everything I touch [global], and I always will [stable]" — he then has reason to expect future losses of control and may therefore experience an enduring sense of helplessness. He is a prime candidate for depression.

If the internal cause to which the student points were more specific ("The way I've behaved the past couple of weeks blew this relationship") and unstable ("I don't know what got into me — I don't usually act like that"), he would not be so likely to anticipate future losses of control. Similarly, if the student were to attribute the breakup to external causes ("That girl never did know what she wanted"), he would be less likely to expect future losses of control, and would probably not experience helplessness and depression.

This attribution factor helps explain why some people react helplessly to losses of control while others do not (Brown & Siegel, 1988). It also suggests that helplessness may be prevented or reversed if people are taught to attribute losses of control to external causes or to internal causes that are specific or unstable. Helplessness reactions were prevented in a group of grade school children in just this way: the children were guided to make alternative attributions for their classroom failures (Dweck, 1976).

Since the helplessness theory was revised, hundreds of studies have tested and supported the relationship between styles of attribution and depressive functioning (Sweeney, Anderson, & Bailey, 1986). In one study, experimenters interviewed sixty-eight subjects, each of whom was caring for a spouse with Alzheimer's disease (Pagel, Becker, & Coppel, 1985). The experimenters determined from the interviews whether the subjects considered their spouse's disease to be uncontrollable and whether they considered themselves to be somehow the cause of it. Those subjects who perceived a greater loss of control and who made internal attributions experienced higher levels of depression over a ten-month period.

In a related study, a group of moderately depressed adults were asked to fill out an adult "Attributional Style Questionnaire" (see Table 8-2) before and after successful therapy (Seligman et al., 1988). Before therapy, their high levels of depression were accompanied by attribution styles that were highly internal, stable, and global. At the end of therapy and again one year later, their depression levels were lower and their attribution styles were significantly less internal, stable, and global.

TABLE 8-1

| INTERNAL AND EXTERNAL ATTRIBUTIONS | | | | |
|---|---|---|---|---|
| Event: "I failed my psych test today" | | | | |
| | Internal | | External | |
| | Stable | Unstable | Stable | Unstable |
| **Global** | "I have a problem with test anxiety." | "Getting into an argument with my roommate threw my whole day off." | "Written tests are an unfair way to assess knowledge." | "No one does well on tests that are given the day after vacation." |
| **Specific** | "I just have no grasp of psychology." | "I got upset and froze when I couldn't answer the first two questions." | "Everyone knows that this professor enjoys giving unfair tests." | "This professor didn't put much thought into the test because of the pressure of her book deadline." |

TABLE 8-2

| SAMPLE ITEM FROM THE ATTRIBUTIONAL-STYLE QUESTIONNAIRE |
| --- |
| **You have been looking for a job unsuccessfully for some time.** |

1. Write down *one* major cause _____ .

2. Is the cause of your unsuccessful job search due to something about you or something about other people or circumstances? (Circle one number.)

Totally due to other people or circumstances         Totally due to me

    1     2     3     4     5     6     7         } **External vs. internal attribution**

3. In the future when looking for a job, will this cause again be present? (Circle one number.)

Will never again be present         Will always be present

    1     2     3     4     5     6     7         } **Unstable vs. stable attribution**

4. Is the cause something that just influences looking for a job, or does it also influence other areas of your life? (Circle one number.)

Influences just this particular situation         Influences all situations in my life

    1     2     3     4     5     6     7         } **Specific vs. global attribution**

5. How important would this situation be if it happened to you? (Circle one number.)

Not at all important         Extremely important

    1     2     3     4     5     6     7

*Source:* Seligman et al., 1979.

***Evaluating the Learned Helplessness Theory*** Although the helplessness model of unipolar depression is a promising and widely applied theory, it poses some problems. First, laboratory-induced helplessness does not parallel depression in every respect. Uncontrollable shocks administered in the laboratory, for example, invariably produce heightened anxiety along with the helplessness effects (Seligman, 1975), but human depression is not always accompanied by anxiety.

A second problem is that much of the research on learned helplessness relies on animal subjects. While the animals' passivity, social withdrawal, and other reactions seems to correspond to the symptoms of human depression, it is impossible to know whether they are true reflections of the same psychological phenomena (Telner & Singhal, 1984).

Finally, the attributional aspect of the helplessness theory has raised important questions. Although numerous studies suggest that depressive reactions are indeed related to internal, stable, and global attributions of negative events (Sweeney et al., 1986; Seligman et al., 1984), equally respectable studies have failed to find such a connection (Brewin & Furnham, 1986; Cochran & Hammen, 1985; Hargreaves, 1985). Moreover, even if we grant that attributions may play an important role in mediating human loss of control, what about the many dogs and rats who learn helplessness? Are they "attributing" their lack of control to internal, general, and stable causes? Can animals make attributions, even implicitly? Or is this an area where animal and human helplessness part company?

These questions notwithstanding, Seligman's learned helplessness theory has provided a compelling model of unipolar depression and has demonstrated an impressive capacity to grow in response to new findings and difficult questions. It has also inspired considerable research and thinking about human depression and human adaptation, from which new insights and ideas continue to emerge.

**The Biological View** Medical researchers have been aware for years that certain diseases, drugs, and toxins produce mood alterations (see Table 8-3), and some have taken this finding to suggest that clinical depression may itself have a biological foundation. Their suspicions have been supported during the past several decades with the emergence of compelling evidence that biological abnormalities also contribute to the development of unipolar depression (Siever, Davis, & Gorman, 1991). The role of biological factors has been implied by genetic studies and more directly supported by investigations that tie unipolar patterns of depression to biochemical dysfunctioning.

**Genetic Factors** Many theorists believe that some people inherit a predisposition to develop unipolar depression. Support for this genetic view has come primarily from family pedigree studies, twin studies, and adoption studies.

In *family pedigree studies,* people with unipolar depression are selected as *probands* (the proband is the person who is the focus of a genetic study), and their close relatives are examined to see whether depression afflicts other members of the family. If a predisposition

to unipolar depression is inherited, relatives should have a higher rate of depression than the population at large. And researchers have found that as many as 18 percent of those relatives are depressed, compared to 6 percent of the general population (Goldin & Gershon, 1988; Vandenberg, Singer, & Pauls, 1986; Nurnberger & Gershon, 1984; Weissman et al., 1984).

If a predisposition to unipolar depression is inherited, one would also expect more cases of depression among the probands' close relatives than among their distant relatives. *Twin studies* of depression among monozygotic (identical) twins and dizygotic (fraternal) twins have found rates consistent with this expectation (Kendler et al., 1986; Nurnberger, 1984). A Danish study determined that when a monozygotic twin has unipolar depression, there is a 43 percent chance that the other twin will have the same disorder, whereas when a dizygotic twin has unipolar depression, the other twin has only a 20 percent chance of developing the disorder (Bertelsen et al., 1977).

Of course, as we have observed in previous chapters, such findings are not proof of a genetic predisposition.

TABLE 8-3

| SUBSTANCES AND CONDITIONS THAT INDUCE SYMPTOMS OF MOOD DISORDERS | | | | | | |
|---|---|---|---|---|---|---|
| **Drug mimickers** | | | | **Medical disease mimickers** | | |
| **Drug** | **Major depression** | **Manic depression** | | **Disease** | **Major depression** | **Manic depression** |
| PCP | + | + | | Narcolepsy | + | |
| Marijuana | + | + | | Huntington's chorea | + | |
| Amphetamines | + | + | | Multiple sclerosis | + | + |
| Cocaine | + | + | | Postconcussion syndrome | + | + |
| Sedative-hypnotics | + | | | Tumors | + | + |
| Heroin | + | | | Hypothyroid | + | + |
| **Toxin mimickers** | | | | Hyperthyroid | + | + |
| **Toxin** | **Major depression** | **Manic depression** | | Hypoglycemia | + | |
| Magnesium | + | | | Cushing's disease | + | + |
| Zinc | + | | | Addison's disease | + | |
| Lead | + | | | Hyperparathyroidism | + | |
| Mercury | + | + | | Hypoparathyroidism | + | |
| Arsenic | + | | | | | |
| Bromides | + | | | | | |

*Source:* Gold, 1988, pp. 89, 104, 127, 141.

Close relatives tend to have similar environments and learning experiences — similar stresses, role models, and family atmospheres — and these shared experiences may account for similar predispositions toward particular disorders (Lewontin, Rose, & Kamin, 1984). Moreover, the data also suggest that even if genetic factors are operating in unipolar depression, they are only contributing factors at best. As the twin studies indicate, the probability that the proband's twin will develop unipolar depression is less than 50 percent even when their genetic structures are identical.

Finally, *adoption studies* suggest that a genetic factor may operate in severe cases of unipolar depression. A study of the families of adopted persons who had been hospitalized for unipolar depression in Denmark determined that the biological parents of these severely depressed adoptees had a higher incidence of severe depression than did the biological parents of a control group of nondepressed adoptees, but not of mild depression (Wender et al., 1986). Theorists who believe that the different patterns of unipolar depression represent distinct disorders with distinct origins have pointed to studies such as this to support their assertion.

***Biochemical Factors***   As we have seen, neurotransmitters are the brain chemicals that carry messages from one nerve cell, or neuron, to another. When an electrical message is received by a neuron, it travels down the cell's long axon to the cell terminals. These nerve endings release a neurotransmitter that travels across a synaptic space to receptors on the receiving neuron, telling that neuron either to fire (transmit the electrical impulse) or to stop firing. Different neurons store and use different neurotransmitters. *Norepinephrine* and *serotonin* are the two neurotransmitters that have been strongly implicated in unipolar patterns of depression (see Figure 8-5).

In the 1950s, several pieces of evidence pointed to low norepinephrine activity in the brain as a possible factor in depression. First, medical researchers discovered that *reserpine,* a drug used to treat high blood pressure, causes depression in some people (Lemieux et al., 1956; Ayd, 1956). An examination of reserpine's effect on the brain indicated that it lowered norepinephrine supplies in the nerve endings of many neurons, thus suggesting to researchers that depression may be related to low supplies of norepinephrine.

A second piece of evidence emerged from the discovery of a family of antidepressant drugs known as *monoamine oxidase (MAO) inhibitors.* These compounds increase the norepinephrine supplies of many neurons. The possibility that this was the means by which MAO inhibitors alleviated depression again fitted in with the

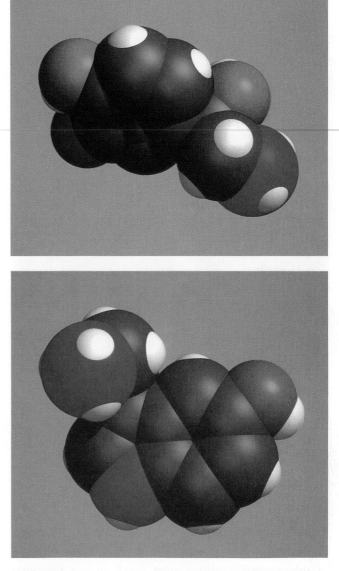

**FIGURE 8-5** Computer-drawn molecules of the neurotransmitters *norepinephrine (top)* and *serotonin (bottom).* Low activity of these neurotransmitters has repeatedly been implicated in unipolar depression.

idea that depression is related to low supplies of norepinephrine.

A third piece of evidence came from the discovery during the 1950s of another group of antidepressant medications, called *tricyclics.* Although these drugs are chemically different from MAO inhibitors, researchers soon learned that they, too, seemed to operate by ultimately increasing norepinephrine supplies in the brain (Axelrod et al., 1961; Snyder, 1984, 1976).

These three lines of investigation led to the tentative conclusion that unipolar depression was a product of low norepinephrine supplies (Schildkraut, 1965; Bunney &

Children whose mothers are depressed are at greater risk of later experiencing depression than are children of nondepressed mothers. Modeling effects, the mother's behavior toward her children, or socioeconomic pressures may partly account for this relationship, but adoption studies suggest that genetic factors may also play a significant role in it.

Davis, 1965). Researchers reasoned that lower supplies of this neurotransmitter must result in less neuronal firing, a concept that certainly fits the slow-motion picture of depression. Because norepinephrine belongs to the class of chemicals called catecholamines, this theory is known as the *catecholamine theory.*

While researchers in the United States were focusing on norepinephrine as the biological key to unipolar depression, British researchers were focusing on the neurotransmitter serotonin (Glassman, 1969; Coppen, 1967). They discovered that serotonin operates much like norepinephrine in a number of ways; that is, the blood pressure medication reserpine lowers supplies of brain serotonin, just as it lowers norepinephrine, and the MAO inhibitors and tricyclic antidepressants increase supplies of serotonin in the brain, just as they increase norepinephrine (Amsterdam & Mendels, 1980). Moreover, the neurons that use serotonin as their neurotransmitter tend to be located in many of the same areas of the

brain as those that use norepinephrine (see Figure 8-6). Given these findings, a number of theorists concluded that serotonin deficiencies may also cause unipolar depression (Golden & Gilmore, 1990). This view is often called the *indoleamine theory,* because serotonin belongs to the class of chemicals known as indoleamines.

***Investigating the Neurotransmitter Theories*** Over the past two decades an enormous amount of research has been devoted to sorting out the contributions of norepinephrine and serotonin to unipolar depression. Several proposals have emerged:

1. *Low norepinephrine and low serotonin combine to cause depression.* According to this argument, unipolar depression will occur only when both norepinephrine and serotonin supplies are low, and it will lift only when the levels of both neurotransmitters are increased. This theory lost its influence when some studies indicated that depression was accompanied sometimes by low norepinephrine levels alone and at other times by low serotonin alone. The blood pressure medicine *alpha-methyldopa* (Aldomet), for example, lowers norepinephrine supplies but does not lower serotonin. Nevertheless, a substantial number of people who take this drug become depressed.

2. *Low levels of either neurotransmitter can lead to depression.* Many findings have been consistent with this proposal (Garver & Davis, 1979). For example, research has been conducted on 3-methoxy-4-hydroxyphenylglycol (MHPG), a chemical by-product of norepinephrine metabolism in the brain (such by-products are called *metabolites*). Because this by-product enters the bloodstream and other parts of the body relatively intact, its level in the urine is thought to reflect the supply of norepinephrine in the brain (McNeal & Cimbolic, 1986). Studies have found that some but not all depressed people excrete low levels of MHPG, suggesting that the norepinephrine levels of depressed individuals are sometimes, but not always, low (Taska & Brodie, 1983; Schatzberg et al., 1982; Hollister, Davis, & Berger, 1980; Maas, 1975; Fawcett & Bunney, 1967).

Studies of 5-hydroxyindoleacetic acid (5-HIAA), a major by-product of serotonin, tell a similar story. Researchers have measured the level of this metabolite in the spinal fluid, believing that it reflects the brain supply of serotonin, and have found that approximately 25 percent of depressed people display very low levels of 5-HIAA, while other de-

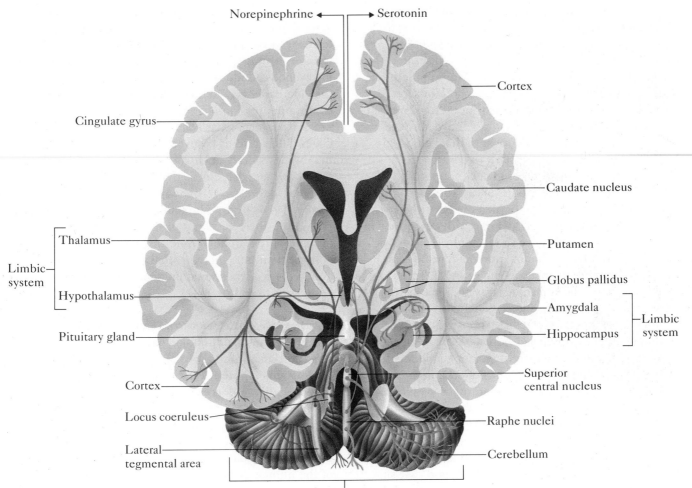

Norepinephrine ← → Serotonin

Cortex

Cingulate gyrus

Caudate nucleus

Thalamus

Putamen

Limbic system

Globus pallidus

Hypothalamus

Amygdala

Limbic system

Pituitary gland

Hippocampus

Cortex

Superior central nucleus

Locus coeruleus

Raphe nuclei

Lateral tegmental area

Cerebellum

Brain stem

**FIGURE 8-6** The cell bodies of neurons that contain norepinephrine and serotonin are located throughout the brain stem. The cell bodies of norepinephrine neurons are found in the locus coeruleus and lateral tegmental area, while the serotonin-containing cell bodies are concentrated in the raphe nuclei. The axons of these neurons extend to various parts of the brain, particularly to the limbic system, the portion that regulates emotion. The norepinephrine pathways are indicated in blue, the serotonin pathways in green. *(Adapted from Snyder, 1986, p. 108.)*

pressed people have normal levels (Leboyer & Plaisant, 1984; Baldessarini, 1983; Taska & Brodie, 1983; Maas, 1975). This finding suggests that unipolar depression is sometimes, but not always, accompanied by low serotonin levels.

Yet another line or research suggests that either low serotonin or low norepinephrine supplies may cause depression. These studies first focused on *tryptophan,* which is a *precursor* of serotonin — that is, a brain chemical that appears early in the chain of reactions that lead to the production of serotonin. Researchers believe that administering tryptophan should increase a person's brain supply of serotonin without increasing that of norepinephrine. That tryptophan often does alleviate depressive symptoms suggests that increases in serotonin alone can improve depression (Meltzer et al., 1987; Van Praag, 1984; Amsterdam & Mendels, 1980; Carroll, 1971). Similarly, when *tyrosine,* a precursor of norepinephrine, is administered to depressed people, it sometimes reduces depressive symptoms, suggesting that norepinephrine increases alone can alleviate depression (Gelenberg et al., 1980).

3. *Norepinpehrine depression is different from serotonin depression.* Some theorists have proposed that uni-

polar depression linked to low norepinephrine is qualitatively different from depression linked to low serotonin (Van Praag, 1984; Asberg et al., 1984, 1976; Maas, 1975). This "two-disease theory" has an intuitive appeal. After all, though norepinephrine and serotonin are both neurotransmitters, they are chemically distinct. Can the depressive reaction caused by the relative absence of one chemical truly be identical to that caused by the absence of the other?

An analogue study that provides support for this view compared three groups of rats, one with their norepinephrine supplies depleted, one with serotonin supplies depleted, and one with depletions of both norepinephrine and serotonin (Ellison & Bresler, 1974). The low-norepinephrine rats showed symptoms that seemed to mimic some characteristics of human depression, notably lethargy, inattentiveness, and reduced hunger. The low-serotonin rats showed reactions that seemed to mimic other symptoms of human depression, such as agitation and an apparent lack of confidence. The rats with lowered supplies of both neurotransmitters showed a combination of these symptoms.

Similarly, in a study of human depressed subjects, Marie Asberg and her colleagues (1976) found that those whose serotonin was depleted were more apathetic and suicidal than those with normal serotonin levels. They also found that suicide attempts made by depressed patients with low serotonin were more frequent and more violent than those made by other depressed people.

4. *Neither norepinephrine nor serotonin supplies are key factors in depression.* Some researchers believe that the biological explanations of unipolar depression have placed too much emphasis on the *supply* of norepinephrine or serotonin available in the brain and that other brain processes are really at the core of unipolar depression (McNeal & Cimbolic, 1986). There are growing suspicions, for example, that the primary biological problem may be defective norepinephrine or serotonin *receptors* that fail to attract and capture sufficient amounts of neurotransmitters, thus creating the impression that the neurotransmitters are depleted in the brain (McNeal & Cimbolic, 1986; Snyder & Peroutka, 1984).

Still other researchers believe that it is wrong to focus exclusively on norepinephrine and serotonin, in terms of either their supplies or their receptors. There is some evidence that high levels of a different neurotransmitter, *acetylcholine,* may also be associated with depression

(McNeal & Cimbolic, 1986; Janowsky, 1980). Exposure to potent insecticides that increase acetylcholine levels causes some adults to undergo a depressive change in mood (Gershon & Shaw, 1961). Similarly, intravenous administration of *physostigmine,* a chemical that increases acetylcholine supplies in the brain, can cause a depressionlike syndrome in previously nondepressed subjects (Risch et al., 1983; Davis et al., 1976). Given such findings, several theorists have proposed that some overall imbalance in norepinephrine, serotonin, *and* acetylcholine activity causes the symptoms of unipolar depression (Ballenger, 1988; Risch & Janowsky, 1984; Charney, Heninger, & Sternberg, 1984; Dumbrille-Ross & Tang, 1983). Finally, a growing number of researchers think that perhaps each of these neurotransmitters plays a role in the operation of a "body clock" whose malfunction is the true source of depression (see Box 8-4).

*Evaluating the Neurotransmitter Theories*    The neurotransmitter theories of depression have deservedly generated much enthusiasm and investigation, but many questions are still unanswered. First, this research, too, has consisted to a large degree of analogue studies that create depressionlike symptoms in laboratory animals. While the symptoms these studies generate are superficially similar to human depression, researchers cannot be certain that they do in fact reflect the quality and substance of the human disorder.

A second problem is that given the limitations of present technology, most studies on human beings must manipulate and measure brain chemical activity indirectly, and as a result the investigator can never quite be certain of the actual biochemical events (Leboyer & Plaisant, 1984; Shopsin & Feiner, 1984). Researchers have assumed, for example, that when they administer certain chemical precursors to human subjects, those precursors are converted into neurotransmitters, whose presence then increases the specific neurotransmitter activity in the brain. It is conceivable, however, that nothing of the kind is happening. Similarly, most estimates of existing supplies of neurotransmitters in a living person's brain have been based on measurements of neurotransmitter metabolites in the person's urine or spinal fluid. Again, it is possible that those measures are not accurate reflections of the supplies of norepinephrine and serotonin in the person's brain (Taska & Brodie, 1983).

These limitations notwithstanding, biological researchers seem to be closing in on a compelling and enlightening understanding of the biological underpinnings of unipolar depression. Their work, along with the work and findings of psychological researchers, has also begun to open doors to the effective treatment of unipolar patterns of depression, an important turn of events that we shall be investigating in Chapter 9.

# BIPOLAR DISORDERS

In contrast to the unrelieved gloom of depression, a person in a state of mania is governed by dramatic, inappropriate, and disproportionate elevation. The symptoms of a manic episode encompass the same areas of functioning — emotional, motivational, behavioral, cognitive, and somatic — as those of depression, but mania affects those areas in an almost diametrically opposite way (see Table 8-4).

## Clinical Picture of Mania

*Manic episodes* are periods of active, expansive *emotion* that seems to be looking for an outlet. The mood of euphoric joy and well-being is out of all proportion to the actual happenings in the person's life. One manic person explained, "I feel no sense of restriction or censorship whatsoever. I am afraid of nothing and no one" (Fieve, 1975, p. 68). Another described his manic experience as "a sense of communion, in the first place with God, and in the second with all mankind" (Custance, 1952, p. 37). Not every manic person is a picture of happiness, however. Some can also become irritable, angry, and annoyed — especially when others get in the way of their ambitions, activities, and plans — like this man:

*All by himself,* he had been building a magnificent swimming pool for his country home in Virginia, working eighteen hours a day at it. He decided to make the pool public and open a concession stand at one end to help defray the mounting costs of the project. When his wife suggested that he might be going overboard, he became furious and threatened to leave her for another woman. Soon afterward, when his wife was out, he took many valuables from the house — his share, he claimed — and sold or pawned them. Complaining that his wife was a stick in the mud, he decided to throw a round-the-clock party, and he invited to the house almost everyone he passed on the street. This psychotic behavior went on for weeks, and during this time he slept only two to four hours a night. He had no time to eat, and he talked continuously, planning grandiose sexual schemes "as soon as someone takes my wife off my hands."

*(Fieve, 1975, p. 148)*

In the *motivational* realm, manic people seem to want constant excitement, involvement, and companionship.

TABLE 8-4

| MANIFESTATIONS OF MANIA AND DEPRESSION | |
| --- | --- |
| **Mania** | **Depression** |
| **Emotional** | |
| Elation | Depressed mood |
| Liking for self | Dislike of self |
| Increased mirth response | Loss of mirth response |
| **Cognitive** | |
| Positive self-image | Negative self-image |
| Positive expectations | Negative expectations |
| Tendency to blame others | Tendency to blame self |
| Denial of problems | Exaggeration of problems |
| Arbitrary decision making | Indecisiveness |
| **Motivational** | |
| Driven and impulsive behavior | Paralysis of the will |
| Action-oriented wishes | Wishes for escape |
| Drive for independence | Increased wishes for dependency |
| Desire for self-enhancement | Desire for death |
| **Behavioral** | |
| Hyperactivity | Inertia/agitation |
| Productivity | Lack of productivity |
| Loudness | Quietness |
| **Physical** | |
| Indefatigability | Easy fatigability |
| Increased libido | Loss of libido |
| Insomnia | Insomnia |

*Source:* Beck, 1967, p. 91.

They enthusiastically seek out new friends and old, new interests and old, and have little awareness that their social approaches are overwhelming, domineering, and excessive:

*He was interested in everything and everyone around him.* He talked familiarly to patients, attendants, nurses, and physicians. He took a fancy to the woman physician on duty in the admission building, calling her by her first name and annoying her with letters and with his familiar, ill-mannered, and obtrusive attentions. . . . He made many comments and asked many questions about other patients and promised that he would secure their discharge. He in-

BOX 8-4

# When Body Clocks Need Resetting

Our lives are structured by cycles and rhythms—daily, monthly, seasonal, and yearly. The 24-hour day provides the cycle to which we adapt our most common activities—sleeping, eating, working, and socializing. Although our daily rhythms are imposed largely by our environment, they are also driven by a kind of internal clock, consisting of recurrent biological fluctuations, called *circadian rhythms,* that must be coordinated with one another and with both cyclic and transient changes in the environment. The daily operation of our internal clock is apparently controlled by at least two self-sustained oscillators. One oscillator is strong and consistent, and rigidly controls regular changes in body temperature, hormone secretions, and *rapid eye movement (REM) sleep*—the near-awake phase of sleep during which we dream. The other oscillator, weaker and more ready to adjust to changes, controls the sleep–wake cycle and activity–rest cycle. Most people can go to sleep late one night and early the next and not have any trouble falling asleep quickly and sleeping soundly; but during this same period their body temperature will rigidly follow its usual pattern, peaking at the same time each afternoon and bottoming out each morning (Gold, 1987).

A series of revealing studies conducted throughout the 1980s has convinced many researchers that depression is often the result of an imbalance, or *desynchronization,* between the body's circadian rhythms and the rhythms of the environment (Healy & Williams, 1988; Zerssen et al., 1985; Campbell et al., 1985; Goodwin et al., 1982). This new view of depression seems to build upon and clarify earlier biological findings on depression. Two parts of the body clock—sleep rhythms and hormone release rhythms—have been implicated in this recent wave of research.

## SLEEP RHYTHMS

The sleep cycle, the most basic rhythm in our lives, consists of four stages of sleep plus REM sleep (Ballenger, 1988; Gold, 1987). As we sleep we cycle through all of these stages every ninety minutes, but the internal pattern of the ninety-minute cycle changes throughout the night. For example, stages III and IV, the deep or slow-wave sleep stages, occupy much of the ninety minutes when we first fall asleep but little of the cycle when we are preparing to wake up. REM sleep, on the other hand, fills only ten minutes or so of the cycle during early sleep and as much as an hour toward morning (Ballenger, 1988; Gold, 1987).

Researchers have learned that these sleep cycles are reversed in depressed people. After falling asleep, they move into REM sleep much more quickly, experience more REM sleep during the early sleep cycles, and have less REM sleep toward morning (Hirschfeld & Goodwin, 1988; Gold, 1987; Gillin et al., 1984; Wehr & Goodwin, 1981). Depressed people also display more frequent rapid eye movements during REM sleep and less deep sleep overall. Some theorists think the body's two oscillators, the rigid one in control of REM sleep and the flexible one in control of the sleep–wake cycle, may be out of harmony (Goodwin et al., 1982).

## HORMONE RELEASE RHYTHMS

Endocrine glands are located throughout the body, working along with the nervous system to regulate such vital activities as growth, reproduction, sexual activity, heart rate, body temperature, energy, and responses to stress. During times of stress, for example, the *adrenal glands,* located on top of the kidneys, secrete *cortisol,* a hormone that helps stimulate body organs to greater activity, and the *thyroid gland,* located in the neck, secretes the *thyroid hormone.* The entire endocrine system is run by the *hypothalamus,* often called the "brain of the brain."

Some researchers used to believe that depression might be related to abnormal hormone activity, particularly to high levels of the stress hormone cortisol and to low levels of the thyroid hormone (Kiellmar et al., 1984; Sachar et al., 1973). Yet abnormal levels of this kind were found in depressed persons only some of the time; at other times, the hormone activity of these same depressed persons seemed to be entirely appropriate (Healy & Williams, 1988). More recent research has revealed that the *timing* of the release of these and other hormones, not hormone production or activity per se, may be disturbed in depressed people (Healy & Leonard, 1987; Healy et al., 1986; Zerssen, 1983). That is, the strong circadian oscillator that controls hormone release may be out of synchrony with the body's weak oscillator and with environmental rhythms. In nondepressed people, cortisol secretions are typically lowest during the night and highest during the early morning and late afternoon. Depressed people display either no such variation at all or reversed variation.

Secretions of the hormone *melatonin* appear to be particularly important in depression (Lam et al., 1990). This hormone is secreted by the brain's *pineal gland* when our surroundings are dark, but not when they are light. The role of melatonin in human biology is not entirely understood, but in animals it seems to help regulate hibernation, activity levels, and sexual and reproductive cycles. As nights grow longer during the fall and winter, animals secrete more and more melatonin, which has the effect of slowing them down and preparing them for an extended seasonal rest. When daytime hours lengthen in the spring and summer, melatonin secretions decrease, raising energy levels and setting the stage for reproduction. Although human activity levels and reproduction cycles do not appear to be so closely tied to light and dark, our pineal glands nevertheless carry on the tradition of secreting greater amounts of melatonin during the dark nights of winter than during the short nights of summer.

Some theorists believe that because of our heightened melatonin secretions, humans slow down, have less energy, and need more rest in the wintertime, much as hibernating animals do (Whybrow & Bahr, 1988). Most people manage to adjust to those internal changes. Researchers believe, however, that some people are extremely sensitive to winter's heightened melatonin secretions and find it impossible to carry on with business as usual (Dilsaver, 1990; Rosenthal & Blehar, 1989; Rosenthal et al., 1988). Their seasonal slowdown takes the form of depression, but a depression characterized by symptoms that are quite consistent with animal hibernation—a big appetite, a craving for carbohydrates, weight gain, oversleeping, and fatigue (Gupta, 1988). Researchers believe that these people are also extremely sensitive to the drop in melatonin secretions that occurs during the longer days of summer. Some, in fact, become overenergized and overactive and display a hypomanic or manic pattern every summer (Carney et al., 1988). Such patterns, often called *seasonal affective disorders* (Rosenthal & Blehar, 1989), or *SAD,* are now described by DSM-III-R.

Research suggests that the *suprachiasmatic nuclei (SCN),* a small cluster of neurons in the hypothalamus, connected to the pineal gland and to the eyes, may be the regula-

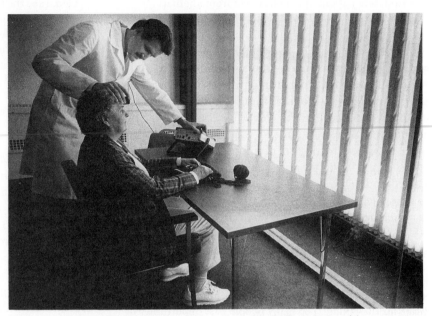

Various techniques have been developed to provide SAD patients with extra amounts of light on short winter days.

tor for circadian rhythms (Ballenger, 1988; Goldner, 1985; Rusak & Zucker, 1979). When light enters the eyes, the "light" message is carried by the neurotransmitter acetylcholine to the SCN. This message is then carried by the neurotransmitter norepinephrine to the pineal gland, which reacts by stopping its manufacture of melatonin. If the pineal gland were to fail to receive this "light" message, it would keep producing melatonin; the melatonin would in turn repeatedly act upon the hypothalamus, thus affecting the timing of hormone secretions throughout the body (Kripke, 1987). Depressed persons may have an abnormality in the SCN or in some other link in this chain, leading to desynchronization and to depressive symptoms (Wehr, 1990; Lewy, 1990; Healy & Waterhouse, 1990).

## LIGHT THERAPY

If in fact darkness is the problem in SAD, the answer may be light, at least in cases characterized by winter depression. One of the most effective treatments for SAD turns out to be light therapy, or *phototherapy,* exposure to extra amounts of synthetic light throughout the winter. When

seasonally depressed patients sit under intense light for several hours every winter day, their depression can be reduced or eliminated (Rosenthal et al., 1988; Lewy et al., 1987, 1980; Wirz-Justice et al., 1986). Some theorists believe that extremely bright light must be applied (an intensity of 2,500 lux as opposed to the normal 250 lux), while others believe that even dim light may be helpful (McIntyre et al., 1990). Some believe that the light must be administered both in the morning and at night, while others consider one administration per day to be sufficient (Doghramji et al., 1990; Lewy et al., 1987).

Of course, there is another, more enjoyable way to get more light— spend a winter vacation in a sunny place. Some theorists go so far as to suggest that people with wintertime blues, and certainly those with SAD, should spend a week or two just before winter begins in a location approximately 34 degrees north or south of the equator, where 70 percent more sunlight is available each day (Whybrow & Bahr, 1988). The effectiveness of this form of "treatment" has yet to be investigated scientifically. The line for volunteer subjects forms to the left.

terfered with their affairs and soon received a blow on the jaw from one patient and a black eye from another.

*(Kolb, 1973, p. 372)*

The *behavior* of manic people is usually described as hyperactive. They move quickly, as though there were not enough time to do everything they want to do. They may talk rapidly and loudly, their conversations filled with jokes and efforts to be clever or, conversely, with complaints and hostile tirades. Flamboyance is another characteristic of manic functioning: dressing in flashy clothes, giving large sums of money to strangers, getting involved in dangerous activities. Several of these qualities are evident in the monologue delivered by Joe to the two policemen who escorted him to the mental hospital:

*You look like a couple of bright, alert, hardworking,* clean-cut, energetic go-getters and I could use you in my organization! I need guys that are loyal and enthusiastic about the great opportunities life offers on this planet! It's yours for the taking! Too many people pass opportunity by without hearing it knock because they don't know how to grasp the moment and strike while the iron is hot! You've got to grab it when it comes up for air, pick up the ball and run! You've got to be decisive! decisive! decisive! No shilly-shallying! Sweat! Yeah, sweat with a goal! Push, push, push, and you can push over a mountain! Two mountains, maybe. It's not luck! Hell, if it wasn't for bad luck I wouldn't have any luck at all! Be there firstest with the mostest! My guts and your blood! That's the system! I know, you know, he, she or it knows it's the only way to travel! Get 'em off balance, baby, and the rest is leverage! Use your head and save your heels! What's this deal? Who are these guys? Have you got a telephone and a secretary I can have in-stanter if not sooner? What I need is office space and the old LDO [long-distance operator].

*(McNeil, 1967, p. 147)*

In the *cognitive* realm, manic people usually display poor judgment and planning, as if they feel too good or move too rapidly to consider consequences or possible pitfalls. Filled with optimism, they rarely listen when others try to slow them down, interrupt their buying sprees, or prevent them from investing money unwisely. They may also hold an inflated opinion of themselves, believing that there are few topics beyond their expertise and few tasks beyond their grasp. Sometimes their self-esteem approaches grandiosity. Writer John Custance (1952) describes his thoughts during a manic episode:

*It seems to me that all my wishes are coming true, that* all my ambitions, in work and in play, political, financial, personal, are going to be realised, that vital secrets of the Universe are being revealed to me and so on. . . . I feel so

close to God, so inspired by His spirit that in a sense I am God. I see the future, plan the Universe, save mankind; I am utterly and completely immortal; I am even male and female. The whole Universe, animate and inanimate, past, present and future, is within me. All nature and life, all spirits, are co-operating and connected with me; all things are possible. I am in a sense identical with all spirits from God to Satan. I reconcile Good and Evil and create light, darkness, worlds, universes.

*(Custance, 1952, pp. 51–52)*

Manic people are easily distracted by random stimuli from the environment. Especially during the acute phases of mania, they may have so much trouble keeping their thoughts on track that they become incoherent (Harrow, 1986). Some manic people also report that their sensory impressions seem sharper, brighter, more colorful, and more pleasurable.

Finally, in the *physical* realm, manic people feel remarkably energetic. They typically get little sleep, yet feel and act wide awake. Even if they miss a night or two of sleep, their energy level seems very high. Clifford Beers wrote:

*For several weeks I believe I did not sleep more than* two or three hours a night. Such was my state of elation, however, that all signs of fatigue were entirely absent; and the sustained and abnormal mental and physical activity in which I then indulged has left on my memory no other than a series of very pleasant impressions.

*(Beers, 1908)*

## Diagnosing Bipolar Disorders

The novelist Saul Bellow captures the expansiveness of a person during a manic episode:

He was a great entertainer but going insane. The pathologic element could be missed only by those who were laughing too hard to look. Humboldt, that grand erratic handsome person with his wide blond face, that charming fluent deeply worried man to whom I was so attached, passionately lived out the theme of Success. Naturally he died a Failure. What else can result from the capitalization of such nouns? Myself, I've always held the number of sacred words down. In my opinion Humboldt had too long a list of them — Poetry, Beauty, Love, Waste Land, Alienation, Politics, History, the Unconscious. And, of course, Manic and Depressive, always capitalized. According to him, America's great Manic Depressive was Lincoln. And Churchill with what he called his Black Dog moods was a classic case of Manic Depression. "Like me, Charlie," said Humboldt. "But think — if Energy is Delight and if Exuberance is Beauty, the Manic Depressive knows more about Delight and Beauty than anyone else. Who else has so much Energy and Exuberance? Maybe it's the strategy of the Psyche to increase Depression. Didn't Freud say that Happiness was nothing but the remission of Pain? So the more Pain the intenser the Happiness. But there is a prior origin to this, and the Psyche makes Pain on purpose. Anyway, Mankind is stunned by the Exuberance and Beauty of certain individuals. When a Manic Depressive escapes from his Furies he's irresistible. He captures History. I think that aggravation is a secret technique of the Unconscious. As for great men and kings being History's slaves, I think Tolstoi was off the track. Don't kid yourself, kings are the most sublime sick. Manic Depressive heroes pull Mankind into their cycles and carry everybody away."

*(Bellow*, Humboldt's Gift*)*

DSM-III-R considers people to be experiencing a manic episode when they display a predominantly elevated, expansive, or irritable mood, along with at least three other symptoms of mania (see Table 8-4). Like Humboldt, those who soar high in a manic episode are expected sooner or later to plunge to the depths of depression and they receive a formal diagnosis of *bipolar disorder* whether or not they have yet taken that plunge.

People who experience rapidly alternating depressive and manic symptoms receive a diagnosis of *bipolar disorder, mixed.* If they are experiencing a depressive episode with no attendant mania but have a past history of mania, they receive a diagnosis of *bipolar disorder, depressed.* Although the current depressive episode may exhibit no trace of mania, such a history suggests that the depressive episode is actually part of a bipolar pattern. People in the grip of a manic episode receive a diagnosis of *bipolar disorder, manic.* Diagnosticians assume the episode to be part of a bipolar pattern even in the absence of additional evidence from the past.

Surveys conducted in the United States and other industrialized nations indicate that between 0.5 and 1 percent of all adults suffer from a bipolar disorder at some time in their lives (Weissman & Boyd, 1984; Boyd & Weissman, 1981). According to most studies, bipolar disorders are equally common in women and men (Weissman & Klerman, 1985) and usually begin between the ages of 15 and 35 years (McGlashan, 1988; APA, 1987; Krauthammer & Klerman, 1979). Some researchers believe that bipolar disorders are more prevalent in the upper socioeconomic classes, while others find no such difference (Robins et al., 1984; Weissman & Boyd, 1984).

The majority of bipolar disorders begin with a manic episode (APA, 1987; Goodwin & Jamison, 1984). In most untreated cases, the manic and depressive episodes last for several months each (Wehr et al., 1988; Jamison & Jamison, 1984; Shopsin, 1979), with intervening periods of normal mood lasting for two or more years

In recent years actress Patty Duke has talked and written about her roller-coaster life with bipolar disorder. Until her disorder was diagnosed and treated, she experienced recurrent episodes of suicidal depression alternating with episodes of normal mood or mania.

(Weissman & Boyd, 1984). In some cases, however, normal mood periods are brief or even absent.

In the absence of treatment, bipolar manic and depressive episodes tend to recur (Goodwin & Jamison, 1990). One team of researchers reviewed the progress of ninety-five recorded cases of untreated bipolar disorders, each spanning an average of twenty-six years, and found that 84 percent of the patients had five or more mood episodes, 65 percent had seven or more, and 42 percent had eleven or more (Angst, Felder, & Frey, 1979). Generally, as episodes recur, the intervening periods of normality grow shorter and shorter (Goodwin & Jamison, 1984).

When the mood swings consist of milder depressive episodes and milder manic (that is, *hypomanic*) episodes, DSM-III-R assigns a diagnosis of *cyclothymia* (see Figure 8-2). Here the milder symptoms continue for two or more years, interrupted occasionally by normal moods that may last up to several months. This disorder, like bipolar disorders, begins in adolescence or early adulthood and is equally common among women and men. Slightly less than 0.5 percent of the population develops cyclothymia. In some of these cases, the milder symptoms eventually blossom into a full bipolar disorder (APA, 1987).

Many people with bipolar disorder describe their life as an emotional roller coaster. They must deal not only with the direct consequences of their reckless euphorias and paralyzing dysphorias, but also with the additional problems brought about simply by the fact that there is so much change in their lives (Goodwin & Jamison,

1990). This roller coaster ride and its impact on relatives and friends is dramatically seen in the following description:

*In his early school years he had been a remarkable student* and had shown a gift for watercolor and oils. Later he had studied art in Paris and married an English girl he had met there. Eventually they had settled in London.

Ten years later, when he was thirty-four years old, he had persuaded his wife and only son to accompany him to Honolulu, where, he assured them, he would be considered famous. He felt he would be able to sell his paintings at many times the prices he could get in London. According to his wife, he had been in an accelerated state, but at that time the family had left, unsuspecting, believing with the patient in their imminent good fortune. When they arrived they found almost no one in the art world that he was supposed to know. There were no connections for sales and deals in Hawaii that he had anticipated. Settling down, the patient began to behave more peculiarly than ever. After enduring several months of the patient's exhilaration, overactivity, weight loss, constant talking, and unbelievably little sleep, the young wife and child began to fear for his sanity. None of his plans materialized. After five months in the Pacific, with finances growing thin, the patient's overactivity subsided and he fell into a depression. During that period he refused to move, paint, or leave the house. He lost twenty pounds, became utterly dependent on his wife, and insisted on seeing none of the friends he had accumulated in his manic state. His despondency became so severe that several doctors came to the house and advised psychiatric hospitalization. He quickly agreed and received twelve electroshock treatments, which relieved his depressed state. Soon afterward he began to paint again and to sell his work modestly. Recognition began to come from galleries and critics in the Far East. Several reviews acclaimed his work as exceptionally brilliant.

This was the beginning of the lifelong career of his moodswing. In 1952, while still in Honolulu, he once again became severely depressed, requiring electroshock treatments. Four years later he returned to London in a high. In this manic state he spent his carefully accumulated lifetime savings, took on several mistresses, divorced his wife, gave away paintings, and gambled. He began to be obsessed by religion and mysticism, and felt he could communicate with the universe through his paintings. When this manic period subsided and he surveyed the wreckage of his life, an eight-month interval of normal mood followed, after which he again switched into a profound depression. During this normal phase he recognized that paintings accomplished during the psychotic high were not as good as he had thought them to be.

During this rebound normal period, he met and married his second wife, who said that at the time he was enthusiastic and irresistibly charming but not in any sense abnormal mentally.

Despite the fact that he was now beginning to achieve international renown for his canvases, he began to feel plagued with frequent and severe suicidal depressions. During these periods he withdrew, refused to paint, lost weight, and slept sixteen hours out of twenty-four. He said that he no longer wanted to live. On one occasion his wife found him walking naked in the middle of the night, about to take a bottle of sleeping pills. This depression lifted spontaneously after six months.

*(Fieve, 1975, pp. 64–65)*

## Explanations of Bipolar Disorders

Throughout the first half of this century, the study of bipolar disorders made little progress. Various models were proposed to explain bipolar mood swings, but research did not support their validity. Psychodynamic theorists suggested that mania, like depression, emerges from the loss of a love object. Whereas some people introject the lost object and become depressed, others deny the loss and become manic. They avoid the terrifying conflicts generated by the loss by escaping into a fast-thinking and fast-moving style of life (Ginsberg, 1979; Lewin, 1950). Although some psychodynamic clinicians have cited case reports that fit this explanation (Krishman et al., 1984; Cohen et al., 1954), few systematic studies have been able to find any relationship between recent loss (real or imagined) and the onset of a manic episode (Dunner & Hall, 1980).

For a long time, manic-depressive cycles seemed to resist all explanations and forms of treatment. Lately, however, some promising clues from the biological realm have led to better understanding. These biological insights come from research into neurotransmitter activity, sodium ion instability, and genetic factors.

**Neurotransmitters**   When researchers first proposed the catecholamine theory, holding that a low norepinephrine supply leads to depression, they also argued that an oversupply of norepinephrine is related to mania (Schildkraut, 1965). Subsequent research has offered some support for this claim. One study measured the norepinephrine level in subjects' spinal fluid, on the assumption once again that this measure would reflect the norepinephrine supply in the brain (Post, 1980, 1978). It found the norepinephrine levels of manic patients to be significantly higher than those of depressed or control subjects. When bipolar patients in another study were given reserpine, the blood pressure drug known to reduce the norepinephrine supply in the brain, a number of the subjects showed a reduction of manic symptoms (Telner, Lapierre, Horn, & Browne, 1986).

The belief that mania is related to high norepinephrine activity has also been supported by research on the

Echoing Shakespeare's observation that "the lunatic, the lover, and the poet are all compact," clinical researchers Frederick Goodwin and Kay Jamison (1990) claim that some of our most famous poets, including Sylvia Plath, have experienced bipolar disorders. Plath committed suicide in 1963 at the age of 31.

1977). Researchers have also found that lithium, the drug that treats mania so successfully, often seems to *increase* brain serotonin activity (Bunney & Garland, 1984; Poitou & Guerinot, 1974; Perez-Cruet et al., 1971). Somehow, depression and mania both seem to be related to a low level of serotonin.

In an effort to make sense of these seemingly contradictory findings, some researchers have proposed a "permissive theory" of mood disorders (Kety et al., 1974; Prange et al., 1974, 1970). According to this theory, low serotonin activity sets the stage for a mood disorder and *permits* the brain's norepinephrine activity to define the particular form of the disorder. Low serotonin activity accompanied by low or normal norepinephrine activity will lead to depression, a notion consistent with the neurotransmitter theories of unipolar depression discussed earlier (pp. 281–285). Conversely, low serotonin activity accompanied by high norepinephrine activity will lead to mania. Although not all researchers are convinced that norepinephrine and serotonin interact in this particular way to produce bipolar disorders, a growing number do believe that the disorders reflect some form of abnormal functioning by both of the neurotransmitter systems (Baraban, Worley, & Snyder, 1989).

action of the drug *lithium*. As we shall see in Chapter 9, clinicians have discovered that lithium is by far the most effective treatment for bipolar disorders, in many cases correcting both the manic and the depressive poles of the cycle. Once researchers became aware of lithium's dramatic impact, they proceeded to study its effects on the brain and soon learned that it reduces norepinephrine activity at key neural sites (Bunney & Garland, 1984; Kuriyami & Speken, 1970; Colburn et al., 1967). Many reasoned that if lithium reduces manic symptoms while reducing norepinephrine activity, mania itself may be related to high norepinephrine activity.

Because serotonin activity often parallels norepinephrine's in relation to depression, theorists initially expected that a large supply of serotonin would also be related to manic functioning. However, this correspondence has not shown up. Instead, research has indicated that mania, like depression, is associated with a *low* supply of serotonin. For example, spinal fluid levels of 5-HIAA, the serotonin metabolite, are no higher in manic patients than in normal control subjects, and in fact are often lower (Post, 1980; Banki, 1977; Sjostrom, 1973). Similarly, when researchers have administered tryptophan to manic patients, they have found that this serotonin precursor sometimes alleviates manic symptoms, again suggesting that a *lack* of serotonin is the problem in mania (Prange et al., 1974, 1970; Van Praag, 1978,

**Sodium Ion Instability**    Another biological explanation of mania and bipolar disorders points to a neural imbalance of sodium ions as the culprit (Hirschfield & Goodwin, 1988). Investigators have arrived at this explanation by working backward from the discovery of lithium's effectiveness as a treatment for bipolar disorders. They already knew that lithium forms mineral salts, is a member of the family of alkali metals, and thus is closely related to sodium (chemical symbol, Na). Reasoning that when lithium is ingested, it may affect the body's use of this alkali relative, researchers began to look closely at the physiological functions of sodium.

Every neuron has electrically charged sodium ions, which play a critical role in carrying incoming messages down a neuron's axon to its nerve endings. The sodium ions sit on both sides of a neuron's membrane (see Figures 8-7 and 8-8). When a neuron is at rest, most of the sodium ions sit on the outer side of the membrane; when the neuron is stimulated by an incoming message at its receptor site, however, a shift occurs in the cell and sodium ions from the outer side of the membrane travel across to the inner side, thus propagating a wave of electrochemical activity that continues down the axon, culminating in the "firing" of the neuron. This activity is followed by the flow of potassium ions from the inside to the outside of the neuron, thus helping the neuron to return to its original resting state.

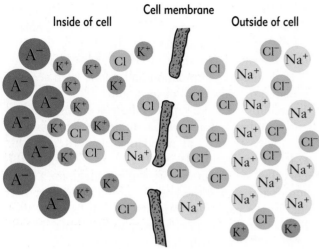

**FIGURE 8-7** The cell membrane, composed of protein and fat, contains small pores that allow the passage of water, sodium ions (Na$^+$), chloride ions (Cl$^-$), potassium ions (K$^+$), and large protein molecules with negative electric charges (A$^-$). Potassium and chloride ions diffuse freely through the pores, but it is much more difficult for sodium ions to do so, and protein molecules can hardly diffuse at all. *(Adapted from Julien, 1985, p. 229.)*

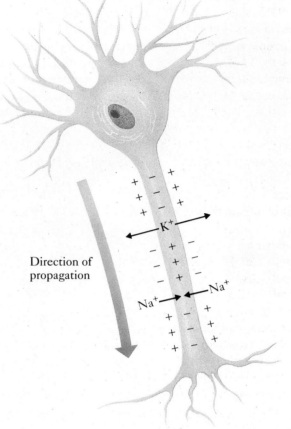

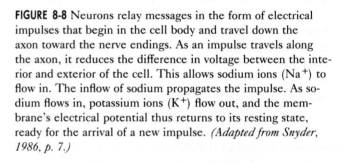

**FIGURE 8-8** Neurons relay messages in the form of electrical impulses that begin in the cell body and travel down the axon toward the nerve endings. As an impulse travels along the axon, it reduces the difference in voltage between the interior and exterior of the cell. This allows sodium ions (Na$^+$) to flow in. The inflow of sodium propagates the impulse. As sodium flows in, potassium ions (K$^+$) flow out, and the membrane's electrical potential thus returns to its resting state, ready for the arrival of a new impulse. *(Adapted from Snyder, 1986, p. 7.)*

If brain messages are to be transmitted properly, the sodium ions on the outside and inside of the neural membrane must be properly aligned. A proper alignment ensures that a neuron will be neither too susceptible nor too resistant to stimulation. Some researchers have focused on this alignment of sodium ions as a possible factor in bipolar disorders. They suspect that manic functioning may result from one kind of misalignment that causes neurons to be fired too easily, while depressive functioning may come from another kind of misalignment that makes it difficult for neurons to fire. Instability in this sodium electrical system may result in shifting misalignments and consequent fluctuations from one mood extreme to the other (Bunney & Garland, 1984).

To test this theory, researchers have looked for signs of sodium ion instability in people with bipolar disorders. One indication of instability would be excessive sodium, and high sodium levels have indeed been found in patients during manic and depressive episodes (Coppen, 1967; Shaw, 1966). Another indication of instability in the sodium electrical system would be a defect in the mechanisms that help transport sodium ions back and forth across a neuron's membrane during firing (Hirschfeld & Goodwin, 1988). Sodium transport mechanisms do seem to function slowly in bipolar patients, particularly during depressive episodes (Naylor et al., 1974; Hokin-Neaverson, Spiegel, & Lewis,

1974). Lithium may achieve its effectiveness by actually substituting for sodium ions, thus perhaps altering the overall transportation of sodium ions in the brain (Bunney & Garland, 1984).

Research in this area has accelerated of late, inspired by the remarkable effectiveness of lithium. As Solomon Snyder (1980) has said, "A drug that normalizes patients, preventing both manic and depressive episodes, would seem to be acting at some site closely linked to the fundamental abnormality of the manic-depressive disorder" (p. 28).

**Genetic Factors**    Many theorists have argued that people inherit a predisposition to develop the biological abnormalities underlying bipolar disorders (Siever et al., 1991; Blehar et al., 1988). Family pedigree studies have provided strong evidence that this is so. Close relatives of people with a bipolar disorder have been found to have a 4 to 20 percent likelihood of developing the same disorder, compared to the less than 1 percent prevalence rate in the general population (Fieve et al., 1984; Dunner et al., 1980; Johnson & Leeman, 1977). If one twin has a bipolar disorder, the likelihood is approximately 70 percent that an identical twin will have it too, compared to the less than 20 percent likelihood for a fraternal twin (Fischer, 1980; Bertelsen et al., 1977). Obviously, the more similar the genetic makeup of two people, the more similar their tendency to develop a bipolar disorder.

Researchers have also conducted ***genetic linkage studies*** to identify possible patterns in the inheritance of bipolar disorders (Hodgkinson et al., 1990). They select extended families that have exhibited high rates of the disorder over several generations, observe the pattern of distribution of the disorder among family members, and determine whether it closely follows the distribution pattern of other family traits, such as color blindness, red hair, or a particular medical syndrome. If, for example, all the family members with a bipolar disorder also were to have a genetically transmitted skin condition while nonbipolar family members did not have this condition, researchers might conclude that a predisposition to bipolar disorders is linked to a predisposition to this skin condition, and that the two predispositions are carried by genes located close together on the same chromosome.

By carefully studying the records of Israeli, Belgian, and Italian families that have shown high rates of bipolar disorder across several generations, a number of researchers have found bipolar disorders linked to red-green color blindness and to a medical abnormality called G6PD deficiency (Baron et al., 1987; del Zompo et al., 1984; Mendelowicz et al., 1981, 1980, 1979, 1975, 1972; Winokur et al., 1969). These two conditions are known to be transmitted by genes on the X chromosome, suggesting that the predisposition to bipolar disorders is also transmitted by a gene on the X chromosome, located "close to and possibly between the two marker loci" (Baron et al., 1987). These researchers further estimate that a third of the bipolar population may inherit a predisposition to develop the disorder in this way.

On the other hand, a genetic examination of Old Order Amish families in Pennsylvania who have also displayed high rates of bipolar disorder across several generations traced the problem to an entirely different chromosomal area (Egeland et al., 1987, 1984). After determining that one extended Amish family had a particularly high prevalence rate of bipolar disorder, the researchers took blood samples from all eighty-one members of the clan. Using new techniques from the field of molecular biology, they isolated DNA (deoxyribonucleic acid, a nucleic acid present in the chromosomes that codes hereditary information) from each sample and cut the DNA into segments. Comparisons of the gene segments from bipolar family members with gene segments from their nonbipolar relatives revealed a discrepancy in a region on chromosome 11 near two known genes — the insulin gene and the Ha-ras-1 gene. On the basis of this discovery, the researchers concluded that a gene or group of genes in this region of chromosome 11 is responsible for a predisposition to develop bipolar disorders.

These two lines of investigation have led some theorists to conclude that at least two different genes may establish a predisposition to develop a bipolar disorder (Hodgkinson et al., 1990; Robertson, 1987). Other theorists, however, have interpreted the very different findings from the two lines of research to mean that the logic behind these genetic studies is faulty and leads to incorrect conclusions about the existence of genetic factors in bipolar disorders (Kelsoe et al., 1989). It is important to remember, after all, that the hypothesized genes pointed to in each line of research have yet to be isolated and analyzed.

## MOOD DISORDERS: THE STATE OF THE FIELD

Because mood disorders are so prevalent in our society, because clinicians treat so many clients with these disorders, and because so much research has been conducted, it seems as though a great deal is known about the subject. In truth, clinicians do have a lot of information about mood disorders, but they do not yet fully understand all that they know.

We know that there are two distinct patterns of mood disorder — unipolar depression and bipolar disorders. Patterns of unipolar depression are quite prevalent; they tend to occur more among women, to subside eventually even without treatment, and to recur periodically. Bipolar disorders are relatively uncommon; they are equally distributed among women and men, are unlikely to subside fully without treatment, and are very likely to recur in the absence of treatment. We also know that both unipolar depression and bipolar disorders are marked by a range of symptoms besides dysfunctional mood, including significant problems in cognitive, motivational, behavioral, and somatic functioning, so that they have a powerful impact on the sufferer's life.

Researchers have also done a remarkable job of identifying important factors that accompany and perhaps cause the mood disorders. In bipolar disorders, only one set of factors has emerged consistently — biological factors. The present assumption is that certain biological abnormalities, perhaps inherited and perhaps precipitated by life stress, cause bipolar disorders.

The situation with unipolar patterns of depression is much more complex. Researchers have identified several factors that are closely tied to these disorders, including a reduction in positive reinforcements, a perception of helplessness, negative ways of thinking, biological abnormalities, and in some cases life stresses such as the loss of a loved one. Precisely how these factors relate to unipolar depression is, to say the least, unclear. It may be that each pattern of unipolar depression represents a distinct disorder, and that each factor causes a particular depressive disorder. Alternatively, the different patterns of unipolar depression may be but variations of the same basic disorder. If so, the factors uncovered by researchers may relate to this single disorder in any of several ways:

1. One of these factors may indeed be the key cause of unipolar depression. That is, one theory may be more useful than any of the others for predicting and understanding how a unipolar depression unfolds. If so, cognitive and biological factors would seem to be the leading candidates, for both have been found to precede and predict depression.

2. Any of the leading factors may be capable of initiating a unipolar pattern of depression (Akiskal & McKinney, 1975, 1973). This initial cause may then trigger problems in other areas of functioning, thus establishing a syndrome of unipolar depression in all its breadth. Some people might begin with low norepinephrine activity, which could predispose them to react helplessly in stressful situations, interpret events negatively, and enjoy fewer pleasures in life. Others may begin by experiencing a severe loss that sets off helplessness reactions, low norepinephrine activity, and reductions in positive reinforcements. Regardless of the initial cause, these people may all move toward a "final common pathway" of unipolar depression.

A number of studies support this interpretation. Some researchers have found that when animals are subjected to uncontrollable negative reinforcements, they not only react helplessly but also develop norepinephrine and serotonin depletions in their brains (Maier, 1984). Other researchers have found that when animals' norepinephrine and serotonin supplies are experimentally reduced, the animals start exhibiting helplessness behavior (Weiss et al., 1976; Weiss, 1970). Clearly, one symptom of depression is capable of engendering or exacerbating others.

3. An interaction between two or more of the factors may be necessary to create an episode of unipolar depression. Perhaps people will become depressed only if they have low norepinephrine activity, feel helpless to control their reinforcements, *and* repeatedly blame themselves for negative events. This would help explain why only some helplessness-trained people actually come to exhibit helplessness in most studies, or why only some of the people with low norepinephrine levels become depressed. These persons may fail to fulfill all of depression's causal requirements.

4. The various factors isolated by researchers may play different roles in unipolar depression. Some may cause the disorder, some may result from it, and some may help maintain it. Peter Lewinsohn and his colleagues (1988) conducted a study aimed at clarifying this issue. They first assessed more than 500 randomly chosen subjects on several key depression factors, then assessed the subjects again eight months later to see who had in fact become depressed and which of the factors had predicted depression. Negative cognitions, life stress, and self-dissatisfaction were found to precede and predict depression; impoverished social relationships and reductions in positive reinforcements did not. The research team concluded that the former factors help cause unipolar depression, while the latter simply accompany or result from depression, and perhaps help maintain it. Given Lewinsohn's seminal role in developing the reinforcement explanation of depression, this study and its conclusion are most compelling.

Because of the work that has been done over the past twenty-five years, mood disorders are now being diagnosed and distinguished with greater precision, with more knowledge about their breadth and course, and with greater awareness of possible contributing factors. Many important puzzle pieces have been gathered. Now the task is to put them together into a meaningful picture that will suggest even better ways to predict, prevent, and treat the disorders.

# SUMMARY

**M**ost people's moods are transient and affect their lives only minimally, but people with mood disorders have moods that tend to last for months or years, dominate their interactions with the world, and disrupt their normal functioning. The victim of *unipolar depression,* the most common pattern of mood disorder, suffers exclusively from depression. In *bipolar* or *manic-depressive disorder,* periods of mania alternate with periods of depression.

**D**epression is characterized by severe and debilitating psychological pain that may keep intensifying over an extended period of time. Women are more likely than men to experience both severe and milder episodes of unipolar depression. Once depressed, a person has an increased risk of becoming depressed again.

The symptoms of depression span five areas of functioning: emotional, motivational, behavioral, cognitive, and physical. Depressed people are also at greater risk for suicidal behavior.

Many unipolar depressions seem to be triggered by stressful life events. Clinicians may distinguish *reactive (exogenous) depression,* which follows clear-cut precipitating events, from *endogenous depression,* which is assumed to be caused by internal factors. This distinction is often difficult to make, however.

Because of growing recognition that unipolar depression may have both situational and biological causes, it is probably best to view each of several theories as offering only a partial account of this disorder. According to the psychodynamic view of depression, a series of unconscious processes are set in motion when people experience real or imagined losses. People who introject feelings for the lost object may come to feel self-hatred and depression. Studies have supported the psychodynamic notion that people who experience early losses and early dependent relationships are more vulnerable to depression later in life.

The behavioral view says that when people experience significant reduction in their total rate of positive reinforcements, they are more likely to develop a depressive style of functioning. As they become less active, their rate of positive reinforcements decreases still further, leading to still fewer positive behaviors and eventually to depression.

According to the cognitive view, depression results from negative thinking about oneself, the world, and the future. Four cognitive processes—*maladaptive attitudes,* the *cognitive triad, errors in thinking,* and *automatic thoughts*—generate the emotional, motivational, behavioral, and physical symptoms of depression, which confirm the negative cognitions and create a vicious cycle.

According to the learned helplessness theory of unipolar depression, people become depressed when they perceive a loss of control over the reinforcements in their lives and when they believe that they themselves are responsible for their helpless state. Three attributional dimensions determine a person's perception of control: internal–external, global–specific, and stable–unstable. People who attribute their loss of control to causes that are internal, global, and stable are more likely to suffer helplessness effects and depression.

According to the biological view, deficiencies in two chemical neurotransmitters, norepinephrine and serotonin, may cause depression. The genetic view suggests that an inherited predisposition to biochemical abnormalities underlies unipolar depression.

**M**ania is a state of dramatic, inappropriate, or disproportionate elevation in mood, a clinical picture almost opposite that of depression. The same five areas are affected: emotional (euphoria), motivational (enthusiasm), behavioral (hyperactivity), cognitive (optimism), and physical (high energy). Manic episodes almost always indicate a bipolar disorder, one in which depressive episodes also occur.

**B**ipolar disorder is much less common than unipolar depression, afflicts women and men equally, emerges between the ages of 15 and 35 years, and tends to recur if it is not treated. The lives of many people with bipolar disorders often fluctuate between extreme highs and lows. Those whose mood swings consist of milder depressive and milder manic episodes receive a diagnosis of *cyclothymia.*

**M**ost clinical models fail to explain bipolar patterns, but biological research has begun to provide clues. Mania has been related to high norepinephrine activity and a low level of serotonin. Researchers also suspect that sodium ions, which play a critical role in the transmission of messages in the brain, may become misaligned along the nerve cell's outer membrane, either causing neurons to be fired too easily, with resultant mania, or making it difficult for the neurons to fire, with resultant depression. And, finally, family pedigree studies suggest that people may inherit a predisposition to the biological abnormalities underlying bipolar disorders. Genetic linkage studies have identified at least two genes that may establish such a predisposition.

# TOPIC OVERVIEW

**TREATMENTS FOR UNIPOLAR
DEPRESSION**

Psychodynamic Therapy

Behavioral Therapy

Interpersonal Psychotherapy

Cognitive Therapy

Electroconvulsive Therapy

Antidepressant Drugs

**TREATMENTS FOR BIPOLAR
DISORDERS**

Lithium Therapy

Adjunctive Psychotherapy

# CHAPTER 9

# TREATMENTS FOR MOOD DISORDERS

When we look at people in the midst of profound depression or mania, it is sometimes hard to believe that their moods can ever return to normal. Nevertheless, many people with mood disorders eventually recover, either spontaneously or through treatment. Others at least learn to carry on effectively in the face of continued depression or mania. Consider two different experiences in the battle to overcome depression:

*It's as if it's all been washed away, as if I* haven't got time to think about the past now. I can't be bothered. I can't imagine ever getting de-

pressed. If it came back again, it would be a hell of a shock. I'm just confident that it's going to stay away.

*(Rowe, 1978, p. 65)*

*Now when I awaken in the morning and feel* so disgusted, I throw off the covers and pull up the window shade. Most of the time I still go back to bed for awhile, but I have made the first step. I then wash my face in cold water and get a cup of coffee. . . . It's a constant effort — this battle against the depression. I know that in the beginning of this illness, I couldn't do these things even if I had wanted to; now I can. With an effort I make condolence calls, visit friends, go to the theater — but I go.

*(Kraines & Thetford, 1977, p. 24)*

Among the things that happy people have in common are spiritual faith, social involvement, productive work that is linked to self-esteem, satisfying sleep, and a satisfying love relationship (Tice, 1990; Erber, 1990; Diener, 1984). It is not always clear, however, whether these are the causes or the effects of their happiness.

Their victories are of different orders, but these two people share an important accomplishment: their lives are no longer governed by their moods. Of the 10 million people with mood disorders in the United States, 20 to 30 percent, or 2 to 3 million, receive treatment in the hope of regaining some measure of control over their moods (Regier et al., 1988; Myers et al., 1984).

## TREATMENTS FOR UNIPOLAR DEPRESSION

A large and diverse group of therapists treat unipolar depression. An average of 10 percent of the clients of psychiatrists, psychologists, and social workers have this kind of disorder (Knesper et al., 1985) — and so do a large number of the therapists. Given the many therapists who treat unipolar depression, it is not surprising that a range of treatment approaches, from global to specific, have been employed.

## Psychodynamic Therapy

Believing that unipolar depression results from unconscious grieving over real or imagined losses compounded by excessive dependence on other people, psychodynamic therapists try to help depressed clients bring these processes to consciousness, so they can understand the source of their pain and learn to leave it behind them. As practitioners of a global therapy, these therapists use the same basic psychodynamic procedures with depressed clients that they use with others: they encourage the client to associate freely during therapy; suggest interpretations of the client's associations, dreams, and displays of resistance and transference; and help the client reexperience and reevaluate past events and feelings. Free association helped one patient recall the early experiences of loss that, according to his therapist, had set the stage for his depression:

> *A mong his earliest memories, possibly the earliest of all,* was the recollection of being wheeled in his baby cart under the elevated train structure and left there alone. Another memory that recurred vividly during the analysis was of an operation around the age of five. He was anesthetized and his mother left him with the doctor. He recalled how he had kicked and screamed, raging at her for leaving him.
>
> *(Lorand, 1968, pp. 325–326)*

In the following case, the therapist interpreted a depressed client's dream to trace his mood problem to early dependence and to real and symbolic losses:

> *T he patient reported a dream in which he was at his* father's gravesite, in which his dead father was lying. In the dream the patient was crying and others were trying to comfort him. He had the feeling that everyone close to him was sick. He woke from the dream crying. In his associations this patient remembered the actual death of his father, stating that at the time, "I felt as if my purpose in life had been extinguished." The patient had had a quasi-symbiotic relationship with his father, who had preferred him over the other children. He followed his father's orders to the letter, in return for which his father lavished praise on him and gave him substantial sums of money. He never dared to cross his father since he had the experience of witnessing what had occurred to his brothers when they disagreed even slightly with the father. This patient had grown up in a rural area where the father, a wealthy and influential business-

man, had ruled over a large estate like a small monarch. Although he had slavishly followed his father's instructions, the patient often had been irresponsible in his own affairs, and had lost moderate sums of money because of his naiveté. He had the dream after losing a considerable sum of money at cards. The dream may have represented an awareness that he was now on his own, yet there remained within him a desperate desire to be taken care of once again by a powerful other. The dream showed his characteristic turning to others to make things right, as his father had done in the past whenever he was in trouble.

*(Arieti & Bemporad, 1978, p. 300)*

At times psychodynamic therapists adjust their usual procedures to address special problems posed by depressed clients. If a client is too dejected even to associate freely early in therapy, the therapist may have to take a more active role than usual in the early therapy discussions (Bemporad, 1982; Spiegel, 1965; Kolb, 1956).

The therapist, by . . . introducing topics which he thinks the patient can discuss, may often help him talk of a wider range of subjects. Also, by asking specific questions the therapist may help the patient overcome his inability to talk about particular subjects. . . . If the therapist is too passive, the patient's silence may increase . . . and after each interview [the patient] may experience a sense of failure with increased depression.

*(Levine, 1968, p. 355)*

By the same token, psychodynamic therapists must deal particularly carefully with the transference behavior of depressed clients. Because of their extreme dependence on important people in their lives, depressed clients may cling to the therapist even more than other clients do, crying out for guidance and relief, and expecting the therapist to take care of them (Bemporad, 1982; Kolb, 1956). In describing her treatment sessions with a depressed client, one therapist wrote:

There followed a long, typical period during which the patient lived only in the aura of the analyst and withdrew from other personal relationships to a dangerous extent. The transference was characterized by very dependent . . . attitudes toward the analyst, but also by growing demands that I display self-sacrificing devotion in return.

*(Jacobson, 1971, p. 289)*

Some psychodynamic theorists believe that the therapist should make the depressed client aware of these extreme transference feelings early in treatment and help the client accept the therapist's limitations (Bemporad, 1982; Arieti & Bemporad, 1978; Jacobson, 1975; Kolb, 1956). Others believe that a transference discus-

sion of this kind should be postponed until "a later phase of the analysis, when the patient can better endure frustration, and can make demands without feeling guilt or fearing dismissal" (Lorand, 1968, pp. 334–335).

Psychodynamic therapists expect that in the course of treatment depressed clients will eventually become less dependent on others, cope with losses more effectively, and make corresponding changes in their daily lives (Bemporad, 1982; Jacobson, 1978). This kind of progress is seen in the case of a depressed middle-aged business executive:

*He had functioned well in the context of a favored* status relationship with his boss. However, he had been transferred to another department where his new boss was aloof and gave his colleagues little feedback. This new superior simply expected everyone to do their jobs and was not concerned with personal niceties. The patient found himself becoming more and more depressed when he failed to elicit the needed reassurance from his new superior. He vacillated between seeing no meaning in his work and getting furious at the company's usually trivial errors, which he now magnified. In therapy, he was able to connect his current plight to his childhood experience of devoting himself to pleasing his father. The latter rarely gave praise and was harshly critical of all the children, but the patient remembered feeling euphoric and important when the father did acknowledge some achievement.

The patient's father was still living and in a nursing home, where the patient visited him regularly. On one occasion, he went to see his father full of high expectations, as he had concluded a very successful business transaction. As he began to describe his accomplishments to his father, however, the latter completely ignored his son's remarks and viciously berated him for wearing a pink shirt, which he considered unprofessional. Such a response from the father was not unusual, but this time, as a result of the work that had been accomplished in therapy, the patient could objectively analyze his initial sense of disappointment and deep feeling of failure for not pleasing the older man. Although this experience led to a transient state of depression, it also revealed to the patient his whole dependent lifestyle — his use of others to supply him with a feeling of worth. This experience added a dimension of immediate reality to the insights that had been achieved in therapy and gave the patient the motivation to change radically his childhood system of perceiving himself in relation to paternal transference figures. This clinical vignette illustrates one of the major objectives of the working-through process: one must perceive usual situations in a new way and then use such insights for the purpose of change.

*(Bemporad, 1982, p. 291)*

Despite successful reports such as this one, researchers have found psychodynamic therapies to be helpful only occasionally in cases of unipolar depression (Prochaska, 1984; Berk & Efran, 1983). Two features of the approach have been cited to explain its limited effectiveness. First, as we noted earlier, depressed clients may be too passive and feel too fatigued to participate fully in therapy discussions and to exercise the subtle insight that psychodynamic therapy requires. Second, clients may become discouraged and end treatment too early when this long-term approach is unable to provide the quick relief that they desperately seek. Despite researchers' findings that psychodynamic therapies are of limited help in treating depression, these approaches continue to be employed widely to combat it (Berk & Efran, 1983; Chessick, 1976).

## Behavioral Therapy

Peter Lewinsohn has developed an influential behavioral treatment for unipolar patterns of depression corresponding to his view that such patterns are related to a decrease in the number of positive reinforcements in a person's life (Teri & Lewinsohn, 1986; Lewinsohn et al., 1984; Lewinsohn, Sullivan, & Grosscup, 1982; Lewinsohn, 1975, 1974, 1973). Therapists who take this approach reintroduce clients to events and activities that the clients once found pleasurable. The therapists also systematically reinforce nondepressive behavior and help clients improve their interpersonal skills.

**Reintroducing Pleasurable Events** The therapist first identifies activities that are reinforcing by having the client monitor his or her daily activities and fill out a Pleasant Events Schedule and an Activity Schedule (see Table 9-1). Given this information, the therapist then selects approximately ten activities that the client considers pleasurable, such as going shopping or taking photographs, and encourages the client to set up a weekly schedule for engaging in them (Lewinsohn,

TABLE 9-1

### SAMPLE ITEMS IN A BEHAVIORAL ACTIVITY SCHEDULE

Make check mark(s) within the parentheses to correspond to the activities of this day.
Only activities that were at least a little pleasant should be checked.

| Activity | Frequency check | Activity | Frequency check |
|---|---|---|---|
| 1. Buying things for myself | ( ) | 17. Having a lively talk | ( ) |
| 2. Going to lectures or hearing speakers | ( ) | 18. Having friends come to visit | ( ) |
| 3. Saying something clearly | ( ) | 19. Giving gifts | ( ) |
| 4. Watching TV | ( ) | 20. Getting letters, cards, or notes | ( ) |
| 5. Thinking about something good in the future | ( ) | 21. Going on outings (to the park, a picnic, or a barbecue, etc.) | ( ) |
| 6. Laughing | ( ) | 22. Photography | ( ) |
| 7. Having lunch with friends or associates | ( ) | 23. Reading maps | ( ) |
| 8. Having a frank and open conversation | ( ) | 24. Wearing clean clothes | ( ) |
| 9. Working on my job | ( ) | 25. Helping someone | ( ) |
| 10. Being helped | ( ) | 26. Talking about my children or grandchildren | ( ) |
| 11. Wearing informal clothes | ( ) | 27. Meeting someone new of the opposite sex | ( ) |
| 12. Being with friends | ( ) | 28. Seeing beautiful scenery | ( ) |
| 13. Reading essays or technical, academic, or professional literature | ( ) | 29. Eating good meals | ( ) |
| 14. Just sitting and thinking | ( ) | 30. Writing papers, essays, articles, reports, memos, etc. | ( ) |
| 15. Social drinking | ( ) | 31. Doing a job well | ( ) |
| 16. Seeing good things happen to my family or friends | ( ) | 32. Having spare time | ( ) |

*Source:* Lewinsohn et al., 1976, p. 117.

1973; Lewinsohn, Weinstein, & Shaw, 1969). Studies have shown that reintroducing selected activities in this way leads to increased participation in the activities and to a better mood (Lewinsohn & Graf, 1973). The following case description exemplifies this process:

*This patient was a forty-nine-year-old housewife whose* children were grown and no longer living at home. Her major interest in life was painting, and indeed she was an accomplished artist. She developed a depression characterized by apathy, self-derogation, and anxiety while she was incapacitated with a severe respiratory infection. She was unable to paint during her illness and lost interest and confidence in her art work when she became depressed. Her therapist thought that she could restitute her sources of "reinforcement" if she could be motivated to return to the easel. After providing a supportive relationship for a month, the therapist scheduled a home visit to look at her paintings and to watch and talk with her while she picked up her brush and put paint to canvas. By the time he arrived, she had already begun to paint and within a few weeks experienced a gradual lessening of her depression.

*(Liberman & Raskin, 1971, p. 521)*

**Reinforcing Nondepressive Behavior**  Behaviorists argue that when people become depressed, old adaptive behavior such as going to work and seeking out pleasurable activities tends to be replaced by negative, depressive behavior such as complaining, crying, and self-deprecation, behavior that serves to keep people and opportunities for positive reinforcement at a distance. To combat this pattern, therapists may use a *contingency management* approach: they systematically ignore a client's depressive behavior while giving attention and other rewards to constructive statements and behavior.

In one case a program of consistent reinforcement was used to speed up the plodding rate of speech that a depressed client had developed (Robinson & Lewinsohn, 1973). Early in therapy, the therapist rewarded faster speech patterns by giving the client increased therapy time when he talked more rapidly. In later sessions, the therapist turned on an irritating buzzer whenever the client talked slowly, and rewarded faster speech by turning the buzzer off. As the client's speech rate increased under this treatment, his depression seemed to lessen as well.

Therapists may also use family members and friends as part of this contingency management approach. Spouses may be instructed to ignore their mates' depressive behaviors and to reward their adaptive behaviors (Liberman & Raskin, 1971). Sometimes a formal contract is even formulated (see Table 9-2), in which the client promises to engage in more pleasant activities and a family member or friend pledges to reward the client for doing so.

TABLE 9-2

## CONTRACT WITH FRIEND OR RELATIVE TO INCREASE POSITIVE ACTIVITIES

My goal for the coming week is to increase the number of pleasant activities which I engage in by . . . . . . . . . . . . . . events or activities. I have explained to . . . . . . . . . . . . . . why this is important for improving my disposition and he/she has agreed to help.

I promise to forfeit . . . . . . . . (put here the amount of money, a valued possession, or a service you might perform for your friend or relative) if I don't achieve the goal of increased activity which I have stated above.

*Signed* . . . . . . . . . . . . . . . . . . . . . . . . . . .
*(your name)*

I understand that . . . . . . . . . . . . . . (your name) is attempting to increase his/her activity in the coming week and I agree to help. Specifically, I agree to provide warmth and encouragement when . . . . . . . . . . . . . . . . . . . (your name) tells me about activities or events which have occurred, and to give . . . . . . . . . . . . . . . . . . (specify some event, amount of money, or other reward you think will motivate you to achieve your goal) to . . . . . . . . . . . . . . . . . (your name) if he/she achieves the goal which he/she has established.

*Signed* . . . . . . . . . . . . . . . . . . . . . . . . . . .
*(friend's name)*

*Source:* Lewinsohn et al., 1976, p. 110.

**Teaching Social Skills**  When depressed people behave despondently in social situations, the people around them are likely to feel uncomfortable and keep their distance; the depressed person is then deprived of an important source of reinforcement for positive social behavior. Thus Lewinsohn and other behavioral therapists argue that it is particularly important for depressed people to be taught, or at least retaught, social skills.

In one program for strengthening the social skills of depressed clients in group therapy, the therapist first observed the interpersonal behavior of group members and determined which areas of social interaction each person needed to work on (Lewinsohn, Weinstein, & Alper, 1970). One individual needed to offer more positive comments to others; another needed to respond more quickly and graciously to praise. As clients practiced their needed social skills, other group members and the therapist provided feedback and reinforcement. In a related group technique, called *personal effectiveness training,* group members are asked to rehearse a variety of social roles with one another as a way of improving "expressive" behaviors such as eye contact, facial expression, tone of voice, and posture. Studies indicate that the social skills of depressed clients improve under such techniques (King, Liberman, & Roberts, 1974).

**Effectiveness of Lewinsohn's Behavioral Treatment** Lewinsohn's behavioral techniques seem to be of little help when only one of them is applied. When one group of depressed people were instructed to increase their pleasant activities over the course of a week and a control group of depressed subjects were told simply to monitor their activities over the same span of time, neither group showed any improvement (Hammen & Glass, 1975).

On the other hand, treatment programs that combine several of Lewinsohn's behavioral techniques do appear to reduce depressive symptoms, particularly if the depression is mild or moderate (Teri & Lewinsohn, 1986; Lewinsohn et al., 1984). A series of studies conducted by Lewinsohn and his colleagues (1982) concluded that moderately depressed clients who received a combination of his behavioral treatments decreased an average of 15 points on the Beck Depression Inventory (a commonly used assessment tool) and 20 points on the MMPI Depression Scale, indicating a shift from moderate to mild levels of depression.

In more recent years Lewinsohn and his colleagues have plotted out a comprehensive group treatment program consisting of lectures, classroom activities, homework assignments, and even a textbook addressed to depressed clients (Teri & Lewinsohn, 1986; Lewinsohn et al., 1984). This group program, which consists of two-hour group sessions scheduled over eight weeks, seems to reduce depressive symptoms substantially in 80 percent of the clients and to help clients maintain these gains. Unfortunately, the approach has, once again, proved less helpful to severely depressed people than to those who are mildly or moderately depressed.

## Interpersonal Psychotherapy

Gerald Klerman and Myrna Weissman have developed an influential and successful form of treatment for unipolar patterns of depression known as *interpersonal psychotherapy,* or *IPT* (Klerman, Weissman, & Rounsaville, 1984), based on the premise that "depression, regardless of symptom patterns, severity, biological vulnerability, or personality traits, occurs in an interpersonal context and that clarifying and renegotiating this context . . . is important to the person's recovery" (Weissman et al., 1982, p. 296).

Borrowing a variety of concepts and techniques from psychodynamic, humanistic, and behavioral therapists, IPT therapists make a concerted effort to rectify the interpersonal problems that they believe accompany depressive functioning (Klerman et al., 1984). Over the course of twelve to sixteen weekly sessions, these therapists help clients to develop insights into their interpersonal conflicts, change their social situations, and acquire social skills.

**Addressing Key Interpersonal Problem Areas** IPT therapists believe that therapy for depressed persons must address at least one of four interpersonal problem areas. First, the depressed person may, as psychodynamic theorists suggest, be experiencing a *grief reaction* over the loss of a significant loved one. In such cases, IPT therapists encourage clients to think about the loss, explore their relationship with the lost person, and acknowledge and express angry feelings toward the departed. As clients formulate new ways of remembering the lost person, they are also expected to develop new relationships to "fill the empty space." IPT therapists often help clients consider alternative ways of becoming involved with other people, such as by dating or through work-related activities (Weissman et al., 1982).

Second, depressed people often find themselves in the midst of an *interpersonal role dispute,* according to IPT therapists. Role disputes occur when two people have different expectations about their relationship and about the roles each should play. Such disputes may lead to open conflicts or smoldering resentments, and to depressed feelings. IPT therapists help clients to explore the role disputes that may exist in their relationship, including how each party contributes to the dispute. Over the course of treatment, therapists may also help clients develop and pursue strategies for solving their role disputes.

Depressed people may also be experiencing *interpersonal role transition.* People can have great difficulty coping with significant life changes, such as divorce or the birth of a child. As with a grief reaction, they may experience the change itself as a loss, but usually what they feel even more keenly is an inability to cope with the *role* change that accompanies the loss, possibly because they perceive the situation as threatening to their self-esteem and sense of identity. Here is an IPT therapist's description of a woman who becomes depressed shortly after her divorce.

*Following the divorce . . . she finds that her married* female friends, who had hitherto been an important source of support for the patient, have now begun to withdraw from her because they perceive her as a threat to their own marriages. In addition, the patient is experiencing feelings of inadequacy (in the mother role) vis-à-vis her children because they seem to blame her for "sending Daddy away." Feeling lonely, abandoned, inadequate, and deprived of her usual social supports, she seeks treatment. What distinguishes this patient's problem from a traditional grief reaction is that she is not mourning her husband so much as her former role of "married woman"; her depression is not related to the separation from her husband, as such, but to her difficulty in coping with the transition from the role of wife and mother to the role of single parent.

*(Weissman et al., 1982, p. 303)*

When unipolar depression is related to role transition, IPT therapists help clients review and evaluate their old roles, explore the opportunities offered by the new roles, and develop the social support system and skills the new roles require. Mastery of the new roles is expected to produce a sense of optimism and to help restore the clients' self-esteem.

The fourth interpersonal problem area that may accompany depression is the existence of some ***interpersonal deficits,*** such as extreme shyness, insensitivity to others' needs, or social awkwardness. According to Weissman and Klerman (1982), depressed people who have a history of inadequate or unsustaining interpersonal relationships often display such deficits. It is common for such people to have experienced a number of severely disrupted relationships as children and never to have established intimate relationships as adults. IPT therapists use psychodynamic procedures to help these clients recognize and overcome past traumas and underlying conflicts that have inhibited their social development. They may also use behavioral techniques such as social skills training or assertiveness training to improve a client's social effectiveness. In the following therapy discussion, the therapist encourages the client to recognize the effect his demeanor has on others.

*Client:* *(After a long pause with eyes downcast, a sad facial expression, and slumped posture)* People always make fun of me. I guess I'm just the type of guy who really was meant to be a loner, damn it. *(Deep sigh)*

*Therapist:* Could you do that again for me?

*Client:* What?

*Therapist:* The sigh, only a bit deeper.

*Client:* Why? *(Pause)* Okay, but I don't see what . . . okay. *(Client sighs again and smiles)*

*Therapist:* Well, that time you smiled, but mostly when you sigh and look so sad I get the feeling that I better leave you alone in your misery, that I should walk on eggshells and not get too chummy or I might hurt you even more.

*Client:* *(A bit of anger in his voice)* Well, excuse me! I was only trying to tell you how I felt.

*Therapist:* I know you felt miserable, but I also got the message that you wanted to keep me at a distance, that I had no way to reach you.

*Client:* *(Slowly)* I feel like a loner, I feel that even you don't care about me — making fun of me.

*Therapist:* I wonder if other folks need to pass this test, too?

*(Young & Beier, 1984, p. 270)*

**Effectiveness of Interpersonal Therapy** Relatively few studies have been conducted to test the effectiveness of IPT, but those few have been comprehensive and methodologically impressive. They provide clear indications that IPT and related interpersonal approaches can be effective treatments for mild to severe cases of unipolar depression (Elkin et al., 1989, 1986, 1985; Nezu, 1986; Weissman et al., 1979). One study found that symptoms almost totally disappeared in 50 to 60 percent of depressed clients who received IPT treatment, compared to 29 percent of those who received placebo therapy (Elkin et al., 1989, 1986, 1985). Another compared the progress of depressed clients who received sixteen weeks of IPT with that of control clients who did not (Weissman et al., 1979; DiMascio et al., 1979). The members of the control group were permitted to see a clinician up to once a month during the sixteen-week period if they felt a real need to do so, and they were in fact removed from the study if their condition worsened before the study's end. On the basis of self-assessments and clinical evaluations, the IPT clients showed a significantly greater reduction of depressive symptoms than the control clients. Moreover, although a comparable improvement in social functioning was not apparent during the treatment period itself, researchers observed one year later that the IPT clients were functioning more effectively than the control clients in their social activities and in their families.

## Cognitive Therapy

In Chapter 8 we saw that in Aaron Beck's view unipolar depression is the result of a chain of cognitive errors. Beck believes that depressed people have ***maladaptive attitudes*** that lead to negatively biased ways of viewing themselves, the world, and their future, the so-called ***cognitive triad.*** These biased views combine with ***illogical ways of thinking*** to produce ***automatic thoughts,*** unrelenting negative thoughts that flood the mind and generate the symptoms of depression.

Beck has developed a cognitive treatment for unipolar depression that helps clients recognize and change their dysfunctional cognitive processes, thus improving both their mood and their behavior (Beck, 1991, 1985, 1967; Beck et al., 1979). The treatment, which usually requires twelve to twenty sessions, is similar to Albert Ellis's rational-emotive therapy (discussed in Chapters 5 and 7), but is tailored more to the specific cognitive errors found in depression. The approach begins with a complete assessment of the client's symptoms (see Box 9-1), followed by four successive phases of treatment.

**Phase 1: Increasing Activities and Elevating Mood** Believing that depressed people could benefit from participating in more activities, therapists set the stage for cognitive therapy by encouraging clients to become more active and confident. A behavioral-like approach is used in which the therapist and client spend time during each session preparing a detailed schedule of hourly activities for the coming week (see Figure 9-1). The initial weekly schedule may be confined to such simple activities as calling a friend and eating dinner with family members. Gradually the assignments become more challenging, but always within the client's grasp. As clients become more active from week to week, their mood is expected to improve. Obviously, this aspect of treatment is similar to Lewinsohn's behavioral approach. Beck, however, believes that the increases in activity and improvements in mood produced by this approach will not by themselves lead a person out of

depressive functioning; cognitive interventions must follow. Inasmuch as Beck incorporates behavioral techniques in the early stage of treatment, it is probably more accurate to call his overall approach a cognitive-behavioral, rather than purely cognitive, intervention.

**Phase 2: Examining and Invalidating Automatic Thoughts** Once clients are somewhat active again and feeling some relief from their depression, they are better able to observe and think about themselves. Cognitive therapists then help educate them about their unrelenting negative automatic thoughts, assigning "homework" in which the client must recognize and record the thoughts as they occur. Some clients are even instructed to use "wrist counters" to help them become aware of how many automatic thoughts they experience in the course of a day.

The automatic thoughts are then reviewed in the therapy session. The client, of course, considers the thoughts realistic, but the therapist questions their validity. In session after session, therapist and client engage in a form of collaborative empiricism in which they test the objective reality behind the thoughts and often conclude that they are groundless. Beck offers the following exchange as an example of this sort of review.

|  | Monday | Tuesday | Wednesday | Thursday | Fr |
|---|---|---|---|---|---|
| 9–10 |  | Go to grocery store | Go to museum | Get ready to go out |  |
| 10–11 |  | Go to grocery store | Go to museum | Drive to Doctor's appointment |  |
| 11–12 | Doctor's appointment | Call friend | Go to museum | Doctor's appointment |  |
| 12–1 | Lunch | Lunch | Lunch at museum |  |  |
| 1–2 | Drive home | Clean front room | Drive home |  |  |
| 2–3 | Read novel | Clean front room | Washing |  |  |
| 3–4 | Clean bedroom | Read novel | Washing |  |  |
| 4–5 | Watch TV | Watch TV | Watch TV |  |  |
| 5–6 | Fix dinner | Fix dinner | Fix dinner |  |  |
| 6–7 | Eat with family | Eat with Family | Eat with family |  |  |
| 7–8 | Clean kitchen | Clean kitchen | Clean kitchen |  |  |
| 8–12 | Watch TV, read novel, sleep | Call sister, watch TV, read novel, sleep | Work on rug, read novel, sleep |  |  |

**FIGURE 9-1** In the early stages of cognitive therapy for depression, the client and therapist prepare a weekly activity schedule such as this. Activities as simple as watching television or calling a friend are specified. *(Adapted from Beck et al., 1979, p. 122.)*

*Therapist:* Why do you think you won't be able to get into the university of your choice?

*Patient:* Because my grades were really not so hot.

*Therapist:* Well, what was your grade average?

*Patient:* Well, pretty good up until the last semester in high school.

*Therapist:* What was your grade average in general?

*Patient:* A's and B's.

*Therapist:* Well, how many of each?

*Patient:* Well, I guess, almost all of my grades were A's but I got terrible grades my last semester.

*Therapist:* What were your grades then?

*Patient:* I got two A's and two B's.

*Therapist:* Since your grade average would seem to me to come out to almost all A's, why do you think you won't be able to get into the university?

*Patient:* Because of competition being so tough.

*Therapist:* Have you found out what the average grades are for admissions to the college?

*Patient:* Well, somebody told me that a B+ average would suffice.

*Therapist:*  Isn't your average better than that?

*Patient:*  I guess so.

*(Beck et al., 1979, p. 153)*

**Phase 3: Identifying Distorted Thinking and Negative Biases**  As clients recognize the fallacies in their automatic thoughts, cognitive therapists point out that illogical thinking processes may be contributing to these thoughts. The depressed student was using "all-or-nothing" (dichotomous) thinking when she concluded that any grade lower than A was a failure.

As clients review their automatic thoughts and thinking errors, therapists also help them to recognize that they are repeatedly interpreting events with a negative bias. Various techniques may be used to help clients identify and change their biased style of interpretation. With self-blaming clients, for example, therapists often use *reattribution techniques* to guide clients to identify possible causes of problems other than themselves. Beck offers the following example of this technique:

*Patient:*  I can't tell you how much of a mess I've made of things. I've made another major error of judgment which should cost me my job.

*Therapist:*  Tell me what the error in judgment was.

*Patient:*  I approved a loan which fell through completely. I made a very poor decision.

*Therapist:*  Can you recall the specifics about the decision?

*Patient:*  Yes. I remember that it looked good on paper, good collateral, good credit rating, but I should have known there was going to be a problem.

*Therapist:*  Did you have all the pertinent information at the time of your decision?

*Patient:*  Not at the time, but I sure found out 6 weeks later. I'm paid to make profitable decisions, not to give the bank's money away.

*Therapist:*  I understand your position, but I would like to review the information which you had at the time your decision was required, not 6 weeks after the decision had been made.

When the therapist and patient reviewed the pertinent information available at the time of his decision, the patient reasonably concluded that his initial decision was based on sound banking principles. He even recalled checking the client's financial background intensively. The patient was helped by the method of reattribution.

*(Beck et al., 1979, p. 188)*

**Phase 4: Altering Primary Attitudes**  In the final phase of therapy, therapists help clients to change their primary attitudes, the central beliefs that have predisposed them to depression in the first place. During the previous three phases of therapy, many clients will already have begun to see the maladaptiveness of their attitudes and started to alter them on their own. By encouraging clients to test their attitudes, therapists can foster further revision, as in the following therapy discussion:

*Therapist:*  On what do you base this belief that you can't be happy without a man?

*Patient:*  I was really depressed for a year and a half when I didn't have a man.

*Therapist:*  Is there another reason why you were depressed?

*Patient:*  As we discussed, I was looking at everything in a distorted way. But I still don't know if I could be happy if no one was interested in me.

*Therapist:*  I don't know either. Is there a way we could find out?

*Patient:*  Well, as an experiment, I could not go out on dates for a while and see how I feel.

*Therapist:*  I think that's a good idea. Although it has its flaws, the experimental method is still the best way currently available to discover the facts. You're fortunate in being able to run this type of experiment. Now, for the first time in your adult life you aren't attached to a man. If you find you can be happy without a man, this will greatly strengthen you and also make your future relationships all the better.

*(Beck et al., 1979, pp. 253–254)*

Therapists expect that repeated tests of and challenges to a client's basic attitudes will help the client form a less self-defeating way of thinking. Thus the cognitive core of the depression is removed.

**Effectiveness of Cognitive Therapy**  Over the past decade more than half of the studies evaluating the effectiveness of unipolar depression therapy have focused on Beck's approach (Weissman, 1984), and most of those studies have concluded that mildly to severely depressed people who receive cognitive therapy do indeed improve significantly more than those who receive placebo treatments or no treatments at all (Beck, 1991; Elkin et al., 1989, 1986, 1985; Blackburn, 1985, 1984; Wilson et al., 1983). Approximately 50 to 60 percent of clients treated with this approach show a total remission of depressive symptoms, compared to 29 percent of those who receive placebo treatments (Elkin et al., 1989, 1986, 1985). Studies also indicate that clients who do respond to this approach display steady improvements in their cognitive functioning (for example, progressively less pessimism) over the course of therapy, and that these improvements correlate strongly with improvements in depression (Seligman et al., 1988).

In view of the strong research support for Beck's approach, increasing numbers of therapists have been employing it. Many have developed group programs to make the therapy more readily available to greater numbers of people (Eidelson, 1985). Thus far, however, research suggests that cognitive therapy may be less effective in groups than in individual therapy sessions (Rush & Watkins, 1981).

## Electroconvulsive Therapy

Two patients describe their experiences with electroconvulsive therapy:

*S*trapped to a stretcher, you are wheeled into the ECT room. The electroshock machine is in clear view. It is a solemn occasion; there is little talk. The nurse, the attendant, and the anesthetist go about their preparation methodically. Your psychiatrist enters. He seems quite matter-of-

---

=== BOX 9-1 ===

# Assessing Depression

If it looks like a duck, walks like a duck, and quacks like a duck, then it probably is a duck. Although many issues in abnormal psychology are more complex than they initially appear, people of all sorts tend to believe that depression is as easily identifiable as a duck. If you look sad, move lethargically, and speak in unhappy tones, then you are probably depressed. However, although there are a number of behavioral signs that a person is suffering from a depressive episode, the actual diagnosis of depression is considerably more difficult than one might expect.

The challenge to clinicians is to develop measures that accurately assess depression. Because strong evidence has been collected in the past ten years suggesting that depression has identifiable biological and cognitive components, it is not surprising that the most widely used diagnostic tools for assessing depression are those that measure physical and cognitive parameters.

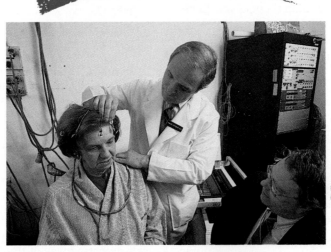

One means of assessing depression is to take electroencephalogram recordings of people while they sleep. Many people who are clinically depressed, especially older persons, demonstrate a shorter-than-average interval between the onset of sleep and the first REM sleep period.

Two prevalent biological assessment techniques are the *dexamethasone suppression test (DST)* and the *phenylethylamine test.* The first test is based on research linking the activity of the hypothalamic-pituitary-adrenal cortical region of the brain to depression. The hormone *cortisol*, which is regulated by this system, is found in higher levels in depressed people than in nondepressed people. A drug called dexamethasone suppresses or reduces the level of cortisol in most people, but does not have that effect on people who are depressed. This finding suggests that their hypothalamic-pituitary-adrenal system is overactive. In any event, the failure of dexamethasone to suppress a person's cortisol level is seen as a positive diagnosis of depression.

More recently depression has also been linked to phenylethylamine (PEA), an amphetaminelike substance found in the brain. A high level of PEA is associated with wakefulness, excitement, and pleasure. Phenyl acetate (PAA) is a chemical by-product of PEA breakdown, and the amount of PEA in the brain is inferred from the amount of PAA excreted in the urine. Studies have linked depression with a low level of PAA in the urine, and hence the test is considered a reliable indicator of depression (Sabelli et al., 1986). Studies showing that the antidepressant phenelzine increases PEA provide further evidence that PAA measurement is a valid indicator of depression (McGrath et al., 1988).

fact, businesslike—perhaps a bit rushed. "Everything is going to be just fine. I have given hundreds of these treatments. No one has ever died." You flinch inside. Why did he say that? But there is no time to dwell on it. They are ready. The electrodes are in place. The long clear plastic tube running from the bottle above ends with a needle in your vein. An injection is given. Suddenly—terrifyingly—you can no longer breathe; and then. . . . You awaken in your hospital bed. There is a soreness in your legs and a bruise on your arm you can't explain. You are confused to find it so difficult to recover memories. Finally, you stop struggling in the realization that you have no memory for

what has transpired. You were scheduled to have ECT, but something must have happened. Perhaps it was postponed. But the nurse keeps coming over to you and asking, "How are you feeling?" You think to yourself: "It must have been given"; but you can't remember. Confused and uncomfortable, you begin the dread return to the ECT room. You have forgotten, but something about it remains. You are frightened.

*(Taylor, 1975)*

*Dr. Persad met us on the sixth floor at seven-forty-five. He tried to calm me down, and I recall his saying that*

---

In the cognitive realm, the Beck Depression Inventory (BDI) is one of the most widely used assessment tools for diagnosing clinical depression (Beck et al., 1961). Originally developed for use in guiding an interview, it eventually became a popular self-report questionnaire in which clients select statements that reflect their attitudes toward themselves. A version containing thirteen items was later introduced as a quick way for family physicians to screen patients for depression (Beck & Beck, 1972), but the original BDI contained twenty-one items, and it is that longer scale that has received the most attention. Studies have shown it to be valid and internally consistent (Beck et al., 1988). Sample items appear below. Examinees are asked to select the response (0, 1, 2, or 3) that best describes their thinking.

The Beck Depression Inventory is clearly not intended as a subtle probe of hidden attitudes. Its questions are direct, aimed at assessing cognitions of which the clients are consciously aware. The items are intended to reflect the types of distorted thinking and disturbances in feeling from which depressed people are thought to suffer (Vredenburg, Krames, & Flett, 1985).

These three assessment tools are only a small sample of the many techniques used to diagnose clinical depression. Because the parameters measured by a test depend on the theoretical assumptions behind it, not all assessment tools yield the same results. A positive DST, for example, may or may not correlate with a high BDI score. The effect of such discrepancies on diagnosis and treatment depends on the orientation of the individual practitioner. Because there is no consensus on the diagnosis, cause, or treatment of depression, different tests may in fact be detecting different problems. Distorted cognitions may constitute one form of depression, for example, while someone with a high PEA level may be suffering from a different depressive syndrome. Although there is no immediate answer to this problem, the best solution for now may be for clinicians to use a battery of tests and diagnose in accordance with what the majority of tests seem to indicate.

## SAMPLE ITEMS FROM THE BECK DEPRESSION INVENTORY

| Item | | Inventory |
|------|---|-----------|
| Suicidal ideas | 0 | I don't have any thought of killing myself. |
| | 1 | I have thoughts of killing myself but I would not carry them out. |
| | 2 | I would like to kill myself. |
| | 3 | I would kill myself if I had the chance. |
| Work inhibition | 0 | I can work about as well as before. |
| | 1 | It takes extra effort to get started at doing something. |
| | 2 | I have to push myself very hard to do anything. |
| | 3 | I can't do any work at all. |
| Loss of libido | 0 | I have not noticed any recent change in my interest in sex. |
| | 1 | I am less interested in sex than I used to be. |
| | 2 | I am much less interested in sex now. |
| | 3 | I have lost interest in sex completely. |

he had never seen anyone so agitated as I. The prospect of ECT really frightened me. . . .

I changed into my pajamas and a nurse took my vital signs [blood pressure, pulse, and temperature]. The nurse and other attendants were friendly and reassuring. I began to feel at ease. The anesthetist arrived and informed me that she was going to give me an injection. I was asked to lie down on a cot and was wheeled into the ECT room proper. It was about eight o'clock. A needle was injected into my arm and I was told to count back from 100. I got about as far as 91. The next thing I knew I was in the recovery room and it was about eight-fifteen. I was slightly groggy and tired but not confused. My memory was not impaired. I certainly knew where I was. I rested for another few minutes and was then given some cookies and coffee. Shortly after eight-thirty, I got dressed, went down the hall to fetch [my wife], and she drove me home. At home I enjoyed breakfast and then lay down for a few hours. Late in the morning I got dressed. I felt no pain, no confusion, and no agitation. I felt neither less depressed nor more depressed than I had before the ECT. . . . After about the third or fourth treatment I began to feel somewhat better. I started perking up. After the third treatment I went up to Dr. Persad's office and spoke to him briefly. He asked me if I had noticed any improvement and to what degree. I believed that I had improved 35 to 40 percent. Dr. Persad believed that the improvement was more likely to be 70 to 75 percent.

*(Endler, 1982, pp. 81–82)*

One of the most controversial forms of treatment for depression is *electroconvulsive therapy,* or *ECT* (Breggin, 1985; Friedberg, 1985). Clinicians and patients alike vary greatly in their opinions of it (see Table 9-3). Some consider it a safe biological procedure with minimal risks and few side effects; others believe it to be an extreme and frightening measure that can cause temporary memory loss and even neurological damage. Despite this heated controversy, ECT is still used, because it is one of the most effective and fastest-acting interventions for severe unipolar depression (Weiner & Coffey, 1988).

**The Treatment Procedure**  In an ECT procedure, one or more electrodes are attached to the patient's head and an electrical current of 65 to 140 volts is sent through the brain for half a second or less. In *bilateral ECT,* two electrodes are applied, one to each side of the forehead, and the current passes through the brain's frontal lobes.

TABLE 9-3

| ARGUMENTS FOR AND AGAINST ELECTROCONVULSIVE THERAPY | |
| --- | --- |
| **Arguments for ECT** | **Arguments against ECT** |
| Theory of ECT is based on correcting a malfunctioning neurophysiological mechanism. | ECT is not corrective and works to the contrary, causing serious neurological destruction. |
| ECT's immediate effectiveness is supported by a large body of well-documented research. | An equally large body of contradictory research can be juxtaposed; ECT's long-term applicability suffers from a high incidence of relapse. |
| Undesired effects are much less troublesome from ECT than from medication in many instances; such effects are typically transient and dissipate over time. | Undesired effects are more profound than acknowledged; potential exists for cognitive dysfunction, personality alteration, and permanent organic changes with repeated treatment. |
| ECT is a useful intervention in life-threatening situations such as suicidal intent. | No data exist to defend ECT's utility in life-threatening situations. |
| State regulations regarding voluntary informed consent are too restrictive and legally impede the necessary administration of ECT under certain conditions. | Specific guidelines for ensuring full informed consent are actually inconsistent from state to state and do not necessarily provide the patient with all essential details surrounding treatment effects and outcome. |

*Source:* Taylor & Carroll, 1987, p. 755.

A method used increasingly in recent years is **unilateral ECT,** in which a single electrode is applied, so that the current passes through only one side of the brain.

The electrical current causes a **convulsion,** or brain seizure, that lasts up to a few minutes. The convulsion itself, not any attendant pain, appears to be the key to ECT's effectiveness (Ottosson, 1985, 1960; Weiner, 1984). Patients can therefore be put to sleep with barbiturates before ECT is administered with no reduction of therapeutic impact. Use of a muscle relaxant, such as succinylcholine or curare, is also routine, to minimize the danger of physical injury from flailing about during the convulsion. Patients awaken approximately ten minutes after the current is applied. A typical program of ECT consists of six treatments administered over a two-week period, at the end of which time most patients feel less depressed than before the treatment was started (Silver & Yudofsky, 1988).

**The Origins of ECT**    The discovery that electric shock can be therapeutic was made by accident. The history of ECT can be traced to 1785, when Dr. W. Oliver, physician to England's royal family, was treating a patient with "mental difficulties." He accidentally gave the man an overdose of **camphor,** a widely used stimulant, and the patient went into a coma and had convulsions. When the patient awakened, Oliver reported, "His senses returned to him, and something like a flash of lightning preceded their return. He now quitted his confinement . . . , he became natural, easy, polite, and in every respect like himself" (Valenstein, 1973, p. 149). On the basis of this accident, a few doctors at the time concluded that convulsions can cure psychological problems and began giving large doses of camphor to other mentally disturbed patients.

Inducing convulsions did not, however, become a common means of treating mental disorders until the early 1930s. At that time a Hungarian physician named Joseph von Meduna observed that schizophrenic and other psychotic people rarely suffered from epilepsy and that epileptic people rarely were psychotic. Moreover, in the few people who were both psychotic and epileptic, epileptic seizures seemed to remove psychotic symptoms temporarily. Believing that the convulsions of epilepsy somehow prevented psychosis, Meduna reintroduced camphor-caused convulsions as a form of treatment for psychosis.

Meduna was leaping to conclusions. A correlation between convulsions and lack of psychotic symptoms does not necessarily imply that one event causes the other. Moreover, subsequent research has challenged his observation that psychosis is inversely related to epilepsy. Nevertheless, whatever the validity of his argument, Meduna pursued and reported success with his convulsion-inducing treatment.

Camphor treatment had serious problems, however. It sometimes caused convulsions so strong that they were fatal; with other patients it would take as long as three hours to produce seizures or could fail to induce convulsions at all. Meduna found that a derivative of camphor, **metrazol,** worked in about fifteen seconds, but it too was very dangerous for some patients and unreliable for others.

At about the same time, Manfred Sakel, a Viennese physician, developed another technique for inducing convulsions in psychotic patients — **insulin coma therapy** (Sakel, 1933). He gave his patients large doses of insulin, causing their blood sugar to drop so dramatically that they went into a coma. This treatment, too, was helpful to some patients, but again quite dangerous, causing intense bodily stress, physical complications, and sometimes death.

A few years later, while looking for more effective and safer ways to induce convulsions in psychotic patients, an Italian psychiatrist named Ugo Cerletti discovered that he could sometimes induce seizures in dogs by attaching electrodes to their mouths and rectums and applying voltage. Still, he feared that placing electrodes on their heads, or on the heads of human beings, would be fatal. One day, however, he visited a slaughterhouse where he observed that before slaughtering hogs with a knife, butchers clamped the animals' heads with metallic tongs and applied an electrical current. The hogs fell unconscious and had convulsions, but they did not die from the current itself. Their comas merely made it easier for the butchers to kill them by other means. Cerletti wrote, "At this point I felt we could venture to experiment on man." Cerletti and his colleague Lucio Bini (1938) did experiment with humans and developed electroconvulsive therapy as a treatment for psychosis. As one might expect, much uncertainty and confusion accompanied their first clinical application of ECT, including doubts about the right of experimenters to impose such an untested treatment against a patient's will:

*The schizophrenic arrived by train from Milan without* a ticket or any means of identification. Physically healthy, he was bedraggled and alternately was mute or expressed himself in incomprehensible gibberish made up of odd neologisms. The patient was brought in but despite their vast animal experience there was great apprehension and fear that the patient might be damaged, and so the shock was cautiously set at 70 volts for one-tenth of a second. The low dosage predictably produced only a minor spasm, after which the patient burst into song. Cerletti suggested another shock at a higher voltage, and an excited and voluble discussion broke out among the spectators. . . . All of the staff objected to a further shock, protesting that the patient would probably die. Cerletti was familiar with committees and knew that postponement would inevitably mean prolonged and possible permanent procrastination, and so he decided to proceed at 110 volts for one-half second. However, before he could do so, the patient who had heard but so far not participated in the discussion sat up and pontifically proclaimed in clear Italian without hint of jargon "Non una seconda! Mortifera!" (Not again! It will kill me!). Professor Bini hesitated but gave the order to proceed. After recovery, Bini asked the patient "What has been happening to you?" and the man replied "I don't know; perhaps I've been asleep." He remained jargon-free and gave a complete account of himself, and was discharged completely recovered after 11 complete and 3 incomplete treatments over a course of 2 months.

*(Brandon, 1981, pp. 8–9)*

ECT soon became popular and was applied to a wide range of psychological problems, as is so often the case with a new technique. Its effectiveness with depressive disorders in particular became quite apparent. But in a final ironic turn of events, clinical researchers concluded that ECT was usually ineffective in cases of psychosis (Taylor & Carroll, 1987).

**Changes in ECT Procedures**    Although Cerletti gained international fame for this procedure, eventually he abandoned ECT and spent his remaining years seeking out alternative treatments for mental disorders (Karon, 1985). The reason: he abhored the broken bones, memory loss, confusion, and neural damage that the convulsions caused. Other clinicians have stayed with the procedure, however, and have modified it to reduce undesirable consequences (Sachs & Gelenberg, 1988; Fink, 1987, 1984, 1978).

In the early years of ECT, fractures and dislocations of the jaw and shoulder sometimes resulted either from the ECT convulsion itself or from excessive restraint by nurses and attendants (Kiloh, 1982). Practitioners avoid this problem today by giving patients muscle relaxants so that restraint is unnecessary and there is no undesirable tension in the body. Similarly, short-term anesthetics (barbiturates) are used to put patients to sleep during the procedure, thus reducing their terror and any consequent trauma. As muscle relaxants and barbiturates have become regular parts of the ECT procedure, they themselves have created new dangers, such as respiratory failure and cardiac arrhythmia, forcing doctors to add still further safeguards, such as the availability of oxygen and artificial respiration.

As a result of these changes, ECT is medically more complex than it used to be, but also less dangerous and

somewhat less frightening (Hamilton, 1986). The number of deaths related to ECT is similar to the mortality rate from general anesthesia—fewer than 3 in 10,000 (Fink, 1984, 1978; Kalinowsky, 1980). Cardiovascular and other physical complications still arise sometimes, though rarely in physically healthy patients (Sachs & Gelenberg, 1988; Weiner & Coffey, 1988; Kiloh, 1982).

Patients given *bilateral ECT* typically have difficulty remembering the period of time just before their ECT treatments, but this memory loss usually clears up after about a month (Sachs & Gelenberg, 1988; Fink, 1984; Price, 1982; Squire, 1982, 1977; Squire, Slater, & Miller, 1981; Campbell, 1961). Some bilateral ECT patients may also experience gaps in more distant memory, and this form of amnesia can be permanent (Price, 1982; Squire, 1982). *Unilateral ECT,* first developed in 1942, has reduced the danger of brain impairment (Liberson, 1945; Friedman & Wilcox, 1942). It requires less electrical current than bilateral ECT and causes less, if any, neural damage (Lancaster, Steinhart, & Frost, 1958; Goldman, 1949) and less memory loss and confusion, especially when the electrode is applied to the nondominant hemisphere of the brain (Sachs & Gelenberg, 1988; Pettinati & Rosenberg, 1984; Lancaster et al., 1958; d'Elia, 1974).

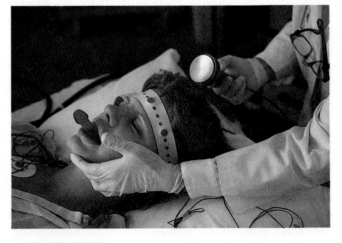

Patients given ECT today are administered barbiturate drugs to help them sleep, muscle relaxants to prevent convulsive jerks of the body and broken bones, oxygen to guard against brain damage, and unilateral, rather than bilateral, applications of electricity to reduce memory loss. After approximately six treatments over the course of two weeks, many severely depressed people find themselves in better spirits. Some do experience a degree of memory loss and confusion, but these effects are usually temporary.

Much of the evidence seems to suggest that unilateral ECT is often just as effective as bilateral ECT, although this issue is hotly debated (Sackeim, 1986; Fontaine & Young, 1984; Squire & Slater, 1978; Squire, 1977; d'Elia & Raotma, 1975). With these generally favorable results, unilateral ECT has increasingly been chosen by many practitioners over bilateral ECT (Asnis, Fink, & Saferstein, 1978).

**Effectiveness of ECT**    Although most studies on the effectiveness of ECT are "characterized by a lack of homogeneity in subject population, number of treatments, severity and subtypes of illness, and measurements of response" (Turek & Hanlon, 1977), properly controlled studies do indicate that ECT is an effective treatment for unipolar depression. In most studies that compare depressed patients receiving ECT with those receiving placebos, the ECT patients consistently improve more than the placebo patients (Janicak et al., 1985; Fink, 1984). Overall, these studies suggest that an average of 72 percent of ECT patients improve, compared to 23 percent of patients who receive placebos (Wechsler, Grosser, & Greenblatt, 1965). The procedure seems to be most effective in severe cases characterized by delusions or by such melancholic symptoms as motor retardation, sleep disturbance, and loss of appetite (Weiner & Coffey, 1988; Weiner, 1979).

How does ECT alleviate unipolar depression? Studies have consistently found that ECT increases neurotransmitter activity in the brain, suggesting to many theorists that the procedure corrects a deficit in norepinephrine and/or serotonin activity in depressed people (Sackeim, 1988; Essman, 1986; Fink, 1984, 1979; Kety, 1974; Fink, Kety, McGaugh, & Williams 1974). Although this is a promising theory, it is important to remember (1) that ECT causes neurons all over the brain to fire, leaving open the possibility that neurons other than the ones that use norepinephrine and serotonin are involved, and (2) that ECT-induced seizures also affect many other systems throughout the body (Sackeim, 1988; Holaday et al., 1986; Fink, 1984). Perhaps one of these other areas of impact is the key to understanding and treating unipolar depression.

**Declining Use of ECT**    Although research has repeatedly established the effectiveness of ECT, and although ECT techniques have improved steadily, the use of this procedure has generally declined since the 1950s. Apparently more than 100,000 patients a year underwent ECT during the 1940s and 1950s. Today as few as

50,000 per year are believed to receive it (Bower, 1985). There are several reasons for ECT's general decline.

1. *It is an extreme measure with undesirable consequences.* Applying an electrical current to the brain is, by any standard, a forceful form of intervention and a frightening prospect to many patients, irrespective of its effectiveness. The reassurances of clinicians and researchers cannot fully relieve this basic and understandable fear. Moreover, while today's techniques reduce the known dangers of ECT, the procedure can still result in confusion and memory loss, particularly in those who receive repeated administrations.
2. *It has a history of abuse.* During its early years, ECT was applied to a wide range of patients for many reasons and in many ways. Some people received literally hundreds of ECT treatments. ECT was also frequently misused as a means of punishing or controlling patients in mental hospitals (Donaldson, 1976; GAP, 1947).

   These abuses reflected a lack of appreciation of the power of this treatment and, many people argue, inadequate self-regulation by the clinical field (Winslade, 1988). In the 1950s and 1960s, motivated by a general atmosphere of increasing concern about social injustice, human rights, and abuse of power in the United States, many lay people and mental health professionals raised critical questions about ECT. By the 1970s, ECT had come under the watchful eye of consumer groups, courts, and state legislatures (Winslade et al., 1984). For example, a 1974 California bill limited the use of ECT, requiring that other treatments be tried first and that patients be assured of the right to refuse ECT (see Box 9-2). Since the 1960s, thirty-seven states have passed laws specifically governing ECT administration (Senter et al., 1984).
3. *There are now medications that treat depression.* The discovery of antidepressant drugs in recent decades has provided an attractive alternative medical tool for relieving unipolar depression. These drugs are effective, relatively inexpensive, and do not have "the same aura of extraordinariness" as ECT does (Heshe & Roeder, 1976).

## Antidepressant Drugs

In the 1950s, two kinds of drugs were discovered that seemed to alleviate depressive symptoms: *monoamine oxidase inhibitors (MAO inhibitors)* and *tricyclics* (see

═══════════════════════ BOX 9-2 ═══════════════════════

# ECT and the Law

Since its introduction in the 1930s, electroconvulsive therapy has increasingly come under the scrutiny of courts and state legislatures throughout the United States. The primary reason: the clinical field has done a poor job of regulating the use of this powerful and frightening procedure. When self-regulation fails, the government and legal system typically step in.

During ECT's first decade, psychiatrists and clinical researchers were left on their own to apply, experiment with, and modify the procedure (Winslade, 1988). Although this work often yielded impressive results, it also elicited numerous complaints from patients and some clinicians (Rothman, 1985). In 1947 a psychiatric task force, the Group for the Advancement of Psychiatry, finally conducted an investigation into "shock therapy" and issued a critical report noting that ECT was being used indiscriminately and excessively, often for punitive rather than therapeutic purposes and for controlling difficult, dangerous, and uncooperative patients (GAP, 1947). The next official report on ECT did not appear until 1978, more than thirty years later, when the American Psychiatric Association issued a task force report titled "Electroconvulsive Therapy." This report endorsed the use of ECT for severe depression when drugs have failed, and made detailed recommendations for *informing* patients about ECT and obtaining their *consent* to the procedure (Winslade, 1988; Winslade et al., 1984). Subsequent psychiatric reports have continued to endorse this procedure as a treatment for people with severe unipolar depression (Winslade, 1988; Rothman, 1985).

Legal regulation of ECT did not begin in earnest until the mid-1970s, when the California state legislature, responding to criticism from patients and former patients, passed a law restricting its use (Senter et al., 1984). All competent mental patients in California — both voluntary and involuntary — were granted the right to be informed about the nature of ECT and to consent to or refuse to undergo it. Thirty-seven states have since passed laws regulating ECT use. Some of these states, such as California and Texas, have strict regulations requiring concurring independent opinions from professionals that ECT is appropriate and necessary and mandating court hearings to determine whether involuntary patients are competent to consent to ECT. Other states, such as Massachusetts, have less restrictive laws that allow hospital superintendents to override a patient's right to refuse ECT simply by documenting that the procedure is being done for "good cause" (Senter et al., 1984).

Typically, state laws fail to specify all of the legal procedures to be used in ECT applications, leaving such specificity to state and federal judges who render decisions in particular cases (Winslade, 1988). Probably the most significant federal court decision regarding ECT has been *Wyatt* v. *Hardin*, which defined the legal standards for ECT treatments in Alabama, specifically forbidding some uses of ECT and establishing fourteen rules that severely restrict its practice (Winslade et al., 1984). This decision dictates, for example, that two psychiatrists (with the hospital director's concurrence) decide in each case that ECT is the most appropriate treatment, that a physical and neurological examina-

tion be conducted ten days before ECT, that anesthesia and muscle relaxants be used, that a psychiatrist and anesthesiologist be present during ECT, and that a single series of treatments be limited to twelve ECT sessions at most in a twelve-month period.

ECT is so widely distrusted by the public at large that some cities have tried to ban it altogether. In 1982 the city council of Berkeley, California, in response to a voter referendum, enacted a city ordinance prohibiting ECT and punishing violators with up to six months' imprisonment or a $500 fine or both (Weidlich, 1982). California's state court later ruled, however, that this city law was unconstitutional because it disregarded the state law permitting the therapeutic use of ECT and because it violated the rights of patients to choose or refuse ECT (*Northern California Psychiatric Society* v. *City of Berkeley*, 1983). At present ECT is not prohibited outright by law anywhere in the United States.

Most states now require that patients be informed about ECT and give their consent to the use of the procedure. But what exactly constitutes informed consent? The psychiatrist Max Fink, a leading authority on ECT, believes that clinicians should offer patients a detailed explanation of the ECT process, its risks and benefits, and its probable mechanism of action (Fink, 1988). He provides this explanation in the following consent form, as well as in broader discussions with the patient and family members and in a demonstration videotape that the patient and family members view.

Legal and judicial restrictions over the use of ECT have stirred heated debate in the clinical community.

## CONSENT FOR ELECTROTHERAPY

I, _____ , M.D.
(and _____ , M.D.) recommend
electrotherapy (brain stimulation, electroconvulsive therapy) for your present mental symptoms. These treatments have been given to thousands of mentally ill patients since 1938, with many improvements in the treatments and greater success in helping patients since then.

Treatments are given in the mornings before breakfast, in a specially equipped treatment room. You will be attended by an anesthetist, a nurse, and a physician.

A needle will be placed in your vein (like you may have had when samples were taken for blood tests) and an anesthetic will be injected. You will become drowsy and fall asleep. Other medicines will be given to relax your muscles. The anesthetist will help you breathe with pure oxygen through a mask.

The treatment is given while you are asleep. Momentary electric currents are passed through electrodes on the scalp to stimulate the brain. When the brain is stimulated, there are muscular contractions for up to a minute, but with proper relaxation, the contractions are barely measurable.

The treatments take only a few minutes. You are then moved to the recovery room where you will gradually wake up as after a deep sleep. You may feel groggy, probably have some muscular aches like after a lot of exercises, and some headache. You will return to your room, usually within an hour of the treatment. You may be hungry and will be given your breakfast and you will spend the rest of the morning on the ward with your nurse or attendant.

Treatments are given every other day for up to 12 treatments. Many patients improve rapidly and require fewer treatments, some require more than 12, but these will not be given without another discussion with you and your family.

There are some risks in the treatment. To provide safe anesthesia, the treatments are given in a room where special equipment and supplies for your protection are available. Patients often become confused, and may not know where they are when they awaken. This may be frightening, but the confusion usually disappears within a few hours. Memory for recent events may be disturbed, and dates, names of friends, public events, telephone numbers and addresses may be difficult to recall. In most patients, the memory difficulty (amnesia) is gone within four weeks after the last treatment, but in about 1 in 200 patients, the problems remain for months and even years. Death is a rare complication, occurring once in 40,000 treatments. Equally uncommon with modern anesthesia are bone fractures, broken or lost teeth, and spontaneous seizures after the treatment is over, but these may occur.

You may discontinue the treatments at any time, although you will be encouraged to continue until an adequate course is completed.

I, _____ , have read this description

of the treatments and these have been explained to me by _____ .

I agree to have the treatments and understand that Dr. _____

will be the physician in charge of my treatment.

_____

Dated: _____

Witness: _____

Agreed: _____

Relationship to Patient: _____

---

Many theorists believe that such protective measures are long overdue (Tenenbaum, 1985; Friedberg, 1976; Tien, 1975). Some would like to make it harder for administrators to override a patient's refusal of ECT, and some would require that all patients be given a complete description of ECT's effects when their consent is obtained (Friedberg, 1976). Others believe that the laws and courts have gone too far, that such requirements as voluntary consent, professional board approval, and full disclosure often slow or prevent the therapeutic administration of ECT, leaving many patients unnecessarily depressed and suicidal (Tenenbaum, 1985; Greenblatt, 1984; Kaufmann & Roth, 1981; Tien, 1975). Like the debate over the value and humaneness of ECT itself, this argument continues with no end in sight (Winslade, 1988; Taylor & Carroll, 1987).

Table 9-4). Before their discovery, the only drugs that brought any relief for depression were amphetamines. Amphetamines stimulated some depressed people to greater activity, but they did not result in greater joy.

**MAO Inhibitors**  As we saw in Chapter 5, the effectiveness of MAO inhibitors as a treatment for unipolar depression was discovered accidentally when physicians noted that *iproniazid* had an interesting effect on many tubercular patients: it seemed to make them happier (Sandler, 1990). It was found to have the same effect on depressed patients (Saunders et al., 1959; Kline, 1958; Loomer et al., 1958).

Iproniazid damages the liver, however, and caused

many deaths. Fortunately, researchers were able to create similar drugs, such as phenelzine (Nardil), isocarboxazid (Marplan), and tranylcypromine (Parnate), that were less toxic than iproniazid but equally powerful in fighting depression. What these drugs all had in common biochemically was that they slowed the body's production of the enzyme *monoamine oxidase (MAO).* Thus they were called *MAO inhibitors.* Research later indicated that approximately half of the mild to severely depressed patients who take MAO inhibitors are helped by them (Davis, 1980; Davis et al., 1967).

During the past few decades, scientists have learned how MAO inhibitors operate on the brain and how they alleviate depression. When the enzyme MAO interacts chemically with molecules of norepinephrine or serotonin, it removes the nitrogen, or amine, component from them by oxidation and destroys their effectiveness as neurotransmitters. People with high MAO levels thus may be left with too little norepinephrine or serotonin and become depressed. MAO inhibitors block this destructive activity of the enzyme MAO and thereby stop the destruction of norepinephrine and serotonin. The MAO inhibitors thus heighten the level of norepinephrine and serotonin activity in depressed people, and their depressive symptoms abate.

As clinicians have gained experience with the MAO inhibitors, they have learned that even the variants of iproniazid are capable of causing liver damage, high blood pressure, and sometimes death. The problem is that the enzyme MAO is essential for certain normal body functions. For example, many of the foods we eat—including cheeses, bananas, and some wines—contain *tyramine,* a chemical that can raise blood pressure dangerously if too much of it accumulates (Silver & Yudofsky, 1988). MAO in the liver and intestines serves the beneficial role of quickly breaking down tyramine into another chemical, and hence keeping blood pressure under control. Unfortunately, when people ingest MAO inhibitors to combat depression, the drugs also block MAO production in the liver and intestine, thus allowing tyramine to accumulate and placing those people in great danger of high blood pressure and perhaps sudden death (Blackwell et al., 1967).

Since becoming aware of this danger, doctors have been careful to restrict the diets of clients who are taking MAO inhibitors, warning them not to eat any of the long list of foods that contain tyramine (see Table 9-5). These restrictions, along with other dangers associated with MAO inhibitors, have reduced clinicians' enthusiasm for these medications, especially since researchers have succeeded in developing another type of antidepressant that is safer and often more effective (White & Simpson, 1981).

### TABLE 9-4

| DRUGS THAT REDUCE DEPRESSION | | |
|---|---|---|
| Class/generic name | Trade name | Usual daily maximum oral dose (mg) |
| **Tricyclics, first generation** | | |
| Imipramine | Tofranil | 300 |
| Amitriptyline | Elavil | 300 |
| Doxepin | Adapin Sinequan | 300 |
| Trimipramine | Surmontil | 300 |
| Desipramine | Norpramin Pertofrane | 300 |
| Nortriptyline | Aventyl Pamelor | 150 |
| Protriptyline | Vivactil | 60 |
| **Tricyclics, second generation** | | |
| Maprotiline | Ludiomil | 225 |
| Amoxapine | Asendin | 600 |
| Trazodone | Desyrel | 400 |
| Fluoxetine | Prozac | 80 |
| Clomipramine | Anafranil | |
| **Monoamine oxidase inhibitors** | | |
| Isocarboxazid | Marplan | 50 |
| Phenelzine | Nardil | 90 |
| Tranylcypromine | Parnate | 50 |

*Source:* Silver & Yudofsky, 1988, pp. 790–791.

## TABLE 9-5

### DIETARY RESTRICTIONS FOR PATIENTS TAKING MAO INHIBITORS

(Avoid these products one day before and two weeks after taking drugs to avoid blood pressure rise)

| Food products | Danger |
|---|---|
| **Foods** | |
| All cheese | Extreme |
| All foods containing cheese, such as pizza, fondue, many Italian dishes, and salad dressing | Extreme |
| Fresh cottage cheese, cream cheese, and yogurt in moderate amounts | Safe |
| All fermented or aged foods, especially aged meats or aged fish, such as aged corned beef, salami, fermented sausage, pepperoni, summer sausage, pickled herring | Moderate |
| Liver (chicken, beef, or pork) | Moderate |
| Liverwurst | Moderate |
| Broad bean pods (English bean pods, Chinese pea pods) | Extreme |
| Meat extracts or yeast extracts, such as Bovril or Marmite | Moderate |
| Baked products raised with yeast, such as bread | Safe |
| Yeast | Safe |
| Spoiled fruit, such as spoiled bananas, pineapples, avocados, figs, raisins | Moderate |
| Fresh fruits | Safe |
| **Drinks** | |
| Red wine, sherry, vermouth, cognac | Moderate |
| Beer and ale | Moderate |
| Other alcoholic drinks, such as gin, vodka, and whiskey, are permitted in true moderation | Safe |

*Source:* Jenicke, 1987.

**Tricyclics** The discovery of tricyclics in the 1950s was also accidental. Researchers had just discovered *phenothiazines,* the first group of drugs found to reduce schizophrenic symptoms, and eagerly began looking for similar drugs to combat schizophrenia. The Swiss psychiatrist Roland Kuhn thought that a drug called *imipramine* might be a possibility because its molecular structure was similar to that of the phenothiazines (Kuhn, 1958).

Imipramine did not turn out to be an effective treat-ment for schizophrenia, but doctors soon discovered that it did relieve unipolar depression in many persons. Imipramine (Tofranil) and related drugs became known as *tricyclic antidepressants* because they all share a three-ring molecular structure. Other well-known tricyclics are amitriptyline (Elavil), nortriptyline (Aventyl), and doxepin (Sinequan).

Research has repeatedly demonstrated the effectiveness of tricyclics for treating unipolar patterns of depression. In hundreds of studies, mild to severely depressed patients taking tricyclics have improved significantly more than similar patients taking placebos (Morris & Beck, 1974; Davis, Klerman, & Schildkraut, 1967). When 387 depressed patients were treated with either tricyclic drugs or placebos for ten weeks, the tricyclic patients showed significantly greater improvement than the placebo patients by the sixth week (Lipman, 1966). Numerous case reports have also described the successful impact of these drugs. The cases of Derek and Beatrice, whom we met in Chapter 8, are typical of the glowing reviews tricyclics often receive:

*D*erek *might have continued living his battleship-gray* life had it not been for the local college. One winter Derek signed up for an evening course called "The Use and Abuse of Psychoactive Drugs" because he wanted to be able to provide accurate background information in future newspaper articles on drug use among high school and college students. The course covered psychiatric as well as recreational drugs. When the professor listed the symptoms of affective disorders on the blackboard, Derek had a flash of recognition. Perhaps he suffered from depression with melancholia.

Derek then consulted with a psychiatrist, who confirmed his suspicion and prescribed imipramine. A week later, Derek was sleeping until his alarm went off. Two weeks later, at 9:00 A.M. he was writing his column and making difficult decisions about editorials on sensitive topics. He started writing some feature stories on drugs just because he was interested in the subject. Writing was more fun than it had been in years. His images of his own violent death disappeared. His wife found him more responsive. He conversed with her enthusiastically and answered her questions without the long delays that had so tried her patience.

*(Lickey & Gordon, 1991, p. 185)*

*F*inally, *after a few tearful months, the psychiatrist . . .* prescribed antidepressant medication for Beatrice. Ten days later, Beatrice told her psychiatrist that a 100-pound weight had suddenly been lifted from her shoulders. For Beatrice, it was not "a beautiful day, but . . ." anymore; it was simply "a beautiful day." No qualifications were necessary. . . . The psychiatrist was almost as delighted as Beatrice.

*(Lickey & Gordon, 1991, p. 182)*

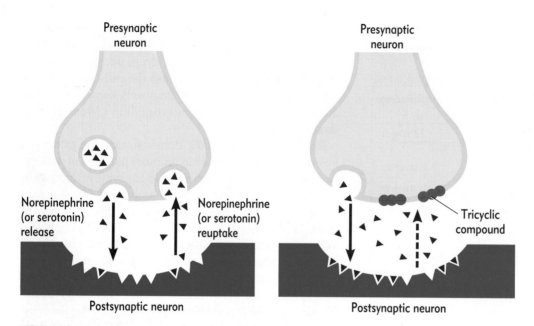

**FIGURE 9-2** *(Left)* When a neuron releases norepinephrine (or serotonin) from its endings, a pumplike reuptake mechanism immediately begins to recapture some of the neurotransmitter molecules before they are received by the postsynaptic (receptor) neuron. *(Right)* Tricyclic drugs block this reuptake process, enabling more norepinephrine (or serotonin) to reach, and thus fire, the postsynaptic (receptor) neuron. *(Adapted from Snyder, 1986, p. 106.)*

Studies also suggest that depressed people who stop taking tricyclics immediately after obtaining relief have a 40 to 50 percent chance of relapse within six to twelve months. If patients continue to take the drugs for several months after being free of depressive symptoms, however, their chances of relapse apparently decrease to approximately 20 percent (Montgomery et al., 1989; Prien & Kupfer, 1986; Klerman, 1978; Weissman & Klerman, 1977).

Many researchers have concluded that tricyclics alleviate depression by acting on neurotransmitter "reuptake" mechanisms (McNeal & Cimbolic, 1986). We saw earlier that a message is carried from a sending neuron to a receiving neuron by means of a neurotransmitter released from the nerve ending of the sending neuron. However, there is a complication in this process. While the nerve ending is releasing a neurotransmitter, a pumplike mechanism in the same ending is trying to recapture it. The purpose of this mechanism is to prevent the neurotransmitter from remaining in the synapse too long and repeatedly stimulating the receiving neuron. Among depressed people, this pumplike reuptake mechanism may be too successful, causing too great a reduction of norepinephrine and serotonin activity and hence of neural firing, and resulting in a clinical picture of depression. Studies have indicated that tricyclics act

to block this reuptake process (see Figure 9-2), preventing nerve endings from recapturing too much norepinephrine and serotonin and therefore increasing neurotransmitter activity (Iversen, 1965; Axelrod et al., 1961).

While many researchers believe that this is why tricyclics are able to alleviate unipolar depression, others have questioned whether this is indeed the key to the drugs' effectiveness (Charney & Heninger, 1983; Charney et al., 1981; Sulser et al., 1978). Critics of the reuptake explanation have observed that although tricyclics inhibit the reuptake process immediately upon being absorbed into the blood, the symptoms of depression usually continue unabated for at least seven to fourteen days after drug therapy is initiated. If the drugs act immediately to increase norepinephrine and serotonin availability, why the lag in clinical improvement?

Further studies conducted with this question in mind have found that after seven to fourteen days of administration, tricyclics seem to alter the sensitivity of norepinephrine and serotonin receptors located on neurons throughout the brain (McNeal & Cimbolic, 1986; Stahl, 1984; Sulser, 1983; Charney et al., 1981; Rosenblatt, 1979). Some of these receptors become more capable of attracting and capturing norepinephrine and serotonin after this period of antidepressant administration, and so better able to receive and transmit messages (Charney et al., 1981); other norepinephrine and serotonin receptors actually become less sensitive after seven to fourteen days of tricyclics (Sulser, 1983). Working backward from these findings, some researchers now suspect that unipolar depression may in fact be caused primarily by neurotransmitter receptors whose sensitivity to norepinephrine and serotonin is disturbed in some manner, and that tricyclics alleviate depression not simply by altering reuptake mechanisms but also by correcting the sensitivity of these receptors (McNeal & Cimbolic, 1986; Jimerson, 1984; Lickey & Gordon, 1991). Some tricyclic drugs primarily correct the sensitivity problem in receptors that receive norepinephrine, while others operate largely on serotonin receptors (Baldessarini, 1983; Simpson et al., 1983).

Today tricyclics are prescribed more often than MAO inhibitors, primarily for two reasons (Davis, 1980). First, although tricyclics have their own undesirable effects, such as tiredness, dry mouth, dizziness, and occasional blurred vision (Cohn, 1990), they are less dangerous than MAO inhibitors and do not require dietary restrictions (Georgotas & McCue, 1986). Second, there is research to suggest that tricyclics are more effective. Numerous studies have shown tricyclics to outperform placebos more often than MAO inhibitors do (Tapia, 1983; Davis et al., 1967; Wechsler et al., 1965). And direct comparisons have found that patients taking tricyclics show higher rates of improvement than those taking MAO inhibitors (Swonger & Constantine, 1983).

On the other hand, discriminating studies conducted in recent years have begun to reveal that different kinds of symptoms may be alleviated by these different kinds of drugs. The MAO inhibitors often seem to be more effective than tricyclics for depressed patients whose symptoms include overeating, oversleeping, and intense anxiety (Zisook, 1985; Pare, 1985; Liebowitz et al., 1984). Tricyclics, on the other hand, may be more effective when the major symptoms are pronounced motor slowdown, loss of appetite, and insomnia (Hirschfeld & Goodwin, 1988). Given these newly emerging distinctions, today's clinicians continue to prescribe MAO inhibitors for some patients, as long as the patients are healthy, willing to be regularly monitored, and capable of adhering to a strict diet (Zisook, 1985; Quitkin et al., 1981).

Finally, a number of new and effective antidepressant drugs, structurally different in certain ways from the traditional tricyclics, have been discovered during the past several years. These so-called *second-generation antidepressants* (which include *maprotiline, amoxapine, trazodone,* and *fluoxetine*) do not seem to inhibit

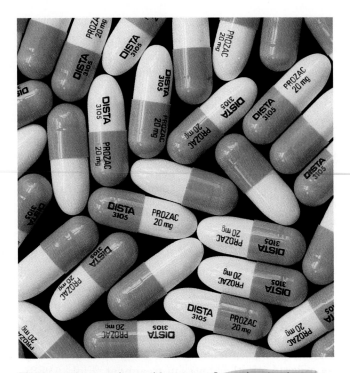

The second-generation antidepressant fluoxetine (trade name Prozac) has become the most often prescribed antidepressant drug. Its 2 to 4 million users throughout the world boosted sales above $500 million in 1990. It is as effective as other antidepressants and seems to have fewer undesirable effects. Although some case reports have linked the drug to suicide and violent behavior, empirical studies have found no such relationship.

MAO activity or primarily to affect reuptake processes (Richelson, 1984; Ananth, 1983; Feighner, 1983), but researchers do suspect that they alter the sensitivity of norepinephrine and serotonin receptors in some way (McNeal & Cimbolic, 1986; Ananth, 1983). Studies directly comparing the effectiveness of these drugs with that of traditional tricyclics find the two groups of drugs to be equally effective.

**Antidepressants versus ECT** A number of studies have found ECT to be more effective than antidepressant drug therapy (Janicak & Davis, 1986; Janicak et al., 1985). One estimate, based on a broad spectrum of controlled studies, is that, on the average, 72 percent of ECT patients improve, while tricyclic drugs and MAO inhibitors yield average improvement rates of 65 percent and 50 percent, respectively (Wechsler et al., 1965). Half of all ECT successes relapse within a year unless that treatment is followed up by treatment with antidepressant medications, a relapse rate similar to that for antidepressant-treated patients who stop taking their medications as soon as their symptoms subside (Perry & Tsuang, 1979; Kay, Fahy, & Garside, 1970).

Some researchers have questioned the fairness of these comparisons (Fogel, 1986; Avery & Lubrano, 1979). When ECT does work, it tends to alleviate unipolar depression within a week or two. Antidepressants, on the other hand, may take as long as three to six weeks and then require yet further weekly adjustments until maximum effectiveness is finally reached (Quitkin et al., 1981). Thus any study comparing ECT with antidepressants after just a few weeks of treatment is likely to favor ECT.

When clinicians today consider a biological treatment for mild to severe unipolar depression, they generally administer antidepressant medications (Cohn, 1990; Extein, Gold, & Pottash, 1984). Sometimes these drugs are even used to help prevent depression in a patient with a history of recurrent episodes (Prien et al., 1984, 1973; Raskin, 1974). Clinicians usually resort to ECT only when patients are severely depressed and unresponsive to all other forms of treatment (Fink, 1988). For example, 95 percent of referrals to the ECT research program at Rush – Presbyterian – St. Luke's Medical Center in Chicago are depressed patients who have not responded to other interventions (Taylor & Carroll, 1987). Studies suggest that ECT is helpful for as many as 80 percent of the severely depressed patients who do not respond to antidepressant drugs (Avery & Lubrano, 1979; Fink, 1978). If a depressed patient seems to be a high suicide risk, the clinician may consider ECT treatment even sooner (Brown, 1974; Hurwitz, 1974). On the other hand, studies have yet to indicate that ECT actually thwarts suicide (Frankel, 1984; Friedberg, 1976).

## Trends in Treatment

For most mental disorders, no more than one treatment or combination of treatments, if any, emerges as highly successful. A unipolar pattern of depression seems to be an exception. Research suggests that unipolar depression may be effectively treated by any of several approaches: cognitive, interpersonal, behavioral, and biological therapy. During the past decade, researchers have conducted several comparative outcome studies to determine whether any of these approaches is more effective than the others. Several patterns have emerged:

1. Cognitive, interpersonal, and biological therapies appear to be the most successful treatments for

Regular exercise has been found to be positively linked to one's level of happiness, and exercise may help prevent or reduce feelings of depression (Diener, 1984). It is not clear, however, whether this relationship is the result of changes in biology, activity level, or cognition, or a combination of factors.

unipolar depression, from mild to severe. In most head-to-head comparisons, these therapies seem to reduce depressive symptoms with equally high levels of effectiveness (Elkin et al., 1989, 1986, 1985; Beck et al., 1985; Weissman, 1984, 1979).

The most ambitious study on this issue was a six-year, $10 million investigation sponsored by the National Institute of Mental Health, the largest therapy outcome study ever conducted in the United States (Elkin et al., 1989, 1986, 1985). Experimenters separated 239 moderately and severely depressed people into four treatment groups. One group was treated with sixteen weeks of Beck's cognitive therapy, another with sixteen weeks of interpersonal therapy, and a third group with the antidepressant drug imipramine. The fourth group received a placebo. A total of twenty-eight therapists conducted these treatments, and each had been carefully chosen, uniformly trained in his or her respective therapy, and then tested for competence (Elkin, 1984; Shaw, 1984; Rounsaville et al., 1984).

The investigators found that each of the three therapies completely eliminated depressive symptoms in 50 to 60 percent of the subjects, whereas only 29 percent of those who received the placebo showed such improvement. Drug therapy reduced the depressive symptoms more quickly than the cognitive and interpersonal therapies, but these psychotherapies had matched the effectiveness of the drug by the final four weeks of treatment. Each of the three treatments appeared to improve all areas of functioning.

These findings are consistent with those of most other comparative outcome studies (Weissman, 1984, 1979; Hersen, 1983). It is important to note, however, that a growing number of studies suggest that cognitive therapy may be even more effective than drug therapy (Beutler et al., 1987; see Figure 9-3), especially with regard to preventing relapses (Hollon & Najavits, 1988; Simons et al., 1986; Rush, 1984; Kovacs et al., 1981; Blackburn et al., 1981; Rush et al., 1979).

2. In head-to-head comparisons, depressed people who receive behavioral therapy have shown less improvement than those who receive cognitive, interpersonal, or biological therapy, although behavioral therapy has proved more effective than placebo treatments or no attention at all (Zeiss et

al., 1981; Wilson et al., 1979; Taylor & Marshall, 1977; Shaw, 1977, 1975). Also, as we have seen, behavioral therapy is of less help to people who are severely depressed than to those with mild or moderate depression.

3. Research suggests that psychodynamic therapies are less effective than these other therapies in treating all levels of unipolar depression (McLean & Hakstian, 1979). Indeed, in several studies psychodynamic therapy has performed no more effectively than placebos, leading to improvement in only 30 percent of the participating subjects (Berk & Efran, 1983). Nevertheless, most people in treatment for depression continue to receive psychodynamic therapy, a reflection of the continuing appeal of this approach to many in the clinical field (Weissman, 1984).

4. Most studies have found that a combination of psychotherapy (usually cognitive or interpersonal psychotherapy) and drug therapy is modestly more helpful to depressed people than either treatment alone (Hirschfeld & Goodwin, 1988; Conte et al., 1986; Teasdale, 1985; Beckham, 1984; Weissman, 1984, 1979). Some studies, however, find combination therapies to be no more effective than either treatment alone (Beck, 1985; Murphy et al., 1984; Rush & Watkins, 1981; Bellack et al., 1981).

## TREATMENTS FOR BIPOLAR DISORDERS

Until recently people with bipolar disorders were usually destined to spend their lives on an emotional roller coaster. Psychotherapists of varying orientations reported almost no success in treating the manic symptoms of bipolar clients and very limited success in treating bipolar depressive symptoms (Lickey & Gordon, 1991). Likewise, biological therapists found that antidepressant drugs and ECT only occasionally relieved the depressive episodes of a bipolar cycle, and that sedatives and antipsychotic drugs failed to affect the grandiosity and accelerated flood of ideas that characterize manic episodes (Prien et al., 1974). For reasons not clearly understood, ECT applied during a manic episode sometimes interrupted the episode and restored normality (Black et al., 1987; Small, 1985), but manic patients usually felt too good to consent to such a frightening and unpleasant procedure.

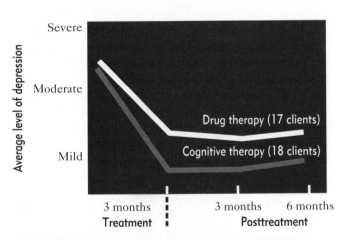

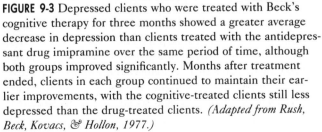

**FIGURE 9-3** Depressed clients who were treated with Beck's cognitive therapy for three months showed a greater average decrease in depression than clients treated with the antidepressant drug imipramine over the same period of time, although both groups improved significantly. Months after treatment ended, clients in each group continued to maintain their earlier improvements, with the cognitive-treated clients still less depressed than the drug-treated clients. *(Adapted from Rush, Beck, Kovacs, & Hollon, 1977.)*

## Lithium Therapy

The drug *lithium* has so dramatically changed this gloomy picture that many people view the silvery-white substance — found in various simple mineral salts throughout the natural world — as a true miracle drug. Moreover, the use of lithium has halved the total cost of treating bipolar disorders, a savings of $270 million a year in the United States alone (Reifman & Wyatt, 1980). The case of Anna, which dates from the 1960s, when lithium was still considered an experimental drug, illustrates the extraordinary impact this drug can have.

*A*nna was a 21-year-old college student. Before she became ill, Anna was sedate and polite, perhaps even a bit prim. During the fall of her sophomore year at college, she had an episode of mild depression that began when she received a C on a history paper she had worked quite hard on. The same day she received a sanctimonious letter from her father reminding her of the financial hardships he was undergoing to send her to college. He warned her to stick to her books and not to play around with men. Anna became

For more than a century, people from around the world have sought to cure their ills by drinking "lithia water," bottled in Lithia Springs, Georgia. The town's mineral-rich spring water is said to alleviate bipolar disorders, alcoholism, and heart and kidney problems, and to act as an aphrodisiac; some people call it "love water."

discouraged. She doubted that she deserved her parents' sacrifice. Anna's depression did not seem unusual to her roommate, to her other friends, or even to Anna herself. It seemed a natural reaction to her father's unreasonable letter and her fear that she could not live up to the standards he set. In retrospect, this mild depression was the first episode of her bipolar illness.

Several months later, Anna became restless, angry, and obnoxious. She talked continuously and rapidly, jumping from one idea to another. Her speech was filled with rhymes, puns, and sexual innuendoes. During Christmas vacation, she made frequent and unwelcome sexual overtures to her brother's friend in the presence of her entire family. When Anna's mother asked her to behave more politely, Anna began to cry and then slapped her mother across the mouth. Anna did not sleep that night. She sobbed. Between sobs she screamed that no one understood her problems, and no one would even try. The next day, Anna's family took her to the hospital. She was given chlorpromazine which calmed her. When she was discharged two weeks later, she was less angry and no longer assaultive. But she was not well and did not go back to school. Her thought and speech were still hypomanic [slightly manic]. She had an exaggerated idea of her attractiveness and expected men to fall for her at the first smile. She was irritated when they ignored her attentions. Depressive symptoms were still mixed with the manic ones. She often cried when her bids for attention were not successful or when her parents criticized her dress or behavior.

Anna returned to school the following fall but suffered another depressive episode, followed by another attack of mania within seven months. She had to withdraw from school and enter the hospital. This time, Anna was fortunate to enter a research unit that was authorized to use lithium. The psychiatrists diagnosed her illness as bipolar disorder. Because she was so agitated, they began treatment with chlorpromazine as well as lithium. The initial sedative action of the chlorpromazine rapidly calmed her agitation, and this drug was discontinued after only a few days. As the effects of chlorpromazine subsided, the lithium began to take effect. After seventeen days on lithium, Anna's behavior was quite normal. She was attractively and modestly dressed for her psychiatric interviews. Earlier, she had been sloppily seductive; hair in disarray, half-open blouse, smeared lipstick, bright pink rouge on her cheeks, and bright green make-up on her eyelids. With the help of lithium, she gained some ability to tolerate frustration. During the first week of her hospital stay, she had screamed at a nurse who would not permit her to read late into the night in violation of the ward's 11:00 P.M. "lights out" policy. On lithium, Anna was still annoyed by this "juvenile" rule, but she controlled her anger. She gained some insight into her illness, recognizing that her manic behavior was destructive to herself and others. She also recognized the depression that was often mixed with the mania. She speculated that the mania was an attempt to cover up depression. She admitted, "Actually, when I'm high, I'm really feeling low. I need to exaggerate in order to feel more important."

Because Anna was on a research ward, the effectiveness of lithium had to be verified by removal of the drug. When she had been off lithium for four to five days, Anna began to show symptoms of both mania and depression. She threatened her psychiatrist, and as before, the threats were grandiose with sexual overtones. In a slinky voice, she warned, "I have ways to put the director of this hospital in my debt. He crawled for me before and he'll do it again. When I snap my fingers, he'll come down to this ward and squash you under his foot." Soon afterward, she threatened suicide. She later explained, "I felt so low last night that if someone had given me a knife or gun, POW." By the ninth day off lithium, Anna's speech was almost incomprehensible: "It's sad to be so putty, pretty, so much like water dripping from a faucet. . . ." Lithium therapy was reinstituted, and within about sixteen days, Anna again recovered and was discharged on lithium.

*(Lickey & Gordon, 1991, pp. 236–239)*

Determining the correct lithium dosage for a given patient is a delicate process, requiring analyses of blood and urine samples and other laboratory tests (Johnson et al., 1984; Swonger & Constantine, 1983). Too low a dosage will have little or no effect on the bipolar mood swings, but too high a dose of lithium can disturb the body's sodium balance and cause kidney dysfunction and even death (Kondziela, 1984). Once the correct dosage is achieved, however, lithium may produce a noticeable change within five to fourteen days, as it did for Anna. Patients may then be placed on maintenance dosages for an indefinite period of time. Patients who are unresponsive to or unable to tolerate lithium sometimes respond better to *carbamazepine* (Tegretol), an anticonvulsant drug discovered to have therapeutic effects in bipolar disorders as well (Post et al., 1984; Ballenger & Post, 1980).

**Origins of Lithium Treatment** The discovery that lithium effectively reduces bipolar symptoms was, like so many other medical discoveries, quite accidental. In 1949 an Australian psychiatrist, John Cade, hypothesized that manic behavior is caused by a toxic level of uric acid in the body. He set out to test this theory by injecting guinea pigs with uric acid, but first he combined the uric acid with lithium to increase its solubility.

To Cade's surprise, the guinea pigs became not manic but quite lethargic after their injections. Cade began to suspect that the lithium had produced this effect. When he later administered lithium to ten manic human beings, he discovered that it calmed and normalized their mood.

Cade's promising findings quickly captured the interest of clinicians and researchers in Australia, Denmark, England, and several other countries, but not in the United States (Kline, 1973). Here lithium had just been declared an illegal drug because its wide use as a salt substitute had led to a number of deaths. Cade later wrote, "One can hardly imagine a less propitious year in which to attempt the pharmacological rehabilitation of lithium." It was not until 1970 that the U.S. Food and Drug Administration approved lithium for use in bipolar disorders.

**Effectiveness of Lithium with Manic Episodes** All manner of research has attested to lithium's effectiveness in treating manic episodes (Bunney & Garland, 1984; Prien, 1978; Bunney et al., 1968). In numerous blind studies, clinicians have given lithium to one group of manic patients and placebo drugs to another; then a different set of clinicians, unaware of what the patients have been taking (blind) and even of the nature of the experiment (blind again), have rated the improvement of all patients in the study. Repeatedly lithium has been found to be much more effective than placebos. Improvement rates of manic patients range upward from 60 percent (Prien, 1978; Goodwin & Ebert, 1973).

Other kinds of studies have demonstrated a still more direct relationship between lithium and the reduction of manic behaviors. In these studies (single-subject, ABAB and multiple-baseline designs, discussed in Chapter 3) manic patients have been given lithium for a while, then placebos, then lithium again, and so on, as Anna was. Manic behavior has consistently decreased under lithium and returned when placebos are substituted (Goodwin, Murphy, & Bunney, 1969; Bunney, Goodwin, Davis, & Fawcett, 1968).

Another frequent finding is that patients with recurrent mania undergo fewer new episodes as long as they are taking lithium (Prieb & Wildgrube, 1990). In one study, only 36 percent of 212 bipolar patients relapsed while taking lithium, compared to a 79 percent relapse rate among 68 bipolar patients on placebos (Davis, 1976). This finding suggests that lithium may also be a *prophylactic* drug, a drug that actually helps prevent symptoms from developing. Accordingly, today's clinicians often recommend that patients continue lithium treatments even after their manic episodes subside (Goodwin & Jamison, 1989; Angst & Grof, 1979).

**Effectiveness of Lithium with Depressive Episodes** Research indicates that lithium also alleviates the depressive episodes of bipolar disorders (Berger, 1978; Basuk & Schoonover, 1977; Goodwin et al., 1969; Fieve et al., 1968). Moreover, maintenance doses of lithium apparently decrease the risk of future depressive episodes, just as they seem to prevent the recurrence of manic episodes (Prien et al., 1984; Prien, 1984; Fieve et al., 1976; Baastrup, 1964).

Given such findings, researchers have naturally wondered whether lithium might also be helpful in cases of unipolar depression. Here the results have been mixed. Although a number of studies suggest that lithium is not very helpful in relieving unipolar depression (Prien, 1984), a few find that it does help a small portion of such patients (Doyal & Morton, 1984; Baron et al., 1975; Noyes, 1974; Goodwin et al., 1972). Some studies also suggest that lithium occasionally prevents recurrences of unipolar depression (Doyal & Morton, 1984; Persson, 1972; Hullin et al., 1972). Of course, it may be that "unipolar" patients helped by lithium in these ways actually have a bipolar disorder whose manic phase is yet to appear.

**Lithium's Mode of Operation**   Researchers do not really understand how lithium operates, but they are beginning to suspect that it alters synaptic activity in neurons that use the neurotransmitters norepinephrine and serotonin, though not in the same way as antidepressant drugs. Recent research indicates that the firing of a neuron actually consists of several phases that unfold at lightning speed. After the neurotransmitter binds to a receptor site on the receiving neuron, a series of cellular changes in the receiving neuron set the stage for firing. These changes are often called "second messengers" because they intervene between the reception of the original message and the actual firing of the neuron (Snyder, 1986). The activity of the second messenger causes sodium ions alongside the neuron's membrane to become active, resulting in a change in the electrical charge of the neuron, the transmission of the message down the cell's axon, and the firing of the neuron (see Figure 8-8). Whereas antidepressant drugs affect the initial reception of neurotransmitters by neurons, lithium appears to affect the second-messenger systems in the neurons.

There are various second-messenger systems in neurons throughout the brain. In one of the most important, chemicals called *phosphoinositides* (consisting of sugars and lipids) are produced after a neurotransmitter is received and lead to other chemical alterations in the neuron (Baraban et al., 1989). A number of studies indicate that lithium has a significant effect on this particular messenger system. That is, the synaptic activity at any neuron that uses this second-messenger system — whether a neuron that receives serotonin or one that receives norepinephrine — may be altered by lithium. Thus, even if bipolar disorders are related to abnormal activity of both serotonin and norepinephrine, as

some theorists argue, one drug — lithium — can correct both kinds of abnormality through its impact on phosphoinositides–producing second-messenger systems.

Alternatively, it may be that lithium effectively treats bipolar functioning by directly altering sodium ion activity in neurons; that is, by correcting the propagation phase of neural firing (Swonger & Constantine, 1983). In Chapter 8 we saw that lithium is related to sodium and we considered the theory that bipolar disorders are triggered by unstable alignments of sodium ions alongside the membranes of certain neurons in the brain. If this instability is indeed the key to bipolar problems, one would expect lithium to have a direct effect of some kind on sodium ion activity. Research suggests that lithium may in fact act in this way. Several studies indicate that lithium ions often substitute, although imperfectly, for sodium ions (Baer, Platman, Kassir, & Fieve, 1971), and others offer evidence that lithium affects sodium concentrations throughout the body (Mendels & Frazer, 1974; Naylor et al., 1974). Still another line of research suggests that lithium alters the transport mechanisms by which sodium ions travel back and forth across the neural membrane (Bunney & Garland, 1984; Thomas, 1972). Any or all of these findings could be the reason that lithium alleviates and prevents the severe mood swings that characterize bipolar disorders. On the other hand, while lithium may in fact affect sodium ion activity, this need not be the primary reason for its effectiveness in relieving bipolar disorders.

## Adjunctive Psychotherapy

Clinicians rarely treat bipolar patients with psychotherapy alone. Ronald Fieve has written, "When the primary treatment of manic depression . . . has required the patient to talk with me about his problems . . . in my experience not very much has happened" (Fieve, 1975, p. 2). There have been virtually no controlled studies on the effectiveness of psychotherapy alone in treating bipolar disorders, a fact that may reflect the clinical community's conviction that such approaches by themselves are simply not sufficient to treat this disorder (Lickey & Gordon, 1991).

At the same time, clinicians have learned that lithium is not always sufficient by itself, either. As we saw earlier, as many as 40 percent of bipolar patients may not respond to lithium or may relapse while taking it (Goodwin & Guze, 1984; Prien et al., 1984; Davis, 1976). There is also evidence that close to 50 percent of patients on lithium do not receive the proper dosage: many are not taking it as prescribed, others stop taking it altogether against medical advice, and some receive prescriptions for incorrect dosages (Gelenberg et al., 1989; Bower, 1987; Jamison, Gerner, & Goodwin, 1979).

Given these problems, many clinicians now advocate psychotherapy as an adjunct to lithium treatment (Miklowitz & Goldstein, 1990; Wulsin, Bachop, & Hoffman, 1988). Individual, group, and family psychotherapies are increasingly being made available to bipolar patients to help them with problems that may affect their recovery. The concerns most commonly addressed in psychotherapy are:

1. *Medication management* The importance of continuing proper lithium treatment is emphasized during therapy, and adherence to the medication regimen may be monitored (Kripke & Robinson, 1985). Patients are also encouraged to discuss their reasons for disliking or rejecting lithium. They may be bothered by the drug's unwanted effects, be feeling too well to recognize the need for ongoing medication, miss the feelings of euphoria they used to have, or complain of being less productive and creative when they take lithium (Wulsin et al., 1988; Jamison, 1987).

2. *Family and social relationships* Bipolar patients who return to critical and overinvolved families are more likely to relapse within nine months than bipolar patients who live in a more supportive and less intrusive family atmosphere (Miklowitz et al., 1988). Thus, helping patients cope with family members and improving family functioning are common focuses in psychotherapy. As they recover, bipolar patients often experience major interpersonal and social difficulties, including the loss of friends and lovers who have been frightened away or repelled during the bipolar episodes (Wulsin et al., 1988; Aleksandrowicz, 1980; Donnelly, Murphy, & Goodwin, 1978). In psychotherapy, bipolar patients may be encouraged to discuss their social problems, recognize their social limitations, and develop social skills and support systems. One study of sixty bipolar patients stabilized on lithium found that social support was the factor most strongly linked to a good treatment outcome (O'Connell et al., 1985).

3. *Education* Many bipolar patients actually know very little about their disorder and need to be given information about causes, common patterns, and practical implications. Psychotherapists may not only provide much important information but also encourage members of therapy groups to share what their firsthand experiences have taught them (Wulsin et al., 1988).

4. *Problem solving* Bipolar disorders can create problems in all aspects of a person's life and interfere in all areas of pursuit. A person may, for example, be unable to stay in school or to hold a job when manic or depressive symptoms strike. Thus one role of therapy may be to help bipolar clients develop solutions for the particular difficulties they encounter (Kripke & Robinson, 1985).

Few controlled studies have tested the effectiveness of psychotherapy as an adjunct to drug therapy, but a growing number of clinical reports suggest that its use leads to less hospitalization, better social functioning, and higher employment rates for bipolar clients (Kripke & Robinson, 1985; Volkmar et al., 1981). Although lithium is clearly the chief agent of genuine improvement in bipolar clients, it is becoming apparent that the drug is most effective when it is combined with other forms of therapy.

# TREATMENTS FOR MOOD DISORDERS: THE STATE OF THE FIELD

Mood disorders are among the most treatable of all mental disorders. More than 60 percent of people who suffer from them can be helped. The symptoms of unipolar patterns of depression can usually be reduced or eliminated in two to twenty weeks; after that, treatment is generally discontinued, to be reinstated if depressive symptoms recur. The symptoms of bipolar disorders can also be reduced within a few weeks, but treatment must be continued indefinitely to help prevent future episodes of depression and mania.

The choice of treatment for bipolar disorders is narrow and simple—lithium (or a related drug), perhaps combined with psychotherapy, is the single most successful approach. The picture for unipolar patterns of depression is broader and more complex, although no less promising. Cognitive therapy, interpersonal therapy, and antidepressant drug therapy are all helpful in cases of any severity; behavioral therapy is helpful in mild to moderate cases; and ECT is useful and effective in severe cases. No single one of the therapies has emerged as clearly superior to the others. Combinations of psychotherapy and drug therapy tend to be modestly more helpful than any one approach alone.

Why should several very different approaches be highly effective in the treatment of unipolar patterns of depression? Although clinicians do not yet know the answer, two explanations have received some credence. First, it seems plausible that removing any one of the factors that contribute to unipolar depression may promote improvements in all areas of functioning, just as it seems possible for one causal factor to trigger several others and create a case of unipolar depression in the first place. Studies supporting this explanation have found that when a given therapy is effective, the client is seen to improve in all areas of functioning (Elkin et al., 1986, 1985). For instance, antidepressant drugs ultimately lead to the same improvements in cognitive functioning as Beck's cognitive therapy does (Simons et al., 1986, 1984; Reda et al., 1985).

The second explanation proposes the existence of various kinds of unipolar depression, each responsive to a different kind of therapy, a possibility noted in Chapter 8. Researchers have in fact found that unipolar depressions with particular features sometimes respond better to one form of treatment than to another. Studies have indicated that interpersonal psychotherapy is more helpful in depressions precipitated by situational factors than in depressions that seem to occur endogenously (Prusoff, Weissman, Klerman, & Rounsaville, 1980), while antidepressant medications are more likely than other treatments to be helpful for cases characterized by appetite and sleep problems, acute onset, and a family history of depression (McNeal & Cimbolic, 1986; Byrne & Stern, 1981; Schatzberg & Rosenbaum, 1980).

Whatever the ultimate explanation, there is no question that the present treatment picture is very promising both for people with unipolar patterns of depression and for those with bipolar disorders. The odds are that one or a combination of the therapies now in use will indeed alleviate their symptoms. On the other hand, the sobering fact remains that as many as 40 percent of people with a mood disorder do not improve under treatment and must suffer their mania or depression until it runs its course.

## SUMMARY

Mood disorders are among the most treatable of all mental disorders: more than 60 percent of people with these disorders can be helped. A wide range of approaches have been employed in the management of unipolar depression. Fewer treatments have been developed for bipolar disorders. There biological interventions rule the field.

Psychodynamic therapists try to help clients with unipolar depression become aware of and work through their real or imagined losses and excessive dependence on others. Although research has shown that psychodynamic therapies are not consistently helpful in cases of unipolar depression, they are still widely employed.

In the behavioral approach, therapists reintroduce their clients to events and activities that the clients once found pleasurable. The therapists also systematically reinforce nondepressive behaviors and teach effective interpersonal skills. If results are to be achieved, several of these behavioral techniques must be applied simultaneously. Such therapy is effective primarily for people who are mildly to moderately depressed.

Interpersonal therapy (IPT) is based on the assumption that depressive functioning stems from interpersonal problem areas. These therapists try to rectify the problem that underlies the depression by helping clients to develop insight into these problem areas, change them, and learn problem-solving skills to protect them in the future. Research suggests that IPT is often an effective treatment for mild to severe cases of unipolar depression.

Cognitive treatment for depression helps clients identify and change their dysfunctional cognitive processes. The four phases of this treatment are (1) increasing activities and elevating mood, (2) examining and invalidating automatic thoughts, (3) identifying distorted thinking and negative biases, and (4) changing primary attitudes. At present, this is one of the most effective approaches to treating depression.

Electroconvulsive therapy (ECT) remains a controversial procedure, although it is one of the most effective and fastest-acting interventions for unipolar depression. Electrodes attached to a patient's head send an electric current through the brain, causing convulsions. The resulting increase in brain norepinephrine and serotonin activity suggests that ECT may correct the neurotransmitter deficiencies of depressed people. ECT is most effective when depression is severe, characterized by delusions, or marked by such symptoms as motor retardation, sleep disturbance, and loss of appetite. Typically six treatments are administered over a two-week period. In recent years, many changes in the way ECT is administered have rendered the treatment more medically complex and at the same time less dangerous and frightening. Despite its established effectiveness and safety, however, the use of ECT is on the decline.

In the 1950s two classes of drugs were discovered that alleviate depressive symptoms: the *MAO inhibitors* and the *tricyclics*. MAO inhibitors block the destruction of norepinephrine and serotonin, allowing the levels of these neurotransmitters to build up and alleviate depressive symptoms. Because MAO is necessary for removing the amino acid tyramine from the body, people taking MAO inhibitors must follow a restricted diet to keep excess tyramine from collecting in the liver and raising their blood pressure to a dangerous level.

Tricyclics may alleviate depression by blocking neurotransmitter reuptake mechanisms, thereby increasing the activity of norepinephrine and serotonin. Today tricyclics are prescribed more often than MAO inhibitors because they are less dangerous, do not require dietary restrictions, and are often more effective. New *second-generation antidepressants* are as effective as traditional tricyclics. Although a number of studies have found ECT to be slightly more effective than antidepressant medication, antidepressants are the more common biological treatments. Usually ECT is administered only when patients are severely depressed and unresponsive to all other forms of treatment.

In sum, many cases of unipolar depression may be effectively treated by a variety of approaches. Cognitive, interpersonal, and biological therapies may be the most successful for mild to severe depression. Behavioral therapy is helpful in mild to moderate cases, and ECT is effective in severe cases. Combinations of psychotherapy and drug therapy tend to be modestly more helpful than any one approach alone.

Lithium has proved to be effective in alleviating and preventing both the manic and the depressive episodes of bipolar disorders. It is generally not very helpful, however, in treating unipolar depression. Although the mechanism by which lithium works is not fully understood, researchers suspect that it may affect second messengers and interact with sodium ions in certain neurons.

In recent years it has become clear that lithium alone is not always sufficient treatment for bipolar disorders and that patients fare better with a combination of drug and other forms of therapy. Therefore, many clinicians now advocate psychotherapy as an adjunct to lithium therapy. The issues most commonly addressed in psychotherapy for bipolar patients are medication management, family and social relationships, information sharing, and problem solving.

# TOPIC OVERVIEW

# CHAPTER *10*

# SUICIDE

I had done all I could and I was still sinking. I sat many hours seeking answers, and all there was was a silent wind. The answer was in my head. It was all clear now: Die. . . .

The next day a friend offered to sell me a gun, a .357 magnum pistol. I bought it. My first thought was: What a mess this is going to make. That day I began to say goodbye to people: not actually saying it but expressing it silently.

Friends were around, but I didn't let them see what was wrong with me. I could not let them know lest they prevent it. My mind became locked on my target. My thoughts were: Soon it will all be over. I would obtain the peace I had so long sought. The will to survive and succeed had been crushed and defeated. I was like a general on a battlefield being encroached on by my enemy and its hordes: fear, hate, self-depreciation, desolation. I felt I had to have the upper hand, to control my environment, so I sought to die rather than surrender. . . .

I was only aware of myself and my plight. Death swallowed me long before I pulled the trigger. The world through my eyes seemed to die with me. It was like I was to push the final button to end this world. I committed myself to the arms of death. There comes a time when all things cease to shine, when the rays of hope are lost.

I placed the gun to my head. Then, I remember a tremendous explosion of lights like fireworks. Thus did the pain become glorious, an army rallied to the side of death to help destroy my life, which I could feel leaving my body with each rushing surge of blood. I was engulfed in total darkness.

*(Shneidman, 1987, p. 56)*

The animal world is filled with seemingly self-destructive behavior. Worker bees lose their stings and die after attacking intrusive mammals. Salmon die after the exhausting swim upstream to spawn. Lemmings are said to rush to the sea and drown. In each of these cases a creature's behavior leads to its death, but it would be inaccurate to say the animal or insect wants to die or is trying to die. If anything, its actions are in the service of life. They are instinctual responses that help the species to survive in the long run. The self-destructive behavior described by the suicide survivor differs radically from these other actions. Only in the human act of suicide do beings knowingly end their own lives.

Suicide has been observed throughout history. It has been recorded among the ancient Chinese, Greeks, and Romans. King Saul's suicide is reported in the Old Testament. Cato threw himself upon his sword. And in more recent times, suicides by such famous people as Ernest Hemingway and Marilyn Monroe have both shocked and fascinated society.

Today suicide ranks among the top ten causes of death in Western society (see Tables 10-1 and 10-2). According to the World Health Organization, approximately 120,000 deaths by suicide occur each year. More than

TABLE 10-2

| NUMBER OF DEATHS FROM SUICIDE IN THE UNITED STATES, 1968–1982 | | | |
|---|---|---|---|
| | | Age (years) | |
| Year | Total, all ages | 5–14 | 15–24 |
| 1982 | 28,242 | 200 | 5,025 |
| 1981 | 27,596 | 167 | 5,161 |
| 1980 | 26,869 | 142 | 5,239 |
| 1979 | 27,206 | 152 | 5,246 |
| 1978 | 27,294 | 153 | 5,115 |
| 1977 | 28,681 | 182 | 5,565 |
| 1976 | 26,832 | 163 | 4,647 |
| 1975 | 26,832 | 170 | 4,736 |
| 1974 | 25,683 | 188 | 4,285 |
| 1973 | 25,118 | 157 | 4,098 |
| 1972 | 25,004 | 120 | 3,858 |
| 1971 | 24,092 | 141 | 3,479 |
| 1970 | 23,480 | 132 | 3,128 |
| 1969 | 22,364 | 136 | 2,731 |
| 1968 | 21,372 | 118 | 2,357 |

*Source: U.S. Monthly Vital Statistics, 1984.*

TABLE 10-1

| THE TEN LEADING CAUSES OF DEATH IN THE UNITED STATES, 1981, BY AGE GROUP | | |
|---|---|---|
| 5–14 years | 15–24 years | All ages |
| 1. Accidents | 1. Accidents | 1. Heart disease |
| 2. Cancer | 2. Homicide | 2. Cancer |
| 3. Congenital anomalies | 3. Suicide | 3. Cerebrovascular disease |
| 4. Homicide | 4. Cancer | 4. Accidents |
| 5. Heart disease | 5. Heart disease | 5. Chronic pulmonary disease |
| 6. Influenza and pneumonia | 6. Congenital anomalies | 6. Influenza and pneumonia |
| 7. Suicide | 7. Cerebrovascular disease | 7. Diabetes mellitus |
| 8. Chronic pulmonary disease | 8. Influenza and pneumonia | 8. Cirrhosis of liver |
| 9. Cerebrovascular disease | 9. Chronic pulmonary disease | 9. Arteriosclerosis |
| 10. Septicemia (blood poisoning) | 10. Nephritis and nephrosis (kidney disease) | 10. Suicide |

*Source: U.S. Monthly Vital Statistics, 1982.*

30,000 suicides are committed annually in the United States alone, by 12.8 out of every 100,000 inhabitants, accounting for almost 2 percent of all deaths in the nation (McIntosh, 1991; National Center for Health Statistics, 1988). It is also estimated that each year more than 2 million other persons throughout the world—600,000 in the United States—make unsuccessful attempts to kill themselves; these people are called *parasuicides* (McIntosh, 1991). Indeed, more than 5 million people now living in the United States have at some time attempted suicide, and still more contemplate such acts without carrying them out (Bagley & Ramsay, 1985; Sherer, 1985). These numbing statistics come to life in the following statement:

Before you finish reading this page, someone in the United States will try to kill himself. At least 60 Americans will have taken their own lives by this time tomorrow. . . . Many of those who attempted will try again, a number with lethal success.

*(Shneidman & Mandelkorn, 1983)*

Actually, it is difficult to obtain accurate figures on suicide. Many investigators believe that the estimates are low, perhaps only half of the actual total (Shneidman, 1981). Because suicide is an enormously stigmatizing act in our society, relatives and friends may refuse to acknowledge that loved ones have taken their own lives. Moreover, it can be difficult for coroners to distinguish suicides from accidental drug overdoses, automobile crashes, drownings, and the like (Lester, 1985). Since relatively few of those who commit suicide actually leave notes (see Box 10-1), only the most obvious cases are categorized appropriately (Shneidman, 1979; Shneidman & Farberow, 1970).

Suicide is not classified as a mental disorder by DSM-III-R, but it does typically involve such clinical variables as a breakdown of coping skills, emotional turmoil, and distorted perspective. Although textbooks often address this topic in conjunction with mood disorders, at least half of all suicides result from other mental disorders, such as alcohol dependence or schizophrenia, or involve no clear mental disorder at all.

Despite the prevalence and long history of suicide, most people are misinformed about its symptoms and causes (see Table 10-3). When researchers administered a suicide fact test to several hundred undergraduates, the average score was only 59 percent correct (McIntosh, Hubbard, & Santos, 1985). Even the clinicians and researchers who have compiled the numerous facts and figures about suicide have a limited understanding of why anyone takes this drastic action. Never-

TABLE 10-3

### FACTS AND FABLES ABOUT SUICIDE

**Fable:** People who talk about suicide don't commit suicide.
**Fact:** Most people who kill themselves have given definite warnings of their suicidal intentions.

**Fable:** Suicide happens without warning.
**Fact:** Suicidal persons typically give many clues regarding their suicidal intentions.

**Fable:** Suicidal people are fully intent on dying.
**Fact:** Most suicidal people are undecided about living or dying, and they "gamble with death," leaving it to others to save them.

**Fable:** Once people are suicidal, they are suicidal forever.
**Fact:** Individuals who wish to kill themselves are suicidal only for a limited period of time.

**Fable:** Improvement following a suicidal crisis means that the suicidal risk is over.
**Fact:** Most suicides occur within about three months following the beginning of "improvement," when the individuals have the energy to put their morbid thoughts and feelings into effect.

**Fable:** Suicide strikes much more often among the rich—or, conversely, it occurs almost exclusively among the poor.
**Fact:** Suicide is very "democratic" and is represented proportionately among all levels of society.

**Fable:** Most suicidal individuals display mental disorders.
**Fact:** Although suicidal people are extremely unhappy, they do not necessarily experience a mental disorder.

*Source:* Adapted from Shneidman et al., 1983.

theless, over the past few decades the study of suicide has become a major focus of the clinical field, and our insights are improving.

## WHAT IS SUICIDE?

Not every self-inflicted death is a suicide. A man who crashes his car into a tree after falling asleep at the steering wheel is hardly trying to kill himself. Thus Edwin Shneidman (1981, 1966), one of the most influential writers on this topic, defines *suicide* as an *intentioned* death—a self-inflicted death in which one makes an *intentional, direct,* and *conscious* effort to end one's life.

Most theorists agree that the term "suicide" should be limited to deaths of this sort.

Intentioned deaths may take various forms. Consider the following three imaginary instances. Although all of these people intended to die, their precise motives, the personal issues involved, and their suicidal actions differed greatly.

**D**ave: *Dave was a successful man. By the age of 50* he had risen to the vice presidency of a small but profitable office machine firm. He was in charge of marketing and sales. True, he had invested most of his time in his work,

and as a result had not developed close family relationships. Still, he was content. He had a devoted wife and two teenage sons who respected him. They lived in an upper-middle-class neighborhood, had a spacious house, and enjoyed a comfortable life. Dave was proud of his professional accomplishments, pleased with his family, and happy in the role of family provider.

In August of his fiftieth year, everything changed. Dave was fired. Just like that, after many years of loyal and effective service. The firm's profits were down and the president wanted to try new, fresher marketing approaches. He wanted to try a younger person in Dave's position.

Dave was shocked. The experience of rejection, loss, and emptiness was overwhelming. He looked for other posi-

---

## BOX 10-1

# Suicide Notes

**D**ear Bill: I am sorry for causing you so much trouble. I really didn't want to and if you would have told me at the first time the truth probably both of us would be very happy now. Bill I am sorry but I can't take the life any more, I don't think there is any goodness in the world. I love you very very much and I want you to be as happy in your life as I wanted to make you. Tell your parents I am very sorry and please if you can do it don't ever let my parents know what happened.

Please, don't hate me Bill, I love you.

Mary

*(Leenaars, 1991)*

A suicide often passes undetected or remains shrouded in mystery because the only person who could tell us the truth has been lost to the world. At the same time, an estimated 12 to 15 percent of people who commit suicide leave notes, providing unequivocal proof of their intentions and a unique record of their psychological state only hours or minutes before they died (Leenaars, 1989).

Each suicide note is a personal document, unique to the writer and the circumstances (Leenaars, 1989). Some are barely a single sentence,

others run several pages. People who leave notes clearly wish to make a powerful statement to those they leave behind (Leenaars, 1989), whether the message be "a cry for help, an epitaph, or a last will and testament" (Frederick, 1969, p. 17). Most suicide notes are addressed to specific individuals.

Suicide notes elicit varied reactions from survivors (Leenaars, 1989). A note can clarify the cause of death, thus saving relatives the ordeal of a lengthy legal inquiry. Friends and relatives may also find that it eases their grief to know the person's reasons for committing suicide (Chynoweth, 1977). On the other hand, suicide notes sometimes add to the guilt and negative emotions that survivors commonly experience, as in the following case:

**R**ather than permit his wife to leave him, twenty-year-old Mr. Jefferson hanged himself in the bathroom, leaving a note on the front door for his wife, saying, "Cathy I love you. You're right, I am crazy . . . and thank you for trying to love me. Phil." Mrs. Jefferson felt

and frequently insisted that she "killed Phil." She attempted suicide herself a week after. . . .

*(Wallace, 1981, p. 79)*

Traditionally, suicide notes have been private documents, read only by relatives, the police, or the courts (Frederick, 1969). During the latter half of this century, however, researchers have asked to study suicide notes for clues that may help them understand the phenomenon of suicide. Several aspects of suicide notes are of interest to researchers: differences between genuine and fake suicide notes; such dimensions as the age and sex of the note writer; the grammatical structure of the note; the type and frequency of words used; the conscious and unconscious content; emotional, cognitive, and motivational themes; and even the handwriting (Frederick, 1969).

Suicide note studies have reached several conclusions about the state of suicidal individuals (Leenaars, 1989):

Suicidal people are in a state of overwhelming anguish. Part of one note read, "There's just this heavy

tions, but found only low-paying jobs for which he was over-qualified. The office machine business was no longer the wide-open field he had started in, nor was he the energetic young man of years past. He began to fear that he would never find a position with the status and salary he was accustomed to.

Each day as he looked for work Dave became more depressed, anxious, and desperate. He was convinced that his wife and sons would not love him if he could not maintain their lifestyle. Even if they did, he could not love himself under such circumstances. He kept sinking, withdrawing from others, and entering a state of hopelessness.

Six months after losing his job, Dave began to consider ending his life. The pain was too great, the humiliation

unending. He hated the present and dreaded the future. He believed his family would be better off with him dead; he was certain he would be better off. He actually discussed these thoughts with friends and listened to their reactions, arguments, and encouragement. Nevertheless, he became increasingly convinced that suicide was a plausible, even desirable, notion.

Throughout February he went back and forth. On some days he was sure he wanted to die. On other days, an enjoyable evening or uplifting conversation might change his mind temporarily. On a Monday late in February he heard about a job possibility and the anticipation of the next day's interview seemed to lift his spirits. But at Tuesday's interview, things did not go well. It was clear to him that he

---

overwhelming—dreading everything. Dreading life." Another said, "I can't handle the responsibility of life. I have tried to cope with the pressures but find that I just can't do it."

Suicidal people are absorbed in interpersonal problems. Notes frequently mention rejection, loss, or disappointment in relationships. One note simply read, "If I haven't the Love I want so badly there is nothing left."

Suicidal people are highly emotional and ambivalent. Notes are charged with both negative and positive feelings. Most common are hostility toward the self—for instance: "I can't help myself, I can't do any more damage than I have already"—and hostility toward others. Positive emotion, including affection and concern for others, are also seen: "I love you so much. Forgive me for doing this."

Suicidal people think in an unusually constricted manner that leads them to perceive their suicide as a logical answer to their problems. One person wrote, "I am tired of failing. If I can do this I will succeed." Notes suggest that the suicidal person still expects to have an influence on others, and so, paradoxically, does not comprehend the finality of death.

Suicide often seems to have unconscious motives.

Suicide shows significant variation with age. Younger persons express more self-directed hostility and interpersonal problems; those between 40 and 49 report being unable to cope with life; those between 50 and 59 rarely cite a reason for their suicide; and those over 60 are motivated by such problems as illness, disability, and loneliness.

The nature of suicide has changed little since the 1940s. Suicide notes written in the 1940s and 1950s are similar in content to those written in the 1980s, with the exception that modern notes show less ambivalence and more constricted thinking.

Notes have also been used to test the validity of various theories of suicide. In such cases, researchers use the theories to predict the content the notes should contain, and then rate the notes for the presence of that content. Theories such as Freud's, which emphasize the importance of relationships, ambivalence, and unconscious motives, have gained relatively strong support in studies of notes.

In addition, suicide notes have been studied to assess how other people perceive those who are suicidal. Unfortunately, most people have a poor

understanding of the suicidal state. When research subjects are asked to generate fake suicide notes, they usually underestimate the weight of interpersonal problems in suicide, use more euphemisms for death, and write much more briefly (Arbitt & Blatt, 1973; Darbonne, 1969). A recent study observed that some suicide notes are more readily judged to be genuine than others (Leenaars & Lester, 1990). Analysis showed, however, that "obvious" notes did not differ from "nonobvious" notes in cognitive constriction, ambivalence, or sense of rejection. The ability to determine precisely how obvious notes differ from notes that are not obvious promises to help us understand what makes others sensitive to and believe in a person's suicidal intentions.

A written note is necessarily only a fragment of the writer's experiences and perceptions, thoughts, and emotions and provides only a partial picture. Moreover, as Edwin Shneidman points out, the writers may not be fully aware of their motives; their cognitive constriction prevents them from being truly insightful. Suicide notes are "not the royal road to an easy understanding of suicidal phenomena" (Shneidman, 1973, p. 380). In conjunction with other sources, however, suicide notes may be a fruitful avenue of research.

would not be offered the job. He went home, took a recently purchased gun from his locked desk drawer, and shot himself.

*Billy: Billy never truly recovered from his mother's* death. He was only 7 years old and unprepared for a loss of such magnitude. His father sent him to live with his grandparents for a time, to a new school with new kids and a new way of life. In Billy's mind, all these changes were for the worse. He missed the joy and laughter of the past. He missed his home, his father, and his friends. Most of all he missed his mother.

He did not really understand her death. His father said that she was in heaven now, at peace, happy. That she had not wanted to die or leave Billy, that an accident had taken her life. His father explained that life would be very hard for a while but that someday Billy would feel better, laugh again, enjoy things again. Billy waited for that day, but it didn't seem to come. As his unhappiness and loneliness continued day after day, he put things together in his own way. He believed that he would be happy again if he could join his mother. He felt that she was waiting for him, waiting for him to come to her. These thoughts seemed so right to him; they brought him comfort and hope. One evening, shortly after saying good night to his grandparents, Billy climbed out of bed, went up the stairs to the roof of their apartment house, and jumped to his death. He was frightened but at the same time happy as he jumped. In his mind he was joining his mother in heaven.

*Margaret: Margaret and Bob had been going together for* a year. It was Margaret's first serious relationship; it was her whole life. She confided all of her feelings to Bob, all of her hopes, ideas, and plans. She loved sharing and doing things with him. She loved their intimacy. She felt that Bob shared these feelings. He said as much and acted like a person who cared. Thus when Bob told Margaret that he no longer loved her and was leaving her for someone else, Margaret was shocked and shaken.

As the weeks went by, Margaret was filled with two competing feelings—depression and anger. On the one hand, she was devastated—wondering how she could continue, fill the void, and bear this rejection. She felt lost and alone. Several times she called Bob, begged him to reconsider, and pleaded for a chance to win him back. At the same time, she felt hatred toward Bob. She didn't deserve this treatment. She had done nothing but love him and give all of herself to him. In return, he had sent her away and destroyed her life. It was he who deserved to suffer, not she. Sometimes when she was talking to him, her pleas would change to demands, her cries to yells. Who did he think he was? He would get his eventually.

Margaret's friends became more and more worried about her. At first they understood her pain, sympathized with it,

and assumed it would soon subside. But as time went on, her depression and anger actually intensified. Then Margaret began to act strangely. When she drove her car, she would suddenly speed around sharp turns. She started drinking heavily and casually mixing her drinks with all kinds of pills. She would pick arguments with friends and even strangers, and wanted to carry these fights to physical blows. She constantly seemed to flirt with danger.

One night Margaret went into her bathroom, reached for a bottle of sleeping pills, and swallowed a handful of them. She wanted to make her pain go away and she wanted Bob to know just how much pain he had caused her. She continued swallowing pill after pill, crying and swearing as she gulped them down. When she began to feel drowsy, she decided to call her close friend Cindy. She was not sure why she was calling, perhaps to say good-bye, to explain her actions, or to make sure that Bob was told; or perhaps to be talked out of it. Cindy, of course, became desperate. She pleaded with Margaret, pointed out the irrationality of her actions, and tried to motivate her to live. Margaret was trying to listen, but she became less and less coherent. She had taken so many pills. She was beyond helping herself. Cindy hung up the phone and quickly called Margaret's neighbor and the police. When reached by her neighbor, Margaret was already in a coma. The police could not revive her and they rushed her to the hospital. Doctors and nurses worked feverishly to save her, but to no avail. Seven hours later, while her friends and family waited for news in the hospital lounge, Margaret died.

While Margaret seemed ambivalent about her death, Dave was clear in his wish to die. And whereas Billy viewed death as a trip to heaven, Dave saw it as an end to his existence. Such differences can be important in assessing, understanding, and treating suicidal clients. Accordingly, Shneidman has distinguished four kinds of people who intentionally end their lives: the *death seeker*, *death initiator, death ignorer,* and *death darer.*

**Death seekers** have a clear intention of ending their lives at the time they attempt suicide. This singleness of purpose is usually of short duration. Such clarity and commitment to act can change to ambivalence the very next hour or day, and then return again in an equally short time.

Dave, the middle-aged executive, was a death seeker. Granted, he had many misgivings about suicide, was ambivalent about it for weeks, and even sought out conversations to dissuade him. Had he been unable to carry out his action on Tuesday, Wednesday might have brought a different frame of mind and perhaps a different ending. On Tuesday, however, he was a death seeker—clear in his desire to die and acting in a manner that guaranteed a fatal outcome.

Some theorists argue that those who use more lethal suicide techniques, such as firearms, have a clearer death-seeking intent than those who use less lethal techniques, such as drug overdose. Shneidman points out, however, that many people who use less lethal techniques are very clear in their wish to die, fully believe that their action will end their lives, and accordingly should be classified as death seekers.

Although *death initiators* also clearly intend to end their lives, they act out of a conviction that the process of death is already under way and that they are simply hastening the process. Some expect that they will die in the near future — a matter of days or weeks. Sometimes they believe that by killing themselves now, they are avoiding the loss of control or suffering that otherwise awaits them. As we shall see later, many suicides among the elderly and sick fall into this category. The novelist Ernest Hemingway, for example, followed the pattern of a death initiator. A strong and proud man, he developed grave concerns about his failing body — concerns that some observers believe were at the center of his suicide.

*Death ignorers* do not believe that their self-inflicted death will mean the end of their existence. They believe they are trading their present life for a better or happier existence. Many child suicides, like Billy, fall into this category, as do adult believers in a hereafter who commit suicide to reach another form of life.

In designating this category, Shneidman was not challenging anyone's belief in the hereafter. Rather, he was distinguishing suicides by people who expect their existence to end from suicides by those who expect some sort of continuation of being. A widower who ends his life because he cannot bear his loneliness has a different intent from a widower who acts so that he may join his wife in heaven.

*Death darers* are ambivalent in their intent to die even at the moment of their attempt, and they show this ambivalence in the act itself. Although to some degree they wish to die, and they often do die, they take actions that do not guarantee death. The person who plays Russian roulette — that is, pulls the trigger of a revolver randomly loaded with one bullet — is a death darer. So is the person who walks along the ledge of a tall building or a nonpilot who flies an airplane without help. Death darers often are as interested in gaining attention, making someone feel guilty, or expressing anger as in dying per se (Brent, Kupfer, Bromet, & Dow, 1988; Hawton et al., 1982).

Margaret, the woman described earlier, might be considered a death darer. Although her unhappiness and anger were pronounced, she was not sure that she

Severely depressed about his progressive illness, Ernest Hemingway shot himself to death in 1961. Two series of electroconvulsive treatments had failed to improve his mood.

wanted to die even as she took an excess of pills. While taking the pills, she called her friend, reported her actions, and listened to her friend's advice and pleas. She carried her ambivalence into the suicidal act itself and remained in conflict until her death.

Although he does not consider such deaths to be suicides, Shneidman (1981) has also distinguished a suicidelike category called *subintentioned death.* Here individuals play *indirect, covert, partial,* or *unconscious* roles in their own deaths. Seriously ill people who consistently mismanage their medicines may belong in this category. In related work, Karl Menninger (1938) has distinguished a category called *chronic suicide.* Here people behave in life-endangering ways over an extended period of time — perhaps consuming excessive alcohol, abusing drugs, indulging in risky activities, or pursuing high-risk occupations. Although their deaths may represent a form of suicide, their true intent is unclear. Thus in this chapter the term "suicide" will refer only to deaths in which the victims intentionally, directly, and consciously end their own lives.

Are daredevils also death darers? Devotees of bungee jumping, a current craze in California and elsewhere, leap headfirst from a tall bridge or crane with their ankles tied to a long, flexible cord, and plunge to within a few feet of the ground. Jumpers sometimes describe the experience as "death survived." Several have been killed when their cords broke.

## The Study of Suicide

Suicide researchers are faced with a major problem— their subjects are no longer alive. How can investigators draw accurate conclusions about the intentions, feelings, and circumstances of people who are no longer available to answer questions about their actions? Two major research strategies have been used, each having certain limitations.

One strategy is *retrospective analysis,* a kind of psychological autopsy in which clinicians and researchers piece together data from the person's past (Robins & Kulbok, 1988). Even when suicide comes as a surprise, relatives and friends may remember past statements, conversations, and behavior that can be revealing in light of the suicide. Other retrospective data may be gathered from psychotherapists' notes and remembrances. Some people who commit suicide were previously in therapy and talked about the issues and problems that led to their lethal action. Finally, retrospective data may also be provided by the suicide notes that some victims leave behind.

Unfortunately, these sources of information are not always available. Less than a quarter of all suicide victims have been in psychotherapy (Fleer & Pasewark, 1982), and at most 15 percent leave suicide notes (Shneidman, 1979). Nor is retrospective information necessarily valid. A grieving, often guilt-ridden relative may be incapable of generating objective and accurate recollections.

Because of these limitations, many researchers also use the strategy of *studying people who survive their suicide attempts* and equating them with those who commit

fatal suicides. Of course, people who survive suicide may differ in important ways from those who actually do kill themselves (Clayton, 1985; Stengel, 1974, 1964). Among adolescents, for example, attempted suicides outnumber fatal suicides by as many as 120 to 1. When the number of incomplete suicides is this high, it may well be that many of these people do not want to die. Although survivors of suicide attempts are an imperfect source of information, suicide researchers have found it useful and informative to study them. We shall therefore consider those who attempt suicide and those who commit suicide as more or less alike.

## Patterns and Statistics

Suicide rates vary from country to country. Hungary, Austria, West Germany, Denmark, Finland, Switzerland, and Sweden have very high rates, more than 20 suicides annually per 100,000 persons (Diekstra, 1990; WHO, 1987). Conversely, Egypt, Mexico, Italy, Ireland, Israel, Greece, and Spain have relatively low rates, fewer than 9 per 100,000. The United States and Canada fall in between, each with a suicide rate of approximately 13 per 100,000 persons (U.S. Bureau of the Census, 1988; WHO, 1987).

One factor often cited to account for these national differences is *religious affiliation and beliefs* (Shneidman, 1979). Countries that are predominantly Catholic, Jewish, or Muslim tend to have lower suicide rates, whereas predominantly Protestant countries have higher rates. It may be that the first three religions, with their relatively strict proscriptions against suicide and heavy integration of members into church and communal life, help to sway people away from suicidal acts. There are, however, exceptions to this interpretation. Austria, for example, a predominantly Roman Catholic country, has one of the highest suicide rates in the world. In fact, research is beginning to suggest that it may not be religious doctrine that militates against suicide, but rather the degree of an individual's devoutness (Holmes, 1985; Martin, 1984). Irrespective of their particular religion, very religious people seem to be less likely to commit suicide. Similarly, it seems that people who hold a greater reverence for life are less prone to contemplate or attempt self-destruction (Lee, 1985).

Suicide rates also differ for men and women (see Figure 10-1). Women attempt three times as many suicides as men; yet men succeed at more than three times the rate of women (McIntosh, 1991; Stillion, 1985). Approximately 20.6 of every 100,000 men in the United States kill themselves each year, an average of 66 men each day; the suicide rate for women, which has been increasing in recent years, is 5.4 per 100,000, an average of 18 women each day (NCHS, 1988).

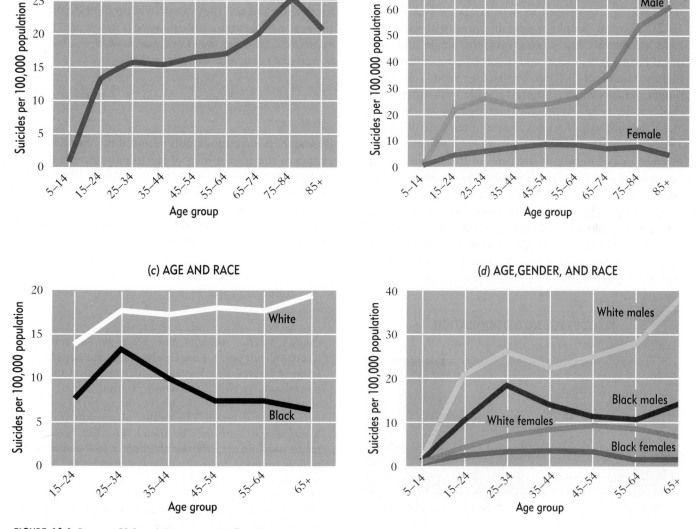

**FIGURE 10-1** Current U.S. suicide rates: *(a)* People over the age of 65 are more likely to commit suicide than those in any other age group; *(b)* males commit suicide at higher rates than females of corresponding ages; *(c)* whites commit suicide at higher rates than blacks of corresponding ages; *(d)* elderly white men have the highest risk of suicide. *(Adapted from McIntosh, 1991, pp. 62–63; U.S. Bureau of the Census, 1987.)*

One reason for these differing rates appears to be the different methods of suicide used by men and women (Kushner, 1985). Men tend to use more violent methods, such as shooting, stabbing, or hanging themselves, while women use less violent methods, such as barbiturate overdose (Kranczer, 1986; Stillion, 1985). Indeed, firearms account for close to two-thirds of the male suicides in the United States, compared to 40 percent of the female suicides (NCHS, 1988; Frederick, 1985). Some observers believe that men are clear in their wish to die more often than women, and that this firmness of purpose accounts for the differential use of these methods. Even if those who use nonviolent techniques are as serious in their wish to die as those who use violent techniques, however, the violent techniques are less reversible and allow less time to change one's mind or for others to intervene (Kushner, 1985; Marks, 1977).

Suicide is also related to marital status (see Figure 10-2). Married people, especially those with children, have a relatively low suicide rate; the single and widowed have higher rates; and divorced people have the highest rate of all (NCHS, 1988). One study compared ninety persons who committed suicide with ninety psychologically troubled patients matched for age, gender, and schooling who had never attempted suicide (Roy, 1982). Only 16 percent of the suicide subjects were married or cohabiting at the time of the suicide, compared to 30 percent of the control subjects. Similarly, an analysis conducted in Canada over three decades has revealed a strong positive correlation between national divorce rates and suicide rates (Trovato, 1987).

Finally, in the United States at least, suicide rates differ markedly among the races (see Figure 10-1c).

The suicide rate of whites in the United States, 14 per 100,000 persons, is twice as high as that of blacks and members of other racial groups (McIntosh, 1991; NCHS, 1988). The major exception to this pattern is the very high suicide rate of Native Americans. Their overall suicide rate is twice the national average; some Native American groups even display rates as high as five to ten times the national average (Willard, 1979; Shore, 1975).

## PRECIPITATING FACTORS IN SUICIDE

Suicidal acts often are tied to contemporaneous events or conditions. While these factors may not fully account for the suicidal act, they do serve to precipitate the drastic action. Common precipitating factors are *stressful events and situations*, *mood and thought changes*, *alcohol use*, *mental disorders*, and *modeling events*.

### Stressful Events and Situations

Researchers have repeatedly counted more undesirable events in the recent lives of suicide attempters than in those of matched control subjects (Paykel, 1990; Isherwood, Adam, & Hornblow, 1982; Slater & Depue, 1981). In one study, suicide attempters reported twice as many stressful events in the year before their attempt as nonsuicidal depressed patients or nondepressed psychiatric patients (Cohen-Sandler et al., 1982). An attempt may be precipitated by a single recent event or, as in the following case, by a series of events that have a combined impact.

*S*ally's suicide attempt took place in the context of a very difficult year for the family. Sally's mother and stepfather separated after 9 years of marriage. After the father moved out, he visited the family erratically. Four months after he moved out of the house, the mother's boyfriend moved into the house. The mother planned to divorce her husband and marry her boyfriend, who had become the major disciplinarian for the children; a fact that Sally intensely resented. Sally also complained of being "left out" in relation to the closeness she had with her mother. Another problem for Sally had been two school changes in the last 2 years which left Sally feeling friendless. In addition, she failed all her subjects in the last marking period.

*(Pfeffer, 1986, pp. 129–130)*

One of the most common kinds of recent stress in cases of suicide is loss of a loved one by death, divorce,

**SUICIDES PER 100,000 POPULATION**

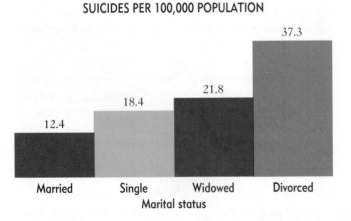

**FIGURE 10-2** In 1986 approximately 37 of every 100,000 divorced persons committed suicide, more than three times the suicide rate of married persons. *(Adapted from McIntosh, 1991, p. 64.)*

breakup, or rejection (Paykel, 1990; Hawton, 1982; McGuire, 1982). In one study of 238 people who were divorcing or recently widowed, it was found that a full 30 percent were contemplating suicide (Jacobson & Portuges, 1978). Another form of loss frequently tied to suicide is loss of a job (Pritchard, 1988; Goldney et al., 1985; Platt, 1984; Stack, 1982). Researchers have found that the rate of suicide attempts in Vienna is significantly higher for unemployed people than for the population in general (Probsting & Till, 1985).

People may also attempt suicide in response to long-term rather than recent or episodic stress. Four long-term stresses are commonly implicated — *serious illness, abusive environment, occupational stress,* and *role conflict.*

**Serious Illness**   The joint suicides in 1975 of Elizabeth and Henry Pitney Van Dusen, church leaders and model religious figures, shocked their friends and followers. She was 80 years old, and he was 77. Elizabeth Van Dusen left the following letter:

> To all Friends and Relations,
>   We hope that you will understand what we have done even though some of you will disapprove of it and some be disillusioned by it.
>   We have both had very full and satisfying lives.
>   Pitney has worked hard and with great dedication for the church. I have had an adventurous and happy life. We have both had happy lives, and our children have crowned this happiness.
>   But since Pitney had his stroke five years ago, we have not been able to do any of the things we want to do and *are* able to do, and my arthritis is much worse.
>   There are too many helpless old people who without modern medical care would have died, and we feel God would have allowed them to die when their time had come.
>   Nowadays it is difficult to die. We feel that this way we are taking will become more usual and acceptable as the years pass.
>   Of course the thought of our children and our grandchildren *make* us sad, but we still feel that this is the best way and the right way to go. We are both increasingly weak and unwell and who would want to die in a Nursing Home.
>   We are not afraid to die.
>   We send you all our love and gratitude for your wonderful support and friendship.
>   "O Lamb of God that takest away the sins of the world Have mercy on us. O Lamb of God that takest away the sins of the world Grant us thy peace."
>
> *(Klinefelter, 1984, pp. 345–346)*

As noted in the earlier discussion of "death initiators," a painful or disabling illness is at the center of many suicide attempts (Mackenzie & Popkin, 1987; Clarke,

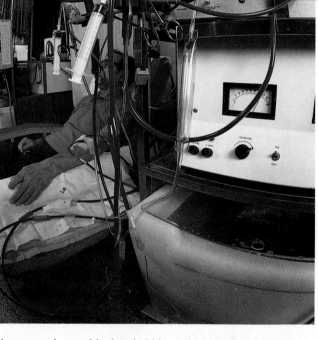

Among patients with chronic kidney disorders who are over the age of 60 and require regular dialysis, one of every six elects to stop treatment (Neu & Kjellstrand, 1986). Without dialysis, most slip into a coma and die within 8 days.

1986; Brown, Henteleff, Barakat, & Rowe, 1986). People with such problems may come to feel that their death is unavoidable and imminent, or that the suffering and problems caused by their illness are more than they can endure. An analysis of the medical records of eighty-eight cancer patients who had died by suicide in Sweden revealed that nearly two-thirds were in an advanced or terminal phase of the disease and had severe symptoms (Bolund, 1985).

Although illness-linked suicides have a long history, they have become more prevalent and controversial in recent years (see Box 10-2). Medical progress is partly responsible. Although physicians can now apply life-sustaining techniques that keep seriously ill people alive much longer, they are seldom able to maintain the quality and comfort of the patients' lives. In such situations some persons try to end their slow and painful decline.

**Abusive Environment**  Suicide is sometimes committed by victims of an abusive or repressive environment from which there is little or no hope of escape. Prisoners of war, victims of the Holocaust, abused spouses, and prison inmates have attempted to end their lives (Counts, 1990; Gaston, 1979). Like those who have serious illnesses, these people may have been in constant psychological or physical pain, felt that they could endure no more suffering, and believed that there was no hope for improvement in their condition.

**Occupational Stress**  Certain jobs create ongoing feelings of tension or dissatisfaction that can precipitate suicide

---

## BOX 10-2

# The Right to Commit Suicide

In the fall of 1989, a Michigan doctor, Dr. J. Kevorkian, built a "suicide device." A person using it could, at the touch of a button, change a saline solution fed intravenously into the arm to one containing chemicals that would bring unconsciousness and a swift death. The following June, under the doctor's supervision, Mrs. J. Adkins took her life. She left a note explaining: "This is a decision taken in a normal state of mind and is fully considered. I have Alzheimer's disease and I do not want to let it progress any further. I do not want to put my family or myself through the agony of this terrible disease." Mrs. Adkins believed that she

Dr. J. Kevorkian and his suicide device.

had a right to choose death and that her choice was a rational one; indeed her husband supported her decision. Meanwhile, Dr. Kevorkian believed that the "device" could be valuable in assisting persons with compelling grounds for suicide. However, Michigan authorities promptly prohibited further use of the device.

*(Adapted from Belkin, 1990; Malcolm, 1990)*

The way a society views suicide depends greatly on its perceptions of life and death. The society of classical Greece valued physical and mental well-being in life and dignity in death; therefore, people with sufficient cause, such as grave illness or mental anguish, had legal recourse to suicide. Athenian citizens could obtain official permission from the Senate to take their own lives, and magistrates were authorized to dispense hemlock to such persons for that purpose (Humphry & Wickett, 1986).

American attitudes toward suicide reflect a tradition that has long discouraged such acts (Siegel, 1988). A "sanctity of life" morality has prevailed, according to which all human existence is valued and should be protected (Eser, 1981). The Bible does not explicitly censure the taking of one's own life, but in the fifth century St. Augustine declared that suicide broke the commandment "Thou shalt not kill." Soon after, the church announced that persons who attempted suicide would be excommunicated (Fletcher, 1981). Christians feared that the restless spirits of suicides would haunt the living and defile holy ground, so a suicide was given an ignominious burial by the highway with a stake through the heart (Fletcher, 1981). Later, in countries such as Britain, suicide was considered a crime against the king or state, a failure to fulfull one's obligations to society (Siegel, 1988). As punishment, the state confiscated a suicide's property, and a person who had attempted suicide faced humiliation in the stocks, a fine, or imprisonment (Fletcher, 1981; Siegel, 1988).

Today we still speak of "committing" suicide as though it were a criminal act (Barrington, 1980). Whereas "natural" and accidental deaths elicit the sympathy of the community, deaths by suicide are more likely

attempts. Research has found particularly high suicide rates among psychiatrists and psychologists, physicians, dentists, lawyers, and unskilled laborers (Richings, Khara, & McDowell, 1986; Stillion, 1985; Roy, 1985). Of course, these correlational data do not establish that occupational pressures are in fact leading to higher suicide rates. There are alternative interpretations. Un-skilled workers may be responding to financial insecurity rather than job stress when they attempt suicide. Similarly, there is the possibility that rather than reacting to the emotional drain of their work, suicidal psychiatrists and psychologists have long-standing emotional problems and that these stimulated their career interest in the first place.

---

to evoke sensationalism, unease, and outright disapproval (Rudestam, 1990). Since the state presumably has an interest in protecting the lives of its citizens, force and involuntary commitment may be used legally to prevent a suicide (Grisez & Boyle, 1979). Assisting suicide, whether by providing advice or encouragement or a place or means for the act, is punishable by law (Francis, 1980). Nevertheless, times and attitudes are changing.

The idea of a "right to suicide" and "rational suicide" is receiving increasing support in our society. Common law traditionally affirms a person's right to self-determination (Miesel, 1989), and some people argue that this right extends to the "liberty right" to end one's life (Battin, 1982; Siegel, 1988). Others consider suicide a "natural right," comparable to the rights to life, ownership of property, and freedom of speech (Battin, 1982). Interpreted in its broadest sense, a right to suicide would apply to everyone. Most proponents, however, would restrict this right to situations in which the act of suicide would be considered "rational," adopting a "quality of life" view that suggests that life is valuable insofar as it is an enriching and fulfilling experience; when it is not, suicide is a reasonable alternative (Eser, 1981; Grisez & Boyle, 1979). In theory, this more conservative stand does not deny the need for measures to prevent suicide, but implies that they should be restricted to "irrational" cases (Battin, 1982, 1980). One clinical theorist argues that persons who seek the assistance of mental health professionals or prevention centers clearly de-sire and require help (Motto, 1980).

Public support for a right to suicide seems strongest in instances of terminal illness (Siegel, 1988). In the United States, the Society for the Right to Die presses for legislation to prevent the "unnecessary prolongation of life"; Concern for Dying educates the public on these issues; and the Hemlock Society supports voluntary euthanasia for the terminally ill. Together these groups boast a membership of about 238,000 persons drawn from all walks of life (Burek, 1990; Siegel, 1988). Polls suggest that about half of the population believes that terminally ill persons should be free to take their lives or to seek assistance from the medical profession in doing so (Malcolm, 1990; Siegel, 1988). Now a legally competent person can write a "living will," declaring in advance the treatment that would be desired or refused in the event of terminal illness (Humphry & Wickett, 1986; Miesel, 1989; Siegel, 1988).

Even in cases of severe medical illness, however, the suicidal person's thinking may be affected by psychological disorders or stress. Though many people face extremely difficult circumstances in which suicide may seem rational, very few choose this option. AIDS and cancer patients who commit suicide, for example, are a very small minority of these populations (Malcolm, 1990). Rather than responses to the negative impact of illness, such suicides may be linked to clinical depression, deficiencies in coping skills, or distress in reaction to the emotional withdrawal of family members. Perhaps these persons would benefit more from treatment and support that help them come to terms with their situation than from being given the "right" to die.

In addition, a medically ill person's right to suicide is questionable *if it impinges* on the lives of others in society. An increased incidence of suicide could enhance the problem of "suicide contagion" in emotionally vulnerable members of society.

Finally, the right to suicide could be gravely abused. Although it is upheld as the ultimate freedom, a right to suicide might trap some people in an "obligation to suicide." An elderly person, for example, might feel unjustified in expecting relatives to support and care for him or her when suicide is a socially approved alternative. The notion of rational suicide may undermine the principle that all members of society have an equal right to life because it suggests that some lives are less worthwhile than others (Sherlock, 1983). A slippery-slope view predicts that if rational suicide is accepted, it might be all too easy for society to slip into accepting such practices as forced euthanasia and infanticide (Battin, 1982).

How are the tensions between the rights of the individual and society, the value of life and dignified death, the nebulous sense that some suicides are rational, and the call for an overarching legal statement to be resolved? The future holds great challenges for those who seek to understand, treat, and prevent suicide, but the question of whether and when we should stand back and do nothing poses just as great a challenge. Whatever one's stand on this issue, it is a matter of life and death.

**Role Conflict** Another long-term stress linked to suicide is role conflict. Everyone occupies a variety of roles in life — spouse, employee, parent, and colleague, to name a few. These roles may conflict and cause considerable stress. In recent years researchers have found that women who hold jobs outside of the home often experience role conflicts — conflicts between their family demands and job requirements, for example, or between their social needs and vocational goals — and that these conflicts are reflected in a higher suicide rate (Stack, 1987; Stillion, 1985; Davis, 1981). Women in professional positions, such as physicians, appear to experience the most role conflict, and they display the highest suicide rate of women in the work force (Arnetz et al., 1987; Stillion, 1985; Pitts et al., 1979). Moreover, professional women who attempt suicide report more conflict between their roles as women and as professionals than nonsuicidal professional women do (Diamond, 1978).

## Mood and Thought Changes

Many suicide attempts are preceded by a shift in the person's mood and thought. Although these shifts may not be severe enough to warrant a diagnosis of a mental disorder, they typically represent a significant change from the person's past mood or point of view.

The mood change most often linked to suicide is an increase in sadness (McGuire, 1982; Tishler, McKenry, & Morgan, 1981). Also common are heightened feelings of anxiety, anger, or shame (Pine, 1981; Weissman, Fox, & Klerman, 1973). Shneidman (1991) characterizes the key to suicide as a feeling of "psychological pain experienced as intolerable, caused by unfulfilled psychological needs." He states, "No one commits suicide out of joy; no suicide is born out of exultation. The enemy of life is pain. Pain is what the suicidal person seeks to escape" (1987, p. 56).

In the cognitive realm, many people on the verge of suicide frequently become preoccupied with their problems, lose perspective, and see suicide as an effective solution to their difficulties (Shneidman, 1987; Chiles et al., 1985). They develop a sense of *hopelessness* — a pessimistic belief that their present circumstances, problems, and negative mood will not change (Hirschfeld & Davidson, 1988; Ellis & Ratliff, 1986; Holden et al., 1985). Some clinicians believe that a feeling of hopelessness is the single most sensitive indicator of suicidal intent (Ellis & Ratliff, 1986; Holden et al., 1985; Beck, 1975), and they take special care to look for signs of hopelessness when they assess the risk of suicide (see Table 10-4). People who contemplate suicide may also develop a pattern of *dichotomous thinking,* viewing their problems and solutions in either/or terms (Shneidman, 1987; Neuringer, 1974, 1976; Wetzel, 1975, 1976). In the following statement a woman who sur-

TABLE 10-4

| HOPELESSNESS SCALE |
|---|
| Hopelessness is indicated when people answer: |
| **True** |
| I might as well give up because there's nothing I can do about making things better for myself. |
| I can't imagine what my life would be like in ten years. |
| My future seems dark to me. |
| I just don't get the breaks, and there's no reason to believe I will in the future. |
| All I can see ahead of me is unpleasantness rather than pleasantness. |
| I don't expect to get what I really want. |
| Things just won't work out the way I want them to. |
| I never get what I want so it's foolish to want anything. |
| It is very unlikely that I will get any real satisfaction in the future. |
| The future seems vague and uncertain to me. |
| There's no use in really trying to get something I want because I probably won't get it. |
| **False** |
| I look forward to the future with hope and enthusiasm. |
| When things are going badly, I am helped by knowing that they can't stay that way forever. |
| I have enough time to accomplish the things I most want to do. |
| In the future I expect to succeed in what concerns me most. |
| I happen to be particularly lucky and I expect to get more of the good things in life than the average person. |
| My past experiences have prepared me well for my future. |
| When I look ahead to the future I expect I will be happier than I am now. |
| I have great faith in the future. |
| I can look forward to more good times than bad times. |

*Source:* Beck, Weissman, Lester et al., 1974.

vived her jump off a building describes her dichotomous thinking at the time of the jump. She saw death as the only alternative to her pain:

*I was so desperate. I felt, my God, I couldn't face this* thing. Everything was like a terrible whirlpool of confusion. And I thought to myself: There's *only* one thing to do. I just have to lose consciousness. That's the *only* way to get away from it. The *only* way to lose consciousness, I thought, was to jump off something good and high. . . .

*(Shneidman, 1987, p. 56)*

## Alcohol Use

Studies indicate that between 20 and 90 percent of those who commit suicide drink alcohol just before the act (Hirschfeld & Davidson, 1989). Autopsies reveal that about one-fifth of these people are legally intoxicated at the time of death (Brent et al., 1987; Center for Disease Control, 1984). In fact, the excessive use of alcohol just before suicide is probably much higher; coroners are more likely to classify deaths as accidental once they detect high alcohol consumption (Crompton, 1985). Such statistics suggest to many clinical researchers that alcohol consumption often contributes to suicidal behavior (Schuckit & Schuckit, 1990).

Some theorists believe that alcohol's disinhibiting effects allow people who are contemplating suicide to overcome the fears that would otherwise restrain them (Patel et al., 1972). Others suggest that alcohol contributes to suicide by lowering an individual's prohibitions against violence and even helping to release covert aggressive feelings (Whitlock & Broadhurst, 1969). Research suggests that the use of other kinds of drugs may have a similar tie to suicide, particularly in teenagers and young adults (Rich, Young, & Fowler, 1986; Shafii et al., 1986). We shall return to this point later in the discussion of suicide by the young.

## Mental Disorders

As we noted earlier, people who attempt suicide do not necessarily have a mental disorder. Although they are troubled, unhappy, or anxious, their feelings may not add up to any disorder defined in DSM-III-R. On the other hand, between 30 and 70 percent of all suicide attempters do display a mental disorder (Litman, 1987; Roy, 1985; Goldney et al., 1985; Miles, 1977). The disorders linked most strongly to suicide are *mood disorders* (unipolar and bipolar depression), *substance use disorders* (particularly alcoholism), and *schizophrenia*. Research suggests that approximately 10 to 15 percent of

people with each of these disorders try to kill themselves (Brent et al., 1987, 1986; Miles, 1977). Mood disorders, the most prevalent of these disorders in the general population, contribute to a greater number of suicides than the others (Clayton, 1985; Bellini et al., 1985).

In Chapter 8 we observed that most people with a major depressive disorder experience suicidal thoughts as part of their syndrome. Those whose disorder includes a strong sense of hopelessness seem most likely to attempt suicide (Fawcett et al., 1987). Even when depressed people are showing improvements in mood, they may remain high suicide risks. In fact, among those who are severely depressed, the risk of suicide may actually increase as their mood improves and they have more energy to act on their suicidal wishes.

Even if suicide is attempted in response to a severe physical illness, an episode of major depression may be playing a key role in the decision. In one case a depressed 26-year-old woman with cerebral palsy initially fought to compel a psychiatric hospital to assist her in committing suicide; when the woman's depression later lifted, she reversed her position (Bursztajn et al., 1986). Similarly, a study of forty-four terminally ill patients revealed that fewer than a quarter of them had thoughts of suicide or wished for an early death, and that those who did were all suffering from major depression (Brown et al., 1986). In the following case a clinically depressed terminally ill woman changes her perspective over time.

*Nancy was a personal friend who had moved away some* months ago, after concluding her divorce and seeing her twin daughters comfortably started in their college careers. With no forewarning, she called one afternoon to say that she was back in town. She realized her request would probably be refused, but could she have 50 seconal tablets? In total seriousness, she said it was important that she do away with herself before the weekend and the arrival home of her daughters. This was no simple "cry for help" or manipulative appeal. She had called from her hospital room, where she later revealed that she had been diagnosed as having advanced lung cancer, with metastases to the skull and back. Her prognosis, with chemotherapy, was for perhaps three or four months before lapsing into a terminal state. She was already pale and withered, breathing with difficulty despite the recent drainage of a quart of fluid from her chest. She was determined to commit suicide, rather than endure the trials of therapy, or see her last financial resources squandered on fruitless medical care. She was the only child of an elderly couple, and was certain the news would strike down her father. Above all, she did not want to face her daughters' pain or her friends' pity and solicitude. "Realistic" suicide? The call for seconal from an unlikely source was still an invitation to debate her fate. Every appeal for time, reflection, and granting her family and friends the opportunity to say goodbye was made and countered. Her only show of sadness came when she was reminded that there were many who would keep some vestige of her in their hearts. She was remarkably free of fear — the determination to act, the focus on how to achieve her aim suppressed all other emotion.

She had her way a day later. Two close friends who accompanied her home managed to provide her with a quantity of medication, which she downed with liberal amounts of alcohol. When she was drowsy, they took their leave, intending to come back a day later to arrange matters before the daughters' return. Some quirk of fate or physiology intervened, for when Nancy was found, in spite of her lethal ingestion, she was still holding to life. She was comatose for several days, and finally returned to a home full of children, parents, her divorced husband, and many friends. She called again that week to vent her anger that she had been "proselytized" to stay alive when she wished only to die, and then to express her deep feelings of thankfulness that she had been given the opportunity to take a more measured and dignified leave of those she loved. She died not long after, spared the agony she had feared, a little afraid, but happier for her manner of leaving. Nancy's attempt may itself have altered the dynamics of her crisis, but it was the working of time that transformed a credibly realistic suicide into an acceptance of death with integrity uncompromised.

*(Kahn, 1982, p. 87)*

In many cases of suicide after alcohol use the individuals actually have a long history of abusing alcohol or some other substance (Brent et al., 1987; Roy & Linnoila, 1986; Miles, 1977). The basis for the link between substance use disorders and suicide is not clear. It may be that the tragic lifestyle resulting from the long-term use of alcohol or other drugs or the sense of being hopelessly trapped by a drug leads to suicidal thinking. Alternatively, both substance abuse and suicidal thinking may be caused by a third factor — by psychological pain, for instance, or desperation (Frances et al., 1987). Nor should the medical complications of chronic substance abuse be overlooked. Most suicides by alcoholic people, for example, occur in the late stages of the disorder when cirrhosis and other medical complications begin, suggesting that at least some of these people may be acting as "death initiators" who believe that a journey toward death has already begun (Miles, 1977; Barraclough et al., 1974).

In Chapter 15 we shall examine schizophrenia, a disorder that causes people to lose touch with reality. Common symptoms include hearing voices that are not actually present (hallucinations) and holding beliefs that are blatantly false and even bizarre (delusions). There is a popular belief that suicides by schizophrenic persons must be in response to imagined voices commanding self-destruction or to a delusion that suicide is a grand and noble gesture. In fact, however, hallucinations and delusions rarely play a role in suicides by schizophrenic persons. These suicides are typically committed by relatively young and unemployed schizophrenic people who have experienced relapses over several years and who now perceive that the disorder will forever disrupt their lives (Drake et al., 1986, 1984; Roy et al., 1986; Waltzer, 1984; Roy, 1982).

## Modeling: The Contagion of Suicide

It is not unusual for people to try to commit suicide after observing or reading about a suicide (Phillips & Carstensen, 1986; Linkowski et al., 1985; Bagley & Ramsay, 1985; Phillips, 1983, 1982, 1980, 1974). Perhaps these people have been struggling with major problems and the other person's suicide seems to reveal a possible solution; or they have been contemplating suicide and the other person's suicide seems to give them permission or finally persuades them to act (Berman & Yufit, 1983). Whatever the specific mechanism may be in such cases, one suicidal act apparently serves as a model for another.

Three kinds of models in particular seem to trigger suicides — suicides by celebrities, highly publicized suicides, and suicides by co-workers or colleagues.

**Celebrities**  In an analysis of suicide data spanning 1948 to 1983, Steven Stack (1987) found that suicides by entertainers and political figures in the United States are regularly followed by unusual increases in the number of suicides across the nation. Shortly after the young comedian Freddie Prinze committed suicide in 1978, for example, a rash of suicides occurred in the United States (Wasserman, 1985). In some cases the victims even left notes in which they mentioned Prinze's suicide.

**Highly Publicized Cases**  The news media often focus on a particular suicide because of its unusual nature, extraordinary circumstances, or special implications. Such highly publicized accounts may trigger suicides that are similar in method or circumstance. In England, a widely publicized suicide by self-immolation was followed within one year by eighty-two suicides in which the victims also set themselves on fire (Ashton & Donnan, 1981). A subsequent examination of inquest reports revealed that most of the suicide victims had histories of emotional problems and that none of the suicides was politically motivated, although the publicized suicide had political overtones. In short, the subjects of the study seemed to be responding to their own problems in a manner precipitated by the suicide they had observed or read about. The frightening impact of well-publicized

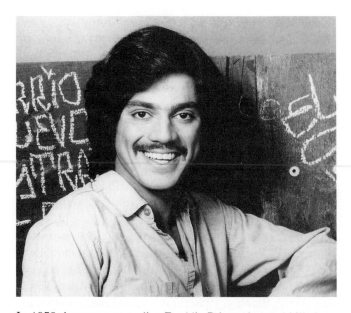

In 1978 the young comedian Freddie Prinze shot and killed himself, shocking millions of fans who had followed his success on the television series *Chico and the Man*. The number of suicide attempts in the United States apparently increased in the aftermath of Prinze's death.

suicides has led some clinicians to call for a code of practice that the news media should follow in reporting such deaths (Motto, 1967).

**Co-workers and Colleagues**  Suicides in a school, workplace, or small community often receive word-of-mouth publicity that may trigger suicide attempts by others in the setting. A suicide by a recruit at a U.S. Navy training school, for example, was followed by another completed and an attempted suicide at the school within a two-week period. To put an end to what threatened to become a suicide epidemic, the school initiated a program of staff education on suicide and group therapy sessions for recruits who had been close to the suicide victims (Grigg, 1988).

## VIEWS ON SUICIDE

Although numerous situations may precipitate suicide, most people who encounter such situations never try to kill themselves. In an effort to explain why some people are more prone to suicide than others, theorists have proposed still broader factors that may set the stage for self-destructive action. The leading theories come from the psychodynamic, biological, and sociocultural per-

spectives. Unfortunately, as we shall see, these explanations have received limited empirical support, and in fact they fail to address all kinds of suicidal acts. Thus it would be inaccurate to conclude that the clinical field currently has a satisfactory understanding of suicide.

## The Psychodynamic View

Psychodynamic theorists believe that suicide usually results from a state of depression and a process of self-directed anger. This theory was first stated by Wilhelm Stekel at a meeting in Vienna in 1910, when he proclaimed that "no one kills himself who has not wanted to kill another or at least wished the death of another" (Shneidman, 1979). Some years later, Sigmund Freud (1920) stated, "No neurotic harbors thoughts of suicide which he has not turned back upon himself from murderous impulses against others."

As we saw in Chapter 8, Freud (1917) and Abraham (1916, 1911) proposed that when people experience the real or symbolic loss of a loved one, they come to "introject" the lost person; that is, they unconsciously incorporate the person into their own identity and feel toward themselves as they had felt toward the other. For a short while, negative feelings they are harboring toward the loved one are experienced as feelings of self-hatred. Introjected feelings become particularly negative and long-lasting in some instances, perhaps in people who have been extremely dependent on and resentful of the lost loved one, or who have experienced childhood losses that were unresolved, causing them to overreact in the face of the present loss. Either way, extreme anger toward the lost loved one turns into unrelenting anger against oneself, and finally into a broad depressive reaction. Suicide is a further expression of this self-hatred. The following description of a suicidal female patient demonstrates how such dynamics may operate:

*A 27-year-old conscientious and responsible woman took* a knife to her wrists to punish herself for being tyrannical, unreliable, self-centered, and abusive. She was perplexed and frightened by this uncharacteristic self-destructive episode and was enormously relieved when her therapist pointed out that her invective described her recently deceased father much better than it did herself.

*(Gill, 1982, p. 15)*

Late in his career, Freud further explained suicide by proposing that human beings have a basic death instinct, which he called ***Thanatos,*** that functions in opposition to their life instinct. According to Freud, while most people learn to redirect their death instinct and aim it toward others, suicidal people, caught in a web of self-anger, direct the instinct squarely upon themselves (Freud, 1955).

In support of Freud's view of suicide, researchers have consistently found a relationship between childhood losses and later suicidal behaviors (Paykel, 1990). One comparison of family histories (Adam et al., 1982) found the incidence of early parental loss to be much higher among 98 suicide attempters (48 percent) than among 102 nonsuicidal control subjects (24 percent). Common losses were death of the father and divorce or separation of the parents, especially during either the earliest years of life (birth to 5 years old) or late adolescence (17 to 20 years old). Of course, although such findings do coincide with the psychodynamic view, they are correlational and do not establish the causal sequence suggested in the model.

Sociological findings, too, are consistent with Freud's proposal that suicidal people are directing a death instinct toward themselves rather than toward others. National suicide rates have been found to drop significantly in times of war, when, onc could argue, people are encouraged to direct their self-destructive energy against others. In addition, societies with high rates of homicide tend to have low rates of suicide, and vice versa (Binstock, 1974). On the other hand, research has failed to establish that suicidal people are in fact dominated by intense feelings of anger. Although hostility is an important component in some suicides, several studies find that other emotional states are even more common (Linehan & Nielsen, 1981; Shneidman, 1979).

By the end of his career, Freud expressed dissatisfaction with his theory of suicide, and other psychodynamic theorists have modified his ideas over the years. Yet themes of loss and self-directed aggression usually remain at the center of their explanations (Pitman, 1982; Kincel, 1981; Furst & Ostow, 1979).

## The Biological View

Until the 1970s the belief that biological factors contribute to suicidal behavior was based primarily on family pedigree studies. Researchers repeatedly found higher rates of suicidal behavior among the parents and close relatives of suicidal people than among those of nonsuicidal people, suggesting to some that genetic, and so biological, factors were at work (Garfinkel et al., 1979; Hauschild, 1968). Studies of twins also were consistent with this view of suicide (Lester, 1986). A study of twins born in Denmark between 1870 and 1920, for example, located nineteen identical pairs and fifty-eight fraternal pairs in which at least one of the twins had committed suicide (Juel-Nielsen and Videbech, 1970). In four of the identical pairs the other twin also committed suicide (21 percent), while the other twin never committed suicide among the fraternal pairs.

Of course, as with all family pedigree research, non-biological interpretations could also be offered for these findings. Psychodynamic clinicians might argue that children whose parents commit suicide are prone to depression and suicide because they have lost a loved one at a critical stage of development. And behavioral theorists might emphasize the modeling role played by parents or close relatives who attempt suicide. Clearly, a genetic or biological conclusion was inappropriate on the basis of family research findings alone.

In the past few years laboratory research has provided more direct support for a biological view of suicide. People who commit suicide are often found to have lower levels of the neurotransmitter *serotonin* (Asberg, 1990; Roy, 1990; Stanley, 1990; Stanley & Mann, 1988; Stanley et al., 1986). The first indication of this relationship came from a study by Marie Asberg and her colleagues (1976). Working with sixty-eight depressed patients, these researchers measured each patient's level of *5-hydroxyindoleactic acid (5-HIAA),* a component of cerebrospinal fluid that is a metabolite, or by-product, of brain serotonin. Twenty of the patients had particularly low levels of 5-HIAA (and presumably low levels of serotonin), while the remaining forty-eight had relatively high 5-HIAA levels. The researchers found that the low 5-HIAA subjects made a total of eight suicide attempts (two lethal), whereas the much larger group of high 5-HIAA subjects made only seven. The researchers interpreted this to mean that a low serotonin level may be "a predictor of suicidal acts." Later studies found that suicide attempters with low 5-HIAA levels are ten times more likely to make a repeated attempt and succeed than are suicide attempters with high 5-HIAA levels (Asberg et al., 1986; Traskman, Asberg, & Bertilsson, 1981).

Studies that examine the autopsied brains of suicide victims point in the same direction (Stanley et al., 1986, 1982; Stanley, Virgilio, & Gershon, 1982; Paul et al., 1984). Such studies usually measure the serotonin level by determining the number of *imipramine receptor sites* in the brain. Recall that imipramine is an antidepressant drug that binds to certain neural receptors throughout the brain (see Chapter 9). It is believed that the degree of imipramine binding reflects a person's usual level of serotonin; the more imipramine binding, the more serotonin activity (Langer & Raisman, 1983). Fewer imipramine binding sites found in the brains of persons who die by suicide than in the autopsied brains of nonsuicides — in fact, approximately half as many binding sites is the usual finding!

At first glance, these studies may appear to tell us little that is new. Given that low serotonin activity is correlated with depression and that depressed people often attempt suicide, we would certainly expect many who are suicidal to have low serotonin activity. On the other hand, there is evidence that the link between low serotonin and suicide is not necessarily mediated by depression. One investigation found low 5-HIAA levels among suicidal subjects who had had no history of depression (Brown et al., 1982). Similarly, researchers have found unusually low 5-HIAA levels among suicide attempters with personality disorders, schizophrenic disorders, anxiety disorders, and substance dependence in addition to those with depressive disorders (Ninan et al., 1984; Van Praag, 1983; Banki & Arato, 1983; Oreland et al., 1981).

How, then, might low serotonin activity act to increase the likelihood of suicidal behavior? Recent research links low serotonin activity with the presence of strong aggressive impulses, and this relationship may mediate serotonin's link with suicide (de Cuyper, 1987; Brown & Goodwin, 1986; Van Praag, 1986). It has been found, for example, that highly aggressive men have significantly lower 5-HIAA levels than less aggressive men (Brown et al., 1982, 1979). Moreover, lower 5-HIAA levels have been found in people who used guns and other violent means to commit suicide than in those who used nonviolent methods, such as drug overdose (Edman et al., 1986; Banki et al., 1985, 1984, 1983; Van Praag, 1983, 1982; Oreland et al., 1981). And finally, one study found that depressed patients with lower 5-HIAA levels both tried to commit suicide more often and displayed higher hostility scores on various personality inventories than did depressed patients with higher 5-HIAA scores (Van Praag, 1987).

Although these studies have been limited to small numbers of subjects (Motto, 1986), the pattern of findings suggests to many theorists that a low serotonin level does indeed produce aggressive feelings (Van Praag, 1986; Brown & Goodwin, 1986; Stanley et al., 1986). In people who are clinically depressed, low serotonin activity may produce aggressive tendencies that leave them particularly vulnerable to suicidal thinking and action. Even in the absence of a depressive disorder, people with low serotonin levels may develop highly aggressive feelings and be dangerous to themselves or others.

## The Sociocultural View

Just before the turn of the century, Emile Durkheim (1897), a sociologist, developed the first comprehensive theory of suicidal behavior. For years Durkheim's theory was the most cited and researched in the area of suicide; even today it continues to be influential in the clinical field. Believing that the societal context is an important influence on individual behavior, Durkheim proposed that scientists should gather epidemiological information about suicide and discern the unique relationships that exist between suicidal people and their society.

According to Durkheim, the probability of suicide is determined by how embedded a person is in such social institutions as the family, the church, and the community. The more a person belongs, the lower the risk of suicide. Conversely, people who are removed from or have poor relationships with society are at greater risk of killing themselves. He defined three categories of suicide based on the individual's relationship with society.

*Egoistic suicides* are committed by people over whom society has little or no control. These people are not concerned with the norms or rules of society; nor are they integrated into the social fabric. According to Durkheim, this kind of suicide is more likely in people who are isolated, alienated, and nonreligious. The larger the number of such people living in a given society, the higher that society's suicide rate.

*Altruistic suicides,* in contrast, occur in people who are very well integrated into the social structure. People who intentionally sacrifice their lives for the well-being of society are committing altruistic suicide. There are many examples of this behavior—soldiers who throw themselves on top of a live grenade to save others, Japanese kamikaze pilots who gave their lives in air attacks, and Buddhist monks and nuns who protested the Vietnam War by setting themselves on fire. According to Durkheim, societies that encourage honorable and altruistic deaths (as Far Eastern societies do) are also likely to have higher suicide rates.

*Anomic suicides,* the third category proposed by Durkheim, are committed by individuals whose social environment fails to provide stable structures, such as family and church, to support and give meaning to life. Such a societal state, called *anomie,* leaves individuals without a sense of belonging and brings about what Durkheim calls a heightened "inclination for suicide." Unlike egoistic suicide, which is the act of an individual who rejects the structures of a society, anomic suicide is the act of a person who has been let down by an inadequate, often a decaying, society.

Durkheim argues that as societies go through periods of anomie, their suicide rates will increase accordingly. Historical research supports this claim. Periods of economic depression bring about relative anomie in a country, and national suicide rates tend to increase during such times (Cormier & Klerman, 1985). Similarly, pe-

According to Emile Durkheim, people who intentionally sacrifice their lives for others are committing altruistic suicide. Betsy Smith, a heart transplant recipient who was warned that she would probably die if she did not terminate her pregnancy, elected to have the baby and died giving birth to a healthy daughter.

riods of population change and increased immigration tend to bring about a state of anomie, and such increases are also reflected in higher suicide rates. Steven Stack (1981) examined the suicide rates and immigration increases of thirty-four countries. After controlling for age and other important factors affecting suicide, he found that immigration and suicide rates were related. Each 1 percent increase in immigration was associated with an increase of 0.13 percent in the suicide rate.

A change in an individual's immediate surroundings, rather than general societal deficiencies, can also lead to anomic suicide. People who suddenly inherit a great sum of money, for example, may go through a period of anomie as their relationship with social, economic, and occupational structures is upset or altered. Thus Durkheim predicts that societies with greater opportunities for change in individual wealth or status will have higher

suicide rates, and this prediction, too, is supported by research (Lester, 1985).

Durkheim's theory of suicide highlights the potential importance of societal factors — a dimension sometimes overlooked by clinicians. On the other hand, his theory by itself is unable to explain why some individuals who experience anomie commit suicide yet the majority do not. Durkheim himself concluded that the final explanation probably involves an interaction between societal and individual factors.

## SUICIDE IN DIFFERENT AGE GROUPS

The likelihood of committing suicide generally increases with age, although individuals of all ages may try to kill themselves (see Figure 10-3). Recently particular attention has been focused on self-destruction in three age groups — *children*, partly because suicide at a very young age contradicts society's perception that childhood is an enjoyable period of discovery and growth; *adolescents and young adults,* because of the steady and highly publicized rise in their suicide rate; and the *elderly,* because suicide is more prevalent in this age group than any other. Although the characteristics and theories of suicide discussed throughout this chapter apply to all age groups, each group faces unique problems that help account for patterns in self-destruction among its members.

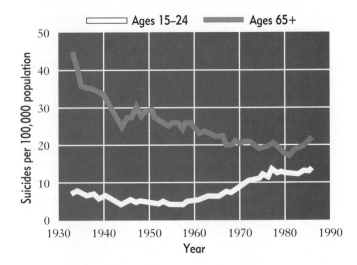

**FIGURE 10-3** Before the 1980s, the suicide rate of elderly people had been declining for at least a half-century, while that of young adults was increasing. Still, older people continue to be at higher risk for suicide. *(Adapted from McIntosh, 1991, 1987, p. 60.)*

# Children

*Tommy [age 7] and his younger brother were playing* together, and an altercation arose that was settled by the mother, who then left the room. The mother recalled nothing to distinguish this incident from innumerable similar ones. Several minutes after she left, she considered Tommy strangely quiet and returned to find him crimson-faced and struggling for air, having knotted a jumping rope around his neck and jerked it tight.

*(French & Berlin, 1979, p. 144)*

*Dear Mom and Dad,*

I love you. Please tell my teacher that I cannot take it anymore. I quit. Please don't take me to school anymore. Please help me. I will run away so don't stop me. I will kill myself. So don't look for me because I will be dead. I love you. I will always love you. Remember me.

Help me.

Love Justin [age 10]

*(Pfeffer, 1986, p. 273)*

Although suicide is relatively infrequent among children, it has been increasing rapidly during the past several decades. Approximately 300 children under 15 years of age in the United States now commit suicide each year (one per 100,000 in this age group), a rate increase of nearly 800 percent since 1950 (Barraclough, 1987; Kranczer, 1986). Boys outnumber girls by three to one. Many other children *try* to kill, or at least hurt, themselves. It has been estimated that as many as 12,000 children may be hospitalized in the United States each year for deliberately self-destructive acts, such as stabbing, cutting, burning, overdosing, or jumping from high places (NIMH, 1986).

One study of suicide attempts by children between 5 and 14 years of age revealed that the majority had taken an overdose of drugs and made their attempt at home, half were living with only one parent, and 25 percent had attempted suicide on a previous occasion (Kienhorst et al., 1987). Researchers have found that suicide attempts by the very young are commonly preceded by such behavioral patterns as running away from home, accident proneness, acting out, temper tantrums, self-deprecation, loneliness, psychophysiological illness (see Chapter 11), extreme sensitivity to criticism, low tolerance of frustration, and morbid fantasies and daydreams (McGuire, 1982). Studies have further linked child suicides to the recent or anticipated loss of a loved one, family stress and parental unemployment, and a clinical level of depression (Kienhorst, 1987; Myers et al., 1985).

Most people find it hard to believe that children fully comprehend the implications of a suicidal act (see Table 10-5). They argue that by virtue of their cognitive limitations, children who attempt suicide fall into Shneidman's category of "death ignorers": like Billy, who sought to join his mother in heaven, they do not appreciate the permanence of death and hold an idealized view of what is to come. Although research indicates that some children who attempt suicide are unclear about the finality of death, especially younger and less mature children, many child suicides are in fact based on a clear understanding of death and on a clear wish to die (Carlson et al., 1987; Pfeffer, 1986).

Suicidal thinking among even normal children is apparently more common than most people once believed. Clinical interviews with 101 schoolchildren between 6 and 12 years of age without any history of mental disorders revealed that 12 percent of the children had contemplated suicide (Pfeffer, 1984). Similarly, a frightening study (Kovacs, 1978) found that 41 percent of 127 children surveyed in Toronto admitted having thoughts about suicide. Other studies suggest that as many as 5 percent of preadolescent children may be seriously self-

TABLE 10-5

## TEN MISCONCEPTIONS ABOUT SUICIDAL BEHAVIOR IN CHILDHOOD

1. Suicide under the age of 6 does not occur.

2. Suicidal behavior is extremely rare between the ages of 6 and 13.

3. True depression is not possible in childhood.

4. Since children do not understand the irreversibility of death, they cannot actually be considered suicidal.

5. Suicide attempts in children are impulsive and are not the result of long-standing preoccupation.

6. Children are too cognitively and physically ineffective to implement a suicide plan successfully.

7. Most suicidal acts in childhood are merely manipulative and not dangerously destructive.

8. Since almost all children periodically make statements such as "If I don't get my way, I'll kill myself," almost all suicidal threats in youngsters need not be taken seriously.

9. Children don't have readily available means to kill themselves.

10. If a self-destructive effort is made by a child, it is almost always in response to a very recent, overwhelming precipitant.

*Source:* Rosenn, 1982, p. 198.

destructive (Paulson, 1978; Puig-Antich, 1978). It is not clear whether such suicidal thinking by young children represents a new phenomenon or was previously undetected by clinical researchers.

## Adolescents and Young Adults

*D**ear Mom, Dad, and everyone else,*
I'm sorry for what I've done, but I loved you all and I always will, for eternity. Please, please, please don't blame it on yourselves. It was all my fault and not yours or anyone else's. If I didn't do this now, I would have done it later anyway. We all die some day, I just died sooner.
Love,
John

John was 17 when he decided to end his brief life. His adolescence was dotted with problems, some typical, others perhaps more hurtful than anyone might have guessed. He kept his pain mostly to himself. Only after his body was found did family and friends begin piecing together the mosaic that John's life was. To the now knowing eyes of survivors, figure and ground shifted to reveal what otherwise had been overlooked, denied, and misinterpreted. Left in the wake of John's death were the inevitable "if only's. . . ."

When John's family was interviewed after his suicide, they claimed he gave no signs of being depressed or suicidal. Their response was not unlike that of others who either were ignorant of the family dynamics or had well-prepared defenses against them. John had an intensely ambivalent, perhaps even symbiotic, relationship with his father. John's father had been depressed since he retired from his job due to a medical disability. He spent much of his day and evening in front of the family television set, drinking until he passed out. John's mother constantly spoke of leaving. There was no love, no sexual involvement, no affection. When John's father interacted with John, it was with anger and rigid control. When John sought his father's permission to be more autonomous, his father found reason to restrict and keep him tied to a childlike role in the family.

John was a child seeking permission to leave the home and join the army. He disliked school, lacking passion for study and performing only marginally. At age 17, he had yet to date and was isolated from friends. Small for his age, he had been bullied by some classmates. As a result of the most recent incident, John dropped out of the one extracurricular activity in which he participated. It was then that he asked to join the military. When his father refused him permission, John threw a temper tantrum and was, consequently, restricted to his room. When his mother checked on him early that evening, his suicide note was found on his pillow. His body was not recovered for 3 days.

In spite of the family's protestations, John had given warnings. He was an impulsive, reckless child who did not know when to stop. He did not give evidence of planned

behavior and was given to violent outbursts. In anger, he threatened to jump from the roof of his house at the age of eight; and he had told a cousin just last year that he would shoot himself one day. In his last week, he had asked his mother whether she thought that people who killed themselves felt pain.

However, perhaps no one could have known that his pain had reached the level of despair and hopelessness. No one bothered to ask. And no one thought to secure his father's shotgun, just in case. There must have been special meaning in John's choice to use his dad's gun when he decided to shoot himself.

*(Berman, 1986)*

Suicidal actions become much more common after the age of 14 than at any earlier age. In the United States more than 6,000 adolescents and young adults kill themselves each year; that is, more than 13 of every 100,000 persons between the ages of 15 and 24 (Center for Disease Control, 1987; Green & Keown, 1986). Because fatal illnesses are relatively rare among the young, suicide has become the third leading cause of death in adolescents and young adults, after accidents and homicides (see Table 10-1), accounting for 13 percent of all deaths in this age range (Pfeffer, 1988; Berman, 1986). In contrast, suicide accounts for less than 2 percent of deaths in the total population. Males commit 83 percent of these suicides (Berman, 1986).

Unlike the rates for other age groups, suicide rates in the 15- to 24-year-old group are becoming more similar across the races in the United States. Although the suicide rate of young whites continues to be considerably higher than that of young blacks, the black rate is growing faster (Earls & Jamison, 1986; Berman, 1986). In many cases the converging rates probably reflect converging pressures on young black and young white persons—competition for grades and college opportunities, for example, is now intense for both groups. In some cases, however, the growth of the young black suicide rate may be linked to unique factors such as increasing unemployment among black teenagers, the numerous anxieties of inner-city life, and the rage among young blacks over racial inequities in our society (Hendin, 1982; Spaights & Simpson, 1986; Stack, 1982).

Although statistical analyses of suicide typically lump 15- to 24-year-olds together, this is hardly a homogeneous group. Clinicians and researchers have often found it important to view separately two subgroups in this category—*teenagers* (15- to 18-year-olds) and *college students* (18- to 22-year-olds).

**Teenagers** Approximately 3,000 teenagers commit suicide in the United States each year, and as many as

250,000 may make attempts (Shaffer & Fisher, 1981). Moreover, in a recent Gallup Poll (1991) a full third of teenagers surveyed said they had considered suicide, and 15 percent said they had thought about it seriously.

Some of the major warning signs of suicide in teenagers are tiredness and sleep loss, loss of appetite, mood changes, decline in school performance, withdrawal, increased smoking, drug or alcohol use, increased letter writing to friends, and giving away valued possessions (Pfeffer, 1988; Neiger & Hopkins, 1988; Berman, 1986; Dykeman, 1984; Gibson, 1982). Drug overdose is the technique by which most adolescents attempt suicide, although shooting oneself leads to the most fatalities (Garfinkel et al., 1982). Attempts usually occur at home and after school (Shafii et al., 1985; Garfinkel et al., 1982).

About half of teenagers' suicides, like those of people in other age groups, have been linked to clinical depression (Robbins & Alessi, 1985; Taylor & Stansfeld, 1984). In addition, adolescents who attempt to kill themselves are often under considerable stress. Many experience such long-term pressures as missing or poor parental relationships, inadequate peer relationships, and social isolation (Neiger & Hopkins, 1988; Stanley & Barter, 1985; McKenry et al., 1982; Tishler & McKenry, 1982). Adolescent suicide also seems to be triggered by more immediate stresses, such as unemployment or financial setbacks in the family or difficulties with a boyfriend or girlfriend (Pfeffer, 1990, 1988; Wright, 1985; Dykeman, 1984; Garfinkel et al., 1982; Hawton et al., 1982).

Stress at school seems to be a particularly common problem in teenagers who attempt suicide. One study found that nearly 60 percent of suicidal teenage subjects had recently been having difficulty keeping up at school (Houston et al., 1982). Still other studies have revealed that suicide is sometimes attempted by academically gifted teenagers, who may feel pressure to be perfect and to stay at the top of the class (Leroux, 1986; Delisle, 1986; Konopka, 1983; Garfinkel and Golombek, 1983).

Nowhere is academic stress more visibly a suicide factor than in Japan. The Japanese suicide rate is very high in the late teenage years (Hawton, 1986). Research suggests that this high rate may be related to *shiken jigoku*, or "examination hell," an extremely competitive testing period that Japanese teenagers must go through if they are to enter college. Many Japanese students who are unsuccessful in this critical testing period try to take their lives.

Beyond depression and stress, teenagers who try to kill themselves appear to struggle with anger more than do suicide attempters in other age groups (Kovacs & Beck, 1977). Aggressive and antisocial behaviors and inade-

The intense training and testing characteristic of Japan's educational system produce very high levels of stress in students. The students in this classroom are participating in summer *juku*, a camp where they receive remedial help, extra lessons, and exam practice 11 hours a day.

quate assertiveness skills have frequently been found in suicidal teenagers (Shaffer & Gould, 1986; Cohen-Sandler et al., 1982; Boswell & Murray, 1981). It may be that unassertive adolescents build up resentment and turn their anger on themselves as the only acceptable target (Rotherman, 1987; Phillip & McCulloch, 1966).

It is important to note that suicide attempts among teenagers greatly outnumber suicide fatalities. Conservative estimates of attempted suicides in this age group have ranged from 57 to 100 attempts per 100,000 population (Solomon & Murphy, 1984). Some theorists believe that there are actually many more attempts, and that the ratio of attempts to fatalities is between 20 to 1 and 120 to 1 (Peck, Farberow, & Litman, 1985; Rosencrantz, 1978; Trautman, 1966). The unusually large number of incomplete attempts by teenagers may mean that they are more often ambivalent than older persons who make such attempts. While some do indeed wish to die, many may simply want to make others understand how desperate they are, get help, or teach others a lesson (Hawton, 1986; Hawton et al., 1982; White, 1974).

Some theorists believe that adolescent life itself engenders a climate conducive to suicidal action (Maris, 1986). Adolescence is a period of rapid growth and development, and in our society it is often marked by conflicts, tensions, and difficulties at home and school. Adolescents tend to react to events more sensitively, angrily, dramatically, and impulsively than people in other age groups, so that the likelihood of suicidal actions during times of stress is increased (Kaplan, 1984; Taylor & Stansfeld, 1984; Davis, 1983). They are also likely to experience depressed feelings, and indeed such feelings appear to be increasing among teenagers in general (Rosenstock, 1985; Teri, 1982). Finally, the highly suggestible nature of adolescents and their eagerness to imitate others may help set the stage for suicidal action (Berman, 1986).

**College Students**    The suicide rate tends to be higher for 18- to 24-year-old college students than for other young people in the same age range. Again, female students are more likely to attempt suicide, but fatal suicides are more numerous among males. Furthermore, studies suggest that as many as 20 percent of college students have suicidal thoughts at some point in their college career (Carson & Johnson, 1985).

One factor underlying these suicides is the challenge of college itself (Lyman, 1961). Academic pressures, examinations, and competition for grades undoubtedly increase the stressfulness of the student's life. Other factors that have been implicated in suicides among these students are the loss of social support felt by those who move away from their families and friends to attend college and the rapid change of values experienced by some students during their college years (Arnstein, 1986; Carson & Johnson, 1985; Berkovitz, 1985).

It may also be that college students bring past problems with them to their new environments, complicating the already difficult task of dealing with college-linked pressures and situations (Hendin, 1988; Curran, 1986; Berkovitz, 1985). Indeed, a third of college students interviewed in one study reported having suicidal thoughts before they entered college (Sherer, 1985). Some clinicians suggest that the college students who consider suicide are those who never learned how to deal with personal problems and emotions before going to college. A study of 218 undergraduates, for example, found that suicidal students did not necessarily experience more stress than other students but had fewer resources for dealing with problems and intense emotions (Carson & Johnson, 1985).

The number and variety of possible contributing factors makes it difficult to interpret studies of suicide among college students. Research in England, for example, has indicated that the number of college suicides increases along with the prestige of the school (Stengel, 1974; Seiden, 1969). How are we to understand this finding? Certainly academic pressures are high at prestigious schools, but these schools also have other characteristics that may contribute to the high rate of suicide. For example, the number of students living away from home — or far from home — usually is higher at these schools than at other institutions. Moreover, these

Adolescent students in Bergenfield, New Jersey, comfort each other after the joint suicides of four classmates. In the weeks following this highly publicized episode in 1987, numerous other teenagers in the United States also attempted to kill themselves — two of them just a week later in the Bergenfield garage where the first four had committed suicide.

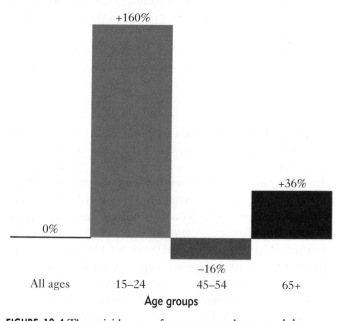

PERCENTAGE OF CHANGE IN SUICIDE RATE SINCE 1955

FIGURE 10-4 The suicide rate of teenagers and young adults has increased a staggering 160 percent since 1955. The rate among middle-aged people has decreased 16 percent, that of elderly persons has increased 36 percent, and that of the total population has remained the same. *(Adapted from Deykin, 1986, p. 280.)*

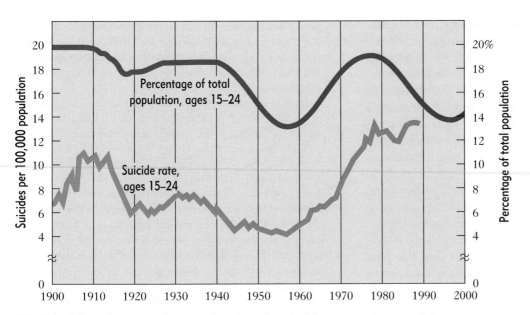

**FIGURE 10-5** Over the years, whenever the proportion of adolescents and young adults in the general population has increased, the suicide rate of this age group has risen as well. *(Adapted from Holinger & Offer, 1991, 1988.)*

schools are noted for encouraging students to work independently. Perhaps the lack of structure introduces a significant amount of stress.

Obviously, many aspects of college life are demanding and stressful. Evidence suggests that students are helped by friendships and by sharing their experiences and problems with others at college (Arnstein, 1986; Brown et al., 1981). In this way, the pressures of college life that sometimes contribute to depression and suicidal behavior may be reduced.

**Rising Suicide Rate**  The suicide rate for adolescents and young adults is not only high but increasing. As Figure 10-4 indicates, the suicide rate for this age group has more than doubled since 1955 (McIntosh, 1991). The rate for young persons peaked in 1977, when 13.6 of every 100,000 adolescents and young adults committed suicide, leveled off to 11.9 per 100,000 by 1983, then increased again to 13.1 in 1986 (NCHS, 1989; Holinger, Offer, & Ostrow, 1987; Center for Disease Control, 1986). This latest upswing suggests that suicide among the young may be on the rise once again (Pfeffer, 1986).

Several theories, each pointing to societal changes, have been proposed to explain why the suicide rate among adolescents and young adults has risen dramatically during the past few decades. First, noting the overall rise in the number and proportion of adolescents and

young adults in the general population since 1950, Paul Holinger and his colleagues (1990, 1988, 1987, 1984, 1982) have suggested that the competition for jobs, college positions, and academic and athletic honors keeps intensifying in this age group, leading increasingly to shattered dreams and frustrated ambitions, which in turn lead to suicidal thinking and behavior (see Figure 10-5). Other theorists, following Durkheim's notion of anomic suicide, hold that weakening ties in the nuclear family during the past few decades have provoked feelings of alienation and rejection in many of today's young persons—emotions that may contribute to suicidal thoughts and actions (Peck, 1982; Miller, 1981).

A third explanation points to the increased availability and use of drugs among the young, as well as to increased pressure to use them (Schuckit & Schuckit, 1990; Hawton, 1986; Arnstein, 1986). Research has in fact uncovered a clear link between drug abuse and suicide attempts in this age group (Rich, Young, & Fowler, 1986). One study found that 70 percent of the teenage suicide attempters abused drugs or alcohol (Shafii et al., 1985). Another found that teenagers and young adults with suicidal thoughts were three to six times more involved with alcohol than nonsuicidal persons of the same age (Wright, 1985).

A final explanation for the rise in suicide rates among the young implicates the broad media coverage attending suicide attempts by teenagers and young adults. As we observed earlier, highly publicized suicides often trigger other suicide attempts. During the past decade, the media and the arts have become particularly interested in the problem of teenage suicide. The detailed descriptions they provide may serve as models for young people who are contemplating suicide. Within days of the highly publicized suicides of four adolescents in a garage in Bergenfield, New Jersey, in 1987, dozens of teenagers across the United States took similar actions (at least twelve of them fatal)—two in the same garage just one week later!

These explanations for the rise in suicide rates among young persons remind us that societal change does not necessarily lead to social progress. People are correctly impressed by our society's advances in medical, industrial, and communication technology during the past several decades. But often there is a significant price to pay for rapid change. And that price may include the mental health and survival of all too many of our youth.

## The Elderly

*R*ose *Ashby walks to the dry cleaner's to pick up her old* but finest dinner dress. Although shaken at the cost of having it cleaned, Rose tells the sympathetic girl behind the counter, "Don't worry. It doesn't matter. I won't be needing the money any more."

Walking through the streets of St. Petersburg, Florida, she still wishes it had been Miami. The west coast of the fountain of youth peninsula is not as warm as the east. If only Chet had left more insurance money, Rose could have afforded Miami. In St. Petersburg, Rose failed to unearth de Leon's promised fount.

Last week, she told the doctor she felt lonely and depressed. He said she should perk up. She had everything to live for. What does he know? Has he lost a husband like Chet, and his left breast to cancer all in one year? Has he suffered arthritis all his life? Were his ovaries so bad he had to undergo a hysterectomy? Did he have to suffer through menopause just to end up alone without family or friends? Does he have to live in a dungeon? Is his furniture worn, his carpet threadbare? What does he know? Might his every day be the last one for him?

As Rose turns into the walk to her white cinderblock apartment building, fat Mrs. Green asks if she is coming to the community center that evening. Who needs it? The social worker did say Rose should come. Since Rose was in such good health, she could help those not so well as she.

Help them do what? Finger-paint like little children? Make baskets like insane people? Sew? Who can see to sew? Besides, who would appreciate it? Who would thank her? Who could she tell about her troubles? Who cares?

When she told the doctor she couldn't sleep, he gave her the prescription but said that all elderly people have trouble sleeping. What does he know? Does he have a middle-aged daughter who can only think about her latest divorce, or grandchildren who only acknowledge her birthday check by the endorsement on the back? Are all his friends dead and gone? Is all the money from his dead husband's insurance used up? What does he know? Who could sleep in this dungeon?

Back in her apartment, Rose washes and sets her hair. It's good she has to do it herself. Look at this hair. So thin, so sparse, so frowsy. What would a hairdresser think?

Then make-up. Base. Rouge. Lipstick. Bright red. Perfume? No! No cheap perfume for Rose today. Remember the bottles of *Joy* Chet would buy for her? He always wanted her to have the best. He would boast that she had everything, and that she never had to work a day in her life for it.

"She doesn't have to lift her little finger," Chet would say, puffing on his cigar. Where is the *Joy* now? Dead and gone. With Chet. Rose manages a wry laugh at the play on words.

Slipping into her dinner dress, she looks into the dresser mirror. "It's good you can't see this face now, Chet. How old and ugly it looks."

Taking some lavender notepaper from the drawer, she stands at the dresser to write. Why didn't anyone warn her that growing old was like this? It is so unfair. But they don't care. People don't care about anyone except themselves.

Leaving the note on the dresser, she suddenly feels excited. Breathing hard now, she rushes to the sink—who could call a sink in the counter in the living room a kitchen?—and gets a glass of water.

Trying to relax, Rose arranges the folds in her skirt as she settles down on the chaise. Carefully sipping the water as she takes all the capsules so as to not smear her lipstick, Rose quietly begins to sob. After a lifetime of tears, these will be her last. Her note on the dresser is short, written to no one and to everyone.

*You don't know what it is like*
*to have to grow old and die.*

*(Gernsbacher, 1985, pp. 227–228)*

Statistics indicate that in Western society the elderly are more likely to commit suicide than people in any other age group (see Figures 10-1*a* and 10-3). Close to 22 of every 100,000 persons over the age of 65 in the United States commit suicide (NCHS, 1989; Turkington, 1987). This rate has been rising steadily since 1981, when 17 of every 100,000 elderly persons took their own lives. While the suicide rate for all men in the United States is 19 per 100,000, it jumps to 38 per 100,000 for men older than 65. Although fewer older women commit suicide, their rate is still much higher than that of younger women. Some investigators believe that suicide is in fact the leading cause of death among the elderly (Simon, 1986).

Many factors contribute to the high suicide rate among

the elderly (Richman, 1991). As people grow older, all too often they become ill, lose close friends and relatives, lose control over their lives, and lose status in our society. Such experiences may result in feelings of hopelessness, loneliness, depression, or inevitability among aged persons, and so increase the likelihood that they will attempt suicide (Osgood, 1987; Kirsling, 1986). Those who have lost a spouse display a much higher suicide rate (Charatan, 1979). Their risk is greatest during the first year of bereavement, but it remains high in later years as well (Adams et al., 1980; Murphy et al., 1979; McMahon & Pugh, 1965).

Elderly persons are typically more resolute than younger persons in their decision to die, so their success rate is much higher (Turkington, 1987). Apparently one out of every four elderly persons who attempts suicide succeeds (McIntosh, 1987). Given this resolve and the obvious physical decline of aged persons, many people argue that older persons who want to die are clear in their thinking and should be allowed to carry out their wishes. As in other age groups, however, clinical depression plays an important role in as many as 50 percent of suicides among the elderly. Robert Simon (1987) suggests that since depressive symptoms frequently impede informed decision making, more elderly persons should be receiving treatment for their depressive disorders. He believes that because their depressive thinking is so readily accepted by relatives and mental health professionals as rational and realistic, older persons often go without needed treatment.

The suicide rate among elderly people in the United States is lower in some minority groups. Although Native Americans have the highest overall suicide rate, for example, the rate among elderly Native Americans is quite low (McIntosh & Santos, 1981). Similarly, the suicide rate among elderly blacks in the United States is only one-third the rate of elderly whites.

Why are suicide rates for the elderly particularly low in some minority groups? The respect afforded elderly Native Americans may help account for their low rate (McIntosh & Santos, 1981). The aged are held in high esteem by Native Americans and looked to for the wisdom and experience they have acquired over the years. This heightened status is quite different from the loss of status often experienced by elderly white persons (Butler, 1975).

The low suicide rate among elderly blacks has been explained in different terms. One theory is that because of the pressures black people live under, "only the strongest survive" (Seiden, 1981). Blacks who reach an advanced age have overcome significant adversity and often feel proud of what they have accomplished. Advancement to old age is not in itself a form of success for whites, and leaves them with a different attitude toward life and age. Another explanation suggests that aged blacks have successfully overcome the rage that characterizes many suicides in younger blacks (Santos & McIntosh, 1981).

# TREATMENT AND SUICIDE

Treatment of people who are suicidal falls into two major categories: (1) *treatment after suicide has been attempted* and (2) *suicide prevention*. Today special attention is also given to relatives and friends (Carter & Brooks, 1991; Farberow, 1991) whose bereavement, guilt, and anger after a suicide fatality or attempt can be intense (see Box 10-3). Although many people require psychotherapy or support groups to help them deal with their reactions to a loved one's suicide, the discussion here will be limited to the treatment afforded suicidal people themselves.

## Treatment after a Suicide Attempt

After a suicide attempt, the victims' primary need is medical care. Some are left with severe injuries, brain damage, or other medical problems. Once the physical damage is reversed, or at least stabilized, a process of psychotherapy may begin. Unfortunately, even after trying to kill themselves, many suicidal people fail to become involved in therapy. In a random survey of 382 teenagers, 9 percent were found to have made at least one suicide attempt, and of those only half had been given subsequent psychological treatment (Harkavy & Asnis, 1985).

Therapy for suicidal people is usually conducted on an outpatient basis (Robinson, 1988; Hawton, 1986). The goal of therapy is to help the client achieve a nonsuicidal state of mind and develop more constructive ways of handling stress and solving problems (Möller, 1990; Lesse, 1988; Möller et al., 1987; Rush & Beck, 1988). Various therapy systems and formats have been employed (Lesse, 1988; Gill, 1982), but relatively little research has compared the effectiveness of the various approaches.

One study compared the results of treatment given two groups of repeated suicide attempters (Liberman & Eckman, 1981). Twelve subjects were treated in a *behavior therapy group* — taught how to improve their verbal and nonverbal expressive skills and instructed in relaxation techniques. They also attended family sessions where they learned to improve family communication and to share responsibilities. The second group of twelve suicide attempters received *insight-oriented treatment* consisting of individual psychodynamic therapy sessions supplemented by group therapy and family therapy sessions. Both treatment programs began during hospitalization and continued on an outpatient basis for nine months.

At first assessment, the subjects who underwent behavior therapy seemed to improve more than those who were given psychodynamic therapy. They showed less depression, less anxiety, and more assertiveness on self-report measures, and twice as many of them were holding full-time jobs at the time of a follow-up review. On the other hand, the number of subsequent suicide attempts was approximately equal in the two groups.

---

## BOX 10-3

# Those Who Are Left Behind

*First Anniversary of Neil's death*

I have something to say:

Exactly one year ago I was deep in an annual contemplation of fall and the significance and approach of winter. I wrote two poems in the midafternoon dealing with the sacrifice and/or suicide of life in the face of an awesome, indefinite, perhaps eternal winter, and the potency of the magic that lies in the uncertainty there.

Magic Sam and Jimi Hendrix were dead. Janis Joplin was either dead or soon to die. Everywhere people would talk about how, in our culture, this was the time that dying took the stage.

Then the phone rang.

My father had a very poor connection. He said something had happened to a member of the family. I could feel my face get hot; I asked who. He said, "Neil is dead . . . can you fill in the rest?"

I envisioned him fallen in a construction pit or in a car accident. I had no idea what my father was asking me. Just three days earlier I'd talked with Neil on the phone about his decision to go to a school to become a forest ranger and about him coming out to stay with me for a few days at Thanksgiving.

Then Dad said Neil had shot himself with a .32. Now I pictured Neil dead in the basement.

He asked me to come home right away — mother and he needed me immediately.

I called Don, and without telling him anything asked him to drive me to the airport. I walked to the Student Co-op and borrowed enough money for fare to New York. I couldn't speak to Don all the way to the terminal. Then I could tell him. He embraced me.

My father met me at Kennedy, where I told him I'd be arriving. He had an overcoat on and was smoking a cigar. I saw him at the bottom of an escalator. He held out his arms and we hugged each other long and hard.

He told me it had happened in Neil's and my room. He told me about the music on loud up in the room when he came home from work. It wasn't unusual for them not to see each other even if they were in the house together a long time. Neil wanted to be by himself, and they let him. He told me about going up into

Three of the insight therapy subjects and two of the behavior therapy subjects attempted suicide again.

## Suicide Prevention

During the past thirty years emphasis has shifted from suicide treatment to suicide prevention (Cantor, 1991; Maltsberger, 1991; Farberow & Litman, 1983; Shneidman, 1982). In some respects this change is most appropriate: the last opportunity to keep many potential suicide victims alive comes before the first attempt.

The emphasis on suicide prevention began in earnest during the mid-1950s with the development of *suicide prevention programs.* The first such program in the United States was the Los Angeles Suicide Prevention

---

the room calling for him because he hadn't come out to take the phone, which was from a worried friend at school, and about Neil lying on his mattress, a pool of blood round his head drying.

I took over the responsibility for the funeral arrangements and all the hassles on the phone and at the door. I also took the job of cleaning Neil's room. I think me being there quickly was very important to my parents. I hadn't wanted to come at all at first. I wanted just to go off somewhere alone for a long time.

In one of the letters Neil left he said those who don't understand what he'd done should ask me, because I was the closest to him. He also said he wanted to be cremated and his ashes given to me in Chicago where I would scatter them. I was perplexed . . . because I partly felt that I did actually know better than anyone what had been going on in him to bring him to suicide; I also felt that I knew almost nothing about Neil or why he would kill himself.

For the superficial, immediate cause, I told my parents it was probably a romantic fantasy that climaxed too precipitously to be stopped at the last moment — that if he'd been able to experience what he was doing instead of dying instantly, or almost instantly, he would have reversed himself.

I told myself that he manifested the climate of the whole country then, of the season.

There were no reasons but huge futile ones. I managed to rail against the school and the city and his pathetically shallow friends. I myself saw dozens of scenes develop from the past where I had failed Neil. I don't know what thing or things could have saved him.

I went back to school. I couldn't get my equilibrium all that year. The smallest things could bring on deep depressions. Don and I drew apart. My father's illness came as an extension of Neil's death, as a consequence of my father's being caught too close to the horror.

And I read the poems over and thought what I was feeling and noticing in the season and the world, and floating on, Neil was feeling and doing and sinking in.

I'm writing this in Florida after a year, where there is no autumn and it is warmer now than it was in "Okeover" in August. I have never before avoided this season and I have been thinking a lot about what it means to go into winter where there is no dying of vegetation and the changes in the earth are small.

It is easy now to imagine my brother, unchanged in his coffin, buried in my clothes. Carefully tended, his long hair, much smoother than mine, combed over the hole in his left temple (He was left-handed so naturally enough he held the little .32 in that hand, the gun barely capable of doing its job), and the unerased look of hurt around his mouth. I share lips that pout like that with him. Will mine express such pain at being unloved as his did, when I die?

*(Rosenfeld & Prupas, 1984, pp. 75–76)*

Center, founded by Norman Farberow and Edwin Shneidman in 1955; the first in England was called the Samaritans, founded by the Reverend Chad Varah in 1953. There are now more than 200 independent, locally funded suicide prevention centers in the United States and over 100 in England, and the numbers are still growing (Lester, 1989; Roberts, 1979). In addition, many mental health centers, hospital emergency rooms, pastoral counseling centers, and poison control centers now include suicide prevention programs among their services.

Suicide prevention centers define suicidal people as people *in crisis*—that is, under great stress, unable to cope, feeling threatened or hurt, and interpreting their situations as unchangeable. Accordingly, the centers try to help suicidal people perceive things more accurately, make better decisions, act more constructively, and overcome their crisis. Because crises can occur at any time, the centers have 24-hour-a-day telephone service ("hot lines") and also welcome clients to walk in without appointments. Those who call reach a counselor, typically a *paraprofessional*—a person without previous professional training who provides services under the supervision of a mental health professional (Heilig et al., 1983).

Although specific features vary from center to center, the general approach used by the Los Angeles Suicide Prevention Center reflects the goals and techniques of many of them (Lester, 1989; Shneidman & Farberow, 1983; Rotherman, 1987; Neville & Barnes, 1985; Boldt, 1985). During the initial contact, the counselor has several tasks: establishing a positive relationship, understanding and clarifying the problem, assessing suicide potential, assessing and mobilizing the caller's resources, and formulating a plan for overcoming the crisis (Shneidman & Farberow, 1963).

*Establishing a Positive Relationship*   Obviously, callers must trust counselors if they are to confide in them and follow their suggestions. Thus counselors try to set a positive and comfortable tone for discussion. They convey that they are listening, understanding, interested, nonjudgmental, and available.

*Understanding and Clarifying the Problem*   Counselors first try to understand the full scope of the caller's crisis, then help the person see the crisis in clear and constructive terms. In particular, counselors try to help callers identify the central issues and the transient nature of their crises and recognize the alternatives to suicidal action.

*Assessing Suicide Potential*   Some callers are in greater crisis than others, and closer to attempt-

ing suicide. The strategy a counselor chooses will depend on the degree of suicidal risk. Thus the development of accurate suicide assessment techniques has become a major concern of clinicians and researchers (Rotherman, 1987; Engelsmann & Ananth, 1981; Pallis et al., 1982).

Crisis workers at the Los Angeles Suicide Prevention Center use a *lethality scale* to estimate the caller's potential for suicide (Table 10-6). It helps them to determine the degree of stress the caller is under, relevant personality characteristics, how detailed the suicide plan is, the severity of symptoms, and the coping resources available to the caller. The crisis workers can then assess whether callers should be hospitalized for their own safety, referred for treatment, or embarked on some other course of action.

*Assessing and Mobilizing the Caller's Resources*   Although they may view themselves as ineffectual and helpless, people who are suicidal usually have some strengths and resources, including such resources as relatives and friends. It is the counselor's job to recognize, point out, and activate those resources.

*Formulating a Plan*   Together the crisis worker and caller formulate a plan of action. In essence, they are agreeing on a way out of the crisis, a constructive alternative to suicidal action. Although both participate in formulating the plan, the counselor may take the lead role, giving suggestions and perhaps even fostering a dependent relationship. If callers are in the midst of a suicide attempt, counselors will also try to ascertain their whereabouts and get medical help to them immediately (Farberow, Heilig, & Litman, 1972).

Most plans of action include a series of follow-up counseling sessions over the next few days or weeks, either in person at the center or by phone. Also counselors usually negotiate a "no suicide" contract with the caller—a promise not to attempt suicide, or at least a promise to reestablish contact if the caller again contemplates suicide. Beyond this, each plan usually requires that the caller make certain changes and take certain actions in his or her personal life. Family members and friends also become involved in some plans.

Although crisis intervention appears to be sufficient treatment for some suicidal people (Hawton, 1986), longer-term therapy is needed for up to 60 percent of them (Farberow, 1974). These are cases in which the suicide crisis has stemmed from chronic problems in

The psychologist Edwin Shneidman, who helped found America's first suicide-prevention center in 1955, has developed techniques to assess suicidal risk, identified various types of suicide, and corrected numerous myths about suicide.

coping and living that are best addressed in extended therapy (Mills, 1985). If the crisis intervention center does not offer this kind of therapy, the counselors will refer these people elsewhere.

As the suicide prevention movement spread during the 1960s, many clinicians concluded that crisis intervention techniques should also be applied to problems other than suicide. They reasoned that nonsuicidal people may also be immobilized by crises and may benefit from an active, problem-solving form of intervention. As we saw in Chapter 5, crisis intervention has emerged during the past three decades as a respected form of treatment for such wide-ranging problems as teenage confusion, drug and alcohol abuse, rape victimization, and spouse abuse (Lester, 1989; Bloom, 1984; Glasscote et al., 1966).

## The Effectiveness of Suicide Prevention

It has been difficult for researchers to assess the effectiveness of suicide prevention centers (Eddy et al., 1987; Bloom, 1984). There are many kinds of centers, each with its own procedures and serving populations that vary in number, age, economic stability, and environmental pressures. Communities with high suicide risk factors, such as an elderly population or economic strife, may continue to have higher suicide rates than other communities irrespective of the effectiveness of their local prevention centers.

Do suicide prevention centers reduce the number of suicides in a community? Clinical researchers do not know (Lester, 1989; Trowell, 1979; Auerbach & Kilmann, 1977). Studies comparing local suicide rates before and after the establishment of community prevention centers have yielded very different findings. Some find a decline in suicide rates (Miller et al., 1984; Dashef, 1984; Bagley, 1968), others no change (Barraclough et al., 1977; Lester, 1974, 1972; Walk, 1967), and still others an increase in suicide rates (Weiner, 1969). It is important to note, however, that the increase in suicide rates found in some studies may reflect society's overall increase in suicidal behavior. One investigation found that although suicide rates did increase in certain cities with prevention centers, they increased even more in cities without such centers (Lester, 1974).

Do suicidal people contact prevention centers? Apparently only a small percentage do. Research has indicated that approximately 2 percent of the people who actually killed themselves in Los Angeles ever contacted the Los Angeles Suicide Prevention Center (Weiner, 1969). Moreover, the typical caller to urban prevention centers appears to be young, black, and female, while the greatest number of suicides are committed by elderly white males (Lester, 1989, 1972).

On the other hand, prevention centers do seem helpful in averting suicide for those high-risk people who do call. Norman Farberow and Robert Litman (1970) identified 8,000 high-risk individuals who contacted the Los Angeles Suicide Prevention Center. Approximately 2 percent of these callers later committed suicide, compared to the 6 percent suicide rate usually found in similar high-risk groups. One implication of such findings is that these centers need to be more visible to and approachable by people who are harboring thoughts of suicide. The growing number of advertisements and announcements in newspapers and on television, radio, and billboards attest to a movement in this direction.

Partly because of the many suicide prevention programs and the data they have generated, today's clinicians have a better understanding of suicide and greater ability to assess suicidal risk than those of the past (McIntosh et al., 1985). Studies reveal that the health care professionals who are most knowledgeable about suicide are psychiatrists, psychologists, and personnel who actually work in prevention centers (Domino & Swain, 1986). The least informed of the professionals who might be contacted by suicidal persons tend to be

TABLE 10-6

| LOS ANGELES SUICIDE PREVENTION CENTER SCALE |
|---|

| Age and sex (1–9)* | Rating for category |
|---|---|
| Male | |
| 50 plus (7–9) | ( ) |
| 35–49 (4–6) | ( ) |
| 15–34 (1–3) | ( ) |
| Female | |
| 50 plus (5–7) | ( ) |
| 35–49 (3–5) | ( ) |
| 15–34 (1–3) | ( ) |

**Symptoms (1–9)**

| | |
|---|---|
| Severe depression: sleep disorder, anorexia, weight loss, withdrawal, despondency, loss of interest, apathy (7–9) | ( ) |
| Feelings of hopelessness, helplessness, exhaustion (7–9) | ( ) |
| Delusions, hallucinations, loss of contact, disorientation (6–8) | ( ) |
| Compulsive gambling (6–8) | ( ) |
| Disorganization, confusion, chaos (5–7) | ( ) |
| Alcoholism, drug addiction, homosexuality (4–7) | ( ) |
| Agitation, tension, anxiety (4–6) | ( ) |
| Guilt, shame, embarrassment (4–6) | ( ) |
| Feelings of rage, anger, hostility, revenge (4–6) | ( ) |
| Poor impulse control, poor judgment (4–6) | ( ) |
| Other (describe): | |

**Stress (1–9)**

| | |
|---|---|
| Loss of loved person by death, divorce, or separation (5–9) | ( ) |
| Loss of job, money, prestige, status (4–8) | ( ) |
| Sickness, serious illness, surgery, accident—loss of limb (3–7) | ( ) |
| Threat of prosecution, criminal involvement, exposure (4–6) | ( ) |
| Change(s) in life, environment, setting (4–6) | ( ) |
| Success, promotion, increased responsibilities (2–5) | ( ) |
| No significant stress (1–3) | ( ) |
| Other (describe): | |
| Acute versus chronic (1–9) | |
| Sharp, noticeable and sudden onset of specific symptoms (1–9) | ( ) |
| Recurrent outbreak of similar symptoms (4–9) | ( ) |
| No specific recent change (1–4) | ( ) |
| Other (describe): | |

**Suicidal plan (1–9)**

| | |
|---|---|
| Lethality of proposed method—gun, jumping, hanging, drowning, knife, pills, poison, aspirin (1–9) | ( ) |
| Specific detail and clarity in organization of plan (1–9) | ( ) |
| Specificity in time planned (1–9) | ( ) |
| Bizarre plan (1–9) | ( ) |
| Rating of previous suicide attempt(s) (1–9) | ( ) |
| No plans (1–3) | ( ) |
| Other (describe): | |

*(continued)*

* *Ratings:*

1    2    3    4    5    6    7    8    9

*Least seriously suicidal*                    *Most seriously suicidal*

TABLE 10-6 *(continued)*

## LOS ANGELES SUICIDE PREVENTION CENTER SCALE

| | Rating for category |
|---|---|
| **Resources (1–9)** | |
| No sources of support (family, friends, agencies, employment) (7–9) | ( ) |
| Family and friends available, unwilling to help (4–7) | ( ) |
| Financial problems (4–7) | ( ) |
| Available professional help, agency or therapist (2–4) | ( ) |
| Family and/or friends willing to help (1–3) | ( ) |
| Stable life history (1–3) | ( ) |
| Physician or clergy available (1–3) | ( ) |
| Employed (1–3) | ( ) |
| Finances no problem (1–3) | ( ) |
| Other (describe): | |
| **Prior suicidal behavior (1–7)** | |
| One or more prior attempts of high lethality (6–7) | ( ) |
| One or more prior attempts of low lethality (4–5) | ( ) |
| History of repeated threats and depression (3–5) | ( ) |
| No prior suicidal or depressed history (1–3) | ( ) |
| Other (describe): | |
| **Medical status (1–7)** | |
| Chronic debilitating illness (5–7) | ( ) |
| Pattern of failure in previous therapy (4–6) | ( ) |
| Many repeated unsuccessful experiences with doctors (4–6) | ( ) |
| Psychosomatic illness, e.g., asthma, ulcer, hypochondria (1–3) | ( ) |
| No medical problems (1–2) | ( ) |
| Other (describe): | |
| **Communication aspects (1–7)** | |
| Communication broken with rejection of efforts to reestablish by both patient and others (5–7) | ( ) |
| Communications have internalized goal, e.g., declaration of guilt, feelings of worthlessness, blame, shame (4–7) | ( ) |
| Communications have interpersonalized goal, e.g., to cause guilt in others to force behavior, etc. (2–4) | ( ) |
| Communications directed toward world and people in general (3–5) | ( ) |
| Communications directed toward one or more specific persons (1–3) | ( ) |
| Other (describe): | |
| **Reaction of significant others (1–7)** | |
| Defensive, paranoid, rejected, punishing attitude (5–7) | ( ) |
| Denial of own or patient's need for help (5–7) | ( ) |
| No feelings of concern about the patient; does not understand the patient (4–6) | ( ) |
| Indecisiveness, feelings of helplessness (3–5) | ( ) |
| Alternation between feelings of anger and rejection and feelings of responsibility and desire to help (2–4) | ( ) |
| Sympathy and concern plus admission of need for help (1–3) | ( ) |
| Other (describe): | |

*Source:* Bassuck, 1982; Beck, Resnik, & Lettieri, 1974, pp. 76–78.

members of the clergy (Domino & Swain, 1986; Domino, 1985). According to research, they, like the general public, continue to demonstrate a relatively weak understanding of the signs and characteristics of suicidal behavior (McIntosh et al., 1985).

Shneidman (1987) has called for broader and more effective public education about suicide as the ultimate form of prevention. And at least some suicide education programs—most of which concentrate on teachers and students—have begun to emerge (Sandoval, Davis, & Wilson, 1987; Deykin, 1986; Berman, 1986; Ross, 1985, 1980). Shneidman reflects the current mood of the clinical field when he states:

> The primary prevention of suicide lies in education. The route is through teaching one another and . . . the public that suicide can happen to anyone, that there are verbal and behavioral clues that can be looked for . . . , and that help is available. . . .
>
> In the last analysis, the prevention of suicide is everybody's business.
>
> *(Shneidman, 1985, p. 238)*

## SUICIDE: THE STATE OF THE FIELD

Once a mysterious and hidden problem, hardly acknowledged by the public and barely investigated by researchers, suicide is today a topic in the limelight. The public's curiosity about this phenomenon is growing, and researchers are actively pursuing information about such acts. During the past two decades in particular, investigators have learned a great deal about the motives, states of mind, social stimuli, and environmental conditions tied to suicide. They have also made impressive progress in identifying its most common precipitants and risk factors.

Perhaps most promising of all, clinicians and educators have begun to enlist the public in the fight against this problem. They now believe that suicide rates can be reduced only if people recognize the enormous scope of this problem and learn how to identify and respond to suicide risks. They are calling for broader public education about suicide—programs aimed at both young and old.

All of this is a promising beginning, but only a beginning. Critical problems remain in this area of study and treatment. First, when all is said and done, clinicians do not yet fully comprehend why people kill themselves.

That is, why do some who are in great pain and at risk take this course of action while others under similar circumstances manage to find alternative ways of addressing their problems? Psychodynamic, biological, and sociological explanations of suicide have received only limited research support and have been unable to predict specific attempts at suicide. Second, clinicians have yet to develop undisputably successful interventions for treating suicidal persons. Suicide prevention programs have been embraced by the clinical community and certainly reflect its commitment to helping suicidal persons, but it is not yet clear that such programs actually reduce the risk or rate of suicide.

It is reasonable to expect that the current commitment by the clinical field to investigate, publicize, and overcome the phenomenon of suicide will lead to a better understanding of suicide and to more successful interventions. Clearly such goals are of importance to everyone. Although suicide itself is typically a lonely and desperate act, the implications and impact of such acts are very broad indeed.

## SUMMARY

Suicide ranks among the top ten causes of death in Western society. It may be defined as a self-inflicted death in which one makes an *intentional, direct,* and *conscious* effort to end one's life. Edwin Shneidman has distinguished four kinds of people who intentionally end their lives: the *death seeker,* the *death initiator,* the *death ignorer,* and the *death darer.* He has also distinguished a suicidelike category called *subintentioned death,* in which people play indirect, covert, partial, or unconscious roles in their own deaths.

The two major research strategies used in the study of suicide are *retrospective analysis,* a kind of psychological autopsy, and the study of people who survive suicide attempts, on the assumption that they are similar to those who commit fatal suicides. Each strategy has certain limitations.

Suicide rates vary from country to country. One reason seems to be cultural differences in religious affiliation, beliefs, or degree of devoutness. Suicide rates also differ according to race and sex. While women make three times as many attempts at suicide as men, nearly four times as many men succeed in killing themselves. Suicide rates are also related to marital status.

Many suicidal acts are tied to contemporaneous events or conditions. While these factors may not fully account for the act, they do serve to precipitate it. Common precipitating factors are *stressful events and situations, mood and thought changes, alcohol use, mental disorders,* and *events that inspire modeling.*

Psychodynamic theorists believe that suicide usually results from a state of depression and a process of self-directed anger. Freud also proposed that human beings have a basic death instinct, which he called *Thanatos.*

The biological view of suicide has focused on the finding that people who commit suicide often have lower activity of the neurotransmitter serotonin. It has been suggested that in people who are clinically depressed, low serotonin activity may produce aggressive tendencies that leave them particularly vulnerable to suicidal thinking and action. Even in the absence of a depressive disorder, people with low serotonin levels may develop highly aggressive feelings and be dangerous to themselves or others.

Emile Durkheim proposed that the probability of suicide is determined by the extent to which a person is embedded in such social institutions as the family, the church, and the community. The more a person belongs, the lower the risk of suicide. Durkheim defined three categories of suicide based on the person's relationship with society: *egoistic suicides, altruistic suicides,* and *anomic suicides.* His theory highlights the potential importance of societal factors, but he concluded that the final explanation probably involves an interaction between societal and individual factors.

The likelihood of committing suicide generally increases with age. Suicide is relatively infrequent among children, although it has been increasing rapidly in that group during the past several decades. Suicidal thinking among normal children is apparently more common than most people once believed.

Suicidal actions become much more common after the age of 14. Suicide has become the third leading cause of death for adolescents and young adults. It is often linked to clinical depression and unusual stress, but some theorists believe that adolescent life itself engenders a climate conducive to suicidal action.

Several theories, each pointing to societal changes, have been proposed to explain why the suicide rate among adolescents and young adults has risen so dramatically during the past few decades. They point to the overall rise in the number and proportion of adolescents and young adults in the general population, the weakening of ties in the nuclear family, the increased availability and use of drugs among the young, and the broad media coverage attending suicide attempts by teenagers and young adults.

In Western society the elderly are more likely to commit suicide than people in any other age group. As people grow older and their health deteriorates, they lose close friends and relatives in their age group, lose control over their lives, and lose status in our society. Resulting feelings of hopelessness, loneliness, depression, or inevitability may increase the likelihood that they will attempt suicide.

After trying to kill themselves, some suicidal people receive therapy. The goal of therapy is to help the client achieve a nonsuicidal state of mind and develop more constructive ways of handling stress and solving problems. Various therapy systems and formats have been employed.

Over the past thirty years, emphasis has shifted from suicide treatment to suicide prevention because the last opportunity to keep many suicidal people alive comes before their first attempt. *Suicide prevention programs* generally consist of 24-hour-a-day "hot lines" and walk-in centers operated by *paraprofessionals.* During their initial contact with someone considered suicidal, these counselors seek to establish a positive relationship, to understand and clarify the problem, to assess the suicide potential, to assess and mobilize the caller's resources, and to formulate a plan for overcoming the crisis. Although such *crisis intervention* may be sufficient treatment for some suicidal people, longer-term therapy is needed for up to 60 percent of them. Apparently, only a small percentage of suicidal people contact prevention centers.

While clinical scientists know a great deal about suicide, they do not yet fully comprehend why people kill themselves. Furthermore, myths about suicide and suicide intervention abound, perhaps contributing to tragedies that might otherwise be averted.

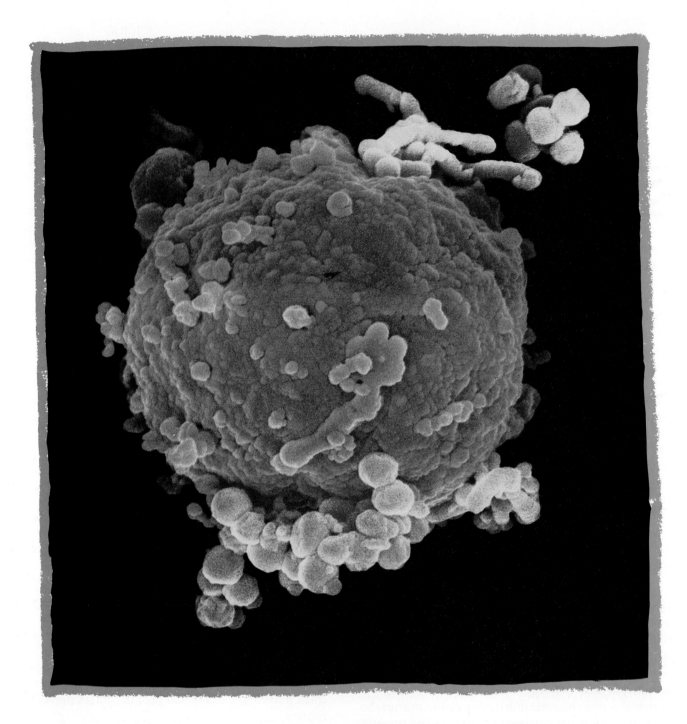

# TOPIC OVERVIEW

**FACTITIOUS DISORDERS WITH PHYSICAL SYMPTOMS**

**SOMATOFORM DISORDERS**

Conversion Disorders

Somatization Disorders

Somatoform Pain Disorders

Hypochondriasis

Body Dysmorphic Disorders

**PSYCHOPHYSIOLOGICAL DISORDERS**

"Traditional" Psychophysiological Disorders

"New" Psychophysiological Disorders

Psychoneuroimmunology

# CHAPTER 11

# PSYCHOLOGICAL FACTORS AND PHYSICAL DISORDERS

Throughout this text we have repeatedly encountered mental disorders that have physical causes. Abnormal neurotransmitter activity, for example, contributes to the development of generalized anxiety disorders, panic disorders, and unipolar patterns of depression. Today's clinicians also recognize that somatic, or bodily, illnesses can have psychological causes. In fact, this notion is not new at all. It can be traced back to the fourth century B.C., when Socrates said, "You should not treat body without soul" (Fiester, 1986; Gentry & Matarazzo, 1981).

Despite its ancient roots, the idea that psychological factors may contribute to somatic illnesses held little appeal before the twentieth century. It was particularly unpopular during the Renaissance, when medicine became a physical science and scientists became committed to the pursuit of objective "fact" (Gatchel & Baum, 1983). At that time the mind was the province of priests and philosophers, the body the realm of physicians and scientists. The seventeenth-century French philosopher René Descartes went so far as to claim that the mind, or soul, was a separate entity from the body, totally unable to affect physical matter or somatic processes. His position, called *mind-body dualism,* dominated medical theory for the next 200 years. Physicians in the nineteenth century followed the tradition of mind-body dualism when they concluded that each organic disease was caused by a distinct microorganism.

During the past 100 years, however, medicine has moved steadily toward an interactive view of physical illness. Clinical research and observations have persuaded medical scientists that many physical illnesses are **psychogenic**—caused by such psychological factors as worry, family stress, and unconscious needs. Some of these physical illnesses, today called *factitious disorders* and *somatoform disorders,* are thought to be caused exclusively by psychological factors. Others, called *psychophysiological disorders,* are believed to result from an interaction of organic and psychological factors.

# FACTITIOUS DISORDERS WITH PHYSICAL SYMPTOMS

People who become physically sick usually go to a physician for medical evaluation, diagnosis, and treatment. Sometimes, however, an illness defies medical assessment, and physicians may suspect some causes other than the physical factors they have been seeking. They may conclude, for instance, that the patient is **malingering**—intentionally feigning illness to achieve some external gains, such as financial compensation or military deferment.

Alternatively, physicians may suspect that the patient is manifesting a **factitious disorder with physical symptoms.** Like malingerers, these people intentionally produce or feign physical symptoms, but they assume the sick role primarily to meet internal psychological needs. They have no external incentives for developing the symptoms.

*A 29-year-old female laboratory technician was admitted* to the medical service via the emergency room because of bloody urine. The patient said that she was being treated for lupus erythematosus by a physician in a different city. She also mentioned that she had had Von Willebrand's disease (a rare hereditary blood disorder) as a child. On the third day of her hospitalization, a medical student mentioned to the resident that she had seen this patient several weeks before at a different hospital in the area, where the patient had been admitted for the same problem. A search of the patient's belongings revealed a cache of anticoagulant medication. When confronted with this information she refused to discuss the matter and hurriedly signed out of the hospital against medical advice.

*(Spitzer et al., 1981, p. 33)*

The physical symptoms of a factitious disorder may be a total fabrication, self-inflicted, or an exaggeration of a preexisting physical condition (APA, 1987). People with the disorder usually describe their medical history dramatically, but become vague when pressed for details. Their knowledge of medical terminology and hospital routine is often extensive. When they are hospitalized they are likely to demand attention from the staff but to disregard hospital regulations. Many eagerly undergo painful testing or treatment, even surgery. They may develop real medical problems, such as the formation of scar tissue from unnecessary surgery, abscesses from numerous injections, or adverse reactions to drugs. If physicians confront them with evidence that their symptoms are factitious, they typically deny the charges and rapidly discharge themselves from the hospital; they are quite likely to enter another hospital the same day.

The best-known form of factitious disorder is called **Munchausen syndrome.** Like Baron Munchausen, an eighteenth-century cavalry officer who journeyed from tavern to tavern in Europe telling fantastical tales about his supposed adventures, people with this syndrome travel from hospital to hospital reciting their symptoms, gaining admission, and receiving treatment (Thompson & Steele, 1985).

Although clinical researchers have yet to determine the prevalence of factitious disorders with physical symptoms, they believe the syndrome to be somewhat more common among men than among women (APA, 1987). Cases usually begin during early adulthood and often develop into a chronic pattern that greatly impairs the person's ability to hold a steady job, maintain family ties, or form enduring social relationships. The disorders seem to be most common among people who (1) received extensive medical treatment and hospitalization as children for a true physical disorder, (2) carry a grudge against the medical profession, (3) have worked as a nurse or other medical professional (but not as a physician), (4) had a significant relationship with a physician in the past, or (5) have underlying dependent, exploitive, or self-defeating personality traits (APA, 1987).

The precise causes of factitious disorders are not really understood. These disorders have received little systematic study, and clinicians have not been able to develop effective treatments for them. DSM-III-R also identifies **factitious disorder with psychological symptoms,** a pattern in which people feign symptoms suggestive of a mental disorder (particularly a psychosis).

# SOMATOFORM DISORDERS

When a physical illness eludes medical assessment, physicians may alternatively suspect that the patient has a *somatoform disorder.* Such patients have physical complaints that are rooted exclusively in psychological causes. In contrast to people with factitious disorders, patients with somatoform disorders experience no sense of willing their symptoms or having control over them. Indeed, they rarely believe that the problems are anything but organic.

In earlier diagnostic systems, somatoform disorders were listed as "neuroses," the Freudian categorization meant to suggest that the disorders resulted from underlying conflicts, intense ongoing anxiety, and ego defense mechanisms that failed to control the anxiety (see p. 178). As we noted earlier, however, DSM-III-R has done away with the category of neurosis, in line with its policy of defining disorders by symptoms and without reference to specific causes. Accordingly, the somatoform disorders now constitute a separate category, unconnected to the anxiety, mood, or dissociative disorders — patterns that were also listed as neuroses in past systems.

Some somatoform disorders, known as *hysterical disorders,* involve an actual loss or alteration of physical functioning. People with *conversion disorders,* for instance, develop one or two dramatic physical symptoms; those with *somatization disorders* experience multiple physical symptoms; and those with *somatoform pain disorders* experience localized pain that is not attributable to an organic cause.

In other somatoform disorders, the *preoccupation disorders,* physical functioning is at most minimally lost or altered. Instead, people with these disorders become preoccupied with the notion that something is wrong with them physically. Those who experience *hypochondriasis* fear that minor fluctuations in their physical functioning indicate a serious disease. Those with *body dysmorphic disorders* worry excessively that some aspect of their physical appearance is defective.

## Hysterical Somatoform Disorders

*Hysterical disorders,* the somatoform disorders that involve altered or lost physical functioning, are often difficult to distinguish from problems with an organic base. The symptoms of these disorders take many forms and typically have a marked impact on patients' lives.

**Conversion Disorders**   A *conversion disorder* is characterized by a significant alteration or loss of one or two areas of physical functioning that is actually an expression of a psychological conflict or need: the psychological problem is converted to a physical symptom. The most dramatic conversion symptoms are those that suggest neurological dysfunctioning, such as paralysis, seizures, blindness, anesthesia (loss of feeling), or aphonia (loss of speech). Symptoms may also suggest autonomic, endocrine, or cardiopulmonary dysfunctioning. One woman developed a conversion symptom of dizziness in apparent response to her unhappy marriage and her inability to deal directly with her abusive husband:

*A 46-year-old married housewife was referred by her hus*band's psychiatrist for consultation. In the course of discussing certain marital conflicts that he was having with his wife, the husband had described "attacks" of dizziness that his wife experienced that left her quite incapacitated.

In consultation, the wife described being overcome with feelings of extreme dizziness, accompanied by slight nausea, four or five nights a week. During these attacks, the room around her would take on a "shimmering" appearance, and she would have the feeling that she was "floating" and unable to keep her balance. Inexplicably, the attacks almost always occurred at about 4:00 P.M. She usually had to lie down on the couch and often did not feel better until 7:00 or 8:00 P.M. After recovering, she generally spent the rest of the evening watching TV; and more often than not, she would fall asleep in the living room, not going to bed in the bedroom until 2:00 or 3:00 in the morning.

The patient had been pronounced physically fit by her internist, a neurologist, and an ear, nose, and throat specialist on more than one occasion. Hypoglycemia had been ruled out by glucose tolerance tests.

When asked about her marriage, the patient described her husband as a tyrant, frequently demanding and verbally abusive of her and their four children. She admitted that she dreaded his arrival home from work each day, knowing that he would comment that the house was a mess and the dinner, if prepared, not to his liking. Recently, since the onset of her attacks, when she was unable to make dinner he and the four kids would go to McDonald's or the local pizza parlor. After that, he would settle in to watch a ballgame in the bedroom, and their conversation was minimal. In spite of their troubles, the patient claimed that she loved her husband and needed him very much.

*(Spitzer et al., 1981, pp. 92–93)*

Most conversion disorders emerge during late adolescence or young adulthood; they are diagnosed twice as often in women as in men (APA, 1987). They usually appear suddenly, at times of extreme psychological stress, and last a relatively short time; at least half of all such symptoms disappear spontaneously within 2 years (APA, 1987; Rachman & Wilson, 1979). Conversion disorders characterized by dramatic neurological symptoms are thought to be quite rare, occurring primarily among soldiers under the stress of combat (APA, 1987; Woodruff et al., 1971). Other kinds of conversion disorders are believed to be more common.

**Somatization Disorders**  Two women known as Ann and Sheila baffled a variety of medical specialists with the wide range of their symptoms:

*A*nn *describes nervousness since childhood; she also spon-*taneously admits to being sickly since her youth with a succession of physical problems doctors often indicated were due to her nerves or depression. She, however, believes that she has a physical problem that has not yet been discovered by the doctors. Besides nervousness, she has chest pain, and has been told by a variety of medical consultants that she has a "nervous heart." She also goes to doctors for abdominal pain, and has been diagnosed as having a "spastic colon." She has seen chiropractors and osteopaths for backaches, for pains in the extremities, and for anesthesia of her fingertips. Three months ago she had vomiting, chest pain, and abdominal pain, and was admitted to a hospital for a hysterectomy. Since the hysterectomy she has had repeated anxiety attacks, fainting spells that she claims are associated with unconsciousness that lasts more than thirty minutes, vomiting, food intolerance, weakness, and fatigue. She has had several medical hospitalizations for workups of vomiting, colitis, vomiting blood, and chest pain. She has had a surgical procedure for an abscess of the throat.

*S*heila *reported having abdominal pain since age 17, ne-*cessitating exploratory surgery that yielded no specific diagnosis. She had several pregnancies, each with severe nausea, vomiting, and abdominal pain; she ultimately had a hysterectomy for a "tipped uterus." Since age 40 she had experienced dizziness and "blackouts," which she eventually was told might be multiple sclerosis or a brain tumor. She continued to be bedridden for extended periods of time, with weakness, blurred vision, and difficulty urinating. At age 43 she was worked up for a hiatal hernia because of complaints of bloating and intolerance of a variety of foods. She also had additional hospitalizations for neurological, hypertensive, and renal workups, all of which failed to reveal a definitive diagnosis.

*(Spitzer et al., 1981, pp. 185, 260)*

When we read the case descriptions of Ann and Sheila, we are struck by the sheer quantity of medical problems these women experienced. People who have 13 or more physical ailments without an organic basis, and whose difficulties continue or recur for several years, are likely to receive a diagnosis of **somatization disorder.** This

pattern, first described by Pierre Briquet in 1859, is also known as **Briquet's syndrome.** The multiple ailments of somatization disorders may include gastrointestinal symptoms (such as vomiting), bodily pain, cardiopulmonary problems (such as shortness of breath), neurological symptoms, sexual symptoms (such as burning sensations in the sex organs), and symptoms associated with the female reproductive system (such as menstrual difficulties).

Patients with somatization disorders usually go from doctor to doctor in search of relief (Cloninger et al., 1984). They often describe their many symptoms in dramatic and exaggerated terms. Most also feel anxious and depressed.

Approximately 1 percent of all women in the United States are believed to develop a somatization disorder during their lives; men almost never receive this diagnosis (APA, 1987; Koran, 1986). The disorder often runs in families (Guze, Cloninger, Martin, & Clayton, 1986). Close female relatives of women with the disorder are ten times more likely than the general population to develop the syndrome (Woodruff et al., 1981). The disorder usually begins during adolescence with no identifiable precipitating event. It lasts considerably longer than a conversion disorder, typically for many years. The symptoms may fluctuate over time but rarely disappear completely without psychotherapy. As many as 70 percent of women with the disorder appear to experience the syndrome for 15 years or more (Coryell & Norten, 1981; Woodruff et al., 1971; Ziegler & Paul, 1954).

**Somatoform Pain Disorder**  People who experience severe and prolonged pain that has no medical explanation or that is disproportionate to a known medical problem may receive a diagnosis of *somatoform pain disorder.* The pain may occur in any part of the body. Patients with conversion or somatization disorders may also experience pain without an organic cause, but it is the dominant symptom of a somatoform pain disorder.

Researchers have not been able to determine the prevalence of somatoform pain disorders, but physicians say they see many such cases in their practices (APA, 1987). Women receive this diagnosis twice as often as men (APA, 1987). The disorder begins most frequently in middle age, usually appearing suddenly, increasing in severity for weeks or months, and in some cases continuing for years. Although the pain is theoretically linked to psychological factors, it is sometimes difficult to discern a precipitating stressful event or conflict.

Often a somatoform pain disorder develops after an accident or during an illness that has caused genuine pain. The pain, however, eventually becomes more severe and enduring than organic factors can explain. Laura, a 36-year-old woman with sarcoidosis, reported pains that far exceeded the usual symptoms of this tubercular disease. In fact, as the following interview indicates, her pain continued even after the sarcoidosis went into complete remission:

*Laura:* Before the operation I would have little joint pains, nothing that really bothered me that much. After the operation I was having severe pains in my chest and in my ribs, and those were the type of problems I'd been having after the operation, that I didn't have before. . . . I'd go to an emergency room at night, 11:00, 12:00, 1:00 or so. I'd take the medicine, and the next day it stopped hurting, and I'd go back again. In the meantime this is when I went to the other doctors, to complain about the same thing, to find out what was wrong; and they could never find out what was wrong with me either. . . .

*Doctor:* With these symptoms on and off over the years, has that interfered with the way you've lived your life?

*Laura:* Yes. At certain points when I go out or my husband and I go out, we have to leave early because I start hurting. . . . A lot of times I just won't do things because my chest is hurting for one reason or another. . . .

*Doctor:* Does it interfere with your work, those pains?

*Laura:* Yes, but I still work. . . .

*Doctor:* Have you had chest x-rays recently? Did they show the sarcoid was the same?

*Laura:* . . . One doctor said he didn't see any signs of sarcoid, but I knew I was still having joint pains. Two months ago when the doctor checked me and another doctor looked at the x-rays, he said he didn't see any signs of the sarcoid then and that they were doing a study now, on blood and various things, to see if it was connected to sarcoid. . . .

*(Green, 1985, pp. 60–63)*

**Identifying Hysterical Symptoms**   In an effort to distinguish hysterical somatoform disorders from "true" medical problems, diagnosticians rely on several distinctions:

*Unusual Emotional Reactions*   People with hysterical disorders usually react to their physical symptoms quite differently from those with identifiable medical problems (Levy, 1985). Whereas most people would be horrified by the onset of blindness, someone with conversion blindness may show relatively little concern about the disability. This nonchalant attitude, sometimes called *la belle indifférence,* appears in as many as one-third of all cases of conversion disorders (Stephens & Kamp, 1962). Similarly, although *la belle indifférence* seldom accompanies somatoform pain disorders, many patients whose symptoms are hysterical in origin express

less concern about their pain than one would expect (APA, 1987).

*Neurological and Anatomical Inconsistencies*   The symptoms of some hysterical disorders do not correspond to what medical scientists know about the anatomical distribution of nerves and the way the nervous system works. Some patients, for example, display a conversion symptom called "glove anesthesia," numbness that begins abruptly at the wrist and extends with uniform intensity throughout the hand to the fingertips. As Figure 11-1 shows, such clearly defined and equally distributed numbness is not characteristic of neurological damage.

*Unexpected Course of Development*   Hysterical disorders do not necessarily lead to the same physical consequences as corresponding organic problems (Levy, 1985). When paraplegia (paralysis from the waist down) is caused by damage to the spinal cord, for example, the leg muscles may atrophy, or waste away, unless the patient receives proper physical therapy and exercise. Someone whose paralysis is a conversion disorder does not ordinarily experience such atrophy; they presumably exercise their muscles to some degree, without being aware that they are doing so.

*Selective Symptomatology*   The physical symptoms of hysterical disease may operate selectively, or inconsistently. People with conversion blindness, for example, have fewer accidents than people who are organically blind, an indication that they have at least some vision even if they are unaware of it.

## Preoccupation Somatoform Disorders

People who have hypochondriasis and body dysmorphic disorders, both characterized as *preoccupation somatoform disorders,* take minimal physical symptoms as signs of serious physical problems. Friends, relatives, and physicians may try to dissuade them from this notion, but usually without success. Although often these kinds of somatoform disorders cause considerable anxiety or depression, they do not affect a person's social or occupational functioning so profoundly as hysterical disorders do (Starcevic, 1988; APA, 1987; Jenike, 1985; Hardy & Cotterll, 1982).

**Hypochondriasis**   People who suffer from *hypochondriasis* unrealistically and fearfully interpret relatively minor physical discomforts as signs of a serious illness. Often the reported ailments are merely normal fluctuations in

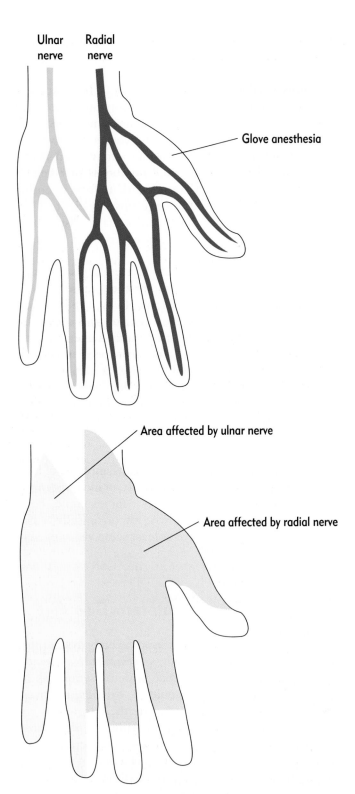

Ulnar nerve    Radial nerve

Glove anesthesia

Area affected by ulnar nerve

Area affected by radial nerve

**FIGURE 11-1** In the conversion symptom called "glove anesthesia," the entire hand extending to the wrist becomes numb. Actual physical damage to the ulnar nerve, in contrast, causes anesthesia in the ring finger and little finger and beyond the wrist partway up the arm; and damage to the radial nerve causes insensitivity only in parts of the ring, middle, and index fingers and the thumb and partway up the arm. *(Adapted from Gray, 1959.)*

*"He didn't really die of anything. He was a hypochondriac."*

(Drawing by George Price; © 1970, *The New Yorker Magazine,* Inc.)

physical functioning, such as occasional coughing, sores, or sweating. Despite repeated diagnostic tests, hypochondriacal patients are not reassured. They may go from doctor to doctor in their efforts to find a helpful intervention.

Hypochondriasis can present a picture very similar to that of a somatization disorder. Each typically involves numerous physical symptoms and frequent visits to doctors, and each causes patients great concern. Although it is often a difficult judgment to make, diagnosticians try to distinguish between the two on the basis of the following criteria: if the anxiety level is significant and the bodily symptoms are relatively minor, a diagnosis of hypochondriasis is in order; if the bodily symptoms are more significant and overshadow the patient's anxiety, they probably indicate a somatization disorder.

Although hypochondriasis can begin at any age, it emerges most commonly between the ages of 20 and 30 years. Some patients eventually overcome their preoccupation, but for most the disorder becomes chronic, the symptoms waxing and waning over the years. Like somatoform pain disorders, hypochondriasis is reportedly very familiar to physicians, but its exact prevalence is unknown. Men and women are equally likely to receive this diagnosis (APA, 1987).

Clinicians sometimes distinguish between two categories of hypochondriacal patients — the *hostile* and the *dependent* (Thompson, 1985). Hostile patients adopt an angry and "untreatable" posture, dwell on their suffering and sacrifices, and try to avoid dependency on physicians. Fyodor Dostoyevsky describes such a person in *Notes from the Underground:*

I am a sick man . . . I am a spiteful man. I am an unattractive man. I believe my liver is diseased. However, I know nothing at all about my disease, and do not know for certain what ails me. I don't consult a doctor for it , and never have, though I have a respect for medicine and doctors. Besides, I am extremely superstitious, sufficiently so to respect medicine, anyway (I am well educated enough not to be superstitious, but I am superstitious). No, I refuse to consult a doctor from spite. . . . My liver is bad, well—let it get worse!

Dependent hypochondriacal patients, by contrast, develop a passive, childlike relationship with a physician, repeatedly visiting the doctor to complain and to seek some reassurance and relief from their physical problems. This form of hypochondriasis is seen in a letter written by a patient to the head of a hospital surgical department:

Dear Dr. . . .

I am writing to you again to see if you can be of any help. I wrote to you in April of this year. You advised me to see one of the gynecologists at your clinic. I did come out to see Dr. Smith. After we talked awhile, he thought I should see a psychiatrist. . . . I didn't even stay to let Dr. Smith examine me I was so disgusted, but he called my husband at work which I didn't exactly appreciate either, and told him that maybe a chiropractor would be of some help. Well, I went to one then and he . . . didn't want to work on me as he didn't feel that he could help me, but advised me to go to a neurosurgeon which I did. He told me that what I really needed was a real good general surgeon. I asked him to recommend one, but he said he couldn't. I am having trouble turning over and getting up and down. Now I have been like this ever since I had my first surgery. . . . I know there is something wrong somewhere. . . . I can feel something move in my lower abdomen. Sometimes so violently that it wakes me up at night. I have about come to the conclusion that they may have left something inside me or I have a fibroid tumor that they missed as he said I have these. Now I do know that it is possible that I could have had one on the outside of the uterus as this happened to a friend of mine. . . . Now another thing is that I have two places in my back that are just like small breaks, something is just pulling my back apart. I was trying to take some physical therapy treatments but they are just killing me. . . . I just can't understand why, with the different doctors I have gone to, someone won't get to the bottom of things. You are just about my last hope. . . .

Thank you,
Mrs. . . .

*(Rhine & Thompson, 1985, pp. 74–75)*

**Body Dysmorphic Disorders** People who experience a *body dysmorphic disorder,* also known as *dysmorphophobia,* become preoccupied with some imagined or exaggerated defect in their appearance. Most commonly they worry about facial flaws such as wrinkles, spots on the skin, excessive facial hair, swelling of the face, or a misshapen nose, mouth, jaw, or eyebrow (APA, 1987). Some worry about the appearance of their feet, hands,

breasts, penis, or another body part. Others are concerned about bad odors coming from sweat, the breath, the genitals, or the rectum (Marks, 1987). Some people are distressed by several body features. Here we see a case of body dysmorphic disorder that centers on body odor:

*A woman of 35 had for 16 years been worried that her* sweat smelled terrible. The fear began just before her marriage when she was sharing a bed with a close friend who said that someone at work smelled badly, and the patient felt that the remark was directed at her. For fear that she smelled, for 5 years she had not gone out anywhere except when accompanied by her husband or mother. She had not spoken to her neighbors for 3 years because she thought she had overheard them speak about her to some friends. She avoided cinemas, dances, shops, cafes, and private homes. Occasionally she visited her in-laws, but she always sat at a distance from them. Her husband was not allowed to invite any friends home; she constantly sought reassurance from him about her smell; and strangers who rang the doorbell were not answered. Television commercials about deodorants made her very anxious. She refused to attend the local church because it was small and the local congregants might comment on her. The family had to travel to a church 8 miles away in which the congregants were strangers; there they sat or stood apart from the others. Her husband bought all her new clothes as she was afraid to try on clothes in front of shop assistants. She used vast quantities of deodorant and always bathed and changed her clothes before going out, up to 4 times daily.

*(Marks, 1987, p. 371)*

It is common for people in our society to be somewhat concerned about their appearance. Adolescents and young adults in particular often worry about such things as acne. The concerns of people with body dysmorphic disorders, however, are extreme and disruptive. Sufferers may even have difficulty looking others in the eye, convinced that their flaws are on display. They may go to great lengths to conceal the "defect"—always wearing sunglasses to hide the shape of their supposedly misshapen eyes, for example, or even seeking plastic surgery to correct the problem (Thomas, 1984; Hay, 1983). Most cases of body dysmorphic disorder begin between adolescence and middle age and persist for several years (APA, 1987). Researchers have not yet determined the prevalence or gender distribution of such disorders (APA, 1987).

## Views on Somatoform Disorders

Theorists usually explain the preoccupation somatoform disorders—hypochondriasis and body dysmorphic disorders—the same way they explain simple phobias (discussed in Chapter 6). Behaviorists, for example, believe that the disproportionate fears displayed by people with these disorders have been acquired earlier in life through classical conditioning or modeling. The hysterical somatoform disorders, however — conversion, somatization, and somatoform pain disorders — are considered to be unique and to require special explanations.

The ancient Greeks believed that hysterical disorders were experienced only by women and came about when the uterus of a sexually ungratified woman wandered throughout her body in search of fulfillment, producing a physical symptom wherever it lodged. (Our word "hysteria" comes from the Greek word for uterus, *hustera*.) Hippocrates suggested marriage as the most effective treatment for hysterical disorders.

The current belief in the clinical field that hysterical ailments are caused by psychological factors dates back to the work of Ambroise-Auguste Liébault and Hippolyte Bernheim in the late nineteenth century. Founders of the Nancy School in Paris — an institution for the study and treatment of mental disorders — these researchers were able to produce such hysterical symptoms as deafness, paralysis, blindness, and numbness in normal people by hypnotic suggestion and could remove these symptoms by the same means (see Chapter 1). Having established that a psychological process — hypnotic suggestion — could both induce and reverse physical dysfunctioning, they concluded that hysterical somatoform disorders are themselves probably caused by psychological processes.

Today's leading explanations for hysterical disorders come from the psychodynamic, behavioral, and cognitive models. As we shall observe, however, none has received much research support, and the disorders are still poorly understood.

**The Psychodynamic View**   As we noted in Chapter 1, Freud's theory of psychoanalysis actually began with his efforts to account for hysterical symptoms. After studying hypnosis in Paris and becoming acquainted with the work of Liébault and Bernheim, Freud became interested in the work of an older physician, Joseph Breuer (1842–1925). Breuer used hypnosis to treat the woman he called Anna O., whom we met in Chapter 2. Recently critics have questioned whether Anna's hysterical deafness, disorganized speech, and paralysis were entirely hysterical and whether Breuer's hypnotic treatment was as helpful to her as he claimed (see Box 11-1). At the time, however, this case, along with others, seemed to confirm the idea that hysterical ailments could be treated effectively by hypnosis. Freud collaborated with Breuer in the 1890s, and together they published an influential book, *Studies in Hysteria.*

Partly because hysterical disorders seemed to respond to hypnosis, Freud (1894) came to believe that these ailments represented a conversion of underlying emotional conflicts into physical symptoms. Observing that most of his patients with these disorders were women, he proposed that the underlying conflicts developed during a girl's phallic stage (ages 3 through 5), when he believed girls develop an **Electra complex:** they experience strong sexual feelings for their father and come to recognize that they must compete with their mother for their father's affection. In deference to their mother's dominant position and to cultural taboos, they repress their sexual feelings and adopt a socially approved abhorrence of such desires.

Freud believed that if a child's parents overreact to her sexual feelings, the Electra conflict will go unresolved and the child may reexperience sexual anxiety throughout her life. Whenever events trigger sexual feelings, the adult may experience an overwhelming, unconscious need to hide them from both herself and the world. Freud concluded that some women hide such reemerging sexual feelings by unconsciously converting them into physical symptoms.

Most of today's psychodynamic theorists have modified Freud's explanation of hysterical disorders, particularly his notion that the disorders can always be traced to unresolved Electra conflicts (Kriechman, 1987). They continue to believe, however, that the disorders reflect (1) an unconscious conflict of some kind that arouses anxiety and (2) a conversion of this anxiety into "more tolerable" physical symptoms that often symbolize the underlying conflict.

Psychodynamic theories have distinguished two mechanisms at work in hysterical somatoform disorders — *primary gain* and *secondary gain* (Colbach, 1987). People are said to be achieving **primary gain** when their hysterical symptoms keep their internal conflicts out of awareness. During an argument, for example, people with inner conflicts about expressing anger may develop a conversion symptom of aphonia (inability to speak) or paralysis of the arm, thus preventing a threatening rage reaction from reaching consciousness. People are said to be achieving **secondary gain** when their hysterical symptoms also enable them to avoid unpleasant activities or to receive kindness or sympathy from others. Both forms of gain help to lock in their symptoms. When, for example, a conversion paralysis allows a soldier to avoid battle duty or conversion blindness prevents the breakup of a relationship, secondary gain may be operating. According to psychodynamic theorists, primary gains initiate hysterical symptoms; secondary gains are by-products of the symptoms. Although such psychodynamic notions are widely accepted, they have received little research support.

## BOX 11-1

# A Closer Look at the Case of Anna O.

Bertha Pappenheim, Josef Breuer's famous "Anna O."

You have read of the groundbreaking case of Anna O., whom Josef Breuer cured through catharsis. He wrote in his famous 1895 report that his "talking cure" relieved her of many bizarre symptoms—paralysis, trances, visual problems, speech problems, and facial disorders. Breuer reported that after he hypnotized Anna O. and traced a symptom back to an original disquieting event, the symptom would disappear. This case is often cited as the basis for Freud's later development of psychoanalysis. The problem is that in reality Anna O. may have never been cured.

In 1925, Carl Jung was told by Sigmund Freud that Anna O. retained many of her original problems and was being treated primarily with morphine. The "talking cure" had failed. Yet this failure was never publicly acknowledged.

In 1972, H. F. Ellenberger tracked down the facts about Anna O. He began by confirming her true identity—Bertha Pappenheim, a well-to-do young woman from Vienna. Breuer treated her from 1880 to 1882, but his renowned report did not emerge until 1895. Ellenberger contacted a sanatorium in Germany where Anna O. stayed in 1882. There he found two fascinating documents: first, the original, previously unknown, report by Breuer, written in 1882, upon which

the later report was based; second, a follow-up report by one of the doctors who treated Anna O. at the sanatorium. They contained a number of discrepancies.

Breuer's 1882 report provides much more detail on Anna O., her family, and her physiological disorders than does his 1895 report and concludes by saying that her symptoms were greatly alleviated. It is presumably an account of his treatment of Anna O., yet it makes no mention of a number of issues that are discussed in detail in the later report. Moreover, the report of the sanatorium doctor

makes no mention of the "talking cure" and instead describes a troubled young woman who was given doses of chloral hydrate and morphine to treat the same symptoms that Breuer claimed to have cured.

Ellenberger concludes that Bertha Pappenheim was not a typical case of hysteria and that there may have been an organic cause for many of her problems. Moreover, the cathartic cure played little, if any, role in her treatment. Proponents of psychoanalysis contend that, like many other apocryphal stories in science, religion, and history, Breuer's dubious report does not affect the merits of the field to which it gave birth. Opponents argue that this "paper tiger" of a case continues to be cited and that relatively little of merit has emerged to substantiate it. As in many other fields, this debate may be of more academic than practical interest. Psychoanalysis is healthy and popular, and its influence permeates our culture. Perhaps this is as it should be, and Anna O.'s continued illness should remain a historical footnote. But, as you learn more about abnormal psychology (or physics, or philosophy, or history), remember the words of a very wise person who, we can almost guarantee, made the following statement—"trust, but verify."

**The Cognitive View**    A number of theorists propose that hysterical disorders are forms of *communication:* through them people manage to express emotions that they can-

not express otherwise (Lipowski, 1987). Like their psychodynamic colleagues, these theorists hold that the emotions of patients with hysterical disorders are being converted into physical symptoms. They suggest, however, that the purpose of the conversion is not to "defend" against anxiety but to communicate some distressing emotion — anger, fear, depression, guilt, jealousy — in a "language" (that is, physical dysfunctioning) that is familiar to the patient and therefore comfortable. Because of its emphasis on language and communication as opposed to underlying conflicts and defenses, this view is generally considered a cognitive perspective.

According to this view, people who have difficulty acknowledging their emotions or expressing them to others are candidates for a hysterical disorder, especially when they are in the midst of a difficult interpersonal situation. Similarly, those who learn the language of physical dysfunctioning through firsthand experience with a genuine physical malady either in themselves or in a relative or friend may then adopt hysterical symptoms as a form of communication (Woodruff, Goodwin, & Guze, 1974; Ziegler & Imboden, 1962). Without any particular awareness on their part, these people may slip into a sick role that distracts them from their own psychological pain while conveying their great distress to others.

This view of hysterical disorders is obviously broader than the psychodynamic explanation. It allows that emotions other than anxiety may contribute to physical dysfunctioning, that defensive functioning is less of a factor in hysterical conversions than poor ability to communicate, and that familiarity with an illness plays a major role in the development of hysterical ailments. Only this last feature of the cognitive explanation has been supported by research, however. Often hysterical disorders emerge after people have had similar medical problems or after close relatives or friends have experienced such maladies (Levy, 1988).

**The Behavioral View** Behavioral theorists propose that the physical symptoms of hysterical disorders bring the sufferer rewards. Perhaps the symptoms keep the sufferer out of a difficult work situation or relationship, or elicit attention that is otherwise withheld (Ullmann & Krasner, 1975). According to behaviorists, such reinforcements operantly condition people into assuming the role of an invalid. Like cognitive theorists, behaviorists hold that a person must be relatively familiar with an illness to be able to adopt its physical symptoms.

The behavioral focus on rewards is similar to the psychodynamic notion that often people with hysterical disorders attain secondary gains from their physical symptoms. The key difference between the two positions is that psychodynamic theorists view such gains as indeed *secondary* — that is, as a feature that develops only after underlying dynamic conflicts produce the disorder. Behaviorists view the gains (or rewards) as the primary factor in the development of the disorder.

Like the psychodynamic and cognitive explanations, the behavioral view of hysterical disorders has received little research support. Even clinical case reports only occasionally support this position. In many cases the pain and upset that accompany the disorders seem to outweigh any rewards the symptoms may bring.

## Treatments for Somatoform Disorders

People with somatoform disorders usually seek psychotherapy only as a last resort. They fully believe that their problems are somatic and reject all suggestions to the contrary. When a physician tells them that their problems have no physical basis, they simply go to another physician.

Eventually some patients with these disorders do try psychotherapy for their problems. Those with preoccupation somatoform disorders typically receive the kinds of treatment that are applied to phobic and obsessive-compulsive disorders, particularly *exposure and response-prevention* interventions (discussed in Chapter 7). The effectiveness of these approaches in treating preoccupation somatoform disorders, however, has yet to be determined.

People with hysterical somatoform disorders receive interventions that stress either *insight, suggestion,* or *confrontation.* The most commonly applied insight approach has been psychodynamic therapy, which helps patients bring their anxiety-arousing conflicts into consciousness so they can work through them, theoretically eliminating the need to convert anxiety into physical symptoms. Approaches that employ suggestion include telling patients persuasively that their physical symptoms will soon disappear (Bird, 1979; Carter, 1979) or suggesting the same thing to them under hypnosis (Ballinger, 1987). Therapists who take a confrontational approach straightforwardly tell patients that their symptoms are without an organic foundation, hoping to force them out of the sick role (Brady & Lind, 1961).

Researchers have been unable to determine the effects of these various forms of psychotherapy on hysterical disorders (Ballinger, 1987). Case studies suggest, however, that conversion disorders and somatoform pain disorders respond better to psychotherapy than do somatization disorders, and that approaches that rely on insight and suggestion bring more lasting improvement than confrontation strategies.

One thing that makes the study and treatment of hysterical disorders difficult is the ever-present possibility that a diagnosis of hysteria may be a misdiagnosis, that the problem under examination may actually have an organic base. Although organic causes must be ruled out before a diagnosis of somatoform disorder is reached, the tools of medical science are too imprecise to eliminate organic factors completely (Merskey, 1986). Some of the medical problems most difficult for doctors to diagnose are those involving vague, multiple, and confusing symptoms, including such conditions as hyperparathyroidism, porphyria, multiple sclerosis, and systemic lupus erythematosis. These problems are often initially misdiagnosed as somatoform disorders. In addition, the organic basis for some physical ailments has simply not yet been discovered. In years past, for example, whiplash was regularly diagnosed as a somatoform pain disorder, because medical scientists had not yet uncovered the physical causes of this painful condition (Merskey, 1986).

In a revealing study on this subject, researchers carefully reassessed a large number of conversion disorder diagnoses and determined that in 25 percent of the cases organic factors may have been involved (Watson & Buranen, 1979). In another study 63 percent of a group of patients diagnosed as having conversion disorders were later found to have organic brain disorders; such brain disorders had developed in only 5 percent of a comparison group of anxious or depressed patients (Whitlock, 1967). Clearly clinicians must be most careful in assessing and treating people with the symptoms of these disorders, and even then, they must always keep in mind that the problems under examination may, as odd as it sounds, be just what they appear — physical problems. Table 11-1 shows some of the factors that distinguish the various types of disorders that involve physical symptoms.

# PSYCHOPHYSIOLOGICAL DISORDERS

Earlier in this century clinicians identified a group of physical illnesses that seemed to result from an *interaction* of psychological and physical factors (Dunbar, 1948; Bott, 1928). These illnesses differed from somatoform disorders in that both psychological and physical factors played significant causal roles and the illnesses themselves brought about actual medical damage. Previous editors of the DSM have labeled these illnesses *psychosomatic* or *psychophysiological*. DSM-III-R uses the label *psychological factors affecting physical condition,* and indicates that this diagnosis is appropriate when (1) "psychologically meaningful environmental stimuli are temporally related to the initiation or exacerbation of a specific physical condition or disorder" and (2) the physical condition involves either demonstrable or known organic pathology. We shall use the more familiar and less cumbersome term "psychophysiological" in our discussion of the disorders.

At first clinicians believed that only a limited number of illnesses were psychophysiological and that these illnesses usually involved dysfunctioning in some part of the patient's autonomic nervous system (see pp. 178–181). The list of such illnesses included ulcers, asthma, and coronary heart disease. In recent years researchers have learned that other kinds of physical illnesses — most notably bacterial and viral infections such as colds, mononucleosis, and cancer — may also be caused by an interaction of psychological and physical factors. Let us focus first on the "traditional" psychophysiological disorders, and then on the newer members of this category.

TABLE 11-1

| DIFFERENTIATING DISORDERS THAT HAVE PHYSICAL SYMPTOMS | | | |
|---|---|---|---|
| Disorder | Voluntary control of symptoms? | Symptoms linked to psychological factors? | An apparent goal? |
| Malingering | Yes | Maybe | Yes |
| Factitious disorder | Yes | Yes | No* |
| Somatoform disorder | No | Yes | Maybe |
| Psychophysiological disorder | No | Yes | Maybe |
| Physical illness | No | Maybe | No |

* *Except for medical attention.*
*Source:* Adapted from Hyler & Spitzer, 1978.

# "Traditional" Psychophysiological Disorders

During the first half of this century, clinicians organized psychophysiological disorders around the various body systems affected by them (APA, 1968). They identified, for example, skin disorders, cardiovascular disorders, gastrointestinal disorders, and musculoskeletal disorders that were psychophysiological. The best-known and most prevalent of the disorders were ulcers, asthma, chronic headaches, hypertension, and coronary heart disease.

*Ulcers* are lesions or holes that form in the wall of the stomach *(gastric ulcers)* or of the duodenum *(peptic ulcers),* resulting in burning sensations or pain in the stomach, occasional vomiting, and stomach bleeding. This disorder is experienced by 5 to 10 percent of all persons in the United States and is responsible for more than 6,000 deaths each year (Suter, 1986; National Center for Health Statistics, 1984). Ulcers are apparently caused by an interaction of psychological factors, such as environmental stress, intense feelings of anger or anxiety, or a dependent personality (Tennant, 1988; Wolf, 1981; Weiner et al., 1957; Wolf & Wolf, 1947),

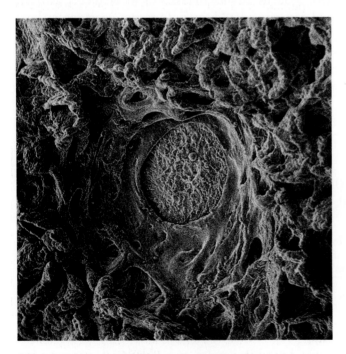

An ulcer in the stomach lining of a rat. Such open sores can occur in the mucous lining of the duodenum as well. For reasons that are not clear, the prevalence of ulcers in human beings has apparently been declining in recent years (Thompson, 1988).

and physiological factors, such as excessive secretions of the gastric juices or a weak lining of the stomach or duodenum (Fiester, 1986; Grossman, 1982; Dragstedt, 1967; Mirsky, 1958; Weiner et al., 1957).

*Asthma* causes the body's airways (the trachea and bronchi) to constrict periodically, so that it is hard for air to pass to and from the lungs. The resulting symptoms are shortness of breath, wheezing, coughing, and a terrifying choking sensation. Approximately 15 million people in the United States suffer from asthma. Most victims are under 15 years of age at the time of the first attack. This disease is the leading cause of illness and disability among children and adolescents (Young, 1980). Approximately 70 percent of all cases appear to be caused by an interaction of such psychological factors as generalized anxiety, heightened dependency needs, environmental stress, or troubled family relationships (Purcell et al., 1969; Rees, 1964; Alexander, 1950) and such physiological factors as allergies to specific substances, a slow-acting sympathetic nervous system, or a weakness of the respiratory system traceable to respiratory infections or biological inheritance (Alexander, 1981; Miklich et al., 1973; Konig & Godfrey, 1973; Rees, 1964).

*Chronic headaches* are frequent intense aches of the head or neck that are not caused by a physical disorder. There are two types of chronic headaches. *Muscle contraction headaches* (also called *tension headaches*), bring a mild to severe pain at the back or front of the head or at the back of the neck. These headaches occur when the muscles surrounding the skull contract, constricting the blood vessels. Approximately 40 million Americans, more women than men, suffer from these headaches. *Migraine headaches* are extremely severe and often immobilizing aches located on one side of the head, often preceded by a warning sensation called an *aura,* and sometimes accompanied by dizziness, nausea, or vomiting. Migraine headaches develop in two phases: (1) blood vessels in the brain constrict, so that the flow of blood to parts of the brain is reduced, and (2) the same blood vessels later dilate, so that blood flows rapidly, stimulating numerous neuron endings and causing pain. Migraines are suffered by about 12 million people in the United States, two-thirds of them women. Research suggests that chronic headaches are caused by an interaction of psychological factors, such as environmental stress, general feelings of helplessness, feelings of hostility, or a passive or depressive personality style (Levor et al., 1986; Williams, 1977), and such physiological factors as vascular weakness or musculoskeletal deficiencies (Blanchard & Andrasik, 1982).

*Hypertension* is a state of chronic high blood pressure. That is, the blood pumped through the body's arteries by

Children who suffer from asthma may use an *aerochamber,* or *inhaler,* to help them inhale helpful medications. The child pumps the medication into the device's plastic tube, then inhales it.

the heart produces too much pressure against the artery walls. Hypertension has few outward symptoms but it plays havoc with the entire cardiovascular system, greatly increasing the likelihood of stroke, coronary heart disease, and kidney problems (Dollery, 1985). It is estimated that 25 million people in the United States have hypertension, at least 60,000 die directly from it annually, and millions more perish because of illnesses brought on by this condition (Rowland & Roberts, 1982). Only 5 to 10 percent of all cases of hypertension are caused exclusively by physiological abnormalities; the remainder are brought about by a combination of psychological and physiological factors and are often designated *essential hypertension* (Rowland & Roberts, 1982). Some of the leading psychological causes of essential hypertension are constant environmental danger, chronic feelings of anger, and an unexpressed need for power (McClelland, 1985, 1979; Harburgh et al., 1973). Leading physiological causes include a diet high in salt and dysfunctional *baroreceptors*—sensitive nerves in the arteries responsible for signaling the brain that blood pressure is becoming too high (Scribner, 1983; Kaplan, 1980; Schwartz, 1977).

*Coronary heart disease* is caused by a blocking of the coronary arteries—the blood vessels that surround the heart and are responsible for providing oxygen to the heart muscle. The term actually refers to any of several specific problems, including *angina pectoris,* extreme chest pain caused when a partial blockage of the coronary arteries prevents a sufficient amount of oxygen from reaching the heart; *coronary occlusion,* a complete

blockage of a coronary artery that halts the flow of blood to various parts of the heart muscle and eventually leads to permanent destruction of heart tissue, or *myocardial infarction* (a "heart attack"). This permanent damage to the heart may lead to death. Together these problems are the leading causes of death in men over the age of 35 and of women over 40 in the United States, accounting for close to 800,000 deaths each year, or 38 percent of all deaths in the nation (Thompson, 1988; Matarazzo, 1984; National Center for Health Statistics, 1984). More than half of all cases of coronary heart disease are related to an interaction of such psychological factors as job stress and the so-called Type A personality style (high levels of impatience, frustration, competitiveness, and hostility, and constant striving for control and success) and such physiological factors as a high level of serum cholesterol, obesity, hypertension, the effects of smoking, and lack of exercise (Thompson, 1988; Williams, 1985; Friedman et al., 1984; Friedman & Rosenman, 1974, 1959).

### The Disregulation Model of Traditional Psychophysiological Disorders

By definition, psychophysiological disorders are caused by an interaction of psychological and physical factors. But how do these factors combine to produce a given illness? Gary Schwartz, a leading researcher, has proposed the *disregulation model* to help account for this phenomenon (see Figure 11-2). Schwartz suggests that our brain and body ordinarily establish *negative feedback loops* that guarantee a smooth, self-regulating operation of the body (Schwartz, 1982, 1977). The brain receives information about external events from

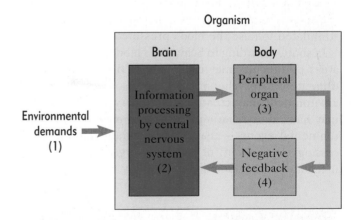

**FIGURE 11-2** In Schwartz's disregulation model, the organism receives environmental pressure (1), the brain processes information about this pressure (2) and then stimulates body organs into action (3), and the organs then provide negative feedback to the brain stating that the stimulation has been sufficient and should cease (4). *(Adapted from Schwartz, 1977.)*

the environment, processes this information, and then stimulates body organs into action. Mechanisms in the organs then provide critical negative feedback, telling the brain that its stimulation has been sufficient and should now stop.

This process can be seen in the blood pressure feedback loop. In one part of this loop the brain receives information that dangers exist in the environment, such as nearby lightning or cars speeding by. In the next part of the loop, the brain processes such information and alerts the nervous system to elevate the blood pressure. And in a later part of the loop, the **baroreceptors,** pressure-sensitive cells surrounding the body's blood vessels, alert the nervous systems when the blood pressure rises too high, and the nervous system then lowers the blood pressure. In short, the various parts of the feedback loop work together to help maintain the blood pressure at an appropriate level.

According to Schwartz, the proper operation of negative feedback loops is essential to a person's health. If one part of a loop falters, the body will enter a state of **disregulation** rather than effective self-regulation, problems will unfold throughout the loop, and a psychophysiological disorder may ultimately develop. Hypertension, for example, may result from problems in any part of the blood pressure feedback loop. Should information from the environment be excessive (as when one is faced with continuous job stress or extended unemployment), should information processing be faulty (as when one keeps misinterpreting or overreacting to everyday events), should a peripheral organ malfunction (as when the aorta narrows abnormally), or should a feedback mechanism fail (as when baroreceptors fail to inform the brain that blood pressure is rising too high), inaccurate information will be fed to the next part of the loop and relayed to the next, until every part in the loop has been stimulated to raise the blood pressure.

In short, according to Schwartz's model, three general areas of difficulty may contribute to disregulation and ultimately to psychophysiological disorders: (1) one's environment may create extraordinary stress; (2) one may have idiosyncratic psychological reactions to environmental events—that is, idiosyncratic ways of processing information; or (3) body organs or feedback mechanisms may function improperly.

### Factors That Contribute to Psychophysiological Disorders

Over the years, theorists have suggested a variety of factors that may contribute to psychophysiological illnesses. These factors may be grouped in accordance with Schwartz's disregulation model.

**Extraordinary Environmental Pressures** Sometimes the demands placed on people are so intense or long-lasting that they prevent negative feedback loops from establishing a comfortable state of self-regulation. Three kinds of environmental events may lead to disregulation and set the stage for psychophysiological disorders—*cataclysmic, personal,* and *background stressors* (Cohen, 1983; Lazarus & Cohen, 1977).

*Cataclysmic stressors* are events that have a powerful and lingering negative effect on a whole population, such as a war or natural disaster. Researchers have determined that populations confronted by such stressors do have an increased likelihood of developing psychophysiological disorders. After the 1979 nuclear accident at Three-Mile Island, for example, people who lived near the nuclear plant were found to experience an unusually high number of psychophysiological disorders (not radiation-linked illnesses), and they continued to do so for years (Baum, 1986).

*Personal stressors* are stressful events that many people are likely to experience at some time in their lives—a severe illness, a death in the family, divorce, loss of one's job. Researchers have linked stressors of this kind too, to the development of psychophysiological disorders (Fryer, 1988). Losing one's job, for example, has been tied to hypertension (Edwards, 1973). One study found that the blood pressure of unemployed men had begun to rise 2 months before they were actually fired or laid off, and it remained high until they found new jobs (Kasl & Cobb, 1970). The investigators found no increase in blood pressure among control subjects who remained employed during the same period of time.

*Background stressors* are ongoing circumstances that produce persistent feelings of tension, such as living in a crime-ridden neighborhood, working in an unsatisfying job, or struggling to keep up with one's schoolwork. Research hints at a relationship between such stressors and psychophysiological disorders (Moos, 1988; Aro et al., 1987). Hypertension, for example, is twice as prevalent among blacks in the United States as among whites (Kaplan, 1974; Freis, 1973). Although physiological factors may help account for this difference, some theorists propose that it is also linked to the dangerous ghetto environments in which so many black Americans live and to the dead-end jobs at which so many must work.

**Idiosyncratic Psychological Reactions** According to some theorists, certain needs, attitudes, and emotions may increase one's chances of developing psychophysiological disorders (Weinberger, 1990; Friedman & Booth-Kewley, 1987). These theorists suggest that such needs or attitudes cause people to overreact repeatedly to stressors, thus setting the stage for psychophysiological dysfunctioning.

Franz Alexander, a leading psychodynamic theorist, proposed that a frustrated dependency need enhances one's chances of developing an ulcer, that unresolved feelings of anger may result in hypertension, and that other unconscious needs may lead to still other psychophysiological disorders (Alexander, French, & Pollock, 1968; Alexander, 1950). Similarly, David Graham proposed that people who see themselves as unjustly treated and who long for revenge may be more likely to develop ulcers; that those who see life as threatening and who keep themselves constantly on guard against danger are prone to develop hypertension (see Figure 11-3); and that those who believe that they are always being left out of things may develop asthma (Graham et al., 1972, 1962). Although these theories have enjoyed some popularity, none has received much research support (Tennant, 1988; Krantz & Glass, 1984; Gatchel, Baum, & Lang, 1982; Weiner et al., 1957).

Other theorists propose that particular styles of personality may lead to psychophysiological disorders (Suls & Rittenhouse, 1990; Friedman & Booth-Kewley, 1987; Dunbar, 1954). The most famous explanation of this kind links the so-called *Type A personality* to the development of coronary heart disease. Meyer Friedman and Raymond Rosenman (1959), both cardiologists, have characterized people with Type A personality as consistently hostile, cynical, driven, impatient, competitive, and ambitious. They propose that this way of assessing and interacting with the world produces continual stress and often leads to cardiovascular deterioration. People with a Type B personality style, by contrast, are thought to be more relaxed, less aggressive, and less concerned about time, and so less likely to develop coronary heart disease. Figure 11-4 indicates the mortality risk associated with Type A and Type B behavior. In reality, of course, most people fall between these two extremes, tending toward one or the other but exhibiting elements of both.

The link between Type A personality style and coronary heart disease has been supported by numerous studies (Wright, 1988; Williams, 1985; Friedman et al., 1984; Cooper et al., 1981). In one well-known investigation of more than 3,000 subjects, Friedman and Rosenman (1974) separated healthy men in their 40s and 50s into Type A and Type B categories and then followed the health of the men over the next 8 years. They found that when physiological factors such as cholesterol level were controlled for, more than twice as many Type A men developed coronary heart disease. Later studies found that this relationship between Type A functioning and heart disease also held among women (Haynes et al., 1980). Recent studies seem to find a

**FIGURE 11-3** When experimenter David Graham asked patients to select the cartoons that reminded them of situations they had been in, both patients with hives and those with hypertension chose these three cartoons, supporting Graham's belief that people with hives feel that they are taking a beating in life and that those with hypertension generally feel threatened. *(Adapted from Roesler & Greenfield, 1962.)*

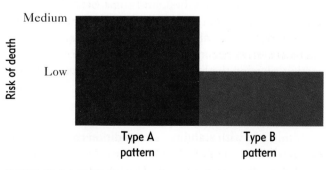

**FIGURE 11-4** All other relevant factors being equal, people who display a Type A behavior pattern have a higher mortality risk than those with a Type B pattern. *(Adapted from Chesney, Eagleston, & Rosenman, 1981.)*

The stresses of working on the New York Stock Exchange and in similar high-pressure environments apparently increase a worker's risk of developing a medical illness, including coronary heart disease.

weaker link between this personality style and heart disease than earlier ones indicated; however, it appears that at least some of the characteristics associated with the Type A style, particularly hostility, are indeed related to heart disease (Williams, 1990; Matthews, 1988; Dembrowski & Costa, 1987; Friedman & Booth-Kewley, 1987).

***Physiological Dysfunctioning*** We saw in Chapter 6 that when the brain stimulates body organs into action it does so through the operation of the ***autonomic nervous system (ANS),*** consisting of the many nerve fibers that connect the central nervous system to the organs. If we see a frightening animal, for example, a group of ANS fibers identified as the ***sympathetic nervous system*** increases its activity and prepares us for action by causing our heart to beat quickly, the pupils of our eyes to dilate, our respiration to speed up, and some blood vessels to constrict and others to dilate. As the danger passes, another group of ANS fibers known as the ***parasympathetic nervous system*** becomes more active in the reverse direction, slowing the heartbeat, respiration, and the like. Essentially, it calms down our functioning. These two subparts of the ANS are constantly working and complementing each other, helping our bodies to operate smoothly and with stability — a condition called ***homeostasis*** (Cannon, 1927).

Hans Selye (1976, 1974, 1946), a leading researcher on the effects of stress, was one of the first to describe the relationship between stress and the ANS. He proposed that people typically respond to stress with a three-stage sequential reaction, which he called the ***general adapta-***

***tion syndrome.*** In the presence of threat, the sympathetic nervous systems increases its activity and arouses responses throughout the body ***(alarm stage).*** The parasympathetic nervous systems next attempts to counteract these responses ***(resistance stage).*** Finally, if exposure to or perceptions of stress continue, the resistance may fail and organs controlled by the ANS may become overworked and break down ***(exhaustion stage).***

Because the ANS is at the center of stress reactions, defects in its operation are believed to contribute to the development of psychophysiological disorders (Friedman & Booth-Kewley, 1987). If, for example, one's ANS is stimulated too easily, it may keep overreacting to situations that most people find only mildly stressful, so that certain organs eventually become damaged. Psychophysiological disorders may then develop.

The ANS is not the only point of connection between stress and bodily reactions. Another is the pituitary-adrenal endocrine system, which when stimulated at times of stress causes the pituitary gland to secrete hormones that affect functioning throughout the body. If this system malfunctions, body organs may be overworked and damaged, and again psychophysiological disorders may develop. Local biological dysfunctioning also may contribute to psychophysiological disorders. People may, for example, have ***local somatic weaknesses*** — particular organs that are either defective or prone to dysfunction under stress (Rees, 1964). Those with a "weak" gastrointestinal system may be candidates for an ulcer. Those with a "weak" respiratory system may develop asthma. Such local somatic weaknesses are thought to be genetically inherited or to result from improper diet or infection.

Organ dysfunctioning may also be caused by ***individual response specificity,*** or idiosyncratic biological reactions to stress. Some people, for example, perspire in response to stress, others develop stomachaches, and still others experience a faster heartbeat or a rise in blood pressure. Although such variations are perfectly normal, the repeated activation of a "favored" system may wear it down and ultimately result in a psychophysiological disorder. It has been discovered, for example, that some infants secrete much more gastric acid under stress than other infants (Weiner, 1977; Mirsky et al., 1958). Over the years, this individual physical reaction may wear down the mucous lining of the stomach or duodenum until an ulcer develops.

Finally, organ dysfunctioning may be the result of ***autonomic learning*** — the inadvertent conditioning of particular responses in the autonomic nervous system (Lachman, 1972). A nervous young boy, for example, may one day secrete excessive gastric acid, which causes him to complain of stomach pain. His parents may respond to his pain by keeping him home from school and seeking to make him comfortable. Though this is certainly an appropriate way to deal with a sick child, a covert process of reinforcement may be taking place. The day at home with tender loving care may serve to reward the child's gastrointestinal activity, conditioning him to secrete excessive amounts of gastric acid in the future, thus increasing his risk of developing an ulcer.

Experimenters have demonstrated that autonomic responses can be conditioned by reward and punishment (Miller, 1969; Kimmel & Kimmel, 1963). After being systematically reinforced for specific changes in heartbeat, blood pressure, or blood vessel dilation, animal subjects have been able to produce such changes voluntarily. One group of researchers, using such rewards as shock avoidance and food, taught baboons to elevate their blood pressure voluntarily for up to 5 minutes at a time, 70 or more times a day (Harris, Goldstein, & Brady, 1977). Similarly, operant conditioning of autonomic responses has been achieved in human subjects by the use of *biofeedback* techniques (discussed on pp. 240–242).

Clearly, then, psychophysiological disorders have strong ties to environmental stress, stressful reactions, and biological dysfunctioning. The interaction of such factors was once considered an unusual occurrence that could occasionally lead to an unusual kind of disorder — a psychophysiological disorder. Such theories as the disregulation model, however, suggest that the interaction of psychological and physical factors is the rule of bodily functioning, not the exception. As the years have passed, more and more illnesses have been added to the list of traditional psychophysiological disorders, until it includes such common ailments as *irritable bowel syndrome* (intermittent episodes of abdominal discomfort), *psoriasis* (a skin disorder involving reddish lesions), *eczema* (a disorder characterized by extremely itchy skin eruptions), *rheumatoid arthritis* (severe inflammation and swelling of the joints), and *hypoglycemia* (a low level of serum glucose).

## "New" Psychophysiological Disorders

For years physicians and clinicians believed that stress could impair physical health only in the form of traditional psychophysiological disorders. In recent years, however, researchers have discovered that stress may contribute to other medical illnesses, particularly to viral and bacterial infections. This discovery came after numerous studies suggested a link between stress and susceptibility to illness in general. Let us look first at how this link was established, and then at the area of study

known as *psychoneuroimmunology,* a new discipline that further ties stress and illness to the body's *immune system.*

**Stress and Susceptibility to Illness** In 1967 Thomas Holmes and Richard Rahe developed a scale that assigned numerical values to the life stresses that many people experience at some time in their lives. The investigators began by asking subjects to estimate, on the basis of their own experiences, how much stress would be elicited by various life events, always using the event of marriage as a point of comparison. If marriage is assigned a stress score of 50, for example, how stressful would they rate trouble with the boss? detention in jail? foreclosure of a mortgage or loan?

The scores of several hundred subjects were then tallied and used as the basis for the Social Adjustment Rating Scale (Table 11-2), which assigns stress values to 43 life changes. The most stressful event on the scale is the death of a spouse, which receives a score of 100 life change units (LCUs). Lower on the scale is retirement (45 LCUs), and still lower is a minor violation of the law (11 LCUs). Even positive events, such as an outstanding personal achievement, are somewhat stressful (28 LCUs). This scale gave researchers a yardstick for measuring the total amount of stress a person has experienced over a period of time. If in the course of a year a businessman started a new business (39 LCUs), sent his son off to college (29 LCUs), moved to a new house (20 LCUs), and witnessed a close friend die in an automobile accident (37 LCUs), his stress score for the year would be 125 LCUs.

The researchers then proceeded to examine the relationship between life stress (as measured in LCUs) and the onset of illness. They found that sick people had much higher LCU scores than healthy people during the year before they fell ill (Holmes, 1979; Rahe, 1979; Holmes & Masuda, 1974; Holmes & Rahe, 1967). A particularly telling cutoff point was a score of 300 LCUs. If someone's life changes totaled more than 300 LCUs over the course of a year, that person was particularly likely to develop a serious health problem, in many cases a viral or bacterial infection.

The first investigations on this topic took the form of *retrospective studies:* subjects were asked to think back over the past year and remember their life events and illnesses. In those circumstances, however, people's illnesses could be serving as time landmarks that actually helped them recall particular life events. In other words, people who had been sick might be more likely to remember events that led up to their illnesses than healthy people were to remember events that occurred during the same span of time. To rule out this possibility, researchers also conducted *prospective studies,* studies

TABLE 11-2

| STRESS AND LIFE EVENTS | | |
|:---:|:---:|:---:|
| Rank | Life event | Stress value |
| 1 | Death of spouse | 100 |
| 2 | Divorce | 73 |
| 3 | Marital separation | 65 |
| 4 | Jail term | 63 |
| 5 | Death of close family member | 63 |
| 6 | Personal injury or illness | 53 |
| 7 | Marriage | 50 |
| 8 | Fired at work | 47 |
| 9 | Marital reconciliation | 45 |
| 10 | Retirement | 45 |
| 11 | Change in health of family member | 44 |
| 12 | Pregnancy | 40 |
| 13 | Sex difficulties | 39 |
| 14 | Gain of new family member | 39 |
| 15 | Business readjustment | 39 |
| 16 | Change in financial state | 38 |
| 17 | Death of close friend | 37 |
| 18 | Change to different line of work | 36 |
| 19 | Change in number of arguments with spouse | 35 |
| 20 | Mortgage over $10,000 | 31 |
| 21 | Foreclosure of mortgage or loan | 30 |
| 22 | Change in responsibilities at work | 29 |
| 23 | Son or daughter leaving home | 29 |
| 24 | Trouble with in-laws | 29 |
| 25 | Outstanding personal achievement | 28 |
| 26 | Wife begins or stops work | 26 |
| 27 | Begin or end school | 26 |
| 28 | Change in living conditions | 25 |
| 29 | Revision of personal habits | 24 |
| 30 | Trouble with boss | 23 |
| 31 | Change in work hours or conditions | 20 |
| 32 | Change in residence | 20 |
| 33 | Change in schools | 20 |
| 34 | Change in recreation | 19 |
| 35 | Change in church activities | 19 |
| 36 | Change in social activities | 18 |
| 37 | Mortgage or loan less than $10,000 | 17 |
| 38 | Change in sleeping habits | 16 |
| 39 | Change in number of family get-togethers | 15 |
| 40 | Change in eating habits | 15 |
| 41 | Vacation | 13 |
| 42 | Christmas | 12 |
| 43 | Minor violations of the law | 11 |

*Source:* Holmes and Rahe, 1967.

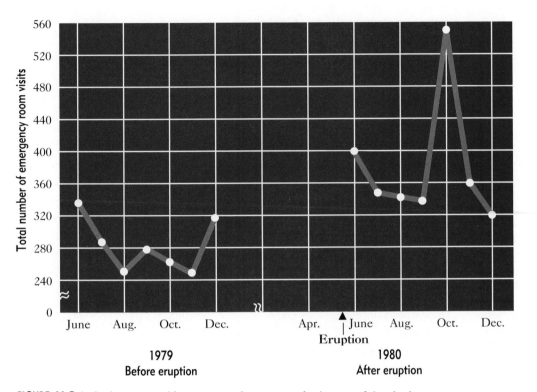

**FIGURE 11-5** A single catastrophic event may increase one's chances of developing a physical ailment. Researchers Paul and Gerald Adams (1984) found that during the months immediately following the eruption of Mount St. Helens on May 18, 1980, there was a 34 percent increase in emergency room visits and 19 percent rise in deaths in nearby Othello, Washington.

that predicted future health changes on the basis of life events.

Rahe (1968), for example, studied 2,500 healthy naval officers and enlisted men who were going to be at sea for at least six months. He divided the naval personnel into a *high-risk group* (the 30 percent with the highest LCU scores over the previous 6 months) and a *low-risk group* (the 30 percent with the lowest LCU scores), and he kept track of and compared the subsequent health changes of the two groups. Twice as many high-risk as low-risk subjects developed illnesses during their first month at sea; in addition, the high-risk group continued to develop more illnesses each month for the next 5 months.

Since Holmes and Rahe's pioneering work, stresses of various kinds (see Figure 11-5 and Box 11-2) have been tied to a wide range of diseases and physical conditions, from trench mouth and upper respiratory infection to cancer (Jemmott, 1987; Lazarus & DeLongis, 1983; McClelland, Alexander, & Marks, 1982). The greater the life stress, the more likely an illness. Researchers have even found a relationship between psychological

stress and death. George Engel (1971, 1968) has concluded that *sudden death*—unexpected death in the wake of psychological trauma—is not uncommon. According to Engel, sudden death may be precipitated by either (1) acute grief, (2) danger, (3) death of a loved one, (4) threatened loss of a loved one, (5) mourning or anniversary of mourning, (6) loss of status or self-esteem, (7) deliverance from danger, or (8) a happy ending. Death during mourning or on the anniversary of mourning is seen in a particularly poignant case, "that of a 70-year-old man who died during the opening bars of a concert held to mark the fifth anniversary of his wife's death. She was a well-known piano teacher, and he had established a music conservatory in her memory. The concert was being given by conservatory pupils" (Engel, 1971).

A striking instance of sudden death at the loss of a loved one is seen in the following case:

*Charlie and Josephine had been inseparable companions* for 13 years. In a senseless act of violence Charlie, in full view of Josephine, was shot and killed in a melee with the

---

BOX 11-2

# Greatest Hassles and Uplifts

Early research indicated that *periodic* significant events, such as the death of a relative or getting married, produce stress. But more recent research has revealed that *daily* events may also cause considerable stress. Studies using the Hassles and Uplifts Scale reveal that concern about one's weight is the most stressful ongoing hassle for middle-aged people; relating well to one's spouse or lover is the most uplifting daily event (Kanner, Coyne, Schaefer, & Lazarus, 1981). The top ten daily hassles and uplifts, in order of impact:

*Hassles*
1. Concerns about weight
2. Family health problems
3. Rising prices of common goods
4. Home maintenance
5. Too many things to do
6. Misplacing or losing things
7. Yard work or outside home maintenance
8. Property, investment, or taxes
9. Crime
10. Physical appearance

*Uplifts*
1. Relating well with your spouse or lover
2. Relating well with friends
3. Completing a task
4. Feeling healthy
5. Getting enough sleep
6. Eating out
7. Meeting your responsibilities
8. Visiting, phoning, or writing someone
9. Spending time with family
10. Home (inside) pleasing to you

---

police. Josephine first stood motionless, then slowly approached his prostrate form, sunk to her knees, and silently rested her head on the dead and bloody body. Concerned persons attempted to help her away, but she refused to move. Hoping she would soon surmount her overwhelming grief, they let her be. But she never rose again; in 15 minutes she was dead. Now the remarkable part of the story is that Charlie and Josephine were llamas in the zoo! They had escaped from their pen during a snow storm and Charlie, a mean animal to begin with, was shot when he proved unmanageable. I was able to establish from the zoo keeper that to all intents and purposes Josephine had been normally frisky and healthy right up to the moment of the tragic event.

*(Engel, 1968)*

The stress of bereavement can be equally fatal to humans (Van Dyke, 1983). When researchers examined the medical records of 4,486 British widowers 55 years of age or older, they discovered that 213 of these men had died during the first 6 months of their bereavement—a fatality rate significantly higher than usual for married men in this age range (Young, Benjamin, & Wallis, 1963). After 6 months the mortality rate of the widowers returned to a normal level. Another study of 903 close relatives of persons who had died in a community in Wales found that almost 5 percent of the relatives died during the first year of their bereavement

(Rees & Lutkins, 1967). The widows and widowers in this group had a mortality rate of 12 percent, compared to a rate of less than 1 percent for age-matched control subjects.

**Psychoneuroimmunology**   How is a stressful event translated into a viral or bacterial infection? Researchers have increasingly focused on our body's *immune system* as the key to this relationship, and have developed a new area of study called *psychoneuroimmunology* to examine the links between stress, the immune system, and health (Jemmott, 1985).

The body's immune system is a complex network of cells that helps protect people from *antigens*—foreign invaders such as bacteria and viruses, which stimulate an immune response—and from cancer cells (Jemmott, 1987; Mims, 1982; Hood, Weissman, & Wood, 1978; Roitt, 1977). Among the most important cells in the system are billions of *lymphocytes,* white blood cells that are manufactured in the lymph system and circulate throughout the bloodstream. Upon stimulation by antigens, lymphocytes spring into action to help the body overcome the invaders.

One group of lymphocytes, called *helper T-cells,* identify antigens and then multiply and trigger the production of still other kinds of immune cells. Another group, *killer T-cells,* seek out and destroy body cells that have already been infected by viruses, thus helping to stop the spread of a viral infection. A third group of lymphocytes, **B-cells,** produce *antibodies,* chemicals that seek out and destroy the antigens.

The functioning of lymphocytes and other cells of the immune system is known to be affected by such factors as age, nutrition, and body temperature (Jemmott & Locke, 1984). Researchers now suspect that stress can also interfere with the activity of lymphocytes, slowing them down and thus increasing a person's susceptibility to viral and bacterial infections (Borysenko & Borysenko, 1982). The notion of a link between stress and deficient functioning by the immune system has been supported by both animal and human studies.

When laboratory animals are subjected to great stress, the concentration of antibodies in their blood decreases (Vessey, 1964) and the response of antibodies to antigens diminishes (Solomon, 1969). Similarly, the lymphocytes of stressed animal subjects reproduce more slowly than normal and respond to and destroy antigens less effectively (Monjan & Collector, 1977; Keller et al., 1981; Joasod & McKenzie, 1976). In one study the immunological functioning of infant monkeys was reduced for up to 2 months after they had been separated from their mothers for a single day (Coe, 1987).

Studies with humans have told a similar story. Scientists who monitored Skylab astronauts during various phases of their extended space mission discovered that their T-cell reactions to antigens decreased within a few hours after the stress of splashdown and returned to normal 3 days later (Kimzey, 1975; Kimzey, Johnson, Ritzman, & Mengel, 1976). The functioning of the immune systems of people who were exposed to simulated combat conditions in a laboratory for 3 days deteriorated significantly (Palmblad et al., 1976).

A relationship has also been found between ordinary life stress and poor immunologic functioning (Jemmott, 1987; Kiecolt-Glaser et al., 1984; Schleifer et al., 1983). In a landmark study, R. W. Bartrop and his colleagues (1977) in New South Wales, Australia, compared the immune systems of 26 people whose spouses had died 8 weeks earlier with those of 26 matched controls whose spouses had not died. Blood samples revealed that lymphocyte functioning was significantly lower in the bereaved subjects than in the control subjects.

These studies seem to be telling a remarkable story. The subjects have all been healthy individuals who happened to experience unusual levels of stress. During the stressful periods, they remained healthy on the surface, but their experiences were apparently slowing their immune systems so that they became susceptible to illness. If stress affects our body's capacity to fight off illness in

this way, we can see why researchers have repeatedly found a relationship between life stress and medical illnesses of various kinds (see Box 11-3).

Researchers are now working to understand exactly how stress alters the immune system, and several have come to focus once again on the autonomic nervous system. As we saw earlier, stress leads to increased activity by the sympathetic nervous system. Studies suggest that this increased autonomic arousal is accompanied by the release of the neurotransmitters norepinephrine and epinephrine throughout the brain and body (McCabe & Schneiderman, 1985; Rose, 1980; Frankenhaeuser, 1975; Mason, 1968). Beyond supporting the activity of the sympathetic nervous system, these chemicals apparently suppress the functioning of the immune system (Jemmott & Locke, 1984; Williams et al., 1981). One study has found that epinephrine injected into volunteers brings about a temporary decrease in the number and circulation of helper T-cells (Crary et al., 1983).

We now know that specific receptors for norepinephrine and epinephrine are located on the membranes of lymphocytes (Borysenko & Borysenko, 1982; Bishopric, Cohen, & Lefkowitz, 1980). When the neurotransmit-

These killer T-cells surround a larger cancer cell and destroy it, thus helping to prevent the spread of cancer. Killer T-cells and other lymphocytes also help fight other illnesses by detecting and destroying bacteria and viruses throughout the body.

=== BOX 11-3 ===

# The Psychological Effects of HIV and AIDS

**H**uman immunodeficiency virus (HIV) is a parasite that leads to the death of its host cell. This virus infects T-4 helper lymphocytes, the cells that protect the body from disease by telling the immune system which invaders to kill (Batchelor, 1988). The lymphocytes in turn transport the killer deep into the immune system. Most sufferers do not die from AIDS per se but instead succumb to opportunistic infections that would not survive in the body if the immune system were not disabled. The psychological suffering of both people who are HIV-positive and people with AIDS, previously overlooked, is now being addressed by researchers and health care workers.

The progression from HIV infection to AIDS may take weeks, months, or

even years (Kiecolt-Glaser & Glaser, 1988); very little is known about how and why persons who are infected with HIV develop AIDS more or less rapidly. One thing is certain, however: an already weakened immune system is less able to defend itself against the virus. In this chapter we have seen that extreme stress, mental dysfunctioning, and environmental pressures can adversely affect the ability of the immune system to ward off illness. For the HIV sufferer there is a deadly interplay between the effect of the disease on the mental health of the patient and the effect of declining mental health on the patient's physical well-being.

Psychological disorders associated with HIV may have either a primarily organic or a primarily psychological cause. The HIV virus

ters bind to these receptors, the lymphocytes apparently receive an inhibitory message to reduce their activity.

Other body chemicals, such as cortisol and endorphins, are also released by the body during times of stress and may have important effects on immunologic processes (Liebeskind et al., 1987; Shavit, 1987; Borysenko & Borysenko, 1982; Ahlquist, 1981; Millan & Emrich, 1981). It is possible that these chemicals will also prove to be important mediators in the stress-illness relationship.

**Perceptions of Control and Immune System Functioning** Does stress inevitably slow the functioning of the immune

system and lead to medical problems? Apparently not. It seems that one's *perceptions* of stress may determine one's vulnerability to immune system dysfunctioning. One study examined the immune reactions of rats who were being subjected to the stress of electric shock (Maier & Laudenslager, 1985). One group of rats (the control subjects) were repeatedly shocked in their cages but could learn to turn off the shocks by turning a wheel in the cage. A second group of rats (the experimental subjects) were also shocked in their cages and could also turn a wheel in the cage, but their wheel-turning had no effect on the shocks; the shocks were delivered at random, whether the rats turned the wheel or not.

may invade the brain, for example, causing AIDS dementia complex (ADC). The virus appears to cross the blood-brain barrier by riding *macrophages,* cells whose normal job is to help fight infection (Joyce, 1988). AIDS dementia complex can result in deep lethargy, manic-depressive symptoms, and psychosis. More commonly, there is a general decrement in cognitive functioning — it takes longer to think or remember. In a vicious and fatal cycle, the patient's psychological well-being diminishes, causing the immune system to weaken further. Not a great deal is known about ADC, but some researchers believe that it may affect 90 percent of AIDS sufferers and that it may be one of the earliest symptoms to develop (Price, Brew, Sidtis, Rosenblum, Scheck, & Cleary, 1988). Unfortunately, the unfamiliarity of clinicians with ADC may interfere with its early detection.

Although not all HIV sufferers will develop AIDS dementia complex, almost all are subjected to a more subtle but equally destructive array of environmental stressors that lead to psychological problems and weaken the ability to fight disease. Society does not provide AIDS sufferers with a supportive environment in which to wage their war. Instead, it attaches considerable stigma to the disease and to the people who contract it. Surveys show that a large part of the population continues to view AIDS as a punishment being visited on a subset of the populace, primarily gay men and intravenous drug users (Herek & Glunt, 1988). Because of these attitudes, patients with AIDS may face discrimination and even harassment, along with a decline in certain services that most of us take for granted, such as health insurance and police protection (Tross & Hirsch, 1988). Major social changes face the victims of AIDS, some of whom must also contend with the loss of friends through social pressure, along with their own imminent demise. This kind of stress can lead to apathy, depression, preoccupation with the illness, and anxiety-related disorders, all of which can directly affect the ability of the immune system to fight off the disease. Once again, a vicious and fatal cycle of events.

No vaccine or cure for HIV infection or AIDS is currently available, but there may soon be a drug therapy that is effective against organic ADC. The experimental drug AZT, which has been found in some cases to slow the progress of AIDS, is able to cross the blood-brain barrier and may be useful in battling the HIV virus in the brain. To help eliminate the psychologically based disorders that accompany HIV, society must learn to give the patient with AIDS what is available to all other sufferers of terminal illness — compassion and hope. It is extraordinarily difficult to overcome deeply felt prejudices against people that some perceive as different and against a disease that is mysterious and deadly. Nevertheless, only when they are accepted as people in need of help and understanding will patients with AIDS find themselves in an environment that may help their recovery rather than accelerate their demise.

The experimenters then injected antigens into the bodies of the rats to see how their lymphocytes would react. The lymphocytes of the control rats multiplied just as they would under unstressful conditions. In the experimental rats, who had had no control over being shocked, lymphocytes multiplied more slowly than usual. In short, stress per se did not cause immunologic dysfunctioning — only stress accompanied by a perceived lack of control. Accordingly, reexaminations of the life change studies discussed earlier are beginning to reveal that uncontrollable life change is more closely linked to the onset of illness than controllable life change (Roll & Theorell, 1987).

***Personality and Immune System Functioning*** Several theorists have proposed that people who generally respond to life stress with optimism, constructive coping strategies, and resilience may experience better immune system functioning and be better prepared to fight off illness (Fischman, 1987; Locke et al., 1985; Scheier & Carver, 1985). As we observed in Chapter 6, some researchers have identified a "hardy" personality style, represented by people who welcome challenge and are willing to commit themselves and take control in their daily encounters (Maddi, 1990; Kobasa, Hiller, & Maddi, 1979; Kobasa, Maddi, & Kahn, 1982; Kobasa et al., 1984). According to studies of telephone company managers,

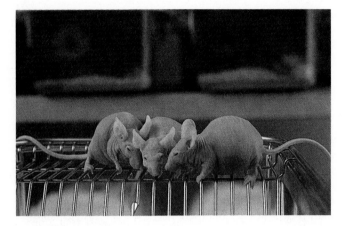

Laboratory animals are widely used in research on the immune system. The destruction of the immune systems of these mice, which has caused their hair to fall out, enables researchers to produce and investigate various invasive cells and viruses.

army officers, bus drivers, printers, and lawyers, people with a "hardy" personality are less likely than others to become ill after stressful events (Kobasa, 1984, 1982). Maddi has even developed a "hardiness course" designed to teach coping strategies to clients, thus increasing their hardiness and lowering their susceptibility to illness (Fischman, 1987).

In a related line of research, David McClelland and his associates have identified a personality style, *the inhibited power motive style,* that they claim contributes to immunologic dysfunctioning (McClelland & Kirshnit, 1988; McClelland, 1985; Jemmott et al., 1981; McClelland et al., 1980). People who display this personality style are thought to have a strong need for power (the desire for prestige or influence over others) but have been taught to inhibit this need (McClelland, 1985, 1979). Instead of seeking powerful positions, cultivating relationships in which they can be dominant, or expressing hostility, they satisfy their need for power in indirect ways — by serving other people or worthy causes, for example, or by upholding high principles.

People with inhibited power motives seem to be more likely than others to develop physical illnesses, particularly upper respiratory infections, in the face of academic and other power-related stresses (Jemmott, 1987; McClelland et al., 1980; McClelland & Jemmott, 1980). According to McClelland, such stressors arouse the power needs of these people; the resulting intense arousal of the sympathetic nervous system increases the amounts of epinephrine and norepinephrine released, which inhibit the functioning of the immune system (McClelland et al., 1980; McClelland, 1979).

In one study designed to test this theory, 64 dental students were examined at five points in the school year: September, November, April, June, and July (Jemmott et al., 1983). September and July were considered to be periods of low academic stress, whereas November, April, and June — months filled with work and exams — were seen as periods of high academic stress. During each of these periods the experimenters collected samples of saliva from the subjects and analyzed them for *secretory immunoglobulin A (s-IgA)* content. S-IgA is an antibody that helps defend people against upper respiratory infections: the lower the s-IgA readings, the poorer the functioning of the immune system.

As expected, the average s-IgA measures of the dental students were normal during the calm of September, dropped significantly during the stressful months of November, April, and June, and rebounded in July. In short, during periods of increased stress, the subjects' immune systems seemed less able to ward off upper respiratory infections. The investigators then looked separately at the s-IgA measures of those dental students who scored high in inhibited power motive. Their s-IgA levels tended to be low even during the relatively calm periods of September and July. That is, these students remained highly susceptible to illness over a longer period of time than those with a low power motive. Their inhibited power drive, then, may account for the relatively high rates of illness among them.

In a related study 132 college students were shown one of two 50-minute films (McClelland & Kirshnit, 1988). Half of the subjects saw a World War II documentary film with a theme of aggressive domination, designed to arouse their power needs. The other group saw a documentary on Mother Teresa, who won the Nobel Peace Prize for her selfless work among the destitute of India. Power needs increased far more among the students who saw the war film than among those who witnessed Mother Teresa's devotion to a peaceful cause. Moreover, among the subjects who viewed the war film, those with a generally higher inhibited power motive showed a greater drop in s-IgA concentrations than did students with a lower power motive.

The work of psychoneuroimmunologists suggests once again that the study of abnormal psychology must extend to behavior and illnesses that once seemed far removed from the clinical domain. Just as abnormal physical functioning may contribute to abnormal mental functioning, mental dysfunctioning may lead to physical problems of various kinds. Again we are reminded that the brain is part of the body, and that the two are inextricably linked for better *and* for worse. On the other hand, even an enlightened perspective such as this can be overstated and can lead to new misunderstandings about illness and causation, as we are reminded in Box 11-4.

## Psychological Treatments for Psychophysiological Disorders

As clinicians have become more aware that psychological factors often contribute to physical disorders, they have increasingly used psychological interventions to help treat such disorders (Stark & Blum, 1986). The most common of these interventions have been *relaxation training, biofeedback training, meditation, hypnosis, cognitive interventions,* and *insight therapy.* Initially these approaches were applied only to the traditional psychophysiological disorders. Today, however, they are used for the fullest range of medical difficulties (Engel, 1986). The field of treatment that combines psychological and physical interventions to treat or prevent medical problems is known as **behavioral medicine.**

**Relaxation Training**    As we saw in Chapter 5, people can be taught to relax their muscles at will, a process that also helps reduce feelings of anxiety, largely by reducing activity in the sympathetic nervous system. Given the effects of relaxation on the nervous system, clinicians believe that **relaxation training** can be of particular help in preventing or treating illnesses that are related to stress and heightened autonomic functioning (Hoffman et al., 1982; Bradley & McCanne, 1981).

Relaxation training has been extensively used in the treatment of essential hypertension (Agras, 1984, 1981). One study assigned hypertensive subjects to one of three forms of treatment: medication, medication plus relaxation training, or medication plus supportive psychotherapy (Taylor et al., 1977). Only those who received relaxation training in combination with medication showed a significant reduction in blood pressure. Still other studies have indicated that the positive effect of relaxation training on patients with hypertension persists for a year or more (Southam et al., 1982; Agras et al., 1980; Braver et al., 1979). Relaxation training has also been of some help in treating headaches, insomnia, asthma, and Raynaud's disease, a disorder of the vascular system characterized by throbbing, aching, and pain (for example, Alexander et al., 1979; Blanchard et al., 1978; Borkovec et al., 1979; Surwit et al., 1978).

**Biofeedback Training**    *Biofeedback training* is conducted by connecting people to machinery that gives them continuous data about their involuntary body activities. This information enables them gradually to gain control over those activities. Moderately helpful in the treatment of anxiety disorders, the procedure has also been applied to a growing number of physical disorders (Miller, 1989). *Electromyograph (EMG)* feedback was used to treat

"Dr. Birnes believes in the holistic approach."

16 patients who were experiencing facial pain caused in part by tension in their jaw muscles (Dohrmann & Laskin, 1978). In an EMG procedure electrodes are attached to a client's muscles so that the electrical activity that accompanies muscular contractions may be detected (see pp. 240–241). The machine then amplifies the bioelectrical potentials and converts them into an audible tone. Changes in the pitch and volume of the tone indicate changes in muscle tension. After "listening" to EMG feedback repeatedly, the subjects learned how to relax their jaw muscles at will and later reported a decrease in facial pain. As a control for this experiment, eight other subjects with the same condition were wired to similar equipment and told that a low-grade electrical current was passing through the affected muscles. These subjects showed little improvement in muscle tension or pain.

EMG feedback has also been used successfully in the treatment of tension headaches and muscular disabilities caused by strokes or accidents (Blanchard et al., 1982; Holroyd, Andrasik, & Noble, 1980). Other forms of biofeedback have been moderately helpful in the treatment of heart arrhythmia, asthma, migraine headaches, high blood pressure, and Raynaud's disease (Engel et al., 1983, 1981; Surwit, 1982; Allen & Mills,

## BOX 11-4

# Psychological Factors in Physical Illness: Has the Pendulum Swung Too Far?

*Benjamin Blech*

*(This essay originally appeared in* Newsweek, *September 19, 1988.)*

It started with a terrible backache. That's when I realized how pervasive the new-age mentality has become. When I read that Shirley MacLaine, its leading practitioner, had convinced her devotees that people create their own reality—"You are God," she said—I assumed she meant nothing more by it than inspirational motivation. After all, isn't that what parents and preachers have been saying all along? Do your best. Aim high. Onward and upward. Every day in every way . . . Be like the little engine that said it could.

Then I discovered the flip side of MacLaine's argument: if I'm sick, it must be my fault. If my life is a mess, I've failed to fulfill my potential. Real life isn't always perfect. Extrapolate

from that to such realities as poverty and pestilence and you have what I view as a contemporary madness: for every misfortune in life, we seem too ready to blame the victim.

But first let me tell you what happened when my back went bad. Remember when sciatica could elicit at least a murmur of sympathy? Well, not anymore. Friends are now Freudians; everyone is "into" psychology. And when I shared the news that I have a herniated disc, all-knowing laymen looked at me and repeatedly asked: "Why are you letting stress get to you that much? Why are you doing this to yourself?"

Believe it or not, wear and tear, age and time, can actually cause damage to bodily parts and functions. Yet in these psychologically sophisticated times, the insight that illness is affected by the mind has so over-

whelmed us that we often forget that it is also physical.

Some years ago Norman Cousins caused a considerable stir in medical circles when he attributed his recovery from a critical arthritic illness to extended exposure to humor. His conclusion deserved widespread circulation. Laughter *is* good medicine. Feelings *can* foster health. Attitude *may* mean the difference between life and death. But—and here is the crucial cautionary but that's often lost in the upbeat literature of our day—disease is still a cruel killer. Cancer victims who truly want to live do nevertheless die. Wishing doesn't necessarily alter dreadful conditions. Yet those who suffer with courage are now stigmatized for failing to recover—even viewed as if they were committing suicide.

I cannot forget the pain of my best

---

1982; Blanchard et al., 1978; Patel, 1977; Feldman, 1976).

**Meditation**  Although meditation has been practiced since ancient times, health-care professionals have only recently become aware of its effectiveness in relieving many forms of physical distress (Milsum, 1984). *Meditation* is a technique of turning one's concentration inward, achieving a slightly altered state of consciousness, and temporarily ignoring all stressors. Meditators go to a quiet place, assume a comfortable posture, utter or think a particular sound (called a *mantra*) to help focus their attention, and allow their minds to turn away from all ordinary thoughts and concerns (Ikemi et al., 1986; Carrington, 1978). Meditation is typically practiced in private for approximately 15 minutes twice a day. Many people who follow a regular schedule of meditation re-

port feeling more peaceful, energetic, and creative, and more capable of enjoying life (Carrington et al., 1980; Carrington, 1978).

Meditation has been used to help treat hypertension, cardiovascular problems, and even viral infections (Shapiro, 1982; Murray, 1982; Carrington, 1978). It has been useful in relieving the stress-related problem of insomnia (see Box 11-5). In one study, people who had suffered from some degree of sleeplessness for 14 years were given four training sessions in meditation (Woolfolk et al., 1976). Thereafter they were able to fall asleep twice as quickly as before and felt more comfortable while doing so (see Figure 11-6). Subjects trained in relaxation showed similar gains, whereas control subjects showed virtually no improvement. These differences were still apparent when the subjects were assessed again 6 months later.

friend in the weeks before he died. Sam faced his imminent demise with dignity. He was able to bear almost everything but he could not forgive himself for his illness. He had been led to believe by the apostles of new age-ism, friends who embraced this cultural perspective, that he had failed. Failed, because if he had really wanted to, the purveyors of these Mary Poppins–style miracles assured him, he would certainly recover. Failed because if he would only try a bit harder he would rid himself of the poisons that were destroying his body. Failed because as a husband and father, his will to live should have overpowered and overcome everything.

Hope is a wonderful tonic, but I fear that these days exhortation has overcome compassion. The result is a kind of indifference and unwillingness to face the fact that some misfortunes will always persist, in spite of our best efforts:

People can be poor not because they didn't try hard enough to pull themselves out of their ghettos but because society really stacked the deck against them so that they literally didn't have a chance.

People can be uneducated because the teachers were not there, because the help which should have been given was not offered, because the "system" failed to work.

People can require welfare and food stamps because, in the words of President Kennedy, life is not fair and there are times when tragedy strikes uninvited and unexpected, even unavoidably.

People can be hungry not because they don't want to work but because the world turns its back on those with unproductive skills and then calls them parasites.

People can even be sick and really need a medical doctor, not a holistic health healer.

Carlyle was of course quite correct when he said, "The greatest of faults is to be conscious of none." Self-awareness demands recognition of personal failings. But it seems we have allowed the pendulum to swing too far. From the blind extreme of "It's always their fault" to the delusionary and self-destructive "It's always my fault," we have veered from truth in equal measure.

Ironically, our obsession with self-incrimination is a product of those very movements which promised peace of mind through an emphasis on personal accountability. Of course in the spirit of est we must "take responsibility for our lives." But must we take as our identities the scripts that all too often are simply handed us?

If I slip on a banana peel that somebody else carelessly left on the ground, I can curse my bad luck and get on with my life. But if I drop the peel myself and was stupid enough to slip on it too, then I will never forgive myself.

Perhaps the time has come for us to call an amnesty in the war on ourselves. No matter what the comic-strip character Pogo may have said, there are times when we have met the enemy — and it isn't us.

When I was a small boy, I loved the story of the little engine that kept telling itself it could and it did. Growing up has taught me that there are times when it can't and maturity demands awareness not only of our abilities, but also of our limits.

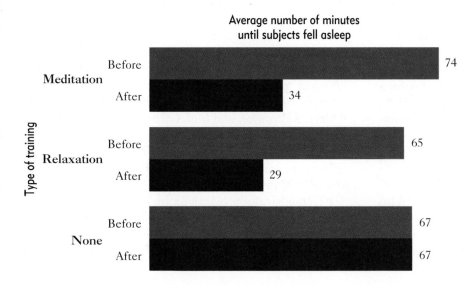

**FIGURE 11-6** After being given training sessions in meditation or in relaxation, insomniac subjects were able to fall asleep twice as quickly as before training. Untrained control subjects continued to take just as long to fall asleep. *(Adapted from Woolfolk et al., 1976).*

**Hypnosis**    As we observed in Chapter 1, subjects who undergo *hypnosis* are guided by a hypnotist into a sleeplike, suggestible state during which they can be directed to act in unusual ways, to experience unusual sensations, to remember seemingly forgotten events, or to forget remembered events. With training some people are able to induce their own hypnotic state *(self-hypnosis)*. Originally developed in the eighteenth century by Franz Mesmer as a treatment for hysterical ailments, hypnosis is now used to supplement psychotherapy, to help conduct research, and to help treat many physical conditions (Barber, 1984).

One common and effective use of hypnosis is to control pain during surgical procedures (Wadden & Anderton, 1982; Werner, Schauble, & Knudson, 1982). Patients appear less likely to have medical complications in response to this procedure than to local or general anesthesia. One patient was reported to have undergone dental implant surgery under hypnotic suggestion (Gheorghiu & Orleanu, 1982): after a hypnotic state was induced, the dentist suggested to the patient that he was in a pleasant and relaxed setting listening to a friend describe his own success at undergoing similar dental surgery under hypnosis. The dentist then proceeded to perform a successful 25-minute operation.

Although only some people are able to undergo surgery when hypnotic procedures alone are used to control pain, hypnosis combined with chemical anesthesia is apparently beneficial to many (Wadden & Anderton, 1982). Given its effectiveness in reducing pain, hypnosis is also used frequently in the treatment of pain disorders (Suter, 1986; Agras, 1988, 1984). Hypnotic procedures have also been successfully applied to combat such problems as skin diseases, asthma, warts, and other forms of infection (Agras, 1984).

Some researchers even propose that hypnosis can be used to help *prevent* bacterial and viral infections. Howard Hall and his colleagues (1987) hypnotized 20 healthy adult subjects, instructing them to visualize their lymphocytes as powerful sharks attacking weak germs in their blood. The subjects were to practice this imagery while hypnotizing themselves twice a day for a week. Blood tests taken before the initial hypnosis, an hour after it, and a week later indicated that the number of lymphocytes in the subjects—particularly the younger adults—actually rose, thus increasing the capacity of these subjects to fight off illness.

**Cognitive Interventions**    People with physical ailments have sometimes been taught new attitudes, or cognitive responses, toward their ailments as part of treatment. In particular, *self-instruction training,* also known as *stress*

*inoculation,* has helped patients to cope with chronic and severe pain disorders (Meichenbaum, 1986, 1977, 1975). As we saw in Chapter 7, stress inoculation therapists systematically teach clients to rid themselves of private negative statements ("Oh, no, I can't take this pain") and to replace them with private coping statements ("When pain comes, just pause; keep focusing on what you have to do").

Researchers gave stress inoculation training to eight burn victims over the course of 5 days, while eight other burn victims (control subjects) received only the routine services provided to burn patients, such as psychiatric consultation, instructions in coping strategies, and pain medication (Wernick, 1983). The stress inoculation subjects were taught to employ private coping statements whenever experiencing pain.

The burn patients who received stress inoculation training significantly reduced their requests for pain medication, while the requests of the control patients actually doubled over the course of the study. In addition, the stress inoculation subjects later complied with other aspects of their treatment better than the control subjects did.

**Insight Therapy**    If stress and anxiety often contribute to physical problems, *insight psychotherapy* designed to reduce general levels of anxiety should alleviate them (House et al., 1988; Varis, 1987). Physicians often recommend insight psychotherapy to patients as an adjunct to medical treatment, but its effectiveness in the medical domain has not been investigated systematically (Agras, 1988). A few studies have been conducted on the treatment of asthma, however, and have indicated that many asthmatic children who receive individual or family therapy become better adjusted to their life situations, experience less panic during asthma attacks, have fewer and milder attacks, and miss fewer days of school (Alexander, 1981).

**Combination Approaches**    A number of studies have found that the various psychological interventions for physical problems often are equal in effectiveness (Agras, 1988; Feuerstein et al., 1986; Shapiro, 1982, 1980). Relaxation and biofeedback training, for example, are equally helpful (and more helpful than placebos) in the treatment of hypertension, tension headaches, migraine headaches, asthma, and Raynaud's disease (Agras, 1988, 1984).

Psychological interventions are often of greatest help when they are combined both with other such treatments and with medical treatment (Lazarus, 1990; Maddi, 1990; Feuerstein et al., 1986). A combination of

Volunteering may affect both physical and psychological processes. Many volunteers experience a "helper's high" while in the act of helping others; they feel stimulated and more energetic.

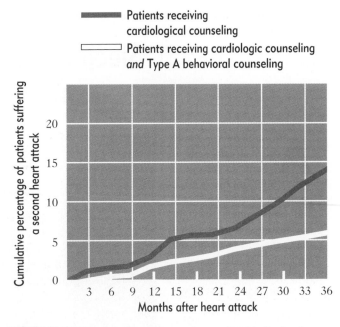

**FIGURE 11-7** Heart attack survivors who received behavioral counseling aimed at reducing their Type A behaviors experienced fewer repeat heart attacks during the 36 months after their attack than did survivors who received only standard medical counseling. *(Adapted from Friedman et al., 1984.)*

relaxation, stress inoculation, and assertiveness training was employed along with medical interventions to treat nine ulcer patients (Brooks & Richardson, 1980). At the completion of treatment, the patients were found to be less anxious, to complain less often about pain, to experience fewer days of symptoms, and to use fewer antacids than a group of eight ulcer subjects who received medication only. Furthermore, a follow-up check 42 months later revealed that five of the medication-only subjects had either required surgery or developed a recurring ulcer problem, whereas only one of the combination-treated subjects had done so.

Combination interventions have also been helpful in changing Type A behavior patterns and in reducing the risk of coronary heart disease among Type A people (Friedman et al., 1986). In one study, 862 patients who had suffered a heart attack within the previous 6 months were assigned to one of two groups (Friedman et al., 1984). The control group was given three years of cardiological counseling regarding diet, exercise, and relevant medical and surgical information. The experimental group received the same counseling plus Type A behavioral counseling over the same period of time. They were taught to identify manifestations of their Type A personalities and to recognize their excessive physiological, cognitive, and behavioral responses in stressful situations. They were also trained in relaxation and taught to change counterproductive attitudes (for example, the belief that achievement is a way of measuring self-worth).

The researchers found that the addition of the Type A

behavioral counseling package led to major differences in lifestyle and health. Type A behavior was reduced in 79 percent of the patients who received both Type A counseling and cardiological counseling for three years, compared to 50 percent of those who received cardiological counseling only. Moreover, fewer of those who received the combined counseling suffered another heart attack — only 7 percent, compared to 13 percent of the subjects who had received cardiological counseling only (see Figure 11-7).

Clearly, the treatment picture for physical illnesses has been changing. Medical interventions continue to predominate, but the use of psychological techniques as adjuncts is clearly on the rise. Psychological interventions already play a major and highly respected role in the treatment of some physical problems. Practitioners at pain centers throughout the world routinely treat chronic and debilitating pain by mixing psychological and medical interventions (Gluck et al., 1985). Though psychological approaches have had a more peripheral role in the treatment of other medical problems, today's scientists and practitioners are traveling a course far removed from the path of mind-body dualism that once dominated medical thinking.

## BOX 11-5

# Sleep and Sleep Disorders

Approximately one-third of one's life is spent in sleep, a state whose importance has been recognized by poets and philosophers throughout history. Homer called sleep the "king of all the gods and of all mortals," and Sophocles called it "the only medicine that gives ease."

Sleep is crucial to health and well-being. Without it people behave oddly and have strange experiences. Studies have found that sleep deprivation for 100 hours or more leads to hallucinations, paranoia, and bizarre behavior. Without sleep, cognitive and motor functioning deteriorate for simple tasks, yet tasks demanding high concentration and skill can be performed with great dexterity (Coleman, 1986). The odd effects of sleep deprivation are completely eliminated once a person is allowed a period of recovery sleep. Physiological recordings indicate that when people remain awake for over 200 hours they frequently experience periods of "microsleep" lasting 2 to 3 seconds. It appears that the body refuses to be entirely deprived of sleep for extended periods.

To study sleep, researchers bring people into the laboratory and record their activities as they sleep. Three types of recording devices are used simultaneously, the *electroencephelograph (EEG)* which records electrical activity in the brain, the *electrooculograph,* which records the movement of the eyes, and the *electromyograph (EMG),* which measures muscle tension and activity.

One of the most important discoveries of sleep research is that a person's eyes move rapidly during certain periods of the night (Aserinsky and

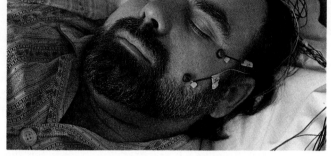

Electrodes attached to a patient's head enable researchers to record and study activity in his brain and muscles as he sleeps.

Kleitman, 1953). This phenomenon, termed *rapid eye movement (REM),* occurs during approximately 25 percent of the time a person is asleep. The rest of the time, eye movements are either slow and regular or nonexistent. The period of rapid eye movement is a distinct stage in the normal sleep cycle. Subsequent research on eye movement and brain activity has helped delineate five identifiable stages that occur during the normal sleep cycle.

*REM Sleep:* Stages 1 through 4 are generally referred to as non-REM (NREM) to distinguish them from the unique activity of REM sleep. As the person cycles through the five stages of sleep several times over the course of a night, they will typically experience 4 to 6 periods of REM sleep. REM sleep is often called "paradoxical sleep" because it resembles both deep sleep and wakefulness. Although there are small movements and muscle twitches during REM, the body is immobilized—essentially paralyzed. At the same time, the eyes are moving back and forth at a high rate. Blood flow to the brain increases and the EEG shows brain wave activity that is almost identical to that of a waking and alert person. Eighty percent of the time that subjects are awakened from REM sleep and asked to report their experiences, they claim to have been dreaming.

When we are deprived of enough sleep or if the normal sleep cycle is disrupted, we suffer. DSM-III-R classifies sleep disorders into two major subgroups: the *dyssomnias,* involving disturbances in the amount or quality of sleep, and the *parasomnias,* involving abnormal events that occur during sleep (APA, 1987). In some cases, sleep disorders occur independent of other psychological or physical disorders; in other cases, the sleep disorders co-occur with mental or physical disorders, either as a result of the disorder itself or as a side effect of drugs used to treat the disorder.

### DYSSOMNIAS

*Insomnia,* also referred to as *disorder of initiating and maintaining sleep (DIMS),* is the most common dyssomnia. Approximately 15 percent of the population reports serious difficulty in falling and staying asleep. Many people experience *transient* insomnia for a few nights, frequently as a result of a stressful life event. A large number of people, however, report an ongoing *chronic* insomnia that lasts months or years (Swanson, 1981). They feel as though they are almost constantly awake. Chronic insomniacs are subject to periods of sleepiness or microsleep during the day, and their ability to function is often impaired.

Five causes of insomnia have been identified:

1. *Biological factors.* Some researchers suggest that a biological predispo-

sition to be a very light sleeper or to have an overactive arousal system may interfere with sleeping (Hopson, 1986). In addition, certain medical disorders can contribute to insomnia.

2. *Psychological disorders.* Many mental disorders, including depression and schizophrenia, are accompanied by difficulties in initiating and maintaining sleep.

3. *Lifestyle.* Sleeping late on weekends, sleeping in a room that is too hot or too cold, exercising just before going to sleep, too much caffeine, and other such acts may cause insomnia.

4. *Bad habits.* People who experience difficulty in falling asleep may try virtually anything to do so. They may develop ritualistic behavior that they believe will allow them to overcome their insomnia. Unfortunately, that behavior may actually become a stimulus for *not* sleeping (Hauri, 1985). Preparing for bed, thinking about sleeping, even counting sheep may condition the person for non-sleep.

5. *Substance misuse.* Many people believe that alcohol and other drugs will help them fall asleep; however, sleeping pills and alcohol often have the opposite effect, leading to shallow sleep and abnormal REM periods.

The treatments for insomnia are as varied as the causes. The most effective treatments address the factors described above.

A less prevalent group of dyssomnias are **hypersomnia disorders,** in which people experience excessive daytime sleepiness; *sleep attacks*—discrete periods of sudden, irresistible sleep; or *sleep drunkenness*—an extended period of disorientation prior to reaching a fully awake state on awakening. Approximately 1 to 2 percent of the population develop one of these disorders. Two of the best-known forms of hypersomnia are *nar-*

*colepsy* and *sleep apnea,* each thought to be caused by biological factors.

**Narcolepsy,** a disorder characterized by sudden onsets of REM sleep during waking hours, is a dyssomnia that afflicts more than 200,000 people in the United States. The person's REM sleep is accompanied by complete or partial paralysis and is generally brought on by strong emotion. Sufferers may find themselves suddenly experiencing REM sleep in the midst of an argument or during an exciting part of a football game. Narcolepsy can be extremely disruptive, particularly for people in professions that require them to perform reliably under pressure. Treatment often includes amphetaminelike drugs.

**Sleep apnea,** a dyssomnia in which the person actually stops breathing for up to 30 or more seconds while asleep, is found predominantly in overweight men and is accompanied by heavy snoring. Hundreds of episodes may occur each night. During an episode, the trachea is partially or fully blocked and the diaphragm is unable to propel air out of the lungs, causing the heart to slow down and the brain to be deprived of oxygen. At the end of an episode, the person awakens very briefly and begins to breathe normally. Sufferers are often unaware of their disorder, but report extreme sleepiness during the day.

## PARASOMNIAS

**Nightmare disorders,** or **dream anxiety disorders,** are the most common of the parasomnias. Periodically during REM sleep, most people experience nightmares, or distressful, frightening dreams that awaken them, but their nightmares are usually infrequent and short-lived and do not affect normal functioning. In some cases, chronic nightmares persist and cause great distress and must be treated with psychotherapy or mild drug therapy. Such nightmares often increase when the people are under stress. In over half of the cases, the problem begins

before age 10 (APA, 1987). Another parasomnia is **night terror disorder,** in which persons awaken suddenly during the first hour of NREM sleep screaming out in extreme fear and agitation. They are in a state of panic, are often incoherent, and have a heartrate to match. Generally the sufferer does not remember the episode in the morning. Night terrors most often appear in young children: approximately 1 to 4 percent experience them at some time (APA, 1987).

People with a **sleepwalking disorder** repeatedly leave their beds and walk around, without being conscious of the episode or remembering it later. The episodes occur when the person is in the stages of deep sleep, and generally consist of sitting up, getting out of bed, and walking around, apparently with a specific purpose in mind. People who are awakened while sleepwalking are confused for several moments. If allowed to continue sleepwalking, they eventually return to bed, and generally do not recall the episode in the morning. Most people who sleepwalk manage to avoid obstacles, climb stairs, and perform complex activities, always in a seemingly emotionless and unresponsive state. Accidents do occur, however: tripping, bumping into objects, and even falling out of windows have all been reported. Approximately 1 to 5 percent of all children have this disorder at some time. As many as 15 percent of children have isolated episodes. The causes of sleepwalking are unknown, and it generally disappears by the age of 20 (APA, 1987).

Sleep and sleep disorders have become popular topics in the last decade, and sleep research laboratories are now found in many major cities. Because sleep is such a crucial component of existence, it is important to understand its underlying mechanisms. The results of sleep studies have implications not only for the treatment of sleep disorders and related psychological problems but for every human activity and endeavor.

# PSYCHOLOGICAL FACTORS AND PHYSICAL DISORDERS: THE STATE OF THE FIELD

In recent years few subjects have wooed the attention of psychologists and clinical researchers more persuasively than physical disorders. Once considered to be outside the field of abnormal psychology, these disorders are being seen increasingly as problems falling squarely within the boundaries of the field. Indeed, clinicians now believe that such psychological factors as internal conflicts and reactions to stress can contribute in some degree to the onset of virtually all physical ailments. In factitious and somatoform disorders, these factors alone account for physical symptoms. In psychophysiological disorders, they interact with organic factors to bring about a physical ailment.

The number of studies devoted to the relationship between psychological dysfunctioning and physical illness has increased steadily during the past 25 years, and our knowledge of this topic has grown substantially. What researchers once saw as a vague tie between stress and physical illness is now understood more precisely as a complicated set of interrelationships involving such factors as idiosyncratic psychological reactions to stress, dysfunction of the autonomic nervous system, activation of neurotransmitters, and suppression of the immune system.

Similarly, insights into treatment techniques have been accumulating rapidly in this area. Psychological approaches such as relaxation training and cognitive therapy are being applied increasingly in cases of physical impairment, usually in combination with traditional medical interventions. Although such approaches have yielded only modest results so far, clinicians are becoming convinced that psychological interventions will eventually play important roles in the treatment of many physical ailments.

The growing insights and applications in this area are exciting less for their acknowledgment of psychological factors as a cause of physical illness than for their emphasis on the interrelationship of the brain and the rest of the body. We have observed repeatedly that mental disorders are best understood and treated when *both* psychological and biological factors are taken into consideration. Now we have seen that medical problems are also best explained by a focus on the way these factors interact. Today's clinicians, no longer hampered by the notion that the mind is a thing apart from the body, are likely to advance our understanding and treatment of physical illness still further in the years ahead.

## SUMMARY

Today's clinicians recognize that somatic, or bodily, illnesses can have psychological causes. This idea received little support before the twentieth century, when medical theory was dominated by *mind-body dualism,* or the belief that the mind and body were totally separate entities. More recently, research has shown that many physical illnesses are *psychogenic*—affected and perhaps even caused by psychological processes.

Patients with *factitious disorders with physical symptoms* feign physical illnesses for gratification. People with *Munchausen syndrome,* the best known of the factitious disorders, travel from hospital to hospital reciting a litany of imaginary ailments and receiving treatment. Less common is *factitious disorder with psychological symptoms.* People with this disorder complain of imaginary psychological problems. At present there is no effective treatment for these disorders.

Patients with a *somatoform disorder* have many vague physical complaints whose causes are exclusively psychological. Unlike people with factitious disorders, these sufferers believe that their illnesses are organic.

*Hysterical somatoform disorders* involve the actual loss or alteration of physical functioning and are often difficult to distinguish from problems with an organic base. They include (1) *conversion disorders,* which are characterized by significant alteration or loss of one or two areas of physical functioning that is actually an expression of a psychological conflict or need; (2) *somatization disorders,* which are characterized by multiple physical symptoms (as in *Briquet's syndrome*); and (3) *somatoform pain disorders,* which are characterized by pain that is not attributable to an organic cause.

People with *preoccupation somatoform disorders* are preoccupied with the notion that something is wrong with them physically. Included in this category are *hypochondriasis,* or a fear that minor fluctuations in physical functioning indicate a serious somatic disease; and *body dysmorphic disorders,* which are characterized by intense concern that some aspect of one's physical appearance is defective.

Theorists explain preoccupation somatoform disorders much as they would simple phobias. Hysterical somatoform disorders, however, are viewed as unique disorders that are still poorly understood. None of the prevailing views has received much support from research.

The psychodynamic view has its roots in Freud's use of hypnosis in the treatment of hysteria. Freud believed that hysterical ailments represented a conversion of underlying psychosexual conflicts into physical symptoms. More recently psychodynamic theorists have focused less on the sexual aspect of the conflict than on the mechanisms of *primary gain* and *secondary gain* at work in hysterical somatoform disorders.

Cognitive theorists propose that hysterical disorders are forms of *communication* that enable people to express their emotions indirectly, by converting them into physical symptoms. Behavioral theorists propose that people with these disorders have been operantly conditioned to assume the role of an invalid.

Therapy for preoccupation somatoform disorders usually includes the kinds of treatments applied to phobic and obsessive-compulsive disorders, particularly *exposure and response-prevention* interventions. Interventions for hysterical somatoform disorders stress either *insight, suggestion,* or *confrontation.*

A third class of psychogenic disorders consists of the *psychophysiological disorders,* in which psychological and physiological factors interact. DSM-III-R uses the label *psychological factors affecting physical condition* to describe illnesses in which psychological factors are clearly related to the patient's physical condition.

Traditional psychophysiological disorders include ulcers, asthma, chronic headaches, hypertension, and coronary heart disease. Researchers have found a clear relationship between these physical disorders and such psychological factors as environmental stress. This link has recently been explained by the *disregulation model,* which proposes that our brain and body ordinarily establish *negative feedback loops* that guarantee a smooth, self-regulating operation of the body. If one part of the loop falters, the body enters a state of disregulation, which causes problems throughout the loop and leads to a psychophysiological disorder. This model identifies three general factors that contribute to disregulation, *extraordinary environmental pressures, idiosyncratic psychological reactions,* and *physiological dysfunctioning.*

Recently several "new" psychophysiological disorders have been identified. Research has revealed a link between stress and viral and bacterial infections. Other serious health problems have also been linked to high levels of stress: even sudden deaths have been recorded in the wake of psychological trauma. Scientists are focusing on the body's *immune system* as the key to these relationships and have developed a new area of study called *psychoneuroimmunology.*

The body's immune system fights off *antigens*—bacteria, viruses, and other foreign invaders. Among the most important cells in this system are the *lymphocytes.* Research has shown that stress can interfere with lymphocyte activity, thereby interfering with the immune system's ability to protect against illness during times of stress.

Other factors that seem to affect immune functioning include *perception of control*—the extent to which people believe they can control their environment—and *personality style.*

*Behavioral medicine,* the most common treatment approach for psychophysiological disorders, combines psychological and physical interventions. Individual interventions include *relaxation training, biofeedback training, meditation, hypnosis, cognitive interventions,* and *insight therapy.*

The use of psychological interventions to treat physical illnesses represents a move away from the mind-body dualism that once dominated medical thinking. What researchers once saw as vague ties between stress and physical illness are now understood more precisely as a complicated set of interrelationships involving such factors as idiosyncratic psychological reactions to stress, autonomic dysfunctioning, neurotransmitter activation, and suppression of the immune system. Physical disorders are best understood when *both* psychological and biological factors are taken into consideration.

# TOPIC OVERVIEW

ANOREXIA NERVOSA
BULIMIA NERVOSA

EXPLANATIONS OF EATING
DISORDERS

TREATMENTS FOR EATING
DISORDERS

# CHAPTER *12*

# EATING
# DISORDERS

People throughout Western society have become extraordinarily conscious of their appearance and weight in recent years. Because thinness is equated with health and beauty, most of us try to control the quantity of the food we eat as well as its quality. One need only count the number of articles about dieting in magazines and newspapers to be convinced that thinness has become a national obsession. Perhaps it is not coincidental that during the past two decades we have also witnessed an increase in two dramatic eating disorders at whose core is a morbid fear of gaining weight. Victims of *anorexia nervosa* relentlessly pursue extreme thinness and lose so much weight that they may starve themselves to death. The term

"anorexia," which means "lack of appetite," is actually a misnomer; sufferers usually continue to have strong feelings of hunger (Neuman & Halvorson, 1983; Garfinkel & Garner, 1982; Crisp, 1980). People with *bulimia nervosa* go on frequent eating binges during which they uncontrollably consume large quantities of food, then force themselves to vomit or take other severe steps to keep from gaining weight.

The news media publish so many reports about these disorders that we may safely assume the public's interest in them. Certainly one reason for this surge in public interest is the frightening medical consequences that can result from anorexic or bulimic behavior. The death in 1982 of Karen Carpenter, the popular singer and entertainer, from the effects of anorexia nervosa serves as a reminder.

Another widespread concern about these disorders is their disproportionate prevalence among adolescent girls and young women. Because we think of adolescence as a time when independence and adulthood should begin to blossom, it is particularly painful to witness young women endangering their development by engaging in bizarre eating habits. It is particularly difficult for their families (Lewis & MacGuire, 1986; Goodwin & Mickalide, 1985). One mother of an anorexic teenager said it this way: "You watch your child deliberately hurting herself, and obviously suffering, and yet you are unable to help her. Another tragedy is that it affects the whole family, for we live in an atmosphere of constant fear and tension" (Bruch, 1978, p. 1).

Up until the past decade, anorexia nervosa and bu-

limia nervosa were viewed as distinct disorders that had different characteristics and causes and required different forms of treatment. Today, however, clinicians and researchers have come to appreciate that often the similarities between the two disorders are as important as the differences between them (Levine, 1988; Vandereycken & Meermann, 1984). Indeed, a number of anorexic persons later develop bulimia nervosa, and vice versa.

## ANOREXIA NERVOSA

Janet Caldwell, 14 years old and in the eighth grade, displays many characteristic symptoms of anorexia nervosa, according to the DSM-III-R classification:

1. Intense fear of gaining weight or becoming fat, even though underweight.
2. Refusal to maintain body weight above minimal normal weight for age and height; for example, weight loss leading to body weight 15 percent below normal or failure to make expected weight gain during period of growth, leading to body weight 15 percent below normal.
3. Disturbance in the way in which body weight, size, or shape is experienced; for example, the person claims to "feel fat" even when emaciated, or believes that one area of the body is "too fat" even when obviously underweight.
4. In females, absence of at least three consecutive menstrual cycles otherwise expected to occur.

*Janet Caldwell was . . . five feet, two inches tall and* weighed 62 pounds. . . . Janet began dieting at the age of 12 when she weighed 115 pounds and was chided by her family and friends for being "pudgy." She continued to restrict her food intake over a two-year period, and as she grew thinner, her parents became increasingly more concerned about her eating behavior. . . .

Janet was the middle child in a family of three children. . . . Her older sister was 17 and a senior in high school, and her brother was 12. Her parents were of Protestant, middle-class background, and the family attended church regularly. . . .

Janet . . . felt that her weight problem began at the time of puberty. She said that her family and friends had supported her efforts to achieve a ten-pound weight loss when she first began dieting at age 12. Janet did not go on any special kind of diet. Instead, she restricted her food intake at meals, generally cut down on carbohydrates and protein intake, tended to eat a lot of salads, and completely

Perhaps the most publicized victim of anorexia nervosa during the past decade was Karen Carpenter, the young singer who developed this disorder at the height of her career and died of related medical problems.

stopped snacking between meals. At first, she was quite pleased with her progressive weight reduction, and she was able to ignore her feelings of hunger by remembering the weight loss goal she had set for herself. However, each time she lost the number of pounds she had set for her goal she decided to lose just a few more pounds. Therefore she continued to set new weight goals for herself. In this manner, her weight dropped from 115 pounds to 88 pounds during the first year of her weight loss regimen.

Janet felt that, in her second year of dieting, her weight loss had continued beyond her control. Her menstrual periods had stopped shortly after she began dieting, and this cessation coincided with the point at which she began to lose weight quite rapidly. However, since her menses had occurred on only two or three occasions, she was not concerned about the cessation of her periods until the past year when her weight loss and change in appearance had become quite noticeable. . . . She became convinced that there was something inside of her that would not let her gain weight. . . . Janet commented that although there had been occasions over the past few years when she had been fairly "down" or unhappy, she still felt driven to keep on dieting. As a result, she frequently went for walks, ran errands for her family, and spent a great deal of time cleaning her room and keeping it in a meticulously neat and unaltered arrangement.

When Janet's weight loss continued beyond the first year, her parents insisted that she see their family physician, and Mrs. Caldwell accompanied Janet to her appointment. Their family practitioner was quite alarmed at Janet's appearance and prescribed a high-calorie diet. Janet said that her mother spent a great deal of time pleading with her to eat, and Mrs. Caldwell planned various types of meals that she thought would be appealing to Janet. Mrs. Caldwell also talked a great deal to Janet about the importance of good nutrition. Mr. Caldwell, on the other hand, became quite impatient with these discussions and tended to order Janet to eat. Janet then would try to eat something, but often became tearful and ran out of the room because she could not swallow the food she had been ordered to eat. The youngster said that she often responded to her parents' entreaties that she eat by telling them that she indeed had eaten but they had not seen her do so. She often listed foods that she said she had consumed which in fact she had flushed down the toilet. She estimated that she only was eating about 300 calories a day.

Mrs. Caldwell indicated that Janet appeared quiet and withdrawn, in contrast to her generally active and cheerful disposition, at the time she began dieting. Mrs. Caldwell recalled that Janet was having difficulties with her girlfriends during that period and Janet had mentioned that it seemed as if her friends were making excuses to avoid coming over when she invited them. Janet became very critical of her girlfriends, and Mrs. Caldwell felt that Janet behaved in an argumentative and stubborn manner with them. On occasions when Janet knew that some friends were coming over to the house, she drew up ahead of time a detailed plan of activities for them that encompassed the entire time period they had planned to spend at her house. She then became angry and uncomfortable if the girls did not want to engage in these activities or did not wish to do so in the order and the amount of time Janet had allotted to each activity. In general, Janet seemed less spontaneous and talked less with her family and others than she had during any previous period that her parents could recall.

*(Leon, 1984, pp. 179–184)*

Approximately 95 percent of all cases of anorexia nervosa occur in females, and although the disorder can appear at any age, the peak age of onset is between 14 and 18 years (Levine, 1988; APA, 1987). Between one and four of every 100 females develop the disorder (Levine, 1988; Pope et al., 1984). Typically, it begins after a person who is slightly overweight or of normal weight decides to "get in shape" or "just lose a few pounds" (Patton et al., 1990; Levine, 1987; Garfinkel & Garner, 1982) and follows a stressful event such as separation of the parents, a move away from home, or an experience of personal failure (APA, 1987; Beumont et al., 1978). Although most victims recover, studies indicate that between 5 and 18 percent of them become so seriously ill that they die, usually of medical problems brought about by starvation (APA, 1987).

Anorexia nervosa seems to be on the increase (Nielsen, 1990; Margo, 1985; Kaye, 1985). The number of diagnosed cases in Monroe County (Rochester), New York, for example, almost doubled during the 1970s (Jones et al., 1980). Certainly one reason for the reported increase is a heightened awareness of the disorder among diagnosticians (Amati et al., 1981). It also appears, however, that the absolute numbers of cases are increasing in the United States, Great Britain, Japan, and Europe (Suematsu et al., 1985).

The central features of anorexia nervosa are (1) a drive for thinness and morbid fear of becoming overweight, (2) certain cognitive disturbances, (3) preoccupation with food, (4) personality and mood problems, and (5) medical dysfunctioning (APA, 1987; Andersen, 1985). As we can see in Table 12-1, these and related features of the disorder can be measured and assessed.

## The Pursuit of Thinness and Fear of Obesity

Becoming thin is life's central goal for the young person with anorexia nervosa, but fear is at the root of her preoccupation: fear of becoming obese, of giving in to her growing desire to eat, and more generally of losing control over the size and shape of her body. In fact, anorexia nervosa has been called a "weight phobia"

TABLE 12-1

| | |
|---|---|
| **ITEMS FROM THE EATING DISORDER INVENTORY II** | |

For each item, decide if the item is true about you ALWAYS (A), USUALLY (U), OFTEN (O), SOMETIMES (S), RARELY (R), or NEVER (N). Circle the letter that corresponds to your rating.

A  U  O  S  R  N     I think that my stomach is too big.

A  U  O  S  R  N     I wish that I could return to the security of childhood.

A  U  O  S  R  N     I eat when I am upset.

A  U  O  S  R  N     I stuff myself with food.

A  U  O  S  R  N     I think about dieting.

A  U  O  S  R  N     I think that my thighs are too large.

A  U  O  S  R  N     I feel ineffective as a person.

A  U  O  S  R  N     I feel extremely guilty after overeating.

A  U  O  S  R  N     I am terrified of gaining weight.

A  U  O  S  R  N     I get confused about what emotion I am feeling.

A  U  O  S  R  N     I feel inadequate.

A  U  O  S  R  N     I have gone on eating binges where I felt that I could not stop.

A  U  O  S  R  N     As a child, I tried very hard to avoid disappointing my parents and teachers.

A  U  O  S  R  N     I am preoccupied with the desire to be thinner.

A  U  O  S  R  N     I have trouble expressing my emotions to others.

A  U  O  S  R  N     I get confused as to whether or not I am hungry.

A  U  O  S  R  N     I have a low opinion of myself.

A  U  O  S  R  N     I think my hips are too big.

A  U  O  S  R  N     If I gain a pound, I worry that I will keep gaining.

A  U  O  S  R  N     When I am upset, I don't know if I am sad, frightened, or angry.

A  U  O  S  R  N     I feel that I must do things perfectly or not do them at all.

A  U  O  S  R  N     I have the thought of trying to vomit in order to lose weight.

A  U  O  S  R  N     I feel empty inside (emotionally).

A  U  O  S  R  N     I think my buttocks are too large.

A  U  O  S  R  N     I eat or drink in secrecy.

A  U  O  S  R  N     I would like to be in total control of my bodily urges.

A  U  O  S  R  N     I say things impulsively that I regret having said.

A  U  O  S  R  N     Eating for pleasure is a sign of moral weakness.

A  U  O  S  R  N     I believe that relaxing is simply a waste of time.

A  U  O  S  R  N     I feel like I am losing out everywhere.

A  U  O  S  R  N     I experience marked mood shifts.

A  U  O  S  R  N     Suffering makes you a better person.

*Source:* Garner, Olmsted, & Polivy, 1984.

(Crisp, 1967). Anorexic people set a weight limit for themselves that is well below the acceptable weight for people of their age and height.

Approximately half of the people with anorexia nervosa reduce weight by restricting their intake of food. Initially they cut out desserts, sweets, and fattening snacks and restrict their intake to foods that are high in protein and low in calories. Gradually other foods join the list of forbidden items, and daily caloric intake settles at approximately 600 to 800 calories (Marshall, 1978; Russell, 1970). The pursuit of thinness becomes a personal test of self-discipline; in many cases there is almost no variability in diet. The other half of anorexic people lose weight by forcing themselves to vomit after meals or by abusing laxatives or diuretics, a pattern that we shall discuss in more detail when we examine bulimia nervosa.

People with anorexia nervosa tend to be in constant motion (Katz, 1986). They hide their fatigue under a display of boundless energy. Janet Caldwell, for instance, was forever going for walks, running errands, and cleaning her room. Some victims follow a rigid regimen of exercise, which, like the diet itself, takes on the character of a test of self-discipline; they refuse to skip a single minute of their routine (Kron et al., 1978; Bruch, 1973; Crisp, 1967). At the same time, most show little interest in sexual activities.

## Cognitive Disturbances

Anorexic persons experience three kinds of cognitive dysfunctioning: (1) distorted body image; (2) distorted internal perceptions; and (3) maladaptive thinking.

**Distorted Body Image**  People with this disorder usually have a low opinion of their body shape and their physical attractiveness (Heilbrun & Witt, 1990; Grant & Fodor, 1986). Most have such a disturbed perception of their body that they fail to recognize their emaciation. Instead, they overestimate their body size. A 23-year-old anorexic woman said:

> I look in a full-length mirror at least four or five times daily and I really cannot see myself as too thin. Sometimes after several days of strict dieting, I feel that my shape is tolerable, but most of the time, odd as it may seem, I look in the mirror and believe that I am too fat.
>
> *(Bruch, 1973)*

A distorted image of this kind complements the person's fear that she is in danger of becoming obese and motivates her to lose even more weight. The tendency to

overestimate body size has been tested in the laboratory (Gardner et al., 1989; Bell, Kirkpatrick, & Rinn, 1986; Slade, 1986; Strober, 1981; Pierloot & Houben, 1978; Fries, 1977). In a popular assessment technique subjects are asked to look at a photograph of themselves through an apparatus with an adjustable anamorphic lens and to manipulate the lens until the image it shows depicts their actual body size. The image can be made to vary from 20 percent thinner to 20 percent larger than actual appearance as the lens is adjusted. In one study more than half of the anorexic subjects were found to overestimate their body size, stopping the lens when the image was larger than they actually were. The majority of control subjects, in contrast, underestimated their body size (Garner et al., 1976).

**Distorted Internal Perceptions**  People with anorexia nervosa often have difficulty identifying internal sensations of hunger and satiety (Bruch, 1978, 1973, 1962). After eating small amounts of food, they report severe bloating, nausea, discomfort, pain, or distension. When asked to describe the internal sensations accompanying fullness, they give vague responses, such as "I don't like it," "I ate too much," "I feel guilty."

This perceptual deficiency may extend to other internal sensations as well (Andersen, 1985). Anorexic people may fail to recognize fatigue, respond to changes in body temperature, or even know how they are feeling. Many confuse emotions with other sensations: when they are anxious, they may believe they are hungry; fullness may be associated, and then confused, with guilt. This inability to recognize motives and feelings

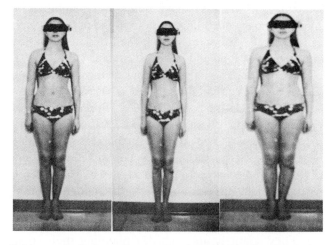

Subjects who look at photographs of themselves through an anamorphic lens can adjust the lens until they see what they believe is their actual image. A subject may alter her actual image (left) from 20 percent thinner (middle) to 20 percent larger (right). Most anorexic subjects overestimate their body size.

creates a "fundamental mistrust of the body" that further encourages anorexic individuals to apply rigid rules for eating and appearance (Levine, 1987).

**Maladaptive Attitudes and Illogical Thinking**    Another cognitive feature of anorexia nervosa is the development of maladaptive attitudes and misperceptions (Garner & Bemis, 1985, 1982; Ben-Tovim et al., 1977). Individuals with the disorder often hold such beliefs as "I must be perfect in every way"; "Self-control and self-discipline must be perfect in life"; "Weight and shape are the most important criteria for inferring one's own worth." From these assumptions grow other notions, such as "I will become a better person if I deprive myself" and "I can avoid guilt by not eating." Gertrude, who recovered from anorexia nervosa, recalls the belief system she developed at age 15 and how it reinforced her motivation to stay thin.

My thought processes became very unrealistic. I felt I had to do something I didn't want to do for a higher purpose. That took over my life. It all went haywire. I created a new image for myself and disciplined myself to a new way of life. My body became the visual symbol of pure ascetic and aesthetics, of being sort of untouchable in terms of criticism. Everything became very intense and very intellectual, but absolutely untouchable.

*(Bruch, 1978, p. 17)*

## Preoccupation with Food

Despite their severe restrictions on food intake, people with anorexia nervosa may spend considerable time thinking and even reading about food and planning their limited meals. Many report that their dreams are filled with images of food and eating (Levitan, 1981, 1979).

This preoccupation with food may be the result of food deprivation more than the cause of it (Yates, 1989; Andersen, 1986; Casper & Davis, 1977). Studies of nonanorexic people placed on extended starvation diets have noted the emergence of similar characteristics. The most prominent starvation study, conducted in the late 1940s, put 36 conscientious objectors who volunteered for the project on a semistarvation diet for 6 months (Keys et al., 1950). Like people with anorexia nervosa, these volunteers became preoccupied with food and eating. They spent hours each day planning their small meals, talked about food more than any other topic, studied cookbooks and recipes, mixed food in odd combinations, and dawdled over their meals. Many also had vivid dreams about food.

## Personality and Mood Problems

Anorexic people tend to be at least mildly depressed and to have low self-esteem (Williams & Manaster, 1990; Devlin & Walsh, 1989; Eckert et al., 1982; Russell, 1981). They may also display symptoms of anxiety beyond their specific fears about body weight, including extreme indecisiveness and a weakening of concentration (Russell, 1981). Some are also troubled by sleep disturbances such as insomnia (Crisp, 1980, 1970).

Anorexia nervosa is often accompanied by obsessive-compulsive patterns of behavior (Rothenberg, 1990, 1986; Hudgens, 1985). It is common for the person to prepare meals in accordance with rigid rules or to cut food into specific shapes. Even broader obsessive-compulsive patterns are common. Recall how Janet Caldwell became decreasingly spontaneous in all spheres of her life. She would make detailed plans for activities to carry out when her friends were coming to her house, and she became angry if they did not wish to engage in the activities precisely as she had planned. In one study anorexic patients and obsessive-compulsive patients were compared by means of tests, psychiatric ratings, and the patients' own self-evaluations, and the two groups earned equally high scores for obsessiveness and compulsiveness (Solyom, Freeman, & Miles, 1982).

Again, studies of normal subjects placed on semistarvation diets have reported similar mood and behavior changes, suggesting that some of these psychological features of anorexia nervosa may be brought about by starvation (Keys et al., 1950; Schiele & Brozek, 1948). The subjects in the conscientious objector study withdrew socially, narrowed their interests, and became increasingly anxious, depressed, and irritable, and some developed noticeable compulsions. Some chewed as many as 60 packages of gum a day, keeping it up even when it failed to alleviate hunger and tension. The subjects were seen to hoard food, cookbooks, coffeepots, hot plates, and even some non-food-related objects such as clothing and old books.

## Medical Problems

The starvation habits of anorexia nervosa cause a range of medical problems (Hall et al., 1989). The most common one in women with the disorder is *amenorrhea*, the cessation of menstruation (Mitchell, 1986; Fries, 1977; Garrow et al., 1975; Russell, 1970). Other medical difficulties include lowered body temperature, low blood pressure, body swelling, and slow heart rate. Metabolic

Thirty-six male subjects who were put on a semistarvation diet for 6 months developed many of the symptoms seen in anorexia nervosa (Keys et al., 1950). Many dawdled over their meals, and a few, like this subject, even licked their plates clean.

and electrolyte imbalances also may occur, and can lead to death by cardiac arrest, congestive heart failure, or circulatory collapse.

The severe nutritional deficiencies related to the disorder may also cause significant changes in the appearance of the skin, hair, and other body parts. The skin becomes rough, dry, and cracked. Nails may become brittle, and hands and feet may be cold and blue. Some people lose hair from their scalp, and some grow lanugo (the fine, silky hair that sometimes covers newborns) on their trunk, extremities, and face.

As the symptoms of this disorder suggest, those with anorexia nervosa are caught in a vicious cycle. Their drive for thinness and fear of obesity — fueled by a distorted body image, mistrust of body cues, and maladaptive attitudes — leads them to starve themselves. Starvation in turn leads to a preoccupation with food, increasing anxiety, depression, obsessive rigidity, and medical dysfunctioning. Then they feel even more afraid that they will lose control over their weight, their eating, and themselves, and so they renew their resolve to achieve thinness and to starve themselves. Michael Levine, a leading theorist on eating disorders, says that "although self-destruction is not the motive, the end result of the battle with starvation is the tightening of a noose" (1987, p. 48).

# BULIMIA NERVOSA

Lindsey Hall, a married woman with bulimia nervosa, describes her day:

*We eat the same breakfast, except that I take no butter on* my toast, no cream in my coffee and never take seconds (until Doug gets out the door). Today I am going to be really good and that means eating certain predetermined portions of food and not taking one more bite than I think I am allowed. I am very careful to see that I don't take more than Doug does. I judge by his body. I can feel the tension building. I wish Doug would hurry up and leave so I can get going!

As soon as he shuts the door, I try to get involved with one of the myriad of responsibilities on the list. I hate them all! I just want to crawl into a hole. I don't want to do anything. I'd rather eat. I am alone, I am nervous, I am no good, I always do everything wrong anyway, I am not in control, I can't make it through the day, I just know it. It has been the same for so long.

I remember the starchy cereal I ate for breakfast. I am into the bathroom and onto the scale. It measures the same, BUT I DON'T WANT TO STAY THE SAME! I want to be thinner! I look in the mirror, I think my thighs are ugly and deformed looking. I see a lumpy, clumsy, pear-shaped wimp. There is always something wrong with what I see. I feel frustrated trapped in this body and I don't know what to do about it.

I float to the refrigerator knowing exactly what is there. I begin with last night's brownies. I always begin with the sweets. At first I try to make it look like nothing is missing, but my appetite is huge and I resolve to make another batch of brownies. I know there is half of a bag of cookies in the bathroom, thrown out the night before, and I polish them off immediately. I take some milk so my vomiting will be smoother. I like the full feeling I get after downing a big glass. I get out six pieces of bread and toast one side in the broiler, turn them over and load them with patties of butter and put them under the broiler again till they are bubbling. I take all six pieces on a plate to the television and go back for a bowl of cereal and a banana to have along with them. Before the last toast is finished, I am already preparing the next batch of six more pieces. Maybe another brownie or five, and a couple of large bowlfuls of ice cream, yogurt or cottage cheese. My stomach is stretched into a huge ball below my ribcage. I know I'll have to go into the bathroom soon, but I want to postpone it. I am in never-never land. I am waiting, feeling the pressure, pacing the floor in and out of the rooms. Time is passing. Time is passing. It is getting to be time.

I wander aimlessly through each of the rooms again tidying, making the whole house neat and put back together. I finally make the turn into the bathroom. I brace my feet, pull my hair back and stick my finger down my throat, stroking twice, and get up a huge pile of food. Three times, four and another pile of food. I can see everything come back. I am glad to see those brownies because they are SO fattening. The rhythm of the emptying is broken and my head is beginning to hurt. I stand up feeling dizzy, empty and weak. The whole episode has taken about an hour.

*(Hall, 1980, pp. 5–6)*

Victims of bulimia nervosa habitually engage in episodes of uncontrollable overeating ("binges") such as the one recalled by Lindsey Hall, who later recovered from the disorder. Like Hall, people with this disorder try to undo the effects of their binges either by forcing themselves to vomit afterward, by taking laxatives or diuretics, by exercising frantically, or by fasting or severely restricting their diet. Although the term "bulimia" comes from the Greek *bous limos,* meaning "cattle hunger," the food is hardly tasted or thought about during binges. The disorder is also known as *binge-purge syndrome, gorge-purge syndrome,* and *dietary chaos syndrome.*

Many adolescents and young adults go on occasional eating binges or experiment with self-induced vomiting or laxatives after they hear about people doing these things from their friends or from the media. In one study, 50 percent of the college students surveyed reported periodic binges, 6 percent had tried vomiting, and 8 percent had experimented with laxatives at least once (Mitchell et al., 1982). In a study of young working women, 41 percent reported binge eating (Hart & Ollendick, 1985). Only some of these subjects, however, satisfied all of the DSM-III-R criteria for a diagnosis of bulimia nervosa:

1. Recurrent episodes of binge eating, averaging at least 2 episodes a week for 3 months or more.
2. A feeling of lack of control over eating behavior during the eating binges.
3. Habitual recourse to self-induced vomiting, use of laxatives or diuretics, strict dieting or fasting, or vigorous exercise in order to prevent weight gain.
4. Persistent overconcern with body shape and weight.

Surveys suggest that between 2 and 6 percent of females develop a full syndrome (Dacey et al., 1990; Levine, 1988, 1987; Mitchell et al., 1982).

Like anorexia nervosa, bulimia nervosa usually occurs in females (again, 90 to 95 percent of the cases), begins in adolescence or young adulthood (most often between 15 and 19 years of age), and unfolds after a period of intense dieting (Patton et al., 1990; Pope et al., 1986). It often lasts for several years, with intermittent letup (APA, 1987).

The weight of people with bulimia nervosa usually stays within a normal range, although it may fluctuate

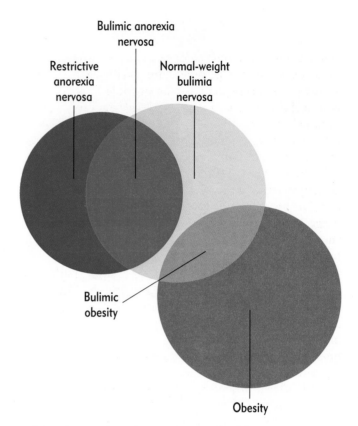

**FIGURE 12-1** Patterns of anorexia nervosa, bulimia nervosa, and obesity may overlap. Some people with anorexia nervosa binge and purge their way to weight loss. Similarly, some obese persons binge-eat. However, only about half of all anorexic people are also bulimic, most bulimic people are not obese, and most overweight people are not bulimic. *(Adapted from Garner & Fairburn, 1986; Russell, 1979.)*

noticeably within that range. Some people with this pattern, however, become dangerously underweight, largely as a result of the repeated purges that follow their binges. These individuals actually receive two diagnoses—anorexia nervosa and bulimia nervosa (see Figure 12-1). This dual pattern is also known as *bulimic anorexia nervosa* and is distinguished from *restrictive anorexia nervosa,* the pattern in which anorexic persons maintain low weight exclusively by restricting their intake of food. Still other bulimic individuals become overweight, largely as a result of their binge eating (Wing et al., 1991; Mitchell et al., 1990). As many as a third of all obese people may be binge eaters (Box 12-1 discusses other causes of obesity). Researchers have become aware in recent years that bulimic individuals of all weights display similar patterns and characteristics. That is, those with bulimic anorexia nervosa are more similar to normal-weight and overweight bulimic individuals than they are to people with restrictive anorexia nervosa.

## Clinical Picture

Binge eating is the central feature of bulimia nervosa. As in Lindsey Hall's case, binges are usually carried out in secret or as inconspicuously as possible. The persons gobble down massive amounts of food very rapidly, with minimal chewing. They tend to select food with a sweet taste, high caloric content, and a soft texture, such as ice cream, cookies, doughnuts, and sandwiches.

In the early stages of the disorder, the binges tend to be triggered by an upsetting life event, hunger, boredom, or an indulgence in a forbidden food. Later the binge becomes a carefully planned event, the food is shopped for, and, as in Lindsey Hall's case, the binge takes on a ritualistic form.

Binges usually begin with feelings of unbearable tension (Lingswiler et al., 1990). Just before the binge, the individual feels irritable, removed from the scene, and powerless to control an overwhelming need to eat "forbidden" foods (Levine, 1987). During the binge, the person usually feels unable to stop eating. The binge typically ends after an hour or more, usually because no more food is available or because of stomach pain, fatigue, interruption by other persons, or self-induced vomiting. Although the binge itself may be experienced as pleasurable in the sense that it relieves unbearable feelings of tension, the episode is followed by feelings of extreme self-reproach, guilt, and depression, and a fear of gaining weight and being discovered (Steere et al., 1990; Devlin & Walsh, 1989; APA, 1987).

Research suggests that persons with bulimia nervosa consume an average of 2,000 to 4,000 calories per binge and have an average of one or two binging episodes per day (Wing et al., 1991; Mitchell & Pyle, 1985, 1982). In one study, 40 bulimic subjects were found to average 12 binge episodes per week, adding up to a weekly total of 14 hours of binging (Mitchell, Pyle, & Eckert, 1981). Binges usually take place around mealtime, most often in the late afternoon or early evening.

After a binge these people feel such physical discomfort and so much guilt, depression, and fear of gaining weight that they seek extreme methods to try to "purge" themselves and undo the effects of the binge. Hall resorted to vomiting. Like many others with bulimia nervosa, she developed great skill at this technique and eventually carried it out in a highly controlled, ritualistic manner that made her feel in control again and relieved her of pain. Actually, vomiting fails to prevent the absorption of at least one-third of the calories consumed during a binge. And ironically, repeated vomiting disrupts the body's satiety mechanisms, making people even hungrier and leading to more frequent and intense binges (Wooley & Wooley, 1985).

Many people with bulimia nervosa purge by using laxatives or diuretics, in addition to or instead of vomiting. Actually, these methods fail almost completely to undo the caloric effects of binging. Even when laxatives are taken immediately after a binge, they do not act until after calories have been absorbed into the small intestine. And diuretics simply do not operate on body fat (Garner et al., 1985).

Finally, many bulimic people try to purge by exercising excessively or by reducing their calorie intake severely, perhaps even fasting, for days. As we shall see, however, such efforts at starvation lead in short order back to a preoccupation with food and to a heightened tendency to binge.

A number of theorists suggest that vomiting and other forms of purging are initially reinforced by (1) the immediate relief they bring to uncomfortable physical feelings of fullness, (2) the fact that they seem to remove "threatening" foods from the body and thus reduce anxiety about gaining weight, (3) the way they help the binger maintain an acceptable appearance that is praised by others, and (4) the fact that they temporarily reduce the feelings of anxiety, self-disgust, and loss of control attached to binge eating (Rosen & Leitenberg, 1985, 1982). Over time, however, a cycle evolves in which purging allows more binging and binging necessitates more purging. The cycle makes bulimic persons feel generally disgusted, powerless, and useless. Most recognize fully that they have an eating disorder, but their anxiety over gaining weight prevents them from stopping the cycle. They feel increasingly depressed, ashamed, and guilty over their secret.

Hall's recollections illustrate how the pattern of binging, purging, and self-disgust may unfold:

*I went away to boarding school at age fourteen with the* nickname, Thunder Thighs. Everyone else from my grammar school class went away to private schools because the local public school was considered "lower class." Without realizing how afraid I was or how to communicate my apprehensions, I left home in tears.

The girls at my boarding school were all so beautiful that they seemed unapproachable. Long fingernails, neat clothes, curly hair and THIN bodies. It was obvious that thin was in right from the start.

Despite my nickname, I wasn't really obese. I weighed 142 pounds and was 5'6" tall. But heavy legs and thighs were the most disgusting form of being overweight. Having a big chest still meant boys wanted to touch you, but being pear-shaped was an unspoken sin. I began to focus on my body as the source of all my unhappiness. Every bite that went into my mouth was a naughty and selfish indulgence, and I became more and more disgusted with myself. . . .

The most devastating thoughts, though, were that other people could eat and I couldn't. I would watch the skin-

BOX 12-1

# Obesity: To Lose or Not to Lose

Fifteen percent of adults between the ages of 30 and 62 in the United States are obese — significantly over the weight that is typical of people of their height. Numerous measures are used to determine whether a person weighs too much. The Body Mass Index (BMI) is the quotient of a person's weight in kilograms and height in centimeters. Various charts list "ideal" weights for people of given ages and heights. The percentage of the body's mass that is fat versus lean is often measured. Although these methods differ in specifics, they all seem to reveal the same fact: many people are significantly overweight.

Obesity has multiple causes. First, genetic and biological factors seem to play a role in it. Researchers have found that children of obese biological parents are more likely to be obese than children whose biological parents are not obese, whether or not the people who raised those children were obese (Theriault et al., 1990). Research has also indicated that there may be a link between the neurotransmitter *serotonin* and obesity — deficits of serotonin in the brain may increase one's craving for carbohydrates and predispose some people to overeat and become obese (Logue, 1991).

Environment also plays a causal role in obesity. Studies have shown that people eat more when they are in the company of others, particularly if the other people are eating (Logue, 1991). It has also been found consistently that people of low socioeconomic environments are more likely to be obese than those of high socio-

economic backgrounds. The same distinction is found between highly developed and Third World countries. Indeed, in countries where food is scarce, overweight is a sign of prosperity.

Mounting evidence indicates that obesity results from a complex set of physiological and social factors and that the overweight person is not to be sneered at as weak and out of control. Despite this evidence, however, societal pressures continue to push obese people to see weight loss as the solution to their problems. The media, people on the streets, and even health professionals often treat obesity as a shameful, avoidable problem. Indeed, obese people are often the unrecognized victims of discrimination and cruelty, an attitude that stems in part from our society's overemphasis on thinness.

Perhaps the primary reason for society's disdain for obese people lies in the web of myths that surround them. One such myth, that overweight people lack character or have personality defects, is, as we have seen, quite inaccurate. So, apparently, are three perceptions that have permeated our society for many years: (1) overweight people are significantly endangering their health; (2) dieting is the best means to lose weight; and (3) weight loss is the appropriate central goal of people who are overweight.

*Health Risk*

Contrary to popular belief, mild to moderately obese people are *not* at greater risk of coronary disease or cancer or any other disease. There is

no hard evidence linking obesity to early death, and in fact quite the opposite may be true — being *underweight* puts one at some health risk (Wilcosky et al., 1991).

*Dieting Is Always Good*

There are scores of diets. Many will produce weight loss over the short term. There is virtually no evidence, however, that any diet yet devised can ensure long-term weight loss. Most studies look only at the weight that obese people have lost during the first year. Any examination of long-term effects generally shows a net *gain* in the person's weight and certainly not any significant loss (Kramer et al., 1989). This rebound effect is common among people who go on very low-calorie diets, which, in addition to failing to keep weight off, frequently are nutritionally deficient and physically dangerous (Stunkard & Lubschitz, 1988).

One reason that dieting fails to achieve long-term weight loss is that the dieter is engaged in a losing battle against his or her own **weight set point** — the weight level that that particular body is organized to maintain. Sensing a deprivation of food and impending loss of weight below the set point, the brain sets in motion various physiological events to counteract the effects of reduced caloric intake. After the initial weight loss, the body increasingly stores energy in its fat cells or adipose cells, rather than in lean muscle mass (Dulloo & Girardier, 1990). Not only does the person's weight return but more of it is now in the form of fat than before the dieting. Furthermore, the body's **metabolic**

niest, most gorgeous girl spread brown sugar and butter on her toast every morning and never get fat — never even feel guilty! I was jealous of everyone who was thinner than I.

The first time I stuck my fingers down my throat was during the last week of school. I saw a girl come out of the bathroom with her face all red and her eyes puffy. She had

*rate* (the rate at which it uses energy) decreases in the course of dieting and remains depressed after dieting stops. This is a natural survival mechanism—as we evolved, it was necessary to expend less energy during times when food was scarce. These physiological changes in the course of dieting are compounded by the fact that the metabolic rate of many obese people is already lower than that of thin people.

Contrary to popular belief, most mildly and moderately obese people do *not* consume more calories than thin people. Most low-calorie dieters shift from weight loss to weight gain, then to loss again, and so on. In the end this yo-yo pattern may itself be a health risk, increasing the likelihood of high blood pressure and cardiovascular disease. As a result of these and other factors, people who are obese often feel that it is impossible to lose weight and keep it off without existing in a permanent state of semistarvation (Garner & Wooley, 1991).

*Lower Body Weight Is the Proper Goal*

Some researchers contend that emphasis should shift away from weight loss and toward improving general health and attitudes. Obesity has often been linked to poor eating habits and, perhaps more important, poor self-concept and distorted body image. Some researchers believe that if the psychological health of obese people can be improved and if they and others can be educated about the myths and truths

regarding obesity, everyone will be better off.

Nevertheless, weight loss may be desired and recommended when obesity is extreme. Several approaches have instigated much discussion about the treatment of extreme obesity, if not actual success. Surgical procedures, for example, have been used to reduce food intake. Gastric surgery involves removal of the lower part of the stomach so that the intestine can be connected directly to the upper stomach. Although this procedure may cause vomiting or ulcers, it frequently does result in weight loss. Similarly, stomach banding involves decreasing the volume of the stomach so that the amount of food that can enter it is restricted.

A nonsurgical procedure sometimes employed in cases of obesity is wiring of the jaw so that it can open only enough to permit liquids to be in-

gested. Another technique, the use of drugs such as amphetamines to reduce appetite, is generally frowned on because of the deleterious side effects. Approaches such as behavioral therapies are able to produce short-term weight loss but rarely result in long-lasting loss. And psychodynamic approaches have been shown to be virtually ineffective in treating obesity. Most of today's programs attempt to use a combination of approaches, since no single treatment is particularly effective. The long-term effectiveness of such combination programs, however, has also been relatively weak.

Oddly enough, a growing number of researchers are beginning to conclude that obesity should be left alone, at least so far as weight loss is concerned. It is certainly desirable to intervene against the environmental and societal factors that may push one toward obesity, but many researchers now counsel that maintaining good physical and psychological health is the most reasonable and useful goal, whatever one's weight. Even if this view persists as the results of ongoing research unfold, it will be a difficult task to re-educate a public that continues to associate obesity with negative personality traits. Regardless of the conclusion reached by scientists in laboratories, it is critical that we overcome our prejudices against people who are overweight, for at worst obesity is a disorder that requires treatment and at best it is simply another version of the normal human condition.

Research does not support the belief that mild or moderate obesity is unhealthy and suggests that the weight appropriate for most women is higher than the current aesthetic ideal.

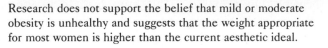

always talked about her weight and how she should be dieting even though her body was really shapely. I knew instantly what she had just done and I had to try it. . . .

I chose to go to a college 3,000 miles from home in a blatant show of independence and bravery, but once alone in my dorm room, I was stunned by the isolation and the enemy relationship I had with my Self. I retreated into eating which was a numbing device in the past, and I learned how to throw up.

I began with breakfasts which were served buffet-style on the main floor of the dorm. I learned which foods I could eat that would come back up easily. When I woke in the morning, I had to make the decision whether to stuff myself for half an hour and throw up before class, or whether to try and make it through the whole day without overeating. There were four stalls in the dorm bathroom and I had to make sure no one caught me in the process. If it was too busy, I knew which restrooms on the way to class were likely to be empty. I always thought people noticed when I took huge portions at mealtimes, but I figured they assumed that because I was an athlete, I burned it off. . . . Once a binge was under way, I did not stop until my stomach looked pregnant and I felt like I could not swallow one more time.

That year was the first of my nine years of obsessive eating and throwing up. . . . I didn't want to tell anyone what I was doing, and I didn't want to stop. I was more attached to being numb than I was to anything else, and though being in love or other distractions occasionally lessened the cravings, I always returned to the food.

*(Hall, 1980, pp. 9–12)*

As in Hall's case, a bulimic pattern typically follows a period of intense dieting in which the individual has tried to address a mild or moderate weight problem. Often that diet has been successful and the weight loss has received praise from family members and friends. Normal subjects placed on very deficient diets also develop a tendency to binge. Some of the subjects in the conscientious objector study, for example, later engaged in binging when they were allowed to return to regular eating, and a number of them continued to be hungry even after large meals (Keys et al., 1950). Thus the intense dieting that typically precedes the onset of bulimia nervosa may itself predispose some people to the disorder.

## Bulimia Nervosa versus Anorexia Nervosa

Bulimia nervosa is similar to anorexia nervosa in many ways. Both disorders typically unfold after a period of intense dieting. People with each disorder are fearful of becoming obese and driven to become thin; they are preoccupied with food, weight, and appearance, grapple with feelings of depression and anxiety, and feel the need to be perfect (Devlin & Walsh, 1989; Marcus et al., 1989). Moreover, like those with anorexia nervosa, bulimic persons believe that they weigh too much, regardless of their actual weight or appearance, and feel dominated by conflicts about what, when, and how much to eat (Dykens & Gerrard, 1986; Post & Crowther, 1985; Pyle, Mitchell, & Eckert, 1981; Abraham & Beumont, 1982; Herzog, 1982). Many also hold disturbed attitudes about eating, and some have difficulty identifying and differentiating internal states such as hunger, fatigue, anxiety, and anger (Steiger et al., 1990; Ruderman, 1986; Post & Crowther, 1985).

Yet bulimic individuals also differ from anorexic persons in important ways (see Table 12-2). They are much more likely to recognize that they are displaying a pathological pattern. They are also more inclined to trust other people and to be interested in pleasing others. Whereas anorexic persons are relatively unconcerned about sexual activity or being sexually attractive, bulimic persons care greatly—indeed, excessively—about being attractive to others and having intimate relationships (Muuss, 1986). Correspondingly, they are more sexually experienced and active than anorexic persons.

Bulimic persons display fewer of the obsessive qualities that enable restrictive anorexic persons to regulate their calorie intake so rigidly (Andersen, 1985; Vandereycken & Meermann, 1984). On the other hand, bulimic persons demonstrate several characteristics that have led some clinicians to think of them as more emotionally labile than anorexic persons. They have long histories of dramatic mood swings and become very easily frustrated or bored. They have enormous difficulty controlling their impulses (Johnson & Maddi, 1986; Garner et al., 1985; Johnson et al., 1984; Gandour, 1984). They find it very hard to control such feelings as anger, they may change friends and relationships very frequently, and they are two to four times more likely than the general population to abuse alcohol and other drugs (Pyle, Mitchell, & Eckert, 1981).

Finally, the medical complications brought about by a bulimic pattern differ from those caused by anorexia nervosa (Hall et al., 1989; Mitchell et al., 1987). Daily repeated vomiting washes the teeth and gums in hydrochloric acid, leading in some cases to serious dental problems, including receding gums, breakdown of enamel, and even loss of teeth (Roberts & Tylenda, 1989; Hellstrom, 1977, 1974). Also, individuals who vomit regularly or have chronic diarrhea may develop a potassium deficiency called *hypokalemia,* which may in turn lead to weakness, paralysis, gastrointestinal disorders, kidney disease, irregular heart rhythms, or heart damage (Mitchell et al., 1990; Hall et al., 1989; Levenkron, 1982; Fohlin, 1977; Russell, 1970). In a few cases, repeated vomiting may damage the wall of the esophagus, causing extensive internal bleeding and possibly even a fatal rupture of the esophagus (Mitchell et al., 1979).

TABLE 12-2

| ANOREXIA NERVOSA VERSUS BULIMIA NERVOSA | |
|---|---|
| **Restrictive anorexia nervosa** | **Bulimia nervosa** |
| Refusal to maintain a minimum body weight for healthy functioning | Underweight, normal weight, near normal weight, or overweight |
| Hunger and illness denied; often proud of weight management and more satisfied with body | Intense hunger experienced and binge-purge considered abnormal; greater body dissatisfaction |
| Less antisocial behavior | Greater tendency to antisocial behavior, such as alcohol abuse |
| Amenorrhea of at least 3 months' duration common | Irregular menstrual periods common; amenorrhea uncommon unless body weight is low |
| Mistrust of others, particularly professionals | More trusting of people who wish to help |
| Tend to be obsessional | Tend to be dramatic |
| Greater self-control, but emotionally overcontrolled with problems experiencing and expressing feelings | More impulsivity and emotional instability |
| More likely to be sexually immature and inexperienced | More sexually experienced and sexually active |
| Females are more likely to reject traditional feminine role | Females are more likely to embrace traditional feminine role |
| Age of onset often around 14–18 | Age of onset around 15–18 |
| Greater tendency for maximum pre-illness weight to be near normal for age | Greater tendency for maximum pre-illness weight to be slightly greater than normal |
| Lesser familial predisposition to obesity | Greater familial predisposition to obesity |
| Greater tendency toward pre-illness compliance with parents | Greater tendency toward pre-illness conflict with parents |
| Tendency to deny family conflict | Tendency to perceive intense family conflict |

*Sources:* Levine, 1987; Andersen, 1985; Garner et al., 1985; Neuman & Halvorson, 1983.

# EXPLANATIONS OF EATING DISORDERS

For years psychodynamic explanations of eating disorders dominated the clinical field (Sayers, 1988; Murray, 1986). Many psychodynamic theorists suggested, for example, that unresolved oral conflicts lead to anorexia nervosa (Lerner, 1986; Bourke, Taylor, & Crisp, 1985; Sugarman, Quinlan, & Devenis, 1981; Meyer & Weinroth, 1957). They argued that some children are unable to separate themselves from their mothers at the appropriate time and become fixated at the oral stage. Such individuals were thought to become especially frightened when they approach adolescence and confront independence, separation from parents, and sexual maturity, and to develop anorexic behavior in an unconscious attempt to return to the early oral relationship by undoing outward signs of maturity. Psychodynamic explanations of this kind, however, have received little research support (Cobb & Rose, 1950).

In recent years theorists and researchers have looked in different directions to understand the eating disorders and have related them to several causal factors, no one of which alone appears to be a necessary or sufficient reason for the disorders to emerge (Vandereycken & Meermann, 1984; Yager, 1982; Bemis, 1978). Today's theorists usually apply a *multidimensional risk perspective* to the disorder, a view that identifies several key factors that place a person at risk for eating disorders (Martin, 1990; Levine, 1987; Johnson & Maddi, 1986; Garfinkel & Garner, 1982). Presumably, the more of these factors that are present, the greater a person's risk of developing the disorders. Some of the leading factors identified to date are *sociocultural pressures, family environment, ego deficiencies and cognitive disturbances, biological factors,* and *mood disorders.*

## Sociocultural Pressures

Many theorists believe that Western society's current emphasis on thinness has contributed to the recent increases in eating disorders (Ogletree et al., 1990; Irving,

*Seated Bather,* by Pierre Auguste Renoir (1841–1919), like other works of art, shows that the aesthetically ideal woman of the past was considerably larger than today's ideal.

Mannequins were once made extra-thin to show the lines of the clothing for sale to best advantage. Today the shape of the ideal woman is indistinguishable from that of a mannequin.

1990; Striegel-Moore, Silberstein, & Rodin, 1986; Swartz, 1985). Western standards of female attractiveness have changed throughout history and now seem to favor a slender figure. As Paul Garfinkel and David Garner (1982) point out, "Favor was shown for a buxom appearance in the early part of the century, followed by the flat chested flapper of the 1920s and the return of bustiness and an hour-glass figure in the 1950s. Recently, preference has once more returned to thinness as attractive for females" (p. 106).

The shift back to a thinner female frame has been steady since the 1950s. One investigation collected data on the height, weight, and age of contestants in the Miss America Pageant from 1959 through 1978 (Garner et al., 1980). After controlling for height differences, they found an average decline of 0.28 pounds per year among the contestants and 0.37 pounds per year among winners. These same researchers examined data on all *Playboy* magazine centerfold models over the past 20 years and found that the average weight, bust, and hip measurements of these women decreased significantly throughout this period. The researchers also found an increased emphasis on dieting when they examined five

popular women-oriented magazines from 1959 through the late 1970s. A total of 385 diet articles appeared over the course of 20 years. During the 1960s the average number of articles was 16 per year, whereas the yearly average for the 1970s was 23.

Because thinness is especially valued and rewarded in subcultures such as that of fashion models, actors, and dancers, members of these groups are likely to be particularly concerned about their weight. As sociocultural theorists would predict, these individuals are more vulnerable than others to eating disorders (Crago et al., 1985; Yates et al., 1983). One study compared the prevalence of anorexia nervosa among 183 ballet students, 56 fashion model students, and 81 female university students. No cases of the disorder were found among the university students, but it did occur in 7 percent of the dancers and 7 percent of the modeling students (Garner & Garfinkel, 1980, 1978).

Varying attitudes toward thinness in different socioeconomic and minority groups may help explain socioeconomic and racial differences in the prevalence of eating disorders (Root, 1990). In past years, white women in the upper classes expressed more concern about thinness and dieting than black women or than white women in the lower classes (Margo, 1985; Stunkard, 1975; Dwyer & Mayer, 1970). Correspondingly, eating disorders were more common among white women higher on the socioeconomic scale. In more recent years the emphasis on thinness and dieting has spread to all classes and minority groups, and, perhaps not so coincidentally, the eating disorders have spread to other groups as well (Root, 1990; Robinson & Andersen, 1985; Garfinkel & Garner, 1982).

Subcultural differences may also help explain the striking gender differences found in the eating disorders. Our society's emphasis on appearance has been aimed at women much more than men during most of our history (see Figure 12-2). Indeed, speaking for an entire culture, Ambrose Bierce (1911) once said:

To men a man is but a mind.
Who cares what face he carries?
Or what form he wears?
But a woman's body is the woman.

Some theorists believe that this double standard of attractiveness has left women much more concerned about being thin, inclined to diet, and vulnerable to eating disorders (Swartz, 1985). It is interesting to note that an increased emphasis on male thinness and dieting in recent years has been accompanied by an apparent increase in the number of eating disorders among males (Striegel-Moore et al., 1986; Herzog et al., 1984).

Western society not only glorifies thinness; it creates a climate of prejudice and hostility against overweight people. Cruel comments and jokes about overweight persons abound on television shows and in movies, books, and magazines, whereas similar slurs based on ethnicity, race, and gender are considered unacceptable. Research also indicates that the prejudice against obese persons is deep-rooted (Levine, 1988, 1987; Garner et al., 1985; Wooley & Wooley, 1982, 1979). In one study prospective parents compared a picture of a chubby child with that of a medium or thin child and rated the former as less friendly, energetic, intelligent, and desirable than the latter. In another study, preschool children, given a choice between a chubby and a thin rag doll, chose the latter, although they could not say why. College students who were asked to compare applicants for a job after reading a description of each candidate recommended a thin applicant over an obese one, even though the descriptions of the two applicants were the same otherwise. Moreover, researchers have found that most female high school and college students of normal weight characterize themselves as overweight, wish to be very thin, and often use dangerous strategies to lose weight (Zellner et al., 1989) (see Figure 12-3).

To a degree, physicians, insurance companies, and health organizations such as the American Heart Association may also contribute to society's bias against obesity by their overstated warnings about the dangers of being overweight (Garner et al., 1985; Bennett & Gurin, 1982; Wooley & Wooley, 1982). Although extreme obesity is indeed unhealthy, mild or moderate obesity is not. Researchers have found no significant differences in mortality among female subjects between 5 feet 3 inches and 5 feet 6 inches who range in weight from 115 to 195 pounds. Similarly, despite the claims of many psychologists, researchers have not found overweight people to be more disturbed psychologically than persons of normal weight (Garner et al., 1985).

Such exaggerated claims about the risks of obesity contribute further to the glorification of thinness and

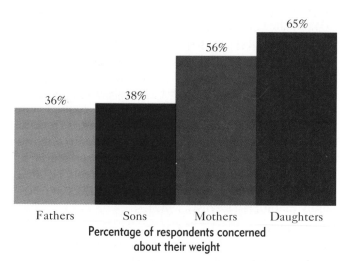

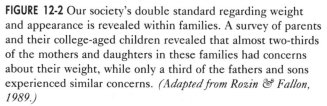

Percentage of respondents concerned about their weight

**FIGURE 12-2** Our society's double standard regarding weight and appearance is revealed within families. A survey of parents and their college-aged children revealed that almost two-thirds of the mothers and daughters in these families had concerns about their weight, while only a third of the fathers and sons experienced similar concerns. *(Adapted from Rozin & Fallon, 1989.)*

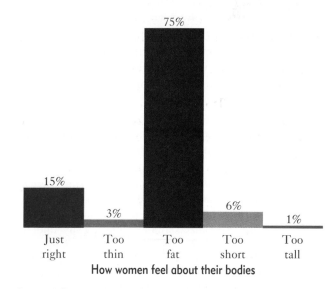

How women feel about their bodies

**FIGURE 12-3** In 1984, 30,000 female readers responded to a survey on body image and eating habits in *Glamour* magazine. The responses, analyzed by the researchers Wayne and Susan Wooley, revealed that 75 percent of the respondents considered themselves "too fat," even though at most a quarter were actually overweight.

prejudice against obesity that pervade Western society. Together these sociocultural pressures establish a climate in which people seek thinness and fear weight gain, thus increasing the likelihood of developing eating disorders.

## Family Environment

As a primary transmitter of societal values, the family often plays a critical role in the development of eating disorders. Research suggests that as many as half of the families of people with eating disorders have a long history of emphasizing thinness, physical appearance, and dieting (Irving, 1990; Schwartz, Barrett, & Saba, 1985; Jones, 1985; Wold, 1985; Rizzuto, 1985; Garfinkel & Garner, 1982).

Families may also set the stage for eating disorders by establishing abnormal and confusing family interactions and forms of communication throughout a child's upbringing (Calam et al., 1990). As we observed earlier, *family systems* theorists view each family as a system of interacting parts. These parts, the family members, interrelate in consistent ways, operate by implicit rules, and maintain a certain balance, or *homeostasis.* Systems theorists argue that the families of people who develop eating disorders are often disturbed to begin with and that the eating disorder of one member is simply a reflection of the larger family pathology (Palazzoli, 1985, 1974; Mirkin, 1985; Levenkron, 1980).

Salvador Minuchin believes that what he calls an *enmeshed* family pattern often leads to eating disorders (Minuchin et al., 1978). In an enmeshed system, family members are overinvolved with each other's affairs and overconcerned about each others' welfare. The members rarely speak about their own ideas and feelings, yet each seems to know what other family members feel and mean. Let us think back to Janet Caldwell, the young woman with anorexia nervosa. Janet's family discouraged individual expression in the manner of enmeshed families, as illustrated by this additional passage from her case description:

*T*he expression of emotions such as anger, fear, or unhappiness was not encouraged at the Caldwell home, and the children were told by their parents that they were being childish if they verbalized strong feelings of any kind. The usual parental approach to dealing with emotional issues was to sit down and spend a great deal of time talking about the precipitating events that led up to a particular emotional feeling or outburst. However, expressing strong feelings was considered to be a sign of immaturity.

*(Leon, 1984, p. 180)*

On the positive side, enmeshed families can be affectionate and loyal. On the negative side, they can be clinging and foster dependency. There is little room in them for individuality and autonomy. Parents are too involved in the lives of their children, and see them not as individuals but as appendages who can make the lives and experiences of the parents more complete.

Minuchin argues that adolescence poses a special problem for these families. The adolescent child's normal push for independence threatens to disrupt the family facade of harmony and closeness. As the family searches for a solution, it subtly forces the child to take on a "sick" role — to develop an eating disorder or some other pattern such as chronic headaches or an ulcer. The child's disorder enables a family to maintain its illusion of living in harmony. A sick child needs her family, and family members can rally round and protect her.

Research has sometimes, but not consistently, lent support to the family systems explanation (Waller et al., 1989; Kog et al., 1985; Gowers, Kadambari, & Crisp, 1985). One study tested the family systems prediction that the families of children with eating disorders would become unstable if the child were to improve (Crisp, Harding, & McGuinness, 1974). They asked parents of anorexic daughters to fill out a psychological inventory before and after their daughters regained their lost weight. Before weight restoration, the parents' scores were comparable to those of parents of nonanorexic individuals. After the daughters regained weight, however, their parents showed a significant increase in depression and anxiety. Although this finding is consistent with family systems theory, it is also possible that the stress of the weight-restoration therapy — itself a source of great conflict and tension — was causing the depressed and anxious feelings of family members.

While the families of both anorexic and bulimic people tend to overemphasize thinness, discourage independence, and operate through a system of enmeshment, those of bulimic individuals pose additional problems. Research indicates that these families may also have higher-than-average levels of stress and conflict and poorer problem-solving skills, and that members tend to support each other less and criticize, reject, and compete with each other more (Levine, 1987; Johnson & Efach, 1985). In such families the child often feels isolated emotionally, yet deeply enmeshed in the lives of other family members (Levine, 1987).

## Ego Deficiencies and Cognitive Disturbances

Hilde Bruch, a pioneer in the study and treatment of eating disorders, has developed an influential theory that incorporates both psychodynamic and cognitive notions (Bruch, 1986, 1981, 1973, 1967). She has argued

Hilde Bruch has called attention to the prevalence of eating disorders and the role of low self-esteem and lack of autonomy. Several interventions developed by her are now included in most eating disorder treatment programs.

that disturbed mother-child interactions lead to serious *ego deficiencies* in the child (including a *poor sense of autonomy and control*) and to severe *perceptual and other cognitive disturbances* that jointly produce disordered eating patterns.

According to Bruch (1974, 1973), parents may respond to their children either effectively or ineffectively. *Effective parents* provide discriminating attention to their children's biological and emotional needs, giving them food when they are crying from hunger and comfort when they are crying out of fear. Children who are responded to in this way develop a sense of control and the ability to differentiate one internal state from another. *Ineffective parents*, by contrast, fail to attend to their children's internal needs and instead impose their own definitions of those needs on the children. The parents arbitrarily decide when their children are hungry, cold, or tired, without correctly interpreting the children's actual condition. They may feed the children at times of anxiety rather than hunger, or comfort them at times of tiredness rather than anxiety. Children who are subjected to this kind of parenting grow up confused and unable to differentiate between their own internal needs, not knowing when they are hungry or satiated and unable to identify their own emotions or levels of fatigue.

Unable to rely on internal standards, these children turn instead to external guides, such as their parents. Some are considered "model children," always trying to do the things that give pleasure to their family, but they fail to develop genuine self-reliance. They feel what Bruch calls a "paralyzing sense of ineffectiveness," and they "experience themselves as not being in control of their behavior, needs, and impulses, as not owning their own bodies, as not having a center of gravity within themselves" (1973, p. 55).

As adolescence approaches, these children are under increasing pressure to establish autonomy but feel unable to do so. To overcome their sense of helplessness, they try to achieve extreme self-control; in particular, they seek control over their body size and shape and over their eating habits. Some individuals are "successful" in this attempt at control, and they march toward restrictive anorexia nervosa. Others are unsuccessful and spiral instead toward the binge-purge patterns that characterize bulimic anorexia nervosa and bulimia nervosa. Helen, an 18-year-old, describes her experience:

*There is a peculiar contradiction—everybody thinks* you're doing so well and everybody thinks you're great, but your real problem is that you think that you are not good enough. You are afraid of not living up to what you think you are expected to do. You have one great fear, namely that of being ordinary, or average, or common—just not good enough. This peculiar dieting begins with such anxiety. You want to prove that you have control, that you can do it. The peculiar part of it is that it makes you feel good about yourself, makes you feel "I can accomplish something." It makes you feel "I can do something nobody else can do."

*(Bruch, 1978, p. 128)*

Clinical reports and research have provided some support for Bruch's theory (Armstrong & Roth, 1989). Clinicians have repeatedly observed that the parents of adolescents with eating disorders tend to define their children's needs for them rather than allow them to define their own needs (Bruch, 1973; Rowland, 1970). When Bruch (1973) interviewed the mothers of fifty-one anorexic patients, many proudly recalled that they had always "anticipated" their young child's needs, never permitting the child to "feel hungry."

Research has also supported Bruch's proposition that people with eating disorders perceive and distinguish internal cues inaccurately, including cues of hunger and emotion. Studies have found that anorexic persons feel "full" sooner after they start to eat than others do (Garner & Bemis, 1982; Garfinkel et al., 1978), and that bulimic subjects often have trouble distinguishing hunger from other bodily needs or emotions. When they are anxious or upset, for example, they mistakenly think they are also hungry, and they respond as they might respond to hunger — by eating. Craig Johnson (1981), a leading researcher on bulimia nervosa, had several hundred bulimic women carry electronic beepers for a week. His staff would beep the subjects randomly throughout the day and week, a signal for the subjects to record whatever emotions they happened to be feeling. Johnson found that the women recorded increasing levels of anger, guilt, and anxiety beginning 2 hours before their binges. The emotions reached peak levels during the binges, at which time they were joined by feelings of disgust and helplessness. If people with bulimia nervosa are indeed mistaking their emotions for hunger, it is not surprising that binges emerge at times of anger, guilt, and anxiety.

Finally, research has supported Bruch's argument that people with eating disorders respond excessively to the opinions and wishes of others. Comparisons of female anorexic and control subjects have indicated that the former are more likely to seek the approval of others, as measured on a social desirability scale, and to score higher on tests of conformity, external locus of control, and lack of responsiveness to their own inner needs (Williams & Manaster, 1990; Strober, 1983, 1981).

Bruch's impact on the study and treatment of eating disorders has been enormous. Her work has moved clinicians to see these disorders as broad-based problems that reflect a variety of deficits. Her theory has brought greater attention to the important issues of autonomy and control. And her work has helped generate enthusiasm for conducting additional controlled research.

## Biological Factors

Over the past decade researchers have tried to determine whether biological factors help cause eating disorders. One influential theory has argued that people with bulimia nervosa have a heightened physiological need for carbohydrates, thus accounting for a strong preference for carbohydrates during binges. Proponents of this position have also proposed that bulimia-prone people are sensitive to high-carbohydrate foods: as they eat carbohydrates, they develop an intensified craving for carbohydrates and eat still more of them to satisfy this craving (Wurtman et al., 1989, 1983; Wurtman & Wurtman, 1984, 1973). However, consistent evidence either for or against this notion has not yet emerged.

More recently biological researchers have focused on the hypothalamus and a concept called *weight set point* as keys to understanding the development and maintenance of eating disorders (Grossman, 1990, 1986; Levine, 1987; Garner et al., 1987). As we saw in Chapter 2, the hypothalamus is a part of the brain that helps maintain various bodily functions and affects the endocrine system by way of the pituitary gland. With its rich supply of blood vessels, it can detect changes in blood chemistry as well as respond to incoming neural information about what is happening throughout the body.

Researchers have located two separate centers in the hypothalamus that control eating (Grossman, 1990; Bray et al., 1981; Stellar, 1954). One, the *lateral hypothalamus,* or *LH,* consisting of the side areas of the hypothalamus, produces hunger when it is activated. When the LH of a laboratory animal is electrically stimulated, the animal eats, even if it has been fed recently. If, on the other hand, the LH is destroyed, the animal will refuse to eat, even if it has been starved by the experimenter. The other hypothalamus center, the *ventromedial hypothalamus,* or *VMH,* consisting of the bottom and middle of the hypothalamus, depresses hunger when it is activated. When the VMH is electrically stimulated, laboratory animals stop eating. When it is destroyed, the stomach and intestines of animals increase their rate of processing food, causing the animals to eat more often and eventually to become obese (Duggan & Booth, 1986; Hoebel & Teitelbaum, 1966).

It is now believed that the LH and VMH work in tandem to help set up a "weight thermostat" in the body that predisposes individuals to keep their body at a particular weight level, called their *weight set point* (Garner et al., 1985; Keesey & Corbett, 1983). When a person's

**FIGURE 12-4** The destruction of this rodent's ventromedial hypothalamus led to extreme overeating and weight gain.

weight falls below his or her particular set point, the LH is activated and seeks to restore the lost weight by producing hunger. It also decreases the body's *metabolic rate,* that is, the rate at which the body expends energy. When a person's weight rises above his or her set point, the VMH is activated, and it seeks to remove the excessive weight by depressing hunger and increasing the body's metabolic rate.

In short, a person's weight set point reflects the range of body weight (or percent of body fat) that is normal for that individual in accordance with such influences as genetic inheritance, early eating practices, and the body's need to maintain internal equilibrium (Levine, 1987). If weight falls significantly below a person's set point, the hypothalamus will act to alter thinking, biological functioning, and behavior in an effort to restore weight to the set point (Polivy & Herman, 1985; Wooley & Wooley, 1985; Garner et al., 1985).

According to weight set point theory, when people pursue a strict diet, their weight eventually moves below their set point and their brain begins compensatory activities. The psychological symptoms that result from starvation, such as preoccupation with food, food hoarding, and desire to binge, are manifestations of the hypothalamus's efforts to reestablish the weight set point. In another compensatory move, the hypothalamus sets in motion a bodily condition known as *hyperlipogenesis,* in which fat cells throughout the body retain abnormally large amounts of fat (Wooley & Wooley, 1985). Once this condition develops, people on extreme diets find it harder and harder to lose weight however little they eat, and they gain weight rapidly as soon as they resume normal eating habits. These compensatory activities address the body's need to maintain internal equilibrium, but they also raise dieters' fears that they are in danger of losing control over their weight and appearance.

Once the brain and body begin acting to restore individuals to their weight set point, dieters enter a battle of sorts against their compensatory activities. Some individuals are apparently "successful" in this battle, manage to shut down and control their eating almost completely, and move toward restrictive anorexia nervosa. For others, the battle spirals toward the binge-purge pattern found in bulimic anorexia nervosa or bulimia nervosa. These people reach a "psychobiological impasse" in which the extreme dieting that they are employing to gain control over their hunger and feelings of tension actually causes them to become more and more hungry, emotionally unstable, and likely to binge (Johnson & Maddi, 1986).

It is not yet clear why some (anorexic) individuals successfully attain control over the body's homeostatic weight mechanisms while others (bulimic) become caught in a cycle of binging and purging. Perhaps the psychological differences between anorexic and bulimic persons are important. Maybe the obsessive style of anorexic persons enables them to stick to a rigid regimen of restrictive eating despite the brain's push for weight gain, while the labile moods and impulsive nature of bulimic individuals make it impossible for them to resist their increasing urge to eat. Alternatively, the different levels of conflict found in the families of the two groups or some kind of biological predisposition may account for the different courses followed by anorexic and bulimic people.

## Mood Disorders

Earlier we noted that many people with eating disorders, particularly those with bulimia nervosa, experience symptoms of depression, such as sadness, low self-esteem, pessimism, and errors in logic (Williams & Manaster, 1990; Beatty et al., 1990). This finding has led some theorists to conclude that mood disorders predispose some individuals to eating disorders (Pope & Hudson, 1988, 1984; Strober & Katz, 1987).

Their claim is supported by four kinds of evidence. First, many more persons with an eating disorder qualify for a clinical diagnosis of major depression than do persons in the general population (Fairburn, 1985). As many as 75 percent of those with bulimia nervosa may experience mood disorders, which are present before the bulimic patterns in at least a third of the cases (Mitchell & Pyle, 1985; Pope & Hudson, 1984). Second, the close relatives of persons with eating disorders have a much higher rate of mood disorders than do close relatives of persons without such disorders. Thirty percent of the first-degree relatives (parents, siblings, and children) of bulimic persons experience major depression, a rate similar to that shown by the first-degree relatives of people with major depression (Johnson & Maddi, 1986). Third, persons with eating disorders, particularly bulimia nervosa, often display low activity of the neurotransmitter serotonin, similar to the serotonin depletions found in depressed people (Goldbloom et al., 1990; Wilcox, 1990). Fourth, persons with eating disorders are often helped significantly by certain antidepressant drugs, the same drugs that alleviate depression. The medications not only reduce the depressive symptoms but also alter the dysfunctional eating patterns in many cases (Johnson & Connors, 1987; Johnson & Maddi, 1986; Robinson et al., 1985; Johnson et al., 1985).

Although such findings are consistent with the notion that depression helps cause eating disorders, alternative explanations are also possible. Sociocultural, familial, and biological factors that contribute to disordered eating patterns may likewise help cause depression, thus accounting for the appearance of both eating and mood disorders in many individuals (McCarthy, 1990; Jimerson et al., 1990). It is also possible that in some cases the pressure and pain of having an eating disorder help cause the mood disorder (Silverstone, 1990). Whatever the correct interpretation, it is clear that many persons grappling with eating disorders also suffer from depression and that treatment must address both forms of dysfunctioning.

## A Multidimensional Perspective

The risk factors linked to eating disorders may be divided into three categories—predispositions, precipitants, and perpetuators (Levine, 1987; Garner & Garfinkel, 1980). *Predispositions* are factors, such as Western society's emphasis on female thinness or a personal sense of ineffectiveness, that produce a general vulnerability to the disorder. *Precipitants* are immediate stressors, such as the pressures of adolescence or insensitive comments about one's appearance, that help transform vulnerability into an actual disorder. And *perpetuators* are the effects of the disorder, such as the hypothalamic changes and increased hunger caused by extreme dieting or by vomiting, that maintain and even worsen the pattern.

According to the multidimensional perspective, these various factors intersect in certain individuals and together encourage eating disorders to unfold (Martin, 1990; Johnson & Maddi, 1986; Garfinkel & Garner, 1983; Garner & Garfinkel, 1980). It is not necessary for a person to display all of the relevant characteristics or to be exposed to all of the relevant influences to develop the syndrome. A combination of sociocultural pressures, autonomy problems, adolescent changes, and biological effects of dieting may bring about and maintain the disorder in some cases, while a different combination, such as a dysfunctional family pattern, depression, and the effects of dieting, may account for other cases. "At this time, the specific interactions between the factors necessary and sufficient . . . is not known. Furthermore, characteristics which protect some . . . vulnerable individuals have not been investigated" (Garfinkel & Garner, 1982, p. 210). Nor is it yet known with certainty why some people develop bulimia nervosa instead of anorexia nervosa, or vice versa, although theorists do suspect that differences in personal characteristics, such as obsessiveness and impulsiveness, and in levels of family conflict may favor the development of one pattern over the other (Levine, 1987; Andersen, 1985; Vandereycken & Meermann, 1984).

David Garner holds, along with colleague Paul Garfinkel, that a combination of risk factors may intersect to produce an eating disorder. Garner is among the pioneers of a multidimensional treatment approach that combines a variety of techniques to help sufferers overcome the disorders.

## TREATMENTS FOR EATING DISORDERS

Today's treatments for eating disorders have two dimensions (Hsu, 1986; Bryant & Bates, 1985). First, they seek to correct as quickly as possible the pathological eating pattern that is endangering the client's health. For anorexic clients this means helping them to eat more and to gain weight; for bulimic persons, it means stopping, or at least reducing, binges and purges. Second, therapists try to address the broader psychological and situational factors that led to and now maintain the dysfunctional eating patterns. In addition, family and friends can play an important role in correcting the disorder (Sherman & Thompson, 1990; see Box 12-2).

### Treatments for Anorexia Nervosa

The immediate aim of treatment is to help anorexic people regain their lost weight, recover from malnourishment, and reestablish normal eating habits. Therapists must then help them to make psychological and situational changes that enable them to maintain their immediate gains.

**Weight Restoration and Resumption of Eating** A number of methods have been used to increase caloric intake and cause anorexic patients to gain weight quickly. These methods, usually applied in a hospital, often restore a patient's health in a matter of weeks.

In life-threatening cases, clinicians may provide nourishment directly by forcing *tube and intravenous feedings* on patients (Martin, 1985; Sours, 1980). Although such feedings help keep patients alive and rapidly reverse the downward trend of weight loss, they are typically applied with minimal cooperation from the patient, breed the

patient's distrust, and set up a power struggle between patient and clinician (Sallas, 1985; Perschuk et al., 1980).

*Antipsychotic drugs* have also been used to help reverse starvation habits (Mitchell, 1989; Condon, 1986; Crisp, 1965). In some cases, their powerful tranquilizing effects appear to reduce food and weight anxiety and also put patients in a more cooperative frame of mind, thus inducing them to accept other aspects of the treatment program. These medications fail to help in most cases, however, and they may have serious undesirable effects, as we shall see in Chapter 16 (Condon, 1986). In addition, their impact tends to be short-lived: patients treated exclusively with the drugs later develop anorexic symptoms once again, as well as other psychological

---

## BOX 12-2

# How Family and Friends Can Help

1. Write down specific instances of the person's problematic behavior or attitudes, and encourage other friends and family members to do the same. [This makes later therapy discussions more precise.]

2. Educate yourself and other family members about eating disorders, and about the nearest resources offering professional and expert treatment.

3. Get support and advice from people you trust — clergy, social workers, friends, family physicians. Don't isolate yourself from people who care about you and who can help. Attend a support group.

4. Arrange for family and friends to speak confidentially with the person about the specifics and consequences of his or her disordered eating and weight management practices. Try to remain calm, caring, and nonjudgmental. Avoid giving simplistic suggestions about nutrition or self-control.

5. Communicate directly to the person the seriousness of your concern, your conviction that treatment is necessary, and your willingness to provide emotional, financial, and other practical support.

6. Exercise responsibility, authority, and authoritative wisdom in obtaining treatment for (a) minors with eating disorders and (b) anyone who is suicidal, very sick, and/or out of control.

7. Reaffirm the importance of yourself and your other family members. Don't allow your life to be disrupted by emotional upheaval — arguments, threats, blame, guilt, bribes, resentment — concerning issues of food, weight, and eating.

8. Sustain the person's sense of importance and dignity by encouraging decision-making and personal responsibility. Don't be manipulated into shielding the person from the consequences of

the disorder, including separation from you.

9. Be patient: Recovery is a long process because treatment must address the physical, psychological, behavioral, social, and cultural dimensions of complex disorders.

10. Love your relative or friend for himself or herself, not for appearance, health, body weight, or achievement. Encourage healthy feelings and interests, and avoid talking about appearance, eating habits, and weight.

11. Remember that families [alone] neither cause nor cure eating disorders, but they can make a major contribution to recovery and future development. Dwelling on guilt or causes is counterproductive.

12. Remember that compassion is "bearing with" a person in distress, not suffering unduly because of their injustices or unwillingness to get help.

*by Michael Levine, 1988*

problems (Dally & Sargent, 1966). Still other clinicians have had some success with *antidepressant medications* (Gwirtsman et al., 1990; Cuixart & Conill, 1979; Moore, 1977). These drugs appear to be particularly helpful in relieving the depressive and obsessive symptoms that often accompany the anorexic syndrome (Gwirtsman et al., 1990; Andersen et al., 1985).

Weight-restoration programs often include an *operant conditioning* approach (Halmi, 1985; Martin, 1985). Patients are given positive reinforcement when they eat properly or gain weight and no reinforcement when they eat improperly or fail to gain weight. Operant conditioning was first used to treat anorexia nervosa in the 1960s in the case of a 37-year-old woman who weighed less than 60 pounds on admission to the hospital, down from a weight of 118 pounds (Bachrach et al., 1965). During treatment she was housed in an unstimulating room without television, books, or visits from staff or family members. She received reinforcements such as attention, conversation, and praise only when she ate. The woman's food intake and weight increased steadily under this program. Since the time of this study, researchers have discovered that it is more effective to reinforce weight gain than food intake per se (Leitenberg et al., 1968). Once again, however, the impact of this approach has proved limited (Halmi, 1985). Studies suggest that patients who are treated with operant conditioning fail to maintain their initial weight gain unless other forms of intervention are also employed (Pertshuk, 1977).

In recent years, *supportive nursing care*, combined with a high-calorie diet, has become the most popular weight-restoration technique (Biley & Savage, 1988; Andersen, 1986; Garfinkel & Garner, 1982). In this approach, well-trained nurses conduct the day-to-day hospital program. They place patients on a low-calorie diet at first and then gradually increase the diet over the course of several weeks to between 2,500 and 3,500 calories a day. The nurses educate patients about the program, give them progress reports, provide encouragement, and help them recognize that their weight gain is proceeding in a deliberate and controlled manner, that they are on their way to health, and that they will not go overboard into obesity. At the same time, the nurses remain firm in carrying out the program and avoid being manipulated into complicity with the patient's anorexic fears and desires. Studies suggest that patients on nursing care programs usually gain weight over 8 to 12 weeks (Garfinkel & Garner, 1982; Russell, 1981).

**Psychological and Situational Changes** Clinical researchers have found that anorexic individuals must address their underlying problems and alter their maladaptive thinking patterns if they are to bring about lasting improvement (Garfinkel, 1985). Therapists typically offer a mixture of therapy and education to achieve this goal, using individual, group, and family therapy formats (Strober & Bowen, 1986; Hall, 1985; Garner, 1985; O'Keefe & Castaldo, 1985; Sallas, 1985; Garfinkel & Garner, 1982).

***Addressing Autonomy Issues*** According to Bruch (1986, 1982, 1973, 1962), anorexic patients need to become more aware of their underlying difficulties with expressing autonomy. Then they can be helped to confront their needs and fears directly, exercise control in more appropriate ways, and develop independence. Bruch believes that the bulk of therapeutic exploration must be initiated by the patient, with the therapist there to listen carefully, provide support, and help probe for insight.

Bruch also recommends that patients carry out *activity programs* such as artwork to "convince patients they do not function only under the influence of others, but that there are things which are truly their own." For similar reasons, occupational therapy has also been included in some treatment programs for anorexia nervosa (Martin, 1985).

***Identifying Internal Sensations and Emotions*** As we discussed earlier, anorexic individuals are typically so ineffective at identifying their internal sensations and emotions that they feel helpless. Thus therapists try to help clients to recognize and trust their own feelings (Bruch, 1973). Therapy in this area is delicate. It would be counterproductive for a therapist to *tell* an anorexic client what he or she is experiencing internally, as that would play into the person's self-distrust and overconcern about others' opinions. Furthermore, therapists must not make guesses about the clients' internal experiences, because the overly conforming anorexic person is likely to agree readily whether the guess is correct or not. Instead, clients must be allowed to discover their own inner sensations — to "say it first" (Bruch, 1973). Then therapists can acknowledge and accept the discovery and probe it further. In the following exchange, a therapist tries to help a 15-year-old client identify and share her feelings:

*Patient:* I don't talk about my feelings; I never did.

*Therapist:* Do you think I'll respond like others?

*Patient:* What do you mean?

*Therapist:* I think you may be afraid that I won't pay close attention to what you feel inside, or that I'll tell you not to feel the way you do — that it's foolish to feel frightened, to feel fat, to doubt yourself, considering how well you do in school, how you're appreciated by teachers, how pretty you are.

*Patient:* *(Looking somewhat tense and agitated)* Well, I was always told to be polite and respect other people, just like a stupid, faceless doll *(Affecting a vacant, doll-like pose)*.

*Therapist:* Do I give you the impression that it would be disrespectful for you to share your feelings, whatever they may be?

*Patient:* Not really; I don't know.

*Therapist:* I can't, and won't, tell you that this is easy for you to do. . . . But I can promise you that you are free to speak your mind, and that I won't turn away.

*(Strober & Yager, 1985, pp. 368–369)*

**Correcting Distorted Cognitions** Changing the misconceptions about eating and weight held by anorexic persons is critical to a full and lasting recovery. Toward this end, Beck's cognitive therapy has been applied to cases of anorexia nervosa, just as it has been applied to depression (Hollin & Lewis, 1988; Fairburn et al., 1986; Garner & Bemis, 1985, 1982). Therapists guide clients to focus on, challenge, and change maladaptive assumptions, such as "I must always be perfect" or "My weight and shape determine my value." The therapist may ask the client to gather evidence to support or refute the truth of such assumptions, weigh the advantages and disadvantages of living by them, and consider their consistency with other values. The therapist may also seek to educate the client about her misconceptions. The following excerpt shows a therapist challenging a common assumption held by anorexic people:

*Patient:* Once I reach my goal weight, or once I get into the habit of eating "non-dietetic" food, I will not be able to stop and I will catapult into obesity.

*Therapist:* Are the only two options emaciation or obesity? If you have maintained "control" at this weight, where is the evidence that you will not be able to exert similar "control" at a normal weight? Recovered patients do not typically indulge in only high-calorie foods, and very few become obese. Could it be that you are feeling this way because you are *currently* starved — that once you get to a normal weight, you won't be sitting on a powder keg of hunger?

*(Garner & Bemis, 1985, pp. 126–127)*

**Correcting Distorted Body Image** Many clinicians believe that anorexic clients' correction, or at least recognition, of their distorted body image is a "precondition to recovery" (Bruch, 1973). Therapists usually educate clients about the body distortions typical of anorexia nervosa and train them to recognize that their own assessments of their size are incorrect (Garner & Bemis, 1982; Garner & Garfinkel, 1982, 1981). Such education often paves the way for more accurate body perceptions. At the very least, a patient may reach a point where she

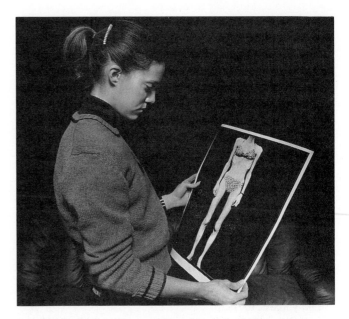

In 1980 a 16-year-old anorexic patient named Jane, 5 feet 8 inches tall, weighed 90 pounds, down 45 pounds from her weight 8 months earlier. After two years of intensive treatment, she gained back 25 pounds. Looking at pictures of anorexic persons helped her to recognize that body distortions are typical of this disorder.

says, "I know that a cardinal feature of anorexia nervosa is a misperception of my own size, so I can expect to feel fat no matter what size I really am," or "When I try to estimate my own dimensions, I'm like a color-blind person trying to coordinate her own wardrobe. I'll have to rely on objective data to determine my actual size." With the aid of such insights, patients are less likely to be driven to extremes of behavior by their distorted body perceptions.

**Changing Interactions within the Family** As we noted earlier, family systems theorists believe that a family structure of enmeshment, along with other forms of family dysfunction, contributes to anorexia nervosa (Eisler, 1988; Sargent, Liebman, & Silver, 1985; Palazzoli, 1985). Thus family therapy is often used in cases of this disorder. As in other family therapy situations, the therapist meets with the family as a whole, observes how the family members interact, points out dysfunctional family patterns, and helps the members make appropriate changes. The therapy of Salvador Minuchin and his colleagues (1978) exemplifies the approach used in many cases of anorexia nervosa. In order to change the common family pattern of enmeshment and help the anorexic individual separate her feelings and needs from those of other family members, Minuchin intervenes in ways that *support the individual space of each family member, protect subsystem boundaries, support the hierarchical organization of the system*, and *create therapeutic crises*.

The therapist supports each family member's personal space by laying down rules that enhance the members' independence and respect for one another. They are encouraged to speak for themselves; for example, checking for approval is strictly prohibited. Members are repeatedly reminded that they may not finish someone else's phrase or story, or request help in an area where they should be competent.

Because children in enmeshed families are often drawn into the conflicts between parents, and parents frequently intrude on sibling interactions, the family therapist is always on guard to protect appropriate family boundaries. Minuchin and his colleagues (1978) regularly remind and question family members during sessions (p. 100):

Did you ask them if they want your participation?

Did you ask for help?

This is an issue that concerns your parents, not you.

Let your children work this out by themselves.

Many parents in enmeshed families abdicate their authority and expect their children to respond with levels of maturity beyond their age. Minuchin tries to counter this tendency by reinforcing respect for each member's unique position within the family and supporting a hierarchy in which parents are higher than children and older children are higher than younger children. As a result, parents are expected to feel more effective in their executive roles, and to respect a child's need to grow and acquire autonomy at a pace appropriate to the child's age.

Finally, the family therapist may find it necessary to instigate therapeutic family crises in order to reveal and then correct hidden conflicts (Minuchin, 1970). Using a strategy called *reframing the symptom*, for example, the therapist may propose to the family that the child's anorexic symptoms are actually voluntary. This redefinition will often serve to unite parents and induce them to stop treating the child as an invalid, and it challenges the anorexic child herself to recognize the power she exerts through her symptoms rather than seeing herself as totally helpless.

In the following excerpt from a family therapy session, the therapist uses these and similar techniques to help change the patterns of enmeshment in the family of an anorexic teenager:

*Mother:*   I think I know what [Susan] is going through: all the doubt and insecurity of growing up and establishing her own identity. *(Turning to the patient, with tears)* If you just place trust in yourself, with the support of those around you who care, everything will turn out for the better.

*Therapist:*   Are you making yourself available to her? Should she turn to you, rely on you for guidance and emotional support?

*Mother:*   Well, that's what parents are for.

*Therapist:*   *(Turning to patient)* What do you think?

*Susan:*   *(To mother)* I can't keep depending on you, Mom, or everyone else. That's what I've been doing, and it gave me anorexia. . . .

*Therapist:*   Do you think your mom would prefer that there be no secrets between her and the kids—an open door, so to speak?

*Older sister:*   Sometimes I do.

*Therapist:*   *(To patient and younger sister)* How about you two?

*Susan:*   Yeah. Sometimes it's like whatever I feel, she has to feel.

*Younger sister:*   Yeah.

*Therapist:*   *(To mother)* How does it make it better for you to be so close and involved with your kids?

*Mother:*   I don't see what's so wrong. You seem to be condemning me for being a conscientious parent. . . .

*Therapist:*   *(To father)* I wonder where you fit in? What stops your wife from turning to you? Again, I wonder if your wife is as sensitive to your needs and what you go through. . . .

*Father:*   I would say, probably not. I'm a pretty reserved fellow.

*Therapist:*   *(To the girls)* Is that the way it is with him?

*Older sister:*   Dad, you need to express what you think more. . . .

*(Strober & Yager, 1985, pp. 381–382)*

**Combining the Approaches**   Today's therapists tend to combine these various techniques for treating anorexia nervosa (Miller & Carlton, 1985; Martin, 1985; Garfinkel & Garner, 1982; Zeller, 1982; Crisp, 1980). The particular combination selected depends on the individual anorexic patient's situation and problems.

Studies suggest that the combining of approaches is indeed often helpful (Martin, 1985; Garfinkel & Garner, 1982; Herson & Detre, 1980). Such programs are now offered in mental health centers, medical and mental hospitals, and private treatment facilities across the United States. Inasmuch as several different pathways may lead to anorexia nervosa, it makes sense that the most effective form of intervention would be a treatment program that is multi-faceted and flexible, able to be tailored to the unique needs of the patient.

**The Aftermath of Anorexia Nervosa** The development of multiple treatment approaches for anorexia nervosa has greatly improved the outlook for people with this disorder in recent years. Nevertheless, many of them still face significant obstacles on the road to recovery. In numerous follow-up studies, certain trends have emerged:

1. Weight restoration often occurs quickly once treatment begins (Andersen et al., 1985; Theander, 1970; Dally, 1969). Complete psychological and physical recovery, however, may take several years. Altogether, approximately 75 percent of patients continue to show improvement when they are examined several years or more after their initial recovery: 45 percent are fully recovered and 30 percent considerably improved. Approximately 25 percent remain seriously impaired or are dead at follow-up (Tolstrup et al., 1985; Martin, 1985; Garfinkel & Garner, 1982; Hsu, 1980).

2. The death rate from anorexia nervosa seems to be declining (Andersen et al., 1985; Crisp, 1981; Hsu et al., 1979). Earlier diagnosis and safer and faster weight-restoration techniques may account for this trend. Deaths are usually caused by starvation and its complications (such as cardiac failure, pneumonia, or renal failure) or by suicide (Tolstrup et al., 1985).

3. Approximately 50 to 80 percent of anorexic females menstruate again when they regain their weight. Others remain amenorrheic at least for a while (Crisp, 1981; Hsu, 1980; Garfinkel et al., 1977).

4. Typically, recovery is not a smooth process (Murray, 1986). At least 15 percent of patients have recurrences of anorexic behavior while they are recovering. These recurrences are usually precipitated by new stresses, such as marriage, pregnancy, or a major relocation (Hsu et al., 1979).

5. At follow-up, many patients continue to express concerns about gaining too much weight. Even years later, approximately 45 to 65 percent say they worry about their weight and appearance (Hsu et al., 1979; Morgan & Russell, 1975). Some patients continue to restrict their diets to some degree, experience anxiety when they eat with other people, or hold some distorted attitudes about food, eating, and weight (Clinton & McKinlay, 1986).

6. Even years later, 40 to 60 percent of anorexic patients continue to experience some emotional problems—particularly depression, social anxiety, and obsessiveness. Such problems are particularly common in those who have not succeeded in attaining a normal weight (Schwartz & Thompson, 1981; Crisp, 1981; Hsu, 1980; Stonehill & Crisp, 1977).

7. Family problems persist for approximately 50 percent of anorexic patients (Hsu, 1980).

8. Most anorexic patients are performing effectively at their jobs at follow-up. As many as 90 percent hold jobs and perform well, and the majority express high job satisfaction (Theander, 1970).

9. Those who recover go on to marry or have intimate relationships at rates comparable to those of nonanorexic populations. Sexual functioning tends to remain impaired in nonrecovered anorexic people (Hsu et al., 1979; Theander, 1970; Dally, 1969).

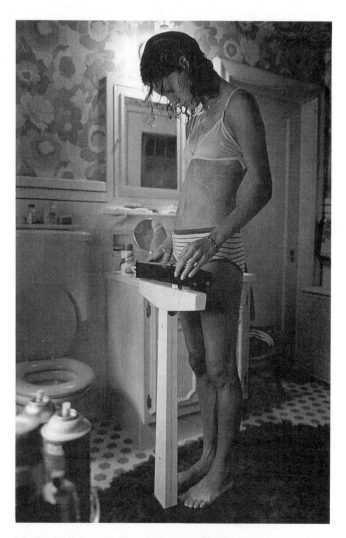

Like many other people who recover from anorexia nervosa, Jane continued to weigh herself every morning and still became anxious each time she observed a weight gain.

10. The more weight patients lose before treatment, the poorer their recovery rate (Burns & Crisp, 1985; Morgan & Russell, 1975).

11. Adolescents seem to have a better recovery rate than older patients (Hsu et al., 1979; Morgan & Russell, 1975; Halmi et al., 1973; Theander, 1970). Females have a better recovery rate than males (Crisp et al., 1977).

12. Those who display psychological, behavioral, or sexual problems before the development of anorexia nervosa tend to have a poorer recovery rate than those without such premorbid problems (Burns & Crisp, 1985; Hsu et al., 1979; Morgan & Russell, 1975; Halmi et al., 1973). Individuals who perform well at school or work before the onset of anorexia nervosa tend to have a higher recovery rate (Garfinkel et al., 1977).

13. The longer an anorexic person goes without successful intervention, the poorer the prognosis (Burns & Crisp, 1985; Hsu et al., 1979; Pierloot et al., 1975).

14. Some anorexic individuals also appear to recover without formal treatment of any kind, but the precise number is not known.

## Treatments for Bulimia Nervosa

Treatment programs tailored to the particular features of bulimia nervosa have been developed only in recent years, but they have already had a meteoric rise in popularity. Most of these programs are offered in eating-disorder clinics, and all share the immediate goal of reducing and eliminating binge-purge patterns and normalizing eating habits and the broader goal of addressing the underlying causes of bulimic behavior patterns. The programs emphasize education as much as therapy. Many programs combine several treatment strategies, including *individual insight therapy, group therapy, behavioral therapy,* and *antidepressant drug therapy* (Fichter, 1990; Pyle et al., 1990; Muuss, 1986).

**Individual Insight Therapy**     Psychodynamic and cognitive approaches have been the most common forms of individual insight therapy for bulimic clients (Fichter, 1990). As in the treatment of other kinds of disorders, psychodynamic therapists use free association and interpretive techniques to help bulimic individuals uncover and eventually resolve their underlying conflicts and issues, including their frustrating tensions, lack of self-trust, need for control, and feelings of powerlessness (Lerner, 1986; Yager, 1985). Case reports suggest that psychodynamic therapy is sometimes helpful for bulimic

persons. Only a few research studies have been conducted to test its effectiveness, but these studies are generally supportive (Yager, 1985; Wilson, Hogan, & Mintz, 1983; Bruch, 1973).

Therapists who take cognitive approaches try to help bulimic people discuss and alter their maladaptive attitudes toward food, eating, weight, and shape, thus eliminating the kinds of thinking that raise anxiety and lead to binging (Hollin & Lewis, 1988; Garner, 1986; Fairburn et al., 1985; Fairburn, 1985, 1981). As in the treatment of anorexia nervosa, the therapists typically teach clients to identify the dysfunctional thoughts that regularly precede their urge to binge — "I have no self-control," "I might as well give up," "I look fat," "I am fat," "I must lose weight," "I must diet" (Fairburn, 1985). They then guide clients to evaluate those thoughts and to draw more appropriate conclusions. Using a combination of therapy and education, the therapists may also guide clients to recognize, question, and eventually change the broader cognitive features of their problem, such as their perfectionistic standards, sense of helplessness, and low self-concept.

Researchers have found cognitive therapy to be relatively effective in cases of bulimia nervosa, reducing binge eating, purging, and feelings of depression (Luka, Agras, & Schneider, 1986; Fairburn et al., 1986; Wilson et al., 1986). Approaches that mix cognitive and psychodynamic techniques also appear to be helpful (Yager, 1985).

**Group Therapy**     Most bulimia nervosa programs now include group therapy, giving sufferers an opportunity to share their thoughts, concerns, and experiences with one another (Pyle et al., 1990; Laube, 1990; Edmands, 1986; Jones, 1985; Mitchell et al., 1985). In these groups they learn that their disorder is not unique or shameful, and they receive much-needed support and understanding from the other members, along with candid feedback and insights (Asner, 1990). Group therapy may also provide a training ground where therapists and bulimic clients can work directly on underlying social fears, such as the fear of displeasing others or being criticized. Research suggests that group therapy is helpful in as many as 75 percent of bulimia nervosa cases, particularly when it is combined with individual insight therapy (Lacey, 1983; Roy-Byrne et al., 1984; Mitchell et al., 1985).

Literally thousands of *self-help support groups* for people with bulimia nervosa or their relatives now exist throughout the world, offering members a mixture of education, therapy, guidance, and support. Perhaps the best-known self-help program is Overeaters Anonymous (OA), a worldwide organization consisting of thousands of groups itself. OA was founded in 1960 to deal with excessive eating and obesity and increasingly has included a focus on bulimia nervosa. As the name implies, it is modeled after Alcoholics Anonymous (see p. 454). Accordingly, it views bulimia nervosa as a debilitating and addictive illness, requires members to acknowledge their disorder and to follow twelve steps to recovery, and emphasizes the spiritual as well as intellectual aspects of recovery.

Despite OA's popularity, some clinical theorists have become uncomfortable with its philosophy and teachings (Levine, 1987; Bemis, 1985; Enright et al., 1985; Garner, 1985). First, these theorists dislike OA's assertion that bulimia nervosa is a lifelong illness of "food addiction" or "compulsive overeating" (Cooper, 1989). In accord with much of the recent research on the disorder, they see it instead as a pattern that emerges as a consequence of multiple factors, including excessive dieting and cognitive distortions (Garner, 1985). Second, they believe that the addiction model used by OA teaches bulimic people to categorize foods into "good" (diet) foods and "bad" (binge) foods, and to use "will power" to help them abstain from the bad food. According to the opponents, such teachings inadvertently encourage bulimic persons to think maladaptively, diet in a counterproductive manner, and aspire to a weight that is too low for them. Although the opponents agree that group treatment is very useful for bulimic persons, they prefer group therapy that is led professionally, offers social support, espouses a multidimensional rather than addictive view of bulimia nervosa, and encourages a normalization of diet—a diet that includes appropriate amounts of sugar and carbohydrates and that allows the person's body to reach its own normal weight, whatever that may be.

**Behavioral Therapy** Behavioral techniques are often employed in cases of bulimia nervosa along with individual insight therapy or group therapy (Nutzinger & deZwaan, 1990; Long & Cordle, 1982). Bulimic clients may, for example, be asked to monitor and keep diaries of their eating behavior, their fluctuations of hunger and satiety, and their other feelings and experiences (Saunders, 1985; Grinc, 1982; Greenberg & Marks, 1982). This strategy helps them to observe their eating patterns more objectively and to recognize the emotional features of their disorder. In another behavioral technique, clients are sometimes instructed actually to plan their binges beforehand. They may be told to set time limits on binges or to binge only at specified times, in certain places, and on certain days (Cauwels, 1983). These steps are expected to help them gain a sense of control over their binge eating.

Members of Overeaters Anonymous acknowlege that they use food self-destructively, and learn to treat their bodies with greater respect. Many members report that the program's twelve steps help them tremendously, but some clinicians believe that OA inadvertently encourages bulimic people to think maladaptively about food.

Behaviorists are increasingly using the technique of *exposure and response prevention* to help break the binge-purge cycle (Gray & Hoage, 1990). As we saw in Chapter 7 (pp. 246–248), this approach has been successfully applied in many cases of obsessive-compulsive disorder. Therapists who take this approach expose people to situations that would ordinarily raise their obsessive anxiety and then prevent them from performing their usual compulsive acts. Over the course of treatment, the clients come to appreciate that the situations are actually quite harmless and that they do not need to resort to their compulsive behaviors as a means of reducing anxiety. Viewing a bulimic person's vomiting as a compulsive act that reduces obsessive fears about eating, these therapists have bulimic clients eat particular kinds and amounts of food and then prevent them from vomiting (Rosen & Leitenberg, 1985, 1982). Studies have found that eating-related anxieties often decrease over the course of this treatment, that patients can eat increasingly large meals without experiencing anxiety, and that binge eating and vomiting decrease substantially (Johnson, Schulundt, & Jarrell, 1986; Wilson, Rossiter, Kleifield, & Lindholm, 1986; Giles, Young, & Young, 1985).

**Antidepressant Medications** During the past decade, antidepressant drugs have often been added to the treatment package for bulimia nervosa (Hudson & Pope, 1990; Mitchell, 1989; Treasure, 1988). In one double-blind study the antidepressant drug imipramine was administered for a 6-week period to 20 bulimic women, while a placebo was given to 10 others (Pope, Hudson, Jonas, & Yurgelun-Todd, 1983). After treatment, 18 of the 20 women treated with antidepressants showed a moderate to marked reduction of binge eating. Indeed, 7 stopped binge eating entirely. In contrast, only 1 of the 10 who were given placebos improved even moderately, 8 showed no improvement, and one became worse.

Although other studies have not always yielded such impressive results, some do indicate that antidepressant medications can be helpful in bulimia nervosa, especially in combination with other forms of therapy (Fava et al., 1990; Pyle et al., 1990; Wilcox, 1990; Walsh, 1985; Hudson, Pope, & Jonas, 1985; Pope, Hudson, & Jonas, 1983). As in the treatment of anorexia nervosa, these drugs appear to be most effective for patients who display severe depression and obsessive-compulsiveness as part of their symptomatology (Yager, 1985). Thus their primary impact may be to relieve those particular aspects of the disorder.

**The Aftermath of Bulimia Nervosa**   Left untreated, bulimia nervosa usually lasts for a number of years, sometimes receding temporarily, but then emerging again (APA, 1987). As with anorexia nervosa, relapses are usually precipitated by a new life stress, such as an impending examination, job change, illness, marriage, or divorce (Abraham & Llewellyn-Jones, 1984).

Approximately 40 percent of bulimic clients show an outstanding immediate response to treatment: they stop their binges or binge less than once a month, stop purging, and stabilize their eating habits and weight, all for at least one year (Fairburn et al., 1986; Pope et al., 1985; Abraham & Llewellyn-Jones, 1984). Another 40 percent show a moderate response — decreased binge eating, decreased purging, and better weight stabilization and meal regularity. The remaining 20 percent show no improvement in their eating patterns.

Research also suggests that treatment helps many bulimic people make significant and lasting improvements in their psychological and social functioning (Herzog et al., 1990). In follow-up studies of between 1 and 3 years, former patients have been found to be less depressed than they were at the time of initial diagnosis, although many continue to experience at least a few depressive symptoms (Brotman et al., 1988; Swift et al., 1987; Norman & Herzog, 1986; Fairburn et al., 1986; Hsu & Holder, 1986). Follow-up studies have also indicated that approximately one-third of former patients interact more healthily with others at work, at home, and in social settings; another third interact effectively in only two of these areas; and the remaining third function well in at best one of these areas (Hsu & Holder, 1986).

Some clinicians have further proposed that several factors will affect the rate and extent of recovery: (1) binge-purge patterns of long duration will be more difficult to change; (2) recovery will be more difficult when a person's daily routine has come to center primarily on binging and when binge-purge patterns have largely taken the place of such activities as sex, socializing, vocational pursuits, and creative endeavors; and (3) change will be more difficult in the face of severe depression, anxiety, and other emotional distress (Levenkron, 1982). However, research has yet to provide clear support for these claims.

# EATING DISORDERS: THE STATE OF THE FIELD

The prevalence of eating disorders has increased in Western society during the past two decades, and public and clinical interest has risen right along with it. Correspondingly, researchers have been studying anorexia nervosa and bulimia nervosa with great fervor and have learned much about these problems.

They have learned, for example, that the two disorders are similar in many important ways. They have uncovered the unusually significant role played by sociocultural pressures in the development of these disorders, and the critical influences of dieting, starvation, and biological factors in precipitating and maintaining them. They have also determined that the disorders are brought about by a host of intersecting factors, which can best be corrected by multiple intervention programs.

At the same time, clinicians have much to learn about the disorders and how to treat them. Indeed, bulimia nervosa was not even formally identified as a clinical disorder until 10 years ago. Every new discovery forces clinicians to adjust their theories and treatment programs. Only recently, for example, have researchers learned that bulimic individuals sometimes feel strangely positive toward their symptoms. A recovered bulimic person raises this point:

It involves all facets of your life, stopping growth completely. It controls your life in a way that only people with other dependencies can understand. It's progressive and makes you feel totally unworthy. Eventually it will kill you. But I still miss my bulimia as I would an old friend who has died.

*(Cauwels, 1983, p. 173)*

Obviously, when such feelings are understood and addressed, treatment programs will become more effective.

While clinicians and researchers strive for more answers about anorexia nervosa and bulimia nervosa and greater effectiveness in treating them, the clinical population itself has begun to take an active role. A number of patient-initiated national organizations now provide information, education, and support to people with eating disorders and to their families through a national telephone hotline, professional referrals, printed information and newsletters, and workshops, seminars, and conferences. These organizations include the National Anorexic Aid Society, American Anorexia and Bulimia Association, National Association of Anorexia Nervosa and Associated Disorders, and Anorexia Nervosa and Related Eating Disorders, Inc.

The very existence of such organizations helps counter the isolation and shame felt by people with eating disorders. By publicizing the broad scope of eating problems and the availability of help, these organizations help countless sufferers to recognize that they are hardly alone or powerless against eating disorders that seem to them to have control over their lives.

## SUMMARY

Eating disorders have increased dramatically since thinness has become a national obsession. Victims of *anorexia nervosa* so relentlessly pursue extreme thinness that they may starve themselves to death. Victims of *bulimia nervosa* go on frequent eating binges, then take laxatives or force themselves to vomit to keep from gaining weight. These eating disorders, which share many important features, are disproportionately prevalent among adolescent girls and young women.

Anorexia most often appears between the ages of 14 and 18 and strikes between 1 and 4 percent of the female population. Between 5 and 18 percent of anorexia's victims die of medical problems related to starvation.

Five central features of anorexia nervosa are a drive for thinness and a morbid fear of becoming overweight, cognitive disturbances, preoccupation with food, personality and mood problems, and medical problems, including *amenorrhea*.

Bulimia, also known as the *binge-purge syndrome, gorge-purge syndrome,* and *dietary chaos syndrome,* usually appears in females between the ages of 15 and 19 years. These young women generally maintain their body weight within a normal range, but may become dangerously underweight. This latter pattern, *bulimic anorexia nervosa,* is distinct from *restrictive anorexia nervosa* in that the weight loss comes from purging rather than from restricting the intake of food. Some bulimics move in the other direction and become dangerously overweight.

The binge periods of bulimic persons are often carefully planned and accompanied by a great deal of tension, followed by guilt and self-reproach. Theorists suggest that purging behavior is initially reinforced by (1) the immediate relief from uncomfortable feelings of fullness, (2) the removal of "threatening" foods from the body, (3) the maintenance of an acceptable appearance, and (4) temporary reduction of the feelings of anxiety, self-disgust, and loss of control attached to binge eating.

Both bulimia nervosa and anorexia nervosa typically begin after a period of intense dieting; affect people who fear becoming obese and are preoccupied with weight, appearance, and food; are associated with feelings of depression and anxiety; and are accompanied by disturbances in the sufferers' attitudes toward eating and in their self-perceptions. The two disorders also differ in important ways. Bulimic persons are more likely to recognize that their behavior is pathological and to be concerned about their attractiveness to others. Bulimic persons display fewer obsessive qualities than anorexic persons, but they tend to have long histories of mood swings and great difficulty controlling their impulses. Additionally, repeated vomiting leads to a unique set of medical problems, including hypokalemia, dental problems, and possible internal bleeding.

Today's theorists usually apply a *multidimensional risk perspective* to explain eating disorders, and identify several key factors that place a person at risk for an eating disorder: sociocultural pressures, family environment, ego deficiencies and cognitive disturbances, biological factors, and mood disorders.

Treatments for eating disorders have two goals: to correct the pathological eating pattern and to address the psychological and situational factors that led to and maintain it.

The first step in treating anorexia nervosa is to increase caloric intake and restore the person's weight quickly, using such strategies as *supportive nursing care.* The second step is to address the underlying problems, so that improvement may be lasting, using a mixture of individual, group, and family therapies.

Treatments for bulimia nervosa are still quite new; they focus on eliminating the binge-purge pattern and addressing underlying causes of the disorder. Often several treatment strategies are combined, including *individual insight therapy, group therapy, behavioral therapy,* and *antidepressant medications.*

# TOPIC OVERVIEW

# CHAPTER 13

## SUBSTANCE USE DISORDERS

Probably just about every substance available in the world has been ingested by human beings somewhere, at some time. Curious and adventuresome, we have learned that a vast variety of substances are edible and nutritious when they are prepared in certain ways, and we have developed a long list of acceptable foods and delicacies. Humans have likewise stumbled upon substances that have interesting effects on the brain and the rest of the body. Many such substances have proved beneficial to health or healing and have gained use as medicines; some have been found to have calming or stimulating effects and are used to enhance social and recreational experiences. Indeed, the use of potent substances is pervasive throughout our society: we may swallow an aspirin to quiet a headache, an antibiotic to fight an infection, or a tranquilizer to calm us down; drink coffee to get going in the morning or wine to relax with friends; or smoke cigarettes to soothe our nerves.

Many of the substances that humans have come across, however, are capable of harming the body or adversely affecting behavior or mood. The misuse of these substances has become one of society's most disabling problems (see Table 13-1).

Technically, the term "drug" applies to any substance other than food that changes our bodily or mental functioning. Henceforth in this chapter, the words "drug" and "substance" will be

TABLE 13-1

## RISKS AND CONSEQUENCES OF DRUG MISUSE

| | Dependency potential | Risk of organ damage or death | Risk of severe social or economic consequences | Risk of severe or long-lasting mental and behavioral change |
|---|---|---|---|---|
| Opioids | High | Low | High | Low to Moderate |
| Sedative-Hypnotics: | | | | |
| Barbiturates | Moderate to High | Moderate to High | Moderate to High | Low |
| Benzodiazepines | Low | Low | Low | Low |
| Stimulants | High | Moderate | Low to Moderate | Moderate to High |
| Alcohol | Moderate | High | High | High |
| Cannabis | Low to Moderate | Low | Low to Moderate | Low |
| Mixed Drug Classes | High | High | High | High |

*Source:* Gold, 1986, p. 28.

used interchangeably with that connotation. In recent years "substance" has gained favor among those who treat substance use disorders, partly because most people think of a drug as being either a medicine (whether prescription or nonprescription) or an illegal substance, and fail to see that potentially harmful substances such as alcohol, tobacco, and caffeine are drugs, too, each with its own set of effects.

Drug misuse may lead to two forms of abnormal functioning. First, ingestion of a drug may bring about a temporary *organic mental syndrome,* a dysfunction of the brain characterized by changes in behavior, emotion, or thought (APA, 1987). An excessive amount of alcohol, for example, may lead to a state of *intoxication* (literally, "poisoning") in which a person exhibits impaired judgment, mood changes, irritability, slurred speech, and loss of coordination. Drugs such as LSD may cause an organic mental syndrome called *hallucinosis,* a state of perceptual distortion and hallucinations.

The regular use of certain substances can also lead to a longer-term pattern of maladaptive behavior called *substance use disorder* (APA, 1987). There are two categories of substance use disorder—substance abuse and substance dependence. People caught in a pattern of *substance abuse* rely on a drug excessively and chronically, and allow its use to occupy a central place in their lives. Because of their loss of control over drug use, substance abusers may seriously damage their family and social relationships, perform unreliably at work, and create physical hazards for themselves or others. People who display *substance dependence,* a more advanced kind of disorder that is known popularly as *addiction,*

develop a *physical* dependence on a drug in addition to a pattern of abusing it — that is, they develop a tolerance for the drug or experience withdrawal symptoms if they suddenly stop taking it, or both. *Tolerance* to a drug means that a person needs increasing doses of it in order to keep obtaining the initial effect. *Withdrawal symptoms* are unpleasant, at times dangerous, reactions — muscle aches and cramps, anxiety attacks, sweating, nausea — that emerge when drug users suddenly stop taking or reduce their dosage of the drug. These withdrawal symptoms can begin within hours of the last dose, often intensifying over a period of days before they subside. Surveys suggest that approximately 7 percent of all adults in the United States currently display a substance use disorder (Myers et al., 1984) but only a fraction of them receive treatment for it (Shapiro et al., 1984).

Many drugs are available in our society, and new ones emerge almost every day. Some are found in nature, others are derived from natural substances, and yet others are synthetically produced. Some, such as anti-anxiety drugs and barbiturates, require a physician's prescription for legal use. Others, such as alcohol and the nicotine found in cigarettes, are legally available to all adults (see Box 13-1). Still others, such as heroin, are illegal under any circumstance, yet are either manufactured or sold in such quantities that they constitute major, albeit underground, industries. Twelve percent of all people in the United States currently use marijuana, cocaine, heroin, or another illegal substance (NIDA, 1985). Thirty-three percent of high school seniors have used an illicit drug within the past year (Johnson et al., 1991).

The drugs that currently are arousing the most concern in the general public fall into three categories: substances that act to depress the central nervous system, such as alcohol and opioids; stimulants of the central nervous system, such as cocaine and amphetamines; and hallucinogens, such as LSD and cannabis, which cause changes in sensory perception.

# DEPRESSANTS

*Depressants* are substances that slow the activity of the central nervous system and in sufficient doses cause a reduction of tension and inhibitions and impair judgment, motor activity, and concentration. The three most widely used groups of depressants are alcohol, sedative-hypnotics, and opioids.

## Alcohol

Two-thirds of the people in the United States drink alcohol-containing beverages, at least from time to time. Indeed, alcohol is by far the most popular drug in the United States, and purchases of beer, wine, liquor, and sundry cocktail ingredients add up to tens of billions of dollars each year. Approximately 11 percent of all adults ingest an ounce or more of alcohol every day, often five drinks in a sitting (APA, 1987). Males who drink outnumber females by a margin of at least two to one, perhaps as much as five to one (APA, 1987).

All alcoholic beverages contain *ethyl alcohol.* This chemical compound is rapidly absorbed into the blood through the lining of the stomach and the intestine, and immediately begins to take effect. The ethyl alcohol is carried in the bloodstream to the central nervous system (CNS), where it acts to depress, or slow, CNS functioning. At first it affects the higher centers of the CNS, those that control judgment and inhibition, and people become less constrained, more talkative, and often more friendly. As their inner control breaks down, they may feel relaxed, safe, self-confident, and happy. Some also experience heightened sexual desire and seek to act upon those feelings. Alcohol's depression of these regions of the CNS also impairs fine motor skills, increases sensitivity to light, and causes the small blood vessels of the skin to dilate, so that the face and neck become flushed and the person feels warm.

As more alcohol is ingested, the effects increase, eventually depressing other areas in the CNS and thus causing changes that are even more problematic. People become still less restrained and more confused. Their

ability to make rational judgments declines, their speech becomes less tasteful and less coherent, and their memory falters (Tucker, Vuchinich, & Schonhaut, 1987). Many become loud, boisterous, and aggressive, their emotions exaggerated and labile; mildly amusing remarks or situations may strike them as hilarious.

Motor impairment also becomes more pronounced as drinking continues, and reaction times slow. People at this stage are unsteady when they stand or walk, and clumsy in performing even simple activities. They may drop things, bump into doors and furniture, and misjudge distances. Their vision becomes blurred, particularly peripheral vision, and they have trouble distinguishing between different intensities of light. Hearing is affected too. As a result of such impairments, people who have drunk too much alcohol may have great difficulty driving or solving simple problems.

The extent of the effect of ethyl alcohol on body chemistry is determined by its *concentration* in the blood. Thus a given amount of alcohol will have less effect on a larger person than on a smaller one (see Table 13-2 and Figure 13-1), because the larger person has a greater volume of blood. Levels of impairment are closely related to the concentration of ethyl alcohol in the blood. When alcohol constitutes 0.06 percent of the blood volume, a person usually feels relaxed and comfortable without yet being intoxicated. However, by the time the blood-alcohol concentration reaches 0.09 percent (3 cocktails, 5 bottles of beer, or 16 ounces of ordinary wine), the drinker crosses the line into a state of intoxication. As the concentration of alcohol in the bloodstream further increases, the drinker becomes even more intoxicated and impaired. If the level goes as high as 0.55 percent, death will probably result. Most people, however, lose consciousness before they can drink enough to reach this level.

The effects of alcohol decline only as the alcohol concentration in the blood declines. Most of the alcohol is broken down, or *metabolized,* by the liver into carbon dioxide and water, which can be exhaled and excreted (Korsten et al., 1975; Raskin, 1975). The average rate of metabolizing is 10 to 15 percent of an ounce per hour, but different livers conduct this process at somewhat different speeds; thus rates of "sobering up" differ. Despite a popular misconception, neither drinking black coffee, splashing cold water on the face, nor "getting hold of oneself" can speed the process up. Only time and metabolism can make a person sober.

Most people become intoxicated at most occasionally, and their use of alcohol remains a matter of personal choice. Many people, however, progress from casual or "social" drinking to a state of uncontrollable alcohol consumption. They develop a long-term pattern of alco-

TABLE 13-2

| RELATIONSHIPS BETWEEN SEX, WEIGHT, ORAL ALCOHOL CONSUMPTION, AND BLOOD ALCOHOL LEVEL | | | | | | | |
| Absolute alcohol (ounces) | Beverage intake* | Blood alcohol level (percent) | | | | | |
| | | Female (100 lb.) | Male (100 lb.) | Female (150 lb.) | Male (150 lb.) | Female (200 lb.) | Male (200 lb.) |
|---|---|---|---|---|---|---|---|
| ½ | 1 oz. spirits† 1 glass wine 1 can beer | 0.045 | 0.037 | 0.03 | 0.025 | 0.022 | 0.019 |
| 1 | 2 oz. spirits 2 glasses wine 2 cans beer | 0.090 | 0.075 | 0.06 | 0.050 | 0.045 | 0.037 |
| 2 | 4 oz. spirits 4 glasses wine 4 cans beer | 0.180 | 0.150 | 0.12 | 0.100 | 0.090 | 0.070 |
| 3 | 6 oz. spirits 6 glasses wine 6 cans beer | 0.270 | 0.220 | 0.18 | 0.150 | 0.130 | 0.110 |
| 4 | 8 oz. spirits 8 glasses wine 8 cans beer | 0.360 | 0.300 | 0.24 | 0.200 | 0.180 | 0.150 |
| 5 | 10 oz. spirits 10 glasses wine 10 cans beer | 0.450 | 0.370 | 0.30 | 0.250 | 0.220 | 0.180 |

\* In 1 hour.
† 100-proof spirits.
*Source:* Ray, 1983, p. 168.

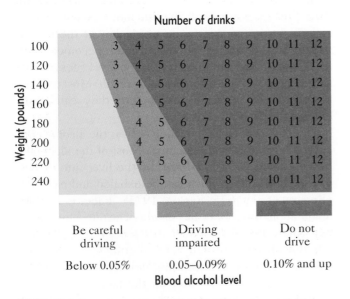

**FIGURE 13-1** Counting a 12-ounce glass of beer as one drink, clinicians estimate that a 100-pound person will reach the usual legal limit for drunk driving, a blood alcohol level of 0.10 percent, after ingesting just four drinks, whereas a 240-pound person will reach this limit only after having seven drinks. The ability to drive is somewhat impaired even when blood alcohol levels are between 0.05 and 0.09 percent, below the legal limit. *(Adapted from Frances & Franklin, 1988.)*

hol abuse or alcohol dependence — patterns collectively known as *alcoholism.* Surveys indicate that between 5 and 6 percent of all adults in the United States currently abuse or are dependent on alcohol (Myers et al., 1984). Approximately 13 percent of the adult population will display one of these patterns at some time in their lives (APA, 1987).

**Alcohol Abuse and Dependence** Alcohol abusers regularly drink excessive amounts of alcohol, feel unable to change their drinking habits, and rely on alcohol to enable them to do things that would otherwise make them anxious. The excessive drinking often interferes with their socializing or with their cognitive ability and work performance (Williams & Skinner, 1990). They may have frequent arguments with family members or friends, miss work repeatedly, and even lose their jobs.

Clinicians have identified three broad patterns of alcohol abuse (APA, 1987). In one, the person drinks large amounts of alcohol every day, keeps drinking until intoxicated, and plans his or her daily life around drinking.

*Drinking made me more relaxed, easier to be with. It* helped me sell, it gave me energy, it gave me courage.

When a man and a woman of identical size drink identical amounts of alcohol, the woman becomes intoxicated more quickly. Apparently women's bodies have so much less *alcohol dehydrogenase,* the enzyme that breaks alcohol down in the stomach, that they absorb 30 percent more alcohol into their blood than men.

Weekends were for drinking, fishing trips were for drinking, holidays were for drinking—everything pleasant was associated with alcohol. And when I stopped drinking for a short time, I couldn't help noticing the difference. I was tired, irritable, vaguely depressed, no fun to be with, a bad father, a worse husband—and so I continued drinking because drinking had come to occupy the center of my life.

. . . By the time I reached my early thirties, though, all pretense at control had gone. Every night was a drinking bout that lasted until I had drained that evening's quart bottle. Then, to get going in the morning, I had to have a couple of bloody Marys. And to keep going during the day, more to drink. Even through the haze of alcohol, I began to feel that things weren't going as well as they had before. My wife and I had nothing to say to each other, I couldn't stand being with the kids for more than a few minutes at a time, and my sales had begun to fall off. I blamed it on the economy, then on the President's policies, then on bad planning at the top of our company—on everybody and everything but me and my drinking. Finally, in a single year, I had three auto accidents, one serious enough to involve injury to the occupants of the other vehicle (needless to say, I'd been drinking before all three). I lost my license for two years. My wife, fed up with life with "a drunken bum," left me and took the children. And my partner called me in and told me that he'd had enough, that if I didn't go on the wagon, he and I were through. . . .

*(Nathan & Harris, 1980, pp. 283–284)*

In a second pattern of alcohol abuse, drinking to excess is limited to weekends or evenings, or both. Dick Van

Dyke, the comedian and actor, displayed this pattern of alcohol abuse.

*I didn't miss work ever because of drinking. And I never* drank at work. Never drank during the day—only at home and only in the evenings. . . . I never craved a drink during the day. I was never a morning drinker—I didn't want one then. The idea made me as sick as it would make anyone else. But evening drinking is a form of alcoholism, just like periodic drinking is a form of alcoholism. . . .

My wife had long gone to bed. I was sitting alone, drinking, lost in what I took to be deep thought. I realized suddenly, "Why I am thinking gibberish here—my mind is completely out of it." When I woke up the next morning, I got up and went to a hospital. Went straight into a treatment center.

*(HEW, 1976, p. 76)*

In a third pattern of alcohol abuse, the person may abstain from drinking for long periods of time, then go on periodic binges of heavy drinking that can last weeks or months. During such binges, the drinker may remain intoxicated for days. Such people experience "blackouts" and later are unable to recall the period of their intoxication.

For some people, the pattern of alcoholism further includes physical dependence. As they use alcohol repeatedly, their body builds up a tolerance for it and they need to drink increasing amounts in order to feel any effects. When they try to stop drinking, within hours their hands, tongue, and eyelids begin to shake noticeably. They feel weak and nauseous. They sweat and vomit. Their heart beats rapidly and their blood pressure rises. They may also become anxious, depressed, or irritable.

A small percentage of people who are alcohol dependent also experience a dramatic withdrawal reaction within three days after they stop or reduce drinking: *alcohol withdrawal delirium* or *delirium tremens (the DT's).* Delirium is abundant mental confusion and clouded consciousness. Alcoholics in the throes of delirium tremens may have terrifying visual hallucinations: they believe they are seeing small frightening animals or objects moving about rapidly, perhaps pursuing them or crawling on them. Here is Mark Twain's classic description of Huckleberry Finn's alcoholic father:

I don't know how long I was asleep, but . . . there was an awful scream and I was up. There was Pap looking wild, and skipping around every which way and yelling about snakes. He said they was crawling up on his legs; and then he would give a jump and scream, and say one had bit him on the cheek—but I couldn't see no snakes. He started and run round . . . hollering "Take him off! he's biting me on the neck!" I never see a man look so wild in the eyes. Pretty

---

BOX 13-1

# Tobacco and Nicotine: A Powerful Addiction

An American Cancer Society anti-smoking poster.

Smoking tobacco has been an accepted practice for centuries, but recently, health professionals have become aware that nicotine, the active substance in tobacco and a stimulant of the central nervous system, is a powerfully addictive substance. The physiological effects and dangers of smoking tobacco are well documented. More than 390,000 people die each year in the United States as a result of smoking (U.S. Surgeon General's Report, 1989). Pregnant women who smoke are more likely than nonsmokers to deliver prematurely and to have babies who are underweight. Smoking is directly associated with hypertension, lung disease, cancer, stroke, and other deadly medical problems. Men who smoke two packs a day are twenty-two times as likely to die from lung cancer as nonsmokers.

Approximately 29 percent of Americans over the age of 12 are regular smokers. Most of the adults among them know that smoking is unhealthy and would rather not do it. So why do they continue to smoke? Because, as the surgeon general declared in 1988, nicotine is as addictive as heroin, perhaps even more so. Inhaling a puff of cigarette smoke delivers a dose of nicotine to the brain faster than it could be delivered by injection into the bloodstream, and is believed to bind directly to receptors in the brain, which soon becomes dependent on it. When regular smokers abstain, they experience withdrawal symptoms—irritability, increased appetite, sleep disturbances, decreased metabolic rate, cognitive difficulties, and a powerful desire to smoke. Smokers also develop a tolerance for nicotine and must increase their consumption in order to achieve the same psychological and physiological results and to avoid withdrawal.

Because smoking is socially accept-

---

soon he was all fagged out, and fell down panting; then he rolled over . . . kicking things every which way, and striking and grabbing at the air with his hands, and screaming . . . there was devils a-hold of him. He wore out by and by. . . . He says . . .

"Tramp-tramp-tramp: that's the dead; tramp-tramp-tramp; they're coming after me; but I won't go. Oh, they're here; don't touch me . . . they're cold; let go . . ."

Then he went down on all fours and crawled off, begging them to let him alone. . . .

*(Twain, 1885)*

Like Pap, people who experience delirium tremens become disoriented; they don't know where they are or what time of the day, month, or year it is. Some also have seizures and lose consciousness. Like most other alcohol withdrawal symptoms, the DT's usually run their course in two to three days. Research suggests that delirium tremens is related to low levels of magnesium and that drinkers with generally low magnesium levels are prone to develop it (Victor & Wolfe, 1973).

Another dramatic and relatively rare withdrawal reaction, *alcoholic hallucinosis,* consists of auditory hallucinations, such as imaginary voices that say demeaning or hostile things, either directly to the alcoholic person or about him or her. This reaction usually develops within 2 days after the person stops drinking and it may last for weeks or months.

## Personal and Social Impact of Alcohol and Alcoholism

Partly because alcohol is legal, accessible, and often portrayed positively in the arts and in advertising, there is little appreciation of the fact that it is one of society's

able (although its acceptability is on the decline), most people are comfortable admitting that they smoke and openly look for ways to quit. This situation has created a ready market for numerous products and techniques for helping people kick the habit. Most of these methods do not work very well. Success rates for *all* approaches depend heavily on the motivation of the smoker. Many seem to find that the immediate pleasure experienced by the smoker often outweigh the fear of long-term consequences. Whether the person succeeds at quitting also depends on factors such as stress, social support, family members who smoke, self-confidence, gender, and availability of information (Tunstal et al., 1985).

In general, self-help kits, informational pamphlets, commercial programs, and support groups are at most modestly helpful. Most people who do stop smoking after receiving such interventions start smoking again within one year (Hall et al., 1985).

The most successful treatments for nicotine addiction have been behavioral therapies and drug interventions.

Using aversive conditioning, therapists have on the average been able to achieve a two-year abstinence from smoking in about 50 percent of cases. The most common form of aversive conditioning is *rapid smoking*. The smoker treated by this technique sits in a closed room and puffs quickly on a cigarette, as frequently as once every six seconds, until the smoker begins to feel ill and is unable to take another puff. The feelings of illness become associated with smoking, and the smoker experiences an aversive reaction to cigarettes (Baker & Brandon, 1988).

The most common drug intervention for smoking is the use of *nicotine gum,* which contains a high level of nicotine that is released as the smoker chews. Theoretically, persons who ingest nicotine by chewing no longer need to smoke, and the reinforcing effects of smoking are removed. Research suggests that this approach does improve a smoker's chances of long-term abstinence, especially when it is combined with behavioral therapies. The more nicotine-dependent the smoker, the more effective

the use of nicotine gum (Jarvik & Schneider, 1984). A primary drawback, however, is that the use of nicotine gum does not lead to a decrease in nicotine consumption.

From the viewpoint of the smoker, most treatments have no effect on one of the critical components of nicotine withdrawal: the craving for a cigarette. Many smokers report that the craving is the most debilitating obstacle to the quitting. The antihypertensive drug *clonidine* has undergone testing as a possible means of reducing this and other symptoms of withdrawal from nicotine and other addictive substances, and has shown some promise (Glossman et al., 1984), but it is no magic pill for quitting. The more one smokes, the harder it is to quit, but on the positive side, five to ten years after quitting, former smokers are at virtually no higher risk for disease and death than people who have never smoked (Jaffe, 1985). For those who are able to take the long view, this assurance may be a powerful motivator. In the meantime, more than 1,000 people die of smoking-related diseases each day.

most dangerous drugs (Futch et al., 1984). Alcoholism destroys millions of families, social relationships, and careers (Steinglass et al., 1985). It is also a factor in nearly half of all suicides, homicides, assaults, rapes, and accidental deaths, including 42 to 50 percent of all fatal automobile accidents in the United States (Alcohol, Drug Abuse, and Mental Health Administration, 1987). Altogether, intoxicated drivers are responsible for 23,000 deaths each year.

Alcohol abuse is also a major problem among the young. Five percent of today's high school seniors report that they drink every day (ADAMHA, 1987). Even 8 percent of surveyed elementary school children admit to some alcohol use (Hutchinson & Little, 1985).

Chronic and excessive alcohol consumption can also seriously damage one's physical health, and it accounts

for medical costs of more than $15 billion annually (ADAMHA, 1987). It can, for example, cause serious, often fatal, damage to the liver. An excessive intake of alcohol overworks the liver, resulting in an accumulation there of excess fat, a condition sometimes called a "fatty liver." If the excessive alcohol intake continues, further liver damage may develop into an irreversible condition called *cirrhosis,* in which the liver becomes scarred, forms fibrous tissue, and begins to change its anatomy and functioning. Blood fails to flow through it properly, and major complications follow. Cirrhosis is the ninth most frequent cause of death in the United States, accounting for 28,000 deaths each year (ADAMHA, 1987). Alcohol can also depress heart functioning and damage heart muscle fibers and over time may lead to heart failure, irregularities of functioning, or blood clots.

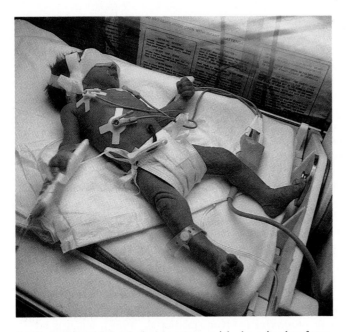

A woman who drinks during pregnancy risks harming her fetus. More than 50,000 babies are born with alcohol-related problems in the United States each year. A fourth of these babies suffer from *fetal alcohol syndrome:* mental retardation, hyperactivity, head and face deformities, heart defects and other organ malfunctions, and retarded growth. Ingestion of cocaine, heroin, and certain other drugs during pregnancy may also severely affect the psychological and physical development of babies.

Chronic excessive drinking also poses major problems in nutrition. Alcohol is high in calories, but because it has virtually no food value—no vitamins, minerals, fats, proteins, or usable carbohydrates—its calories are often described as "empty." They satiate people, lower their desire for other foods, and lead them to eat less than they should. As a result, chronic drinkers are likely to become malnourished, their bodies weak, tired, and highly vulnerable to disease.

The vitamin and mineral deficiencies of alcoholics may also cause certain organic mental disorders. An alcohol-related deficiency of vitamin B (thiamine), for example, may cause **Wernicke's encephalopathy,** a potentially fatal neurological disease characterized by confusion, excitement, delirium, double vision, and other eye-movement abnormalities. Untreated, Wernicke's encephalopathy may on occasion develop into **Korsakoff's syndrome** (also called *alcohol amnestic disorder*), a disorder marked by extreme confusion, memory impairment, and other neurological symptoms. These people cannot remember the past or learn new information, and may make up for their memory losses by *confabulating*—spontaneously reciting made-up events to fill in the gaps.

## Sedative-Hypnotic Drugs

Sedative-hypnotic drugs produce feelings of relaxation and drowsiness. At relatively low dosages, they have a calming or "sedative" effect. At higher ones, they are sleep inducers—or "hypnotics." The two most widely used sedative-hypnotics are antianxiety drugs and barbiturates.

**Antianxiety Drugs**   As we saw in Chapter 6, *benzodiazepines,* the antianxiety drugs discovered in the 1950s, are now the most popular sedative-hypnotic drugs. These drugs, which include Valium, Xanax, Halcion, and Librium, can relieve anxiety without making people as drowsy as other kinds of sedative-hypnotics. They have less impact on the brain's respiratory center than barbiturates, so they involve less risk of depressed respiratory functioning and death as a result of an overdose.

When benzodiazepines first emerged, they seemed so safe and effective that physicians prescribed them quite readily, and their use proliferated in our society. It became easy to get prescriptions for benzodiazepines or to obtain them illegally; it was therefore easy to take them in high dosages (APA, 1987). This widespread and heavy use showed clinicians that the drugs can, in fact, cause intoxication in high dosages and lead to a pattern of abuse or dependence. It is now estimated that more than 1 percent of the adult population in the United States will abuse or be dependent on antianxiety drugs at some point in their lives (APA, 1987).

**Barbiturates**   First discovered in Germany more than 100 years ago, barbiturates were widely prescribed by physicians throughout the first half of this century to combat anxiety and to help people sleep (Cooper, 1977). Although the emergence of benzodiazepines has reduced the use of these drugs in recent years, some physicians still prescribe them, especially for sleep problems. Barbiturates can indeed be helpful for tension and insomnia, but clinicians have become aware that there are also many dangers involved in their use, not the least of which is their potential for abuse and dependence. Disproportionate use of barbiturates among middle-aged women in our society has made them the chief victims of this problem. In addition, approximately 5,000 deaths per year are caused by accidental or suicidal overdoses of the drug. A number of other sedative-hypnotic drugs, including *methaqualone* (trade name Quaalude), act upon the brain in barbituratelike ways and can lead to similar forms of abuse or dependence.

Barbiturates are usually taken in pill or capsule form. In low doses, like benzodiazepines, they reduce the person's level of excitement by increasing the synaptic activity of the inhibitory neurotransmitter GABA (see pp. 200–201, but apparently they do so through different biological channels than benzodiazepines (Vellucci, 1989). At higher doses, barbiturates depress the firing of neurons that bring messages into the *reticular formation*. Since the reticular formation is the body's arousal center and responsible for keeping people awake and alert, the person gets sleepy. At still higher doses, barbiturates depress spinal reflexes and muscles, and are often used as a surgical anesthetic. If a barbiturate dose reaches too high a level, the resulting respiratory failure and low blood pressure can lead to coma and even death.

Barbiturates are actually more similar to alcohol than to benzodiazepines in their action on the brain and the rest of the body. In fact, before the development of barbiturates, alcohol and its derivatives were the most widely used sedative-hypnotic drugs. People can get intoxicated from high dosages of barbiturates, just as they do from alcohol. They become increasingly impulsive, talkative, and in some cases irritable. Their judgment declines and their moods swing rapidly. Coordination is affected, speech is slurred, and attention and memory are impaired.

Even in cases in which physicians prescribe barbiturates for their hypnotic effects, patients soon discover their sedative qualities and may start taking the drug to help them cope with daily problems rather than to help them sleep. Repeated usage of this kind can quickly lead to a pattern of barbiturate abuse. A person may feel unable to stop or reduce the use of barbiturates and may spend much of the day intoxicated. Social and occupational functioning may be disrupted by quarrels, alienation, and poor job performance, all stemming from the effects of the drug.

Barbiturate abuse can further lead to dependence. Tolerance for the drugs increases very rapidly in people who overuse them; increasing amounts become necessary to calm those people down or put them to sleep. Moreover, abstaining from the drug may cause withdrawal symptoms that are similar to those seen in alcoholism: nausea, vomiting, weakness, malaise, and feelings of anxiety and depression. In extreme cases the withdrawal reaction may resemble delirium tremens (here called *barbiturate withdrawal delirium*). Barbiturate withdrawal is one of the most dangerous forms of drug withdrawal, as some barbiturate addicts experience convulsions when they abstain from the drug.

One of the great dangers of barbiturate dependence is that the lethal dose of the drug remains the same even while the body is building up a tolerance for its other effects (Gold, 1986). In a common and tragic scenario, once the initial barbiturate dosage prescribed by a physi-

cian stops working, a person decides independently to keep increasing the dose every few weeks. Eventually the person ingests a dose that may very well prove fatal.

## Opioids

Opioids include opium and the drugs derived from it, such as heroin, morphine, and codeine. A natural substance from the sap of the opium poppy seed, *opium* itself has been in use for thousands of years. In the past it was used widely in the treatment of medical disorders because of its ability to reduce both physical and emotional pain. Physicians eventually discovered, however, that the drug was physically addictive.

In 1804, a new substance—*morphine*—was derived from opium by the German chemist Frederic Serturner. It, too, was an effective pain reliever, even more effective than opium. In addition, morphine made people quiet and helped put them to sleep (thus its name, derived from Morpheus, the Greek god of sleep). Believing that morphine was free of opium's addictive properties, physicians began to use it widely soon after its discovery. In the United States its use accelerated during the Civil War, when many wounded soldiers received morphine injections. Although the drug helped alleviate their pain, it soon became clear that repeated administrations could also lead to addiction. In fact, morphine addiction became known as "soldiers' disease."

Near the end of the 19th century, scientists were trying to derive a nonaddictive pain reliever from morphine by removing its addictive components and retaining the

The more things change, the more they stay the same. Opium users used to get high at opium dens, such as this one in New York City's Chinatown, photographed in 1926. Today many crack users gather at "crack houses" to drug themselves into near oblivion.

pain-relieving ones. In 1898 morphine was converted into a new pain reliever — *heroin* — that was believed to achieve this goal. In fact, for several years heroin was viewed as a wonder drug. It was used as a cough medicine and for other medicinal purposes and to relieve the discomforts of morphine withdrawal. Eventually physicians recognized that heroin itself is extremely addictive, and in fact leads to more rapid tolerance than the other opioids. By 1917 the U.S. Congress concluded that all drugs derived from opium were addictive and passed a law making opioids illegal except for medical purposes.

New derivatives of opium have been discovered, and synthetic (laboratory-blended) opioids such as methadone have also been developed. These various opioid drugs are known collectively as *narcotics.* Each has its own potency, speed of action, and tolerance level. Morphine and codeine have become the primary medical narcotics, usually prescribed to relieve pain. Heroin has remained illegal in the United States under all circumstances.

Narcotics may be smoked, inhaled ("snorted"), injected by needle just beneath the skin ("skin popped"), or injected directly into the bloodstream ("mainlined"). An injection quickly brings on a *rush*—a spasm of warmth and ecstasy that is sometimes compared with a sexual orgasm. This spasm is short-lived and is followed by several hours of a pleasant feeling called a *high* or *nod.* During a high, the drug user feels relaxed and euphoric. Worries, tensions, and pains subside. The person becomes lethargic and unconcerned about food, sex, or other bodily needs.

Heroin and other opioids create these effects by depressing the central nervous system, particularly the centers that generate emotion. The drugs are received at brain receptor sites that ordinarily receive *endorphins*—neurotransmitters that help relieve pain and reduce emotional tension (Snyder, 1991, 1986; Trujillo & Akil, 1991). When opioids are received by neurons at these receptor sites, the neurons fire and produce pleasurable and calming feelings just as they would if they were receiving endorphins. In addition to pain relief, sedation, and mood changes, opioids cause nausea, constriction of the pupils of the eyes ("pinpoint pupils"), and constipation, bodily reactions that can also be brought about by the release of endorphins in the brain.

**Heroin Abuse and Dependence**   It takes only a few weeks of repeated heroin use for people to be caught in a pattern of abuse: the drug becomes the center of their lives, and social and occupational functioning deteriorates significantly. Most abusers also develop a dependence on heroin, quickly building up a tolerance for it

and experiencing withdrawal symptoms when they abstain.

Addicted individuals start to experience withdrawal symptoms right after the several-hour high. They begin to feel anxious and restless, and have a profound craving for heroin. After a few more hours, they start to perspire profusely, breathe more rapidly, and develop the symptoms of a head cold. These withdrawal symptoms become progressively more serious for approximately two or three days. They may be accompanied by severe twitching, constant aches, painful gastrointestinal and muscle cramps, fever, acute vomiting and diarrhea, loss of appetite, elevated blood pressure, dehydration, and weight loss of up to 15 pounds.

Withdrawal distress usually peaks by the third day, then gradually subsides and disappears by the eighth day. A person in withdrawal can either wait the symptoms out (an extremely difficult and unpleasant ordeal) or end withdrawal by taking more heroin. Heroin taken at any time during withdrawal will quickly restore a feeling of physical and emotional well-being.

The character of drug taking eventually changes for people dependent on heroin. They soon need the drug just to maintain normal functioning and to avoid the distress of withdrawal, and they must continually increase their doses in order to achieve that state. The temporary high becomes less intense and less important (Julien, 1985). What started as a search for pleasure develops into a fight for survival.

Because they must be on a steady diet of heroin, addicts soon organize their lives around plans for getting their next dose. The habit can cost more than $200 a day, because heroin is available only through illegal channels, and many addicts turn to criminal activities, such as theft and prostitution, to support their "habit." It has been estimated that heroin addicts commit as many as 50 million crimes in the United States each year (Ball et al., 1982).

**Dangers of Heroin**   The most direct danger of heroin abuse is an overdose. An overdose of this drug depresses the respiratory center in the brain, virtually paralyzing it and in many cases causing death. Death is particularly likely during sleep, when a person is unable to fight the effect by consciously working at breathing. People who resume the use of heroin after having abstained for a period of time run a special risk of overdosing. They often make the fatal mistake of taking the dosage they used when they were last addicted. Because their bodies have been free of heroin for some time, however, they can no longer tolerate this high level. Between 1 and 2 percent of heroin addicts die under the drug's influence, usually from an overdose (APA, 1987; DuPont, 1971).

Opioids may be taken by mouth, inhaled (snorted), injected just beneath the surface of the skin, or, as here, injected intravenously. Those who share needles to inject themselves run the risk of developing AIDS or hepatitis; those using unsterile equipment may develop skin abscesses.

Users run risks aside from the effects of the drug itself. Often profit-minded pushers mix heroin with cheaper drugs, such as barbiturates, LSD, or local anesthetics, or even deadly substances such as cyanide and battery acid. Addicts who use dirty needles and other unsterile equipment when they inject heroin are vulnerable to AIDS, hepatitis, and skin abscesses (O'Rourke, 1990; NIDA, 1987). The drug *quinine* is often added to heroin to counteract the dangers of infection. While this does help to some extent, an excess of quinine may itself cause flooding of the lungs and death. Many deaths attributed to heroin may actually have been caused by a quinine-induced flooding of the lungs.

Surveys suggest that as many as 1 percent of the adult population become addicted to heroin or other opioids at some time in their lives (APA, 1987). The number of opioid addicts took its sharpest turn upward during the 1960s and 1970s, and by the late 1970s it had reached more than half a million. Although recent studies suggest a decline during the 1980s, there are still more than 400,000 addicts in the United States (Gold, 1986). Of course, such statistics may be understated, given the reluctance of many people to admit to an illegal activity (Maurer & Vogel, 1978).

## STIMULANTS

*Stimulants* are substances that act to increase the activity of the central nervous system, resulting in increased blood pressure and heart rate and in intensified behavioral activity, thought processes, and alertness. Two of the best-known and most troublesome stimulants are cocaine and amphetamines. The effects of these substances on the brain are virtually indistinguishable (Snyder, 1986). When users report different effects from the two, it is because they have ingested different amounts of the drugs. Inhaled cocaine, for example, acts more quickly than an amphetamine taken in pill form.

## Cocaine

*Cocaine*—the central active ingredient of the coca plant, found in South America—is the most powerful natural stimulant now known. The drug was first isolated from the plant in 1865. South American natives, however, have chewed the leaves of the plant since prehistoric times for the energy and alertness the drug content provides. Processed cocaine *(hydrochloride powder)* is an odorless, white, fluffy powder. For recreational use, it is most often inhaled ("snorted") so that it is absorbed through the mucous membrane of the nose. Some users prefer the more powerful effects of injecting cocaine intravenously or smoking cocaine "base" in a pipe or cigarette.

Sherlock Holmes took his bottle from the corner of the mantelpiece, and his hypodermic syringe from its neat morocco case. With his long white nervous fingers, he adjusted the delicate needle and rolled back his left shirtcuff. For some little time his eyes rested thoughtfully upon the sinewy forearm and wrist, all dotted and scarred with innumerable puncture-marks. Finally, he thrust the sharp point home, pressed down the tiny piston, and sank back into the velvet-lined armchair with a long sigh of satisfaction.

Three times a day for many months I had witnessed this performance, but custom had not reconciled my mind to it. . . .

"Which is it today," I asked, "Morphine or cocaine?"

He raised his eyes languidly from the old black-letter volume which he had opened.

"It is cocaine," he said, "a seven-per-cent solution. Would you care to try it?"

"No, indeed," I answered brusquely. "My constitution has not got over the Afghan campaign yet. I cannot afford to throw any extra strain upon it."

He smiled at my vehemence. "Perhaps you are right, Watson," he said. "I suppose that its influence is physically a bad one. I find it, however, so transcendently stimulating and clarifying to the mind that its secondary action is a matter of small moment."

"But consider!" I said earnestly. "Count the cost! Your brain may, as you say, be roused and excited, but it is a pathological and morbid process which involves increased tissue-change and . . . a permanent weakness. You know, too, what a black reaction comes upon you. Surely, the game is hardly worth the candle."

(Doyle, 1938, pp. 91–92)

For years the prevailing opinion of cocaine was that aside from causing temporary intoxication and occasional psychosis, it posed few significant problems (see Box 13-2). Like Sherlock Holmes, many people believed that the benefits outweighed the costs. Only in recent years have researchers recognized its potential for harm and developed a clearer understanding of how cocaine produces its effects. This insight was triggered by a dramatic increase in the drug's popularity and in problems related to its use. In the early 1960s an estimated 10,000 persons in the United States had tried cocaine; in the early

1970s the number was 100,000; and by the early 1980s it was 15 million. Today approximately 24 million people in the United States have tried cocaine, including 30 percent of all college students (Allen, 1985; NIDA, 1985). Close to 6 million people are currently using cocaine at least once a month — 390,000 teenagers, 2.5 million young adults, and 2.9 million persons over 25 years of age (NIDA, 1985).

Cocaine brings on a euphoric rush of well-being and confidence. Given a high enough dose, this rush can be almost orgasmic, like that produced by heroin. Initially cocaine stimulates the higher centers of the central nervous system, making its users feel excited, energetic, talkative, and even euphoric. As more is taken, it also stimulates other centers of the CNS, producing a faster

---

══════ BOX 13-2 ══════

# "A Big Wild Man Who Has Cocaine in His Body"

**S**igmund Freud's contributions to the understanding and treatment of mental disorders are second to none. Even his detractors acknowledge his brilliance, his wisdom, and his cleverness. Yet Freud, like so many people before and after him, was played for a fool by a drug — in his case, cocaine. Freud fell into the familiar trap of wishful thinking, prematurely concluding that cocaine was free of danger, largely because he enjoyed it and wanted it to be safe. His colossal misjudgment almost brought down his career before it had really begun.

In 1884 Freud's reputation as an effective neurologist and skillful researcher of neuroanatomy was growing. Having read about the stimulating effects of coca leaves on Peruvian Indians and about the isolation of pure cocaine, he wondered whether the substance might be an effective treatment for nervous exhaustion, and he proceeded to ingest it himself. He quickly experienced a powerful reaction — euphoria, energy, alertness,

strength, and disinterest in food. He seemed more than a little smitten with cocaine when he wrote to his fiancée, "Woe to you my princess when I come. I will kiss you quite red and feed you until you are plump. And if you are forward, you shall see who is stronger, a gentle little girl who doesn't eat enough or a big wild man who has cocaine in his body" (Freud, 1885).

Freud proceeded to study the effects of cocaine on numerous subjects and soon proclaimed to the medical community of Western Europe:

Cocaine brings about an exhilaration and lasting euphoria. . . . You perceive an increase of self-control and possess more vitality and capacity for work. . . . In other words, you are simply normal, and it is soon hard to believe that you are under the influence of any drug. . . . Long intensive mental or physical work is performed without any fatigue. . . . This result is enjoyed without any of the unpleasant after effects that follow exhilaration brought about by alcohol.

(Freud, 1885)

Freud's professional influence grew, as did the use of cocaine by patients with anxiety or depression.

A rude awakening occurred when Freud recommended to a close friend, Erst Fleischl von Marxow, that he take cocaine to relieve him of his addiction to morphine. Fleischl injected himself with increasingly higher doses of cocaine until finally he became a victim of cocaine psychosis.

The plight of his friend was more than a personal tragedy for Freud. Soon reports of cocaine psychosis from all over Europe led to severe criticism of Freud by the continent's most eminent medical authorities and dealt a heavy blow to Freud's reputation. It was not at all clear that he would be able to continue his medical career. But then he became interested in hypnosis and began to develop the theories and techniques of psychoanalysis, and this time his provocative and daring ideas served him and the clinical field very well indeed.

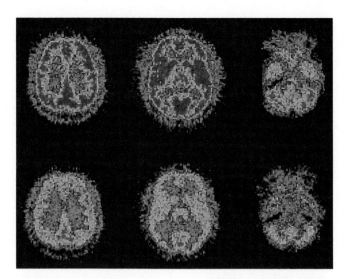

Although cocaine stimulates the central nervous system, it decreases activity in some areas of the brain. The PET scans of a cocaine user (bottom row) reveal a drop in glucose metabolism—indicated by the color blue—in some brain regions. PET scans of a nonuser (top row) reveal a high level of activity—indicated by the color red—in the same areas.

pulse, higher blood pressure, faster and deeper breathing, and further arousal and wakefulness. Cocaine apparently produces these effects by stimulating the release of the neurotransmitters dopamine and norepinephrine from neurons throughout the brain; supplies of these neurotransmitters at receiving neurons become excessive and the CNS is overstimulated (Kleber & Gawin, 1987; Olds & Forbes, 1981; Gallistel et al., 1981).

If a very high dose of cocaine is taken, the stimulation of the CNS will result in poor muscle coordination, grandiosity of manner, declining judgment, and a changeable temper—all symptoms of *cocaine intoxication.* People in a severe state of intoxication may also become confused, anxious, rambling, and incoherent. Some people experience hallucinations and delusions, a condition known as *cocaine psychosis* (Spotts & Shontz, 1983).

*A young man described how, after freebasing, he went to* his closet to get his clothes, but his suit asked him, "What do you want?" Afraid, he walked toward the door, which told him, "Get back!" Retreating, he then heard the sofa say, "If you sit on me, I'll kick your ass." With a sense of impending doom, intense anxiety, and momentary panic, the young man ran to the hospital where he received help.

*(Allen, 1985, pp. 19–20)*

As the symptoms caused by cocaine subside, the user will often experience a depressionlike letdown. The feeling of depression—popularly called "crashing"—may be accompanied by headaches, dizziness, and fainting. For occasional users, the effects of cocaine usually disappear within 24 hours. Those who have taken an excessive dose, however, may sink into stupor, deep sleep, or coma.

**Cocaine Abuse and Dependence** An extended period of cocaine use may lead to a pattern of abuse in which the person feels unable to stop using cocaine, is intoxicated throughout the day, and functions poorly in social and occupational spheres. Dependence on cocaine may also develop: more cocaine is needed to achieve the desired effects, and abstinence results in deep depression, intense fatigue or deep sleep, irritability, tremulousness, and anxiety (Washton, 1987). These withdrawal symptoms may last for weeks or even months.

In the past, cocaine abuse and dependence were limited by the high cost of processed cocaine and by the fact that it was usually snorted—a means of ingestion that has less powerful effects than injection (Spotts & Shontz, 1983). Since 1984, however, newer, more powerful, and sometimes cheaper forms of cocaine have gained favor among users and have produced an enormous increase in abuse and dependence (APA, 1987; Manschreck, 1985). Currently one user in five falls into a pattern of abuse or dependence. Many people now use the technique of *free-basing,* in which the pure cocaine basic alkaloid is chemically separated or "freed" from processed cocaine, vaporized by heat from a flame, and inhaled with a pipe (Cohen, 1980). And millions more use *crack,* a powerful ready-to-smoke free-base cocaine

Crack, a powerful form of free-base cocaine, is produced by boiling cocaine down into crystalline balls and is smoked with a special crack pipe.

(Cohen, 1985). Crack is produced by boiling cocaine down into crystalline balls, like baking soda, packaged for consumers, and smoked with a special crack pipe. This form of cocaine makes a crackling sound when it is smoked, hence the name. Crack is sold in small quantities at a typical cost of between $10 and $20. Some cities have seen veritable crack epidemics among people who previously could not have afforded cocaine. As Figure

13-2 indicates, approximately 4 percent of high school seniors report using crack and other forms of cocaine to some extent (NIDA, 1987).

**Dangers of Cocaine**  Cocaine poses serious dangers for users. As we have already noted, it may cause users to become irritable, depressed, paranoid, and unable to control their emotions. In addition, cocaine turns out to be highly dangerous to one's physical well-being. Its widespread use in increasingly powerful forms caused the number of cocaine-related emergency-room incidents in the United States to more than quadruple between 1982 and 1986, from 4,243 cases to 18,202 cases. During the same period, medical examiners' reports of cocaine-related deaths increased fivefold, from 217 to 1,080 (NIDA, 1986).

The most obvious danger of cocaine use comes from overdosage (Allen, 1985). Excessive doses have a strong effect on the respiratory center of the brain, at first stimulating it and then depressing it, possibly to the point of respiratory failure and death. Cocaine also stimulates the brain center that controls body temperature: while the drug raises a person's temperature, it may also constrict the blood vessels in the skin — and throughout the rest of the body — making it impossible for the person to perspire. The dangerously high body temperature that results can lead to death.

Cocaine can also create significant, even fatal, heart problems. The heart, beating rapidly and irregularly under the drug's influence, must also work harder to pump blood through cocaine-constricted blood vessels. For some people, this strain on the heart causes a brain seizure that brings breathing or heart functioning to a sudden halt. These effects may be more common in people who have taken a high dose of cocaine and who have a history of cocaine abuse, but they also occur in casual cocaine users (Gold, 1987). Such was the case with Len Bias, the well-known college basketball player who died of these effects a few years back, apparently after ingesting only a moderate amount of cocaine.

## Amphetamines

The amphetamines are stimulant drugs that are manufactured in the laboratory. Some common ones are amphetamine (Benzedrine), dextroamphetamine (Dexedrine), and methamphetamine (Methedrine). First synthesized by the chemist Gordon Alles in the 1930s for use in the treatment of asthma, these drugs soon became popular among people trying to lose weight; athletes seeking an extra burst of energy; soldiers, truck drivers, and pilots trying to stay awake; and students

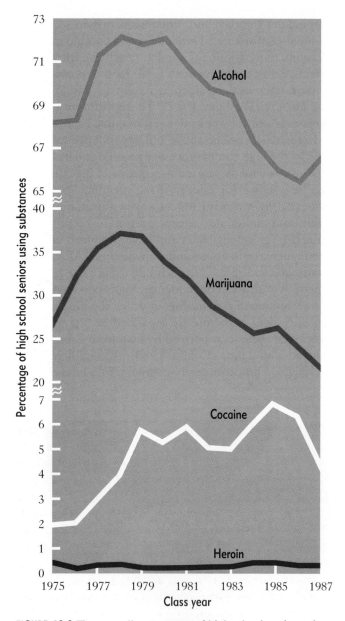

**FIGURE 13-2** The overall percentage of high school seniors who admitted to using drugs illicitly at least once within 30 days of being surveyed rose in the 1970s and then declined in the 1980s. The rate of marijuana use has been falling ever since it peaked in 1978, cocaine use has been falling since 1985, alcohol use has started to rise again recently, and heroin use has remained relatively stable. *(Adapted from Jaffe, 1989, p. 645.)*

studying for exams throughout the night. They are still frequently used in these ways (Johnson et al., 1982) — now, however, with significantly less approval and help from medical practitioners. The drugs are far too dangerous to be used so casually.

Amphetamines are most often taken in pill or capsule form, although some people inject the drug intravenously for a quicker, more powerful impact. Others ingest the drug in such forms as "ice" and "crank," counterparts of free-basing cocaine and crack, respectively.

Like cocaine, amphetamines increase energy and alertness and reduce appetite in low doses, produce intoxication and psychosis in high doses, and cause an experience of crashing as they leave the person's body. Also like cocaine, amphetamines stimulate the CNS by increasing the release of the neurotransmitters dopamine and norepinephrine from neurons throughout the brain. Because of their chemical resemblance to these neurotransmitters, amphetamine molecules are able to enter the nerve endings where the neurotransmitters are stored and push them out of their storage sites and across the synaptic space to stimulate the firing of nearby neurons (Bhakthavatsalam et al., 1985).

Tolerance to amphetamines builds so quickly that it is easy to become ensnared in a pattern of amphetamine dependence. People who start using amphetamines to reduce their appetite and weight may soon find they are as hungry as ever, and increase their amphetamine dosage in response. Athletes who initially use amphetamines to increase their energy may find before long that larger and larger amounts of the drug are needed. As their tolerance of amphetamines increases, they are also pushed toward a greater expenditure of energy than their bodies can afford, and so subject themselves to more injuries and illness. So-called speed freaks who pop pills all day for days at a time have built a tolerance so high that they now take as much as 200 times their initial amphetamine dosage. When chronic abusers stop taking amphetamines, they enter the state of deep depression and extended sleep that also characterizes withdrawal from cocaine.

## HALLUCINOGENS

*Hallucinogens* are substances that cause changes primarily in sensory perception. They may differ from one another both structurally and in the other effects they produce. They include so-called *psychedelic drugs* such as LSD, powerful drugs whose profound perceptual changes may extend to hallucinations, and *cannabis drugs,* a group of drugs produced from varieties of the hemp plant *Cannabis sativa,* that cause a mixture of hallucinogenic, depressant, and stimulant effects.

## Psychedelic Drugs

Our brain receives and interprets sensations of sight, sound, smell, taste, and touch that combine to give us the information we need about the world around us. If these sensations or their processing become disturbed, our perceptions of the world can be distorted. Psychedelics are chemical substances that affect these sensory experiences, producing sensations so novel that they are sometimes called "trips." The trips may be exciting or frightening, enhancing or dangerous, depending on how a person's mind interacts with the psychedelics. This interaction may vary greatly from person to person, or even for one person at different times.

The psychedelic drugs include LSD (lysergic acid diethylamide), mescaline, psilocybin, MDMA ("ecstasy"), DOM, DMT, morning-glory seeds, bufotenine, and PCP. Many of these substances come from plants or animals; others are laboratory-produced rearrangements of natural psychedelics.

*LSD* is one of the most famous and most powerful hallucinogens. It was derived by the Swiss chemist Albert Hoffman in 1938 from a group of naturally occurring drugs called *ergot alkaloids.* For years LSD remained in limited use while researchers struggled to understand its action and medicinal value. Then during the 1960s, a decade of social rebellion and experimentation, it found a home. Millions of persons turned to the drug as a means of expanding their experience.

Within two hours of being swallowed, LSD brings on a state of *hallucinogenic hallucinosis,* a general intensification of perceptions, particularly visual perceptions. People may focus on minute details of objects — pores of the skin, for example, or individual blades of grass. Colors may seem enhanced or take on a shade of purple. Objects may seem distorted, and inanimate objects may appear to move, breathe, or change shape. A person under the influence of LSD may see people, objects, or geometric forms that are not actually present.

Hallucinations involving the other senses may include hearing sounds more clearly, often with new or previously undetected qualities, and feeling tingling or numbness in the arms or legs or altered sensations of hot and cold. Some people have been badly burned after touching flames that felt cool to them under the influence of LSD. LSD may also cause the senses to cross, an effect called *synesthesia.* A loud noise may be experienced as visible fluctuations in the air. Colors may be "heard" or "felt."

LSD can also cause emotional changes, ranging from euphoria to anxiety or depression. The perception of time may slow down dramatically. Long-forgotten thoughts and feelings may resurface. Physical symptoms can include dilation of the pupils, sweating, palpitations, blurred vision, tremors, and loss of coordination. All these effects take place while the user is fully awake and alert. The overall experience can seem either mystical or horrifying (Moody, 1969). Whether pleasant or frightening, the immediate effects wear off in about 6 hours.

It seems that LSD produces these symptoms by interfering with neurons that use the neurotransmitter serotonin (Jacobs, 1984; Aghajanian, 1984). These neurons are ordinarily involved in the brain's transmission of visual information and (as we observed in Chapter 8) emotional experiences; thus LSD's interference produces a range of visual and emotional symptoms. Ordinarily when serotonin-containing neurons are activated, they release serotonin, whose action helps the brain to filter incoming sensory messages. Without the action of serotonin, the brain would be flooded by perceptual and emotional input — particularly visual input — and people would experience more sensations, see more details, distort visual images, and even see things not actually there. This is the very effect created by LSD, which apparently binds to the surface of serotonin-containing neurons and essentially prevents them from releasing serotonin (Jacobs, 1984).

Although tolerance for LSD is minimal and no withdrawal symptoms occur when one stops the drug, it poses distinct dangers for both one-time and long-term users (Hollister, 1991, 1984). First, LSD is so remarkably potent that any dosage, no matter how small, is likely to elicit powerful perceptual, emotional, and behavioral reactions. Sometimes these powerful reactions to LSD are extremely unpleasant, an experience described in the drug vernacular as a "bad trip":

> *A 21-year-old woman was admitted to the hospital along* with her lover. He had had a number of LSD experiences and had convinced her to take it to make her less constrained sexually. About half an hour after ingestion of approximately 200 microgm., she noticed that the bricks in the wall began to go in and out and that light affected her strangely. She became frightened when she realized that she was unable to distinguish her body from the chair she was sitting on or from her lover's body. Her fear became more marked after she thought that she would not get back into herself. At the time of admission she was hyperactive and laughed inappropriately. Stream of talk was illogical and affect labile. Two days later, this reaction had ceased.
>
> *(Frosch et al., 1965)*

Reports of LSD users who injure themselves or commit suicide or murder usually involve a severe panic reaction of this kind.

Another danger is that LSD has an extended impact on some individuals. They may, for example, develop a *hallucinogen delusional disorder* in which they confuse their hallucinations with reality and develop bizarre ideas to support their disturbed perceptions (Bower, 1977). Or they may develop a *hallucinogen mood disorder,* in which they experience extreme guilt, fearfulness, tension, or restlessness. Many fear that they have destroyed their brains and driven themselves crazy, and worry that they will never return to normal.

Finally, about a quarter of LSD users experience lingering effects called *flashbacks* — sensory and emotional changes that recur long after the LSD has left the body (Hollister, 1991, 1984; Wesson & Smith, 1976). Flashbacks may occur as long as several months after the last LSD experience; eventually, however, they become less severe and disappear. Flashbacks are entirely unpredictable. A one-time LSD user may have multiple flashbacks, and a regular user with no history of flashbacks may suddenly start to experience them.

## Cannabis

*Cannabis sativa,* the hemp plant, grows in warm climates throughout the world. Its main active ingredient, *tetra-*

Psychedelic art seemed all-pervasive in the 1960s. Displayed on advertisements, clothing, record albums, and book covers, it tried to convey the kinds of images and sensations produced by psychedelic drugs such as LSD.

*hydrocannabinol (THC),* is found in the resin exuded by its leaves and flowering tops. The drugs produced from the different varieties of hemp are collectively called *cannabis.* The most powerful of them is *hashish;* drugs of intermediate strength include *ganja;* and the weaker ones include the best-known form of cannabis, *marijuana,* a mixture of the crushed leaves and flowering tops. Actually, each of these cannabis drugs is found in various strengths because the potency of a cannabis drug is greatly affected by the climate in which the plant is grown, the way the drug was prepared, and the manner and duration of its storage.

Although cannabis contains several hundred active compounds, THC appears to be the ingredient most responsible for its effects. The greater the THC content, the more powerful the cannabis: hashish contains a high portion, while marijuana's is relatively low.

Cannabis is smoked. At low doses it typically produces feelings of inner joy and relaxation and may lead people to become either contemplative or talkative (Wilson & Maguire, 1985). Some smokers, however, feel anxious, suspicious, apprehensive, or irritated, especially if they have been in a bad mood or are smoking in an upsetting environment. Many smokers report experiencing sharper perceptions and great preoccupation with the intensified sounds and sights around them. Time seems to slow down, and distances and sizes seem greater than they actually are. This overall state of *cannabis intoxication* is known more commonly as a "high."

The physical changes induced by cannabis include reddening of the eyes (the blood vessels in the conjunctiva become engorged), a faster heartbeat, an increase in appetite, dryness in the mouth, dizziness, and nausea. Some people become drowsy and may even fall asleep.

In high doses, cannabis produces visual distortions, alterations of body image, and hallucinations. Smokers may become confused or impulsive; some panic and fear that they are losing their minds. Some smokers develop delusions in which they believe others are trying to hurt them *(cannabis delusional disorder).* Most of the effects of cannabis last for three to six hours. The changes in mood, however, may continue for a longer time (Chait et al., 1985).

**Marijuana Abuse and Dependence** Until the early 1970s, the use of the weak form of cannabis, marijuana, rarely led to a pattern of abuse or dependence. Most people who used the substance seemed able to do so recreationally without letting it become the center of their lives. Since then the picture has changed. Many people, including large numbers of high school students, are now caught in a pattern of marijuana abuse — getting high on marijuana every day and finding their social and occupational or academic lives significantly affected by their heavy usage. Many chronic users also develop a tolerance for marijuana (Comptom, Dewey, & Martin, 1990), and some experience flulike withdrawal symptoms when they try to stop smoking, including hot flashes, loss of appetite, runny nose, sweating, diarrhea, and hiccups (Jones, 1977).

Why have patterns of marijuana abuse and dependence emerged in the last two decades? Mainly because the drug has changed. The marijuana available in the United States today is two to ten times as powerful as that used in the early 1970s. The THC content of today's marijuana is as much as 10 to 15 percent, compared to 1 to 5 percent in the late 1960s (APA, 1987). Apparently marijuana is now cultivated in locations — both foreign and domestic — whose hot and dry climates produce higher THC content (Weisheit, 1990).

**Dangers of Marijuana** As the potency and use of marijuana have increased, researchers have discovered that smoking this substance may pose significant problems and dangers. It occasionally elicits panic reactions similar to the ones caused by psychedelics. People with emotional problems are thought to be more vulnerable to such reactions, but others may also experience them. Typically the panic reaction ends in 3 to 6 hours, along with marijuana's other effects.

Earlier research suggested that marijuana did not interfere with automobile driving as much as alcohol did (Crancer et al., 1969) and that drivers were able to compensate for their perceptual changes through concentration and increased caution (Crancer et al., 1969). It seems, however, that marijuana's impact on driving has increased along with its potency. Studies have implicated marijuana in numerous automobile accidents (Marijuana Research Findings, 1980). Apparently cannabis intoxication interferes with performance of the complex sensorimotor tasks involved in driving.

Marijuana also appears to interfere with cognitive functioning (Hooker & Jones, 1987). People on a marijuana high often fail to remember information, especially recently acquired information, no matter how hard they try to concentrate. Clearly, heavy marijuana smokers are operating at a considerable disadvantage at school and in the workplace.

Evidence has mounted that chronic marijuana smoking may lead to a number of long-term problems. It may, for example, contribute to lung disease. Studies have indicated that marijuana smoking reduces one's ability to expel air from the lungs even more than tobacco smoking does. One marijuana cigarette is equivalent to

16 tobacco cigarettes in this regard (Tashkin et al., 1978). In addition, research indicates that marijuana smoke contains significantly more tar and benzopyrene than tobacco smoke. Both of these substances have been linked to cancer.

Another concern is the effect of chronic marijuana smoking on human reproduction. Although early studies found reductions in the male hormone testosterone among marijuana smokers, the reductions were very small and researchers concluded at that time that chronic marijuana use had no effect on reproduction (Kolodny, 1974). Studies since the late 1970s, however, have discovered lower sperm counts and reduced spermatozoa activity in men who are chronic smokers of marijuana, and irregular and abnormal ovulation has been found among women (Hembree et al., 1979).

Finally, research has suggested that THC has a mild and temporary suppressive effect on the functioning of the immune system (Ray, 1983). Although this suppression is not clinically significant and marijuana smokers have not displayed higher rates of infection, some researchers suspect that the effect may have longer-term implications.

Recent efforts to educate the public about the changing nature and impact of regular marijuana use appear to be paying off: 4 percent of today's high school seniors smoke marijuana on a daily basis, down from 11 percent in 1978 (NIDA, 1987). Moreover, a survey in the late 1980s found that 71 percent of high school seniors believed that regular marijuana smoking posed a serious risk, more than double the percentage in 1978 (NIDA, 1987)—but probably fewer than held this belief 50 years earlier (see Box 13-3). Still other surveys show both junior high and senior high school students reporting little peer pressure to smoke marijuana (Shepperd, Wright, & Goodstadt, 1985; Kohn et al., 1985).

## COMBINATIONS OF SUBSTANCES

Because people often take more than one drug at a time, researchers have had to study the ways in which drugs interact with one another. Two important concepts have emerged from this work: cross-tolerance and synergistic effects.

### Cross-tolerance

Sometimes two or more drugs are so similar in their actions on the brain and the rest of the body that as people build up a tolerance for one drug, they are simultaneously developing a tolerance for the others, even if they have never taken them. When users display such *cross-tolerance,* they can reduce the symptoms of withdrawal from one drug by taking one of the others. Because alcohol and antianxiety drugs are cross-tolerant, for example, it is sometimes possible to alleviate the alcohol withdrawal reaction of delirium tremens by administering antianxiety drugs, along with vitamins and electrolytes.

### Synergistic Effects

When different drugs are in the body at the same time, they may potentiate, or enhance, each other's effects. The combined impact, called a *synergistic effect,* is often greater than the sum of the effects of each drug taken alone: a small dose of one drug mixed with a small dose of another can produce an enormous change in body chemistry.

One kind of synergistic effect occurs when two or more drugs have *similar actions.* For instance, alcohol, antianxiety drugs, barbiturates, and opioids—all depressants of the central nervous system—may produce a severe depression of the CNS when mixed (Miller & Gold, 1990). Combining them, even in small doses, can lead to extreme intoxication, coma, or even death.

Many tragedies have been caused by synergistic effects of this kind. A young man may drink just a few alcoholic beverages at a party, for example, and shortly afterward take a normal dose of barbiturates to help him fall asleep. He believes he has acted with restraint and good judgment—yet he may never wake up.

A different kind of synergistic effect results when drugs have *opposite (antagonistic) actions.* Stimulant drugs, for example, interfere with the liver's usual disposal of barbiturates and alcohol. Thus people who combine barbiturates or alcohol with cocaine or amphetamines may build up toxic, even lethal, levels of the depressant drugs in their systems. Students who take amphetamines to help them study late into the night and then take barbiturates to help them fall asleep are unwittingly placing themselves in serious danger.

### Polydrug Use

Each year tens of thousands of people are admitted to hospitals with a multiple-drug emergency, and several thousand of them die (Kosten et al., 1987; Robins & Przybeck, 1985). Sometimes the cause is carelessness or ignorance: a "wired" student who later takes sleeping

= BOX 13-3 =

# Cannabis and Society

For centuries cannabis played a respected role in the field of medicine. It was recommended as a surgical anesthetic by Chinese physicians 2000 years ago and was used in other lands to treat cholera, malaria, coughs, insomnia, and rheumatism. In the mid–19th century, Western European physicians used it to treat neuralgia, menstrual pain, and migraine. Cannabis entered the United States in the early 20th century, mainly in the form of marijuana. The U.S. drug company Parke-Davis became a leading importer of marijuana and distributed it for medical purposes.

The positive view of cannabis began to change quite quickly, however. For one thing, more effective medicines replaced it. As morphine, aspirin, barbiturates, and other drugs were developed, physicians used cannabis less and less. Second, cannabis acquired some notoriety as a recreational drug early in the century, and its illegal distribution became a concern for law enforcement agencies. Authorities associated marijuana with alcohol and other disreputable drugs, assumed it was highly dangerous, and communicated this "fact" to the public. The "killer weed" was outlawed in 1937. The following 1937 magazine report was typical:

> In Los Angeles, Calif., a youth was walking along a downtown street after inhaling a marijuana cigarette. For many addicts, merely a portion of a "reefer" is enough to induce intoxication. Suddenly, for no reason, he decided that someone had threatened to kill him and that his life at that very moment was in danger. Wildly he looked about him. The only person in sight was an aged bootblack. Drug-crazed nerve centers conjured the innocent old shoe-shiner into a destroying monster. Mad with fright, the addict hurried to his room and got a

Marijuana is made from the leaves of the hemp plant *Cannabis sativa*. The plant is an annual herb, reaches a height of between 3 and 15 feet, and is grown in a wide range of altitudes, climates, and soils.

> gun. He killed the old man, and then, later, babbled his grief over what had been wanton, uncontrolled murder. . . .
> That's marijuana!
> *(Anslinger & Cooper, 1937, p. 153)*

Marijuana resurfaced with renewed vigor in the 1960s. It seemed to fit right in with that decade's mood of disillusion, protest, and self-exploration. Young people in particular discovered the pleasures of getting high, and smoking marijuana became a popular form of recreation. Many saw marijuana as a symbol of the government's low credibility: the drug was hardly the killer weed the government claimed it to be, and the harsh legal punishments for smoking it seemed unreasonable.

In the 1970s marijuana use continued to expand throughout the United States. By the end of the decade 16 million people reported using it at least once, 11 percent of the population identified themselves as recent users, and 11 percent of high school seniors said they smoked marijuana every day (NIDA, 1982).

These rates declined considerably during the 1980s. The marijuana that was imported to the United States became more powerful and dangerous than the earlier form and people stopped using it so often and so casually. At the same time, marijuana and other kinds of cannabis returned to their roots, so to speak, and once again found respect as a form of medical treatment.

In the late 1970s and 1980s, cannabis researchers developed precise techniques for measuring and controlling THC content and for extracting pure THC from cannabis. They also developed synthetic analogues of THC. These newly acquired abilities opened the door to a number of new medical applications for cannabis (Ray, 1987). For example, cannabis became helpful in treating glaucoma, a severe eye disease in which fluid from the eyeball is obstructed from flowing properly. Oral THC combats glaucoma by lowering the pressure of fluid in the eye. Cannabis was also found to help patients with asthma, by causing the bronchi to dilate. And because THC helps prevent nausea and vomiting, it gained use among cancer patients whose chemotherapy elicited such reactions (Gunby, 1981). Although cannabis and THC are not yet conventional forms of medical treatment, their therapeutic potential is such that most states in the United States now allow their use in experimental medical treatments.

The comedian John Belushi often made jokes about the use of drugs on *Saturday Night Live*. His polydrug use, particularly his taste for a mixture of cocaine and opioids, eventually proved fatal.

pills may simply be unaware of the synergistic effects created by the combination. Often, however, the person uses a combination of drugs precisely because he or she enjoys the synergistic effects. This kind of multiple drug use, called *polydrug use*, appears to be on the rise — so much so that a condition of *general* drug dependence is becoming as common as dependence on one specific drug (Miller et al., 1990; Weisheit, 1990). The following excerpt from a group therapy session for crack users illustrates this point:

Okay. Now, can you give me a list of all the drugs you've used? Gary?

*Gary:* Pot. Coke. Crack. Mescaline. Acid. Speed. Crystal meth. Smack. Base dust. Sometimes alcohol.

*Dennis:* Alcohol. Pot. Coke. Mescaline. LSD. Amyl nitrate. Speed and Valium.

*Davy:* Coke. Crack. Reefer. Alcohol. Acid. Mescaline. Mushrooms. Ecstasy. Speed. Smack.

*Rich:* Alcohol. Pot. Ludes [Quaaludes]. Valium. Speed. Ups [amphetamines]. Downs [barbiturates]. Acid. Mesc [mescaline]. Crack. Base. Dust. That's about it.

*Carol:* Alcohol. Pot. Cocaine. Mescaline. Valium. Crack.
*(Chatlos, 1987, pp. 30–31)*

Teenagers and young adults seem particularly likely to use drugs in combination (Wright, 1985; Gould et al., 1977). Research suggests that 27 percent of the young adults who currently use marijuana also use cocaine, often at the same time; that 84 percent of the teenagers

who use marijuana also drink alcohol; and that 37 percent of the teenagers who drink alcohol also use marijuana (NIDA, 1985).

Some famous people have been the victims of polydrug use. Elvis Presley's delicate balancing act of stimulants and depressants eventually went awry. Janis Joplin's propensity for mixing wine and heroin was ultimately fatal. And John Belushi's liking for the combined effect of cocaine and opioids ("speedballs") also ended in tragedy. Obviously, whether it is intentional or accidental, mixing drugs is a hazardous undertaking.

# EXPLANATIONS OF SUBSTANCE ABUSE AND DEPENDENCE

Clinicians have proposed a number of theories to explain why people abuse or become dependent on various substances. Although such theories are often presented with considerable passion and conviction, none has gained unqualified research support (Peele, 1989). Like other forms of mental dysfunctioning, excessive and chronic drug use is increasingly being viewed as a consequence of a combination of biological, psychological, and sociocultural factors.

## The Genetic and Biological View

For years studies of twins and of adoptees have suggested that people can inherit a predisposition to substance abuse and dependence (Gabrielli & Plomin, 1985; Goodwin, 1984, 1980, 1979, 1976; Vaillant, 1983). As we noted in Chapter 3, twin studies compare the concordance rates of genetically identical (monozygotic) twins with those of fraternal (dyzygotic) twins. If a predisposition to drug taking is indeed inherited, then the drug-abuse concordance rate of identical twins should be higher than that of fraternal twins. Studies seem to indicate that it is. For example, an alcohol-abuse concordance rate of 54 percent was found in one group of identical twins; that is, in 54 percent of the cases in which one identical twin abused alcohol, the other twin also abused alcohol. In contrast, a group of fraternal twins had a concordance rate of only 28 percent (Kaij, 1960). Of course, as we have observed previously, such findings do not rule out other interpretations. For one thing, parents may act more similarly toward identical twins than toward fraternal twins.

A stronger indicator that there may be a genetic factor in drug abuse and dependence has come from adoption studies (APA, 1987). In one investigation, for example, alcoholism rates of people who had been adopted shortly

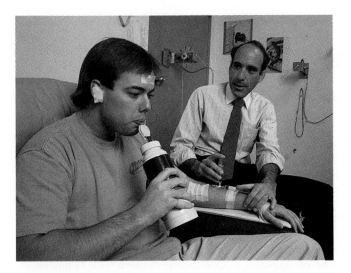

In studies to help determine whether the effects of alcohol and other drugs are linked to genetic factors, the children of drug-dependent parents and control subjects ingest various substances in the laboratory while researchers systematically observe the effects of these substances on brain and body functioning.

after birth were examined (Goodwin et al., 1973). One group of adoptees had biological parents who were alcoholic, while the other group's biological parents were not. By the age of 30, those with alcoholic biological parents showed significantly higher rates of alcohol abuse than those with nonalcoholic biological parents. Since all adoptees were reared in nonalcoholic environments, the different alcoholism rates suggest that a predisposition to develop alcoholism may be inherited.

Research involving the breeding of animals has also implicated genetic factors in the development of drug dependence (George, 1990). Researchers who have selected animals that prefer alcohol to other beverages and mated them have found that their offspring display the same preference. Similarly, researchers have mated rats from strains with different levels of alcohol preference and found the alcohol preferences of the offspring to be intermediate between those of the parents.

For years genetic studies provided the only evidence for the position that biological factors play a key role in the development and maintenance of drug misuse. However, advances in technology have recently enabled researchers to explore the biological underpinnings of drug dependence more directly and to pinpoint some of the biological factors that may contribute to excessive and chronic drug use (Miller & Giannini, 1990).

Even more direct evidence that a genetic factor may be at play in drug abuse and dependence has recently been provided by the "gene mapping" techniques that we discussed in Chapter 8. Using this new technology, investigators locate genes that are tied to various characteristics and disorders. Gene-mapping investigations are beginning to find links between aberrant genes and drug use disorders. For example, one study found that an aberrant form of the so-called $D_2$ receptor gene was present in 69 percent of alcoholic subjects but in only 20 percent of nonalcoholic subjects (Blum & Noble, 1990). The samples in this and related studies have been small, but should the relationship hold in larger investigations, it would provide the strongest evidence to date that genes play at least some role in the development of alcoholism and other drug use disorders.

One line of study has pinpointed some of the biological processes that produce drug tolerance and withdrawal symptoms (see Box 13-4). In many cases, the excessive and chronic ingestion of a particular kind of drug causes the brain to reduce its production of a particular neurotransmitter that would ordinarily act to sedate, alleviate pain, lift mood, or increase alertness. Because the drug acts to produce such a reaction, action by the neurotransmitter is less necessary. As the drug is taken increasingly, the body's production of the corresponding neurotransmitter decreases, leaving the person in need of more and more of the drug to achieve its initial effects. In short, the person builds tolerance for the drug. Moreover, as persons become increasingly reliant on the drug rather than on their own neurotransmitter, they must continue to ingest the drug in order to feel reasonably calm, comfortable, happy, or alert. If they suddenly stop taking the drug, for a while they will have a deficient supply of the neurotransmitter needed for feeling well; they will in fact feel terrible. That is, they will experience uncomfortable withdrawal symptoms until the brain resumes its normal production and release of the necessary neurotransmitter.

Research has found that a chronic and excessive ingestion of benzodiazepines eventually lowers the brain's production of the inhibitory neurotransmitter GABA (Tallman, 1978), setting the stage for insufficient GABA activity when a benzodiazepine abuser suddenly stops using the drug. Similarly, a chronic use of opioids eventually reduces the brain's own production of endorphins, leaving an abstinent addict with an inadequate supply of this neurotransmitter for sedating and for reducing pain (Snyder, 1991, 1986, 1977; Goldstein, 1976). And a chronic use of cocaine or amphetamines eventually lowers the brain's own production of dopamine and norepinephrine, leaving abstinent users with fewer of these chemicals to stimulate their brains and the rest of their bodies (Kleber & Gawin, 1987; Dackis & Gold, 1987; Snyder, 1986; Julien, 1985).

Even if biological factors do predispose certain people to develop and maintain drug problems, most people

BOX 13-4

# The Body's Own Opioids

Some of science's most important discoveries are the result of serendipity. Others read like a good detective story. And still others have the character of a breathless race to the finish line. And then there are those discoveries that have elements of all three, such as the discovery of *endorphins,* the natural opioids manufactured by our brains and bodies.

This discovery actually began in the 1960s with the discovery of *narcotic antagonists*—drugs that seemed to block and even undo the effects of heroin and other opioids (Ray, 1983). People who were near death from an opioid overdose were sometimes returned to normal functioning by injections of narcotic antagonists. Moreover, people dependent on opioid drugs were suddenly thrown into severe withdrawal by injections of an antagonist.

Researchers already knew that whenever a drug's effects can be totally countered by an antagonist, the drug itself must operate at selective sites in the brain and elsewhere in the body—sites that receive the drug and its antagonist as specifically as a lock receives a key. Researchers therefore began a search for the specific sites that receive opioid drugs.

By 1973 the work of several researchers made it possible to map out the body's receptor sites for opioid drugs (Snyder, 1991, 1986). Sites were found in the central nervous system and intestines that seemed consistent with the impact of opioids. Opioid receptors were found in the area of the brain that regulates pupil dilation, for example, and one effect of opioid drugs is to constrict the pupils of the eye.

Investigators were then ready to ask another question: Why do our bodies have highly specific receptors for foreign substances such as heroin, opium, and morphine? In 1974 John Hughes and Hans Kosterlitz, researchers in Aberdeen, Scotland, boldly suggested that perhaps our bodies produce natural opioids that ordinarily operate at these receptor sites. A frantic search began for these hypothesized natural opioids, and in 1975 natural opioidlike substances were discovered in the brains of pigs (Kosterlitz & Hughes, 1975) and calves (Simantov & Snyder, 1976). Some researchers labeled these natural opioids *enkephalins* (Greek for "in the head"), while others called them *endorphins* (contracted from "endogenous morphine"). Today the natural opioids are collectively referred to as endorphins (Snyder, 1986).

Once endorphins were discovered, a flurry of investigations followed. One line of research tried to find endorphins in other animals, including human beings. A second sought to determine just how similar these natural opioids were to opioid drugs. Both lines of research yielded eye-opening results. Vertebrates of all kinds, including humans, apparently produce endorphins that operate at opioid receptors (Snyder, 1986), and endorphin effects consistently parallel those of opioid drugs (Amalric et al., 1987; Akil & Watson, 1979). Concentrated endorphin injections can cause analgesia, for example, and lead to addiction in various animals. On the basis of such findings, researchers concluded that our bodies ordinarily produce and depend on endorphins to help alleviate the pains and stresses of daily life. Without them, life would be extraordinarily unpleasant.

Theorists have also offered a tenta-

---

with such predispositions never fall into the trap of drug abuse and dependence. Why do some, and not others, develop these grossly dysfunctional problems? Psychological theorists—particularly psychodynamic and behavioral theorists—and sociocultural theorists have tried to suggest factors that may help push biologically predisposed people to take drugs and produce a pattern of misuse.

## The Psychodynamic View

Psychodynamic theorists believe that people who ultimately abuse substances have inordinate dependency needs traceable to their early years (Shedler & Block, 1990; Ward, 1985; Abadi, 1984). They theorize that when parents fail to satisfy a child's need for nurturance, the child is likely to go through life in a dependent manner—relying too much on others for support, help, and comfort—in an effort to find the nurturance he or she did not receive as a child. If this search for external sources of support includes experimentation with a drug, such a person is likely to develop a dependent relationship with the substance.

Some psychodynamic theorists also believe that certain people develop a "substance abuse personality" that makes them particularly vulnerable to drugs. To investigate this proposition, researchers have typically

tive explanation of opioid dependence based on these findings (Snyder, 1991, 1986, 1977; Trujillo & Akil, 1991; Goldstein, 1976). When people first take opioids, the drugs fill endorphin receptor sites that are unoccupied, thus reducing tensions and pains and bringing on a pleasant high. As people continue to take these drugs over time, their bodies have less need for endorphins, and their endorphin production decreases. They thus become chemically less equipped to cope with daily pains and stresses and need ever-larger doses of opioids to help them cope. As they take greater and greater amounts of opioids, their endorphin production continues to decrease. Obviously, this increasing need for opioids corresponds to the clinical picture of tolerance.

Eventually endorphin production ceases entirely and these people become fully dependent on opioid drugs to cope with pain and distress. If they stop taking opioids at this point, their receptor sites will remain empty for as long as it takes their body to resume endorphin production. Meanwhile they have no means of fighting pain and stress and may experience tremendous discomfort — a state consistent with the clinical picture of withdrawal.

Researchers are currently trying to evaluate the therapeutic implications of this theory. Can endorphin produc-

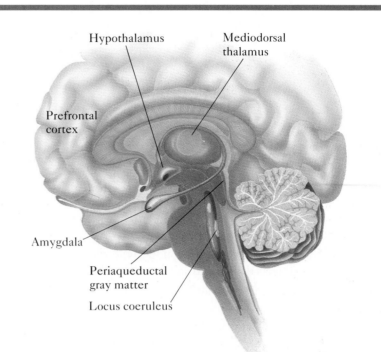

The neural receptors to which opioids bind are most concentrated in the brain's emotion center, which includes the amygdala, hypothalamus, and locus coeruleus, and the pain center, which includes the mediodorsal thalamus and periaqueductal gray matter. *(Adapted from Snyder, 1986, p. 49.)*

tion be manipulated so that addicts' natural opioids can fight their addiction to opioid drugs? Researchers are also examining the role played by endorphins in other kinds of problems, such as the effectiveness of placebos, the nature of pain, and the efficacy of acupuncture (Snyder, 1991). Similarly, efforts are under way to explore the possible links between endorphins and schizophrenia, depression, and other abnormal patterns. Certainly the discovery of endorphins has been one of the clinical field's most dramatic and exciting breakthroughs in recent times.

---

selected a population of chronic users of a particular drug, administered a battery of interviews and personality tests, determined the personality characteristics of each participant, and compared these personality profiles with those of control subjects who do not take the drug. Such studies have found that people who abuse or depend on drugs tend to be more dependent, antisocial, impulsive, and depressive than other people (Shedler & Block, 1990; Grinspoon & Bakalar, 1987; Labouvie & McGee, 1986; Gilbert & Lombardi, 1967).

Researchers have tried to determine the causal sequence of such correlations by repeating the personality tests at intervals during the subjects' lives. One such longitudinal study measured the characteristics of a large group of nonalcoholic young men and then kept track of each man's development (Jones, 1971, 1968). The profiles of those men who subsequently developed alcohol problems in middle age were compared with the profiles of those who did not. The men who developed alcohol problems had been more impulsive as adolescents, and continued to be so as middle-aged men, suggesting that impulsive men are indeed more prone to develop alcohol problems.

A major problem in these studies is that a suspiciously wide range of personality traits has been linked to drug abuse and dependence; in fact, different studies point to different "key" traits. Given that some addicted people are apparently dependent, others impulsive, and still others antisocial, researchers have been unable to conclude that any one personality trait or cluster of traits stands out as a factor in substance abuse and dependence (Lang, 1983).

## The Behavioral View

According to reinforcement theorists, the reduction of tension, raising of spirits, or sense of well-being produced by a drug has a reinforcing effect and increases the likelihood that the user will seek this reaction again, especially when under stress (Lewis, 1990; Steele & Josephs, 1990; Ward, 1985).

In support of this theory, studies have found that both human and animal subjects do in fact drink more alcohol when they are under stress (Young & Herling, 1986; Stewart et al., 1984; Marlatt, 1977; Higgins & Marlatt, 1975, 1973). One group of experimenters had social drinkers work on a difficult anagram task while being unfairly criticized and belittled by another person (Marlatt, Kosturn, & Lang, 1975). These subjects were then asked to participate in an "alcohol taste task": their job was supposedly to compare and rate various alcoholic beverages. The harassed subjects drank significantly more alcohol during the taste task than did control subjects who had not been criticized during the anagram task. Another group of subjects were harassed while doing the anagrams but were given the opportunity to retaliate against their critics. These subjects drank relatively little during the tasting. Their retaliatory behavior had apparently reduced their tension and lessened their need for alcohol.

In a manner of speaking, the reinforcement theorists and researchers are arguing that many people take drugs to medicate themselves when they feel tense and upset. If so, one would expect elevated rates of drug abuse and dependence among people with high levels of anxiety, depression, or anger (Khantzian, 1985). This expectation has in fact been supported by research (APA, 1987). In a study of 835 clinically depressed patients, for example, more than one-fourth were found to abuse drugs during episodes of their disorders (Hasin, Endicott, & Lewis, 1985). Another study found that 50 percent of cocaine abusers met the diagnostic criteria for a depressive disorder (Gawin & Kleber, 1986).

On the other hand, a number of studies indicate that many people do not find drugs pleasurable or reinforcing when they first take them. Some volunteers who are administered heroin in laboratory settings, for example, initially dislike the drug or feel indifference to it (Alexander & Hadaway, 1982; Beecher, 1959). Similarly, a number of addicts report that their initial opium experiences were anything but pleasurable:

*We slept most of the day until late afternoon, and when I* woke up she got up and got a tray out of the dresser drawer and brought it over and placed it on the bed. . . . She told me she was [an opium] smoker and asked me if I had ever smoked hop. I told her I never had and she said that I ought to try it once, as she was sure I would like it. . . . [After smoking it] I suddenly became very nauseated and had to leave to vomit. I vomited till there was nothing left on my stomach and I was still sick so I went to bed.

*(Lindesmith, 1972, p. 85)*

Even when a drug does initially produce pleasant feelings and reward the user with a reduction in tension, the picture seems to change later when the person takes the drug excessively and chronically. As we saw earlier, many people become increasingly anxious and depressed over time as they take more and more drugs (Nathan et al., 1971, 1970). Why, then, do they keep ingesting them?

Some behaviorists use Richard Solomon's **opponent-process** theory to answer this question. Solomon (1980) holds that the brain is structured in such a way that pleasurable emotions, such as drug-induced euphoria, inevitably lead to opponent processes — negative aftereffects — that leave the person feeling worse than usual. People who continue to use pleasure-giving drugs inevitably develop opponent aftereffects, such as cravings for more of the drug, withdrawal responses, and an increasing need for the drug. According to Solomon, the opponent processes eventually dominate and suppress the pleasure-giving processes, and avoidance of the negative aftereffects replaces pursuit of pleasure as the individual's primary motivation for taking drugs. Although a highly regarded theory, the opponent-process explanation has not received systematic research support (Peele, 1989).

Other behaviorists have proposed that classical conditioning may also contribute to certain aspects of drug abuse and dependence (Pomerleau & Pomerleau, 1984; Siegel, 1983, 1979; Wikler, 1980, 1973, 1965; Lindesmith, 1968). They hold that objects present at the time drugs are taken may act as conditioned stimuli and come to elicit some of the same pleasure brought on by the drugs themselves. Just the sight of a hypodermic needle or a regular supplier, for example, have been known to comfort a heroin or amphetamine addict and help relieve withdrawal symptoms.

In a similar manner, objects that are present during withdrawal distress may elicit withdrawal-like symptoms. One former heroin addict experienced nausea and other withdrawal symptoms when he returned to the neighborhood where he had gone through withdrawal in the past—a reaction that led him to start taking heroin again (O'Brien, 1975). Similarly, after eight addicted human subjects were repeatedly exposed to a peppermint odor during their withdrawal reactions, they experienced withdrawal-like symptoms (tearing eyes, sick feelings, running nose) whenever someone near them ate peppermint candy (O'Brien & Ternes, 1979).

Although these studies demonstrate that withdrawal responses *can* be classically conditioned, other studies suggest that such conditioning is not at work in most cases. In interviews with 40 addicts who had previously gone through heroin withdrawal, only 11 reported having withdrawal symptoms during later encounters with environments and objects associated with their withdrawal, and only 5 of these individuals actually relapsed into heroin use (McAuliffe, 1982). In short, the classical conditioning explanations of drug abuse and dependence, like the reinforcement explanations, have received at best mixed support.

## The Sociocultural View

Sociocultural theorists propose that the people most likely to develop a pattern of drug abuse or dependence are those whose societies create an atmosphere of stress and whose families value, or at least tolerate, drug taking. Epidemiological studies have provided some support for these claims. One study found, for example, that regions in the United States where daily life is relatively more stressful (states where divorce is more common or where more people are laid off from work) report higher rates of alcoholism (Linsky et al., 1985). Similarly, hunting societies, in which people presumably experience greater danger, uncertainty, and tension, have more alcohol problems than agrarian societies (Bacon, 1973; Horton, 1943); city dwellers have higher alcoholism rates than residents of small towns and rural areas (Cisin & Calahan, 1970); and lower socioeconomic classes and minority groups display higher drinking rates than other classes and ethnic groups (Beauvais & LaBeueff, 1985; McCord, McCord, & Gudeman, 1950). Studies have similarly found higher heroin addiction rates among people who live in stressful environments. For example, as we noted in Chapter 6, heroin use was very common among American soldiers in Vietnam during the 1960s. About 40 percent of army enlisted men there used heroin at least once, half of them so often that they had a withdrawal reaction when they stopped (Grinspoon & Bakalar, 1987).

Studies also support the claim that family attitudes may play a role in the development of patterns of drug misuse. Problem drinking is more common among teenagers whose parents and peers drink (Jessor & Jessor, 1975; Braucht, Brakarsh, Follingstad, & Berry, 1973). Similarly, relatively lower rates of alcohol abuse are found among Jews and Protestants—groups in which the boundaries of drinking are clearly defined and drinking to the point of intoxication is less common (Calahan, Cisin, & Crossley, 1969; McCord et al., 1960; Snyder, 1955). Conversely, alcoholism rates are high among the Irish and Eastern Europeans, who less clearly define the boundaries of acceptable drinking (Vaillant & Milofsky, 1982).

Epidemiological findings of these kinds are consistent with the sociocultural view of drug abuse and dependence, but as we noted earlier, they are subject to nonsociocultural interpretations as well. In fact, as we have seen, none of the models has provided undisputed evidence to support its position on drug use disorders and certainly none by itself has been able to account for dysfunctional patterns of drug use (Peele, 1989). Thus at present drug misuse remains a complex phenomenon that is far from being fully understood.

# TREATMENTS FOR SUBSTANCE USE DISORDERS

A wide variety of treatments have been applied to substance use disorders, sometimes with great success, at other times with only moderate effectiveness (Walburg, 1985). The treatments may be applied on either an outpatient or an inpatient basis. Although inpatient treatment for these disorders seems to be on the rise, research does not suggest that this more expensive format is more effective than outpatient treatment (Miller & Hester, 1986).

Investigators of treatment programs for people with substance use disorders confront several problems. First, different substance use disorders often pose different treatment problems (Kleber & Gawin, 1986).

Second, some people recover from their drug problems without any intervention at all (Biernacki, 1990; Walburg, 1985), particularly people dependent on heroin, most of whom are young. Yet other people appear to recover and then relapse, or fail to recover from their disorder even after intensive treatment, and continue to lead a drug-involved life for the time that is left to them. Thus it can be extremely difficult to determine at any given time whether a treatment is succeeding, failing, or irrelevant to a given person's progress.

Finally, as with other mental disorders, the different criteria and goals employed by different clinical researchers make it difficult to draw broad conclusions about a treatment's effectiveness (Woody, Luborsky, McLellan & O'Brien, 1988). How long, for example, must a person refrain from drug use in order to be categorized as a treatment success? And is total abstention the only criterion, or is a reduction of drug use considered significant? Different answers to these questions will lead to markedly different research conclusions.

These problems notwithstanding, clinicians have worked diligently to find ways to correct substance use disorders. Most of the approaches fall into one of three groups: insight, behavioral, and biological therapies.

## Insight Therapies

Insight therapists try to help people with substance use disorders to become aware of and address the psychological factors that contribute to their pattern of drug use (Jungman, 1985). Psychodynamic therapists, for example, first help clients to uncover and resolve their underlying conflicts, and then try to help them alter their drug- or alcohol-related styles of living (Levinson, 1985). Client-centered therapists guide clients to accept the feelings and thoughts that, according to their theory, they have hidden from themselves while turning to drugs.

Although these approaches are often applied to substance use disorders, research has not found them to be highly effective (Meyer et al., 1989; Cooper, 1987; Miller & Hester, 1980). Their lack of success may indicate that drug abuse or dependence eventually becomes a stubborn and independent problem irrespective of its causes, and that the maladaptive pattern must be the primary target for change if people are to become drug-free. Thus insight therapies tend to be of greater help when they are combined with other approaches in a multidimensional treatment program for substance abuse and dependence (Bucher & Costa, 1985). They have been combined successfully with behavioral and biological therapies (Phillips et al., 1987; Weidman, 1985) and are offered most often in group-therapy formats.

## Behavioral and Cognitive-Behavioral Therapies

A widely used behavioral treatment for substance use disorders is *aversive conditioning,* an approach based on the principles of classical conditioning. Here individuals are repeatedly presented with an unpleasant stimulus (for example, an electric shock) at the same time that they are taking a drug. After repeated pairings, the individuals are expected to start reacting negatively to the substance itself and to lose their craving for it.

Aversive conditioning has been applied to alcohol abuse and dependence more than to other substance use disorders (Callner, 1975). In the past, the protocols for aversive conditioning were sometimes drastic and controversial. In one treatment program alcoholic people were injected with *succinylcholine,* a drug that actually paralyzed their bodies while they tasted alcoholic beverages (Sanderson, Campbell, & Laverty, 1963). These individuals did develop an aversion to alcohol, but many clinicians understandably worried about the safety and ethics of the program. Moreover, the effectiveness seemed to be short-lived. Electrical aversive conditioning, which pairs electrical shock with drinking, also raised ethical questions while proving to have limited effectiveness (Wilson, 1987, 1978).

Today's aversive conditioning techniques tend to be somewhat less severe. In one approach, drinking behavior is paired with drug-induced nausea and vomiting (Wiens & Menustik, 1983; Wilson, 1987, 1977). Another, called *covert sensitization,* requires alcoholic people to imagine extremely upsetting, repulsive, or frightening scenes while they are drinking (Miller & Dougher, 1984; Elkins, 1980; Cautela, 1979, 1966). The supposition is that the pairing of these imagined scenes with liquor will elicit negative responses to liquor itself. One of the main limitations of the aversive conditioning approaches is that they can be successful only when clients are sufficiently motivated to continue with such a program despite its unpleasantness.

Another behavioral approach focuses on teaching *alternatives* to drug taking. This approach, too, has been applied to alcohol abuse and dependence more than to other substance use disorders. Problem drinkers may be taught to use relaxation, meditation, or biofeedback instead of alcohol to reduce their tensions (Rohsenow, Smith, & Johnson, 1985). Some are also given assertiveness training or taught social skills to help them both express their anger more directly and withstand social pressures to drink (Rioux & VanMeter, 1990; Chaney, O'Leary, & Marlatt, 1978; Miller, 1978).

The behavioral treatments for substance abuse and dependence have had at most limited success (Meyer et al., 1989). They generally work best in combination with cognitive approaches (Washton & Stone-Washton, 1990; Washton, 1987; Marlatt & Gordon, 1980). In one cognitive-behavioral approach, *behavioral self-control training (BSCT),* therapists first instruct clients to self-monitor their drinking behavior (Miller, 1983). When clients record the times, locations, emotions, bodily changes, and other circumstances that accompany their drinking, they become more sensitive to the cues they associate with increased drinking. Clients are then taught to set appropriate limits on their drinking, to recognize when the limits are being approached, to control their rate of drinking (perhaps by spacing their drinks or by sipping them rather than gulping), and to apply alternative coping behaviors, such as relaxation techniques, in situations that would otherwise elicit drinking. Approximately 70 percent of the clients who complete this program have been assessed as showing some improvement (Miller & Hester, 1980). The program appears to be more effective in cases of alcohol abuse than in cases of alcohol dependence (Meyer et al., 1989).

In a similar combination approach, *relapse-prevention training,* heavy drinkers again use self-monitoring to identify the situations and emotional changes that place them at risk for heavy drinking, then learn coping strategies to use in such situations (Marlatt & Gordon, 1985, 1979; Marlatt, 1983; Cummings, Gordon, & Marlatt, 1980). Clients are also taught to plan ahead of time how much drinking is appropriate, what they will consume, and under what circumstances, and they practice their adaptive strategies in either real or imagined high-risk situations. In the following explanation, the basic principles of this approach are presented to a client:

We know that you would like to be totally abstinent for life, but our knowledge of alcoholics generally and of you in particular suggests that however hard you try, you are likely to drink on some occasion or occasions after you leave hospital. This is not being pessimistic, but simply realistic. We are not suggesting that your task is hopeless—far from it—but we do want you to anticipate future events and work out ways of coping. We have already told you that some drink will be given to you during your stay in hospital and that your aim is to stop after a certain amount when you feel like continuing. In this way we believe that you will gradually break the compulsion to continue and will develop your willpower. This should have two effects when you leave hospital. First, when you attempt to drink, your experience of resisting temptation in the hospital will give you greater control. Second, if you do drink you will find it easier to pull out before you explode into a heavy-drinking binge. . . .

*(Hodgson & Rankin, 1982, p. 213)*

As this statement suggests, relapse-prevention training, like BSCT, seeks to give clients control over their drinking behaviors. Research indicates that the approach only sometimes reduces the frequency of intoxication (Annis et al., 1988; Ito et al., 1988; Chaney et al., 1978). As with BSCT, relapse-prevention training is apparently more effective for alcohol abusers than for those who are physically dependent on alcohol (Meyer et al., 1989).

## Biological Treatments

Biological techniques play a variety of roles in the treatment of substance use disorders (Madden, 1984). They may be directed at helping individuals withdraw from substances, abstain from them, or simply maintain their existing substance use without further escalation. Research suggests that biological approaches alone rarely lead to long-term improvement but can sometimes be a helpful component of broader treatment programs (Kleber, 1985).

**Detoxification** *Detoxification* is systematic and medically supervised withdrawal from a drug (Wartenberg et al., 1990). Many detoxification programs are set up in hospitals or clinics, as drug users often seem more motivated to persevere through withdrawal in those settings. Inpatient detoxification programs of this kind may also offer individual and group therapy, a "full-service" institutional approach that has become increasingly popular in recent years.

One detoxification strategy, used most often with sedative-hypnotic drug dependence, is to have clients withdraw *gradually* from the drug, taking ever-decreasing doses until they are off the drug completely. Although withdrawal symptoms still occur with this technique, they are likely to be milder. Another detoxification strategy is to administer other drugs that help reduce the symptoms of withdrawal. As we noted earlier, antianxiety drugs are sometimes used to reduce severe alcohol withdrawal reactions.

Detoxification programs have proved effective in helping motivated people to withdraw from drugs. For people who fail to pursue psychotherapy after withdrawal, however, relapse rates tend to be high (Weinberg, 1977).

**Antagonist Drugs** After successful withdrawal from a drug, the next challenge is to avoid a recurrence of drug abuse or dependence. In one biological technique, people with substance use disorders are given *antagonist drugs,* drugs that block or change the effects of the addictive drug (Gold, 1987). *Disulfiram (Antabuse),* for example, is often given to people who are trying to refrain from drinking alcohol (Phillips, 1986). By itself this drug is believed to have relatively few negative effects; but, a person who drinks alcohol while taking disulfiram will experience intense nausea, vomiting, blushing, faster heart rate, dizziness, and perhaps fainting. Theoretically, people who have taken disulfiram will refrain from alcohol, knowing the terrible reaction that awaits them should they have even one drink. Disulfiram has proved helpful but again only with people who are highly motivated (Meyer et al., 1989; Becker, 1979; Weinberg, 1977). After all, they can stop taking the disulfiram and return to alcohol at any time.

*Narcotic antagonists,* such as naloxone, cyclazocine, and naltrexone, are sometimes used with people who are dependent on opioids. These drugs attach to opioid receptor sites throughout the brain and make it impossible for the opioid to have its usual euphoric effect. Theoretically, without the rush or high, continued drug use becomes pointless. Although narcotic antagonists have been helpful in emergencies to rescue people from an overdose of opioids, they are usually considered too dangerous for treatment of opioid dependence. The antagonists must be administered very carefully because of their ability to throw addicts into severe withdrawal reactions (Kleber, 1985).

**Drug Maintenance Therapy**  A person's drug-related lifestyle may be a greater problem than the drug's direct effects. Much of the damage caused by heroin addiction, for example, comes from overdoses, unsterile needles, harmful mixtures, and an accompanying life of crime. Thus clinicians were initially very enthusiastic when *methadone maintenance programs* were developed in the 1960s to treat heroin addiction (Dole & Nyswander, 1967, 1965). In these programs, addicted clients are given the synthetic opioid methadone as a substitute for heroin. Although the clients then become dependent on methadone, their addiction is maintained under legal and safe medical supervision. The programs' creators believed methadone to be preferable to heroin because it can be taken orally, thus eliminating the dangers of needles, and it needs to be taken only once a day.

The initial methadone programs appeared to be very effective, and some of them claimed success rates as high as 80 to 100 percent (McGlothlin et al., 1978; DeLong, 1975). These programs also offered vocational and social rehabilitation so that some opioid users could live relatively normal and constructive lives. As a result of these successes, numerous methadone maintenance programs were established throughout the United States, Canada, and England (Payte, 1989). These programs are less popular today, largely because of the addictiveness of methadone itself (Peachey & Franklin, 1985; Etzioni, 1973). Many clinicians believe that substituting one addiction for another is not an acceptable "solution" for drug dependence, and addicts themselves have often complained that methadone addiction creates an additional drug problem that simply complicates their original drug problem and leaves them with a far from drug-free existence. In fact, methadone is apparently harder to withdraw from than heroin.

## Self-help Programs

Given the cost and limited success of clinical interventions, many drug users have organized among themselves to help one another recover without professional assistance. The drug self-help movement dates back to 1935, when two alcoholic men from Ohio met to discuss alternative treatment possibilities. The first discussion led to others and to the eventual formation of a self-help group for alcoholics. The members discussed alcohol-related problems, offered suggestions, and provided support. The organization became known as *Alcoholics Anonymous (AA).*

Today AA has more than 650,000 members in 22,000 chapters across the United States and nearly 100 other countries. It provides peer support therapy with moral and religious features to help people overcome alcoholism (Moos & Finney, 1983). Different members apparently find different aspects of AA helpful. For some it is the peer support and identification that helps them gain control over drinking behavior (Galanter et al., 1990). For others it is the religious dimension. Meetings take place regularly, and members are available to help each other 24 hours a day. By establishing guidelines for living, the organization helps members abstain "one day at a time," urging them to accept as "fact" the idea that they are powerless over alcohol and that they must stop drinking entirely and permanently if they are to live normal lives.

A related self-help organization is AlAnon, which offers support groups for people who live with and care about alcoholic persons. In these groups, people share their painful experiences and learn how to cope with the impact of the alcoholic persons in their lives and how to stop reinforcing their drinking and related behavior.

Self-help programs have also been developed for other substance use disorders, particularly heroin and cocaine dependence. Many programs, such as Daytop Village and Phoenix House, have further expanded into *residential treatment centers,* or *therapeutic communities,* where former heroin and cocaine addicts live, work, and socialize in a drug-free environment while undergoing individual, group, and family therapies and making a transition back to community life. The actual success of the self-help and residential treatment programs has been difficult to determine (Meyer et al., 1989). Some of the programs keep no records of members who failed to be helped and dropped out. Moreover, self-help and residential treatment programs are often distrustful of researchers and deal with them very selectively (Vaillant, 1983). This attitude may be changing, though, and collaborations now under way between such programs and researchers may eventually yield a more precise

At *Via Avanta*, a residential treatment center in Los Angeles, a therapist leads a parenting session for women dependent on opioids. Addicts live, work, and socialize in such centers while receiving treatment for their substance dependence.

picture of the programs' effectiveness. In the meantime, the evidence that keeps self-help and residential treatment programs going comes in the form of individual testimonials. Many tens of thousands of persons unabashedly reveal that they are members of these programs and credit them with turning their lives around (Galanter et al., 1990).

## Controlled Drug Use versus Abstinence

Is total abstinence the only cure for drug abuse and dependence, or can people with substance use disorders learn to keep drug use under better control? This issue has been debated for years, especially when the drug in question is alcohol.

As we saw earlier, many cognitive-behavioral theorists believe that people can continue to drink in moderation if they learn to set more appropriate drinking limits. These advocates of controlled drinking argue that a goal of strict abstinence may in fact encourage people to abandon self-control entirely if they should have a single drink (Peele, 1985; Heather et al., 1982). On the other hand, those who view alcoholism as a disease take the AA position, "Once an alcoholic, always an alcoholic," and hold that relapse is almost inevitable when alcoholic people believe that they can safely take a single drink (Pendery, Maltzman, & West, 1982). They hold that this misguided belief will sooner or later open the door to alcohol once again and lead back to uncontrollable drinking.

Feelings about this issue are so strong that the people on one side have at times challenged the motives and

integrity of those on the other (Sobell & Sobell, 1984, 1982, 1976, 1973; Pendery et al., 1982). Research indicates, however, that both controlled drinking and abstinence may be viable treatment goals, depending on personality and on the nature of the individual's particular drinking problem (O'Leary & Wilson, 1987). Studies suggest, for example, that abstinence is a more appropriate goal for people who are physically dependent on alcohol, while controlled drinking can be helpful to younger abusive drinkers, who may simply need to be taught a nonabusive form of drinking (Marlatt, 1985; Miller, 1983, 1982). Studies also suggest that abstinence is more appropriate for people who believe that they are alcoholic and that abstinence is the only answer for them. These people are more likely to relapse after having just one drink (Brugman, 1985; Heather et al., 1983; Miller, 1982; Skinner et al., 1982). The results of these studies may apply to other drug disorders as well.

It is important to keep in mind that, generally speaking, both abstinence and controlled drinking are extremely difficult for alcoholics to achieve (Watson, 1987; Vaillant, 1983; Enrich & Hansen, 1983). Although treatment may help heavy drinkers to improve for a while, follow-up studies indicate high relapse rates. A study that followed the progress of 110 alcoholics found that 30 years after treatment, 20 percent had become moderate drinkers, 34 percent had become abstinent, and the rest continued to display significant drinking problems (Vaillant, 1983). Other findings are even gloomier, suggesting that recovery rates may be as low as 5 to 10 percent (Peele, 1985; Vaillant, 1983; Enrich & Hansen, 1983), a harsh reminder that substance abuse and dependence continue to be among our society's most durable and disabling problems.

## SUBSTANCE USE DISORDERS: THE STATE OF THE FIELD

In certain respects the story of the misuse of drugs is the same today as it was in past years. Substance use is still rampant, and it creates some of society's most prevalent psychological disorders and debilitating problems. New drugs keep emerging and the public continues to go through periods of naiveté regarding their use, believing for a time that the drugs are "safe" and only gradually learning that they pose significant problems and dangers. And treatments for substance use disorders continue to have only limited effect.

Yet there are some important new wrinkles in this

familiar story. Researchers have begun to develop a clearer understanding of the way many drugs act on the body and of the biological reasons for drug tolerance and withdrawal symptoms. In the treatment sphere, self-help groups and rehabilitation programs are flourishing. Preventive education to make people aware of the seduction of drugs and the dangers of drug misuse is also on the upswing and seems to be making a dent in the public's drug behavior, especially among teenagers, whose use of drugs has declined somewhat in recent years. And clinicians have discovered a number of drug antagonists that seem to hold promise as future forms of biological intervention.

These recent developments are encouraging. Meanwhile, however, enormous quantities of drugs are being distributed and used, more every year. New drugs and drug combinations are discovered almost daily. And with them come new problems, new questions, and requirements for new research and new interventions. Thus despite their efforts, clinical practitioners and investigators find it difficult to make a sizable impact on this problem. As drugs proliferate, perhaps the most valuable lesson to be learned from clinical research and from our society's drug-taking history is an old one: There is no free lunch. High psychological and biological costs are attached to the pleasures associated with many of these substances. Not all the costs are yet known, but costs do inevitably seem to emerge.

# SUMMARY

The term "drug" applies to any substance other than food that changes our bodily and mental functioning. Drug misuse may lead to a temporary *organic mental syndrome,* such as intoxication or hallucinosis. Chronic excessive use can lead to a *substance use disorder* — either *substance abuse,* a pattern in which people rely heavily on a drug and structure their lives around it, or *substance dependence,* in which they show all the symptoms of substance abuse plus physical dependence on the drug (often called *addiction*). People who become dependent on a drug develop a *tolerance* to it or experience unpleasant *withdrawal symptoms* when they abstain from it, or both. It is believed that approximately 7 percent of all adults in the United States currently display some form of substance use disorder.

**D**epressants are drugs that slow the activity of the central nervous system. The most widely used depressants are alcohol, sedative-hypnotic drugs, and opioids. Alcoholic beverages contain *ethyl alcohol,* which is carried to the central nervous system (CNS), depressing its func-

tion and leading to impairment of fine motor skills and other physiological effects. These effects become more pronounced as consumption increases. Intoxication occurs when the concentration of alcohol in the bloodstream reaches 0.09 percent. Alcohol abuse generally follows one of several patterns: large amounts of alcohol daily, excessive amounts only during evenings and weekends, and occasional binges. Severe alcohol abuse may further lead to alcohol dependence. Excessive alcohol intake can lead to *cirrhosis* of the liver and to organic disorders related to vitamin and mineral deficiencies, including *Wernicke's encephalopathy* and *Korsakoff's syndrome.* Alcohol misuse affects millions of families, is a factor in numerous accidents and crimes, and leads to enormous medical costs.

*Sedative-hypnotic drugs* produce feelings of relaxation and drowsiness. *Antianxiety drugs* are the most popular of these drugs, and *barbiturates* are the most dangerous and widely abused. Chronic excessive use of barbiturates often leads to an increase in tolerance and very severe withdrawal symptoms, including convulsions in some instances.

*Opioids* include opium and drugs derived from it, such as heroin, morphine, and codeine. The opium derivatives and synthetic opioids, collectively known as *narcotics,* depress the central nervous system, reducing tension and pain and causing other bodily reactions. They are received at brain receptor sites that normally receive endorphins. Dependence on powerful opioids such as heroin develops after only a few weeks of use, an overdose can easily lead to respiratory failure.

**S**timulants are substances that act to increase the activity of the central nervous system. The best known are cocaine and amphetamines. *Cocaine* produces a euphoric effect by stimulating the release of dopamine and norepinephrine in the brain. Ingestion of high doses of cocaine leads to *cocaine intoxication* and may lead to *cocaine psychosis.* Cocaine abuse often leads to dependence, marked by tolerance and by withdrawal symptoms that include depression, fatigue, and irritability. Cocaine can lead to respiratory failure, irregular heartbeat, high body temperature, and heart attack.

*Amphetamines* are stimulant drugs that are manufactured in a laboratory. They are usually either taken in pill form or injected intravenously. As with cocaine, tolerance to amphetamines develops quickly, and depressive withdrawal symptoms occur when an addicted person stops taking the drug.

*Hallucinogens* are substances that primarily cause changes in sensory perception. They include psychedelic drugs and cannabis. *Psychedelic drugs,* such as LSD, cause profound perceptual changes and hallucinations by disturbing the normal processing of perceptual information. LSD interferes with neurons that use serotonin, which is critical in the filtering of incoming perceptual information. LSD is extremely potent, and ingestion of the drug may lead to a "bad trip," *hallucinogen delusional disorder, hallucinogen mood disorder,* or flashbacks.

*Cannabis sativa* is a hemp plant whose main ingredient is *tetrahydrocannabinol (THC).* The most powerful form is *hashish;* the most popular, and weakest, is *marijuana.* Today's marijuana is more powerful than in past years, and regular use can lead to patterns of abuse and dependence. Marijuana smoking can impair motor and cognitive functioning and may contribute to lung disease.

Many people take more than one drug at a time, and the drugs interact with each other. Sometimes two drugs display *cross-tolerance.* They act similarly on the brain, and taking one drug will affect the person's tolerance for the other. When different drugs enhance each other's effects, they have a combined impact known as a *synergistic effect.* The use of two or more drugs at the same time — *polydrug use* — has become increasingly common.

Although a number of explanations for substance abuse and dependence have been put forward, none has gained unqualified research support. The *biological view* of substance misuse has made considerable strides in recent years. Studies of twins and adoptees suggest that people may inherit a predisposition to substance dependence. Biological researchers have further learned that drug tolerance and withdrawal symptoms are related to a common sequence of biological events. Chronic ingestion of a drug causes the brain to reduce its production of a particular neurotransmitter that ordinarily acts to alleviate pain or increase alertness. When the drug is taken regularly, the body decreases its production of the neurotransmitter, leaving the person in need of more and more of the drug (tolerance), and defenseless against pain or depressive functioning when drugtaking is stopped suddenly (withdrawal).

The *psychodynamic view* proposes that people who turn to substance abuse have inordinate dependency needs traceable to the oral stage of life. Some theorists also believe that certain people have a "substance abuse personality" that makes them vulnerable to drugs. However, efforts to link particular personality traits to substance abuse have been largely unsuccessful.

The *behavioral view* proposes that drug use is reinforced because it reduces tension and raises spirits. Research has supported the behavioral view that people ingest drugs to alleviate stress. In many instances, however, the initial experience is not pleasurable, and even when it is, subsequent drug use often leads to dramatically unpleasant experiences.

Classical conditioning is also believed to play a role in substance abuse — the drug-taking act itself and surrounding events may become conditioned stimuli and may elicit some of the same pleasure as actual ingestion of the drug. Both the reinforcement and the classical conditioning explanations of drug abuse have received only limited research support.

The *sociocultural view* proposes that the people most likely to develop a pattern of drug abuse are those whose societies create an atmosphere of stress and whose families value or tolerate drug taking. Epidemiological studies provide some support for these claims.

Treatments for substance abuse vary as widely as explanations for its cause. Frequently one approach is more effective with one type of substance use disorder than another. *Insight therapies* try to help clients become aware of and address the psychological factors that contribute to their pattern of drug use. Research has not found these approaches to be highly effective, although they do appear to be useful in combination with others.

A common *behavioral technique* is *aversive conditioning,* in which an unpleasant stimulus is paired with the drug that the person is taking. A mild form of this technique is *covert sensitization,* in which people imagine upsetting or unpleasant stimuli while they ingest the drug. Behavioral approaches have had limited success on their own but are apparently useful in combination with cognitive techniques in such forms to *behavioral self-control training (BSCT)* and *relapse-prevention training.*

*Biological treatments* by themselves rarely lead to long-term improvement but can sometimes be a helpful component of a broader treatment program. *Detoxification* is systematic and medically supervised withdrawal from a drug. *Antagonist drugs* are sometimes used to block or change the effects of the addictive drug. And *drug maintenance therapy,* in which clients are given a synthetic drug as a substitute for their addictive drug, has been used to control and maintain a client's addiction under safe and legal medical supervision.

*Self-help groups* have emerged as a popular means to combat substance abuse and dependence. Alcoholics Anonymous provides peer support for alcohol abusers, establishing guidelines for living and overcoming the addiction. Similar programs have been started for other substance use disorders. Many of these programs have expanded into *residential treatment centers,* or *therapeutic communities,* where former addicts live, work, and socialize in a drug-free environment while receiving treatment. The effectiveness of self-help groups and residential treatment centers has been difficult to gauge.

# TOPIC OVERVIEW

# CHAPTER *14*

# SEXUAL DISORDERS

*Joseph LoPiccolo*

*(The section on paraphilias was written by Ronald J. Comer.)*

Few areas of functioning are of more interest to human beings than sexual behavior. Because sexual feelings are so much a part of our development and daily functioning, because sexual activity is so tied to the satisfaction of our basic needs, and because sexual performance is so linked to our self-esteem, sexual behavior is a major focus of both private thoughts and public discussions.

Correspondingly, abnormal sexual behavior is of more interest to people than almost all other forms of abnormal functioning. Most people are fascinated by the sexual problems of others and worry about the normality of their own sexuality. Our society is so curious about abnormal sexual behavior and attaches so much shame to it that many people who have problems in this realm are also burdened with feelings of anxiety, guilt, or self-disgust as a consequence.

There are two kinds of sexual disorders: sexual dysfunctions and paraphilias. People with *sexual dysfunctions* are unable to function normally in some area of the human sexual response cycle. They may not be able to become sexually aroused, for example, or to achieve orgasm. People with *paraphilias* have recurrent and intense sexual urges and sexually arousing fantasies in response to sexual objects or situations that society deems inappropriate. They may, for example, be aroused by sexual activity with a child or by exposure of their genitals to strangers, and may act on these urges.

## SEXUAL DYSFUNCTIONS

Many psychological disorders affect only a small percentage of people. Sexual dysfunctions, in contrast — problems in sexual functioning, such as failure to achieve an erection in men and difficulties with orgasm in women — are very common, and are very distressing to those who experience them. Sexual frustration, guilt about failure, loss of self-esteem, and emotional problems with the sexual partner are typically the psychological effects of sexual dysfunction. Sexual dysfunction is a common cause of divorce — unfortunately, for most dysfunctions can be treated successfully in relatively brief therapy.

Sexual dysfunctions will be described here in the context of heterosexual couples in long-term relationships, because this is the context in which the majority of cases are seen in therapy. Both male and female homosexual couples are subject to the same dysfunctions, however, and therapists use the same basic techniques when they treat these couples. When a man's penis will not become erect, it does not matter whether the intended partner is a woman or another man.

A word about terminology: people often speak vaguely when they talk of sex; they say "sleep with" when they mean "have sex with." Here the term "intercourse" will be used only to refer to penile-vaginal thrusting. Other sexual activities will also be specified precisely — "genital caressing," for instance, rather than the less clear "petting."

## Types of Sexual Dysfunctions

DSM-III-R classifies sexual dysfunctions according to the phases of the sexual response cycle, as first described by the pioneering sex researchers William Masters and Virginia Johnson (1966), with additions by the noted sex therapist Helen Kaplan (1977, 1974). In this classification, sexual dysfunctions are defined as "psychophysiological disorders which make it impossible for the individual to have and/or enjoy coitus." The sexual response cycle and the physical changes that occur during each phase are shown in Figures 14-1, 14-2, and 14-3. Dysfunctions can affect any of the first three phases of the cycle, the *desire phase*, the *arousal phase*, and the *orgasm phase*. There is also a fourth phase, the *resolution phase*, but as it consists simply of the relaxation and decline in arousal that follow orgasm, there are no sexual dysfunctions associated with it.

The desire phase consists of feeling an urge to have

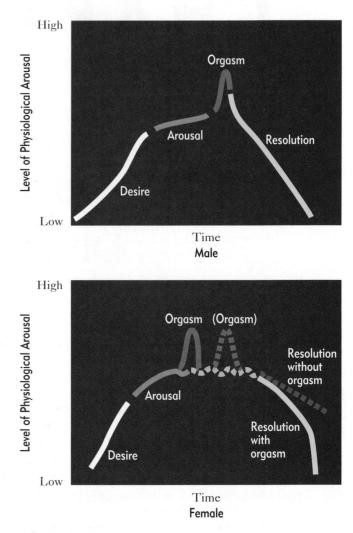

**FIGURE 14-1** Masters and Johnson found a similar sequence of phases in the normal sexual response cycle of both males and females. Sometimes, however, women do not experience orgasm, which leads to a somewhat different resolution phase. And sometimes women experience two or more orgasms in succession before the resolution phase. *(Adapted from Masters & Johnson, 1970, 1966; Kaplan, 1974.)*

sex, having sexual fantasies or daydreams, and feeling sexually attracted to others. Two dysfunctions are associated with the desire phase. ***Hypoactive sexual desire*** is a lack of interest in sex, and, as a result, a low level of sexual activity. When a person with hypoactive sexual desire does have sex, however, he or she often functions normally and may even enjoy the experience, or at least does not find it unpleasant. Patients with ***sexual aversion,*** in contrast, find sex actively unpleasant. Instead of experiencing arousal and pleasure, these patients often feel revulsion, disgust, anxiety, and fear.

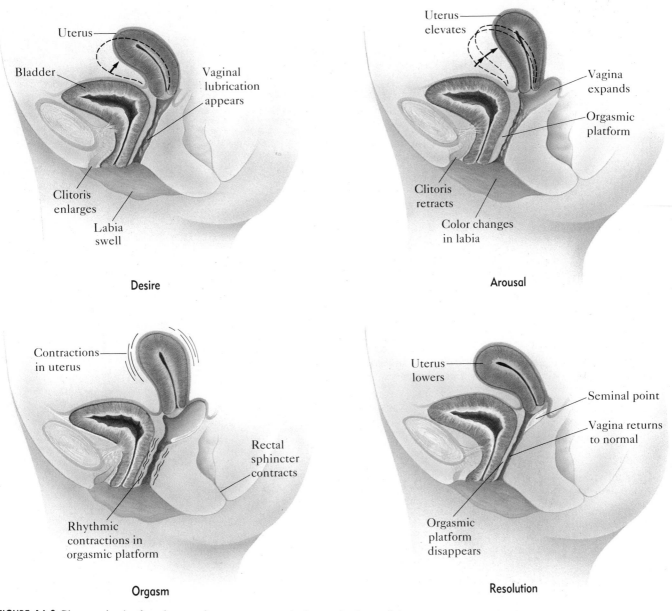

Uterus
Bladder
Vaginal lubrication appears
Clitoris enlarges
Labia swell

**Desire**

Uterus elevates
Vagina expands
Orgasmic platform
Clitoris retracts
Color changes in labia

**Arousal**

Contractions in uterus
Rectal sphincter contracts
Rhythmic contractions in orgasmic platform

**Orgasm**

Uterus lowers
Seminal point
Vagina returns to normal
Orgasmic platform disappears

**Resolution**

**FIGURE 14-2** Changes in the female sexual anatomy occur during each phase of the sexual response cycle. *(Adapted from Hyde, 1990, p. 200.)*

The *sexual arousal* phase is marked by general physical arousal, increases in heart rate, muscle tension, blood pressure, and respiration, and specific changes in the pelvic region. Blood pooling in the pelvis, called *pelvic vasocongestion,* leads to erection of the penis in men, and to swelling of the clitoris and labia and the production of vaginal lubrication in women. Dysfunctions during this phase are *male erectile disorder* (previously called *impotence*) and *female arousal disorder* (previously referred to as *frigidity*). Earlier versions of the DSM did not differentiate between physical arousal and the subjective experience of emotional arousal, and sex therapists pointed out that a more detailed classification system was needed (Schover et al., 1982). As one of my own patients put it, "Oh, I get very aroused and excited, the problem is just that my damn penis won't get hard!" Conversely, there are patients (more typically women) who report the occurrence of all the physiological components of arousal but do not experience any accompanying excitement, pleasure, or arousal. In recognition of

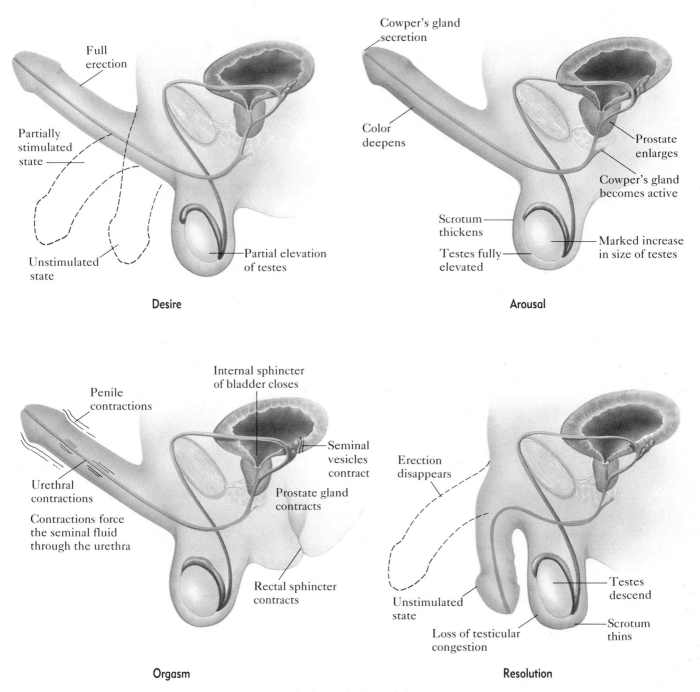

**FIGURE 14-3** Changes in the male sexual anatomy occur during each phase of the sexual response cycle. *(Adapted from Hyde, 1990, p. 199.)*

this distinction, DSM-III-R defines *sexual arousal disorders* as involving either a failure of lubrication or genital swelling in women, the absence of penile erection in men, or the lack of a subjective sense of sexual excitement and pleasure in either men or women.

The *orgasm phase* of the sexual response cycle consists of reflexive muscular contractions in the pelvic re-

gion. The most common male sexual dysfunction in this phase is *premature ejaculation,* defined as "ejaculation with minimal sexual stimulation or before, upon, or shortly after penetration and before the person wishes it" (APA, 1987, p. 295). Much rarer is a man's inability to reach orgasm despite adequate stimulation, called *inhibited male orgasm* in DMS-III-R, but usually referred to as *inhibited ejaculation, ejaculatory incompetence,* or *retarded ejaculation* by sex therapists.

DSM-III-R calls the female disorder of the orgasm phase *inhibited female orgasm.* As we shall see, there is some disagreement as to whether a woman's lack of orgasm during intercourse per se is a sexual dysfunction, provided she can reach orgasm with her partner during direct stimulation of the clitoris, with caressing by her partner's hand or mouth. Almost all contemporary sex therapists and researchers feel that the evidence is clear that women who have such "clitoral" orgasms are entirely normal and healthy (LoPiccolo & Stock, 1987).

DSM-III-R lists two other dysfunctions as *sexual pain disorders.* They do not fit neatly into a specific phase of the sexual response cycle. *Vaginismus,* spastic contractions of the muscles around the outer third of the vagina, prevents entry of the penis. Severe cases of vaginismus can result in "unconsummated marriage," which means that the couple have never been able to have intercourse. *Dyspareunia* (from Latin words meaning "painful mating") refers to pain in the genitals during sexual activity. Dyspareunia does occasionally occur in men, but it is much more common in women.

As the DSM-III-R categories of sexual dysfunction are rather broad, two additional dimensions are often used to clarify a patient's specific problem. The dysfunction may be described as either *lifelong* or *not lifelong,* and as either *global* or *situational.* Thus a woman with lifelong, global orgasmic dysfunction has never experienced an orgasm during any form of sexual activity. A man with not lifelong, situational erectile failure previously had erections during sex with his wife, but now has erections only during solitary masturbation or with another partner.

## Prevalence of Sexual Dysfunctions

It is difficult to arrive at an accurate figure for the rates of occurrence of sexual dysfunction. Many people who are troubled by sexual dysfunctions are too embarrassed to seek treatment. Researchers have attempted to circumvent this problem by contacting a random sample of the general, nonpatient population and asking them to fill out questionnaires or to be interviewed about their sexual adjustment. Many people contacted in such studies refuse to participate, however, feeling that sex is a very private matter. Typical refusal rates are in the 25 percent range, and it appears that those who do volunteer to participate in sex research are more liberal, more sexually experienced, and more unconventional, and hence do not constitute a representative sample (Catania, Gib-

son, Chitwood, & Coates, 1990). As sexual conservatism and lack of experience are often considered to be factors leading to sexual dysfunction, the research studies on volunteers may underestimate the rate of sexual dysfunction in the general population.

**Prevalence of Male Dysfunctions** Estimates of the prevalence of sexual dysfunctions can be derived from several studies conducted on the general population: the famous "Kinsey reports" on several thousand American men and women, which were conducted in the 1930s and 1940s (Kinsey, Pomeroy, Martin, & Gebhard, 1953; Kinsey, Pomeroy, & Martin, 1948); more recent American surveys (Frank, Anderson, & Rubinstein, 1978; Hunt, 1974; Hite, 1970); and surveys of large samples of men and women in England (Sanders, 1987, 1985).

In spite of the cultural stereotype that all men want all the sex they can get, hypoactive sexual desire is found in about 15 percent of men studied. Aversion to sex, in contrast, seems to be so rare in men as not to appear in these studies, although sex therapists do see occasional cases.

In the last several years there has been a large increase in the number of men seeking therapy for hypoactive sexual desire. One study reports that from 1974 to 1976, only 30 percent of hypoactive sexual desire patients were male (LoPiccolo & Friedman, 1988); in 1981 and 1982, in contrast, 55 percent of all patients in therapy for hypoactive sexual desire were male. Some social commentators have suggested that the women's liberation movement has made women competitors with men for jobs, status, and power, and this competition has caused a rise in the incidence of male hypoactive sexual desire. Sex therapists tend not to agree with this idea, however. Rather, what seems to account for the increase in male cases is our culture's increasing acceptance of women's sexuality. In the past, when our society considered "nice" women to be uninterested in sex, a woman married to a man with hypoactive sexual desire would be unlikely to complain and to suggest that they enter sex therapy. As the women's movement legitimized female sexuality, women became more likely to pressure their husbands for more frequent sex and to initiate sex therapy. It is pressure from sexually deprived wives that brings men with hypoactive sexual desire into sex therapy, as the men themselves typically do not feel very distressed about their lack of sex drive and are not eager to enter therapy (LoPiccolo & Friedman, 1988).

Erectile failure occurs in about 8 to 10 percent of the general male population. Because of its association with several of the diseases that afflict older adults, erectile failure is most often seen in older men; the majority of cases involve men over the age of 50 (Bancroft, 1989).

The rates of premature ejaculation found in population studies have varied between 10 and 25 percent, probably because definitions of the problem vary. In terms of actual duration of intercourse, the Kinsey report found that "for perhaps three-quarters of all males, orgasm is reached within two minutes" (Kinsey, Pomeroy, & Martin, 1948, p. 580), but Morton Hunt's 1974 study found that the average duration of intercourse had increased dramatically, to 10 to 14 minutes, in the intervening 26 years.

This dramatic change has increased the distress of men who suffer from premature ejaculation, which is primarily a younger man's problem; the majority of cases involve men under the age of 30 (Bancroft, 1989). Premature ejaculation is typical of young men in their first sexual experiences, but they often blame themselves and think of themselves as dysfunctional, as they have no history of successful sexual relationships as a basis for sexual self-esteem. With continued sexual experience, most men spontaneously get over their initial premature ejaculation. Along with the effects of experience, the time required for a man to reach orgasm will increase as a normal physiological change in aging, but this is a slow change that occurs over many years. A young man whose premature ejaculation is not resolved with greater sexual experience would have to wait 20 to 30 years for normal aging processes to solve his problem.

Inhibited male orgasm is a relatively uncommon disorder, occurring in less than 1 percent of the general population and in only about 3 percent of patients seeking sex therapy.

**Prevalence of Female Dysfunctions** Hypoactive sexual desire is found in 20 to 35 percent of the general population of women, and sex therapists report that low sex drive is now the most commonly seen problem in clinical practice. Sexual aversion remains a less common problem, although precise prevalence figures on this form of dysfunction are not available.

Lack of arousal alone is not often a focus of either sex therapy or research, as this condition almost always coexists with orgasmic dysfunction, but there has been a great deal of research on female orgasm rates. Studies indicate that 10 to 15 percent of women have never had an orgasm, and that another 10 to 15 percent only rarely experience orgasm. Interestingly enough, the prevalence of global, lifelong lack of orgasm does not seem to have changed over the last 40 years, though change might have been expected, given the sexual revolution and the increased acceptance of female sexuality. In addition, a number of women display a situational lack of orgasm, a term that covers a wide range of behavior patterns. As we saw earlier, sex therapists agree that lack of orgasm during intercourse is not itself a dysfunction, provided the woman enjoys intercourse and can reach orgasm during genital caressing. On the other hand, traditional psychoanalytic theory did hold lack of orgasm during intercourse to be pathological (see Box 14-1).

Various studies have indicated that altogether 30 to 77 percent of women do have orgasm during intercourse. Differences in methodology probably account for this wide range of results. A reasonable current estimate is that perhaps 50 percent of women experience orgasm in intercourse at least fairly regularly (LoPiccolo & Stock, 1987).

Not many data are available on the prevalence of vaginismus and dyspareunia. While perhaps 20 percent of women occasionally experience pain during intercourse, vaginismus probably occurs in less than 1 percent of the population. Among patients of one British sex therapy clinic, 10 to 15 percent complained of vaginismus or dyspareunia as their main problem (Bancroft, 1989). This figure is higher than is typical of clinics in the United States. Perhaps these disorders are less common in America, or perhaps American women are more likely to consult their gynecologist for these problems than to go to a sex therapy clinic.

## Causes of Sexual Dysfunctions

Theories of the causes of sexual dysfunctions focus on the influence of childhood learning about sex, attitudes and beliefs that are problematic, biological causes such as the effect of diseases and medications, individual psychodynamic factors, and relationship issues. Our knowledge of causation is incomplete, and much more research is needed in this area.

**Hypoactive Sexual Desire and Sexual Aversion** The definition of low sexual desire is somewhat problematic. DSM-III-R defines this dysfunction as "persistently or recurrently deficient or absent sexual fantasies and desire for sexual activity" (p. 293), but does not specify what a "deficient" level is. Large-scale surveys (Blumstein & Schwartz, 1983; Hunt, 1974) indicate that the average frequency of sex is two to three times per week for married couples, but these figures are not very meaningful. Age, years married, education, social class, and race, to mention just a few variables, all influence this average figure. Furthermore, frequency of occurrence does not necessarily indicate level of desire, as sexual activity may occur because of pressure from the spouse or a sense of obligation. Moreover, disagreement about how often partners want to have sex does not

## BOX 14-1

# The Vaginal Orgasm Controversy

Sigmund Freud (1905) began the controversy about what constitutes sexual health for women. As we saw in Chapter 2, a child's sexuality progresses through an innate, biologically programmed series of phases, in Freud's theory. During the oral phase, in infancy, sexual pleasure is focused on the mouth. Later, during the anal phase, about age 2, erotic feelings center on the anus. Around age 4 or so, in the phallic phase, the little girl's clitoris becomes erotically charged and is her main source of sexual arousal and pleasure.

During the phallic phase, the girl develops an Electra complex: she experiences sexual feelings toward her father and rivalry with her mother. According to Freud, she feels women are inferior because they lack a penis, and develops penis envy. In healthy resolution of the Electra complex, the child identifies with her mother, accepts her femininity, and loses interest in her clitoris, which is essentially a small substitute for a penis. When she becomes a mature woman, she reaches

the genital stage, and gets her sexual arousal from vaginal stimulation. Women who failed to make this shift in focus from the clitoris to the vagina were considered, by classical psychoanalytic theory, to be fixated at an immature, neurotic, and masculine level. They were even considered to be "frigid," since the orgasms they had from clitoral stimulation were not thought to be mature and healthy (Sherfey, 1973).

What is the evidence for this theory? Essentially, it was pure speculation, without any experimental work to support it. During Freud's time, virtually nothing was known about the anatomy and physiology of female sexual response.

In the past 25 years, the weight of the evidence has been very heavily against Freud's theory. It has been shown that in comparison with the clitoris, the vagina is poorly supplied with nerve endings (Kinsey et al., 1953). The clitoris and penis both develop from the same structure in the embryo, so expecting a woman to lose

clitoral sensitivity makes as much sense as expecting a man's sexual focus to somehow switch from his penis to his scrotum. Masters and Johnson, in their pioneering studies of the female sexual response, showed that all orgasms are identical, regardless of the body part being stimulated. Furthermore, their research demonstrated that when orgasm occurs during vaginal intercourse, it does so primarily because of indirect stimulation of the clitoris (Masters & Johnson, 1966). In essence, then, there actually is no difference between a "clitoral" and a "vaginal" orgasm. Finally, decades of research have failed to demonstrate any differences in mental health, maturity, femininity, or sexual adjustment between women who have orgasms during vaginal intercourse and those who have their orgasms during direct clitoral stimulation (Sherfey, 1973; Fisher, 1973; LoPiccolo & Stock, 1987). Modern sex therapists are virtually unanimous in rejecting Freudian ideas about clitoral and vaginal orgasms.

necessarily indicate that one of them has low sexual desire. The wife may desire sex daily, for example, and the husband may want to have sex only three times a week. Both of these desired frequencies are in the normal range, and neither partner may have any psychological problems that are related to their desired frequency. This couple is just badly matched in regard to the desired frequency of intercourse. If they had chosen different partners, this might not be a problem for them. Table 14-1 shows the results of a survey of 93 happily married couples, who were asked to report their actual frequency of sex and their desired frequency. These data show there is a wide range of desired frequency, and that anything between once a day and twice a week is typical of many of the subjects surveyed. On the basis of these results and of clinical experience, it has been sug-

gested that the diagnosis of hypoactive sexual desire is not warranted unless the patient desires sex less frequently than once every two weeks (LoPiccolo & Friedman, 1988).

Actually most of the cases seen in sex therapy do not involve merely hypoactive sexual desire but virtually *nonexistent* sexual desire (LoPiccolo & Friedman, 1988). These patients typically have no interest whatsoever in having sex with their partner, do not masturbate, and do not have sexual fantasies. Typical statements from these patients include:

If my husband didn't mention it, it would probably be a year before it even occurred to me that we hadn't had sex lately.

TABLE 14-1

| DESIRED VERSUS ACTUAL FREQUENCY OF SEXUAL INTERCOURSE FOR MALES AND FEMALES IN 93 HAPPILY MARRIED COUPLES* | | | | |
| --- | --- | --- | --- | --- |
| | Percentage reporting as "desired" | | Percentage reporting as "actual" | |
| Frequency | Males | Females | Males | Females |
| More than once a day | 12.2% | 3.3% | 2.2% | 1.1% |
| Once a day | 28.9 | 19.8 | 2.2 | 1.1 |
| 3–4 times a week | 42.4 | 50.6 | 35.6 | 39.6 |
| Twice a week | 12.2 | 16.5 | 30.0 | 24.2 |
| Once a week | 4.4 | 9.9 | 15.6 | 20.9 |
| Once every 2 weeks | 0 | 0 | 8.9 | 8.8 |
| Once a month | 0 | 0 | 2.2 | 2.2 |
| Less than once a month | 0 | 0 | 3.3 | 0 |
| Not at all | 0 | 0 | 0 | 0 |

\* Mean age, 34 for men, 32 for women; married mean of 9 years; mean number of children, 2.6; mean family income, $33,000.
*Source:* LoPiccolo & Friedman, 1988.

When we have sex, I enjoy it and everything works fine. I tell myself that I should remember to do it more often. Then a month goes by, my wife gets upset with me, and I realize it slipped my mind again.

When I haven't eaten in a while, I get hungry. But it doesn't seem to matter how long it's been since we had sex, I never get hungry for sex.

Questions about the normal range of sexual desire do not enter the picture in sexual aversion disorders, patterns marked by "persistent or recurrent extreme aversion to, and avoidance of, all or almost all genital sexual contact with a partner" (APA, 1987, p. 293). The strong negative emotions that these patients experience, up to and including panic attacks or nausea and vomiting, make fine diagnostic distinctions a nonissue.

A person's sex drive is determined by a combination of physical and psychological factors, any of which may play a part in reducing sexual desire. Most cases of low sexual desire are attributable primarily to psychological factors, but certain physical conditions can lower a person's sex drive severely.

To begin with, a number of hormones are involved in the physiology of sex, and abnormalities in their levels can help cause low sex drive (Segraves, 1988a). *Testosterone,* the major male sex hormone, is an important factor in the sex drive of both men and women (in women, testosterone is produced by the adrenal glands). If testosterone is low, sex drive is usually impaired. *Luteinizing hormone,* produced in the brain by the pituitary gland, stimulates testosterone production, so an abnormally low level of this hormone is another cause of low sex drive. *Estrogen,* the primary female sex hormone, is also important for sex drive. In women, any marked deviation in the estrogen level, whether excessively high or excessively low, can result in low sex drive. There were high levels of estrogen in many of the early oral contraceptives, and many of the women who took them did have their sex drive repressed. While this effect is rarer with the low-dose pills prescribed today, it does still occur in some women. Women who are postmenopausal can have an insufficient level of estrogen, and a lowered sex drive as a result. In men, estrogen levels above the small amount normally present in their system interfere with sex drive. Men produce a small amount of estrogen, but it is usually metabolized in the liver, and so has no effect. However, in men whose liver is not functioning normally, such as men with alcoholic liver damage, estrogen levels will be elevated and sex drive reduced. Elevated levels of *prolactin,* another pituitary hormone, will interfere with sex drive in both men and women. This elevation is most often caused by a prolactin-secreting tumor in the pituitary. Abnormally high or low levels of several of the hormones secreted by the thyroid gland will also reduce sex drive. All these hormonal conditions can be treated with replacement hormones or drugs. It appears, however, that abnormal hormone levels are the cause of only a very small percentage of cases of hypoactive sexual desire (LoPiccolo & Friedman, 1988).

A number of drugs, both prescription and illicit, suppress sex drive (Segraves, 1988b). Many medications used to treat high blood pressure reduce sexual interest, as do drugs used to treat ulcers, glaucoma, allergies, heart disease, and convulsions. Many psychotropic drugs, including antianxiety, antidepressant, and antipsychotic agents, also have this effect. Most of these drugs influence the level of a neurotransmitter such as dopamine or serotonin, which seems to be involved in sexual desire. Sedative and pain-reducing medications often have the effect of lowering sex drive. While many illicit drugs, such as cocaine, marijuana, amphetamines, and heroin, may initially increase sexual interest at low doses, sex drive is uniformly very reduced in chronic users and at higher dose levels, despite the great differences in the other effects of these drugs. Alcohol may also enhance sex drive at a low level, presumably by lowering psychological inhibitions, but with higher levels and chronic use, sex drive is diminished. This outcome reflects both the sedating effect of alcohol and the liver damage that comes with long-term use. While any number of drugs are known to suppress sex drive, centuries of searching have failed to find a true aphrodisiac, a substance that increases sexual drive (Bancroft, 1989).

Not surprisingly, chronic physical illness can also suppress sex drive (Bullard, 1988). A low sex drive can be a direct result of the illness, an effect of medication on sex hormones, or a consequence of the stress, pain, and depression that often accompany chronic illness.

The psychological causes of hypoactive sex drive and sexual aversion are even more varied and complex. Situational factors such as divorce, a death in the family, job stress, or the increased life stress of having a baby when both parents are employed often lead to hypoactive sexual desire (Kaplan, 1979).

Personal beliefs and characteristics can also be important determinants. A number of traits are commonly found in association with hypoactive sexual desire and sexual aversion. Being raised in a severely antisexual religion or culture is one such factor. Having an exaggeratedly hardworking, serious approach to life and thinking of sex as frivolous or self-indulgent is another. People with mild obsessive-compulsive traits may find contact with another person's body fluids and odors to be unpleasant and aversive. People who are basically homosexually oriented may marry, either as a way of ensuring social acceptance or as a means of escaping from impulses they regard as unacceptable, and then find their sexual desire to be low in this heterosexual relationship. Some low-desire patients have been hurt in past relationships in which they felt strong sexual desire. These people may now fear loss of control over their sexual urges, and therefore suppress them completely. Occasionally patients with low sexual desire actually have a sexual deviation, or paraphilia, and are therefore not very interested in normal sexual activity. For example, men who are transvestites (aroused by dressing up in women's clothes, wigs, and makeup) often marry without admitting their transvestism to their wives, and then appear to have hypoactive sexual desire, because their interest in conventional sex is low. Simple fear of pregnancy can inhibit sexual desire, and so can even a mild level of depression. Because our culture defines sexual attractiveness in terms of youth, many aging men and women lose interest in sex as their self-esteem and attraction to their partner diminish with age.

There are also many relationship-based causes of hypoactive sexual desire and sexual aversion. Simply being in an unhappy, conflicted relationship is sufficient to suppress sex drive or make sex unpleasant. If one partner gains a large amount of weight or becomes careless about personal hygiene, this can make sex unappealing or unpleasant for the other. If one partner is a very unskilled, unenthusiastic lover, the other can begin to lose interest in sex. Sometimes people in an otherwise happy marriage differ in their needs for closeness and "personal space." The one who needs more personal space may develop hypoactive sexual desire as a way of creating the necessary distance. A person who feels powerless in a relationship and very dominated by the other can also lose sexual interest. Finally, some men, having adopted our culture's double standard, are unable to feel sexual desire for a woman they love and respect. Some of these men lose sexual interest when their wife has their first child, as they cannot see a mother as a sexually exciting woman.

While all of these factors can lead to either hypoactive sexual desire or sexual aversion, the experience of having been molested or assaulted is especially likely to result in sexual aversion (Browne & Finklehor, 1986). Women are infinitely more likely than men to be raped as adults or molested as children; thus the majority of people with sexual aversion disorder are female. Research has indicated that sexual aversion is extremely common in victims of sexual abuse and persists for years, even decades, afterward (Becker, 1989; Maltz & Holman, 1987). These people typically have very specific aversions to whatever happened to them during the assault. For example, a woman who as a child was forced to fondle her father's penis may be unable to look at or touch her husband's genitals without strong feelings of revulsion and disgust. In extreme cases, these patients may experience vivid flashbacks during adult sexual activity, and visual memories of the assault overwhelm them.

**Erectile Failure**   As the following case history illustrates, erectile failure is often caused by a combination of physiological and psychological factors.

> *Robert, a 57-year-old man, came to sex therapy with his* wife because of his inability to get erections. He had not had a problem with erections until 6 months earlier, when they attempted to have sex after an evening out, during which he had had several drinks. They attributed his failure to get an erection to his being "a little drunk," but he found himself worrying over the next few days that he was perhaps becoming impotent. When they next attempted intercourse, he found himself unable to get involved in what they were doing because he was so intent on watching himself to see if he would get an erection. Once again he did not, and they were both very upset. His failure to get an erection continued over the next few months. Robert's wife was very upset and sexually frustrated, accusing him of having an affair, or of no longer finding her attractive. Robert wondered if he was getting too old, or if his medication for high blood pressure, which he had been taking for about a year, might be interfering with erection. Robert was a heavy smoker and was overweight—two factors that contributed to his high blood pressure. When they came for sex therapy, they had not attempted any sexual activity for over 2 months.

Until recently, cases of erectile failure were customarily categorized as *either* psychogenic *or* organic, as if these were two mutually exclusive categories. Current thinking acknowledges that many cases—perhaps the majority—involve some partial organic impairment of the erection response, which in turn makes the man more vulnerable to the psychological factors that inhibit erection (LoPiccolo, 1985). One recent study found that only 10 of 63 cases of erectile failure were caused by purely psychogenic factors, and only 5 were the result of organic impairment alone (LoPiccolo, 1991).

The same hormonal abnormalities that can cause hypoactive sexual desire can also produce erectile failure. However, abnormal levels of testosterone, estrogen, prolactin, or thyroid hormones are found in only a small percentage of cases. Vascular abnormalities are much more common. Since an erection occurs when the chambers in the penis fill with blood, erectile failure can result from heart disease, restriction of blood flow into the penis by atherosclerosis (clogging of the arteries,

which can result from years of heavy smoking), or excessive drainage from abnormally large penile veins. Leakage of blood out of the penile chambers through holes or tears can also cause erectile failure, as can disease or damage to the nervous system. Perhaps 50 percent of diabetic men experience erectile failure, as diabetes often damages the peripheral nerves involved with erection. Spinal cord injuries, kidney failure, and renal dialysis (treatment with an artificial kidney machine) can each produce erectile failure. Many of the medications that lower sexual drive also interfere with erection, so men who take medication for high blood pressure, allergies, ulcers, anxiety, or depression may experience erectile failure as a result (Tanagho, Lue, & McClure, 1988).

Medical procedures for diagnosing organic causes of erectile failure have become very sophisticated in the past few years. With *Doppler ultrasound recording,* blood flow in the penis can be measured very accurately and vascular abnormalities located. Hormonal factors can be evaluated from simple blood tests.

Neurological damage is more difficult to assess, but

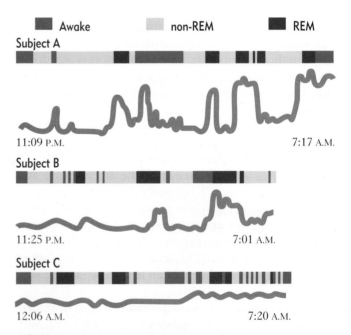

**FIGURE 14-4** Measurements of erections during sleep help reveal the sources of erectile problems. Subject A, a man without erectile problems, has normal erections during REM sleep. Subject B has erectile failure problems that seem to be at least partly psychogenic—otherwise he would not have any erections during REM sleep. Subject C's erectile failure disorder is related to severe organic problems, an interpretation supported by his lack of erections during REM sleep. *(Adapted from Bancroft, 1985.)*

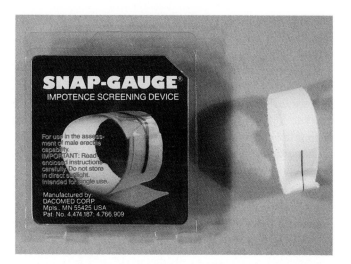

The *snap-gauge,* worn around the penis at night, is a fabric band with three plastic filaments. If the filaments are broken in the morning, the man knows that he has experienced normal erections during REM sleep and that erectile failures during intercourse are probably due to psychological factors. If the filaments are still intact, his erection problems may be due to organic impairment.

evaluation of *nocturnal penile tumescence (NPT),* or erections during sleep, in a sleep laboratory is very useful. Men typically have erections during rapid eye movement (REM) sleep, the phase that corresponds with dreaming (see p. 390). A healthy man will have two to five REM periods each night, with perhaps two to three hours of nocturnal penile erections (see Figure 14-4). Abnormal or absent NPT usually indicates some organic basis for erectile failure (Mohr & Beutler, 1990). Because it is expensive to have the patient sleep in a hospital-based sleep laboratory, portable take-home recorders are available, as are simple "snap gauge" bands that the patient fastens around his penis before going to sleep and then checks the next morning. Broken bands indicate that penile erection has occurred during the night. These snap gauges are only rough screening devices; indeed the lack of NPT may indicate an abnormal lack of REM sleep rather than organic impairment of erection (Mohr & Beutler, 1990).

Psychological factors underlying erectile failure can be quite complex. Any of the individual or interpersonal causes of hypoactive sexual desire, such as marital conflict, lack of attraction to the partner, or fear of closeness, can also interfere with arousal and lead to erectile failure. Certain psychological and behavioral issues, however, are particularly likely to be associated with erectile failure.

A major psychological mechanism emphasized by Masters and Johnson (1970) is *performance anxiety* and *the spectator role.* Once a man begins to experience erectile problems, for whatever initial reason, he becomes anxious about failing to have an erection and worries during each sexual encounter. Instead of relaxing and enjoying the sensations of sexual pleasure, he remains somewhat distanced from the activity, watching himself and focusing on the goal of reaching erection. Instead of being an aroused participant, he becomes a self-evaluative spectator. Whatever the initial reason for erectile failure, the resulting anxious, self-evaluative spectator role becomes the reason for the ongoing problem. In this self-perpetuating vicious cycle, the original cause of the erectile failure becomes less important than fear of failure.

The performance-anxiety theory has been tested by David Barlow (1986) in a series of laboratory analogue experiments. In these studies, erotic films are shown both to men with erectile failure and to normal control subjects, and their erection responses are recorded by a gauge around the penis called a *plethysmograph* (see Figure 14-5). Before viewing the films, the men are given either a "performance demand" instruction (for example, a request that they try to get the best erection they can or a threat that they will receive an electric shock if an erection does not occur) or a "no demand" instruction that simply asks them to watch the films. Interestingly, normal men tend to respond to performance demands with *increased* erection, while erectile-failure patients show the pattern predicted by Masters and Johnson: their best erections occur in the absence of a performance demand. Barlow suggests that it is not performance demand per se that causes erectile failure, but the way a man cognitively processes a perceived performance demand. Performance demands cause nondysfunctional men to focus on the sexually stimulating aspects of the encounter, increasing their arousal, but cause anxiety and fear of failure in dysfunctional men. Barlow also compared the men's subjective ratings of their erections with actual physiological measurements of the penis, and found that normal men perceive their erections accurately, but dysfunctional men underestimate the degree of their erections. This finding supports the idea that negative self-evaluation has a role in erectile failure. While these studies have identified interesting differences between erectile-failure patients and the control group, they don't explain how the differences developed. It is possible that the earlier experience of erectile failure leads these patients to respond to performance cues with anxiety, rather than the reverse order of causation suggested by Barlow.

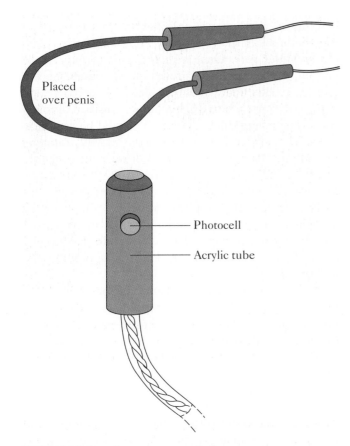

**FIGURE 14-5** Experimenters use a plethysmograph to measure sexual arousal in subjects. A penile plethysmograph *(above)*, a rubber tube filled with mercury is placed around the penis. The diameter of the column of mercury increases as the subject becomes aroused. A vaginal plethysmograph, a tampon-shaped device with a light at its end, is inserted in the vagina. It reflects more and more light as the arteries of the vaginal wall receive additional blood—as the subject becomes increasingly aroused.

Another major psychological factor in erectile failure is the nature of the sexual relationship between a male patient and his wife (LoPiccolo, 1991). There are two relationship patterns that may contribute to erectile failure. In one, the wife provides inadequate physical stimulation to the husband. As a man ages, more intense, direct, and lengthy physical stimulation of the penis is required for erection to occur. This is a normal change and does not necessarily lead to erectile failure, but many older wives, raised in a more conservative time, have never engaged in much stimulation of the husband's penis, and the husbands have never asked them to. When they were younger, the psychological stimulation of kissing his wife and caressing her breasts and genitals led to good erections in the husband. Now that they are aging, he needs more physical stimulation, and

because they are not aware of these normal changes, he may begin to develop the anxieties that lead to erectile failure. The second relationship pattern may occur when a couple believes that only intercourse can give the wife an orgasm. This idea increases the pressure on the man to have an erection and makes him more vulnerable to erectile failure. If the wife reaches orgasm through oral or manual caressing of her genitals, she does not depend on his erection for her sexual gratification, and his performance pressure is reduced.

**Premature Ejaculation**    Eddie's case history is typical of many men with premature ejaculation:

*Eddie, a 20-year-old student, sought treatment after his* girlfriend ended their relationship because his premature ejaculation left her sexually frustrated. Eddie had had only one previous sexual relationship, during his senior year in high school. With two friends he would drive to a neighboring town and find a certain prostitute. After picking her up, they would drive to a deserted area and take turns having sex with her, while the others waited outside the car. Both the prostitute and his friends urged him to hurry up because they feared discovery by the police, and besides, in the winter it was cold. When Eddie began his sexual relationship with his girlfriend, his entire sexual history consisted of this rapid intercourse, with virtually no foreplay. He found caressing his girlfriend's breasts and genitals and her touching of his penis to be so arousing that he sometimes ejaculated before complete entry of the penis, or after at most only a minute or so of intercourse.

Research has failed to connect premature ejaculation to organic factors, or to the complex individual and relationship factors associated with hypoactive sexual desire or erectile failure. Rather, premature ejaculation seems to be typical of young, sexually inexperienced men who simply have not *learned* to slow down, modulate their arousal, and prolong the pleasurable process of making love. Men who have sex only infrequently are also prone to ejaculate prematurely, as the sensory threshold in the penis varies with the frequency and recency of sexual activity (LoPiccolo, 1985). Because both anxiety and ejaculation involve activation of the sympathetic nervous system, the anxiety aroused by efforts to delay ejaculation can make the problem worse (Bancroft, 1989).

Masters and Johnson (1970) proposed that men learn to be rapid ejaculators during adolescent masturbation, when they often hurry to ejaculate because of fear of being discovered by their parents. Such experiences, however, seem to have been equally common in men who are not premature ejaculators (Heiman, Gladue, Roberts, & LoPiccolo, 1986). Helen Kaplan (1974) proposed that premature ejaculators cannot accurately perceive their own arousal level and therefore cannot control their ejaculation. However, a laboratory study that compared premature ejaculators and age-matched normal control subjects actually found that the premature ejaculators were *more* accurate when their self-ratings were compared with objective measures of physiological arousal (Spiess, Geer, & O'Donohue, 1984). It may be that premature ejaculators, who because of their problem keep their attention focused on how close they are to ejaculation throughout the sex act, have trained themselves to be unusually accurate self-observers in this regard. Some evolutionary biologists have even speculated that rapid ejaculation may have been selected for during primate evolution, through a "survival of the fastest" process (Hong, 1984). A male who could ejaculate rapidly would be more likely to reproduce successfully, as there would be less chance that the female would escape, another male would interrupt, or a predator would attack before coitus was completed. None of these theories is well supported by research.

**Inhibited Ejaculation**    A number of physiological factors can inhibit ejaculation. A low testosterone level can interfere, and so can any neurological disease that reduces peripheral sensation or impairs functioning of the sympathetic nervous system. Men with multiple sclerosis or with neuropathy caused by diabetes may first experience inhibited ejaculation and then later develop erectile failure, as the ejaculation reflex seems to be more fragile than the erection reflex. Drugs that inhibit sympathetic arousal, such as alcohol, certain medications for high blood pressure, some antidepressants, and most antianxiety and antipsychotic agents can also inhibit ejaculation (Bancroft, 1989). Men who suffer a concussion may develop inhibited ejaculation, but the mechanism for this effect is not known (LoPiccolo, 1985).

Psychological causes of inhibited ejaculation are thought to be similar to those for erectile failure. The concept of performance anxiety and the spectator role has been stressed: once a man begins to focus on reaching orgasm, he stops being an aroused participant in his sexual activity and instead becomes an unaroused, self-critical observer. Inhibited ejaculation may also be secondary to hypoactive sexual desire (LoPiccolo & Friedman, 1988). A man who engages in sex primarily because of pressure from his partner, without any real desire for sex, simply may not get aroused enough to reach orgasm.

Myths aside, people do not lose interest in sex as they age. Most middle-aged and elderly women and men remain fully capable of sexual performance and orgasms, although the speed and intensity of their sexual response may lessen somewhat.

**Female Arousal and Orgasm Dysfunctions**    Stephanie and Bill, married for three years, came for sex therapy because of her total lack of orgasm.

*Stephanie had never had an orgasm in any way, but* because of Bill's concern, she had been faking orgasm during intercourse until recently. Finally she told him the truth, and they sought therapy together. Stephanie had been raised by a strictly religious family. She could not recall ever seeing her parents kiss or show physical affection for each other. She was severely punished on one occasion when her mother found her looking at her own genitals, at about age 7. Stephanie received no sex education from her parents, and when she began to menstruate, her mother told her only that this meant that she could become pregnant, so she mustn't ever kiss a boy or let a boy touch her. Her mother restricted her dating severely, with repeated warnings that "Boys only want one thing." While her parents were rather critical and demanding of her (asking her why she got one B among otherwise straight A's on her report card, for example), they were loving parents and their approval was very important to her.

Stephanie's history seems to provide a clear example of the causes of orgasm problems in women. However, things are not quite this simple. Until recently there was a major weakness in the theory of female arousal and orgasm dysfunctions proposed by sex therapists. The traditional theory considered these dysfunctions to result from our culture's double standard, which demands that women suppress and deny their sexuality. According to this view, women are raised with negative messages about what it means to be sexual, and sexual dysfunction is a direct result of this learning (Masters & Johnson, 1970). The flaw in this theory is that it doesn't explain why some women develop healthy sexuality and others become dysfunctional, since all of them are exposed to the same cultural message. Most inorgasmic women who come for therapy report that they, like Stephanie, were raised in a sexually restrictive manner, which suggests that factors such as religious upbringing, punishment for childhood masturbation, lack of preparedness for onset of menstruation, restrictions placed on adolescent dating, and being told that "nice girls don't" are indeed likely causes of orgasmic dysfunction. Research has demonstrated, however, that this kind of history is just as common among sexually functional women (LoPiccolo and Stock, 1987; Morokoff, 1978; Fisher, 1973). Unfortunately, the "protector factors" that make some women immune to these negative cultural and familial messages about female sexuality have yet to be identified. It is also unclear just how powerful the cultural script is that says nice women are nonsexual. One study did find that 88 percent of inorgasmic women, but only 30 percent of orgasmic women, reported they had been "good girls" as children — that is, they were obedient, did well in school, and never had major conflicts with their parents (O'Connor, 1979).

Psychological factors known to reduce arousal and interfere with orgasm in women include all the individual and relationship factors listed earlier as factors in hypoactive sexual desire and sexual aversion. Fifty to seventy-five percent of women molested as children or raped as adults have arousal and orgasm dysfunctions (Browne & Finklehor, 1986).

Kinsey's study in 1953 found that orgasm was more frequent in women who were better educated, came from upper-class families, had been married longer, and had more experience with adolescent masturbation or premarital petting. Kinsey also found that women born later in the century had a higher orgasm rate than those born earlier, presumably a reflection of the sexual liberalization that occurred during the 1920s and 1930s. Morton Hunt's large-scale study in 1974, however, did not find that any of these differences still existed some 20 years later. He concluded that the widespread social revolution of the last generation, with its increased acceptance of female sexuality, had wiped out the effects of education, social class, and so on. A very comprehensive study by Seymour Fisher (1973) found no relationship between orgasm rates and such personality traits as femininity, aggressiveness, passivity, guilt, impulsivity,

and narcissism. Fisher did find, however, that positive memories of a good father-daughter relationship during childhood and adolescence were related to attainment of orgasm in adulthood.

When a large number of sexually dysfunctional women in sex therapy were compared with a matched control group of highly sexually responsive women, some interesting factors related to orgasm consistency were brought to light (Heiman, Gladue, Roberts, & LoPiccolo, 1986). Childhood memories of a positive relationship with mother, affection between parents, mother's positive personality qualities, and mother's expression of positive emotions were all shown to be related to orgasm. Even more strongly related were the degree of emotional involvement and the length of the relationship at the time of the woman's first experience of coitus, the pleasure she obtained during that experience, her current attraction to her partner's body, and marital happiness. Interestingly, it was also found that use of sexual fantasies during sex with the current partner was much more common in orgasmic than in dysfunctional women.

Some physiological conditions can also affect women's arousal and orgasm. Diabetes can damage the nervous system in ways that interfere with arousal, vaginal lubrication, and possibly orgasm. Similarly, many women with multiple sclerosis or some other neurological disease are inorgasmic (Schover & Jensen, 1988). The same medications and drugs that inhibit ejaculation in men interfere with orgasm in women. Postmenopausal changes in skin sensitivity and in the structure of the clitoris and the vaginal walls can lead to either dyspareunia or orgasmic dysfunction in some women (Morokoff, 1988).

A number of theories have related female orgasm to the size of the clitoris, the presence of adhesions between clitoral shaft and hood, the distance from the clitoris to the vaginal opening, and the strength of the *pubococcygeal (PC) muscle* (part of the pelvic floor). However, research has failed to support these ideas (LoPiccolo & Stock, 1987).

**Vaginismus** Vaginismus has no physiological cause; it is a psychological condition in which the muscles around the vagina involuntarily contract. It is considered to be a conditioned fear response, set off by anticipation that vaginal penetration will be painful and damaging. Vaginismus can result from general anxiety and ignorance about sexual intercourse, specific fears caused by exaggerated stories about how painful and bloody the first occasion of intercourse is for women, trauma caused by an unskilled, impatient lover who forces his penis into the vagina before the woman is aroused and lubricated, and, of course, the trauma of childhood sexual abuse or adult rape. Women who experience painful intercourse because of an infection of the vagina or urinary tract or a gynecological disease such as herpes simplex, or after menopause, can develop a "rational" vaginismus, as it is true that insertion of the penis *will* be painful for them unless they obtain medical treatment for these conditions. Most women who have vaginismus also have other dysfunctions, such as sexual aversion or orgasmic dysfunction, but this is not always the case. Some women with vaginismus enjoy sex, have a high sex drive, and have orgasm from clitoral stimulation. In these women, the negative emotions are specific to fear of vaginal penetration.

**Dyspareunia** Painful intercourse in women usually has a physical cause. Sex therapists have learned to be skeptical about patients referred for treatment of "psychogenic dyspareunia," as the majority of such diagnoses reflect the referring gynecologist's ignorance about physical causes of painful intercourse rather than an absence of organic cause (LoPiccolo & Stock, 1987). Damage caused by childbirth is the most common cause of dyspareunia, as delivery can injure the vagina, cervix, uterus, or the pelvic ligaments. Similarly, the scar left by an episiotomy (a cut often made to enlarge the vaginal entrance and ease delivery) can be a source of pain. The penis hitting remnants or strands of the hymen can cause dyspareunia; so can an undiagnosed vaginal infection; and wiry pubic hair can abrade the labia when penile thrusting drags it into the vagina. Pelvic diseases such as endometriosis (a condition in which tissue migrates from the lining of the uterus and becomes attached to internal organs), tumors, and cysts are also possible causes, as are allergic reactions to the chemicals in vaginal douches, spermicidal contraceptive creams, the rubber in condoms or diaphragms, or the protein in male semen (Lo-Piccolo & Stock, 1987).

Dyspareunia that is truly psychogenic usually reflects a simple lack of arousal: it is painful to have a penis forced into an unaroused, unlubricated vagina. In other words, psychogenic dyspareunia is synonymous with female sexual arousal disorder. Women who suffer from organically based dyspareunia usually report that they enjoy sex and get aroused, but their sex life is being ruined by the pain that accompanies what used to be an unreservedly positive event.

# Treatment of Sexual Dysfunctions

The last twenty years have brought a remarkable change in the psychotherapeutic procedures used to treat sexual dysfunction. Since early in this century, the major treatment approach had been long-term, intensive Freudian psychoanalysis, on the assumption that sexual dysfunction was caused by failure to progress through the stages of childhood psychosexual development. To advance through the developmental stages, the patient had to reexperience childhood (more successfully this time) by means of the transference relationship with the analyst, which functions as a substitute for the original parent-child relationship. A major personality reorganization was considered necessary, since in psychoanalytic theory, sexual dysfunctions are symptomatic of a much larger failure of personality development. It was thought that analytic therapy four to five times a week over many months or even years would be required to increase sexual functioning. This idea led analysts to conclude that "as a mass problem, the question of frigidity is unfortunately not to be solved" (Bergler, 1951).

In the 1950s and 1960s, behavioral therapists began to offer alternative treatments for sexual dysfunctions. In behavioral theory, sexual dysfunctions are considered to result from anxiety, which is known to block sexual response. Therapeutic procedures consisted of training in muscle relaxation, which reduces anxiety, and systematic desensitization (Lazarus, 1965; Wolpe, 1958). In systematic desensitization of erectile failure, for example, patients would become deeply relaxed and then imagine or visualize sexual scenes, beginning with mild activities such as kissing and working up to images of intercourse. When the patients could imagine a sexual activity without becoming anxious and tense, they would be permitted to try the activity at home, in actual sexual interaction with their partner. This anxiety-reduction approach was moderately successful but did not work when the major causes of dysfunction were misinformation, a negative attitude, and lack of effective sexual technique.

A revolution in the treatment of sexual dysfunctions occurred with the publication of Masters and Johnson's *Human Sexual Inadequacy* in 1970. Their approach came to be known as "sex therapy." Over the years their procedures have been modified and some entirely new ones added, so that today's sex therapy is a complex treatment approach with several different components, including cognitive, behavioral, and communication skill–building techniques. At the same time, modern sex therapy is short term, focused specifically on the sexual problem rather than on personality reorganization, and directive in nature. Fifteen to twenty sessions of weekly therapy are typical for treatment of most dysfunctions.

The first component of sex therapy is the *assessment and conceptualization* of the problem. Along with a medi-

The extensive research, theories, and clinical reports of William Masters and Virginia Johnson have dramatically changed the way clinicians understand and treat sexual functioning and dysfunctioning.

cal examination to uncover possible organic problems, the patient is interviewed concerning his or her "sex history." The emphasis is on understanding both past life events and current factors that cause the dysfunction. Masters and Johnson (1970) spent several hours taking histories from each patient, but modern practice is to spend much less time on the past than on the current emotions, attitudes, and behavior that maintain the dysfunction (LoPiccolo, 1990). When discussing these causative factors with patients, sex therapists stress the principle of **mutual responsibility.** Both partners in a relationship share the sexual problem, regardless of who has the actual dysfunction. The husband of an inorgasmic woman, for example, is partially responsible for creating or maintaining their problem, and he is also a patient who needs to make changes if she is ever to be able to have an orgasm. Because of the principle of mutual responsibility, sex therapists much prefer to have both members of a sexual partnership in therapy, and indeed, treatment is generally more successful

when that is the case (Heiman, LoPiccolo, & LoPiccolo, 1981). Often the partner who does not have a dysfunction is reluctant to enter therapy, claiming that "it's not my problem." The sex therapist's response is that assigning blame is not the issue, and while the nondysfunctional partner may have had nothing to do with *causing* the problem, he or she clearly has a crucial role to play in *solving* it. Masters and Johnson (1970) suggested that patient couples would feel more comfortable with a male-female therapy team, since each would then have an advocate in the therapist who knows what intercourse is like for a person of her or his sex. Masters and Johnson considered this "dual sex co-therapy team" to be crucial for therapeutic success, but research comparing the success rates of single therapists and dual sex co-therapy teams has not shown any differences in effectiveness (LoPiccolo, Heiman, Hogan, & Roberts, 1985). Because of the greater expense of co-therapy, most sex therapy today is done by one therapist working alone.

A second major component of sex therapy is the provision of *accurate information* about sexuality. Many patients who suffer from sexual dysfunction know very little about the anatomy and physiology of sexual response. They may be misinformed about effective techniques of sexual stimulation, the role of the clitoris in a woman's orgasm, or the need for more physical stimulation to produce penile erection as men age. Sex therapists assess and supplement their patients' knowledge through discussion, instructional books and videotapes, and professional educational films.

The third component of sex therapy is work to *change problematic attitudes, cognitions, and beliefs* about sexuality. Family attitudes toward sex, past traumatic experiences, and the patients' own emotional reaction to dysfunction in themselves or their partners can all create strongly negative thoughts and emotions that prevent sexual arousal and pleasure, and our socially imposed sex roles are accompanied by a set of sex-role myths or cognitive distortions that can also lead to sexual dysfunctions. Some of these widespread myths are listed in Box 14-2. Helping patients to examine these myths critically can be very therapeutic.

Another important component of sex therapy is the *elimination of performance anxiety and the spectator role* through **sensate focus** and **nondemand pleasuring.** Since pressure to attain an erection or orgasm interferes with arousal, sex therapy begins with a ban on intercourse and genital caressing. Couples are instructed that for a time, sexual activity at home is to be restricted to kissing, hugging, and sensual whole-body massage, not including breasts or genitals. Over successive weeks their sexual repertoire is gradually rebuilt, with a constant emphasis on enjoying the experience of sensual pleasure and not striving for results. Although the sensate focus principle is associated with Masters and Johnson (1970), who systematized it, a British physician, Sir John Hunter, is known to have suggested the same approach over 200 years ago. Sir John told a man with erectile failure to "'go to bed with this woman, but first resolve to himself that he would not have any connection with her, for six nights. . . . He told me that his resolution had produced such a total alteration in the state of his mind that the powers [erection] soon took place, for instead of going to bed with the fear of inability, he went with fears that he would be possessed with too much desire, too much power'" (Hunter & MacAlpine, 1963).

The fifth component of sex therapy is to *increase communication and the effectiveness of sexual technique.* Because it is embarrassing or uncomfortable for most dysfunctional patients to tell their partners what they find pleasurable in sexual activity, they do not learn from each other, but instead engage in the same ineffective sexual techniques over and over. During therapy the couple are told to use their sensate focus sessions at home to try sexual positions in which the person being caressed can guide the other's hands and regulate the speed, pressure, and location of the caressing. Couples are also taught to give verbal instructions in a nonthreatening, informative manner ("It feels better over here, with a little less pressure"), instead of in a threatening manner that doesn't tell the partner what to do differently ("The way you're touching me doesn't turn me on").

The last general component of sex therapy is to *change destructive lifestyles and marital interactions.* Sex is the lowest priority in the schedule of many dysfunctional patients, and if sex is left until late at night, in bed, when both partners are exhausted, they are unlikely to feel any sensuality and pleasure. The sex therapist will suggest that couples rearrange their priorities, and have their sensate focus sessions when they are relaxed, not tired out or under time pressure. Similarly, if the couple's marriage is in conflict, or if there is little emotional connection between them, trying to build a good sexual relationship is virtually impossible. In such cases the therapist will help the couple restructure their relationship to reduce conflict and build more closeness.

Specific techniques have been developed to treat each of the sexual dysfunctions.

### Hypoactive Sexual Desire and Sexual Aversion

Because of the many difficult psychological issues that are likely to underlie hypoactive sexual desire and sexual aversion, these dysfunctions require a longer and more complex program of treatment than others. Jerry Friedman and I (1988) have described a four-element sequential treatment model for hypoactive drive and aversion that is widely used.

The first stage of therapy, called *affectual awareness,* focuses on helping the client become aware of his or her negative emotions regarding sex. Therapy sessions during which the patient visualizes sexual scenes help uncover feelings of anxiety, fear, resentment, vulnerability, and so forth. Many patients claim that they have overcome negative ideas about sex, but such changes are likely to be superficial, leaving a negative affectual (emotional or gut-level) residue hidden under a bland umbrella feeling of lack of interest in sex. The purpose of the affectual awareness stage of therapy is to get under this umbrella and make the patient aware that he or she is not just naturally uninterested in sex, but that something is blocking the normal biological sex drive that all people have.

The second phase of therapy, the *insight* phase, helps patients understand why they have the negative emotions identified in the affectual awareness phase. Negative messages from their religion, culture, family, and current and past relationships are explored. In a sense, this and the previous step are preparatory. The more active treatment follows.

The third phase of therapy fosters *cognitive and emotional change.* In this phase, cognitive techniques are applied to the irrational thoughts and emotions that inhibit sexual desire. Patients generate "coping statements" that help them change their negative emotions and thoughts. Typical statements might be "If I allow myself to enjoy sex, it doesn't mean I'll lose control," and "When I was younger I learned to feel guilty about sex, but I'm a grownup now, and I don't have to feel that way anymore."

The fourth stage of treatment consists of *behavioral interventions.* It is at this stage that sensate focus, skill training, and other general sex therapy procedures are introduced. Sex drive is heightened in a number of ways: having patients keep a "desire diary" in which they record sexual thoughts and feelings, having them read books and view films with good erotic content, and encouraging them to develop their own sexual fantasies. All of these activities make sexual thoughts and cues more readily available to the patient. Nonsexual affection, consisting of simple hugs, squeezes, and pats, and pleasurable shared activities such as dancing and walking together are also encouraged, to help strengthen feelings of sensual enjoyment and sexual attraction.

For sexual aversion resulting from sexual assault or childhood molestation, additional therapeutic procedures are used. The patient is encouraged to remember the assault, and to talk and think about these memories until they are no longer traumatic. In another procedure, the patient writes letters to the molester or has an "empty-chair" mock dialogue with the molester, in order to finally express the feelings of rage and power-

═══════ BOX 14-2 ═══════

# Sex-Role Myths

## MYTHS OF MALE SEXUALITY

1. *Men should not have certain emotions.* Men believe they are supposed to be strong, aggressive, competitive, unemotional, and in control. All of these emotions interfere with the tenderness, closeness, sensuality, openness, and emotional expressiveness that contribute to good sex.

2. *In sex, it's performance that counts.* Men take a goal-oriented approach to sex, equating erections and orgasm with success, and are unable to relax and enjoy sex as a pleasurable process rather than as an end to be achieved.

3. *The man must take charge and orchestrate sex.* Men who think this way do not let the woman guide them to do what she likes to have done to her. This attitude also leads a man to focus on what he is doing to the woman, rather than learning to receive pleasure from what she does to him.

4. *A man always wants and is always ready to have sex.* This myth pressures men to try to have sex in situations or relationships in which they are not emotionally comfortable, with predictably unpleasant results.

5. *All physical contact must lead to sex.* This notion prevents men from simply enjoying kissing, hugging, cuddling, and caressing, as they see these activities as only a prelude to "the real thing."

6. *Sex equals intercourse.* This myth is especially destructive to men with erectile problems. If a man and his partner can derive sexual pleasure and orgasm from manual or oral genital caressing, any performance anxiety that might interfere with erection will be greatly reduced.

7. *Sex requires an erection.* This is a corollary to myth 6. The truth is that the penis is not the only sexual part of the man's body, and couples can have very pleasurable sex without an erection.

8. *Good sex is a linear progression of increasing excitement terminated only by orgasm.* Acceptance of this myth eliminates the pleasure of leisurely, playful sex, which may include breaks to talk, rest, and enjoy each other fully as people rather than as just genital organs.

9. *Sex should be natural and spontaneous.* This myth prevents couples from teaching each other what they like during sex. For today's typical couple, with both partners working, sharing child-rearing responsibilities, and living high-stress lives, it is often necessary to make very nonspontaneous plans for sex, designating a time when both are likely to be relaxed, not exhausted, and capable of responding sexually.

10. *In this enlightened age, myths 1–9 no longer have any influence on us.* While the sexual liberalization of the past 30 years has eliminated some sexual inhibitions, it has caused us to worry much more about being good enough at sex and to strive to emulate the supersexual role models in

---

lessness the assault created. During the cognitive phase, patients are encouraged not to allow the offender to continue to harm them by inhibiting their sex life now, but rather to fight back by recovering the sexuality that was taken from them by the molestation. Sensate focus is carefully structured so that location, context, and sexual actions do not set off flashbacks to the assault.

This type of program seems to be fairly successful. In one study of the approach, frequency of sex increased from once a month to once a week for men who had experienced hypoactive sexual desire, and from once every two weeks to more than once a week for female patients. Women who had experienced sexual aversion increased sexual intercourse from less than once every two weeks to more than once a week (Schover & LoPiccolo, 1982).

**Erectile Failure**    Treatment of erectile failure also consists of reducing performance anxiety and increasing stimulation. During sensate focus, the couple learns the "tease technique," in which, if he gets an erection in response to her caressing, they stop until he loses it. This exercise teaches them that erections occur naturally in response to stimulation, as long as the couple doesn't focus on performance. When they are ready to resume intercourse, the man lies on his back and the woman

current literature, films, and music.

*(Zilbergeld, 1978)*

## MYTHS OF FEMALE SEXUALITY

1. *Sex is only for women under 30.* Many women don't reach their peak of sexual responsiveness until their mid-30s, and there is no real decline thereafter.

2. *Normal women have an orgasm every time they have sex.* Even for easily orgasmic women, 70 to 80 percent of the time is the average rate of orgasm.

3. *All women can have multiple orgasms.* Research indicates that 20 percent of women are multiply orgasmic. There is no relationship between sexual adjustment or satisfaction and the number of orgasms a woman has each time she has sex.

4. *Pregnancy and delivery reduce women's sexual responsiveness.* While discomfort during the last months of pregnancy and just after delivery can temporarily inhibit sex, the increased blood supply to the pelvis that de-

velops during pregnancy can actually increase sexual responsiveness.

5. *A woman's sex life ends with menopause.* While vaginal dryness can interfere with enjoyment of intercourse in some postmenopausal women who do not receive estrogen therapy, many women, freed from concerns about contraception and pregnancy, experience increased sexual arousal and interest after menopause.

6. *There are different kinds of orgasm related to a woman's personality. Vaginal orgasms are more feminine and mature than clitoral orgasm.* An orgasm is an orgasm, not a personality trait.

7. *A sexually responsive woman can always be turned on by her partner.* Fatigue, anger, worry, and many other emotions suppress sexuality in even the most responsive women.

8. *Nice women aren't aroused by erotic books or films.* Research indicates that women are just as aroused by erotica as men are.

9. *You are frigid if you don't like the more exotic forms of sex.* Many

very sexual women aren't interested in oral or anal sex, sex toys such as vibrators, or group sex.

10. *If you can't have an orgasm quickly and easily, there's something wrong with you.* The threshold for orgasm varies naturally among women. Just as some women can run faster than others, some have orgasm more rapidly.

11. *Feminine women don't initiate sex or become wild and unrestrained during sex.* This is a holdover of the Victorian double standard.

12. *Double jeopardy: you're frigid if you don't have sexual fantasies and a wanton woman if you do.* Many, but not all, sexually responsive women do have sexual fantasies.

13. *Contraception is a woman's responsibility, and she's just making up excuses if she says contraceptive issues are inhibiting her sexually.* Many highly sexual women find their sexual enjoyment interfered with by contraceptive technology. Many couples who feel their families are complete find vasectomy to be a good solution.

*(Heiman & LoPiccolo, 1988)*

kneels above him and uses her fingers to push his *non-erect* penis into her vagina. This procedure, known as the "stuffing technique," frees him from having to have a rigid penis to accomplish entry. The couple are instructed to achieve the woman's orgasms through manual or oral sex, again reducing pressure on the male to perform.

This set of procedures seems to work well in cases in which there is no severe organic impairment of erection. Physical intervention is often indicated, however, for men with major physical problems underlying or complicating their difficulty with erection. For these men, a common approach is surgical implantation of a *penile*

*prosthesis,* which produces an artificial erection. This device consists of a semirigid rod made of rubber and wire. It can be bent down so that the man can wear normal clothing, but bent up to an erect position when the man wants to have sex. Another type of prosthesis consists of inflatable hollow cylinders inserted into the penis, a reservoir of fluid placed under the abdominal wall, and tubing connecting the penile cylinders to a pump inserted in the scrotum. When the man wants to have sex, he squeezes the pump, forcing fluid from the reservoir to the penile cylinders, which expand and produce an erection. These surgically implanted prostheses are expensive (between $5,000 and $15,000, depending on the type), but over 25,000 were installed in 1988 in the United States. This kind of treatment is uncommon elsewhere in the world, primarily because of the expense (LoPiccolo, 1991).

A nonsurgical approach to erectile failure is the use of a *vacuum erection device (VED).* A hollow cylinder is placed over the penis and pushed against the body to create an airtight seal. The cylinder is connected to a hand pump, which pumps the air out of the cylinder and leaves the penis in a partial vacuum. This draws blood into the penis and produces an erection. The cylinder is removed and a rubber constriction ring is placed around the base of the penis to maintain the erection. The VED is less expensive ($300 to $600), but interferes with the spontaneity of sex, as the man must take time to use it during lovemaking.

Vascular surgery to remove blockages in the arteries, repair leaks in the penile chambers, or tie off excessively large penile veins is also useful in some cases. For men with neurologic damage but an intact blood circulation system, injection of drugs that dilate the penile arteries is often useful. Long-term use of these drugs can damage the penis, however, so they are now used more as a short-term "confidence booster" for men with acute erectile failure that is situational in nature (Bancroft, 1989).

**Premature Ejaculation**     Premature ejaculation is treated with almost a 100 percent success rate by direct behavioral retraining procedures (Masters and Johnson, 1970; Semans, 1956). In the "stop-start" or "pause" procedure, the penis is manually stimulated until the man is fairly highly aroused. The couple then pause until his arousal subsides, then the stimulation is resumed. This sequence is repeated several times before stimulation is carried through to ejaculation, so the man ultimately experiences much more total time of stimulation than he has ever experienced before and learns to have a higher threshold for ejaculation. The "squeeze" procedure is much like the "stop-start" procedure, except that when stimulation stops, the woman firmly squeezes the penis between her thumb and forefinger, at the place where the head of the penis joins the shaft. This squeeze seems to reduce arousal further. After a few weeks of this training, the necessity of pausing diminishes. Then the couple progress to putting the penis in the vagina, but without any thrusting movements. Again, if the man rapidly becomes highly aroused, the penis is withdrawn and the couple waits for arousal to drop off. When good tolerance for inactive containment of the penis is achieved, the training procedure is repeated during active thrusting. Generally, 2 to 3 months of practice are sufficient to enable a man to enjoy prolonged intercourse without any need for pauses or squeezes.

**Inhibited Ejaculation**     Inhibited male orgasm is treated by reducing performance anxiety and ensuring adequate stimulation. The couple are instructed that during sex the penis is to be caressed manually (and, if acceptable to them, orally) until the man is aroused, but that stimulation is to stop whenever he feels he might be close to having an orgasm. This paradoxical instruction reduces goal-focused anxiety about performance and allows the man to enjoy the sexual pleasure provided by the caressing. An electric vibrator may be used to increase the intensity of stimulation. For men with neurological damage or a history of concussion, therapy is likely to include some physiological treatment, possibly a drug that increases arousal of the sympathetic nervous system or stimulation of the anus with a vibrator or electric current to trigger the ejaculation reflex (Murphy & Lipshultz, 1988).

**Female Arousal and Orgasm Dysfunctions**     Specific treatment techniques for female arousal and orgasm dysfunctions include self-exploration, body awareness, and directed masturbation training (Heiman & LoPiccolo, 1988). These procedures are especially useful for women with global, lifelong lack of orgasm. Masters and Johnson stressed the use of couple sensate-focus procedures for such cases, but later experience showed that it is more effective for the woman to learn to have orgasm by herself first, and then share this knowledge with her partner.

The directed masturbation program has 9 steps. In the first step, the woman uses diagrams and reading material simply to learn about her body, her genitals, and the female sexual response. In step 2 she explores her whole body by touch. Step 3 consists of locating erotically sensitive areas, with a focus on the breasts and genitals, especially the clitoris. Actual stimulation of these areas, masturbation, is step 4. Step 5 is erotic masturbation accompanied by sexual pictures, stories, and the woman's own fantasies.

Step 6 has three elements. First, if the woman has not yet experienced an orgasm, she will begin to use an electric vibrator to increase the intensity of stimulation. Second, she will be instructed to act out or role-play a very exaggerated orgasm, to overcome any fears about losing control or looking silly when she has a real orgasm. Finally, she will use "orgasm triggers," such as holding her breath, contracting her pelvic muscles, tensing her leg muscles, and thrusting her pelvis.

Step 7 integrates the Masters and Johnson sensate-focus procedure with the woman's individual progress. This training in communication and sexual skill teaches her to demonstrate for her partner how she likes to be touched and how she can have orgasm. In step 8 her partner brings her to orgasm with manual, oral, or vibrator stimulation. In the last step, the woman and her partner practice intercourse in positions that permit one or the other of them to continue to stimulate her clitoris while the penis is in the vagina.

This training program has been found to be very effective: over 90 percent of women learn to have orgasm during masturbation, about 80 percent during caressing by their partner, and about 30 percent during intercourse (Heiman & LoPiccolo, 1988). As it is a structured program, it works equally well in group therapy, and even as a self-treatment: the woman can go through the program without a therapist, using a self-help book and instructional videotape (LoPiccolo, 1990).

Treatment for situational lack of orgasm includes a gradual stimulus generalization procedure, to help the woman expand the ways in which she reaches orgasm. If the woman can masturbate to orgasm when she is alone, for example, but only by pressing her thighs together, and can't have orgasm in any way when her partner is present, the therapist will help her to identify a number of small, intermediate steps between the way she has orgasm now and the wished-for orgasm during sex with her partner. In this example, intermediate steps might include using thigh pressure but also putting her fingers on her clitoris, direct stimulation of the clitoris with the thighs spread apart, thigh pressure with her partner present, thigh pressure with his fingers on her clitoris, his direct stimulation of her clitoris without thigh pressure, and direct clitoral stimulation during insertion of the penis (Zeiss, Rosen, & Zeiss, 1977). This approach is quite effective in helping women learn to have orgasm with a partner. As we saw earlier, sex therapists do not consider lack of orgasm during intercourse to be a problem, provided the woman enjoys intercourse and can have orgasm when her partner caresses her. For this reason, reassurance about their normality, not treatment, is indicated for women whose only concern is situational lack of orgasm during intercourse.

**Vaginismus** Vaginismic patients practice contracting and relaxing the pubococcygeal muscle, which, as we noted earlier, is part of the pelvic floor and surrounds the vagina, until they have acquired voluntary control over their vaginal muscles. They overcome their fear of penetration by using a set of gradually larger dilators, which they insert in their own vagina at home and at their own pace, so that they are not frightened or traumatized. Later, when the woman can comfortably insert the largest dilator, she begins to guide her partner as he slowly and gently inserts the dilators. Finally, as he lies passively on his back and she kneels above him, she gradually inserts his penis. The therapist stresses the need for effective stimulation, so that she learns to associate pen-

etration with vaginal lubrication, pleasure, and arousal, instead of with fear. Some therapists use muscle-relaxing drugs or hypnosis during dilation, but this does not seem to be a necessary part of the treatment. Therapy for vaginismus is highly successful; over 90 percent of the women treated become able to have pain-free intercourse (LoPiccolo, 1990).

**Dyspareunia** There are no specific treatment procedures for psychogenic dyspareunia. Since psychogenic dyspareunia is actually caused by lack of arousal, the general sex therapy procedures and the specific techniques for enhancing female arousal and orgasm are used. When the pain is caused by scars or lesions, the couple can be taught positions for intercourse that do not put pressure on the traumatized sites.

# PARAPHILIAS

People with *paraphilias* have recurrent and intense sexual urges and sexually arousing fantasies involving either nonhuman objects, children or nonconsenting adults, or experiences of suffering or humiliation on the part of themselves or their partners (APA, 1987). According to DSM-III-R, only those who repeatedly act on these urges or feel extreme guilt, shame, or some other kind of distress over them warrant a diagnosis. In many cases people with a paraphilia become aroused *only* when a paraphiliac stimulus is present, acted out, or fantasized about. In other cases, the paraphilia seems to be occasional, occurring and being acted on only during times of stress, for example. Some clinicians hold that, with the exception of nonconsensual paraphilias, paraphiliac activities should be considered a disorder only when they are the exclusive or preferred means of achieving sexual excitement and orgasm (Becker & Kavoussi, 1988). People with one kind of paraphilia often display others as well (Abel et al., 1985).

Actually, relatively few people receive a formal diagnosis of paraphilia, but the large market in paraphiliac pornography and items leads clinicians to suspect that the disorders may be quite prevalent. Those who do receive a diagnosis are almost always men. When the paraphilia involves children or nonconsenting adults, the individual often winds up in legal trouble. Although theorists have proposed various explanations and applied various treatments to paraphilias, research has revealed relatively little about the causes and treatments of most of these disorders (APA, 1987).

## Fetishism

The key feature of *fetishism* is recurrent intense sexual urges and sexually arousing fantasies that involve the use of an inanimate object or body part, often to the exclusion of all other stimuli. Usually the disorder begins in adolescence. Almost any object can be the focus of a fetish, from earlobes to underwear (Raphling, 1989). Some fetishists commit petty thievery for the purpose of collecting as many objects of their desire as possible or collect photographs of the favorite body part. The objects or photos are generally touched, smelled, or somehow used while the person masturbates, or fetishists may ask their partners to wear the object. In the 19th century Richard von Krafft-Ebing ([1886] 1965) described a case of this disorder:

> *A lady told Dr. Gemy that in the bridal night and in the* night following her husband contented himself with kissing her, and running his fingers through the wealth of her tresses. He then fell asleep. In the third night Mr. X produced an immense wig, with enormously long hair, and begged his wife to put it on. As soon as she had done so he richly compensated her for his neglected marital duties. In the morning he showed again extreme tenderness, whilst he caressed the wig. When Mrs. X removed the wig she lost at once all charm for her husband. . . . The result of this marriage was, after five years, two children and a collection of 72 wigs.

Researchers have not been able to clarify the causes of fetishism (Wise, 1985). Psychodynamic theorists have proposed that fetishes are defense mechanisms to help the person avoid anxiety associated with normal sexual contact. Behaviorists have proposed that they are acquired through classical conditioning. In one behavioral study male subjects were made to look at slides of nude women interspersed with slides of boots (Rachman, 1966). After numerous trials, the subjects became aroused by the boot photos alone. If early sexual experiences similarly occur in conjunction with a particular object, the stage may be set for development of a fetish.

Behaviorists have sometimes treated fetishism with aversion therapy (Kilmann et al., 1981). In one study, an electric shock was administered to the arms or legs of subjects with fetishes while they imagined their objects of desire (Marks & Gelder, 1967). After two weeks of therapy all subjects in the study showed at least some improvement. In another aversion technique, *covert sensitization,* fetishists are guided to imagine the pleasurable but unwanted object and repeatedly to pair this image with an imagined aversive stimulus, until the object of erotic pleasure is no longer desired.

Another behavioral treatment for fetishism is *masturbatory satiation* (Quinsey & Earls, 1990; Marshall,

1979; Marshall & Lippens, 1977). In this method, the client masturbates to orgasm while fantasizing aloud about a sexually appropriate object, then switches to fantasizing in detail about fetishistic objects while masturbating, and continues to elaborate on the fetishistic fantasy for an hour. The procedure is meant to produce a feeling of boredom, which in turn becomes associated with the fetishistic object.

## Transvestic Fetishism

*Transvestic fetishism,* also known as *transvestism* or *cross-dressing,* involves the recurrent need or desire to dress in clothes of the opposite sex in order to achieve sexual arousal. The typical transvestite, almost always a heterosexual male, begins cross-dressing in childhood or adolescence. He is the picture of unremarkable masculinity in everyday life, and cross-dresses only in relative privacy. A small percentage of such men cross-dress to visit bars or social clubs. Some transvestites wear a single item of women's apparel, such as underwear or hosiery, under their masculine clothes. Others wear makeup and dress fully as women. Many married transvestites involve their wives in their cross-dressing behavior (Kolodny, Masters, & Johnson, 1979). Transvestic fetishism is often confused with transsexualism, but the two are entirely separate disorders (see Box 14-3).

The development of transvestic fetishism sometimes seems consistent with the principles of operant conditioning. Several case studies describe transvestites who

*Crossroads* is a self-help group for men with transvestic fetishism, a recurrent need to dress in women's clothing as a means to achieve sexual arousal. These men are *not* transsexuals; they never question their identity as men and have no wish to be women.

were reinforced for cross-dressing as children, openly encouraged and supported by parents or other adults for this behavior. In one case, a woman was delighted to discover that her young nephew enjoyed dressing in girls' clothes; for she had always wanted a niece, and she proceeded to buy him dresses and jewelry and sometimes dressed him as a girl and took him out shopping.

## Pedophilia

A person who is subject to *pedophilia,* literally "love of children," obtains sexual gratification by watching, touching, or engaging in simple or complex sexual acts with prepubescent children, usually those 13 years old or younger. Some pedophiles are satisfied by child pornography; others are driven to watching, fondling, or engaging in sexual intercourse with children (Grinspoon, 1986). One study found 4 percent of pedophilia victims to be 3 years old or younger, 18 percent 4 to 7, and 40 percent 8 to 11 (Mohr et al., 1964). In addition, studies suggest that the victim usually knows the molester and that 15 to 30 percent of sexual molestation cases are incestuous (Gebhard et al., 1965; Mohr et al., 1964). Victims may be boys or girls (APA, 1987).

Pedophiles usually develop their disorder during adolescence. Many were themselves sexually abused as children (APA, 1987). Many are married and have sexual difficulties or other frustrations in life that lead them to seek an arena in which they can be masters. Alcohol abuse is another factor that figures prominently in a number of such cases (Rada, 1976).

Some clinicians suggest that immaturity is often the primary cause of this disorder (Groth & Birnbaum, 1978). Social and sexual skills may never have been acquired, so that the person feels intense anxiety at the very thought of a normal sexual relationship. Some pedophiles also display faulty thinking, such as "It's all right to have sex with a child as long as they agree" (Abel et al., 1984).

Most pedophilic offenders are imprisoned or forced into treatment if they are caught. The various treatments include those already mentioned for other paraphilias, such as aversion therapy and masturbatory satiation (Enright, 1989; Kilmann et al., 1982). Another, also used for other paraphilias, is *orgasmic reorientation* (Enright, 1989). This procedure conditions clients to new, more appropriate sources of erotic stimuli. They are shown conventional stimuli while they are responding to the other, unconventional objects. For example, a pedophile may be instructed to obtain an erection from pictures of young children and then begin masturbating to a picture of a nude adult. If he starts to lose the erection, he must return to the original stimulus until he

is masturbating effectively, then change back to the accepted stimulus. When orgasm becomes imminent, all focus should be on the more appropriate stimulus. This training continues for a period of several weeks and may be supplemented by covert sensitization, social skills training, or psychodynamic intervention.

Finally, a cognitive-behavioral treatment for pedophilia is *relapse-prevention training.* Modeled after the relapse-prevention programs used in the treatment of drug dependence (see p. 453), this approach helps clients to identify the problematic situations that typically precede their pedophilic fantasies and actions (such as depressed mood or distorted thinking) and to develop strategies to avoid or cope more effectively with these situations, thus preventing the pedophilic behavior (Pithers, 1990). One study of 147 pedophiles found only a 4 percent relapse rate over a five-year period among offenders who received this treatment (Pithers & Cumming, 1989).

## Exhibitionism

The person who engages in *exhibitionism* has sexually arousing fantasies of exposing his genitals to another person, almost always a member of the opposite sex, and recurrent intense urges to act the fantasies out (Abel, 1989). Further sexual activity with the other person is not usually attempted or desired. What is often desired, however, is a reaction of shock or surprise. Sometimes a so-called flasher will frequent a particular neighborhood or exhibit at particular hours. Exhibitionists' urges to expose themselves typically intensify when they have free time or are under significant stress (Abel, 1989).

Generally, the disorder begins before age 18, and almost all exhibitionists are males. Exhibitionists are immature in their approaches to the opposite sex and have difficulty in interpersonal relationships. Over half of exhibitionists are married, but their sexual relationships with their wives are not satisfactory (Blair & Lanyon, 1981; Mohr, Turner, & Jerry, 1964). Many have doubts or fears about their masculinity, and some apparently have a strong bond to a possessive mother.

Treatment, again, is the same as that for other paraphilias, including covert sensitization, masturbatory satiation, and relapse-prevention training, possibly combined with arousal reorientation, social skills training, or psychodynamic intervention. One unusual, apparently successful version of covert sensitization pairs the unpleasant smell of valeric acid with images of self-exposure (Maletzky, 1980). Clinicians have also reported some success with hypnotherapy (Polk, 1983; Epstein, 1983; Mutter, 1980; Ritchie, 1968; Roper, 1967).

## Voyeurism

In *voyeurism* a person has recurrent and intense sexual desires to observe people in secret as they undress or to spy on couples engaged in intercourse. The risk of being discovered often adds to the person's excitement. The voyeur does not seek to have sex with the person being spied on.

Voyeurs may masturbate either during the act or when thinking about it afterward. The vulnerability of the people being observed and the possibility that they would be humiliated if they found out are often part of the voyeur's enjoyment. Voyeurism usually begins before the age of 15 and tends to be chronic.

Both exhibitionism and voyeurism can play a role in normal sexuality, but in such instances they are engaged in with the consent or understanding of the partner. The clinical disorder of voyeurism is marked by the repeated invasion of another's privacy. Some voyeurs are unable to have normal sexual interplay; others, however, maintain normal sexual relationships apart from their voyeurism.

Many clinicians believe that voyeurs are seeking by their actions to exercise power over others, possi-

---

## BOX 14-3

# Transsexualism

One of the most fascinating disorders related to sexuality is *transsexualism,* a disorder in which people persistently feel that a vast mistake has been made — they have been assigned to the wrong sex. Such persons are preoccupied with getting rid of their primary and secondary sex characteristics — often finding their own genitals repugnant — and acquiring the characteristics of the other sex (APA, 1987). They usually feel uncomfortable wearing the clothes of their own sex and dress instead in clothes of the opposite sex. They are not, however, transvestites. Transvestites cross-dress in order to become sexually aroused; transsexuals have much deeper reasons for cross-dressing, reasons of sexual identity. In addition to cross-dressing, transsexuals often engage in activities that are traditionally associated with the other sex.

Some transsexuals seek to alter their sexual characteristics by hormone treatments. The hormone prescribed for male transsexuals, who outnumber female transsexuals by more than three to one, is the female hormone estrogen. It causes breast development, loss of body and facial hair, and change in the distribution of body fat, it may also lead to such unwanted effects as hypertension, weight gain, depression, and liver abnormalities. Similar treatments, using the male sex hormone testosterone are given to female transsexuals.

Given their cross-dressing, activity preferences, and hormone-induced physical changes, many transsexuals become virtually indistinguishable from the other sex.

It is estimated that one in 30,000 men and one in 100,000 women have this disorder. Various psychological theories have been proposed to explain it, but research in this area has been limited and generally weak. Some clinicians suspect that the disorder has largely biological causes, but studies of hormonal, EEG, and other physiological measures have not found any differences between transsexuals and nontranssexuals.

Some children have a similar disorder called *gender identity disorder of childhood.* These children, too, feel uncomfortable about their assigned sex and thoroughly wish to be a member of the opposite sex. This childhood disorder usually disappears by adolescence or adulthood, but in some cases it develops into adult transsexualism. Thus most adult transsexuals have had a childhood gender identity disorder, but most children with a gender identity disorder do not become adult transsexuals.

For many transsexuals, drug therapy and psychotherapy are sufficient to enable them to lead a satisfactory existence in the gender role that they believe represents their true identity. For others, however, this is not enough, and their dissatisfaction leads them to undergo one of the most controversial practices in medicine: sex-change surgery.

The first sex-change operation actually took place in 1931, but the procedure did not gain acceptance until 1952, when an operation converted an ex-soldier named George Jorgensen into a woman, renamed Christine Jorgensen. This made headlines around the world and sparked the interest of people everywhere.

By 1980, sex-reassignment surgery was routine in at least forty medical centers in the western hemisphere (Arndt, 1991). This surgery is preceded by one to two years of hormone therapy, after which the operation itself involves (for men) amputation of

bly because they feel inadequate or are sexually or socially inhibited. Psychodynamic theorists have explained voyeurism as an attempt to reduce castration anxiety, orginally generated by the sight of adult genitals. Theoretically, voyeurs are repeating the behavior that produced the original fright, so that they can be reassured there is nothing to fear (Fenichel, 1945). Behaviorists explain the disorder as a learned behavior that can be traced to a chance and secret observation of a sexually arousing scene. If such observations are repeated on several occasions in conjunction with masturbation, a voyeuristic pattern may develop.

## Frotteurism

In *frotteurism,* a person has recurrent and intense sexual urges and sexually arousing fantasies of touching and rubbing against a nonconsenting person. As with other paraphilias, the person must act on these urges or be very distressed by them in order to warrant a diagnosis. Frottage (from French *frotter,* to rub) is usually committed in a crowded place, such as a subway or a busy sidewalk. The person, almost always a male, may rub his genitals against the victim's thighs or buttocks or fondle her genitalia or breasts with his hands. Typically he fanta-

the penis, creation of an artificial vagina, and face-altering plastic surgery. For women, surgery may include bilateral mastectomy and hysterectomy. The procedure for creating a functioning penis is not yet perfected and not recommended. Approximately 1,000 sex change operations are performed each year in the United States.

Clinicians have heatedly debated the legitimacy of surgery as a treatment for transsexualism. Some consider it a humane solution, indeed the only completely satisfying one to transsexuals. Others have argued that transsexual surgery is a "drastic nonsolution" for a purely psychological problem, akin to lobotomy (Restak, 1979). Research has not yet been able to settle the matter. The long-term outcome of surgical sex reassignment, either by itself or in combination with psychotherapy and hormone treatments, is not well established (APA, 1987). Many people seem to function well for years after such treatments, but some have experienced serious psychological difficulties. Without any form of treatment, transsexualism is usually chronic, but some cases of spontaneous remission have reportedly occurred.

Our gender is so fundamental to our sense of our identity that it is difficult for most of us to imagine wanting to change it, much less the feelings of

Feeling like a woman trapped in a man's body, the English writer James Morris *(left)* underwent sex-reassignment surgery, described in his 1974 autobiography *Conundrum.* Today Jan Morris *(right)* is the successful author of more than a dozen books and numerous travel articles and seems comfortable with her change of gender.

conflict and stress experienced by those who do question their gender. Whether the underlying cause is biological or psychological, transsexual-

ism represents a dramatic psychological dysfunction that shakes the foundations of the sufferer's existence.

sizes during the act that he is having a caring relationship with the victim (APA, 1987).

Frotteurism usually begins in adolescence or earlier, often after the person observes others committing an act of frottage. After the person reaches the age of 25, the acts gradually decrease and often disappear.

## Sexual Masochism

*Sexual masochism* is a pattern in which people repeatedly have intense sexual urges and fantasies that involve being humiliated, beaten, bound, or otherwise made to suffer. Although many people have fantasies (while they masturbate or have intercourse) of being forced into sexual acts against their will, only those who are markedly distressed by the fantasies would receive this diagnosis (Reik, 1989). Many with the disorder act on the masochistic urges by themselves, perhaps binding, sticking pins into, or even mutilating themselves. Others have their sexual partners restrain, tie up, blindfold, spank, paddle, whip, beat, electrically shock, "pin and pierce," or humiliate them (APA, 1987).

In most cases, the masochistic sexual fantasies begin in childhood. Acting out the urges does not take place until later, usually by early adulthood. The disorder typically continues over the course of many years. The masochistic acts of some people remain at the same level of severity over the years; others keep increasing the potential dangerousness of their acts over time or show an increase during times of particular stress.

In many cases the pattern of sexual masochism seems to have developed through classical conditioning. One case study tells of a teenage boy with a broken arm who was caressed and held close by an attractive nurse as the physician set his fracture without anesthesia (Gebhard, 1965). He experienced a powerful combination of pain and sexual arousal that may have been the cause of his later masochistic urges and acts.

## Sexual Sadism

*Sexual sadism* is a pattern in which a person, usually male, is intensely sexually aroused by the act or thought of inflicting physical or psychological suffering on others, such as by dominating, restraining, blindfolding, cutting, strangling, mutilating, or even killing the victim. The label is derived from the name of the Marquis de Sade (1740–1814), who inflicted severe cruelty on other people in order to satisfy his sexual desires. Eventually he was confined in a mental institution. People who fantasize about sadism typically imagine that they have total control over a sexual victim who is terrified by

Sexual masochists and sexual sadists often achieve sexual satisfaction with each other. Although many such relationships stay within safe bounds and are often portrayed with humor in photos, novels, and movies, they sometimes cross the line and can result in severe physical or psychological damage.

the prospect of the sadistic act. Many carry out sadistic acts with a consenting partner, often a person who is sexually masochistic. Some act out their urges on nonconsenting victims (see Box 14-4). In all cases, the real or fantasized victim's suffering is the key to the sadist's arousal.

As in sexual masochism, fantasies of sexual sadism may appear in childhood, and sadistic acts, when they occur, develop by early adulthood. The pattern is chronic. The acts sometimes stay at the same level of cruelty, but more often they increase in severity over the years. Obviously, people with severe forms of the disorder may be highly dangerous to others.

The pattern has been associated with a number of causal factors. Behaviorists suggest that classical conditioning often plays a role in its development. While inflicting pain, perhaps unintentional, on an animal or person, an adolescent may feel intense emotions, sometimes with the inclusion of sexual arousal. The associa-

## BOX 14-4

# Rape: Sexual Assault, Psychological Trauma

Rape—forced sexual intercourse or another sexual act upon a nonconsenting or underage person—is prevalent in our society and leaves the victim psychologically traumatized and vulnerable. More than 100,000 rapes are reported annually (Senate Judiciary Committee, 1991), but they represent only a small fraction of the number of rapes committed (Freiberg, 1990; Koss, 1990). Many victims are reluctant to report a rape because they are ashamed or because they feel that dealing with police or the courts will compound their trauma.

Most rapists are men and most victims are women. About 61 percent of reported rapes are committed by strangers, 31 percent by persons known to the victims, and 8 percent by close relatives of the victims (Sadock, 1989); rapes by close acquaintances are particularly likely to go unreported. Twenty percent of reported rapes involve more than one attacker.

A discussion of rape is actually out of place in a chapter on sexual disorders. Although rape does by definition involve a sexual act, the motivation for this act is often not primarily sexual. The typical rapist's motivation is aggression or anger rather than sexual desire, and his sexual gratification is usually limited during the rape. Between a third and a half of all rapists fail to have an erection or to ejaculate (Sadock, 1989; Burgess & Baldwin, 1981).

Rapists fall into four categories: *sexual sadists,* who are sexually aroused by seeing a victim suffer; *sexual exploiters,* who impulsively use victims as objects of gratification; *inadequate aggressors,* who believe that no woman would voluntarily have sex with them; and *angry abusers,* who seem to displace their rage against women in general upon the victim.

The psychological impact of rape on a victim is enormous and may last a long time. Even years later, many rape victims continue to be highly anxious, depressed, guilt-ridden, and unable to sleep well (Burnam et al., 1988; Kilpatrick et al., 1985; Burgess & Holmstrom, 1979, 1974). Victims who have a strong psychological foundation and who are bolstered by a strong support system are more likely to make an adequate psychological recovery, but the trauma of the sexual assault and its aftermath (including a harsh legal system and a judgmental society) may overwhelm even the healthiest and most well supported of women.

Victims who can express their fear and rage to believing family members, doctors, and police seem to make the most progress (Sadock, 1989). But researchers have not systematically evaluated the effect of such community services (Koss, 1990). Several kinds of rape have received special attention during the past decade: spouse rape, date rape, and incest.

**Spouse Rape** Until recently the law presumed that sexual intercourse was a contractual part of marriage, and a woman could not accuse her husband of rape. That situation changed in 1982, when a Florida man was convicted of the crime of raping his wife. The legal exemption for marital rape has now been eliminated in twenty-five states.

**Date Rape** Rape by a date or close acquaintance is a major social problem, according to several large surveys of college students (Koss et al., 1988; Muehlenhard & Linton, 1987). These surveys suggest that 15 percent of women have been forced into intercourse against their will by acquaintances, either in high school or in college. Although date rape may occur on a first or early date, many students say that they knew or dated the person who raped them for a year or more before.

**Father-Daughter Incest** Incest, from the Latin *incestus,* "impure," is sexual intercourse between persons closely related by blood or marriage. About 75 percent of reported cases involve father-daughter (or stepfather-stepdaughter) relationships (Sadock, 1989). These cases represent a form of statutory rape (unlawful intercourse between a man over 16 years old and a female under the state's age of consent) as well as a psychological assault on the victim that may last a lifetime. Research suggests that 50,000 to 200,000 children are sexually abused in the United States each year (Green, 1989), but it is difficult to know how many of them are victims of father-daughter incest. Daughters are reluctant, ashamed, or afraid to tell what has happened to them (Kilpatrick et al., 1987).

Most of the statistical information about incest comes from adult subjects who are surveyed anonymously about sexual abuse that they experienced during childhood. Because many incidents have been reported in such studies, clinicians have become increasingly interested in studying and treating victims of incest (Koss, 1990). They have in particular become aware of the profound feelings of depression, guilt, and shame that victims of father-daughter incest often carry into adulthood, and of the difficulties that these early experiences may pose for later intimacy and interpersonal trust (Conte, 1991; Arndt, 1991; Gold, 1986; Owens, 1984). Therapy and self-help groups for adult women who have experienced incest as children and adolescents have proliferated rapidly in recent years and are reportedly helpful to many victims.

tion between inflicting pain and being aroused sexually sets the stage for a pattern of sexual sadism. Behaviorists also propose that many cases result from modeling, when adolescents observe others achieving sexual satisfaction by inflicting pain. The ubiquitous sexual magazines, books, and videotapes in our society make such models readily available. Psychodynamic and cognitive theorists have suggested that people with sexual sadism may have underlying feelings of sexual inadequacy or insecurity and that they inflict pain in order to achieve a sense of power, which in turn increases their sexual arousal. None of these explanations has been systemati-

cally investigated or consistently supported by empirical research (Breslow, 1989).

Sexual sadism has been treated by aversive conditioning. The public's view of, and perhaps distaste for, this procedure has been influenced by the description of treatment given to a cruel and sadistic character in Anthony Burgess's novel (later a movie) *A Clockwork Orange:* simultaneous presentation of sadistic images and electrical shocks. It is not clear that aversive conditioning is consistently helpful in sexual sadism. Relapse-prevention training, used in some criminal cases, seems somewhat effective (Pithers & Cumming, 1989).

BOX 14-5

# Homosexuality and Society

In 1948 Alfred Kinsey and his associates conducted one of the first extensive studies of male sexuality. They found that 4 percent of the male population were exclusively homosexual and that 37 percent had had a homosexual experience that led to orgasm. Half of the unmarried men over the age of 35 had had a homosexual experience to the point of orgasm. In a subsequent study, the occurrence of homosexuality among women was found to be approximately one-half to one-third that of men (Kinsey et al., 1953). These findings shocked and astonished many people.

Homosexuality has always existed in all cultures. It is not new, nor is the controversy that surrounds it. Most cultures do not openly advocate homosexuality, but historically few have condemned it so fiercely as Western culture has since the Victorian era. Nevertheless, research shows a soci-

ety's acceptance or rejection of people who engage in homosexual activity does not affect the incidence of homosexual behavior.

Before 1973, the DSM listed homosexuality as a sexual disorder. Protests by gay activist groups and many psychotherapists eventually led to its elimination from the manual as a sexual disorder per se, but the DSM did retain a category called *ego dystonic homosexuality* — the experience of extreme distress over one's homosexual preference. DSM-III-R has dropped even this category, and the issue of

homosexuality is no longer mentioned. Most clinicians now accept homosexuality as a variant of normal sexual behavior and not a disorder.

Despite the growing acceptance of homosexuality by clinicians, many people in Western society continue to foster anti-homosexual attitudes and to propagate myths about the lifestyles of homosexuals. The facts are that homosexuals do *not* suffer from gender confusion. They are *not* prone to psychopathologies (Paul et al., 1982). There is *not* an identifiable "homosexual personality" (Wilson, 1984). And children raised in a homosexual household are *not* more likely than others to become homosexual (Green et al., 1986).

To cope with the stress, discrimination, and even danger they encounter, many homosexual people have chosen to live on streets or in neighborhoods that are predominantly homosexual.

## Final Thoughts

The definitions of the various paraphilias, like those of sexual dysfunctions, are closely tied to the norms of the particular society in which they occur rather than to fixed medical criteria (Brown, 1983). It could be argued that except when people are hurt by them, many paraphilic behaviors are not disorders at all (Grinspoon, 1986). Especially when one considers the stigma associated with sexual disorders and the self-revulsion that many people experience when they believe they have such a disorder, we need to be very careful about applying such labels to others or to ourselves. Keep in mind that homosexuality was for years considered a paraphilia by clinical professionals and that this judgment helped to justify laws and even police actions against homosexual persons (see Box 14-5). Only when the gay rights movement helped change society's understanding of and attitudes toward homosexuality did clinicians stop considering it a disorder. In the meantime, the clinical field had inadvertently contributed to the persecution, anxiety, and humiliation of millions of people because of personal sexual behavior that differed from its conventional norms.

---

Certain bars or restaurants serve as gathering places where gays exchange information and socialize. Organizations exist to support and lobby for issues affecting homosexual people, demanding equal treatment under the law and in society at large.

Homosexuals are represented in every socioeconomic group, every race, and every profession. It is impossible to identify a characteristic that consistently separates them from the rest of the population, other than their sexual preference. Moreover, heterosexual and homosexual relationships do not differ dramatically. AIDS is presently striking hundreds of thousands of male homosexuals, moving an increasing number of previously promiscuous individuals toward monogamy and long-term relationships, but it is important to note that commitments of this sort have always existed among homosexual persons.

Given that sexual preference is the only variable that consistently distinguishes homosexual from heterosexual couples, gay couples have increasingly demanded that they be accorded the same rights as heterosexuals. Marriages are performed for same-sex couples. Homosexual couples are demanding access to housing reserved for couples only, and recent court cases are supporting their right to have the same rights as heterosexual couples. Other cases have focused on health insurance coverage: should the partner of a gay person receive "spouse" coverage? These issues affect the day-to-day lives of homosexual couples in the same way that they affect heterosexual couples. The goal of the homosexual community is simple. They wish to be treated exactly as male-female couples are treated. They point out that the critical issues in any relationship whether homosexual or heterosexual, are commitment, love, interdependence—gender need *not* be an important consideration.

Often the most powerful tool for changing popular attitudes against homosexuality is a popular public figure, either a politician or an entertainment personality, who reveals his or her homosexuality. The effectiveness of such revelations has led to a controversial practice in recent years: some gay activist groups make public the homosexuality of public figures who have not previously announced their status. "Outing," as this practice is called, is defended by the activists as necessary to gain public acceptance of homosexuality. They feel that public figures are obligated to come forward and use their fame for the benefit of other homosexual people. For the person who has thus been identified, however, the timing of the disclosure may be inappropriate at the very least, and the "outing" may be psychologically devastating and disruptive both personally and professionally. The right to privacy versus obligation to a cause—this debate often leads to acrimony among groups that have the same ultimate goal: acceptance and an end to discrimination.

Obviously, homosexuality continues to be a lifestyle that many people adopt, whether through choice, environment, genetics, or psychosocial development. Now that clinical concerns about homosexuality have been put aside, one of the key remaining issues is how society will deal with a significant proportion of its population that typically does not differ from the rest in any way other than sexual preference. So far, Western society cannot claim to have dealt very effectively or fairly with this question, but at least a trend toward understanding and equality seems to be emerging.

## SEXUAL DISORDERS: THE STATE OF THE FIELD

Because there is so much public interest in and discussion about sexual disorders, it sometimes appears as if much is known about these problems; this is not the case. Clinical theorists and practitioners have only recently begun to understand the nature and origins of sexual dysfunctions and to develop effective treatments for them. Moreover, they have made rather limited progress in explaining and treating paraphilias, the other group of sexual disorders.

Yet this picture is changing rapidly, at least in the realm of sexual dysfunctions. For years, our explanations and treatments for sexual dysfunctions were influenced largely by popular myths and by the dominating perspective of the psychodynamic model. Then in 1970 William Masters and Virginia Johnson published their research on human sexual functioning and dysfunctioning and began a veritable revolution in the clinical field that continues today. Over the past two decades, sexual functioning has been one of the most broadly investigated subjects in clinical research, with systematic studies revealing enlightening and useful information about the nature and causes of various sexual dysfunctions. Correspondingly, clinicians have developed extraordinarily helpful treatments for people with sexual dysfunctions — people previously doomed to a lifetime of sexual frustration and distress. Today sex therapy is typically a complex approach with multiple components tailored to the particular problems and personality of an individual and couple. The breadth of current research undertakings and therapy programs suggests that our understanding and treatment of sexual dysfunctions will continue to progress in the coming years.

One of the most important insights to emerge from all this work concerns the need for proper education about sexual dysfunctions. Popular myths and judgments still abound in this area, often leading to feelings of shame, self-dislike, isolation, and hopelessness — and often contributing directly to the sexual difficulty. Sex therapists have come to recognize that even a modest amount of proper education about sexual functioning can help persons who are in treatment. In fact, most people, not just those who seek treatment, can benefit from a clearer, more accurate understanding of sexual functioning. Public education about sexual functioning — through books, television and radio, school programs, group presentations, and the like — has become a new focus of clinical scientists in recent years. Broad interventions of this kind appear to be as important as private treatment or continued research efforts. It is to be hoped that they too will continue and increase in the coming years.

## SUMMARY

There are two kinds of sexual disorders: sexual dysfunctions and paraphilias. People with *sexual dysfunctions* are unable to function normally in some area of the human sexual response cycle. People with *paraphilias* have recurrent and intense sexual urges and sexually arousing fantasies in response to objects or situations that society deems inappropriate.

DSM-III-R classifies sexual dysfunctions according to the phase of the sexual response cycle affected — the *desire, arousal, orgasm,* or *resolution* phase. During the desire phase, the two most common dysfunctions are *hypoactive sexual desire,* or a lack of interest in sex, and *sexual aversion,* in which sex is found to be actively unpleasant. The two most common dysfunctions involving the arousal phase are *male erectile disorder* and *female arousal disorder.* DSM-III-R distinguishes between lack of physical arousal and lack of emotional excitement. During the orgasm phase the most common dysfunctions are *premature ejaculation* and *inhibited male or female orgasm.* DSM-III-R also identifies the dysfunctions of *vaginismus,* spastic contractions of the muscles around the outer vagina, and *dyspareunia,* pain in the genitals during sexual activity. Disorders may further be viewed as *lifelong* or *not lifelong* and either *global* or *situational.*

Studies suggest that approximately 15 percent of men suffer from hypoactive sexual desire, 10 to 25 percent suffer from premature ejaculation, 8 to 10 percent experience inhibited male orgasm, and less than 1 percent suffer from erectile failure. Among women, hypoactive sexual desire is found in 20 to 35 percent; 10 to 30 percent experience either no or very few orgasms; and vaginismus occurs in less than 1 percent of the female population.

Sex drive is determined by a combination of physical and psychological functions. It varies so widely that it is difficult to specify a "normal" level of sexual desire and activity. The dysfunctions associated with sexual arousal may be related to the hormones involved in the physiology of sex, to various prescription and illicit drugs, and to stress, strict religious upbringing, obsessive-compulsive traits, or a history of painful relationships.

The causes of erectile failure are also both physiological and psychological. Frequently a mild organic impairment can make a man more vulnerable to the psychological factors that inhibit erection. The physiological factors include vascular abnormalities that restrict blood flow to the penis, damage to the penile chambers, spinal cord injuries, kidney failure, and many of the drugs that affect arousal. Psychological factors affecting erectile failure are generally the same as those that affect arousal. In addition, *performance anxiety* and *the spectator role* are psychological phenomena believed to contribute to erectile failure.

Premature ejaculation is generally attributable to psychological factors and is typical of young, inexperienced men. Inhibited ejaculation may be caused by a low testosterone level, by drugs that inhibit sympathetic arousal, by many of the drugs that are associated with hypoactive sex arousal, and perhaps by psychological factors similar to those that cause erectile failure.

Female arousal and orgasm dysfunctions were traditionally believed to result from our culture's double standard, which until recently demanded that women suppress their sexuality; but this view has received little research support. Psychological causes apparently include those that lead to hypoactive sexual desire. A woman's sexual responsiveness has been linked to childhood memories of a positive relationship with her mother; issues related to her current partner, such as attraction and emotional commitment; and the use of sexual fantasies.

Vaginismus is considered to be a conditioned fear response developed through negative sexual experiences or because of gynecological diseases that have caused pain during sex. Dyspareunia, on the other hand, usually has a physical cause, such as damage caused by childbirth, undiagnosed vaginal infections, pelvic diseases, and allergies to chemicals introduced into the vagina.

Until recently the major treatment for sexual dysfunctions was long-term psychoanalysis, based on the assumption that sexual dysfunction was caused by failure to progress through the stages of psychosexual development. This approach proved minimally successful. Behavioral treatments focusing on relaxation and *systematic desensitization* were somewhat more successful. In the 1970s the work of William H. Masters and Virginia E. Johnson led to the development of *sex therapy.* The major components of this therapeutic approach are assessment and conceptualization; accurate information; change of problematic attitudes, cognitions, and beliefs; the elimination of performance anxiety and the spectator role; improvements in communication and sexual technique; and a change in destructive lifestyles and marital interactions.

Treatments for hypoactive sexual desire and sexual aversion disorders involve four elements: affectual awareness, insight, cognitive and emotional changes and behavioral interventions. This approach has met with a fair degree of success. Premature ejaculation is treated with almost a 100 percent success rate by direct behavioral retraining procedures. Inhibited male orgasm is treated by reducing performance anxiety and ensuring adequate stimulation. Treatment for erectile failure also consists of reducing performance anxiety and increasing stimulation. In addition, if the cause of erectile dysfunction is physiological, surgical implantation of a *penile prosthesis* may be undertaken. A nonsurgical alternative is the use of a *vacuum erection device.*

Treatments for female arousal and orgasm dysfunction include self-exploration, body awareness, and directed masturbation training. Vaginismus is treated by having patients practice contracting and relaxing the pubococcygeal muscles, while inserting progressively larger dilators, in order to acquire voluntary control.

Paraphilias are characterized by intense sexual urges and sexually arousing fantasies involving either nonhuman objects, children or nonconsenting adults, or experiences of suffering or humiliation. These behaviors are generally classified as disorders if they are the only or primary source of arousal for the person or if the person feels shame, guilt, or distress over them. Paraphilias are found primarily in men. Little is known about what causes or how to treat the disorders.

*Fetishism* is characterized by recurrent, intense sexual urges and sexually arousing fantasies that involve the use of an inanimate object or body part. *Transvestic fetishism,* or *transvestism,* is the recurrent need or desire to dress in clothes of the opposite sex in order to achieve sexual arousal. *Pedophilia* involves sexual gratification by watching, touching, or engaging in sexual acts with prepubescent children. *Exhibitionism* consists of recurrent intense urges to act out sexually arousing fantasies of exposing one's genitals to another person.

*Voyeurism* involves recurrent intense desire to secretly observe people undressing or during intercourse. *Frotteurism* is a recurrent and intense desire to touch and rub one's genitals against a nonconsenting adult. *Sexual masochism* is a pattern in which people repeatedly have intense sexual urges and fantasies of being humiliated, beaten, bound, or otherwise made to suffer. *Sexual sadism* is a pattern in which people are intensely sexually aroused by the act or thought of inflicting physical or psychological suffering on others. The definitions of paraphilias are closely tied to the norms of the particular society in which they occur, and some people argue that paraphilic behaviors are not disorders at all unless people are hurt by them.

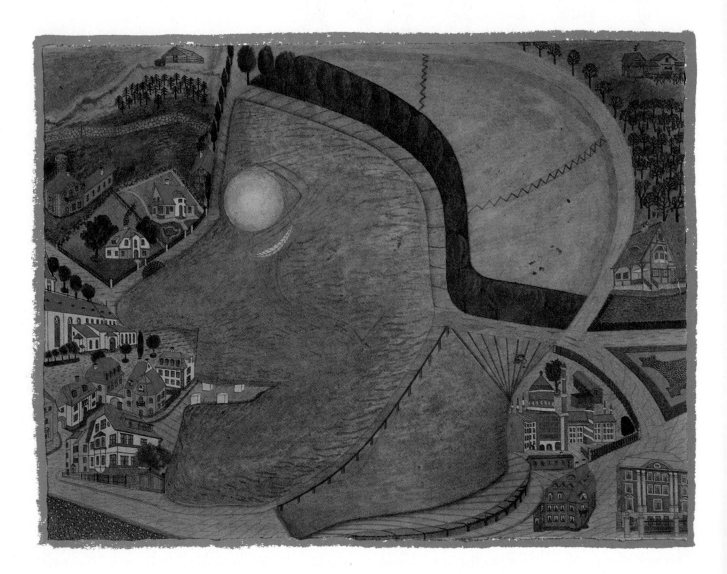

# TOPIC OVERVIEW

# CHAPTER *15*

# SCHIZOPHRENIA

**P**sychosis is a condition in which individuals lose contact with reality. Typically, their capacity to perceive, process, and respond to environmental stimuli becomes so impaired and distorted that they may be unable to achieve even marginal adaptive functioning. Individuals in a state of psychosis may have hallucinations (false sensory perceptions) or delusions (false beliefs) or may withdraw into a private world that is almost totally unaffected by the persons and events around them (see Box 15-1).

Psychosis may result from various factors. As we noted in Chapter 13, taking LSD, abusing amphetamines or cocaine, or ingesting certain toxic substances may produce psychosis. Simi-

larly, aging, brain injuries, or brain diseases may cause psychotic disorders. Most commonly, psychosis appears in the form of *schizophrenia,* a disorder in which personal, social, and occupational functioning that had previously been adaptive deteriorates into a welter of distorted perceptions, disturbed thought processes, deviant emotional states, and motor abnormalities.

*What . . . does schizophrenia mean to me? It* means fatigue and confusion, it means trying to separate every experience into the real and the unreal and sometimes not being aware of where the edges overlap. It means trying to think straight when there is a maze of experiences getting in the way, and when thoughts are continually being sucked out of your head so that you become embarrassed to speak at meetings. It means feeling sometimes that you are inside your head and visualizing yourself walking over your brain, or watching another girl wearing your clothes and carrying out actions as you think them. It means knowing that you are continually "watched," that you can never succeed in life because the laws are all against you and knowing that your ultimate destruction is never far away.

*(Rollin, 1980, p. 162)*

Approximately one of every 100 people on earth meets the DSM-III-R criteria for schizophrenia

(Gottesman, 1991; Jablensky, 1988; APA, 1987). Equal numbers of men and women receive the diagnosis (APA, 1987). More than two million people currently living in the United States have been or will be diagnosed as suffering from schizophrenia (Locke & Regier, 1985; Torrey, 1983). Some 200,000 new cases are reported each year (Kramer, 1983). The President's Commission on Mental Health (1978) brought such figures to life with the observation "There are as many schizophrenics in America as there are people in Oregon, Mississippi and Kansas, or in Wyoming, Vermont, Delaware and

---

## BOX 15-1

# An Array of Psychotic Disorders

"Schizophrenia" is often used as a synonym for "psychosis." Although schizophrenia is indeed the most common kind of psychosis, it is but one of several. Psychotic functioning actually comes in all sizes and shapes, and may be caused by a variety of factors. In addition to schizophrenia, DSM-III-R distinguishes the following psychotic disorders.

### DELUSIONAL DISORDER

When people have persistent, nonbizarre delusions that are not part of a larger schizophrenic pattern, they may receive a diagnosis of *delusional,* or *paranoid, disorder.* Aside from their delusions, they do not act in a particularly odd way and rarely show prominent hallucinations.

*Persecution, jealous, grandiose,* and *somatic* delusions are common in this disorder. Lately public attention has been drawn to *erotomanic* delusions. People with these delusions believe, without any basis whatsoever, that they are loved by another person, such as an acquaintance, or even a complete stranger. Increasingly, celebrities and other famous people are complaining to police about being incessantly telephoned, harassed, and stalked by a particular person — someone at first considered an avid

fan but later recognized as having a serious disorder. In a few cases the erotomanic delusions have led to tragedy, as when Rebecca Schaeffer, the young star of the television series *My Sister Sam*, was killed by a man who wanted her affection, and when John Hinckley shot President Ronald Reagan to prove his love to actress Jodie Foster.

### BRIEF REACTIVE PSYCHOSIS

If psychotic symptoms appear suddenly after a very stressful event or period of emotional turmoil and last anywhere from a few hours to a month, a diagnosis of *brief reactive psychosis* may be called for. The psychotic symptoms may include delusions, hallucinations, loose associations, incoherence, catatonia, or disorganized behavior.

### SCHIZOPHRENIFORM DISORDER

People with *schizophreniform disorder* experience all of the key features of schizophrenia, but the symptoms last less than six months. In short, this diagnosis applies if the disorder lasts longer than a brief reactive psychosis but is less persistent than schizophrenia. Emotional turmoil, fear, confusion, and very vivid

hallucinations often characterize this psychotic pattern.

### SCHIZOAFFECTIVE DISORDER

Sometimes people display symptoms of both schizophrenia and a mood disorder without meeting the full diagnostic criteria of either. In such cases, they may receive a diagnosis of *schizoaffective disorder.* To receive this diagnosis, however, the individual must have a history of at least one episode of concurrent schizophrenia and mood disturbance and another episode of psychotic symptoms only. Some clinicians dislike this category, believing it to be a wastebasket category that is generally used when diagnosticians have a hard time determining whether a client's mood problems are resulting from a schizophrenic disorder or vice versa.

### INDUCED PSYCHOTIC DISORDER

When persons embrace the delusions held by another individual, they may qualify for a diagnosis of *induced psychotic disorder.* They usually have a close relationship with the person (called the primary person) whose psychotic thinking they come to believe. When the disorder is found in a two-person relationship, as it usually

Hawaii combined." The financial cost of the disorder is enormous — estimated at between $10 and $20 billion annually, including the cost of hospitalization, lost wages, and disability benefits (Cancro, 1985; Gunderson & Mosher, 1975). The catastrophic impact of this disorder on families represents an even greater emotional cost. Moreover, schizophrenia is associated with increased risk for suicide and for physical — often mortal — illness (McGlashan, 1988).

Although it appears in all socioeconomic groups, schizophrenia is more likely to be found in people of the lower socioeconomic classes (APA, 1987). It was once thought that the stress of poverty was itself a cause of schizophrenia. Although this may indeed be part of the reason for the statistical link between schizophrenia and membership in the lower socioeconomic classes, lately other factors have been cited as well (APA, 1987). Schizophrenia may actually cause a person to migrate from a higher to a lower socioeconomic class (Scottish Schizophrenia Research Group, 1988; Silverton & Mednick, 1984). Victims of schizophrenia may be less able to maintain previously high levels of functioning

In one or two of every 1,000 births, a mother suffers *postpartum psychosis*, marked by hallucinations, severe depression, and, in some cases, impulses to kill herself or her child or both. This disorder, different from the much more common postpartum major depression, appears to be a variation of schizophreniform disorder, schizoaffective disorder, or major depression with psychotic features.

is, it is known as *folie à deux.* If the relationship with the primary person is broken, the second person's delusional beliefs usually subside or disappear. Sometimes the disorder occurs in a whole family or group.

### ORGANIC DELUSIONAL SYNDROME

If a specific organic factor is causing delusions, a person may receive a diagnosis of *organic delusional syndrome.* There are many possible organic causes of delusions, including substances such as amphetamines, cocaine, cannabis, and LSD; temporal lobe epilepsy; Huntington's chorea; and certain cerebral lesions.

### ORGANIC HALLUCINOSIS

When a specific organic factor causes hallucinations, a person may qualify for a diagnosis of *organic hallucinosis.* The most common causes are use of hallucinogenic drugs and extended use of alcohol. The syndrome may also result from the sensory deprivation of blindness or deafness, or from certain types of seizure. Particular organic factors may produce particular kinds of hallucinations. Hallucino-genic drugs, for example, typically induce visual hallucinations, while alcohol tends to cause auditory hallucinations. People who become blind may develop visual hallucinations, while those who become deaf may experience auditory hallucinations.

after they become impaired. Similarly, those born into lower socioeconomic classes may find an upward economic climb interrupted by the onset of this disorder.

Schizophrenia has been with us throughout history; it is the condition commonly described by the word "madness" (Cutting, 1985). The Bible speaks of King Saul's mad rages and terrors and of David's efforts to feign madness in order to escape his enemies. Hippocrates considered this syndrome to be a form of mental deterioration, caused by an imbalance of the body's humors, and the Roman physician Galen (A.D. 130–200), who referred to it as "dementia," blamed it on "rarefaction" and "diminution" of a person's normal "animal spirits," and on coldness and excess humidity in the brain.

In 1865 a Belgian psychiatrist named Benedict Morel (1809–1873) used the label *démence précoce* ("precocious dementia") to describe a 14-year-old-boy who showed progressive apathy, mutism, withdrawal, and emotional instability. Although previously a brilliant student, the boy had lost interest in academics and seemed to forget everything he had known. *Démence* was meant to describe the serious intellectual and mental deterioration and *précoce* to convey that the deterioration began relatively early in life. Similarly, in 1899 Emil Kraepelin used the Latin form of Morel's label, *dementia praecox*, to describe such disorders.

In 1911 the Swiss psychiatrist Eugen Bleuler (1857–1939) gave the name "schizophrenia" to disorders of this kind. It is a combination of Greek words that means "split within the mind." Bleuler used the term to imply (1) a fragmentation of thought processes, (2) a split between thoughts and emotions, and (3) a withdrawal from reality. It was not meant to convey a split into two or more personalities, although many lay people continue to misinterpret it in this way (see Chapter 18). Bleuler improved on Morel's descriptions by correctly observing that intellectual deterioration was not an inevitable feature of schizophrenia, nor was progressive mental deterioration the rule. He noted, on the contrary, that many individuals eventually stabilized and a few even improved.

Today theorists and researchers continue to try to understand the nature and causes of schizophrenia. The general public shows great interest in the disorder, flocking to movies (including the remarkably popular horror movies) and plays whose plots center on schizophrenia. Yet all too many schizophrenic people are virtually neglected in our country, and their needs almost entirely ignored. Although practicable and effective therapies have been developed for the disorder, most of these people live without adequate treatment and without even partially fulfilling their potential as human beings.

# THE CLINICAL PICTURE OF SCHIZOPHRENIA

Among people who are diagnosed as schizophrenic, there is considerable variation in symptoms, in the apparent cause and course of the disorder, and in responsiveness to treatment (APA, 1987). In fact, there is a growing belief among clinicians that schizophrenia is actually a group of many distinct disorders that share some common features (Carpenter et al., 1988; APA, 1987). DSM-III-R, however, now classifies schizophrenia as a single disorder with numerous faces. To illustrate the variety of forms schizophrenia may take, let us consider three people who were diagnosed as suffering from it. The cases are taken from the files of Silvano Arieti (1974), a prominent theorist on schizophrenia.

### *Ann, 26 years old*

Ann graduated from high school and from a school for commercial art. She was a very persistent student, very punctual in her study habits, and even in her early childhood showed a talent for drawing and painting. Following her studies in commercial art she obtained several jobs which were not commensurate with her ability. She even did factory work.

. . . At the age of 18 she met a man ten years her senior with whom she became infatuated. They went out on frequent dates, but the man was inducted into the army. The patient then began going out with Henry, the younger brother of the inducted man. . . .

They became engaged shortly thereafter and went out together frequently until their marriage. . . . Married life was considered a boring routine by both Ann and Henry. There was very little conversation between them. . . .

Ann's disappointment in Henry increased. They had nothing in common; she was artistically inclined, whereas he had only an ordinary, conventional outlook toward life. It was at this time that she started to go dancing and then met Charles. Her interest in him increased, but she knew that she was married and that a divorce was not compatible with the precepts of the Catholic church. Her conflict grew and put her in a state of great agitation. . . .

. . . One evening she came home from dancing and told her mother that she was going to give up her husband Henry, marry Charles, go to Brazil with him, and have twenty babies. She was talking very fast and saying many things, several of which were incomprehensible. At the same time she also told her mother that she was seeing the Virgin Mary in visions. She then went to her mother-in-law and told her to take back her son Henry, because he was too immature. The following day Ann went to work and tried to get the entire office down on their knees with her to recite the rosary. A few days later, her mother took her to a priest, whom she "told off" in no uncertain terms. She finally spit at him. A psychiatrist was consulted, and he recommended hospitalization.

. . . When the patient was first seen in the ward by the examiner, she was dashing around the room, singing and laughing. She was markedly agitated; frequently she would cry one minute and then laugh in a silly, impulsive manner, or suddenly slump over and become mute. Her speech would be incoherent at one time because she mumbled and at another time she would shriek very loudly. She would be irrelevant, or circumstantial, and she frequently rambled, her thoughts being completely unrelated to one another. Her affect would vary from extreme lability to complete flatness. She was hallucinating in auditory and visual spheres quite vividly. She was saying:

I was judged insane and others felt that this was the place for me. I am too weak. You look to me like Uncle Joe, and he is so far away. He knew how much I loved him. We could always get along. I never meant to be disobedient to you. The darn son of a bitch, you couldn't smile at me. You are the Pope and I must be obedient to the Pope. He is the only one I must be obedient to. You didn't flinch when I said "son of a bitch." You are trying to help me. All the others are different. That I can't fake in your presence, my Lord. You will understand me as my friends didn't. Russia is the only Catholic country. Russia is to the rest of the world what God is to the Pope.

Later the patient became more agitated and required strong sedation. Her illness seemed to proceed toward more advanced disintegration. She laughed in an inappropriate manner, and her whole behavior appeared silly. She was restless, confused, and talked to imaginary persons.

*(Arieti, 1974, pp. 173–177)*

## *R*ichard, *23 years old*

In high school, Richard was an average student. After graduation from high school, he was drafted into the army, where he felt unhappy. . . . After his discharge, he wanted to enter some kind of musical career, but gave up the idea because it did not offer financial security. He had several jobs, for example, as a delivery boy, elevator man, and hospital helper. He could not keep a job for any length of time because he was very sensitive to criticism and was always afraid that he would not satisfy his bosses.

Richard remembered this period, after his discharge from the army, as one of the worst in his life, even worse than his childhood. Throughout his life he had been very sensitive and had always taken things too much to heart, but after his discharge, when he was supposed to do things on his own and show what he was able to do, his sensitivity increased. He was "eating his heart out" for unimportant reasons; any, even remote, anticipation of disappointment was able to provoke attacks of anxiety in him. He could never be indifferent or detached, but was very much involved in everything. After his discharge from the army his life had become a series of crises.

Approximately two years after his return to civilian life, Richard left his job because he became overwhelmed by these feelings of lack of confidence in himself, and he refused to go look for another one. He stayed home most of the day. His mother would nag him that he was too lazy and unwilling to do anything. He became slower and slower in dressing and undressing and taking care of himself. When he went out of the house, he felt compelled "to give interpretations" to everything he looked at. He did not know what to do outside the house, where to go, where to turn. If he saw a red light at a crossing, he would interpret it as a message that he should not go in that direction. If he saw an arrow, he would follow the arrow interpreting it as a sign sent by God that he should go in that direction. Feeling lost and horrified, he would go home and stay there, afraid to go out because going out meant making decisions or choices that he felt unable to make. He reached the point where he stayed home most of the time. But even at home, he was tortured by his symptoms. He could not act; any motion that he felt like making seemed to him an insurmountable obstacle, because he did not know whether he should make it or not. He was increasingly afraid of doing the wrong thing. Such fears prevented him from dressing, undressing, eating, and so forth. He felt paralyzed and lay motionless in bed. He gradually became worse, was completely motionless, and had to be hospitalized.

. . . Even in the hospital, he had to interpret everything that occurred. If a doctor asked him a question, he had a sudden impulse to answer, but then feared that by answering he would do the wrong thing. He tried desperately to find signs that would indicate to him whether he should answer or not. An accidental noise, the arrival of another person, or the number of words the questions consisted of were indications of whether he should reply or not.

Being undecided, he felt blocked, and often would remain mute and motionless, like a statue, even for days. He had always been more or less afraid of being with people because he did not feel strong enough to take their suggestions or to refuse them; in the hospital such fear increased.

*(Arieti, 1974, pp. 153–155)*

## *L*aura, *40 years old*

Laura's desire was to become independent and leave home as soon as possible. Throughout her childhood she attended dancing schools, and she became a professional dancer at the age of 20. . . . She was very successful and was booked for vaudeville theaters in many European countries, but she performed mostly in Germany. . . .

It was during one of her tours in Germany that Laura met her husband. He was a French tourist, a businessman, who became interested in her acting. He would often go to Germany from France just to see her. He overwhelmed her with his consideration and interest, and Laura felt that she liked his attention. She had some qualms about leaving her theatrical career and marrying him, but finally she decided to do so. They were married and went to live in a small provincial town in France where the husband's business was. Laura felt like a stranger immediately; she was in an environment very different from her own and was not accepted by his family. There were realistic grounds for her feelings. They considered her a foreigner and could not forgive her for having been a dancer, and not a "regular girl." She spent a year in that town and was very unhappy. She felt that when there were arguments or controversies, her husband always took the side of his family and never took her part.

Finally . . . Laura and her husband decided to immigrate to the United States, along with her husband's sister. Laura did not get along well with her sister-in-law and again felt that her husband showed favoritism toward his sister.

The years spent in America had not been easy ones. Laura and her husband had not been happy together. They had different points of view about many things, and the gap caused by their different backgrounds was never closed. Laura's husband became more and more intolerant of her attitude and started to neglect her. Nothing would irritate her more than his lavish attentions to his sister. They had no children, and Laura . . . showed interest in pets. She had a dog to whom she was very devoted. The dog became sick and partially paralyzed, and veterinarians felt that there was no hope of recovery. The dog required difficult care, and her husband, who knew how she felt about the animal, tolerated the situation for several weeks. But finally he broached the problem to his wife, asking her "Should the dog be destroyed or not?" From that time on Laura became restless, agitated, and depressed. . . .

. . . Later Laura started to complain about the neighbors. A woman who lived on the floor beneath them was knocking on the wall to irritate her. According to the husband, this woman had really knocked on the wall a few times; he had heard the noises. However, Laura became more and more concerned about it. She would wake up in the middle of the night under the impression that she was hearing noises from the apartment downstairs. She would become upset and angry at the neighbors. Once she was awake, she could not sleep for the rest of the night. The husband would vainly try to calm her. Later she became more disturbed. She started to feel that the neighbors were now recording everything she said; maybe they had hidden wires in the apartment. She started to feel "funny" sensations. There were many strange things happening, which she did not know how to explain; people were looking at her in a funny way in the street; in the butcher shop, the butcher had purposely served her last, although she was in the middle of the line. During the next few days she felt that people were planning to harm either her or her husband. In the neighborhood she saw a German woman whom she had not seen for several years. Now the woman had suddenly reappeared, probably to testify that the patient and her husband were involved in some sort of crime.

Laura was distressed and agitated. She felt unjustly accused, because she had committed no crime. Maybe these people were really not after her, but after her husband. In the evening when she looked at television, it became obvious to her that the programs referred to her life. Often the people on the programs were just repeating what she had

thought. They were stealing her ideas. She wanted to go to the police and report them.

*(Arieti, 1974, pp. 165–168)*

## Symptoms of Schizophrenia

Ann, Richard, and Laura each regressed from a normal level of functioning to become significantly ineffective in dealing with the world. Ann, a promising art student, became unhappy and discontented, and finally totally disoriented; Richard, a sensitive and talented young man, became so indecisive that he literally stopped moving; and Laura, once so independent and competent, became restless and agitated and eventually consumed by bizarre suspicions. Among them, these three individuals demonstrate the range of symptoms associated with schizophrenia: disturbances in content of thought, form of thought, perception and attention, affect, sense of self, relationship to the outside world, volition, and psychomotor behavior. Although several such disturbances are usually present in any given case of schizophrenia, no single symptom is present in every case.

**Disturbances in Content of Thought**    Many schizophrenic people develop disturbances in their thought content — that is, in their ideas and beliefs. They have *delusions,* ideas that they believe fervently but that have no basis in fact and are often absurd. These beliefs may be elaborate and internally consistent or fragmented and capricious; they may appear to the believer as either enlightening or confusing. Some people with schizophrenia hold a single delusion that dominates their life and behavior, while others have many delusions. The most common are delusions of persecution, reference, grandiosity, and control.

People who have *delusions of persecution* believe that they are being plotted or discriminated against, spied on, slandered, threatened, attacked, or deliberately victimized. Laura believed that her neighbors were trying to irritate her and that other people were trying to harm her and her husband. When she saw an old acquaintance from Germany, she thought the woman had come to testify against her.

People who have *delusions of reference* attach special and personal significance to the actions of others, or to various objects or events. A man may believe, for example, that the words spoken in a movie are referring to him, that a radio announcer is secretly mocking him, or that a sudden weather change is a sign to change jobs. Laura believed that strangers were looking at her in a funny way and Richard interpreted arrows on street signs as indicators of the direction he should take.

People with *delusions of grandeur* believe themselves to be great inventors, historical figures, religious saviors, or other specially empowered persons. One patient recalled, "I felt that I had power to determine the weather, which responded to my inner moods, and even to control the movement of the sun in relation to other astronomical bodies."

*Delusions of control* are beliefs that one's impulses, feelings, thoughts, and actions are being controlled by other people. A woman may believe that external forces are regulating her need to eat, the speed at which she drives, and her behavior toward people. Often people with such delusions believe that they are somehow "wired" to the outside forces or receiving radio signals from them. In the following letter about his hospital experience, a man describes his desperate concerns about being controlled:

*T*he *inmates, here, hate me extremely because I am* sane. . . . They talk to me telepathically, continuously and daily almost without cessation, day and night. (Inmates and employees talk to me telepathically, daily, and continuously without cessation, day and night). . . . By the power of their imagination and daily and continuously, they create extreme pain in my head, brain, eyes, heart, stomach and in every part of my body. Also by their imagination and daily and continuously, they lift my heart and stomach and they pull my heart, and they stop it, move it, twist it and shake it and pull its muscles and tissues . . . they force one another to talk orally and to send their voices to my head, forehead, temples and heart. . . . By telepathy and imagination, they force me to say orally whatever they desire, whenever they desire and as long as they desire. I never said a word of my own. I never created a thought or image of my own.

*(Arieti, 1974, pp. 404–405)*

Somewhat less common are somatic and religious delusions. People with *somatic delusions* believe that they have horrible diseases, that they are deteriorating rapidly, turning to dust, or even being eaten away. Those with *religious delusions* develop bizarre religious notions and guidelines.

**Disturbances in Form of Thought**   *Formal thought disorders,* disturbances in the very production and organization of thought, may also accompany schizophrenia. These abnormalities can cause the sufferer great confusion and make communication with others extremely difficult (Liddle & Barnes, 1988). Formal thought disorders are revealed by peculiarities of verbal expression, such as loose associations, neologisms, perseveration, clang, and blocking.

People who manifest *loose associations,* the most common formal thought disorder, rapidly shift from one

The renowned ballet artist Vaslav Nijinsky, performing here in *Schéhérazade,* developed severe schizophrenia and spent the last years of his life in a mental institution.

topic to another, making inconsequential and incoherent statements and apparently believing them to make sense. For example, a schizophrenic man, asked about his itchy arms, responded:

*T*he *problem is insects. . . . My brother used to collect* insects. . . . He's now a man 5 foot 10 inches. . . . You know, 10 is my favorite number. . . . I also like to dance, draw, and watch television.

In this man's speech, associations between one block of words and the next are oblique: a relatively unimportant word from each sentence becomes the focus of the next.

Loose associations often convey great emotion but very little meaning, reflecting what is termed *poverty of content.* Vaslav Nijinsky, one of the century's great ballet dancers, wrote the following diary entry on February 27, 1919, as his schizophrenia was becoming increasingly apparent:

*I do not wish people to think that I am a great writer or that I am a great artist nor even that I am a great man.* I am a simple man who has suffered a lot. I believe I suffered more than Christ. I love life and want to live, to cry but cannot—I feel such a pain in my soul—a pain which frightens me. My soul is ill. My soul, not my mind. The doctors do not understand my illness. I know what I need to get well. My illness is too great to be cured quickly. I am incurable. Everyone who reads these lines will suffer—they will understand my feelings. I know what I need. I am strong, not weak. My body is not ill—it is my soul that is ill. I suffer, I suffer. Everyone will feel and understand. I am a man, not a beast. I love everyone, I have faults, I am a man—not God. I want to be God and therefore I try to improve myself. I want to dance, to draw, to play the piano, to write verses, I want to love everybody. That is the—object of my life. I know that Socialists would understand me better—but I am not a Socialist. I am a part of God, my party is God's party. I love everybody. I *do not* want war or frontiers. The world exists. I have a home everywhere. I live everywhere. I do not want to have any property. I do not want to be rich. I want to love. I am man. I am man. God is in me. I am in God. I want Him, I seek Him. I want my manuscripts to be published so that everybody can read them. I hope to improve myself. I do not know how to, but I feel that God will help all those who seek Him. I am a seeker, for I can feel God. God seeks me and therefore we will find each other.

*(Nijinsky, 1936)*

*Neologisms* are made-up words that have meaning only to the person using them. The following statement illustrates one patient's use of such words:

*I am here from a foreign university . . . and you have to* have a "plausity" of all acts of amendment to go through for the children's code . . . and it is no mental disturbance or "putenence" . . . it is an "amorition" law . . . there is nothing to disturb me . . . it is like their "privatilinia" . . . and the children have to have this "accentuative" law so they don't go into the "mortite" law of the church.

*(Vetter, 1969, p. 189)*

Schizophrenic individuals may also display formal thought disorders by *perseverating*—that is, repeating their words and statements again and again. They may also use *clang,* or rhyme, as a guide to formulating thoughts and statements. When asked how she was feeling, one schizophrenic person replied, "Well, hell, it's well to tell." Another described the weather as "So hot, you know it runs on a cot." Finally, schizophrenic people may display the formal thought disorder of *blocking.*

Their thoughts disappear from memory, and their statements end in silence before they can be completed. One patient describes how this problem feels to him:

*I may be thinking quite clearly and telling someone something and suddenly I get stuck.* You have seen me do this and you may think I am just lost for words or that I have gone into a trance, but that is not what happens. What happens is that I suddenly stick on a word or an idea in my head and I just can't move past it. It seems to fill my mind and there's no room for anything else. This might go on for a while and suddenly it's over. Afterwards I get a feeling that I have been thinking very deeply about whatever it was but often I can't remember what it was that has filled my mind so completely.

*(McGhie & Chapman, 1961)*

Formal thought dysfunctioning is not unique to schizophrenia. Loose associations and perseverations are common in cases of severe mania. Even people who function normally may organize statements loosely or may on occasion use words that others fail to understand, especially when they are fatigued or feeling ill; but the formal thought disorders of schizophrenia are much more severe and pervasive (Holzman, 1979).

It may be that some degree of disordered thinking appears long before a full pattern of schizophrenic symptoms unfolds (Walker & Lewine, 1990). A number of researchers have conducted ***high-risk studies*** to investigate schizophrenia—studies in which people hypothesized to be "at greater risk" for developing the disorder (such as people whose parents are schizophrenic) are followed throughout their childhood. These studies have indicated that high-risk people who later develop schizophrenia show significantly more disordered thinking when tested at the age of 15 than similar high-risk subjects who do not later develop schizophrenia (Parnas et al., 1982).

**Disturbances in Perception and Attention**   A *heightened sensitivity to sounds and sights* is reported by many people with schizophrenia, and has long been associated with "madness." The deranged protagonist in Edgar Allan Poe's "Tell-Tale Heart" asks, "Have I not told you that what you mistake for madness is but the overacuteness of the senses?" Some schizophrenic people feel that their senses are being *flooded* by all the sights and sounds that surround them, so that it is almost impossible for them to attend to anything important:

*Everything seems to grip my attention although I am not* particularly interested in anything. I am speaking to you just now, but I can hear noises going on next door and in the corridor. I find it difficult to shut these out, and it makes it more difficult for me to concentrate on what I am saying to you. Often the silliest little things that are going on seem to interest me. That's not even true; they don't interest me, but I find myself attending to them and wasting a lot of time this way.

(McGhie and Chapman, 1961)

Laboratory studies of schizophrenic subjects have repeatedly demonstrated this kind of dysfunctioning (Goldberg, Gold, & Braff, 1991; Harvey et al., 1990, 1988; Rund, 1988; Posner et al., 1988). In one study, schizophrenic and nonschizophrenic subjects were instructed to listen for and identify a target syllable on a recording while background speech was also being played on the recording (Harris et al., 1985). As long as the background speech was kept simple, the two groups were equally effective at picking out the target syllable; but when the background speech was made more distracting, the schizophrenic subjects became less able than the others to identify the target syllable. Related studies of high-risk subjects suggest that attention problems of this kind may also develop years before a full schizophrenic pattern unfolds (Cornblatt & Erlenmeyer-Kimling, 1985).

Other schizophrenic people may suffer from *sensory blunting,* a significant reduction in the strength of their physical sensations. They feel as if a blanket were covering their senses, making it impossible for them to see, hear, feel, taste, or smell clearly. Perhaps blunting is a compensatory mechanism for heightened sensitivity. It is as if overloaded senses, unable to filter and organize the influx of sensory experiences, simply close down.

*Hallucinations,* perceptions that occur in the absence of external stimuli, are an even more severe perceptual disturbance found in many cases of schizophrenia. In *auditory* hallucinations, by far the most common kind in schizophrenia (Mueser, Bellack, & Brady, 1990), people hear sounds and voices that seem to come from outside their heads. The voices may be familiar or unfamiliar, single or multiple, complimentary or critical, and may be heard frequently or only on occasion. Often they talk directly to the hallucinator, perhaps giving commands or warning of dangers. In other cases, they are experienced as being overheard.

*The voices . . . were mostly heard in my head, though I* often heard them in the air, or in different parts of the room. Every voice was different, and each beautiful, and generally, speaking or singing in a different tone and measure, and resembling those of relations or friends. There appeared to be many in my head, I should say upwards of fourteen. I divide them, as they styled themselves, or one another, into voices of contrition and voices of joy and honour.

("Perceval's Narrative" in Bateson, 1974)

*For about almost seven years—except during sleep—I* have never had a single moment in which I did not hear voices. They accompany me to every place and at all times; they continue to sound even when I am in conversation with other people, they persist undeterred even when I concentrate on other things, for instance read a book or a newspaper, play the piano, etc.; only when I am talking aloud to other people or to myself are they of course drowned by the stronger sound of the spoken word and therefore inaudible to me. But the well-known phrases recommence at once, sometimes in the middle of a sentence, which tells me that the conversation had continued during the interval, that is to say that those nervous stimuli or vibrations responsible for the weaker sounds of the voices continue even while I talk aloud.

(Schreber, 1955, p. 225)

Researchers have found that schizophrenic subjects who are unskilled at voluntarily imagining sounds are more likely than other schizophrenic people to experience auditory hallucinations (Heilbrun et al., 1983; Starker & Joli, 1982; Seitz & Molholm, 1947). Studies have also suggested that auditory hallucinations are more likely to occur during times of idleness, inattention, or sensory isolation. One study noted increases in hallucinations when schizophrenic people listened to a bland noise over headphones and wore goggles to restrict visual information (Margo et al., 1981). As a patient once observed, "Isn't it funny, when I'm shoveling snow I don't hear voices" (Strauss et al., 1981).

Hallucinations can also involve the other senses. *Tactile* hallucinations may take the form of tingling, burning, or electrical-shock sensations, or the feeling of insects crawling over one's body or just beneath the skin. *Somatic* hallucinations convey the sensation that something is happening inside the body, such as an organ shifting position or a snake crawling inside one's stomach. *Visual* hallucinations run the gamut from vague perceptions of colors or clouds to distinct visions of people, objects, or scenes that are not there. They are different from the range of normal mental images experienced by adults and children. People with *gustatory* hallucinations regularly find that their food or drink tastes strange, and people with *olfactory* hallucinations smell odors that no one else does, being haunted, for example, by the smell of poison, smoke, or decay.

Hallucinations and delusional ideas often go hand in hand. A woman who hears voices issuing commands, for example, may have the delusion that the commands are being placed in her head by someone else. Similarly, a man with delusions of persecution may hallucinate the smell of poison in his bedroom or the taste of poison in his coffee. Regardless of which comes first, the hallucination and delusion eventually feed into each other.

**Disturbances in Affect**   Schizophrenic people may suffer various forms of emotional disturbance. Many schizophrenic people have a ***blunted affect*** — they manifest less anger, sadness, joy, or other feelings than other people — and some show almost no emotions at all, a condition known as ***flat affect.*** The faces of these subjects are typically immobile and their voices are monotonous. One young schizophrenic man told his father, "I wish I could wake up feeling really bad — it would be better than feeling nothing" (Wechsler, 1972, p. 17).

The emotions expressed by a person with ***inappropriate affect*** are unsuited to the situation. Schizophrenic individuals may, for example, smile inappropriately when making a somber statement or on being told terrible news, or become upset in situations that should make them happy. They may also undergo inappropriate shifts in mood. During a tender conversation with his wife, for example, a schizophrenic man suddenly started yelling obscenities at her and complaining about her inadequacies.

Many clinicians believe these affective symptoms arise from the other features of schizophrenia, such as disturbances in perception. Consider a schizophrenic woman who smiles when told of her husband's serious illness. Although her apparent joy is an inappropriate reaction to bad news, we do not know that she is indeed happy about this news or that she is even hearing or comprehending it. Instead, she may be responding to another of the many thoughts and stimuli flooding her senses, or to a joke she is hearing from an auditory hallucination.

**A Disturbed Sense of Self**   At some point in our lives most of us grapple with such important questions as "Who am I?" or "What am I?" Confronting such questions can eventually lead to our feeling unique and self-directed. Schizophrenic people, however, tend to be haunted by a much more difficult question: "Am I?" They become extremely confused about their identity, the reality of their existence, and their ability to discover and express who they are.

*I am in no small degree, I find, a sham — a player to the* gallery. Possibly this may be felt as you read these analyses.

In my life, in my personality, there is an essence of falseness and insincerity. A thin, fine vapor of fraud hangs always over me and dampens and injures some things in me that I value. . . .

. . . It may be that the spirit of falseness is itself a false thing — yet true or false, it is with me always. . . . This element of falseness is absolutely the very thinnest, the very finest, the rarest of all the things in my many-sided character.

It is not the most unimportant.

I have seen visions of myself walking in various pathways. I have seen myself trying one pathway and another. And always it is the same: I see before me in the path, darkening the way and filling me with dread and discouragement, a great black shadow — the shadow of my own element of falseness.

*(MacLane, 1902)*

Schizophrenic people may also find that parts of their bodies seem strange and foreign:

*I get shaky in the knees and my chest is like a mountain in* front of me, and my body actions are different. The arms and legs are apart and away from me and they go on their own. That's when I feel I am the other person and copy their movements, or else stop and stand like a statue. I have to stop to find out whether my hand is in my pocket or not. I'm frightened to move or turn my head. Sometimes I let my arms roll to see where they will land.

*(Chapman, 1966)*

**Disturbed Relationships with the External World**   If one cannot comfortably be with oneself, one is likely to have difficulty being with others. Schizophrenic people often withdraw emotionally and socially from their environment and become totally preoccupied with their own ideas and fantasies (Bellack & Morrison, 1987; Faloon et al., 1984). They may distance themselves from other people and even avoid looking at or talking to them. Because their ideas are illogical and distorted, this withdrawal helps distance them still further from reality. In fact, one study found that 75 percent of schizophrenic subjects were less knowledgeable about everyday social issues than were people with other psychological disorders (Cutting & Murphy, 1990, 1988).

**Disturbances in Volition**   As schizophrenic people, in their isolation, struggle to function in a grossly distorted world, many undergo changes in volition. They start to feel drained of energy and interest in normal goals, unable to make decisions, and unable to complete a course of action. This problem is particularly common in those who have had the disorder for many years, as if they have been worn down by it. Ambivalence was so common among the subjects Bleuler studied that he proclaimed this feature one of the central symptoms of schizophrenia.

Richard, in the case study we discussed earlier, was overwhelmed by his indecisiveness. He stayed at home because going out required him to make decisions, but even in his house, every motion involved a tortuous choice. Should he move his body or not? Was he following "signs" correctly? Daily activities such as eating, dressing, and undressing eventually became impossible ordeals.

**Disturbances in Psychomotor Behavior** Loss of spontaneity in movement and the development of odd grimaces, gestures, and mannerisms are also symptoms of schizophrenia. Such movements tend to be repetitive and often seem to be purposeful for the individual, like a ritualistic or magical act.

Sometimes the psychomotor symptoms of schizophrenia take extreme forms collectively called *catatonia.* People in a *catatonic stupor* become totally unresponsive to their environment, remaining motionless and silent for long stretches of time. Recall how Richard would lie motionless and mute in bed for days. Some people show *catatonic rigidity,* maintaining a rigid, upright posture for hours and resisting efforts to be moved. Others exhibit *catatonic posturing,* assuming awkward, bizarre positions for long periods of time. They may spend hours holding their arms out at a 90-degree angle or balancing in a squatting position. Some subjects also display *waxy flexibility,* indefinitely maintaining postures into which they have been placed by someone else. If a nurse raises a patient's arm or tilts the patient's head, for example, the individual will remain in that position until moved again.

People who display *catatonic excitement,* a different form of catatonia, move excitedly, sometimes with wild waving of arms and legs. When such patients are extremely hyperactive and uncontrolled, they pose a danger to themselves and others.

## The Course of Schizophrenia

Schizophrenia usually emerges during adolescence or early adulthood (APA, 1987). Although the course of this disorder varies widely from person to person (McGlashan, 1988; Harding & Strauss, 1984), many patients seem to go through three phases — prodromal, active, and residual (APA, 1987).

During the *prodromal phase* schizophrenic symptoms are not yet prominent, but the person has begun to deteriorate from previous levels of functioning. The person may withdraw socially; have trouble completing tasks and fulfilling responsibilities; acquire peculiar habits, such as collecting garbage or picking fights; neglect personal hygiene and grooming; or display blunted or inappropriate affect. Difficulties in communication, thought, and perception may emerge in such forms as digressive, vague, elaborated, or metaphorical speech, strange ideas, superstitions, or belief in a "sixth sense."

During the *active phase,* schizophrenic symptoms become prominent. In some instances this phase is triggered by stress in the person's life. For Ann, the confused and disoriented woman we read about earlier, the immediate precipitant was falling in love with a man she met dancing. Similarly, reality unraveled for Laura, the Austrian woman, when her dog had to be destroyed. Richard's symptoms, on the other hand, could not be traced to a particular stressful event.

The *residual phase* is marked by a return to the prodromal level of functioning. The florid symptoms of the active phase recede, but the individual usually remains in a general state of decline. Emotions are typically blunted or flat, and the person is still unable to carry out previous functions and responsibilities.

Each of these phases may last for days or for years. Although complete recoveries from schizophrenia may occur, the majority of patients continue indefinitely to show at least some residual impairment (APA, 1987). After months or even years in a residual state, many people have a recurrence of their active phase, followed again by another residual phase. Recovery from schizophrenia is more complete and more likely in subjects who functioned quite adequately before the disorder appeared (had good *premorbid* functioning), or when the disorder was precipitated by stressful events, was abrupt in onset (short prodromal phase), or developed during middle age (APA, 1987).

## Diagnosing Schizophrenia

For years schizophrenia was the "wastebasket category" for diagnosticians, especially in the United States, where the disorder was defined more broadly than elsewhere. A person who acted unpredictably or strangely was often given this label, even if the behavior was transient or did not include the major symptoms of schizophrenia. A popular slogan among clinicians in the 1950s was "Even a trace of schizophrenia is schizophrenia" (Lewis & Piotrowski, 1954).

To avoid an overuse of this diagnostic category, the writers of DSM-III-R have carefully specified the diagnostic criteria for schizophrenia. The manual now calls for a diagnosis of schizophrenia when:

1. The person has shown continuous signs of schizophrenia for six months or more. For at least one week of this pattern, the person has displayed an active phase of schizophrenia which includes two major symptoms of the disorder.
2. The person has deteriorated from a previous level of functioning in such areas as work, social relations, and self-care.
3. A depressive or manic syndrome, if present, developed *after* the psychotic symptoms, or was brief in comparison with the duration of psychotic symp-

toms. This criterion enables clinicians to differentiate schizophrenia from a mood disorder.

4. The symptoms are not due to other physical disorders that could produce similar symptoms, such as cerebral tumors, brain traumas, epilepsy, multiple sclerosis, carbon monoxide poisoning, thallium poisoning, Vitamin $B_{12}$ deficiency, or drug overdose.

**DSM-III-R's Categories of Schizophrenia**   As we have seen, schizophrenia is a heterogenous disorder. Some people with schizophrenia are troubled by delusions and hallucinations but remain coherent in their conversations. Others display very confused thought processes but do not seem to be having systematized delusions. Kraepelin, writing in 1896, distinguished three patterns of schizophrenia—hebephrenic, catatonic, and paranoid schizophrenic. The writers of DSM-III-R continue to find his categories descriptive of patient behavior, and have labeled the different types of schizophrenia disorganized (hebephrenic), catatonic, paranoid, undifferentiated, and residual.

**Disorganized Type**   The central symptoms of *disorganized schizophrenia* are confusion and incoherence. Fragmentary delusions or hallucinations may be present, but the disorganization of thought is so extreme that broad and systematized ideas and perceptions do not develop. Formal thought disturbances and perceptual problems make for difficult communication, which leads in turn to extreme social withdrawal. Grimaces, odd mannerisms, and flat and inappropriate affect are common in this type of schizophrenia. "Silliness" is also a common feature; some patients giggle constantly without apparent reason. This is why the pattern was first called "hebephrenic," after Hebe, the Greek goddess of youth, who according to Greek mythology often acted like a clown to make the other gods laugh. Not surprisingly, people with disorganized schizophrenia usually function very poorly. They are unable to take adequate care of themselves, to maintain social relationships, or to hold a job.

**Catatonic Type**   The central feature of *catatonic schizophrenia* is a psychomotor disturbance of some sort. Some of the people in this category spend their time in a catatonic stupor, mute and unresponsive; others are seized with catatonic excitement, waving their arms and acting in an uncontrolled manner; in still other cases, the extremes of stupor and excitement alternate. Richard, the unemployed young man who became mute and statue-like, would receive a diagnosis of "schizophrenia, catatonic type."

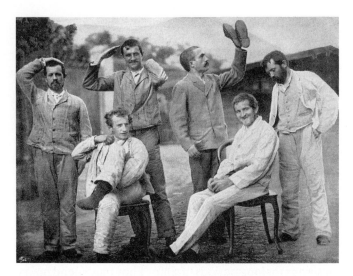

Each of these schizophrenic patients, photographed at the turn of the century, displays features of catatonia, including *catatonic posturing*, in which they assume bizarre postions for long periods of time. The prevalence of catatonic schizophrenia has declined considerably during the past forty years.

Although catatonic schizophrenia was relatively common up until the 1950s, it has become rare in Europe and North America (APA, 1987). Some clinicians believe that its decline is due to the particular ability of antipsychotic drugs (which we shall discuss in Chapter 16) to reverse this pattern of symptoms. Others believe that catatonia is actually a sign of mood disorder rather than schizophrenia, and suggest that its decline is related to the effectiveness of treatments best suited to mood disorders, such as electroconvulsive therapy, antidepressant drugs, and antibipolar drugs (Magrinat et al., 1981).

**Paranoid Type**   The most prominent symptom of *paranoid schizophrenia* is an organized system of delusions and hallucinations that guides the person's life. Laura would receive this diagnosis. She believed that her neighbors, a past acquaintance, and people on the street were out to get her (delusions of persecution). People on television programs were supposedly stealing her ideas (delusions of reference). And she heard noises from the apartment downstairs (auditory hallucinations) and experienced "funny sensations" that further supported her beliefs. Increasingly her delusions and hallucinations took center stage.

Anxiety or anger may accompany the delusional thoughts and hallucinatory perceptions in this type of schizophrenia, especially when the thoughts and perceptions are questioned or denied by others. On the other hand, some people, particularly those whose paranoia is marked by delusions of grandeur, remain cool and aloof. Confident and impressed by their special knowledge, they find other people's "naiveté" laughable. DSM-III-R suggests that persons with a paranoid type of schizophrenia are more likely to improve than those who manifest other forms of schizophrenia.

***Undifferentiated Type*** Many people who are diagnosed as schizophrenic do not fall neatly into one category; in these cases, the schizophrenic disorder is classified as ***undifferentiated type.*** Over the years, this vague diagnosis has been particularly abused, and a range of schizophrenic and nonschizophrenic patterns have been incorrectly assigned to it. Although such misassignments are less common today because of DSM-III-R's detailed clinical criteria, some misuse of the category continues.

***Residual Type*** When the florid symptoms of schizophrenia lessen in intensity and number yet remain with the patient in a residual form, the diagnosis is usually changed to ***residual type*** of schizophrenia. As we noted earlier, people with this type of schizophrenia may continue to display blunted or inappropriate emotional reactions, social withdrawal, eccentric behavior, and some illogical thinking. If less than two years have passed since schizophrenic symptoms first appeared, the residual type of schizophrenia is called ***subchronic.*** After two years, the residual type is labeled ***chronic.***

**Other Categorizations of Schizophrenia** Although DSM-III-R favors the distinctions described above, clinicians have also used other schemas to subtype schizophrenia over the years. Before DSM-III, for example, *acute* cases of schizophrenia, those characterized by sudden onset of symptoms and good premorbid functioning, were commonly distinguished from *chronic* cases, those marked by an insidious and early onset and poor premorbid functioning (Serban & Gidynski, 1975). In recent years a distinction between so-called Type I and Type II schizophrenia has caught the attention of clinicians (Crow, 1985, 1982, 1980). The label ***Type I schizophrenia*** is applied to cases dominated by such ***positive symptoms*** as delusions, hallucinations, and florid formal thought disorders (Ragin, Pogue-Geile, & Oltmans, 1989; Pogue-Geile, 1989; Andreasen et al., 1985; Crow, 1985, 1982, 1980). The symptoms are called "positive" because they seem to represent "pathological excesses," bizarre additions to a normal repertoire of behavior. Cases of ***Type II schizophrenia*** are those characterized by ***negative symptoms,*** symptoms that seem to reflect "pathological deficits," such as flat affect, poverty of speech, motor retardation, and loss of volition. In other words, negative symptoms represent characteristics that seem to be lacking in certain schizophrenic personalities.

The distinction between Type I and Type II schizophrenia has been gaining favor among clinicians because researchers have found it to be more useful than other kinds of distinctions in predicting the course and prognosis of the disorder. As we shall see shortly, Type I patients generally have a better premorbid adjustment, greater likelihood of improvement, and better responsiveness to antipsychotic drugs than do Type II patients. Moreover, the positive symptoms of Type I schizophrenia seem to be closely linked to biochemical abnormalities in the brain, while the negative symptoms of Type II schizophrenia have been tied to structural abnormalities in the brain (Weinberger & Kleinman, 1986).

# VIEWS ON SCHIZOPHRENIA

As with many other kinds of psychological disorders, sociocultural, biological, and psychological factors each contribute to the development of schizophrenia. In the sociocultural realm, the very label "schizophrenia" has been found to create societal expectations and reactions that may exacerbate schizophrenic behavior. In the biological realm, biochemical and structural abnormalities appear to increase the likelihood of a person's developing the disorder. And in the psychological realm, schizophrenia has been associated with intrapsychic, social environmental, and family problems. In fact, many theorists hold that an interaction of factors contributes to schizophrenia — for example, that people with a biological predisposition to develop the disorder may do so in response to certain societal pressures and expectations and in the face of key psychological stressors (Cutting, 1985).

## The Sociocultural View

Sociocultural theorists believe that many features of schizophrenia are caused by the diagnosis itself (Goldstein & Strochan, 1987; Szasz, 1987, 1964; Brody, 1976; Murphy, 1968; Scheff, 1967). They propose that the label "schizophrenia" is assigned by society to people who deviate from certain behavioral norms. Justified or not, once the label is assigned, a self-fulfilling prophecy unfolds that helps ensure the development of many schizophrenic symptoms. People who are called schizophrenic are viewed and reacted to as "crazy," and expected and encouraged to take on a schizophrenic style of behavior. Increasingly, they accept their assigned role and learn to play it convincingly.

At one level, this theory constitutes a general warning about the dangers of psychiatric labeling. As such, it has appeal for many clinicians, a number of whom have observed for themselves that diagnoses are often made on the basis of inadequate data, stick once they are made, influence the way subsequent behavior is perceived, and lead to other behaviors implied by the diagnosis.

Perhaps the most influential demonstration of these dangers has been offered in the famous Rosenhan (1973) study, which we first encountered in Chapter 2 (see p. 62). When eight normal people presented themselves at various mental hospitals complaining that they had been hearing voices utter the words "empty," "hollow," and "thud," they were readily diagnosed as schizophrenic and hospitalized. Although the pseudopatients then dropped all symptoms and proceeded to behave normally, they had great difficulty getting rid of the label. Throughout their hospitalization, their diagnosis of schizophrenia influenced the way they were viewed and treated by the hospital staff. A pseudopatient who paced the corridor out of boredom was thought to be "nervous." Pseudopatients who kept notes on the ward to document their experiences received the daily nursing notation, "Patient engages in writing behavior."

The pseudopatients also reported that staff members spent limited time interacting with them or with other patients, usually responded briefly to patients' questions, frequently acted authoritarian, and often treated patients as though they were invisible. Rosenhan reports, "A nurse unbuttoned her uniform to adjust her brassiere in the presence of an entire ward of viewing men. One did not have the sense that she was being seductive. Rather, she didn't notice us. A group of staff persons might point to a patient in the dayroom and discuss him animatedly, as if he were not there." The pseudopatients described feeling powerless, depersonalized, and bored, and often behaved in a listless and apathetic manner.

The controversial design of this study has aroused the emotions of clinicians and researchers, pro and con. Even those who are outraged by it agree with its conclusion that a diagnosis of schizophrenia can itself have a negative effect on the way people are perceived and treated, and on the way the people themselves feel and behave.

Some theorists go so far as to assert that schizophrenia is largely the creation of society and that as a product of norms and expectations, the disorder can be expected to vary from society to society as norms and expectations vary. According to this more extreme sociological hypothesis, each society will define bizarreness differently and will attach different role prescriptions to the label. In short, symptoms that Western society calls schizophrenic should be different from the schizophrenic symptoms defined by other countries and cultures.

This prediction of variability has not been borne out by research (Smith, 1982). In fact, most societies have a label that approximates the Western category of schizophrenia, and the behavior implied by this label tends to be remarkably the same from society to society. Anthropologist Jane Murphy (1976), for example, studied two non-Western societies — the Yupik-speaking Eskimos on an island in the Bering Sea and the Egba Yorubas of rural, tropical Nigeria — and found that the Eskimos have a disorder called *nuthkavihak* while the Yorubas have a disorder called *were*, each of which loosely translates into English as "insanity" and has symptoms (hallucinations, delusions, disorientation) that are remarkably similar to those of the Western disorder of schizophrenia. The symptoms of *nuthkavihak* include

> talking to oneself, screaming at someone who does not exist, believing that a child or husband was murdered by witchcraft when nobody else believes it, believing oneself to be an animal, refusing to eat for fear eating will kill one, refusing to talk, running away, getting lost, hiding in strange places, making strange grimaces, drinking urine, becoming strong and violent, killing dogs, and threatening people.
>
> *(Murphy, 1976, p. 1022)*

Similarly, the Yoruba disorder of *were* involves

> hearing voices and trying to get other people to see their source though none can be seen, laughing when there is nothing to laugh at, talking all the time or not talking at all, asking oneself questions and answering them, picking up sticks and leaves for no purpose except to put them on a pile, throwing away food because it is thought to contain juju, tearing off one's clothes, setting fires, defecating in public and then mushing around in the feces, taking up a weapon and suddenly hitting someone with it, breaking things in a state of being stronger than normal, believing that an odor is continuously being emitted from one's body.
>
> *(Murphy, 1976, p. 1022)*

## Genetic and Biological Views

What is arguably the most prolific and enlightening research on schizophrenia during the past few decades has come from the genetic and biological realms of inquiry. These studies have underscored the important role of genetic and biological factors in the development of schizophrenia and, just as important, have opened the door to important changes in its treatment.

**The Genetic View** Genetic researchers believe that some people inherit a biological predisposition to schizophrenia and, in accordance with a diathesis-stress model, come to develop the disorder when they are confronted by extreme stress, usually during early adulthood (Gottesman, 1991; Holzman & Matthysse, 1990; Gottesman, McGuffin, & Farmer, 1987; Scharfetter, 1985). The genetic viewpoint has been supported by studies of (1) relatives of schizophrenic people, (2) twins who are schizophrenic, (3) schizophrenic people who are adopted, and (4) chromosomal mapping.

*Relatives of Schizophrenic People* Studies have found repeatedly that schizophrenia is more common among relatives of schizophrenic people than among relatives of nonschizophrenic people (Gottesman, 1991; Eaves et al., 1988; Kendler et al., 1985; Gottesman & Shields, 1982). Moreover, the more closely related the relatives are to the schizophrenic proband, the greater their likelihood of developing the disorder (see Figure 15-1).

As we saw earlier, approximately 1 percent of the general population develops schizophrenia. This rate increases to an average of 10 percent among first-order relatives (parents, siblings, and children) of schizophrenic people (Gottesman, 1991; Eaves et al., 1988; Gottesman & Shields, 1982). Approximately 6 percent of the parents, 9 percent of the siblings, and 13 percent of the children of schizophrenic people also manifest schizophrenia. Similarly, the schizophrenia prevalence rate rises to 3 percent among second-order relatives; that is, half siblings, uncles, aunts, nephews, nieces, and grandchildren of schizophrenic people (Gottesman & Shields, 1982).

Of course, this trend by itself does not establish a genetic basis for the disorder. The prominent neuroscientist Solomon Snyder (1980) points out, "Attendance at Harvard University also runs in families but would hardly be considered a genetic trait." Family members are exposed to many of the same environmental influences as the schizophrenic person, and it may be these influences that lead to schizophrenia.

*Twins Who Are Schizophrenic* As we have noted previously, if both members of a pair of twins have a particular trait, they are said to be *concordant* for that trait. For a trait that is transmitted genetically, identical twins (who share identical genes) will show a higher concordance rate than fraternal twins (who share only some genes). Thus if genetic factors are at work in schizophrenia, identical twins should have a higher concordance rate for schizophrenia than fraternal twins. This expectation has

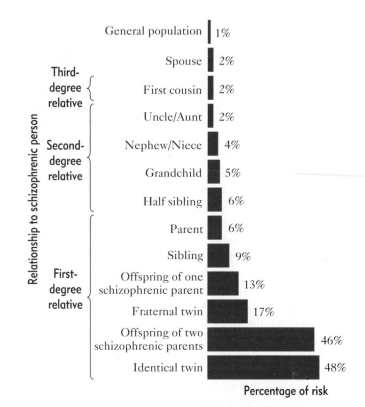

**FIGURE 15-1** People who are biologically related to schizophrenic people have a heightened risk of developing the disorder during their lifetime. The closer the biological relationship (that is, the more similar the genetic structure), the greater the risk of developing the disorder. *(Adapted from Gottesman, 1991, p. 96.)*

been supported repeatedly by research (Gottesman, 1991; Gottesman & Shields, 1982). Studies have found that if one identical twin develops schizophrenia, there is a 40 to 60 percent chance that the other twin will do so as well. If one fraternal twin is schizophrenic, in contrast, the other twin has approximately a 17 percent chance of developing the disorder.

*Schizophrenic People Who Are Adopted* Adoption studies have pointed convincingly to a genetic factor in schizophrenia (Gottesman, 1991, 1982; Kety, 1974; Rosenthal, 1971; Heston, 1966). These studies look at schizophrenic adults who were adopted as infants and determine whether their behavior is more similar to that of their biological relatives or to that of their adoptive relatives. Because the schizophrenic subjects were reared apart from their biological relatives, similar schizophrenic symptoms in those relatives would indicate genetic influences. Conversely, schizophrenic similarities in their adoptive relatives would suggest environmental influences.

Seymour Kety and his colleagues (1988, 1978, 1975, 1974, 1968) conducted an extensive study on this subject in Copenhagen, Denmark, where detailed records of adoptions and mental disorders are available. In a sample of nearly 5,500 adults who had been adopted early in life, they found 33 who were schizophrenic. Matching control subjects were also selected from the same large sample — 33 normal adoptees of similar age, sex, and schooling as the schizophrenic subjects. Next the investigators located a total of 365 biological and adoptive relatives (parents and siblings) of these 66 adoptees and separated the relatives into four groups: (1) biological relatives of schizophrenic adoptees; (2) adoptive relatives of schizophrenic adoptees; (3) biological relatives of normal adoptees; and (4) adoptive relatives of normal adoptees. A psychiatrist, unaware of who was related to whom, conducted an in-depth interview with each relative. His interview summaries were then read and evaluated by independent psychiatric judges who were again unaware of each person's status. On the basis of these interviews and evaluations, each relative was given a psychiatric diagnosis.

Of the 365 relatives, a total of 37 received a diagnosis of either *definite schizophrenia* or *uncertain schizophrenia* (schizophrenialike patterns that did not fully warrant a clinical diagnosis). Most of these 37 turned out to be biological relatives of schizophrenic adoptees, a result that strongly supports the hypothesis that there is a genetic factor in schizophrenia. Almost 14 percent of the biological relatives of the schizophrenic adoptees were classified as schizophrenic (either definite or uncertain schizophrenia), whereas only 2.7 percent of their adoptive relatives received this classification. The biological and adoptive relatives of the normal adoptees had schizophrenic prevalence rates of 3.4 percent and 5.5 percent, respectively. Clearly the biological relatives of schizophrenic adoptees were most likely to develop schizophrenia.

Some critics of Kety's work have argued that it is misleading to include the category "uncertain schizophrenia" in the study's results. After all, individuals in this category are *not* schizophrenic. In response to this criticism, Kety also conducted data analyses in which only individuals who were judged to manifest definite schizophrenia received the diagnosis. Using these stricter criteria, he found that the schizophrenia prevalence rate for biological relatives of schizophrenic adoptees became 6.4 percent, still significantly higher than the revised prevalence rates shown by their adoptive relatives (1.4 percent) or by the biological and adoptive relatives of normal adoptees (1.7 percent and 2.2 percent, respectively). More recently Kety (1988) conducted a similar analysis of the relatives of schizophrenic persons living in other parts of Denmark, and found a strikingly similar pattern of results.

Such findings have led many researchers to conclude that the genetic factor in schizophrenia is significant, at least as great as that found in such illnesses as diabetes, hypertension, coronary artery disease, and ulcers, which are all acknowledged to have a genetic component (Kendler, 1983). Few, however, believe that this is the only factor involved (Crow, 1988). Kety himself has said, "These data do not imply, nor do I believe, that genetic factors . . . are the only important influences in the etiology and pathogenesis of schizophrenia" (1974, p. 961).

**Chromosomal Mapping**    As with bipolar disorders (see Chapter 8), researchers have conducted *chromosomal mapping* research to identify more precisely the possible genetic factors in schizophrenia (Eaves et al., 1988). In this new strategy, they select large families in which schizophrenia is unusually common, take blood samples from all members of the families, isolate the DNA from each sample and "cut" it into segments, and then compare the gene segments from schizophrenic family members with the gene segments from nonschizophrenic members using a technique called *restriction fragment-length polymorphism (RFLP)*. Applying RFLP to five families from Iceland and two families from England, Hugh Gurling and his colleagues (1988) have found that a particular area on chromosome 5 of schizophrenic family members has a different appearance from the same area on chromosome 5 of nonschizophrenic family members. The researchers concluded from this study of 39 schizophrenic and 65 nonschizophrenic family members that an abnormal gene or cluster of genes in this area of chromosome 5 establishes a predisposition in at least some cases of schizophrenia.

Although this research has been greeted as a possible breakthrough in the study of schizophrenia, major problems remain to be solved (Holzman & Matthysse, 1990). For example, the area of chromosome 5 implicated in the study is very large, containing more than 1,000 genes. Researchers have yet to isolate the gene or cluster of genes that may contribute to schizophrenia. In addition, another study, applying the same approach to schizophrenic and nonschizophrenic members of a large family in Sweden, has found no consistent discrepancy on chromosome 5 (Kidd et al., 1988). It may be that the findings of the Gurling study are misleading or being misinterpreted. Alternatively, as researchers from both studies propose, different kinds of schizophrenia may have different causes. Gurling's subjects may have a kind of schizophrenia caused by a chromosome 5 defect, while the schizophrenia symptoms in the Swedish family may be caused by gene defects on other chromosomes or by factors that are entirely nongenetic.

**Biological Views**   How might genetic factors lead to the development of schizophrenia? Biological research has pointed to two kinds of biological abnormalities, each of which apparently contributes to schizophrenia and each of which could conceivably be inherited — biochemical abnormalities and abnormal brain structure.

**Biochemical Abnormalities**   Remember our earlier discussions of neurons, neurotransmitters, and synapses. The brain consists largely of neurons. When an impulse (or "message") travels from neuron to neuron in the brain, it is received by a neuron's dendrites (antennae), travels down the neuron's axon, and reaches its nerve ending. The nerve ending then releases a chemical neurotransmitter from its storage vessels, and these neurotransmitter molecules cross the synaptic space and attach to receptors on the dendrites of another neuron, thus relaying the message and causing that neuron to fire. Research conducted over the past two decades has suggested that in schizophrenic persons, the neurons that use the neurotransmitter dopamine fire too often and transmit too many messages, thus producing the symptoms of the disorder. Like the biological explanations of anxiety, depression, and mania, this so-called *dopamine hypothesis* of schizophrenia was arrived at by a mixture of serendipity, painstaking experimental work, and clever theorizing. The chain began with the accidental discovery of *antipsychotic medications,* drugs that help remove the symptoms of schizophrenia.

As we shall see in Chapter 16, the first group of antipsychotic medications, the *phenothiazines,* were discovered in the 1950s by researchers who were looking for effective antihistamine drugs to combat allergies. Although phenothiazines failed as antihistamines, their effectiveness in reducing schizophrenic symptoms soon became apparent, and clinicians began prescribing them for most schizophrenic people. Eventually researchers learned that these drugs also produce a very troublesome effect, muscular tremors identical to those seen in Parkinson's disease. Normally this disabling neurological disease emerges after the age of 50; when schizophrenic patients were given an antipsychotic drug, the young were as likely to develop Parkinsonian symptoms as the old.

This effect of antipsychotic drugs gave researchers their first important clue to the biology of schizophrenia. Medical scientists already knew that people with Parkinson's disease have abnormally low levels of the neurotransmitter dopamine in some areas of the brain as a result of the destruction of dopamine-containing neurons, and that insufficient dopamine is the reason for their uncontrollable shaking. In fact, administration of the chemical L-dopa — a precursor of dopamine — is a

somewhat helpful treatment for Parkinson's disease precisely because it helps to raise dopamine levels.

Scientists put these pieces of information together and came up with a pair of important hypotheses. If antipsychotic drugs generate Parkinsonian symptoms while alleviating schizophrenia, perhaps they operate by reducing dopamine activity. And if lowering dopamine activity alleviates the symptoms of schizophrenia, perhaps schizophrenia is related to excessive dopamine activity in the first place.

**Establishing the Dopamine-Schizophrenia Link**   Since the 1960's research has both supported and enlarged upon the dopamine hypothesis. It has been found, for example, that some people with Parkinson's disease develop schizophrenic symptoms if they take too much L-dopa (Davis, Comaty, & Janicak, 1988). Presumably the L-dopa raises their dopamine activity to schizophrenia-inducing levels. Correspondingly, when schizophrenic patients have been given L-dopa by researchers, their schizophrenic symptoms have worsened considerably (Angrist, Sathananthan, & Gershon, 1973). Presumably their high dopamine activity becomes even higher.

Support for the dopamine hypothesis has also come from research on amphetamines, drugs that, as we saw in Chapter 13, stimulate the central nervous system (Davis et al., 1988). Researchers first became aware of close links between amphetamines and schizophrenia during the 1970s when they noticed that people who take high doses of amphetamines over an extended period of time may develop *amphetamine psychosis* — a syndrome that closely mimics schizophrenia and includes hallucinations and motor hyperactivity. They later found that antipsychotic drugs can correct amphetamine psychosis, just as they are able to alleviate the symptoms of schizo-

A computer-drawn molecule of dopamine. Excessive activity of this neurotransmitter has been linked to schizophrenia and to amphetamine and cocaine psychosis, while low dopamine activity has been related to Parkinson's disease.

phrenia, and furthermore, that even small doses of amphetamines exacerbate the symptoms of schizophrenia (Janowsky & Davis, 1976; Janowsky, 1973). Researchers eventually traced these links between amphetamines, schizophrenia, and antipsychotic drugs to dopamine activity (Biel & Bopp, 1978; Snyder, 1973). They found that amphetamines increase dopamine synaptic activity in the brain, thus inducing or exacerbating schizophrenic symptoms.

The dopamine hypothesis gained its widest acceptance once researchers developed a procedure that enabled them to pinpoint sites in the brain that have high concentrations of dopamine receptors (Seeman, Lee, Chau-Wong, & Wong, 1976; Snyder, 1976). In this procedure, a small area of an animal's brain is removed and its neurons are spread out in a dish filled with fluid. Radioactive dopamine is added to the fluid, and any radioactivity that subsequently concentrates at the neurons is measured. If a neuron's radioactivity reading is high, dopamine binding is presumed to have taken place, and the neuron is presumed to possess dopamine receptors. Conversely, no radioactivity at a neuron indicates no dopamine binding and no dopamine receptors. By systematically applying this test to neurons from all parts of the brain, researchers were able to map the brain's dopamine receptor sites.

Researchers then repeated the procedure, substituting antipsychotic drugs for dopamine. That is, they determined which neuroreceptors throughout the brain would accumulate radioactive antipsychotic drugs. They found that antipsychotic drugs bind to the same receptors as dopamine (Creese, Burt, & Snyder, 1978; Snyder, Burt & Creese, 1976; Burt, Creese, & Snyder, 1976). On the basis of this finding, they concluded that phenothiazines and other antipsychotic drugs are *dopamine antagonists* — drugs that bind to dopamine receptors, prevent dopamine from binding there, and so prevent dopamine-receiving neurons from firing (Iversen, 1977; Kebabian et al., 1972).

*Overactive Dopamine Synapses* Given such findings, researchers now believe that the dopamine synapses of many schizophrenic people are overactive, that messages from dopamine-sending neurons to dopamine-receiving neurons are transmitted too readily or too often. This theory has an intuitive appeal because dopamine neurons have been found to play an active role in guiding and sustaining attention (Cohen et al., 1988). People whose attention mechanisms are grossly impaired might well be expected to suffer from the abnormalities of attention, perception, and thought that characterize schizophrenia.

It has sometimes been proposed that excessive activity of other neurotransmitters, such as norepinephrine or serotonin, may also help produce schizophrenia (Kornhuber et al., 1984). However, research has usually found dopamine activity to be the main culprit (Resnick et al., 1988; Mass et al., 1988). In one study, investigators found elevated dopamine but normal norepinephrine levels in the autopsied brains of seven schizophrenic subjects, compared to normal levels of both dopamine and norepinephrine in the brains of fourteen control subjects (Oke et al., 1988).

Why might the dopamine synapses of schizophrenic people be overactive? Researchers used to think that the dopamine-sending neurons of these individuals produce and store too much dopamine, but studies have failed to support this hypothesis (Seidman, 1990; Carlsson, 1978; Von Praag, 1977; Sedvall, 1975; Bowers, 1974). Currently theorists believe that the cause of the synaptic overactivity is a larger than usual number of dopamine receptors (Sedvall, 1990; Seidman, 1990; Kleinman et al., 1989; Owen et al., 1987). Remember that when dopamine carries a message to a receiving neuron, it binds to receptors on the membrane of the neuron. Apparently schizophrenic people have a larger number of dopamine receptors on their receiving neurons than other people do. Inasmuch as more receptors lead to more firing, the numerous dopamine receptors ensure greater dopamine synaptic activity and overtransmission of dopamine messages. Researchers have in fact found that the autopsied brains of many schizophrenic people contain more dopamine receptors than those of nonschizophrenic people (Owen et al., 1987, 1978; Lee & Seeman, 1980). In some cases the use of antipsychotic drugs appears to be partly responsible for the production of these extra dopamine receptors, but autopsies have also revealed larger numbers of dopamine receptors in schizophrenic people who have never taken antipsychotic drugs.

*Questioning the Dopamine Hypothesis* Although these studies are helping to unravel the biology of schizophrenia, their results may not be as clear-cut as they first appear. To begin with, the dopamine hypothesis may be overstated (Meltzer, 1987). Most dopamine studies concentrate on dopamine activity in and near one specific area of the brain, the striatum. However, there are also dopamine neurons in other parts of the brain. Perhaps a high level of dopamine activity in one area does not mean a high level of dopamine activity in another (see Figure 15-2). Similarly, the activity of dopamine neurons or the number of dopamine receptors may not be as central a problem as most researchers have concluded. Some theorists, for example, suggest that the central problem in schizophrenia may be the production of problematic vi-

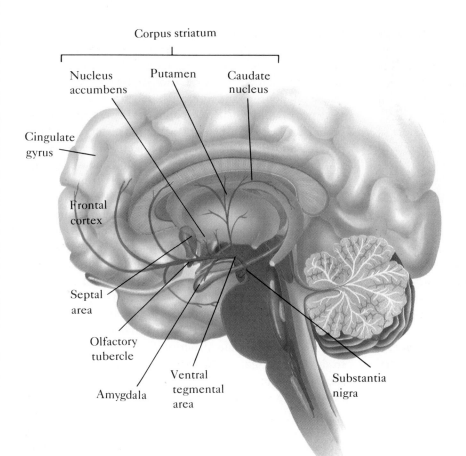

**FIGURE 15-2** Some of the neurons that release the neurotransmitter dopamine have cell bodies in the substantia nigra with axons extending all the way to the corpus striatum, the part of the brain that functions to produce smooth coordination and movement in the arms and legs. When these neurons release too little dopamine, the muscular tremors and other symptoms of Parkinson's disease occur. Another group of neurons that release dopamine have cell bodies in the ventral tegmental area with axons extending to the olfactory tubercle, nucleus accumbens, amygdala, and cingulate gyrus — areas that apparently function to link sensory perceptions to memories and emotions. It may be that when these neurons are excessively active and release too much dopamine, the symptoms of schizophrenia result. Other dopamine pathways do not appear to be linked to Parkinson's disease or schizophrenia. *(Adapted from Snyder, 1986, p. 85.)*

ruses or antibodies that act to stimulate dopamine receptors (Eaves et al., 1988; Knight, 1985).

A number of theorists are also beginning to suspect that excessive dopamine activity may contribute only to Type I schizophrenia (Crow, 1985, 1982, 1980). As we saw earlier, cases of Type I schizophrenia are those characterized by positive symptoms such as delusions and hallucinations, whereas Type II cases are marked by negative symptoms such as flat affect and loss of volition. Because Type I cases seem to be more responsive than Type II cases to antipsychotic drugs, the dopamine hypothesis may be relevant only to the former (Ragin et al., 1989; Crow, 1980). Type II schizophrenia has been

linked increasingly to a totally different kind of biological abnormality — abnormal brain structure.

***Abnormal Brain Structure*** Ever since Kraepelin, clinicians have suspected that schizophrenia is caused by abnormalities in brain structure. Only during the past decade, however, have researchers been able to link this disorder, particularly Type II schizophrenia, to specific structural abnormalities (Johnson, 1989; Buchsbaum & Haier, 1987). This development has been made possible by improvements in postmortem tissue analyses and by the development of computerized technologies (such as computerized axial tomography, positron emission

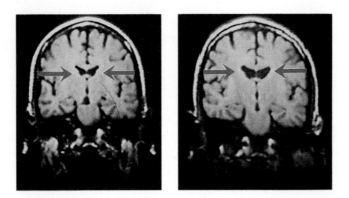

In a study of fifteen pairs of identical twins in which one of each pair was diagnosed as schizophrenic, *magnetic resonance imaging* revealed that the brain of the schizophrenic twin *(right)* almost always had larger ventricles—butterfly-shaped spaces filled with fluid and located between the lobes—than the other *(left)*.

tomography, and magnetic resonance imaging) that can produce pictures of brain structure and brain activity without harming the brain in the process (see pp. 112–113).

The most consistent finding of research using these newer technologies has been that many schizophrenic people have enlarged ventricles—the brain cavities that contain cerebrospinal fluid (Hyde et al., 1991; Suddath et al., 1990; Meltzer, 1987; Weinberger & Kleinman, 1986; Shelton & Weinberger, 1986). In particular, the ventricles on the left side of their brains seem much larger than the ventricles on the right (Losonczy et al., 1986). In addition, these enlargements appear at the onset of schizophrenia and before drug treatment, indicating that they are not produced by antipsychotic drugs (Schultz et al., 1983; Weinberger et al., 1982). Various studies have collected evidence that such enlargements may be caused by genetic factors, birth complications, viral infections, immune reactions, or toxins (DeLisi et al., 1986; Andreasen et al., 1986; Reveley, Reveley, & Murray, 1984).

Patients with such ventricle enlargements tend to display more negative and fewer positive symptoms of schizophrenia, a poorer premorbid social adjustment, and poorer responses to antipsychotic drugs (Weinberger & Kleinman, 1986). On the other hand, enlarged ventricles have also been found in cases of mood disorder and of alcoholism, so that researchers cannot be certain about the precise implications of the relationship of enlarged ventricles to schizophrenia (Pearlson et al., 1984; Ron et al., 1982).

Other kinds of structural abnormalities, quite possibly related to enlarged ventricles, have also been found in the brains and in the skulls of Type II schizophrenic patients. Some studies suggest that these people have smaller frontal lobes, cerebrums, and craniums than nonschizophrenic people (Suddath et al., 1990; Black et al., 1988; Meltzer, 1987). Other studies reveal a lower density of neurons and reduced blood flow in their brains (Sagawa et al., 1990; Buchsbaum & Haier, 1987; Weinberger et al., 1986). One investigation observed schizophrenic and nonschizophrenic subjects who were performing a simple card-sorting task, and measured the rate at which blood was flowing to their frontal lobes (Weinberger, 1983). The rate of blood flow dropped sharply for approximately half of the schizophrenic subjects, whereas blood flow actually increased for most of the nonschizophrenic control subjects.

Although the precise nature and meaning of these brain structure abnormalities have yet to be clarified, this research has already indicated that the biological underpinnings of schizophrenia are more complex and more subtle than anyone had imagined. Together the biochemical and brain structure findings are beginning to shed much light on the mysteries of schizophrenia. At the same time, it is important to recognize that many people who manifest these biochemical and structural abnormalities never develop schizophrenia. Why not? Possibly, as we noted earlier, because biological factors merely set the stage for schizophrenia, while key psychological factors must be present for the disorder to unfold (see Box 15-2).

## Psychological Views

When investigators began having success identifying genetic and biological factors in schizophrenia during the 1950s and 1960s, many clinicians abandoned psychogenic explanations of the disorder. During the past decade, however, the tables have been turned once again and psychological factors are increasingly being considered an important piece of the puzzle of schizophrenia. This turnaround has occurred partly because biology alone has proved unable to account for schizophrenia and partly because research has increasingly provided support for certain psychological theories. The leading psychological explanations of schizophrenia have come from the psychodynamic, behavioral, family systems, existential, and cognitive perspectives.

**The Psychodynamic View**   Psychodynamic theorists have generally followed Freud's (1924, 1915) view that the development of schizophrenia involves a two-part psychological process: (1) *regression* to a pre-ego stage and (2) *restitutive efforts* to reestablish ego control. After very limited contact with schizophrenic persons, Freud proposed that schizophrenia, like neurosis, stems from a basic conflict between a person's self-gratifying impulses and the demands of the real world. When their external world is particularly harsh or withholding (for example, when their parents are consistently cold or unnurturing), those who become schizophrenic, like people who develop a neurosis, regress to an early period in their functioning. According to Freud, neurotic people regress partially and become overly dependent on ego defense mechanisms to deal with real-world demands; schizophrenic people, with egos that are even less stable, regress to the earliest point in their development, a point before the formation of the ego and before their recognition of the external world as existing outside of and apart from them.

Ultimately, schizophrenic persons regress to a state of *primary narcissism,* like that of infants, in which only their own needs are felt. This near-total regression leads to self-indulgent symptoms such as neologisms, loose associations, and delusions of grandeur. Freud also believed that upon regressing to a pre-ego stage these people start trying to reestablish ego control and contact with reality. Their restitutive efforts give rise to yet other schizophrenic symptoms. Auditory hallucinations, for example, may represent an unconscious attempt to substitute for a lost sense of reality.

Freud's general position that schizophrenia involves extreme regression and restitutive efforts has been retained by many psychodynamic theorists throughout the twentieth century (Blatt & Wild, 1976; Fenichel, 1945). However, their views have received virtually no research support (Maher, 1966). As a result, psychodynamic explanations of this disorder have commanded less attention than psychodynamic theories about such problems as anxiety and mood disorders.

**The Behavioral View**  Behaviorists point primarily to *operant conditioning* in their explanation of schizophrenia (Liberman, 1982; Ullman & Krasner, 1975). They propose that most people are taught by their environment (family, neighbors, social institutions) to attend to social cues — for example, to other people's smiles, frowns, and comments. When they respond to these stimuli in a socially acceptable way, they are better able to satisfy their emotional needs and to achieve their goals. Some people, however, do not receive such reinforcements. Unusual circumstances may prevent their encountering social cues in their environment, or important figures in their lives may be socially inadequate and unable to provide proper reinforcements. Either way, these people stop attending to social cues and focus instead on other, often irrelevant cues — the brightness of light in a room, a bird flying above, or the sound of a word rather than its meaning. As they attend more and more to such inappropriate signals, their responses become increasingly bizarre. Such responses in turn elicit heightened attention or other types of reinforcement from the environment, thus increasing the likelihood that they will be repeated.

Support for the behavioral position has been circumstantial. As we shall see in Chapter 16, researchers have found that schizophrenic patients are often "capable" of learning appropriate verbal responses and social behaviors if their bizarre responses are consistently ignored by hospital personnel while normal responses are reinforced with cigarettes, food, attention, or other rewards (Belcher, 1988; Foxx et al., 1988; Braginsky, Braginsky, & Ring, 1969; Ayllon & Michael, 1959). The fact that verbal and social responses can be successfully altered by such reinforcements suggests to some theorists that the behavioral patterns of schizophrenia may be acquired through operant conditioning in the first place. On the other hand, as we know, an effective treatment for a disorder does not necessarily imply the cause of the disorder. Entirely different factors may be responsible for the development of schizophrenic behavior.

Today the behavioral view is usually treated as only a partial explanation for schizophrenia. Although it may help explain why a given person displays more schizophrenic behavior in some situations than in others, it is too limited, in the opinion of many people, to account for schizophrenia's origins and its many symptoms.

**Family Views**  In the psychological views discussed so far, the environment is thought to play a central role in schizophrenia. Psychodynamic theorists believe that inadequate early relationships set the stage for schizophrenia. Similarly, behaviorists believe that environmental reinforcements help produce and maintain schizophrenic behavior. This collective focus on the environment has led some theorists to look particularly closely at the families of schizophrenic people.

*The Schizophrenogenic Mother*  Some theorists have suggested that the parents of schizophrenic individuals have a particular personality style. The noted psychodynamic clinician Frieda Fromm-Reichmann (1948), for example, used the term *schizophrenogenic mother* (meaning schizophrenia-causing mother) to describe the mothers of schizophrenic individuals, saying that such mothers are cold, domineering, and impervious to the needs of others. According to Fromm-Reichmann, they appear to be self-sacrificing, but are actually using their children to address their own needs. At once overprotective and rejecting, they confuse their children and set the stage for schizophrenic functioning.

Although this notion has appealed to many clinicians, years of research have challenged its validity. The majority of schizophrenic people do *not* appear to have had mothers who fit the schizophrenogenic description. In fact, some studies have suggested that quite a different personality style may prevail among the mothers of schizophrenic persons. In one study the mothers of schizophrenic subjects were found to be shy, inadequate, withdrawn, anxious, suspicious, and incoherent, while the mothers of nonschizophrenic control subjects seemed more likely to display what Fromm-Reichmann would have called a schizophrenogenic maternal style (Waring & Ricks, 1963).

**Double-bind Communications**   One of the best-known family theories is the ***double-bind hypothesis*** (Bateson, 1978; Weakland, 1960; Haley, 1959; Bateson, Jackson, Haley, & Weakland, 1956), which maintains that some parents repeatedly communicate pairs of messages that are mutually contradictory, thus placing the children in double-bind situations: the children cannot avoid displeasing their parents; nothing they do is right. Children who are repeatedly caught in such contradictions may react by developing schizophrenic symptoms.

According to Gregory Bateson and his colleagues, both a primary communication and a metacommunication are contained in any message. The ***primary communication*** is the semantic content of the message; the ***metacommunication*** encompasses the tone, context, and gestures attached to the message. Although primary communications and metacommunications may be congruent, they can also be incongruent and therefore confusing. If one person says to another, "I'm glad to see you," yet frowns and avoids eye contact, the two aspects of the message are incongruent. Usually double-bind messages arise from a contradiction between a primary communication and the accompanying metacommunication. In the following double-bind situation little Leo cannot be clear whether his mother is telling him to stay away, as her frozen posture suggests, or "Come to me," as her spoken words require.

*M*omma goes out shopping leaving three-year-old Leo with Daddy. As she returns and opens the door, Leo runs over to greet his mother. Whereupon the woman involuntarily freezes. Leo sees this and stops. Whereupon his mother says, "Leo, baby, what's the matter, don't you love your Mommy? Come and give me a big kiss." 
If baby Leo ignores his first perception and runs up to the woman again, she freezes and takes his kiss in an off-hand, angry way. If baby Leo refuses to budge, she scolds him for being a bad boy. Because of his age or inexperience Leo can't comment on what is happening, or if he does, either his mother or father scolds him for being naughty: "Don't

talk to your mother/father that way or you will be punished." The net result is that Baby Leo is reduced to an impotent rage whereupon he is sent to bed for being bad.
*(Barnes & Barnes, 1973, p. 85)*

Adults can escape the confusion caused by incongruent messages by avoiding people who give such messages. Or they may point out incongruities by asking such questions as "Are you happy to see me or not? Then why do you flinch when I go near you?" Unfortunately, children in double-bind families rarely have such opportunities. Avoiding their parents is impossible, and if they try to point out incongruities, they may be rebuked for being "fresh." Such children are forced to try to respond to the double-bind communications, and of course, no matter how they respond, they incur the parent's displeasure.

According to this theory, a child who is repeatedly exposed to double-bind situations may adopt a *special life strategy* for coping with the environment. Unfortunately, some such strategies can lead to schizophrenic symptoms. One strategy might be always to ignore primary communications and respond only to metacommunications. That is, always be suspicious of what a person is saying, wonder about its true meaning, look for clues in the person's gestures or tones, and respond accordingly. People who increasingly respond to messages in this way may be on their way to manifesting symptoms of paranoid schizophrenia.

Another strategy might be to respond to primary communications exclusively, interpreting everything literally. People who adopt this strategy will not learn to appreciate the subtleties of communication. They will often miss the intent of others' communications and respond inappropriately, in ways that may seem hyperliteral and only loosely relevant. Such behavior may develop into the symptoms of disorganized schizophrenia.

Finally, a third strategy is to ignore the messages coming from others. If one does not hear incongruent messages, one will not be confused by them. People who consistently employ this strategy of coping with their environment may become more and more removed from the external world. Eventually they may become withdrawn, perhaps even mute, displaying the symptoms of catatonic schizophrenia.

The double-bind hypothesis is closely related to the schizophrenogenic-mother explanation of schizophrenia. When Fromm-Reichmann describes schizophrenogenic mothers as both overprotective and rejecting at the same time, she is in fact describing someone who is likely to offer double-bind communications. Similarly, the mothers in Bateson's case examples of double-bind communications, such as Leo's mother, typically fit the description of schizophrenogenic mother. Like the schizophrenogenic-mother theory, the double-bind hypothesis has been popular in the clinical field since its inception (Cronen et al., 1983), but investigations into the theory have been few and in fact unsupportive (Shuhan, 1967). In one study, clinicians read and evaluated letters written by parents to their children in the hospital (Ringuette & Kennedy, 1966). One group of parents had schizophrenic children; the other had nonschizophrenic children. Rating each letter on a seven-point scale according to the double-bind messages it contained, the clinicians found the letters of both groups of parents to offer similar degrees of double-bind communication.

***Family Structure*** Theodore Lidz (1973, 1963) has proposed that disturbed patterns of interaction and communication evolve in certain families and may push offspring toward schizophrenic functioning. According to Lidz, either of two kinds of family alignments can lead to schizophrenia: marital schism or marital skew.

*Marital schism,* in Lidz's view, is more often associated with schizophrenia in women. It is seen in families in which the mother and father are in open conflict, with each spouse trying to undercut the other and compete for the daughter's loyalty. The mother is constantly denigrated by the father and develops low self-esteem. She tries to counteract it by becoming increasingly aloof toward her family; nevertheless, the father succeeds in making her nervous about raising her daughter. Because the father feels unfulfilled by the mother, he turns to the daughter, implicitly asks her to take her mother's place, and develops a heightened emotional relationship with her.

The daughter is caught in the middle in this family structure. Any attempt to please one parent will be viewed as a rejection by the other. She also experiences intense internal conflict. Although attached to her father, she also identifies with his foe, her mother. In defense, she adopts a posture of massive confusion that allows her to avoid acknowledging or resolving the conflicts. In other words, she retreats into schizophrenia.

Lidz claims that schizophrenic men come from families with a ***marital skew*** structure. Here there is no overt hostility. The mother, following Fromm-Reichman's stereotype of the schizophrenogenic mother, is impervious to the needs of others and dominates family life. The father keeps peace by continually yielding to her wishes. The mother develops a heightened emotional relationship with her son, implicitly asking him to be different from his father.

Like the daughter who is confused by marital schism, the son in a marital skew situation is also full of conflict.

He wants to identify with this father, yet must reject all that his father stands for in order to please his mother. Again, he takes refuge in the pathology of schizophrenia, nonfunctional behavior that effectively distances him from his family dynamics and his own internal turmoil.

Although Lidz's theory has attracted widespread interest, it is actually based on very small and possibly unrepresentative family samples. Indeed, the studies that yielded this theory examined a total of only 40 families, all from the upper socioeconomic classes (Lidz, 1973, 1963; Lidz, Cornelison, & Fleck, 1965; Lidz & Fleck, 1960; Lidz, Cornelison, Fleck, & Terry, 1957). Without wider sampling and appropriate control groups, it is impossible to know how common these family patterns are in cases of schizophrenia.

***The Status of Family Theories*** So far no single family explanation of schizophrenia has received impressive research support. This is not to suggest, however, that the behaviors of family members have little to do with the development of schizophrenia. On the contrary, it has been found that schizophrenia, like other mental disorders, is often precipitated by stressful family situations, including emotional instability of some kind in a parent (Leff & Vaughn, 1975; Tsuang, Fowler, Cadoret, & Monnelly, 1974; Birley & Brown, 1968; Kaufman et al., 1960). Moreover, studies keep pointing to the presence of family conflict of one kind or another in the backgrounds of most people with schizophrenia (Falloon & Liberman, 1985; Doane et al., 1981). Thus many clinicians continue to suspect that family behaviors contribute in some way to the onset of schizophrenia (Goldstein, 1988, 1985; Howells & Guirguis, 1984; McFarlane & Beels, 1983; Wynne, 1981; Liem, 1980).

One informative technique for investigating familial influences has been the ***revealed-differences approach,*** first developed in the field of social psychology. Here parents and their children are brought together by an investigator and told to reach an agreement on selected issues about which they have previously disagreed. Their interactions, as they try to reach a consensus, are taped and later analyzed by judges. In numerous studies of the families of schizophrenic persons using this and similar techniques, three family trends have emerged. The parents of schizophrenic people (1) *display more conflict,* (2) *have greater difficulty communicating with one another,* and (3) *are more critical of and overinvolved with their children* than other parents (Holte & Wichstrom, 1990; Manrique-Solana, 1988; McFarlane & Beels, 1983; Liem, 1980; Hirsch, 1979; Vaughn & Leff, 1976; Brown et al., 1972, 1962; Fontana, 1966). Certainly these trends suggest that negative family experiences may contribute to the development of schizophrenia;

## BOX 15-2

# Howling for Attention

It's when I was bitten by a rabid dog. . . . When I'm emotionally upset, I feel as if I am turning into something else: my fingers go numb, as if I had pins and needles right in the middle of my hand; I can no longer control myself. . . . I get the feeling I'm becoming a wolf. I look at myself in the mirror and I witness my transformation. It's no longer my face; it changes completely. I stare, my pupils dilate, and I feel as if hairs are growing all over my body, as if my teeth are getting longer. . . . I feel as if my skin is no longer mine.

*(Benezech et al., 1989)*

**Lycanthropy,** the delusion of being an animal, is a rare psychological syndrome. The word "lycanthropy" comes from the Greek *lykos,* wolf, and *anthropos,* man. Accounts have been found all over the world of people who take

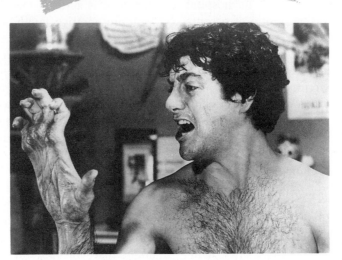

In the film *An American Werewolf in London*, a possessed man watches in terror as his hand stretches into the forepaw of a wolf.

on the characteristics and behavior of wolves or other animals. Belief in these tales has persisted for centuries, though the perceptions about causation have changed. In the Middle Ages, lycanthropy was attributed to

demonic possession (Lehmann, 1985). In the sixteenth and seventeenth centuries, the accepted causes were physical illness and satanic influence. In some societies where lycanthropy was frequently reported, it occurred after special ointments, probably potent hallucinogenic drugs, were applied, often for religious purposes (Lévi-Strauss, 1977). In other societies, cases of lycanthropy were closely linked to mental disorders, including schizophrenia, severe mood disorders, and certain forms of brain damage.

Mention of lycanthropy continues to evoke an image of a werewolf baring its fangs at a terrified villager on a fog-shrouded Scottish moor, all because the former was bitten by another werewolf in the unbroken chain

---

however, it is also possible that schizophrenic individuals themselves disrupt family life and help cause the family problems that clinicians and researchers keep observing (Asarnow & Horton, 1990; Parker et al., 1988; Scottish Schizophrenia Research Group, 1988; Mishler & Waxler, 1968).

**The Existential View**   R. D. Laing (1967, 1964, 1959) adopted key components of the sociological and family theories of schizophrenia, combined them with the existential principles that were his hallmark, and formulated the most controversial view of schizophrenia in the clinical field. Laing believed that schizophrenia is actually a constructive process in which people try to cure themselves of the confusion and unhappiness caused by their social and family environment. He believed that, left alone to complete this process, people with schizophre-

nia would indeed achieve a healthy level of integration.

Laing's theory begins with the existential position that in order to give meaning to their lives, all human beings must be in touch with their true selves. If they are not, their lives will be inauthentic, unstable, and anxious. Unfortunately, says Laing, it is difficult to achieve this inner discovery and lead a meaningful existence in present-day society. Typically, social interactions require us to develop a false self rather than a true one in order to satisfy the expectations, demands, and standards of others.

Laing asserted that the people who become schizophrenic have even greater obstacles than these to deal with. Like the double-bind theorists, he believed that the families of schizophrenic people communicate and act in particularly confusing ways, convey contradictory expectations, and make paradoxical demands. Not only

that passes such a legacy on, but there are now more plausible explanations for this type of behavior. One explanation is that people afflicted with lycanthropy suffer from *porphyria,* an inherited blood disease whose victims sprout extra facial hair and are vulnerable to sunlight. People with porphyria can be treated successfully with blood pigment. Another current explanation associates lycanthropy with a disturbance in the activity of the temporal lobe of the brain. The posterior region of the temporal lobe is close to other areas of the brain that are linked to visual functions and may be the source of visual hallucinations. Abnormal brain activity in the temporal lobe combined with a psychotic thought disorder may account for many of the symptoms of lycanthropy.

One of the most interesting recent instances of lycanthropy happens to differ somewhat from the classical mold. A 26-year-old man had been convinced that he was a cat for more than fifteen years at the time his case was reported. He was a research sci-

entist who had a history of alcohol abuse, major depression, and several other problems. While being treated for these disorders, he revealed to the clinician that as a child he had discovered that he was a cat. He was able to communicate with other cats, he reported, and his true identity was confirmed by the family cat, Tiffany. It should be noted that this man had apparently been neglected, if not outright abused, by his parents. In addition, there was a history of severe mental and emotional disorders in his immediate family.

When the boy made his discovery, he began to hunt with cats and to eat raw meat. He also reported that he had had a series of monogamous sexual relationships with cats. At the age of 17 he refined his view of his feline existence and concluded that in fact he was a tiger. He fell in love with Dolly, a tiger at the zoo. His plans to orchestrate Dolly's escape from the zoo and live with her were dashed when she was sold to an Asian zoo, and he fell into a major depression.

At the time of the clinical interview,

the young man looked normal except for his attire—striped clothes, primarily—and his long fingernails. He had a number of friends, and except for his cat delusions, his thought processes were normal.

The clinician's explanation for this extreme and persistent case of lycanthropy was that the patient had "failed to form an adequate self-identification with either parent, due to their own disturbances, and subsequently targeted his favorite cat as an idealized self-object during childhood. This process, perhaps superimposed on a medical or neurological vulnerability, may have produced his remarkably persistent lycanthropic delusion" (Kulick, Pope, & Beck, 1990, p. 136).

Modern cases of lycanthropy, like those of lunacy, make a powerful point about human nature: ideas and beliefs play major roles in shaping behavior. Though our explanations for abnormal behavior evolve as we become more sophisticated about the workings of the human mind, age-old myths are difficult to put to rest.

are children in these families unable to discover their true selves, they cannot even develop a false self that succeeds in meeting the demands of others. Everything they do or say is unsatisfactory.

The situation becomes so bad that out of desperation these people undertake an inner search for a sense of strength and purpose. They withdraw from others and attend increasingly to their own inner cues as they try to recover their wholeness as human beings. Laing argued that these people would emerge stronger and less confused if they were simply allowed to continue this inner search. Instead, however, society and its clinicians tell them that they are sick and even list signs and symptoms of schizophrenia that seem to prove this assertion. The victims, who are already experiencing themselves as "things" instead of "beings," become further objectified as "schizophrenics." Expected by society to behave

as sick, they assume the role of schizophrenic patient, submitting to efforts at treatment that actually serve to produce further schizophrenic symptoms. In an effort to cure these people, society dooms them to suspension in an inner world.

It is easy to understand why Laing's theory is so controversial. Most theorists reject his notion that schizophrenia is a positive or constructive process. They see it as a problem that brings extensive suffering and no benefit. Laing acknowledged the pain and terror experienced by schizophrenic persons, but he maintained that their suffering grows largely from society's inadequacies and from its inappropriate response to the inward searches of individuals. The debate continues, and for the most part research has not resolved the controversy (Howells & Guirguis, 1984). Laing's phenomenological ideas do not lend themselves to empirical research

(Hirsch & Leff, 1975). Moreover, the existentialists who embrace his view have little confidence in traditional research approaches.

**The Cognitive View** The cognitive explanation of schizophrenia incorporates the biological findings of the past few decades. It proposes that biological problems arise first, causing strange sensory experiences; then further features of schizophrenia emerge as a result of the individuals attempts to understand and explain their unusual experiences. When first confronted by voices, visions, or other sensations, these individuals turn to friends and relatives to help them clarify what is happening, only to have the existence of their new sensory experiences denied. Eventually they come to believe that their friends and relatives are trying to hide the truth from them, they reject all feedback from others, and they develop beliefs (delusions) that they are being manipulated or persecuted (Frith, 1979; Maher, 1974). In short, they take what is sometimes called a "rational path to madness" (Zimbardo, 1974).

This cognitive theory has not been tested directly among schizophrenic subjects, but a link between sensory dysfunctioning and delusional thinking has often been observed in persons who lose their hearing (Zimbardo et al., 1981; Maher, 1974; Reed, 1974). Most people who lose their hearing for an organic reason are not immediately aware of what is happening to them. When their hearing begins to deteriorate, they tend to think that the people around them are whispering; when told this is just not so, hearing-impaired persons sometimes conclude that they are being deceived and plotted against. As long as they are unaware of their growing deafness, their logical processes lead them to delusional conclusions. This is a common phenomenon and helps to account for the relatively high prevalence of persecutory delusions among the elderly (Kay, 1972; Post, 1966).

The cognitive view of schizophrenia is newer than the other psychological explanations of the disorder. Admittedly, it focuses primarily on one piece of the schizophrenia puzzle — delusions — and research to evaluate it has been limited and indirect. The emergence of this explanation, however, reflects a growing tendency to see schizophrenia as a disorder determined by multiple interacting factors. In contrast to many psychological theories of past years, this cognitive theory explicitly acknowledges the role of biological factors and tries to understand how psychological processes may interact with such factors. Similar interactionist perspectives are being adopted increasingly by today's psychodynamic, behavioral, and family theorists. Given the complexity

and elusiveness of schizophrenia, such efforts at integration seem most appropriate and welcome.

# SCHIZOPHRENIA: THE STATE OF THE FIELD

Schizophrenia, one of our species' most bizarre and frightening disorders, has been studied intensively throughout this century. Only since the discovery of antipsychotic drugs in the 1950s, however, have clinicians gained significant insight into its causes. Although theories about schizophrenia abounded before that time, they typically lacked empirical support, contributed to inaccurate stereotyping of the parents of schizophrenic people, and resulted in ineffective forms of treatment. With effective antipsychotic medications in hand, however, researchers have been able to work backward to identify important biological factors in the development of schizophrenia, and have begun to understand better the role of psychological and sociological factors.

Investigators have also begun to learn much about the nature and course of schizophrenia. As a result, the prevailing view of schizophrenia as a single disorder with numerous faces seems to be changing. Research is increasingly suggesting that the different types of schizophrenia may in fact represent entirely different disorders, each with a distinct course; distinct biological, genetic, and perhaps psychological origins; and a distinct response to treatment.

Most clinical theorists now agree that schizophrenia, in whatever form, is probably caused by a combination of factors. Many believe, for example, that genetic and biological factors establish a predisposition to develop the disorder, that psychological factors such as personal or familial stress help bring the disorder to fruition, and that other psychological and sociological factors, such as individual misinterpretations or societal labeling, help maintain and exacerbate the symptoms.

The precise ways in which heredity, biology, psychology, and society combine to cause schizophrenia are still being uncovered. Certainly there have been exciting, at times spectacular, findings in each of these spheres, including findings from the recent studies of chromosome markers, brain chemistry, and brain structure, but much remains to be learned. What are the precise, determining causes of schizophrenia, how does each contribute to the disorder, how do they interact, and how should various forms of schizophrenia be viewed and treated? The considerable progress now being made should impress us, but it must not blind us to the significant gaps, uncertainties, and confusions that continue to obscure our view.

# SUMMARY

*Psychosis* is a state in which individuals lose contact with reality. It frequently appears in the form of *schizophrenia,* a disorder in which previously adaptive levels of social, personal, and occupational functioning deteriorate into distorted perceptions, disturbed thought processes, deviant emotional states, and motor abnormalities. Approximately 1 percent of the world's population suffers from this disorder. Many clinicians believe that schizophrenia is a group of distinct disorders that share some common features.

The symptoms associated with schizophrenia fall into several categories. Disturbances in the *content* of thought usually take the form of *delusions.* Disturbances in the *form* of thought *(formal thought disorders),* include loose associations, neologisms, perseveration, clang, and blocking. Disturbances in *perception* and *attention* include *hallucinations.* Disturbances in *affect,* or emotions, include blunted affect, flat affect, and inappropriate affect. A disturbed *sense of self* is characterized by doubt in the reality of one's existence. A disturbed *relationship with the external world* is manifested in emotional and social withdrawal and preoccupation with ideas and fantasies. Disturbances in *volition* include ambivalence and loss of interest. Disturbances in *psychomotor behavior* are typically characterized by *catatonia.*

*Schizophrenia* usually emerges during adolescence or early adulthood and tends to go through three phases. A *prodromal phase,* characterized by a deterioration in functioning, is followed by an *active phase,* in which schizophrenic symptoms become more prominent. The *residual phase* is marked by a return to functioning similar to that of the prodromal phase. Patients may be placed in 5 categories of schizophrenia, according to DSM-III-R criteria: *disorganized type, catatonic type, paranoid type, undifferentiated type,* and *residual type.* In addition, clinicians have begun to distinguish between *Type I* and *Type II schizophrenia,* which refer to a prevalence of positive and negative symptoms, respectively.

*A*n interaction of sociological, biological, and psychological factors seem to contribute to schizophrenia. The *sociocultural view* is based on the principle that society has certain expectations in regard to the behavior of a person who is labeled as schizophrenic, and that these expectations may promote the development of symptoms.

*T*he *genetic view,* based on the principle that some people inherit a biological predisposition to schizophrenia, is supported by studies of several kinds, including twin studies, adoption studies, and chromosomal mapping studies.

*T*he *biological view* attempts to identify the biological abnormalities that are inherited or developed by persons with schizophrenia. The two most likely candidates are biochemical abnormalities and abnormal brain structures. The predominant biochemical explanation of schizophrenia focuses on an unusually high level of activity in neurons that use the neurotransmitter dopamine. There is evidence that the brains of schizophrenic people contain an unusually large number of dopamine receptors. In addition, modern brain imaging techniques have detected abnormal brain structures in schizophrenic people. The most typical abnormality is the presence of enlarged ventricles.

*T*he *psychological view* is based on the principle that psychological factors are critical in the development of schizophrenia. The leading psychological explanations have come from the psychodynamic, behavioral, family, existential, and cognitive perspectives. Psychodynamic theorists believe that schizophrenia involves *regression* to a pre-ego state of *primary narcissism* and *restitutive* efforts to reestablish ego control. Behaviorists theorize that schizophrenic people fail to attend to relevant social cues and as a result develop bizarre responses to the environment. The family explanation for schizophrenia holds that the family environment contains such confusing elements as a *schizophrenic mother, double-bind communications, marital schism,* and *marital skew.* R. D. Laing's theory states that schizophrenia is actually a constructive process by which people try to cure themselves of the confusion and unhappiness caused by their social and family environment. Cognitive theorists contend that when schizophrenic people try to explain their biologically induced hallucinations or other strange sensations, they develop delusional thinking. Their logical processes lead them to delusional conclusions. Most clinical theorists now agree that schizophrenia, in whatever form, can probably be traced to a combination of factors such as these.

# TOPIC OVERVIEW

# CHAPTER *16*

# TREATMENTS
# FOR
# SCHIZOPHRENIA

**T**he symptoms of schizophrenia seem by their very nature to defy treatment. What possible help can there be for people whose thoughts and perceptions are so profoundly confused and distorted? What kind of communication can take place between a patient and a therapist who speak virtually different languages? For years, efforts at treating schizophrenia brought only frustration. Lara Jefferson, a young schizophrenic woman, wrote of her treatment experience:

*They call us insane*—*and in reality they are as* inconsistent as we are, as flighty and changeable. This one in particular. One day he derides and

ridicules me unmercifully; the next he talks to me sadly and this morning his eyes misted over with tears as he told me of the fate ahead. Damn him and all of his wisdom!

He has dinned into my ears a monotonous dirge—"Too Egotistical—too Egotistical—too Egotistical. Learn to think differently."—And how can I do it? How—how—can I do it? How the hell can I do it? I have tried to follow his suggestions but have not learned to think a bit differently. It was all wasted effort. Where has it got me?

*(Jefferson, 1948)*

For much of human history, schizophrenic patients were considered hopeless. The disorder is

519

Francisco de Goya's early nineteenth century painting *The Madhouse*, depicting a typical mental hospital of his day, is strikingly similar to the portrayal in Ken Kesey's 1950s novel (later a play and film), *One Flew Over the Cuckoo's Nest*. Institutions of both the distant and the recent past were overcrowded, often negligent, and concerned primarily with keeping order.

still extremely difficult to treat, but clinicians are much more successful today than they were in the past. Much of the credit goes to the recently discovered antipsychotic drugs, which help many people with schizophrenia think more rationally, thus making it possible for them to engage in therapeutic programs that previously had a limited effect at best. Clinicians still have far to go in the treatment of schizophrenia, but finally, after years of failure, they have made strides in developing an array of therapeutic approaches that offer considerable promise for the future.

## INSTITUTIONALIZATION

For more than half of this century, society's response to schizophrenia was *institutionalization,* usually in a public facility. Because schizophrenic patients failed to respond to traditional therapies and remained thoroughly incapacitated by their disorder, the principal goals of these establishments were patient restraint and custodial care (provision of food, shelter, and clothing). Patients rarely saw therapists and were largely neglected.

Many were abused. Oddly enough, this tragic state of affairs unfolded in an atmosphere of good intentions.

### Past Institutional Care

The move toward institutionalization began in 1793 when the French physician Philippe Pinel "unchained the insane" from virtual imprisonment at La Bicêtre asylum and began the practice of "moral treatment" (as we saw in Chapter 1). For the first time in centuries, severely disturbed patients were viewed as human beings who should be cared for with sympathy and kindness. Pinel's ideas spread throughout Europe and the United States, and led to the creation of large mental hospitals rather than asylums to care for mentally disturbed individuals (Goshen, 1967).

These new mental hospitals, typically located in isolated, relatively inexpensive areas, were developed with the noblest of goals (Grob, 1966). They were to provide a haven from the stresses of daily life and offer a healthful psychological environment in which patients could work closely with therapists. It was believed that such institutional care should be available to both the poor and the rich. Thus states throughout the United States were required by law to establish public mental institutions, *state hospitals,* to serve as a supplement and alternative to the private ones.

Starting in the mid–nineteenth century, the state hospital system developed serious problems. Wards became increasingly overcrowded, admissions kept rising, and state funding was unable to keep up with the increasing need for professional therapists. Too many aspects of treatment became the responsibility of nurses and attendants whose knowledge and experience at that time were limited. Between 1845 and 1955, the number of state hospitals and mental patients rose steadily while the quality of care declined. During this period, close to 300 state hospitals were established in the United States. The number of hospitalized patients on any given day rose from 2,000 in 1845 to nearly 600,000 in 1955.

The priorities of the public mental hospitals changed during this span of 110 years. In the face of overcrowding and understaffing, the emphasis shifted from humanitarian care to order-keeping and efficiency. In a throwback to the asylum period, disruptive patients were physically restrained, isolated, and punished; individual attention diminished. Upon first entering a state hospital, most patients were given solicitous attention and care, but they were soon transferred to chronic wards, or "back wards," if they failed to improve (Bloom, 1984). These back wards were in fact human warehouses that were filled with an aura of hopelessness. Staff members often relied on mechanical restraints such as straitjackets and handcuffs to deal with difficult patients. More "advanced" forms of intervention included medically debilitating approaches such as hydrotherapy and lobotomy (see pp. 157–158). In the late 1950s it was estimated that 94 percent of the state hospitals could not meet the standards that had been set by the American Psychiatric Association (Roche, 1964). Most of the patients in these institutions were schizophrenic (Hafner & an der Heiden, 1988).

Many patients not only failed to improve under these conditions but developed additional symptoms, apparently as the result of institutionalization itself. The most common pattern of deterioration was the *social breakdown syndrome:* extreme withdrawal, anger, physical aggressiveness, and loss of interest in personal appearance and functioning (Gruenberg, 1980; American Public Health Association, 1962). Often more troublesome than the original symptoms of their disorders, this new syndrome made it impossible for patients to return to society, even if they somehow recovered from the difficulties that first brought them to the hospital.

## Improved Institutional Care

As we noted in Chapter 5, the 1950s saw the development and spread of humanistic and behavioral treatments for various kinds of mental disorders. Clinicians of the time also developed two institutional interventions, *milieu therapy* and the *token economy program*—the former based primarily on humanistic principles and the latter on behavioral principles—that finally offered some help to schizophrenic and other patients who had been languishing in institutions for years (Bloom, 1984). These approaches were particularly helpful in addressing the personal-care and self-image problems exacerbated by institutionalization. They were soon adopted by many institutions, and are now standard features of institutional care.

**Milieu Therapy** Humanistic theorists propose that institutionalized patients deteriorate mainly because they are deprived of opportunities to develop self-respect, independence, and responsibility and to engage in meaningful activity, all experiences basic to healthy human functioning. This deprivation begins as a result of their disorder and intensifies in response to institutional depersonalization and neglect. Thus the premise behind *milieu therapy* is that the social milieu of institutions must change if patients are to make clinical progress, that institutional climates conducive to self-respect, individual responsibility, and meaningful activity must be established.

***Origins of Milieu Therapy*** The pioneer of this approach was Maxwell Jones, a London psychiatrist who in 1953 converted a psychiatric ward of patients with various disorders into a ***therapeutic community.*** Patients were referred to as "residents" of the community and were treated as persons capable of running their own lives and making their own decisions. Residents participated in institutional planning and government, attending community meetings where they worked with staff members to establish rules and determine sanctions. In fact, patient–staff distinctions were almost eliminated in Jones's therapeutic community. Everyone was valued as an important therapeutic agent, in the belief that patients could benefit from interactions with other patients as well as from discussions with staff members. Similarly, staff members could gain insights from talking with patients. The atmosphere was one of mutual respect, interdependence, support, and openness. Patients were involved in a variety of constructive activities, including special projects, semipermanent jobs, occupational therapy, recreation, and community government. In short, their daily schedule resembled life outside the hospital.

**The Spread of Milieu Therapy** Milieu-style programs were soon developed in institutions throughout the Western world. Even clinicians who did not agree with Jones's humanistic perspective on mental disorders agreed that milieu therapy was superior to custodial care for most institutionalized mental patients. They were excited about its potential for improving the attitudes of staff members toward patients, reducing apathy among staff and patients, exposing patients to real-world opportunities and demands, and motivating them to be active participants in life.

Milieu approaches have varied from setting to setting. In some institutions, "milieu therapy" simply means that staff members try to facilitate interactions (especially group interactions) between patients and staff, keep patients active, and establish higher expectations of what patients should be able to accomplish. Other milieu programs actually create patient councils to administer ward affairs, give patients considerable responsibility in guiding their lives, and offer meaningful work opportunities. A few institutions, such as R. D. Laing's Kingsley Hall, have been fully converted into therapeutic communities where staff and patients are equals, and the social milieu is indeed the central feature of the treatment received there.

**The Effectiveness of Milieu Therapy** Because milieu approaches vary so greatly among institutions and have been applied to patients with various disorders, researchers have had difficulty assessing their effectiveness. So far the only conclusion that can be drawn is that some milieu approaches do indeed help institutionalized schizophrenic patients. Chronic patients in some milieu hospital programs have improved and left the hospital at higher rates than chronic patients in custodial programs (Paul & Lentz, 1977; Artiss, 1962; Cumming & Cumming, 1962). On the other hand, many of these patients remain impaired and must live in sheltered settings after their release. In addition, as we shall see shortly, milieu approaches tend to be less effective in treating institutionalized schizophrenic patients than are other approaches, such as token economy programs and antipsychotic drugs.

Despite these limitations, milieu therapy continues to be practiced in many institutions. It has also had an impact on community treatment programs. We shall see later that halfway houses trying to ease schizophrenic individuals back into community residential life often incorporate resident self-government, work schedules, and other features of milieu therapy into their programs.

**The Token Economy** In the 1950s behaviorists had little status in mental institutions and were permitted to work only with patients whose problems seemed virtually hopeless. At the time, the "hopeless" included chronic schizophrenic patients. Through years of experimentation, behaviorists found that the systematic application of operant techniques could help alter the dysfunctional patterns of these patients (Ayllon & Haughton, 1964; Ayllon, 1963; Ayllon & Michael, 1959). Programs that apply such techniques have been given the name *token economy programs*.

Teodoro Ayllon and Nathan Azrin (1968, 1965) set up the first token economy program for schizophrenic patients in an Illinois hospital. Patients were rewarded whenever they behaved acceptably according to an established set of criteria and were not rewarded when they behaved unacceptably. The immediate rewards for acceptable behavior were *tokens* that could later be used to purchase desired objects or opportunities. Thus the name "token economy."

As a first step Ayllon and Azrin selected a series of target behaviors that patients would be rewarded for. The patients could earn tokens by performing on-the-ward tasks such as making their beds, serving meals, and doing laundry, and for off-ward jobs such as kitchen work and telephone duty. They could also earn tokens by speaking more normally, abiding by ward rules, and showing self-control in social interactions.

The researchers then selected a range of reinforcements that patients would find appealing. Tokens could be redeemed for any of the following rewards:

1. *Privacy.* A single-bed room cost 30 tokens, a two-bed room 15, and a four-bed room 8 tokens.
2. *Privileges.* Patients could go on an escorted walk on the hospital grounds at a cost of 2 tokens. An accompanied trip downtown cost 100 tokens.
3. *Staff interactions.* An extended private discussion with the social worker cost 100 tokens.

4. *Religious activities.* For 1 token patients could purchase an extra religious service on the ward. They could purchase one off the ward for 10 tokens. Private discussions with the chaplain remained free.

5. *Recreation.* Patients could chose their own television programs for 3 tokens. They could attend a movie on the ward for 1 token.

6. *Shopping.* Candy, beverages, and cigarettes cost from 1 to 5 tokens. Toiletries ranged from 1 to 10 tokens. Clothing cost from 12 to 400 tokens.

Although some clinicians had predicted that such a program would prove too complicated for schizophrenic patients, Ayllon and Azrin found that most learned the system and began to behave more appropriately. They also conducted a series of experiments to determine the range and limits of token economy programs, and found that the most effective payoff time was immediately after patients performed a task properly. Tokens given before a task resulted in poor performance. Today token economy programs are being used in many hospital settings (Paul & Lentz, 1977; Kazdin, 1977, 1975; Schaefer & Martin, 1975; Atthowe & Krasner, 1968).

To keep widening a patient's repertoire of appropriate behaviors, clinicians must periodically introduce new target behaviors and reinforcements. Some hospitals actually set up several token economy programs, called *leveled programs,* each representing a different level of difficulty. When patients learn to perform the target behaviors of one program consistently, they are transferred to another program where more demanding behaviors are now required; target behaviors from the former program no longer earn tokens. Ideally, the patients progress from level to level until they are ready for discharge (Kazdin, 1978).

### The Effectiveness of Token Economy Programs

Research suggests that token economies do help change schizophrenic patterns and related inappropriate behaviors (Belcher, 1988). In one of the most successful such programs, Gordon Paul and R. L. Lentz (1977) applied operant principles to twenty-eight chronic schizophrenic patients whose dysfunctional behaviors included mutism, repeated screaming, incontinence, smearing feces on walls, and physical assault. The program addressed every aspect of the patients' lives. Tokens could be earned for proper appearance, bedmaking, bathing, appropriate meal behavior, contributions in class, acceptable social behavior, and normal talk—all of which were explained and rehearsed in regular training sessions. The list of reinforcements was long and varied, and even included certain necessities,

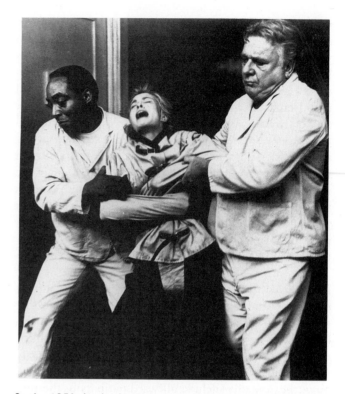

In the 1950s institutions began to rely less on restraints such as the straitjacket (depicted in the film biography *Frances*) in favor of milieu therapy programs, which encouraged patients to control their own lives, or of token economy programs, which used systematic reinforcements to change patients' behavior.

such as breakfast, lunch, and dinner. If patients did not earn enough tokens to buy meals, they were given a free "medical meal"—a healthful but unappetizing blend of nutrients.

Most patients improved significantly under this program. After seven months, many were regularly demonstrating appropriate behavior in each target area. By the end of the program, four and a half years later, 98 percent of the subjects had been released, usually to shelter care facilities. At a follow-up eighteen months later, only two patients had been rehospitalized.

Paul and Lentz also set up two other kinds of programs for purposes of comparison. A *custodial program,* consisting of custodial care, medication, and limited psychotherapy, was administered to a control group of twenty-eight chronic schizophrenic patients closely matched to the token economy patients in symptoms, age, and background. In addition, a *milieu program* was administered to twenty-eight other matched patients. This last group was organized as a community, with a patient council to make important decisions about patients' activities and community events. Staff members repeatedly communicated positive expectations and encouragement ("I know you can get that job done"), while also conveying negative feedback for inappropriate behavior and making it clear that they expected to see improvement.

In all three programs, staff members observed patients' behavior on an hourly basis, thus enabling Paul and Lentz to compare the patients' progress. They found that after seven months the token economy patients made more improvements than the milieu patients, and both groups improved significantly more than the custodial patients. In addition, only 71 percent of the milieu patients and 45 percent of the custodial patients were released by the end of their four-and-a-half-year programs, compared to 98 percent of the token economy patients.

***Problems Facing Token Economies***    A number of important questions and problems have been raised regarding token economy programs and the studies that have been done to evaluate them. One problem is that many token economy studies, unlike the Paul and Lentz study, are uncontrolled. When administrators set up a token economy, they usually include all ward patients in the program rather than dividing the patients into a token economy group and a control group. As a result, patients' improvements can be compared only with their own past behaviors, and that comparison may be confounded by variables other than the program's operant principles (a new physical setting, for example, or a general increase in staff attention could be the cause of improvement).

Some clinicians have also questioned the quality of the improvement achieved under token economy programs. Are behaviorists altering a patient's schizophrenic thoughts and perceptions or simply improving the patient's ability to mimic normal behavior? This issue is illustrated in the case of a middle-aged schizophrenic man named John, who had the delusion that he was the United States government. Whenever he spoke to others, he spoke as the government. "We are happy to see you. . . . We need people like you in our service. . . . We are carrying out our activities in John's body." When John's hospital ward was converted into a token economy, the staff members targeted his delusional statements, requiring him to identify himself properly to earn tokens. If he called himself John, he would receive tokens; if he maintained that he was the government, he would receive nothing.

After a few months on the token economy program, John stopped presenting himself as the government. When asked his name, he would say, "John." Although staff members were understandably pleased by his improvement, John himself had a different view of the situation. In a private discussion he said:

*We're tired of it. Every damn time we want a cigarette, we* have to go through their bullshit. "What's your name. . . . Who wants the cigarette. . . . Where is the government?" Today, we were desperate for a smoke and went to Simpson, the damn nurse, and she made us do her bidding. "Tell me your name if you want a cigarette. What's your name?" Of course, we said, "John." We needed the cigarettes. If we told her the truth, no cigarettes. But we don't have time for this nonsense. We've got business to do, international business, laws to change, people to recruit. And these people keep playing their games.

*(Comer, 1973)*

Critics of the behavioral approach would argue that John was still delusional and therefore as "schizophrenic" as before. Behaviorists, however, would defend John's progress, arguing that he had improved by learning to keep his delusion to himself and at the very least had improved in his judgments about the consequences of his behavior. They also might see this as an important step toward changing his private thinking.

Finally, getting patients to make a satisfactory transition from token economy hospital programs to community living has presented a difficult problem for behaviorists. In an environment where rewards are contingent on proper behaviors, proper behaviors become contingent on continued rewards. Patients who find that the real world doesn't reward them so concretely will sometimes abandon their newly acquired behaviors. Behaviorists have adopted two strategies to facilitate the transition from token economy hospital programs to community living: (1) *changing hospital programs* so that they resemble real life more closely and (2) *changing community residences* into token economy programs.

In one approach to changing a hospital program, administrators gradually adjust the token economy so that it increasingly reflects life outside the hospital. At a certain point, they may institute **social reinforcements,** such as attention from staff members, praise, enjoyable discussions, and social events — the kind of reward that normal behavior elicits in the outside world. Another approach is gradually to change the token economy toward a ***partial reinforcement schedule.*** Instead of receiving tokens every time they perform target behaviors, patients may receive them only some of the time. In this way they learn to keep performing the desired behaviors even in the absence of immediate reinforcements; they learn that the behaviors will pay off eventually (Koegel & Rincover, 1977; Atthowe, 1973). In still another procedure, token economy administrators may adopt a ***fading*** process for phasing out tokens (Rimm & Masters, 1979). For example staff members may gradually lengthen the time interval between a patient's performance of a target behavior and the token payment, thus loosening the close association of target behaviors and rewards. Research suggests, however, that such program changes have at best a limited effect on the long-term progress of schizophrenic patients (Paul & Lentz, 1977).

Experience has shown that the other strategy for easing the transition from hospital token economy programs to the community, running community homes as token economies, is also fraught with difficulties. Patients have far more freedom in community homes than they do in the hospital, and it is no simple matter to control the way they spend their time, energy, and money. Moreover, many clinicians are uncomfortable with the idea of controlling people's lives to such an extent after they leave an institution. They believe that a return to the community should mean a return to independence and self-regulation. Accordingly, most prefer to adopt the salient features of milieu therapy, such as support, self-government, and job placement, as the focus of community residential programs.

All these issues notwithstanding, token economy programs have had a most important effect on the treatment of people with schizophrenia. They were among the first hospital treatment techniques that actually helped change schizophrenic symptoms, got chronic patients moving again, and enabled some of them to be released from the hospital. Today token economies are employed in mental hospitals throughout the United States, usually along with medication, and in some community residences as well. The token economy approach has also been applied to other clinical problems, including mental retardation, delinquency, and hyperactivity, as well as in other fields, such as education and business.

# ANTIPSYCHOTIC DRUGS

Milieu therapy and token economy programs helped to improve the gloomy prognosis for schizophrenia, but it was the discovery of antipsychotic drugs in the 1950s that truly revolutionized its treatment (Weinberger, 1991; Bloom, 1984). These drugs eliminate many schizophrenic patients' symptoms and today are almost always a part of treatment. What is more, as we noted in Chapter 15, they have also influenced the way clinicians diagnose and view schizophrenia (see Box 16-1).

The discovery of antipsychotic medications dates back to the discovery of *antihistamine drugs.* In the 1940s medical researchers found that certain drugs blocked the release of histamine—a chemical stored in cells

throughout the body—and brought remarkable relief to people suffering from allergies such as hay fever. Although the drugs also produced considerable tiredness and drowsiness, they were so effective at quelling allergic reactions that they quickly rose in popularity. Many antihistamines were developed, some more effective for allergy sufferers than others.

During the same period, researchers in the area of surgical anesthesia were looking for a way to prevent anesthetized patients from experiencing a sudden drop in blood pressure and going into shock. The French surgeon Henri Laborit came to believe that the new antihistamine drugs, given along with general anesthesia, might prevent such a drop in blood pressure. He administered one group of antihistamines, *phenothiazines,* to his surgical patients. Although the drugs actually had no effect on blood pressure, Laborit noticed that they did have an effect that might be useful in helping to calm patients before surgery—they made patients sleepy and relaxed, while allowing them to remain awake. Laborit and others experimented with several phenothiazine antihistamines and became most impressed with one called *chlorpromazine.* Laborit reported, "It provokes not any loss of consciousness, not any change in the patient's mentality but a slight tendency to sleep and above all 'disinterest' for all that goes on around him." Before long, this drug gained wide acceptance as a preoperative medication.

Laborit and other researchers also suspected that, because of its relaxing effect, chlorpromazine might be helpful in the treatment of mental disorders. The psychiatrists Jean Delay and Pierre Deniker (1952) soon tested the drug on six psychotic patients and reported a sharp reduction in their symptoms. In 1954, after a series of laboratory and clinical tests, chlorpromazine began to be marketed in the United States as an antipsychotic medication under the trade name Thorazine.

Since the discovery of chlorpromazine, numerous antipsychotic drugs have been developed (see Table 16-1). Collectively they are known as *neuroleptic drugs,* because they often produce effects similar to the symptoms of neurological diseases. Some of the drugs, like chlorpromazine, are from the phenothiazine group, including *thioridazine* (Mellaril), *mesoridazine* (Serentil), *fluphenazine* (Prolixin), and *trifluoperazine* (Stelazine). Others, such as *haloperidol* (Haldol) and *thiothixene* (Navane), belong to different chemical classes (see Table 3-1).

As we saw in Chapter 15, these drugs apparently manage to reduce schizophrenic symptoms by reducing excessive activity of the neurotransmitter dopamine in the brains of schizophrenic persons (Davis et al., 1988; Carlsson & Lindquist, 1963). Remember that many

TABLE 16-1

| ANTIPSYCHOTIC DRUGS | | |
|---|---|---|
| Class/generic name | Trade name | Usual daily oral dose (mg) |
| Chlorpromazine | Thorazine | 200–600 |
| Triflupromazine | Vesprin | 50–150 |
| Thioridazine | Mellaril | 200–600 |
| Mesoridazine besylate | Serentil | 150 |
| Piperacetazine | Quide | 20–40 |
| Trifluoperazine | Stelazine | 2–4 |
| Fluphenazine hydrochloride | Prolixin Permitil | 2.5–10 |
| Perphenazine | Trilafon | 16–64 |
| Acetophenazine maleate | Tindal | 60 |
| Chlorprothixene | Taractan | 75–200 |
| Thiothixene | Navane | 6–30 |
| Haloperidol | Haldol | 2–12 |
| Loxapine | Loxitane | 20 |
| Molindone hydrochloride | Moban Lidone | 15–60 |
| Pimozide | Orap | 2–10 |
| Clozapine | Clozaril | 200–900 |

*Source:* Silver & Yudofsky, 1988, pp. 771–773.

schizophrenic persons, particularly those with Type I schizophrenia, have an excessive number of receptors on their dopamine-receiving neurons, which lead to excessive dopamine activity at those brain sites and so to the symptoms of schizophrenia. After a patient takes antipsychotic drugs for a period of time, the dopamine-receiving neurons apparently grow additional dopamine receptors (Riederer et al., 1989; Muller & Seeman, 1978; Burt, Creese, & Snyder, 1977). It is as if the neurons recognize that dopamine transmission is being blocked at the usual receptors and compensate by developing new ones. Now the patient has two groups of dopamine receptors — the many original ones, which are now blocked, and a normal number of new ones, which produce normal synaptic activity rather than schizophrenic symptoms.

## Effectiveness of Antipsychotic Drugs

Research has repeatedly shown that antipsychotic drugs reduce schizophrenic symptoms in many patients (Davis, Comaty, & Janicak, 1988; Lindstrom, 1988; Cutting, 1985). An early comprehensive study examined 344 schizophrenic patients from nine hospitals (Cole, 1964; Cole et al., 1964). Patients were randomly assigned to one of four treatment groups. Each of the first three groups was treated with a different antipsychotic drug, while the fourth group received a placebo. In this double-blind study, neither the patients nor the hospital staff knew who was taking real drugs and who was taking the placebos. After six weeks of treatment, the patients were evaluated by the hospital staff. More than 75 percent of the patients taking actual antipsychotic medications were evaluated as "much improved." Only 25 percent of the placebo patients improved to this degree. In fact, 50 percent of the patients taking antipsychotic drugs were now rated as "normal" or "borderline normal," compared to only 15 percent of the placebo patients (see Figure 16-1).

Further research has suggested that antipsychotic drugs are the single most effective intervention for schizophrenic patients *during hospitalization*. May and his colleagues conducted a well-known and well-

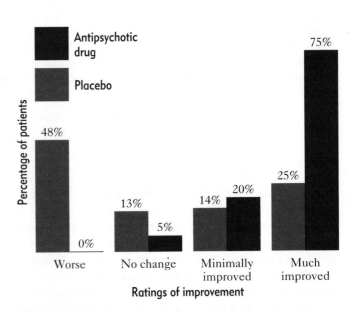

FIGURE 16-1 After 6 weeks of treatment, 75 percent of schizophrenic patients who were given antipsychotic drugs were much improved, compared to only 25 percent of patients given placebos. In addition close to half of those on the placebos worsened. *(Adapted from Cole et al., 1964.)*

=== BOX 16-1 ===

# A Diagnostic and Treatment Dilemma

Depending on how we hold a close-up photograph of the moon, we can perceive the formations on its surface either as mounds or as craters. Sometimes diagnosing a mental disorder can also seem a matter more of perspective than of clear-cut differences in symptoms. Clinicians are frequently confronted with patients who display symptoms that suggest both schizophrenia and a bipolar disorder. Differentiating between them is sometimes easier said than done.

Schizophrenic people often exhibit severe mood changes, and patients suffering from a bipolar disorder may have distorted perceptions and bizarre cognitive experiences. Yet if clinicians are to fully understand the nature and possible course of a client's problems and choose an appropriate treatment, they must decide on one diagnosis. Schizophrenia, for example, will respond well to antipsychotic drugs, while a bipolar disorder will respond to lithium. There is growing evidence that clinicians frequently make mistakes when they diagnose these two disorders. Apparently, many persons hospitalized for schizophrenia are actually experiencing a bipolar disorder, and vice versa (Lipton & Simon, 1985).

What are clinicians to do in the face of such confusion? One solution is not to choose between schizophrenia and bipolar disorders at all when a clear choice cannot be made. DSM-III-R lists *schizoaffective disorder* as a possible diagnosis when people exhibit both schizophrenic symptoms and signs of mood disorders. This category is very controversial, however. Many clinicians argue that there is no such disorder, and that the name should really be read as "I don't know."

Yet another way to distinguish schizophrenia from a bipolar disorder might be to observe how the patient responds to treatment. If lithium works, the problem is mania. If antipsychotic medication works, it is schizophrenia. Haphazard as this procedure may sound, some clinicians believe it to be the most efficient way to arrive at a correct diagnosis. They suggest that it is also a powerful means to learn to differentiate between disorders that appear not in black and white but in shades of gray.

The better a clinician learns to make these distinctions, the more reliably he or she will be able to prescribe proper treatment for a given disorder at its earliest and most treatable stage. It is important to keep in mind, however, that diagnosis by treatment is always a risky venture. Headaches caused by a brain tumor may be alleviated temporarily by aspirin, but people whose headaches respond to aspirin are not necessarily suffering from a brain tumor.

Today there is no totally satisfactory solution to the diagnostic dilemma. The problem exists because our current state of knowledge about these mental disorders is limited, and the situation will improve only as our knowledge of psychopathology grows. In the meantime, perhaps the most useful approach to the problem is for clinicians to pay closer attention to the diagnostic standards of DSM-III-R. Studies suggest that diagnoses of schizophrenia and bipolar disorder become at least more accurate when these criteria are followed with meticulous care (Pulver, Carpenter, Adler, & McGrath, 1988).

---

constructed hospital study on this subject (May, Tuma, & Dixon, 1981; May, 1968; May & Tuma, 1964). A total of 228 hospitalized schizophrenic patients were assigned to one of five treatment groups: (1) antipsychotic medications only, (2) psychodynamic psychotherapy only, (3) antipsychotic medications plus psychotherapy, (4) milieu therapy, or (5) electroconvulsive therapy. The patients' progress was assessed by the staff's evaluations, the patients' performances on psychological tests, and length of hospitalization. Patients treated with drugs alone and those treated with drugs plus psychodynamic psychotherapy improved equally and showed significantly more improvement than all other subjects in the study. The least improvement occurred among those receiving psychodynamic psychotherapy only or milieu therapy only. Patients receiving electroconvulsive therapy fell in between.

The patients in the study subsequently received treatments that were determined individually by their therapists. A follow-up assessment conducted two to five years later indicated that those who had received antipsychotic drug treatment in the hospital, with or without psychodynamic therapy, continued to do better than the other patients after release from the hospital. They were rehospitalized less frequently and spent fewer days in the hospital during the intervening years.

These results suggest that antipsychotic drugs may be superior to other forms of treatment for many hospitalized schizophrenic patients. While drugs alone seemed to be quite helpful to the schizophrenic patients in the study, psychodynamic therapy alone and milieu therapy alone were of less help. Furthermore, psychodynamic therapy added little to the positive effect of the drugs. The superior showing by antipsychotic drug treatments has held up in other studies of hospitalized schizophrenic patients, including studies in which psychotherapy was conducted by highly experienced therapists (Grinspoon et al., 1972, 1968).

Research has also indicated that schizophrenic symptoms typically return if the patients stop taking antipsychotic drugs too soon (Cutting, 1985). One study examined the continued progress of people who had been helped by antipsychotic medications (Hogarty et al., 1974, 1973). Soon after improving, one group of patients was switched to placebo drugs, while a second group continued to receive real antipsychotic medication for at least several months more. A follow-up two years later revealed that the placebo group went on to have a rehospitalization rate of 80 percent, while the real medication group relapsed at a 45 percent rate.

As we noted in Chapter 15, recent research has indicated that antipsychotic drugs alleviate the *positive symptoms* of schizophrenia, such as hallucinations, delusions, and florid thought disorders, more completely, or at least more quickly, than the *negative symptoms*, such as flat affect, poverty of speech, and motor retardation (Breier et al., 1991; Petrie et al., 1990; Kay & Singh, 1989). Correspondingly, people dominated by positive symptoms display generally higher recovery rates from schizophrenia, while those with negative symptoms are less affected by drug treatment and have a much poorer prognosis (Pogue-Geile, 1989; Ragin et al., 1989; Crow, 1980; Mackay, 1980).

Antipsychotic drugs have now achieved widespread acceptance in the treatment of schizophrenia (Lindstrom, 1988). Patients often dislike taking these powerful drugs, and some refuse to take them; but like Edward Snow, a writer who overcame schizophrenia, many are greatly helped by the medications.

*I*n my case it was necessary to come to terms with a specified drug program. I am a legalized addict. My dose: 100 milligrams of Thorazine and 60 milligrams of Stelazine daily. I don't feel this dope at all, but I have been told it is strong enough to flatten a normal person. It keeps me — as the doctors agree — sane and in good spirits. Without the brain candy, as I call it, I would go — zoom — right back into the bin. I've made the institution scene enough already to be familiar with what it's like and to know I don't want to go back.

*(Snow, 1976)*

## Unwanted Effects of Antipsychotic Drugs

Unfortunately, in addition to their impact on schizophrenic symptoms, antipsychotic drugs can produce disturbing movement abnormalities that may affect appearance and functioning (Pickar, Owen, & Litman, 1991; Woggon, 1985). These effects are called ***extrapyramidal effects*** because they appear to be caused by the drugs' impact on the extrapyramidal areas of the brain, areas that regulate motor activity. They include *Parkinsonian symptoms, dystonia, akathisia,* and *tardive dyskinesia.*

**Parkinsonian Symptoms**    As we saw in Chapter 15, antipsychotic drugs sometimes produce effects that resemble the symptoms of the neurological disorder Parkinson's disease. Patients may experience such severe and continuous muscle tremors and muscle rigidity that they shake, move very slowly, shuffle their feet, and show little facial expression. These drug effects are sometimes mistakenly viewed as further symptoms of the schizophrenic disorder.

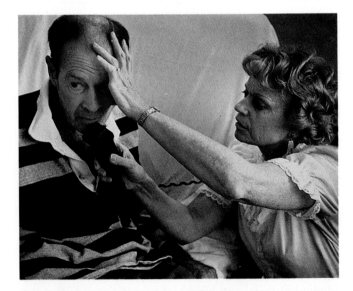

This man has a severe case of Parkinson's disease, a disorder caused by low dopamine activity, and his muscle tremors prevent him from shaving himself. Antipsychotic drugs often produce similar Parkinsonian symptoms.

Parkinson's disease is caused by low dopamine activity in the substantia nigra, a part of the midbrain that coordinates movement and posture. Apparently when antipsychotic drugs block dopamine activity throughout the brain, activity of the neurotransmitter in the substantia nigra ceases, thus causing Parkinsonian symptoms (Pickar et al., 1991). In most cases the unwanted effects can be reversed by an anti-Parkinsonian drug (such as benztropine, trade name Cogentin) along with the antipsychotic drug.

**Dystonia**  Dystonia is a condition in which involuntary muscle contractions cause bizarre and uncontrollable movements of the face, neck, tongue, and back. Apparently this drug effect is also related to the reduction of dopamine synaptic activity in the substantia nigra and responds well to treatment with anti-Parkinsonian drugs.

**Akathisia**  Akathisia is marked by a very high degree of restlessness and agitation, sometimes mistaken for schizophrenic agitation. People who suffer from this effect of antipsychotic drugs experience great discomfort in the limbs and continually move their arms and legs in an effort to relieve it. Like the Parkinsonian symptoms and dystonia, akathisia seems to be related to reduced dopamine activity in the substantia nigra, but it is not so easy to control by anti-Parkinsonian medications (Pickar et al., 1991). Sometimes the only recourse is to reduce the dosage of the antipsychotic drug.

**Tardive Dyskinesia**  "Tardive dyskinesia" means "late-appearing movement disorder." Whereas the other undesirable drug effects appear within days, tardive dyskinesia usually does not unfold until a person has taken antipsychotic drugs for more than a year. It consists of involuntary writhing or ticlike movements of the tongue, mouth, face, or whole body, and may include involuntary chewing, sucking, and lip smacking and jerky, purposeless movements of the arms, legs, or entire body. In some people it is accompanied by memory impairment (Sorokin et al., 1988).

Although most cases of tardive dyskinesia are mild and involve a single symptom such as tongue flicking, some are severe and socially debilitating and include such features as continual rocking back and forth, irregular breathing, and grotesque contortions of the face and body. It is believed that between 10 and 20 percent of those who take antipsychotic drugs for an extended period of time develop tardive dyskinesia to some degree (Torrey, 1983).

Apparently people over 55 years of age are especially vulnerable to tardive dyskinesia, although younger patients may also develop the problem. The highest incidence occurs in those who take antipsychotic drugs for longer than two years (Smith & Baldessarini, 1980; May & Simpson, 1980). There are also some research indications that Type II schizophrenic people, whose negative symptoms are relatively unresponsive to antipsychotic drugs anyway, may have a higher risk of developing tardive dyskinesia (Barnes & Braude, 1985).

Tardive dyskinesia is considered the most dangerous effect of antipsychotic drugs because it can be difficult, sometimes impossible, to eliminate (Berger et al., 1989; Berger & Bridges, 1984). If it is discovered early and the antipsychotic drugs are stopped immediately, it will usually disappear (Smith & Baldessarini, 1980; May & Simpson, 1980). Early detection, however, is elusive. Some of the symptoms are so similar to schizophrenic symptoms that clinicians may overlook them, continue or even increase antipsychotic drug therapy, and inadvertently create a more stubborn case of tardive dyskinesia. The longer these patients continue taking antipsychotic drugs, the less likely it is that their tardive dyskinesia will disappear when the antipsychotic drugs are finally stopped. No drug has yet been discovered that consistently eliminates tardive dyskinesia. Thus early detection and cessation are at present the only effective treatment for this problem (Pickar et al., 1991).

Researchers do not yet understand why antipsychotic drugs cause tardive dyskinesia in some patients. One popular theory focuses on the drugs' effect on dopamine receptors in the substantia nigra. Remember that when dopamine receptors are blocked by antipsychotic drugs, the receiving neurons apparently produce a small number of new receptors. This process of blocking old receptors and producing new receptors works well for many schizophrenic persons, but for some the newly formed dopamine receptors may actually make the receiving neurons extrasensitive to dopamine and yield a new kind of dopamine overactivity. It is this overactivity, particularly in the substantia nigra, that may produce tardive dyskinesia.

Despite the risk of tardive dyskinesia, antipsychotic medications continue to be prescribed for most schizophrenic patients, particularly those with positive symptoms. Clinicians argue that without the drugs these patients would be doomed to lives of schizophrenic dysfunctioning. They also point out that most patients who take antipsychotic drugs do not develop tardive dyskinesia and that it can usually be reversed if it is detected early. At the same time, they are now careful to prescribe the lowest effective dosage of antipsychotic drugs for each patient and to reduce or halt medication weeks or at most months after the patient reestablishes nonpsychotic functioning (Kane, 1990, 1987; Muller, 1983). Clinical researchers are currently trying to develop new drugs to counter the symptoms of tardive dyskinesia. Still others are working to develop new antipsychotic drugs that are free from this and other undesirable consequences (Carpenter et al., 1988; Kane et al., 1988; Kane, 1987). One recently developed antipsychotic drug, *clozapine*, is being hailed by some clinical researchers as such a drug (Kane et al., 1988).

# PSYCHOTHERAPY

Before the discovery of antipsychotic drugs, psychotherapy was not really a viable option as a treatment for schizophrenia. Most schizophrenic patients were simply too far removed from reality to profit from therapy. A further complication was that successful therapy is based on a trusting relationship with a therapist, and people with schizophrenia tend to react to therapists and everyone else with suspicion and avoidance. In these circumstances, it was remarkable indeed that a handful of therapists, blessed with extraordinary patience and skill, did specialize in the treatment of this disorder and reported some success with it (Will, 1967, 1961; Sullivan, 1962, 1953; Fromm-Reichmann, 1954, 1952, 1950).

These therapists believed that the primary task of therapy was to win the trust of schizophrenic patients and build a close relationship with them. Frieda Fromm-Reichmann, for example, would initially tell her patients that they could continue to exclude her from their private world and hold onto their disorder as long as they wished. She reported that eventually, after much testing and acting out, schizophrenic patients would accept, trust, and grow attached to her, and begin to examine relevant issues with her. Similarly, Otto Will offered patients total acceptance, love, and understanding. Sometimes he would even enter into their distorted world and use their language, symbols, and logic.

Although there was no consistent research into the effectiveness of such psychotherapeutic approaches, people who later recovered from schizophrenia often confirmed that trust and emotional bonding had been important to them throughout therapy. Here a woman tells her therapist how she had felt during their early interactions:

*At the start, I didn't listen to what you said most of the time* but I watched like a hawk for your expression and the sound of your voice. After the interview, I would add all this up to see if it seemed to show love. The words were nothing compared to the feelings you showed. I sense that you felt confident I could be helped and that there was hope for the future. . . .

The problem with schizophrenics is that they can't trust anyone. They can't put their eggs in one basket. The doctor will usually have to fight to get in no matter how much the patient objects. . . .

Loving is impossible at first because it turns you into a helpless little baby. The patient can't feel safe to do this until he is absolutely sure the doctor understands what is needed and will provide it.

Hating is like shitting. If you shit, it shows you are alive but, if the doctor can't accept your shit, it means he doesn't want you to be alive. It makes him like a mother who can't accept her child's mess. . . . It used to terrify me to sit and watch you, to see if you could handle all my hate and shit, or whether you would be choked by it the way I was.

*(Hayward & Taylor, 1965)*

Psychotherapy is now successfully employed in many more cases of schizophrenia, thanks to the discovery and effectiveness of antipsychotic drugs (Goldstein, 1991; Karon, 1990, 1985). By helping to relieve their thought and perceptual disturbances, the drugs enable people with schizophrenia to examine themselves and make changes in their behavior (Bartko et al., 1988). Although psychotherapy tends to be of limited help during the earliest stages of the disorder, especially during hospitalization (May, 1968), research suggests that it becomes very useful later on. The most helpful forms of psychotherapy include *insight therapy*, *social therapy*, and *family therapy*.

## Insight Therapy

A variety of insight therapies are now applied to schizophrenia (Ernst, 1985; Auerhahn & Moskowitz, 1984; Knobel, 1983). Studies suggest that insight therapists who are more experienced with schizophrenia have greater success, often regardless of their particular orientation (Karon, 1990, 1985; Karon & Vandenbos, 1981; Lamb, 1982; Schwartz, 1978).

According to one study of therapists and their success rates with schizophrenic patients, successful therapists tend to take a more active role with their patients, setting limits, expressing opinions, challenging patients' statements, and guiding patients to make specific life adjustments (Whitehorn & Betz, 1975). In addition, they regularly convey confidence in the patients' potential for independence and mastery of life skills. Therapists who are more passive and permissive tend to have less success with schizophrenic patients. An active mode of therapy is evident in the following case report:

*A 36-year-old married woman had been hospitalized five* times for acute psychotic episodes between the ages of twenty and thirty-one. For the past five years she had been doing well in outpatient psychotherapy: no hospitalizations and no overt psychosis. Her therapy, which initially had been once a week, was now once a month.

She was on vacation, visiting her mother in a distant city, when she called the therapist, obviously disturbed and in the incipient stages of a psychotic episode. Unraveling the story over the phone, the therapist finally ascertained that she had been going through her mother's cedar chest bringing out all kinds of momentos from the past. Finally she had come across a birthday card she had received from her now dead father on her eleventh birthday. He had written "Happy birthday to a good little girl who is doing the dishes on her own birthday." She was being flooded with memories of the deprivation she had experienced as a child, the unreasonable demands that had been placed upon her, and the feelings of loss for her dead father, about whom she still felt quite ambivalent.

The therapist's response was, "Put all those things back and close that cedar chest." The patient complied. When she called back an hour later, she was much less distraught; she now felt in control of the situation and a psychotic decompensation had been averted. In succeeding visits over the years, she did not reopen the cedar chest either literally or figuratively.

*(Lamb, 1982, p. 130)*

## Social Therapy

Clinicians now make practical advice and life adjustment a central focus of treatment for schizophrenic people (Bellack et al., 1989). Although they are still concerned with the removal of symptoms, many direct therapy toward such issues as self-management, problem solving, decision making, and the development of social skills (Wixted, Morrison, & Bellack, 1988). Therapists may also help their clients find work, financial assistance, and proper housing. This kind of intervention has been labeled *social therapy,* or *sociotherapy* (Hogarty et al., 1986, 1974; Meyer, 1984; Fairweather, 1964), and it is now offered in a group therapy format as well as individual therapy format (Wilson, Diamond, & Factor, 1990).

Research suggests that social therapy helps keep patients out of the hospital. Gerard Hogarty and his colleagues (1986, 1974) compared the progress of four groups of schizophrenic patients after their discharge from state hospitals. One group received both antipsychotic medications and social therapy in the community,

while the other groups received medications only, social therapy only, or no treatment of any kind. The researchers' first finding was that patients needed medication in the community to avoid rehospitalization. Over a two-year period, 80 percent of those who did not take medication needed to be hospitalized again, compared to 48 percent of those taking medication. They also found that among the patients on medication, those who also received social therapy adjusted to the community and avoided rehospitalization most successfully. Clearly, social therapy played an important role in their recovery.

## Family Therapy

Between 25 and 40 percent of recovering schizophrenic patients in the community live with their parents, siblings, spouses, and children (Torrey et al., 1988; Bocker, 1984; Lamb & Goertzel, 1977). Such unions create special pressures for both the patients and the family members.

Recovering schizophrenic patients are greatly affected by the behavior and reactions of family members, even if family dysfunctioning was not a factor in the onset of the patients' disorder (Kreisman et al., 1988). It has been found, for example, that released schizophrenic patients whose relatives are emotionally expressive and demanding often have a higher relapse rate than those who return to cooler, more detached relatives (Brown et al., 1972).

Family members, for their part, are often greatly affected by the behavior of a schizophrenic relative living at home. In an enlightening series of interviews with eighty British families that had a schizophrenic family member living at home, investigators found most family members to be greatly disturbed by the social withdrawal of their schizophrenic relative (Creer & Wing, 1974). They found it hard to carry on normally with a schizophrenic relative who conversed minimally with others, performed tasks very slowly, or showed little interest in anything. A number of family members were also disturbed by the schizophrenic person's socially embarrassing behaviors, such as restlessness, pacing, odd posturing, and talking to him- or herself. One relative complained, "In the evening you go into the sitting room and it's in darkness. You turn on the light and there he is just sitting there, staring in front of him."

To address such family issues and enhance the chance of recovery, clinicians now often include family therapy in the treatment of schizophrenia (Goldstein, 1991, 1987, 1981; Berkowitz et al., 1990, 1989, 1981; Wing, 1988; Faloon, 1988; Hemsley, 1987; Anderson et al., 1986; McFarlane, 1983; Vaughn & Leff, 1976). Over the course of treatment, they try to help schizophrenic individuals cope with the pressures of family life, guiding them to make better use of family resources and to avoid problematic interactions with family members. Family therapists also provide family members with guidance, training, practical advice, education about schizophrenia (called psychoeducation), and emotional support and empathy. They try to help the family members become more realistic in their expectations, more tolerant of deviant behavior, less guilt-ridden and confused, and more willing to try new patterns of interaction and communication. Such approaches often succeed in reducing family tensions and reducing relapse rates. They are the principles at work in the following case:

*M*ark was a 32-year-old single man living with his parents. He had a long and stormy history of schizophrenia with many episodes of psychosis, interspersed with occasional brief periods of good functioning. Mark's father was a bright but neurotically tormented man gripped by obsessions and inhibitions in spite of many years of psychoanalysis. Mark's mother appeared weary, detached, and embittered. Both parents felt hopeless about Mark's chances of recovery and resentful that needing to care for him would always plague their lives. They acted as if they were being intentionally punished. It gradually emerged that the father, in fact, was riddled with guilt and self-doubt; he suspected that his wife had been cold and rejecting toward Mark as an infant and that he had failed to intervene, due to his unwillingness to confront his wife and the demands of graduate school that distanced him from home life. He entertained the fantasy that Mark's illness was a punishment for this. Every time Mark did begin to show improvement—both in reduced symptoms and in increased functioning—his parents responded as if it were just a cruel torment designed to raise their hopes and then to plunge them into deeper despair when Mark's condition deteriorated. This pattern was especially apparent when Mark got a job. As a result, at such times, the parents actually became more critical and hostile toward Mark. He would become increasingly defensive and insecure, finally developing paranoid delusions, and usually would be hospitalized in a panicky and agitated state.

All of this became apparent during the psychoeducational sessions. When the pattern was pointed out to the family, they were able to recognize their self-fulfilling prophecy and were motivated to deal with it. As a result, the therapist decided to see the family together. Concrete instances of the pattern and its consequences were explored, and alternative responses by the parents were developed. The therapist encouraged both the parents and Mark to discuss their anxieties and doubts about Mark's progress, rather than to stir up one another's expectations of failure. The therapist had regular individual sessions with Mark as well as the family sessions. As a result, Mark has successfully held a job for an unprecedented 12 months.

*(Heinrichs & Carpenter, 1983, pp. 284–285)*

In addition to family therapy, a number of *family support groups* have been organized to address the needs of the close relatives of schizophrenic people (Wing, 1988). Family members come together with others in the same situation and share their thoughts and emotions. Although research has yet to determine the usefulness of these groups, either to family members or indirectly to their schizophrenic relatives, such approaches are becoming increasingly common as professionals try to address this long-neglected area of need.

## THE COMMUNITY APPROACH

During the 1950s the United States government established a Joint Commission on Mental Illness and Mental Health, part of whose purpose was to study the deplorable conditions prevailing in public mental institutions. In 1960 the commission issued a report, *Action for Mental Health*. Because the isolated state hospitals had failed so miserably to address the needs of chronic mental patients, the commission called for the development of local mental health services and recommended the transfer of care of patients from the state institutions to local hospitals and mental health clinics. As we saw in Chapter 5, President John F. Kennedy put the weight of his office behind these recommendations in 1963, calling for a "bold new approach" to mental illness, and Congress passed the Community Mental Health Act.

According to this act, mental patients were to receive a range of mental health services—including outpatient therapy, inpatient treatment, emergency care, preventive care, and aftercare—right in their communities rather than far from home. Although the act was intended to address a variety of psychological disorders, schizophrenic patients, especially those who had been institutionalized for years, were targeted and affected more than most (Hafner & an der Heiden, 1988). The government was ordering that these patients be released and treated in the community. Other countries around the world put similar community care programs into action shortly after (Torrey, 1988; Hafner & an der Heiden, 1988).

Thus began three decades of *deinstitutionalization,* an exodus of hundreds of thousands of schizophrenic and other chronic mental patients from state institutions into the community (Perris, 1988; Lee & Goodwin, 1987). On a given day in 1955 close to 600,000 patients were living in state institutions; today fewer than 125,000 patients reside there (NIMH, 1985). During this period of deinstitutionalization, clinicians have learned much about how to care for these new community residents, and have clarified that recovering schizophrenic patients can profit greatly from community-based programs. Unfortunately, as we shall see in more detail later, the quality and funding of community care for schizophrenic patients have been grossly inadequate throughout the United States, leading to a "revolving door" syndrome in which patients are repeatedly released to the community, readmitted to an institution within months, released again, readmitted yet again, and so on.

# Effective Community Care

Recovering schizophrenic patients living in the community need medication, psychotherapy, help in handling daily pressures and responsibilities, guidance in making decisions, training in social skills, residential supervision, and vocational counseling and training. According to research, patients whose communities systematically address these needs make greater progress than patients living in other communities. One study compared the one-year progress of thirty schizophrenic patients whose community in Vancouver, British Columbia, offered outstanding community services with that of thirty matched subjects in a community in Portland, Oregon, that offered fewer services (Beiser et al., 1985). The Vancouver patients were found to have fewer hospital readmissions and a higher employment rate and to report a greater sense of general well-being than the Portland group. Some of the key elements in effective community care programs are coordination of patient services by a community mental health center, short-term hospitalization, partial hospitalization, halfway houses, and occupational training.

**Coordinated Services** The Joint Commission on Mental Illness and Mental Health proposed that the cornerstone for community care should be a *community mental health center,* a treatment facility that would provide medication, psychotherapy, and inpatient emergency care to severely disturbed people. In addition, the community mental health center was to coordinate the patient services offered by other community agencies. Each center was expected to serve a designated "catchment area," a geographic area with a population of 50,000 to 200,000 people.

When community mental health centers do in fact place a high priority on the treatment of schizophrenic patients, and do develop and coordinate a range of community services for them, the patients often make steady and significant progress (Beiser et al., 1985). Among the most effective centers in the United States are those

serving Prairie View, Kansas; Dane County, Wisconsin; Weber County, Utah; Range, Minnesota; and Sacramento, California.

**Short-term Hospitalization** As Rosenhan's 1972 study of pseudopatients confirmed (see p. 62), institutional life may lead patients to feel powerless, bored, and even doomed by their diagnostic labels. At the same time, as the Group for the Advancement of Psychiatry (1970–1971) has pointed out, schizophrenic patients can profit greatly from the routine diagnostic evaluation, close observation, supervision, and precise monitoring of medication that are uniquely available in hospitals.

Clinicians have grappled with the problem of providing the positive features of hospitalization while minimizing its negative effects. The solution developed by the community mental health movement has been to provide patients who seem to need hospitalization with a short-term program of inpatient treatment that lasts a few weeks, rather than months or years, followed by a program of posthospitalization care and treatment out in the community, called *aftercare* (Lamb, 1988). Countries throughout the world now favor this policy of short-term hospitalization (Hafner & an der Heiden, 1988).

When people develop schizophrenic symptoms, today's clinicians first try to treat them on an outpatient basis, usually administering antipsychotic medication and perhaps psychotherapy. If these interventions prove inadequate, a short-term hospitalization may be tried (Davis et al., 1988). As soon as stabilization has been achieved, the patients are released to the community for aftercare. Short-term hospitalization of this kind usually leads to a greater reduction of symptoms and a lower rehospitalization rate than extended institutional care (Caton, 1982; Herz et al., 1977, 1975).

**Partial Hospitalization** For individuals whose needs fall somewhere between full hospitalization and outpatient therapy sessions, some communities offer partial hospitalization at facilities called *day centers* or *day hospitals* (Hoge et al., 1988). These programs originated in Moscow in 1933 when a shortage of hospital beds necessitated the premature release of many mental patients. Day hospitals were formed to provide these patients with hospital-type care during the day, followed by a return home for the night. The concept was later accepted in Canada and England and still later was adopted by community treatment programs in the United States. Today's day centers provide daily activities and specific treatment programs for patients, and social rehabilitation programs to help them improve their social skills.

Several studies suggest that recovering schizophrenic patients in day centers often do better than those in such programs as extended hospitalization and traditional outpatient therapy. Day center patients are more likely to stay out of the hospital, find and keep a job, and show improvements in self-esteem, independence, and family relationships over a period of one or more years (Herz et al., 1971; Meltzoff & Blumenthal, 1966). Degree of success may depend on the quality and type of care given at particular day centers and on the availability of other community programs, such as halfway houses and occupational training (Creed, Black, & Anthony, 1989).

**Halfway Houses** Halfway houses are residences for people who do not require hospitalization but cannot live either alone or with their families. These residences typically shelter between one and two dozen people, often in a large house located in an area of the community where housing is inexpensive. Although outside professionals, such as a psychologist, may be available to residents, the live-in staff usually consists of *paraprofessionals* — lay people who have received some training in providing emotional support and practical guidance about matters of daily living. Various patient populations reside in halfway houses; schizophrenic patients are among the most common.

The atmosphere of most halfway houses is supportive. The residents interact with one another, discussing their day-to-day problems and trying to help each other adjust to life in the community. The houses are usually organized around a milieu therapy philosophy: residents are encouraged to set up their own rules and governing mechanisms, to be responsible and independent, and to contribute to the welfare of the halfway house by doing chores, helping other residents, and behaving properly.

In the following passage, a woman describes how living in a halfway house contributed to her recovery from schizophrenia. She entered the house on a court order, after ten hospitalizations over a twelve-year period.

*The halfway house changed my life. First of all, I discov-*ered that some of the staff members had once been clients in the program! That one single fact offered me hope. For the first time, I saw proof that a program could help someone, that it was possible to regain control over one's life and become independent. The house was democratically run; all residents had one vote and the staff members, outnumbered 5 to 22, could not make rules or even discharge a client from the program without majority sentiment. There was a house bill of rights that was strictly observed by all. We helped one another and gave support. When residents were in a crisis, no staff member hustled them off or in-creased their medication to calm them down. Residents could cry, be comforted and hugged until a solution could be found, or until they accepted that it was okay to feel bad. Even anger was an acceptable feeling that did not have to be feared, but could be expressed and turned into constructive energy. If you disliked some aspect of the program or the behavior of a staff member, you could change things rather than passively accept what was happening. Choices were real, and failure and success were accepted equally. Although I was incredibly suspicious, I could find little about which to be "paranoid." I could read my file at any time. All problems were discussed at house meetings so nothing was kept secret. Bit by bit, my distrust faltered and the fears lessened. I slept better and made friends. I was treated with respect and respected others, so gradually I began to respect myself. My life became more manageable as I learned the "tools" I needed. I learned about stress, how to recognize symptoms of stress in my life, and how to control or cope with the stressors. Other residents and staff members who had hallucinated for years and now were able to control their hallucinations shared with me some of the techniques that had worked for them. Things like diet, bioenergetic "grounding," and interpersonal relationships became a few of my tools.

*(Lovejoy, 1982, pp. 605–609)*

Research indicates that halfway houses often help recovering schizophrenics adjust to community life (Simpson, Hyde, & Faragher, 1989; Canton, 1975). One of the most effective programs was set up in the 1960s by a team of clinicians headed by George Fairweather (1969). A group of hospitalized schizophrenic patients were discharged together to a "lodge," actually a converted motel. There they were largely responsible for their own lives, including their finances, the buying and preparing of food, and the dispensing of medication. As a group, they operated an independent business that offered custodial services, painting, hauling, and gardening to the community.

During its three-year existence the lodge was a great success. The business turned a total profit of $52,000 and the lodge residents shared these earnings as wages in accordance with each individual's work contribution. New patients were eventually admitted as the program expanded and the lodge was relocated to two houses in a middle-class neighborhood.

The progress of lodge residents was compared with that of similar individuals who had gone to live in community boardinghouses or apartments after leaving the hospital. During their three years at the lodge and even after they left it, the residents were better integrated into the community and less likely to be rehospitalized (see Figure 16-2). Moreover, by the time that the lodge closed, almost 40 percent of its residents had established

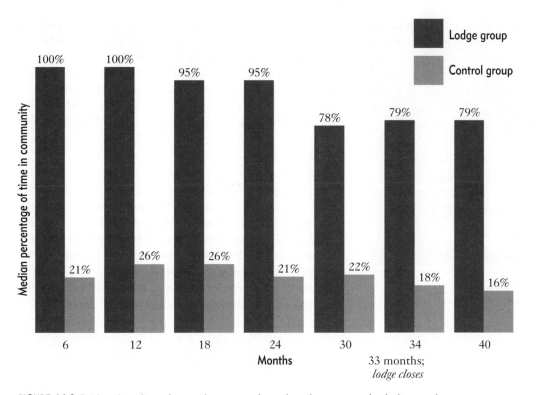

**FIGURE 16-2** Schizophrenic patients who were released to the community lodge established by George Fairweather and his associates adjusted better than schizophrenic people who were released directly to a boardinghouse or an apartment, remained in the community longer, and avoided rehospitalization more successfully, and they continued this trend even after the lodge closed. *(Adapted from Fairweather et al., 1969.)*

full-time employment, compared with only 3 percent of the control group.

Few halfway house programs have been as extensive or well evaluated as Fairweather's. Even houses with less comprehensive programs, however, can help recovering schizophrenic persons avoid rehospitalization and remain in the community. The number of halfway houses has grown steadily throughout the United States, from 2 in 1950 to more than 1,000 today.

**Occupational Training** Regular employment enables people to support themselves, exercise independence, gain self-respect, and learn to work with others. It also helps bring companionship and order to a person's daily life. For these reasons, occupational training and placement are important aspects of community treatment for schizophrenic people. Many community mental health centers work with vocational rehabilitation agencies to place clients in appropriate training programs.

Many people recovering from schizophrenia begin their occupational training in a *sheltered workshop* — a

protected and supervised workplace for employees who are not ready for competitive or complicated jobs. The workshop tries to establish a typical work environment: products such as toys, home furnishings, or simple appliances are manufactured and later sold, workers are paid according to performance, and all are expected to be at work regularly and on time. For some the sheltered workshop becomes a permanent workplace. For others it is an important step toward better-paying and more complex outside employment or a return to their previous job or its equivalent.

Unfortunately, in the United States vocational rehabilitation is not consistently available to people with schizophrenia. The Department of Labor and its programs focus more on other needy groups, such as minority groups, lower socioeconomic groups, and the poorly educated. Sheltered workshop opportunities are more available to long-term mental patients in Sweden, England, the Netherlands, and Russia, among other countries, than they are in the United States (Black, 1977).

Sheltered workshops, such as the one at New York City's Fountain House, provide job training and jobs and teach independence, self-respect, and social skills. Unfortunately, there is a severe shortage of such workshops for people with schizophrenia.

## Inadequacies in Community Treatment

The community mental health movement has had a major impact on the treatment of mental disorders. In 1955 only 23 percent of all patients in treatment were receiving outpatient care in the United States. As we saw in Chapter 1, approximately 74 percent of all treated patients receive outpatient services today. The shift to community care for schizophrenic individuals accounts for much of this overall change (Rosenstein et al., 1989).

As we have observed, effective community programs clearly can help schizophrenic patients recover. Moreover, in comparison with institutionalized patients, patients who are treated by effective community programs report that they are happier and more satisfied with their lives (Test & Stein, 1978). Unfortunately, however, less than half of all schizophrenic persons receive appropriate community mental health services (Von Korft et al., 1985). Two factors are primarily responsible: *poor coordination of services* and *shortage of services.*

**Poor Coordination of Services**   Often there is no communication between the various agencies in a community and no overall strategy dictating the care that a schizophrenic person receives from them. The advice that a patient receives in a day center may differ from that dispensed at the community mental health center; simi-

larly, there could be an opening at a nearby halfway house and the therapist at the community mental health center might not even know about it.

This problem is exemplified by one study's finding that out of sixty-five schizophrenic persons living in a California residential facility, only 51 percent attended a social rehabilitation program located a block away (Lamb, 1979). Moreover, when the rehabilitation program was moved to a more distant location, only 29 percent made use of a van that was available to take them to the program. Although some patients themselves decide not to use available community services, many community agencies are to blame for the failure to use services. Their systems for contacting patients and getting them involved in available programs may simply be inadequate (Brown, 1980; McNees, et al., 1977).

Poor communication between state hospitals and the state's various community mental health centers is also a source of inefficiency and poor mental health care (McShane & Redoutey, 1987). Often community agencies are not informed when patients are discharged from the hospital. This problem had its beginning in the early days of the community mental health movement, when hospitals were forced to discharge patients before many of the community mental health centers were open and ready to receive them. The hospitals developed habits of independence that have continued to the present day. In 1969 a full third of the schizophrenic patients discharged from state hospitals were never even referred to an outpatient care program. Although the situation is better today, the problem still exists in many communities (Goldman et al., 1980).

**Shortage of Services**   The number of community programs in existence for schizophrenic people falls decidedly short of the number needed. Although there are now close to 800 community mental health centers in the United States the Joint Commission on Mental Illness and Mental Health had estimated that nearly three times that many would be necessary to serve communities throughout the nation properly. There is also a severe shortage of halfway houses and sheltered workshops.

Perhaps even more disturbing, most of the community mental health centers that do exist have failed to provide adequate and coordinated services for the schizophrenic people they do purport to treat. Although the primary function of community mental health centers was to "concentrate on providing psychiatric treatment for acute mental illness cases and for patients who can be helped either short of admission to a mental hospital or following discharge," most centers have given little time, attention, or financial priority to these patients over the past three decades. Increasingly the larger part of the centers' resources has been devoted to providing outpatient psychotherapy, education, and prevention services for people with less dysfunctional problems, such as anxiety and depressive disorders or problems in social adjustment. For the past fifteen years only about 10 percent of the patients treated by community mental health centers have been schizophrenic (Rosenstein 1990, 1989; Torrey, 1988). Several factors appear to be responsible.

First, most mental health professionals simply prefer to work with people whose problems are less severe than schizophrenia (Kirk & Therrien, 1975; Hogarty, 1971). Providing sociotherapy and related services for recovering schizophrenic patients means spending a great deal of time on such issues as daily schedules and self-care. From a professional standpoint, this tends to be less interesting than therapy for the anxious and depressed. Moreover, the progress of schizophrenic patients is usually slower and more frustrating than that of less disturbed patients.

Second, community residents often object to the presence of community programs for recovering schizophrenic patients in their neighborhoods (NIMH, 1974), often going so far as to picket, protest, and even vandalize halfway houses, day centers, and other community facilities. Community resistance is one of the major problems facing halfway houses and similar programs today.

But perhaps the primary reason for shortages and inadequacies in community care for schizophrenia is economic. On the one hand, more public funds are allocated for people with mental disorders now than in the past. In 1963 a total of $1 billion was spent in this area, whereas today more than $17 billion is spent on people with mental disorders, 53 percent of it supplied by state governments, 38 percent by the federal government, and 9 percent by local governments (Torrey, 1988). On the other hand, little of this new money is going to community treatment programs for the severely disturbed. The states continue to direct most of their money into staff salaries at state hospitals, despite the fact that the daily census of these hospitals has decreased more than 80 percent since 1963 (NASMHP, 1987). Indeed, in many states the number of staff members at state hospitals has actually increased since the 1960s (Torrey, 1988). The federal government directs its aid into monthly subsistence payments for the severely disturbed (supplemental security income, or SSI, and social security disability income, or SSDI), subsidies for the mentally disturbed residing in nursing homes and in general hospitals (Medicaid and Medicare), and subsidies to community mental health centers (which, as we know, direct most of their services to people who are less disturbed). Thus much of the financial burden of providing community treatment for the severely disturbed falls on the local governments, whose resources are simply too limited to meet the challenge effectively.

Clearly it is in the state governments' best financial interest to keep moving schizophrenic patients away from state hospitals (where the states bear most of the expense) and out into the community (where the states bear only a portion of the cost). Critics claim that this stark financial reality provides state officials and state hospital administrators with a powerful incentive to overlook the shortages and inadequacies of community programs (see Box 16-2).

**Consequences of Inadequate Community Treatment** What happens to schizophrenic patients whose communities do not provide necessary services and whose families cannot afford private treatment? After a short time in a state hospital, many are discharged prematurely, often without benefit of adequate follow-up treatment (Torrey et al., 1988; Pepper & Ryglewicz, 1982; Lamb & Goertzel, 1977). Between 25 and 40 percent of all schizophrenic patients return to their families, under

E. Fuller Torrey has spent the past three decades pointing out the failures of deinstitutionalization and lobbying for greater resources and better treatment facilities for schizophrenic people.

whose care many receive medication, perhaps some emotional and financial support, but little else in the way of treatment. Another 5 to 11 percent leave the state hospital to enter an alternative institution such as a nursing home or rest home. Here they typically receive little more than custodial care and medication (Smyer, 1989; Torrey, 1988; Torrey et al., 1988). An additional 21 to 35 percent are placed in single-room-occupancy hotels or in privately run boarding homes, large rooming houses, or converted hotels typically found in run-down inner-city neighborhoods (Torrey et al., 1988). Although some boarding homes are legitimate "bed-and-care" facilities, providing meals, medication reminders, and a certain amount of staff supervision, most fail to offer even these minimal services. Rather, the patient lives in a small room under conditions that are substandard and unsafe. At times, a media report such as the following newspaper account focuses on the abominable conditions in such dwellings; usually they receive no public attention.

> Hundreds of mentally ill patients throughout Dade County are being packed into aging hotels and homes that are little better than slums, according to health officials who say the appalling living conditions virtually ensure patients will sink deeper into insanity.
>
> Florida's policy of emptying its mental institutions, a paucity of appropriate "halfway houses," and lax inspections of existing homes have left many mentally ill without the care that might ease them back into normal life.
>
> It also has left them without protection. Released from hospitals into overburdened halfway houses, the indigent patients eventually are shunted to landlords, some of whom jam them, perhaps three to a room, into decaying and dangerous buildings and then collect their welfare payments as rent.

---

## BOX 16-2

# Forsaking the Mentally Ill

**O**liver Sacks is a neurologist whose beautifully written books and articles about mental patients have gained him considerable fame as a writer. In 1990 his book *Awakenings*, which told about the joys and frustrations of caring for patients in a state hospital, was made into a successful movie. Ironically, about the same time that *Awakenings* was being seen and applauded by millions of people, Sacks's job at Bronx Psychiatric Center, where he had worked for twenty-five years, was eliminated, part of New York State's continuing policy of reducing institutional treatment for severely disturbed mental patients. Sacks discussed his feelings about deinstitutionalization in an editorial published in *The New York Times* on February 13, 1991:

There will be substantial layoffs this month of physicians, nurses, therapists, treatment aides and others at state hospitals throughout New York State. Some 1,200 jobs, including my own, will be eliminated for budgetary reasons.

Apart from the hardship this will cause, I am deeply concerned, even fearful, for our patients. As a neurologist who has worked since 1966 at Bronx Psychiatric Center, I daily encounter the reality of how disabled many of these patients are and how little their needs could be met in any setting but a residential one.

When deinstitutionalization was first undertaken in the 1960s, it seemed a noble aim. Coupled with the use of such "wonder drugs" as Thorazine, it was perceived as a humane way of returning patients to their communities while cutting the costs of their treatment.

In practice, deinstitutionalization did not work. The vast majority of the patients discharged from state hospitals were not looked after by the community, were not adequately treated by outpatient facilities and rapidly drifted into homelessness, destitution, misery and sometimes death. Indeed, the late Seymour Kaplan, the psychiatrist who pioneered deinstitutionaliza-

tion in New York State, often said later that it was the gravest error he had ever made.

Under ideal conditions, that is, in communities where there may be a very exceptional communal sense of responsibility, deinstitutionalization can work. But in a large, bustling, indifferent city, such as New York, it has no chance of success.

There is indeed a "hard core"— perhaps 25,000 in New York State alone— of very disabled patients who have to live in chronic hospitals. Most are deeply psychotic and lacking in social skills; many in addition have medical, physical and neurological problems: retardation, autism, epilepsy, AIDS, Alzheimer's.

In addition to these permanently ill people, there are others, another 25,000, who do very well outside, for years at a time, with adequate support and crisis facilities and medication— but then relapse, become deeply psychotic again and have to be readmitted, often forcibly, to the hospital. City and university hospitals have limited capacity and can admit psychiatric patients for only short periods. The re-

The worst buildings, found scattered throughout Little Havana and the dying hotel district in South Miami Beach, contain the stuff of nightmares. Piles of trash and feces litter the floors. Half-naked men wander purposelessly through hallways, and doors swing open into hot and fetid rooms where others, gazing vacantly at the ceiling, lie neglected on dirty cots.

In some cases, the state Department of Health and Rehabilitative Services places patients in substandard homes. HRS officials concede there is a problem, but say they are doing the best they can in an overloaded and underfunded system.

In one instance, HRS released patients to a Little Havana house run by a landlord who three years earlier lost his state license to operate a group home because of its life-threatening conditions.

The landlord, Ulpaiano Talavera, didn't apply for a license for his latest home at 218 SW Eighth Ave. Instead, he used plywood sheets to divide the coral rock house into 12-foot by 14-foot boxes and then told HRS workers he would take in the mentally ill.

Each of the boxes, strung along trash-strewn passageways in the two-story house, contains a narrow bed, a fan and a chest of drawers. Hot meal containers and plastic forks fill waste bins. Most of the boxes also contained people like Vallant Garez, a timid 55-year-old whose bed sores attest to hours spent in bed, staring at a paint-chipped wall a foot from his pillow.

*(Miami Herald, August 10, 1984)*

Few attempts are made to engage such boarding home residents in therapeutic activities, and they have few opportunities for vocational rehabilitation, sheltered work, or job placement. Most survive on government disability payments and spend their days wandering through neighborhood streets. Their sad plight is open

lapsed schizophrenic, however, needs months to restabilize, and only state hospitals can provide such long-term care.

Nothing has been sadder than the steady deterioration of the state hospital system since the mid-1970's. The hospitals are not only underpopulated but dirty and dilapidated. They have come to labor more and more heavily under the costly burden of a huge administrative, nonmedical machinery. There has not been a medically qualified director of the Bronx Psychiatric Center, for example, for a decade; the present administration never visits the wards, has no experience, no idea, of the needs and realities of medical care.

And yet, precisely at this juncture, further cuts are being made. Massive lay-offs have been announced, not only in the huge, bureaucratic machinery, which is the real drain on state resources, but among the few physicians, therapists, and treatment aides left. With this, the state hospitals will lose their last care-giving capacity and become little more than warehouses for the sick.

Outpatient clinics, the last resource for deinstitutionalized patients, are also being closed all over the country. For example, the huge crisis center at Mt. Zion Hospital in San Francisco, which looks after 10,000 patients a year, is scheduled to close next month. All psychiatric care in the U.S. is being dangerously cut back now.

There are 80,000 desperately ill and wretched people on our streets, not only homeless and endangered, and perhaps dangerous to others, but often in a nightmare of their own psychoses. These people need institutional care. We must not reduce the state hospitals to shadows of themselves, but restore and adapt them into streamlined, economically efficient strongholds of care. We need to restructure our state hospitals, not close them.

to inspection in inner cities throughout the nation (Lamb et al., 1976). It is often said that these schizophrenic patients are now being dumped and warehoused in the community, just as they were once warehoused in institutions. Not surprisingly, most of them go through repeated cycles of hospitalization, discharge, and readmission—the "revolving door" syndrome. Although the daily census of patients in state hospitals has fallen by 80 percent since 1963, the number of annual hospital admissions has actually increased by 80 percent, from 178,000 to more than 326,000 (Rosenstein et al., 1990). The majority of these admissions are in fact readmissions. Approximately half of the mental patients released from state hospitals are rehospitalized within a year of discharge.

Finally, and perhaps saddest of all, a great number of released schizophrenic patients have become homeless (Torrey et al., 1988). During the past twenty years, cities throughout the United States have undertaken redevelopment and gentrification programs designed to revitalize inner-city life by replacing low-income housing and single-room-occupancy hotels with office buildings, shopping centers, convention centers, and expensive condominiums and hotels. As a result, more than a million single-room units have disappeared nationwide since 1970, almost half of the previous total (Knesper, Wheeler, & Pagnucco, 1984). New York City alone has lost 110,000, or 87 percent, of its low-rent single-room housing. In the process schizophrenic people have been turned out into the streets (see Figure 16-3). They take refuge in hallways, subways, and vacant buildings, and sleep on park benches or heating grates. The "lucky" ones find beds in public shelters. Certainly deinstitutionalization and the community mental health movement have failed these people.

There are between 350,000 and 1 million street people in the United States. At least one-third of them have a severe mental disorder, most commonly schizophrenia (Gelberg, Linn, & Leake, 1988; Conference of Mayors, 1986; Torrey et al., 1985; Arce et al., 1983; Bassuk et al., 1984). One study followed a sample of 132 patients after their release from the Central Ohio Psychiatric Hospital in 1985. Over a third of the patients became homeless within six months of their release—this in a state whose mental health system has been ranked among the best in the country (Belcher, 1988). Perhaps the ultimate irony for such individuals is described by E. Fuller Torrey, one of the clinical field's leading figures in the treatment of schizophrenia:

During the 1960s and 1970s, many buildings at Manhattan State Hospital were closed as patients were deinstitution-

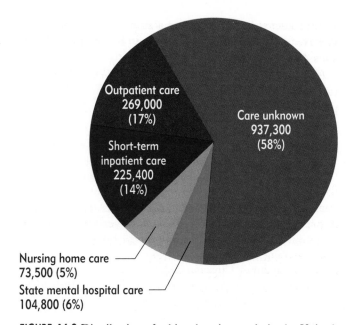

**FIGURE 16-3** Distribution of schizophrenic people in the United States. When the National Institute of Mental Health sought to ascertain the care given to schizophrenic people throughout the United States in 1986, it was unable to find most of them. Only 42 percent of schizophrenic people were receiving care. *(Adapted from Torrey, 1988, p. 35; NIMH, 1986.)*

alized. As the number of homeless individuals in the city climbed rapidly, however, one of these buildings was reopened as a men's shelter, operated on a city contract by the Volunteers of America. Some of the same mentally ill individuals who once used that building as hospitalized patients now use it as shelter residents. The difference is that now there are no nurses, no doctors, no medication, and no treatment.

*(Torrey, 1988, p. 10)*

## The Promise of Community Treatment

Despite these very serious problems, the demonstrated success and potential of proper community care for people recovering from schizophrenia continue to capture the interest of both clinicians and many government officials, who press for further development of community services. In 1977 a program called the Community Support Program (CSP) was initiated by the National Institute of Mental Health to provide local communities and states with funds to develop wide-ranging and coordinated support systems for chronic and severely disturbed mental patients. This has now grown into a $15-million-a-year program and is beginning to help some states make significant progress in planning proper services for schizophrenic and other severely disturbed persons (Torrey, 1988).

Another important development has been the formation of two national interest groups that are successfully promoting community treatment for schizophrenic and other chronic patients (Rosenstein et al., 1989). One, the National Alliance for the Mentally Ill, began in 1979 with 300 members and has expanded to include more than 60,000 members in 900 chapters. Comprising family members of people with severe mental disorders (particularly schizophrenia, bipolar disorders, and major depression), this group has become a powerful lobbying force in many state legislatures, has established inspection procedures for state hospitals, and has pressured community mental health centers to provide treatment for schizophrenic persons. The other interest group is the National Mental Health Consumers Association, comprising patients who lobby for better services, living conditions, and job opportunities and who fight the stigmatization often associated with severe mental dysfunctioning (Rogers & Centifanti, 1988).

Finally, community care has also become the major form of treatment for recovering schizophrenic patients in countries throughout the world (Perris, 1988; Madianos & Economou, 1988). Some have in fact tried to learn from the problems of deinstitutionalization in the United States. Sweden, for example, has gradually dismantled its public mental hospitals, taking care to have community resources available before releasing chronic hospitalized patients and to give patients adequate preparation for release (Perris, 1988). By following this more deliberate strategy, Sweden has steadily reduced the patient census in its public mental hospitals without disproportionately increasing the numbers of patients readmitted to hospitals, living in nursing homes, or wandering the streets. Clearly, both in the United States and abroad, effective, wide-ranging, and coordinated community treatment is viewed as an important part of the solution to the problem of schizophrenia.

# TREATMENTS FOR SCHIZOPHRENIA: THE STATE OF THE FIELD

After years of frustration and failure in treating schizophrenia, clinicians now have an arsenal of weapons with which to fight it — medication, institutional programs,

psychotherapy, and community programs. These approaches are usually combined in ways that are tailored to the needs of the individual (Meyer, 1984).

Today, at the first sign of schizophrenic symptoms, a person is usually given treatment on an outpatient basis, starting with antipsychotic drugs, perhaps accompanied by psychotherapy and enrollment in appropriate community programs (Davis et al., 1988). Although this outpatient approach is helpful to many patients, short-term hospitalization may be necessary for others (Davis et al., 1988; Naka, 1985). At the hospital, psychiatrists try to stabilize patients on medication and then release them to the community, where ideally they can participate in community programs, live in a supportive environment, pursue psychotherapy, and continue on medication as long as necessary.

This combined approach has greatly improved a schizophrenic person's chances of returning to functional living. When Kraepelin first described schizophrenia at the turn of the century, he estimated that only 13 percent of patients with this disorder improved and that the improvements were usually temporary. Today, even with the current shortages and inadequacies in community programs, many more schizophrenic people show improvement. Somewhere between 4 and 30 percent are believed to recover completely and permanently. Another 30 percent return to relatively independent lives, although their occupational and social functioning may continue to fall short of earlier levels. And still another 30 percent remain out of the hospital most of the time and a number are able to maintain some level of employment, although they need considerable help in caring for themselves. Sadly, however, between 10 and 30 percent continue to require hospitalization for much of their lives (Wing, 1988; Lehmann, 1980; Hollister, 1977; Tsuang, Woolson, & Fleming, 1979; Bland, Parker, & Orn, 1976).

Certainly the clinical field has advanced considerably in the treatment of schizophrenia. On the other hand, the field has far to go in this area of treatment. It is intolerable that the majority of schizophrenic people receive few or none of the effective community interventions that have been developed over the past three decades, worse still that tens of thousands have become homeless vagrants deserted by society. Although many factors have contributed to this state of affairs, neglect by clinical practitioners has certainly played a big role. It is now the mandate of these professionals, prodded in part by the newly developed interest groups, to address the needs of all schizophrenic people by more systematically applying the treatment interventions and insights that have emerged in recent years.

# SUMMARY

For years, efforts to treat schizophrenia brought only frustration. The disorder is still difficult to treat, but today's therapies are more successful than those of the past.

For more than half of this century, the main treatment for schizophrenia was *institutionalization* and custodial care. Schizophrenic patients, because they failed to respond to traditional therapies, were usually placed in institutions, typically in the back wards of public institutions where the primary goal was to restrain them. They rarely saw therapists. Most were neglected, and many were abused. Many patients not only failed to improve under these conditions but developed additional symptoms as a result of institutionalization itself.

Between 1845 and 1955, the number of state hospitals and mental patients rose steadily while the quality of care declined. Subsequently, following humanistic and behavioral principles, clinicians developed two in-hospital interventions—*milieu therapy* and the *token economy program*—that finally offered some help to schizophrenic and other patients who had been institutionalized for years. These approaches were particularly helpful in addressing the personal-care and self-image problems brought about by schizophrenia and by institutionalization. They were soon adopted by many institutions and are now standard features of institutional care.

The discovery of antipsychotic drugs in the 1950s revolutionized the treatment of schizophrenia. In many cases, these drugs, also called *neuroleptic drugs,* helped to eliminate the symptoms of schizophrenia. Today they are almost always a part of treatment. Research suggests that antipsychotic drugs are the single most effective intervention for schizophrenic patients during hospitalization. Patients may experience a return of symptoms, however, if they stop taking the drugs too soon.

Recent evidence indicates that antipsychotic drugs alleviate the so-called positive symptoms of schizophrenia more than the negative ones. Many theorists believe that the drugs operate by reducing excessive dopamine activity in the brains of schizophrenic persons. Unfortunately, antipsychotic drugs can also produce dramatic, unwanted effects. The most visible are movement abnormalities, called *extrapyramidal effects,* that affect appearance and functioning. Effects such as *Parkinsonian symptoms, dystonia,* and *akathisia* respond in most cases to anti-Parkinsonian drugs, enabling individuals to continue taking antipsychotic drugs. *Tardive dyskinesia,* however, considered the most dangerous effect of antipsychotic drugs, is often difficult—at times impossible—to eliminate, and early detection is elusive because of its similarities to some of the symptoms of schizophrenia.

Before the discovery of antipsychotic drugs, psychotherapy was of little help in treating schizophrenia. Now, however, psychotherapy is often employed successfully in conjunction with antipsychotic drugs, and research suggests that it can be very useful over the course of the disorder. The most helpful forms of psychotherapy include insight therapy, social therapy, and family therapy.

Recently, a *community approach* has been applied to the treatment of schizophrenia. A policy of *deinstitutionalization* has brought about a mass exodus of hundreds of thousands of schizophrenic and other chronic mental patients from state institutions into the community, leading to an urgent need for community service programs designed to help integrate them back into society.

Recovering schizophrenic patients living in the community need medication, psychotherapy, help in handling daily pressures and responsibilities, guidance in making decisions, social skills training, residential supervision, and vocational counseling and training. Among the key elements of effective community care programs are coordination of patient services by a *community mental health center, short-term hospitalization* (followed by *aftercare*), *day centers, halfway houses,* and *occupational training.*

The community mental health movement has had a major impact on the treatment of mental disorders. Unfortunately, the quality of and funding for community care for these patients has been grossly inadequate throughout the United States, resulting in a "revolving door" syndrome in which patients who have been released to the community are readmitted to an institution within months, released again, readmitted yet again, and so on. Fewer than half of all schizophrenic persons receive effective community mental health services. Two factors are primarily responsible for this state of affairs: poor coordination of services and shortage of services.

One result of the inadequacy of community treatment is that a great number of released schizophrenic patients have become homeless. At least one-third of the street people in the United States suffer from a severe mental disorder, most commonly schizophrenia.

Despite very serious problems, the success and potential of proper community care for recovering schizophrenics continue to capture the interest of both clinicians and government officials. One major development in this area has been the formation of *national interest groups* that are successfully promoting community treatment for schizophrenic and other chronic patients. Moreover, community care has become the major form of treatment for recovery schizophrenic people in countries throughout the world.

# TOPIC OVERVIEW

# CHAPTER *17*

# PERSONALITY DISORDERS

*Theodore Millon and George S. Everly, Jr.*

*(Boxes 17-2 and 17-3 were written by Professor Comer.)*

The term "personality" refers to the unique pattern of behavior, perception, and emotion displayed by each individual. Usually, a personality is unified, and integrated; it gives consistency to the way the person acts at different times, in different situations, and with different people. The enduring consistencies with which we react to and act upon our surroundings — often called our *personality traits* — are viewed by many theorists as intrinsic characteristics that each of us brings to the situations we confront in life.

According to DSM-III-R, people with *personality disorders* display inflexible and maladaptive personality traits that impair their social or occupational functioning or cause them intense distress. Because these disorders involve the entire personality, they typically have a pervasive impact on the person's thoughts and behavior. The disorders usually develop by adolescence and continue through adulthood, though they sometimes become less apparent as old age approaches (APA, 1987). One survey has concluded that nearly 10 percent of the general adult population and over one-half of those in treatment may suffer from one of the personality disorders (Merikangas & Weissman, 1986).

By including personality disorders in the clinical field's classification system, the formulators of DSM-III-R have acknowledged that personality may indeed play an important role in abnormal behavior (see Box 17-1). By requiring clinicians

━━━━━━━━━━━━━━━ BOX 17-1 ━━━━━━━━━━━━━━━

# Personality Disorder: A Legitimate Category

Although clinicians have increasingly embraced the category of personality disorder since it was first introduced, not everyone is comfortable with the notion. Some take issue with the assumption that human beings have stable personality traits, and they point to research indicating that behavior is often greatly influenced by immediate situational factors. We agree that situational pressures influence behavior and should be recognized and studied, but not at the expense of personality. Research also reveals that people's actions and perceptions are consistent across many spheres of their life, and it seems to us that such consistencies figure at least as prominently in behavior as situational factors do. Moreover, clinicians repeatedly report seeing clients whose psychological dysfunctioning is really best viewed as a maladaptive orientation toward the world rather than as a set of specific symptoms. The broad personality dimensions of their problems simply should not be ignored.

Another concern in regard to the DSM-III-R category of personality disorder is that normal personality traits may be confused too readily with abnormal ones and wrongly diagnosed as pathological. Clinicians cannot really identify a point at which normal patterns of personality become so inflexible, maladaptive, and distressful that they constitute a disorder; the boundaries between normal and abnormal personality traits *are* imprecise. Hence, this is an appropriate concern. However, we hold that it argues for increased research to help clinicians better identify, distinguish, and understand personality disorders, not for abolition of the category.

In the meantime, it is important that students and others avoid the trap of overapplying this category to themselves or to the people they know. Indeed, it is all too easy to catch glimpses of oneself or of one's acquaintances in the descriptions of the various personality disorders. In the vast majority of cases, such interpretations are unwarranted. We all display personality traits; that is part of being human. And many of these traits inevitably resemble those that are characteristic of personality disorders. Only rarely are they so inflexible, maladaptive, and distressful that they can be considered examples of the disorders we describe within this chapter.

━━━━━━━━━━━━━━━━━━━━━━━━━━━━━━━━━━━━━━

to search for evidence of a personality disorder in each diagnostic assessment, they have made an even stronger statement about the possible role of personality in abnormal behavior.

As we saw in Chapter 4, DSM-III-R distinguishes two kinds of mental disorders—Axis I disorders, the many vivid and discrete psychological problems that have been examined thus far in this book, and Axis II disorders, the longer-standing forms of dysfunctioning, primarily personality disorders, that usually begin in childhood and persist in stable form into adulthood. According to DSM-III-R's multiaxial assessment procedure, whenever clinicians decide that a person qualifies for an Axis I diagnosis, such as generalized anxiety disorder or major depression, they must also determine whether the person's problem is accompanied by a longer-standing personality disorder in Axis II. If so, the person receives a diagnosis of a personality disorder right along with the Axis I diagnosis. In short, symptoms are not viewed as isolated forms of aberrant behavior in DSM-III-R, at least not until the broader context of the client's personality is first taken into consideration.

We would go even further and suggest that most Axis I disorders are pathological extensions of personality disorders and that personality disorders themselves should be viewed as extremes of normal personality traits (Libb et al., 1990; Hogg et al., 1990). We believe that most behavior—normal and abnormal—is ultimately anchored in the personality, and that personality patterns are the best single predictors of (1) mental disorders of various kinds, (2) responsiveness to psychotherapy and drug therapy, and (3) the overall course of any mental disorder. The notion that personality is central to functioning in these ways has been referred to as the principle of *personologic primacy* (Everly, 1987).

## MODELS OF PERSONALITY DISORDERS

DSM-III-R recognizes eleven formal personality disorders and groups them in three major clusters. Odd or eccentric qualities characterize the *Cluster A personal-*

*ity disorders* — the schizoid, paranoid, and schizotypal personality disorders. Patients with these disorders share a certain detached quality that in their extreme forms may resemble psychotic disorders. ***Cluster B personality disorders*** are characterized by behavior that is overly dramatic, overly reactive, extremely emotional, or highly erratic. The antisocial, narcissistic, histrionic, and borderline personalities are in this cluster. People with these disorders share a remarkable intrinsic instability often characterized by mood fluctuation, interpersonal vacillation, grandiosity, and exhibitionism. They can be generally impulsive, although they are not usually dominated by one specific impulse control problem as are people with an impulsive control disorder (see Box 17-2). Pervasive anxiety is found in the ***Cluster C personality disorders*** — the dependent, passive-aggressive, obsessive compulsive, and avoidant personality disorders. The disorders are linked by the common themes of fearfulness and obsessiveness. These eleven disorders are listed on Axis II. In addition, DSM-III-R describes two other personality disorders that its framers believe require further study — the sadistic and the self-defeating personality disorders.

The clustering schema used in DSM-III-R is widely accepted. At the same time, it can be criticized for failing to consider the possibility that the personality disorders may have underlying causes or themes in common. A related shortcoming is that it gives no consideration to the various levels of severity that may differentiate the disorders. Certainly, clustering by symptom saliency is not the only way to categorize personality disorders. The study of the human personality may be approached from many perspectives. Consider, for example, Theodore Millon's perspective on the subject.

Millon (1990, 1988, 1981, 1969) proposes that the simplest and clearest way to understand an individual's personality is to understand the reinforcements that pervade his or her life. Specifically, what *types* of reinforcements does the person typically seek, what are the usual *sources* of these reinforcements, and what *instrumental processes*, or strategies, does the person use to obtain the reinforcements? As Figures 17-1 and 17-2 show, this information may be summarized on a graph consisting of three polarities.

1. ***Type: positive vs. negative*** The type of reinforcements that people seek may be primarily positive (R+) — likely to enhance their lives or to bring pleasure — or negative (R−) — likely to prevent or relieve psychological pain or suffering. From a broader evolutionary perspective, the type of reinforcement people pursue may be viewed as their "aim of survival," and they may pursue pleasure or, conversely, avoid pain.

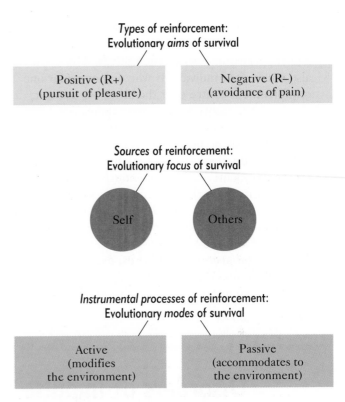

**FIGURE 17-1** Millon's personality polarities.

2. ***Sources: self vs. others*** People may typically look to themselves or to others as the potential source of their reinforcements. Again from an evolutionary perspective, the source of reinforcement may be thought of as one's "focus of survival" and will be either to depend on and promote oneself or to depend on and nurture others. Those who rely on themselves for reinforcement tend to be independent self-starters who at the extreme may have difficulty developing trust in and empathy for others. They may have a need to control themselves, others, and their environment. People who rely on

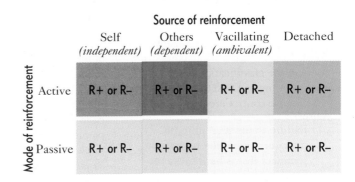

**FIGURE 17-2** This grid summarizes the sources, modes, and types of reinforcement that define the various personality patterns, according to Theodore Millon. The sources of reinforcement are listed on the horizontal axis; the modes, or processes, of reinforcement are found on the vertical axis; and the sustaining types of reinforcement are indicated within the cells.

others for reinforcement may demonstrate in a variety of ways a strong need for affection, affiliation, and support from outside themselves. There are also ambivalent individuals who do not prefer one reinforcement source over the other. As a result, they vacillate between relying on themselves and relying on others for reinforcement. In extreme cases they may go beyond a healthy vacillation and become so distressingly ambivalent that a need to act independently and autonomously is frustrated by insecurity and self-doubt. Finally, some individuals have great difficulty obtaining reinforcement from sources of any kind, and often appear withdrawn and detached.

3. *Instrumental processes: active vs. passive* People may pursue reinforcements by using an active strategy, characterized by initiative and alertness,

or a passive strategy, characterized by reactivity and inertness. In evolutionary terms, one's "mode of survival" will tend toward behaving in a modifying and controlling manner or toward accommodating and reacting to others.

## THE BASIC PERSONALITY DISORDERS

Just as the three polarities help to describe normal personality patterns (see Figure 17-3), they may also be used to categorize and describe the various personality disorders and to provide insight into how the disorders are developed and sustained. The personality disorders

============ BOX 17-2 ============

# Disorders of Impulse Rather than Personality

Some maladaptive behavior is guided and dominated by a single powerful pathological *impulse* that overtakes the individual. Impulses that misguide behavior are narrower and more spontaneous than broad personality traits, and they are frequently experienced as urges that defy control rather than as consistent characteristics or preferred modes of action. DSM-III-R has identified several disorders of impulse control, including *pyromania, kleptomania,* and *pathological gambling,* and distinguishes them from the personality disorders and indeed from all other disorders in the classification system.

According to DSM-III-R, disorders of impulse control are marked by

1. Failure to resist an impulse, drive, or temptation to perform some act that is harmful to the person or others.

2. A mounting sense of tension or arousal before the act is committed.

3. Pleasure, gratification, or relief at the time the act is committed. Afterward the person may or may not feel genuine remorse, shame, or guilt.

The disorders that meet these criteria often cause enormous distress to the sufferer and the community. Although they arouse much curiosity and are portrayed in numerous movies and television programs, they have in fact received relatively little research attention.

*Pyromania* is the deliberate setting of fires to achieve intense pleasure or relief. The fires are not set for monetary or any other apparent gain. Pyromania sometimes accompanies alcoholism, mental retardation, or a paraphilia. Research on the disorder has been hampered by the difficulty of separating cases of pyromania from those of arson — the setting of fires for revenge or gain or because of a psychotic delusion. The largest study undertaken so far surveyed the records

of the National Board of Fire Underwriters and found that many of the firesetters described themselves as experiencing an "irresistible impulse" to set fires (Lewis & Yarnell, 1951). More recent studies have found few, if any, cases of pyromania (Kosson & Dvosking, 1982), suggesting that the criteria for diagnosis, or perhaps the diagnostic category itself, may not be very useful.

The story is similar with respect to *kleptomania* — recurrent failure to resist the impulse to steal. People with this disorder do not steal for gain. In fact, they often have more than enough money to pay for the articles they steal. Apparently, it is the tension before the act and the sense of relief afterward that drive their behavior.

Little research has been done on kleptomania. What is known has been drawn from case studies of shoplifting and stealing, yet researchers do not agree on what percentage of these cases represent kleptomania. Some

## Source of reinforcement

| | Self *(independent)* | Others *(dependent)* | Vacillating *(ambivalent)* | Detached |
|---|---|---|---|---|
| Active | Forceful personality | Sociable personality | Sensitive personality | Inhibited personality |
| Passive | Confident personality | Cooperative personality | Respectful personality | Introversive personality |

*Mode of reinforcement*

**FIGURE 17-3** Normal personality patterns.

have been formally recognized for only a short time, so the amount of research that has been conducted on most of them is limited. In this section, we will discuss what we think of as the eight basic personality disorders. The next sections will address the three more severe personality disorders and, then, the two personality disorders proposed by the DSM-III-R for further study.

## Antisocial Personality Disorder

The characteristics of a person with an antisocial personality disorder are vividly seen in the case of a young man named Tom:

*T*om looks and is in robust physical health. His manner and appearance are pleasing. . . . Evidence of his maladjustment became distinct in childhood. He appeared to be a reliable . . . fellow but could never be counted upon to keep at any task or to give a straight account of any situation. He was frequently truant from school. . . . Though

clinical theorists argue that kleptomania, like pyromania, may not be a useful clinical category.

The most common of the impulsive disorders is *pathological gambling.* The American Psychological Association estimates that 2 to 3 percent of the adult population may suffer from this disorder (APA, 1987). Clinicians are careful to distinguish pathological from social gambling, for unlike pyromania and kleptomania, this behavior occurs in mild forms that are not only legal but socially encouraged. Pathological gambling is defined less by the amount of time or money spent in gambling than by the *addictive* nature of the behavior. Pathological gamblers are unable to walk away from a wager and are restless and irritable if gambling is denied them. Repeated loss of money leads to more gambling in an effort to win the money back, and the gambling continues even in the face of financial, social, and health problems.

Pathological gambling differs from the other impulse disorders in one very important way. Because this disorder is more prevalent than the others and because the behavior resembles alcoholism, a great deal of attention has been directed to its treat-

ment. Treatments that combine approaches tend to be more effective than any one approach alone. Pathological gamblers who join self-help support groups, such as Gambler's Anonymous, a network patterned after Alcoholics Anonymous, seem to have a higher recovery rate, perhaps in part because they have admitted that they have a problem and are seeking to conquer it.

A major difficulty in understanding these impulsive disorders is to distin-

guish them from other disorders. Because some of their features overlap with those of obsessive compulsive and other anxiety disorders and with depression, theorists commonly explain the origin of the abnormalities in terms of similar or related disorders. When they are looked at closely, however, firesetting, stealing, and pathological gambling do not fit readily into existing categories of abnormal behavior. Further research is necessary before they will be understood.

he was generously provided for, he stole some of his father's chickens from time to time, selling them at stores downtown. Pieces of table silver would be missed. These were sometimes recovered from those to whom he had sold them for a pittance or swapped them for odds and ends which seemed to hold no particular interest or value for him.

. . . At fourteen or fifteen, having learned to drive, Tom began to steal automobiles with some regularity. . . . Tom continued to forge his father's name to small checks and steal change, pocketknives, textbooks, etc., at school. Occasionally, on the pretext of ownership he would sell a dog or a calf belonging to some member of the community.

. . . Tom was sent to a federal institution in a distant state, where a well-organized program of rehabilitation and guidance was available. He soon impressed authorities at this place with his attitude and in the way he discussed his past mistakes and plans for a different future.

. . . He found employment in a drydock at a nearby port and talked modestly but convincingly of the course he would now follow, expressing aims and plans few could greatly improve. . . . His employers found him at first energetic, bright, and apparently enthusiastic about the work. Soon evidence of inexplicable irresponsibility emerged and accumulated. Sometimes he missed several days and brought simple but convincing excuses of illness. As the occasions multiplied, explanations so detailed and elaborate were made that it seemed only facts could have produced them. Later he sometimes left the job, stayed away for hours, and gave no account of his behavior except to say that he did not feel like working at the time. . . .

Sometimes he was arrested for fomenting brawls in low resorts, provoking fights, or for such high-handed and disturbing behavior as to constitute public nuisance. Though not a very regular drinker or one who characteristically drank to sodden confusion or stupefaction, he exhibited unsociable and unprepossessing manners and conduct after taking even a few beers or highballs.

. . . This young man has, apparently, never formed any substantial attachment for another person. Sexually he has been desultorily promiscuous under a wide variety of circumstances.

*(Cleckley, 1976, pp. 84–85)*

Three percent of men and 1 percent of women in the United States habitually engage in antisocial behavior; the distress they cause themselves and society has commanded clinicians' interest in this disorder for years. People who display an ***antisocial personality disorder,*** also known as ***psychopathy*** or ***sociopathy,*** have a lifelong history of misconduct. As children they may play truant, vandalize or damage property, get into brawls, and show cruelty to animals or people. As adults they are often unable to hold a steady job, do not meet financial obligations, and are inadequate parents. Many engage in illegal activities. Destroying property, stealing, holding illegal occupations, and assaulting and abusing others are

Charles Manson, who directed his followers to kill nine people in 1969, fits many of the criteria of an antisocial personality disorder, including failure to conform to social and legal norms of behavior and aggressiveness, impulsivity, disregard for truth, and lack of remorse.

common among people with this disorder. These individuals are indifferent to others and have no qualms about lying for gain or pleasure, and little remorse over the pain they inflict. Antisocial personality patterns may be found in all walks of life, but given the extremely debilitating consequences of the disorder on the individual's functioning, it winds up being more prevalent in the lower classes. The disorder also runs in families: among people who have the disorder, males are five times and females ten times more likely than average to have biological relatives who also have the disorder.

**Reinforcement Pattern** Millon's (1981, 1969) reinforcement scheme views people with an antisocial personality disorder as *active, self-focused,* and sustained primarily by *positive* reinforcement (see Figure 17-4). That is, they actively pursue pleasure and do so by depending on themselves.

*Type of Reinforcement: Positive* The primary type of reinforcement that sustains the antisocial personality disorder is the pursuit of pleasure (R+), even though that pleasure may be extremely short-lived and may result in some form of punishment. Antisocial people believe that following the rules imposed by society has brought them nothing but failure. Therefore, they say, they have no choice but to violate the boundaries of socially accept-

## Source of reinforcement

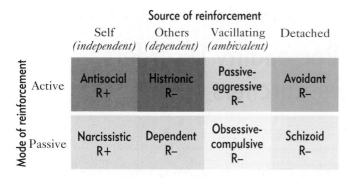

FIGURE 17-4 Millon's reinforcement matrix, summarizing source, mode, and type (R+ or R−) of reinforcement for the *eight basic personality disorders.*

able behavior if they are ever to attain the pleasures that life has to offer. In their view, they may either behave in an acceptable manner and lead a life of deprivation and frustration or behave antisocially—with little or no regard for the long-term consequences of this behavior—and enjoy some of life's rewards, if only fleetingly.

*Source of Reinforcement: Self*   People with antisocial personality disorders are independent in the extreme: they rely exclusively on themselves for survival. They are intensely egocentric, untrustworthy, and unreliable, either violating existing codes of social behavior outright or mentally rewriting them in a self-serving way. A hallmark of the person with antisocial personality disorder is general insensitivity and lack of empathy toward others.

*Reinforcement Process: Active*   The antisocial personality disorder conforms to an active instrumental process of reinforcement. Not only do such people tend to take action to procure their reinforcements, but they do so impetuously and irresponsibly. Such spontaneous restlessness exceeds the boundaries of constructive active behavior and may be thought of as shortsightedness and as resistance to planning ahead, examining alternative actions, and considering the consequences of actions.

**Causes and Treatments**   Researchers have studied the nature and causes of antisocial personality disorder more than the other personality disorders (see Box 17-3) and have learned that biological factors may play a role in its development. It has been suggested, for example, that neuronal hypersensitivity in the amygdala of the limbic system may establish a biological predisposition to develop the disorder by lowering an individual's biological threshold for impulsive, aggressive, and egocentric behavior (Everly, 1988).

Research has suggested that environmental factors may also contribute to the problem. Parental hostility toward a child is likely to engender hostility in return and may also serve as a model that the child learns to copy. Parental hostility teaches a child that he or she can rely on no one but him- or herself for protection, affiliation, and support. A similar lesson may be learned when parenting is simply deficient. Under these circumstances, a child is likely to learn to fight for survival no matter what the cost and may never learn how to behave within socially appropriate bounds. Severe socioeconomic hardship may add to these problems of parenting. Finally, any child who is the target of parental or societal abuse or neglect may not only learn to overcompensate for these factors but also develop a vindictive cast to his or her personality. Such people may essentially attempt to get even with those who have hurt or neglected them.

Thus far, all attempts at treating antisocial personality disorders have failed. A review by the American Psychiatric Association concluded, "There is virtually no note of optimism for treating sociopaths in outpatient settings without external controls over their behavior" (APA, 1989, p. 2745). In fact, even external controls, such as parole guidance, halfway houses, and partial hospitalization programs, do little to improve the prognosis. Behavioral therapy programs have been applied with minimal success, and the use of psychotropic medications has yielded inconsistent results. The existing data suggest that drug therapy may have some value in diminishing the explosive, aggressive, and impulsive symptoms of this personality disorder, but this effect cannot be considered overall improvement in the personality disorder itself. So far, any improvements achieved through therapy appear to be fragile and short-lived (APA, 1989).

## Narcissistic Personality Disorder

The narcissistic personality disorder can be seen in the case of 30-year-old Steven, an artist who is married and has one child:

*Steven came to the attention of a therapist when his wife* insisted that they seek marital counseling. According to her, Steve was "selfish, ungiving and preoccupied with his work." Everything at home had to "revolve about him, his comfort, moods and desires, no one else's." She claimed that he contributed nothing to the marriage, except a rather meager income. He shirked all "normal" responsibilities and kept "throwing chores in her lap," and she was "getting fed up with being the chief cook and bottlewasher, tired of being his mother and sleep-in maid."

On the positive side, Steven's wife felt that he was basically a "gentle and good-natured guy with talent and intelli-

BOX 17-3

# Investigating Antisocial Personality Disorders: A Model for Researchers

Personality disorders have received less study than most other mental disorders. Part of the reason is that diagnosticians traditionally have had difficulty distinguishing several of the personality disorders from each other. Although they would usually agree that a given person was indeed manifesting a personality disorder, they might disagree as to whether it was an avoidant, schizoid, or some other personality disorder. In short, the personality disorder had little diagnostic reliability (Beck et al., 1962). The lack of specificity in diagnosing these disorders hampered any efforts to study their nature, origins, and treatment.

The diagnostic reliability of personality disorders is now changing for the better. In the past decade clinicians have developed structured interviews (Widiger et al., 1988; Loranger et al., 1987) and assessment scales (Millon, 1990; Overholser, 1990) that are specifically designed to identify personality disorders and have found that the disorders can indeed be distinguished reliably with the use of these new procedures. As a result researchers have at last begun to study the various disorders more effectively.

What can we expect from this coming wave of research on personality disorders? Certainly we can anticipate more systematic lines of investigation rather than one-shot studies that leave us curious but unconvinced. Actually, in-depth research in which one study

builds upon the findings of another has already been conducted on antisocial, or sociopathic, personality disorders. Because the symptoms of this personality disorder are rather distinct from the symptoms of other personality disorders, it has received much more study than the others over the years, and we have gained some important clinical insights. A look at one line of research into antisocial personality disorders may offer us a sneak preview of the kinds of research about to unfold with regard to the other personality disorders.

Until the 1950s, clinicians observed that people with an antisocial personality disorder seemed unable to profit from experience; that is, they could not learn to avoid problems the way others learn. Researchers set out to determine the nature of this learning deficiency. David Lykken (1957) hypothesized that sociopathic people may experience *less anxiety* than other people and thus may lack an ingredient that is essential for learning a number of important behaviors. He argued that people ordinarily learn socially appropriate behaviors, for example, in order to avoid or reduce the anxiety brought on by others' disapproval. Sociopathic people, however, cannot learn from feelings of anxiety, because they do not experience those feelings.

In a clever study, Lykken (1957) tested the relationships between anxiety and learning in sociopathic people.

In the first part of the study, Lykken asked whether sociopathic subjects experience the same anxiety as normal subjects in response to real-life situations. He constructed a questionnaire in which subjects read thirty-three pairs of activities and were asked which of each pair they would rather do. While both items in each pair described an unpleasant event, the events differed in the amount of anxiety they provoked. One activity was unpleasant because it was tedious ("getting up to go to work in the morning," say, or "cleaning out a cesspool") and the other activity was unpleasant because it provoked anxiety ("standing on a ledge on the 25th floor" or "knocking over a glass in a restaurant"). Lykken reasoned that if sociopaths were not deterred by anxiety, they would be more likely than the normal subjects to choose the anxiety-producing alternative over the tedious alternative. This was in fact the case. These findings suggest that sociopathic people do experience less anxiety than other people.

Next Lykken examined the role that anxiety plays in learning for sociopathic and normal subjects. He had subjects try to learn a mental maze that consisted of twenty choice points or steps. At each choice point, the subject was required to press one correct switch out of four choices in order to move to the next step. Subjects were instructed to get through the maze with as few errors as pos-

gence." But this wasn't enough. She wanted a husband, someone with whom she could share things. In contrast, he wanted, according to her, "a mother, not a wife"; he didn't want "to grow up, he didn't know how to give affection, only to take it when he felt like it, nothing more, nothing less."

Steve presented a picture of an affable, self-satisfied and somewhat disdainful young man. He was employed as a commercial artist, but looked forward to his evenings and weekends when he could turn his attention to serious painting. He claimed that he had to devote all of his spare time

sible. The learning of the twenty correct responses was the "manifest" task. But embedded in this task was an avoidance-learning "latent" task. One of the three incorrect responses at each choice point was paired with an electric shock. That is, when subjects made this incorrect response, they were shocked. Lykken reasoned that in addition to learning correct responses (the manifest task), subjects would learn to avoid shocked incorrect responses (the latent task) and would eventually err only on unshocked responses. The anxiety reduction associated with making the unshocked response was expected to increase the frequency of unshocked errors and decrease the frequency of shocked errors. Lykken found that sociopaths learned the manifest task as well as normal subjects, but failed to learn the anxiety-motivated avoidance task. In short, when learning depended on anxiety, they failed to learn.

Next Lykken placed all of his subjects in a classical conditioning experiment in which an unconditioned stimulus (an electric shock) was paired with a conditioned stimulus (the sound of a buzzer) to condition an anxiety response (heightened galvanic skin response) to the sound of the buzzer alone. Lykken was unable to condition an anxiety response in the sociopathic subjects. Taken together, these findings support the notion that people with an antisocial personality disorder are devoid of the normal anxiety concomitants needed to learn certain behaviors.

Are sociopathic people ever capable of learning avoidance responses? Apparently yes. A few years later Frank Schmauk (1970) used Lykken's maze-learning problem and found that sociopathic subjects did in fact learn to make the avoidance response when failure to do so resulted in a loss of money rather than a shock. This finding suggests that one focus of subsequent research should be on the identification of those factors that do motivate sociopathic people.

Why should people with antisocial personality disorders experience less anxiety than other people? Biological researchers picked up the ball here and tried to locate a biological cause for the anxiety deficits of these individuals. In a series of studies they found that sociopathic subjects respond to expectations of stress with a pair of distinct biological reactions: large increases in heart rate and small increases in skin conductance. J. Lacey (1967) contended that this pattern of responding was associated with *low cortical arousal.* In addition, the pattern was indicative of decreased sensory response to environmental stimulation. Robert Hare (1978) suggested that this physiological pattern enables sociopaths to "tune out" or repress anxiety arousal. Consequently, emotional situations have less impact on them than on non-sociopathic individuals, and failure to learn anxiety-motivated avoidance responses is inevitable.

A second implication of Hare's reasoning is that sociopaths' chronic un-derarousal may lead them to engage in sensation-seeking behavior. Sociopaths may in fact be drawn to antisocial activity precisely because it meets their need for excitement. Herbert Quay (1965) speculated that sociopathic people may need excitement for one of two reasons. First, they may need increased sensory input to produce a desired level of stimulation. Second, they may quickly become habituated to stimulation and require frequent sensory change. In support of this thinking, several researchers subsequently found that sociopathy is often related to sensation-seeking behavior (Zuckerman, 1978; Blackstein, 1975). Simply put, sociopathic persons generally take risks and seek thrills.

This line of investigation is still continuing. For example, more recent research has determined that sociopathic persons can be influenced by anxiety and can learn avoidance tasks if they are forced to pay attention to the risks involved in a given task or if the punishments involved in a task are made more vivid (Newman, Kosson, & Patterson, 1987; Newman & Kosson, 1986).

Obviously, antisocial personality disorder can be studied systematically and precisely, and clinical researchers can make significant contributions to our understanding of this disorder. It is reasonable to expect that in coming years researchers can and will play just as valuable a role in clarifying the nature, causes, and treatments of the other personality disorders.

---

and energies to "fulfill himself," to achieve expression in his creative work. . . .

His relationships with his present co-workers and social acquaintances were pleasant and satisfying, but he did admit that most people viewed him as a "bit self-centered,

cold and snobbish." He recognized that he did not know how to share his thoughts and feelings with others, that he was much more interested in himself than in them and that perhaps he always had "preferred the pleasure" of his own company to that of others.

*(Millon, 1969, pp. 261–262)*

The self-absorption of people with a narcissistic personality is apparent even when they pretend to be interested in others.

The Greek myth has it that Narcissus died enraptured by the beauty of his own reflection in a pool, pining away while longing for his own image. His name has come to be synonymous with extreme self-involvement. While we all may aspire to greatness, the person with **narcissistic personality disorder** lives a life pervaded by fantasies of success, beauty, or remarkable talent. These individuals are so self-focused that they look to other people only to further their own goals and are rarely attentive to others' needs. Despite their rosy vision, they can be swamped by feelings of worthlessness, easily wounded by criticism, and envious of those who fare better than they. Some may be driven enough to achieve, but others are bogged down in depression and dysfunction.

**Reinforcement Pattern**   People with a narcissistic personality disorder are *passive, self-focused,* and sustained primarily by *positive* reinforcement (Millon, 1981, 1969). That is, they pursue pleasure, and do so in a passive manner and by depending on themselves.

***Type of Reinforcement: Positive***   The narcissistic personality disorder is sustained primarily by positive reinforcement (R+). This is quite contrary to the traditional perception that the narcissist acts out of a deep-seated sense of inadequacy; in that case the primary sustaining reinforcement would be negative. Actually, however, the narcissistic disorder is characterized by an overly expansive egocentrism and sense of entitlement; this, rather than insecurity, propels the patterns of behavior designed to extract praise, admiration, and special consideration from others. Consonant with this pattern, achievements are often unrealistically exaggerated to the point of boastful arrogance, facile rationalization, and frank prevarication.

***Source of Reinforcement: Self***   The narcissist, like the individual with an antisocial personality disorder, is in-

dependent and self-reliant, and confidently exhibits a self-importance and self-absorption that exclude any consideration for others. This self-absorption can become an immature preoccupation with indulgent illusions and fantasies of fame and fortune. The narcissist intends no harm to others but may harm them through benign neglect. Such an individual often assumes that rules and morals are for the other guy. While from Millon's perspective narcissism is a manifestation of an expanded sense of self rather than an inadequate one, this view does not overlook the fact that narcissists are vulnerable to **narcissistic injury,** a condition in which the person is temporarily overwhelmed by personal failure or rejection. In such cases, however, the resultant depression or shame abates relatively rapidly; the inherent ego strength is soon reharnessed.

***Reinforcement Process: Passive***   People with a narcissistic personality disorder differ from those with an antisocial personality disorder in that their reinforcement process is passive. They expect special favors from others without feeling a need to reciprocate, and may extract such favors by exploitation or insensitivity to others' needs. In their minds, just *being* gives them the right to receive reinforcements. Their demeanor ranges from cool nonchalance and imperturbability to buoyant optimism.

In sum, the narcissistic personality disorder is a passive, independent disorder, positively reinforced. The narcissistic person's expansive sense of self and egocentric self-absorption result in a flagrant lack of empathy and a disdain for traditional rules of shared social cooperation and living.

**Causes and Treatments**   Millon hypothesizes that the narcissistic personality disorder is founded in excessive, unconditional parental valuation of the child (Millon, 1981, 1969). This could account for the unjustified sense of self-worth, disdain for rules of social conduct, and expansive sense of self-importance. Similarly, parental overindulgence and failure to set limits could account for the lack of a sense of respect for others and the absence of self-control.

At present there is no compelling evidence that drug therapies have any lasting effects on people with a narcissistic personality. Some clinical reports suggest, however, that long-term psychotherapy, particularly psychodynamic therapy, may have value in the treatment of these people. In addition, some clinicians have reported that social skills training can be helpful in removing the veil of narcissistic self-absorption so that the patient can be helped to cultivate interest in and empathy toward others. As the American Psychiatric Association's (1989) review of the treatment of personality disorders notes, however, "The literature on the treatment of narcissistic personality disorder is so new that empirical studies do not exist to support the efficacy of any treatment approach" (p. 2742).

## Histrionic Personality Disorder

A histrionic personality disorder can complicate life considerably, as we see in the case of Suzanne:

*Suzanne, an attractive and vivacious woman, sought* therapy in the hope that she might prevent the disintegration of her third marriage. The problem she faced was a recurrent one, her tendency to become "bored" with her husband and increasingly interested in going out with other men. She was on the brink of "another affair" and decided that before "giving way to her impulses again" she had "better stop and take a good look" at herself. . . .

Suzanne was quite popular during her adolescent years. . . Rather than going on to college, Suzanne attended art school where she met and married a fellow student—a "handsome, wealthy ne'er-do-well." Both she and her husband began "sleeping around" by the end of the first year, and she "wasn't certain" that her husband was the father of her daughter. A divorce took place several months after the birth of this child.

Soon thereafter she met and married a man in his forties who gave both Suzanne and her daughter a "comfortable home, and scads of attention and love." It was a "good life" for the four years that the marriage lasted. . . . In the third year of this marriage she became attracted to a young man, a fellow dancing student. The affair was brief, but was followed by a quick succession of several others. Her husband learned of her exploits, but accepted her regrets and assurances that they would not continue. They did continue, and the marriage was terminated after a stormy court settlement.

Suzanne "knocked about" on her own for the next two years until she met her present husband, a talented writer who "knew the scoop" about her past. He "holds no strings" around her; she is free to do as she wishes. Surprisingly, at least to Suzanne, she had no inclination to venture afield for the next three years. She enjoyed the titillation of "playing games" with other men, but she remained loyal to her husband, even though he was away on reportorial assignments for periods of one or two months. The last trip, however, brought forth the "old urge" to start an affair. It was at this point that she sought therapy.

*(Millon, 1969, p. 251)*

People with a *histrionic personality disorder* live in dramatic emotionality and fervent pursuit of attention. They react to even the smallest event with an elaborate show of emotion, sobbing at a trivial disappointment and becoming exuberant at a minor success (APA, 1987). Yet these feelings are shallow and short-lived. The individuals are bent on being at center stage and they attempt to be charming, attractive, and seductive. However, they are typically controlling in relationships, look to authority figures to solve all their problems, and are constantly in need of praise and reassurance.

**Reinforcement Pattern**  People with this disorder are *active, other-focused,* and sustained primarily by *negative* reinforcement. That is, they actively try to avoid pain, and do so by depending on others.

*Type of Reinforcement: Negative*  The extraordinary need of people with a histrionic personality disorder for affection, affiliation, and support goes well beyond the life-enhancing qualities of positive reinforcement. It is a pathologically extreme and seemingly insatiable craving for interpersonal stimulation, apparently to *avoid* the boredom and pain of emotional emptiness (R—). It is this terrifying, deeply embedded emotional abyss that motivates histrionic persons to actively, vigorously, and unceasingly pursue novelty, stimulation, and especially interpersonal attention, usually of a facile (and hence ultimately unfulfilling) nature.

*Source of Reinforcement: Others*  Histrionic people are extremely dependent on others. Self-dramatizing, vain, and seductively exhibitionistic, they *perform* in a manner calculated to solicit attention, praise, reassurance, and approval. They have no taste for introspection and enter into relationships frivolously, with no thought of commitment. These people are quick to form friendships but soon become excessively demanding, pushing the limits of interpersonal affiliation.

*Reinforcement Process: Active*  Histrionic people tend to be impulsive and often hedonistic in their active, never-ending pursuit of praise and attention and their single-minded avoidance of boredom and emotional emptiness. Thus their behavior tends to be highly theatrical, adventurous, lively, and seductive.

**Causes and Treatments** The histrionic personality disorder seems to arise out of a combination of biological and behavioral mechanisms. Persons with the disorder appear to have a lower threshold of excitability and a propensity to overreact, characteristics that may emanate from hypersensitivity in the limbic and hypothalamic areas of the brain (Weil, 1974). A low threshold of excitability in the ascending reticular formation has also been implicated in the disorder.

Behaviorists have traditionally pointed to three parental behavior patterns as possible factors: (1) minimal punishment, leading to an underdeveloped inclination to self-restraint; (2) frequent positive reinforcement for overly dramatic social performing, leading to a continuation of such behavior; and (3) unusual or inconsistent positive reinforcement for socially acceptable behavior. Dramatic and exciting behavior by histrionic parent models may also set the stage for development of histrionic traits in the child.

Some clinicians suggest that the treatment of histrionic patients should focus on their core, deep-rooted dependency needs. Just how their extraordinary neediness is to be addressed depends on the orientation of the therapist. Psychotropic medications are apparently of value in treating the depression that often accompanies the histrionic personality disorder.

## Dependent Personality Disorder

People with dependent personality disorder are so reliant on others that they cannot make the smallest decision for themselves. Mr. G. is a case in point.

*Mr. G. was a rather short, thin and nicely featured but* somewhat haggard man who displayed a hesitant and tense manner when first seen by his physician. His place of employment for the past 15 years had recently closed and he had been without work for several weeks. He appeared less dejected about the loss of his job than about his wife's increasing displeasure with his decision to "stay at home until something came up." She thought he "must be sick" and insisted that he see a doctor. . . .

Mr. G. was born in Europe, the oldest child and only son of a family of six children. . . . His mother kept a careful watch over him, prevented him from engaging in undue exertions and limited his responsibilities; in effect, she precluded his developing many of the ordinary physical skills and competencies that most youngsters learn in the course of growth. . . .

A marriage was arranged by his parents. His wife was a sturdy woman who worked as a seamstress, took care of his home, and bore . . . four children. Mr. G. performed a variety of odds-and-ends jobs in his father's tailoring shop.

His mother saw to it, however, that he did no "hard or dirty work," just helping about and "overlooking" the other employees. As a consequence, Mr. G. learned none of the skills of the tailoring trade. . . .

During the ensuing years, he obtained employment at a garment factory owned by his brothers-in-law. Again he served as a helper, not as a skilled workman. Although he bore the brunt of essentially good-humored teasing by his co-workers throughout these years, he maintained a friendly and helpful attitude, pleasing them by getting sandwiches, coffee and cigarettes at their beck and call.

He married again to a hard-working, motherly type woman who provided the greater portion of the family income. Shortly thereafter, the son of his first wife emigrated to this country. Although the son was only 19 at the time, he soon found himself guiding his father's affairs, rather than the other way around.

*(Millon, 1969, p. 242)*

Two is more than just company for people with a ***dependent personality disorder;*** it is an absolute must. Women receive this diagnosis more often than men. People with this disorder are unable to undertake any project alone, from choosing a gift to choosing a career. Needy of praise, they are sensitive to any rebuff and fearful of losing a relationship. They may wish for something but never speak up, know a partner's views are wrong yet never disagree, demean themselves to please others, and even tolerate abuse. Should an abusive relationship end, they are out of the frying pan and into the fire — devastated, helpless, unable to cope.

**Reinforcement Pattern** Persons with a dependent personality disorder are *passive, other-focused,* and sustained primarily by *negative* reinforcement. That is, they seek to avoid psychologically painful circumstances, doing so in a passive manner and by depending on others.

*Type of Reinforcement: Negative* As with the histrionic personality disorder, an extraordinary need for affection, support, and security permeates the dependent personality disorder. Again like people with a histrionic personality disorder, those with a dependent personality disorder try primarily to avoid pain (R−). Dependent people see themselves as weak, incompetent, and fragile. Their dependent and submissive behavior is a strategy to avoid losing the support of the people they rely on.

*Source of Reinforcement: Others* Individuals suffering from dependent personality disorder turn away from themselves and toward others as the source of happiness and rewards in life. They characteristically subordinate their own needs to those of stronger and (they hope) nurturing individuals on whom they wish to rely for security, happiness, and protection against a myriad of real and imagined threats in the environment. Dependent individuals are passive, obliging, and even conciliatory in their relations with others because asserting themselves or making direct demands would jeopardize their sense of security. With their need to depend on others at all costs, they tend to be unsuspicious and gullible, sometimes even blithe in their refusal to acknowledge interpersonal conflict.

**Reinforcement Process: Passive**   Ill equipped to function as autonomous adults, dependent people assume a passive, docile posture marked by timidity and noncompetitiveness — a style the reverse of the active, impulsive, and hedonistic approach of histrionic people. These persons abdicate most aspects of independent functioning in their rush to embrace a role of pacific immaturity.

**Causes and Treatments**   Deficient physical stature or health status often contributes to the development of dependent personality disorders. Thin and frail or heavy and cumbersome individuals have a greater tendency to develop dependent qualities because they feel a need to rely on others for protection and social patronage.

Environmental factors may also play a role in the development of this personality disorder. Parental overprotection may serve to inhibit the natural formation of interpersonal competence, even in the absence of physical health problems. Similarly, general feelings of unattractiveness or lack of intelligence or some other perceived disadvantage may set the stage for the development of this disorder, beginning as early as childhood.

In sum, any physical or social deficit, real or imagined, can set the stage for the formation of the dependent personality disorder. Once again, however, the way the environment shapes these factors and the way the person responds will serve as the ultimate determinants of adaptive or maladaptive personality development.

There is general agreement among psychotherapists that dependent patients should be encouraged to express their feelings, opinions, and preferences in therapy without fear of rejection (APA, 1989). Successful treatment of persons with the disorder typically includes having patients engage in repeated exercises in assertiveness, both in the therapeutic setting and in the everyday world. In many ways, both histrionic and dependent patients can be viewed as adults whose psychological growth and progression toward autonomy and independence have been halted at the level of adolescence. Thus the successful treatment of both these personality disorders requires development of the social skills, assertiveness, and mature sense of self that are associated with independent adulthood.

# Passive-Aggressive Personality Disorder

People with a passive-aggressive personality seek to control the lives of the people close to them by indirect means, and in the process complicate their own:

*A*nn *had withdrawn from her husband sexually, implored* him to seek a new job in another community despite the fact that he was content and successful in his present position, disliked the neighborhood in which they lived and had become increasingly alienated from their friends in past months. . . . A similar sequence of events had occurred twice previously, resulting in her husband's decision to find new employment as a means of placating his wife. This time Ann's husband was "getting fed up" with her complaints, her crying, her sexual rebuffs, her anger and her inability to remain on friendly terms with people. He simply did not want to "pick up and move again, just to have the whole damn thing start all over."

When Ann first was seen by her therapist she appeared contrite and self-condemning; she knew the physical problems she had been experiencing were psychosomatic, that she caused difficulties for her husband and that she precipitated complications with their friends. This self-deprecation did not last long. Almost immediately after placing the burden of responsibility on her own shoulders, she reversed her course, and began to complain about her husband, her children, her parents, her friends, her neighborhood and so on. Once she spilled out her hostility toward everyone and everything, she recanted, became conscience-smitten and self-accusing again. . . .

Ann's marriage has mirrored many of the elements she experienced and observed in her childhood. She is submissive and affectionate, then sickly, demanding and intimidating of her husband, a pattern not unlike the one she saw her mother use to control her father. Ann's husband spent much of his energies trying to placate her, but "Ann is never content." During the six years of their marriage, she seemed satisfied only when they first moved to a new location. But these "bright periods" dimmed quickly, and the same old difficulties emerged again.

*(Millon, 1969, pp. 288–289)*

Rather than assertively express anger or a difference of opinion, individuals with a ***passive-aggressive personality disorder*** protest in a passive, maladaptive fashion. They usually resent even the most reasonable requests, become sulky or irritable, and criticize or scorn superiors. Forgetting to do a job, procrastinating, and being inefficient are some of the tactics they may unconsciously employ. Such reactions undermine their performance in the workplace, yet they fail to recognize the poor quality of the work they do and may be upset by their "inexplicable" failure.

**Reinforcement Pattern** People with a passive-aggressive personality disorder are *active, ambivalent* in regard to the source of their reinforcement, and sustained primarily by *negative* reinforcement. These patients use a covert form of aggression to resist situations and people who threaten their sense of self-determination or control.

*Type of Reinforcement: Negative* Passive-aggressive people are always trying to avoid the psychological pain of confirming their underlying suspicion that they are impotent in comparison with others (R−). Thus they are characteristically cynical, skeptical, untrusting, pessimistic, and generally misanthropic. Sulky, moody, obstinate, and resentful of others, they find a cloud in every silver lining. By being contrary, obstinate, caustic, and resentful, they manage to maintain a sense of efficacy and power over others. When faced with personal frustrations and others' perceived successes, passive-aggressive individuals respond by rationalizing their own inadequacies and denigrating the successes of those around them.

*Source of Reinforcement: Vacillating between Self and Others* The passive-aggressive individual vacillates between a desire to be assertive and independent and a perceived need to be acquiescent and dependent. This is an ambivalent posture, a conflicted pattern that results in frustration, anger, and often pessimism. To others the individual may seem withdrawn, combative, intolerant, and intent on demoralizing and even undermining others.

*Reinforcement Process: Active* People with a passive-aggressive personality disorder tend to be active, impulsive, and impatient. They hide behind a passive veneer, however, using indirect means to discharge their anger and discontent. They resort to such strategies as forgetfulness, blaming others, and procrastination to express disagreement or anger, to preserve a modicum of self-determination, or simply to prevent the feeling that someone else is in control.

**Causes and Treatments** Pronounced cyclical hormonal or neurotransmitter fluctuations may set the stage for the mood changes seen in the active, ambivalent style displayed by people with passive-aggressive personality disorders. We think it likely, however, that the ambivalent posture is a function more of learning than of biological factors.

In particular, family influences seem to help generate this disorder. Parental inconsistency often confuses a child as to what behaviors are appropriate and what behaviors are not. The child, desiring to receive reinforcement, learns to shift quickly from one extreme to the other according to what the parent seems to want at any given moment. Passive-aggressive traits may also be engendered by a conflicted family environment in which the child plays the role of moderator between the family members in conflict. The need to assume this role often encourages children to develop a vacillating, ambivalent personality style. Finally, a child can acquire passive-aggressive traits copying the traits modeled by a parent. Given these familial factors, it is not surprising that passive-aggressive personality disorders are often observed in close relatives (Millon & Everly, 1985).

Efforts to treat the passive-aggressive personality disorder are characteristically impeded by the patient's seemingly unending resistance to the therapy process, with the therapist becoming the focus of direct and indirect gestures of hostility and anger. These patients most commonly show their resistance by being late for appointments, not paying the bill, missing sessions, and making excuses for not complying with the treatment program (APA, 1989). It has been suggested that the therapist should anticipate resistance issues and address them in therapy before they actually arise (Malinow, 1981). Effective therapy for people with a passive-aggressive personality disorder should also include social skills training and general assertiveness training designed to teach patients how to express their feelings constructively rather than through their habitual avenues of suppression, passive hostility, and self-defeating power struggles.

## Obsessive Compulsive Personality Disorder

People with an obsessive compulsive personality are so intent on doing everything right that their efforts impair both their productivity and their relationships, as in the case of Wayne:

*Wayne was advised to seek assistance from a therapist* following several months of relatively sleepless nights and a growing immobility and indecisiveness at his job. When first seen, he reported feelings of extreme self-doubt and guilt and prolonged periods of tension and diffuse anxiety. It was established early in therapy that he always had experienced these symptoms. They were now merely more pronounced than before.

The precipitant for this sudden increase in discomfort was a forthcoming change in his academic post. New administrative officers had assumed authority at the college, and he was asked to resign his deanship to return to regular departmental instruction. In the early sessions, Wayne spoke largely of his fear of facing classroom students again, wondered if he could organize his material well, and doubted that he could keep classes disciplined and interested in his lectures. It was his preoccupation with these matters that he believed was preventing him from concentrating and completing his present responsibilities.

At no time did Wayne express anger toward the new college officials for the "demotion" he was asked to accept. He repeatedly voiced his "complete confidence" in the "rationality of their decision." Yet, when face-to-face with them, he observed that he stuttered and was extremely tremulous.

Wayne was the second of two sons, younger than his brother by three years. His father was a successful engineer, and his mother a high school teacher. Both were "efficient, orderly and strict" parents. Life at home was "extremely well planned," with "daily and weekly schedules of responsibilities posted" and "vacations arranged a year or two in advance." Nothing apparently was left to chance. . . . Wayne adopted the "good boy" image. Unable to challenge his brother either physically, intellectually or socially, he became a "paragon of virtue." By being punctilious, scrupulous, methodical and orderly, he could avoid antagonizing his perfectionistic parents, and would, at times, obtain preferred treatment from them. He obeyed their advice, took their guidance as gospel and hesitated making any decision before gaining their approval. Although he recalled "fighting" with his brother before he was six or seven, he "restrained his anger from that time on and never upset his parents again."

*(Millon, 1969, pp. 278–279)*

People with an *obsessive compulsive personality disorder* are perfectionists, so bent on meeting high standards that they may be unable to finish a task because the work never seems good enough, and unable to make a decision for fear of being mistaken. They are governed by rules and details; if a list is lost, for example, rather than make a new one, they may waste considerable time looking for it (APA, 1987). These people insist that others do things their perfectionistic way. They are workaholics, and leisure is just another task to be planned and perfected. They can be emotionally cold and moralistic. This disorder is often encountered in the general population, mostly in men. Few people find the obsessive compulsive personality endearing.

**Reinforcement Pattern** People with an obsessive compulsive personality disorder are *passive, ambivalent* in regard to the source of their reinforcement, and sustained by *negative* reinforcement. That is, they use a passive approach to try to avoid pain, vacillating between depending on themselves and depending on others in the pursuit of this goal.

***Type of Reinforcement: Negative*** People with obsessive compulsive personality disorders typically resort to obsessive compulsive behavior to protect themselves from behaving in a socially unacceptable manner or making a mistake that might injure someone (R—). Their rigid, perfectionistic, highly disciplined, and emotionally constricted style is a defense against a flood of primal, angry, undisciplined impulses that they are striving to keep suppressed or repressed, fearing that the impulses would be uncontrollable if they were ever released. Thus everyday relationships have a formal and serious quality for these people. They are constantly concerned about being organized, structured, and efficient. They are conscientious about schedules and deadlines. This preoccupation with details interferes with their ability to see issues from a broad, or global, perspective.

***Source of Reinforcement: Vacillating between Self and Others*** People with an obsessive compulsive personality disorder have, on the one hand, a desire to be assertive and to act autonomously, yet, on the other hand, a need to derive support and comfort through conformity. Thus they routinely second-guess their own actions and decisions, and wind up seeking approval and confirmation from others.

They exhibit unusual adherence to social conventions; are obsequious, loyal, and deferent in most interpersonal transactions; and prefer to keep relationships polite but formal. While these individuals desire personal and professional advancement, they are hesitant to take on roles or positions that require unusual creativity or risk taking or that give them the final authority in important decision-making processes. Obsessive compulsive people often make good followers and team players. They follow their chosen pursuits with an almost workaholic dedication, but they usually lack the self-confidence required for a top leadership role.

***Reinforcement Process: Passive*** Obsessive compulsive people operate in a passive manner, although their passivity emerges as a perfectionistic adherence to the rules, regulations, and general expectations promulgated by society. Such behavior is passive in the sense that should a desired outcome not be achieved, the person who has conscientiously followed the dictates of others is absolved of personal responsibility, blame, and guilt.

**Causes and Treatments** Historically, environmental factors have been suggested as the primary determinant of this personality disorder. Interviews with obsessive compulsive people often reveal that in their childhood at least one of their parents was overcontrolling and un-

TABLE 17-1

## COMPARISON OF PERSONALITY DISORDERS AND SIMILAR AXIS I DISORDERS

| Personality disorder | Resembling disorder | Difference |
|---|---|---|
| Histrionic | Somatization disorder | In a somatization disorder, complaints of physical illness dominate the person's histrionic symptoms. |
| Obsessive compulsive | Obsessive compulsive disorder | True obsessions and compulsions are not present in obsessive compulsive personality disorder. |
| Paranoid | Delusional disorder<br>Schizophrenia, paranoid type | Persistent psychotic symptoms, such as delusions and hallucinations, are never part of a paranoid personality disorder. |
| Schizotypal | Schizophrenia, residual type | When psychotic symptoms occur in schizotypal personality disorder, they are transient and less severe. Ongoing psychotic symptoms are experienced by those with schizophrenia, residual type. |
| Sadistic | Sexual sadism | Those with sexual sadism display sadistic behavior only to achieve sexual arousal. |
| Self-defeating | Sexual masochism | Those with sexual masochism seek humiliation or suffering only to achieve sexual arousal. |
| | Depressive disorder | Self-defeating behavior is but one symptom of a depressive disorder. |

skilled at expressing love and affection. Many family histories have also revealed parents who neglected or abused their children, and it is not unusual to find parents who were psychologically handicapped by illness, drugs, or alcohol. In these families the children often developed an extraordinary sense of responsibility, if only as a survival mechanism. Forced to grow up too quickly, they became easy prey for guilt-inducing parents. In addition, as with other personality disorders, some children apparently develop obsessive compulsive symptoms through modeling.

There is also growing evidence of a biological basis for the development of obsessive compulsive personality disorder (APA, 1989). Like obsessive compulsive anxiety disorders (see Table 17-1), this personality disorder has been linked to inappropriate activity of the neurotransmitter serotonin at key receptor sites in the brain.

Given that obsessive compulsive people use their personality traits as defenses against social impropriety and against the release of angry, primal urges, they can be viewed as being consumed by a never-ending struggle to control themselves and their environment. It would then be logical to target therapy at the individual's propensity to be overcontrolling as well as his or her cognitive rigidity. Clinicians have reported that social skills training,

relaxation training, encouragement of risk taking, and cognitive techniques for engendering cognitive flexibility are sometimes helpful. Not surprisingly, people with obsessive compulsive disorders prefer highly structured, goal-oriented methods of therapy and tend to drop out if they find the process too ambiguous or too threatening. Because they fear change, however, people with this disorder are generally unreceptive to the overriding goals of treatment.

## Avoidant Personality Disorder

People with an avoidant personality disorder are so fearful of being rejected that they give no one an opportunity to reject them — or to accept them either.

*James was a bookkeeper for nine years, having obtained* this position upon graduation from high school. He spoke of himself as a shy, fearful and quiet boy ever since early childhood. . . .

James was characterized by his supervisor as a loner, a peculiar young man who did his work quietly and efficiently. They noted that he ate alone in the company cafeteria and never joined in coffee breaks or in the "horsing around" at the office. . . .

As far as his social life was concerned, James had neither dated nor gone to a party in five years. . . . He now spent most of his free time reading, watching TV, daydreaming and fixing things around the house.

James experienced great distress when new employees were assigned to his office section. Some 40 people worked regularly in this office and job turnover resulted in replacement of four or five people a year. . . . In recent months, a clique formed in his office. Although James very much wanted to be a member of this "in-group," he feared attempting to join them because "he had nothing to offer them" and thought he would be rejected. In a short period of time, he, along with two or three others, became the object of jokes and taunting by the leaders of the clique. After a few weeks of "being kidded," he began to miss work, failed to complete his accounts on time, found himself unsure of what he was doing and made a disproportionate number of errors. . . . Although he did not connect his present discomfort to the events in his office, he asked if he could be reassigned to another job where he might work alone.

*(Millon, 1969, pp. 231–232)*

Encumbered by timidity and sensitivity, people with an *avoidant personality disorder* suffer the pain of being unable to establish the social ties for which they yearn. What if I embarrass myself by crying, blushing, or saying something foolish? These are the doubts that hold the individual back. Unlike people with social phobia, who fear specific social contexts, avoidant individuals fear relationships themselves. Easily hurt by criticism, they are unwilling to risk entering unfamiliar situations and often imagine that formidable obstacles lie in their path. Apparently this crippling disorder is not uncommon (APA, 1987).

**Reinforcement Pattern**  People with an avoidant personality disorder are *active* and sustained by *negative* reinforcement, but *unable to obtain reinforcement* either from themselves or from others. They actively avoid the pain of social rejection or humiliation by withdrawal.

***Type of Reinforcement: Negative***  Avoidant individuals are hypersensitive to scrutiny, embarrassment, and rejection, and avoid the psychological pain of these experiences by withdrawing from people and society (R—). They actually desire affection and affiliation, but the fear of rejection is so great that no one is ever trusted and risks are never taken.

***Source of Reinforcement: Detached***  Avoidant persons are *detached*, unable to obtain reinforcement because of their inability to execute either self-directed or other-directed behavior. They will often pay lip service to the desirability of seeking social affiliation but persist in maintaining

social distance and privacy. At the same time, they experience only loneliness, emptiness, conflict, and tension, rather than solace in their isolation because of their frustrated desire to receive affection. In sum, anxiety is always present for these people. They are too fearful of rejection to seek friendship, yet are reminded by a sense of emptiness that their avoidant traits are simply not making them happy.

***Reinforcement Process: Active***  Although it may sound like a contradiction in terms, people with avoidant personality disorders are active in their avoidance of others. They warily scan their environment for potential threats, actively reading between the lines in search of insults or derogations and overreacting to what are often innocuous events. Because these people manage to extract personal humiliation from virtually any occurrence, they are motivated to spend considerable energy avoiding the worry and pain of social exchange; ever withdrawing, they never really attain a satisfying social demeanor.

**Causes and Treatments**  Biological factors seem to play a role in the development of avoidant personality disorders. In particular, dysfunctioning in the brain's limbic area may make it difficult for people with this disorder to dampen incoming stimulation and so may make it necessary for them to detach themselves from external sources of stimulation. This argument is consistent with the finding that some babies display anxious, avoidant-like behavior almost immediately after birth.

That is not to say that environmental factors contribute nothing to avoidant disorders. People who possess a hypersensitivity to stimulation may find themselves severely uncomfortable when they are confronted by particular kinds of interpersonal interactions, such as rejection by a parent or by the peer group at early critical stages in psychosocial development. In sum, avoidant patients may have a biological vulnerability to social stimuli, which may blossom into an avoidant personality disorder under the stress of rejection, humiliation, or ridicule by a parent, a sibling, or the peer group.

The best way to treat people with an avoidant personality disorder appears to be with a combination of two or more strategies. Treatment must first include procedures aimed at reducing the ever-present anxiety of these individuals. In this regard, antianxiety medications and stress-reduction interventions such as biofeedback may be of initial value. These approaches set the stage for other therapy procedures that may reduce the patients' ongoing overreactivity. Patients may, for example, undergo desensitization in an effort to reduce their specific sensitivity to and fear of rejection. Finally, interventions such as assertiveness training, social skills training, and perhaps cognitive therapy may help to replace the avoidant, withdrawing behavior in social situations with more effective interpersonal approaches (Renneberg et al., 1990).

## Schizoid Personality Disorder

Unlike people with an avoidant personality disorder, those with a schizoid personality disorder do not yearn for close ties with anyone. They avoid social contact because they genuinely prefer to be alone.

*R*oy *was a successful sanitation engineer involved in the* planning and maintenance of water resources for a large city; his job called for considerable foresight and independent judgment but little supervisory responsibility. In general, he was appraised as an undistinguished but competent and reliable employee. There were few demands of an interpersonal nature made of him, and he was viewed by most of his colleagues as reticent and shy and by others as cold and aloof.

Difficulties centered about his relationship with his wife. At her urging they sought marital counseling for, as she put it, "he is unwilling to join in family activities, he fails to take an interest in the children, he lacks affection and is disinterested in sex."

The pattern of social indifference, flatness of affect and personal isolation which characterized much of Roy's behavior was of little consequence to those with whom a deeper or more intimate relationship was not called for; with his immediate family, however, these traits took their toll.

*(Millon, 1969, p. 224)*

People with avoidant and schizoid personality disorders often spend much of their time alone. The former yearn for but fear social relationships, whereas the latter are indifferent to social relationships and truly want to be alone.

People with a *schizoid personality disorder* show lifelong indifference to other people. They find little pleasure in being with relatives or friends. While most of us glow with praise or blush at criticism, schizoid persons are unruffled by others' comments. "Lone wolves," they often show no interest in either sex or marriage. Just as people with this personality disorder find company unappealing, so others find them cold, unsympathetic, and humorless. In the game of life, schizoid people choose to play solitaire; some fare well, especially in occupations that necessitate independence and being alone; but when they must associate with others, the disorder is debilitating.

**Reinforcement Pattern**   People with a schizoid personality disorder are *passive, unable to obtain reinforcement* either from themselves or from others, and sustained by *negative* reinforcement. Their schizoid pattern of behavior enables them to avoid the pain of overstimulation of any kind.

***Type of Reinforcement: Negative***   Negative reinforcement (R−) appears to be the primary form of reinforcement for people with this disorder. Unlike avoidant persons, whose withdrawal helps them to defend against the pain of interpersonal rejection, schizoid people are hypersensitive to stimulation no matter what its origin. Whereas avoidant persons desire social affiliation, persons with schizoid personality disorders have no such need. The schizoid person is characteristically apathetic, listless, and aloof, incapable of experiencing normal pleasure or pain, and knowing little if any happiness, sadness, anger, or even anxiety. When they encounter overstimulating environmental conditions, schizoid people tend to lose the ability to function normally, so they avoid all potential forms of overstimulation.

***Source of Reinforcement: Detached***   Like people with an avoidant personality disorder, those with a schizoid personality disorder are detached. They seem deficient both in self-reliance and in the ability or inclination to rely on others. Social exchange is aversive to them, so they remain aloof, indifferent, remote, and unresponsive. They have difficulty giving and receiving affection, express few social interests, and have few if any close friendships. This lack of external interest is matched by an equal absence of introspective qualities. Life for those with a schizoid personality disorder is a mechanistic function, void of emotional highs and lows.

***Reinforcement Process: Passive***   Lethargic and chronically fatigued, schizoid patients are classic pictures of passivity. They lack spontaneity and initiative and display little need for social or sexual activity, appearing to others as passive observers content to let life make a detour around them.

**Causes and Treatments**   Of all the personality disorders, it is in the schizoid type that biology seems to exert its strongest influence (Millon, 1990; Everly, 1988). Although the specific mechanisms are not fully understood, abnormal activity of the neurotransmitter dopamine seems to predispose individuals to develop this personality disorder. The role played by dopamine here is not unlike its role in the development of schizophrenia. Inasmuch as dopamine plays a key role in the brain's processing of sensory stimulation, it is not surprising that this brain chemical has been linked to a personality disorder whose sufferers seem hypersensitive to various kinds of stimulation.

Environmental factors also appear to play a role in the development of the schizoid personality disorder. Early childhood trauma, abuse, and neglect have been implicated, as have less extreme factors, such as a fragmented pattern of family communication, a very rigid home environment, and reinforced social isolation.

The schizoid patient's intrinsic resistance to self-disclosure, introspection, and the forging of psychologically intimate relationships poses a difficult challenge to the therapist. Perhaps the best first step is for the therapist to establish an empathic relationship with the patient, acknowledging the patient's resistance to self-disclosure and the intrinsic difficulty that the patient may have in dealing with emotionally laden issues. Both patient and therapist must remember that therapy will progress slowly at best. As yet there are no medications that seem to benefit persons with a schizoid personality disorder.

# THE SEVERE PERSONALITY DISORDERS

Unlike DSM-III-R's method of classifying the personality disorders, Millon's scheme takes the severity of the disorders into account. The paranoid, borderline, and schizotypal personality disorders are distinguished from the basic personality disorders by their severity. Although these three disorders are more severe disturbances, they may also be, to some degree, extensions of the basic disorders (see Figure 17-5).

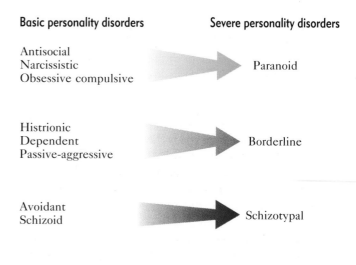

| Basic personality disorders | Severe personality disorders |
|---|---|
| Antisocial Narcissistic Obsessive compulsive | Paranoid |
| Histrionic Dependent Passive-aggressive | Borderline |
| Avoidant Schizoid | Schizotypal |

## Paranoid Personality Disorder

People with a paranoid personality disorder shun close relationships—not because they fear rejection, as in avoidance personality disorder, or overstimulation, as in schizoid personality disorder, but because they suspect everyone of intending them harm. Their trust in their own ideas and abilities, though, can be excessive, as we see in the case of Charles.

*Charles, an only child of poorly educated parents, had been* recognized as a "child genius" in early school years. He received a Ph.D. degree at 24, and subsequently held several responsible positions as a research physicist in an industrial firm.

His haughty arrogance and narcissism often resulted in conflicts with his superiors; it was felt that he spent too much time working on his own "harebrained" schemes and not enough on company projects. Charles increasingly was assigned to jobs of lesser importance than that to which he was accustomed. He began to feel, not unjustly, that both his superiors and his subordinates were "making fun of him" and not taking him seriously. To remedy this attack upon his status, Charles began to work on a scheme that would "revolutionize the industry," a new thermodynamic principle which, when applied to his company's major product, would prove extremely efficient and economical. After several months of what was conceded by others as "brilliant thinking," he presented his plans to the company president. Brilliant though it was, the plan overlooked certain obvious simple facts of logic and economy.

Upon learning of its rejection, Charles withdrew to his home where he became obsessed with "new ideas," proposing them in intricate schematics and formulas to a number of government officials and industrialists. These resulted in new rebuffs which led to further efforts at self-inflation.

*(Millon, 1969, pp. 329–330)*

No man, it is said, is an island. Yet for someone with a *paranoid personality disorder,* the other people around seem like a threatening sea. Expecting to be hurt and deceived, such a person reads the worst into the actions of others, believing, for example, that a friend who cancels a dinner date because of illness is doing so on purpose. People with the disorder are watchful and quick to react to any perceived threat; they ruminate at length when they are wronged and find it difficult to forgive. Putting great store on independence, they rarely establish close relationships with family or friends, and doubt the trustworthiness of even the people closest to them. Fear that a spouse is being unfaithful or a friend insincere is pervasive. At best the individual's relationships and career may be problematic. The disorder is most common in men, and few seek professional help.

**Reinforcement Pattern**    We view the paranoid personality disorder as an *active, self-focused* style of functioning, sustained by *negative* reinforcement. It is actually an extension, or caricature, of either the antisocial, narcissistic, or obsessive compulsive personality disorder.

***Type of Reinforcement: Negative***    Paranoid people are constantly vigilant, as if to anticipate and defend against expected attacks and perceived threats. Given this defensive posture, we consider deeply embedded negative reinforcement (R−) to be the primary mechanism of reinforcement. The view of the world as a malevolent place falls short of being a full-blown delusion, but it does possess irrational qualities. People with this disorder desperately and maladaptively engage in a never-ending quest for control over an environment they perceive as threatening and malevolent.

***Source of Reinforcement: Self***    Paranoid people rely on themselves for survival. In interactions with other people, they are provocative, quarrelsome, and often abrasive, anticipating deception and resistant to external authority and control. They often "test" the loyalty of the people close to them, tending to be skeptical, doubting, and mistrustful of others.

Paranoid individuals are pridefully independent, often with grandiose notions of their own importance, and quick to perceive injury and insults in innocuous events. Perhaps what frightens them most is the possibility of losing self-determination. This is why they construct such a highly vigilant, protective mechanism for staying in control.

***Reinforcement Process: Active***    Behaviorally defensive, interpersonally provocative, and cognitively suspicious, people with paranoid personality disorders are highly active. They are often edgy, jealous, impulsive, and quick to react with anger to environmental cues that they perceive as threatening. Even more, the paranoid pattern expresses itself as quarrelsome and quick to test the limits and loyalties of personal relationships.

**Causes and Treatments**    The paranoid personality disorder is best thought of as a syndromal extension—an exaggeration or caricature—of either the antisocial, the narcissistic, or the obsessive compulsive personality disorder. Therefore, there may well be at least three variants of the paranoid personality disorder, and likewise three sets of causal factors at work.

In the case of the paranoid-antisocial variant, harsh environmental conditions, abusive or neglectful parental behavior, or both serve to facilitate the development of the paranoid disorder. The personality of the paranoid-narcissist may be rooted in parental overvaluation and the need for control. The paranoid-compulsive patient may have experienced persistent parental criticism and conspicuous lack of parental approval, which led to an extraordinary need to be in control and to strive for perfection.

Perhaps the most critical point to be made about the relationship between the paranoid personality disorder and the three basic personality disorders is that the paranoid personality disorder is most likely to emerge when a person with one of the less severe disorders is faced with extreme stress at a critical developmental juncture.

The literature on the treatment of paranoid people is sparse. Except during periods of extreme stress and acute dysfunction, they are unlikely to seek treatment. Those who are referred for treatment through some external source may resist and even sabotage therapy. Their self-focus, defensive guardedness, and tendency to test the therapist can all undermine the therapeutic process.

Perhaps the most powerful strategy therapists can employ in treating paranoid patients is to form a *therapeutic alliance* in which the therapist agrees that the world is indeed a threatening place at certain times and in certain ways. This strategy will go a long way toward establishing initial rapport. The task of the therapist is then to help the person become more competent at discriminating real threats from perceived ones. The final step is to teach the patient to respond in adaptive ways to real and even ambiguous threats. All in all, however, therapy with the paranoid patient is beset by numerous hurdles, not the least of which are these patients' litigious propensities—their tendency to sue or to threaten to sue perceived enemies. This tendency is often aroused by concerns about confidentiality in therapy, but the threat of litigation may also be just a strategy the patient uses to control the therapist.

# Borderline Personality Disorder

People with a borderline personality disorder are so unstable that their relationships cannot help but be dysfunctional, as in the case of Helen.

*Helen decompensated over several years . . . following* persistent quarrels with her exasperated husband, a man she married in her teens who began to spend weeks away from home in recent years, presumably with another woman. For brief periods, Helen sought to regain her husband's affections, but these efforts were for naught, and she became bitterly resentful, guilt-ridden and self-deprecating. Her erratic mood swings not only increased feelings of psychic disharmony, but further upset efforts to gain her husband's attention and support. As she persisted in vacillating between gloomy despondency, accusatory attacks and clinging behaviors, more of her sources of support were withdrawn, thereby intensifying both separation anxieties and the maladaptive character of her behaviors. The next step, that of a regression to invalidism, was especially easy for her since it was consistent with her lifelong pattern of passive-dependence. Along with it, however, came discomforting feelings of estrangement and the collapse of all self-controls, as evidenced in her ultimate infantile-like behaviors and the total disorganization of her cognitive processes.

*(Millon, 1969, pp. 360–361)*

Instability is the hallmark of the ***borderline personality disorder***. Individuals with this disorder are painfully uncertain of themselves, their image, sexual orientation, life goals, and values. They complain of feeling "empty" or "bored" (APA, 1987). This confusion extends to relationships. Those with this personality disorder fear being alone, yet are ambivalent about others—at one moment describing associations in glowing terms, the next being wholly dissatisfied with them. The individual is prone to depression, anxiety, anger, and impulsive behavior, such as binging, drinking, or even attempting suicide (Levitt et al., 1990; Alnaes & Torgersen, 1990). Most people with borderline personality patterns are individuals who find both their work and their relationships marred.

The borderline personality disorder, marked by dysfunctions in interpersonal relationships and a marked instability of mood, is one of the most frequently diagnosed personality disorders, in part because clinicians have a tendency to diagnose this disorder when they are unsure of the nature of the case before them.

**Reinforcement Pattern** We consider this disorder to be a syndromal extension of the histrionic, dependent, or passive-aggressive personality disorder. It is perhaps the most egregiously ambivalent variant on the reinforcement matrix. Borderline persons are *ambivalent* not only about whether to rely on themselves or on others for reinforcement, but about whether the pattern of reinforcement they prefer is positive or negative and about whether to use an actual or a passive mode of behavior to attain it.

*Type of Reinforcement: Vacillating* The borderline personality disorder is characterized by an ambivalent approach to reinforcement. Burdened by an uncertain and often paradoxical self-image, people with the disorder display a vacillating pattern of behavior that combines self-indulgence and impulsive decadence with expressions of guilt, self-punishment, self-rejection, and extreme dependency.

*Source of Reinforcement: Vacillating* The borderline patient also vacillates between striving for self-reliance and demanding the support of others in the pursuit of reinforcement. This uncertainty is clearly an outgrowth of the person's paradoxical self-concept. Self-assurance to the point of grandiose self-importance is intermixed with self-deprecation, guilt, and a virtual absence of a clearly defined sense of self. This person may abdicate personal rights and virtually plead for interpersonal affiliation or support, then resentfully spurn it when it is offered. Perhaps the trait most characteristic of the borderline person is manipulativeness and exploitiveness. Some theorists believe that the borderline patient's greatest fear is abandonment. Consistent with this notion, the history of these people is often replete with evidence of anxiety about interpersonal separations.

*Reinforcement Process: Vacillating* People with a borderline personality disorder are characteristically ambivalent about whether to approach life in an active, initiative-taking manner or in a passive, reactive one. Thus the disorder is marked by impulsive, abrupt, and unexpected outbursts interspersed with periods of withdrawal, sullenness, depression, and even suicidal thoughts and behavior. Much of the time, a general mood of apathy may prevail. In sum, the borderline patient displays an amalgam of conflicting, contradictory, and generally paradoxical behavior, moods and inclinations.

**Causes and Treatments** The borderline personality disorder is almost certainly linked to dysfunction in the family: parental neglect, parental inconsistency, contradictory parental communications, physical and emotional trauma, and so on. It may be that when these factors are present during key developmental periods, neurons within the limbic system develop dysfunctionally (Everly, 1988). In support of this hypothesis, fascinating parallels have been drawn between post-traumatic stress disorder and the borderline personality disorder: there is evidence that trauma at an early age can lead to a dysfunction of personality that mimics the borderline personality, suggesting that the dysfunction may in fact be a result of altered limbic neurology (Van der Kolk, 1987).

Whether the borderline personality disorder is a set of learned behaviors or the result of an alteration in neurological structure or function, it is clear that this personality disorder begins to develop at a physiological and psychosocial stage that far precedes maturation. It is also clear that such factors as neglect, parental inconsistency, and physical and psychological trauma can undermine normal psychological development and create at the very least ambivalence in regard to the core issues of self-concept and the nature and source of reinforcement.

This disorder can be remarkably resistant to treatment, and controversies abound with regard to the way to approach it in therapy. Nevertheless, there are several points of agreement (Waldinger, 1986):

1. It is important to establish a stable environment within which therapy may proceed. Given the intrinsic instability of the disorder, establishing stable, predictable boundaries is critical to the successful treatment of this personality disorder.
2. The therapist must assume an active role in therapy and provide assurance of support, especially in times of crisis. At the same time, the therapist must remain alert to the possibility that the patient is using crisis as a manipulative technique.
3. The therapist should help the patient recognize self-destructive, maladaptive aspects of his or her behavior, such as promiscuity and drug abuse, and help the patient identify adaptive replacements for these behavior patterns.
4. The patient needs help in identifying the needs and motives behind his or her behavior patterns, especially those that are self-defeating.
5. Perhaps most important of all, the therapist needs to monitor the tenor and effects of any countertransference that occurs during therapy. The borderline patient is a demanding, challenging, crisis-prone individual, adept at manipulating others. This behavior inevitably antagonizes the therapist and often evokes negative countertransference. Faced with such a patient, even experienced therapists may feel the need to seek advice and moral support from their institutions and peers.

# Schizotypal Personality Disorder

The schizotypal personality disorder is so dysfunctional that those who suffer from it are greatly handicapped in all interactions with other people, as we see in the case of Harold:

*Harold was the fourth of seven children. . . . "Duckie,"* as Harold was known, had always been a withdrawn, frightened and "stupid" youngster. The nickname "Duckie" represented a peculiar waddle in his walk; it was used by others as a term of derogation and ridicule. Harold rarely played with his sibs or neighborhood children; he was teased unmercifully because of his "walk" and his fear of pranksters. Harold was a favorite neighborhood scapegoat; he was intimidated even by the most innocuous glance in his direction.

His father's brutality toward the other children of the family terrified Harold. Although Harold received less than his share of this brutality, since his father thought him to be a "good and not troublesome boy," this escape from paternal hostility was more than made up for by resentment and teasing on the part of his older siblings. By the time Harold was 10 or 11, his younger brothers joined in taunting and humiliating him.

Harold's family was surprised when he performed well in the first few years of schooling. He began to falter, however, upon entrance to junior high school. At about the age of 14, his schoolwork became extremely poor, he refused to go to classes and he complained of a variety of vague, physical pains. By age 15 he had totally withdrawn from school, remaining home in the basement room that he shared with two younger brothers. Everyone in his family began to speak of him as "being tetched." He thought about "funny religious things that didn't make sense"; he also began to draw "strange things" and talk to himself. When he was 16, he once ran out of the house screaming "I'm gone, I'm gone, I'm gone . . . ," saying that his "body went to heaven" and that he had to run outside to recover it; rather interestingly, this event occurred shortly after his father had been committed by the courts to a state mental hospital. By age 17, Harold was ruminating all day, often talking aloud in a meaningless jargon; he refused to come to the family table for meals.

*(Millon, 1969, pp. 347–348)*

Approximately 3 percent of Americans have symptoms that, though milder than schizophrenia, are eccentric and dysfunctional (APA, 1987). These persons, who display a *schizotypal personality disorder,* have thoughts unusual to their culture. The belief that others are watching or talking about them is common, as are paranoia and magical thinking, such as a belief in mind reading and clairvoyance. Peculiar perceptions, such as hallucinations of talking with a dead relative (APA, 1987), are frequent. Behavior is equally unusual. These people tend to be slovenly, to talk to themselves, to speak in a vague, rambling manner, or to be taciturn. Their emotions are often blunted or inappropriate; they may laugh at a funeral, for example. Socially anxious and lacking appropriate skills, they find it difficult to interact with others. Thus people with a schizotypal personality disorder are both isolated and impaired in everyday functioning.

**Reinforcement Pattern**    Many clinicians regard the schizotypal personality disorder as a nonpsychotic personality variant of schizophrenia. We see the disorder as an extension of the avoidant and schizoid personality disorders. Those with the disorder tend to display striking deficits in each of the three reinforcement polarities.

*Type of Reinforcement: None or Negative*    People with the schizotypal personality disorder are cognitively autistic, behaviorally aberrant, interpersonally peculiar, chronically distraught, and possessed of a rather chaotic sense of self. It is difficult to see how such patterns of expression are in any way reinforcing, and indeed, Millon has argued that the schizotypal patient has great difficulty obtaining reinforcement of any kind. This could be viewed as compelling evidence—perhaps more than exists for any of the other personality disorders—that the schizotypal personality disorder has anchors in aberrant biological phenomena. If one were to attempt to fit the reinforcement scheme onto this disorder, however, it would most likely be a pattern of negative reinforcement (R—). Perhaps the schizotypal patterns of withdrawal, fantasy, and other eccentric behavior are an escape mechanism by which the person avoids overstimulation or otherwise unmanageable levels of stress.

*Source of Reinforcement: None*    Schizotypal persons also seem to lack any source of reinforcement. Secretive and withdrawn, they form few relationships, and even those are tenuous and may be marked by bizarre behavior. They are inclined to see themselves as incomplete, estranged, and burdened with a life of emptiness. Their mood may shift from unhappiness (when they focus on their deficits) to insentience (when they retreat into fantasy). This is a major factor differentiating the schizotypal patient from the schizoid patient.

*Reinforcement Process: None*    These individuals also usually seem to lack instrumental reinforcement mechanisms. They seem paralyzed—void, or incapable, of meaningful action—and self-absorbed, are often lost in daydreams, and are prone to magical thinking. Apathetic, joyless, spiritless, and often drab, the personality

of the schizotypal patient is best described in terms of what it lacks.

**Causes and Treatments**    The schizotypal personality disorder appears to grow from an intertwining of biological and psychosocial causes. The resemblance of schizotypal processes to schizophrenic processes has led some theorists to propose abnormalities in the activity of the neurotransmitter dopamine as a partial cause of the schizotypal constellation (Everly, 1988). Others have suggested that excessive dampening of signals in the ascending reticular activating system may also help account for this disorder (Siever et al., 1990; Millon, 1969). At the same time, psychosocial factors—including parental abuse, neglect, and psychological malnourishment in general—may also play an important role in the development of this disorder.

Psychotherapy can be of value in repairing some of the schizotypal person's deficiencies, especially when dissociation and magical thinking are minimal and when the patient does not elude reality by frequently escaping into fantasy. In fact, it has been noted that milder variations of this disorder sometimes respond rather well to treatment (APA, 1989).

Progress in psychotherapy depends on the therapist's ability to develop a viable relationship with the patient at the outset. The most helpful psychotherapeutic tactics appear to be those that include social skills training, assertiveness training, and training in the attending to the here and now.

# THE PROVISIONAL PERSONALITY DISORDERS

The sadistic and self-defeating personality disorders have been assigned "provisional" status by the DSM-III-R task force, pending further study.

## Sadistic Personality Disorder

While we all occasionally battle or exchange angry words with others, people with a *sadistic personality disorder* make active attempts to hurt and humiliate others, including those with whom they have intimate or working relationships. They are enthralled by violence and feed their imaginations either by consuming books and movies that have themes of violence and torture or by collecting guns, knives, and other weapons. Many are violent, and police assistance and medical attention are often necessary for victims of their cruelty.

People with this disorder want to control people and often also bring psychological coercion to bear on others. They embarrass children or subordinates by disciplining them in public and by using punishments that far outweigh the misdemeanor. They restrict others' freedom; for instance, a husband with this pattern may forbid his wife from going out without him. And they hurt others with deliberate untruths; for example, a sadistic wife may pretend to be having an affair with another man.

Extreme as they are, this kind of behavior by no means pricks the conscience of people with this personality disorder. They find it pleasurable and amusing to cause suffering in others. Many also enjoy the suffering of animals. Sadistic personalities are often men who were themselves the victims of abuse as children or witnessed a parent being abused. Their generally hurtful behavior is differentiated in DSM-III-R from problems such as spouse abuse, where a single person is victimized, and sexual sadism, which is directed at achieving sexual pleasure rather than dominance (APA, 1987).

**Reinforcement Pattern**   People with this disorder are *active, self-focused,* and sustained primarily by *positive* reinforcement, similar in many ways to people with an antisocial personality disorder. Those with a sadistic personality disorder, however, further demonstrate *discordance* in their personality: their perceptions of pain and pleasure are distorted, so that they receive pleasure by inflicting pain.

**Type of Reinforcement: Positive**   Acts of intimidation, abuse, and other forms of cruelty are experienced as pleasurable to sadistically aggressive people. Thus the sustaining type of reinforcement is positive (R+).

**Source of Reinforcement: Self**   People with a sadistic personality pattern are remarkably self-focused. Having learned that no one is truly trustworthy, they look with disdain upon others and enjoy intimidating and dominating them. Domination can easily erode into humiliation, as well as physical and psychological abuse. Sadistic individuals display social intolerance and malicious prejudice. They are characteristically cold-blooded and apparently unable to act with humane consideration, although they may feign it as a means to an end.

**Reinforcement Process: Active**   People with sadistic personality disorder employ an active reinforcement strategy. They are energetic, action-oriented, and often impulsive, tending to act reflexively without thinking ahead.

They enjoy high-risk endeavors and appear undaunted by pain, danger, or even punishment. They do not see the rules of fair play as applying to them. Power seems to be the only thing they respect. Weakness, in themselves and especially in others, is contemptible.

## Self-defeating Personality Disorder

While sadistic persons cause pain in others, those with a *self-defeating personality disorder* seem to be their own worst enemy. Habitually self-sacrificing, these people thwart their own potential for enjoyment, success, and caring relationships. They shy away from pleasurable activities—taking a vacation seems impossible—and find little enjoyment in normal pastimes. They seem uncomfortable when things go well for them, react with guilt or depression at success, and may even go so far as to counter it. For example, a businessman praised by his boss for good work may deliberately commit a mistake soon afterward or may continually underachieve.

Individuals with a self-defeating personality disorder are attracted to people who are exciting yet uncaring. Women with this disorder regularly date men who are unfeeling and self-centered. They decline reasonable offers of help from others and often alienate or annoy other people, either by being overly demanding of attention or so self-sacrificing that others are uncomfortable around them. The majority of people with this disorder are women; they are likely to have been abused as children, and many suffer deep depression and distress. The diagnosis is not made, however, if the self-defeating behavior occurs only when the person is depressed. In the past, the disorder has been called *masochistic personality disorder,* but the framers of DSM-III-R changed the name to avoid the historic association of that term with the notion that the person derives unconscious pleasure from suffering (APA, 1987).

Although the category of self-defeating personality disorder is new to DSM-III-R, the study of this disorder can be traced back to the early days of psychoanalysis, when it was referred to as *masochism.* Its principal traits are a sense of martyrdom and behavior that is self-effacing and servile.

The framers of DSM-III-R relegated this personality disorder to the appendix, partly because they were concerned that its formal recognition might indirectly promote bias against women and against victims of violence and abuse.

There is some concern that the self-defeating . . . diagnosis may result in blaming the victim of abusive relationships, ignoring the threatening dominance of the spouse, and denigrating the loyalty and commitment of a wife to marriage. Masochism was associated with "feminine nature" in the early psychoanalytic literature. The DSM-III-R title was changed from masochistic to self-defeating in order to minimize the association of the diagnosis with this early literature.

*(Frances, 1988, p. 644)*

**Reinforcement Pattern** People with a self-defeating personality disorder are *passive*, focused on *others*, and at times sustained by *negative* reinforcement, similar in some ways to people with a dependent personality disorder. However, those with a self-defeating personality disorder further demonstrate discordance in their personality: their perceptions of pain and pleasure are distorted in a way that causes them to accept pain and suffering passively rather than to avoid them and pursue pleasure.

*Type of Reinforcement: Positive or Negative* Actually, both positive and negative reinforcement mechanisms may be at work in the self-defeating personality, depending on the person (Millon, 1990). In some instances, for example, willingness to accept exploitation, ridicule, and psychological and physical abuse and to engage in self-sabotaging behavior may actually lead to a desired goal, such as love, intimacy, affection, affiliation, or support from others; that is, self-defeating behavior may have a positively reinforcing (R+) consequence. In other cases a person might resort to self-defeating behavior as a means of preventing the current bad situation from worsening (Berglas, 1986). Thus present failures and present suffering may serve a negatively reinforcing (R−) function by virtue of their promise to prevent more dreaded outcomes.

*Source of Reinforcement: Others* People with a self-defeating personality pattern tend to be other-oriented, with a demeanor that accepts being used, humbled, and debased and that may even encourage others to use and abuse them. They act in an unassuming manner, preferring to place themselves in an inferior position and present themselves in a self-abasing light. They passively accept exploitation and abuse as if they believe they deserve nothing better.

*Reinforcement Process: Passive* People with self-defeating personality disorders tend to assume a predominantly mournful, self-sacrificing posture, and willfully accept mistreatment and abuse from others, as well as undeserved blame and criticism. They typically avoid or abstain from any effort that could lead to a truly positive outcome (such as a gift, assistance, opportunities, favors, and so on).

Thus the discordant self-defeating personality disorder is characterized by passively self-effacing, self-sabotaging, and self-sacrificing patterns of behavior that sustain self-injurious relationships in which the person is exploited and abused.

# PERSONALITY DISORDERS: THE STATE OF THE FIELD

Psychologists' attitudes toward the concept of personality have shifted over the years. For the first half of this century, theorists and researchers believed deeply in the legitimacy of the concept and tried to identify stable personality traits that would account for behavior. Then they discovered the importance of situational factors and a backlash developed — "personality" became almost an obscene word in some circles. The category of personality disorders has suffered the same fate among clinicians. When psychodynamic and humanistic theorists dominated the clinical field, neurotic character disorders, the precursors to personality disorders, were considered useful clinical categories; but the popularity of these categories declined as the behavioral, cognitive, biological, and sociocultural models gained ascendancy. During the 1960s and 1970s, only the antisocial personality disorders received much attention.

Personality and personality disorders have rebounded during the past decade and have gained the rapt attention of numerous researchers and practitioners. Researchers have increasingly noted the inability of situational factors alone to account for behavior, and clinicians have seen case after case in which rigid personality traits, or consistencies in behavior, are more problematic for a client than specific biochemical, behavioral, or cognitive deficiencies. Consequently, the concept of personality disorders is now once again receiving considerable respect among clinicians and unprecedented levels of study.

A major problem that once hindered the study of personality disorders was the difficulty of identifying these broad problems. In recent years, however, some clinical theorists have proposed unifying principles and themes that help define and distinguish the personality disorders, and diagnosticians have developed effective objective tests for assessing the various personality disorders. Such advances have in turn contributed to the wave of systematic research that we are currently witnessing.

So far, only the antisocial and borderline personality disorders have received much study, but in the current research climate we can expect the other personality disorders to attract considerable attention in the coming years. Then clinicians should be better able to answer some pressing questions: How prevalent are the various personality disorders? How do they interrelate? How are they related to other kinds of mental disorders? And what interventions will make a dent in these disorders?

We also expect research to point to various limitations in the present categorizations of personality disorders, and some categories may well change. Any alterations, however, are likely to be based on systematic research rather than, as in the past, on the intuitions, frustrations, or mood changes of clinicians and theorists. To the many people who are impaired and distressed by inflexible and maladaptive personality traits, this change in direction will be most welcome.

# SUMMARY

**E**ach individual has a unique *personality,* or pattern of behavior, perception, and emotion. *Personality traits* are enduring consistencies with which we relate to our surroundings, and are often viewed as intrinsic characteristics. People with *personality disorders* display inflexible and maladaptive personality traits that impair their social or occupational functioning or cause them intense distress.

DSM-III-R recognizes eleven formal personality disorders, which are grouped into three major clusters. In an alternative method for organizing personality disorders developed by Theodore Millon, an individual's personality is revealed by the types of reinforcements the person seeks, the sources of those reinforcements, and the instrumental processes that the person uses to obtain the reinforcements. This information may be indicated along three polarities: *type* (positive or negative), *source* (self or others), and *instrumental processes* (active or passive).

People who display an *antisocial personality disorder* have a lifelong history of misconduct. They are indifferent to others and have no qualms about lying for gain and little remorse over the pain they inflict on others. In Millon's reinforcement scheme, these people are seen as active, self-focused, and sustained by positive reinforcement. This disorder is believed to be caused by both biological and environmental factors. Thus far, all attempts to treat antisocial personality disorders have failed.

*Narcissistic personality disorder* is characterized by fantasies of success, beauty, or remarkable talent. People with this disorder are passive, self-focused, and sustained primarily by positive reinforcement. At present there is little evidence of success in the treatment of this disorder.

*Histrionic personality disorder* is characterized by dramatic emotionality and fervent pursuit of attention. People with this disorder are active, other-focused, and sustained primarily by negative reinforcement. Psychotropic medications have been of some value in the treatment of this disorder.

People suffering from *dependent personality disorder* rely totally on others to make decisions for them and provide emotional and psychological support. People with this disorder are passive, other-focused, and sustained primarily by negative reinforcement. Clinicians who treat people with dependent personality disorder generally encourage them to engage in excercises of assertiveness.

People with a *passive-aggressive personality disorder* resent reasonable requests and criticize or scorn superiors. These people are active, ambivalent, and sustained primarily by negative reinforcement. Treatment is generally met with resistance and is most effective if it includes training in social skills and assertiveness.

People with *obsessive compulsive personality disorder* are perfectionists who are often unable to finish a task because the work never seems good enough. They are passive, ambivalent, and sustained by negative reinforcement. Treatment includes training in social skills and relaxation.

*Avoidant personality disorder* is characterized by timidity and sensitivity. People with this disorder are active and sustained by negative reinforcement. Treatment focuses on reducing anxiety and on teaching social skills and assertiveness.

People with *schizoid personality disorder* display lifelong indifference to other people. People with this disorder are passive, unable to obtain reinforcement from themselves or others, and sustained by negative reinforcement. Causes of this disorder appear to be primarily biological, involving the neurotransmitter dopamine; but no drug therapies have yet been developed to treat schizoid personality disorder.

People with *paranoid personality disorder* expect to be hurt and deceived by others and rarely develop close relationships. The disorder may be characterized as active, self-focused, and sustained by negative reinforcement. It may be viewed as an extension of some of the basic personality disorders and may emerge when a person is faced with extreme stress at a critical developmental juncture. Treatment may include the formation of a *therapeutic alliance* between patient and therapist. In general, however, therapy is not often successful.

The *borderline personality disorder* is marked by dysfunction in interpersonal relationships and instability of mood. This disorder is ambivalent on all dimensions of reinforcement. Its causes, including parental neglect and physical and emotional trauma, are linked to the dysfunctional family. Treatment is remarkably difficult. The therapist strives to establish a stable therapeutic environment and assumes an active role in helping the patient recognize self-destructive behavior, identifying the needs or motives behind the behavior, and monitoring the effects of countertransference.

Many clinicians believe that *schizotypal personality disorder,* which is characterized by unusual thoughts, beliefs, and behavior, is a nonpsychotic variant of schizophrenia. People with this disorder appear to have no source of reinforcement and no reinforcement processes and to be sustained by either negative reinforcement or none. Causes of this disorder appear to be both biological and psychosocial, and are probably related to factors associated with schizophrenia. Treatment with psychotherapy has been found to be fairly successful.

A DSM committee is studying two other personality disorders with a view to their possible inclusion in the diagnostic system in the future. People with *sadistic personality disorder* have distorted perceptions that cause them to receive pleasure by inflicting pain. These people are active, self-focused, and sustained primarily by positive reinforcement. People with *self-defeating personality disorder* experience distorted perceptions that cause them to accept pain and suffering passively. They are passive, focused on others, and at times sustained by negative reinforcement.

# TOPIC OVERVIEW

# CHAPTER *18*

# DISSOCIATIVE
# DISORDERS

As we observed in Chapter 17, the term "personality" encompasses the unique pattern of behavior, motives, and emotions that each individual person is known by. Ordinarily a personality has unity; its facets are integrated, so that the person can act with some degree of consistency. Many factors help us to maintain this personal unity; two important ones are memory and identity.

Our *memory* links our past, present, and future. The recollection of past experiences helps us make sense of and react to present events and guides us in making decisions about the future. We recognize our friends and relatives, teachers and employers, and respond to them in appropriate and consistent ways. Without a memory we

would always be starting over; with it, life has progression and continuity. The Spanish film-maker Luis Buñuel wrote, "Our memory is our coherence, our reason, our feeling, even our action. Without it, we are nothing."

Memory also provides us with an *identity,* a sense of who we are. We know ourselves as a unique person with particular preferences, abilities, characteristics, and needs. Others recognize our particularities and expect certain things of us. Even more important, we recognize ourselves and develop our own expectations, values, and goals.

People with *dissociative disorders* experience a breakdown in this integration and self-recognition; they experience a *significant alteration in their memory or identity*, often conceptualized as a dissociation, or separation, of one part of their identity from another. The three most prominent dissociative disorders are psychogenic amnesia, psychogenic fugue, and multiple personality disorder. The principal symptom of **psychogenic amnesia** is an inability to recall important personal events and information. A person with **psychogenic fugue** not only forgets the past but travels to a new location and assumes a new identity. And an individual with **multiple personality disorder** has two or more distinct personalities and periodically switches from one to another.

Several memorable books and movies have dealt with dissociative disorders. Two of the best known are *The Three Faces of Eve* and *Sybil*. It is such an intriguing topic that the majority of television drama series seem to include at least one case of dissociative functioning each season, creating the impression that the disorders are very common. In actuality, they are relatively rare.

DSM-III-R also lists **depersonalization disorder** as a dissociative disorder. This listing is controversial among diagnosticians because the memories and identities of people with this problem seem to remain united and intact. It is their sense of self and of the reality of the self that becomes altered. Their mental processes or bodies feel unreal and foreign to them. The reason given for the DSM-III-R classification is that one's sense of self is an important component of one's identity, so depersonalization disorders qualify as a dissociation in identity. To be consistent with the current diagnostic system, deper-

People with dissociative disorders are able to "get away from it all," including themselves, by totally forgetting many of their actions, thoughts, and events.

sonalization disorders will be discussed at the close of this chapter. Outside of that discussion, however, "dissociative disorders" will refer exclusively to problems that involve clear alterations in memory and identity: psychogenic amnesia, psychogenic fugue, and multiple personality disorder.

## PSYCHOGENIC AMNESIA

People with **psychogenic amnesia** are suddenly unable to recall important personal information or past events in their lives. The loss of memory is much more extensive than normal forgetting and cannot be attributed to an organic disorder. Very often it is precipitated by extreme emotional stress.

*B*rian was spending the day sailing with his wife, Helen. The water was rough but well within what they considered safe limits. They were having a wonderful time and really didn't notice that the sky was getting darker, the wind blowing harder, and the sailboat becoming more difficult to control. After a few hours of sailing, they found themselves far from shore in the middle of a powerful and dangerous storm.

The storm intensified very quickly. Brian had trouble controlling the sailboat amidst the high winds and wild waves. He and Helen tried to put on the safety jackets they had neglected to wear earlier, but the boat turned over before they were finished. Brian, the better swimmer of the two, was able to swim back to the overturned sailboat, grab the side, and hold on for dear life, but Helen simply could not overcome the rough waves and reach the boat. As Brian watched in horror and disbelief, his wife disappeared from view.

After a time, the storm began to lose its strength. Brian managed to restore the sailboat to its proper position and sail back to shore. Finally he reached safety, but the personal consequences of this storm were just beginning. The next days were filled with pain and further horror: the Coast Guard finding Helen's body . . . discussions with authorities . . . breaking the news to Helen's parents . . . funeral plans . . . the funeral itself . . . conversations with friends . . . self-blame . . . grief . . . and more—the start of a nightmare that wouldn't end.

There are four kinds of psychogenic amnesia— *localized, selective, generalized,* and *continuous*. Any can be triggered by a traumatic experience such as Brian's, but each represents a distinct pattern of forgetting.

Let us imagine that on the day after the funeral Brian awakens and cannot recall any events from the past difficult days, beginning with the time of the boating tragedy. He remembers everything that occurred before the accident and can now recall everything from the morning after the funeral forward, but the intervening days remain a total blank. In this case, Brian would be suffering from *localized,* or *circumscribed, amnesia,* the most common type of psychogenic amnesia. Here a person forgets *all* events that occurred over a *limited* period of time, beginning almost always with an event that was very disturbing.

People with *selective amnesia,* the second most common form of psychogenic amnesia, remember *some, but not all,* events occurring over the circumscribed period of time. Brian may remember his conversations with friends and breaking the news to his parents-in-law, for example, but have no recollection of making funeral plans or of the funeral itself.

The forgotten or partially forgotten period is called the *amnestic episode.* During an amnestic episode, people sometimes act puzzled and confused and may even wander about aimlessly. They are already experiencing memory difficulties, but seem to be unaware of them. Later, however, when they try and fail to recall the events of the amnestic episode, they are quite aware of their memory disturbance and upset by it.

In some cases the forgetting extends back to a time before the traumatic period. Brian may awaken after the funeral and find that, in addition to the preceding few days, he cannot remember other events in his past life. In this case, he is experiencing *generalized amnesia.* In extreme cases, people with this form of amnesia do not even remember who they are and fail to recognize relatives and friends. At the same time, they remember how to write, read, solve problems, drive a car, and so on.

In the forms of psychogenic amnesia discussed so far, the period affected by the amnesia has an end; but in *continuous amnesia,* a relatively rare disorder, forgetting continues into the present, and new and ongoing experiences fail to be retained. Brian's loss of memory, for example, may extend indefinitely into his life after the accident. He may remember what happened before the tragedy but keep forgetting events that occur since then. He is caught in a prolonged amnestic episode. Although rare as a psychogenic form of amnesia, continuous amnesia is more common in cases of amnesia that have an organic basis (see Box 18-1).

Many cases of psychogenic amnesia occur during wartime or in natural disasters, when a person's health or safety is significantly threatened (Loewenstein, 1991; APA, 1987). In fact, between 5 and 14 percent of all mental disorders that emerge during military combat are cases of psychogenic amnesia. More than a third of these combat amnesia cases arise in soldiers who have endured prolonged marching and fighting under heavy enemy fire; soldiers who have engaged in periodic fighting

make up 13 percent of the cases; soldiers whose experience has been confined to base camp make up only 6 percent of the cases (Sargent & Slater, 1941).

The disorder may also arise under more ordinary circumstances (APA, 1987). The sudden loss of a loved one through rejection, abandonment, or death can lead to psychogenic amnesia (Loewenstein, 1991). In other cases, guilt over behavior that a person considers immoral or sinful (such as an extramarital affair) may precipitate the disorder.

The personal impact of psychogenic amnesia depends on the extent and importance of what is forgotten. Obviously, an amnestic episode of two years is more disabling than one of two hours. Similarly, an amnestic episode during which a person undergoes major life changes causes more difficulties than one that is largely uneventful. The impairment from psychogenic amnesia is usually temporary. In most cases the amnesia ends as abruptly as it began, and the person recovers completely and does not experience any recurrence of the disorder (APA, 1987).

## PSYCHOGENIC FUGUE

When a loss of memory takes on the added dimension of actual physical flight, it is labeled a psychogenic fugue. People with this disorder forget their personal identity and all details of their past life, flee to an entirely different location, and establish a new identity. In most cases they travel only a short distance, their new identity is not a complete one, and they have few social contacts (APA, 1987). Usually the fugue is brief — a matter of hours or days — and ends suddenly.

In some cases, however, the fugue is quite extensive. Such persons establish a well-integrated new identity, adopt a new name, engage in complex social interactions, and even pursue a new line of work. In their new identity they may have personal characteristics they never displayed previously. Usually they are more outgoing and less inhibited (APA, 1987). Despite a missing personal history, they give no outward appearance of abnormal functioning. Fugues of this kind usually last longer than a few hours, and the distance traveled is more than a few miles. Indeed, some people have been known to travel to foreign countries thousands of miles away. This kind of fugue is seen in the case of the Reverend Ansel Bourne, described by the famous psychologist William James at the turn of the century:

*The Rev. Ansel Bourne, of Greene, R.I., was brought up to* the trade of a carpenter; but . . . he became converted from Atheism to Christianity just before his thirtieth year, and has since that time for the most part lived the life of an itinerant preacher. . . . He is of a firm and self-reliant disposition, a man whose yea is yea and his nay, nay; and his character for uprightness is such in the community that no person who knows him will for a moment admit the possibility of his case not being perfectly genuine.

On January 17, 1887, he drew 551 dollars from a bank in Providence with which to pay for a certain lot of land in Greene, paid certain bills, and got into a Pawtucket horse-car. This is the last incident which he remembers. He did not return home that day, and nothing was heard of him for two months. He was published in the papers as missing, and foul play being suspected, the police sought in vain his

whereabouts. On the morning of March 14th, however, at Norristown, Pennsylvania, a man calling himself A. I. Brown who had rented a small shop six weeks previously, stocked it with stationery, confectionery, fruit and small articles, and carried on his quiet trade without seeming to any one unnatural or eccentric, woke up in a fright and called in the people of the house to tell him where he was. He said that his name was Ansel Bourne, that he was entirely ignorant of Norristown, that he knew nothing of shop-keeping, and that the last thing he remembered—it seemed only yesterday—was drawing the money from the bank, etc. in Providence. He would not believe that two months had elapsed. The people of the house thought him insane; and so, at first, did Dr. Louis H. Read, whom they

===

## BOX 18-1

# Anterograde Amnesia: The Long and the Short of It

Although psychogenic amnesia can take any of several specific forms, it most often affects a person's ability to recall autobiographical information from the past. This is generally known as *retrograde amnesia*—a lack of memory about events that occurred before the event that caused the amnesia. Localized, selective, and generalized amnesias are all forms of retrograde amnesia. In contrast, people who suffer organic injury to the brain often exhibit *anterograde amnesia,* characterized by inability to learn new information. Continuous amnesia is a form of anterograde amnesia. People newly met are almost immediately forgotten, and problems solved one day must be tackled again the next. Patients may not remember any of the changes that have taken place since the time of their organic trauma. A patient from a bygone era, for example, may continue to believe that Richard Nixon is president in 1992, a full twenty years after suffering his or her trauma.

The sufferer may retain all other cognitive skills, including verbal skills and problem-solving abilities. The IQ

is not changed. It is as though information from short-term memory, the psychological "work space" that holds information for a few minutes or so, can no longer cross over into long-term memory. Thus, some believe that anterograde amnesia is a case of short-term memory gone awry.

An alternative explanation for anterograde amnesia is that it involves a problem with retrieval. Perhaps the new information—the president's name, for example—*does* move from short-term memory to long-term memory, but the injury has interfered with the way the information is coded. If you think of a piece of information as a book that is to be put on a library shelf, anterograde amnesia might be equivalent to shelving the book without a call number or title, so that it becomes impossible to find the book and review its contents.

To make matters even more complicated, there is evidence that people suffering from organic anterograde amnesia may learn new information even though they are *entirely unaware* that they have done so. This was re-

vealed by a clever doctor after he had been introduced on several consecutive days to a patient who each time greeted the doctor as though they had never met. One day the doctor concealed a pin in his hand and pricked the patient as they shook hands. The following day during the ritual of the daily introduction, the patient refused to shake the doctor's hand but was unable to explain why. The patient apparently had learned a valuable lesson that affected his behavior even though he was not aware of it (Kopelman, 1987). Other researchers have studied this phenomenon and discovered that people with anterograde amnesia may be able to learn procedural information, such as how to solve a puzzle, but not factual information.

The mind is a wondrous machine. Researchers learn as much about it when it malfunctions as when it operates smoothly. Organic amnesia continues to offer insight into the inner workings of our memory, at the same time furnishing some of the clinical field's oddest and most interesting case histories.

called in to see him. But on telegraphing to Providence, confirmatory messages came, and presently his nephew, Mr. Andrew Harris, arrived upon the scene, made everything straight, and took him home. He was very weak, having lost apparently over twenty pounds of flesh during his escapade, and had such a horror of the idea of the candystore that he refused to set foot in it again.

The first two weeks of the period remained unaccounted for, as he had no memory, after he had once resumed his normal personality, of any part of the time, and no one who knew him seems to have seen him after he left home. The remarkable part of the change is, of course, the peculiar occupation which the so-called Brown indulged in. Mr. Bourne has never in his life had the slightest contact with trade. "Brown" was described by the neighbors as taciturn, orderly in his habits, and in no way queer. He went to Philadelphia several times; replenished his stock; cooked for himself in the back shop, where he also slept; went regularly to church; and once at a prayer-meeting made what was considered by the hearers a good address, in the course of which he related an incident which he had witnessed in his natural state of Bourne.

*(James, 1890, pp. 391–393)*

Like psychogenic amnesia, a fugue usually follows a severely stressful event, such as a wartime experience or a natural disaster, though it also can be triggered by personal stress (Loewenstein, 1991; APA, 1987). Some common characteristics of the experiences that precipitate fugues are (1) perceived danger that can neither be fought nor escaped, (2) perceived or actual loss of important objects, and (3) overwhelming homicidal or suicidal impulses (Putnam, 1985). Some adolescent runaways are suspected to be cases of fugue (Loewenstein, 1991; Goodwin et al., 1990).

Fugues tend to end abruptly. In some cases, the recovery of past memories is spontaneous, as with the Reverend Mr. Bourne. The person "awakens" in an unfamiliar place, surrounded by strangers, and wonders how he or she got there. In other cases the lack of personal history may arouse curiosity or suspicion, a traffic accident or legal difficulty may lead police to discover the false identity, or friends may search for and find the missing person. When these people are found, it may be necessary to ask them extensive questions about the details of their lives, repeatedly remind them who they are, and even involve them in psychotherapy before they recover their memories.

Most people who experience a fugue regain all of their memories and never have a recurrence. Interestingly, though, as they recover their past, many of them forget the events of the fugue period. Some, like the Reverend Mr. Bourne, never have even a temporary recollection of the fugue period; their awareness of it may come entirely from other people's accounts.

In 1980 a Florida park ranger found a woman naked and starving in a shallow grave. Unaware of her identity and in an apparent fugue state, she was hospitalized as "Jane Doe." Five months later, the woman was recognized on *Good Morning, America* by Irene Tomiczek *(right)* as her 34-year-old daughter, Cheryl Ann, who had been missing for seven years. With the help of sodium amobarbital treatment and reunion with her family, Cheryl Ann's fugue at last began to lift.

Since most fugues are brief and totally reversible, impairment and aftereffects are usually minimal (Keller & Shaywitz, 1986). People who have been away for months or years, however, often do have trouble adjusting to family, social, or occupational changes that have occurred during their flight. Moreover, some people commit illegal or violent acts in their fugue state and later must face the consequences of those acts.

## MULTIPLE PERSONALITY DISORDER

Multiple personality disorder is as dramatic as it is disabling, as we see in the case of Eric:

*Dazed and bruised from a beating, Eric, 29, was discov*ered wandering around a Daytona Beach shopping mall on Feb. 9. He had no ID and acted so oddly that ambulance workers, who took him to a nearby hospital, assumed he was retarded. Transferred six weeks later to Daytona Beach's Human Resources Center, Eric began talking to doctors in two voices: the infantile rhythms of "young Eric," a dim and frightened child, and the measured tones of "older Eric," who told a tale of terror and child abuse. According to "older Eric," after his immigrant German parents died, a harsh stepfather and his mistress took Eric from his native South Carolina to a drug dealers' hideout in a Florida swamp. Eric said he was raped by several gang members and watched his stepfather murder two men.

One day in late March an alarmed counselor watched Eric's face twist into a violent snarl. Eric let loose an unearthly growl and spat out a stream of obscenities. "It sounded like something out of *The Exorcist*," says Malcolm Graham, the psychologist who directs the case at the center. "It was the most intense thing I've ever seen in a patient." That disclosure of a new personality, who insolently demanded to be called Mark, was the first indication that Graham had been dealing with a rare and serious emotional disorder: true multiple personality. . . .

Eric's other manifestations emerged over the next weeks: quiet, middle-aged Dwight; the hysterically blind and mute Jeffrey; Michael, an arrogant jock; the coquettish Tian, whom Eric considered a whore; and argumentative Phillip, the lawyer. "Phillip was always asking about Eric's rights," says Graham. "He was kind of obnoxious. Actually, Phillip was a pain."

To Graham's astonishment, Eric gradually unfurled 27 different personalities, including three females. . . . They ranged in age from a fetus to a sordid old man who kept trying to persuade Eric to fight as a mercenary in Haiti. In one therapy session, reports Graham, Eric shifted personality nine times in an hour. "I felt I was losing control of the sessions," says the psychologist, who has eleven years of clinical experience. "Some personalities would not talk to me, and some of them were very insightful into my behavior as well as Eric's."

(*Time*, October 25, 1982, p. 70)

A person with multiple personality disorder displays two or more distinct personalities, often called *subpersonalities,* each with a unique set of memories, behaviors, thoughts, and emotions. At any given time, one of the subpersonalities dominates the person's consciousness and interactions with the environment. Usually one subpersonality, the *primary,* or *host, personality,* appears more often than the others.

The transition from one subpersonality to another is usually sudden and often dramatic (Dell & Eisenhower, 1990; Putnam, 1988; APA, 1987). Eric, for example, twisted his face, growled, and yelled obscenities while changing personalities. Transitions are usually precipitated by a stressful event, although artificial precipitants, such as hypnotic suggestion, can also bring about the change (Brende & Rinsley, 1981).

Multiple personality was first reported almost four centuries ago (Bliss, 1986, 1980). It is considered to be a rare disorder, but recent reports suggest that it may be more common than was previously believed (Kluft, 1991; Bliss, 1985). Most cases are first diagnosed in late adolescence or young adulthood, but the symptoms usually begin to develop in early childhood, typically after

episodes of abuse (Ament, 1987; Sachs, 1986). Indeed, studies suggest that as many as 97 percent of these patients have been physically, often sexually, abused during their early years (Ross et al., 1990, 1989; Chu & Dill, 1990; Dell & Eisenhower, 1990; Schultz et al., 1989; Putnam et al., 1986). The disorder is diagnosed in women between four and nine times as often as it is diagnosed in men (Ross & Norton, 1989; APA, 1987; Putnam et al., 1986). In a number of cases, the parents of people with multiple personality disorder appear to have themselves displayed some kind of dissociative disorder (Dell & Eisenhower, 1990; Ross, Norton, & Wozney, 1989).

## The Subpersonalities

The subpersonalities relate to one another in ways that vary from case to case. Generally, however, there are three kinds of relationships: mutually amnesic, mutually cognizant, and one-way amnesic.

In *mutually amnesic relationships,* the subpersonalities have no awareness of one another (Ellenberger, 1970). Conversely, in *mutually cognizant patterns,* each subpersonality is well aware of the rest. They may hear one another's voices and even talk among themselves. Some are on good terms, relating as friends would and sharing opinions and goals. Others do not get along at all. Eric's subpersonalities were mutually cognizant:

*M*ost of the personalities interacted. Cye, a religious mystic, once left a comforting note for Eric. The pushy Michael, who loved rock music, hated Eric's classical records so much that he yanked the wires from a stereo. Eric defended the menacing Mark: "Mark never hurt anybody," he said one day. "He is just there to scare other people off when they get too close." Eric referred to his troupe of personalities as his "talking books." One of the characters was a librarian named Max who occasionally announced a sudden personality change by saying, "One of the books just fell off the shelf."

(*Time*, October 25, 1982, p. 70)

Other patterns fall between these two extremes. The most common multiple personality pattern is the *one-way amnesic relationship:* some subpersonalities are aware of others, but the awareness is not reciprocated. Those that are aware are called *co-conscious subpersonalities.* They are "quiet observers" that watch the actions and thoughts of the other subpersonalities but do not interact with them. Sometimes they make themselves known while another subpersonality is dominating consciousness through such indirect means as "automatic writing": the conscious personality finds itself writing down words over which it experiences no control.

A one-way amnesic relationship was at work in the case of Miss Christine Beauchamp, one of the earliest reported and most famous examples of multiple personality (Prince, 1924, 1906). In therapy, this woman initially manifested three subpersonalities. Her therapist labeled them the Saint (a religious, even-tempered subpersonality), the Woman (irreligious and bad-tempered), and the Devil (mischievous and cheerful). The Saint, Miss Beauchamp's primary personality, knew nothing of the Woman or the Devil. The Woman knew of the Saint but not of the Devil. The Devil knew of both the Saint and the Woman but in different ways: she had direct access to the Saint's thoughts, but her knowledge of the Woman was based solely on her observations of the Woman's behavior.

Investigators used to believe that cases of multiple personality disorder usually involved two or three subpersonalities. Studies now suggest, however, that the average number of subpersonalities per patient may be as high as thirteen or fourteen (Ross et al., 1989; Kluft, 1984). In fact, there have been cases in which 100 or more subpersonalities were observed (APA, 1987). The subpersonalities tend to emerge in groups of two or three at a time (APA, 1987). The subpersonalities within such groups tend to be relatively close in age and interdependent. Often one of the subpersonalities will take on the role of protecting the others in the group.

Therapists typically become aware of the greater number of subpersonalities only as therapy progresses. In the case of Miss Beauchamp, the Saint, the Woman, and the Devil were joined by other personalities during the course of treatment (Rosenzweig, 1988, 1987; Prince, 1924, 1906). A more recent example is the full story of "Eve White," the woman made famous in the book and movie *The Three Faces of Eve.* The book reported that Eve had three personalities—Eve White, Eve Black, and Jane (Thigpen & Cleckley, 1957). Eve White, the primary personality, was colorless, quiet, and serious; Eve Black was carefree, mischievous, and uninhibited; and Jane was mature and intelligent. According to the book, these three subpersonalities eventually merged into Evelyn, a stable and enduring personality who represented an integration of the other three.

It turned out, however, that this was not the end of Eve's dissociation. Twenty years later, in the mid-1970s, she identified herself in an autobiography. Now named Chris Sizemore, she described her pre- and posttherapy life more fully and said that altogether twenty-two subpersonalities had emerged, including nine subpersonalities after Evelyn! Usually they emerged in groups of three, with each group displaying a range of characteristics, abilities, and tastes. Apparently the authors of *The Three Faces of Eve* had worked with her during the ascen-

Chris Sizemore, the subject of the film *The Three Faces of Eve,* is now an accomplished author, artist, and mental health spokesperson who no longer manifests a multiple personality disorder. The variety of her portraits reflects the many subpersonalities Sizemore displayed.

dancy of one such group, and never knew about her previous and subsequent subpersonalities. It appears that this woman has now overcome her disorder and achieved a single, stable identity. She has been Chris Sizemore for nearly 20 years (Sizemore & Huber, 1988).

**Differences between Subpersonalities** Subpersonalities usually have their own names. This seems strangely appropriate, given the extent to which they differ from one another in personality characteristics, vital statistics, abilities and preferences, and even physiological responses.

*Personality Characteristics* Subpersonalities usually differ greatly in their personal styles (Dell & Eisenhower, 1990; Putnam, 1989). A look once again at the three personalities first displayed by Miss Beauchamp highlights this diversity (Prince, 1906). The primary personality, the Saint, was a fragile, prim, and humorless woman who also was very religious and cared for children and older people. She was overly conscientious and idealistic, and often experienced severe guilt and depression. The subpersonality called the Woman was an irreligious person who disliked children and older people. She had a bad temper and was very ambitious. Finally, the Devil, also named Sally, had a mischievous and "playfully wicked" personality and a corresponding sense of humor. She tended to be childlike, impulsive, and seductive, and was filled with energy and the joy of life. Even when the Saint became depressed and suicidal, Sally remained cheerful and functional. Not surprisingly, Sally had little patience with the other two subpersonalities. To her the Saint was weak and sentimental, and she truly hated the Woman.

**Vital Statistics** The subpersonalities may differ in features as basic as age, sex, race, and family history (Coons, Bowman, & Milstein, 1988), as in the famous case of Sybil Dorsett. Sybil's multiple personality disorder has been described in fiction form, but the novel is based on an actual case and both the therapist and patient have attested to its accuracy (Schreiber, 1973). Sybil manifested seventeen subpersonalities, all with different identifying features. They included adults, a teenager, and a baby named Ruthie; and while most of her personalities were female, two were male, named Mike and Sid. The subpersonalities had distinct physical images of themselves and of each other. The subpersonality named Vicky, for example, saw herself as an attractive blonde, while another, Peggy Lou, was described as a pixie with a pug nose. Mary was plump with dark hair, and Vanessa was a tall redhead with a willowy figure. Mike's olive skin and brown eyes stood in contrast to Sid's fair skin and blue eyes.

**Abilities and Preferences** It is not uncommon for the different subpersonalities to have different abilities. One may be able to drive, speak a foreign language, or play a musical instrument, while the others cannot (Coons et al., 1988). Their handwriting styles can also differ (Coons, 1980). Usually a person's subpersonalities will have different tastes in food, friends, music, and literature, as in Sybil's case.

*Among outsiders Vanessa claimed to like everybody who* wasn't a hypocrite. Peggy Lou vented her spleen against what she called "showoffs like Sybil's mother." Vicky favored intelligent and sophisticated persons. Both Mary and Sybil had a special fondness for children. Mary, indicating oneness rather than autonomy, remarked about a woman they all knew, "None of us liked her."

Excited by conversations about music, Peggy Lou often shut her ears in the course of other conversations. Bored by female conversation in general, Mike and Sid sometimes succeeded in making Sybil break an engagement or nagged throughout the visit.

. . . Marjorie told Dr. Wilbur, "I go with Sybil when she visits her friends, but they talk about things they like and I don't care about—houses, furniture, babies. But when Laura Hotchkins comes, they talk about concerts, and I like that."

*(Shreiber, 1973, p. 288)*

Chris Sizemore ("Eve") displayed similar differences in abilities and preferences. She later pointed out, "If I had learned to sew as one personality and then tried to sew as another, I couldn't do it. Driving a car was the same. Some of my personalities couldn't drive" (1975, p. 4). She also reported, "I had at one time about every kind of [phonograph] record you could imagine because each personality had its own taste" (1975, p. 26).

**Physiological Responses** Clinical researchers have discovered that subpersonalities may also differ in their physiological responses, such as their autonomic nervous system activity, blood pressure levels, and menstrual cycles (Putnam, Zahn, & Post, 1990). One study examined the stress responses of Jonah, a man with four subpersonalities (Ludwig et al., 1972). The experimenters asked each of Jonah's subpersonalities to choose two words that had special emotional meaning for it. Then they composed a list of twenty words—the eight emotion-laden words selected by the four subpersonalities plus twelve neutral words. The list was read to each subpersonality individually, and the subpersonality's galvanic skin response (GSR) was measured after each word. Jonah, the primary personality, showed heightened GSRs to all eight emotionally charged words; but each of the other subpersonalities responded in a heightened manner only to the pair of words it had chosen. In short, each personality seemed to have its own stressors and experienced intensive physiological reactions to those stressors only.

Another study investigated the brain activities of different subpersonalities by measuring their *evoked potentials*—that is, the brain response patterns recorded on an electroencephalograph as the subject observed a flashing light (Putnam, 1984). When this evoked-potential test was administered to four subpersonalities of each of ten people with multiple personality disorder, it showed that the brain activity patterns of the subpersonalities differed greatly within each individual. This was a dramatic finding. The brain response patterns to a specific stimulus are usually unique and stable for a given individual. The subpersonalities of these ten subjects showed the kinds of variations usually found in totally different people.

This study also made use of control subjects who pretended to have different subpersonalities. They were instructed to create and rehearse their alternate personalities in detail and were then given the same evoked-potential test for each of their simulated subpersonalities. The brain reaction patterns of these control subjects did not vary for the different simulated subpersonalities. This is evidence that the significant variations in brain reaction patterns from subpersonality to subpersonality in cases of multiple personality cannot be brought about by simple faking.

## The Prevalence of Multiple Personality Disorder

As we noted earlier, multiple personality has traditionally been thought of as a rare disorder. By 1970 only 100 cases had ever been reported in professional journals, and many clinicians challenged the legitimacy of even these cases. They argued that the patients' therapists had unintentionally helped create the disorder by subtly suggesting the existence of alternate personalities during therapy or by eliciting the personalities while patients were under hypnosis (Larmore et al., 1977). This argument seemed to be supported by the fact that many cases did initially come to the attention of a therapist while the client was being treated for a less serious problem (Allison, 1978).

In recent years, the number of people diagnosed with multiple personality disorders has been increasing more and more rapidly. By the mid-1970s, 200 cases had been reported; the number reached 300 by the late 1970s and then doubled by the early 1980s (Kluft, 1983). In recent years, thousands of contemporary cases have been identified in the United States and Canada alone (Ross et al., 1989; APA, 1987; Kluft, 1987; Bliss, 1985; Putnam, 1985; Braun, 1984). Although the disorder is still relatively rare, the prevalence rate appears to have increased dramatically.

What accounts for this recent increase in the number of cases reported? At least two factors seem to be involved. First, there is a growing belief in the authenticity of this disorder and hence in the willingness to diagnose it (French, 1987). It has become clear to many investigators, after careful evaluation of the literature and careful observations of clients, that cases of multiple personality are not necessarily *iatrogenic* — that is, unintentionally caused by practitioners (Braun, 1984; Kluft, 1982). Many of the so-called iatrogenic cases actually involved people who had finally sought treatment after having experienced losses of time throughout their lives, a symptom that is very consistent with multiple personality disturbances (Putnam, 1989; Schacter et al., 1989). Moreover, in many of these cases, it turned out that the subpersonalities had already been observed by friends or relatives, or noticed by the individuals themselves, before the therapist was first consulted.

The increased number of multiple personality cases reported may also reflect recent changes in diagnostic biases and criteria. As we saw in Chapter 15, from 1910 to 1978 schizophrenia was one of the most popular diag-

One of the cinema's best-known fictional sufferers of multiple personality disorder, Norman Bates, is horrified to discover his mother has stabbed a woman to death in the shower. Later in the movie *Psycho* we learn his mother died years ago and now "exists" as one of Bates's subpersonalities.

noses in the clinical field (Rosenbaum, 1980). Because the criteria for that disorder tended to be vague and flexible, the diagnosis was readily applied to a wide range of unusual and mysterious patterns of abnormality. It is possible that many cases of multiple personality were incorrectly diagnosed as schizophrenia during that period. Under the stricter criteria of DSM-III and DSM-III-R, diagnosticians have applied the label of schizophrenia with greater accuracy, allowing multiple personality cases to be recognized and assessed more readily (Coons & Fine, 1990; French, 1987).

Despite such changes in viewpoint and in the diagnostic system, many clinicians remain reluctant to make this diagnosis. In fact, people suffering from this disorder still receive an average of four different diagnoses, such as schizophrenia and depression, and average nearly seven years of contact with health services, before a diagnosis of multiple personality disorder is finally made (Putnam et al., 1986). The problem is that most therapists have little direct experience with this disorder (Bliss, 1988) and some are apparently frightened away from the diagnosis by the skepticism of their colleagues (Dell, 1988; Davidson, Allen, & Smith, 1987).

This problem is reflected in the following statement, made by a clinician who has treated patients with multiple personality disorder:

> Most of the psychiatrists and other mental health professionals I have met who have diagnosed and treated patients with multiple personality disorder have found little initial support from their colleagues. Some have found the going very difficult. Many have been told, in various ways, by their colleagues, their supervisors, and others, that they were simply wrong, that there was no such thing as multiple personality disorder, or, if the diagnosis was considered accurate, that it was probably basically a seizure disorder or an affective disorder and should be treated primarily with medication. Worse, many have experienced quite derisive criticism or ridicule, either directly or indirectly. In one instance a member of a nursing staff told a multiple personality disorder patient that the patient's doctor was crazy and diagnosed everyone as having multiple personality disorder.
>
> Certainly, multiple personality disorder evokes some very strong emotions. I know of no other illness that stimulates such strong denials of the possibility of its existence, and an absence of interest in many very capable clinicians who have very intense spontaneous curiosity about other clinical phenomena!
>
> *(Hicks, 1985, pp. 243–244)*

# EXPLANATIONS OF DISSOCIATIVE DISORDERS

Relatively few researchers have investigated the origins of the dissociative disorders, although a variety of theories have been offered to explain them. Proponents of older perspectives especially, such as the psychodynamic and behavioral viewpoints, have gathered little systematic data. On the other hand, newer theories, which combine cognitive, behavioral, and biological principles and highlight such factors as *state-dependent learning* and *self-hypnosis,* have begun to capture the enthusiasm of clinical scientists.

## The Psychodynamic View

Psychodynamic theorists believe that dissociative disorders represent an extreme use of *repression,* the most fundamental defense mechanism: people ward off anxiety by unconsciously preventing painful memories, thoughts, or impulses from reaching awareness. Every-

one uses repression to a degree, but those people diagnosed as having dissociative disorders are thought to repress their memories excessively and dysfunctionally (Terr, 1988).

*Psychogenic amnesias* and *fugues* are each seen as representing a single episode of massive repression in which a person unconsciously blocks the memory of an extremely upsetting event to avoid the pain of confronting it (Putnam, 1985). Such a reaction has its roots in childhood. When parents overreact to a child's expressions of id impulses (for example, to signs of sexual impulses), some children become excessively afraid of those impulses, defend against them, and develop a strict code prohibiting such "immoral" desires. Later in their lives, when they act in a manner that violates their moral code — by having an extramarital affair, for example — they are brought face to face with their most unacceptable impulses. They may be forced to repress the whole situation as the only means of protecting themselves from overwhelming anxiety.

If amnesia and fugue conceal a single repressed event, multiple personality disorders bespeak a lifetime of excessive repression. Dependence on this ongoing style of coping is thought by psychodynamic theorists to be triggered by extremely traumatic childhood experiences, particularly abusive parenting. Young Sybil, for example, was repeatedly made to suffer unspeakable tortures by her disturbed mother, Hattie:

> *A favorite ritual . . . was to separate Sybil's legs with a* long wooden spoon, tie her feet to the spoon with dish towels, and then string her to the end of a light bulb cord, suspended from the ceiling. The child was left to swing in space while the mother proceeded to the water faucet to wait for the water to get cold. After muttering, "Well, it's not going to get any colder," she would fill the adult-sized enema bag to capacity and return with it to her daughter. As the child swung in space, the mother would insert the enema tip into the child's urethra and fill the bladder with cold water. "I did it," Hattie would scream triumphantly when her mission was accomplished. "I did it." The scream was followed by laughter, which went on and on.
>
> *(Schreiber, 1973, p. 160)*

According to psychodynamic theorists, children who are exposed to such traumas and abuses may come to fear the dangerous world they live in and take to flight symbolically by regularly pretending to be another person who is safely looking on from afar. This flight is much more desperate and pathological than the flights of fantasy and daydreaming that all people engage in on occasion. Sybil's psychotherapist concluded, "She had sought rescue from without until, finally recognizing that this rescue would be denied, she resorted to finding rescue from within. . . . Being a multiple personality was the ultimate rescue" (Schreiber, 1973, p. 158).

Abused children may also become afraid of the impulses that they believe are leading to their punishments. They may strive to be "good" and "proper" all of the time and keep repressing the impulses they consider "bad" and "dangerous." Whenever "bad" thoughts or impulses do break through, such children may feel bound to disown and deny them, and may unconsciously assign all unacceptable thoughts, impulses, and emotions to other personalities. This situation would lead to an inhibited and drab primary personality that is accompanied by bold and colorful subpersonalities.

Most of the support for the psychodynamic position is drawn from case histories. Such brutal childhood experiences as beatings, cuttings, burnings with cigarettes, imprisonment in closets, rape, and extensive verbal abuse have often been reported in multiple personality cases. On the other hand, the backgrounds of some individuals with multiple personality disorders do not seem to be markedly deviant (Bliss, 1980). Moreover, child abuse appears to be far more prevalent than multiple personality disorder. Why then do only a small fraction of abused children develop this form of dysfunctioning?

## The Behavioral View

Behaviorists believe that dissociation is a response acquired through operant conditioning. People who experience a horrifying event may later find temporary relief when their mind drifts to other subjects. For some, this momentary forgetting, leading to a reduction in anxiety, increases the likelihood of future forgetting. In short, they are reinforced for the act of forgetting and learn— without being aware that they are learning—that forgetting lets them avoid or escape anxiety.

The behavioral explanation of dissociative disorders shares several features with the psychodynamic view. Both hold that dissociative disorders are precipitated by traumatic experiences, that the disorders represent ways of avoiding extreme anxiety, and that the individuals themselves are unaware that their disorder is actually protecting them from facing a painful reality. The explanations do, however, differ in some important ways. Psychodynamic theorists believe that the disorders represent attempts at forgetting that, although unconscious, are purposeful from the start, whereas behaviorists believe the initial development of dissociative reactions to be more accidental. Furthermore, behaviorists believe that a subtle reinforcement process rather than a hard-

working unconscious is keeping the individual unaware that he or she is using dissociation as a means of escape.

Like the psychodynamic explanation, the behavioral explanation has certain shortcomings. Behaviorists too have been forced to rely largely on case histories to support their position. While case descriptions do typically support the behavioral viewpoint, they are often equally consistent with other kinds of explanations as well, offering no evidence that one explanation is superior to the other. A case that seems to reflect the reinforcement of forgetting, for example, can usually also be interpreted as an example of unconscious repression.

The behavioral explanation does not yet explain precisely how temporary distractions from painful memories grow into acquired responses or why, since temporary acts of forgetting are frequently reinforced in life, more people do not develop dissociative disorders. Nor has it yet described how reinforcement can account for the complicated interrelationships of subpersonalities found in multiple personality disorders.

## State-Dependent Learning

What people learn when they are in a particular state or situation they tend to remember best when they are returned to that same state or situation. Something learned under the influence of alcohol, for example, is likely to be recalled better under the influence of alcohol than in an alcohol-free condition (Overton, 1966). Similarly, people given a learning task to do while they smoke cigarettes will later recall the learned material better when they are smoking.

This association between state and recall is called *state-dependent learning.* It was initially observed in experimental animals that were administered certain drugs, taught to perform certain tasks, and later tested on those tasks under various conditions. Researchers repeatedly found that the animals' subsequent test performances were better in corresponding drug states and poorer in drug-free states (Pusakulich & Nielson, 1976; Spear, 1973; Overton, 1966, 1964). Research with human subjects later showed that state-dependent learning could be associated with psychological states as well as physiological ones. One study found mood to be influential (see Figure 18-1): material learned during a happy mood was recalled best when the subject was again in a happy mood, and sad-state learning was recalled best during sad states (Bower, 1981). Similarly, people who commit crimes of passion or violence often recall the details of their crimes more completely when hypnotists cause them to return to a similar state of arousal (Fischer & Landon, 1972).

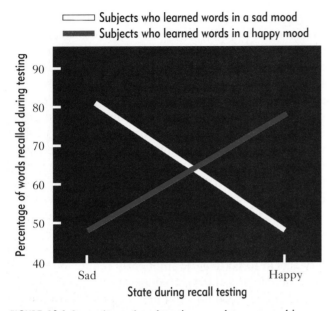

**FIGURE 18-1** State-dependent learning was demonstrated in a study by Bower (1981). Subjects who learned a list of words while in a hypnotically induced happy state remembered the words better if they were in a happy mood when tested later than if they were in a sad mood. Conversely, subjects who learned the words when in a sad mood recalled them better if they were sad during testing than if they were happy.

One way of interpreting the phenomenon of state-dependent learning is to see it as an indication that *arousal levels* are an important part of memory processes. That is, a particular level of arousal will have a set of remembered events, thoughts, and skills attached to it. When a situation elicits that particular level of arousal, the person is more likely to recall the memories associated with it. Skill performances may be enhanced at levels of arousal that correspond to the states in which they were acquired and practiced. Some research even suggests that the *amygdala,* the structure in the brain's limbic system that originates emotional behavior (see Chapter 6), may also regulate the link between arousal and memory (Mishkin, 1981).

For most people state-dependent learning is a relative phenomenon. They can recall many past events across a range of arousal states, but will remember each better in some states than in others. Perhaps some people — those prone to develop dissociative disorders — have state-to-memory links that are extremely rigid and narrow. Their thoughts, memories, and skills may be tied exclusively to particular states of arousal. They recall past events only when they experience arousal states almost identical to the states in which the memory was acquired.

According to proponents of this view, changes in arousal may be at the core of dissociative disorders (Silberman et al., 1985). In psychogenic amnesia, for example, extreme anxiety may be experienced during an upsetting event and relative calm at a later time. In dissociation-prone people, this contrast in arousal states may interfere with the ability to recall the upsetting event. Similarly, in psychogenic fugue, the shift from a harrowing environment and anxious state to a peaceful environment and calmer state may make past events irretrievable for certain individuals.

Multiple personality disorders may also be accounted for by the principles of state-dependent learning. Different arousal levels may elicit different clusters of memories, thoughts, and abilities — that is, different subpersonalities. When a person experiences a particular mood or level of arousal, the memories, thoughts, and abilities acquired previously under a similar level of arousal may surge into consciousness. Later, when the person undergoes a major shift in arousal, a different set of memories and abilities may emerge. This explanation is consistent with our earlier observation that personality transitions in multiple personality disorders tend to be rapid and stress-related.

Efforts to tie state-dependent learning to dissociative disorders keep running into a major problem: theorists do not yet agree about the nature of the contribution of state to memory. Many believe that arousal does not have a special role in remembering and that state-dependent learning can be explained in other ways. Researchers already know that several kinds of cues present at the time of learning will act as memory aids (Tulving & Watkins, 1977). Objects, smells, and sounds can help elicit memories of past events to which they are tied. It is possible that a state of arousal is just another such cue, albeit an internal one. Proponents of this view argue that the notion of state-dependent learning has little new to say about memory itself and less still about the active forgetting involved in dissociative disorders.

## Self-hypnosis

As we first noted in Chapter 1, the word "hypnosis" describes the deliberate induction of a sleeplike state in which a person shows a very high degree of suggestibility. While in this state, the person can behave, perceive, and think in ways that would ordinarily seem impossible. Hypnotized subjects can, for example, be made to suspend their sensory functioning so that they become temporarily blind, deaf, or insensitive to pain (Wallace & Fisher, 1979; Evans, 1968).

Hypnosis can be employed to help people remember events that occurred and were forgotten years ago, a capability of which many psychotherapists make frequent use. Conversely, it can also be used to make people forget facts, events, and even their personal identity—a phenomenon that is called *hypnotic amnesia* (Tkachyk, Spanos, & Bertrand, 1988; Simon & Salzberg, 1985; Hilgard, 1977; Nace, Orne, & Hammer, 1974).

Most investigations of hypnotic amnesia follow similar formats (Hilgard, 1987, 1977; Radtke-Bodorik et al., 1980, 1979; Spanos & Bodorik, 1977). Subjects are asked to study a word list or other material until they are able to repeat it correctly. Under hypnosis, they are then instructed to forget the material until they receive a cancellation signal (such as the snap of a finger), at which time they will suddenly recall the learned material once again. Repeatedly these experiments have shown the subjects' memories to be severely impaired during the period of hypnotically suggested amnesia and then restored after the cancellation signal is given (Spanos & Bodorik, 1977; Hilgard, 1977). It appears that memories of specific events such as a birthday party or an accident are more readily forgotten under hypnotic suggestion than memories of basic knowledge such as how to read, add, or spell (Kihlstrom, 1980).

The parallels between hypnotic amnesia and dissociative disorders are striking (Evans, 1988; Bliss, 1986). Both are conditions in which people forget certain material for a period of time yet later recall it to mind. In both, the people forget without any insight into why they are forgetting or any awareness that something has been forgotten. Finally, in both situations, events are more readily forgotten than basic knowledge. These parallels have led some theorists to conclude that dissociative disorders may represent a form of *self-hypnosis:* people actively induce themselves to forget unpleasant events (Bliss, 1986, 1980; Hilgard, 1977). Psychogenic amnesia, for example, may occur in people who, consciously or unconsciously, go so far as to hypnotize themselves into forgetting horrifying experiences that have recently occurred in their lives. If the self-induced amnesia extends to all memories of a person's past and identity, that person may undergo a psychogenic fugue. As in experimental hypnosis, the forgotten material is fully retrievable and is remembered completely when the fugue ends.

Self-hypnosis can also be used to explain multiple personality disorders. In fact, in a report on fourteen women diagnosed with the disorder, Eugene Bliss (1980) argued that "the crux of the syndrome of multiple personalities seems to be the patient's unrecognized abuse of self-hypnosis" (p. 1395). Each of the women in Bliss's investigation appeared to be very susceptible to hypnosis and to be capable of hypnotic amnesia. More-

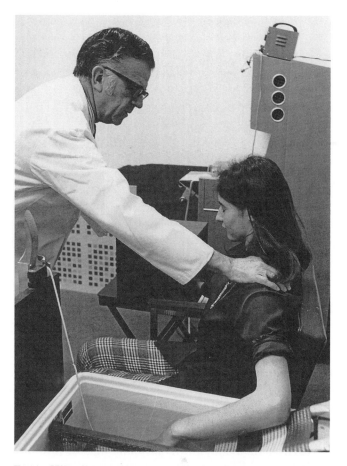

Ernest Hilgard hypnotizes subjects into experiencing tepid water as painfully cold or ice water as comfortably warm. Work by Hilgard and other researchers on hypnotic amnesia has helped convince many clinicians that dissociative disorders represent a form of self-hypnosis.

over, most of them reported long histories of what could be construed as self-hypnosis, dating back to the age of 4, 5, or 6. As one of these women described her early childhood, "Now that I know what hypnosis is, I can say that I was in a trance often. There was a little place where I could sit, close my eyes and imagine, until I felt very relaxed just like hypnosis" (p. 1392). Other studies have similarly suggested great susceptibility to hypnosis and an early history of self-hypnosis among multiple personality patients (Braun & Sacks, 1985).

On the basis of investigations such as this, a number of theorists now believe that multiple personality disorders usually begin at the young age of 4 to 6, when children are generally very suggestible (see Figure 18-2) and excellent hypnotic subjects (Kluft, 1987; Bliss, 1986, 1980; Beahrs, 1983). They suggest that some traumatized or abused children manage to escape their threatening world by self-hypnosis, mentally separating them-

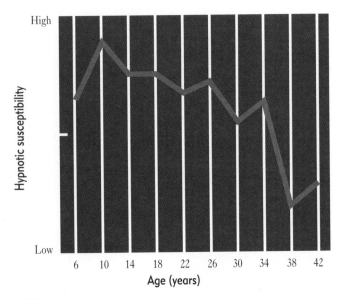

**FIGURE 18-2** Multiple personality disorder is thought to begin between the ages of 4 and 6, when the child's hypnotic susceptibility is on the rise. A person's hypnotic susceptibility steadily increases until pre-adolescence, then generally declines with age. *(Adapted from Morgan & Hilgard, 1973.)*

selves from their body and its surroundings and fulfilling their wish to become some other person or persons. According to Bliss, "self-hypnosis becomes the primary mode of coping. Unpleasant experiences are henceforth forgotten or delegated to a personality by the switch into a hypnotic state."

There are two schools of thought about the nature of hypnosis, each with distinctive implications for dissociative disorders. Some theorists see hypnosis as a *special process* or *trance*, an out-of-the-ordinary kind of psychological and physiological functioning (Hilgard, 1987, 1977; Kihlstrom, 1978; Evans, 1968; Bowers, 1966). The special-process viewpoint holds (1) that people with dissociative disorders place themselves in internal trances during which their conscious functioning is significantly altered, (2) that their forgetting during this self-hypnosis is automatic and complete, and (3) that their willingness to develop new identities (fugue) or become different personalities (multiple personality disorder) is fostered by the heightened capacity for illogical thinking that occurs under hypnosis. Special-process theorists might also argue that people with high, stable levels of susceptibility to hypnosis are strong candidates for dissociative disorders (Sarbin & Coe, 1979).

Other theorists believe that hypnotic behaviors, and hypnotic amnesia in particular, can be explained by *common processes* such as attention and expectation (Spanos, 1982; Barber, 1969). According to these theorists, hypnosis consists simply of motivated people performing tasks that are asked of them. Because of their high motivation, heightened attention, and receptiveness to hypnosis, these individuals actively work to carry out the instructions of the hypnotist to the letter. Yet, because of their strong belief in hypnosis, they fail to recognize their own contributions and report instead that they are behaving automatically and without purposeful effort.

Nicholas Spanos (1991, 1990, 1986) believes that hypnotized subjects manage to forget and then to recall material by *first diverting and then refocusing their attention* at critical times during testing. He argues that hypnotized subjects actively distract themselves during testing and keep their attention focused away from rather than on the test material. He and his colleagues have conducted studies comparing the test performances of hypnotized subjects with those of highly motivated nonhypnotized subjects (Spanos, 1986, 1982; Spanos & D'Eon, 1980; Spanos et al., 1980). In one, a group of subjects were taught a word list and then hypnotized and instructed to forget it. A second group of nonhypnotized subjects were taught the same word list and then asked to recall the words while performing a distracting task (counting backward by threes). The experimenters found that the self-distracted nonhypnotized subjects displayed the same kinds of memory problems as the hypnotized subjects, and to the same extent. Other studies have found that nonhypnotized task-motivated subjects can also be induced to perform like hypnotized subjects in experiments involving, variously, pain reduction, hallucinations, and time distortion (Spanos et al., 1983, 1979; Spanos, Ham, & Barber, 1973).

Thus, according to the common-process view of hypnosis, people with dissociative disorders provide themselves with powerful suggestions to forget and to imagine, and earnestly follow those suggestions. These persons are not faking, just as hypnotized subjects are not faking. Rather, they are very thoroughly fooling themselves.

Whether hypnosis involves special or common processes, hypnosis research effectively demonstrates the power and potential of our normal thought processes, while rendering the idea of dissociative disorders somewhat less remarkable. At the same time, hypnosis research has raised a number of questions, and until these questions are addressed, the possible tie between hypnosis and dissociative disorders remains unsettled (Evans, 1988; Pettinati, 1988; Spanos, 1986).

# TREATMENTS FOR PSYCHOGENIC AMNESIA AND FUGUE

As we saw earlier, cases of psychogenic amnesia and fugue usually end spontaneously and lead to complete recovery. Sometimes, however, they linger and require treatment (Lyon, 1985). *Psychodynamic therapy* is commonly applied to both disorders (Loewenstein, 1991). Therapists guide patients to free-associate and search their unconscious in the hope of bringing the forgotten experiences back to the level of consciousness. Actually, the focus of psychodynamic therapy is very much in harmony with the treatment needs of people with dissociative disorders. After all, people with amnesia and fugue need to recover lost memories, and psychodynamic therapists generally strive to uncover memories — as well as other psychological entities — that have been repressed. Thus many theorists, including some who do not espouse the psychodynamic perspective ordinarily, believe that psychodynamic therapy may be the most appropriate and effective approach for these disorders.

Another common treatment for psychogenic amnesia and fugue, used either in conjunction with or instead of psychodynamic therapy, is **hypnotic therapy,** or **hypnotherapy.** Therapists hypnotize patients and then guide them to recall the forgotten events (MacHovek, 1981; Garver, Fuselier, & Booth, 1981; Bliss, 1980). Experiments have repeatedly indicated that hypnotic suggestion can successfully elicit forgotten memories, and experience has shown that people with dissociative disorders are usually highly susceptible to hypnosis (Putnam et al., 1986; Bliss, 1986, 1980). Moreover, if, as some theorists argue, amnesia and fugue involve self-hypnosis, then hypnotherapy may be a uniquely relevant intervention for them. It has been applied both alone and in combination with other approaches.

Sometimes intravenous injections of **sodium amobarbital** (Amytal) or **sodium pentobarbital** (Pentothal) are used to help patients regain lost memories (Ruedrich et al., 1985). At the proper dosage, these barbiturates can put people into a near-sleep state during which they may recall forgotten events (Kluft, 1988; Perry & Jacobs, 1982). The nickname "truth serum" is sometimes applied to the drugs, but the key to their success is their capacity for sedating people and lowering their inhibitions.

Several problems with this biological approach have limited its use by clinicians. First, it often fails to work; a large percentage of treated clients fail to recall past events. Second, the drugs cannot be used safely for more than a few sessions, because as barbiturates they may lead to physical dependence. Finally, even when one of the drugs does help someone recall past events, the recollection may last only as long as the interview session itself. After they awaken, many people forget much of what they have said and experienced under the drug's influence. For these reasons, sodium amobarbital and sodium pentobarbital tend to be used in conjunction with other treatment approaches, if they are used at all.

# TREATMENTS FOR MULTIPLE PERSONALITY DISORDER

Unlike the victims of psychogenic amnesia and fugue, people with multiple personality disorder rarely recover spontaneously. Therapists usually try to help people with this more chronic disorder to (1) recover the gaps in their memory, (2) recognize the full breadth of their disorder, and (3) integrate their subpersonalities into one (Kluft, 1991, 1983; Dell & Eisenhower, 1990; Bliss, 1986, 1980; Coons & Bradley, 1985).

To help these patients recover the missing pieces of their past, therapists use many of the same approaches applied to the other dissociative disorders, including psychodynamic therapy, hypnotherapy, and sodium amobarbital (Kluft, 1991, 1985; Bliss, 1986; Herzog, 1984). At best, these techniques work slowly for multiple personality patients. After all, past events not only are actively forgotten by the primary personality but often are embedded exclusively in the minds of alternate personalities. Such "separate ownership" presents a formidable obstacle to the task of remembering.

Multiple personality patients are also slow to recognize the full scope and nature of their disorder. The notion of having more than one personality may seem as strange to them as it does to everyone else. Although patients "have lived in this twilight state for years, experienced amnesias, and been told by others about strange behaviors, the reality has not been confronted" (Bliss, 1980, p. 13). Some therapists actually introduce the subpersonalities to one another under hypnosis, and some have patients look at videotapes of their other personalities (Ross & Gahan, 1988; Sakheim, Hess, & Chivas, 1988). The process of opening the patient's eyes to the extent of the problem is usually intensely emotional for the patient (Bliss, 1980).

Even when the past has been reconstructed and remembered and the subpersonalities made known to one another, many patients are reluctant to pursue the final treatment goal—integration of the subpersonalities into one (Kluft, 1991, 1988). The subpersonalities themselves are likely to distrust the idea. As one subpersonality said, "There are too many advantages to being multiple. Maybe we're being sold a bill of goods by therapists" (Hale, 1983). It is not unusual for subpersonalities to view integration as a form of death.

Therapists have used a range of approaches to help integrate the personalities, including psychodynamic (Sutcliffe & Jones, 1962), supportive (Cutler & Reed, 1975), hypnotic (Herzog, 1984), cognitive (Caddy, 1985), and drug therapies (Fichtner, Kuhlman, Gruenfeld, & Hughes, 1990). One woman's primary personality was given assertiveness training: as she learned to express anger in more functional and satisfying ways, her aggressive and hostile subpersonality began to disappear. Some therapists have even conducted discussions and interactions among the subpersonalities, as if they were conducting group therapy.

In Sybil's case, the progress toward full integration was slow and halting and required eleven years of therapy. Her progress can be traced in the following excerpts from different stages of her treatment (Shreiber, 1973):

*1957* Integration? Far from it. As the past flooded back, there was all the more reason to regress into the other selves, defenses against the past. (p. 270)

*1958* Peggy Lou's memories were becoming Sybil's. By responding to Peggy Lou's memory as it if were her own, . . . Sybil had been able to recall an incident from the childhood of the alternating self. And all at once Sybil realized that at that moment she felt not merely *like* Peggy Lou: she was *one* with her. (p. 272)

*1962* "Am I going to die?" each of the selves asked Dr. Wilbur. For some of the selves integration seemed synonymous with death. The doctor's assurances that, although one with Sybil, the individual selves would not cease to be seemed at best only partly convincing. "There are many things I have to do," Vanessa told Marcia. "You see, I won't be here very long." (p. 316)

*1965* Sybil's attitude toward these selves . . . had completely changed, from initial denial to hostility to acceptance—even to love. Having learned to love these parts of herself, she had in effect replaced self-derogation with self-love. This replacement was an important measure of her integration and restoration. . . . Dr. Wilbur hypnotized Sybil and called for Vicky Antoinette. "How are things going, Vicky?" the doctor asked. "What progress is there underneath?" "I'm part of Sybil now, you know," Vicky replied. "She always wanted to be like me. Now we are one." (p. 337)

Some therapists report high success rates in treating multiple personality disorder (Wilbur, 1984; Kluft, 1984; Allison, 1978), but others find that most patients continue to resist full and final integration. A few therapists have in fact questioned the need for full integration, arguing that patients may be able to function with reasonable effectiveness as long as they rid themselves of their more disturbed subpersonalities (Hale, 1983).

The relatively small number of reported multiple personality cases has prevented researchers from assessing and comparing the effectiveness of the various treatment approaches. As the number of case reports continues to grow, it may soon be possible to conduct statistical evaluations. Meanwhile, individual case reports remain the primary source of information about treatment methods and their outcomes.

# DEPERSONALIZATION DISORDER

The following case study describes a young man who received a diagnosis of a depersonalization disorder.

*A 24-year-old graduate student sought treatment because* he felt he was losing his mind. He had begun to doubt his own reality. He felt he was living in a dream in which he saw himself from without, and did not feel connected to his body

Unlike the extreme avoidance that occurs in dissociative disorders, daydreaming and fantasizing are normal, healthy, and constructive processes. They may serve as flights of fancy or help us analyze or resolve problems.

or his thoughts. When he saw himself through his own eyes, he perceived his body parts as distorted—his hands and feet seemed quite large. As he walked across campus, he often felt the people he saw might be robots; he began to ruminate about his dizzy spells—did this mean that he had a brain tumor? . . . He often noted that he spent so much time thinking about his situation that he lost contact with all feelings except a pervasive discomfort about his own predicament.

In his second session, he was preoccupied with his perception that his feet had grown too large for his shoes, and fretted over whether to break up with his girlfriend because he doubted the reality of his feelings for her, and had begun to perceive her in a distorted manner. He said he had hesitated before returning for his second appointment, because he wondered whether his therapist was really alive. He was very pessimistic that he could be helped, and had vague suicidal ideation. A thorough medical and neurological evaluation found no organic etiology. Medications were without significant impact. The symptoms gradually diminished in the course of a five-year intensive psychoanalytic psychotherapy, at the end of which the patient . . . appeared to experience himself and external reality fairly directly.

*(Kluft, 1988, p. 580)*

As we noted earlier, DSM-III-R categorizes this pattern of symptoms as a dissociative disorder, even though it is quite different from the other patterns discussed in this chapter. Its central symptom is *depersonalization,* an alteration in one's experience of the self in which one's mental functioning or body feels unreal or foreign. Like the graduate student in the example above, people with this symptom feel as though they have become separated from their body and are observing themselves from outside. Occasionally their mind seems to be floating a few feet above them—a sensation known as *doubling.* Their body parts seem foreign, the extremities smaller or bigger than usual. Many of them describe their emotional state as "mechanical," "dreamlike," or "dizzy." Throughout the whole depersonalization experience, however, they are aware that their perceptions are distorted, and in that sense they remain in contact with reality.

In some cases this sense of unreality extends to other sensory experiences, mental operations, and behavior. Some people experience distortions in their sense of touch or smell or their judgments of time or space, or feel that they have lost control over their speech or actions. Depersonalization is often accompanied by an experience of *derealization*—the feeling that the external world, too, is unreal and strange. Objects may seem to change shape or size; other persons may seem removed, mechanical, or even dead. The graduate student, for example, began to perceive his girlfriend in a distorted

manner, and he hesitated to return for a second session of therapy because he wondered whether his therapist was really alive.

Depersonalization symptoms by themselves do not indicate a depersonalization disorder. Transient depersonalization experiences are fairly common (Putnam, 1991), but a depersonalization disorder is not (APA, 1987; Myers & Grant, 1970; Roberts, 1960). Up to 70 percent of adolescents and young adults occasionally experience these symptoms of depersonalization and derealization (APA, 1987; Putnam, 1985). Young children may experience depersonalization from time to time as part of the process of developing their capacity for self-awareness. People sometimes have feelings of depersonalization after practicing meditation (Castillo, 1990). And individuals who travel to new places often report a temporary sense of depersonalization. Impairment from these temporary experiences is rare; social or occupational activities are minimally affected (Castillo, 1990). The person is able to compensate for the distortion, and continues to function with reasonable effectiveness until the episode eventually ends.

The symptoms of a depersonalization disorder, in contrast, are persistent or recurrent, and cause marked distress and impairment in the social and occupational realms. The disorder occurs most frequently in adolescents and young adults, hardly ever in people over 40 (APA, 1987). It usually comes on suddenly, precipitated by experiences such as extreme fatigue, physical pain, intense stress, anxiety, depression, or recovery from substance abuse. Survivors of traumatic experiences, such as internment in a concentration camp or an automobile accident, and people caught in life-threatening situations, such as hostages or kidnap victims, seem to be particularly vulnerable (APA, 1987; Putnam, 1985; Bettelheim, 1979; Noyes & Kletti, 1977). The disorder tends to be chronic; the symptoms may improve and even disappear for a time, only to return or intensify during periods of mild anxiety or depression (APA, 1987). Not surprisingly, people with this disorder often feel anxious or depressed. Like the graduate student, many believe that they are losing their minds and become obsessed with worry about their symptoms (APA, 1987). If the symptoms appear as a part of a pattern of schizophrenia or some other disorder, a diagnosis of depersonalization disorder is not made.

Relatively few theories have been offered to explain depersonalization disorders, and as yet little research has been conducted on the problem. Despite its separate listing in DSM-III-R, many clinical theorists reject the notion that this pattern of symptoms ever appears as a distinct disorder (Kluft, 1988).

*Psychodynamic theorists* view depersonalization as a

primitive, highly pathological defense mechanism (Nemiah, 1989). They propose that people who are unable to control unacceptable impulses through repression, denial, or other defenses may resort to more extreme strategies such as unconsciously separating themselves from their body, mental processes, and behavior. Some psychodynamic theorists believe that people with disturbed ego functioning, especially disturbances in the ego's capacity to identify with external beings and objects, are more likely to develop such pathological defenses (Nemiah, 1989).

*Cognitive theorists* argue that adaptive interactions with the world require a balance of focus between internal and external events. Attending to one sphere exclusively and excessively may so skew a person's perceptions that they become alarmingly inaccurate. For example, subjects in **sensory deprivation** experiments who are prevented from seeing, hearing, or touching any external stimulus for an extended period of time, and whose entire attention is therefore directed inward, often develop depersonalization-type symptoms. Thus proponents of a cognitive perspective suggest that people who attend excessively to their bodily sensations and inner thoughts are more prone to develop a depersonalization disorder.

These explanations are vague and fall far short of explaining the origin and nature of depersonalization disorders. Correspondingly, although various treatment approaches have been tried with these disorders, including drug therapy, hypnotherapy, and psychodynamic therapy, none has emerged as clearly effective (Steinberg, 1991; Kluft, 1988; Blue, 1979).

# DISSOCIATIVE DISORDERS: THE STATE OF THE FIELD

Periodically, a phenomenon comes along that interests the public but is scoffed at by scientists. In medicine, for example, the chronic fatigue syndrome received little respect or attention from medical scientists until recent years. They used to believe that reports of this disabling pattern of weakness either were exaggerated or could be explained by reference to a broader medical syndrome. The growing number of carefully reported cases, however, eventually convinced most scientists that this is indeed a serious and distinct medical ailment, and serious efforts to investigate and treat the disorder have increased in recent years.

In the field of clinical psychology, dissociative disorders have suffered a similar fate. Until recent years, investigations into psychogenic amnesia and fugue fell short of the studies into their organic counterparts, multiple personality disorder failed to stir the interest of empirical researchers, and depersonalization disorders were likewise ignored. This picture of scientific disinterest and skepticism has changed greatly during the past decade. The growing number of reported cases of dissociative disorders, particularly of multiple personality disorder, has increasingly convinced researchers that the patterns do in fact exist and often lead to significant dysfunctioning.

In the last ten years there has in fact been a veritable explosion of research seeking to help clinicians recognize, understand, and treat these disorders. Although this research has yet to lead to comprehensive insights or highly effective treatments, it has already established that the disorders are more common than anyone previously believed and may in fact be rooted in processes, such as state-dependent learning or self-hypnosis, that are well known to clinical scientists from other contexts. Given this new wave of research enthusiasm, we shall probably witness significant growth in our understanding and treatment of these disorders in the coming years.

Researchers' growing interest in these disorders has led to still greater interest by the public. In addition to a continuing rise in the use of these disorders as plot devices in television shows, movies, and novels, the legal profession now frequently employs them as a form of defense for persons accused of crimes ranging from burglary to murder. Similarly, the growing interest of researchers has enhanced many clinicians' belief in and respect for these disorders. More and more therapists are now reporting that their patients have multiple personality disorders, and they are trying to provide an appropriate course of treatment.

A number of persons in the clinical field now worry that the interest and belief in dissociative disorders is swinging too far in the other direction (Kelley & Kodman, 1987). They believe, for example, that at least some of the legal defenses based on multiple personality disorder are contrived or inaccurate and that many current diagnoses of dissociative disorder have more to do with the increasing popularity of the disorders than with a careful assessment of symptoms. Such possibilities serve to underscore even further the importance of continued investigations into all aspects of these disorders.

# SUMMARY

Memory plays a central role in personality by linking us to the past, present, and future and providing us with a sense of identity. People with dissociative disorders experience a significant alteration in their memory or identity. The three most prominent dissociative disorders are psychogenic amnesia, psychogenic fugue, and multiple personality disorder. A fourth, controversial dissociative disorder is depersonalization disorder.

People with *psychogenic amnesia* are suddenly unable to recall important personal information or past events in their lives. There are four kinds of psychogenic amnesia: *localized, selective, generalized,* and *continuous.* People with *psychogenic fugue* not only lose their memory of their personal identity but flee to an entirely different location and establish a new identity. *Multiple personality disorder* is a rare, dramatic disorder in which a person displays two or more distinct *subpersonalities.* A *primary personality* appears more often than the others, but transitions to the subpersonalities may occur frequently and suddenly. Most people with multiple personality disorder have been abused as children. The subpersonalities often have complex relationships with one another and usually differ from one another in *personality characteristics, vital statistics, abilities and preferences,* and even *physiological responses.* The number of subpersonalities varies from case to case, but it appears to average around thirteen or fourteen, although cases of more than 100 have been reported. The number of people diagnosed with multiple personality disorder has increased in the past two decades, perhaps primarily because it has come to be more widely recognized as a legitimate disorder.

Although several theories have been advanced, few researchers have investigated the origins of dissociative disorders. Psychodynamic theorists believe that dissociative disorders represent extreme *repression.* Behavioral theorists believe that dissociation is a response acquired through operant conditioning. Some cognitive theorists suggest that dissociative disorders may be tied to the phenomenon of *state-dependent learning;* that is, information is best recalled when a person experiences the same *arousal level* or the same state of mind as that experienced when the information was originally learned. This link is particularly strong and rigid in people with dissociative disorders, and entire sets of memories, even personalities, are elicited when the person reenters a particular mood or level of arousal.

*Self-hypnosis* has emerged as a promising explanation for dissociative disorders. Hypnosis has been used to induce *hypnotic amnesia,* which bears a striking resemblance to the memory losses seen in dissociative disorders. On the basis of several studies, a number of theorists now believe that multiple personality disorders usually begin around the age of 4 to 6, when children are generally very susceptible to hypnosis. After some trauma or abuse, the child mentally separates from his or her body through self-hypnosis.

Psychogenic amnesia and fugue often end spontaneously, but when they do not, *psychodynamic therapy* is commonly used to help persons recover their lost memories. Therapists may also *hypnotize* patients and then guide them to recall the forgotten events. In a few cases, intravenous injections of *sodium amobarbital* or *sodium pentobarbital* help patients regain lost memories. Recovery from a multiple personality disorder is rarely spontaneous. Therapists usually try to help people to recover the missing pieces of their past, recognize the full scope and nature of their disorder, and integrate the subpersonalities into one.

*Depersonalization disorder* is characterized by an alteration in a person's experience of self. The mental functioning or body of a person with this disorder feels unreal or foreign. Many such persons feel as though they have been separated from their body and are observing themselves from outside. Most people experience transient feelings of depersonalization at one time or another, but the persistent and recurrent feelings of dissociation experienced by people with depersonalization disorder are rare.

The growing number of cases of dissociative disorders has spurred new research into their causes and treatments. The result is an increasing acceptance of the belief, scoffed at by scientists for many years, that these disorders do indeed exist.

# TOPIC OVERVIEW

**NORMAL STAGES OF DEVELOPMENT**

**ABNORMAL DEVELOPMENTS OF CHILDHOOD AND ADOLESCENCE**

Childhood Anxiety Disorders

Childhood Depression

Conduct Disorders

Attention-Deficit Hyperactivity
Disorder

Elimination Disorders

Specific Developmental Disorders

Autistic Disorder

Mental Retardation

# CHAPTER *19*

# PROBLEMS OF CHILDHOOD AND ADOLESCENCE

Many psychological disorders have their onset during childhood or early adolescence. Some seem to be caused in part by the pressures that are a natural part of early life, others by unique traumatic experiences, and still others by biological abnormalities. Some of the disorders subside without treatment or can be corrected during childhood, some seem to evolve into distinctly adult psychological problems, and some continue virtually unchanged throughout the life span.

Many theorists think of life as a series of stages through which people pass on the way from birth to death. The stages that they propose are typically traversed in fixed order, although the rate and nature of the passage may vary from person to person. The stages give clinicians a useful picture of normal development and help them detect deviations from the norm.

In Chapter 2 we discussed Freud's theory of personality development and his proposal that each child passes through psychosexual stages—the oral, anal, phallic, latency, and genital stages. Although Freud also talked about stages of adulthood, he offered little insight into their nature. A more comprehensive developmental theory has been provided by Erik

Erikson, the ego psychologist whom we discussed in Chapter 2 (see pp. 44–45).

# NORMAL STAGES OF DEVELOPMENT

Erikson divides life into eight stages, each marked by a particular developmental crisis. To Erikson a "crisis" is not a cataclysmic event but rather a turning point, a time when heightened potential coincides with heightened vulnerability. The passage from stage to stage can be marked by enhanced functioning, if the transition is made successfully, or by maladjustment, if the transition is incomplete or unsuccessful. Erikson suggests that people experience new drives and needs at each stage, new kinds of social interactions, and new reactions from society. The way one experiences each stage is directly related to the way one has resolved earlier crises. Failure to master the developmental tasks of one stage produces a pattern of pathology in the next.

### Stage 1: Crisis of Trust vs. Mistrust
The psychosocial crisis that occurs during the first year of life is the infant's need to develop a sense of trust. The developing infant is ready to take in the world through its senses, but he or she needs help to do so. If all goes well, the infant is nurtured, provided for, and satisfied by the parents, and so develops a general sense of trust and hope. If all does not go well, however, either because gratification is repeatedly and excessively delayed or because the parents fail to provide the needed satisfaction, the child may suffer a defect in basic trust, which may lead to a childhood disorder or set the stage for a disorder later in life.

### Stage 2: Crisis of Autonomy vs. Shame and Doubt
In the second year of life, children experience rapid growth in motor activity, speech, sensory discrimination, and other areas of functioning. This growth serves the child's need for increased *autonomy,* or sense of independence and self-control. According to Erikson, there is a tension in both child and parent during this stage, as the parent's wish to protect the child clashes with the child's efforts to become autonomous. If parents resist the demands for autonomy too strongly, they may produce shame or doubt in the child. Children who successfully meet the challenges of this stage develop willpower and a balance between the exercise of free will and self-restraint. Those who are overwhelmed by parental restraints, however, may come to display compulsive overcompliance or impulsive defiance; in other words, overcontrolled or undercontrolled behavior.

### Stage 3: Crisis of Initiative vs. Guilt
In the third or fourth year, children begin to understand how parents expect them to behave, and role playing begins. They start to associate with peers, enter into games and other forms of cooperative play, and develop a sense of initiative. Sex roles also emerge. During this stage, children learn that unbounded initiative is not acceptable but must often be inhibited or repressed. As they play various roles in the context of the family and develop a sense of what is allowed and what is not, they develop a conscience and an ability to feel guilt. Children who move through this stage successfully ultimately arrive at a state of equilibrium in which their sense of initiative, the courage to pursue tangible goals, is guided by an appropriate degree of conscience. Those whose initiative is stifled too much may be paralyzed by guilt.

### Stage 4: Crisis of Industry vs. Inferiority
Erikson's fourth stage starts with the child's entrance into school and lasts until adolescence. During this stage, children discover the importance of work and develop a sense of industry. At the same time, they are in danger of acquiring feelings of inadequacy. If children judge themselves to be inferior to their peers, they may be discouraged from further work or learning. They are also at risk of working too much, to the detriment of imagination and playfulness. The major rules and laws of society are incorporated during these years. Erikson

According to Erik Erikson, children discover the importance of work and develop a sense of industry during their early school years. However, he adds, they must also make room for imagination, play, and experimentation if they are to obtain a balanced perspective and be properly prepared for adolescence.

views this as a most decisive stage. Successful passage results in a sense of competence that serves as the basis for cooperative participation in the workings of society. Unsuccessful passage leaves children with lingering feelings of inferiority.

### Stage 5: Identity vs. Role Confusion

The fifth stage lasts through adolescence. The primary concern during this stage is *psychosocial identity,* a sense of inner sameness and continuity. The adolescent strains for inner coherence and a durable set of values. A successful transition through adolescence results in fidelity, an ability to be true to oneself at the same time that one is true to others. Adolescents typically join with others in their efforts to define themselves, and in doing so, are often cruel and exclusionary to outsiders. When such cruelty and exclusion are carried to extremes, they may result in delinquency, temporary or permanent. Other pathological patterns that may develop during adolescence result from the individual's inability to form a cohesive identity.

### Stage 6: Intimacy vs. Isolation

During early adulthood, people use the consolidated identity that they developed during adolescence to form intimate relationships and sexual unions that call for self-sacrifice and compromise. The goal of this period is to attain love. The ethical conviction developed in adolescence and the sense of moral obligation formed in childhood contribute to ethical strength in young adulthood. People who are unable to meet the challenges of this stage may become isolated, some actually avoiding the contacts that create and sustain intimacy. Their insularity and isolation can lead to various psychological problems, such as irrational fears or depression.

### Stage 7: Generativity vs. Stagnation

During middle adulthood, people ordinarily turn their attention to the next generation. Their focus becomes procreativity, or, to use Erikson's term, generativity. Caring for younger people, whether through parenthood or by mentoring junior colleagues at work, is a primary concern. This process enriches the individual who engages in it. People who fail to develop such activities may, according to Erikson, experience stagnation and boredom.

### Stage 8: Integrity vs. Despair

The last of Erikson's stages, old age, brings accumulated knowledge and understanding and mature judgment along with a decline in bodily and mental functioning. The goal of the period is to attain wisdom, a detached yet active concern with life in the face of death. Wisdom is achieved through the integration of insights gained from the past and the present regarding one's place in the stream of life. Those who do not effectively meet the challenges of this stage may experience an extreme fear of death or despair, show bitterness and disgust, and feel that time is too short. Such persons are prone to develop depression, hypochondriasis, or paranoia during their final years.

Although theorists sometimes disagree with the details of Erikson's scheme, most agree with his belief that people pass through successive stages, confront key pressures during each one, and either grow or decline, depending on how they and their environment meet these pressures. As Erikson repeatedly points out, there are many opportunities for failure and maladaptiveness during each developmental stage, whether because of psychological inadequacy, biological abnormality, or extraordinary environmental stress. In this chapter we shall discuss the abnormal patterns and dysfunctions that develop when people have problems during the first five of Erikson's stages — those from birth through adolescence. In Chapter 20 we shall examine the abnormal patterns that are linked to Erikson's last three stages, particularly the final stage — old age.

# ABNORMAL DEVELOPMENTS OF CHILDHOOD AND ADOLESCENCE

People often think of childhood as a carefree and happy period. However, it can also be a frightening and upsetting time during which one is regularly confronting new people, situations, and obstacles. In fact, most children experience at least some emotional and behavioral problems in the normal course of development (see Box 19-1). As Figure 19-1 indicates, worrying, bed-wetting, nightmares, temper tantrums, and restlessness are common problems among children. In most cases these problems seem to resolve themselves as children get older (Crowther, Bond, & Rolf, 1981; Achenbach, 1978; Lapouse & Monk, 1964, 1959; MacFarlane, Allen, & Honzik, 1954).

Nor is adolescence necessarily the upbeat period that many people think it is. The physical and sexual changes, social and academic pressures, personal doubts, and temptations that characterize this time of transition leave many teenagers anxious, confused, and depressed, and these feelings, too, are a normal experi-

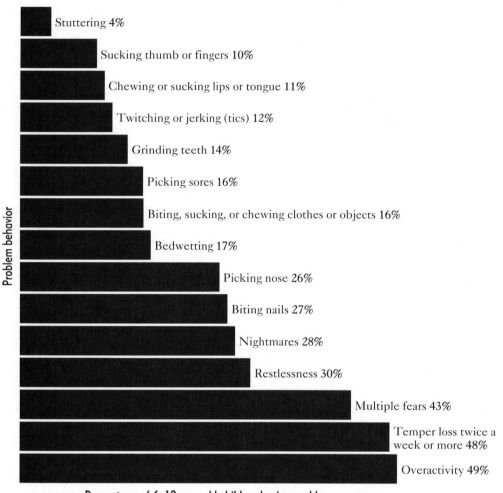

Stuttering 4%

Sucking thumb or fingers 10%

Chewing or sucking lips or tongue 11%

Twitching or jerking (tics) 12%

Grinding teeth 14%

Picking sores 16%

Biting, sucking, or chewing clothes or objects 16%

Bedwetting 17%

Picking nose 26%

Biting nails 27%

Nightmares 28%

Restlessness 30%

Multiple fears 43%

Temper loss twice a week or more 48%

Overactivity 49%

*Problem behavior*

**Percentage of 6–12-year-old children having problem**

**FIGURE 19-1** Problem behaviors are prevalent among 6- to 12-year olds. In a classic study, interviews with the mothers of 482 children indicated that close to 50 percent of the children were overactive, lost their temper at least twice a week, and had multiple fears, and nearly 30 percent had nightmares, were restless, and bit their nails. *(Adapted from Lapouse & Monk, 1959.)*

ence (see Table 19-1). In fact, the "normal" psychological state of adolescents seems to be deteriorating in the United States. Surveys reveal that today's teenagers, although generally happy, feel less confident, secure, and trusting, less affectionate toward their families, and less in control of their inner feelings and impulses than adolescents did just a few decades ago (Offer, Ostrov, & Howard, 1981). Today's teenagers also report more problems, are more worried about their bodies, and describe themselves as more easily hurt than did teenagers of the past.

Beyond these common psychological difficulties, 15 to 20 percent of all children and adolescents in the United States experience a diagnosable mental disorder (Saxe, Cross, & Silverman, 1988, 1987). Boys with mental disorders outnumber girls, a most interesting difference

in view of the fact that the prevalence rate of adult psychological disorders is usually higher among women than among men. Some believe that the shift in rates of psychological disorders from childhood to adulthood reflects the special and increased pressures placed on women in Western society. Others suggest that it may reflect biases against women in diagnosis.

The perception of childhood disorders has changed over the course of this century. Initially clinicians viewed children as small adults and treated their disorders as downward extensions of adult disorders. Now, however, clinicians recognize that there are often important differences between adult and childhood disorders.

Some of the disorders of children—childhood anxiety disorders, childhood depression, and conduct disorders—do have similarities to their adult counterparts,

TABLE 19-1

| STRESSORS REPORTED BY ADOLESCENTS | |
|---|---|
| **Stressors** | **Percentage Reporting** |
| Receiving failing grades on a report card | 28 |
| Arguments between parents | 28 |
| Serious illness of a family member | 28 |
| Breaking up with a boyfriend or a girlfriend | 24 |
| Death in the family | 22 |
| Problems with brothers or sisters | 21 |
| Arguments with parents | 21 |
| Personal illness or injury | 16 |

*Source:* Meer (1985).

but they are also distinct in important ways. Other childhood disorders—attention-deficit hyperactivity disorder and elimination disorders—usually disappear or radically change form by adulthood. A third category, the developmental disorders—those involving disturbances in the acquisition of cognitive, language, motor, or social skills—persist in stable forms into adult life. Given their long-term nature, the developmental disorders are listed on DSM-III-R's Axis II. They are the specific developmental disorders (so-called learning disabilities), autistic disorder, and mental retardation.

## Childhood Anxiety Disorders

Anxiety is a common problem among children; in fact, surveys suggest that close to half of all children have multiple fears. These fears tend to disappear over time—they seem to be almost "a passing episode in a normal developmental process" (Emmelkamp, 1982)—and clinicians believe that formal treatment for them is unnecessary (Schwartz & Johnson, 1985). Three forms of anxiety cause severe suffering for certain children, however, and are listed as special categories in DSM-III-R. These are *separation anxiety disorder, avoidant disorder*, and *overanxious disorder* (APA, 1987).

**Separation Anxiety Disorder** Carrie, a 9-year-old girl suffering from a separation anxiety disorder, was referred to a local mental health center by her school counselor.

*T*he counselor indicated that he perceived the girl's problem to be a fear of school. He reported that the problem seemed to begin about 2 months ago when Carrie seemed to become excessively anxious while at school for no apparent reason. She initially reported feeling sick to her stomach and later became quite concerned over being unable to get her breath. She stated that she was too nervous to stay at school and that she wanted her mother to come get her and take her home. Upon being called, Carrie's mother seemed extremely concerned and came to get her. The counselor indicated that a similar incident occurred the next day with Carrie ending up going home again. She had not returned to school since. The counselor reported having spoken to Carrie's mother over the phone, who stated that the family doctor was unable to find anything wrong with her daughter but that Carrie still resisted the idea of going to school.

At the time of the intake evaluation the mother indicated that she felt Carrie was just too nervous to go to school. She stated that she had encouraged her daughter to go to school on numerous occasions but that she seemed afraid to go and appeared to feel bad, so she had not forced her. In inquiring about Carrie's activities while not in school, the mother reported that she watched some TV and that the two of them found a lot of things to do together, such as visiting relatives or going shopping. When asked if Carrie went places by herself, the mother stated that Carrie didn't like to do that and that the two of them typically did most everything together. The mother went on to note that Carrie really seemed to want to have her (the mother) around all the time and tended to become upset whenever the two of them were separated.

*(Schwartz & Johnson, 1985, p. 188)*

Children with a *separation anxiety disorder* experience excessive anxiety, often panic, whenever they are separated from a parent. They have great trouble traveling independently away from home, and often refuse to visit friends' houses, go on errands, or attend camp or school. Many cannot even stay alone in a room, and cling to their parent around the house. The children may fear that they will get lost when they are separated or that their parent will meet with an accident or illness.

Although this disorder is very familiar to clinicians, exact figures on its prevalence are not available. If it is going to emerge, it always does so before 18 years of age, often in the preschool years, and then waxes and wanes over the course of childhood. In many cases the disorder is precipitated by a traumatic incident or by separation. It is equally common among boys and girls.

As in Carrie's case, a separation anxiety disorder sometimes takes the form of a *school phobia,* or *school refusal,* a common problem in which children experience extreme anxiety about attending school and often stay home for an extended period of time. Some cases of school phobia, however, may involve factors other than separation, such as social fears, anxiety about academic performance, depression, and fears of specific objects or persons at school.

===== BOX 19-1 =====

# The Etiology and Treatment of Childhood

*Jordan W. Smoller*

*This "clinical review" of the "disorder" called childhood originally appeared in Glen C. Ellenbogen (Ed.),* Oral Sadism and the Vegetarian Personality. *New York: Brunner/Mazel, 1986.*

Childhood is a syndrome that has only recently begun to receive serious attention from clinicians. The syndrome itself, however, is not at all recent. As early as the eighth century, the Persian historian Kidnom made reference to "short, noisy creatures," who may well have been what we now call "children." The treatment of children, however, was unknown until this century, when so-called child psychologists and child psychiatrists became common. Despite this history of clinical neglect, it has been estimated that well over half of all Americans alive today have experienced childhood directly (Seuss, 1983). In fact, the actual numbers are probably much higher, since these data are based on self-reports which may be subject to social desirability biases and retrospective distortion.

Clinicians are still in disagreement about the significant clinical features of childhood, but the proposed DSM-IV will almost certainly include the following core features:

1. Congenital onset
2. Dwarfism
3. Emotional lability and immaturity
4. Knowledge deficits
5. Legume anorexia

· **Congenital Onset** In one of the few existing literature reviews on childhood, Temple-Black (1982) has

noted that childhood is almost always present at birth, although it may go undetected for years or even remain subclinical indefinitely. This observation has led some investigators to speculate on a biological contribution to childhood. As one psychologist has put it, "we may soon be in a position to distinguish organic childhood from functional childhood" (Rogers, 1979).

**Dwarfism** This is certainly the most familiar clinical marker of childhood. It is widely known that children are physically short relative to the population at large. Indeed, common clinical wisdom suggests that the treatment of the so-called small child (or "tot") is particularly difficult. These children are known to exhibit infantile behavior and display a startling lack of insight (Tom & Jerry, 1967).

**Emotional Lability and Immaturity** This aspect of childhood is often the only basis for a clinician's diagnosis. As a result, many otherwise normal adults are misdiagnosed as children and must suffer the unnecessary social

stigma of being labeled a "child" by professionals and friends alike.

**Knowledge Deficits** While many children have IQs within or even above the norm, almost all will manifest knowledge deficits. Anyone who has known a real child has experienced the frustration of trying to discuss any topic that requires some general knowledge.

**Legume Anorexia** This last identifying feature is perhaps the most unexpected. Folk wisdom is supported by empirical observation—children will rarely eat their vegetables (see Popeye, 1957, for review).

## CAUSES OF CHILDHOOD

Now that we know what it is, what can we say about the causes of childhood? Recent years have seen a flurry of theory and speculation from a number of perspectives. Some of the most prominent are reviewed below.

### Sociological Model

Emile Durkind was perhaps the first to speculate about sociological causes of childhood. He points out two key observations about children: (1) the vast majority of children are unemployed, and (2) children represent one of the least educated segments of our society. In fact, it has been estimated that less than 20 percent of children have had more than a fourth-grade education. . . . One promising rehabilitation program (Spanky &

Alfalfa, 1978) has trained victims of severe childhood to sell lemonade.

## Biological Model

The observation that childhood is usually present from birth has led some to speculate on a biological contribution. An early investigation by Flintstone and Jetson (1939) indicated that childhood runs in families. Their survey of over 8,000 American families revealed that over half contained more than one child. Further investigation revealed that even most nonchild family members had experienced childhood at some point. . . .

## Psychological Models

A considerable number of psychologically based theories of the development of childhood exist. They are too numerous to review here. Among the more familiar models are Seligman's "learned childishness" model. According to this model, individuals who are treated like children eventually give up and become children. As a counterpoint to such theories, some experts have claimed that childhood does not really exist. Szasz (1980) has called "childhood" an expedient label. In seeking conformity, we handicap those whom we find unruly or too short to deal with by labeling them "children."

## TREATMENT OF CHILDHOOD

Efforts to treat childhood are as old as the syndrome itself. Only in modern times, however, have humane and systematic treatment protocols been applied.

The overwhelming number of children has made government intervention inevitable. The nineteenth century saw the institution of what remains the largest single program for the treatment of childhood — so-called public schools. Under this colossal program, individuals are placed into treatment groups on the basis of the severity of their condition. For ex-

ample, those most severely afflicted may be placed in a "kindergarten" program. Patients at this level are typically short, unruly, emotionally immature, and intellectually deficient.

Unfortunately, the "school" system has been largely ineffective. Not only is the program a massive tax burden, but it has failed even to slow down the rising incidence of childhood.

Faced with this failure and the growing epidemic of childhood, mental health professionals are devoting increasing attention to the treatment of childhood. . . . The following case (taken from Gumbie & Pokey, 1957) is typical.

Billy J., age 8, was brought to treatment by his parents. Billy's affliction was painfully obvious. He stood only 4'3" high and weighed a scant 70 pounds, despite the fact that he ate voraciously. Billy presented a variety of troubling symptoms. His voice was noticeably high for a man. He displayed legume anorexia and, according to his parents, often refused to bathe. His intellectual functioning was also below normal — he had little general knowledge and could barely write a structured sentence. Social skills were also deficient. He often spoke inappropriately and exhibited "whining behavior." His sexual experience was nonexistent. Indeed, Billy considered women "icky." . . .

After years of this kind of frustration, startling new evidence has come to light which suggests that the prognosis in cases of childhood may not be all gloom. . . . Moe, Larrie, and Kirly (1974) began a large-scale longitudinal study. These investigators studied two groups. The first group comprised 34 children currently engaged in a long-term conventional treatment program. The second was a group of 42 children receiving no treatment. . . .

The results . . . of a careful 10-year follow-up were startling. . . . Shemp (1984) found subjects improved. Indeed, in most cases, the subjects appeared to be symptom-free. Moe et al. report a spontaneous remission rate of 95 percent, a finding

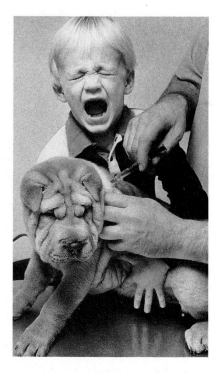

that is certain to revolutionize the clinical approach to childhood.

These recent results suggest that the prognosis for victims of childhood may not be so bad as we have feared. We must not, however, become too complacent. Despite its apparently high spontaneous remission rate, childhood remains one of the most serious and rapidly growing disorders facing mental health professionals today. And beyond the psychological pain it brings, childhood has recently been linked to a number of physical disorders. Twenty years ago, Howdi, Doodi, and Beauzeau (1965) demonstrated a sixfold increased risk of chickenpox, measles, and mumps among children as compared with normal controls. Later, Barbie and Kenn (1971) linked childhood to an elevated risk of accidents — compared with normal adults, victims of childhood were much more likely to scrape their knees, lose their teeth, and fall off their bikes.

Clearly, much more research is needed before we can give any real hope to the millions of victims wracked by this insidious disorder.

**Avoidant Disorder**    Children who experience an *avoidant disorder* shrink from all contact with unfamiliar people. Although they may interact warmly with family members and friends, they become extremely withdrawn, embarrassed, and timid in the presence of strangers, no matter how trivial the contact. Some even become inarticulate or mute. Children with this disorder may have great difficulty developing social skills and become quite isolated and depressed.

Typically an avoidant disorder appears during the early school years, when children are confronted with many new persons. It may, however, develop as early as 2½ years (APA, 1987). It seems to be rather uncommon, and it is more prevalent among girls than among boys (APA, 1987). Again, however, precise figures are not available.

**Overanxious Disorder**    Children with an *overanxious disorder* experience excessive or unrealistic levels of anxiety or worry for a period of six months or longer (APA, 1987). They tend to be very self-conscious and to worry about future events, possible injuries, group activities, meeting expectations and deadlines, and even past behavior. Many are overly concerned about their competence in various kinds of tasks and about others' evaluations of their performance. As with the other childhood anxiety disorders, some children also experience physical symptoms of fear, such as stomach distress, a lump in the throat, headaches, shortness of breath, nausea, or dizziness.

This disorder can appear at any point during childhood. Precise figures are unknown, but it is apparently not uncommon. It is equally common in boys and girls. The disorder seems to be more common in eldest children, in small families, in upper socioeconomic groups, and in achievement-oriented families (APA, 1987).

Childhood anxieties can be caused by society's warnings of possible catastrophes. These kindergartners in San Francisco dive for cover during an earthquake drill. Their parents participated in similar nuclear drills in kindergarten.

Childhood anxieties may be the result of developmental traumas, such as the increasingly common experience of having to share a parent's affection with a new stepparent. The face of this boy after his mother's remarriage says it all.

**Causes and Treatments of Childhood Anxiety Disorders**
Proponents of the various models explain childhood anxiety in much the same way they account for adult anxiety (discussed in Chapter 6). Childhood fears, for example, are caused by classically conditioned fear responses, according to behaviorists; by excessive use of repression and displacement, according to psychodynamic theorists; and by physiological abnormalities, according to biological theorists.

In addition, features unique to childhood have been cited as important to the development of childhood anxiety disorders. Since children have had fewer past experiences than adults, many aspects of their world are new, unpredictable, and scary to them. They may be frightened by common developmental changes, such as a mother's return to work (see Figure 19-2), the birth of a sibling, or the beginning of school, or by special traumas, such as moving to a new residence, losing a parent, or becoming seriously ill (Kashani et al., 1981). Although most children seem to overcome the effects of such events, some are unable to recover and develop an abnormal pattern of anxiety or some other form of psychopathology (Long & Vaillant, 1984).

Children are highly dependent on their parents for emotional support and guidance, and may be greatly influenced by parental inadequacies. If, for example, parents themselves react to events with high levels of anxiety or overprotect their child, the child is more likely to develop anxiety problems. Similarly, if parents repeatedly reject, disappoint, avoid, or abuse their children, the world may become an unpleasant and anxious place for the child.

PERCENTAGE OF ALL MOTHERS OF PRESCHOOLERS
WORKING OUTSIDE THE HOME

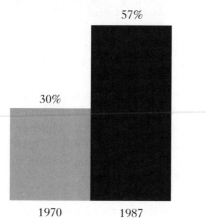

57%

30%

1970    1987

**FIGURE 19-2** More than half the mothers of preschoolers in the United States work outside the home, compared to 30 percent in 1970. The majority of mothers with children under 1 also work outside the home. *(Adapted from Child Care Inc., 1990; U.S. Census Bureau.)*

Finally, our culture often presents children with dark notions and images that may frighten them and set the stage for anxiety disorders. Today's children are repeatedly warned, both at home and at school, about the dangers of kidnapping and drugs. Although these discussions and reminders may be necessary for the children's safety, they hardly breed feelings of psychological security. Similarly, television shows, movies, and news programs are often filled with violent and scary images that can heighten anxiety levels. Investigators have even noted that many of our time-honored fairy tales and nursery rhymes contain frightening images that may upset children.

As with adult anxiety problems, childhood anxiety disorders may be treated by a variety of approaches. Psychodynamic therapists try to help anxious children, as well as those with other kinds of psychological problems, bring their unconscious conflicts to the surface and resolve them. Because children have a limited capacity for analyzing and reflecting on their feelings and motives, therapists typically use *play therapy* to help achieve these goals. They have the children express their conflicts and feelings indirectly by playing with toys, drawing, and making up stories. The therapists then interpret these activities and, through continued play and fantasy, try to help the children develop relevant insights, resolve conflicts, and alter their emotions and behavior. As with adult anxiety disorders, a number of case studies have indicated that psychodynamic therapy is effective in the treatment of childhood anxiety disorders (Schwartz & Johnson, 1985; Elmhirst, 1984;

White et al., 1972; Freud, 1909). However, only a limited number of empirical studies have tested and supported its effectiveness (Barrios & O'Dell, 1989). Similarly, family therapy and drug therapy for childhood anxiety disorders have been applied widely but have received relatively limited empirical support to date (Gittelman & Klein, 1985, 1973, 1971; Barker, 1984; Herbert, 1984).

Behaviorists have used exposure techniques to treat childhood anxiety disorders, including desensitization and modeling (Morris & Kratochwill, 1983; Graziano & Mooney, 1980). Studies suggest that behavioral approaches, particularly when combined with each other, significantly reduce children's fears and anxieties, just as they help to reduce adult fears (Barrios & O'Dell, 1989). Approaches that combine behavioral with cognitive techniques, such as helping children to identify anxiety cues and to employ coping skills, have also helped reduce childhood anxiety (Kendall et al., 1990, 1989; Kendall, 1989; Kane & Kendall, 1989).

Until the 1980s, clinicians generally assumed that young children were incapable of severe depression (Hochman, 1986). They believed that the depressive patterns observed among some children were simply a normal

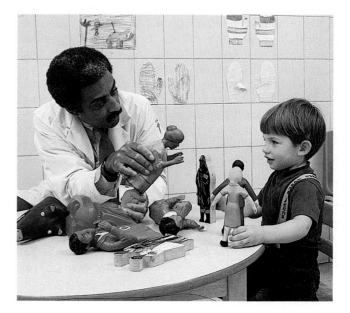

Therapists may use special techniques such as play therapy to assess the functioning of children and to help children express their feelings and thoughts and understand themselves and others.

lowering of mood or a part of another psychological disorder (Cantwell, 1982; Pearce, 1977). Studies conducted throughout the 1980s, however, indicated that many children do in fact experience a constellation of depressive symptoms that are severe and not attributable to other problems—such symptoms as persistent crying, negative self-concept, decreased activity, social withdrawal, and suicidal thoughts (Schwartz & Johnson, 1985). Clinicians now estimate that more than 400,000 children in the United States between the ages of 7 and 12, as well as some who are even younger, are clinically depressed (Hochman, 1986). Bobby is one such child:

*When seen for an interview, Bobby appeared as a rather* dejected looking 10-year-old who seemed to be much more serious than one would expect for a child of his age. Bobby indicated that his parents had brought him to the clinic because "they think I have emotional problems." When asked to elaborate, Bobby said that he wasn't sure what emotional problems really were but that he thought they were upset because "I cry sometimes." In observing Bobby in the playroom it was obvious that his activity level was well below that expected for a child of 10. He showed a lack of interest in the toys that were available to him, and the interviewer was unable to get him interested in any play activity for more than a few minutes. In questioning him about home and school, Bobby indicated that he didn't like school because he didn't have any friends, and he wasn't good at playing games like baseball and soccer like the other kids were, stating "I'm not really very good at anything." He stated that, at home, things were "OK" except that "my parents work most of the time, and we never do anything together like other families." When asked what he would wish for if he could have any three wishes granted he indicated, "I would wish that I was the type of boy my mother and father want, I would wish that I could have friends, and I would wish that I wouldn't feel sad so much."

In speaking with the parents, the mother reported that she and her husband had become increasingly concerned about their son during the past year. She indicated that he always seemed to look sad and cried a lot for no apparent reason and that he appeared to have lost interest in most of the things that he used to enjoy doing. The mother confirmed Bobby's statements that he had no friends, indicating that he had become more and more of a loner during the past 6 to 9 months. She stated that his schoolwork had also suffered in that he is unable to concentrate on school assignments and seems to have "just lost interest." The mother notes, however, that her greatest concern is that he has recently spoken more and more frequently about "killing himself," saying that the parents would be better off if he wasn't around.

*(Schwartz & Johnson, 1985, p. 214)*

Explanations of childhood depression are similar to those offered for adult depression (see Chapter 8).

Theorists have pointed to such factors as loss, learned helplessness, negative cognitive bias, and low norepinephrine activity to account for the disorder (Schwartz & Johnson, 1985). Moreover, like adult depression, childhood depression often seems to be precipitated by a negative life event, major change, rejection, or ongoing abuse (see Box 19-2).

Research has uncovered a relatively high rate of depression and other forms of mental dysfunctioning among the parents of depressed children (Brumback et al., 1980). As with all such family correlations, however, it is not clear whether this relationship suggests hereditary or environmental factors.

Research also indicates that childhood depression responds best to the kinds of treatment that are highly successful for adult depression—cognitive-behavioral therapy, drug therapy, and social skills training—as well as to family therapy (Stark, Rouse, & Livingston, 1990; Kazdin, 1989; Puig-Antich et al., 1987, 1983; Reynolds & Coats, 1986). Treatments that combine these approaches according to the needs of a particular child may often be more helpful than any one alone (Kazdin, 1989).

## Conduct Disorders

It is common for children to flout social rules, misbehave, or act aggressively or defiantly. In one study, teachers were asked to rate aggression and noncompliance in hundreds of normal day-care students (Crowther, Bond, & Rolf, 1981). As Figure 19-3 indicates, at age 2 almost 29 percent of the boys were considered to be at least moderately aggressive and 57 percent were rated as at least moderately noncompliant. These rates fell as the children grew older.

Some children, however, further display patterns of negativity, hostility, and defiance that are more frequent, intense, and disruptive than common aggressiveness, and they receive a diagnosis of either oppositional defiant disorder or conduct disorder. Children with *oppositional defiant disorder* argue repeatedly with adults, lose their temper, and swear, and feel great anger and resentment. They frequently defy adult rules and requests, annoy others, and blame others for their own mistakes and problems. These behaviors are always apparent at home, and sometimes at school and elsewhere. The disorder typically begins by 8 years of age and is more common in boys than in girls, at least before puberty.

*Conduct disorder* is a more severe pattern. Children with this disorder go further and repeatedly violate the basic rights of others. They are often aggressive and may

The death of a parent may lead to childhood depression. Edvard Munch's painting *The Dead Mother and the Little Girl* captures the devastating impact of such a loss.

in fact be physically cruel to persons or animals, deliberately destroy others' property, lie and cheat, skip school, or run away from home. Many steal from and threaten or even harm their victims, committing such crimes as shoplifting, forgery, breaking into houses, buildings, or cars, mugging, extortion, and armed robbery. As they get older their physical violence may extend to rape, assault, even homicide (APA, 1987).

Conduct disorders usually begin before puberty. Children with milder conduct symptoms may improve over time, but in severe cases the disorder often continues into adulthood. Nine percent of boys under 18 and 2 percent of girls display this disorder.

About a third of the children seen at child guidance clinics are referred there for conduct disorders. Large numbers of adult criminals have been seen earlier in their lives in child guidance clinics for conduct problems, or placed in correctional institutions. Children with conduct disorders are often suspended from school, placed in foster homes, or incarcerated.

When children between the ages of 8 and 18 break the law, they are often labeled *juvenile delinquents* by the legal system. Each state provides its own definition of delinquency. More than half of the juveniles who are arrested each year are *recidivists,* or persons who have records of previous arrests. Males are more involved in juvenile crime than females, although rates for females are on the increase. Females are more likely to be arrested for drug use, sexual offenses, and running away,

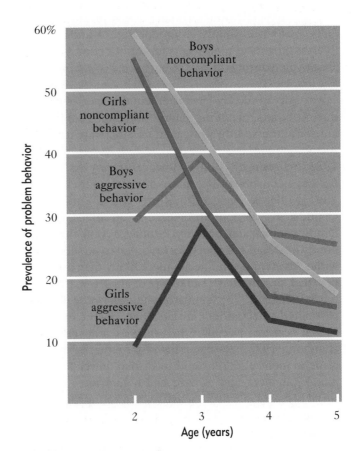

**FIGURE 19-3** Teacher evaluations of more than 700 preschoolers indicated that the rates of both noncompliant and aggressive behavior dropped as the children grew older. *(Adapted from Crowther, Bond, & Rolf, 1981.)*

The aggressive behavior of 2-year-olds is considered quite normal. It is expected to become significantly less frequent and less intense as a child grows older. If it does not, the child may be displaying an oppositional deficit disorder or conduct disorder.

males for drug use and crimes against property. Arrest statistics typically underestimate actual juvenile crime rates; many acts simply go unreported or undetected. Even so, arrests of adolescents for serious crimes have at least tripled during the past twenty years (*Uniform Crime Reports,* 1981).

A variety of factors have been cited as causes of conduct disorders, including genetic and biological factors, antisocial traits, drug abuse, and membership in a lower socioeconomic class (Linz et al., 1990; Rutter & Giller, 1983; Schulsinger, 1980). However, *family dysfunctioning* has been pointed to most often (Fendrich et al., 1991; Miller & Prinz, 1990; Rutter & Quinton, 1984). Conduct disorders often emerge in an atmosphere of family conflict and hostility. Studies reveal that children whose parents reject, leave, or fail to provide them with consistent discipline are more likely than others to lie, steal, or run away (Lefkowitz et al., 1977; Pemberton & Benady, 1973). Similarly, children whose parents, particularly their fathers, are alcoholic, violent, or absent a great deal are more likely to display a conduct disorder (Bandura, 1973). Research has also found that parents of delinquent children tend to display lower levels of moral judgment and to have had higher rates of antisocial behavior and hyperactivity when young than other parents (Schachar, 1990; Moore & Arthur, 1983).

Generally, treatments for conduct disorders have been more effective with children under 13 years of age than with those over 13 (McMahon & Wells, 1989). The most effective approaches appear to be *family interventions* in which (1) parents are taught more effective ways to deal with their children (for example, to consistently

reward appropriate behaviors), or (2) parents and children meet together in behavior-oriented family therapy (Wells, 1985; O'Dell, 1985, 1974; Griest & Wells, 1983). These approaches, however, tend to bring about greater change in the child's behavior in the home than outside of the home. Community-based residential programs for children with conduct disorders, school-based interventions, and skill training techniques (training the child to cope with anger) have had at most limited effectiveness (McMahon & Wells, 1989).

Dealing effectively with juvenile offenders has been a troubling problem for the courts. Institutionalization in so-called juvenile training centers has not met with much success. In fact, such institutions frequently serve to solidify the delinquent culture rather than resocialize the individuals who are detained. While the rate of repeated arrests for adolescents sent to training centers varies with the type of crime and the type of treatment, the overall rate has been estimated to be as high as 80 percent. When therapy, particularly behavior therapy, has replaced or accompanied juvenile institutionalization, improvements in behavior have sometimes been observed. Immediate probation as an alternative to institutionalization has been more successful in cases involving crimes of a less serious nature. The success of such a course of action apparently depends in part on adequate supervision and on the sensitivity of probation officers.

Critics of the penal system claim that the greatest promise for delinquents lies in *prevention* programs. Preventive measures might include increasing training opportunities for young people who are disaffected by school, increasing the quality and quantity of recreational facilities, and alleviating the conditions of poverty and family disorganization.

## Attention-Deficit Hyperactivity Disorder

Children who display an *attention-deficit hyperactivity disorder (ADHD),* commonly called *hyperactivity* or *hyperkinesis,* attend very poorly to tasks, behave impulsively, and are excessively overactive. An ADHD pattern often appears before the child starts school, as seen in the case of Steven.

*Steven's mother cannot remember a time when her son was* not into something or in trouble. As a baby he was incredibly active, so active in fact that he nearly rocked his crib apart. All the bolts and screws became loose and had to be tightened periodically. Steven was also always into forbidden places, going through the medicine cabinet or under the kitchen sink. He once swallowed some washing detergent and had to be taken to the emergency room. As a matter of fact, Steven had many more accidents and was more clumsy than his older brother and younger sister. Even though Steven was less well-coordinated and more clumsy than other children, he always seemed to be moving fast. His mother recalls that Steven progressed from the crawling stage to a running stage with very little walking in between.

Trouble really started to develop for Steven when he entered kindergarten. Since his entry into school, his life has been miserable and so has the teacher's. Steven does not seem capable of attending to assigned tasks and following instructions. He would rather be talking to a neighbor or wandering around the room without the teacher's permission. When he is seated and the teacher is keeping an eye on him to make sure that he works, Steven's body still seems to be in motion. He is either tapping his pencil, fidgeting, or staring out the window and daydreaming. Steven hates kindergarten and has few long-term friends; indeed, school rules and demands appear to be impossible challenges for him. The effects of this mismatch are now showing in Steven's schoolwork and attitude. He has fallen behind academically and has real difficulty mastering new concepts; he no longer follows directions from the teacher and has started to talk back.

*(Gelfand, Jenson, & Drew, 1982, p. 256)*

The symptoms of ADHD often feed into one another. A child who has trouble focusing attention may be pulled in several directions at once. Similarly, a constantly moving child is likely to have difficulty attending to tasks or exercising careful judgment. Often one of these areas of disturbance is more prominent than the others. ADHD symptoms tend to be highly visible at home, school, and work, and in social situations (Biederman et al., 1990), and less apparent when the child enters a novel setting or one-on-one situation or receives frequent reinforcement or strict control.

About half of the children with ADHD also experience learning problems (Lahey et al., 1978), many perform poorly in school, and about 80 percent misbehave, often quite seriously (APA, 1987; Satterfield et al., 1972). In fact, ADHD is often seen in conjunction with conduct disorders (Paniagua et al., 1990).

Between 1 and 6 percent of schoolchildren display ADHD, most of them boys (APA, 1987; Ross & Ross, 1982). The disorder spans all cultures (Ross & Ross, 1982) and usually persists through childhood. Many individuals show a lessening of symptoms as they move into adolescence, but in a number of these cases some forms of learning and perceptual problems remain (Hoy et al., 1978; Ross & Ross, 1976). ADHD continues into adulthood for about a third of affected individuals. Those children whose parents manifested this problem are more likely than others to develop it (APA, 1987).

Research has not pointed to clear causes of hyperactivity. Some investigators have argued that biological dysfunctioning leads to the attention deficits and other features of the disorder, but they have not yet determined the precise nature of the dysfunctioning (Loge et al., 1990; Hynd et al., 1990; Ferguson et al., 1981). One popular theory holds that hyperactivity reflects some form of brain damage — indeed, the disorder was once referred to as *minimal brain damage* — but this notion has failed to receive consistent support (Loney, 1981).

Other theorists believe that hyperactivity is caused by psychological factors (Amsel, 1990), such as stress. Some research does suggest that parents of hyperactive children display more personality disorders than other parents, and that hyperactive children and their parents often get along poorly (Fendrich et al., 1990; Morrison, 1980; Barkley & Cunningham, 1979). Once again, however, such family correlates are as likely to be the result of a child's hyperactive pattern as the cause of it.

Given this state of research, today's clinicians generally view hyperactivity as a disorder with multiple and interacting causes (Bloomingdale, 1984). They also recognize that hyperactive symptoms and a diagnosis of hyperactivity may create still further difficulties and generate additional symptoms in the child. Research suggests, for example, that hyperactive children are often viewed more negatively than other children by their peers, their parents, and the children themselves (King & Young, 1981; Arnold, 1973).

There is considerable disagreement about the most effective treatment for ADHD. The most common approach has been stimulant drugs, such as methylphenidate, known by the brand name Ritalin (Safer & Krager, 1984). These have a quieting effect upon many ADHD children and increase their ability to solve complex problems, perform academically, and control aggressive behavior (Hinshaw et al., 1989; Douglas et al., 1988). It is believed that they achieve such effects by neurologically enhancing the child's ability to profit from reinforcement (Barkley, 1989). Drug therapy appears to be somewhat beneficial in half to two-thirds of the cases in which it is used. However, data on the efficacy of drugs are sometimes contradictory, and many clinicians express great concern over the long-term effects of drug use.

A biological treatment that gained a vocal and devoted following in the late 1970s was a diet that eliminates food containing certain additives. Specifically, the Feingold diet eliminates artificial flavoring or coloring, preservatives, and natural salicyclates (Feingold, 1975). This treatment, however, has received little or no research support and has lost most of its early popularity.

## BOX 19-2

# Child Abuse

Honoré Daumier's *Fatherly Discipline.*

Child abuse is the intentional use of physical or psychological force by an adult on a child, often aimed at hurting, or destroying the child (Gil, 1970). It has been estimated that 1.9 million cases of child abuse occur each year, at least 2,000 to 4,000 of which result in a child's death (Green, 1989). In fact, physical child abuse is currently believed by some to be the leading cause of death among young children. Surveys suggest that each year one in ten children are subjected to severe violence, such as kicking, biting, hitting or trying to hit with an object, beating, threatening with a knife or gun, or using a knife or gun (Gelles & Straus, 1987).

> What I remember most about my mother was that she was always beating me. She'd beat me with her high-heeled shoes, with my father's belt, with a potato masher. When I was eight, she black-and-blued my legs so badly, I told her I'd go tell the police. She said, "Go, they'll just put you into the darkest prison." So I stayed. When my breasts started growing at 13, she beat me across the chest until I fainted. Then she'd hug me and ask forgiveness. . . . Most kids have nightmares about being taken away from their parents. I would sit on our front stoop crooning softly of going far, far away to find another mother.
>
> (Time, *September 5, 1983, p. 20)*

Although child abuse occurs in all socioeconomic groups, it is apparently more common among the poor. The abusers are usually the parents. Girls and boys are abused at approximately the same rate. Physical injury is more likely to occur during the preschool years and adolescence (American Humane Association, 1984). Babies who are fussy and irritable and cry a great deal are apparently at particu-

larly high risk of being abused (Gil, 1970).

Two other forms of child abuse have been receiving special attention in recent years: psychological abuse and sexual abuse. ***Psychological abuse*** may include severe rejection; coercive, punitive, and erratic discipline; scapegoating and ridicule; unrealistic expectations; and refusal to provide help for an emotionally disturbed child (Hart & Brassard, 1987; Hart et al., 1987). This form of mistreatment probably accompanies all cases of physical abuse and neglect, and occurs by itself in about 200,000 cases each year (Hart & Brassard, 1987; AHA, 1986). The legal system has devoted little attention to this form of child abuse, but the mental health field has become increasingly concerned about the effects of and treatments for this problem (Garrison, 1987).

***Child sexual abuse,*** the use of a child as an object of gratification for adult sexual desires, does not usually

result in physical injury but causes the victim enormous psychological damage, including long-term feelings of mistrust, poor self-image, depression, guilt, social withdrawal, poor school performance, and difficulties with sexual intimacy. It may occur outside of or in the home. It is estimated that 50,000 to 200,000 new cases occur each year in the United States. In surveys of adult women, 20 to 35 percent reported having been forced into sexual contact with an adult male as children, many of them with their father or stepfather (Green, 1989). Both legal and mental health professionals have become interested in this problem during the past decade because of a number of highly publicized cases of alleged sexual abuse at child-care centers around the United States.

Before the turn of the century, the legal system tried to avoid intervention in family life, even in instances of child abuse (Garrison, 1987). Medical reports of suspected cases of child abuse did not begin to receive widespread attention until the 1960s (Newberger, 1983), and medical and legal authorities did not become actively involved in detecting and intervening in such cases until 1974, when states adopted laws requiring physicians to report cases of suspected child abuse and the Federal Child Abuse Prevention and Treatment Act was passed (Garrison, 1987). Since then media accounts have kept this staggering social problem in the public eye. Numerous federal and state legislatures and court systems have also sprung into more protective and punitive action; and mental health professionals have contributed by developing numerous research and therapy programs.

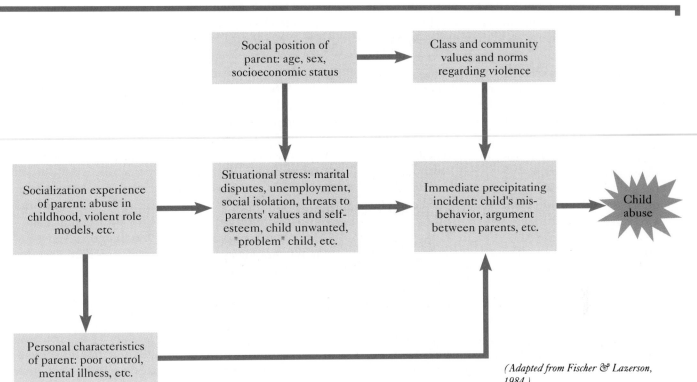

(*Adapted from Fischer & Lazerson, 1984.*)

Since entering into this area, clinical researchers have learned that a number of factors may interact to produce child abuse, including such parental characteristics as poor impulse control and low self-esteem, such parental background factors as having been abused as children and having had poor role models, such situational stresses as marital disputes or family unemployment, and such immediate precipitants as child misbehavior (see chart). Because the type and combination of factors vary from case to case, clinicians must carefully assess the parents, child, and family dynamics of a case before planning a treatment program (Azar & Wolfe, 1989).

A number of interventions have been tried in cases of child abuse. Parents may develop insight about themselves and their behavior in self-help groups such as Parents Anonymous. They may learn more effective child interaction and management skills through such behavioral interventions as modeling, role playing, and feedback (Barth et al., 1983). They may receive cognitive therapy to help correct misperceptions about their children or themselves (Azar, 1984).

Many parents who abuse their children believe that the children actually intend to upset them, and some have unrealistic expectations in regard to their children's behavior (Azar & Rohrbeck, 1986; Plotkin, 1983). A number of treatments are also aimed at helping parents deal more effectively with the situational stresses that often trigger their abuse, such as unemployment, marital discord, or depressed feelings (Campbell et al., 1983). Some treatment programs combine various therapy interventions, in accordance with the needs of a particular family (Wolfe et al., 1981). The effects of such approaches on the parents' behavior, the child's self-esteem and psychological recovery, and family harmony have yet to be fully determined (Azar & Wolfe, 1989).

Obviously, the treatments developed by clinicians for cases of child abuse have focused on the parents more than the abused child. Recent clinical studies suggest, however, that many victims of child abuse may suffer pervasive long-term psychological effects that probably should be anticipated and addressed in early child-

focused interventions. Cathy Spatz Widom (1991) is currently conducting a longitudinal study that compares the later development of 908 people who were abused or neglected before the age of 11 with that of 607 similar people who were not abused or neglected as children. She has found that those who were abused as children later (1) had a 53 percent higher arrest record as teenagers and a 38 percent higher arrest record as adults; (2) had a greater risk of becoming criminally violent; (3) had a higher unemployment rate, lower-paying jobs, less education, and lower IQ scores; and (4) had a higher suicide rate. Similarly, the child psychologist Byron Egeland (1991) has found in another longitudinal study that people who had been abused as children later showed lower achievement scores in school, poorer work and study skills, lower social acceptance, and more psychological problems such as anxiety, misbehavior, aggression, defiance, and hyperactivity-distractibility. Clearly, many victims of child abuse are even more victimized than anyone previously had imagined.

Behaviorists have treated ADHD primarily by teaching parents and teachers how to systematically reinforce the children for paying attention or behaving appropriately at home or school. Such operant conditioning treatments have been relatively successful, especially when applied in combination with drug therapy (Hinshaw & Erhardt, 1990). Some therapists have further combined behavioral approaches with self-instruction training for the ADHD children, similar to the adult-oriented cognitive approach that we discussed in Chapter 7 (Reid & Borkowski, 1987). However, the effectiveness of such cognitive strategies in treating ADHD children has yet to be fully clarified by researchers (Hinshaw & Erhardt, 1990).

## Elimination Disorders

Children with elimination disorders—functional enuresis and functional encopresis—repeatedly and involuntarily urinate or pass feces, respectively, in their clothes, in bed, or on the floor, after an age at which control of these bodily functions is expected.

*Functional enuresis* is involuntary or intentional bed-wetting or wetting of one's pants. It may be nocturnal (occurring primarily at night) or, less commonly, diurnal (occurring primarily during daytime). Nocturnal enuresis usually occurs during the first third of the night, when the child is not yet dreaming. Children under 7 who have at least two enuretic experiences per month qualify for this diagnosis; for children 7 and older the criterion is one or more experiences per month.

The condition may represent a continuation of the habits of infancy (called *primary enuresis*) or may reflect a return to earlier behavior after a period of having been dry (called *secondary enuresis*). Often children who have been dry for a time return to bed-wetting as an apparent response to stress. Predisposing stresses include hospitalization between ages 2 and 4, the birth of a sibling, and entrance into school.

The point at which it is no longer considered "normal" to wet one's bed or pants depends on the society. In the United States, it is estimated that 10 to 16 percent of all children between the ages of 3 and 4 wet their beds. Yet the clinical theorist Bruno Bettelheim (1969) reported that 40 percent of the 9-year-olds on an Israeli kibbutz wet their beds, and that no one seemed to regard this as much of a problem.

Psychodynamic theorists explain bed-wetting as a symbol of other conflicts and therefore as a symptom of a more general disorder (Olmos-de-Paz, 1990). Family systems theorists attribute the disorder to disturbed family interactions that produce sustained anxiety or hostility. Behaviorists suggest that bed-wetting repre-

sents a failure of toilet training. Training may have been attempted too early, or may have been lax or improperly reinforced.

Treatments for enuresis based on behavioral principles have enjoyed much success (Friman & Warzak, 1990; Whelan & Houts, 1990). In a widely used and apparently helpful classical conditioning approach, a bell and a battery are wired to a pad consisting of two metallic foil sheets, and the entire apparatus is placed under the child at bedtime (Mowrer & Mowrer, 1938). A single drop of urine acts as an electrolyte that sets off the bell. The child is awakened immediately after he or she starts to wet. Thus the bell (unconditioned stimulus) paired with the sensation of a full bladder (conditioned stimulus) produces the conditioned response of waking. For the procedure to be successful, parents must administer it accurately and supportively, and the child must cooperate.

*Functional encopresis,* or involuntary defecating, is less common than functional enuresis and less well researched. Like enuresis, it may be primary or secondary. It usually starts between the ages of 4 and 8. The disorder affects about 1 percent of 5-year-olds, a rate that drops to near zero by the age of 16 (APA, 1987). It is more common in boys than in girls and in children of disadvantaged socioeconomic status (APA, 1987; Schaefer, 1979).

Encopresis is accompanied by enuresis about 25 percent of the time and frequently by constipation as well. Unlike enuresis, encopresis occurs mainly during the day, usually late in the afternoon after school, and seldom at night (Levine, 1975). Some theorists have attributed it to inadequate or inconsistent toilet training or to stressful events such as the birth of a sibling.

Encopresis is regarded as more serious than enuresis. The disorder typically causes social problems, shame, and embarrassment. Children who suffer from it often try to conceal their condition from others and try to avoid situations, such as camp or school, in which they might become embarrassed (APA, 1987; Ross, 1981). The most common and successful treatments are behavioral, medical, and combinations of the two (Dawson et al., 1990; Gumaer, 1990; Parker & Whitehead, 1982). Family therapy has also been helpful (Wells & Hinkle, 1990).

## Specific Developmental Disorders

Children who display grossly inadequate development and functioning in specific academic, language, speech, or motor skills may receive a diagnosis of *specific developmental disorder,* a group of disorders also known as *learning disabilities,* because they often impair one's ability to learn particular skills, such as reading and writing. The disorders typically cause impaired performance in school and daily living, and are at least twice as common in boys as in girls (APA, 1987). Often, similar problems are seen in a child's close biological relatives. The specific developmental disorders include academic skills disorders, language or speech disorders, and coordination disorder.

The classification of these learning problems as mental disorders has been controversial in the clinical field (APA, 1987). Many clinicians view them as primarily educational problems, typically detected and addressed within the school — problems that should remain outside of the mental health system. The framers of DSM-III-R have reasoned, however, that the dysfunctioning caused by the disorders and their frequent occurrence in association with other psychological problems justify their classification as mental disorders.

In our society, women have traditionally been blamed for the psychological disorders of their children. Psychologist Paula Caplan and her colleagues (1989) found that mothers were blamed much more than fathers or others for more than seventy kinds of problems, from schizophrenia to enuresis.

**Academic Skills Disorders**    Children may receive a diagnosis of *developmental arithmetic disorder* when their arithmetic skills are markedly below their intellectual capacity and interfere with academic achievement or daily activities. The disorder is usually apparent by the third grade (APA, 1987).

The expressive writing skills of a child with a *developmental expressive writing disorder* are so far below the child's intellectual capacity that they lead to impaired functioning in the academic and personal realms. Specific deficits include extreme and repeated errors in spelling, grammar, punctuation, and paragraph organization. Severe cases are usually apparent by the second grade.

Children with a *developmental reading disorder,* also known as *dyslexia,* show marked impairment in the ability to recognize words and to comprehend what they read, though they have no visual or hearing defects, their schooling is adequate, and their intellectual functioning is at least average. These children omit, distort, or substitute words when they read, and read slowly and haltingly. The disorder is usually apparent by the second grade. It is estimated that 2 to 8 percent of school-age children experience dyslexia. Mild cases can be greatly helped by reading therapy, and the problem may virtually disappear by adulthood. However, in severe cases symptoms may continue into adulthood despite treatment.

**Language and Speech Disorders**    Children who consistently fail to make correct speech sounds at an appropriate age receive a diagnosis of *developmental articulation disorder* if the problem is not due to a defect of hearing or of the speech mechanism or to a neurological disorder. The child's misarticulations, substitutions, and omis-

sions of speech sounds give an impression of baby talk. It is estimated that 10 percent of children under 8 years of age and 5 percent of those 8 years and over experience this disorder (APA, 1987). Speech therapy results in complete recovery in virtually all cases; in milder cases the problem may disappear without treatment by the age of 8 years.

Children who display a *developmental expressive language disorder* have great difficulty using language to express themselves. They may have a very limited or inaccurate vocabulary, have trouble acquiring new words, regularly shorten sentences, omit critical parts of sentences, order words in an unusual manner, or develop language slowly. Between 3 and 10 percent of all school-age children display this problem. Most children with the disorder eventually acquire normal language abilities. As many as half catch up before they reach school age, the remainder by late adolescence. Specialized help is often useful.

Children with a *developmental receptive language disorder* have such difficulty comprehending language that it interferes with their academic achievement or daily activities. In mild cases, the children may have difficulty understanding particular words or complex statements, such as "if–then" sentences. In more severe cases, they may be poor at understanding basic vocabulary or simple sentences, or at processing auditory information. They may have difficulty discriminating sounds, associating sounds and symbols, or storing, recalling, or sequencing information. Between 3 and 10 percent of schoolchildren may display this problem (APA, 1987). Many eventually acquire adequate language abilities, but some severely affected persons do not.

**Developmental Coordination Disorder**    Children with a *developmental coordination disorder* show very poor motor coordination that is not explainable by mental retardation or physical problems. Young children with the disorder are clumsy and show delays in motor activities such as tying shoelaces, buttoning shirts, and zipping pants. Older sufferers may have great difficulty assembling puzzles, building models, playing ball, and printing or writing. It is estimated that 6 percent of children between 5 and 11 years may experience this disorder (APA, 1987). In some cases the lack of coordination continues into adulthood.

**Causes of Specific Developmental Disorders**    Studies have linked learning disabilities to such factors as genetic defects, birth injuries, lead poisoning, inappropriate diet, sensory dysfunctioning, and poor teaching (Gelfand et al., 1982). Yet none of these relationships has been found consistently, and the precise causes of the specific developmental disorders remain unclear.

A leading explanation, the *perceptual deficit theory,* sees learning disabilities as products of problems in perceptual processing (Wong, 1979). Dyslexia, for instance, is thought to be caused by a perception deficit in which the letters are actually perceived in reverse in mirror image. Another explanation, the *academic instruction theory,* suggests that learning disabilities reflect deficiencies in teaching rather than in perception, that certain children receive poor instruction in particular areas of cognitive functioning (Englemann, 1969). Proponents of this position have tried to develop better ways of teaching learning-disabled children. They break down arithmetic, reading, and other learning areas into component skills and teach these skills in small increments. In one study a behaviorist worked individually with reading-disabled seventh-graders who had been reading from 1½ to 4½ years below their grade level (Schwartz, 1977). He awarded points and positive reinforcements to the students for progress in reading words, then sentences, then paragraphs. The students' reading levels improved an average of 2.6 grades, compared to 1.6 grades for control students who received other forms of treatment. Improvements were observed not only in reading levels but in the amount of spontaneous reading, attention span, and self-confidence.

## Autistic Disorder

A little boy named Mark presents a typical picture of autistic disorder:

*In retrospect [Susan, Mark's mother] can recall some* things that appeared odd to her. For example, she re-

members that . . . Mark never seemed to anticipate being picked up when she approached. In addition, despite Mark's attachment to a pacifier (he would complain if it were mislaid), he showed little interest in toys. In fact, Mark seemed to lack interest in anything. He rarely pointed to things and seemed oblivious to sounds. . . . Mark spent much of his time repetitively tapping on tables, seeming to be lost in his own world.

After his second birthday, Mark's behavior began to trouble his parents. . . . Mark, they said, would "look through" people or past them, but rarely at them. He could say a few words but didn't seem to understand speech. In fact, he did not even respond to his own name. Mark's time was occupied examining familiar objects, which he would hold in front of his eyes while he twisted and turned them. Particularly troublesome were Mark's odd movements — he would jump, flap his arms, twist his hands and fingers, and perform all sorts of facial grimaces, particularly when he was excited — and what Robert [Mark's father] described as Mark's rigidity. Mark would line things up in rows and scream if they were disturbed. He insisted on keeping objects in their place and would become upset whenever Susan attempted to rearrange the living room furniture. . . .

Slowly, beginning at age five, Mark began to improve. . . . The pronoun in the sentence was inappropriate and the sentence took the form of a question he had been asked previously, but the meaning was clear.

*(Wing, 1966)*

Mark was manifesting an *autistic disorder,* also called *autism,* a disorder first identified by the American psychiatrist Leo Kanner in 1943. Children with this disorder are extremely unresponsive to others, show poor communication skills, and often respond bizarrely to their environment. The symptoms appear very early in life, before 3 years of age. When the same symptoms unfold at a later age, the pattern is called a *pervasive developmental disorder.* Autism is actually a particular kind of pervasive developmental disorder (APA, 1987).

Autism affects only 4 children out of every 10,000 (APA, 1987). Approximately 75 percent of autistic children are boys. Four autistic children in six remain severely impaired into adulthood and are unable to lead independent lives. Only one in six makes an adequate adjustment and is able to maintain social relationships, perform regular work, and lead an independent life. Another one in six makes a fair adjustment. Autistic people with a higher IQ and better language skills tend to have a more promising future. Since the disorder begins in childhood and usually persists in a stable form into adult life, it is listed on Axis II in DSM-III-R.

**Unresponsiveness to Others**    Aloofness, lack of responsiveness, and lack of interest in other people have long formed the cornerstone of the diagnosis of autism

(Walters et al., 1990). Like Mark, autistic children typically do not reach for their parents during infancy, and may arch their backs when they are held. They often treat adults interchangeably or cling mechanically to a select person.

Autistic children often fail to recognize or acknowledge those around them. They may offer no eye contact or facial responsiveness to their parents. As Mark's parents noted, he "would look through people or past them, but rarely at them."

In early childhood, autistic children also show indifference to children of their own age. They do not form friendships or play cooperatively. As they grow older, some become more aware and sociable, form attachments, and become involved in games and physical activities with other children. However, such social activities tend to be passive and superficial.

**Language and Communication Deficits**    Between 50 and 60 percent of autistic children fail to speak or develop language skills (Rutter, 1966). Those who do talk may show peculiarities in their speech. One of the most common speech problems is *echolalia,* the exact echoing or parroting of phrases said by others. The children repeat words with the same accent or inflection, but without comprehension. It has been found that autistic children echo questions and commands more often when they do not know proper responses. If they are taught to say "I don't know," the echoing decreases (Carr, Schreibman, & Lovaas, 1975). Sometimes the children use echoing as a form of assent. That is, they repeat a phrase instead of saying "Yes." In addition to immediate echolalia of this kind, many display *delayed echolalia,* that is, they repeat a sentence hours or days after they have heard it.

Autistic children may also display other speech oddities. In *pronominal reversal* they confuse pronouns, using "you" instead of "I." When Mark was hungry, he would say, "Do you want dinner?" Many also use words that have idiosyncratic and unclear meanings *(metaphorical language).* Some have difficulty naming objects *(nominal aphasia),* and others cannot use abstract speech. The children may also employ incorrect speech inflections, ending statements with a questionlike rise in tone, for example. And finally, they may fail to use properly the facial expressions and gestures that ordinarily accompany speech.

Autistic children also have difficulty understanding speech and using it spontaneously. A slight change in sentence structure may prevent them from understanding a familiar question or request. Even those with relatively effective speech and comprehension have difficulty initiating or making spontaneous conversation.

**Deviant Responses to the Environment**    Autistic children interact with the environment in unusual ways. Typically they are very resistant to change and become very upset at minor changes in objects or persons, or in their routine. Many also display ritualistic and repetitive behaviors. Mark, for example, would line things up, and would scream if they were disturbed. Similarly, autistic children may react with tantrums if a parent wears an unfamiliar pair of glasses, a chair is moved to a different part of the room, they are told to clean up after dinner instead of before, or a word in a song is changed. Kanner (1943) labeled this characteristic a **perseveration of sameness.** Conversely, the same children may fail to react to major life changes.

Autistic children often become strongly attached to particular objects, such as plastic lids, rubber bands, cards, buttons, parts of the body, or water. They may collect these objects, carefully arrange them, carry them, or play with them constantly. Objects that can be taken apart or have a certain texture are particular favorites. Some children are fascinated by movement, and may observe spinning objects such as fans or records for hours.

The motor movements of autistic children may also be unusual. Mark would jump, flap his arms, twist his hands and fingers, and perform various facial grimaces. In addition to these *self-stimulatory behaviors,* the children may perform *self-injurious behaviors,* such as repeatedly lunging or banging their heads against walls, pulling their hair, or biting parts of their body.

The perceptual reactions of autistic children are often disturbed and paradoxical (Wing, 1976; Wing & Wing, 1971). Sometimes the children appear overstimulated by sights and sounds and try to block them out, while at other times they seem understimulated and perform self-stimulatory actions. The may fail to react to loud noises, yet turn around when they hear soda being poured. They may fail to recognize that they have reached the dangerous edge of a high place, yet immediately spot something out of place in their room.

**Views on Autism**    A variety of explanations have been offered for autism, including perceptual-cognitive, biological, and environmental. Although each of these views has received some support, none is without limitations and problems.

*Perceptual-Cognitive Views*    According to some theorists, autistic children have primary perceptual or cognitive disturbances that make normal communication, interpersonal relationships, and environmental interactions impossible (Goodman & Ashby, 1990). Several kinds of disturbance have been suggested.

One of the oldest perceptual explanations holds that autistic children have a fundamental impairment in their ability to *comprehend sounds* (Rutter, 1971, 1968). Theoretically, the children hear sounds but cannot make sense of them as other children can. This inability, in turn, hinders their understanding of the world around them and makes them asocial. In support of this theory, several studies have found that autistic children do not respond appropriately to sounds, sometimes react to a sound as if they hear more than one, and sometimes remember meaningful speech no better than meaningless speech (Webster & Konstantareas, 1978; Codon, 1975).

In another perceptual-cognitive explanation, the psychiatrist Ivar Lovaas has postulated that autism stems from *stimulus overselectivity*—attending to only one dimension of a stimulus (Lovaas et al., 1971). A lemon, for example, has a certain shape, color, smell, taste, and texture, all of which help us identify it. If you attended only to the color of a lemon, you might confuse it with a banana, a lawn chair, the sun, or some other yellow object. Similarly, you would not be able to identify a black-and-white picture of a lemon. This is precisely the experience of autistic children, according to Lovaas. As a result, they have difficulty associating human beings with all the things they represent—security, food, warmth, gratification of needs, and the like—and they fail to develop a proper affection and desire for social interactions. Similarly, they cannot associate words with the objects they represent.

Some theorists believe that a central difficulty for autistic children is *abstract thinking,* specifically abstracting and coding information (Hermelin, 1976). Although the children have effective short-term memories, they seem to be unable to analyze information and store the main idea. Research has consistently suggested that autistic children have problems with abstract tasks, such as discriminating between a square, a circle, and other abstract symbols (Prior & Chen, 1975). Certainly a deficit in grasping of abstract concepts and in information coding is consistent with many features of autism. For example, it may help explain the children's inability to associate the concept of height with danger or their tendency to answer questions by repeating the questions themselves.

**Biological Views** During the past few decades, researchers have tried to determine the role of biological factors in autism. Biological explanations have been popular for two reasons. First, the disorder unfolds so early in life—often at birth—that environmental factors have relatively little time to operate. Second, underlying biological factors sometimes seem to offer the only possible explanation for symptoms that are so diverse and paradoxical. Yet research has yet to provide a clear biological understanding of this disorder.

Examinations of the relatives of autistic children are consistent with the possibility of a *genetic factor* in this disorder. Studies find that siblings of autistic children have an increased risk of developing the disorder (APA, 1987). The prevalence of autism among these siblings is between 1 and 2 per 100 (Rutter, 1968), a rate fifty times higher than the general population's 4 per 10,000. Moreover, identical twins of autistic siblings demonstrate the highest risk of all.

Some studies suggest a link between autism and *prenatal difficulties* or *birth complications* (Goodman, 1990; Steffenburg et al., 1989). The rate of maternal rubella (German measles), for example, is ten times higher in pregnancies that produce autistic children (Chess, 1971). Similarly, more labor and delivery complications have been reported in births of autistic children than in births of other children. Illnesses during the first three years of life have also been linked to the disorder in a number of studies (DeMyer, 1979).

Research also suggests that *organic brain dysfunctioning* may be involved in autism. Several studies find that autistic children have a higher number of neurological problems than other children (Gillberg et al., 1990). And some researchers have found differences between the electroencephalograms (EEGs) of autistic and non-autistic children (James & Barry, 1980; White, 1964).

Behaviorist Ivar Lovaas is one of the field's most influential theorists on autism. His behavioral treatment approaches have been in thousands of educational and clinical settings.

Between 40 and 90 percent of autistic children register abnormal EEG readings.

A number of theorists have suggested that all biological factors (genetic, prenatal, birth, and postnatal) eventually lead to a common problem in the brain—a "final common pathway" that leads to autistic patterns (DeMyer et al., 1981; Coleman, 1979). Some of the leading candidates for this final pathway are disturbances in the *brain stem* (Tanguay & Edwards, 1982; Skoff et al., 1980); abnormalities in the *reticular activating system,* the area that ascends from the brain stem and arouses electrical activity in the cortex (Kootz et al., 1982; Hutt et al., 1964); abnormalities in the *cortex* of the brain, the area that deals with higher-order processing, integration, coding, and language (Maurer & Damasio, 1982; DeMyer et al., 1981; Hauser, DeLong, & Rosman, 1975); and *neurotransmitter imbalances,* such as high activity of *serotonin* (Cook et al., 1990; Young et al., 1982) or *dopamine* (Cohen, Carapulo, Shaywitz, & Bowers, 1977).

***Environmental and Family Views*** Many theories of autism have implicated the environment, and specifically the family, as a cause. These theories have undergone an interesting transition since autism was first identified. Initially, most theorists believed that environmental factors were wholly or largely responsible for the disorder. As the years passed, however, focus on the environment diminished considerably. Research failed to offer much support for this view of autism, and promising perceptual-cognitive and biological interpretations increasingly captured the attention of researchers and clinicians. Although less influential today, environmental explanations continue to make a significant impact on the clinical field and to generate many studies. Theories and research focus on three areas of causation—characteristics of parents, family interactions, and early stress.

From the time he first identified autism, Kanner (1954, 1943) argued that particular personality *characteristics of the parents* of autistic children contribute to the disorder. He saw these parents as very intelligent people, yet obsessive and cold—"refrigerator parents." Once children are confronted by such parents, certain innate deficiencies are exacerbated and blossom into a full autistic syndrome of withdrawal and isolation.

Although such claims have had enormous influence on the public's impression of these parents and on the self-image of the parents themselves, research has failed to support a picture of rigid, cold, or disturbed parents (McAdoo & DeMyer, 1978; Schriebman, 1975). In fact, they have proved to be warmer and more sociable in many comparisons with parents of normal children and with parents of deaf, mentally retarded, and dysphasic children (who exhibit language deficits as a result of a brain injury) (Gonzales et al., 1977; Cox et al., 1975). Even the claim of higher parental intelligence has not been borne out (Gillberg & Schaumann, 1982; Tsai et al., 1982).

Other theorists argue that it is not the parents' characteristics but *parent interactions with the child* that lead to autistic patterns (Bettelheim, 1967; Ferster, 1961). According to them, the parents interact with their children in ways that are negative, angry, rejecting, or nonreinforcing.

Bruno Bettelheim's (1967) family interaction theory of autism was for years very influential in the field. Bettelheim explained that parents of autistic children reject them and fail to respond to their emotional needs. The children sense the parents' negative feelings and can do nothing to get a positive response. Feeling powerless, they withdraw to protect themselves. They become totally passive and seek a simple world filled with sameness.

Like the theories that point to characteristics or maladjustment of the parents, the family interaction explanations have received little empirical support. Most studies suggest that the parents of autistic children are as supportive and accepting of their children as the parents of normal, mentally retarded, brain-damaged, or dysphasic children are of their children (Cantwell, Baker, & Rutter, 1978; Cox et al., 1975; DeMyer et al., 1972).

Finally, some clinicians suspect that unusual *environmental stress* helps cause autism. They propose that events that occur very early in life traumatize the children, stifle their development, and lead them into lives of near-total withdrawal. Once again, however, research has not supported this notion. Aside from the birth and postnatal factors described earlier, no relationship has been found between stressful life events and autism (Folstein & Rutter, 1977; Cox et al., 1975). One study compared autistic and dysphasic children and found no differences in the incidence of parental death, divorce, separation, financial problems, or environmental deficits (Cox et al., 1975).

***Treatment*** Treatments for autism try to help the children adapt better to their environment within their limitations. At present there is no treatment that totally reverses the autistic pattern. It is often possible, however, to help the children attain more effective functioning and contact with the world. The most prominent treatment approaches for autistic children are drug, psychodynamic-humanistic, behavioral, and educational approaches.

***Drug Therapy***  Given alone, psychotropic medications have been of limited help to autistic children. In conjunction with other treatments or with educational programs, however, they may be effective. Among the more helpful drugs are ***haloperidol*** and ***fenfluramine*** (Stern et al., 1990; Campbell et al., 1982, 1978). Because of its positive impact on attention and learning, haloperidol has been particularly helpful when it is used in conjunction with the learning approaches of behavioral therapists.

***Psychodynamic-Humanistic Treatment***  Believing that autism is primarily the result of severe disturbances in early mother-child relationships (Bettelheim, 1967; Goldfarb, 1967; Mahler, 1965), psychodynamic and humanistic therapists have tried to provide corrective environmental experiences, marked by great warmth and acceptance, which theoretically help the child form a bond with the mother or a mother figure (Bettelheim, 1967; Goldfarb, 1969; Mahler, 1965).

Although several clinicians have reported considerable success with psychodynamic-humanistic treatments of this kind (Bettelheim, 1967), such claims have been challenged by research (Brown, 1963, 1960). The reports of success often seem to be based on a therapist's subjective ratings.

***Behavioral Treatment***  Behavioral approaches have been used with autistic children for more than thirty years (Harris & Milch, 1981; Lovaas et al., 1974; Ferster & DeMyer, 1961). These approaches teach the children new, appropriate behaviors, including speech, social skills, classroom skills, and self-help skills, and try to reduce negative, dysfunctional ones.

In modeling techniques, the children imitate behaviors that therapists demonstrate. In operant conditioning, the children are reinforced when they perform desired behaviors. Neither of these behavioral procedures is easy to employ, because autistic children often have difficulty imitating and find it hard to make connections between behaviors and rewards. Nevertheless, with careful planning and execution, therapists apparently can help the children learn new behaviors. For successful learning to occur, the desired behaviors must be ***shaped***—broken down and learned step by step—and the reinforcements must be explicit and consistent (Harris & Milch, 1981; Lovaas, Schreibman, & Koegel, 1974).

Behaviorists have also developed techniques for eliminating undesirable behaviors from the autistic child's repertoire (Foxx & Faw, 1990; Foxx et al., 1988). These efforts have centered on self-injurious behaviors, such as head-banging or biting oneself, which often

Behaviorists have had considerable success teaching autistic children to speak. The therapist systematically models how to position the mouth and how to make appropriate sounds, and then rewards the child's accurate imitations.

place the children in danger, and self-stimulatory behaviors, such as repeated rocking or hand-flapping, which may interfere with learning and with cooperative play (Koegel et al., 1974; Koegel & Covert, 1972).

Some behavioral programs ignore inappropriate behaviors while reinforcing alternative behaviors. However, this approach can be cumbersome and slow to take effect, and does not always work with self-injurious or self-stimulatory behaviors (Harris & Ersner-Hershfield, 1978). Other behavioral programs use punishment to help eliminate negative behaviors. The punishments range from restraint to electric shock (Saposnek & Watson, 1974). It turns out, however, that self-injurious behaviors often resume or even increase after the restraint or electric shocks are discontinued (Harris & Ersner-Hershfield, 1973).

The use of punishment in the treatment of autistic children has understandably concerned many people and stirred debate. Although these procedures may help achieve important goals, they prompt a number of questions. First, does punishment belong under the heading of treatment? Some people believe that the pain and suffering brought about by these approaches are unacceptable. Others counter that treatments in the medical sphere are often painful, yet necessary to improve a person's health. Second, how does a clinician determine when punishment is necessary? Does biting one's arm justify the interventions, or must the behavior be life-threatening? And finally, who has the right to make these judgments? When children are involved, consent must be obtained from parents or guardians. But do they have the right to authorize painful procedures? Some clinicians argue that punishments such as shock should be used only after an impartial review board has been consulted (Oppenheim, 1976).

Behavioral programs also have other limitations and difficulties. Behavioral packages do not "cure" autistic children (Browning, 1971). Although children in these programs sometimes make considerable progress at learning new skills and reducing inappropriate behavior, they do not suddenly become "normal." Furthermore, behavioral contingencies must also be set up in the home to ensure that newly acquired behaviors generalize outside of the school program. It is critical that children taught to say "I want milk" in school also say it at home and in other settings, day in and day out.

Despite these difficulties, behavioral programs often bring results that other approaches do not. In research comparisons, autistic children in behavioral classrooms were found to make more progress in academic, social, and behavioral development than those in psychodynamic therapy or psychodynamic-humanistic classrooms (Rutter & Bartak, 1973). Thus many clinicians now consider behavioral programs and schools to offer the preferred treatment for autism (Waters, 1990).

**Educational Approaches** Many therapies for autistic children, particularly behavioral therapies, are conducted in a school setting. The children attend special classes, often at special schools, where education and therapy are pursued simultaneously. Specially trained teachers help the children improve their skills, behaviors, and interactions with the world.

**Treatment and Training for Parents** Professionals no longer view parents of autistic persons as the enemy. Increasingly they are recognizing the parents' needs for information, guidance, and support, and are trying to address these needs (Schopler, 1976).

Each treatment model now tries to involve parents in the treatment program. Psychodynamic therapists often work to establish a link between mother and child. Behavioral programs include parent-training components to help parents learn and apply behavioral techniques at home (Love et al., 1990; Lovaas et al., 1973). Furthermore, some treatment programs now include instruction manuals, and home visits by professionals. In some cases, the entire program of treatment is conducted in the child's home.

Individual therapy and support groups for parents also are becoming increasingly available. Here they can explore their feelings and have their own problems and needs addressed. In addition, parent associations and lobbies such as the National Society for Children and Adults with Autism provide emotional support and practical help.

**Group Homes** Clinicians are now developing new ideas and programs to improve the opportunities of autistic children as they grow older (Wall, 1990; Schopler & Hennike, 1990). Educational and home programs, for example, are becoming increasingly concerned with teaching self-help, living, and work skills to autistic children as early as possible. In addition, carefully run group homes are being established for many autistic adolescents and young adults. These homes, along with sheltered workshops, address the dilemma of parents who are aging and children who are maturing but will always need supervision (Van-Bourgondien & Schopler, 1990; Schopler, 1981; Wing, 1981). Such efforts demonstrate the field's awareness that the needs and problems of autistic individuals usually last a lifetime.

## Mental Retardation

Ed Murphy, aged 26, can tell you what it's like to be diagnosed as retarded:

*What is retardation? It's hard to say. I guess it's having* problems thinking. Some people think that you can tell if a person is retarded by looking at them. If you think that way you don't give people the benefit of the doubt. You judge a person by how they look or how they talk or what the tests show, but you can never really tell what is inside the person.

Take a couple of friends of mine, Tommy McCan and PJ. Tommy was a guy who was really nice to be with. You could sit down with him and have a nice conversation and enjoy yourself. He was a mongoloid. The trouble was people couldn't see beyond that. If he didn't look that way it would have been different, but there he was locked into what the other people thought he was. Now PJ was really something else. I've watched that guy and I can see in his eyes that he is aware. He knows what's going on. He can only crawl and he doesn't talk, but you don't know what's inside. When I was with him and I touched him, I know that he knows.

*(Bogdan & Taylor, 1976, p. 51)*

For much of his life Ed was labeled mentally retarded and was educated and cared for in special institutions. During his adult years, his clinicians came to suspect that Ed's intellect in fact surpassed that ordinarily implied by this term. Nevertheless, Ed did live the childhood and adolescence of a person labeled retarded, and his recollections illustrate the issues often confronted by mentally retarded persons.

Mentally retarded individuals are those who are significantly below average in intelligence and adaptive ability. As Ed's description suggests, the term has been applied to a wide range of persons, including children in institutional wards who rock vacantly back and forth, young adults who work daily in special job programs, and adult men and women who raise and support their families by working at undemanding jobs (APA, 1987).

Approximately one out of every 100 persons receives a diagnosis of mental retardation (APA, 1987), with 100,000 to 150,000 infants born each year destined to receive this diagnosis (President's Committee on Mental Retardation, 1980). Sixty percent of them are boys. As we shall see, the vast majority are considered mildly retarded (APA, 1987).

In 1905 Alfred Binet developed the first widely used intelligence test and proposed that testing should serve as the first step in treating mental retardation. He wrote, "After the illness, the remedy." Unfortunately, the remedy for this problem proved elusive, and for much of the twentieth century mentally retarded persons were considered beyond help. During the past few decades, professionals have taken a more positive attitude, worked to prevent or improve the disorder, and developed special interventions and educational approaches for those who are mentally retarded (Fiedler & Antonak, 1991).

A major turning point came in the 1960s, when President John Kennedy publicly acknowledged that one of his sisters was retarded and established a panel to make recommendations for improved services to mentally retarded persons. The panel's recommendations and organized lobbying efforts by parents of retarded persons resulted in laws that mandated more research and rehabilitation in this area. Indeed, since the 1960s the federal government has trained and supported thousands of mental retardation specialists, whose efforts have led to a clearer understanding and better education and treatment of persons with this disorder (Grinspoon et al., 1986).

According to DSM-III-R, a diagnosis of **mental retardation** should be made when a person *manifests significant subaverage general intellectual functioning (an IQ of 70 or below), displays concurrent deficits or impairments in adaptive behavior*, and *develops these symptoms before the age of 18* (APA, 1987). Although these criteria may seem straightforward, they are in fact hard to apply.

**Intelligence**    As we observed in Chapter 4, clinicians and educators rely largely on *intelligence tests* to define and distinguish different levels of intelligence. These tests contain numerous questions or tasks chosen to represent different dimensions of intelligence, such as knowledge, reasoning, and judgment. An *intelligence quotient (IQ)* score, derived from the individual's test performance,

theoretically indicates the person's overall intellectual capacity.

*It's funny. You hear so many people talking about IQ. The first time I ever heard the expression was when I was at Empire State School. I didn't know what it was or anything, but some people were talking and they brought the subject up. It was on the ward, and I went and asked one of the staff what mine was. They told me 49. Forty-nine isn't fifty, but I was pretty happy about it. I mean I figured that I wasn't a low grade. I really didn't know what it meant, but it sounded pretty high. Hell, I was born in 1948 and 49 didn't seem too bad. Forty-nine didn't sound hopeless. I didn't know anything about the highs or the lows, but I knew I was better than most of them.*

*(Ed Murphy, in Bogdan & Taylor, 1976, pp. 48–49)*

Theorists have often questioned whether IQ tests are *valid*—that is, whether they measure and predict what they are supposed to measure and predict. If IQ scores reflect intelligence, they should predict a person's performance on tasks that seem to rely on intelligence, such as school tasks (Smith & Smith, 1986). Correlations between IQ and school performance range from .45 to .75, indicating that children with lower IQs do indeed often perform poorly in school while those with higher IQs often perform better (Smith & Smith, 1986; Anastasi, 1982; Achenbach, 1974; Matarazzo, 1972). At the same time, these correlations also suggest that the relationship is far from perfect. Educators frequently find a particular child's school performance to be at odds with his or her IQ. Moreover, IQ scores do not correlate at all highly with job productivity or social effectiveness—areas of performance that also seem to rely on intellectual ability (Anastasi, 1982).

In another kind of validity problem, intelligence tests appear to be culturally biased, as we first noted in Chapter 4 (Anastasi, 1982; Klineberg, 1963; Lee, 1951). Children reared in middle and upper socioeconomic households tend to have an advantage in the tests because they are regularly exposed to the kinds of vocabulary, problem sets, and challenges that the tests measure (Tulkin, 1968). The tests rarely reflect the "street sense" needed for survival by persons who live in poor, crime-ridden areas—a kind of know-how that would seem to require intellectual skills.

Validity is also a problem when intelligence tests are given to members of cultural minorities and in a language in which the person being tested is not fluent (Elliott et al., 1985). Studies suggest that people score significantly higher when they are tested in their native languages, an opportunity rarely afforded immigrants in educational settings in the United States (Edgerton, 1979).

Such concerns have direct implications for the diagnosis of mental retardation (Heflinger, Cook, & Thackrey, 1987; Whitaker, Rueda, & Prieto, 1985). It may be that some persons receive this diagnosis primarily because of cultural differences, discomfort in the testing situation, or the bias of a tester. In fact, one investigator found that school psychologists are more likely to recommend lower-socioeconomic Mexican-American children to special classes for the retarded even when their IQs are the same as those of nonminority children of a higher socioeconomic class (Mercer, 1973).

**Adaptive Functioning**    Diagnosticians have chosen a cutoff IQ score of 70 for mental retardation because individuals with scores below 70 tend to be deficient in their adaptive functioning — that is, in their ability to be personally independent and socially responsible, to communicate, and to fulfill daily living requirements (APA, 1987). This relationship between IQ and adaptive skills does not always hold, however, especially for those whose IQs are close to 70. These individuals are sometimes quite capable of managing their lives and functioning independently. Both Brian and Jeffrey have an IQ score of 60.

> *Brian comes from a lower-income family. He always has* functioned adequately at home and in his community. He dresses and feeds himself and even takes care of himself each day until his mother returns home from work. He also plays well with his friends. At school, however, Brian refuses to participate or do his homework. He seems ineffective, at times lost, in the classroom. Referred to a school psychologist by his teacher, he received an IQ score of 60.

> *Jeffrey comes from an upper-middle-class home. He was* always slow to develop, and sat up, stood, and talked late. During his infancy and toddler years, he was put in a special stimulation program and given special help and attention at home. Still Jeffrey has trouble dressing himself today and cannot be left alone in the backyard lest he hurt himself or wander off into the street. Schoolwork is very difficult for him. The teacher must work slowly and provide individual instruction for him. Tested at age 6, Jeffrey received an IQ score of 60.

Brian seems well adapted to his environment outside of school. He is the kind of child that the President's Committee on Mental Retardation once called the "six-hour retarded child." He fits the IQ criterion for mental retardation, but perhaps not the adaptive criterion. Jeffrey's limitations are more pervasive. His low IQ score is complemented by poor adaptive behaviors at home and elsewhere. A diagnosis of mental retardation may be more appropriate for Jeffrey than for Brian.

Various scales have been developed to assess adaptive

"You can't build a hut, you don't know how to find edible roots and you know nothing about predicting the weather. In other words, you do *terribly* on our IQ test."

behavior (Leland, 1991; Britton & Eaves, 1986). For example, the *Vineland Social Maturity Scale* rates a child's ability to dress, bathe, and perform other daily functions (Doll, 1953). The *AAMD Adaptive Behavior Scales* cover still more areas, including independent functioning, physical development, economic activity, language, number and time concepts, vocational activity, self-direction, responsibility, and socialization (Nihira, Foster, Shellhaas, & Leland, 1974).

Although helpful, such scales are not always accurate predictors of ability to function independently. Some children function more effectively than the scales predict; others fall short. Thus clinicians themselves must observe and judge the effectiveness of individuals, paying attention both to their background and to community standards. This too can be a subjective process. The clinicians are not always familiar with a particular culture's or community's standards, and may at times be biased against such standards.

**Characteristics of Mentally Retarded Individuals**    The most important and consistent difference between retarded and nonretarded people is that the retarded person learns more slowly (Hale & Borkowski, 1991; Israely, 1985). When retarded and nonretarded people of comparable mental age approach the same learning task, the retarded person usually employs relevant behavior, skills, and insights at a slower pace than the nonretarded. Other areas of difference include attention, short-term memory, and language (Chamberlain, 1985; Yabe et al., 1985; Mineo & Cavalier, 1985; Smith, 1974).

*When I was at school, concentrating was almost impos-*
sible. I was so much into my own thoughts — my daydreams — I wasn't really in class. I would think of the
cowboy movies — the rest of the kids would be in class and I
would be on the battlefield someplace. The nuns would yell
at me to snap out of it, but they were nice. That was my
major problem all through school that I daydreamed. . . . I
don't think I was bored. I think all the kids were competing
to be the honor students, but I was never interested in that. I
was in my own world — I was happy.

*(Ed Murphy in Bogdan & Taylor, 1976, p. 48)*

Difficulties in attention and memory are particularly
characteristic of institutionalized retarded persons, and
clinicians suspect that institutionalization itself contributes to the cognitive difficulties of retarded persons. It
may be, for example, that the limited number of adult-
child interactions in institutions contributes to slow language development. Similarly, institutional factors may
be partly responsible for the tendency to rely on others
that inhibits the task performances of retarded children.

Educators and clinicians have found it useful to distinguish four levels of mental retardation: *mild* (IQ 50–
70), *moderate* (IQ 35–49), *severe* (IQ 20–34), and *profound* (IQ below 20). The persons who function at these
various levels differ markedly from each other. In addition, their intellectual and adaptive impairments are
often the result of very different factors.

**Mild Retardation**   Approximately 85 percent of all retarded persons fall into the category of *mild retardation*
(IQ 50–70) (APA, 1987). They are sometimes called
"educably retarded" because they can benefit from an
academic education. They can develop social and communication skills during their preschool years; academic
skills up to approximately the sixth-grade level during
adolescence; and social and vocational skills adequate
for self-support during adulthood (APA, 1987; Schalock
et al., 1981). Still, they typically need assistance when
they are under unusual social or economic stress. Their
jobs tend to be unskilled. Some work in sheltered workshops.

Mild mental retardation is not usually detected until a
child enters school, at which time school evaluators assign the label. Interestingly, the intellectual performance of individuals in this category often seems to improve with age; some even lose the label once they leave
the academic setting, and function adequately in the
community (APA, 1987).

Research has linked mild mental retardation primarily
to environmental factors and, to a lesser extent, to genetic and biological factors.

***Environmental Causes***   Environmental understimulation,
inadequate parent-child interactions, and insufficient
early learning experiences may each contribute to mild
mental retardation. These relationships have emerged
in studies of deprived environments and enriched environments.

The majority of mildly retarded individuals come from
poor and *deprived home environments* (see Figure 19-4)
(Robinson & Robinson, 1970). In many cases, one of the
parents and perhaps a sibling also display low intelligence. The greater health problems and inadequate
diets common in poorer homes may partly account for
this relationship. A study of impoverished environments, however, suggests that the poor quality of parent
modeling and low stimulation that exist in some of these

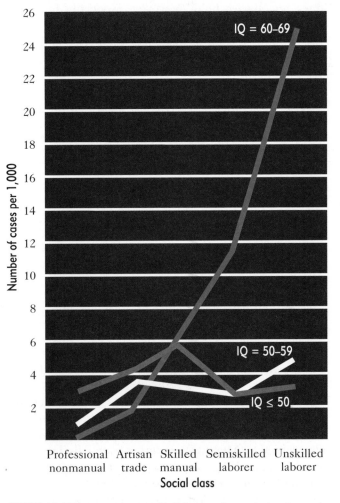

**FIGURE 19-4** The prevalence of mild mental retardation is much
higher in the lower socioeconomic classes than in the upper
classes. In contrast, more impaired forms of mental retardation
are evenly distributed. *(Adapted from Popper, 1988; Birch et al.,
1970.)*

homes may be the overriding factors in the development of mild mental retardation (Heber, 1979). The investigator in this study examined the IQ scores of mothers and children living in a poor Milwaukee neighborhood. Children whose mothers had IQs under 80 seemed to decline in intellectual functioning as they got older. While only 20 percent of 6-year-olds with such mothers themselves had IQ scores under 80, 90 percent of adolescents with such mothers had IQ scores under 80. On the other hand, neighborhood children whose mothers had IQs over 80 showed no decline in their IQ scores as they got older.

Some of the strongest evidence for environmental factors in mental retardation comes from projects that alter the environment of retarded children (Marfo & Kysela, 1985). In 1939, for example, two clinicians transferred thirteen very young children from an unstimulating orphanage to another institution where they were regularly played with and given attention (Skeels & Dye, 1939). The children's IQs increased an average of 30 points and eventually most of them were adopted. In contrast, eleven children who remained in the orphanage continued to decline in IQ. In a follow-up study twenty-five years later, the same clinicians found that the thirteen transferred individuals were now holding good jobs and raising families (Skeels, 1966). In contrast, those who had remained in the orphanage were still institutionalized or holding menial jobs.

**Genetic Causes**  Because environmental factors seem to play such an important causal role in mild mental retardation, this kind of retardation has also been called *cultural, familial,* or *environmental retardation.* Yet at least some genetic and biological factors also seem to be operating. Some researchers who have compared the IQ scores of adopted children, their adoptive parents, and their biological parents have found higher IQ correlations between the children and their biological parents than between the children and their adoptive parents (Vernon, 1979; Munsinger, 1975; Skodak & Skeels, 1949). These findings have suggested to many people that heredity plays a major role in intellectual functioning and in the development of mild mental retardation.

At the same time, however, other adoption studies have highlighted the important role of environmental factors in IQ. One study examined families in which parents were raising adopted children along with their own biological children (Scarr & Weinberg, 1977). The researchers computed IQ correlations between the mothers and their biological child, and between the mothers and their adopted child. The two sets of correlations turned out to be approximately the same, suggesting that IQ is often influenced more by environment

than by heredity. The environmental influence shown in this study merited particular notice because the children in all of the families were of different races — that is, the parents and biological children were white while the adopted children were black.

Another team of investigators conducted a similar study and in addition obtained the IQ scores of the adopted children's biological mothers (Horn et al., 1979). The IQ scores of these women averaged six points lower than those of the adoptive mothers. Yet the adopted children earned IQ scores similar to those of the other children in their new family (average IQ of 112).

**Biological Causes**  Early biological events may also contribute to mild mental retardation. Studies suggest, for example, that a mother's moderate drinking, drug use, or malnutrition during pregnancy may impair her child's intellectual potential (AMA, 1982; Harrell, Woodyard, & Gates, 1955; Stein et al., 1972). Similarly, malnourishment during childhood increases the risk of a person developing mild mental retardation (Davison & Dobbing, 1966). One study found an unusually low number of cells in the autopsied brains of children who had died from malnutrition (Winick, Rosso, & Waterlow, 1970).

It appears that the effect of malnourishment on intellectual development is at least partly reversible. One investigation compared the intellectual growth of three groups of children: severely malnourished Korean children who were adopted at 18 months of age and reared in middle-class American homes, properly nourished Korean children adopted by American families, and malnourished children who remained in their native environment (Winick, Meyer, & Harris, 1975). At age 6, the previously malnourished children who had been adopted scored an average IQ of 102, whereas the malnourished children who had remained in their native environment scored forty points lower. Although the scores of these adopted children were still lower than the scores of adopted children who had always been properly nourished, their IQs improved significantly after the children had been on regular, proper diets for years.

**Moderate, Severe, and Profound Retardation**  The approximately 10 percent of the retarded population who function at a level of *moderate retardation* (IQ 35–49) are sometimes known as "trainable" because the dominant part of their education involves training in self-care and social and vocational skills. At the same time, these individuals can also profit to some degree from an academic curriculum (APA, 1987). Although they may learn to talk in their preschool years, their retardation is usually evident from infancy. When they reach adulthood, many can work in supervised jobs, and with careful training some can work with relative independence in unskilled or semiskilled jobs. Most moderately retarded persons have lifelong difficulty with social skills, and some are institutionalized.

The approximately 5 percent of the retarded population who are *severely retarded* (IQ 20–34) display poor motor coordination and little speech during the preschool years. During the school-age years they can learn some speech and self-care skills with concentrated teaching and training (APA, 1987). Their understanding of communication is usually better than their speech. They usually require careful supervision, profit somewhat from vocational training, and can perform only basic vocational tasks in structured and sheltered settings.

Less than 1 percent of the retarded population is *profoundly retarded* (IQ below 20). In their preschool years these individuals display minimal capacity for almost any kind of activity requiring sensorimotor functioning. With training they may learn to walk and say a few words or phrases, feed themselves, or use the toilet. Relatively few go further than the acquisition of such basic skills. Profoundly retarded individuals require close supervision and help throughout their lives. Many have a short life span.

The primary causes of moderate, severe, and profound retardation are biological, although individuals who function at these levels of retardation are also enormously affected by their environment (President's Committee on Mental Retardation, 1980). The leading biological causes are chromosomal and metabolic disorders (Pueschel & Thuline, 1991), prenatal and birth complications (Menke et al., 1991), and postnatal diseases and injuries.

***Chromosomal Causes*** *Down syndrome,* named after Langdon Down, the British physician who first identified this syndrome, is the most common of the chromosomal disorders leading to mental retardation (Evans & Hamerton, 1983). Approximately 1 out of every 640 live births results in Down syndrome (Smith & Wilson, 1973). The incidence increases to 1 in 100 when the mother's age is over 35 (Somasundaram & Papakumari, 1981). Older fathers, especially those over 50 years of age, also are at greater risk of having a child with Down syndrome (Stene et al., 1981). Many older mothers are now encouraged to undergo *amniocentesis,* testing of the amniotic fluid that surrounds the fetus, during the fourth month of pregnancy to detect Down syndrome and other chromosomal abnormalities.

Three types of chromosomal aberrations may cause Down syndrome. In the most common type, called *trisomy 21,* the individual has three twenty-first chromo-

Until the 1970s, clinicians were pessimistic about the potential of children with Down syndrome. Today these children are viewed as individuals who can learn and accomplish many things.

somes instead of two (Pueschel & Thuline, 1991). In *mosaicism,* both normal and trisomic cells are found. And in a third type, *translocation,* the twenty-first and fifteenth chromosomes are fused.

Individuals with Down syndrome have a distinct appearance, with a small head, a flat face with slanted eyes, high cheekbones, and protruding tongue. Their hands are broad and thick with short fingers and only a single palm crease. Because their eyes and high cheekbones suggest those of Asians, the disorder has sometimes been called *mongolism.*

Individuals with Down syndrome may also articulate poorly and be difficult to understand (Mahoney, Glover, & Finger, 1981). Although they are often affectionate with family members, the stereotype of them as being "always" placid, cheerful, and cooperative appears to be an exaggeration. In fact, they display the usual range of individual personality characteristics.

Most Down syndrome individuals range in IQ from 35 to 55; they account for about a third of the people who are moderately retarded (Grinspoon et al., 1986). Those with mosaicism have IQs closer to 70. The aging process appears to occur more quickly in these individuals, and some even show signs of senility as they approach 40 (see Figure 19-5). As we discussed in Chapter 8, scientists are now able to observe chromosomes under a microscope by using chemical "staining" techniques and in turn are beginning to map the genes on each of the body's twenty-three pairs of chromosomes. They suspect that Down syndrome is linked to genes located on the lower third of chromosome 21 (Epstein & Groner, 1989). When the child inherits three copies of chromosome 21 instead of the usual two, the extra genes on the lower part of the chromosome apparently produce the symptoms of Down syndrome. Scientists have previously determined that the genes of many people with Alzheimer's disease are located on the middle third of chromosome 21 and that one of the Alzheimer-producing genes is located particularly close to the Down-syndrome-producing genes (Tanzi et al., 1989). Thus, it may well be that Down syndrome and early dementia co-occur because the genes producing each of these disorders are located close to each other on chromosome 21.

***Metabolic Causes***   Metabolic disorders that affect intelligence and development are typically caused by the pairing of two defective ***recessive genes,*** one from each parent. Although one such gene would have no influence if it were paired with a normal dominant gene, its pairing with another defective gene leads to disturbed enzyme production in the child and thus to disturbed metabolic processes.

The most common retardation-causing metabolic disorder is ***phenylketonuria (PKU).*** Approximately 1 out of every 15,000 children has this disorder. Babies with PKU appear normal at birth but are unable to metabolize the amino acid ***phenylalanine*** into ***tyrosine.*** The phenylalanine accumulates and is converted into substances that poison the system, causing severe retardation. Persons with PKU have light coloring and often have eczema

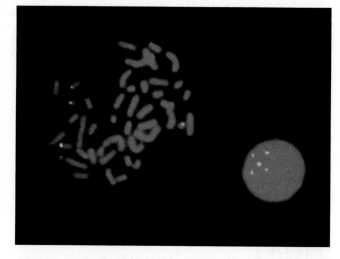

Clinicians are now able to identify Down syndrome and other chromosomal disorders early. They obtain fetal cells by amniocentesis and apply a fluorescent dye that binds only to certain chromosomes. The large red spot at the right is actually a cell with an extra chromosome, suggesting the presence of Down syndrome; to the left are chromosomes of a dividing cell.

and epilepsy. They sometimes display odd behavior and movements and may be hyperactive.

Infants can now be screened for PKU. If the disorder is diagnosed early enough, affected children can be given a diet low in phenylalanine (Manolascino & Egger,

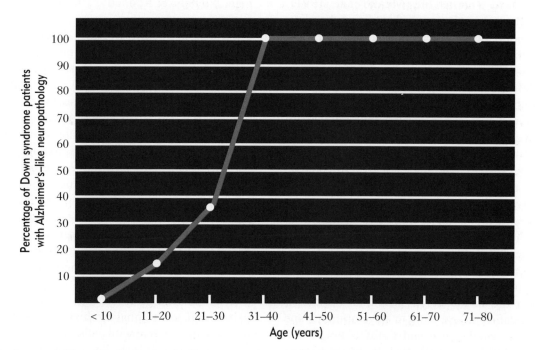

**FIGURE 19-5** By the age of 35 to 40, all people with Down syndrome show *some* of the neuropathological changes characteristic of Alzheimer's disease. Both Down syndrome and Alzheimer's disease are linked to abnormalities on chromosome 21. *(Adapted from Popper, 1989; Wisniewski et al., 1985.)*

1978). If the diet is started before three months of age, the children may develop normal intelligence. Eventually, after age 6, they may, under careful supervision, be able to increase the phenylalanine in their diet.

In *Tay-Sachs disease,* another metabolic disorder resulting from a pairing of recessive genes, an enzyme missing from the infant's nerve cells leads to an excessive accumulation of fats, which in turn causes progressive mental deterioration and loss of visual functioning over the course of two to four years, followed by death. The disease is most common among Jewish persons (Carter, 1970). One out of every 30 persons of Eastern European Jewish ancestry carries the recessive gene responsible for this disorder, meaning that 1 out of every 900 Jewish couples is at risk for having a child with Tay-Sachs disease.

Carriers of these metabolic disorders (those who may pass on the defective recessive genes) can often be detected with blood tests. If a couple are identified as carriers, the prospective mother can undergo amniocentesis during her pregnancy to determine whether the child is going to have the disorder. If the test is positive, the couple may choose to undergo a therapeutic abortion to avoid the painful degeneration and early death that await the victims of some of these disorders (Pueschel & Goldstein, 1991).

**Prenatal Causes** As a fetus develops, significant physical problems in the pregnant mother can endanger the child's prospects for a normal life (Menke et al., 1991). When a pregnant woman has too little iodine in her diet, for example, her child may develop *cretinism.* Her low supplies of iodine may lead to a severe deficiency in the manufacture of the hormone *thyroxin,* which in turn can result in a defective thyroid gland in the baby. As the baby's thyroid gland deteriorates, development slows down and mental retardation occurs. Individuals with cretinism have a dwarflike appearance — a large head, swollen abdomen, and short, stubby limbs. The disorder is rare today because the salt in most diets now contains iodine. Also, any infant born with this disorder may quickly be given thyroid extract to bring about a relatively normal development.

Children whose mothers abuse alcohol or other drugs during pregnancy are also at risk for mental retardation. As we observed in Chapter 13, such children may be born with a cluster of serious problems called *fetal alcohol syndrome:* the infant weighs less than normal, is intellectually deficient and slow in development, and has irregularities of the face and limbs (Abel, 1984; Jones & Smith, 1975, 1973; NIMH, 1978). It has been estimated that as many as 3 of 1,000 newborn children may display the fetal alcohol syndrome (Hanson et al., 1978).

Maternal infections during pregnancy may cause a number of childhood abnormalities. *Rubella,* or German measles, is one of the best-known infections of this kind. If a mother contracts this otherwise minor illness, particularly in the first three months of pregnancy, mental retardation, heart disease, deafness, and a host of other abnormalities may develop in the child (Barlow, 1978). A vaccine taken during pregnancy now reduces the likelihood of this infection, but some mothers contract rubella before they even realize that they are pregnant.

Another prenatal maternal infection that can cause mental retardation is *syphilis.* Children of mothers with syphilis often die within weeks after birth or even before birth. The effects on those who survive may include mental retardation, blindness, and deafness. The blood of pregnant women is now automatically tested to detect syphilis, so that this disease is a less common cause of mental retardation today than it was in the past.

**Birth-Related Causes** Two birth complications that can lead to mental retardation are *anoxia* (loss of oxygen to the baby) and *extreme prematurity* (Menke et al., 1991). A prolonged period without oxygen during or after delivery can cause brain damage and retardation (Schwartz & Johnson, 1986). Similarly, although premature birth does not necessarily pose problems for children, researchers have found that a very low birth weight (less than 3.5 pounds) resulting from prematurity may cause some degree of mental retardation (Broman, Nichols, & Kennedy, 1975).

**Disease- and Injury-Related Causes** After birth, particularly up to age 6, certain injuries and illnesses can lead to mental retardation. Poisonings, serious head injuries caused by an accident or child abuse, highly frequent exposure to X rays, and excessive use of certain drugs pose special dangers in this regard.

One of the most serious childhood diseases is *meningitis,* an inflammation of the meninges of the brain (Scola, 1991). This infection can cause brain damage and mental retardation, but such effects can be prevented with proper early treatment. Similarly, *encephalitis* during early childhood can cause serious brain damage unless it is treated quickly and effectively. Approximately 10 to 20 percent of children who experience these diseases are left mentally retarded (Koch, 1971).

Lead poisoning, associated with eating lead-based paints and with inhaling high levels of automobile fumes, can interfere with cellular metabolism and cause retardation in children. The exact blood levels that are dangerous have not yet been determined. Similarly, mercury, radiation, nitrate, and pesticide poisoning may each cause retardation.

Some forms of moderate, severe, and profound mental retardation have multiple biological causes. ***Microencephaly***—characterized by a small, unusually shaped head—can be caused by a combination of hereditary, prenatal, birth, and postnatal factors. Twenty percent of institutionalized retarded people suffer from this disorder (Citryn & Louriel, 1974). Another disease with multiple causes is ***hydrocephalus,*** characterized by an increase in cerebrospinal fluid and resultant head enlargement. If this disease is treated quickly and successfully, its effect on intellectual functioning may be less severe; if not, the disease may even be fatal.

### Care, Education, and Treatment for Mentally Retarded People

The prognosis for mentally retarded persons is influenced by several factors: (1) Where do they live? (2) What kinds of educational and treatment programs do they participate in? (3) What growth opportunities are offered by their family and community?

***Residential Alternatives*** Until the middle of the nineteenth century, retarded people in the United States were cared for at home (Grinspoon et al., 1986). Later in the century, public institutions—***state schools***—were established (Grinspoon et al., 1986). Parents were encouraged to send their retarded child to live in these institutions as soon as possible, theoretically to afford them proper care, treatment, and education. Unfortunately, in practice these overcrowded institutions offered only custodial care, and retarded persons in these settings were neglected, often abused, and isolated from society. Ed Murphy recalls his experiences in a state school:

*To me there never was a State School. The words State* School sound like a place with vocational training or you get some sort of education. That's just not the way Empire State School is. . . . If you looked at individuals and see what they said they were supposed to do for that person and then what they actually did, you would find that many of them were actually hurt—not helped. I don't like the word vegetable, but in my own case I could see that if I had been placed on the low grade ward I might have slipped to that. I began feeling myself slip. They could have made me a vegetable. If I would have let that place get to me and depress me I would still have been there today. Actually, it was one man that saved me. They had me scheduled to go to P-8—a back ward—when just one man looked at me. I was a wreck. I had a beard and baggy State clothes on. I had just arrived at the place. I was trying to understand what was happening. I was confused. What I looked like was P-8 material. There was this supervisor, a woman. She came on to the ward and looked right at me and said: "I have him scheduled for P-8." An older attendant was there. He looked over at me and said, "He's too bright for that ward. I think we'll keep him.". . .

Of course I didn't know what P-8 was then, but I found out. I visited up there a few times on work detail. That man saved my life. Here was a woman that I had never known who they said was the building supervisor looking over me. At that point I'm pretty positive that if I went there I would have fitted in and I would still be there.

*(Bogdan & Taylor, 1976, p. 49)*

During the 1960s and 1970s a parent lobby, legal actions, and heightened public awareness led to a series of institutional reforms (Fiedler & Antonak, 1991). A number of newly established small institutions for mentally retarded persons encouraged self-sufficiency, devoted more staff time to patient care, and offered educational and medical services. Persons in these institutions began to show gains in IQ and reported being happier than in the past (Klaber, 1969; King & Raynes, 1967).

During this same period of time, Denmark and Sweden began ***normalization*** treatment programs in their institutions for mentally retarded persons. These programs offered conditions of everyday life that closely resembled those available to the mainstream of society (Baldwin, 1985; Marlett, 1979). Persons in such programs were provided with flexible routines, normal developmental experiences, opportunities to make their own decisions, the right to develop a sexual identity, and normal economic freedoms. Today many institutions operate normalization programs. Moreover, care for mentally retarded persons has spread to community settings (Baldwin, 1985).

As part of the ***deinstitutionalization*** movement of the 1960s and 1970s (see pp. 532–533), large numbers of retarded individuals were released from institutions (Beyer, 1991). Many had to make the transition to community life without special education or guidance, even without adequate residential placement. Like deinstitutionalized schizophrenic persons, they were virtually dumped into the community. Not surprisingly, many failed to adjust to a life without help or supervision and required reinstitutionalization.

In recent years, more community programs and residences have been set up to address the needs of retarded persons (Jacobson & Schwartz, 1991; Clarke, Clarke, & Berg, 1985; Surah & Rizzo, 1983). These programs take such forms as small local branches of larger institutions, group homes, halfway houses, and even independent residences. In these settings community staff members may be available to assist the retarded residents, and the residents are given education and training on how to get along in the community. Under programs of this kind, a number of retarded persons have been able to live successfully in the community (Jacobson & Schwartz, 1991; Repp, Barton, & Brulle, 1986). Ed Murphy states his preference for community life:

*I don't have it that bad right now. I have my own room and* I get my meals at the house. The landlord is going to up the rent though — $45 a week for room and board. I'll be able to pay it, but I don't know what Frank and Lou across the hall will do. They wash dishes at the steak house and don't take home that much.

*(Bogdan & Taylor, 1976, p. 50)*

With the development of such programs, most mentally retarded persons now live their adult lives in the community (APA, 1987). Virtually all who function at a level of mild mental retardation can reside successfully in the community, often independently. Those with a moderate level of retardation may live in group homes that provide either evening supervision *(supported living arrangements)* or twenty-four-hour supervision *(community living families).* Severely retarded persons live either with their families, in supervised houses, or in community nursing homes that provide close supervision *(intermediate care facilities).* And although some profoundly retarded individuals still must spend their adult lives in an institution, many are able to live in a community facility (APA, 1987; Landesman-Dwyer, 1981).

Today most retarded children live at home rather than in an institution until they are ready to enter a community residence (APA, 1987; Grinspoon et al., 1986; Tizard & Grad, 1961). On the other hand, even with strong support systems, approximately 8 percent of parents cannot cope with a handicapped child (Grenscheff, 1975). In such circumstances, the child typically spends his or her early years in an institution.

As retarded persons approach adulthood, the family home may become a lonely and restricted place for them (Seenger, 1957). As their parents grow older and less energetic, they may no longer be able to address the needs of the retarded individual. Accordingly, a community residence often becomes most appropriate for retarded children moving into late adolescence.

**Educational Programs**    Ed Murphy found school a difficult experience after he had been labeled retarded.

*I kind of stood in the background — I kind of knew that I* was different — I knew that I had a problem, but when you're young you don't think of it as a problem. A lot of people are like I was. The problem is getting labeled as being something. After that you're not really seen as a person. It's like a sty in your eye — it's noticeable. Like that teacher and the way she looked at me. In the fifth grade — in the fifth grade my classmates thought I was different, and my teacher knew I was different. One day she looked at me and she was on the phone to the office. Her conversation was like this, "When are you going to transfer him?" This was the phone in the room. I was there. She looked at me

and knew I was knowledgeable about what she was saying. Her negative picture of me stood out like a sore thumb.

*(Bogdan & Taylor, 1976, p. 48)*

In 1975 Congress passed the Education for All Handicapped Children Act, calling upon each state to provide mentally retarded children with "free appropriate public education in the least restrictive environment." Appropriate education depends on the severity of the child's retardation (Cipani, 1991). Mildly retarded children, for example, must initially be taught preschool readiness skills (sitting and attending), self-help skills, and language; later they are instructed in academic subjects and adaptive behaviors; and still later they receive vocational training (Marlett, 1979; Goldstein, 1975). At the other end of the spectrum, education for severely and profoundly retarded children must focus more on survival, self-help, language, and sensorimotor skills. Teachers of these children may also need to concentrate on reducing inappropriate behavior such as rocking or tantrums.

One of the great debates in the field of education centers on the correct educational environment for mentally retarded individuals. Some educators favor special classes while others advocate mainstreaming (Gottlieb et al., 1991). In the *special education* approach, retarded children are grouped only with other retarded children and given a curriculum designed specially for them. It has been argued that special classes help prevent a sense of failure, make special attention available, and provide a more appropriate curriculum for the children. In the *mainstreaming* approach, retarded children are placed in regular classes with nonretarded students. Proponents argue that this format provides more normal educational experiences, helps underscore the many similarities between retarded and nonretarded children, reduces stigmatization, facilitates interactions between retarded and nonretarded children, and places greater emphasis on academics (Turner & Small, 1985). In addition, some educators interpret "least restrictive environment" as a call for placement in regular classes. Mainstreaming approaches, however, are difficult to initiate and run effectively (Lieberman, 1982).

Researchers have not been able to determine which approach is superior (Gottlieb, 1981). Children generally perform the same under both educational formats (Budoff & Gottlieb, 1976). Moreover, although some studies find that children who are mainstreamed have a better self-image than children in special classes, others find either no such difference or else a better self-image among special-class children (Haywood et al., 1982; Zigler & Muenchow, 1979). Finally, mainstreamed children appear to be just as stigmatized in the eyes of their peers as special-class children (Gottlieb & Budoff, 1973). Perhaps mainstreaming is better for some children, special classes for others. The issue may also depend on the subjects being taught and on the skill, planning, and attitude that particular teachers bring to their work (Ascione & Borg, 1983; Haywood et al., 1982).

*Operant learning principles* are regularly applied in the education of retarded individuals (Kiernan, 1985; Kazdin, 1979; Gabrowski & Thompson, 1977). Teachers break learning tasks down into small steps and give positive reinforcement as each small step is accomplished. Tasks taught to mentally retarded persons in this way include self-help skills, proper verbal responding, appropriate social responding, and academic tasks (Matson & Gorman-Smith, 1986). Computer programs that apply reinforcement principles have been used increasingly to help educate mentally retarded persons (Mineo & Cavalier, 1985; Ager, 1985). Many institutions, schools, and even homes have instituted **token economy programs** — the larger-scale operant learning programs that have also been used with institutionalized schizophrenic patients.

Parents often play an active role in their retarded child's education. Indeed, the Education for All Handicapped Children Act mandates parents' participation in developing "individualized education programs," a privilege not afforded to the parents of nonretarded children. This high level of involvement has resulted from the hard work and lobbying of parent associations in courts and legislatures across the United States.

In addition to their involvement in school programs, parents must often serve as teachers at home (Reese & Serna, 1986; Chamberlain, 1985). To help parents in their teaching role, parent-training manuals and courses have been developed. Although parents often prove to be effective and dedicated teachers, working with their own retarded child is a slow and sometimes discouraging task, and encouragement and support from therapists and teachers continue to be needed (Gordon & Davidson, 1981).

**Therapy** Retarded persons often experience emotional and behavioral problems. It is estimated that a quarter of the severely and profoundly retarded persons in the United States manifest such problem behaviors as self-injury, vandalism, aggression, tantrums, and stereotyped repetitive movements (Grinspoon et al., 1986). Moreover, mentally retarded persons at all levels may experience such problems as low self-esteem, interpersonal difficulties, and difficulty in adjusting to community life (Lubetsky, 1986; Reiss, 1985; Reiss & Benson, 1985; Reiss, Levitan, & McNally, 1982).

The interpersonal and sexual needs of retarded persons are normal, and many demonstrate considerable ability to express intimacy. Yet most retarded persons receive poor preparation and excessive restriction in these areas.

Insight therapies have been used to help mentally retarded individuals deal with issues of this kind (Hurley & Hurley, 1986; Ginsberg, 1984). Research suggests, however, that these therapies are helpful only some of the time. Apparently the greatest success comes from insight approaches that are structured, directive, and problem solving, help retarded individuals cope and interact with their environment, enhance their feelings of self-worth, and encourage them to persevere (Grinspoon et al., 1986). Group therapy has also become a popular and often effective format for retarded individuals (Richards & Lee, 1972).

Close to half of all institutionalized retarded persons also take medication for emotional or behavioral problems, and a third take medication for epileptic seizures (Grinspoon et al., 1986). As many as 20 percent of the mildly retarded persons in the community take such medications. Yet research has not clearly indicated that medications are in fact helpful to retarded persons (Aman & Singh, 1991; Grinspoon et al., 1986), nor has it established the long-term effects of such medications on retarded persons. Indeed, many clinicians suggest that the medications are often used simply to keep retarded persons docile (Grinspoon et al., 1986).

**Opportunities for Personal, Social, and Occupational Growth** In addition to a proper residence, education, and treatment, retarded persons must be given opportunities for *personal, social,* and *vocational growth*. Personal growth begins with the family. Parents can unintentionally stifle a retarded child's self-sufficiency and independence by remaining too helpful, too protective, and too available as the child grows older. Ed Murphy recalls his mother:

*When I was growing up she never let me out of her sight.* She was always there with attention. If I yelled she ran right to me. So many children who are handicapped must be in that position—they become so dependent on their mother. Looking back I don't think she ever stopped protecting me even when I was capable of being self-sufficient. I remember how hard it was to break away from that. She never really believed that after I had lived the first six months that I could be like everybody else. . . .

My mother protected me. It wasn't wrong that she protected me, but there comes a time when someone has to come in and break them away. I can remember trying to be like the others kids and having my mother right there pulling me away. She was always worried about me. You can't force yourself to say to your mother: "Stop, I can do it myself." Sometimes I think the pain of being handicapped is that people give you so much love that it becomes a weight on you and a weight on them. There is no way that you can break from it without hurting them—without bad feelings—guilt. It is like a trap because of the fact that you are restricted to your inner thoughts. After a while you resign yourself to it. The trap is that you can't tell them, "Let me go." You have to live with it and suffer. It has to do with pity. Looking back on it I can't say it was wrong. She loved me. You do need special attention, but the right amount.

*(Bogdan & Taylor, 1967, pp. 47–48)*

The community must also provide retarded persons with opportunities for personal growth. Denmark and Sweden, the originators of the normalization movement, have once again led the way in this area (Perske, 1972). These countries have developed youth clubs for retarded persons that encourage risk-taking experiences and encourage members to find their way around independently, cope with minor emergencies, and, in some cases, locate and set up their own apartments.

Socializing, sex, and marriage are among the most difficult issues for retarded persons and their families. Typically, society does a poor job preparing retarded individuals in these areas. Institutions are usually careful to separate male and female patients, and indeed, many parents prevent their retarded adolescents and young adults from socializing with persons of the opposite sex. This lack of education and experience may create even more problems for retarded individuals than IQ level when they first encounter social and sexual relationships. Local chapters of the National Association for Retarded Citizens now provide guidance in this re-

spect. Ed Murphy describes his attraction to Joan and his lack of knowledge in this domain:

*I first met Joan in 1970. It was when I started working at* the ARC workshop. I sat there and maybe the second or third day I glanced over and saw her there. The first time I noticed her was in the eating area; I was having lunch. I looked around and she was the only one there that attracted me. There was just something about her. . . .

It took awhile for her to understand how she felt. She didn't want to be too friendly. She didn't like me putting my arm around her. We went for walks during lunch and she got pretty fond of me and I got pretty fond of her. One day I asked her, "Well, how about a movie?" She said, "All right," but she had to get her mother's permission. Then one day she said she could go. It was a Saturday matinee gangster movie. We arranged to meet at the bus stop downtown. . . .

Being at the State School and all you never have the chances romantically like you might living on the outside. I guess I was always shy with the opposite sex even at Empire. We did have dances and I felt that I was good looking, but I was bashful and mostly sat. I was bashful with Joan at the movie. In my mind I felt funny, awkward. I didn't know how to approach her. Should I hug her? You can't hug the hell out of her because you don't know how she would take it. You have all the feeling there, but you don't know what direction to go in. If you put your arm around her she might scream and you're finished. If she doesn't scream you're still finished.

*(Bogdan & Taylor, 1976, p. 50)*

A number of states have laws restricting marriage for retarded persons on the grounds that many cannot understand the obligations of marriage. These laws are rarely enforced, however, and in fact between a quarter and half of all mildly retarded persons eventually marry (Grinspoon et al., 1986). Despite public stereotypes, the marriages can be very successful. Research suggests that mildly retarded persons encounter on the average only slightly more marital discord than nonretarded couples (Robinson & Robinson, 1976). While some retarded persons are able to raise children without unusual difficulty, others need special help and community services; still others may be incapable of raising children.

It was once common for retarded persons to be sterilized involuntarily, often at the request of their parents (Grinspoon et al., 1986). However, laws that permit this practice have been increasingly challenged as unconstitutional, and such procedures have become very restricted (Beyer, 1991). The current feeling among many clinicians is that with proper training and experience, retarded individuals can usually learn to use contraceptives, carry out responsible family planning, and in many cases rear children effectively.

Finally, retarded adults need the self-satisfaction, structure, social stimulation, and financial rewards that come from holding a job. Studies suggest that many retarded persons do indeed want to work, but often have difficulty finding a job without government or agency intervention (Friedman, 1976). Many work in *sheltered workshops,* where the pace and type of work are tailored to their skills and where supervision is available. After training in these workshops, mildly or moderately retarded individuals often move out into the regular work force. Studies indicate that between 63 and 86 percent of mildly retarded adults hold jobs (Edgerton, 1979; Edgerton & Bercovici, 1976; Baller, Charles, & Miller, 1967; Kidd, 1970). In the case of severely and profoundly retarded individuals, the sheltered workshop tends to be the highest level of employment they can achieve, and enables them to be at least partly self-supporting.

Although training programs for mentally retarded persons have improved greatly in both number and quality over the past twenty-five years, much remains to be accomplished. Indeed, it is estimated that the majority of today's mentally retarded persons fail to receive the full range of educational and vocational training services from which they could profit (Tyor & Bell, 1984). To help ensure that the lives of mentally retarded persons are as complete, independent, and meaningful as possible, the United States federal government has funded numerous *university-affiliated facilities* whose job is to support research and provide model service programs for retarded and other developmentally disabled persons around the country (Grinspoon et al., 1986). It is hoped that programs of this kind will lead to further innovations in education, treatment, and vocational training, as well as for better public education on the issue of mental retardation. Only with such progress will retarded persons be able truly to cross the barrier created by their label. Once again Ed Murphy movingly and eloquently conveys the importance of this issue:

*I never thought of myself as a retarded individual but who* would want to. You're not knowledgeable about what they are saying behind your back. You get a feeling from people around you; they try to hide it but their intentions don't work. They say they will do this and that—like they will look out for you—they try to protect you but you feel sort of guilty. You get the feeling that they love you but that they are looking down at you. You always have that sense of a barrier between you and the ones that love you. By their own admission of protecting you you have an umbrella over you that tells you that you and they have an understanding that there is something wrong—that there is a barrier.

*(Bogdan & Taylor, 1976, p. 50)*

# PROBLEMS OF CHILDHOOD AND ADOLESCENCE: THE STATE OF THE FIELD

Early in this century, children and adolescents were largely ignored by researchers, except for the insights they seemed to offer about adult functioning and dysfunctioning. Similarly, clinicians usually viewed children as little adults rather than as individuals who may experience unique kinds of problems and require special interventions.

All that has changed over the course of the past sixty years, and today children are a major focus of both researchers and clinicians. Numerous studies now concentrate exclusively on the problems of children and adolescents, and numerous clinicians specialize in the treatment of this population. As a result, many childhood problems have been identified and clinical theorists have proposed various explanations for them: the unique cognitive and emotional structure of young persons, the ordinary pressures of youth, special childhood traumas, parenting deficiencies and family dysfunction, biological factors. In addition, disorders of childhood and adolescence have been distinguished from such life-span (or developmental) disorders as autism and mental retardation, which begin early and impair their victims' functioning throughout their lives.

Child-focused researchers and clinicians have generally followed a path that parallels the one pioneered by adult-focused researchers and practitioners. That is, they have identified and distinguished a large number of childhood disorders and developed a variety of specialized treatment interventions. They have learned that although some of these disorders appear straightforward, they are in fact anything but simple in their causes, treatments, and implications. And they have discovered at first hand the powerful negative influence that labels may have on the expectations and reactions of parents, teachers, clinicians, and the public at large, and have correspondingly become sensitive to the dangers of overdiagnosing children's problems. They now recognize that some degree of dysfunctioning and pain is a normal part of the human condition and that overreaction to it by clinicians may create extra problems for children and their families.

In recent years clinicians and researchers have also increasingly recognized the relative powerlessness of children, and have enlisted the aid of government agencies to protect the rights and safety of this population and to call to society's attention such problems as child abuse and neglect, child sexual abuse, child malnourishment, and the fetal alcohol syndrome. Clinicians have helped to determine the psychological impact of such problems and developed interventions designed to prevent and treat them.

The study and treatment of childhood problems may have been relatively slow to get started, but they are now moving rapidly. With the clinical field's growing recognition of children as important beings and with its growing insights and effectiveness, developments in this area of abnormal psychology are likely to continue at an impressive pace. A greater knowledge and better understanding of childhood problems are likely to be achieved in the coming years, and new problems, issues, and areas of concern are likely to be identified and studied. As the tongue-in-cheek box on the "disorder called childhood" implies, childhood has been around for a long time; now that clinicians have discovered it, they are unlikely to underestimate the complexity of its special issues or the extent of its importance ever again.

## SUMMARY

**M**any theorists think of life as a series of stages through which people pass in a fixed order. Erik Erikson has provided a comprehensive developmental theory in which life is divided into eight stages, each marked by a particular developmental crisis and a new set of drives and needs. Erikson's stages are based on the following eight crises: *trust vs. mistrust, autonomy vs. shame and doubt, initiative vs. guilt, industry vs. inferiority, identity vs. role confusion, intimacy vs. isolation, generativity vs. stagnation,* and *integrity vs. despair.* Abnormal behavior may appear during each developmental stage as a result of psychological inadequacy, biological abnormality, or extraordinary environmental stress.

**U**p to 15 to 20 percent of all children and adolescents in the United States experience a mental disorder. Clinicians who initially viewed children as small adults now recognize that there are often important differences between adult and childhood disorders.

Close to half of all children have multiple fears. In addition to the normal fears that disappear over time, three *childhood anxiety disorders* are more persistent and may cause severe suffering in children. *Separation anxiety disorder* is characterized by excessive anxiety, often panic, whenever the child is separated from a parent. This disorder sometimes takes the form of *school phobia.* Children with *avoidant disorder* shrink from all contact with unfamiliar people and are extremely withdrawn, timid, and embarrassed in the presence of strangers. Children with *overanxious disorder* experience excessive or unrealistic levels of anxiety or worry for six months or longer. Proponents of the various models explain childhood anxiety disorders in much the same way they account for adult anxiety. In addition, features unique to childhood have been cited as important to the development of these disorders, including the unpredictable, new, and scary nature of the child's world, as well as such significant changes as starting school, moving, and losing a parent.

Only recently have clinicians recognized that children experience severe *depressive* symptoms. Explanations of childhood depression are similar to those offered for adult depression. Research has uncovered a relatively high rate of depression and other forms of mental dysfunctioning among the parents of depressed children.

Some children exceed the normal breaking of rules and act very aggressively. Children who display an *oppositional defiant disorder* argue repeatedly with adults and lose their temper. Those with a *conduct disorder,* a more severe pattern, repeatedly violate the basic rights of others. These children often are violent and cruel, and may lie, cheat, steal, and run away. Causes of conduct disorders are believed to include biological and genetic factors, modeling, antisocial traits, drug abuse, and, perhaps most important, family dysfunctioning.

Children who display *attention-deficit hyperactivity disorder (ADHD),* commonly called *hyperactivity* or *hyperkinesis,* attend poorly to tasks, act impulsively, and move around excessively. Approximately half of the children with this disorder also experience learning problems. Causes of the disorder are not fully understood but appear to include biological and environmental factors.

Children with *elimination disorders*—*functional enuresis* and *functional encopresis*—repeatedly and involuntarily urinate and pass feces, respectively, during the day or at night while sleeping or both. The behavioral bell-and-battery technique is an effective treatment for enuresis.

Children who display grossly inadequate development and functioning in specific academic, language, speech, or motor skills may receive a diagnosis of *specific developmental disorder,* also frequently known as a *learning disability.* These problems include *academic skills disorders, language and speech disorders,* and *developmental coordination disorder.* Studies have linked learning disabilities to such factors as genetic defects, birth injuries, lead poisoning, diet, sensory dysfunctioning, and poor teaching. Current leading explanations are *perceptual deficit theory,* which sees learning disabilities as products of problems in perceptual processing, and *academic instruction theory,* which considers learning disabilities to be a reflection of inadequate teaching.

People with *autistic disorder (autism)* display a broad set of dysfunctional behaviors early in life. They are unresponsive to others, have language and communication deficits (including echolalia, pronominal reversal, nominal aphasia, and metaphorical language), and exhibit deviant responses to the environment, such as perseveration of sameness and strong attachments to objects, self-stimulatory behaviors, and self-injurious behaviors. There are several views on the causes of autism, including the *perceptual-cognitive view,* the *biological view,* and the *environmental and family view.* Treatment for autism seeks to help the children adapt to their environment. Although no treatment totally reverses the autistic pattern, some help has been found through the use of drug therapy, behavioral treatments, educational approaches, treatment and training for parents, and group homes.

Individuals with *mental retardation* are significantly below average in intelligence (as measured on *intelligence tests*), display concurrent deficits or impairments in adaptive behavior (as measured on *adaptive functioning tests* or in clinical interviews) and develop these symptoms before the age of 18. Approximately 1 out of every 100 persons receives a diagnosis of mental retardation. Controversy, however, surrounds these criteria.

The most important and consistent difference between retarded and nonretarded individuals is that retarded people learn more slowly. Educators and clinicians have found it useful to distinguish four levels of mental retardation: mild, moderate, severe, and profound.

*Mild retardation,* the most common level, has been linked primarily to environmental factors such as environmental understimulation, inadequate parent-child interaction, and insufficient early learning experiences; it has also been referred to as *cultural, familial,* or *environmental retardation.* There is growing evidence that genetic factors and biological factors may also contribute to mild mental retardation.

The dominant causes of *moderate, severe,* and *profound mental retardation* are biological, although individuals who function at these levels of retardation are also enormously affected by their environment. The leading biological causes are *chromosomal disorders* (for example, Down syndrome), *metabolic disorders* that typically are caused by the pairing of two defective recessive genes (for example, phenylketonuria, or PKU, and Tay-Sachs disease), disorders related to *prenatal problems* (cretinism and fetal alcohol syndrome), disorders related to *birth complications,* such as anoxia or extreme prematurity, and disorders that result from *postnatal diseases and injuries,* such as head injuries, poisonings, meningitis, or encephalitis.

In recent decades treatment for mental retardation has begun to focus on *normalization* programs that offer conditions of everyday life in an institutional or community setting. Halfway houses, group homes, and residences of various kinds provide education and training on how to get along in the community.

One of the most intense debates in the field of education centers on the correct educational environment for mentally retarded individuals, pitting proponents of *special classes* against proponents of *mainstreaming.* Research has not yet favored one approach over the other. In general, the use of operant learning principles has been successful in educating retarded individuals.

# TOPIC OVERVIEW

# CHAPTER 20

# PROBLEMS OF AGING

*Dolores Gallagher-Thompson*
*and*
*Larry W. Thompson*

*(The section on Early and Middle Adulthood and Box 20-2 were written by Ronald J. Comer.)*

I n Chapter 19, we saw that many psychological disorders have their onset during childhood or early adolescence. At the other end of the spectrum, a number of disorders develop as old age approaches or advances. As with childhood disorders, some of the disorders of later life seem to be caused primarily by the pressures that are natural at that time of life, others by unique traumatic experiences, and still others by biological abnormalities.

Chapter 19 focused on the first five of the eight developmental stages proposed by Erik Erikson—those from birth through adolescence.

These stages, according to Erikson, are followed by the stages of *early adulthood*, in which people ideally attain intimacy and love rather than isolation; *middle adulthood*, in which people strive for generativity, and care for younger people through parenthood or mentoring of junior colleagues or coworkers; and *old age*, in which the goal is to integrate and to pass along all of one's insights from the past and present. Erikson believes that the developmental stages of adulthood, like those of childhood and adolescence, are filled with opportunities for either growth or maladaptiveness.

## EARLY AND MIDDLE ADULTHOOD

Several theorists have elaborated upon Erikson's descriptions of the stages of early and middle adulthood (Levinson, 1986; Gould, 1978; Vaillant, 1977; Neugarten, 1968). Gail Sheehy's *Passages,* one of the most successful books of the 1970s and 1980s, presented their views in popular form. Like Erikson, these theorists believe that the stages are marked by repeated change, stress, and adjustment (see Box 20-1).

One of the most extensive descriptions and investigations of the stages of early and middle adulthood is that of Daniel Levinson (1986, 1984, 1980, 1977). According to Levinson, the stage of *early adulthood,* lasting from about age 22 to 40, is characterized simultaneously by high energy and abundance and by contradiction and stress. Typically, people are in their peak biological form during this stage. Their aspirations are youthful, they establish a niche in society, they may raise a family, and ultimately they reach a relatively "senior" position in the adult world. For many, this period brings great satisfaction and creativity. But the period of early adulthood can also be one of enormous stress. The burden of becoming a parent, undertaking an occupation, incurring financial obligations, and making other critical decisions about marriage, family, work, and lifestyle often fills people with intense feelings of anxiety and tension.

Levinson describes the stage of *middle adulthood,* lasting from about age 45 to 60, as a period in which biological functioning, although less than optimal, is still

---

BOX 20-1

# Suddenly I'm the Adult?

### *Richard Cohen*

*(This essay originally appeared in* Psychology Today, *May 1987.)*

Several years ago, my family gathered on Cape Cod for a weekend. My parents were there, my sister and her daughter, too, two cousins, and, of course, my wife, my son and me. We ate at one of those restaurants where the menu is scrawled on a blackboard held by a chummy waiter and had a wonderful time. With dinner concluded, the waiter set the check down in the middle of the table. That's when it happened. My father did not reach for the check.

In fact, my father did nothing. Conversation continued. Finally, it dawned on me. Me! I was supposed to pick up the check. After all these years, after hundreds of restaurant meals with my parents, after a lifetime of thinking of my father as the one with the bucks, it had all changed. I reached for the check and whipped out my American Express card. My view of myself was suddenly altered. With a stroke of a pen, I was suddenly an adult.

Some people mark off their life in years, others in events. I am one of the latter, and I think of some events as rites of passage. I did not become a young man at a particular year, like 13, but when a kid strolled into the store where I worked and called me "mister," I turned around to see whom he was calling. He repeated it several times—"Mister, mister"—looking straight at me. The realization hit like a punch: Me! He was talking to me. I was suddenly a mister.

There have been other milestones. The cops of my youth always seemed to be big, even huge, and of course they were older than I was. Then one day they were neither. In fact, some of them were kids—short kids at that. Another milestone.

The day comes when suddenly you realize that all the football players in the game you're watching are younger than you. Instead of being big men, they are merely big kids. With that milestone goes the fantasy that someday, maybe, you too could be a player—maybe not a football player but certainly a baseball player. I had a good eye as a kid—not much power, but a keen eye—and I always thought I could play the game. One day I realized that I couldn't. Without having ever reached the hill, I was over it.

For some people, the most momentous milestone is the death of a parent. This happened recently to a friend of mine. With the burial of his father came the realization that he had moved up a notch. Of course, he had known all along that this would happen, but until the funeral, the knowledge seemed theoretical at best. As long as one of your parents is alive, you stay in some way a kid. At the very least, there remains at least one person whose love is unconditional.

For women, a milestone is reached when they can no longer have children. The loss of a life, the inability to create one—they are variations on the same theme. For a childless woman who could control everything in life but the clock, this milestone is a cruel one indeed.

I count other, less serious milestones—like being audited by the Internal Revenue Service. As the au-

sufficient for an "energetic, personally satisfying and socially valuable life." During this stage, people usually become "senior members" of their particular world, and take responsibility for their own work, that of others, and the development of younger adults. Although this too can become a period of self-satisfaction and peace of mind, one's growing biological problems, numerous responsibilities, and anticipation of upcoming old age may also produce considerable stress and tension and some degree of psychological dysfunctioning.

Although the stages of early and middle adulthood may themselves be a source of stress, Levinson believes that the periods of *transition* that people must pass through as they move from one stage to another are even more unstable and wrenching and likely to produce tension and psychological dysfunctioning. During such

transitional periods, people confront particularly difficult career, marital, and family issues and reflect on and adjust their dreams.

In the *early adult transition,* for example, a period lasting from age 17 to 22 that bridges adolescence and early adulthood, people typically go through a very unsettled time. Although they take steps toward individuation and they modify their relationships with family, friends, and social institutions, they typically feel insecure in these efforts and, correspondingly, may experience repeated anxiety and confusion.

Even more traumatic is *middle life transition,* a period lasting from age 40 to 45 that bridges early and middle adulthood. During this period, individuals experience significant changes in the character of their lives. On the positive side, they may ultimately become more com-

ditor caught mistake after mistake, I sat there pretending that really knowing about taxes was for adults. I, of course, was still a kid. The auditor was buying none of it. I was a taxpayer, an adult. She all but said, Go to jail.

There have been others. I remember the day when I had a ferocious argument with my son and realized that I could no longer bully him. He was too big and the days when I could just pick him up and take him to his room/isolation cell were over. I needed to persuade, reason. He was suddenly, rapidly, older. The conclusion was inescapable: So was I.

One day you go to your friends' weddings. One day you celebrate the birth of their kids. One day you see one of their kids driving, and one day those kids have kids of their own. One day you meet at parties and then at weddings and then at funerals. It all happens in one day. Take my word for it.

I never thought I would fall asleep in front of the television set as my father did, and as my friends' fathers did, too. I remember my parents and their friends talking about insomnia and they sounded like members of a different species. Not able to sleep? How ridiculous. Once it was all I did. Once it was what I did best.

I never thought that I would eat a food that did not agree with me. Now I

"You take all the time you need, Larry—this certainly is a big decision."

(Drawing by Eric Teitelbaum; © 1990, *The New Yorker Magazine,* Inc.)

meet them all the time. I thought I would never go to the beach and not swim. I spent all of August at the beach and never once went into the ocean. I never thought I would appreciate opera, but now the pathos, the schmaltz and, especially, the combination of voice and music appeal to me. The deaths of Mimi and Tosca move me, and they die in my home as often as I can manage it.

I never thought I would prefer to stay home instead of going to a party, but now I find myself passing parties up. I used to think that people who watched birds were weird, but this

summer I found myself watching them, and maybe I'll get a book on the subject. I yearn for a religious conviction I never thought I'd want, exult in my heritage anyway, feel close to ancestors long gone and echo my father in arguments with my son. I still lose.

One day I made a good toast. One day I handled a headwaiter. One day I bought a house. One day—what a day!—I became a father, and not too long after that I picked up the check for my own. I thought then and there it was a rite of passage for me. Not until I got older did I realize that it was one for him, too. Another milestone.

A new father prepares for his daughter's feeding and a new mother says good-bye before going off to war in the Persian Gulf. Although the specific responsibilities change from generation to generation, early adulthood — a period lasting until about age 40 — is filled with numerous stresses that can sometimes lead to anxiety and tension.

passionate, reflective, and judicious, less conflicted, and more accepting and loving of themselves and others during these years. On the negative side, however, they may feel overwhelmed as they increasingly recognize that they are no longer young and vibrant, that time is passing quickly, that life's heaviest responsibilities are falling on them, that they must prepare for the future, and that their dreams may not be met. They may question their accomplishments in life and conclude that they have achieved and will continue to achieve too little. During this period of transition, some persons even try to deny the passage of time and to recapture their youth. Close to 80 percent of men interviewed by Levinson reported that this transition, popularly labeled the *midlife crisis,* was truly tumultuous and painful and that feelings of anxiety and depression were common.

Another line of theorizing about early and middle adulthood proposes that the values and expectations of one's cohorts may also affect and place stress on a person (Neugarten, 1968). *Cohorts* are groups of people born in the same year or time period — that is, people of the same generation. Generally, members of a given cohort group are influenced by many of the same historical and personal events. The cohort group born in 1920, who experienced prohibition, the Great Depression of the 1930s, and the "good war" of the 1940s (World War II), is likely to have a different set of attitudes than the cohort group born in the 1950s, who have directly experienced the Vietnam War and the women's liberation movement. Moreover, each cohort group establishes its own values, expectations, and implicit timetables for accomplishing life tasks. Surveys suggest, for example, that the members of the cohort group born around 1920 believed as adults that the "right" time to get married was between 19 and 25 years of age and that the "right" age to finish school and go to work was between 20 and 22; by contrast, only a minority of the cohorts born in 1940 believed as adults that these life tasks should be completed at such an early age (Easterlin, 1987). In the older cohort group, people who married and completed school in their thirties might find themselves much more isolated, unsupported, and, in turn, stressed than people from the younger group. Research suggests that people whose values, expectations, and social clique are "in sync" with their cohorts' often have relatively less stressful and less tense lives than those who are out of sync with their cohorts.

In short, stress is built into the normal experiences, stages, and climate of early and middle adulthood. For some adults these normal stresses feel overwhelming and lead to high levels of anxiety and depression and other forms of dysfunctioning. In addition to these natural sources of stress, abnormal behavior may also result from traumatic occurrences during early and middle adulthood such as losing one's job or being abused by one's spouse (see Box 20-2). Moreover, abnormal behavior during these years can also be caused by all the other psychological and biological factors that have been a primary focus of this textbook.

## LATER LIFE

Like the problems of children and adolescents, those of elderly persons received little attention until recent years. The field of *geropsychology* is concerned with the mental health of elderly people. It has developed almost entirely within the last twenty years, mainly to explore whether or not methods of assessment and treatment of the mental health problems of later life should be similar to the methods applied to younger and middle-aged persons or whether this age group requires different approaches. It studies the influence of socioeconomic status, ethnic affiliation, and history (both personal and generational) on the psychological functioning of people as they age and the impact of special challenges such as dwindling income and failing health, which often accompany old age.

"Old age" is arbitrarily defined in our society as referring to people who are 65 years old and above. Clinicians further distinguish between the *young-old,* people between the ages of 65 and 74; the *old-old,* those between 75 and 84; and the *oldest-old,* individuals 85 and above. In 1989, 31 million people in the United States were over 65; they accounted for nearly 13 percent of the total U.S. population, or about one in every eight Americans

(see Figure 20-1). This figure reflected a tenfold increase in the older population since 1900. Another surge of growth is anticipated between the years 2010 and 2030, when members of the baby-boom generation will be reaching old age (AARP, 1990).

Life expectancy in the United States has been increasing since 1900. Childhood diseases and illnesses have become less common than they used to be, and infant deaths are correspondingly fewer. In addition, as people age they learn to take better care of themselves, so that those who survive to adulthood are likely to live fairly long lives. Persons who reach the age of 65 have an average life expectancy of an additional 17 years (19 years for women and 15 years for men).

Data from the American Association of Retired Persons (1990) and the U.S. Census Bureau (1988) indicate that today's older men are nearly twice as likely to be married as older women — 77 percent of men compared to 42 percent of women. Half of all older women are widows. Indeed, there are five times as many widows as widowers, largely because most women of the present generation of elders married men older than themselves. There are about 145 older women for every 100 older men.

Two-thirds of older adults live with their families, usually with a spouse but sometimes with a child, a sibling, or another relative. Close to a third of all noninstitutionalized older persons live alone. This category has been increasing rapidly during the past decade, perhaps because families are on the move and thus less nuclear than they used to be.

Older persons head approximately 20 million households, with 75 percent of these owning their own homes and 25 percent renting. Only about 5 percent of the total older population live in nursing homes, but the percentage increases dramatically with age, from 1 percent of the young-old to 6 percent of the old-old and 22 percent of the oldest-old.

About 90 percent of the elderly in the United States are Caucasian, 8 percent are black, and about 2 percent are of other races. Persons of Hispanic origin (of whatever race) represent about 3 percent of the older population. For the past decade, however, the minority elderly population has been growing rapidly, and by the year 2050, 20 percent of the elderly will be nonwhite.

About half of the population of older adults live in nine states. California, New York, and Florida each have over 2 million elders, and Pennsylvania, Texas, Illinois, Ohio, Michigan, and New Jersey have over 1 million each. More elders are moving to Sunbelt states such as Florida, California, Arizona, and New Mexico in search of a warm climate.

In 1989, households headed by older adults in this

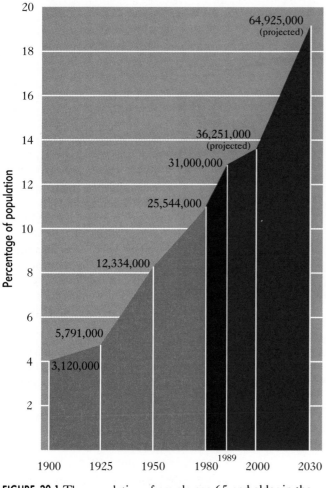

**FIGURE 20-1** The population of people age 65 and older in the United States has been climbing throughout the twentieth century. The percentage of elderly people in the population has increased from 4 percent in 1900 to 13 percent in 1989 and is expected to be 19 percent in 2030. *(AARP, 1990; U.S. Bureau of the Census, 1988.)*

country reported a median income of $23,179 ($23,817 for whites, $15,766 for blacks, and $19,310 for Hispanics). Elders who lived alone reported the lowest incomes. The major sources of income for older individuals are social security, personal savings, earnings, and pension plans. Only about 12 percent of older Americans are in the labor force, and about half of these are employed only part-time.

The educational level of the older population has been steadily increasing. More than half have earned a high school diploma, and 11 percent have graduated from college.

Older people tend to have more health problems than younger people (see Figure 20-2). About 29 percent assess their health as failing or poor compared to 7 per-

cent of those under the age of 65, and most older adults report one or more chronic health conditions, such as arthritis, hearing loss, or heart disease. Older persons account for a third of all hospital stays. Altogether, people over 65 account for 36 percent of total personal expenditures for health care.

The population of older adults is actually quite heterogeneous. We need to be mindful of the fact that older adults are more *unlike* than similar to one another (Cavanaugh, 1990). Elders have very different life experiences, adapt to change in uniquely personal ways, and age at different rates. The field of geropsychology distinguishes between *chronological age* and *functional age.* *Chronological age,* or the number of years one has lived since birth, is regarded as nothing more than a "short-

---

## BOX 20-2

# Spouse Abuse

In Stamford, Conn., a woman married to a Fortune 500 executive locked herself into their Lincoln Continental every Saturday night to escape her husband's kicks and punches. She did not leave him because she mistakenly feared he could sue for divorce on grounds of desertion and she, otherwise penniless, would get no alimony.

Barbara, 30, a middle-class housewife from South Hadley, Mass., was first beaten by her husband when she was pregnant. Last summer Barbara's husband hurled a dinner plate across the kitchen at her. His aim was off. The plate shattered against the wall and a piece of it struck their four-year-old daughter in the face, blinding the child in one eye.

In Miami, Diane, 27, a receptionist, said she married "a real nice guy," a Dr. Jekyll who turned into Mr. Hyde a week after the wedding. "Being married to this man was like being a prisoner of war. I was not allowed to visit my family. I couldn't go out on my own. He wouldn't even let me cry. If I did, it started an 'episode.'"

In a Duluth shelter for battered women, Lola, who married 19 years ago at age 18, said her husband was losing control more frequently: "He gets angry because he's coming home with a bag full of groceries and I didn't open the door fast enough. Because he didn't like the way I washed the clothes. Because the supper's not ready. Because supper's ready too soon."

(Time, *September 5, 1983, p. 23*)

Spouse abuse, the mistreatment or misuse of one spouse by the other, can take various forms, from shoving to battering (Sadock, 1989). In most

cases wives are abused by their husbands. It is estimated that spouse abuse occurs in between 4 and 10 million homes in the United States each year and is responsible for more than 8 to 10 percent of all homicides. Between a fourth and a third of all U.S. women have been abused at least once by their husbands. In addition, many unmarried women are battered by the persons they live with or date.

Spouse abuse cuts across all races, religions, and socioeconomic groups (Straus et al., 1980). It is most frequent in families with alcohol or other substance-abuse problems (Browne & Frieze, 1988). For years this behavior was viewed as a private matter, and even the legal system avoided involvement. Indeed, until 1874 a husband had a legal right to beat his wife in the United States. Even after that date abusers were rarely arrested or prosecuted. Police were reluctant to do anything other than calm down do-

hand variable" because it is not a true indicator of a person's functional capacities. *Functional age,* on the other hand, is a reflection of three interrelated aspects of aging—biological, social, and psychological (Birren & Cunningham, 1985).

*Biological age* represents one's present position with respect to one's potential life span. Clinicians determine biological age by assessing the functioning of various vital organ systems, such as the cardiovascular system. With increasing age, the systems' capacity for self-regulation diminishes, resulting in an increased probability of death. *Social age* refers to a person's roles, habits, and behavior in comparison with those of other members of his or her society. A person's manner of dress, language, and interpersonal style, for example,

will reflect a particular social age. *Psychological age* refers to a person's capacity to adapt his or her behavior to the changing environment. This aspect of aging will be influenced by the person's cognitive functioning, motivation, and self-esteem. To fully understand older persons, it is necessary to consider all of these aspects of aging.

Older people are frequently stereotyped by younger ones (including younger clinicians), who react to them strictly in terms of their chronological age rather than their functional capabilities (Kimmel, 1988; Gatz & Pearson, 1988). One study asked over 500 college students to evaluate photos of the same men at various ages (25, 52, or 73) on such characteristics as activity level, competence, intelligence, creativity, flexibility, and en-

---

mestic violence, the number-one source of police fatalities. And the courts rarely prosecuted an abuser. The emphasis on civil rights in the 1970s and the efforts of women's groups finally revealed the magnitude of the problem, and in the past two decades state legislatures have passed more laws to prosecute abusers and protect victims; police have become more oriented toward intervention; and the clinical profession has increasingly studied and treated the problem.

Many abusive husbands consider their wives to be their private property and become most assaultive when the wife shows independence. They are extremely jealous and possessive, and often inflict more abuse when the wife pursues outside friendships or even attends to the children's needs before the husband's. Beyond assault, they tend to belittle and isolate their wives, and repeatedly make them feel inept, worthless, and dependent. Although an abusive husband may show genuine remorse for a time after beating his wife, he is likely to repeat the behavior (Walker, 1984, 1979). Many such men were themselves beaten as children or saw their mothers beaten (Pagelow, 1981).

Victims of abuse typically feel very dependent on their spouses, unable to function on their own, and even unable to experience an identity separate from their spouse. This sense of dependence and their feeling that they are helpless to change the situation help keep them in the relationship despite the obvious physical dangers. The large majority of victims are not masochistic, as many clinical theorists once believed (Walker, 1984; Finkelhor et al., 1983). About 50 percent of victims grew up in homes where they or their mothers were abused, and most come from families that saw male and female roles in stereotyped ways. Many victims have very low self-esteem (Cornell & Gelles, 1983), blame themselves for the abuse, and agree with their spouse that they did something bad to provoke it. Usually the pattern of abuse does not emerge until after the couple is married.

Initially clinicians proposed family therapy as the treatment of choice for spouse abuse. But they have learned that as long as a woman continues to be abused at home, such an intervention is only a charade. The steps of treatment now preferred are (1) separating a woman from her abusive hus-

band and situation; (2) therapy for the victim to help her recognize her plight, see her options, and experience a more positive self-image and greater autonomy; (3) therapy for the abuser to help him cope with life more effectively, develop more appropriate attitudes toward his wife, and develop more appropriate avenues for expressing anger and frustration (Saunders, 1982; Ganley, 1981); and (4) couple therapy, if both spouses have made satisfactory progress in their individual therapies. A number of community programs have been set up to help provide these intervention services, including hot lines, emergency shelters or "safe houses" for women, and public organizations and self-help groups to aid abused spouses and provide education on the problem. The very fact that treatment programs for spouse abuse now exist is an important development for both victims and our society, and clinicians believe that many of these programs are on the right track. Because relatively little empirical evaluation of the programs has been undertaken, however, it is not yet possible to know precisely how helpful the various interventions are or how to improve upon them.

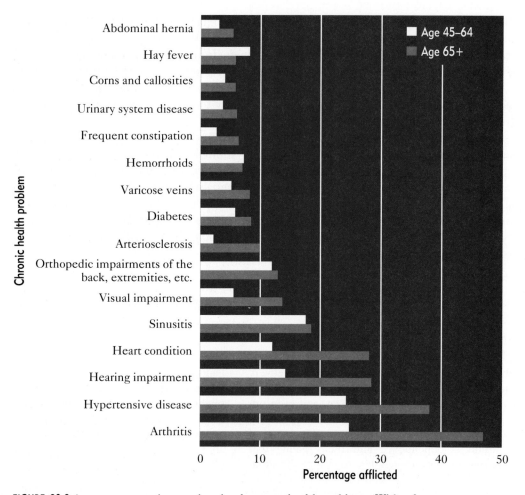

**FIGURE 20-2** As persons age, they tend to develop more health problems. With a few exceptions, chronic medical problems are more prevalent among elderly persons than among the middle aged. *(Adapted from U.S. Senate Special Committee on Aging, 1983, p. 59.)*

ergy (Levin, 1988). Students consistently evaluated the same men at 73 more negatively than at younger ages, suggesting that it may be difficult for younger persons to see older persons in their true light. As the negative images of aging continue to be countered by the media and by direct experience, it is to be hoped that such attitudes will change.

## SUCCESSFUL AGING: A STRESS-AND-COPING MODEL

As we age, important changes occur both physically and psychologically. On the negative side, our bodies experience continued wear and tear, and we become more prone to illness and injury than when we were younger.

We are also more likely to experience certain kinds of psychological stress. Significant losses, for example, occur with greater frequency in later life. Older people lose persons close to them (spouse, friends, adult children), and many lose a sense of purpose in life after they retire or experience other role shifts. If they live long enough, they lose bodily integrity through chronic illness. And not to be overlooked is the loss of favored pets and possessions through relocation and the like.

Despite these common experiences of change and stress, older people need not deteriorate rapidly, physically or psychologically (Rowe & Kahn, 1987). In fact, a growing body of literature challenges the assertion that the aging body and mind are programmed to fall apart (Rowe & Kahn, 1987). Extensive research on the prevention of heart disease, for example, has shown that when older patients take control over key risk factors such as cigarette smoking, cholesterol intake, and blood pressure, this major cause of death is substantially reduced. Such findings suggest that prudent living and new health technology may enable older adults to remain healthy and vigorous for longer periods of time.

Similarly, psychological stress need not necessarily result in mental dysfunction among elderly people (Lewinsohn, 1990). While losses and other stressful experiences do contribute to depression in a number of older adults, for others such situations apparently become opportunities to learn more about themselves and to grow as people.

Why do some older people succumb to the stresses that accompany aging and develop physical and psychological problems, while others, indeed the majority, manage to endure? The answer seems to lie in the notion of coping. Some people manage to cope with stress better than others (Horn & Meer, 1987).

What does it mean to cope effectively? The *stress-and-coping model* developed by Richard Lazarus and Susan Folkman (1984) suggests that the key to coping is how one cognitively appraises a given situation or event. According to this model, when people confront a potentially stressful situation, they make certain evaluations, either consciously or unconsciously. First, they make a *primary appraisal* — they judge the situation to be either irrelevant, positive, or stressful. If they determine that the event is stressful, they then make a *secondary appraisal,* and judge what might and can be done in response. They evaluate what coping options are available to them, whether the options will accomplish what they are supposed to do, and whether they will be able to apply the coping strategies effectively. As the situation develops further and as they apply their coping responses, the individuals are likely to make *reappraisals* — they repeatedly change their perceptions of the situation based on the flow of new information.

People's appraisals of a situation and of their coping options determine how they will react to it. If they evaluate a given event as being extraordinarily taxing or their coping options as inadequate, they may feel overwhelmed by the stress, either physically or psychologically. If, on the other hand, they determine that they have effective coping options available to them and apply these options, they may address the threat effectively and even profit from the challenge that it provides.

According to research, older persons use a wide range of strategies to cope with negative life events (McCrae, 1982; Folkman et al., 1987). Lazarus and Folkman (1984) have had subjects fill out the "Ways of Coping" checklist, a self-report measure that they developed, and have found that some people are more inclined to use coping strategies that are *problem-focused* — cognitive or behavioral problem-solving strategies, such as trying

Exercise and physical fitness are needed to maintain one's health and vigor in old age. Members of the Sun City Poms combine the playfulness of childhood with the serious needs of old age, and manage at the same time to provide entertainment throughout Arizona.

to come up with several solutions, gathering information, and making a plan of action — while others prefer *emotion-focused* strategies such as seeking emotional support, distancing, avoiding, and self-blame. In general, the older people who cope most effectively with loss and other stressors tend to use problem-focused strategies more than emotion-focused strategies. Studies have also found, however, that some emotion-focused strategies may be useful in old age, particularly when one is diagnosed as having a serious physical illness. In fact, health-care professionals often encourage some form of avoidance or denial, because it may be seen as adaptive in that circumstance (Cavanaugh, 1990).

A common strategy for coping in old age that does not quite fit the problem-focused versus emotion-focused distinction is to turn to religion and spirituality (Cox & Hammonds, 1988). Older people who cope successfully are more likely than younger persons to attend a house of worship. Many of them seem to hold a strong belief in a higher power and benefit from the social aspects of religion, such as attending services with friends or family members and receiving support from the clergy and members of the congregation, as well as from the theology itself. It is likely that if we are fully to understand coping in older adults, we must include the study of religious beliefs and practices in addition to the more traditional methods of coping.

In short, even though older adults do not have much control over the stressful events that occur in their environment, they do have control over their responses to those events: how they appraise them and what behav-

Geropsychologists point out that old age is more than a loss of youth or a march toward death. Elderly persons are filled with a mixture of past memories, present needs, and future goals, all of which must be addressed if they are to achieve fulfillment and psychological peace.

iors they activate to deal with the situation. By using more problem-focused modes of coping such as direct action, seeking information, and cognitive techniques, many older people are able to weather these challenges and even learn a great deal from them. This perspective has led clinical geropsychologists to place strong emphasis on the development of cognitive and behavioral interventions to help older people cope with the stresses they confront. In the cognitive realm they often help older people identify those perceptions and thoughts that are overly pessimistic and stress-inducing. In the behavioral realm, they help people reengage with family and friends and put a certain amount of pleasant activity and control into their lives.

A considerable body of recent research has found that a range of problems among elderly people respond well to cognitive and behavioral therapies, including depression (Thompson, Gallagher, & Breckenridge, 1987), anxiety disorders (McCarthy, Katz, & Foa, 1991), prolonged or atypical grieving (Gantz, Gallagher-Thompson, & Rodman, 1991), and chronic functional limitations due to physical health problems (Rybarczyk et al., 1991). Our work with family members experiencing stress in their role of primary caregiver to a frail elder relative also supports the usefulness of this kind of practical approach (Gallagher-Thompson, Lovett, & Rose, 1991). In some instances, however, family members, whether caregivers or not, find that their stress exceeds their capacity, and what results is neglect of their elder spouse or parent, or actual abuse of the person (see Box 20-3.)

Cognitive and behavioral therapies are generally accepted well by older individuals, perhaps because they are less threatening than more traditional psychotherapies and do not carry the risks associated with psychotropic medications (Thompson et al., 1986). This factor may place cognitive and behavioral therapies at an advantage over other approaches that have also proved beneficial to elderly persons, such as group therapy, family therapy, and psychoeducational approaches.

# COMMON CLINICAL PROBLEMS IN LATER LIFE

Studies indicate that as many as 50 percent of the elderly would benefit from mental health services (MacDonald & Schnur, 1987), yet fewer than 20 percent actually receive such help. A number of barriers explain this gap (Butler & Lewis, 1986). First, many older individuals do not define their problems in psychological terms. They tend to hold a highly stigmatized view of mental health problems and assume that help-seeking will result in prolonged care or even hospitalization. Thus they prefer to go to their primary-care physician when they are troubled rather than to a mental health practitioner. Second, relatively few clinicians are equipped to work with the psychological problems of later life. Few graduate or medical school programs even offer a course or provide supervised field experience in gerontology. Though this situation is slowly being remedied, it will be some time before gerontology courses are required of all health-care professionals. Third, the limitations on insurance reimbursement to providers of mental health care for the elderly have been a barrier. Medicare has only recently raised its ceiling on mental health benefits, and private insurance firms tend to provide little reimbursement for mental health care (an average of about $1,000 per person annually). Thus there is not much financial incentive for clinicians to give quality mental health care to older adults.

Taken together, these factors make it very difficult to serve the mental health needs of the elderly. Changes are needed both in the way elderly people perceive stress and mental health care and in the way professionals are trained and reimbursed.

## Depression

*B*ernice Anderson is a 78-year-old woman who is beginning to feel that life is not worth living. She recently became widowed, has severe arthritis, and sometimes finds it diffi-

= BOX 20-3 =

# Abuse of the Elderly

A 78-year-old New York woman . . . was assaulted and beaten by her 36-year-old grandson a dozen times, even though she was confined to a wheelchair. Although hospitalized seven times, the woman still refused to testify against her grandson. . . .

A 68-year-old South Carolina woman was kept by her daughter in "conditions of unspeakable squalor." . . . Living under a pile of filthy blankets, the woman was kept in an unheated portion of the house that got so cold that the urine from the woman's catheter was frozen when a social worker discovered her.

A 64-year-old Florida man, his health failing, was swindled out of his 40-acre orange grove and everything else he owned by a relative he trusted. "I signed too many papers," the man told social workers. "I still fear for my life."    *(Ryan, 1981)*

The abuse of elderly persons is a major problem in our society. A survey of more than 2,000 elderly persons in the Boston metropolitan area revealed that 3 percent had been subjected to physical violence, verbal aggression, and neglect (Pillemer & Finkelhor, 1988). Similarly, a compilation of current records, documents, and mental health surveys has suggested that approximately 4 percent of elderly people living in the United States have been "moderately to severely" abused in forms ranging from theft of social security checks to neglect, beatings, druggings, torture, and rape (House Select Committee on Aging, 1981).

Abuse of an elderly person is usually committed by a close relative, in most cases by the spouse, but in many cases by the person's adult child. Some cases of elder abuse by spouses are continuations of long-term patterns of spouse abuse, but often they represent new behaviors triggered by the special pressures and frustrations of old age or sickness. Similarly, elder abuse by children may represent continuations of long-term patterns or new responses. Once it begins, however, the abuse usually becomes a chronic pattern.

Although both men and women are victims of elder abuse, more women are victimized than men and women usually suffer more serious abuse. It is believed that the prevalence rates indicated by the survey underestimate the actual extent of the problem. Older people may hesitate to report abuse because of the guilt and shame attached to it. Also, many victims are confused by the abuse because of the love they feel for the abusive relative. And many victims, dependent on their abusers, are terrified of being abandoned or retaliated against if they report the pattern of abuse.

There is little literature on the treatment of this pervasive problem other than some clinical reports that attempt to remedy the situation by moving the elder out of the home and into a nursing home. Obviously, however, this solution is inappropriate for those older individuals who are not really so functionally impaired that they require a nursing home; it severely limits their independence and in a sense punishes the victim. Besides, some elders are physically abused in nursing homes, too.

More effective interventions might include the establishment of safe apartments where abused elders could take refuge, the creation of the kind of self-help groups that have been successful for younger abused wives, and education of the elderly so that they will recognize abuse when it occurs and be less likely to use denial as a means of coping with the situation (Pillemer & Finkelhor, 1988).

A great deal of abuse springs from strong feelings of anger that the caregiver has difficulty controlling (Gallagher et al., 1989). The teaching of cognitive-behavioral skills in the management of anger, such as relaxation training, appropriate assertiveness, development of alternative responses to anger, and the use of positive self-talk to reward oneself for developing alternative responses, can modify this behavior significantly, sometimes in a relatively short time.

---

cult to take care of herself. Her daughter Sarah, aged 50, recently told her that she may have to go to live in a senior housing situation of some kind. Sarah, a very busy professional woman with a husband and family, recognizes that her mother probably cannot continue to live alone, but she also feels that she cannot have her mother living with her. Since these events occurred, Bernice has not been eating well, is having difficulty sleeping, and has lost interest in her hobbies of gardening and swimming at a local club, where she also used to meet with friends regularly.

Depression is the most common mental health problem of older adults (Blazer, 1990). A range of depressive feelings, from profound unhappiness to feelings of being blue and dissatisfied with life, have been reported by as many as 60 percent of older adults in self-report questionnaires. Between 1 and 20 percent of older adults meet DSM-III-R's criteria for clinical depression. Those who have recently experienced a trauma such as the loss of their spouse and those with serious physical illnesses

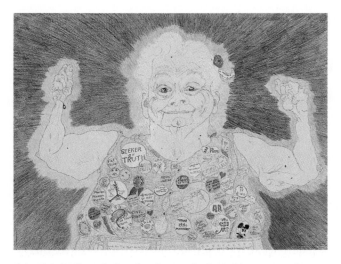

A key to feeling vital and upbeat, whether old or young, is to be active, committed, and interested in one's surroundings. Elderly people with this life posture maintain a relatively young *psychological* age.

have the highest rate of depression (Philpott, 1990; Bliwise, McCall, & Swan, 1987). The prevalence of depression also is high in older individuals with cognitive impairment: as many as 30 percent of older adults who are diagnosed as cognitively impaired, or demented, also have a significant clinical depression to contend with (Reifler et al., 1986).

Finally, the prevalence of depression is higher in older women than in older men, although, as with younger persons, it is unclear whether men genuinely experience less depression or simply underreport the symptoms they do experience. Men may also express their depression through physical rather than psychological symptoms (Blazer, 1990).

**Assessment**    Depression is best assessed in older adults through a structured clinical interview rather than through a self-report questionnaire. An interview gives the older person an opportunity to explain more about his or her symptoms and gives the interviewer an opportunity to be sure that the client really understands the questions being asked. Since some elderly people have less than a high school education, they can and do misunderstand self-report questionnaires. Also, there can be confusion about whether the specific symptoms uncovered by a questionnaire, such as fatigue, poor appetite, and sleep disturbances, really reflect depression or some other health problem, such as undiagnosed cancer or heart disease. Greater understanding can be achieved in a clinical interview, since there is opportunity to clarify such questions and concerns.

Nevertheless, two self-report questionnaires have been widely used as screening devices with older adults in both medical and mental health settings. One is the Geriatric Depression Scale (GDS) (Yesavage et al., 1983), a 20-item measure that asks whether each statement such as "I find it hard to get up in the morning" and "I tend to avoid people at social gatherings" is true or false. The GDS was specifically developed to emphasize the psychological aspects of depression and to deemphasize its physiological aspects. Its validity and reliability have been demonstrated with older adults, even those with concurrent health or cognitive problems. Also, its simple true/false response format makes it relatively easy for older adults with less education, those from disadvantaged backgrounds, and those for whom English is not the primary language to comprehend the items and answer accurately.

The other popular scale, used with older adults who have a higher reading level and greater comprehension of English, is the Beck Depression Inventory (BDI) (Beck et al., 1961). This 21-item measure, which was first described in Chapter 9, asks about sadness, appetite, sleep problems, low energy, libido problems, self-evaluation, ideas about the future, and the like. Its validity and reliability with older adults have also been demonstrated (Gallagher, 1986), and its scores are easily interpreted.

It is also important for older depressed people to have a thorough physical evaluation by a geriatrician familiar with the common health problems of old age. It is crucial to review all medications that the person is taking, since many older adults unintentionally abuse both over-the-counter and prescription medications, using compounds that interact badly with one another or taking more or less than the optimal amount. These practices can make it very difficult to prescribe proper antidepressant medication, even if that seems warranted.

Finally, it is important to assess the cognitive functioning of older people who have symptoms of depression. Cognitive impairment, or dementia, has a number of symptoms in common with depression, and an older client may be incorrectly diagnosed as having one or the other if the full picture is not obtained. This situation has implications for treatment because there are no known treatments for dementia, whereas clinical depression responds to a variety of both short- and long-term interventions. When a thorough evaluation by a neuropsychologist is not possible, many practitioners use Folstein's Mini-Mental State Examination (Folstein, Folstein, and McHugh, 1975). This is a well-validated measure for assessing orientation and common cognitive processes such as memory and reasoning. Although it can be affected by levels of education and anxiety, an experienced clinician is usually able to evaluate the findings appropriately.

**Treatment** Like younger depressed patients, older persons who are depressed may be helped by a number of treatments. Drug therapy is sometimes viewed as the treatment of choice for clinical depression, partly because psychotherapy for older adults is a relatively recent development. Until about ten years ago, antidepressant medications were the most readily available form of treatment, and therefore the most heavily used. At the same time, however, it is difficult to use drug treatment effectively with older persons (Blazer, 1990). The biological mechanisms for the breakdown and absorption of these chemicals are not the same in later life as in the earlier years: the overall metabolic rate is slower in older adults, so that drugs remain in the system longer and can accumulate to toxic levels more quickly. In addition, older adults often find that the undesirable effects of the common antidepressant medications are very difficult to tolerate. For example, as we saw in Chapter 9, the tricyclic antidepressants often cause dry mouth, dizziness upon getting up, constipation, and other annoying effects that may reach such severe proportions in some older individuals that they discontinue the medication. These effects may be controlled by reducing the usual dosage and helping the patient to monitor them and to take practical steps to minimize them, such as increasing the amount of bran in their diet to control constipation (Vieth, 1982). Nevertheless, it may be very difficult to find exactly the right antidepressant medication for a given patient or to manage the undesired effects so successfully.

The use of psychotherapy with clinically depressed older adults has focused on relatively short-term treatments such as cognitive-behavioral therapy or brief psychodynamic therapy. Our own research has indicated that about 75 percent of clinically depressed elderly outpatients respond well to about 20 sessions of psychotherapy alone, and respond equivalently to both types that we investigated. Their depression either disappeared completely or improved substantially, and they maintained these gains for at least two years (Gallagher-Thompson, Hanley-Peterson, & Thompson, 1989; Thompson et al., 1987). The cognitive-behavioral therapy that we have evaluated follows the models of Aaron Beck (1991) and Peter Lewinsohn (1975, 1973) and helps clients identify thoughts and behaviors that have a negative effect on their mood, as well as teaching them specific skills for challenging and modifying these thoughts and behaviors (see Chapter 9). The psychodynamic approach that we have evaluated helps clients identify a core conflict and explore how that past conflict is affecting them in the present (Horowitz & Kaltreider, 1979). Elderly clients who respond best to psychotherapy alone tend to be those whose depression is situationally caused, who have no concurrent personality disorder, and who have the ability to plan for and to experience pleasant activities regularly.

In current ongoing studies we have compared cognitive-behavioral psychotherapy with drug therapy and are finding that the combination of the two tends to be more effective than either of them alone, particularly for older people with a physiologically caused type of depression (Gantz et al., 1991). About 65 percent of older depressed subjects are responding extremely well to the combined condition versus about 50 percent for the cognitive-behavioral therapy alone or the medication alone. In our studies the medication used most often is desipramine, which produces relatively few undesirable effects. We also found that the highest dropout rate occurs when patients are given medication alone, and that in order to use medication in combination with therapy successfully, clinicians must be extremely well versed in the management of the undesirable effects that typically occur (Roose, 1991).

In addition, clinicians in our setting have been exploring the use of long-term cognitive-behavioral therapy with older individuals who are experiencing both depression and a personality disorder such as an avoidant personality disorder. We have found that extending treatment to approximately fourty or fifty sessions rather than the usual twenty enables more persons with this dual diagnosis to improve in both mood and general functioning. The additional sessions focus on identifying and challenging the core beliefs or schemas that underlie the personality structure for most of the person's adult life (Beck et al., 1990). Several other treatment approaches have also been used in cases of elderly depression. Although these interventions are used less frequently and have received less research attention than the cognitive-behavioral, short-term psychodynamic, and drug therapies. Some depressed older persons apparently respond well to family therapy, partly because their families unintentionally reinforce negative rather than positive adaptive behaviors, and family therapy is able to channel the energy of family members in more appropriate directions. Some older depressed persons also appear to profit from group therapy, particularly supportive (Finkel, 1991) or cognitive-behavioral group therapy (Yost, Beutler, Corbishley, & Allender, 1986). And for some older adults with a very severe depression that has been unresponsive to other interventions, electroconvulsive therapy (ECT) is sometimes applied. Its administration is considered safer and freer from harmful effects than it was in the past, even for older patients, as long as they are in good physical health (Blazer, 1990). As with younger adults, a course of six to ten treatments is administered, and in most cases improvement occurs by the time they are all completed. There is some debate over whether "maintenance" ECT is useful or advisable to prevent further severe depression in older adults.

As we saw in Chapter 10, depression is often accompanied by suicidal thoughts or actions. Suicide is particularly likely to occur in older white males who have a combination of clinical depression and a sense of severe hopelessness regarding the future (Fry, 1986). Suicidal older persons often profit from inpatient care, followed by various forms of therapy to help them resolve the crisis and find hope for the future. Once again, we and others have found that cognitive-behavioral therapy with such patients can effectively marshal their resources and help them develop a different perspective on their current problems and on future opportunities, once the suicidal crisis is past (Osgood, 1985).

**Psychoeducational Programs**   Psychoeducational programs began as a series of weekly "Coping with Depression" classes offered to older adults in the community who were interested in acquiring skills to improve their mood. The classes focused on the same kind of cognitive-behavioral skills used in therapy, but they were packaged differently, with equal emphasis on didactic learning of the material and its practical application. Skills such as mood monitoring, increasing the frequency of engagement in pleasant activities, and learning to reward oneself for new behaviors were featured. This series of classes has now been successfully used with nonclinically depressed elders for more than a decade and has been described by some as "just what they needed" to prevent a clinical depression from developing (Thompson, Gallagher, Nies, & Epstein, 1983).

More recently, classes with a different content have also been developed to help family members reduce the stress associated with providing long-term care for older persons. These caregivers are themselves often elderly; as many as 50 percent are older than 60, and 18 percent are older than 70 (Melcher, 1988). The classes teach family caregivers how to solve problems, manage their anger, assert themselves with recalcitrant family members, and relax in stressful situations. Class participants have less depression and more perceived social support than control subjects evaluated at comparable time intervals (Lovett & Gallagher, 1988). Additional programs geared to other needs of caregivers, such as decision making in regard to nursing home placement and preparing for their loved one's death, are now in the planning stages. The psychoeducational approach

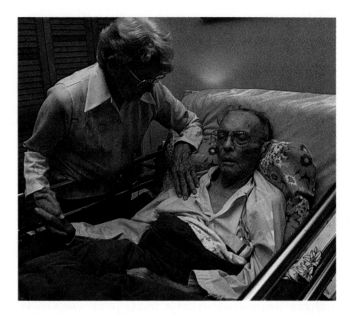

The burden of providing care at home for a spouse or parent who is impaired physically or psychologically can arouse feelings of anxiety, depression, and anger. Newly developed *psychoeducation* programs for caregivers appear to prevent or reduce such feelings.

seems to appeal to a broad range of older persons and is acceptable to them, in part because it does not share the stigma of mental health services.

## Anxiety Disorders

Anxiety is a common human emotion experienced throughout life, including old age. Yet anxiety and anxiety disorders are relatively undefined and poorly studied in the elderly. As in younger persons, anxiety often coexists with depression in elderly people. In fact, it can be very difficult to determine which is the major disorder (Shamoian, 1991). In a study conducted in our laboratory, we examine the degree of overlap between anxiety and depression in a group of close to 100 older individuals who were seeking treatment for depression and found relatively high correlations between the anxiety and depression measures (Kilcourse et al., 1991).

Not much was known about the prevalence of anxiety disorders in the elderly until recently, when data from surveys conducted in several major cities indicated that generalized anxiety disorder is found in about 7 percent of elders, agoraphobia in about 2 to 5 percent, simple phobias in 1 to 12 percent, and panic disorders in less than 1 percent (Bliwise et al., 1987). These surveys also suggested that the prevalence of most anxiety disorders actually decreases with age among both men and women

(Blazer, George, & Hughes, 1991), although the rate is generally higher in women than in men, regardless of age. There is a possibility that anxiety disorders are underreported by the elderly. Perhaps they must reach a higher level of discomfort before they will actually seek help, or they may attribute symptoms of anxiety such as heart palpitations and sweating to medical conditions (Blazer et al., 1991).

**Assessment**   Assessing anxiety in older people is similar in many ways to assessing depression. Although several self-report questionnaires may be used to give a rough estimate of the severity of anxiety experienced, most geropsychologists prefer to gather this information through a structured clinical interview. This way, additional probes can be used and ambiguous issues clarified.

One of the most important tasks facing assessors is determining whether the anxiety experienced by an older adult is in fact an appropriate response to objective conditions. The fear of an older person who dreads being alone in his or her apartment in a high-crime neighborhood, for instance, may be quite realistic. Such a person should be helped to relocate rather than given clinical treatment.

**Treatment**   Traditionally, older adults with anxiety disorders have been treated with antianxiety medication, particularly benzodiazepines. Although they are effective, these drugs must be used very carefully because persons over the age of 60 respond to them quite differently from younger adults. Lower doses are necessary, and the potential for unpleasant effects is much greater (Pomara et al., 1991). It is also important to note that these drugs can cause cognitive impairment, which may be mistaken for mental deterioration. The drugs may also cause drowsiness, headaches, low energy level, and loss of coordination. In addition, most geropsychiatrists try to avoid the long-term use of these drugs because of the potential for the patient to become addicted to them (Pomara et al., 1991). Such behavioral techniques as relaxation training (for generalized anxiety disorder) and systematic desensitization (for phobias) have also been applied in cases of older persons with anxiety disorders. An effective cognitive-behavioral approach called *anxiety management techniques (AMT)* seeks to reduce anxiety through the development of skills for controlling fear (McCarthy et al., 1991). Chief among these skills are progressive muscle relaxation, controlled breathing, and a cognitive focus on identifying and correcting maladaptive thought patterns through such techniques as self-talk and imagery. Social skills training may also be incorporated in the package. This treatment

approach seems to be well tolerated by older individuals and effective for simple phobias and generalized anxiety, the two anxiety disorders that are most common in the elderly. And finally, psychodynamic approaches in which anxious older patients review their lives to help them understand and reduce underlying conflicts have also met with some success (Johnson, 1991).

In contrast to the extensive empirical literature on the treatment of late-life depression, few controlled research studies have been done to support the efficacy of various treatments for anxiety. Given the overlap of depression and anxiety, it seems particularly important to design clinical studies that will assess the effectiveness of the various methods of intervention both for the anxiety disorders themselves and for the anxiety component of depressive disorders. Further research is also needed to develop safer drug therapies for anxious older adults (Zimmer & Gershon, 1991).

## Cognitive Impairments

Fear that we are losing our mental abilities occasionally strikes all of us, perhaps after we have rushed out the door without our keys, when we meet a familiar person and cannot remember her name, or when in the middle of a critical test our mind seems to go blank. Now if we are inclined to think the worst, at such times we may well believe we are experiencing the first stages of *dementia,* an organic mental syndrome (cluster of symptoms) marked by impaired cognitive functioning in such areas as memory, abstract thinking, and judgment, which interferes significantly with work or social behavior. Rest assured that such mishaps are quite common and normal. Indeed, as people progress through middle age, such memory difficulties and lapses of attention are likely to increase, and by age 60 or 70 they may occur with alarming regularity. Intellectual changes of this kind are, however, associated with the normal process of aging, and for the most part they are not severe enough to be considered a sign of dementia. Sometimes, however, people experience intellectual changes that are broad, severe, and excessive. Like Harry, they manifest dementia.

*Harry seemed in perfect health at age fifty-eight, except* that for a couple of days he had had a touch of flu. He worked in the municipal water treatment plant of a small city, and there, while responding to a minor emergency, Harry seemed to become confused about the order in which the levers controlling the flow of fluids were to be pulled. Several thousand gallons of raw sewage was discharged into a river. Harry had been an efficient and diligent worker and after puzzled questioning, his error was overlooked. Then, several weeks later, he came home with a baking dish that his wife had asked him to pick up; he had forgotten that he had brought the identical dish home two nights before. Later that month, on two successive nights, he went to pick up his daughter at her job in a restaurant, apparently forgetting that she had changed shifts and was working days. A week later he quite uncharacteristically became argumentative with a clerk at the phone company; he was trying to pay a bill that he had already paid three days before.

By this time his wife had become alarmed about the changes in Harry. When she discovered that he had been writing little notes to himself on odd scraps of paper, to serve as reminders, and that these included detailed instructions about how to operate machinery at work if various problems arose, she insisted that he see a doctor. Harry himself realized that his memory had been failing for perhaps as long as a year and he reluctantly agreed with his wife. The doctor did a physical examination and ordered several laboratory examinations, plus an electroencephalogram (a brain wave test). The examination results were normal and the doctor thought that the problem might be depression. He prescribed an antidepressant drug but, if anything, it seemed to make Harry's memory worse. It certainly did not make him feel better. Then the doctor thought that Harry had hardening of the arteries of the brain.

Months passed and Harry's wife was beside herself. Now fully aware of the problem, she could see that it was worsening. Not only had she been unable to get effective help, but Harry himself was becoming resentful and even suspicious of her attempts. He now insisted there was nothing at all wrong with him and she would catch him watching her every movement. From time to time he accused her of having the police watch him. He would draw all of the blinds in the house and once he ripped the telephone out of the wall; it was "spying." These episodes were tolerable because they were short lived; besides, there didn't seem to be dangerous intensity to any of Harry's ideas. His wife, who had the summer off from her position as a fourth grade teacher, began checking on him at his job at least once a day. Soon she was actually doing most of his work; his supervisor, an old friend of the family, looked the other way. Harry seemed to be very grateful that his wife was there.

Approximately eighteen months had passed since Harry had first allowed the sewage to escape and he was clearly a changed man. Most of the time he seemed preoccupied; he had a vacant smile on his face and what little he said seemed empty of meaning. He had entirely given up his main interests, golf and woodworking. Sometimes he became angry—sudden storms of anger without apparent cause. This was quite unlike him. He would shout angrily at his wife and occasionally would throw or kick things, although his actions never seemed directed at anyone. He became careless about his person, and more and more he slept in his clothes. Gradually his wife took over—getting him up, toileted and dressed each morning.

Harry himself still insisted that nothing at all was wrong, but by now no one tried to explain things to him. He had long since stopped reading; he would sit vacantly in front of

the television. He was no longer suspicious of television, but neither could he describe any program that he had watched. One day the county supervisor stopped by to tell Harry's wife that Harry just could not work any longer. He would be sixty-two in a few months and was eligible for early retirement. Of course he hadn't really worked for a long while anyhow, and he had become so inattentive that he was a hazard around the machinery.

Slowly Harry's condition worsened. He stayed alone at home through the day since his wife's school was in session. Sometimes he would wander out. He would greet everyone he met, old friends and strangers alike, with "Hi, it's so nice." That was the extent of his conversation, although he might repeat "nice, nice, nice . . ." over and over again. He had promised not to drive, but one day he did take the family automobile out and, fortunately, promptly got lost. The police brought him home; his wife took the keys to the automobile and kept them. When he left a coffee pot on a unit of the electric stove until it melted, his wife, who by this time was desperate for any help, took him to see another doctor.

Harry could no longer be left at home alone, so his daughter began working nights and caring for him during the day until his wife came home after school. He would sit all day, but sometimes he would wander aimlessly. He seemed to have no memory at all for events of the day and very little recollection of occasions from the distant past, which a year or so before he had enjoyed describing. His speech consisted of repetitions of the same word or phrase over and over, for example, "Hooky then, hooky then, hooky then."

Because Harry was a veteran, she took him to the nearest Veteran's Administration Hospital which was 150 miles away. After a stay of nine weeks, the doctors said that Harry had a chronic brain syndrome. They advised long-term hospitalization in a regional veterans hospital about 400 miles away from Harry's home. His wife could not manage Harry and apparently no one else would. Desperate, five years after the accident at work, she accepted with gratitude hospitalization at the veterans hospital which was so far away.

The nursing staff at the hospital sat Harry up in a chair each day and, aided by volunteers, made sure that he ate enough. Still he lost weight and became weaker. When his wife came to see him he would weep, but he did not talk and he gave no other sign that he recognized her. After a year he stopped weeping. His wife could no longer bear to visit. He lived on until just after his sixty-fifth birthday when he choked on some food, developed pneumonia, and died.

*(Heston & White, 1991, pp. 1–5)*

According to DSM-III-R, persons must display a number of features in order to qualify for the diagnosis of dementia:

1. There must be evidence of impairment in short- and long-term memory, as when a person cannot learn new information or cannot remember important information of a long-standing and personal

nature, such as birthday or birthplace. Since most people experience some memory loss as they get older, a diagnosis of dementia is only applied when the loss is unusually severe. For example, an older person who is having difficulty remembering who was at a recent family reunion may be suffering from age-related memory changes, whereas a person who fails to remember having been there at all is most likely suffering from dementia.

2. At least one of the following must also be present:
   (a) Impaired abstract thinking, such that the person cannot explain what related objects (an apple and a banana, say) have in common (they are both fruits).
   (b) Impaired judgment in handling interpersonal and other social and vocational problems.
   (c) Other disturbances of higher cognitive functioning, such as impaired performance on a variety of simple psychomotor tests (copying three-dimensional figures or assembling blocks according to prearranged designs, for instance).
   (d) Noticeable personality changes.
3. The disturbances must significantly interfere with occupational or typical social activities, including relationships with others in one's social network.
4. There must be evidence from medical history, physical examination, or laboratory tests that there is an organic basis for the behavioral disturbances observed.

How many people suffer from dementia at any one time? The first thing to note about this organic mental syndrome is its remarkable relationship to age. Studies indicate that among people around the age of 65, the prevalence of dementia ranges from 2 to 4 percent. There is a gradual increase over the next ten years of the life span to a rough range of 10 to 15 percent, and a jump to 30 percent for all people over the age of 80. Since dementia is age-related and since the average life span continues to increase, we can expect the prevalence eventually to reach catastrophic proportions in our society unless preventive and curative treatments are developed soon (see Figure 20-3). In 1980 over 1.5 million persons displayed dementia in the United States, and the incidence, or number of new cases during that year, was around 350,000. By the year 2020, the incidence will exceed 600,000, and the total number of persons with dementia is projected to be about 3.5 million (Schoenberg, Kokmen, & Okazaki, 1987). This growing prevalence means increasing health-care costs, greater stress and burdens placed on the families that care for these frail persons, and a serious public health problem that requires a coordinated national policy effort.

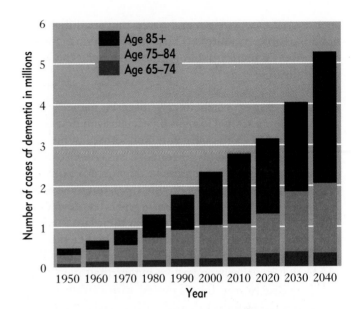

**FIGURE 20-3** The number of people suffering from dementia in the United States has increased each decade, along with increases in the average life span. As the number of people reaching the age of 80 and beyond keeps increasing, so does the number of persons vulnerable to dementia. Nearly a third of all people over 80 suffer some form of dementia. *(Adapted from Office of Technology Assessment, 1987; Cross & Gurland, 1986.)*

**Disorders That Produce Dementia**   As we have noted, dementia refers to an *organic mental syndrome*—a cluster of related, organically caused symptoms. Dementia is often confused with another organic mental syndrome called *delirium,* a clouded state of consciousness in which a person has great difficulty concentrating, focusing attention, and maintaining a straight-forward stream of thought. Although some symptoms of delirium are similar to those of dementia, and although delirium is also more common in elderly people than in people of other ages, the two syndromes are usually caused by different factors and follow a different course. Delirium may be caused by drug intoxication, stress, nutritional imbalance, fever, infection, or certain neurological disorders, and often follows major surgery (Lipowski, 1980). It is often totally reversible if the cause is addressed quickly.

Sometimes dementia, too, has an underlying cause that is reversible. It has been estimated that up to 20 percent of first-time patients who complain of dementia symptoms may respond to appropriate medical treatments if the cause can be pinpointed (Katzman, 1981). Some elders, for example, may be suffering from metabolic or nutritional disorders that can be corrected. For others, improvement in sensory functions such as vision and hearing can lead to a substantial improvement in cognitive performance. Unfortunately, however, most cases of dementia are caused by neurological problems, such as *Alzheimer's disease* and *stroke,* that are difficult, if not impossible, to address. Thus, in the opinion of many, dementia is a more troubling problem among the aged than delirium.

**Alzheimer's Disease**  Alzheimer's disease, named after Alois Alzheimer, the German physician, who first identified it in 1907, is the most common form of dementia, accounting for at least 50 percent of cases (Bliwise et al., 1987). This gradually progressive degenerative process can occur in middle age *(presenile type),* but most often it occurs after the age of 65 *(senile type).* Its prevalence increases markedly among people in their late 70s and early 80s. Some studies have reported higher rates of this disease in women, but this finding may be due simply to the fact that women live longer than men. Alzheimer's disease can be diagnosed with certainty only by postmortem studies that identify specific structural changes within the brain tissue. In living people it can only be suspected on the basis of typical symptoms (Winograd, 1988). The course of the illness ranges from two years to as many as fifteen years. Dysfunction progresses insidiously over this time, usually beginning with mild memory problems and lapses of attention that are virtually unnoticed or ignored at first. As time passes, these symptoms increase in frequency and severity, and at some point it becomes clear that the individual is having difficulty in completing complicated tasks, such as balancing the checkbook, or is forgetting extremely important appointments. Later the individual begins to have difficulty with simple tasks, and changes in personality often become much more noticeable. A man who for most of his life was quite controlled may make inappropriate sexual advances toward a family friend, say.

Deterioration of cognitive skill and performance is steady and dramatic in Alzheimer's disease. The wife of this Alzheimer's sufferer said, "I used to work with him with a calendar every night, take about 15, 20 minutes to do the days of the week. Then it got too stressful for him. . . . So that's why you see him swishing around with paint, with the crayons — to relieve that stress."

During the early stages of Alzheimer's disease, people tend to deny that they have a problem, but when it becomes more obvious, many become anxious or depressed about their impaired thinking. As the dementia progresses, however, they show less and less concern about it. While they may display a burst of anger at their inability to accomplish a task or at a caregiver's efforts to restrain them, in general they show little acknowledgment of or concern about their limitations. During the late stages of this process there is less interpersonal involvement, increased disorientation as to time and place, frequent wandering, and extremely poor judgment in matters important to safety and hygiene. They become more and more agitated at night and take frequent naps during the day. During this stage, which can last anywhere from two to five years, the individuals require constant care and supervision (Mace & Rabins, 1991).

Despite the serious changes in cognitive functioning that occur over this time, Alzheimer's victims usually remain in fairly good health until the later stages of the disease. As their mental facilities decline, their activity level decreases markedly and they tend to spend more time just sitting or lying in bed. At this point they begin to have more physical ailments, and often they develop complicating illnesses, such as pneumonia, that can result in death.

**Multi-infarct Dementia**  In *multi-infarct dementia* the symptoms of dementia are due to a cerebrovascular accident or stroke that caused a loss of blood flow to certain areas of the brain and in turn damaged focal, or specific, areas of the brain. The patient may be aware of these strokes, or they may be "silent"—that is, the patient is unaware that anything has happened. The more strokes a person has, or the more massive each one is, the greater the extent of the brain damage. This condition is unlike Alzheimer's disease, in which large areas of the brain atrophy, with correspondingly greater loss of cognitive function. Multi-infarct dementia is the second most common type of dementia among the elderly, with prevalence rates estimated to range from 8 to 29 percent (Katzman, 1981). It has been found more often in men than in women. This finding may be related to the documented higher prevalence of cardiovascular disease and hypertension in men as they age, so that the risk of strokes increases. This disease, too, is progressive, but its clinical course differs quite a bit from that of Alzheimer's disease. Its symptoms develop abruptly, rather than gradually, as they do in Alzheimer's disease, since they result from strokes. Behavioral changes occur in a stepwise rather than global fashion, with greater fluctuations in function: persons with multi-infarct dementia usually maintain very intact cognitive function in areas governed by parts of the brain that have not been affected, whereas Alzheimer's patients generally are impaired, at least to some extent, in all areas of cognitive functioning because larger areas of their brains are nonfunctional (see Table 20-1). Sometimes people with multi-infarct dementia are very difficult for their caregivers to manage because they are often not able to discriminate between types of cognitive processes that they perform well and those that are significantly impaired. Families generally have to make these decisions for the individual, which leads to more overt conflict than is generally encountered with Alzheimer's victims, who more often recognize their limitations.

Sometimes Alzheimer's disease and multi-infarct are present in the same individual. It is estimated that between 10 and 20 percent of patients who have one of these disorders also have the other. These patients tend to be more difficult to treat because the rate and types of decrements they will experience are highly unpredictable. Many are placed in extended-care facilities because they present an overwhelming management problem for the family.

**Other Dementias**  Several other disorders that produce dementia among the elderly are less common but have had considerable influence on the development and evaluation of models devised to explain Alzheimer's disease. *Pick's disease,* for example, is a rare progressive impairment that is difficult to differentiate from Alzheimer's disease clinically, but the distinction becomes clear at autopsy. For every 100 patients with Alzheimer's disease there are five with Pick's disease. The strong suggestion of genetic inheritance in Pick's disease has provided impetus for continued investigations of a genetic basis for Alzheimer's disease. *Jakob-*

*Creutzfeldt* disease, also a rare progressive dementia, has a rapid course and often includes spasmodic movements that are rarely seen in Alzheimer's patients. An interesting feature of this condition is that it is caused by a slow-acting virus that has been isolated.

*Huntington's chorea,* which usually has its onset during the middle years, typically starts with a movement disorder, which is later followed by dementia. A unique feature of this disease is its clearly dominant pattern of inheritance. An affected person will have transmitted it to 50 percent of his or her offspring. The gene carrying the disease has been located on chromosome 4.

Finally, as we saw in Chapters 15 and 16, *Parkinson's disease* is an age-related disorder of the central nervous system experienced by as many as 400,000 persons in the United States. This disease involves loss of motor control and disturbances in activities that require psychomotor coordination, such as walking and writing. It is often accompanied by dementia, particularly in the later stages (Boller, 1983). Clinicians disagree, however, as to whether this form of dementia is qualitatively similar to or different from that of Alzheimer's disease.

**Theories of Alzheimer's Disease and Experimental Pharmacological Treatments**  A review of the prevalence rates and clinical course of the various dementias that can strike during the later years leaves little question that Alzheimer's disease most urgently requires attention by researchers. We still have little information about the cause of this devastating disease, but theories abound.

**Neurotransmitter Theories**  At least two common neurotransmitters—*acetylcholine* and *L-glutamate*—are depleted in the brains of Alzheimer victims. In numerous studies, clinical researchers have tried to increase the activity of these neurotransmitters to see whether this would alleviate the symptoms of Alzheimer's disease.

Several experimental procedures have been designed to increase the brain availability of *acetylcholine*—a neurotransmitter implicated in high-level cognitive processes such as learning, memory, and abstract thinking. One strategy has been to administer choline, an essential component of acetylcholine, or lecithin, a choline precursor, to Alzheimer's patients, but this procedure has not proved particularly beneficial. Another strategy has been to prevent the breakdown of acetylcholine in the brain by blocking the action of the enzyme acetycholinesterase. At first, clinicians used the drug *physostigmine* to achieve this goal. Preliminary findings indicated small improvements in memory function, but the drug's other effects have precluded its use in a practical treatment program. More recently a major experimental trial involving the drug *tetrahydroaminoacridine (THA)* has

TABLE 20-1

| A COMPARISON OF ALZHEIMER'S DISEASE AND MULTI-INFARCT DEMENTIA | | |
| --- | --- | --- |
| Characteristic | Alzheimer's Disease | Multi-infarct Dementia |
| Age of onset | 60s–80s | 40s–50s |
| Sex most affected | Possibly females | Males |
| Nature of onset | Gradual | Abrupt |
| Course of disease | Progressive | Stepwise |
| Physical impairments | Few, appear late in life | Frequent |

shown positive results. The effects of this drug are fairly specific, however, and promise only limited benefits at the clinical level, with a high risk of severe undesirable effects. Nevertheless, there has been some interest in marketing this drug, since no other viable treatment is available. Treatments that combine the strategies of providing choline and disrupting acetylcholinesterase function have also resulted in some fairly specific memory improvement, but again the improvements have been minimal and the risks are high. Nevertheless, research continues into the efficacy of these and other medications to treat both the underlying causes and the symptoms of Alzheimer's disease.

*L-glutamate* is a neurotransmitter that plays an important role in the transmission of impulses from a specific part of the cortex to the hippocampus, the part of the brain that is essential for the storage and retrieval of new information. The role of L-glutamate depletions in Alzheimer's disease is thought to be significant because memory is often the first and most severely affected cognitive ability in patients. Research on this drug has been limited as yet. Other drugs and drug therapies—including the use of vasopressin and piracetam—to address other kinds of neurotransmitter activity have also been studied in an attempt to improve the cognitive functioning of Alzheimer's patients (Bondareff, Mountjoy, & Roth, 1982). However, no truly effective compound has yet been discovered (Crook, 1986).

**Genetic Theories**   The hypothesis that mental deterioration in the elderly may have a genetic basis has interested researchers for several decades, and evidence in its favor has emerged over the years. Researchers have found, for example, a concentration of progressive dementias in some families (Matsuyama, Jarvik, & Kumar, 1985). They have also discovered that the risk of a sibling developing Alzheimer's disease is inversely related to the patient's age at the onset of the disease (Heston, Mastri, Anderson, & White, 1981). That is, the younger a patient is at the onset of the disease, the greater the likelihood that a sibling may also develop it. And, finally, as noted in Chapter 19, an association between Alzheimer's disease and Down syndrome has led researchers to propose that some genes on chromosome 21 may contribute to Alzheimer's disease (see Figure 20-4).

On the other hand, the genetic research to date has not ruled out alternative explanations. Two close relatives who both develop Alzheimer's disease may, for example, be exposed to similar environmental toxins rather than to the same gene. Moreover, the vast majority of persons with Alzheimer's disease come from families without a strong pattern of this disease.

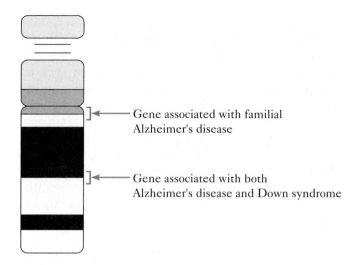

**FIGURE 20-4** A gene abnormality located toward the top of chromosome 21 is commonly found in patients with a *familial* form of Alzheimer's disease. In addition, scientists have located a gene lower on the chromosome responsible for the production of the *beta-amyloid protein*, found in abnormal deposits in the brains of both people with Alzheimer's disease and those with Down syndrome. *(Adapted from Tanzi et al., 1989.)*

**Other Theories**   A number of other hypotheses have also stimulated research on the underlying mechanisms of Alzheimer's disease. The fact that a viral agent has been isolated in other dementias, such as in Jakob-Creutzfeldt disease, has encouraged scientists to look for a slow-acting infectious agent in Alzheimer's disease as well. Researchers have also investigated the hypothesis that the immune systems of people who develop Alzheimer's disease fail to recognize neural tissue and attack it as though it were a foreign body. Clinical researchers who favor vascular theories continue to seek evidence that the structural changes characteristic of Alzheimer's disease may result from inadequate delivery of oxygen and sugar to the brain, or from the disruption of other metabolic processes by poor exchanges at the capillary level. High concentrations of aluminum in the brains of some Alzheimer's victims have encouraged some investigators to look for heavy metals or other toxic substances in the brain of Alzheimer's patients, perhaps as a result of a breakdown in the blood-brain barrier. And finally, a growing number of theorists believe that any number of factors may precipitate the structural changes characteristic of Alzheimer's disease. The disease may simply be the final common pathway of expression for many different causal agents whose common theme is the disruption of cerebral metabolic processes, which in turn triggers permanent structural and biochemical changes and leads to massive dysfunction (Glenner, 1985).

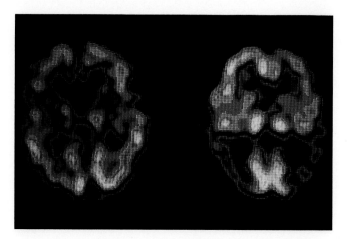

A PET scan of the brain of an Alzheimer's disease sufferer *(right)* indicates diminished blood flow and degeneration of brain tissue; a PET scan of a normal subject's brain appears at the left.

### Psychological Treatments for Alzheimer's Victims and Their Families

The first step in treating a person suspected of having Alzheimer's disease is to make as accurate a diagnosis as possible. This requires a thorough examination by an interdisciplinary team of physicians and other health specialists to ascertain the basis of the recurring problems. A detailed medical history and complete physical examination, along with additional laboratory tests, are nearly always essential because the type of dementia a person is suffering from usually cannot be established on the basis of the behavioral symptoms alone. In some cases, the condition can be diagnosed for certain only after an autopsy.

Once an accurate diagnosis has been made, various therapies may be employed. Although there is no medical cure for Alzheimer's disease, a variety of interventions can alleviate some of the distress and problematic behaviors that it causes. These interventions cannot eliminate cognitive impairment or return individuals to their earlier level of functioning, but they can improve the quality of life for both patients and members of their families.

Behavioral interventions are often applied in cases of Alzheimer's disease. Typically, behaviorists identify specific everyday actions performed by the Alzheimer's victim that are stressful for the family, such as wandering at night, being incontinent, and demanding frequent attention. They may also identify behavioral deficits that the family would like to see increased, such as the ability to participate in some self-care activities (Fisher & Carstensen, 1990). Behavioral therapists next teach family members how to shape positive behaviors and how and when to apply reinforcement, using a combination of role-playing techniques, modeling, and in-home

practice (Pinkston & Linsk, 1984). Research has indicated that behavioral principles and techniques can also be taught to staff members in long-term care facilities and nursing homes, to improve the quality of life for both them and their patients and to reduce the need for such offensive practices as keeping hard-to-manage patients in restraints (Fisher & Carstensen, 1990). These behavioral approaches have been particularly effective in treating such problems as wandering, inappropriate sexual behavior, incontinence, and refusal to feed oneself.

A very different behavioral approach focuses on developing programs to treat the feelings of depression experienced by approximately 30 percent of victims in the early to middle stages of the disease (Teri & Reifler, 1987). Behaviorists guide the caregiver and patient together to develop a list of potentially pleasant activities to share, so that more pleasurable interactions can be built into their daily routine (Teri & Logsdon, 1991). Research has indicated that this approach is quite effective in reducing symptoms of depression in both the patient and the family caregiver.

Caregiving takes a very heavy toll on the close relatives of Alzheimer's victims. In fact, one of the most frequent reasons for the institutionalization of victims is that overwhelmed caregivers can no longer cope with the demands of the situation (Colerick & George, 1986). Caretakers frequently report experiencing anger and depression (Gallagher et al., 1989), and a number of empirical studies have demonstrated the negative impact of caregiving on caregivers' physical and mental health (Schulz, Visintainer, & Williamson, 1990).

Given the high psychological and medical costs of caregiving, clinicians now recognize that one of the most important aspects of treating Alzheimer's disease is to identify and treat the needs of caregivers and to improve their well-being, often without involving the patient at all (Zarit, Orr, & Zarit, 1985).

Our work has concentrated on helping caregivers reduce their own depression and acquire skills for more adaptive management of the frustration and anger that they experience. This effort includes such programs as inpatient and outpatient respite care, which emphasizes that regular time-out should be planned for (Berman et al., 1987); the psychoeducational programs that we described earlier; individual counseling and psychotherapy for very distressed family members; and support groups of various kinds to meet a wide variety of needs (Gallagher, Lovett, & Rose, 1991).

The support-group movement is very strong in this as in many other areas of human suffering. A national organization called the Alzheimer's Association provides a leadership role in setting up chapters throughout the United States and Europe. It was founded by a woman whose husband had Alzheimer's disease at a time when few people even knew what the term meant and still fewer services were available for patients and their families. More specialized support groups exist for families of brain-damaged people whose impairment is attributable to other causes, such as Parkinson's disease and frequent strokes. Caregivers typically report that they gain the most from support groups that are made up of people in situations very similar to their own, thus therapists now encourage them to shop around until they find a support group where they feel comfortable.

Finally, interventions need to be developed to help caregivers maintain their physical as well as mental health. Some studies reveal that caregivers show significantly greater signs of deficient immune system functioning than noncaregivers (Kiecolt-Glaser et al., 1987). And other research has found other negative physiological consequences of prolonged caregiving, such as increased cardiovascular distress in female caregivers (Vitaliano, Maiuro, Ochs, & Russo, 1989). This area is just beginning to be investigated, however.

Fortunately, just as patients seem to adapt to their impairment and to at least some of its functional limitations over time (Burnside, 1988), family caregivers do too (Rabins et al., 1990). Moreover, work in our laboratory, reminiscent of the hardiness research discussed in Chapters 6 and 11, indicates that there is a subgroup of caregivers who tend to remain high in positive affect, low in perceived burden and depression, and high in morale throughout their caregiving experience, despite the fact that their frail elder relative continues to deteriorate. Researchers have not, however, determined what factors enable some caregivers to be such good copers.

**Special Concerns about Dementia**    One area about which very little is known is the influence of ethnicity on assessment and treatment of people with dementia and their families. Although a large increase in the minority population of persons over the age of 65 is expected in the next twenty years, there has been very little research on or clinical attention paid to their special needs (Valle, 1989; Baker, 1988). We know, for example, that proportionately fewer Asians and Pacific Islanders than people of European descent are placed in nursing homes, but we do not really know why. And we do not know the extent to which other cultures view caregiving as a burden, as it is almost uniformly viewed in the Anglo culture. Moreover, because only a few assessment instruments have been appropriately translated or validated in the native language of many minority elders, it is difficult to conduct standardized assessments for diagnosing cases of dementia in members of those minority groups.

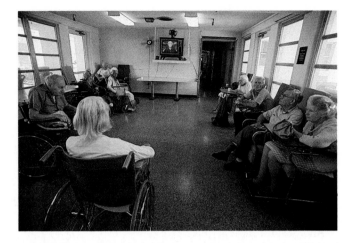

Many of today's nursing homes are unstimulating settings in which elderly patients may be neglected, mistreated, and overmedicated.

A second area of concern is that serious abuses exist in the nursing-home industry. Indeed, health-care professionals may soon find it necessary to lobby for reform in nursing homes, or more forcefully to promote the development of a continuum of care that permits the cognitively impaired elder to remain at home as long as possible. If appropriate services were available to support elders and their families at home, expensive and impersonal care might not be needed—at least not to the extent that is now projected for the future. Such services would include in-home health care; in-home support services such as assistance in meal preparation, bathing, and medication; and day-care facilities that can offer rehabilitation programs and social activities. It is a tremendous relief to caregivers to have these services and to know that their frail elder relative is in a safe and supervised environment whose cost is substantially less than a stay in a nursing home. The nursing-home industry has been slow to develop such alternatives, probably largely because services of this kind would lower the demand for the profitable institutional care the nursing homes provide.

A final concern is the growing cost of long-term care. As the proportion of elders in the population increases in the next twenty to forty years, it is younger persons who will have to bear most of the burden of financing these various programs (Hewitt & Howe, 1988). Careful planning must be done now if the problem is to be solved in an equitable fashion.

## Substance Abuse

*Chuck and Sandra Clemens are elderly neighbors of yours* who are becoming increasingly withdrawn from other people. Chuck's speech seems to be slurred fairly often lately, and Sandra's appearance is not as neat as it used to be. You frequently see them at the local convenience store buying beer and lots of over-the-counter medicines, such as antihistamines, but they really never seem that sick to you. You hear some other neighbors talking about the deplorable condition of their apartment and you wonder what is wrong. The next thing you know, Sandra has been taken to the hospital: she broke her hip in a fall, because she was unsteady on her feet. When the visiting nurse inspects the apartment in preparation for Sandra's return from the hospital, she finds a stash of unused medications, many empty beer cans and wine bottles, and little food. Chuck is immediately brought in for counseling, and both he and his wife are strongly encouraged to join the chapter of Alcoholics Anonymous in their area.

Accurate data about the prevalence of alcohol and other forms of drug abuse among older adults is difficult to determine, because many older people do not admit that they have such a problem—some regard it as shameful, others fail to realize that their drinking has become a problem, and a number misuse their medications without being aware of it.

Although alcohol and other forms of drug abuse are certainly a problem for many older persons, the prevalence of drug abuse actually appears to decline after age 60, perhaps as a consequence of changes in health and reduced financial status (Maddox, 1988). It seems that the majority of older adults do not misuse alcohol, prescription drugs, and other substances despite the fact that aging is widely perceived as a time of frequent stress, and that in our society alcohol and drugs are widely used to reduce stress.

Recent surveys suggest that about 5 percent of the older adult population, particularly men, have alcohol-related problems (Maddox, 1988). Men under 30 are four times as likely as men over 60 to exhibit a behavioral problem associated with alcohol abuse, such as repeated falling, spells of dizziness or blacking out, secretiveness about drinking, and increasing social withdrawal (Butler & Lewis, 1986). These studies fail to show a consistent relationship between older adults' alcohol abuse and their socioeconomic status, though younger adults' alcohol abuse is associated with lower socioeconomic status. Older patients who are institutionalized for either medical or psychological reasons do, however, display relatively high rates of problem drinking. For example, alcohol problems among older persons admitted to general and mental hospitals ranged from a reported low of 15 percent to a high of 49 percent, and estimates of alcohol-related problems among patients in nursing homes have ranged from 25 to 60 percent (Maddox, 1988).

Surveys and descriptive studies often distinguish two major categories of older problem drinkers: early-onset and late-onset alcohol abusers. *Early-onset* drinkers are aging alcoholics who have experienced significant alcohol-related problems for many years, often since their 20s or 30s. Many of these people are well known to the health and to social services professionals in their community. *Late-onset* alcohol abusers, in contrast, may not have started the pattern until their 50s or 60s. Their abusive drinking typically begins as a reaction to the frequent negative events associated with growing older, such as the death of a spouse, retirement, moving away from their original home or state, reduction in income, and impaired health. Researchers disagree about the relative numbers of late- and early-onset alcohol abusers, and particularly about the extent to which women fall into the late-onset category.

Another leading form of drug abuse in the elderly stems from the unintentional or, less commonly, intentional misuse of prescription drugs, particularly from combining them with alcohol (Gottheil, 1987). A very poignant letter by a 72-year-old woman was published in the magazine *Aging* in 1990. She revealed that because of problems earlier in her life, her physician prescribed first tranquilizers, then a stimulant, and then medication for severe headaches. Eventually she increased the dosage of these various medications, noting that the drugs no longer had the same effect and that she did not feel well. She said she felt no guilt about what happened because "after all I was only following the doctor's orders at all times" (Reynolds, 1990, p. 27). Her functioning became so impaired, however, that she needed hospitalization and therapy to end her addiction.

A major national survey has indicated that among persons who receive prescriptions from a physician, the average number of prescriptions is 7.5, but it is 14.2 for people over the age of 60. Among those living in the community, 85 percent indicated that they used prescription drugs regularly; 67 percent took at least one drug everyday and 25 percent took three or more drugs daily, whereas for younger persons the corresponding figures were 43 percent and 9 percent (Lipton, 1988, p. 74). Over 95 percent of the residents of nursing homes take two or more medications each day, sometimes more for the convenience of the nursing home staff than for the good of the resident. Research is beginning to suggest that there is a problem of some magnitude here, and it is likely to get worse as the population of elders increases.

Finally, research indicates that the use of "hard drugs" or "street drugs" by the elderly is very unusual (Petersen, 1988). Those who have been heroin users in their youth typically completely stop by their 50s or 60s, often because of concurrent serious health problems and lack of money. There have been very few studies on the use of cocaine, LSD, PCP, or other such drugs among the elderly.

## BOX 20-4

# À Votre Santé

One school of thought says that alcohol can be very helpful to those older people who are able to drink in moderation, and can add pleasure and meaning to their lives. Robert Kastenbaum (1988) cites data indicating that small servings of alcoholic beverages may stimulate appetite and digestion by both physiological and sensory enhancement, in contrast to large quantities of alcohol, which have the opposite effect. Several studies in nursing homes found that persons who participated in a "pub" and had a glass or so of alcohol each day reported such positive benefits, as improved social interaction, morale, and mutual support. Kastenbaum suggests that the moderate use of alcohol be encouraged in long-term-care settings, since the good feeling that it induces seems to reduce fatigue, anxiety, and depression and thus enhances the quality of life. He suggests that beverages of low ethanol content, such as beer and wine, may have their place in the lifestyles of some older adults, whether they live independently or in a retirement community or a nursing home.

**Assessment**    An older person's abuse of alcohol or prescription drugs may be discovered when a physician evaluate the physical status of the individual or when the family detects changed behavioral patterns and increased use of substances. Sometimes older people themselves realize that they have a problem. Unfortunately, relatively few mental health professionals have acquired the skills necessary to assess and deal with the alcohol and prescription drug problems of elderly people. Some younger clinicians, for example, find it difficult to ask older persons direct questions about alcohol intake, feeling presumptuous or intrusive when they do so. We find, however, that older adults will provide information about alcohol consumption and alcohol-related behaviors if they are asked about them straightforwardly. In addition, many professionals mistakenly believe that they should not deprive older persons of one of their "few remaining joys."

It has also been difficult to find a good screening measure for identifying alcohol and other forms of drug abuse in the elderly. Clinical theorists Mark Willenbring and William Spring (1988) recommend giving elderly clients the "HEAT," a mnemonic device for a series of four questions: one subjective, open-ended question designed to elicit subtle defensiveness and three questions that have been found to successfully identify the majority of alcoholics in hospitals:

*How* do you use alcohol?

Have you ever thought you use to *Excess?*

Has *Anyone* else ever thought you used too much?

Have you ever had any *Trouble* resulting from your use?

Any other substance may be mentioned in place of alcohol. Willenbring and Spring advise that clinicians should suspect a drug problem if clients appear excessively defensive, angry, embarrassed, or uncomfortable in their answers to any of these questions. They also suggest that for persons between 55 and 75 years of age, two drinks a day and three per occasion are probably reasonable maximum safe usages, while for those over 75, one drink per day and two per occasion may be safe, although this has not yet been established empirically (1988, p. 31). Some people in the field of gerontology further think that it is good to encourage older adults to have a small amount of alcohol daily, to promote socialization and relaxation (see Box 20-4).

To detect misuse of medications, it is first necessary to find out exactly what medications older persons are taking. A number of therapists ask their clients to put all of their medications in a bag and bring them to the next evaluation session (Lesage & Zwygart-Stauffacher, 1988). This strategy typically leads to more accurate information than questioning alone, since many older people are forgetful and may easily omit some medications or get the dosages mixed up. If older persons are responsible for taking their own medications, clinicians need to also determine whether they understand how to take each one (Gottheil, 1987). Medications will be taken most carefully and accurately by older people who understand the purposes behind them and the exact procedures for taking them, and who recognize the "red flags"—such as alterations in sensory or perceptual functioning—that can signify their unintentional misuse.

**Treatment**    Alcohol abuse among elderly people is treated in many of the same ways as alcohol abuse among younger adults (see pp. 451–453), including such approaches as detoxification, Antabuse, and Alcoholics Anonymous (Schiff, 1988). While most AA meetings are attended by people of varying ages, specialized groups called Golden Years have been organized largely to attract older adults and make the experience more comfortable for them.

An important component of many treatment programs for older alcohol abusers is a group therapy format which includes a focus on the social and psychological stresses associated with aging (Zimberg, 1979). The Florida Mental Health Institute has a number of cognitive-behavioral group programs for the treatment of older drinkers. These groups, targeted to people aged 55 and over, teach older drinkers how to solve problems, enhance their social support networks, and manage themselves in high-risk situations, and they provide education and information on alcohol. Research has indicated that these programs are successful in helping older persons attain sobriety and remain free of alcohol and medication misuse for as long as one year after completing the programs (Schonfeld & Dupree, 1990).

A variety of strategies appear to be useful in reducing medication misuse among elderly people. First, it is helpful when clinicians make sure that older patients have accurate information about their medications and understand it, and when pharmacists or nurses take time to clarify directions and to develop a system for taking the medications as prescribed. Second, it is helpful when a medication regimen is simplified as much as possible so that the patient is more able to follow it accurately. Third, older individuals tend to receive better health care when taught to tell their various physicians just what medications they are on and from whom they are receiving them; many physicians do not realize how easy it is for elders to misuse their medications. Finally, it is beneficial when clinicians instruct older persons to monitor the undesired effects of medications and to distinguish those that are potentially serious from those that are inconveniences, so that serious effects can be reported immediately to the physician and the medication regimen can be changed (Ascione & Shimp, 1988). More active collaboration among pharmacists, physicians, and older patients can also greatly reduce the likelihood of unintentional drug misuse.

## Psychotic Disorders

*Schizophrenia* is more common in younger persons than in older ones. In fact, many schizophrenic persons find that their symptoms become attenuated in later life (APA, 1987). Improvement can occur in people who have been schizophrenic thirty or more years, particularly in such areas as social skills and work capacity

(Cohen, 1990). New symptoms do not commonly appear in old age; the majority of symptoms remain throughout life but are experienced in a less severe form after the age of 50.

Most older schizophrenic people require some sort of structured care (Cavanaugh, 1990). Having had this severe disorder for many years, they tend to function best at relatively low-level jobs; a number experience repeated hospitalizations. As a result of the trend toward deinstitutionalization in the United States over the past few decades, many older schizophrenic people end up in nursing homes, where they do not receive appropriate treatment, or homeless on the streets, a situation discussed in Chapter 16.

Another psychotic disorder, *delusional,* or *paranoid disorder,* is relatively rare among adults of all ages (3 out of every 10,000) but tends to increase slightly with age (Cavanaugh, 1990). Some geriatric clinicians believe that a mild form of delusional disorder can sometimes be a healthy adaptation to a stressful world that may in fact really be out to get the individual in one way or another. There is, however, little in either the clinical or the research literature to support this view.

The psychotic disorders are often treated with antipsychotic drugs. As we have seen previously, however, these medications may produce serious undesired motor effects in adults of all ages, particularly in elderly patients, and so they must be used sparingly. In other interventions, clinicians may try to develop a strong therapeutic alliance so that patients can trust at least one person in the world, offer supportive counseling, encourage patients to identify and discount their delusional ideas, and work with family members to increase their tolerance for their older psychotic relatives (Blazer, 1990). So far few controlled studies have investigated the efficacy of treatment of psychotic disorders among the elderly.

## OTHER FACTORS IN THE MENTAL HEALTH OF THE ELDERLY

As geropsychologists, we are continually struck by the amount of new knowledge that is developing in our field, and constantly wrestle with it to determine its clinical implications. Among issues of increasing interest today are the role of ethnicity in the mental health of the elderly, the problems raised by long-term care, and the necessity of health maintenance in an aging world.

### Ethnicity

Gerontologists must be aware of their patients' ethnicity as they try to diagnose and treat the mental health problems of older people. An *ethnic group* is a collection of people who share some common ancestry, memories of specific historical events that were unique to them, and a cultural focus on symbolic elements that are important to their identity as a people. These elements include kinship patterns, lifestyles, religious beliefs, race, and common physical features. The term "ethnic minority" is often used to refer to persons of a race and cultural background that differ from those of the majority of the population in a given country.

Discrimination based on ethnicity has always been a problem in the United States, and many people have suffered disadvantages as a result, particularly those who are now old (Cavanaugh, 1990). The term "double jeopardy" has been used to describe the problem of being simultaneously old and a member of a minority racial or ethnic group. "Triple jeopardy" describes the dilemma of the person who is old, a member of an ethnic minority, and female, since many more older women than older men live alone, are widowed, and have incomes below the poverty level.

The language barrier is the most significant difficulty for many ethnic elders, as well as cultural beliefs that prevent them from seeking the services of medical and mental health professionals. Many members of minority groups simply do not trust the establishment, and rely instead on remedies traditional in their immediate social network. Ethnic elders may also lack information about available services that are sensitive to their culture and particular needs (Ralston, 1991; Jackson, 1988).

A significant challenge for the next twenty to forty years will be the development of appropriate outreach, diagnostic, and intervention programs that older minority adults and their families will find culturally relevant. This task is not easy, given the number of minority groups in this country, the multitude of languages they speak, and the scarcity of information currently available about how these elders respond to stress and about what they perceive as a stressful event. A concerted effort in this regard is needed, because the minority population is the fastest-growing segment within the over-65 group in the United States today.

## Long-Term Care

The term "long-term care" is applied to a variety of forms of extended care provided to older adults. Long-term care may be provided in a partially supervised apartment or housing complex for seniors who are not as independent as they used to be or in a nursing home or other institutional setting where skilled medical and nursing care are available around the clock. Since the majority of elders have at least one chronic health prob-

lem and may live alone, there is and will continue to be a need for settings where elders can live safely and with as high a quality of life as possible when they are no longer able to function independently.

Investigations indicate that the quality of care provided in long-term residences varies widely. Persons should make a careful review of their own situation as well as the pluses and minuses of the facility before choosing to enter a program of long-term care, particularly in respect to a nursing home. That decision, however, is often made not by the elderly persons themselves, but by physicians or family members.

At any given time only about 5 percent of the elderly population actually reside in nursing homes, but fear of being "put away" in a nursing home is a significant factor in the lives of most older adults (Butler & Lewis, 1986). Many fear having to move, as well as the impersonal environment and the emphasis on disabilities that exist in long-term-care settings. Others fear losing their independence, or have known people who died shortly after being admitted to such a facility and thus are very pessimistic about their ability to adjust.

A number also worry about the economic implications of moving to a long-term-care facility. Because families are trying to keep their elders at home longer (and using a variety of services to help them do so) most elders do

When long-term-care institutions are stimulating and comfortable, allow patients to control their lives as much as possible, and facilitate involvement by family members and friends, elderly persons are generally happier and show better cognitive functioning.

not enter nursing homes until they are in the last stages of a disease and in need of almost total care. This means that nursing homes will be dealing increasingly with terminally ill patients and their families. Since round-the-clock nursing care is always going to be expensive, nursing home costs will continue to rise. The health insurance plans that are currently available do not even begin to cover the costs of permanent placement. All of these issues can affect the mental health of older adults in very significant ways, from causing depression and anxiety in the individual to arousing conflict in the family. Research focused on improving the quality of life for both patients and staff in long-term-care facilities is sorely needed. A related issue of interest to clinicians is the need for continued training of the staff and management of such facilities so that any advances in knowledge can be quickly shared and implemented.

## Health Maintenance

Because of the increasing longevity of older persons and the increasing cost of health care, it would seem prudent for the current generation of young adults to take a wellness or health-promotion approach to their own aging process. By this we mean doing things that are important for maintaining both physical and mental health, such as not smoking, eating well-balanced and sensible meals, and exercising regularly—not only to look good but also to manage stress. Although research data are lacking at present, it is reasonable to assume that older adults will adapt more readily to changes and negative events if their health is good. Good health may serve as a buffer against depression, since the ability to enjoy one's good health encourages engagement in enjoyable activities in general.

By the same token, mental health professionals should be encouraging lifelong participation in prevention programs, such as the various psychoeducational approaches we discussed earlier. It is also important to urge people to seek treatment promptly for any psychological problems that they do develop as they grow older, and to help them overcome their prejudices against doing so.

# PROBLEMS OF AGING: THE STATE OF THE FIELD

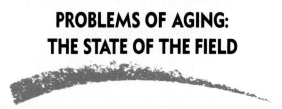

For many years elderly persons, like children and adolescents, received little attention from clinical practitioners and researchers. It was as if these professionals believed that the broadly studied psychological problems of early and middle adulthood disappeared when people reached the age of 65, or that elderly people were immune to developing new problems. Clinicians now recognize that quite the opposite is true. Because of the losses and other stresses elders face, stresses brought about by a changing brain and body and the changes in lifestyle attached to old age, elderly people are vulnerable to a range of psychological problems. Some of the problems—depression, anxiety, alcoholism—are familiar, but their emergence in old age is often the result of the special stresses of later life. Other problems are disproportionately common in the elderly population, such as dementia and the abuse of prescription drugs. Either way, it is now clear to clinicians that elderly people often experience various mental disorders and problems, and they have started to study and treat these problems in earnest during the past two decades.

This shift in clinical priorities has occurred for a variety of reasons. First, the number and percentage of people who are elderly in our society is steadily increasing, so that the needs of this age group are becoming more and more visible. Second, as the elderly population grows larger, greater caretaking pressures are being placed upon middle-aged and young-old children, and these people have lobbied for more clinical help and research. Third, as the number of elderly persons in our society rises, young and middle-aged adults are increasingly recognizing that the problems of old age await them as well, and they understand that they have a vested interest in the study and treatment of these problems. And fourth, as the number of elderly people grows, the number of aging-related psychological disorders continues to grow as well. The prevalence of aging-related psychological disorders is higher now than it ever was before, and it keeps rising.

Thus the public and the mental health field are currently devoting considerable attention to the psychological problems of aging. As the study and treatment of elderly persons advance in the coming years, a number of puzzles will probably be resolved. Dementia, depression, anxiety, and other disorders among the aged are likely to be better understood and treated. The special concerns of caretakers will probably be better appreciated and addressed. And it is hoped that more humane and comforting solutions for the residential needs of aged persons will be developed.

Another important trend in the study and treatment of elderly people is the current emphasis on prevention and preparation. Given that the stresses and biological changes of old age are largely predictable, clinical educators are now developing programs aimed at preventing them or preparing people for them before they occur. Young adults are being encouraged to start planning for a financially secure retirement, middle-aged persons are advised to take proper care of their health, and clinical educators organize groups to help middle-aged and young-old persons understand the changes that await them in their later years. These are all important forms of "treatment" for the psychological problems of old age. Such efforts are really just beginning, but their value is already becoming clear. We may not be able to stop the aging process, but we can and should use every weapon in our arsenal to prevent and reduce the psychological pain attached to it.

# SUMMARY

In the course of aging, adults pass through the stages of *early adulthood, middle adulthood,* and *old age,* or *later life.* Each of these stages, and the transition from one to another, contains a variety of stresses.

The problems of later life have received considerable attention only in recent years. In fact, the field of *geropsychology* has developed almost entirely within the last twenty years to explore whether methods of assessment and treatment of the mental health problems of later life should be similar to the methods appropriate for younger persons. Clinicians distinguish the *young-old* (age 65–74), the *old-old* (age 74–84), and the *oldest-old* (age 85 and up). The field of geropsychology also distinguishes *chronological age,* the number of years a person has been alive, from *functional age,* which is a reflection of three interrelated aspects of aging: *biological age, social age,* and *psychological age.* A distinction is also made between chronological age and one's *cohort,* or the particular generation a person belongs to.

A common source of psychological stress for older people is their frequent experience of loss as friends, spouses, and relatives die. Some also lose a sense of meaning or purpose after retirement or as chronic illness afflicts them. Most older adults, however, do not develop mental health problems despite the many stresses in their lives. Lazarus and Folkman's *stress-and-coping* model suggests that most older people cope effectively with these stresses, using such approaches as *primary appraisal, secondary appraisal,* and *reappraisal.* A person's coping responses may be *problem-focused* or *emotion-focused* or both. By using more problem-focused modes of coping, many older adults are able to weather the challenges facing them. Research has found that cognitive-behavioral interventions, which tend to be problem-focused techniques, are particularly helpful in the treatment of mental health problems in older patients.

Although as many as 50 percent of the elderly would benefit from mental health services, fewer than 20 percent seek help. Many elderly people have a highly stigmatized view of mental health problems and prefer to see their primary-care physician for all their difficulties. Too, few clinicians are trained specifically to deal with the mental health problems of the elderly.

Depression is the most common mental health problem of older adults; as many as 20 percent meet the DSM-III-R criteria for clinical depression. The prevalence is higher among women than men. The most accurate assessment can be made through a clinical interview, although several self-report questionnaires also are used widely as screening devices. It is also important to assess the physical and cognitive functioning of older persons to distinguish symptoms of depression from similar symptoms that accompany decline in other areas. The most common treatment for depression among the elderly is drug therapy, but it is less effective for older depressed patients than for younger ones because the biological mechanisms for the breakdown and absorption of these drugs change with age. Cognitive-behavioral therapy and brief psychodynamic therapy appear to be helpful. In some cases, electroconvulsive therapy (ECT) has been used successfully. Group therapy may also be effective.

Prevention programs for nondepressed older adults that focus on ways to cope with the pressures of aging have been found to be effective in preventing depression. Similar training for caregivers has also helped to prevent depression among them.

Approximately 7 percent of elderly people suffer from *generalized anxiety disorder,* 2 to 5 percent from *agoraphobia,* 1 to 12 percent from *simple phobias,* and less than 1 percent from *panic disorders.* Overall, the prevalence of anxiety disorders actually decreases with age. The assessment of anxiety problems is similar to that of depression. Clinicians use self-report questionnaires to get a rough estimate of the severity of anxiety but ideally rely more heavily on clinical interviews. Again, the diagnostician must distinguish symptoms of anxiety disorders from similar symptoms associated with physical or cognitive decline. Treatment for anxiety disorders among the elderly has traditionally included *antianxiety* medications, although these drugs may cause cognitive impairments that are sometimes mistaken for mental deterioration. *Psychotherapy* also appears to be helpful with anxiety disorders, particularly behavioral techniques such as systematic desensitization and cognitive-behavioral therapies such as *anxiety management tech-*

niques *(AMT),* in which the client learns cognitive skills to help control fear.

**A**lthough minor lapses in memory or intellectual functioning increase as one gets older, these problems are usually not severe enough to warrant a diagnosis of cognitive dysfunction, or *dementia.* Around the age of 65, the prevalence of dementia ranges from 2 to 4 percent, followed by a gradual increase over the next ten years to a range of 10 to 15 percent; it jumps to 30 percent among persons over the age of 80. Dementias may stem from either progressive mental impairment or an underlying medical condition, such as a metabolic or nutritional disorder or diminished sensory functioning. The most common form of dementia among the elderly is *Alzheimer's disease.* It can be definitively diagnosed only on the basis of a postmortem study that identifies structural changes in the brain. This disorder is characterized by an insidious progression of dysfunction that increases in frequency and severity. Despite the serious changes in cognitive functioning, Alzheimer's victims usually remain in good health until the later stages of the disease. The second most common form of dementia among the elderly is *multi-infarct dementia,* characterized by damage to very specific areas of the cerebral cortex that have been caused by a cerebrovascular accident (or stroke). This disorder differs from Alzheimer's disease in that it develops abruptly and may affect some areas of cognitive functioning but not others. Other forms of dementia are found in cases of *Pick's disease, Jakob-Creutzfeldt disease, Huntington's chorea,* and *Parkinson's disease.*

Because of its high prevalence, Alzheimer's disease has received much research attention. A number of theories have been proposed to explain its occurrence. *Neurotransmitter theories* propose that the depletion of *acetylcholine* may be responsible. Correspondingly, some clinicians treat Alzheimer's disease by increasing the amount of acetylcholine in the brains of patients. *L-glutamate,* which plays an important role in the transmission of impulses in the brain, has also been tied to Alzheimer's disease. *Genetic theories* suggest that the more relatives one has who have had Alzheimer's, the greater one's risk of developing the disease. Finally, some theorists have proposed that Alzheimer's disease may be the result of a slow-acting *infectious agent.*

Although there is no medical cure for Alzheimer's disease, a variety of interventions alleviate some of its distress and problematic behaviors. *Behavioral therapists* focus on teaching family members how to encourage and reward specific behaviors, primarily using techniques of classical conditioning. Because of the heavy strain placed on caregivers, some programs have focused on alleviating their anger and depression in order to help them cope with the Alzheimer's patient. *Self-help support groups* have been formed by the friends and families of Alzheimer's sufferers to help them learn to cope in the caregiver role.

**A**pproximately 5 percent of the older adult population exhibit *alcohol-related problems.* Clinicians distinguish between older problem drinkers whose alcohol-related problems began when they were much younger and those who developed problems in their 50s or 60s in response to the negative events associated with growing older. Treatment for alcohol abuse in the elderly is similar to that used with younger patients, including *detoxification, group therapy, support-group therapy* (such as Alcoholics Anonymous), and *training in developing better coping skills.* The *abuse of street drugs* is unusual among older persons, but the *abuse of prescription drugs* is alarmingly common. To reduce abuse of prescription drugs, patients must be informed of the effects of their medications and then helped to monitor and administer the appropriate medication in the appropriate dosages.

**E**lderly persons may also manifest *psychotic disorders* such as *schizophrenia.* It is rare, however, for new symptoms of schizophrenia to appear in old age, and in fact schizophrenic persons usually show a reduction in their residual symptoms as they reach later life. *Paranoid disorder* is also relatively uncommon among elderly adults. In general, schizophrenic and paranoid disorders in the elderly are treated much the same as they are in younger patients.

**M**any factors must be considered if we are to understand mental disorders among older adults. Geropsychologists are looking at *ethnicity,* for example, and the role that discrimination may play in mental dysfunctioning among the elderly. Another issue of major importance is the *long-term* care of the elderly. Long-term-care facilities have not typically been effective in addressing the needs of older persons. In fact, the fear of inadequate care or being "put away" in a nursing home weighs heavily on the minds of most elderly persons. Finally, *health maintenance* of the elderly requires more attention. Prevention of medical problems in older adults may circumvent later problems and help them cope with stress more effectively.

# TOPIC OVERVIEW

# CHAPTER *21*

# LAW, SOCIETY, AND THE MENTAL HEALTH PROFESSION

Throughout this book we have seen the importance of the roles clinical scientists and practitioners play in our society: they gather and impart knowledge about psychological dysfunctioning, and they treat people who are experiencing psychological problems. They do not, however, perform these functions in a vacuum. Their relationship with their science, their clients, and the public unfolds within a complex social system. It is that society, in fact, which assigns them their professional responsibilities and regulates them in the performance of their duties.

Earlier chapters have highlighted a number of the ways clinical scientists and practitioners interact with the public at large and with specific social agencies. They described how clinicians have helped carry out the government's policy of deinstitutionalization, how the government has regulated clinicians' use of electroconvulsive therapy, and how clinicians have called to society's attention the psychological ordeal of Vietnam veterans. The relationship between the field of abnormal psychology and the other institutions of our society is complex. Just as we must understand the social context of abnormal behavior in order to appreciate its nature and consequences, so must we understand the context in which this behavior is studied and treated.

The mental health profession and the legislative and judicial professions—the institutions charged with promoting and protecting both the public good and the rights of individuals — have had an interesting relationship dating back many years. Sometimes the relationship has been harmonious, and the two fields have worked in concert to protect the rights and address the needs of mentally disturbed individuals and society. At other times one field has imposed its will on the other and overridden its judgments, and the relationship has been stormy.

This relationship has two distinct facets. One consists of the role played by mental health professionals in the criminal justice system. Clinicians have, for example, been called upon to evaluate the mental stability of many people accused of crimes and to determine their culpability. The second facet of this relationship consists of the role played by the legislative and judicial systems in regulating some aspects of mental health care. Legal channels have been established that can force individuals to receive psychological treatment, even against their will. At the same time, the courts have become watchdogs over patients' rights in the mental health system.

# CLINICAL INFLUENCES ON THE CRIMINAL JUSTICE SYSTEM

Our courts mete out what they consider just and appropriate punishment on the assumption that individuals are *responsible* for their crimes and are *capable* of defending themselves in court. If *either* of these features is lacking, it is considered inappropriate to find individuals guilty or incarcerate them in the usual manner. The courts have decided that *mental instability* is one mediating factor that can indeed render individuals incapable of being responsible for their actions and of defending themselves in court. Although the courts make the final judgment of mental instability, their decisions are guided largely by the opinions of mental health professionals.

When individuals accused of crimes are judged to be mentally unstable, they are typically sent to a mental institution for treatment, a process called **criminal commitment.** Actually there are two forms of criminal commitment. In one, individuals are judged *mentally unstable at the time of their crime* and accordingly are found innocent of wrongdoing. Those who plead not guilty by reason of insanity are permitted to bring mental health professionals into court to support their claim. If they are found not guilty on this basis, they are committed for treatment until they improve enough to be released.

In a second form of criminal commitment, individuals are judged *mentally unstable at the time of their trial* and accordingly are considered to be incapable of understanding the procedures and defending themselves in court. They are committed for treatment until they are competent to stand trial. Once again, the testimony of mental health professionals is relied on to help determine the defendant's mental incompetence.

Such judgments of mental instability have generated many arguments over the years. Many people consider the judgments to represent unfortunate loopholes in the legal system that allow criminals to escape proper punishment for their wrongdoing. Others argue that a legal system simply cannot be just unless it allows for extenuating circumstances, such as mental instability.

# Criminal Commitment and Insanity during Commission of a Crime

In March 1981 the actress Jodie Foster received the following letter:

Dear Jodie:
   There is a definite possibility that I will be killed in my attempt to get Reagan. It is for this very reason that I am writing you this letter now. As you well know by now, I love you very much. The past seven months I have left you dozens of poems, letters and messages in the faint hope you would develop an interest in me. . . . Jodie, I would abandon this idea of getting Reagan in a second if I could only win your heart and live out the rest of my life with you, whether it be in total obscurity or whatever. I will admit to you that the reasons I'm going ahead with this attempt now is because I just cannot wait any longer to impress you. I've got to do something now to make you understand in no uncertain terms that I am doing all of this for your sake. By sacrificing my freedom and possibly my life I hope to change your mind about me. This letter is being written an hour before I leave for the Hilton Hotel. Jodie, I'm asking you please to look into your heart and at least give me the chance with this historical deed to gain your respect and love. I love you forever.

                                      JOHN HINCKLEY

Are these the ravings of an insane man? Or are they the heartfelt emotions of a calculating murderer? Soon after writing this letter, John W. Hinckley stood waiting, pistol ready, outside the Washington Hilton Hotel. Moments later, President Ronald Reagan emerged from the hotel, and the popping of pistol fire was heard. As Secret Service men propelled Reagan into the limousine, a policeman and the president's press secretary fell to the pavement. The president had been shot, and by nightfall most of America had seen the face and heard the name of the young man from Colorado.

Few courtroom decisions have spurred as much debate or legislative action as the jury's verdict that John Hinckley was not guilty by reason of insanity in his attempt to kill President Ronald Reagan. As a consequence of this verdict, Congress and half of the state legislatures changed their criteria for such a verdict.

Was John Hinckley insane at the time of the shooting? If insane, should he be held responsible for his actions? On June 21, 1982, fifteen months after he shot four men in the nation's capital, a jury pronounced Hinckley not guilty by reason of insanity. Hinckley thus joined the ranks of Richard Lawrence, a house painter who shot at Andrew Jackson in 1835, and John Schrank, a saloon-keeper who shot former president Teddy Roosevelt in 1912. Each of these would-be assassins was found not guilty by reason of insanity.

For most Americans, the Hinckley verdict was a shock. For those familiar with the characteristics of the insanity defense, the verdict was less surprising. In the Hinckley case, as in other federal court cases, the prosecution had the burden of proving that the defendant was *sane* beyond a reasonable doubt. Approximately half of the state courts place a similar responsibility on the prosecution. Such a clear-cut demonstration of sanity can be a difficult task, especially when the defendant has exhibited bizarre behavior in other domains.

A jury's acquittal of a criminal defendant by reason of insanity has been a part of the British legal tradition since 1505 (Robitscher & Haynes, 1982). The most important precursor of the modern insanity defense occurred in 1843 in response to the Daniel M'Naghten murder case. M'Naghten shot and killed Edward Drummond, the secretary to British Prime Minister

Robert Peel, while trying to shoot Peel. Because of M'Naghten's apparent delusions of persecution, the jury found him to be not guilty by reason of insanity. The public was appalled by this decision, and their angry outcry forced the British law lords to present a new clarification of the insanity defense. This clarification has come to be known as the *M'Naghten rule:*

> To establish a defense of insanity, it must be proved that at the time of committing the act, the party accused was laboring under such a defect of reason, from disease of the mind, as *not to know the nature and quality of the act he was doing,* or if he did know it, that he did *not know he was doing what was wrong.*

In essence, the M'Naghten test asked, "Did the defendant know right from wrong?" In the late nineteenth century some state and federal courts, dissatisfied with the M'Naghten rule, adopted an alternative test—the *irresistible impulse test.* This test, which had first been applied in Ohio in 1834, emphasized inability to control one's actions. Individuals who committed crimes during a "fit of passion" were considered insane and not guilty under this test.

Until recent years, state and federal courts chose between the M'Naghten test and the irresistible impulse test in determining the sanity of criminal defendants; most courts used the M'Naghten criteria. For a while a third test, called the *Durham test,* was popular, but it was soon replaced in most courts. This test, based on a decision handed down by the Supreme Court in 1954 in *Durham* v. *United States,* stated that individuals are not criminally responsible if their "unlawful act was the product of mental disease or mental defect." This test was meant to offer more flexibility in decisions regarding insanity, but the general criterion of "mental disease" or "mental defect" proved too broad. It could refer to such problems as alcoholism, drug dependence, and conceivably even headaches or ulcers, which were listed as psychophysiological disorders in DSM-I. The Durham test forced courts to rely even more on the interpretations and opinions of clinicians—and these were often contradictory.

In 1955 the American Law Institute (ALI) formulated a penal code that combined elements of all three tests—M'Naghten, irresistible impulse, and Durham. For a short time this code became the most widely accepted legal test of insanity. All federal courts and most state courts applied its criteria, including the court that had jurisdiction over the Hinckley case. The code indicated that

> a person is not responsible for criminal conduct if at the time of such conduct as a result of mental disease or defect he

lacks substantial capacity either to appreciate the criminality (wrongfulness) of his conduct or to conform his conduct to the requirements of law.

The ALI test also clarified a very important point:

> As used in this Article, the term "mental disease or defect" does not include an abnormality manifested only by repeated criminal or otherwise antisocial conduct.

Under previous tests, a defendant's criminal behavior could be cited as a demonstration of "mental disease" or "irresistible impulse." A defense attorney might attempt to demonstrate, for example, that a client's life of crime was sufficient evidence that the client was a "disturbed sociopath." Under the ALI guidelines, there had to be independent indicators of an individual's mental instability.

After the Hinckley verdict, however, there was a public uproar over the ALI guidelines, and a movement to toughen the standards gained momentum among elected officials, lawyers, and mental health professionals. In 1983 the American Psychiatric Association recommended removal of the provision that absolved people of responsibility for criminal acts if they were unable to conform their behavior to the requirements of law, and advised retention only of the wrongfulness criterion — essentially a return to the M'Naghten standard:

> A person charged with a criminal offense should be found not guilty by reason of insanity if it is shown that, as a result of mental disease or mental retardation, he was unable to appreciate the wrongfulness of his conduct at the time of his offense.

> *(APA, 1983, p. 685)*

This revised criminal insanity test was passed by Congress the same year, and now applies to all cases tried in federal courts and about half the state courts. The broader ALI standard is still used in the remaining state courts, except those in Idaho, Montana, and Utah, which have abolished the insanity plea altogether.

Approximately two-thirds of defendants who are acquitted of a crime by reason of insanity receive a diagnosis of schizophrenia when they are hospitalized after their acquittal (Pasewark et al., 1979). Less severe disorders, such as personality disorder, post-traumatic stress disorder, and paraphilia, are not usually considered to support an insanity defense (Wettstein, 1988; Rachlin et al., 1984). Defendants who successfully plead insanity are disproportionately older, white, and female (Zonana, Wells, & Getz, 1990). The crimes for which defendants are found not guilty by reason of in-

sanity vary greatly, but the majority of such acquittals occur in cases of murder (see Figure 21-1).

**Criticisms of the Insanity Defense** Despite the recent revisions of the criteria for a decree of insanity, criticism of the insanity defense continues. One concern arises out of seemingly incompatible assumptions of United States law and the science of human behavior. While United States law assumes that individuals have free will and thus are responsible for their actions, several models of human behavior rest on the assumption that behavior is determined by situational or biological forces acting on the individual. Since "insanity" in criminal cases is a legal and moral judgment and not a scientific one, critics argue that the goals and philosophy of law are incompatible with those of behavioral science (Winslade, 1983).

A second criticism questions the validity of current scientific knowledge of abnormal behavior. During a typical insanity defense trial, the testimony of defense clinicians conflicts with the testimony of clinicians hired by the prosecution (Otto, 1989). To make matters worse, expert clinical witnesses hired by one side may contradict each other. The jury can be faced with a situation in which no two "experts" altogether agree on their diagnostic assessments. Some people see this lack of

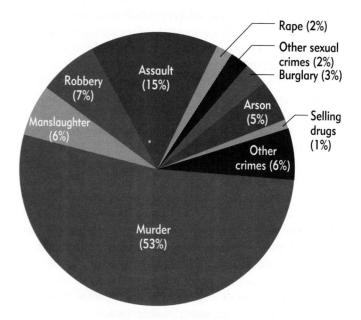

**FIGURE 21-1** Crimes for which persons are found not guilty by reason of insanity. An examination of 239 defendants who were ruled not guilty by reason of insanity in New York State between 1965 and 1976 reveals that 53 percent of these acquittals occurred in cases of murder, 15 percent in assault cases, 7 percent in robbery cases, 2 percent in rape cases, and 1 percent in cases of selling drugs. *(Adapted from Pasewark & Pasewark, 1982; Pasewark et al., 1979.)*

professional consensus as evidence that the clinical field is still too primitive to be influencing the outcome of important legal proceedings. Thomas Szasz (1963) has argued, "The presence or absence of mental illness in an offender cannot be ascertained simply because there are no workable standards of mental health" (p. 137). Many mental health professionals would counter, however, that DSM-III-R now provides a "workable standard" of mental health.

Perhaps the most widespread criticism of the insanity defense is that it systematically allows dangerous criminals to escape punishment. This view was held by former president Richard Nixon, for example, who advocated that the insanity defense be abolished. It is true that some individuals who successfully plead insanity are in fact released from treatment facilities within months of their acquittal. And some legal scholars have argued that unless the insanity defense is abolished throughout the nation, a small but significant number of dangerous criminals will continue to slip through our criminal justice system (Winslade, 1983). Yet it is important to keep in mind that the number of such cases is quite small. In fact, the number of criminal defendants who even enter insanity pleas is relatively small, approximately one in every 1,000 cases. Moreover, research suggests that only a minority of these defendants fake or exaggerate their psychological symptoms (Grossman & Wasyliw, 1988).

During most of our history, the successful insanity plea amounted to the same thing as a long-term prison sentence — indeed, often a longer sentence than a verdict of guilty would have brought (Finkel, 1988; Steadman, 1980). Treatment in a mental hospital wrought little, if any, improvement, and mental health professionals were therefore reluctant to assert that the offender was unlikely to commit a crime again. (As we shall see, the ability to predict dangerousness or the lack of it is not notably widespread among clinicians.) However, the increasing effectiveness of drug therapy in institutions, the growing bias against extended institutionalization, and greater emphasis on patients' rights have led of late to much earlier releases of offenders from mental hospitals — releases that sometimes have proved tragically premature. In Idaho, for example, a young man raped two women and was found not guilty by reason of insanity. After receiving less than a year of treatment, he was released. Soon he was arrested again for shooting a nurse, and convicted of assault with intent to kill. This 1981 case caused an uproar in Idaho that led to the state's abolition of the insanity plea.

**Recent Trends** In recent years several states (Michigan, Indiana, New Mexico, Georgia, Illinois, and Delaware) have started to permit a verdict of "guilty but mentally ill," and almost half of the remaining states are now considering the adoption of a similar option. Defendants who receive this verdict are found to have had a mental illness at the time of their crimes, but the illness was not sufficiently related to the crime to acquit them of the offense. The "guilty but mentally ill" option allows jurors to convict a person they perceive as dangerous while attempting also to ensure that the individual's psychotherapeutic needs will be met.

Unlike the traditional insanity verdict, this new verdict assigns moral blame to the defendant. Defendants found to be guilty but mentally ill are given a prison term with the provision that they will also undergo psychological treatment if necessary. Advocates of this new option see it as a better means of maintaining and defending our society's standards of behavior. Critics of the concept believe that appropriate mental health care should be made available to all prisoners anyway, without any special designation, and point out that there is a much higher prevalence of mental disorders among people in prison than among nonprisoners (see Figure 21-2). Moreover, the new verdict may only confuse a jury already faced with an enormously complex task (Morris, 1983).

Some states allow still another kind of verdict, "guilty with diminished responsibility." Here a defendant's mental instability is viewed as an extenuating circumstance that should be taken into consideration during sentencing. Such a verdict might lead to conviction for a lesser offense, but would not replace conviction altogether. The famous case of Dan White, who killed Mayor George Moscone and City Supervisor Harvey Milk of San Francisco in 1978, illustrates the use of this verdict.

*On the morning of November 27, 1978, Dan White loaded* his .38 caliber revolver. White had recently resigned his position as a San Francisco supervisor because of family and financial pressures. Now, after a change of heart, he wanted his job back. When he asked Mayor George Moscone to reappoint him, however, the mayor refused. Supervisor Harvey Milk was among those who had urged Moscone to keep White out, for Milk was America's first openly gay politician, and Dan White had been an outspoken opponent of measures supporting gay rights.

White avoided the metal detector at City Hall's main entrance by climbing through a basement window after telling construction workers who recognized him that he had forgotten his keys. After they unlocked the window for him, he went straight to the mayor's office. There Moscone greeted him and poured a couple of drinks, perhaps hoping to soothe White's rage at not being reappointed. Neither man had a chance to touch his drink before White pulled out his gun and shot the mayor once in the arm and once in the

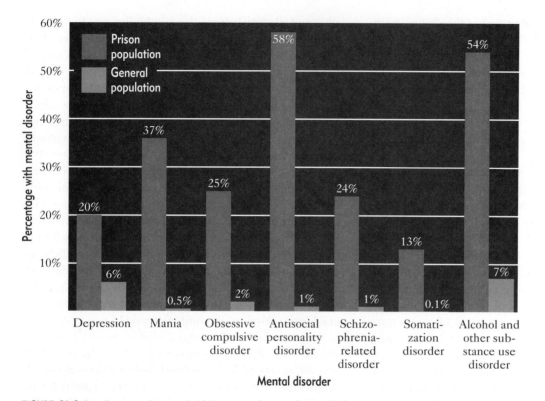

**FIGURE 21-2** Studies reveal a much higher prevalence of mental disorders among prisoners than in the general population. According to one study of 6,350 inmates from federal prisons, depression is three times more common among prisoners, schizophrenia twenty-four times more common, mania thirty-seven times more common, and antisocial personality disorder fifty-eight times more common. *(Adapted from Megargee, 1986, 1977; Megargee & Bohn, 1977.)*

chest. As Moscone lay bleeding on the floor, White walked over to him and, from only inches away, fired twice into Moscone's head.

White then reloaded his gun, ran down the hall, and spotted Harvey Milk. White asked to talk with him. Right after the two men went into White's former office, three more shots rang out. Milk crumpled to the floor. Once again White from point-blank range fired two more bullets into his victim's head. Shortly afterward he turned himself in to the police. Several months later the jury rendered its verdict: Dan White was not guilty of murder, only voluntary manslaughter.

Murder is the illegal killing of a human being with malice aforethought, that is, with the intent to kill. Manslaughter is the illegal killing of a human being *without* malice aforethought. The attacker may intend to harm the victim, but not to kill. If the victim nonetheless dies, the crime is voluntary manslaughter. Involuntary manslaughter is an illegal killing from negligence rather than intentional harm.

How could a man who loaded his pistol with cartridges that explode on impact, who made a conscious effort to avoid the metal detector, and who, finally, walked over to the prone, wounded men and shot each one twice more in

the head — how could such a man be said to have no murderous intent?

The answer lies in the role psychiatry played in the trial. Defense attorney Douglas Schmidt argued that a patriotic, civic-minded man like Dan White — high school athlete, decorated war veteran, former fireman, policeman, and city supervisor — could not possibly have committed such an act unless something had snapped inside him. The brutal nature of the two final shots to each man's head only proved that White had lost his wits. White was not fully responsible for his actions because he suffered from "diminished capacity." Although White killed Mayor George Moscone and Supervisor Harvey Milk, he had not planned his actions. On the day of the shootings, White was mentally incapable of planning to kill, or even of wanting to do such a thing.

Well known in forensic psychiatry circles, Martin Blinder, professor of law and psychiatry at the University of California's Hastings Law School in San Francisco, brought a good measure of academic prestige to White's defense. White had been, Blinder explained to the jury, "gorging himself on junk food: Twinkies, Coca-Cola . . . The more he consumed, the worse he'd feel and he'd respond to his ever-growing depression by consuming ever more junk food." Schmidt later asked Blinder if he could elaborate on this. "Perhaps if it were not for the ingestion of this junk food," Blinder responded, "I would suspect that these homicides would not have taken place." From that moment on, Blinder became known as the author of the Twinkie Defense.

The next psychiatrist, George F. Solomon, further drove home the idea that it was not Dan White but an irritating extraneous influence — something outside himself — that made White do these terrible things. Did White have the capacity to premeditate and deliberate murder? "No," Solomon responded. "Why not?" he was asked. "I don't think that he was capable of permitting himself to plan something so awful." The killings, Solomon told the jury, were the result of "a dissociated state of mind, which means a disruption of the normal integrated functions." White had, Solomon continued, "blocked out of his mind his awareness of his duty to uphold the right."

Dan White was convicted only of voluntary manslaughter, and was sentenced to seven years, eight months. (He was released on parole January 6, 1984.) Psychiatric testimony convinced the jury that White did not wish to kill George Moscone or Harvey Milk.

The angry crowd that responded to the verdict by marching, shouting, trashing City Hall, and burning police cars was in good part homosexual. Gay supervisor Harvey Milk had worked well for their cause, and his loss was a serious setback for human rights in San Francisco. Yet it was not only members of the gay community who were appalled at the outcome. Most San Franciscans shared their feelings of outrage.

*(Coleman, 1984, pp. 65–70)*

Because of possible miscarriages of justice, many legal experts have argued vociferously against the "diminished capacity" defense (Coleman, 1984), and a number of states have eliminated it.

**Sex Offender Statutes**  Ever since 1937, when Michigan enacted the first "sex psychopath" statute, many states have given a special designation to sex offenders (Monahan & Davis, 1983). These states presume that persons who are repeatedly found guilty of certain sex crimes are mentally ill and categorize them as "mentally disordered sex offenders." The Michigan statute, for example, classifies as "sexually delinquent" any person "whose sexual behavior is characterized by repetitive or compulsive acts . . . , by the use of force upon another person in attempting sexual relations . . . , or by the commission of sexual aggression against children under the age of 16." In California 78 percent of the persons designated as mentally disordered sex offenders have been convicted of pedophilia or incest (Sturgeon & Taylor, 1980).

Unlike defendants who have been found not guilty by reason of insanity, individuals classified as mentally disordered sex offenders have been convicted of a criminal offense and are thus judged to be morally responsible for their actions. Nevertheless, the status of a sex offender, like that of a person found not guilty by reason of insanity, implies that commitment to a mental health facility is a more appropriate sentence than imprisonment. In part, such statutes reflect society's conception of sex offenders as sick people. On a practical level, the provisions help prevent the physical abuse that sex offenders sometimes face as ostracized members of prison society.

In 1977 the Group for the Advancement of Psychiatry recommended the repeal of mentally disordered sex offender statutes, and in recent years a growing number of states have modified or abolished such statutes and programs. There are several reasons for this trend. First, many states have found these statutes difficult to act on. Some state statutes, for example, require that a candidate for sex offender status be found "sexually dangerous beyond a reasonable doubt" — a judgment that often goes beyond the clinical field's expertise. Also, there is evidence that racial bias can significantly affect the assignment of sex offender status (Sturgeon & Taylor, 1980). Whites are twice as likely to be granted sex offender status as blacks and Hispanics who have been convicted of similar crimes.

## Criminal Commitment and Incompetence to Stand Trial

Regardless of their state of mind at the time of a crime, defendants may be held to be mentally incompetent to stand trial. The competence provisions have been established to ensure that defendants understand the charges and proceedings they are facing and have "sufficient present ability to consult with" their counsel in preparing and conducting an adequate defense. This minimum standard for competence was specified by the Supreme Court in *Dusky* v. *United States* (1960).

Competence issues typically are raised by the defendant's attorney, although prosecutors and arresting police officers may bring the issue before the court as well. In order to ensure due process, all parties (including the presiding judge) are usually careful to recommend a psychological examination for any defendant who seems to exhibit signs of mental dysfunctioning. They prefer to err on the side of caution because a number of convictions have been reversed on appeal when a defendant's competence was not initially established. When the issue of competence is raised, the judge orders a psychological evaluation, usually on an inpatient basis. Most such evaluations take more than a month to complete (Wexler, 1976). The examiner then presents a written or oral report to the court at a hearing to determine the mental state of the accused. If the court holds that the defendant is incompetent to participate in his or her defense, the individual is assigned to a mental health facility until he or she is competent to stand trial (Bennett & Kish, 1990). It is important to note that many more cases of criminal commitment result from decisions of mental incompetence than from verdicts of not guilty by reason of insanity. On the other hand, the majority of criminals currently institutionalized for psychological treatment in the United States are prison and jail inmates whose mental problems have led officials of correctional institutions to send them to special mental health units within the prison or to mental hospitals for treatment (Monahan & Steadman, 1983; Steadman et al., 1982).

A risk inherent in competence provisions is that an innocent defendant may spend years in a mental health facility without having the opportunity to disprove accusations of criminal conduct in court. Some defendants have served longer "sentences" in mental health facilities than they would have in prison if they had been convicted. The possibility of such abuses was curbed by an important Supreme Court ruling in the case of *Jackson* v. *Indiana* (1972). In this case the Court ruled that a chronically disordered defendant cannot be *indefinitely* committed under criminal status. After a reasonable amount of time, a criminally committed defendant should be either found competent and tried, set free, or transferred to a mental health facility under *civil* commitment procedures. Furthermore, the Court noted that criminal charges may be dismissed if, as in any case, the defendant's right to a speedy trial has been violated.

Until the early 1970s, most states followed the practice of requiring the commitment of mentally incompetent defendants to maximum security institutions for the "criminally insane" (Winick, 1983). Under current law, the courts have greater flexibility in such matters. In some cases, particularly when the charge is a minor one, the defendant may be treated on an outpatient basis.

# LEGAL INFLUENCES ON THE MENTAL HEALTH SYSTEM

The legal system also has had a significant impact on clinical professionals. First, courts and legislatures have developed the process of *civil commitment,* whereby certain individuals can be forced to undergo mental health treatment. Although many persons who show signs of mental disturbances seek treatment voluntarily, a large number are not aware of their problems or are simply not interested in receiving treatment. What are clinicians to do for these individuals? Should they force treatment upon them? Or do people have the right to feel miserable and function ineffectively? The law has addressed this question by providing civil commitment guidelines under which certain persons can be forced into treatment.

Second, the legal system, on behalf of the state, has also taken on the responsibility of specifying and protecting *patients' rights* during treatment. The protection of patients' rights is obviously important for those disturbed individuals who have been involuntarily committed, but it is also important for those who have voluntarily sought institutionalization or even outpatient therapy. The rights that have received the most attention in recent years are the right to receive treatment and the right to refuse treatment.

## Civil Commitment

Every year in the United States large numbers of mentally disturbed persons are involuntarily committed to mental institutions. These commitments have long been a focus of controversy and debate. As you will see, the laws that currently govern the treatment of mentally disturbed persons during civil commitment proceedings bear a resemblance to those governing the treatment of criminal defendants. In some ways, however, the law provides greater protection for the suspected criminal than for the suspected psychotic (Burton, 1990).

**Why Commit?**　When does society allow the involuntary commitment of disturbed individuals? Generally our legal system permits such commitment when one is considered to be in *need of treatment* and *dangerous to oneself or others.* The state's authority to commit disturbed individuals rests on two principles: *parens patriae* and police power (Wettstein, 1988). Under the principle of *parens patriae* ("father of the country"), the state can make decisions, including involuntary hospitalization, that promote the *individual's* best interests and protect him or her from self-harm or self-neglect. Conversely, police power enables the state to protect society from the harm that may be inflicted by a person who is violent or homicidal. Seeking to protect the assumed interests of the individual and society, the state provides treatment to those persons whose disabilities are so severe that they are unable to recognize their needs and to seek treatment voluntarily.

**Current Procedures and Rights**   Statutes governing the civil commitment process vary from state to state. Some basic procedures and rights, however, are common to most of these statutes.

In many cases, formal commitment proceedings are initiated by family members. In response to a son's suicide attempt, for example, his parents may try to persuade him to commit himself to a mental institution. If the son refuses, the parents may go to court and seek an involuntary commitment order. If the son is a minor, the process is simple. The Supreme Court, in the case of *Parham* v. *J.R.* (1979), ruled that a due process hearing is not necessary in such cases. It need only be demonstrated that a mental health professional considers such commitment warranted. If the son is an adult, however, the process is more elaborate. The court will usually order a mental examination and provide the individual with the opportunity to contest the commitment attempt in court. In many states the person has a right to a jury trial on the matter, and the right to be represented by legal counsel.

Although the Supreme Court has offered few guidelines on the procedural aspects of civil commitment, one important decision, rendered in the case of *Addington* v. *Texas* (1979), has outlined the *minimum standard of proof* necessary for commitment. Before this case was decided, each state developed its own standard of proof for commitment. Many states vaguely required a "preponderance of evidence" that commitment was necessary. Some had stricter requirements. Texas, for example, required the presentation of "clear, unequivocal and convincing evidence" of the necessity of commitment. Many persons felt that even this standard was not strict enough and argued that the need for civil commitment should be established "beyond a reasonable doubt" — the standard in criminal cases. This was the standard at issue in *Addington* v. *Texas.* When Addington's mother attempted to have him committed by the state of Texas, he argued that the standard of proof for commitment in Texas was not strict enough. Addington asked the Supreme Court to overturn the state court by mandating that the "beyond a reasonable doubt" standard employed in criminal cases should be applied to his civil commitment case. Addington lost his appeal, but in the course of its decision, the Supreme Court established a Texas-style standard as the appropriate minimum standard for all states. Specifically, it ruled that in order for an individual to be committed, there must be "clear and convincing" proof that the individual is mentally ill and has met the state's criteria for involuntary commitment. The Court was concerned that the "beyond a reasonable doubt" standard employed in criminal cases was too strict for civil commitment cases, given the "fallibility of psychiatric diagnosis." Nevertheless, the Court did establish a new minimum standard of proof for commitment cases that in fact was stricter than the standards then employed in many states.

It is important to note that the Court's "clear and convincing" standard of proof can be applied to a variety of criteria. The ruling does not suggest *what* criteria should be used. This matter is left to the discretion of each state. The ruling determines only the minimum standard of proof that should be applied to whatever commitment criteria the state chooses to enforce.

**Emergency Commitment**   Many situations require immediate action; no one can wait for formal commitment proceedings when a life is at stake. An emergency room patient who is suicidal or suffering from auditory hallucinations that order hostile actions against others may need immediate treatment and round-the-clock supervision. If treatment could not be applied in such situations without the patient's full consent, the consequences could be tragic.

Most states acknowledge that such circumstances may arise. Therefore, many state laws provide attending physicians with the right to order temporary commitment and medication of a patient who is behaving in a bizarre or violent manner. Usually the states require certification by two physicians that such patients are in a state of mind that makes them dangerous to themselves or others. Such certifications are often referred to as

Each segment of the clinical field has its own *forensic specialists* who represent it in the courts and houses of legislature. Forensic psychologists, psychiatrists, and social workers typically receive special training in such duties as evaluating the functioning of criminal defendants, making recommendations concerning patients' rights, and assessing the psychological trauma experienced by crime victims.

*two-physician certificates,* or "2 PCs." Limitations on the length of such emergency commitments vary from state to state. Should the attending physicians determine that a longer period of commitment is necessary, formal commitment proceedings may be initiated.

**Who Is Dangerous?**    Despite popular stereotypes, research suggests that mentally disturbed persons are not generally violent or dangerous (Monahan, 1981; Rabkin, 1979). Because a determination of dangerousness frequently is required for judicial approval of involuntary civil commitment, the reliable and valid determination of who *is* dangerous is of major importance.

Can mental health professionals accurately *predict* who will commit violent acts? The data gathered to date are not very encouraging (Educational Conference on Psychiatry, Psychology, and the Law, 1989; Monahan, 1978; Cocozza & Steadman, 1976; Stone, 1975). Research suggests that psychiatrists and psychologists are wrong more often than right when they predict violence, and even when predicting violence against themselves (see Box 21-1). They frequently overestimate the likelihood that a patient will engage in violent behavior. This body of research is not conclusive, however, because it has usually examined long-term predictions for institutionalized patients who are later released. It may be that the experience of institutionalization reduces such patients' tendency to behave violently.

Are accurate predictions of violent behavior impossible? If so, should dangerousness be excluded as a criterion for commitment? John Monahan (1984), an authority on mental health law, has cautioned against premature conclusions. Monahan points out that much more research is needed before firm conclusions can be drawn. In particular, more studies of short-term predictions of violence — that is, predictions of imminent violence — are needed. It may well be that short-term predictions are more accurate than long-term predictions.

Whether or not practicing clinicians are now accurate predictors of violent behavior, it may be possible to develop new assessment and prediction techniques that are relatively accurate. One group of researchers, for example, conducted a study of short-term predictions of violence among patients in an acute-care psychiatric unit (Werner, Rose, & Yesavage, 1983). Consistent with earlier research, they found that predictions made by individual clinicians were very inaccurate (psychologists and psychiatrists were equally likely to be wrong). The clinicians apparently viewed suspicious, excited, and uncooperative patients as dangerous, although these characteristics are not actually related to violent behavior. The researchers also found that the accuracy of predictions remained low when the predictions of several clinicians were combined. Nevertheless, the investigators were able to demonstrate that clinicians did have

---

BOX 21-1

# Violence against Therapists

Is therapy hazardous to one's health? Indeed it is for some patients. Now it appears that many therapists are at risk as well. Between 12 and 14 percent of therapists have been targets of patients' violence at least once in private therapy, and an even larger percentage have been assaulted in mental hospitals (Tryon, 1987; Bernstein, 1981). The likelihood of being assaulted appears to be equal for female and male therapists.

Patients have used a variety of weapons in their attacks, including such common ones as shoes, lamps, fire extinguishers, and canes. In very serious cases, the ones we occasionally read about in newspapers, patients have used guns or knives and have severely wounded or even killed a therapist.

What are the causes of these attacks? More research is needed, but the surveys conducted to date indicate that some therapists consider themselves at fault; they feel that they may have had a role in provoking the attack (Tryon, 1987; Madden et al., 1976). Inexperienced therapists are more likely to be victims. Many of the assailants have displayed violent behavior before, but only a small minority of therapists were able to anticipate the attacks.

Many therapists who have been attacked, like victims of other kinds of assault, are deeply affected by the incident. They feel anxious and insecure in their work for a long time. They may try to be more selective in accepting patients and look for cues that signal an impending attack. One therapist even studied karate for a year and a half (Tryon, 1987). Unfortunately, lingering feelings of anxiety may affect the outcomes of new therapy cases. Therapists who are focusing on their own safety are concentrating less on the problems of their patients, rendering the patients unwitting victims of the crime as well.

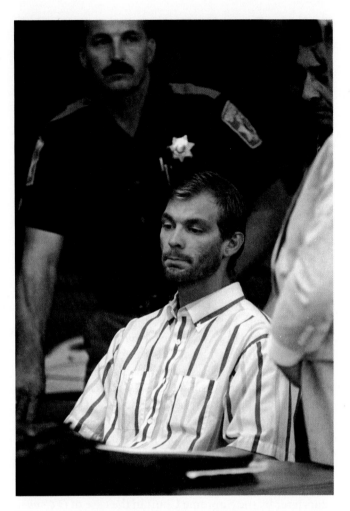

The criminal justice system's ability to predict dangerousness is often tragically inadequate, as we are reminded by the case of Jeffrey Dahmer. In 1988 Dahmer was imprisoned for sexually molesting a 13-year-old boy. In 1990, despite his own father's stated concerns, Dahmer was released with only limited followup. By his own admission, he proceeded to drug, strangle, and dismember at least seventeen additional victims.

information available to them that could increase the accuracy of their predictions if they used it. In particular, individuals who experience hallucinations and exhibit relatively little emotional withdrawal are more likely to assault other people. This research indicates that it may be possible to develop objective assessment techniques that have more predictive power than the subjective judgments of clinicians.

**Criticisms of Civil Commitment** Civil commitment has been criticized on several grounds. The criterion of dangerousness is one bone of contention. If judgments of dangerousness are often inaccurate, why should such judgments be used as grounds to deprive someone of liberty? The American Civil Liberties Union has

strongly criticized the use of such assessments in commitment cases (Ennis & Emory, 1978).

A related problem is that legal definitions of "mental illness" and "dangerousness" are frequently vague. The terms may be defined so broadly that they can be applied to individuals whom the evaluators view as simply undesirable or inferior. It has been argued that involuntary commitment standards have sometimes been applied to people whose only offenses are bouncing checks, spending too much money, living unconventional lifestyles, and holding unpopular political opinions (Wexler, 1981).

A further problem with involuntary civil commitment lies with the sometimes questionable therapeutic value of commitment itself. Research suggests that many persons committed involuntarily do not respond well to psychotherapy (Wanck, 1984). Perceptions of choice and control and personal commitment may be important determinants of successful outcome in a therapeutic setting (Langer 1983; Cooper & Axsom, 1982).

On the basis of these and other arguments, Thomas Szasz (1977, 1963) has argued that involuntary commitment should be abolished. As we saw earlier, Szasz views the label of mental illness as arbitrary and usually unjustified. Because of the ambiguities of diagnosis, he says, the biases of the practitioner and of the society rather than scientific facts are the major determinants of clinical evaluations. He and others believe that individuals who demonstrate by their behavior that they are truly dangerous are best dealt with through the criminal justice system.

Many civil libertarians are sympathetic to Szasz's argument that involuntary commitment can be abused for purposes of coercive control (Morse, 1982; Ennis & Emory, 1978). Indeed, such abuses by the state have been reported frequently in the Soviet Union and other countries, where mental hospitals have been used routinely to incarcerate political dissidents (Bonnie, 1990).

**Trends in Civil Commitment** The acceptance of broad involuntary commitment statutes probably reached its peak in 1962, when a Supreme Court ruling encouraged placement in mental health facilities instead of prisons for individuals whose unacceptable behavior seemed to be caused by psychological dysfunctioning. In the case of *Robinson* v. *California*, the Court ruled that the sentencing of drug addicts to correctional institutions may violate the Constitution's ban on cruel and unusual punishment, and it recommended involuntary civil commitment to a mental hospital as a more reasonable action. This ruling encouraged the application of civil commitment proceedings against many kinds of "social deviants" at a time when the laws governing such procedures were vague or nonexistent.

In the years immediately following this ruling civil commitment procedures granted far fewer rights to "defendants" than did criminal courts. It was particularly difficult for involuntarily committed patients to obtain their release. Substantial legal assistance was often needed. The persistent overprediction of dangerousness by clinicians exacerbated this problem.

During the late 1960s, the plight of the committed was increasingly publicized by reporters, novelists, and civil libertarians who were convinced that numerous persons were being committed unjustifiably. As the public became more aware of the problems surrounding involuntary commitment, state legislatures started to enact narrower standards for commitment. These statutory revisions of the late 1960s and early 1970s had a significant impact on the rate of involuntary commitment (Wanck, 1984). Commitment rates declined while release rates increased. Furthermore, the bulk of court decisions favored the broadening of patients' rights, including an elaboration of the commitment hearing process.

Criticisms of the criteria for dangerousness also increased during this time, and many jurisdictions modified their commitment standards to require the demonstration of *imminent* dangerousness. Short-term predictions of dangerousness are now used in most states as justification for short-term emergency commitment. In addition, many states adopted more specific definitions of dangerousness itself, in some cases spelling out the specific types of behavior that must be observed before such a diagnosis can be made.

These changes have continued to influence commitment rates and procedures; however, recent rulings and statutes suggest that the pendulum may be swinging back in the other direction. Concerned that commitment criteria have become too narrow, some states have started to broaden their criteria once again (Belcher & Blank, 1990; Fernandez & Nygard, 1990; Wanck, 1984; Wexler, 1983). Whether this movement actually represents a return to the vague commitment procedures of past years and whether such a trend is in fact advantageous for disturbed individuals and society will become clearer in the coming years.

## Protecting Patients' Rights

Over the past two decades the legal rights of mental patients have been significantly expanded by influential court decisions and state and federal legislation. The rights that have received the most attention have been the *right to treatment* and the *right to refuse treatment*.

**The Right to Treatment** Theoretically, some individuals are so mentally disturbed that they are unable to recognize their need for treatment. Involuntary commitment procedures afford the state a means to provide care for these individuals. A risk inherent in such provisions, however, is that individuals may be deprived of their liberty without receiving any beneficial treatment. If the state does not provide the treatment that motivated commitment in the first place, mental institutions become mere prisons for the unconvicted.

Faced with the inadequacies of large state mental institutions, some patients and their legal representatives began in the 1960s and 1970s to demand the treatment they felt the state was obligated to provide. A suit filed on these grounds on behalf of institutionalized patients in Alabama led to an important landmark in the battle for patients' rights. In the 1972 case of *Wyatt* v. *Stickney*, a federal court ruled that the state was constitutionally obligated to provide "adequate treatment" to all persons who had been committed involuntarily. Because conditions in the state hospitals were so deplorable, the presiding judge laid out specific goals that had to be met by state administrators. The court ordered Alabama to provide more therapists, better living conditions, more privacy, opportunities for heterosexual interaction and physical exercise, and a more judicious use of physical restraint and medication. Many of these standards have since been adopted in other court jurisdictions.

Another important decision was handed down three years later by the Supreme Court in the case of *O'Connor* v. *Donaldson*. After being confined in a Florida mental institution for fourteen years, Kenneth Donaldson sued for release. Throughout his confinement Donaldson had repeatedly sought release but had been overruled by the institution's psychiatrists. Indeed, Donaldson and his fellow patients had been largely ignored by the staff and allowed a bare minimum of personal freedom. His only communication with the outside world had been through the few letters he received and the ones he was able to smuggle out. Furthermore, Donaldson had been initially committed on highly questionable grounds. Despite evidence to the contrary, his father had claimed that his son was dangerous.

Donaldson argued that he was not dangerous and that the facility in which he was confined did not provide adequate treatment. The Supreme Court ruled in favor of Donaldson, fined the hospital's superintendent, and ruled that such institutions must engage in periodic reviews of their patients' cases. The justices also stated unanimously that the state "cannot constitutionally confine . . . a nondangerous individual who is capable of surviving safely in freedom by himself *or with the help of willing and responsible family members or friends.*"

Donaldson did have a friend who had repeatedly agreed to take him into his custody. The *Donaldson* case attracted a great deal of publicity. In addition to setting an important legal precedent, it helped focus attention on the plight of people committed to mental institutions.

A more recent case of importance, *Youngberg* v. *Romeo* (1982), provided support for the right to treatment while cautioning courts against becoming too involved in the exact methods of treatment. The Supreme Court ruled that persons committed involuntarily have a constitutional right to "reasonably non-restrictive confinement conditions" as well as conditions of "reasonable care and safety." In contrast to the earlier lower-court decision in *Wyatt* v. *Stickney*, however, this decision provided only a crude outline of minimum standards for institutions.

Some people were concerned that the *Youngberg* decision signaled a slowing of the pace of court-mandated reforms and of the Supreme Court's involvement in mental health issues. In this decision the Court noted the expertise of mental health professionals and suggested that treatment decisions should be assumed to be valid until proved otherwise. Such a perspective seemed to indicate that the justices were unwilling to support a significant expansion of the judicial system's involvement in the daily affairs of mental health institutions. The ruling also suggested that mental health professionals could rely largely on their professional judgment when they formulated systematic treatment procedures. To make sure that mental patients did not lose the rights they had gained throughout the 1970s, Congress passed the Protection and Advocacy for Mentally Ill Individuals Act in 1986 (Woodside & Legg, 1990). This law established *protection and advocacy* systems in all states and U.S. territories and gave advocates and lawyers who worked for patients within the system the power to investigate possible cases of patient abuse and neglect, and to address these problems legally. In recent years public advocates have argued that the right to treatment should be extended to the tens of thousands of severely mentally disturbed persons who keep being released from hospitals after a short stay and are essentially sent to the streets to care for themselves. The advocates are suing federal and state agencies across the country, demanding that they fulfill the promises of the community mental health movement.

**The Right to Refuse Treatment**   During the past two decades the courts have also established that patients, particularly those in institutions, have the right to refuse certain forms of treatment. The courts have been reluctant to issue a single general ruling on this issue because the range of treatment methods is so broad. A ruling based on one form of treatment would be likely to affect other treatments in unintended ways. Thus specific treatments have been targeted in various court rulings.

Most of the "right to refuse treatment" rulings have centered on *biological treatments* — treatments that are easier to impose on patients without their cooperation and that often seem more intrusive, aversive, and hazardous than psychotherapy. For example, state rulings have consistently granted patients the right to refuse psychosurgery, the form of physical treatment considered most clearly irreversible and therefore most dangerous.

As we saw in Chapter 9, some states have also acknowledged a patient's right to refuse electroconvulsive therapy (ECT), the treatment used in many cases of unipolar depression. The issue is much more arguable with regard to ECT than with respect to psychosurgery. ECT is highly effective for many severely depressed persons. On the other hand, ECT is an aversive form of treatment that has been criticized by a number of recipients and that has a potential for misuse and abuse, as many media reports, books, and movies have made clear. Stories such as Nan's are not uncommon:

*W*henher private psychiatrist told her to enter a psychiatric hospital for shock treatment, she reluctantly agreed. After entering the hospital, however, she changed her mind. Despite her protests, she was given shock treatment and experienced the usual effects of confusion and memory loss. After a few shocks, however, her wish to stop the treatment became so strong that she said to a nurse, "I just have to get out of here. I'm leaving no matter what you say." It was then that she escaped.

When the psychiatrist who had sent her to the hospital found out that Nan had run away, he telephoned her at home and said he would call the police if she did not return to the hospital. Under this pressure she returned, telling the nurses, "I really don't want to be here; I feel like I'm being forced to have shock. The doctor said if I didn't come back he'd send the police after me." Despite these events, her readmission was called voluntary, with no mention of her documented fear of shock treatment, of her desire not to be in the hospital, or of the threat of police intervention. She received more shock treatment during her second hospitalization, until she fled once more.

*(Coleman, 1984, pp. 166–167)*

Today states vary in the degree to which they allow patients to refuse ECT. Some continue to permit ECT to be imposed on committed patients, others require the consent of a third party in such cases, and still others grant patients — particularly voluntary patients — the right to refuse ECT. In these latter states ECT can usually be administered only after patients are informed fully about the nature of the treatment and give their written consent to it.

In the past, patients have not had the right to refuse psychotropic *medications*. States viewed these drugs as a benign form of treatment that often helped and rarely hurt patients. As we have seen repeatedly, however, this perception of drug treatments turns out to have been naive. Many psychotropic drugs, particularly antipsychotic drugs, are exceedingly powerful and sometimes produce such dangerous effects as tardive dyskinesia. As these unwanted effects have become more apparent, some states have granted patients the right to refuse medication.

Two leading federal cases have led the way on the "right to refuse medication" issue—*Rennie* v. *Klein* (1979, 1981) in New Jersey and *Rogers* v. *Okin* (1979, 1980, 1981) in Massachusetts. Typically in states that recognize a patient's right to refuse medication, the purpose and intent of medications must be explained to patients and written consent obtained from them. If the patient's refusal is considered incompetent, dangerous, or irrational, it can be overturned by an independent psychiatrist, medical committee, or local court (Wettstein, 1988). However, the refusing patient is supported in this review process by legal counsel or a patient advocate.

**Other Rights of Patients**     The rights to receive treatment and to refuse treatment have attracted the most attention, but they are not the only patient rights to have been safeguarded by court decisions over the past few decades. In the 1973 case of *Sounder* v. *Brennan,* for example, a district court ruled that patients who perform work in mental institutions must receive payment in accordance with the Fair Labor Standards Act. In 1976 the Supreme Court ruled that this right applied in private mental institutions but not in state hospitals.

A district court ruled in the 1974 case of *Stoner* v. *Miller* that patients released from state mental hospitals have a right to live in community "adult homes." As we discussed earlier, many patients released under the policy of deinstitutionalization have encountered inadequate treatment and poor residential opportunities in the community. As an extension of their guaranteed right to treatment, *Stoner* v. *Miller* and other court decisions during the 1970s have acknowledged the right of such individuals to aftercare and to an appropriate community residence.

Finally, a district court ruled in the 1975 case of *Dixon* v. *Weinberger* that individuals whose mental dysfunction is not severe enough to require confinement in a mental institution have a right to treatment in less restrictive facilities. If an available community mental health

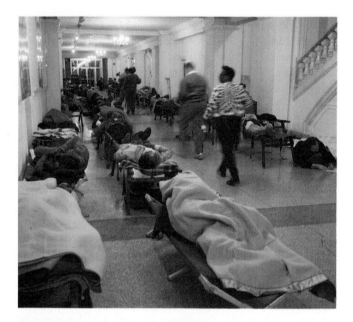

Although "guaranteed" the right to live in community adult homes, chronic mental patients often receive no treatment or guidance and wind up on the streets or in public shelters, such as this shelter for the homeless in Washington, D.C.

center inpatient program or halfway house is the appropriate treatment facility, then that is the facility to which the individual should be committed, not a mental hospital.

**The "Rights" Debate**     Few would argue with the intent of these guaranteed patient rights. Obviously, disturbed people do not cease to be human beings, and as such they have civil rights that must be considered and protected at all times. However, many clinicians express concern that these guaranteed rights sometimes lead to undesirable outcomes and may even serve to deprive patients of opportunities for effective recovery. Consider the right to refuse medication. Many clinicians believe that this right or the procedures needed to safeguard it may deprive some patients of a faster, more complete recovery. If medications can help bring about a schizophrenic patient's recovery, does not the patient have the right to that recovery? If confusion guides patients to refuse medication, can clinicians in good conscience go along with that refusal and delay medication while legal channels are cleared? Psychologist Marilyn Whiteside (1983) raises similar concerns in her description of a 25-year-old mentally retarded patient:

*He was 25 and severely retarded. And after his favorite* attendant left, he became self-abusive. He beat his fists against the side of his head until a football helmet had to be ordered for his protection. Then he clawed at his face and gouged out one of his eyes.

The institution psychologists began a behavior program that had mildly aversive consequences: they squirted warm water in his face each time he engaged in self-abuse. When that didn't work, they requested permission to use an electric prod. The Human Rights Committee vetoed this "excessive and inhumane form of correction" because, after all, the young man was retarded, not criminal.

Since nothing effective could be done that abridged the rights and negated the dignity of the developmentally disabled patient, he was verbally reprimanded for his behavior—and allowed to push his thumb through his remaining eye. He is now blind, of course, but he has his rights and presumably his dignity.

*(Whiteside, 1983, p. 13)*

Similar questions can even be raised about the right of patients to a minimum wage. Although this court ruling correctly tries to protect patients from being taken advantage of by institutions, it may also disrupt the effectiveness of reputable behavioral token economy programs (Glynn, 1990). These hospital programs may wish to reward patients' work with hospital privileges, social rewards, and other nonmonetary rewards. While monetary reinforcement may be effective for some patients, nonmonetary rewards may be more effective for others. By depriving such programs of a highly flexible reward system, a mandated minimum wage may reduce a patient's chances for recovery.

On the other side of the argument, it must be pointed out that the clinical field has not always monitored itself in these areas of patients' rights. Over the years, many treatment programs have administered medications and other biological treatments carelessly, excessively, or harmfully (Garber, 1979; Crane, 1973). Similarly, many institutions have misused patients' labor. So the courts and state legislatures have stepped in. Legislator William Keating, describing the initial reactions of clinicians to his proposed regulations in California, said, "There were a lot of bruised egos, a lot of people saying that doctors should regulate themselves. I said, That's right, you should, but haven't been. That's why we are."

One must also ask whether the field's present state of knowledge and expertise justifies allowing clinicians to override patients' rights. That is, can clinicians confidently say that certain treatments will indeed help patients? And can they predict and overcome the potential unwanted effects of certain forms of treatment? Since today's clinicians themselves often are in conflict concerning these issues, it seems appropriate that patients, their advocates, and impartial evaluators continue to play significant roles in the decision-making process.

# OTHER CLINICAL-LEGAL INTERACTIONS

Mental health and legal professionals may also influence each other's work in other ways. During the past two decades, for example, their paths have crossed in three new areas: malpractice suits, jury selection, and the scope of clinical practice.

## Malpractice Suits

The number of lawsuits against therapists has risen so sharply in recent years that clinicians have coined new terms for the fear of being sued: they now are increasingly subject to "litigaphobia" and "litigastress." About 16 percent of psychiatrists have been sued (AMA, 1987), although the percentage of psychologists and social workers who have been sued appears to be much smaller. Events that precipitate claims against clinicians include attempted suicide, sexual activity with a patient, failure to obtain informed consent for a treatment, negligent drug therapy, improper termination of treatment, and wrongful commitment.

Improper termination of treatment was at issue in a highly publicized case involving an Alabama state hospital in 1985. Two and a half months after a man being treated for alcohol-related depression was released from the hospital, he shot and killed a new acquaintance in a motel lounge. He was convicted of murder and sentenced to life in prison. The victim's father, claiming negligence, filed a civil suit against a psychologist, physician, and social worker at the state hospital, and after two years of legal action was awarded a total of almost $7 million by a jury. The state supreme court later overturned the verdict, saying that a state hospital is entitled to a certain degree of immunity in such cases.

Two investigators studied the effects of this case on subsequent decisions to release patients from the state hospital (Brodsky & Poythress, 1990). They found that the hospital had released 11 percent of its patients during the six months before the lawsuit was filed and 10 percent during the two years it was being litigated, compared to a release of only 7 percent of its patients during the six months following the verdict. Although judgments about a patient's improvement are supposed to be made on their own merits, they were apparently being affected by a heightened fear of litigation at this hospital. Clearly civil malpractice suits are capable of having significant effects on clinical decisions and practice, for better or for worse.

## Jury Selection

During the past fifteen years more and more lawyers have been turning to clinicians for advice on conducting trials (Gottschalk, 1981). A relatively new breed of clinical specialists, often known as "jury specialists," now advise lawyers on which prospective jurors are likely to favor their side and on what procedures and strategies are likely to win jurors' support during trials. The clinical specialists make their suggestions on the basis of surveys, interviews, statistical analyses of correlations between jurors' backgrounds and attitudes, and laboratory simulations of upcoming trials. It is not clear that such clinical advice is more valid than a lawyer's instincts, or indeed that either group's judgments are particularly accurate. Because some lawyers believe that clinical advice is useful, however, clinical professionals are influencing these legal procedures and decisions.

## The Scope of Clinical Practice

During the past few years the legislative and judicial systems have also helped to alter the boundaries that distinguish one clinical profession from another. In particular, they have given more authority to psychologists and effectively blurred the line that once separated psychiatry from psychology. In late 1989 Congress passed a group of bills that permitted psychologists to receive direct reimbursements from Medicare for treating elderly and disabled people. Until then, only psychiatrists received such payments. In late 1990 the California Supreme Court ruled that psychologists could admit patients to the state's hospitals, a power previously held only by psychiatrists *(California Association of Psychology Providers* v. *Rank)*. And in 1991 Congress empowered the Department of Defense (DOD) to explore the most significant boundary of all between the two professions — the authority to prescribe drugs, heretofore denied to psychologists. DOD has set up a two-year training program for Army psychologists in which they are prescribing drugs for a broad range of mental problems while under supervision. Independent practitioners will assess the performance at the end of the trial period and recommend to Congress that they expand or curtail the program. Right now, the issue centers on the military, where there is a severe shortage of mental health services. The Army, for instance, has only 110 psychologists and 180 psychiatrists to serve 700,000 persons on active military duty. But everyone in the clinical field recognizes the much larger implications of the trial program and of Congress's ultimate decision.

This blurring of professional boundary lines is not just a matter of the legislative and judicial systems taking it upon themselves to alter the activities of clinical professionals. In fact, psychologists have actively organized around this issue, built their case, and lobbied for each of the decisions that have increased their power, and psychiatrists have lobbied just as hard against the decisions. In each instance clinicians have sought the involvement of other institutions, and each demonstrates how intertwined the mental health system is with the various other institutions of society.

# SELF-REGULATION: ETHICS AND THE MENTAL HEALTH FIELD

Discussions of the legal and mental health systems may sometimes give the impression that clinicians are uncaring practitioners who address patients' rights and needs only when being monitored by outside forces. This, of course, is not the case. Most clinicians are very much aware of and concerned about the subtle human issues that pervade their work. They strive to help clients and at the same time respect their rights and dignity.

But clinicians do face considerable obstacles in the pursuit of these goals. First, patients' rights and proper care raise complex questions that do not have simple or obvious answers. Different clients and therapists, the latter guided by their diverse perspectives, may indeed arrive at different answers to such questions. Second, clinicians, like other professionals, often have difficulty appreciating the full impact of their actions or altering the system in which they work. For example, the quality of institutional care afforded mental patients during the first half of this century is now viewed as a dark chapter in the field's history. But although the poor therapy, the inhumanity, and the abuses that characterized such care may be apparent now, they were not so obvious then. Indeed, thousands of conscientious and caring clinicians contributed to this very system — partly because they did not appreciate how misguided the system was and partly because they felt helpless to change it.

A third problem is that some clinicians are indeed self-serving and even immoral. Like other professions, the clinical field includes at least a few practitioners who place their own needs and wishes above those of others. For the integrity of the profession and the protection of individuals, such professionals need to be monitored and regulated.

Clinicians do not rely exclusively on the legislative and court systems to address such obstacles to proper and effective clinical practice. They also regulate themselves by continually thinking about, developing, and revising ethical guidelines for members of the field. Often legal decisions simply place the power of law behind these professional guidelines.

Each profession within the mental health field has a code of ethics. The code of the American Psychological Association exemplifies the kinds of issues with which the various mental health professions are concerned. The psychologists' code of ethics begins with a basic principle: "Psychologists know that they bear a heavy social responsibility because their recommendations and professional actions may alter the lives of others" (APA, 1981). The code, revised in 1981 and further amended in 1990, addresses a number of specific points.

1. *Psychologists are now permitted to offer advice* in self-help books, television and radio programs, newspaper and magazine articles, and other nontraditional settings, provided they do so responsibly and professionally and use the most current relevant data. Past codes sanctioned only the traditional formats of psychotherapy.
2. *The amended code (APA, 1990) prohibits psychologists from engaging in fraudulent research or distorting, fabricating, misrepresenting, or biasing their results.* They may not suppress disconfirming data, and should acknowledge alternative hypotheses and explanations of their findings. During the past fifteen years a number of cases of scientific fraud or misconduct have been uncovered in all of the sciences, including abnormal psychology. These acts have led to misunderstandings of important issues, led scientific inquiries in the wrong direction, and undermined public trust. Unfortunately, the effects of research misconduct are hard to undo, even after a retraction. The impressions created by false findings may continue to influence the thinking of both the public and other scientists for years (Pfeifer & Snodgrass, 1990).
3. *Psychologists are also prohibited from exploiting the trust and dependency of clients and students, sexually or otherwise.* This guideline is meant to address the broad societal problem of sexual harassment, as well as the problem of therapists who take sexual advantage of clients in therapy. In the amended ethics code (APA, 1990), psychologists are specifically prohibited from engaging in sexual intimacies with either current or former therapy clients.

    Recent years have seen an increase in the number of clients who have told state licensing boards of sexual misconduct by their therapist or sued their therapist for such behavior. Some cases in point:

Two women patients brought claims against the same male psychologist in the mid-1980s for having sex during treatment, which he claimed was for "therapeutic benefit." In the first case, settled out of court in 1985, the patient sued for sexual misconduct, emotional distress, pain and loss of self-esteem. . . . In the second case, the patient sued the therapist for sexual misconduct, breach of contract and assault and battery. The cases were settled out of court.

A woman sued a husband-and-wife psychotherapy team for sexual misconduct and mental and physical discomfort. The patient said sex with the male therapist resulted in a pregnancy and subsequent abortion, and that the woman therapist also inappropriately cuddled her. The case was settled out of court.

*(Youngstrom, 1990, p. 21)*

Clients may suffer extensive emotional damage from such betrayals of trust. Indeed, a growing number of therapists are now treating clients whose primary problem is that they have previously been sexually abused in some manner by a therapist (Pope & Vetter, 1991).

How many therapists actually have a sexual relationship with a client? A 1977 study found that 12.1 percent of male and 2.6 percent of female psychologists admitted having sexual conduct with patients (Holroyd & Brodsky, 1977). In a survey conducted ten years later, 3.6 percent of male psychologists and 0.5 percent of female psychologists anonymously reported sexual relationships with patients (Pope, Tabachnick, & Keith-Spiegel, 1987). And a 1989 survey of 4,800 therapists revealed that 0.9 percent of male therapists and 0.2 percent of female therapists had sexual contact with patients (Borys & Pope, 1989).

The steady decline in sexual misconduct by therapists revealed in these studies may indicate that fewer therapists are in fact having sexual relationships with patients, either because of a growing recognition of the inappropriateness of such behavior or because of growing fear of the legal and professional consequences of such actions (Pope & Bouhoutsos, 1986; Walker & Young, 1986). Alternatively, today's therapists may simply be less willing to admit, even anonymously, the misbehavior that is a felony in a growing number of states.

As we have seen, the amended code of ethics (APA, 1990) prohibits psychologists to enter into sexual relationships with past patients as well as those they are currently treating. Some therapists make a distinction on this point, however, and believe that a sexual relationship with a former client may be acceptable under certain circumstances, especially when therapy ended at least a year before the relationship began. In one survey, 11 percent of 395 randomly selected psychologists admitted having had a sexual relationship with a former patient (Akamatsu, 1989).

Although the vast majority of therapists control and keep their sexual conduct within appropriate professional bounds, their ability to control private feelings and thoughts is apparently another story. In one survey, 72 percent of therapists reported engaging in sexual fantasy about a client, although most said that this was a rare occurrence (Pope et al., 1987). In another survey close to 90 percent reported having been sexually attracted to a client, at least on occasion (Pope et al., 1986). Although relatively few of these therapists acted on their feelings, 63 percent felt guilty, anxious, or concerned about the attraction.

4. *Confidentiality* has long been one of the most important features of therapy. For a client's peace of mind and to facilitate effective therapy, clients must be able to trust that their private exchanges with a therapist will not be disclosed to others. *Thus the APA code of ethics states, "Psychologists have a primary obligation to respect the confidentiality of information obtained from persons in the course of their work as psychologists."*

There are times, however, when the principle of complete confidentiality must be compromised. A therapist in training, for example, may need to discuss cases on a regular basis with a supervisor. This practice is common, and clients are usually informed when such procedures are in effect. A second exception may arise in cases of outpatients who are clearly dangerous, even homicidal. In such cases, a therapist may breach confidentiality to initiate involuntary commitment proceedings.

A further qualification of the confidentiality principle has been added as the result of a 1974 ruling by the California Supreme Court in the case of *Tarasoff* v. *Regents of the University of California,* considered one of the most important court decisions affecting client–therapist relationships. The *Tarasoff* case concerned a mental health outpatient at a University of California hospital who confided to his therapist that he wanted to harm his former girlfriend, Tanya Tarasoff. Several days after terminating therapy, the former patient fulfilled his promise. He stabbed Tanya Tarasoff to death.

Should confidentiality have been breached in this case? The therapist, in fact, felt that it should. Campus police were notified, but the patient was released after some questioning. In their suit

against the hospital and therapist, the victim's parents argued that these measures were insufficient. They argued that *they* and *their daughter* should have been *warned by the therapist* that the patient intended to harm Ms. Tarasoff. The court agreed. According to the court, "The protective privilege ends where the public peril begins."

In addition to mandating a breach of confidentiality, this ruling requires the therapist to perform an extremely difficult feat: to determine when "a patient poses a serious danger of violence to others." In partial concession to the *Tarasoff* ruling, the APA code of ethics declares that therapists should

reveal confidential information only with the formal consent of the person or the person's legal representative, except in those unusual circumstances in which a psychologist reasonably determines that releasing the information is necessary to prevent a clear danger to the person or other persons or if warranted and appropriate to comply with a legal requirement.

Since the *Tarasoff* ruling, California's courts have further clarified the therapist's duty to protect unsuspecting people from a client (Greenberg, 1987). The courts have held that this duty applies only when the intended victim is identified or readily identifiable, rather than a member of the general public *(Thompson* v. *County of Alameda).* The courts have also held that therapists are obligated to protect persons who are in close proximity to a client's intended victim and thus in danger *(Hedlund* v. *Collson).* A child, for example, is likely to be endangered when a client assaults the child's mother. Finally, the California courts have held that the duty does not apply when violence is unforeseeable or when the object of a client's intended violence is property rather than a person. Although the *Tarasoff* principles technically apply only to therapists in California, a number of other states have either adopted the courts' rulings or modified them (Pietrofesa et al., 1990; Bloom, 1990). Some states, however, have rejected them.

Many therapists were initially resistant to this whole notion, but surveys indicate that most now accept the legitimacy and ethics of breaking confidentiality in order to prevent danger (Pope et al., 1987). More than 90 percent of surveyed psychologists view this action as ethical in cases involving suicide, child abuse, or homicide. Moreover, 79 percent report having broken confidentiality in their own cases when the client was suicidal, 62 percent when child abuse was occurring, and 58 percent when the client was homicidal.

# MENTAL HEALTH, BUSINESS, AND ECONOMICS

The legislative and judicial systems are not the only institutions with which mental health professionals interact. Among the others that influence and are influenced by clinical practice and study are the business and economic institutions.

## Business and Mental Health

The National Institute for Occupational Safety and Health (NIOSH) lists psychological disorders as among the ten leading work-related diseases and injuries in the United States (Millar, 1984). The business world has worked closely with mental health professionals to help identify the extent of psychological problems in the work force and their influence on workers' performance (Millar, 1990, 1984). It has also turned to clinical professionals to help develop programs to prevent and rem-

edy such problems (NIOSH, 1988, 1985). Two programs that have gained broad acceptance in the past decade are employee assistance programs and stress-reduction and problem-solving seminars.

*Employee assistance programs* are run either by mental health professionals who are employed directly by a company or by consulting mental health agencies. Companies publicize the availability of such services in the workplace, educate workers about mental dysfunctioning, and teach supervisors how to identify and refer workers who are in psychological trouble. Businesses believe that employee assistance programs save them money in the long run by preventing psychological problems from interfering with work performance and by cutting down on the costs of mental health insurance.

In *stress-reduction* and *problem-solving seminars,* mental health professionals run workshops or group sessions to teach employees coping, problem-solving, and stress-reduction techniques. Programs are just as likely to be organized for higher-level executives as for middle-level managers and assembly-line workers. Often groups of workers are required to attend such workshops, which may run for several days, and given

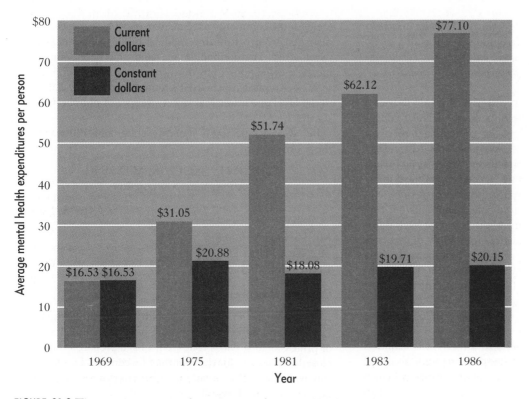

**FIGURE 21-3** The average amount of money spent for mental health services annually per person in the United States increased almost fivefold from $16.53 in 1969 to $77.10 in 1986. However, when adjustments are made for inflation and expenditures are stated in 1969 dollars, the amount spent per person rose more modestly, from $16.53 to $20.15 in 1986. *(Adapted from Witkin et al., 1990, p. 8.)*

time off from their jobs in order to do so. Again, the expectation of businesses is that these programs will save money by helping workers develop coping skills that led to a healthier state of mind, less dysfunctioning on the job, and better job performance.

## Economics and Mental Health

We have already seen how government-level economic decisions influence the mental health field's treatment of schizophrenic people. The desire by state and federal governments to reduce expenses has been a major consideration in the deinstitutionalization programs around the country, which have contributed to the premature release of hospital patients to communities unprepared to provide the needed treatment. Economic considerations affect other kinds of clients and forms of treatment as well.

At first glance, funding for mental health services seems to have risen sharply in the United States over the past two decades. A total of $18.5 billion was spent on such services in 1986, compared to $3.3 billion in 1969 (Witkin et al., 1990). However, if adjustments are made for inflation and findings are stated in 1969 dollars, the 1986 expenditure is $4.8 billion, a relatively modest rise from the 1969 total (see Figure 21-3). Thus, although the number of persons in need of or seeking therapy has increased significantly, funding for such services is not currently increasing. In fact, it peaked in 1975. This

---

**BOX 21-2**

# The Itemized Statement in Clinical Psychiatry: A New Concept in Billing

*(In this article, by Robert S. Hoffman, M.D., which originally appeared in* The Journal of Irreproducible Results, *1980, the psychiatrist's biting wit is equaled only by his sense of outrage over the growing demands made by insurance companies.)*

Due to the rapidly escalating costs of health care delivery, there has been increasing pressure on physicians to document and justify their charges for professional services. This has created a number of serious problems, particularly in the field of psychiatry. Chief among these is the breach of confidentiality that arises when sensitive clinical information is provided to third-party insurance carriers, e.g. the patient's diagnosis or related details about his/her psychiatric disorder. Even when full disclosure of such information is made, insurance carriers frequently deny benefits because the description of the treatment appears imprecise or inadequate. There also has been some criticism of the standard hourly fee-for-service, the argument being that psychiatrists, like other medical specialists, should be required to adjust their fees depending upon the particular treatment offered.

In view of these considerations, a method is required which will bring psychiatric billing in line with accepted medical practice. The procedure illustrated below, which we have successfully employed in our clinic for the past two years, achieves this goal. It requires only a modest investment in time and effort: the tape-recording of all psychotherapy sessions, transcription of tapes, tabulation of therapeutic interventions, and establishment of a relative value scale for the commonly used maneuvers. This can easily be managed by two full-time medical billing personnel per psychiatrist. The method, in our hands, has been found to increase collections from third-party carriers by 65% and to raise a typical psychiatrist's annual net income almost to the level of a municipal street sweeper or plumber's assistant.

Below is a specimen monthly statement illustrating these principles:

CALVIN L. SKOLNIK, M.D., INC.
A Psychiatry Corporation

Jan. 5, 1978

Mr. Sheldon Rosenberg
492 West Maple Dr.
East Orange, N.J.

Dear Mr. Rosenberg:

In response to the request by your insurer, Great Lakes Casualty and Surety Co., for more precise documentation of professional services rendered, I have prepared the enclosed itemization for the month of December. I trust that this will clarify the situation sufficiently for your benefit payments to be resumed.

Until next Tuesday at 11:00, I remain

Cordially,
CALVIN L. SKOLNIK, M.D.

imbalance inevitably affects the length and frequency of services mental health professionals can supply.

In response to such financial realities, more and more individuals have to pay for mental health services themselves, and private insurance companies have become a major source of support for such services. Only 56 percent of all mental health services are now government-supported; 44 percent are paid for by direct client fees and private insurance reimbursements (see Figure 21-4).

The growing economic role of private insurance companies has a significant effect on the way clinicians go about their work. In an effort to reduce their expenditures and to monitor what they are paying for, these companies have, for example, instituted a *peer review*

*system* in which a panel of clinicians who essentially work for the insurance companies may periodically review a therapist's report of a client's treatment and recommend that insurance benefits be either continued or terminated. Many therapists and clients dislike this system, claiming that the reports that therapists must make breach confidentiality, even when efforts are made to safeguard anonymity, and that the value of therapy in a given case is sometimes difficult to convey in a brief report (see Box 21-2). Some also argue that peer review inevitably works to shorten therapy, even if longer-term treatment would be advisable in particular cases. And others worry that the system could be a step toward wider regulation of therapy by insurance companies rather than by therapists.

Charges

| | | | | |
|---|---|---|---|---|
| 140 | clarifications | @ | .25 | 35.00 |
| 157 | restatements | @ | .25 | 39.25 |
| 17 | broad-focus questions | @ | .35 | 5.95 |
| 42 | narrow-focus questions | @ | .30 | 12.60 |
| 86 | reflections of dominant emotional theme | @ | .35 | 30.10 |
| 38 | resolutions of inconsistencies | @ | .45 | 17.10 |
| 22 | pointings out of nonverbal communications | @ | .40 | 8.80 |
| 187 | encouragements to say more | @ | .15 | 28.05 |
| 371 | sympathetic nods with furrowed brow | @ | .10 | 37.10 |
| 517 | acknowledgements of information reception (Uh-huhs, Um-hmmm, etc.) | @ | .08 | 41.36 |
| 24 | interpretations of unconscious defense configurations | @ | .30 | 7.20 |
| 16 | absolution for evil deeds | @ | .50 | 8.00 |
| 2 | pieces of advice | @ | .75 | 1.50 |
| 6 | expressions of personal feelings | @ | .50 | 3.00 |
| 2 | personal reminiscences | @ | .65 | 1.30 |
| 35 | misc. responses (sighs, grunts, belches, etc.) | @ | .20 | 7.00 |
| 7 | listening to remarks disparaging therapist's appearance, personal habits, or technique | @ | 1.75 | 12.25 |
| 12 | listening to sarcastic remarks about psychiatry | @ | 1.00 | 12.00 |
| 3 | listening to psychiatrist jokes | @ | .80 | 2.40 |
| 3 | telephone calls to therapist | @ | .15 | .45 |
| 1 | telephone call to therapist at especially inopportune moment | @ | 10.50 | 10.50 |

| | | | | |
|---|---|---|---|---|
| 22 | Kleenex tissues | @ | .005 | .11 |
| 1 | ashtray | @ | 3.50 | 3.50 |
| 1 | filling and repainting of 1 ashtray-size dent in wall | @ | 27.50 | 27.50 |
| 1 | shampooing of soft drink stain on carpet | @ | 15.00 | 15.00 |
| 1 | letter of excuse from work | @ | 2.50 | 2.50 |
| 2 | surcharges for unusually boring or difficult sessions | @ | 35.00 | 70.00 |
| | Subtotal: charges | | | $438.52 |

Credits

| | | | | |
|---|---|---|---|---|
| 4 | unusually interesting anecdotes | @ | .45 | 1.80 |
| 3 | good jokes | @ | .50 | 1.50 |
| 1 | item of gossip about another patient which was found useful in her therapy | @ | 3.50 | 3.50 |
| 1 | apology for sarcastic remark | @ | 1.00 | 1.00 |
| 1 | use of case history at American Psychiatric Association convention | | | 10.00 |
| ½ | chicken salad sandwich on whole wheat c/mayo | @ | 1.75 | .88 |
| 7 | bummed cigarettes (65¢/pack) | | | .23 |
| 1 | damaged Librium tablet, returned unused | | | .10 |
| | Subtotal: credits | | | $18.99 |
| | Total: PLEASE REMIT— | | | $419.53 |

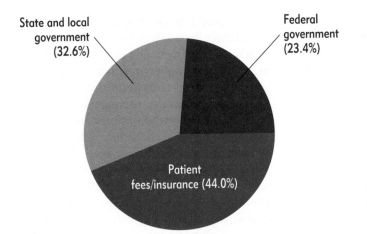

**FIGURE 21-4** Sources of mental health expenditures. Forty-four percent of all mental health services in the United States in 1980 were reimbursed by direct client fees and private insurance companies. In contrast, direct client fees and private insurance reimbursed 62 percent of all other health services. *(Adapted from Taube, 1990, p. 219; Freeland & Schlender, 1983.)*

## THE PERSON WITHIN THE PROFESSION

The actions and goals of clinical researchers and practitioners not only influence and are influenced by other institutions in society but are closely tied to their own needs and goals as individuals. Abnormal psychology is a discipline in which the human strengths, imperfections, wisdom, and clumsiness of its professionals combine to influence the effectiveness of the profession as a whole. We have seen that the needs and preferences of these human beings influence their responses to clients' concerns, their theoretical orientations, and the kinds of clients they choose to work with. And we have also noted that personal leanings sometimes overcome professional standards and lead in extreme cases to instances of research fraud by clinical scientists and sexual misconduct by therapists.

A survey on the mental health of therapists found that 71 percent of 509 psychotherapists reported being in therapy at least once, about a fifth of them three or more times (Norcross et al., 1987). Most of those who received treatment spent more than 100 hours with therapists. Their reasons for seeking therapy were largely the same as those of other clients: mental problems, depression, and anxiety topped the list.

Another survey revealed that all therapists feel like imposters at some point in their career, 87 percent feel like fakes at least occasionally, and 18 percent feel this way frequently (Gibbs & DeVries, 1987), not unlike the imposter phenomenon found in other professions (see p. 189). The survey also seemed to suggest that such feelings are not related to the fact that therapists must appear well adjusted and highly educated, but stem from personal anxieties and traits.

The science and profession of abnormal psychology has lofty goals: to understand, predict, and alter abnormal functioning. But we must not lose sight of the context in which its activities are conducted. Mental health researchers and clinicians are human beings, within a society of human beings, working to serve human beings. The mixture of discovery, misdirection, promise, and frustration that we have encountered in these chapters is thus to be expected. When one thinks about it, could the study and treatment of human behavior really proceed in any other way?

## LAW, SOCIETY, AND THE MENTAL HEALTH PROFESSION: THE STATE OF THE FIELD

Clinical researchers and professionals once conducted their work in relative isolation. Today, however, their activities are intimately tied to other institutions of society, such as the legislative, judicial, and economic systems. The main reason for this growing interconnectedness is that the clinical field has achieved a remarkable level of acceptance in our society. It now provides direct services to millions of people; it has much to say about almost every aspect of society, from education to ecology; and it is looked to as a source of information and expertise by government agencies, journalists, and people in general. When a field achieves such acceptance, it almost inevitably has some influence on the way other institutions are run. It also runs the risk of becoming so influential that other institutions jump in to monitor and restrict its activities.

To an extent, the interrelationship that has evolved between the mental health field and other institutions in our society is a healthy system of checks and balances. It allows the mental health profession to continue providing many useful services, yet helps ensure that its influence does not become excessive or misguided. Given the importance of such checks and balances, the close ties between the clinical field and other institutions are likely to continue and even to grow in the coming years.

The enormous growth and impact of the mental health profession make it all the more important that people hold an accurate perception of its strengths *and* weaknesses. As we have seen throughout this book, the field has acquired an impressive body of knowledge, especially during the past several decades; however, what it does not know and what it cannot do still outweigh what it does know and can do. Indeed, everyone who turns to the field directly or indirectly must recognize this important fact. A society cannot be faulted for being vastly curious about and regularly seeking the input of a field of study—even when the field is young and imperfect—as long as the members of society fully appreciate the actual *state of the field*.

# SUMMARY

The mental health profession interacts with the legislative and judicial institutions in two primary ways. First, clinicians may be called upon to evaluate the mental stability of people accused of crimes. Second, the legislative and judicial branches of government help regulate various aspects of mental health care.

Criminal punishment depends on the assumption that individuals are *responsible* for their crimes and are *capable* of defending themselves in court. If, as a result of clinical testimony, persons are judged to have been mentally unstable at the time of a crime, they may be found not guilty by reason of insanity and placed in a treatment facility rather than a prison. If, on the basis of clinical testimony, a person is judged mentally unstable at the time of the trial, the trial itself may be delayed while the individual receives treatment. Each of these situations represents a form of *criminal commitment.*

Until the late nineteenth century, all federal courts and most state courts in the United States judged insanity in accordance with the *M'Naghten rule,* which holds that defendants are insane at the time of a criminal act if they do not know the nature or quality of the act or do not know right from wrong at the time of the act. Some states later abandoned this test in favor of the *irresistible impulse test,* which holds that defendants are insane at the time of a crime if they are unable to control their actions during the crime. In the 1950s a third test became popular: the *Durham test* states that people are not responsible if their criminal acts are the result of mental disease. In 1955 the American Law Institute proposed a penal code that combined elements of all three tests, and this code gained widespread use in federal and state courts. In 1983, however, after John Hinckley was found not guilty of shooting the president and several aides by reason of insanity, the federal courts and half of the state courts adopted a more stringent code that essentially reestablished the M'Naghten standard.

The insanity defense has been criticized on several grounds, and in recent years several states have started to permit a verdict of "guilty but mentally ill." This new verdict assigns moral blame to defendants but recognizes their mental illness. They are given a prison term with the provision that they will also undergo psychological treatment. Similarly, in many states sex offenders are found to be mentally ill and assigned to treatment. By such innovations society tries to balance moral responsibility and mental illness.

Regardless of their state of mind at the time of the crime, defendants may be mentally incompetent to stand trial; that is, incapable of fully understanding the charges and legal proceedings that confront them. If they are ruled incompetent upon clinical evaluation, they are typically sent to a mental hospital until they are competent to stand trial. In some cases, the period of time spent in the mental institution can be longer than the prison sentence would have been. A ruling by the Supreme Court now ensures that incompetent persons cannot be *indefinitely* committed.

The legal system also has significant influence on the clinical profession. First, legal channels may be used to commit noncriminals to mental hospitals for treatment—a process called *civil commitment.* Society allows involuntary commitment when one is considered *in need of treatment and is dangerous to oneself or others.* Statutes governing civil commitment procedures vary from state to state, but a *minimum standard of proof* — clear and unequivocal evidence of the necessity of commitment — must be provided for commitment, as defined in the case of *Addington* v. *Texas.*

Second, courts and legislatures have significantly affected the clinical profession by specifying a number of legal rights to which mental patients are entitled. The rights that have received the most attention are the *right to treatment* and the *right to refuse treatment.* Other rights gained by patients in recent years include the right to receive payment for work performed in a mental institution, the right to aftercare and an appropriate community residence upon release from an institution, and the right to treatment in the least restrictive facility available.

Mental health and legal professionals also cross paths in three other areas. First, malpractice suits against therapists have risen in recent years, charging such offenses as sexual activity with a patient, wrongful commitment, and improper termination of treatment. Second, lawyers now frequently solicit the advice of mental health professionals regarding the selection of jurors and case strategies. Finally, the legislative and judicial systems have played a role in defining the scope of clinical practice. For example, legislation now permits psychologists as well as psychiatrists to receive Medicare payments for therapy services and to admit patients to certain state hospitals.

Clinicians are not simply guided by laws, courts, and legal processes. They regulate themselves by regularly thinking about, developing, and revising ethical guidelines for members of the field. Each clinical profession has a code of ethics. The code for psychologists, for example, sets guidelines for offering advice to the public in books and on television; prohibits psychologists from engaging in fraudulent research; prohibits them from exploiting the trust and dependence of clients and students, sexually or otherwise; and establishes guidelines for respecting patient confidentiality. Although the code of ethics states generally that "psychologists have a primary obligation to respect the confidentiality of information obtained from persons in the course of their work," there are times when this principle must be compromised. Perhaps the most important court case affecting client–therapist confidentiality has been *Tarasoff* v. *Regents of the University of California,* which has led to clarifications of the circumstances under which therapists must break confidentiality in order to protect the public.

Clinical practice and study also intersect with the business world. The two institutions have worked closely together to identify and address psychological problems in the workplace. Similarly, the mental health system often interacts with the economic institutions of our society. For example, because government funding for mental health services has risen only modestly in the past two decades, more and more private insurance companies are reimbursing therapists for their services and are setting up reimbursement procedures that may indirectly influence the duration and focus of therapy.

Finally, mental health activities are affected by the personal needs, values, and goals of the human beings who provide the clinical services. Therapists and researchers are themselves grappling with psychological issues that inevitably affect the choices, direction, and even quality of their work.

**Abnormal psychology** The scientific study of abnormal behavior in order to describe, predict, explain, and ultimately learn to prevent or to alter abnormal patterns of functioning.

**Acetylcholine** A neurotransmitter that when present in high levels may be associated with depression.

**Acute schizophrenia** A form of schizophrenia characterized by sudden onset of symptoms, good premorbid functioning, prominent affective symptoms or confusion, and good response to treatment.

**Addiction** Physical dependence on a drug. See also **Tolerance** and **Withdrawal symptoms.**

**Affect** A subjective experience of emotion or mood.

**Affectual awareness** The first stage of sexual therapy in which the client becomes aware of his or her negative emotions regarding sex.

**Aftercare** A program of posthospitalization care and treatment out in the community.

**Agoraphobia** A fear of leaving the home and entering public places.

**Agoraphobia without history of panic disorder** An agoraphobic pattern that does not have its origin in a panic attack.

**Akathisia** A Parkinsonian symptom consisting of a very high degree of restlessness and agitation and great discomfort in the limbs.

**Alarm stage** An increase of activity in the sympathetic nervous system in the presence of a perceived threat. See also **General adaptation syndrome.**

**Alcohol** Any beverage containing ethyl alcohol, including beer, wine, and liquor.

**Alcohol withdrawal delirium** A dramatic reaction experienced by some people who are alcohol-dependent. It occurs within three days of cessation or reduction of drinking and consists of mental confusion, clouded consciousness, and terrifying visual hallucinations. Also known as delirium tremens (DTs).

**Alcoholics Anonymous (AA)** A self-help organization that provides support and guidance for alcoholic persons.

**Alcoholism** A pattern of behavior in which a person abuses or develops a dependence on alcohol.

**Alpha waves** Brain waves characteristic of relaxed wakefulness.

**Alprazolam** A benzodiazepine drug, also shown to be effective in the treatment of panic disorders. Marketed as Xanax.

**Altruistic suicides** Suicides committed by people very well integrated into the social structure who intentionally sacrifice their lives for the well-being of society.

**Alzheimer's disease** The most common form of dementia, sometimes occurring well before old age.

**Amenorrhea** The cessation of menstruation that often accompanies anorexia nervosa in women.

**Amnesia** Loss of memory. See also **Anterograde, Psychogenic,** and **Retrograde Amnesia.**

**Amphetamine** A stimulant drug that is manufactured in the laboratory.

**Amphetamine psychosis** A syndrome caused by a high dose of amphetamines that closely mimics schizophrenia and includes hallucinations and motor hyperactivity.

**Amygdala** The structure in the brain's limbic system that gives rise to emotional behavior and that may also regulate the link between arousal and memory.

**Anaclitic depression** A pattern of behavior that includes sadness, withdrawal, weight loss, and trouble sleeping and that is associated with separation from one's mother before the age of 6 years.

**Anal stage** In psychoanalytic theory, the second 18 months of life, during which the child's focus of pleasure shifts to the anus, and libidinal gratification comes from retaining and passing feces.

**Analogue experiment** An investigation in which the experimenter induces laboratory subjects to behave in ways that resemble real-life abnormal behavior.

**Anatomical brain disorders** Problems stemming from abnormal size or shape of certain brain regions.

**Anesthesia** A lessening or loss of sensation for touch or pain.

**Anomic suicides (anomie)** Suicides committed by individuals whose social environment fails to provide stability.

**Anorexia nervosa** A disorder characterized by the relentless pursuit of extreme thinness and by an extreme loss of weight.

**Anoxia** A complication of birth in which the baby is deprived of oxygen. It may lead to mental retardation.

**Antagonist drug** Any drug that blocks or changes the effects of another drug.

**Anterograde amnesia** The inability to learn new information. It sometimes follows a shock or trauma.

**Anthropology** The study of human cultures and institutions.

**Antianxiety drugs** Psychotropic drugs that reduce tension and anxiety.

**Antibipolar drug** A drug that helps stabilize the moods of people suffering from bipolar mood disorder. See also **Lithium.**

**Antibodies** Bodily chemicals that seek out and destroy antigens such as bacteria or viruses.

**Antidepressant drugs** Psychotropic drugs that lift the mood of severely depressed people.

**Antigens** Foreign invaders such as bacteria and viruses that stimulate an immune response.

**Antipsychotic drugs** Psychotropic drugs that help correct grossly confused or distorted thinking.

**Antisocial personality disorder** A personality disorder characterized by a lifelong history of misconduct. Individuals suffering from this disorder are indifferent to others and have little remorse over the pain they cause in others.

**Anxiety** Emotional state characterized by fear, apprehension, and physiological arousal.

**Anxiety disorders** Disorders in which anxiety is a central symptom.

**Anxiolytics** See Antianxiety drugs.

**Arbitrary inference** An error in logic in which a person draws negative conclusions on the basis of little or even contrary evidence. It may contribute to some cases of depression.

**Arousal phase** The second phase in the sexual response cycle, characterized by general physical arousal, increases in heart rate, muscle tension, blood pressure, and respiration, and specific changes in the pelvic region.

**Assertiveness Training** A cognitive-behavioral approach to increasing assertive behavior that is socially desirable.

**Assessment** The collection of relevant information about a client or subject.

**Asthma** Constricting of the trachea and bronchi resulting in shortness of breath, wheezing, coughing, and choking.

**Asylum** A type of institution first established in the sixteenth century to provide care for the mentally ill. Most became virtual prisons in which patients endured degrading conditions.

**Attention deficit hyperactivity disorder** Childhood disorder characterized by the inability to focus attention.

**Attribution** The explaining of the things we see going on around us as the result of particular causes that then influence the way we feel about ourselves and others.

**Auditory hallucination** A hallucination in which a person hears sounds and voices that seem to come from outside the head.

**Aura** A warning sensation that frequently precedes a migraine headache.

**Autism** A pervasive developmental disorder characterized by the failure to respond to other people and situations in a socially appropriate way.

**Automatic thought** Unbidden cognitions that come into the mind, some comforting and some upsetting.

**Autonomic learning** The inadvertent conditioning of particular responses in the autonomic nervous system.

**Autonomic nervous system (ANS)** The extensive network of nerve fibers that connects the central nervous system to all the other organs of the body.

**Aversion therapy** A behavioral technique that helps clients acquire anxiety responses to stimuli that they have been finding too attractive.

**Avoidance behavior** Behavior that removes or avoids anxiety-producing objects or situations.

**Avoidant disorders of childhood** A disorder in which children shrink from all contact with unfamiliar people.

**Avoidant personality disorder** A personality disorder characterized by an extreme fear of being rejected.

**Axon** The long fiber that extends from the body of the neuron.

**Barbiturates** Addictive sedative-hypnotic drugs used to reduce anxiety or to help persons fall asleep.

**Baroreceptors** Sensitive nerves in the arteries responsible for alerting the brain when blood pressure becomes too high.

**Baseline measurement** An individual's initial response level on a test or scale.

**Basic irrational assumptions** Inappropriate assumptions guiding the way in which one acts that prejudice a person's chances for happiness and success.

**Basic personality disorders** Antisocial, narcissistic, histrionic, dependent, passive-aggressive, obsessive-compulsive, avoidant, and schizoid personality disorders.

**Battery** A comprehensive group of tests, each of which targets a specific skill area.

**B-cell** Lymphocyte that produces antibodies.

**Behavior** The response that an organism makes to the stimuli in its environment.

**Behavioral assessment** The collection of information about specific dysfunctional behaviors a person engages in.

**Behavioral model** A theoretical perspective that emphasizes ingrained behavior and the ways in which it is learned.

**Behavioral self-control training (BSCT)** An approach to treating alcohol abuse in which clients are taught to monitor their own drinking behavior, set appropriate limits on their drinking, control their rate of drinking, and apply alternative coping behaviors.

**Behavioral therapy (also Behavior modification)** A therapeutic approach that views the goal of therapy as identifying the client's specific problem-causing behaviors and either modifying them or replacing them with more appropriate ones.

**Benzodiazepines** The most common antianxiety drugs. The group includes Valium, Xanax, and Librium.

**Bereavement** The process of working through the grief that one feels when a loved one dies.

**Bilateral electroconvulsive therapy (ECT)** A form of electroconvulsive therapy in which two electrodes are used, and electrical current is passed through both sides of the brain.

**Binge-purge syndrome** See **Bulimia nervosa.**

**Biochemical brain disorders** Problems that stem from abnormal activity of the chemicals that enable neurons to operate.

**Biofeedback** A treatment technique in which the client is given systematic information about key physiological responses as they occur and learns to control the responses voluntarily.

**Biological model** The theoretical perspective that cites organic processes as the key to human behavior.

**Biological therapy** The use of physical and chemical procedures to help people overcome psychological difficulties.

**Bipolar disorder** A disorder marked by alternating periods of mania and depression.

**Birth complications** Biological conditions during birth, including anoxia and extreme prematurity, that can compromise the physical and mental well-being of the child.

**Blind design** An experiment in which subjects do not know whether they are in the experimental or the control condition.

**Blocking** A symptom associated with schizophrenia in which thoughts disappear from memory and statements end in silence before they can be completed.

**Blunted affect** A symptom of schizophrenia in which a person displays less emotion — anger, sadness, joy — than other people.

**Body dysmorphic disorder (dysmorphobia)** Excessive worry that some aspect of one's physical appearance is defective.

**Body mass index (BMI)** The quotient of one's weight in kilograms and height in centimeters, used to determine whether a person weighs too much.

**Borderline personality disorder** A personality disorder characterized by extreme instability in relationships.

**Brain stem** The region of the central nervous system that connects the spinal cord with the cerebrum.

**Brain wave** The oscillations of electrical potential, as measured by an electroencephalograph, that are created by neurons in the brain.

**Brief reactive psychosis** Psychotic symptoms that appear suddenly after a very stressful event or a period of emotional turmoil and last anywhere from a few hours to a month.

**Briquet's syndrome** See **Somatization disorder.**

**Bulimia nervosa** A disorder characterized by frequent eating binges, during which the person uncontrollably consumes large quantities of food followed by forced vomiting or other extreme steps to avoid gaining weight.

**Bulimic anorexia nervosa** A pattern of behavior that combines features of both bulimia and anorexia.

**Cannabis drugs** Drugs produced from the different varieties of hemp plant. They cause a mixture of hallucinogenic, depressant, and stimulant effects.

**Case study** A detailed account of one person's life and psychological problems.

**Catatonia** Extreme psychomotor symptoms found in some forms of schizophrenia.

**Catatonic excitement** A form of catatonia in which a person moves excitedly, sometimes with wild waving of the arms and legs.

**Catatonic schizophrenia** Schizophrenia characterized by a severe psychomotor disturbance.

**Catatonic stupor** A symptom associated with schizophrenia in which a person becomes totally unresponsive to the environment, remaining motionless and silent for long stretches of time.

**Catecholamine theory** The view that unipolar depression is related to low activity of norepinephrine (a catecholamine) in the brain and less neuronal firing.

**Catharsis** The reliving of past repressed feelings in order to settle internal conflicts and overcome problems.

**Central nervous system** The brain and spinal cord.

**Cerebral cortex** The outer layer of the cerebrum, or upper portion of the brain, also known as the gray matter. It is associated with higher cognitive functions.

**Checking compulsion** A compulsion in which people feel compelled to check the same things over and over.

**Child abuse** The intentional, nonaccidental use of physical or psychological force by an adult on a child, often aimed at hurting, injuring, or destroying the child.

**Chlorpromazine** A phenothiazine drug commonly used for treating schizophrenia. Marketed as Thorazine.

**Chromosomal mapping** A research strategy for studying the DNA of a large extended family in which a particular trait (schizophrenia, for example) is unusually common.

**Chromosomes** The structures within a cell that contain genes.

**Chronic schizophrenia** A category of schizophrenia characterized by insidious and early onset, poor premorbid functioning, affective blunting, social isolation, and poor responsiveness to treatment.

**Chronological age** The number of years one has lived since birth.

**Circadian rhythms** Internal "clocks" consisting of recurrent biological fluctuations.

**Cirrhosis** An irreversible condition, often caused by excessive drinking, in which the liver becomes scarred and begins to change its anatomy and functioning.

**Civil commitment** The legal process by which individuals can be forced to undergo mental health treatment.

**Clang** A rhyme used by schizophrenic individuals as a guide to formulating thoughts and statements.

**Classical conditioning** A process of learning by temporal association in which two events that repeatedly occur close together in time become fused in a person's mind.

**Cleaning compulsion** A common compulsion in which people feel compelled to keep cleaning themselves, their clothing, their homes, and anything they might touch.

**Client-centered therapy** The therapeutic approach associated with Carl Rogers that focuses on a patient's unique subjective perspective rather than on someone's definition of objective reality. Rogers proposed that clients would respond better if therapists were particularly warm, genuine, and understanding.

**Clinical psychologist** A professional who earns a doctorate in clinical psychology by completing four years of graduate training in abnormal functioning and its treatment as well as a one-year internship at a mental hospital or mental health agency.

**Clinical psychology** The study, assessment, treatment, and prevention of abnormal behavior.

**Clitoris** The female sex organ located in front of the urinary and vaginal openings. It becomes enlarged during sexual arousal.

**Cocaine** A drug that is the most powerful natural stimulant known.

**Cognition** The intellectual capacity to think, remember, and anticipate.

**Cognitive behavior** Thoughts and beliefs, many of which remain private.

**Cognitive-behavioral model** A theoretical perspective that attributes psychological problems to cognitive behaviors.

**Cognitive model** A theoretical perspective that emphasizes the process and content of the thinking that underlies behavior.

**Cognitive therapy** A therapeutic system constructed on the premise that abnormal functioning is caused by counterproductive assumptions and thoughts. Its goal is to help people recognize and change their faulty thinking processes.

**Cognitive triad** The three forms of negative thinking that Aaron Beck says encompass one's experiences, one's view of oneself, and one's view of the future.

**Cohort** A person who is born in the same time period or year as another.

**Coitus** Sexual intercourse.

**Community mental health center** A treatment facility for persons with psychological dysfunctions that provides outpatient psychotherapy and medication and inpatient emergency care.

**Community mental health movement** A sociopolitical trend emphasizing community care for people with severe psychological disturbances.

**Compulsion** A repetitive and rigid activity that a person feels compelled to perform.

**Computerized axial tomography (CAT scan)** A composite image of the brain created by compiling X-ray images taken from many angles.

**Concordance** A statistical measure of the frequency with which both members of a pair of twins have the same particular trait.

**Conditioned response (CR)** A response previously associated with an unconditioned stimulus that comes to be elicited by a conditioned stimulus.

**Conditioned stimulus (CS)** A previously neutral stimulus that comes to be associated with nonneutral stimulus.

**Conditioning** A simple form of learning in which a given stimulus comes to evoke a given response.

**Conditions of worth** The internal standards by which a person judges his or her own lovability and acceptability, determined by the standards (i.e., conditions of worth) to which the person was held as a child.

**Conduct disorder** A pathological pattern of childhood behavior in which the child repeatedly violates the basic rights of others, displaying aggression and sometimes destroying others' property, lying, cheating, or running away from home.

**Confabulation** A spontaneously made-up event fabricated to fill in a gap in one's memory. Characteristic of alcoholics suffering from Korsakoff's syndrome.

**Confederate** An experimenter's accomplice who plays a role in creating a believable counterfeit situation in an experiment.

**Confidentiality** The commitment on the part of a professional person not to divulge the information he or she obtains from a client.

**Confound** A variable other than the independent variable that is also acting on the dependent variable.

**Conjoint family therapy** A family therapy approach in which the therapist focuses primarily on communication within the family system, helping members to recognize harmful patterns of communication, to appreciate the impact of such patterns on other family members, and to change the patterns.

**Continuous amnesia** A disturbance of memory in which forget-ting continues into the present and new and ongoing experiences fail to be retained.

**Control group** In an experiment, a group of subjects who are not exposed to the independent variable.

**Conversion disorder** A somatoform disorder characterized by significant alteration or loss of one or two areas of physical functioning.

**Coronary heart disease** Illness caused by a blocking of the coronary arteries.

**Correlation** The degree to which events or characteristics vary in conjunction with each other.

**Counseling psychology** A mental health specialty similar to clinical psychology that requires completion of its own graduate training program.

**Countertransference** A phenomenon of psychotherapy in which therapists unintentionally allow their own feelings, history, and values to subtly influence the way they interpret a patient's problems.

**Couples therapy** See **Marital therapy.**

**Covert desensitization** Desensitization training that focuses on imagining confrontations with the frightening objects or situations while in a state of relaxation. See also **In vivo desensitization.**

**Covert sensitization** A behavioral treatment for eliminating unwanted behavior by pairing the behavior with unpleasant mental images.

**Crack** A powerful, ready-to-smoke free-base cocaine. See also **Free-base.**

**Cretinism** A congenital disorder characterized by mental retardation and other physical abnormalities and caused by low levels of iodine in a pregnant woman's diet.

**Criminal commitment** A legal process by which individuals accused of crimes are judged to be mentally unstable and are sent to a mental institution for treatment.

**Crisis intervention** See **Suicide prevention program.**

**Cross-tolerance** Tolerance for a drug one has never taken, as a result of using another similar drug.

**Culture** A people's common history, values, institutions, habits, technology, and arts.

**Cyclothymia** A disorder characterized by mood swings that consist of mild depressive and manic episodes.

**Date rape** Rape by a date or close acquaintance.

**Day center (day hospital)** A treatment center that provides day-long therapeutic activity and cure.

**Defense mechanisms** See **Ego defense mechanisms.**

**Deinstitutionalization** The practice begun in the mid-twentieth century to release hundreds of thousands of patients from public mental hospitals.

**Delirium** A state of mental confusion characterized by disorientation, restlessness, and often hallucinations.

**Delirium tremens (DTs)** See **Alcohol withdrawal syndrome.**

**Delusion** A blatantly false belief firmly held despite evidence to the contrary.

**Delusion of control** The belief that one's impulses, feelings, thoughts, and actions are being controlled by other people.

**Delusion of grandeur** The belief that one is a great inventor, historical figure, religious savior, or other specially empowered person.

**Delusion of persecution** The belief that one is being plotted or discriminated against, spied on, slandered, threatened, attacked, or deliberately victimized.

**Delusion of reference** Attaching special and personal significance to the actions of others or to various objects or events.

**Delusional (paranoid) disorder** A disorder consisting of persistent, nonbizarre delusions that are not part of a larger schizophrenic pattern.

**Dementia** A severe decline of intellectual and other mental faculties, first described by early Greek and Roman philosophers and physicians.

**Demonology** The belief that abnormal behavior results from supernatural causes such as evil spirits.

**Dendrite** The extensions, or antennae, located at one end of a neuron that receive impulses from other neurons.

**Dependent personality disorder** A personality disorder characterized by dependence on others to the extent that the person cannot make the smallest decision alone.

**Dependent variable** The variable in an experiment that is expected to change as the independent variable is manipulated.

**Depersonalization disorder** A disorder characterized by an alteration in a person's experience of self so that the person feels unreal and alien.

**Depression** A low, sad state in which life seems bleak and its challenges overwhelming.

**Derealization** The feeling that the external world is unreal and strange.

**Desire phase** The first phase of the sexual response cycle, characterized by an urge to have sex, sexual fantasies, and feelings of sexual attraction to others.

**Desynchronization** An imbalance between the body's circadian rhythms and the rhythms of the environment.

**Detoxification** Systematic and medically supervised withdrawal from a drug.

**Developmental disorder** A childhood disorder characterized by deficits in language comprehension, speech, and responses to other people.

**Deviance** Variance from accepted patterns of behavior.

**Dexamethasone suppression test (DST)** A biological assessment technique that indirectly measures cortisol levels in patients in order to diagnose depression.

**Diagnosis** The process of determining whether a person's dysfunction constitutes a particular psychological disorder.

**Diathesis-stress perspective** The view that a person must first have a biological, psychological, or sociocultural predisposition to a disorder and then be subjected to an immediate form of psychological stress to develop and maintain it.

**Diazepam** A benzodiazepine drug marketed as Valium.

**Disorganized schizophrenia** Schizophrenia characterized by confusion and incoherence. Also known as hebephrenic schizophrenia.

**Displacement** An ego defense mechanism that channels unacceptable id impulses toward another, safer target.

**Disregulation model** A theory that explains psychophysiological disorders as breakdowns in the body's negative feedback loops, resulting in an interruption of the body's smooth, self-regulating operation.

**Dissociative disorder** Disorder characterized by fugue, amnesia, multiple personality, or depersonalization.

**Dizygotic twins** Twins who develop from separate eggs.

**Dopamine** The neurotransmitter whose high activity has been shown to be related to schizophrenia.

**Dopamine hypothesis** The theory that schizophrenia results from excessive firing of neurons that use the neurotransmitter dopamine and, hence, from their transmitting too many messages.

**Dopper ultrasound recording device** A device that measures the blood flow in the penis.

**Double depression** A sequence in which dysthymia leads to a major depression.

**Double-bind communication** Simultaneous messages that are mutually contradictory.

**Double-bind hypothesis** A family systems theory that says some parents cause schizophrenic symptoms in their children by repeatedly engaging in double-bind communications, thus placing the children in the dilemma of being unable to please them.

**Double-blind procedure** Experimental procedure in which neither the subject nor the experimenter knows whether the subject has received the experimental treatment or a placebo.

**Down Syndrome** A form of mental retardation related to a chromosomal abnormality.

**Drug abuse** The excessive intake of a substance that results in emotional, social, occupational, or functional impairment.

**Drug maintenance therapy** An approach to treating substance abuse in which addicted clients are given legally and medically supervised doses of a substitute drug with which to satisfy their addiction.

**Drug therapy** The use of psychotropic drugs to alleviate the symptoms of mental disorders.

**DSM-III-R (Diagnostic and Statistical Manual-III-Revised)** A system for classifying psychological problems and disorders. Developed by the American Psychiatric Association, it is the most widely used system in the United States.

**Durham test** A legal test for determining the responsibility of a person committing a crime. It asks whether the unlawful act is a product of a mental disease or defect. This test was used only for a short period.

**Dyslexia** Any one of several developmental impairments in the ability to read.

**Dyspareunia** Pain in the genitals during sexual activity.

**Dyssomnias** Sleep disorders in which the amount or quality of sleep is disturbed.

**Dysthymia** A mood disorder that is similar to but less disabling than depression.

**Dystonia** A Parkinsonian symptom in which involuntary muscle contractions cause bizarre and uncontrollable movements of the face, neck, tongue, and back.

**Echolalia** A symptom of schizophrenia in which a person responds to being spoken to by repeating some of the other person's words.

**Educational psychology** A mental health specialty that focuses on behavior and problems particularly in educational settings.

**Ego** One of the three psychological forces proposed by Freud as central to shaping the personality. The ego operates in accordance with the reality principle, employing reason and deliberation to guide us in recognizing when the expression of id impulses would have negative consequences.

**Ego defense mechanisms** According to psychoanalytic theory, these are strategies developed by the ego to control unacceptable id impulses and to avoid or reduce the anxiety they arouse.

**Ego-dystonic homosexuality** A homosexual preference accompanied by extreme distress.

**Ego ideal** A composite image of the values one has acquired—the kind of person one believes in striving to become.

**Ego psychology** Outgrowth of Freudian theory that focuses on the importance of the ego.

**Egoistic suicides** Suicides committed by people over whom society has little or no control.

**Ejaculation** Contractions of the muscles at the base of the penis that causes sperm to be ejected.

**Electra complex** According to Freud, the pattern of desires all girls experience in which they develop a sexual attraction for their father, rooted in the fantasy that by seducing him they can have his penis.

**Electroconvulsive therapy (ECT)** See **Bilateral ECT** and **Unilateral ECT.**

**Electroencephalograph (EEG)** A device that records electrical impulses in the brain.

**Electromyograph (EMG)** A device that provides feedback about the level of muscular tension in the body.

**Electrooculograph** A device that records the movement of the eyes.

**Emergency commitment** Temporary commitment to a mental hospital of a patient who is behaving in a bizarre or violent way. See also **Two-physician certificates.**

**Employee assistance programs** Mental health programs a company offers its employees. They may be run either by mental health professionals employed directly by the company or by consulting mental health agencies.

**Encephalitis** An early-childhood disease that can cause serious brain damage if untreated.

**Encopresis** Childhood disorder characterized by uncontrolled bowel movements.

**Encounter group** A small group guided by a leader through intensive experiences designed to develop participants' self-awareness and, as a consequence, their skill in human relationships.

**Endogenous** A depression that develops without apparent antecedents and is assumed to be caused by internal factors.

**Endorphin** A neurotransmitter that helps relieve pain and reduce emotional tension.

**Enkephalin** See **Endorphin.**

**Enmeshed family pattern** A family system in which members are overinvolved with each other's affairs and overconcerned about each other's welfare.

**Enuresis** Involuntary bedwetting.

**Epidemiological study (epidemiology)** An investigation that determines the incidence and prevalence of a disorder in a given population.

**Epilepsy**  A disorder of the brain characterized by seizures, alterations in consciousness, and impairment of sensory, mental, or motor skills.

**Epinephrine**  Hormone secreted by the medulla during emotional arousal.

**Erectile failure**  See **Male erectile disorder.**

**Ergot alkaloid**  A naturally occurring compound from which LSD is derived.

**Erogenous zones**  Body areas that Freud considered representative of the child's sexual drives and conflicts at each of the normal stages of development.

**Essential hypertension**  Chronic high blood pressure brought about by a combination of psychological and physiological factors.

**Estrogen**  The primary female sex hormone.

**Ethyl alcohol**  The chemical compound in all alcoholic beverages that is rapidly absorbed into the blood and immediately begins to affect the person's functioning.

**Evoked potential**  The brain response patterns recorded on an electroencephalograph.

**Exhaustion stage**  The failure of the parasympathetic nervous system to resist a sustained response of the sympathetic nervous system, leading to a breakdown in the control of the autonomic nervous system over the organs of the body. See also **General adaptation syndrome.**

**Exhibitionism**  A disorder in which persons have sexually arousing fantasies about exposing their genitals to another person and act upon or are distressed by these fantasies.

**Existential anxiety**  A pervasive fear of the limits and responsibilities of one's existence.

**Existential model**  See **Humanistic-existential model.**

**Existential therapies**  Like humanistic therapies, existential therapies emphasize the validity of the individual's phenomenological world and the importance of the here and now, but they also place great emphasis on making choices and on the relationship between therapist and client.

**Exorcism**  The practice in early societies of treating abnormality by coaxing evil spirits to leave the person's body.

**Experiment**  A scientific procedure in which a situation is manipulated and the effect of the manipulation is observed.

**Experimental group**  In an experiment, the group of subjects who are exposed to the independent variable.

**Exposure and response prevention**  A treatment for obsessive compulsive disorder in which clients are exposed to anxiety arousing thoughts or situations and then prevented from performing their compulsive acts.

**Exposure-based treatment**  Behavioral approaches to treating simple phobias in which clients are exposed to the dreaded object or situation.

**External validity**  The degree to which the results of a study may be generalized beyond the immediate investigation.

**Extinction**  The decrease in conditioned response that occurs when the unconditioned stimulus is no longer paired with the conditioned stimulus.

**Extrapyramidal effect**  Undesirable movement, such as severe shaking, bizarre-looking contractions of the face and body, and extreme restlessness, induced by some antipsychotic drugs, resulting from the effect of certain drugs on the extrapyramidal areas of the brain.

**Factitious disorder**  An illness with no identifiable physical cause in which the patient is believed to be intentionally producing or feigning physical or psychological symptoms.

**Family pedigree study**  The method used by biological researchers to see how many members of a given family have a particular disorder.

**Family systems theory**  An approach to human behavior that views the family as a system of interacting parts and proposes that members of a given family interact in consistent ways and operate by implicit rules.

**Family systems therapy**  A therapy format in which therapists meet with all members of a family, point out problematic behavior and interactions between the members, and help the whole family to change.

**Fear**  The central nervous system's physiological and emotional response to danger.

**Fear hierarchy**  A list of the objects or situations that frighten a person, starting with those which are minimally feared and ending with those which are feared the most. Used in desensitization.

**Fetal alcohol syndrome**  A cluster of problems in a child, including low birth weight, irregularities in the hands and face, and intellectual deficits, caused by excessive alcohol intake by its mother during gestation.

**Fetishism**  A recurrent sexual urge and sexually arousing fantasy that involves the use of an inanimate object or body part.

**Fixation**  According to Freud, a condition in which the id, ego, and superego do not mature properly and are frozen at an early stage of development.

**Flashback**  The recurrence of LSD-induced sensory and emotional changes long after the drug has left the body. Or in post-traumatic stress disorder, the re-experiencing of past traumatic events.

**Flat affect**  A symptom of schizophrenia in which the person shows almost no emotions at all.

**Flooding**  A treatment for phobias in which clients are exposed repeatedly and intensively to the feared object and made to see that it is actually quite harmless. See also **Implosive therapy.**

*Folie à deux*  A psychotic disorder in which a delusion is shared by two people.

**Forebrain**  The top area of the brain, consisting of the cerebrum, thalamus, and hypothalamus.

**Forensic science**  The study of legal issues relating to medicine or psychology.

**Formal thought disorder**  A disturbance in the production and organization of thought.

**Free association**  A psychodynamic technique in which the patient describes any thought, feeling, or image that comes to mind, even if it seems unimportant.

**Free-base**  A technique for ingesting cocaine in which the pure cocaine basic alkaloid is chemically separated from processed cocaine, vaporized by heat from a flame, and inhaled with a pipe.

**Free-floating anxiety**  Chronic and persistent feelings of nervousness and agitation that are not clearly attached to a specific, identifiable threat.

**Frontal lobe**  The region of each cerebral hemisphere that governs motor function and abstract thinking.

**Frotteurism**  A disorder in which recurrent and intense sexual urges and sexually arousing fantasies center on touching and rubbing against a nonconsenting person.

**Fugue**  See **Psychogenic fugue.**

**Functional age**  A measure that reflects three interrelated aspects of aging, the biological, the social, and the psychological.

**Functional mental disorders**  Abnormal behavior patterns that have no clear link to physical abnormalities in the brain.

**Galvanic Skin Response (GSR)**  Changes in the electrical resistance of the skin.

**GABA**  The neurotransmitter gamma aminobutyric acid, whose low activity has been linked to generalized anxiety disorders.

**Ganja**  A recreational drug of at least intermediate strength derived from varieties of the hemp plant.

**Gender identity disorder of childhood**  A childhood disorder in which the child feels uncomfortable about his or her assigned sex and strongly wishes to be a member of the opposite sex.

**Gene**  A structure within the chromosome that carries a discrete piece of hereditary information.

**General adaptation syndrome**  A three-stage reaction to stress proposed by Hans Selye to describe the relationship between stress and the autonomic nervous system.

**General paresis**  An irreversible, progressive disorder with both physical and mental symptoms, including paralysis and delusions of grandeur.

**Generalized amnesia**  A disorder in which a person forgets both the period beginning with a traumatic event and all other events before the onset of this period.

**Generalized anxiety disorder**  A disorder characterized by general and persistent feelings of anxiety that are not associated with specific objects or situations.

**Genetic linkage study**  A research approach in which extended families with high rates of a disorder over several generations are observed in order to determine whether the disorder closely follows the distribution pattern of other family traits.

**Genital stage**  In Freud's theory, the stage beginning at approximately 12 years old, when the child begins to find sexual pleasure in heterosexual relationships.

**Gerontology**  The study of the physical, emotional, and psychological changes, as well as the disorders, that accompany old age.

**Geropsychology**  The field of psychology concerned with the mental health of elderly people.

**Gestalt therapy**  A humanistic form of therapy developed by Fritz Perls in which life is viewed as a series of figure-ground relationships. Therapists try to move their clients toward self-recognition and self-acceptance by frustrating and challenging them.

**Glia**  Brain cells that support the neurons.

**Grief**  The reaction one experiences when a loved one is lost.

**Group home**  Special homes where people with disorders or disabilities are taught self-help, living, and working skills.

**Group therapy**  A therapeutic approach in which a group of people with similar problems meet together with a therapist and discuss the problems or concerns of one or more of the members. The therapist usually follows the principles of his or her preferred theoretical model in conducting the group.

**Guided participation**  A modeling technique in which the therapist and client first construct a fear hierarchy and the client then observes and imitates the therapist, experiencing the least feared item in the hierarchy, a more feared item, and so on.

**Halfway house**  A group home that has a live-in staff to offer support, guidance, and practical advice to residents.

**Hallucination**  The experiencing of imagined sights, sounds, or other sensory experiences as if they were real.

**Hallucinogen**  A substance that primarily causes changes in sensory perception.

**Hallucinosis**  A state of perceptual distortion and hallucination.

**Hardiness**  A set of positive attitudes in response to stress that enable a person who has been exposed to life-threatening situations to carry on with a sense of fortitude, control, and commitment.

**Hashish**  The most powerful drug produced from varieties of the hemp plant.

**Hebephrenic schizophrenia**  See **Disorganized schizophrenia.**

**Helper T-cell**  A lymphocyte that identifies antigens and then both multiplies and triggers the production of other kinds of immune cells.

**Helplessness**  See **Learned helplessness.**

**Heroin**  A highly addictive substance derived from opium.

**High**  The pleasant feeling of relaxation and euphoria that follows the rush from certain recreational drugs.

**High-risk study**  A study in which people hypothesized to be at greater risk for developing a disorder are followed throughout their childhood and compared with controls who are considered not to be at risk.

**Hindbrain**  The lower rearward portion of the brain comprised of the medulla, pons, and cerebellum.

**Histrionic personality disorder**  A personality disorder characterized by dramatic emotionality and fervent pursuit of attention.

**Homeostasis**  A state in which the parts of a system interact in ways that enable the system to maintain itself and survive.

**Homosexuality**  Sexual preference for a person of one's own gender.

**Humanistic-existential model**  A theoretical point of view that stresses the role of values and choices in determining human individuality and fulfillment.

**Humanistic-existential therapy**  A system of therapy that tries to help clients view themselves and their situations more accurately and acceptingly and move toward actualizing their full potential as human beings.

**Huntington's chorea**  A disease inherited through a dominant gene. Its onset, usually during the middle years, is later followed by dementia.

**Hydrocephalus**  A disease characterized by an increase in cerebrospinal fluid and resultant head enlargement.

**Hypertension**  Chronic high blood pressure.

**Hypnosis**  A sleeplike, suggestible state during which a person can be directed to act in unusual ways, to experience unusual sensations, to remember seemingly forgotten events, or to forget remembered events.

**Hypnotic amnesia**  A condition in which a person forgets facts, events, and even his or her identity in obedience to an instruction received under hypnosis.

**Hypnotic therapy (hypnotherapy)**  A treatment for psychological problems, such as amnesia and fugue, in which the patient undergoes hypnosis and is then guided to recall forgotten events.

**Hypnotism**  The inducing of a trancelike mental state in which a person becomes extremely suggestible.

**Hypoactive sexual desire**  A lack of interest in sex.

**Hypochondriasis**  A somatoform disorder in which a person fears that minor fluctuations in his or her physical functioning indicate a serious disease.

**Hypoglycemia**  A psychophysiological disorder characterized by a low level of serum glucose.

**Hypomania**  A mood disorder characterized by mild episodes of mania.

**Hypothalamus**  A part of the brain that helps maintain various bodily functions, including hunger and eating.

**Hypothesis**  A tentative explanation advanced to provide a basis for an investigation.

**Hysteria**  A term once used to describe what is now known as conversion disorder.

**Hysterical disorder**  A somatoform disorder in which physical functioning is altered or lost.

**Iatrogenic disorders**  Disorders that are unintentionally caused by practitioners.

**Id**  One of the three psychological forces proposed by Freud as central to shaping personality; the id is the source of instinctual needs, drives, and impulses.

**Idiographic understanding**  An understanding of the abnormal behavior of a given individual.

**Illogical thinking**  Habitual illogical ways of thinking that may lead to self-defeating and even pathological conclusions.

**Imipramine**  A tricyclic drug that has been found to be effective in treating unipolar depression.

**Immune system**  The sum of complex bodily systems that detect and destroy antigens.

**Implosive therapy**  A treatment for phobias in which clients are exposed repeatedly to the feared object and made to see that such exposure is harmless. See also **Flooding.**

**Impulse control disorders**  Disorders in which a person is driven by a powerful impulse to perform a certain act. This disorder is marked by failure to resist the impulse, a sense of tension before committing the act, and pleasure or relief at the time the act is committed.

**In vivo desensitization**  Desensitization training that makes use of actual physical situations, as opposed to imagined ones. See also **Covert desensitization.**

**Inappropriate affect**  A symptom of schizophrenia in which a person expresses emotions that are unsuited to the situation.

**Incest**  Sexual relations between close relatives.

**Incidence**  A statistical measure of the number of new cases of a problem or disorder that occur over a specific period of time.

**Independent variable**  The variable in an experiment that is manipulated to determine whether it has an effect on another variable that is held constant.

**Individual therapy**  A therapeutic approach in which a therapist sees a client alone for sessions that may last from fifteen minutes to two hours.

**Indoleamine theory**  The view that unipolar depression is caused by deficiencies in the level of the neurotransmitter serotonin (an indoleamine).

**Induced psychotic disorder**  A disorder in which a person embraces delusions held by another individual.

**Informed consent**  A person's consent to participate in an experiment or procedure, given with full knowledge of the potential benefits and risks.

**Inhibited ejaculation**  See **Inhibited male orgasm.**

**Inhibited female orgasm**  A woman's inability to reach orgasm despite adequate stimulation.

**Inhibited male orgasm** A man's inability to reach orgasm despite adequate stimulation.

**Inhibited power motive style** A personality style linked to a tendency to develop physical illness and characterized by a strong but inhibited need for power.

**Insanity defense** A legal defense in which persons charged with a criminal offense claim to be not guilty by reason of insanity and try to show that, as a result of mental dysfunctioning, they were unable to appreciate the wrongfulness of their conduct at the time of their offense.

**Insight therapy** Psychotherapeutic approach that helps the patient achieve a greater understanding of his or her motives and coping mechanisms.

**Insomnia** The most common dyssomnia, characterized by lack of sleep during the night and periods of microsleep during the day.

**Instrumental conditioning** See **Operant conditioning.**

**Intelligence quotient (IQ)** A score derived from intelligence tests that represents the ratio of a person's mental age to his or her chronological age.

**Intelligence test** A test designed to measure a person's intellectual ability.

**Internal validity** The accuracy with which a study can pinpoint one out of various possible factors as being the cause of a phenomenon.

**Interpersonal psychotherapy (IPT)** A treatment for unipolar patterns of depression. It is based on the premise that because depression occurs in an interpersonal context, clarifying and renegotiating that context is important to a person's recovery.

**Intoxication** A drug-induced state, or organic mental syndrome, in which a person exhibits impaired judgment, mood changes, irritability, slurred speech, and loss of coordination.

**Introjection** According to psychodynamic theory, people who have lost a loved one may introject, or fuse, their own identity with that of the person they have lost. Also, in depression, the unconscious incorporation of parental values that leads to the development of the superego in the child.

**Irresistible impulse test** A legal criterion for determining a person's responsibility for committing a crime. This test asks whether the person was unable to control his or her actions.

**Irritable bowel syndrome** A psychophysiological disorder characterized by intermittent episodes of abdominal discomfort.

**Isolation** An ego defense mechanism in which people unconsciously isolate and disown undesirable and unwanted thoughts, experiencing them as foreign intrusions from undetermined parts of the mind. This mechanism has been invoked as an explanation of obsessive compulsive disorder.

**Jakob-Creutzfeldt disease** A rare, rapidly progressive dementia that often includes spasmodic movements rarely seen in Alzheimer's patients.

**Juvenile delinquents** Children between the ages of 8 and 18 who break the law.

**Killer T-cell** A lymphocyte that seeks out and destroys body cells that have been infected by viruses.

**Kleptomania** Recurrent failure to resist the impulse to steal.

**Koro** A pattern of anxiety found in Southeast Asia in which a man suddenly becomes intensely fearful that his penis will withdraw into his abdomen and that he will die as a result.

**Korsakoff's syndrome (alcohol amnestic disorder)** An alcohol-related disorder marked by extreme confusion, memory impairment, and other neurological symptoms.

**L-dopa** A precursor of dopamine, given to patients suffering from Parkinson's disease, a disease in which dopamine is low.

**L-glutamate** A common neurotransmitter that is depleted in the brains of Alzheimer's victims.

*La belle indifférence* A nonchalant attitude about one's symptoms that often accompanies conversion disorders.

**Latency stage** In psychoanalytic theory, the stage children enter at 6 years of age in which their sexual desires apparently subside and their libidinal energy is devoted to developing new interests, activities, and skills.

**Latent content** The symbolic meaning of a dream.

**Lateral hypothalamus (LH)** The region of the hypothalamus that produces hunger when activated.

**Law of effect** The principle which states that when a response leads to a satisfying consequence, it is strengthened and is likely to be repeated.

**Learned helplessness** The perception, based on subjective experience, that one has no control over events and circumstances.

**Learning disability** A developmental disorder marked by impairments in cognitive skills such as reading, mathematics, or language.

**Lesion** Localized damage to tissue.

**Lethality scale** A scale used by crisis prevention centers to estimate a caller's potential for suicide.

**Leveled programs** A token economy system that incorporates different levels of difficulty.

**Libido** In Freudian theory, the sexual energy that fuels the id and other forces of personality.

**Life change units (LCUs)** A system for measuring the stress associated with various life events.

**Light therapy** A treatment for seasonal affective disorders in which patients are exposed to intense light for several hours.

**Limbic system** Region of the brain at the lower part of the cerebrum that controls bodily changes associated with emotions.

**Lithium** A metallic element that occurs in nature as a mineral salt and is the most effective antibipolar drug.

**Lobotomy** Psychosurgery that severs the connections between the cortex of the brain's frontal lobes and the lower centers of the brain.

**Localized (circumscribed) amnesia** In this, the most common form of psychogenic amnesia, a person forgets all events that occurred over a limited period of time.

**Logotherapy** A treatment that focuses on changing clients' attitudes toward their existence. Developed by Viktor Frankl. See **Paradoxical intention.**

**Longitudinal study** An investigation in which the characteristics or behavior of the same subjects is observed on many different occasions over a long period of time.

**Loose association** A common thought disorder of schizophrenia, characterized by rapid shifts from one topic of conversation to another, through inconsequential and incoherent statements that the schizophrenic person apparently believes make sense.

**LSD (lysergic acid diethylamide)** A psychedelic drug derived from ergot alkaloids that brings on a state in which perceptions in general, but particularly visual perceptions, are intensified.

**Luteinizing hormone** The chemical produced by the pituitary gland that stimulates testosterone production.

**Lycanthropy** A condition in which a person believes himself or herself to be possessed by wolves or other animals.

**Lymphocytes** White blood cells that are manufactured in the lymph system and circulate throughout the bloodstream, helping the body overcome antigens.

**M'Naghten rule** A test for determining a person's responsibility for committing a crime. First used in the mid-nineteenth century, it is based on whether the person was able to determine right from wrong.

**Mainstreaming** An approach to educating mentally retarded persons in which retarded children are placed in regular classes with nonretarded children.

**Major depression** Severe episode of depressed mood that is not complicated by hallucinations or delusions.

**Male erectile disorder (impotence)** A dysfunction of the arousal phase of the sexual response cycle in men.

**Mania** A state or episode of euphoria, frenzied activity, or related episodes.

**Manic-depressive disorder** See **Bipolar disorder.**

**Manifest content** The consciously remembered features of a dream.

**Mantra** A sound, uttered or thought, used to focus one's attention to turn away from ordinary thoughts and concerns during meditation.

**MAO inhibitor**  An antidepressant drug that inhibits the action of the enzyme monoamine oxidase.

**Marijuana**  One of the drugs derived from the varieties of the hemp plant.

**Marital schism**  A family situation in which the father and mother are in open conflict, with each trying to undercut the other in competition for the loyalty of the daughter. Some theorists believe this conflict can lead to schizophrenic behavior in the daughter.

**Marital skew**  A family situation in which a so-called schizophrenogenic mother dominates the family, and the father keeps peace by continually yielding to her wishes. Some theorists believe this conflict can lead to schizophrenic behavior in the son.

**Marital therapy**  A therapeutic approach in which the therapist works with two people who share a long-term relationship. It focuses on the structure and communication patterns in the relationship.

**Masked depression**  A childhood depression disorder in which the child's primary depressive reaction appears to be hidden by other symptoms such as very active behavior, aggressiveness, psychophysiological problems, or delinquency behavior.

**Masochism**  A paraphilia in which a person becomes sexually aroused by suffering physical pain or humiliation.

**Masturbation**  Self-stimulation of the genitals to achieve sexual arousal.

**Mean**  The average of a group of scores.

**Meditation**  A technique of turning one's concentration inward and achieving a seemingly altered state of consciousness. Often used to relieve emotional and physical stress.

**Melancholia**  A condition described by early Greek and Roman philosophers and physicians as consisting of unshakable sadness. Today it is known as depression.

**Melatonin**  A hormone that appears to have a role in regulating mood. Melatonin is secreted when a person's surroundings are dark, but not when they are light.

**Meningitis**  A childhood disease marked by inflammation of the meninges of the brain. It can lead to brain damage and mental retardation if not treated.

**Mental age**  The age level at which a person performs on a test of intellectual skill, independent of his or her chronological age.

**Mental retardation**  A condition of impaired intellectual ability, generally characterized by scores below 70 on IQ tests and a poor ability to adapt.

**Mescaline**  A psychedelic drug.

**Mesmerism**  The method employed by Austrian physician F. A. Mesmer to treat hysterical disorder. It was a precursor to hypnotism.

**Metabolism**  The chemical and physical processes that go on in any living organism that break down food and convert it into energy.

**Metabolize**  The biochemical transformation of substances in the cells of living things, as when the liver breaks down alcohol into acetylaldehyde.

**Metacommunication**  The context, tone, and gestures attached to any message. See also **Primary communication.**

**Methadone**  A substitute drug for heroin. See also **Drug maintenance therapy.**

**Microencephaly**  A biological disorder characterized by a small, unusually shaped head, resulting from a combination of hereditary, prenatal, birth, and postnatal factors.

**Midbrain**  The middle region of the brain.

**Middle life transition**  A period lasting from approximately ages 40 to 45 that bridges early and middle adulthood and may be characterized by significant changes in a person's life.

**Midlife crisis**  The tumultuous and painful feelings of anxiety and depression that often accompany the changes associated with middle life transition.

**Migraine headache**  An extremely severe headache that occurs on one side of the head and is often immobilizing.

**Milieu therapy**  A humanistic approach to institutional treatment based on the premise that institutions help patients recover by creating a climate conducive to self-respect, individual responsibility, and meaningful activity.

**Mind-body dualism**  The view that the mind is a separate entity from the body, totally unable to affect physical matter or somatic processes.

**Minnesota Multiphasic Personality Inventory (MMPI)**  A widely used personality inventory consisting of a large number of statements which subjects mark as being true or false for them.

**Minor tranquilizers**  See **Antianxiety drugs.**

**Mitral valve prolapse (MVP)**  A cardiac malfunction marked by periodic episodes of heart palpitations.

**Mixed design**  A research design in which correlation analysis is used in concert with other types of analyses. See also **Quasi-experiment.**

**Model**  A set of concepts taken from one domain and applied analogously to another. It helps scientists explain and interpret observations. See also **Paradigm.**

**Modeling**  A form of learning in which an individual acquires responses by observing and imitating others.

**Monoamine oxidase (MAO)**  A body chemical that destroys the neurotransmitter norepinephrine.

**Monoamine oxidase (MAO) inhibitors**  Antidepressant drugs that lower MAO activity and thus increase the level of norepinephrine activity in the brain.

**Monozygotic twins**  Twins who have developed from a single egg.

**Mood disorder**  Disorder affecting one's emotional state, including depression and manic-depression.

**Moral anxiety**  According to Freud, anxiety that results from being punished or threatened for expressing id impulses, rather than following superego standards, so that a person eventually comes to perceive the id impulses themselves as threatening.

**Moral treatment**  An approach to treating mentally ill people, that was originated by Phillippe Pinel and William Tuke in the early nineteenth century. It emphasized moral guidance, humane and respectful intervention, and kindness.

**Morphine**  A substance derived from opium that is even more effective than opium in relieving pain.

**Multi-infarct dementia**  Dementia caused by cerebrovascular accident or stroke that restricted the blood flow to certain areas of the brain.

**Multiaxial system**  A classification system in which different "axes," or categories, represent different kinds of diagnostic information. DSM-III-R is a commonly used multiaxial system for diagnosing psychological problems.

**Multidimensional risk perspective**  A theory about eating disorders that identifies several different kinds of risk factors—sociocultural pressures, family environment, ego deficiencies and cognitive disturbances, biological factors, and mood disorders.

**Multiple personality disorder**  A dissociative disorder in which a person displays two or more distinct personalities.

**Münchausen syndrome**  A factitious disorder in which a person travels from hospital to hospital reciting symptoms, gaining admission, and receiving treatment.

**Muscle-contraction headache**  A chronic headache caused by the contraction of muscles surrounding the skull.

**Narcissistic personality disorder**  A personality disorder in which the person's life is pervaded by fantasies of success, beauty, or remarkable talent.

**Narcolepsy**  A dyssomnia characterized by sudden onsets of REM sleep during waking hours.

**Narcotic**  Any natural or synthetic derivative of opium.

**Narcotic antagonist**  A substance that counteracts the effects of opioids. See **Antagonist drug.**

**Natural experiment**  An experiment in which nature rather than an experimenter manipulates an independent variable and the experimenter systematically observes the effects.

**Naturalistic observation (in vivo observation)**  A method for observing behavior in which clinicians or researchers observe clients or subjects in their everyday environment.

**Negative feedback loops**  A physiological process in which the brain receives information about external events from the environment, processes this information, and then stimulates body organs into action. Mechanisms in the organs then provide negative feedback, telling the brain that its stimulation has been sufficient and should now stop.

**Negative symptoms (of schizophrenia)**  Symptoms that seem to reflect pathological deficits or characteristics that seem to be lacking—flat affect, poverty of speech, motor retardation, and loss of volition.

**Neologism**  A made-up word that has meaning only to the person using it.

**Nerve ending**  The region at the neuron's terminus from which an impulse that has traveled through the neuron is transmitted to a neighboring neuron.

**Neuroleptic drug**  See **Antipsychotic drugs.**

**Neurological**  Relating to the structure or activity of the brain.

**Neuron**  A nerve cell. The brain contains billions of neurons.

**Neuropsychological test**  A test that detects brain damage by measuring a person's cognitive, perceptual, and motor performances.

**Neurosis**  Freud's term for disorders characterized by intense anxiety, attributed to failure of a person's ego defense mechanisms to cope with his or her unconscious conflicts.

**Neurotic anxiety**  In Freudian theory, anxiety is experienced by people who are repeatedly and excessively prevented, by their parents or by circumstances, from expressing their id impulses.

**Neurotransmitter**  A chemical that, released by one neuron, crosses the synaptic space to be received at receptors on the dendrites of adjacent neurons.

**Night terror disorder**  A parasomnia in which a person awakens suddenly during the first hour of non-REM sleep, screaming out in extreme fear and agitation.

**Nightmare disorder**  A common parasomnia in which a person experiences chronic distressful, frightening dreams.

**Nomothetic understanding**  A general truth about the nature, causes, and treatments of abnormality.

**Norepinephrine**  A neurotransmitter whose low activity is linked to depression.

**Normalization program**  A treatment program for mentally retarded persons that provides everyday conditions that closely resemble life in the mainstream of society.

**Norms**  A given culture's explicit and implicit rules for appropriate conduct.

**Nuclear magnetic resonance (NMR) imaging**  The use of the magnetic property of certain atoms in the brain to create a detailed picture of the brain's structure.

**Observer drift**  The tendency of an observer who is rating subjects in an experiment to gradually and involuntarily change criteria, thus making the data unreliable.

**Obsession**  A repetitive thought, impulse, or mental image that seems to invade a person's consciousness.

**Obsessive compulsive disorder**  A disorder in which a person has recurrent and unwanted thoughts or the need to perform repetitive and ritualistic actions, and the experience of intense anxiety whenever these behaviors are suppressed.

**Obsessive compulsive personality disorder**  A disorder characterized by such a need to do everything right that one's productivity and relationships are impaired.

**Oedipus complex**  In Freudian theory, the pattern of desires in which boys become attracted to their mother as a sexual object and see their father as a rival they would like to push aside.

**Operant conditioning**  The process of learning through reinforcement.

**Oppositional defiant disorder**  A disorder in which children argue repeatedly with adults, lose their temper, and swear, feeling great anger and resentment.

**Operationalization**  The translating of an abstract variable of interest to an investigator into discrete, observable entities or events.

**Opioid**  Opium or any of the drugs derived from opium, including morphine, heroin, and codeine.

**Opium**  A highly addictive substance made from the sap of the opium poppy seed. It has been widely used for thousands of years to reduce physical and emotional pain.

**Opponent-process theory**  An explanation for drug addiction based on the interplay of positive, pleasurable emotions that come from ingesting the drug and negative aftereffects that leave a person feeling even worse than usual.

**Oral stage**  In this earliest developmental stage in Freud's conceptualization of psychosocial development, the infant's main libidinal gratification comes from feeding and from the body parts involved in it.

**Organic amnesia**  Amnesia that has an identifiable physiological cause.

**Organic delusional syndrome**  A disorder in which a specific organic factor is causing delusions.

**Organic hallucinosis**  A disorder in which a specific organic factor is causing hallucinations.

**Organic mental disorders**  Mental disorders that have clear physical causes.

**Organic mental syndrome**  A cluster of symptoms caused by a dysfunction of the brain. Characterized by changes in a person's behavior, emotion, or thought.

**Organicity**  The quality of being caused primarily by damage to the brain or alterations in brain activity.

**Orgasm**  The third stage of the sexual response cycle, consisting of reflexive muscular contractions in the pelvic region.

**Orgasm phase**  The third phase in the sexual response cycle, characterized by reflexive muscular contractions in the pelvic region.

**Orgasmic reorientation**  A procedure for treating pedophilia or certain other paraphilias in which clients are conditioned to new, more appropriate sources of erotic stimuli.

**Outpatient**  A setting for treatment in which persons visit a therapist's office as opposed to remaining in a hospital.

**Overanxious disorder**  A disorder of childhood defined as excessive or unrealistic levels of anxiety or worry for a period of six months or longer.

**Overt behavior**  Observable actions or clear verbalizations.

**Panic attack**  A discrete period of panic that usually occurs unpredictably and without apparent provocation.

**Panic disorder**  An anxiety disorder characterized by recurrent attacks of terror.

**Panic disorder with agoraphobia**  A panic disorder in which panic attacks lead to agoraphobic patterns of behavior.

**Panic disorder without agoraphobia**  A panic disorder in which agoraphobia is absent.

**Paradigm**  An implicit theoretical framework that arises out of an explicit set of basic assumptions. A scientist's paradigm affects the way he or she interprets observations and other data.

**Paradoxical intention**  A technique used in logotherapy in which the therapist employs direct and sometimes humorous confrontation to help clients embrace the very thoughts, fears, and behaviors that are causing problems for them.

**Paranoia**  A psychosis characterized by delusions.

**Paranoid disorder**  See **Delusional disorder.**

**Paranoid personality disorder**  A personality disorder characterized by the shunning of close relationships because of mistrust in other people.

**Paranoid schizophrenia**  A form of schizophrenia in which an organized system of delusions and hallucinations guides the person's life.

**Paraphilias**  Disorders in which the person has recurrent and intense sexual urges and sexually arousing fantasies in response to sexual objects or situations that society deems inappropriate.

**Paraprofessional**  A person without previous professional training who provides services under the supervision of a mental health professional.

**Parasomnias**  Sleep disorders characterized by the occurrence of abnormal events during sleep.

**Parasympathetic nervous system**  The group of nerve fibers of the autonomic nervous system that helps maintain normal organ functioning. It also slows organ functioning after stimulation and returns other body processes to normal.

**Parens patriae**  The principle by which the state can make decisions—such as to hospitalize a person against his or her wishes—that are believed to promote the individual's best interests and protect him or her from self-harm or neglect.

**Parkinson's disease**  An age-related disorder of the central nervous system that seems to be cause by decreased dopamine activity.

**Parkinsonian symptom**  Dystonia, akathisia, tardive dyskinesia, and other symptoms similar to those found in Parkinson's disease. Schizophrenic patients taking antipsychotic medication that blocks the activity of dopamine may display one or more of these symptoms.

**Partial reinforcement schedule**  A token economy system in which people receive tokens only some of the times that they perform target behaviors. This is thought to encourage them to perform a behavior for its own sake.

**Passive-aggressive personality disorder**  A personality disorder characterized by the need to control the lives of people close to oneself by indirect means.

**Pathological gambling**  The inability to resist wagering, marked by irritability and restlessness if gambling is prevented.

**PCP**  Phencyclidine, a psychedelic drug.

**Pedophilia**  A disorder in which a person obtains sexual gratification by watching, touching, or engaging in simple or complex sexual acts with prepubescent children.

**Peer review**  A process in which a panel of clinicians reviews a therapist's reports of a client's treatment and recommends that insurance benefits be either continued or terminated.

**Penile prosthesis**  A surgical implantation consisting of a semirigid rod made of rubber and wire that produces an artificial erection.

**Penis envy**  The Freudian theory that girls wish to overcome their feelings of inferiority during the phallic phase by having a penis.

**Performance anxiety**  The fear of performing inadequately and a consequent tension experienced during sex. See also **Spectator role.**

**Perseveration**  The persistent repetition of words and statements often seen in schizophrenia or autism.

**Personality**  The unique pattern of behavior, perception, and emotion displayed by each individual.

**Personality assessment**  The gathering of information about the components of someone's personality and any unconscious conflicts he or she may be experiencing.

**Personality disorder**  A disorder in which inflexible and maladaptive personality traits impair social or occupational functioning or cause intense distress.

**Personality test**  A device, such as pencil-and-paper inventory, that is used to describe and measure aspects of a subject's personality.

**Personality trait**  An enduring consistency with which a person reacts to and acts upon his or her surroundings.

**Phallic stage**  In psychoanalytic theory, the period between the third and fourth years when the focus of sexual pleasure shifts to the genitals.

**Phenomenology**  One's personal experiences and perspectives of the world.

**Phenothiazine**  A group of antihistamine drugs, originally prescribed for allergic reactions, that were found to be effective antipsychotic medications.

**Phenylethylamine test**  A biological assessment technique that indirectly measures the level of phenylethylamine, a chemical linked to depression, in the brain.

**Phenylketonuria (PKU)**  A metabolic disorder that if untreated, causes retardation.

**Phobia**  A persistent and irrational fear of a specific object, activity, or situation.

**Phototherapy**  See **Light therapy.**

**Physostigmine**  A drug used to prevent the breakdown of acetylcholine in an effort to reduce the effects of Alzheimer's disease.

**Pick's disease**  A rare progressive impairment that is often difficult to differentiate from Alzheimer's disease.

**Placebo**  A sham treatment that the subject believes to be genuine.

**Play therapy**  An approach to treating childhood anxiety disorders that helps children express their conflicts and feelings indirectly by drawing, playing with toys, and making up stories.

**Pleasure principle**  In Freudian theory, the pursuit of gratification that motivates the id.

**Plethysmograph**  A device used to measure sexual arousal.

**Polydrug use**  The misuse of combinations of drugs to achieve a synergistic effect.

**Positive symptoms (of schizophrenia)**  Symptoms that seem to represent pathological excesses or bizarre additions to a normal repertoire of behavior. They include delusions, hallucinations, and florid formal thought disorders.

**Positron emission tomography (PET scan)**  A computer-produced motion picture showing rates of metabolism throughout the brain.

**Post-traumatic stress disorder**  Fear and related symptoms experienced long after a traumatic event.

**Poverty of content**  A lack of meaning in spite of high emotion that is often found in the speech of schizophrenics who display loose associations.

**Predisposition**  An inborn or acquired vulnerability (or inclination or diathesis) for developing certain symptoms.

**Premature ejaculation**  Ejaculation with minimal sexual stimulation or before, upon, or shortly after penetration and before the person wishes it.

**Premorbid**  The period prior to the onset of an illness.

**Preparedness**  A predisposition to acquire certain fears.

**Presenile**  Occurring in middle age.

**Presenile dementia**  Dementia occurring in middle age. See also **Dementia.**

**Prevalence**  The total number of cases of a problem or disorder occurring in a population over a specific period of time.

**Prevention**  A key aspect of community mental health programs, which strive to prevent or at least minimize mental disorders.

**Primary communication**  The semantic content in any message. See also **Metacommunication.**

**Primary gain**  In psychodynamic theory, part of a mechanism for explaining hysterical somatoform disorder. It is the goal achieved by hysterical symptoms of keeping internal conflicts out of awareness.

**Primary process**  In Freudian theory, a source of id gratification that consists of activating a memory or image of a desired object.

**Principle of reinforcement**  B. F. Skinner's version of the law of effect, believed by him to be the primary mechanism for explaining and controlling human behavior.

**Proband**  The person who is the focus of a genetic study.

**Prodromal phase.**  The period during which symptoms of schizophrenia are not yet prominent, but the person has begun to deteriorate from previous levels of functioning.

**Prognosis**  A prediction on the course and outcome of a disorder.

**Projection**  An ego defense mechanism in which a person attributes to others undesirable characteristics or impulses in himself or herself.

**Projective test**  A test that consists of unstructured or ambiguous material to which people are asked to respond.

**Prolactin**  A pituitary hormone that can interfere with the sex drive.

**Prophylactic drug**  A drug that actually helps prevent symptoms from developing.

**Prospective analysis**  A study that predicts future changes on the basis of past and present events.

**Protection and advocacy system**  The system by which lawyers and advocates who work for patients may investigate possible cases of patient abuse and neglect and then address any problems they find.

**Psilocybin**  A psychedelic drug.

**Psychedelic drug**  A substance, such as LSD, that causes profound perceptual changes.

**Psychiatric social worker**  A mental health specialist who is qualified to conduct psychotherapy upon earning a Masters degree or Doctorate in social work.

**Psychiatrist**  A physician who in addition to medical school has completed three to four years of training in the treatment of abnormal mental functioning.

**Psychoanalysis**  Either the theory or the treatment of abnormal mental functioning that emphasizes unconscious conflicts as the cause of psychopathology.

**Psychodrama**  A group therapy technique that calls for group members to act out dramatic roles as if they were participating in an improvised play in which they express their feelings and thoughts, explore new behaviors and attitudes, and empathize with the feelings and perspectives of others.

**Psychodynamic model**  The theoretical perspective that sees all human functioning as being shaped by dynamic psychological forces and looks at people's unconscious internal conflicts in order to explain their behavior.

**Psychodynamic therapy**  A system of therapy whose goals is to help clients uncover past traumatic events and the inner conflicts that have resulted from them; resolve, or settle, those conflicts; and resume interrupted personal development.

**Psychogenesis**  The development of abnormal functioning from psychological causes.

**Psychogenic amnesia**  A memory disruption in which the inability to recall important personal events and information is not due to organic causes.

**Psychogenic fugue**  A psychologically caused disorder in which a person travels to a new location and assumes a new identity, simultaneously forgetting his or her past.

**Psychogenic illness**  An illness caused by psychological factors such as worry, family stress, and unconscious needs.

**Psychological autopsy** A procedure used to analyze information about a deceased person to determine whether the person's death was self inflicted.

**Psychological report** A clinician's write-up of information collected and interpreted, creating a clinical picture framed in the language of the clinician's particular theoretical orientation.

**Psychoneuroimmunology** The study of the connections between stress, illness, and the body's immune system.

**Psychopathology** Any abnormal pattern of functioning that may be described as deviant, distressful, dysfunctional, or dangerous.

**Psychopathy** See **Antisocial personality disorder.**

**Psychophysiological disorders** Illnesses believed to result from an interaction of organic and psychological factors.

**Psychosexual stages** The developmental stage defined by Freud in which the id, ego, and superego interact. Each stage is marked by a different source of libidinal pleasure.

**Psychosis** A state in which an individual loses contact with reality.

**Psychosomatic illnesses** Illnesses that have both psychological and physical causes.

**Psychotherapy** A treatment system in which words, acts, and rituals are used by sufferer and healer to overcome psychological difficulties.

**Psychotropic drugs** Drugs that primarily affect the brain.

**Pubococcygeal (PC) muscle** The primary pelvic muscle in women, used during sexual activity

**Pyromania** The deliberate setting of fires to achieve intense pleasure or release tension.

**Q-sort** A widely used self-report instrument in which subjects are given a set of cards containing statements about personality or performance and are asked to sort them into piles describing different aspects of themselves.

**Quasi-experiment** An experiment in which investigators do not randomly assign the subjects to control and experimental groups but instead make use of groups that already exist in the world at large.

**Quinine** A drug that is often added to heroin to counteract the dangers of infection.

**Random sample** Subjects who have (1) been randomly selected from the population and then (2) randomly placed either in the control condition or in the experimental condition.

**Rape** Forced sexual intercourse against the will of the victim.

**Rapid eye movement (REM) sleep** The period of the sleep cycle during which the eyes move quickly, back and forth, indicating that the person is dreaming.

**Rapprochement** An effort to delineate a set of "common therapeutic strategies" that characterize the work of all effective therapists.

**Rational emotive therapy** A therapeutic technique developed by Albert Ellis that helps clients to discover the irrational assumptions governing their emotional responses and to change those assumptions into constructive ways of viewing the world and themselves.

**Rationalization** Ego defense mechanism in which one creates acceptable reasons for unwanted or unacceptable behavior.

**Reaction formation** An ego defense mechanism in which a repressed desire is instead expressed by opposite personality traits (such as when an anal desire to be messy and rebellious is repressed and expressed as neatness and conformity).

**Reactive depression** A depression that appears to follow on the heels of clear-cut precipitating events.

**Reactivity** The extent to which the very presence of an observer affects a person's behavior.

**Reality principle** In Freudian theory, the knowledge we acquire through experience and from the people around us that it can be dangerous or unacceptable to express our id impulses outright.

**Receptor** A site on a neuron that receives a neurotransmitter.

**Reciprocal inhibition** A desensitization process in which a fear response is stopped by pairing fear-arousing stimuli with responses (such as relaxation) that are incompatible with fear.

**Reflex gratification** In Freudian theory, a direct source of id grati-

fication, as when an infant seeks and receives milk from the mother's breast to satisfy its hunger.

**Regression** An ego defense mechanism in which a person returns to a more primitive mode of interacting with the world.

**Reinforcement** The desirable or undesirable stimuli that follows as a result of an organism's behavior.

**Relapse-prevention training** A treatment technique in which heavy drinkers are taught to use self-monitoring to identify the situations and emotional changes that place them at high risk for heavy drinking.

**Relaxation training** A procedure in which clients are taught to release all the tension in their bodies on cue.

**Reliability** A measure of the consistency of test or research results.

**Repression** An ego defense mechanism that prevents unacceptable impulses from reaching consciousness.

**Reserpine** A drug originally used to treat high blood pressure but later discovered to cause depression in some people.

**Residential treatment center** A place where former drug addicts live, work, and socialize in a drug-free environment.

**Residual schizophrenia** A condition in which the florid symptoms of schizophrenia have lessened in intensity and number yet remain with the patient in a residual form.

**Resistance** An ego defense mechanism that blocks a patient's free associations or causes the patient to change subjects to avoid a potentially painful discussion.

**Resistance stage** The parasympathetic nervous system's attempt to counteract the response of the sympathetic nervous system in the presence of a threat. See also **General adaptation syndrome.**

**Resolution phase** The fourth phase in the sexual response cycle, characterized by relaxation and a decline in arousal following orgasm.

**Respondent conditioning** See **Classical conditioning.**

**Response prevention** See **Exposure and response prevention.**

**Response set** A particular way of responding to questions or statements on a test, such as always selecting "true," regardless of the content of the questions.

**Restriction fragment-length polymorphism (RFLP)** A technique used in chromosomal mapping in which gene segments from members of a family are compared in order to locate the gene responsible for an inherited disorder, such as schizophrenia.

**Reticular formation** The body's arousal center located in the brain.

**Retrograde amnesia** A lack of memory about events that occurred before the event that caused the amnesia.

**Retrospective analysis** A kind of psychological autopsy in which clinicians and researchers piece together data from the past of a person who has committed suicide.

**Revealed differences approach** A technique for investigating familial influences in which parents and their children are brought together by an investigator and told to reach an agreement on issues about which they disagree.

**Reversal design (ABAB)** An experimental design in which behavior is measured to achieve a baseline (A), then again after the treatment has been applied (B), then again after the conditions during baseline have been reintroduced (A), and then once again after the treatment is reintroduced (B).

**Reward** A pleasurable stimulus given to an organism to encourage a specific behavior.

**Rorschach test** A projective test using a subject's reactions to inkblots to examine the psychological condition of the subject.

**Risk study** A research method that surveys the biological relatives of a patient who has been diagnosed with a specific abnormality to see which and how many of them have the same disorder.

**Role play** A therapy technique in which clients are instructed to act out roles assigned to them by the therapist.

**Rosenthal effect** The general finding that the results of any experiment often conform to the expectations of the experimenter. It is attributed to the inescapable effects of bias.

**Rush** A spasm of warmth and ecstasy that occurs when certain drugs, such as heroin, are ingested.

**Sadism** Sexual pleasure achieved through inflicting physical or emotional pain.

**Sadistic personality disorder**  A personality disorder characterized by a need to control people and to bring psychological coercion to bear on others.

**Sample**  A group of subjects that is representative of the larger population about which a researcher wishes to make a statement.

**Schizoaffective disorder**  A disorder in which symptoms of both schizophrenia and a mood disorder are present without meeting the full diagnostic criteria of either.

**Schizoid personality disorder**  A personality disorder characterized by a desire to avoid social contact and to be alone.

**Schizophrenia**  A psychotic disorder in which personal, social, and occupational functioning that were previously adaptive deteriorate as a result of distorted perceptions, disturbed thought processes, deviant emotional states, and motor abnormalities.

**Schizophreniform disorder**  A disorder in which all of the key features of schizophrenia are present but last less than six months.

**Schizophrenogenic mother**  A mother who is supposedly cold, domineering, and impervious to the needs of others. It has been suggested by some theorists that this type of behavior in the mother may be associated with schizophrenia in the child.

**Schizotypal personality disorder**  A personality disorder characterized by marked egocentric thoughts and perceptions and avoidance of others.

**School phobia**  Extreme anxiety about attending school.

**School refusal**  See **School phobia.**

**Scientific method**  The process of systematically acquiring and evaluating information through observation to gain an understanding of specific phenomena.

**Seasonal affective disorder (SAD)**  A mood disorder in which mood episodes are related to changes in season. It appears to be related to shifts in the overall amount of light one is exposed to, and correspondingly, to shifts in melatonin secretions.

**Second-generation antidepressants**  Antidepressant drugs that differ structurally from tricyclics and MAO inhibitors and affect the sensitivity of norepinephrine and serotonin receptors.

**Secondary gain**  In psychodynamic theory, part of a mechanism for explaining hysterical somatoform disorder. Hysterical symptoms not only keep internal conflicts out of awareness (primary gain) but also result in the person's receiving kindness or sympathy from others (secondary gain).

**Secondary process**  In Freudian theory, the ego's mode of operation, consisting of assessing new situations, weighing in past experiences, anticipating consequences, and planning how best to obtain gratification.

**Sedative-hypnotic drug**  A drug used in low doses to reduce anxiety and in high doses to help people sleep.

**Selective amnesia**  A disorder in which the person remembers some but not all events occurring over a circumscribed period of time.

**Self psychology**  A variation of psychoanalysis developed by Heinz Kohut that focuses on a person's self-worth.

**Self-actualization**  The humanistic process by which people fulfill their potential for goodness and growth.

**Self-defeating personality disorder**  A personality disorder characterized by a sense of martyrdom and by behavior that is self-effacing and servile.

**Self-help group (mutual help group)**  A therapy group made up of people who have similar problems and come together to help and support one another without the direct leadership of a professional clinician.

**Self-hypnosis**  The induction by oneself of a hypnotic state.

**Self-instruction training**  A cognitive therapy that helps people solve problems and cope with stress by teaching them how to make helpful statements to themselves and how to apply such statements in difficult circumstances.

**Self-monitoring**  A technique for monitoring behavior in which clients observe themselves.

**Self-report inventory**  A test consisting of lists of items that people are asked to evaluate as characteristic or uncharacteristic of them.

**Self-statement**  A statement about oneself, sometimes counterproductive, that comes to mind during stressful situations.

**Senile**  Typical of or occurring in people over the age of 65.

**Senile dementia**  See **Dementia.**

**Sensate focus**  A treatment for sexual disorders that instructs couples to take the focus away from intercourse and instead spend time concentrating on mutual massage, kissing, and hugging. This approach reduces the pressure to achieve erection and orgasm.

**Sensitivity training group**  A small group in which a "trainer," or leader, helps participants to observe and think about their own interactions and, as a result, to develop greater insight about and skill in human communications and relationships.

**Sensory blunting**  A significant reduction in the strength of one's physical sensations.

**Separation anxiety disorder**  A childhood disorder characterized by excessive anxiety, even panic, whenever the child is separated from a parent.

**Serotonin**  A neurotransmitter whose low activity is linked to depression.

**Sex offender statute**  The presumption by legislators that people who are repeatedly found guilty of certain sex crimes are mentally ill and should be categorized as "mentally disordered sex offenders."

**Sexual arousal disorder**  A failure of lubrication or genital swelling in women or an absence of penile erection in men, or the lack of a subjective sense of sexual excitement and pleasure in either men or women.

**Sexual aversion**  An intense dislike of sexual activity in which the person feels revulsion, disgust, anxiety, and fear.

**Sexual dysfunction**  A disorder in which a person is unable to function normally in some area of the human sexual response cycle.

**Sexual masochism**  A pattern in which a person has repeated and intense sexual urges and fantasies that involve being humiliated, beaten, bound, or otherwise made to suffer.

**Sexual pain disorder**  A dysfunction in which a person experiences pain during arousal or intercourse. See also **Dyspareunia** and **Vaginismus.**

**Sexual response cycle**  The generalized sequence of behavior and feelings that occur during sexual intercourse, consisting of desire, arousal, orgasm, and resolution.

**Sexual sadism**  A pattern in which a person, usually a male, is intensely sexually aroused by the act or thought of inflicting physical or psychological suffering on others, and acts on or is disturbed by such thoughts.

**Shaping**  A learning procedure in which successive approximations of the desired behavior are rewarded.

**Sheltered workshop**  A protected and supervised workplace that offers clients occupational training.

**Simple phobia**  A persistent fear of an object or situation (excluding social phobia and agoraphobia).

**Single-subject experimental design**  A research method in which a single subject is observed and measured both before and after the manipulation of an independent variable.

**Situation (or state) anxiety**  Anxiety experienced in particular situations or environments.

**Sleep apnea**  A dyssomnia in which the person actually stops breathing for thirty or more seconds while asleep.

**Sleepwalking disorder**  A parasomnia in which people leave their beds and walk around without being conscious of the episode or remembering it later.

**Social breakdown syndrome**  A pattern of deterioration resulting from institutionalization and characterized by extreme withdrawal, anger, physical aggressiveness, and loss of interest in personal appearance.

**Social phobia**  A persistent fear of some form of social evaluation and humiliation.

**Social skills training**  A therapeutic approach used by behavioral therapists to help people acquire or improve their social skills and assertiveness through the use of role playing and rehearsing of desirable behaviors.

**Social therapy**  An approach to therapy in which the therapist makes practical advice and life adjustment a central focus of treatment for schizophrenia.

**Sociocultural model**  The theoretical perspective that emphasizes the effect of society and culture on individual behavior.

**Sociology**  The study of human relationships and social groups.

**Sociopathy**  See **Antisocial personality disorder.**

**Sociotherapy**  See **Social therapy.**

**Sodium amobarbital (amytal)**  A drug used to put people into a near-sleep state during which they may recall forgotten events.

**Sodium pentobarbital (Pentothal)**  See **Sodium amobarbital.**

**Somatization disorder**  A somatoform disorder characterized by numerous physical ailments without an organic basis.

**Somatoform disorder**  A physical illness that eludes medical assessment. It differs from a factitious disorder in that the patient experiences no sense of willing the symptoms or of having control over them.

**Somatoform pain disorder**  A somatoform disorder characterized by severe and prolonged pain that has no medical explanation.

**Somatogenesis**  The development of abnormal functioning from physical causes.

**Spectator role.**  A psychological position in which a person's focus on his or her sexual performance is so pronounced that sexual performance and enjoyment are impeded.

**Standardization**  The process in which a test is administered to a large group of subjects whose performance then serves as a common standard or norm.

**State dependent learning**  Learning that becomes associated with conditions in which it occurred, so that it is best remembered under the same conditions. For example, information learned when under the influence of alcohol is better recalled when the person is again under the influence of alcohol.

**State hospital**  A public mental institution.

**Statistical analysis**  The application of principles of probability to the findings of a study to learn how likely it is that the findings have occurred by chance.

**Statistical significance**  A measure of the probability that an observed event occurred by chance rather than as the result of experimental manipulation.

**Statutory rape**  Sexual intercourse with a minor.

**Stimulant drug**  A drug that induces physical agitation.

**Stimulus generalization**  A phenomenon in which responses to one stimulus are also elicited by similar stimuli.

**Stress inoculation**  See **Self-instruction training.**

**Stress management training**  An approach to treating generalized anxiety disorders that focuses on teaching clients to reduce and control stress.

**Structural family therapy**  A family systems treatment approach in which the therapist pays particular attention to the family power structure, the role each member plays within the family, and the alliances between family members.

**Structured observation**  A method of observing behavior in which people are monitored in artificial settings created in clinicians' offices or in laboratories.

**Subintentioned death**  A death in which the victim plays an indirect, covert, partial, or unconscious causal role.

**Subject**  An individual chosen to participate in a study.

**Sublimation**  In psychoanalytic theory, the rechanneling of narcissistic impulses into endeavors that are both socially acceptable and personally gratifying.

**Subpersonalities**  The distinct personalities found in individuals suffering from multiple personality disorder.

**Substance abuse**  A pattern of behavior in which a person relies on a drug excessively and chronically, allowing it to occupy a central position in his or her life.

**Substance dependence**  A pattern of behavior typical of a person with a physical addiction to a drug.

**Substance use disorder**  A long-term pattern of maladaptive behavior centered around the dependence on or use of certain substances.

**Sudden death**  Unexpected death in the wake of psychological trauma.

**Suicide**  A self-inflicted death in which the person acted intentionally, directly, and consciously.

**Suicide prevention programs**  Programs found in many hospitals and counseling centers that try to identify people who are at the point of killing themselves and to help them perceive their situation more accurately and constructively in order to overcome the crisis.

**Superego**  One of the three psychological forces proposed by Freud as central to shaping the personality. The superego emerges from the ego and embodies the values and ideals taught to us by our parents.

**Support group**  A therapylike group of people with a common psychological problem who meet and work on their difficulties together.

**Supportive nursing care**  A treatment, applied to anorexia nervosa in particular, in which well-trained nurses conduct a day-to-day hospital program.

**Symbolic loss**  A Freudian concept developed to explain depression in cases where the person has not lost a loved one. In symbolic loss any valued lost object (for example, a loss of employment) is unconsciously interpreted as the loss of a loved one.

**Sympathetic nervous system**  The nerve fibers of the autonomic nervous system that quicken the heartbeat and produce other changes experienced as fear or anxiety.

**Symptom**  A physical or psychological sign of a disorder.

**Synapse**  The tiny space into which neurotransmitters are released, between the nerve ending of one neuron and the dendrite of another.

**Syndrome**  A cluster of symptoms that usually occur together.

**Synergistic effect**  An enhancement of effects that occurs when more than one drug is having an effect on the body at any one time.

**Synesthesia**  A crossing over of sensory perceptions, caused by LSD and other psychedelic drugs. For example, a loud sound may be experienced as visible fluctuation in the air.

**Systematic desensitization**  A process in which phobic clients learn to react calmly instead of with intense fear to the objects or situations they dread.

**T-group**  A small group guided by a leader and similar to an encounter group in intensity but concerned primarily with educating people.

**Tarantism**  Also known as St. Vitus's dance, this was a phenomenon that occurred throughout Europe between A.D. 900 and 1800 in which groups of people would suddenly start to jump around, dance, and go into convulsions.

**Tardive dyskinesia**  Extrapyramidal effects, such as involuntary smacking of the lips or wagging of the chin, that appear in some patients after they have taken antipsychotic drugs for a few years. It is more common in older patients, and it is sometimes difficult or impossible to eliminate. See also **Extrapyramidal effects.**

**Tay-Sachs disease**  A metabolic disorder resulting from a pairing of recessive genes that causes mental deterioration, loss of visual functioning, and death.

**Tension headache**  See **Muscle-contraction headache.**

**Testosterone**  The principal male hormone.

**Tetrahydroaminoacridine (THA)**  A drug used to prevent the breakdown of acetylcholine and reduce the effects of Alzheimer's disease.

**Tetrahydrocannabinol (THC)**  The main psychoactive ingredient of the hemp plant.

**Thalamus**  The region of the brain that acts as a relay station for sensory information, sending it to the cerebrum.

**Thanatos**  According to the Freudian view, thanatos is the basic *death* instinct that functions in opposition to the *life* instinct.

**Thematic Apperception Test**  A projective test using pictures that depict people in somewhat unclear situations.

**Therapist**  A person who implements a system of therapy to help a person overcome psychological difficulties.

**Therapies**  Special, systematic processes for helping people overcome their psychological difficulties.

**Thought stopping**  A cognitive-behavioral technique for treating obsessions in which therapists teach clients to interrupt their obsessive thoughts, based on the assumption that doing so will keep them from occurring so often.

**Token economy**  A program in which a person's desirable behavior is reinforced systematically throughout the day by the awarding of tokens that can be exchanged for goods or privileges.

**Tolerance**  The adjustment the body makes to the habitual presence of certain drugs so that larger and larger doses are required to achieve the initial effect.

**Trait**  A characteristic of an individual that may be observed and measured.

**Trait anxiety**  A person's general level of anxiety.

**Tranquilizer**  A drug that reduces anxiety.

**Transference**  A phenomenon that occurs during psychotherapy, in which the patient acts toward the therapist as he or she did toward important figures, particularly parents, as a child.

**Transsexualism**  A disorder characterized by the intense belief that one was born into the "wrong" gender and is trapped in an anatomically incorrect body.

**Transvestic fetishism (transvestism, or cross-dressing)**  The recurrent need or desire to dress in clothes of the opposite sex to achieve sexual arousal.

**Trephination**  An ancient operation in which a stone instrument was used to cut away a circular section of the skull. It is believed to have been a Stone Age treatment for abnormal behavior.

**Trichotillomania**  An extremely painful and upsetting compulsion in which people repeatedly pull at and even yank out their hair, eyelashes, and eyebrows.

**Tricyclic drug**  An antidepressant drug such as imipramine that has three rings in its molecular structure.

**Trisomy**  Three chromosomes of one kind rather than the usual two.

**Tube and intravenous feeding**  Forced nourishment provided to sufferers of eating disorders when their condition becomes life-threatening.

**Two-physician certificates (2 PCs)**  Certification by two physicians that a person is in such a state of mind as to be dangerous to himself or herself or to others and may be committed involuntarily.

**Type A personality**  A personality pattern characterized by hostility, cynicism, drivenness, impatience, competitiveness, and ambition.

**Type I schizophrenia**  Schizophrenia that is dominated by positive symptoms.

**Type II schizophrenia**  Schizophrenia that is dominated by negative symptoms.

**Tyramine**  A chemical that, if allowed to accumulate, can raise blood pressure dangerously. It is found in many common foods and is broken down by MAO. See also **MAO inhibitor.**

**Tyrosine**  The chemical that most people produce by metabolizing the amino acid phenylalanine, a process that fails to occur in children with phenylketonuria.

**Ulcer**  Lesions or holes that form in the wall of the stomach or of the duodenum.

**Unconditional positive regard**  Full, warm acceptance of a person regardless of what he or she says, thinks, or feels; a critical component of client-centered therapy.

**Unconditioned response (UCR)**  The natural, automatic response elicited by an unconditioned stimulus.

**Unconditioned stimulus (UCS)**  A stimulus that elicits an automatic, natural response.

**Unconscious**  The deeply hidden mass of memories, experiences, and impulses that is viewed in Freudian theory as the wellspring of most behavior.

**Undifferentiated schizophrenia**  A diagnosis assigned to people who are considered schizophrenic but who do not fall neatly into one of the categories of schizophrenia.

**Undoing**  An ego defense mechanism used by psychoanalytic theorists to explain obsessive compulsive disorder. The compulsive act

is thought to implicitly cancel out the person's undesirable impulses.

**Unilateral electroconvulsive therapy (ECT)**  A form of electroconvulsive therapy in which only one electrode is used and electrical current passes through only one side of the brain. Unilateral ECT causes less confusion and memory loss than bilateral ECT and is equally effective.

**Unipolar depression**  Depression without a history of mania which is followed by a return to a normal or nearly normal mood.

**Vacuum erection device (VED)**  A device consisting of a hollow cylinder that is placed over the penis connected to a hand pump. The pump is used to create a partial vacuum around the penis, which fills with blood as a result and becomes erect.

**Vaginismus**  Spasmodic contractions of the muscles around the outer third of the vagina, preventing entry of the penis.

**Validity**  The accuracy of a test's or study's results i.e., the extent to which the test or study actually measures or shows what it claims to. See also **External validity** and **Internal validity.**

**Valium**  A minor tranquilizer.

**Variable**  Any characteristic or event that can vary, whether from time to time, from place to place, or from person to person.

**Ventromedial hypothalamus (VMH)**  The region of the hypothalamus that when activated depresses hunger.

**Vicarious conditioning**  Acquiring fear or other reactions through modeling.

**Visual hallucinations**  Hallucinations in which a person may either experience vague perceptions, perhaps of colors or clouds, or have distinct visions of people, objects, or scenes that are not there.

**Voyeurism**  A disorder in which a person has recurrent and intense sexual desires to observe people in secret as they undress or to spy on couples engaged in intercourse.

**Wayy flexibility**  A catatonia in which a person will maintain a posture into he or she has been placed by someone else.

**Weight set point**  The weight level that a person is predisposed to maintain, set up by a "weight thermostat" that is governed by the lateral and ventromedial hypothalamus.

**Wernicke's encephalopathy**  A potentially fatal neurological disease characterized by confusion, excitement, delirium, double vision, and other eye-movement abnormalities, and caused by an alcohol-related deficiency of vitamin B.

**Windigo**  A disorder once common among Algonquin hunters who believed in a supernatural monster that ate human beings and had the power to bewitch them and turn them into cannibals.

**Wish fulfillment**  In psychodynamic theory, the gratification of id instincts by primary process thinking.

**Withdrawal symptoms**  Unpleasant, sometimes dangerous reactions that occur when drug users suddenly stop taking or reduce their dosage of a drug.

**Working through**  The process during psychoanalysis of confronting repressed conflicts, reinterpreting memories and feelings, and overcoming their negative effects.

# REFERENCES

## JOURNAL ABBREVIATIONS

Acta Psychiatr. Scandin. *Acta Psychiatrica Scandinavica*
Adol. Psychiat. *Adolescent Psychiatry*
Adv. Behav. Res. Ther. *Advances in Behavior Research and Therapy*
Amer. J. Clin. Hyp. *American Journal of Clinical Hypnosis*
Amer. J. Ment. Def. *American Journal of Mental Deficiency*
Amer. J. Orthopsychiat. *American Journal of Orthopsychiatry*
Amer. J. Psychiat. *American Journal of Psychiatry*
Amer. J. Psychother. *American Journal of Psychotherapy*
Amer. J. Pub. Hlth. *American Journal of Public Health*
Amer. Psychol. *American Psychologist*
Ann. Clin. Psychiat. *Annals of Clinical Psychiatry*
Annu. Rev. Neurosci. *Annual Review of Neuroscience*
Annu. Rev. Psychol. *Annual Review of Psychology*
Arch. Gen. Psychiat. *Archives of General Psychiatry*
Austral. New Zeal. J. Psychiat. *Australian and New Zealand Journal of Psychiatry*
Austral. J. Clin. Exp. Hyp. *Australian Journal of Clinical and Experimental Hypnosis*
Behav. Mod. *Behavior Modification*
Behav. Psychother. *Behavioural Psychotherapy*
Behav. Res. Ther. *Behavior Research and Therapy*
Behav. Sci. *Behavioral Science*
Behav. Ther. *Behavior Therapy*
Biofeed. Self-Reg. *Biofeedback and Self-Regulation*
Bio. Psychiat. *Biological Psychiatry*
Brit. J. Cog. Psycother. *British Journal of Cognitive Psychotherapy*
Brit. J. Psychiat. *British Journal of Psychiatry*
Bull. Menninger Clin. *Bulletin of the Menninger Clinic*
Bull. Psychosom. Soc. *Bulletin of the Psychosomatic Society*
Canad. J. Psychiat. *Canadian J. Psychiatry*
Child Dev. *Child Development*
Clin. Pharm. Ther. *Clinical and Pharmacological Therapy*
Child Psychiat. Human Dev. *Child Psychiatry and Human Development*
Cog. Emot. *Cognitive Emotions*
Cog. Ther. Res. *Cognitive Therapy and Research*
Comprehen. Psychiat. *Comprehensive Psychiat.*
Dis. Nerv. Sys. *Diseases of the Nervous System*
Drug Alc. Dep. *Drug and Alcohol Dependence*
Eur. Arch. Psychiat. Neurol. Sci. *European Archives of Psychiatry and Neurological Science*
Gen. Hosp. Psychiat. *General Hospital Psychiatry*
Hosp. Comm. Psychiat. *Hospital and Community Psychiatry*
Individ. Psychol. J. Adlerian Res. Prac. *Individual Psychology: A Journal of Adlerian Theory, Research and Practice*
Integ. Psychiat. *Integrated Psychiatry*
Inter. J. Addic. *International Journal of Addiction*
Inter. J. Clin. Exp. Hyp. *International Journal of Clinical and Experimental Hypnosis*
Inter. J. Eat. Dis. *International Journal of Eating Disorders*
Inter. J. Offend. Ther. Compar. Crimin. *International Journal of Offender Therapy and Comparative Criminology*
Inter. J. Psychoanal. *International Journal of Psychoanalysis*
Inter. J. Psychosom. *International Journal of Psychosomatics*
J. Abnorm. Child Psychol. *Journal of Abnormal Child Psychology*
J. Abnorm. Psychol. *Journal of Abnormal Psychology*
J. Abnorm. Soc. Psychol. *Journal of Abnormal and Social Psychology*

J. Affect. Dis. *Journal of Affective Disorders*
J. Amer. Acad. Child Adol. Psychiat. *Journal of the American Academy of Child and Adolescent Psychiatry*
J. Amer. Acad. Psychoanal. *Journal of the American Academy of Psychoanalysis*
JAMA *Journal of the American Medical Association*
J. Appl. Behav. Anal. *Journal of Applied Behavior Analysis*
J. Appl. Behav. Sci. *Journal of Applied Behavioral Sciences*
J. Appl. Soc. Sci. *Journal of Applied Social Sciences*
J. Autism Child. Schizo. *Journal of Autism and Childhood Schizophrenia*
J. Autism Dev. Dis. *Journal of Autism and Developmental Disorders*
J. Behav. Ther. Exp. Psychiat. *Journal of Behavior Therapy and Experimental Psychiatry*
J. Child Psychol. Psychiat. Allied Disc. *Journal of Child Psychology, Psychiatry and Allied Disciplines*
J. Clin. Psychiat. *Journal of Clinical Psychiatry*
J. Cons. Clin. Psychol. *Journal of Consulting and Clinical Psychology*
J. Exp. Anal. Behav. *Journal of Experimental Analysis of Behavior*
J. Exp. Psychol. *Journal of Experimental Psychology*
J. Hlth. Soc. Behav. *Journal of Health and Social Behavior*
J. Learn. Dis. *Journal of Learning Disorders*
J. Nerv. Ment. Dis. *Journal of Nervous and Mental Diseases*
J. Neurochem. *Journal of Neurochemistry*
J. Pers. Assess. *Journal of Personality Assessment*
J. Pers. Dis. *Journal of Personality Disorders*
J. Pers. Soc. Psychol. *Journal of Personality and Social Psychology*
J. Psychiat. Res. *Journal of Psychiatric Research*
J. Psychosom. Med. *Journal of Psychosomatic Medicine*
J. Psychosom. Res. *Journal of Psychosomatic Research*
J. Rehab. *Journal of Rehabilitation*
J. Soc. Behav. Pers. *Journal of Social Behavior and Personality*
J. Soc. Psychol. *Journal of Social Psychology*
Med. Aspects Human Sex. *Medical Aspects of Human Sexuality*
NY St. J. Med. *New York State Journal of Medicine*
Profess. Pyschol. *Professional Psychologist*
Prog. Neuropsychopharm. *Progressive Neuropsychopharmacology*
Psychiat. Ann. *Psychiatric Annals*
Psychiat. Clin. N. Amer. *Psychiatric Clinics of North America*
Psychiat. Hosp. *Psychiatric Hospital*
Psychiat. J. Univ. Ottawa *Psychiatric Journal of the University of Ottawa*
Psychiat. Quart. *Psychiatric Quarterly*
Psychol. Bull. *Psychological Bulletin*
Psychol. Med. *Psychological Medicine*
Psychosom. Med. *Psychosomatic Medicine*
Psych. Rec. *Psychological Record*
Psych. Rep. *Psychological Reports*
Psych. Rev. *Psychological Review*
Psych. Today *Psychology Today*
Psychother. Priv. Prac. *Psychotherapy in Private Practice*
Psychother. Theory Res. Prac. *Psychotherapy: Theory, Research and Practice*
Quart. J. Stud. Alcohol. *Quarterly Journal on the Studies of Alcoholism*
Scientif. Amer. *Scientific American*
Schizo. Bull. *Schizophrenic Bulletin*
Soc. Behav. Pers. *Social Behavior and Personality*
Soc. Psychiat. *Social Psychiatry*
Soc. Sci. Med. *Social Science and Medicine*
Suic. Life-Threat. Behav. *Suicide and Life-Threatening Behavior*

---

Abadi, S. (1984). Adiccion: la eterna repeticion de un desencuentro (Acerca de la dependencia humana) [Addiction: The endless repetition of a disencounter]. *Revista de Psicoanalisis, 141*(6), 1029–1044.

Abel, E. L. (1984). Prenatal effects of alcohol. *Drug Alc. Dep., 14*(1), 10.

Abel, G. G. (1976). Assessment of sexual deviation in the male. In M. Hersen & A. S. Bellack (Eds.), *Behavioral assessment: A practical handbook*. Oxford: Pergamon.

Abel, G. G. (1989). Paraphilias. In H. I. Kaplan & B. J. Sadock (Eds.), *Comprehensive textbook of psychiatry* (Vol. 1, 5th ed.). Baltimore: Williams & Wilkins.

Abel, G. G., Becker, J. V., & Cunningham-Rathner, J. (1984). Complications, consent, and cognitions in sex between children and adults. *Inter. J. Law Psychiat., 7,* 89–103.

Abel, G. G., Mittelman, M. S., & Becker, J. V. (1985). Sexual offenders: Results of assessment and recommendations for treatment. In H. H. Ben-Aron, S. I. Hucker, & C. D. Webster (Eds.), *Clinical criminology.* Toronto: MM Graphics.

Abraham, K. (1927). Notes on the psychoanalytic investigation and treatment of manic-depressive insanity and allied conditions. In *Selected papers on psychoanalysis.* London: Hogarth.

Abraham, K. (1927). The first pregenital stage of the libido. In *Selected papers on psychoanalysis.* London: Hogarth.

Abraham, S., & Llewellyn-Jones, D. (1984). *Eating disorders: The facts.* New York: Oxford Univ.

Abramson, L., Seligman, M. E., & Teasdale, J. D. (1978). Learned helplessness in humans: Critique and reformulation. *J. Abnorm. Psychol., 87*(1), 49–74.

Achenbach, T. M. (1974). *Developmental psychopathology.* New York: Ronald.

Achenbach, T. M. (1978). Developmental aspects of psychopathology in children and adolescents. In M. E. Lamb (Ed.), *Social and personality development.* New York: Holt, Rinehart & Winston.

Ackerman, N. (1965). Interlocking pathologies in family relationships. In S. Rado & G. Daniels (Eds.), *Changing concepts in psychoanalytic medicine.* New York: Grune & Stratton.

Adam, K. S., Bouckoms, A., & Streiner, D. (1982). Parental loss and family stability in attempted suicide. *Arch. Gen. Psychiat., 39*(9), 1081–1085.

Adams, H. E., Doster, J. A., & Calhoun, K. S. (1977). A psychological based system of response classification. In A. R. Ciminero, K. S. Calhoun, & H. E. Adams (Eds.), *Handbook of behavioral assessment.* New York: Wiley.

Adams, N. et al. (1978). The eating behavior of obese and nonobese women. *Behav. Res. Ther., 16,* 225–232.

Adams, P. R., & Adams, G. R. (1984). Mount Saint Helen's ashfall: Evidence for a disaster stress reaction. *Amer. Psychol., 39,* 252–260.

Adcock, N. V., & Ross, M. W. (1983). Early memories, early experiences and personality. *Soc. Behav. Pers., 11*(2), 95–100.

Aden, G. C., & Thein, S. G. (1980). Alprazolam compared to diazepam and placebo treatment of anxiety. *J. Clin. Psychiat., 41*(7), 245–248.

Adesso, V. J. et al. (1974). Effects of a personal growth group on positive and negative self-references. *Psychother. Theory, Res. Prac., 11*(4), 354–355.

Adler, A. (1927). *Individual psychology.* London: Kegan Paul, Trench, Trubner & Co.

Adler, T. (1989, Dec.). Integrity test popularity prompts close scrutiny. *APA Monitor,* 7.

Ager, A. (1985). Recent developments in the use of microcomputers in the field of mental handicap: Implications for psychological practice. *Bull. Brit. Psychol. Society, 38,* 142–145.

Agras, W. S. (1985). *Panic: Facing fears, phobias, and anxiety.* New York: Freeman.

Agras, W. S. (1987). So where do we go from here? *Behav. Ther., 18,* 203–217.

Agras, W. S., Sylvester, D., & Oliveau, D. (1969). The epidemiology of common fears and phobias. *Comprehen. Psychiat., 10*(2), 151–156.

Agras, W. S., Taylor, O. B., Kraemer, H. C., Allen, R. A., & Schneider, M. S. (1980). Relaxation training: Twenty-four hour blood pressure reductions. *Arch. Gen. Psychiat., 37,* 859–863.

Ahlquist, J. (1981). Hormonal influences on immunologic and related phenomena. In R. Ader (Ed.), *Psychoneuroimmunology.* New York: Academic.

Aiken, L. R. (1985). *Psychological testing and assessment* (5th ed.). Boston: Allyn & Bacon.

Akamatsu, T. J. (1989, June). Cited in B. Fischman, "Sex on the couch: maybe later." *Psych. Today.*

Akhtar, S., Wig, N. N., Varma, V. K., Pershad, D., & Verma, S. K. (1975). Phenomenological analysis of symptoms in obsessive-compulsive neurosis. *Brit. J. Psychiat., 127,* 342–348.

Akil, H., & Watson, S. (1979). Endorphins: Basic science issues. In R. W. Pickens & L. L. Heston (Eds.), *Psychiatric factors in drug abuse.* New York: Grune & Stratton.

Akiskal, H. S., & McKinney, W. T. (1973). Depressive disorders: Toward a unified hypothesis. *Science, 182,* 20–28.

Akiskal, H. S., & McKinney, W. T. (1975). Overview of recent research in depression: Integration of ten conceptual models into a comprehensive clinical frame. *Arch. Gen. Psychiat., 32,* 285–305.

Akiyama, M. (1968). Relation between extinction techniques and extinction of avoidance response in albino rats. *Japanese Ann. of Animal Psychol., 19,* 15.

Albee, G. W. (1982). Primary prevention: Insights for rehabilitation psychology. *Rehab. Psychol., 27*(1), 13–22.

Alcohol, Drug Abuse and Mental Health Administration (Fall 1987). *Update: Facts from the sixth special report to Congress on alcohol and health.* Washington, DC: Author.

Alden, L., & Safran, R. (1978). A comparison of cognitive and skills training strategies in the treatment of unassertive clients. *Behav. Ther., 9,* 843–846.

Alden, L., Safran, J., & Weideman, R. (1978). A comparison of cognitive training and response cost procedures in modifying cognitive styles of impulsive children. *Cog. Ther. Res., 2,* 183–188.

Alevizos, P., DeRisi, W., Liberman, R., Eckman, T., & Callahan, E. (1978). The behavior observation instrument: A method of direct observation for program evaluation. *J. Appl. Behav. Anal., 11,* 243–257.

Alexander, A. B. (1975). An experimental test of assumptions relating to the use of electromyographic biofeedback as a general relaxation training technique. *Psychophysiology, 12,* 656–662.

Alexander, A. B., Cropp, G. J., & Chai, H. (1979). Effects of relaxation training on pulmonary mechanics in children with asthma. *J. Appl. Behav. Anal., 12,* 27–35.

Alexander, B. (1981). Behavioral approaches to the treatment of bronchial asthma. In C. K. Prokop & L. A. Bradley (Eds.), *Medical psychology: Contributions to behavioral medicine.* New York: Academic.

Alexander, B. K., & Hadaway, P. F. (1982). Opiate addiction: The case for an adaptive orientation. *Psychol. Bull., 92*(2), 367–381.

Alexander, F. (1930). About dreams with unpleasant content. *Psychiat. Quart., 4,* 447–452.

Alexander, F. (1936). The sociological and biological orientation of psychoanalysis. *Ment. Hyg. of New York, 20,* 232–248.

Alexander, F. (1950). Analysis of the therapeutic factors in psychoanalytic treatment. *Psychoanal. Quart., 19,* 482–500.

Alexander, F. (1950). *Psychosomatic medicine.* New York: Norton.

Alexander, F., French, T. M., & Pollack, G. H. (1968). *Psychosomatic specificity: Experimental study and results.* Chicago: Univ. Chicago.

Alexopoulos, G. S. (1991). Anxiety and depression in the elderly. In C. Salzman & B. D. Lebowitz (Eds.), *Anxiety in the elderly.* New York: Springer.

Alford, B., & Norcross, J. (1991). Cognitive therapy as integrative therapy. *J. Integ. Psychother.*

Allderidge, P. (1979). Hospitals, madhouses and asylums: Cycles in the care of the insane. *Brit. J. Psychiat., 134,* 321–334.

Allen, R. A., & Mills, G. K. (1982). The effects of unilateral plethysmographic feedback of temporal artery activity during migraine head pain. *J. Psychosom. Res., 26*(2), 133–140.

Allison, R. B. (1978). A rational psychotherapy plan for multiplicity. *Svensk Tidskrift Hyp., 3,* 9–16.

Allodi, F., & Cowgill, G. (1982). Ethical and psychiatric aspects of torture: A Canadian study. *Canad. J. Psychiat., 27*(2), 98–102.

Alloy, L. B. (Ed.). (1988). *Cognitive processes in depression.* New York: Guilford.

Alnaes, R., & Torgerson, S. (1990). MCMI personality disorders among patients with major depression with and without anxiety disorders. *J. Pers. Dis., 4*(2), 141–149.

Amalric, M., Cline, E. J., Martinez, J. L., Bloom, F. E. et al. (1987). Rewarding properties of β-endorphin as measured by conditioned place preference. *Psychopharmacology, 91*(1), 14–19.

Aman, M. G., & Singh, N. N. (1991). Pharmacological intervention. In J. L. Matson & J. A. Mulick (Eds.), *Handbook of mental retardation.* New York: Pergamon.

Amati, A., Celani, T., del Vecchio, M., & Vacca, L. (1981). Anorexia nervosa: l'iter attraverso la medicine generale e l'approccio differito in psichiatria. [Anorexia nervosa: The connection between general medicine and the approach in psychiatry.] (Ital) *Medicina Psicosomatica, 26*(4), 357–363.

Ament, A. (1987). Rape and multiple personality disorder. *Amer. J. Psychiat., 144*(4), 541.

American Assoc. of Retired Persons. (1990). *A profile of older Americans.* Washington, DC: Author.

American Humane Assoc. (1986). *Highlights of official child neglect and abuse reporting 1984.* Denver: Author.

American Psychiatric Assoc. (1987). *Diagnostic and statistical manual of mental disorders* (3rd rev. ed.). Washington, DC: Author.

American Psychiatric Assoc. (1989). *Treatments of psychiatric disorders.* Washington, DC: Author.

American Psychiatric Assoc. (1991). *DSM-IV options book.* Washington, DC.

American Psychological Assoc. (1981). *Specialty guidelines for the delivery of services.* Washington, DC: Author.

American Psychological Assoc. (1987). Ethical principles of psychologists. *Amer. Psychol., 45,* 390–395.

American Psychological Assoc. (1990). Ethical principles of psychologists (amended June 2, 1989). *Amer. Psychol., 45*(6), 390–395.

American Public Health Assoc. (1962). *Mental disorders: A guide to control methods.* New York: Author.

Amsel, A. (1990). Arousal, suppression, and persistence: Frustration theory, attention, and its disorders [Special Issue]. *Cog. Emot., 4*(3), 239–268.

Amsterdam, J. D., Brunswick, D. J., & Mendels, J. (1980). The clinical application of tricyclic antidepressant pharmacokinetics and plasma levels. *Amer. J. Psychiat., 137*(6), 653–662.

Ananth, J. (1983). New antidepressants. *Comprehen. Psychiat., 24,* 116–124.

Ananth, J., Pecknold, J. C., Van den Steen, N., & Engelsmann, F. (1981). Double-blind study of clomipramine and amitryptyline in obsessive neurosis. *Prog. Neuropsychopharm., 5,* 257–262.

Anastasi, A. (1982). *Psychological testing* (5th ed.). New York: Macmillan.

Anderson, A. E. (1985). *Practical comprehensive treatment of anorexia nervosa and bulimia.* Baltimore: Johns Hopkins Univ.

Anderson, A. E. (1986). Sexuality and fertility: Women with anorexia nervosa and bulimia. *Med. Aspects of Human Sexuality, 20,* 138–143.

Anderson, A. E., Morse, C., & Santmyer, K. (1985). Inpatient treatment for anorexia nervosa. In D. M. Garner & P. Garfinkel (Eds.), *Handbook of psychotherapy for anorexia nervosa and bulimia.* New York: Guilford.

Anderson, B. L. (1983). Primary orgasmic dysfunction: Diagnostic considerations and review of treatment. *Psychol. Bull., 93*(1), 105–136.

Anderson, C. M., Hogarty, G. E., & Reiss, D. J. (1986). *Schizophrenia and the family.* New York: Guilford.

Anderson, N. (1923). *The hobo: The sociology of the homeless man.* Chicago: Univ. Chicago.

Andrasik, F., Blanchard, E. B., & Neff, D. F. (1984). Biofeedback and relaxation training for chronic headaches: A controlled comparison of booster treatments and regular contacts for long-term maintenance. *J. Cons. Clin. Psychol., 52*(4), 609–615.

Andreasen, N. C. (1980). Mania and creativity. In R. H. Belmaker & H. M. van Praag (Eds.), *Mania: An evolving concept.* New York: Spectrum.

Andreasen, N. C. (1985). Positive vs. negative schizophrenia: A critical evaluation. *Schizo. Bull., 11*(3), 380–389.

Andreasen, N. C., Hoffman, R. E., & Grove, W. M. (1985). *Mapping abnormalities in language and cognition, in "Controversies in Schizophrenia: Changes and Constancies."* New York: Guilford.

Andreasen, N. C., Nasrallah, H. A., Dunn, V. et al. (1986). Structural abnormalities in the frontal system in schizophrenia: A magnetic resonance imaging study. *Arch. Gen. Psychiat., 43,* 136–144.

Angrist, B., Lee, H. K., & Gershon, S. (1974). The antagonism of amphetamine-induced symptomatology by a neuroleptic. *Amer. J. Psychiat., 131,* 817–819.

Angrist, B., Sathananthan, G., & Gershon, S. (1973). Behavioral effect in schizophrenic patients. *Psychopharmacologia, 31,* 507.

Angst, J., & Dobler-Mikola, A. (1983). Anxiety states, panic and phobia in a young general population. *World psychiatry congress proceedings, Vienna.* New York: Plenum.

Angst, J., & Dobler-Mikola, A. (1985). The Zurich study: A prospective epidemiological study of depressive, neurotic and psychosomatic syndromes: IV. Recurrent and nonrecurrent brief depression. *Eur. Arch. Psychiat. Neurol. Sci., 234*(6), 408–416.

Annas, G. J., Glants, L. H., & Katz, B. F. (1977). *Informed consent to human experimentation: The subject's dilemma.* Cambridge, MA: Ballinger.

Annis, H. M., Davis, C. S., Graham, M. et al. (1989). *A controlled trial of relapse prevention procedures based on self-efficacy theory.* Unpublished manuscript. Toronto: Addiction Research Foundation.

Anslinger, H. J., & Cooper, C. R. (1937). Marijuana: Assassin of youth. *American Magazine, 124,* 19, 153.

Arbitt, S. A., & Blatt, S. J. (1973). Differentiation of simulated and genuine suicide notes. *Psych. Rep., 33,* 283–297.

Arce, A. A., Tadlock, M., Vergare, M. J., & Shapiro, S. H. (1983). A psychiatric profile of street people admitted to an emergency shelter. *Hosp. Comm. Psychiat., 34*(9), 812–817.

Arieti, S. (1974). An overview of schizophrenia from a predominantly psychological approach. *Amer. J. Psychiat., 13*(3), 494.

Arieti, S. (1974). *Interpretation of schizophrenia.* New York: Basic.

Arieti, S., & Bemporad, J. (1978). *Severe and mild depression: The psychotherapeutic approach.* New York: Basic.

Arieti, S., & Bemporad, J. R. (1980). The psychological organization of depression. *Amer. J. Psychiat., 137,* 1360–1365.

Aring, C. D. (1974). The Gheel experience: Eternal spirit of the chainless mind! *JAMA, 230*(7), 998–1001.

Aring, C. D. (1975). Gheel: The town that cares. *Family Health, 7*(4), 54–55, 58, 60.

Arkowitz, H., Christensen, A., & Royce, S. (1975). *Treatment of social inhibition by real-life practice.* Paper to American Association of Behavior Therapy.

Arlow, J. A. (1989). Psychoanalysis. In R. J. Corsini & D. Wedding (Eds.), *Current psychotherapies.* Itasca, IL: Peacock.

Armstrong, J. G., & Roth, D. M. (1989). Attachment and separation difficulties in eating disorders: A preliminary investigation. *Inter. J. Eat. Dis., 8*(2), 141–155.

Arndt, W. B., Jr. (1991). *Gender disorders and the paraphilias.* Madison, CT: International Univ.

Arnetz, B. B., Horte, L. G., Hedberg, A., Theorell, T. et al. (1987). Suicide patterns among physicians related to other academics as well as to the general population: Results from a national long-term prospective study and a retrospective study. *Acta Psychiatr. Scandin., 75*(2), 139–143.

Aro, H., Paronen, O., & Aro, S. (1987). Psychosomatic symptoms among 14- to 16-year-old Finnish adolescents. *Soc. Psychiat., 22*(3), 171–176.

Arrindell, W. A., Emmelkamp, P. M., & Van-der-Ende, J. (1984). Phobic dimensions: I. Reliability and generalizability across samples, gender and nations. *Adv. Behav. Res. Ther., 6*(4), 207–254.

Artiss, K. L. (1962). *Milieu therapy in schizophrenia.* New York: Grune & Stratton.

Asarnow, J. R., & Horton, A. A. (1990). Coping and stress in families of child psychiatric inpatients: Parents of children with depressive and schizophrenic spectrum disorders. *Child Psychiat. Human Dev., 21*(2), 145–157.

Asberg, M. (1986). Therapeutic effects of serotonin uptake inhibitors in depression. *J. Clin. Psychiat., 47*(Suppl.) 23–35.

Asberg, M. et al. (1984). CSF monoamine metabolites in melancholia. *Acta Psychiatr. Scandin., 89*(3), 201–219.

Asberg, M., Traskman, L., & Thoren, P. (1976). 5 HIAA in the cerebrospinal fluid: A biochemical suicide predictor? *Arch. Gen. Psychiat., 33*(10), 1193–1197.

Ascione, F. R., & Borg, W. R. (1983). A teacher training program to enhance mainstreamed, handicapped pupils' self concepts. *J. School Psychol., 21*(4), 297–309.

Aserinsky, E., & Kleitman, N. (1953). Eye movements during sleep. *Federal Process, 13,* 6–7.

Ashton, J. R., & Donnan, S. (1981). Suicide by burning as an epidemic phenomenon: An analysis of 82 deaths and inquests in England and Wales in 1978–9. *Psychol. Med., 11*(4), 735–739.

Asner, J. (1990). Reworking the myth of personal incompetence: Group psychotherapy for bulimia nervosa. *Psychiat. Ann., 20*(7), 395–397.

Asnis, G. M., Fink, M., & Saferstein, S. (1978). ECT in metropolitan New York hospitals: A survey of practice, 1975–76. *Amer. J. Psychiat., 135,* 479–482.

Athanasiou, R., Shaver, P., & Tavris, C. (1970, July). Sex. *Psych. Today,* 39–52.

Atthowe, J. M. (1973). Token economies come of age. *Behav. Ther., 4*(5), 646–654.

Atthowe, J. M., Jr., & Krasner, L. (1968). Preliminary report on the application of contingent reinforcement procedures (token economy) on a "chronic" psychiatric ward. *J. Abnorm. Psychol., 73,* 37–43.

Auerbach, S. M., & Kilmann, P. R. (1977). Crisis intervention: A review of outcome research. *Psychol. Bull., 84,* 1189–1217.

Auerhahn, N. C., & Moskowitz, M. B. (1984). Merger fantasies in individual inpatient therapy with schizophrenic patients. *Psychoanal. & Psychol., 1*(2), 131–148.

Avery, D., & Lubrano, A. (1979). Depressions treated with imipramine and ECT: The DeCarolis study reconsidered. *Amer. J. Psychiat., 136*, 559–569.

Ayd, F. J., Jr. (1956). A clinical evaluation of Frenquel. *J. Nerv. Ment. Dis., 124*, 507–509.

Ayllon, T. (1963). Intensive treatment of psychotic behavior by stimulus satiation and food reinforcement. *Behav. Res. Ther., 1*, 53–62.

Ayllon, T., & Azrin, N. H. (1965). The measurement and reinforcement of behavior of psychotics. *J. Exp. Anal. Behav., 8*, 357–383.

Ayllon, T., & Azrin, N. H. (1968). *The token economy: A motivational system for therapy and rehabilitation.* New York: Appleton.

Ayllon, T., & Haughton, E. (1964). Modification of symptomatic verbal behaviour of mental patients. *Behav. Res. Ther., 2*, 87–97.

Ayllon, T., & Michael, J. (1959). The psychiatric nurse as a behavioural engineer. *J. Exp. Anal. Behav., 2*, 323–334.

Ayllon, T., & Roberts, M. D. (1974). Eliminating discipline problems by strengthening academic performance. *J. Appl. Behav. Anal., 7*(1), 71–76.

Azar, S. T., & Wolfe, D. A. (1989). Child abuse and neglect. In E. J. Mash & R. Barkley (Eds.), *Treatment of childhood disorders.* New York: Guilford.

Azar, S. T., Fantuzzo, J. W., & Twentyman, C. T. (1984). An applied behavioral approach to child maltreatment: Back to basics. *Adv. Behav. Res. Ther., 8*(1), 3–11.

Azar, S. T., Rohrbeck, C. A. (1986). Child abuse and unrealistic expectations: Further validation of the Parent Opinion Questionnaire. *J. Cons. Clin. Psychol., 54*, 867–868.

Baastrup, P. C. (1964). The use of lithium in manic-depressive psychosis. *Comprehen. Psychiat., 5*, 396–408.

Bachrach, A. J., Erwin, W. J., & Mohr, P. J. (1965). The control of eating behavior in an anorexic by operant conditioning techniques. In L. Ullmann & L. Krasner (Eds.), *Case studies in behavior modification.* New York: Holt, Rinehart & Winston.

Bacon, S. D. (1973). The process of addiction to alcohol: Social aspects. *Quart. J. Stud. Alcohol., 34*(1, Pt. A), 1–27.

Baekland, F., Lundwall, L., & Kissin, B. (1975). Methods for the treatment of chronic alcoholism: A critical appraisal. In R. Gibbins, Y. Israel, H. Kalant, R. Popham, W. Schmidt, & R. G. Smart (Eds.), *Research advances in alcohol and drug problems.* New York: Wiley.

Baer, L., Platman, S. R., Kassir, S., & Fieve, R. R. (1971). Mechanisms of renal lithium handling and their relationship to mineralcorticoids: A dissociation between sodium and lithium ions. *J. Psychiat. Res., 8*(2), 91–105.

Bagby, E. (1922). The etiology of phobias. *J. Abnorm. Psychol., 17*, 16–18.

Bagley, C. (1968). The evaluation of suicide prevention schemes by an ecological method. *Soc. Sci. Med., 2*, 1–14.

Bagley, C., & Ramsay, R. (1985). Psychosocial correlates of suicidal behaviors in an urban population. *Crisis, 6*(2), 63–77.

Baker, T., & Brandon, T. H. (1988). Behavioral treatment strategies. In *A report of the Surgeon General: The health consequences of smoking: Nicotine addiction.* Rockville, MD: U.S. Dept. Health and Human Services.

Baldessarini, R. J., & Tarsey, D. (1980). Dopamine and the pathophysiology of dyskinesias induced by antipsychotic drugs. *Annu. Rev. Neurosci., 3*, 23–41.

Baldwin, S. (1985). Sheep in wolf's clothing: Impact of normalisation teaching on human services and services providers. *Inter. J. Rehab. Res., 8*(2), 131–142.

Balint, M. (1952). New beginning and the paranoid and the depressive syndromes. *Inter. J. Psychoanal., 33*, 214–224.

Ball, J. C., Rosen, L., Flueck, J. A., & Nurco, D. N. (1982). Lifetime criminality of heroin users in the United States. *J. Drug Issues*, 225–239.

Ballenger, J. C. (1988). The clinical use of carbamazepine in affective disorders. *J. Clin. Psychiat., 49*(Suppl.), 13–19.

Ballenger, J. C., & Post, R. M. (1980). Carbamazepine in manic-depressive illness: A new treatment. *Amer. J. Psychiat., 137*(7), 782–790.

Ballenger, J. C., Burrows, G. D., DuPont, R. L., Lesser, I. M. et al. (1985). Alprazolam in panic disorder and agoraphobia: Results from a multicenter trial: I. Efficacy in short-term treatment. *Arch. Gen. Psych., 45*(5), 413–422.

Ballinger, S. E. (1987). Uses and limitations of hypnosis in treating a conversion overlay following somatic trauma. *Austral. J. Clin. Exp. Hyp., 15*(1), 29–37.

Bancroft, J. (1989). *Human sexuality and its problems.* New York: Churchill-Livingstone.

Bancroft, J., Jones, H. G., & Pullan, B. R. (1966). A single transducer for measuring penile erection, with comments on its use in the treatment of sexual disorders. *Behav. Res. Ther., 9*, 239–241.

Bandura, A. (1973). *Aggression: A social learning analysis.* Englewood Cliffs, NJ: Prentice-Hall.

Bandura, A. (1977). Self-efficacy: Toward a unifying theory of behavioral change. *Psych. Rev., 84*(2), 191–215.

Bandura, A. (Ed.). (1979). *Psychological modeling.* Chicago: Atherton.

Bandura, A., & Rosenthal, T. (1966). Vicarious classical conditioning as a function of arousal level. *J. Pers. Soc. Psychol., 3*, 54–62.

Bandura, A., Adams, N. E., & Beyer, J. (1977). Cognitive processes mediating behavioral change. *J. Pers. Soc. Psychol., 35*(3), 125–139.

Bandura, A., Blanchard, E. B., & Ritter, B. (1969). Relative efficacy of desensitization and modeling approaches for inducing behavioral, affective, and attitudinal changes. *J. Pers. Soc. Psychol., 13*, 173–199.

Bandura, A., Ross, D., & Ross, S. (1963). Imitation of film-mediated aggressive models. *J. Abnorm. Soc. Psychol., 66*, 3–11.

Banki, C. M. (1977). Correlation between cerebrospinal fluid amine metabolites and psychomotor activity in affective disorders. *J. Neurochem., 28*, 255–257.

Banki, C. M., & Arato, M. (1983). Amine metabolites and neuroendocrine responses related to depression and suicide. *J. Affect. Dis., 5*(3), 223–232.

Baraban, J., Worley, P., & Snyder, S. (1989). Second messenger systems and psychoactive drug action: Focus on the phosphoinositide system and lithium. *Amer. J. Psychiat., 146*(10), 1251–1259.

Barahal, H. S. (1958). 1000 prefrontal lobotomies: Five to ten year follow-up study. *Psychiat. Quart., 32*, 653–678.

Barber, T. X. (1969). *Hypnosis: A scientific approach.* New York: Van Nostrand Reinhold.

Barclay, C. R. (1981). A component view of memory development. *Psychol. Quart. J. Human Behav., 18*(4), 35–52.

Barker, P. (1984). Family dysfunction and anxiety in children. In V. P. Varma (Ed.), *Anxiety in children.* London: Croom Helm.

Barkley, R. A. (1989). Attention deficit-hyperactivity disorder. In E. J. Mash & R. Barkley (Eds.), *Treatment of childhood disorders.* New York: Guilford.

Barkley, R. A., & Cunningham, C. E. (1979). Stimulant drugs and activity level in hyperactive children. *Amer. J. Orthopsychiat., 49*, 491–499.

Barlow, C. F. (1978). *Mental retardation and related disorders.* Philadelphia: Davis.

Barlow, D. H. (1986). Causes of sexual dysfunction: The role of anxiety and cognitive interference. *J. Cons. Clin. Psychol., 54*, 140–148.

Barlow, D. H. (1988). Current models of panic disorder and a view from emotion theory. In A. J. Frances & R. E. Hales (Eds.), *American Psychiatric Press review of psychiatry* (Vol. 7). Washington, DC: American Psychiatric.

Barlow, D. H. (1989). Treatment outcome evaluation methodology with anxiety disorders: Strengths and key issues. *Adv. Behav. Res. Ther., 11*(3), 121–132.

Barlow, D. H., & Beck, J. G. (1984). The psychosocial treatment of anxiety disorders: Current status, future directions. In J. B. W. Williams & R. L. Spitzer (Eds.), *Psychotherapy research: Where are we and where should we go?* New York: Guilford.

Barlow, D. H., & Craske, M. G. (1988). The phenomenology of panic. In S. Rachman & J. Maser (Eds.), *Panic: Psychological perspectives.* Hillsdale, NJ: Erlbaum.

Barlow, D. H., & Waddell, M. T. (1985). Agoraphobia. In D. H. Barlow (Ed.), *Clinical handbook of psychological disorders.* New York: Guilford.

Barlow, D. H., & Wolfe, B. E. (1981). Behavioral approaches to anxiety disorders: A report on the NIMH-SUNY, Albany, research conference. *J. Cons. Clin. Psychol., 49*(3), 448–454.

Barlow, D. H., Craske, M. G., Cerny, J. A., & Klosko, J. S. (1989). Behavioral treatment of panic disorder. *Behav. Ther., 20*(2), 261–282.

Barlow, D. H. et al. (1984). Panic and generalized anxiety disorders: Nature and treatment. *Behav. Ther., 15*(5), 431–449.

Barlow, D. H., O'Brien, G. T., & Last, C. G. (1984). Couples treatment of agoraphobia. *Behav. Ther., 15*(1), 41–58.

Barmann, B. C., & Murray, W. J. (1981). Suppression of inappropriate sexual behavior by facial screening. *Behav. Ther., 12*(5), 730–735.

Barnes, G. E., & Prosen, H. (1985). Parental death and depression. *J. Abnorm. Psychol., 94*(1), 64–69.

Barnes, T. R., & Braude, W. M. (1985). Akathisia variants and tardive dyskinesia. *Arch. Gen. Psychiat., 42*(9), 874–878.

Baron, M., Barkai, A., Gruen, R., Peselow, E. et al. (1987). Platelet sup 311 imipramine binding and familial transmission of affective disorders. *Neuropsychobiology, 17*(4), 182–186.

Baron, M., Gershon, E. S., Rudy, V., Jonas, W. Z., & Buchsbaum, M. (1975). Lithium carbonate response in depression: Prediction by unipolar/bipolar illness, average-evoked response, catechol-O-methyl transferase, and family history. *Arch. Gen. Psychiat., 32,* 1107–1111.

Barrett, J. E. (1984). Naturalistic change after two years in neurotic depressive disorders (RDC categories). *Comprehen. Psychiat., 25*(4), 404–418.

Barrington, M. R. (1980). Apologia for suicide. In M. P. Battin & D. J. Mayo (Eds.), *Suicide: The philosophical issues.* New York: St. Martin's.

Barrios, B. A., & O'Dell, S. L. (1989). Fears and anxieties. In E. J. Mash & R. Barkley (Eds.), *Treatment of childhood disorders.* New York: Guilford.

Barry, H., III. (1982). Cultural variations in alcohol abuse. In I. Al-Issa (Ed.), *Culture and psychopathology.* Baltimore: Univ. Park.

Barth, R. P., Blythe, B. J., Schinke, S. P., Stevens, P., & Schilling, R. F. (1983). Self-control training with maltreating parents. *Child Welfare, 62,* 313–324.

Bartko, G., Herczeg, I., & Zador, G. (1988). Clinical symptomatology and drug compliance in schizophrenic patients. *Acta Psychiatr. Scandin., 77*(1), 74–76.

Barton, E. J., & Osborne, J. G. (1978). The development of classroom sharing by a teacher using positive practice. *Behav. Mod., 2*(2), 231–250.

Barton, R. (1965). Diabetes insipidus and obsessional neurosis. *Lancet, 1,* 133–135.

Bartrop, R. W., Lockhurst, E., Lazarus, L., Kiloh, L. G., & Penny, R. (1977). Depressed lymphocyte function after bereavement. *Lancet, 1,* 834–836.

Bass, C., & Gardner, W. (1985). Diagnostic issues in the hyperventilation syndrome. *Brit. J. Psychiat., 146,* 101–102.

Bassuk, E. L., Rubin, L., & Lauriat, A. (1984). Is homelessness a mental health problem? *Amer. J. Psychiat., 141*(12), 1546–1550.

Batchelor, W. F. (1988). AIDS 1988. *Amer. Psychol., 43*(11), 853–858.

Bateson, G., Jackson, D., Haley, J., & Weakland, J. (1956). Toward a theory of schizophrenia. *Behav. Sci., 1,* 251–264.

Battin, M. P. (1980). Manipulated suicide. In M. P. Battin & D. J. Mayo (Eds.), *Suicide: The philosophical issues.* New York: St. Martin's.

Battin, M. P. (1980). Suicide: A fundamental human right? In M. P. Battin & D. J. Mayo (Eds.), *Suicide: The philosophical issues.* New York: St. Martin's.

Battin, M. P. (1982). *Ethical issues in suicide.* Englewood Cliffs, NJ: Prentice Hall.

Baucom, D. H. (1982). A comparison of behavioral contracting and problem-solving/communication training in behavioral marital therapy. *Behav. Ther., 13,* 162–174.

Bauer, M. S., & Whybrow, P. C. (1988). Thyroid hormones and the central nervous system in affective illness: Interactions that may have clinical significance. *Integ. Psychiat., 6*(2), 75–85.

Baxter, L. R., Schwartz, J. M., Guze, B. H., Bergman, K. et al. (1989). PET imaging in obsessive compulsive disorder with and without depression. Symposium: Serotonin and its effects on human behavior (1989, Atlanta, GA). *J. Clin. Psychiat., 51*(Suppl.), 61–69.

Beahrs, J. O. (1983). Co-consciousness: A common denominator in hypnosis, multiple personality, and normalcy. *Amer. J. Clin. Hyp., 26*(2), 100–113.

Beatty, W. W., Wonderlich, S. A., Stanton, R. D., & Ternes, L. A. (1990). Cognitive functioning in bulimia: Comparison with depression. *Bull. Psychonom. Society, 28*(4), 289–292.

Beaty, E. T., & Haynes, S. N. (1979). Behavioral treatment of muscle-contraction headache. *Psychosom. Med., 41,* 165–180.

Beauvais, F., & LaBoueff, S. (1985). Drug and alcohol intervention in American Indian communities. *Inter. J. Addic., 20*(1), 139–171.

Beck, A. (1988). Cognitive approaches to panic disorder. In S. Rach-

man & J. Maser (Eds.), *Panic psychological perspectives.* Hillsdale, NJ: Erlbaum.

Beck, A. T. (1967). *Depression: Causes and treatment.* Philadelphia: Univ. Penn.

Beck, A. T. (1967). *Depression: Clinical, experimental and theoretical aspects.* New York: Harper & Row.

Beck, A. T. (1976). *Cognitive therapy and the emotional disorders.* New York: International Univ.

Beck, A. T. (1985). Is behavior therapy on course? *Behav. Psychother., 13*(1), 83–84.

Beck, A. T. (1985). Theoretical perspectives on clinical anxiety. In A. H. Tuma & J. D. Maser (Eds.), *Anxiety and the anxiety disorders.* Hillsdale, NJ: Erlbaum.

Beck, A. T. (1987). Cognitive therapy. In J. K. Zeig (Ed.), *The evolution of psychotherapy.* New York: Brunner/Mazel.

Beck, A. T. (1988). Cognitive approaches to panic disorder: Theory and therapy. In S. Rachman & J. Maser (Eds.), *Panic: Psychological perspectives.* Hillsdale, NJ: Erlbaum.

Beck, A. T. (1991). Cognitive therapy: A 30-year retrospective. *Amer. Psychol., 46*(4), 368–375.

Beck, A. T. et al. (1985). Treatment of depression with cognitive therapy and amitriptyline. *Arch. Gen. Psychiat., 42*(2), 142–148.

Beck, A. T., & Beck, R. W. (1972). Screening depressed patients in family practice: A rapid technique. *Postgraduate Med., 52,* 81–85.

Beck, A. T., & Emery, G., with Greenberg, R. L. (1985). Differentiating anxiety and depression: A test of the cognitive content-specificity hypothesis. *J. Abnorm. Psychol., 96,* 179–183.

Beck, A. T., & Greenberg, R. L. (1988). Cognitive therapy with children and adolescents. In A. J. Frances & R. E. Hales (Eds.), *American Psychiatric Press review of psychiatry* (Vol. 7). Washington, DC: American Psychiatric.

Beck, A. T., & Sokol-Kessler, L. (1986). *A test of cognitive dysfunction in panic attacks.* Paper presented at the research conference, Univ. Pennsylvania, Philadelphia.

Beck, A. T., Emery, G., & Bohnert, M. (1974). Ideational components of anxiety neurosis. *Arch. Gen. Psychiat., 31,* 319–325.

Beck, A. T., Emery, G., & Greenberg, R. (1985). *Anxiety disorders and phobias: A cognitive perspective.* New York: Basic.

Beck, A. T., Epstein, N., & Harrison, R. (1983). Cognitions, attitudes and personality dimensions in depression. *Brit. J. Cog. Psychother., 1*(1), 1–16.

Beck, A. T., Freeman, A. & Assoc. (1990). *Cognitive therapy of personality disorders.* New York: Guilford.

Beck, A. T., Laude, R., & Bohnert, M. (1974). Ideational components of anxiety neurosis. *Arch. Gen. Psychiat., 31,* 319–325.

Beck, A. T., Rush, A. J., Shaw, B. F., & Emery, G. (1979). *Cognitive therapy of depression.* New York: Guilford.

Beck, A. T., Steer, R. A., & Garbin, M. G. (1988). Psychometric properties of the Beck Depression Inventory: Twenty-five years of evaluation. *Clin. Psychol. Rev., 8*(1), 77–100.

Beck, A. T., Ward, C. H., Mendelson, M., Mock, J. E., & Erbaugh, J. (1962). Reliability of psychiatric diagnosis. 2: A study of consistency of clinical judgments and ratings. *Amer. J. Psychiat., 119,* 351–357.

Beck, A. T., Ward, C. H., Mendelson, M., Mock, J. E., & Erbaugh, J. (1961). An inventory for measuring depression. *Arch. Gen. Psychiat., 4,* 561–571.

Beck, A. T., Weissman, A., Lester, D. et al. (1974). The measurement of pessimism: the hopelessness scale. *J. Cons. Clin. Psychol. 42,* 861–865.

Becker, J., & Kleinman, A. (Eds.). (1991). *Psychological aspects of depression.* Hillsdale, NJ: Erlbaum.

Becker, C. E. (1979). Pharmacotherapy in the treatment of alcoholism. In J. Mendelson & N. Mello (Eds.), *The diagnosis and treatment of alcoholism.* New York: McGraw-Hill.

Becker, E. (1962). Toward a theory of schizophrenia: External objects and the creation of meaning. *Arch. Gen. Psychiat., 7*(9), 170–181.

Becker, H. S. (1973). *Outsiders: Studies in the sociology of deviance.* New York: Free.

Becker, J. V. (1989). Impact of sexual abuse on sexual functioning. In S. R. Leiblum & R. C. Rosen (Eds.), *Principles and practice of sex therapy* (2nd ed.). New York: Guilford.

Becker, J. V., & Kavoussi, R. J. (1988). Sexual disorders. In J. A. Talbott, R. E. Hales, & S. C. Yudofsky (Eds.), *American Psychiatric Press textbook of psychiatry.* Washington, DC: American Psychiatric.

Beckham, E. E. (1984). The comparative efficacy of psychotherapy and pharmacotherapy in depression: Implications for clinical practice. *Psychother. Priv. Prac., 2*(2), 31–37.

Bednar, R. L., & Kaul, T. J. (1978). Experiential group research: Current perspectives. In A. E. Berin & S. Garfield (Eds.), *Handbook of psychotherapy and behavior change* (2nd ed.). New York: Wiley.

Bednar, R. L., & Kaul, T. J. (1979). Experiential group research: What never happened. *J. Appl. Behav. Sci., 11*, 311–319.

Bednar, R. L., & Moeschl, M. J. (1981). Conceptual and methodological considerations in the evaluation of group psychotherapies. In P. McReynolds (Ed.), *Advances in psychological assessment* (Vol. 5). San Francisco: Jossey-Bass.

Beech, H. R., & Vaughan, M. (1978). *Behavioral treatment of obsessional states.* New York: Wiley.

Beecher, H. K. (1959). *Measurement of subjective responses: Quantitative effects of drugs.* New York: Oxford Univ.

Begley, S. (1989, Aug. 14). The stuff that dreams are made of. *Newsweek,* 41–44.

Beitman, B. D. (1989). Why am I an integrationist (not an eclectic). *Brit. J. Guid. Couns., 17*(3), 259–273.

Belcher, J. R. (1988, Nov.). Defining the service needs of homeless mentally ill persons. *Hosp. Comm. Psychiat.*

Belcher, J. R. (1988). The future role of state hospitals. *Psychiat. Hosp., 19*(2), 79–83.

Belcher, J. R., & Blank, H. (1989). Protecting the right to involuntary commitment. *J. Appl. Soc. Sci., 14*(1), 95–115.

Belkin, L. (1990, Jun. 6). Doctor tells of first death using his suicide device. *New York Times,* A1, p. 3.

Bell, C., Kirkpatrick, S. W., & Rinn, R. C. (1986). Body image of anorexic, obese, and normal females. *J. Clin. Psychol., 42*(3), 431–439.

Bell, J. E. (1961). Family group therapy: A method for the psychological treatment of older children, adolescents, and their parents. *Public Health Monograph, 64.* Washington, DC: GPO.

Bellack, A. S., & Hersen, M. (1980). *Introduction to clinical psychology.* New York: Oxford Univ.

Bellack, A. S., Hersen, M., & Himmelhoch, J. (1981). Social skills training compared with pharmacotherapy and psychotherapy in the treatment of unipolar depression. *Amer. J. Psychiat., 138*(12), 1562–1567.

Bellack, A. S., Hersen, M., & Turner, S. M. (1976). Generalization effects of social skills training in chronic schizophrenics: An experimental analysis. *Behav. Res. Ther., 14*(6), 391–398.

Bellack, A. S., Morrison, R. L., & Mueser, K. T. (1989). Social problem solving in schizophrenia. *Schizo. Bull., 15*(1), 101–116.

Bellak, L., & Bellak, S. (1952). *Children's apperception test.* New York: Psychology Corp.

Bellini, M. et al. (1985). Suicidalita e diagnosi DSM III [On suicidal behavior patterns and the DSM III system]. *Revista Sperimentale di Freniatria e Medicina Legale delle Alienazioni Mentali, 109*(2), 253–270.

Bellow, S. *Humboldt's gift.*

Belser, M., Shore, J. H., Peters, R., & Tatum, E. (1985). Does community care for the mentally ill make a difference? A tale of two cities. *Amer. J. Psychiat., 142*(9), 1047–1052.

Bemis, K. M. (1978). Current approaches to the etiology and treatment of anorexia nervosa. *Psychol. Bull., 85*, 593–617.

Bemporad, J. R. (1983). Cognitive, affective and psychologic changes in the depressed process. *J. Amer. Acad. Psychoanal., 11*, 159–172.

Ben-Tovim, D. I., Hunter, M., & Crisp, A. H. (1977). Discrimination and evaluation of shape and size in anorexia nervosa: An exploratory study. *Res. Communication Psychol. Psychiat. & Behav. 2*(5–6), 241–257.

Benassi, V. A., Sweeney, P. D., & Dufour, C. L. (1988). Is there a relation between locus of control orientation and depression? *J. Abnorm. Psychol., 97*(3), 357–367.

Bender, B. (1976). Duo therapy: A method of casework treatment of children. *Child Welfare, 55*(2), 95–108.

Bender, L. (1938). *A visual motor gestalt test and its clinical use.* New York: American Orthopsychiatric Assoc.

Benedict, R. (1934). Anthropology and the abnormal. *J. Gen. Psychol., 10,* 59–82.

Benedict, R. (1934). *Patterns of culture.* New York: Houghton Mifflin.

Benezech, M., DeWitte, J. J. E., & Bourgeois, M. (1989). A lycanthropic murderer [letter to the editor]. *Amer. J. Psychiat., 146*(7), 942.

Benne, K. D. (1964). History of the T-group in the laboratory setting. In L. P. Bradford, J. R. Gibb, & K. D. Benne (Eds.), *T-group theory and laboratory method.* New York: Wiley.

Bennett, G. T., & Kish, G. R. (1990). Incompetency to stand trial: Treatment unaffected by demographic variables. *J. Forensic Sci., 32*(2), 403–412.

Benson, H., Arns, P. A., & Hoffman, J. W. (1981). The relaxation response and hypnosis. *Inter. J. Clin. Exp. Hyp., 29*(3), 259–270.

Berger, F. M. (1963). The similarities and differences between meprobamate and barbiturates. *Clin. Pharm. Ther., 4,* 209–231.

Bergin, A. E., & Lambert, M. J. (1978). The evaluation of therapeutic outcomes. In S. L. Garfield & A. E. Bergin (Eds.), *Handbook of psychotherapy and behavior change: An empirical analysis.* New York: Wiley.

Berglas, S. (1986). *The success syndrome.* New York: Plenum.

Bergler, E. (1951). *Neurotic counterfeit sex.* New York: Grune & Stratton.

Bergman, G. W. (1985). Indicaties voor gecontroleerd drinken als behandelingdoel bij clienten met alcoholproblemen [Indications for controlled drinking as treatment goal for clients with alcohol problems]. *Gedragstherapie, 18*(1), 47–52.

Bericco, D. A., Brigham, T. A., & Garlington, W. K. (1977). Development and evaluation of treatment paradigms for the suppression of smoking behavior. *J. Appl. Behav. Anal., 10*(2), 173–181.

Berk, S. N., & Efran, J. S. (1983). Some recent developments in the treatment of neurosis. In C. E. Walker et al. (Eds.), *The handbook of clinical psychology: Theory, research, and practice* (Vol. 2). Homewood, IL: Dow Jones-Irwin.

Berkovitz, I. H. (1985). The adolescent, schools, and schooling. *Adol. Psychiat., 12,* 162–176.

Berkowitz, R., Kuipers, L., Eberlein-Vries, R., & Leff, J. (1981). Lowering expressed emotion in relatives of schizophrenics. In M. J. Goldstein (Ed.), *New developments in interventions with families of schizophrenics.* London: Jossey-Bass.

Berkowitz, R., Shavit, N., & Leff, J. P. (1990). Educating relatives of schizophrenic patients. *Soc. Psychiat. Psychiatr. Epidemiology, 25,* 216–220.

Berman, A. L. (1986). Helping suicidal adolescents: Needs and responses. In C. A. Corr & J. N. McNeil (Eds.), *Adolescence and death.* New York: Springer.

Berman, S., Delaney, N., Gallagher, D., Atkins, P., & Graeber, M. (1987). Respite care: A partnership between a Veterans Administration nursing home and families to care for frail elders at home. *Gerontologist, 27,* 581–584.

Bertelsen, A., Harvald, B., & Hauge, M. (1977). A Danish twin study of manic depressive disorders. *Brit. J. Psychiat., 130,* 330–351.

Bettelheim, B. (1967). *The empty fortress: Infantile autism and the birth of the self.* New York: Free, Collier-Macmillan.

Beumont, P. J., Abraham, S. F., Argall, W. J., George, C. W., & Glaun, D. E. (1978). The onset of anorexia nervosa. *Austral. New Zeal. J. Psychiat., 12*(3), 145–149.

Beutler, L. E. (1983). *Eclectic psychotherapy.* New York: Pergamon.

Beutler, L. E., Daldrup, R. J., Engle, D., Oro-Beutler, M. E. et al. (1987). Effects of therapeutically induced affect arousal on depressive symptoms, pain and beta-endorphins among rheumatoid arthritis patients. *Pain, 29*(3), 325–334.

Bhakthavatsalam, P., Kamatchi, G. L., & Ghosh, M. N. (1985). Tolerance pattern to amphetamine anorexia after selective lesions in the hypothalamic dopaminergic projection. *Life Sciences, 37*(7), 635–643.

Bibring, E. (1953). The mechanisms of depression. In P. Greenacre (Ed.), *Affective disorders.* New York: International Univ.

Bickman, L., & Dokecki, P. (1989). Public and private responsibility for mental health services. *Amer. Psychol., 44*(8), 1133–1137.

Biederman, J., Keenan, K., & Faraone, S. V. (1990). Parent-based diagnosis of attention deficit disorder predicts a diagnosis based on teacher report. *J. Amer. Acad. Child Adol. Psychiat., 29*(5), 698–701.

Bierman, K. L., & Furman, W. (1984). The effects of social skills training and peer involvement on the social adjustment of preadolescents. *Child Dev., 55*(1), 151–162.

Biernacki, P. (1990). Recovery from opiate addiction without treatment: A summary. *National Institute on Drug Abuse Research Monograph Series, 98,* 113–119.

Bilsbury, C., & Morley, S. (1979). Obsessional slowness: A meticulous replication. *Behav. Res. Ther., 17*(4), 405–408.

Binet, A., & Simon, T. (1916). *The development of intelligence in children (The Binet-Simon Scale).* Baltimore: Williams & Wilkins.

Binik, Y. M., Servan-Schreiber, D., Freiwald, S., & Hall, K. S.

(1988). Intelligent computer-based assessment and psychotherapy: An expert system for sexual dysfunction. *J. Nerv. Ment. Dis.*, *176*(7), 387–400.

Binstock, J. (1974). Choosing to die: The decline of aggression and the rise of suicide. *The Futurist, 8*(2), 68–71.

Birch, H. G., Richardson, S. A., Baird, D. et al. (1970). *Mental subnormality in the community—A clinical and epidemiological study.* Baltimore: Williams & Wilkins.

Bird, J. (1979). The behavioral treatment of hysteria. *Brit. J. Psychiat., 143*, 127–129.

Birley, J. L. T., & Brown, G. W. (1968). Crises and life changes and the onset of schizophrenia. *J. Hlth. Soc. Behav., 9*(3), 203–214.

Birren, J., & Cunningham, W. (1985). Research on the psychology of aging: Principles, concepts and theory. In J. Birren & K. W. Schaie (Eds.), *Handbook of the psychology of aging* (2nd ed.). New York: Van Nostrand Reinhold.

Bishopric, N. J., Cohen, H. J., & Lefkowitz, R. J. (1980). Beta-adrenergic receptors in lymphocyte subpopulations. *J. Allergy & Clin. Immun., 65*, 29–33.

Black, A. (1974). The natural history of obsessional neurosis. In H. R. Beech (Ed.), *Obsessional states.* London: Methuen.

Black, B. J. (1977). Substitute permanent employment for the deinstitutionalized mentally ill. *J. Rehab., 43*, 32–35.

Black, D. W., Yates, W. R., & Andreasen, N. C. (1988). Schizophrenia, schizophreniform disorder, and delusional (paranoid) disorders. In J. A. Talbott, R. E. Hales, & S. C. Yodofsky, *Textbook of psychiatry.* Washington, DC: American Psychiatric.

Blackburn, I. M. (1985). Depression. In B. P. Bradley & C. T. Thompson (Eds.), *Psychological applications in psychiatry.* Chichester: Wiley.

Blackburn, I. M., Bishop, S., Glen, A. I. M. et al. (1981). The efficacy of cognitive therapy in depression: A treatment trial using cognitive therapy and pharmacotherapy, each alone and in combination. *Brit. J. Psychiat., 139*, 181–189.

Blackstein, K. R. (1975). The sensation seeker and anxiety reactivity. Relationship between sensation-seeking scales and the activity preference questionnaire. *J. Clin. Psychol., 31*, 677–681.

Blackwell, B., Marley, E., Price, J., & Taylor, D. (1967). Hypertensive interactions between monoamine oxidase inhibitors and foodstuffs. *Brit. J. Psychiat., 113*, 349–365.

Blair, C. D., & Lanyon, R. I. (1981). Exhibitionism: Etiology and treatment. *Psychol. Bull., 89*(3), 439–463.

Blanchard, E. B., & Andrasik, F. (1982). Psychological assessment and treatment of headache: Recent developments and emerging issues. *J. Cons. Clin. Psychol., 50*(6), 859–879.

Blanchard, E. B., & Epstein, L. H. (1978). *A biofeedback primer.* Reading, MA: Addison-Wesley.

Blanchard, E. B., & Young, L. D. (1973). Self-control of cardiac functioning: A promise as yet unfulfilled. *Psychol. Bull., 79*(3), 145–163.

Blanchard, E. B., Andrasik, F., Ahles, T. A., Teders, S. J., & O'Keefe, D. (1980). Migraine and tension headache: A meta-analytic review. *Behav. Res. Ther., 2*, 469–481.

Blanchard, E. B. et al. (1982). Biofeedback and relaxation training with three kinds of headache: Treatment effects and their prediction. *J. Cons. Clin. Psychol., 50*(4), 562–575.

Blanchard, E. B., Theobald, D. E., Williamson, D. A. et al. (1978). Temperature biofeedback with treatment of migraine headaches. *Arch. Gen. Psychiat., 35*, 581–588.

Bland, R. C., Parker, J. H., & Orn, H. (1976). Prognoses in schizophrenia: A ten-year follow-up of first admissions. *Arch. Gen. Psychiat., 33*(8), 949–954.

Blank, A. S. (1979). *Vietnam veterans—Operation Outreach. First Training Conference Papers.* St. Louis: U.S. Veterans Admin.

Blank, A. S. (1982). *Apocalypse terminable and interminable: Operation Outreach for Vietnam veterans. Hosp. Comm. Psychiat., 33*(11), 913–918.

Blass, J. P. et al. (1989). *Report of the Advisory Panel on Alzheimer's Disease.* Washington, DC: GPO.

Blatt, S. J., & Berman, W. M. (1984). A methodology for the use of the Rorschach in clinical research. *J. Pers. Assess., 48*, 226–239.

Blazer, D. (1990). *Emotional problems in later life.* New York: Springer.

Blazer, D., George, L. K., & Hughes, D. (1991). The epidemiology of anxiety disorders: An age comparison. In C. Salzman & B. D. Lebowitz (Eds.), *Anxiety in the elderly.* New York: Springer.

Blehar, M. C., Wessman, M. M., & Cerehon, E. S. (1988). Family and genetic studies of affective disorders. National Institute of Mental Health: Family and genetic studies of affective disorders. *Arch. Gen. Psychiat., 45*(3), 288–292.

Bliss, E. L. (1980). Multiple personalities: A report of 14 cases with implications for schizophrenia and hysteria. *Arch. Gen. Psychiat., 37*(12), 1388–1397.

Bliss, E. L. (1980). *Multiple personality, allied disorders and hypnosis.* New York: Oxford Univ.

Bliss, E. L. (1985). "How prevalent is multiple personality?": Dr. Bliss replies. *Amer. J. Psychiat., 142*(12), 1527.

Bliss, E. L. (1988). Professional skepticism about multiple personality: Commentary. *J. Nerv. Ment. Dis., 176*(9), 533–534.

Bliwise, N., McCall, M. E., & Swan, S. J. (1987). In E. E. Lurie & J. H. Swan & Assoc. (Eds.), *Serving the mentally ill elderly: Problems and perspectives.* Lexington, MA: Heath.

Bloch, S. (1986). Therapeutic factors in group psychotherapy. In A. J. Frances & R. E. Hales (Eds.), *American Psychiatric Association annual review* (Vol. 5). Washington, DC: American Psychiatric.

Bloom, B. L. (1984). *Community mental health: A general introduction* (2nd ed.). Monterey, CA: Brooks/Cole.

Bloom, J. D. (1990). The Tarasoff decision & gun control legislation. *Inter. J. Offend. Ther. Compar. Criminol., 34*(1), v–viii.

Bloom, L. J., & Trautt, G. M. (1977). Finger pulse volume as a measure of anxiety: Further evaluation. *Psychophysiology, 14*, 541–544.

Bloomingdale, L. M. (1984). Whither ADD (Attention Deficit Disorder)? *Psychiat. J. Univ. Ottawa, 9*(4), 175–186.

Blue, F. R. (1979). Use of directive therapy in the treatment of depersonalization neurosis. *Psych. Rep., 45*(3), 904–906.

Blumenfield, M., & Thompson, T. L., II (1985). The psychological reactions to physical illness. In R. C. Simons (Ed.), *Understanding human behavior in health and illness* (3rd ed.). Baltimore: Williams & Wilkins.

Blumstein, P., & Schwartz, P. (1983). *American couples.* New York: Morrow.

Bocker, F. M. (1984). Soziale Integration und Kontakte zu Bezugspersonen des gewohnten sozialen Umfeldes wahrend stationarer Behandlung im psychiatrischen Krankenhaus. Eine prospektive katamnestische Untersuchung an erstmals aufgenommenen Patienten mit schizophrenen und cyclothymen Psychosen [Social integration and contact with people in the normal social environment during treatment in a psychiatric hospital: A follow-up of first-admission inpatients with schizophrenia and affective disorders]. *Eur. Arch. Psychiat. Neurol. Sci., 234*(4), 250–257.

Bockoven, J. S. (1963). *Moral treatment in American psychiatry.* New York: Springer.

Bogdan, R., & Taylor, S. (1976, Jan.). The judged, not the judges: An insider's view of mental retardation. *Amer. Psychol.*

Boldt, M. (1985). A systematic and integrated interagency model for providing coordinated and comprehensive suicide prevention services. *Crisis, 6*(2), 106–118.

Bolgar, H. (1965). The case study method. In B. B. Wolman (Ed.), *Handbook of clinical psychology.* New York: McGraw-Hill.

Boller, F. (1983). Alzheimer's disease and Parkinson's disease: Clinical and pathological associations. In B. Reisberg (Ed.), *Alzheimer's disease: The standard reference.* New York: Free.

Bolund, C. (1985). Suicide and cancer: II. Medical and care factors in suicides by cancer patients in Sweden, 1973–1976. *J. Psychol. Oncology, 3*(1), 31–52.

Bondareff, W., Mountjoy, L. Q., & Roth, M. (1982). Loss of neurons of origin of the adrenergic projection to cerebral cortex (nucleus locus coeruleus) in senile dementia. *Neurology, 32*, 164–168.

Borkovec, T. D. (1985, Dec.). What's the use of worrying? *Psych. Today.*

Borkovec, T. D. (1985). Worry: A potentially valuable concept. *Behav. Res. Ther., 23*(4), 481–482.

Borkovec, T. D., & Hu, S. (1990). The effects of worry on cardiovascular response to phobic imagery. *Behav. Res. Ther., 28*(1), 69–73.

Borkovec, T. D., & Inz, J. (1990). The nature of worry in generalized disorder: A predominance of thought activity. *Behav. Res. Ther., 28*(2), 153–158.

Borkovec, T. D., & Sides, J. K. (1979). Critical procedural variables related to the physiological effects of progressive relaxation: A review. *Behav. Res. Ther., 17*, 119–125.

Borkovec, T. D., & Sides, J. K. (1979). The contribution of relaxation and expectancy to fear reduction via graded, imaginal exposure to feared stimuli. *Behav. Res. Ther., 17*(6), 529–540.

Bornstein, P. H., Hamilton, S. B., & Bornstein, M. T. (1986). Self-monitoring procedures. In A. R. Ciminero, K. S. Calhoun, & H. E.

Adams (Eds.), *Handbook of behavioral assessment* (2nd ed.). New York: Wiley.

Borys, D. S., & Pope, K. S. (1989). Dual relationships between therapist and client: A national study of psychologists, psychiatrists and social workers. *Profess. Psychol., 20,* 283–293.

Borysenko, M., & Borysenko, J. (1982). Stress, behavior, and immunity: Animal models and mediating mechanisms. *Gen. Hosp. Psychiat., 4,* 59–67.

Boswell, P., & Murray, E. J. (1981). Depression, schizophrenia and social attribution. *J. Cons. Clin. Psychol., 495,* 641–647.

Boudewyns, P. A., Tanna, V. L., & Fleischman, D. J. A. (1975). A modified shame aversion therapy for compulsive obscene telephone calling. *Behav. Ther., 6,* 704–707.

Boulougouris, J. C. (1977). Variables affecting outcome in obsessive-compulsive patients treated by flooding. In J. C. Boulougouris & A. D. Rabavilis (Eds.), *Treatment of phobic and obsessive compulsive disorders.* Oxford: Pergamon.

Boulougouris, J. C., Marks, I. M., & Marset, P. (1971). Superiority of flooding to desensitization as a fear reducer. *Behav. Res. Ther., 9,* 7–16.

Boulougouris, J. C., Rabavilas, A. D., & Stefanis, C. (1977). Psychophysiological responses in obsessive-compulsive patients. *Behav. Res. Ther., 15*(3), 221–230.

Bourke, M. P., Taylor, G., & Crisp, A. H. (1985). Symbolic functioning in anorexia nervosa. *J. Psychiat. Res., 19*(2–3), 273–278.

Bourne, P. G. (1970). *Men, stress & Vietnam.* Boston: Little, Brown.

Bowen, M. (1987). Psychotherapy, past, present & future. In J. K. Zeig (Ed.), *The evolution of psychotherapy.* New York: Brunner/Mazel.

Bowen, M. A. (1960). A family concept of schizophrenia. In D. D. Jackson (Ed.), *The etiology of schizophrenia.* New York: Basic.

Bower, B. (1987, June). What's in the cards for manic depression? The surprisingly harsh and long-lived mood swings of manic depression are charted in a closetful of cards. *Science News.*

Bower, E. M. (1969). Slicing the mystique of prevention with Occam's razor. *Amer. J. Pub. Hlth., 59,* 478–484.

Bower, G. H. (1981). Mood and memory. *Amer. Psychol., 15*(6), 60–69.

Bowers, M. B. (1974). Central dopamine turnover in schizophrenic syndromes. *Arch. Gen. Psychiat., 31*(1), 50–54.

Bowers, M. B. (1977). Psychoses precipitated by psychomimetic drugs. *Arch. Gen. Psychiat., 34,* 832–835.

Bowlby, J. (1973). *Separation: Anxiety and anger.* New York: Basic.

Bowlby, J. (1977). The making and breaking of affectional bonds: I. Aetiology and psychopathology in the light of attachment theory. *Brit. J. Psychiat., 130,* 201–210.

Bowlby, J. (1977). The making and breaking of affectional bonds: II. Some principles of psychotherapy. *Brit. J. Psychiat., 130,* 421–431.

Bowlby, J. (1980). By ethology out psychoanalysis: An experiment in interbreeding. *Animal Behav., 28*(3), 840–850.

Boyd, J. H., & Weissman, M. M. (1981). Epidemiology of affective disorders: A reexamination and future directions. *Arch. Gen. Psychiat., 38*(9), 1030–1040.

Bradley, B. W., & McCanne, T. R. (1981). Autonomic responses to stress: The effects of progressive relaxation, the relaxation response, and expectancy of relief. *Biofeed. Self-Reg., 6*(2), 235–251.

Brady, J. P., & Lind, D. L. (1961). Experimental analysis of hysterical blindness: Operant conditioning techniques. *Arch. Gen. Psychiat., 4,* 331–339.

Brady, J. P., Thornton, D. R., & deFisher, D. (1962). Deleterious effects on anxiety elicited by conditioned preaversive stimuli in the rat. *Psychosom. Med., 24,* 590–595.

Brady, J. V., Porter, R. W., Conrad, D. G., & Mason, J. W. (1958). Avoidance behavior and the development of gastroduodenal ulcers. *J. Exp. Anal. Behav., 1,* 69–73.

Brady, J. V. (1958). Ulcers in "executive" monkeys. *Scientif. Amer., 199,* 95–100.

Braestrup, C., Albrechtsen, R., & Squires, R. F. (1977). High densities of benzodiazepine receptors in human cortical areas. *Nature, 269*(5630), 702–704.

Braestrup, C., Schmiechen, R., Neef, G., Nielson, M., & Petersen, E. N. (1982). Interactions of convulsive ligands with benzodiazepine receptors. *Science, 216,* 1241–1243.

Braginsky, B. M., Braginsky, D. D., & Ring, K. (1969). *Methods of madness: The mental hospital as a last resort.* New York: Holt.

Brandon, S. (1981). *The history of shock treatment, in "Electroconvulsive therapy: An appraisal."* Oxford: Oxford Univ.

Braucht, G. N., Brakarsh, D., Follingstad, D., & Berry, K. L. (1973). Deviant drug use in adolescence: A review of psychosocial correlates. *Psychol. Bull., 79*(2), 92–106.

Braun, B. G. (1984). Hypnosis creates multiple personality: Myth or reality? *Inter. J. Clin. Exp. Hyp., 32*(2), 191–197.

Bray, G. A., Dahms, W. T., Atkinson, R. L. et al. (1980). Factors controlling food intake: A comparison of dieting and intestinal bypass. *Amer. J. Clin. Nutrition, 33,* 376–382.

Breggin, P. R. (1979). *Electroshock: Its brain-disabling effects.* New York: Springer.

Bregman, E. (1934). An attempt to modify the emotional attitudes of infants by the conditioned response technique. *J. Genetic Psychol., 45,* 169–198.

Brende, J. O., & Parson, E. R. (1985). *Vietnam veterans.* New York: Plenum.

Brende, J. O., & Parson, E. R. (1987). Mulitiphasic treatment of the Vietnam veterans. *Psychother. Priv. Prac., 5*(2), 51–62.

Brende, J. O., & Rinsley, D. B. (1981). A case of multiple personality with psychological automatisms. *J. Amer. Acad. Psychoanal., 9*(1), 129–151.

Breslau, N., Meltzer, H. Y. (1988). Validity of subtyping psychotic depression: Examination of phenomanology and demographic characteristics. *Amer. J. Psychiat., 145*(1), 35–40.

Breslow, N. (1989). Sources of confusion in the study and treatment of sadomasochism. *J. Soc. Behav. Pers., 4*(3), 263–274.

Brewin, C. R., & Furnham, A. (1986). Attributional versus preattributional variables in self-esteem and depression: A comparison and test of learned helplessness theory. *J. Pers. Soc. Psychol., 50*(5), 1013–1020.

Brier, A., Schreiber, J. L., Dyer, L. et al. (1991). NIMH longitudinal study of chronic schizophrenia: prognosis and predictor of outcome. *Arch. Gen. Psychiat.*

Britton, W. H., & Eaves, R. C. (1986). Relationship between the Vineland Adaptive Behavior Scales — Classroom Edition of the Vineland Social Maturity Scales. *Amer. J. Ment. Def., 91*(1), 105–107.

Brodsky, L., Doerman, A. L., Palmer, L. S., Slade, G. F. et al. (1990). Post-traumatic stress disorder: An eclectic approach. *Inter. J. Psychosom., 37*(1–4), 89–95.

Brodsky, S., & Pothyress, N. (1990). *Presentation.* American Psychological Association Convention, Boston.

Broman, S. H., Nichols, P. L., & Kennedy, W. A. (1975). *Preschool IQ: Prenatal and early developmental correlates.* Hillsdale, NJ: Erlbaum.

Bromet, E. J. (1984). Epidemiology. In A. S. Bellack & M. Hersen (Eds.), *Research methods in clinical psychology.* New York: Pergamon.

Bromet, E. J., Schulberg, H. C., & Dunn, L. (1982). Reactions of psychiatric patients to the Three Mile Island nuclear accident. *Arch. Gen. Psychiat., 39*(6), 725–730.

Brooks, G. R., & Richardson, F. C. Emotional skill training: A treatment program for duodenal ulcer. *Behav. Ther., 11*(2), 198–207.

Brotman, A. W., Herzog, D. B., & Hamburg, P. (1988). Long-term course of bulimic patients treated with psychotherapy. *J. Clin. Psychiat., 49,* 157.

Broverman, I. K., Broverman, D. M., Clarkson, F. E., Rosenkrantz, P. S., & Vogel, S. R. (1970). Sex role stereotypes and clinical judgments of mental health. *J. Cons. Clin. Psychol., 34,* 1–7.

Brown, B. (1974). Depression roundup. *Behav. Today, 5*(17), 117.

Brown, B. S. (1976). Obstacles to treatment for blue-collar workers. In *New dimensions in mental health.* Washington, DC: U.S. Dept. Health, Education and Welfare.

Brown, B. S. (1983). The impact of political and economic changes upon mental health. *Amer. J. Orthopsychiat., 53*(4), 583–592.

Brown, C. W., Harris, T. O., & Peto, J. (1973). Life events and psychiatric disorders: II. Nature of causal link. *Psychol. Med., 3*(2), 150–170.

Brown, E. (1972). Assessment from a humanistic perspective. *Psychother. Theory Res. Prac., 9,* 103–106.

Brown, G., Birley, J., & Wing, J. (1972). Influence of family life on the course of schizophrenic disorders: A replication. *Brit. J. Psychiat., 121,* 241–258.

Brown, G. L., & Goodwin, F. K. (1986). Special Issue: Suicide and life-threatening behavior. *Suic. Life-Threat. Behav., 16*(2), 223–243.

Brown, G. W., & Harris, T. O. (1978). *Social origins of depression.* London: Tavistock.

Brown, G. W., Bone, M., Dalison, B., & Wing. J. K. (1966). *Schizophrenia and social care.* London: Oxford Univ.

Brown, J. C. (1983). Paraphilias: Sadomasochism, fetishism, transvestism and transsexuality. *Brit. J. Psychiat., 143,* 227–231.

Brown, J. D., & Siegel, J. M. (1988). Attributions for negative life events and depression: The role of perceived control. *J. Pers. Soc. Psychol., 54*(2), 316–322.

Brown, J. H., Henteleff, P., Barakat, S., & Rowe, C. J. (1986). Is it normal for terminally ill patients to desire death? *Amer. J. Psychiat., 143*(2), 208–211.

Brown, J. L. (1960). Prognosis from presenting symptoms of preschool children with atypical development. *Amer. J. Orthopsychiat., 30,* 382–390.

Brown, J. L. (1963). Follow-up of children with atypical development (infantile psychosis). *Amer. J. Orthopsychiat., 33,* 855–861.

Brown, L. T., & Weiner, E. E. (1979). *Introduction to psychology.* Boston: Winthrop.

Brown, W. R., & McGuire, J. M. (1976). Current psychological assessment practices. *Profess. Psychol., 7*(4), 475–484.

Browne, A., & Finklehor, D. (1986). Impact of child sexual abuse: A review of the research. *Psychol. Bull., 99*(1), 66–77.

Browne, A., & Frieze, I. H. (1988). Violence in marriage. In L. Ohlin & M. Tonry (Eds.), *Crime and justice: An annual review of research: Family violence.* Chicago: Univ. Chicago.

Browning, R. M. (1971). Treatment of a total behavior modification program with five autistic children. *Behav. Res. Ther., 9,* 319–327.

Bruch, H. (1962). Perceptual and conceptual disturbances in anorexia nervosa. *Psychosom. Med., 24,* 187–194.

Bruch, H. (1973). *Eating disorders: Obesity, anorexia nervosa and the person within.* New York: Basic.

Bruch, H. (1973). Psychiatric aspects of obesity. *Psychiat. Ann., 3*(7), 6–10.

Bruch, H. (1978). *The golden cage: The enigma of anorexia nervosa.* Cambridge, MA: Harvard Univ.

Bruch, H. (1981). Developmental considerations of anorexia nervosa and obesity. *Canad. J. Psychiat., 26,* 212–217.

Brudny, J. et al. (1974). Sensory feedback therapy as a modality of treatment in central nervous system disorders of voluntary movement. *Neurology, 24*(10), 925–932.

Brumback, R. A., Jackoway, M. K., & Weinberg, W. A. (1980). Relation of intelligence to childhood depression in children referred to an educational center. *Percep. & Motor Skills, 50*(1), 11–17.

Bryant, R., & Bates, B. (1985). Anorexia nervosa: Aetiological theories and treatment methods. *J. Adol., 8*(1), 93–103.

Buchbaum, M. S., & Haier, R. J. (1987). Functional and anatomical brain imaging: Impact on schizophrenia research. *Schizo. Bull., 13*(1), 115–132.

Bucher, R. E., & Costa, P. F. (1985). A abordagem terapeutica do toxicomano [The treatment of drug addicts]. *Acta Psiquiatrica y Psicologica de America Latina, 31*(2), 113–130.

Budoff, M., & Gottlieb, J. (1976). Special class students mainstreamed: A study of an aptitude (learning potential) multiplied by treatment interaction. *Amer. J. Ment. Def., 81,* 1–11.

Bugental, J. F. (1965). The existential crisis in intensive psychotherapy. *Psychother. Therapy Res. Prac., 2*(1), 16–20.

Bugental, J. F. T. (1964). The third force in psychology. *J. Humanistic Psychol., 4*(1), 19–26.

Bullard, D. G. (1988). The treatment of desire disorders in the medically and physically disabled. In R. C. Rosen & S. R. Leiblum (Eds.), *Sexual desire disorders.* New York: Guilford.

Bunney, W. E., & Davis, J. M. (1965). Norepinephrine in depressive reactions: A review. *Arch. Gen. Psychiat., 13*(6), 483–493.

Bunney, W. E., & Garland, B. (1981). Receptor function in depression. *Adv. in Bio. Psychiat., 7,* 71–84.

Bunney, W. E., & Garland, B. L. (1983). Possible receptor effects of chronic lithium administration. *Neuropharm., 22*(38), 367–372.

Bunney, W. E., Goodwin, F. K., Davis, J. M., & Fawcett, J. A. (1968). A behavioral-biochemical study of lithium treatment. *Amer. J. Psychiat., 125,* 499–512.

Burbach, D. J., & Borduin, C. M. (1986). Parent-child relations and the etiology of depression: A review of methods and findings. *Clin. Psychol. Rev., 6*(2), 133–153.

Burek, D. M. (Ed.) (1990). *Encyclopedia of associations* (25th ed.). Detroit, MI: Gale Research.

Burgess, A. W., & Holmstrom, L. L. (1974). Rape trauma syndrome. *Amer. J. Psychiat., 131*(9), 981–986.

Burgess, A. W., Holmstrom, L. L., & McCausland, M. P. (1979). Sexual disruption and recovery. *Amer. J. Orthopsychiat., 49*(4), 648–657.

Burke, J. D. (1986). Diagnostic categorization by the diagnostic interview schedule (DIS): A comparison with other methods of assessment. In J. E. Barrett & R. M. Rose (Eds.), *Mental disorders in the community: Findings from psychiatric epidemiology.* New York: Guilford.

Burke, J. D., & Regier, D. A. (1988). Epidemiology of mental disorders. In J. A. Talbott, R. E. Hales, & S. C. Yudofsky (Eds.), *American Psychiatric Press textbook of psychiatry,* Washington, DC: American Psychiatric.

Burnam, M. A., Stein, J. A., Golding, J. M., Siegel, J. M., Sorenson, S. B., Forsythe, A. B., & Telles, C. A. (1988). Sexual assault and mental disorders in a community population. *J. Cons. Clin. Psychol., 56,* 843–850.

Burns, T. P., & Crisp, A. H. (1985). Factors affecting prognosis in male anorexics. *J. Psychiat. Res., 19*(2–3), 323–328.

Burnside, I. (1988). Nursing care. In L. F. Jarvik & C. H. Winograd (Eds.), *Treatments for the Alzheimer patient: The long haul.* New York: Springer.

Bursztajn, H., Gutheil, T. G., Warren, M. J., & Brodsky, A. (1986). Depression, self-love, time, and the "right" to suicide. *Gen. Hosp. Psychiat., 8*(2), 91–95.

Burt, D. R., Creese, I., & Snyder, S. H. (1977). Antischizophrenic drugs: Chronic treatment elevates dopamine receptor binding in brain. *Science, 196*(4287), 326–328.

Burton, V. S. (1990). The consequences of official labels: A research note on rights lost by the mentally ill, mentally incompetent, and convicted felons. *Comm. Ment. Hlth. J., 26*(3), 267–276.

Buss, A. H. (1962). Two anxiety factors in psychiatric patients. *J. Abnorm. Soc. Psychol., 65*(6), 426–427.

Butcher, J. N. (Ed.), (1979). *New developments in the use of the MMPI.* Minneapolis: Univ. Minnesota.

Butcher, J. N. (1981, Mar.). Evaluating the MMPI. Presented at the International MMPI Symposium, Minneapolis, MN.

Butcher, J. N., & Graham, J. R. (1988). *The MMPI restandardization project.* Tampa, FL: Univ. Minnesota Continuing Education Project.

Butcher, J. N., Graham, J. R., Dahlstrom, W. G., Tellegen, A. M., & Kaemmer, B. (1989). *MMPI-2 manual for administration and scoring.* Minneapolis: Univ. Minnesota.

Butler, G., & Matthews, A. (1983). Cognitive processes in anxiety. *Adv. Behav. Res. Ther., 5,* 51–62.

Butler, G., Cullington, A., & Munby et al. (1984). Exposure and anxiety management in the treatment of social phobia. *J. Cons. Clin. Psychol., 52,* 642–650.

Butler, R. N., & Lewis, M. I. (1986). *Aging and mental health* (3rd ed.). Columbus, OH: Merrill.

Butler, R. W., & Satz, P. (1989). Psychological assessment of personality of adults and children. In H. I. Kaplan & B. J. Sadock (Eds.), *Comprehensive textbook of psychiatry* (Vol. 1, 5th ed.). Baltimore: Williams & Wilkins.

Byrne, K., & Stern, S. L. (1981). Antidepressant medication in the outpatient treatment of depression: Guide for nonmedical psychotherapists. *Profess. Psychol., 12*(3), 302–308.

Caddy, G. R. (1985). Cognitive behavior therapy in the treatment of multiple personality. *Behav. Mod., 9*(3), 267–292.

Calahan, D., Cisin, I. H., & Crossley, H. M. (1969). *American drinking practices: A national study of drinking behaviors and attitudes.* New Brunswick, NJ: Rutgers Center of Alcohol Studies.

Calam, R., Waller, G., Slade, P., & Newton, T. (1990). Eating disorders and perceived relationships with parents. *Inter. J. Eat. Dis., 9*(5), 479–485.

Callner, D. A. (1975). Behavioral treatment approaches to drug abuse: A critical review of the research. *Psychol. Bull., 82*(2), 143–164.

Campbell, D. T., & Stanley, J. C. (1963). Experimental and quasi-experimental designs for research. In N. L. Gage (Ed.), *Handbook of research on teaching.* Chicago: Rand McNally.

Campbell, I. T., Jarrett, R. J., & Keen, H. (1975). Diurnal and seasonal variation in oral glucose tolerance: Studies in the antarctic. *Diabetologia, 11,* 139–145.

Campbell, M., Anderson, L. T., Small, A. M., Perry, R., & Green, W. H. (1982). The effects of haloperidol on learning and behavior in autistic children. *J. Autism Dev. Dis., 12,* 167–175.

Campbell, M., Geller, B., Small, A. M., Petti, T. A., & Ferris, S. H. (1978). Minor physical anomalies in young psychotic children. *Amer. J. Psychiat., 135,* 573–575.

Campbell, R. V., O'Brien, S., Bickett, A. D., & Lutzker, J. R. (1983).

In-home parent training of migraine headaches and marital counseling as an ecobehavioral approach to prevent child abuse. *J. Behav. Ther. Exp. Psychiat., 14,* 147–154.

Cane, D. B., & Gotlib, I. H. (1985). Depression and the effects of positive and negative feedback on expectations, evaluations, and performance. *Cog. Ther. Res., 9*(2), 145–160.

Canero, R. (1985). University/state collaboration. Special Issue: The renaissance of the state psychiatric system. *Psychiatr. Quart., 57* (3–4), 182–186.

Cannon, D. S., Baker, T. B., & Wehl, C. K. (1981). Emetic and electric shock alcohol aversion therapy: Six- and twelve-month follow-up. *J. Cons. Clin. Psychol., 49*(3), 360–368.

Cannon, W. B., & Lewis, J. T. (1927). Physiological maximum heart rate as artefact. *Amer. J. Physiol., 82,* 67–74.

Cannon, W. B., & Rosenblueth, A. (1933). Studies on conditions of activity in endocrine organs. *Amer. J. Physiol., 104,* 557–574.

Canter, A., Kondo, C. Y., & Knott, J. R. (1975). A comparison of EMG feedback and progressive muscle relaxation training in anxiety neurosis. *Brit. J. Psychiat., 127,* 470–477.

Cantwell, D., Baker, L., & Rutter, M. (1978). A comparative study of infantile autism and specific developmental receptive language disorder: IV. Analysis of syntax and language function. *J. Child Psychol. Psychiat., 19,* 351–362.

Cantwell, D. P. (1982). Childhood depression. In B. B. Lahe & A. E. Kazdin (Eds.), *Advances in clinical child psychology* (Vol. 5). New York: Plenum.

Caplan, G. (1964). *Principles of preventive psychiatry.* New York: Basic.

Caplan, P. J. (1989). *Don't blame mother: Mending the mother-daughter relationship.* New York: Harper & Row.

Carey, G., & Gottesman, I. I. (1981). Twin and family studies of anxiety, phobic, and obsessive disorders. In D. K. Klein & J. Rabkin (Eds.), *Anxiety: New research and changing concepts.* New York: Raven.

Carlson, G. A., Asarnow, J. R., & Orbach, I. (1987). Developmental aspects of suicidal behavior in children: I. *J. Amer. Acad. Child Adol. Psychiat., 26*(2), 186–192.

Carlsson, A. (1978). Antipsychotic drugs, neurotransmitters, and schizophrenia. *Amer. J. Psychiat., 135*(2), 104–173.

Carlsson, A. (1978). Does dopamine have a role in schizophrenia? *Bio. Psychiat., 13*(1), 3–21.

Carlsson, A., & Lindquist, M. (1963). Effect of chlorpromazine or haloperidol on formation of 3-methoxytyramine and normetanephrine in mouse brain. *Acta Pharmacologia Toxicologica, 20,* 140.

Carney, P. A., Fitzgerald, C. T., & Monaghan, C. E. (1988). Influence of climate on the prevalence of mania. *Brit. J. Psychiat., 152,* 820–823.

Carpenter, W. T., & Kirkpatrick, B. (1988). The heterogeneity of the long-term course of schizophrenia. *Schizo. Bull., 14*(4), 845–852.

Carpenter, W. T., Heinrichs, D. W., & Wagman, A. M. (1988). Deficit and nondeficit forms of schizophrenia: The concept. *Amer. J. Psychiat., 145*(5), 578–583.

Carr, E. G., Schreibman, L., & Lovaas, O. I. (1975). Control of echolalic speech in psychotic children. *J. Abnorm. Child Psychol., 3,* 331–351.

Carrington, P., Collings, G. H., Jr., Bensen, H., Robinson, H., Wood, L. W., Lehrer, P. M., Woolfolk, R. L., & Cole, J. W. (1980). The use of meditation relaxation techniques for the management of stress in a working population. *J. Occupational Med., 22*(4), 221–231.

Carroll, M. E. (1990). PCP and hallucinogens. *Adv. in Alchohol & Substance Abuse, 9*(1–2), 167–190.

Carson, N. D., & Johnson, R. E. (1985). Suicidal thoughts and problem-solving preparation among college students. *J. Coll. Stud. Personnel, 26*(6), 484–487.

Carter, C. H. (1970). *Handbook of mental retardation syndromes.* Springfield, IL: Thomas.

Cartwright, R. (1961). The effects of psychotherapy on self-consistency: A replication and extension. *J. Cons. Clin. Psychol., 29,* 376–382.

Cartwright, R., & Vogel, J. (1960). A comparison of changes in psychoneurotic patients during matched periods of therapy and no therapy. *J. Cons. Clin. Psychol., 28,* 121–127.

Castillo, R. J. (1990). Depersonalization and meditation. *Psychiatry, 53*(2), 158–168.

Catania, J. A., Gibson, D. R., Chitwood, D. D., & Coates, T. J. (1990). Methodological problems in AIDS behavioral research: Influences on measurement error and participation bias in studies of sexual behavior. *Psychol. Bull., 108,* 339–362.

Caton, C. L. (1982). Effect of length of inpatient treatment for chronic schizophrenia. *Amer. J. Psychiat., 139*(7), 856–861.

Cattell, R. B., & Scheier, I. H. (1961). *The meaning and measurement of neuroticism and anxiety.* New York: Ronald.

Cattell, R. B., & Warburton, R. W. (1961). A cross-cultural comparison of patterns of extraversion and anxiety. *Brit. J. Psychol., 52,* 3–15.

Cautela, J. R. (1966). Treatment of compulsive behavior by covert sensitization. *Psych. Rec., 16*(1), 33–41.

Cautela, J. R. (1977). Covert conditioning: Assumptions and procedures. *J. Mental Imagery, 1*(1), 53–64.

Cautela, J. R., & Kastenbaum, R. (1967). A reinforcement survey schedule for use in therapy, training, and research. *Psych. Rep., 20,* 1115–1130.

Cautela, J. R., & Upper, D. (1976). The behavioral inventory battery. In M. Hersen & A. Bellach (Eds.), *Behavioral assessment: A practical handbook.* New York: Pergamon.

Cauwels, J. M. (1983). *Bulimia: The binge-purge compulsion.* New York: Doubleday.

Cavanaugh, J. C. (1990). *Adult development and aging.* Belmont, CA: Wadsworth.

Cerletti, U., & Bini, L. (1938). L'elettroshock. *Archiv. Gen. Neurol. Psychiat. & Psychoanal., 19,* 266–268.

Cerney, M. S. (1988). "If only . . ." Remorse in grief therapy. *Psychotherapy-Patient, 5*(1–2), 235–248.

Chait, L. D., Fishman, M. W., & Schuster, C. R. (1985). "Hangover" effects the morning after marijuana smoking. *Drug Alc. Dep., 15*(3), 229–238.

Chamberlain, P. (1985). Increasing the attention span of five mentally handicapped children using their parents as agents of change. *Behav. Psychother., 13*(20), 142–153.

Chambless, D. L. (1988). Cognitive mechanisms in panic disorder. In S. Rachman & J. Maser (Eds.), *Panic: psychological perspectives.* Hillsdale, NJ: Erlbaum.

Chambless, D. L., Foa, E. B., Groves, G. A., & Goldstein, A. J. (1979). Flooding with Brevital in the treatment of agoraphobia: Countereffective? *Behav. Res. Ther., 17*(3), 243–251.

Chambless, D. L., Foa, E. B., Groves, G. A., & Goldstein, A. J. (1982). Exposure and communications training in the treatment of agoraphobia. *Behav. Res. Ther., 20*(3), 219–231.

Chaney, E. F., Blane, H. T., Abran, H. S., Gotner, J., Lacy, E., McCourt, W. F., Clark, E., & Myers, E. (1978). Skill training with alcoholics. *J. Cons. Clin. Psychol., 46,* 1092–1104.

Chapman, J. (1966). The early symptoms of schizophrenia. *Brit. J. Psychiat., 112,* 225–251.

Charatan, F. B. (1979). Psychiatric syndromes in the aged. *Hillside J. Clin. Psychiat., 1*(2), 143–160.

Charney, D. S., & Heninger, G. R. (1983). Monoamine receptor sensitivity and depression: Clinical studies of antidepressant effects of serotonin and noradrenergic function. *Psychopharm. Bull., 19,* 490–495.

Charney, D. S., Heninger, G. R., & Redmond, E. D. (1984, May). Neurobiological mechanism. From *Abstracts of the APA Annual Meeting* (Abstract 30C). Los Angeles.

Charney, D. S., Heninger, G. R., & Sternberg, D. E., Jr. (1983). Yohimbine induced anxiety and increased noradrenergic function in humans: Effects of diazepam and clonidine. *Life Science, 33,* 19–29.

Charney, D. S., Heninger, G. R., & Sternberg, D. E. (1984). The effect of mianserin on alpha 2 adrenergic receptor function in depressed patients. *Brit. J. Psychiat., 144,* 407–418.

Charney, D. S., Menkes, D. B., & Heninger, G. R. (1981). Receptor sensitivity and the mechanism of action of antidepressant treatment. *Arch. Gen. Psychiat., 38*(10), 1160–1180.

Chesney, M. A., Eagleston, J. R., & Rosenman, R. H. (1981). Type A behavior: Assessment and intervention. In C. K. Prokop & L. A. Bradley (Eds.), *Medical psychology: Contributions to behavioral medicine.* New York: Academic.

Chess, S. (1971). Autism in children with congenital rubella. *J. Autism Child. Schizo., 1,* 33.

Chiles, J. A., Strosahl, K. D., McMurtray, L., & Linehan, M. M. (1985). Modeling effects on suicidal behavior. *J. Nerv. Ment. Dis., 173*(8), 477–481.

Chiu, L. H. (1971). Manifested anxiety in Chinese and American children. *J. Psychol., 79,* 273–284.

Chodorkoff, B. (1954). Self-perception, perceptual defense, and adjustment. *J. Abnorm. Soc. Psychol.*, 49, 508–512.

Christensen, A., Johnson, S. M., & Phillips, S. (1980). Cost effectiveness in behavioral family therapy. *Behav. Ther.*, 11(2), 208–226.

Chu, J. A., & Dill, D. L. (1990). Dissociative symptoms in relation to childhood physical and sexual abuse. *Amer. J. Psychiat.*, 147(7), 887–892.

Churgin, M. J. (1983). Prisoners transferred to mental hospitals. In J. Monahan & H. J. Steadman (Eds.), *Mentally disordered offenders: Perspectives from law and social science.* New York: Plenum.

Chynoweth, R. (1977). Significance of suicide notes. *Austral. New Zeal. J. Psychiat.*, 11, 197–200.

Ciminero, A. R. (1986). Behavioral assessment. An overview. In A. R. Ciminero, K. S. Calhoun, & H. E. Adams (Eds.), *Handbook of behavioral assessment* (2nd ed.). New York: Wiley.

Cipani, E. (1991). Educational classification and placement. In J. L. Matson & J. A. Mulick (Eds.), *Handbook of mental retardation.* New York: Pergamon.

Cisin, I. H., & Calahan, D. (1968). Comparison of abstainers and heavy drinkers in a national survey. *Psychiat. Res. Rep.*, 24, 10–22.

Cisin, I. H., & Calahan, D. (1970, Jul. 6). The big drinkers. *Newsweek*, 57.

Claghorn, J. L., McBee, G. W., & Roberts, L. (1976). Trends in hospital versus community treatment of mental illness: A Texas example. *Amer. J. Psychiat.*, 133(11), 1310–1312.

Clance, P. R. (1985, Apr.). Cited in J. Meer, Will the real impostor please stand up? *Psych. Today*, 24–25.

Clance, P. R., & O'Toole, M. A. (1987). The impostor phenomenon: An integral barrier to empowerment and achievement [Special Issue]. *Women & Therapy*, 6(3), 51–64.

Clark, D. A., Beck, A. T., & Stewart, B. L. (1990). Cognitive specificity and positive negative affectivity: Complementary or contradictory views on anxiety and depression? *J. Abnorm. Psychiat.*, 99(2), 140–155.

Clark, D. F. (1988). The validity of measures of cognition: A review of the literature. *Cognitive Ther. Res.*, 12, 1–20.

Clark, D. M. (1988). A cognitive model of panic attacks. In S. Rachman & J. Maser (Eds.), *Panic: Psychologic perspectives.* Hillsdale, NJ: Erlbaum.

Clark, D. M., & Salkovskis, P. M. (1986). A cognitive-behavioural treatment for panic attacks. In W. Huber (Ed.), *Proceedings of the SPR: European conference on psychotherapy research.* Belgium: Louvain-la-Neuve Univ.

Clark, D. M., Salkovskis, P. M., & Chalkley, A. J. (1985). Respiratory control as a treatment for panic attacks. *J. Behav. Ther. Exp. Psychiat.*, 16(1), 23–30.

Clarke, A. M., Clarke, A. D. B., & Berg, J. M. (Eds.). (1985). *Mental deficiency: The changing outlook.* London: Methuen.

Clarke, D. B. (1986). Voluntary euthanasia and the Hemlock Society. *Amer. J. Psychiat.*, 143(11), 1503.

Clayton, P. J. (1985). Suicide [Special Issue]. *Psychiat. Clin. N. Amer.*, 8(2), 203–214.

Cleckley, H. (1976). *The mask of sanity* (5th ed.). St. Louis: Mosby.

Cline, V. B., & Richards, J. M. (1961). The generality of accuracy of interpersonal perception. *J. Abnorm. Soc. Psychol.*, 62, 446–449.

Clinton, D. N., & McKinlay, W. W. (1986). Attitudes to food, eating and weight in acutely ill and recovered anorectics. *Brit. J. Clin. Psychol.*, 25(1), 61–67.

Clipp, E., & George, L. (1990). Psychotropic drug use among caregivers of patients with dementia. *J. Amer. Geriatric Society*, 38, 228–235.

Cloninger, C. R., Martin, R. L., Guze, S. B., & Clayton, P. J. (1986). A prospective follow-up and family study of somatization in men and women. *Amer. J. Psychiat.*, 143(7), 873–878.

Cloninger, C. R., Sigvardsson, S., von Knorring, A. L., & Bohman, M. (1984). An adoption study of somatoform disorders: II. Identification of two discrete somatoform disorders. *Arch. Gen. Psychiat.*, 41(9), 863–871.

Cocarro, E. F. (1991). Psychodynamic aspects of mental disorders. In K. Davis, H. Klar, & J. T. Coyle (Eds.), *Foundations of psychiatry.* Philadelphia: Saunders.

Coche, E. B., & Dies, R. R. (1981). Integrating research findings into the practice of group psychotherapy. *Psychother. Theory Res. Prac.*, 18, 410–415.

Cockran, S. D., & Hammen, C. L. (1985). Perceptions of stressful life events and depression: A test of attributional models. *J. Pers. Soc. Psychol.*, 48(6), 1562–1571.

Cocozza, J. J., & Steadman, M. J. (1978). Prediction in psychiatry: An example of misplaced confidence in experts. *Social Problems*, 25, 265–270.

Cohen, C. I. (1990). Outcome of schizophrenia into later life: An overview. *Gerontologist*, 30, 790–797.

Cohen, D. J., Caparulo, B. K., Shaywitz, B. A., & Bowers, M. B. (1977). Dopamine and serotonin metabolism in neuropsychiatrically disturbed children. *Arch. Gen. Psychiat.*, 34, 545–550.

Cohen, M. B., Baker, G., Cohen, R. A., Fromm-Reichmann, F., & Weigert, E. V. (1954). An intensive study of twelve cases of manic-depressive psychosis. *Psychiatry*, 17, 103–137.

Cohen, R. (1987). Suddenly, I'm the adult. *Psych. Today*, 70–71.

Cohen, R. M., Semple, W. E., Gross, M., & Nordahl, T. E. (1988). From syndrome to illness: Delineating the pathophysiology of schizophrenia with PET. *Schizo. Bull.*, 14(2), 169–176.

Cohen, R. M., Semple, W. E., Gross, M. et al. (1989). Dysfunction in a prefrontal substrate of sustained attention in schizophrenia. *Life Sciences*, 40, 2031–2039.

Cohen, S. (1980). Coca paste and freebase: New fashions in cocaine use. *Drug Abuse & Alcoholism Newsletter*, 9(3).

Cohen, S. (1984). Cocaine: Acute medical and psychiatric complications. *Psychiat. Ann.*, 14(10), 728–732.

Cohen-Sandler, R., Berman, A. L., & King, R. A. (1982). A follow-up study of hospitalized suicidal children. *J. Amer. Acad. Child Psychiat.*, 214, 398–403.

Cohn, E. G. (1990). Weather and violent crime: A reply to Perry and Simpson. *Environment & Behav.*, 22(2), 280–294.

Cohn, J., Katon, W., & Richelson, E. (1990, Jul. 15). Choosing the right antidepressant. *Patient Care*, 88–116.

Colbach, E. M. (1987). Hysteria again and again and again. *Inter. J. Offend. Ther. Compar. Crim.*, 31(1), 41–48.

Colby, K. M., Faught, W. S., & Parkison, R. C. (1979). Cognitive therapy of paranoid conditions: Heuristic suggestions based on a computer simulation model. *Cog. Ther. Res.*, 3(1), 159.

Cole, J. O., Klerman, G. L., Goldberg, S. C. et al. (1964). Phenothiazine treatment in acute schizophrenia. *Arch. Gen. Psychiat.*, 10, 246–261.

Coleman, L. (1984). *The reign of error: Psychiatry, authority, and law.* Boston: Beacon.

Coleman, M. (1979). Studies of the autistic syndromes. In R. Katzman (Ed.), *Congenital acquired cognitive disorders.* New York: Raven.

Colerick, E. J., & George, L. K. (1986). Predictors of institutionalization among caregivers of patients with Alzheimer's Disease. *J. Amer. Geriatric Society*, 34, 493–498.

Comer, R. (1973). *Therapy interviews with a schizophrenic patient.* Unpublished manuscript.

Compton, D. R., Dewey, W. L., & Martin, B. R. (1990). Cannabis dependence and tolerance production. *Adv. in Alcohol & Substance Abuse*, 9(1–2), 129–147.

Condon, J. T. (1986). Long-term neuroleptic therapy in chronic anorexia nervosa complicated by tardive dyskinesia: A case report. *Acta Psychiatr. Scandin.*, 73(2), 203–206.

Conger, J. J. (1951). The effects of alcohol on conflict behavior in the albino rat. *Quart. J. Stud. Alcohol.*, 12, 1–29.

Conte, H. R., Plutchik, R., Wild, K. V., & Karasu, T. B. (1986). Combined psychotherapy and pharacotherapy for depression: A systematic analysis of the evidence. *Arch. Gen. Psychiat.*, 43(5), 471–479.

Conte, J. R. (1991). Overview of child sexual abuse. In A. Tasman & S. M. Goldfinger (Eds.), *American Psychiatric Press review of psychiatry* (Vol. 10). Washington, DC: American Psychiatric.

Conway, J. B. (1977). Behavioral self-control of smoking through aversive conditioning and self-management. *J. Cons. Clin. Psychol.*, 45(3), 348–357.

Cook, E. H., Leventhal, B. L., Heller, W., Metz, J. et al. (1990). Autistic children and their first-degree relatives: Relationships between serotonin and norepinephrine levels and intelligence. 35th Annual Meeting of the American Academy of Child and Adolescent Psychiatry (1988, Seattle, WA). *J. Neuropsychiat. Clin. Neurosci.*, 2(3), 268–274.

Cook, M. L., & Peterson, C. (1986). Depressive irrationality. *Cog. Ther. Res.*, 10(3), 293–298.

Cook, T. D., & Campbell, D. T. (1979). *Quasi-experimentation: Design and analysis issues for field settings.* Chicago: Rand McNally.

Cookerly, J. R. (1980). Does marital therapy do any lasting good? *J. Marital Fam. Ther.*, 6(4), 393–397.

Coons, P. M. (1980). Multiple personality: Diagnostic considerations. *J. Clin. Psychiat.*, 41(10), 330–336.

Coons, P. M. (1990). Accuracy of the MMPI in identifying multiple personality disorder. *Psych. Rep.*, 66(3, Pt 1), 831–834.

Coons, P. M., & Bradley, K. (1985). Group psychotherapy with multiple personality patients. *J. Nerv. Ment. Dis.*, 173(9), 515–521.

Coons, P. M., Bowman, E. S., & Milstein, V. (1988). Multiple personality disorder: A clinical investigation of 50 cases. *J. Nerv. Ment. Dis.*, 176(9), 519–527.

Cooper, J., & Axsom, D. (1982). Effort justification in psychotherapy. In G. Weary & H. L. Mirels (Eds.), *Integrations of clinical and social psychology*. New York: Oxford Univ.

Cooper, J. R. (Ed.). (1977). *Sedative-hypnotic drugs: Risks and benefits*. Washington, DC: GPO.

Cooper, S. E. (1989). Chemical dependency and eating disorders: Are they really so different? *J. Couns. Dev.*, 68(1), 102–105.

Coppen, A. (1967). The biochemistry of affective disorders. *Brit. J. Psychiat.*, 112, 1237–1264.

Corder, B. F. et al. (1981). An experimental study of the effect of structured videotape feedback on adolescent group psychotherapy process. *J. Youth Adol.*, 10(4), 255–262.

Cormier, H. J., & Klerman, G. L. (1985). Unemployment and male-female labor force participation as determinants of changing suicide rates of males and females in Quebec. *Soc. Psychiat.*, 20(3), 109–114.

Cornblatt, B. A., & Erlanmeyer-Kimling, L. (1985). Global attentional deviance as a marker of risk for schizophrenia: Specificity and predictive validity. *J. Abnorm. Psychol.*, 94(4), 470–488.

Cornell, C. P., & Gelles, R. J. (1983). *Intimate violence in families*. Beverly Hills, CA: Sage.

Corson, S. A., & Corson, E. D. (1978). Pets as mediators of therapy. *Current Psychiat. Ther.*, 18, 195–205.

Coryell, W., & Norten, S. G. (1981). Briquet's syndrome (somatization disorder) and primary depression: Comparison of background and outcome. *Comprehen. Psychiat.*, 22(3), 249–256.

Costa, E. (1983). Are benzodiazepine recognition sites functional entities for the action of endogenous effectors or merely drug receptors? *Adv. In Biochem. & Psychopharm.*, 38, 249–259.

Costa, E. (1985). Benzodiazepine-GABA interactions: A model to investigate the neurobiology of anxiety. In A. H. Tuma & J. Maser (Eds.), *Anxiety and the anxiety disorders*. Hillsdale, NJ: Erlbaum.

Costa, E., & Guidotti, A. (1979). Molecular mechanisms in the receptor action of benzodiazepines. In G. R. Okun & A. K. Cho (Eds.), *Annual Review of Pharmacology and Toxicology* (Vol. 19). Palo Alto, CA: Annual Review.

Costa, E., Guidotti, A., & Toffano, G. (1978). Molecular mechanisms mediating the action of benzodiazepines on GABA receptors. *Brit. J. Psychiat.*, 133, 239–248.

Costa, E., Guidotti, A., Mao, C. C., & Suria, A. (1975). New concepts on the mechanism of action of benzodiazepines. *Life Sciences*, 17(2), 167–185.

Costello, C. G. (1972). Depression: Loss of reinforcers or loss of reinforcer effectiveness? *Behav. Ther.*, 3, 242–247.

Coursey, R. D. (1975). Electromyograph feedback as a relaxation technique. *J. Cons. Clin. Psychol.*, 43(6), 825–834.

Coursey, R. D. (1975). Personality measures and evoked responses in chronic insomniacs. *J. Abnorm. Psychol.*, 84(3), 239–249.

Cowen, E. L. (1973). Social and community interventions. *Annu. Rev. Psychol.*, 24, 135.

Cox, A., Rutter, M., Newman, S., & Bartak, L. (1975). A comparative study of infantile autism and specific developmental receptive language disorder: II. Parental characteristics. *Brit. J. Psychiat.*, 126, 146–159.

Cox, H., & Hammonds, A. (1988). Religiosity, aging, and life satisfaction. *J. Religion & Aging*, 5, 1–21.

Coyne, J. C. (1976). Depression and the response of others. *J. Abnorm. Psychol.*, 85(2), 186–193.

Coyne, J. C. (1985). Studying depressed persons interactions with strangers and spouses. *J. Abnorm. Psychol.*, 94(2), 231–232.

Crago, M., Yates, A., Beutler, L. E., & Arizmendi, T. G. (1985). Height-weight ratios among female athletes: Are collegiate athletics the precursors to an anorexic syndrome? *Inter. J. of Eat. Dis.*, 4, 79–87.

Crancer, A., Dille, J., Wallace, J., & Haykin, M. (1969). Comparison of effects of marijuana and alcohol on simulated driving experience. *Science*, 164, 851–854.

Crancer, A., Jr., & Quiring, D. L. (1969). The mentally ill as motor vehicle operators. *Amer. J. Psychiat.*, 126(6), 807–813.

Crary, B., Borysenko, M., Sutherland, D. C., Kutz, I., Borysenko, J. Z., & Benson, H. (1983). Decrease in mitogen responsiveness of mononuclear cells from peripheral blood after epinephrine administration in humans. *J. Immunol.*, 130, 694–697.

Crary, B., Hauser, S. L., Borysenko, M., Kutz, I., Hoban, C., Ault, K. A., Weiner, H. L., & Benson, H. (1983). Epinephrine induced changes in the distribution of lymphocyte subsets in the peripheral blood of humans. *J. Immunol.*, 131, 1178–1181.

Craske, M. G. (1988). Cognitive-behavioral treatment. In A. J. Frances & R. E. Hales (Eds.), *American Psychiatric Press review of psychiatry* (Vol. 7). Washington, DC: American Psychiatric.

Craske, M. G., & Barlow, D. H. (1988). A review of the relationship between panic and avoidance. *Clin. Psychol. Rev.* 8(6), 667–685.

Craske, M. G., Rapee, R. M., & Barlow, D. H. (1988). The significance of panic-expectancy for individual patterns of avoidance. *Behav. Ther.* 19(4), 577–592.

Creed, F., Black, D., & Anthony, P. (1989). Day-hospital and community treatment for acute psychiatric illness: A critical appraisal. *Brit. J. Psychiat.*, 154, 300–310.

Creer, C., & Wing, J. K. (1974). *Schizophrenia at home* [monograph]. London: National Schizophrenia Fellowship.

Creese, I., Burt, D. R., & Snyder, S. H. (1963). Biochemical actions of neuroleptic drugs. In L. L. Iversen, S. D. Iversen, & S. H. Snyder (Eds.), *Handbook of psychopharmacology* (Vol. 10). New York: Plenum.

Crisp, A. H. (1966). A treatment regime for anorexia nervosa. *Brit. J. Psychiat.*, 112, 505–512.

Crisp, A. H. (1967). The possible significance of some behavioral correlates of weight and carbohydrate intake. *J. Psychosom. Res.*, 11, 117–131.

Crisp, A. H. (1980). *Anorexia nervosa: Let me be*. New York: Grune & Stratton.

Crisp, A. H. (1981). Anorexia nervosa at a normal weight?: The abnormal-normal weight control syndrome. *Inter. J. Psychiat. Med.*, 11, 203–233.

Crisp, A. H., Harding, B., & McGuinness, B. (1974). Anorexia nervosa: psychoneurotic characteristics of parents: relationship to prognosis. *J. Psychosom. Res.*, 18, 167–173.

Cronbach, L. J., & Meehl, P. E. (1955). Construct validity in psychology tests. *Psychol. Bull.*, 52, 281–302.

Cronen, V. E., Johnson, K. M., & Lannamann, J. W. (1983). Paradossi, doppi-legami e circuiti riflessivi: una prospettiva teorica alternativa. *Terapia-Familiare*, 14, 87–120.

Crook, T. (1986). Drug effects in Alzheimer's Disease. In T. L. Brink (Ed.), *Clinical gerontology: A guide to assessment and intervention*. New York: Haworth.

Crook, T., & Eliot, J. (1980). Parental death during childhood and adult depression: A critical review of the literature. *Psychol. Bull.*, 87(2), 252–259.

Crooks, R., & Baur, K. (1990). *Our sexuality* (4th ed.). New York: Benjamin-Cummings.

Crow, M. J., Marks, I. M., Agras, W. S., & Leitenberg, H. (1972). Time-limited desensitization implosion and shaping for phobic patients: A cross-over study. *Behav. Res. Ther.*, 10, 319–328.

Crow, T. J. (1980). Positive and negative schizophrenic symptoms and the role of dopamine: II. *Brit. J. Psychiat.*, 137, 383–386.

Crow, T. J. (1985). The two-syndrome concept: Origins and current status. *Schizophrenic Bull.*, 11(3), 471–486.

Crow, T. J. (1988). Genes and viruses in schizophrenia: the retrovirus/transposon hypothesis. In C. N. Stefanis & A. D. Rabavilis (Eds.), *Schizophrenia: Recent biosocial developments*. New York: Human Sciences.

Crow, T. J. (1988). Sex chromosomes and psychosis: The case for a pseudoautosomal locus. *Brit. J. Psychiat.*, 153, 675–683.

Crow, T. J., Cross, A. J., Johnstone, E. C., & Owen, F. (1982). Two syndromes in schizophrenia and their pathogenesis. In F. A. Henn & H. A. Nasrallah (Eds.), *Schizophrenia as a brain disease*. New York: Oxford Univ.

Crowther, J. H., Bond, L. A., & Rolf, J. E. (1981). The incidence, prevalence, and severity of behavior disorder among preschool-age children in day care. *J. Abnorm. Child Psychol.*, 9, 23–42.

Cumming, J., & Cumming, E. (1962). *Ego and milieu: Theory and practice of environmental therapy*. New York: Atherton.

Cummings, C., Gordon, J., & Marlatt, G. A. (1980). Relapse: Prevention and prediction. In W. Miller (Ed.), *The addictive behaviors*. Oxford: Pergamon.

Curran, D. K. (1986). Adolescent suicidal behavior. *Issues in Ment. Hlth. Nursing, 8*(4), 275–477.

Curran, J. P. (1977). Skills training as an approach to the treatment of heterosexual-social anxiety: A review. *Psychol. Bull., 84*(1), 140–157.

Curran, J. P., & Gilbert, F. S. (1975). A test of the relative effectiveness of a systematic desensitization program and an interpersonal skills training program with date-anxious subjects. *Behav. Ther., 6,* 510–525.

Cutting, J. (1985). *The psychology of schizophrenia.* Edinburgh: Churchill-Livingstone.

Cutting, J., & Murphy, D. (1988). Schizophrenic thought disorder: A psychological and organic interpretation. *Brit. J. Psychiat., 152,* 310–319.

Cutting, J., & Murphy, D. (1990). Impaired ability of schizophrenics, relative to manics or depressives, to appreciate social knowledge about their culture. *Brit. J. Psychiat., 157,* 355–358.

Cyr, J. J., & Kalpin, R. A. (1988). Investigating the lunar-lunacy relationship: A reply to Rotton and Kelly. *Psych. Rep., 62*(1), 319–322.

Cytryn, L., & Lourie, R. D. (1967). Mental retardation. In A. M. Freedman & H. I. Kaplan (Eds.), *Comprehensive textbook of psychiatry.* Baltimore: Williams & Wilkins.

D'Elia, G. (1974). Unilateral electroconvulsive therapy. In M. Fink, S. S. Kety, J. McGaugh, & T. D. Williams (Eds.), *Psychobiology of convulsive therapy.* Washington, DC: Winston.

D'Elia, G., & Raotma, H. (1975). Is unilateral ECT less effective than bilateral ECT? *Brit. J. Psychiat., 126,* 83–89.

Dacey, C. M., Nelson, W. M., & Aikman, K. G. (1990). Prevalency rate and personality comparisons of bulimic and normal adolescents. *Child Psychiat. Human Dev., 20*(4), 243–251.

Dailey, C. A. (1952). The effects of premature conclusions upon the acquisition of understanding a person. *J. Psychol., 33,* 133–152.

Dally, P. (1969). *Anorexia nervosa.* New York: Grune & Stratton.

Dally, P., & Sargant, W. (1960). A new treatment of anorexia nervosa. *Brit. Med. J., 1,* 1770–1773.

Dashef, S. S. (1984). Active suicide intervention by a campus mental health service: Operation and rationale. *J. Amer. Coll. Hlth., 33*(3), 118–122.

Daty, S. S. et al. (1976). Mental illness in the biological and adoptive families of adopted individuals who have become schizophrenic. *Behav. Genetics, 8*(3), 218–225.

Davanloo, H. (Ed.) *Short-term dynamic psychotherapy.* New York: Aronson.

Davidson, J., Allen, J. G., & Smith W. H. (1987). Complexities in the hospital treatment of a patient with multiple personality disorder. *Bull. Menninger Clinic, 51*(6), 561–568.

Davies, J., Nasar, S., Spira, N., & Vogel, C. (1981). Anxiety: differential diagnosis and treatment from a biological perspective. *J. Clin. Psychiat., 42,* 4–14.

Davis, J. M. (1975). Overview: Maintenance therapy in psychiatry: I. Schizophrenia. *Amer. J. Psychiat., 132*(12), 1237–1245.

Davis, J. M. (1976). Overview: Maintenance therapy in psychiatry: II. Affective disorders. *Amer. J. Psychiat., 133,* 1–13.

Davis, J. M. (1980). Antidepressant drugs. In H. I. Kaplan, A. M. Freedman, & B. J. Sadock (Eds.), *Comprehensive textbook of psychiatry III.* Baltimore: Williams & Wilkins.

Davis, J. M., & Dysken, M. (1989). The pharmacology of psychotropic drugs and drug-drug interactions. In H. I. Kaplan & B. J. Sadock (Eds.), *Comprehensive textbook of psychiatry V.* Baltimore: Williams & Wilkins.

Davis, J. M., Comaty, J. E., & Janicak, P. G. (1988). The psychological effects of antipsychotic drugs. In C. N. Stefanis & A. D. Rabavilis (Eds.), *Schizophrenia: Recent biosocial developments.* New York: Human Sciences.

Davis, J. M., Klerman, G., & Schildkraut, J. (1967). Drugs used in the treatment of depression. In L. Efron, J. O. Cole, D. Levine, & J. R. Wittenborn (Eds.), *Psychopharmacology: A review of progress.* Washington, DC: U. S. Clearinghouse of Mental Health Information.

Davis, R. A. (1981). Female labor force participation, status integration and suicide, 1950–1969. *Suic. Life-Threat. Behav., 11*(2), 111–123.

Dawson, P. M., Griffith, K., & Boeke, K. M. (1990). Combined medical and psychological treatment of hospitalized children with encopresis. *Child. Psychiat. Human Dev., 20*(3), 181–190.

de Cuyper, H. (1987). (Auto) aggression and serotonin: A review of human data. *Acta Psychiatrica Belgica, 87*(3), 325–331.

Dean, A., & Ensel, W. M. (1983). The epidemiology of depression in young adults: The centrality of social support. *J. Psychiat. Treatment & Evaluation, 5*(2–3), 195–207.

DeFazio, V. J., Rustin, S., & Diamond, A. (1975). Symptom development in Vietnam-era veterans. *Amer. J. Orthopsychiat. 45*(1), 158–163.

Deitz, S. M. (1977). An analysis of programming DRL schedules in educational settings. *Behav. Res. Ther., 15*(1), 103–111.

Dekker, J., & Everaerd, W. (1988). Attentional effects on sexual arousal. *Psychophysiology, 25*(1), 45–54.

Del Zempo, M., Bocchatta, A., Goldin, L. R., & Corsini, C. U. (1984). Linkage between X chromosome markers and manic depressive illness: Two Sardinian pedigrees. *Acta Psychiatr. Scandin., 70*(3), 282–287.

DeLisi, L. E., & Crow, T. J. (1986). Is schizophrenia a viral or immunologic disorder? *Psychiat. Clin. No. Amer., 9*(1), 115–132.

DeLisi, L. E., Smith, S. B., & Hamovit, J. R. (1986). Herpes simplex virus, cytomegalovirus and Epstein-Barr virus antibody titres in sera from schizophrenic patients. *Psychol. Med., 16*(4), 757–763.

Delisle, J. R. (1986). Death with honors: Suicide among gifted adolescents [Special Issue]. *J. Couns. Dev., 64*(9), 558–560.

Dell, P. F. (1988). Professional skepticism about multiple personality. *J. Nerv. Ment. Dis., 176*(9), 537–538.

Dell, P. F., & Eisenhower, J. W. (1990). Adolescent multiple personality disorder: A preliminary study of eleven cases. *J. Amer. Acad. Child Adol. Psychiat., 29*(3), 359–366.

DeLong, F. L. (1975). Cognitive effects of long-term marijuana use. *Dissertation Abstracts Inter., 36*(5-B), 2444–2445.

Deluty, B. M., Deluty, R. H., & Carver, C. S. (1986). Concordance between clinicians and patients ratings of anxiety and depression as mediated by private self-consciousness. *J. Pers. Assess., 50*(1), 93–100.

Dembroski, T. M., & Costa, P. T. (1987). Coronary prone behavior: Components of the Type A pattern and hostility. *J. Personal., 55*(2), 211–235.

DeMyer, M. K. (1979). *Parents and children in autism.* Washington, DC: Winston.

DeMyer, M. K., Alpern, G. D., Barton, S., DeMyer, W., Churchill, D. W., Hingtgen, J. N., Bryson, C. Q., Pontius, W., & Kimberlin, C. (1972). Imitation in autistic, early schizophrenic, and nonpsychotic subnormal children. *J. Autism Child. Schizo., 2,* 264–287.

DeMyer, M. K., Hingtgen, J. N., & Jackson, R. K. (1981). Infantile autism reviewed: A decade of research. *Schizo. Bull., 7,* 388–391.

Den Boer, J. A., Westenberg, H. G., & Verhoeven, W. M. (1990). Biological aspects of panic anxiety. *Psychiat. Ann., 20*(9) 494–500.

Dept. Health Education and Welfare. (1976). Even my kids didn't know I was an alcoholic: An interview with Dick Van Dyke. (ADM) 76–348. Washington, DC: GPO.

Depue, R. A., & Kleiman, R. M. (1979). Free cortisol as a peripheral index of central vulnerability to major forms of polar depressive disorders: Examining stress-biology interactions in subsyndromal high-risk persons. In R. A. Depue (Ed.), *The psychobiology of the depressive disorders.* New York: Academic.

Derry, P. A., & Stone, G. L. (1979). Effects of cognitive-adjunct treatments on assertiveness. *Cog. Ther. Res., 3,* 213–222.

DeSilva, P., Rachman, S., & Seligman, M. (1977). Prepared phobias and obsessions: Therapeutic outcome. *Behav. Res. Ther., 15,* 65–77.

Deutsch, A. (1949). *The mentally ill in America.* New York: Columbia Univ.

Devlin, M. J., & Walsh, B. T. (1989). Eating disorders and depression [Special Issue]. *Psychiat. Ann., 19*(9), 473–476.

Deykin, E. Y. (1986). Adolescent suicidal and self-destructive behavior: An intervention study. In *Suicide and depression among adolescents and young adults.* American Psychiatric.

Dial, T. H., Tebbutt, R., Pion, G. M., Kohout, J, VandenBos, G., Johnson, M., Schervish, P. H., Whitting, L., Fox, J. C., & Merwin, E. I. (1990). Human resources in mental health. In R. W. Manderscheid & M. A. Sonnenschein (Eds.), *Mental Health, United States, 1990,* DHHS Pub. No. (ADM) 90–1708. Washington, DC: GPO.

Diener, E. (1984). Subjective well-being. *Psychol. Bull, 95,* 542–575.

Dies, R. R. (1979). Group psychotherapy: Reflections on three decades of research. *J. Appl. Behav. Sci., 15,* 361–373.

DiLoreto, A. O. (1971). *Comparative psychotherapy: An experimental analysis.* Chicago: Aldine-Atherton.

Dilsaver, S. C. (1990). Onset of winter depression earlier than generally thought? *J. Clin. Psychiat., 51*(6), 258.

DiMascio, A., Weissman, M. M., & Prusoff, B. A. et al. (1979). Differential symptom reduction by drugs and psychotherapy in acute depression. *Arch. Gen. Psychiat., 36,* 12450–12456.

DiNardo, P. A. (1975). Social class and diagnostic suggestion as variables in clinical judgment. *J. Cons. Clin. Psychol., 43,* 363–368.

Doane, J., West, K., Goldstein, M. J., Rodnick, E., & Jones, J. (1981). Parental communciation deviance and affective style as predictors of subsequent schizophrenia spectrum disorders in vulnerable adolescents. *Arch. Gen. Psychiat., 38,* 679–685.

Dobson, K. S. (1985). An analysis of anxiety and depression scales. *J. Pers. Assess., 49*(5), 522–527.

Dobson, K. S., & Shaw, B. F. (1986). Cognitive assessment with major depressive disorders. *Cog. Ther. Res., 10*(1), 13–20.

Doghramji, K., Gaddy, J. R., Stewart, K. T., Rosenthal, N. E. et al. (1990). 2- versus 4-hour evening phototherapy of seasonal affective disorder. *J. Nerv. Ment. Dis., 178*(4), 257–260.

Doherty, W. J., & Jacobson, N. S. (1982). Marriage and the family. In B. B. Wolman (Ed.), *Handbook of developmental psychology.* Englewood Cliffs, NJ: Prentice-Hall.

Dohrenwend, B. P., & Dohrenwend, B. S. (1982). Perspectives on the past and future of psychiatric epidemiology. *Amer. J. Pub. Hlth., 72,* 1271–1279.

Dohrenwend, B. P., Dohrenwend, B. S., Gould, M. S., Link, B., Neugebauer, R., & Wunsch-Hitzig, R. (1980). *Mental illness in the United States: Epidemiological estimates.* New York: Praeger.

Dohrenwend, B. P., Shrout, P. E., Egri, G., & Mendelsohn, F. S. (1980). Nonspecific psychological distress and other dimensions of psychopathology. *Arch. Gen. Psychiat., 37*(11), 1229–1236.

Dole, V. P., & Nyswander, M. (1965). A medical treatment for heroin addiction. *JAMA, 193,* 646–650.

Dole, V. P., & Nyswander, M. Heroin addiction, a metabolic disease. *Arch. Inter. Med., 120,* 19–24.

Doll, E. A. (1953). A manuel for the Vineland Social Maturity Scale. In E. A. Doll, *The measurement of social competence.* Minneapolis, MN: Educational Test Bureau.

Domino, G. (1985). Clergy's attitudes toward suicide and recognition of suicide lethality. *Death Studies, 2*(3–4), 187–199.

Domino, G., & Swain, B. J. (1985–86). Recognition of suicide lethality and attitudes toward suicide in mental health professions. *Omega: J. Death & Dying, 16*(4), 301–308.

Donaldson, K. (1976). Insanity inside out. New York: Crown.

Donnelly, E. F., Murphy, D. L., & Goodwin, F. K. (1978). Primary affective disorder: Anxiety in unipolar and bipolar depressed groups. *J. Clin. Psychol., 34,* 621–623.

Dooley, C., & Catalano, R. (1980). Economic change as a cause of behavioral disorder. *Psychol. Bull., 87*(3), 450–468.

Dos Santos, J. (1985). La nevrose d'angoisse [Anxiety neurosis]. *Revue Francaise de Psychanalyse, 49*(1), 27–106.

Douglas, V. I., Barr, R. G., Amin, K., O'Neill, M. E., & Britton, B. G. (1988). Dosage effects and individual responsivity to methylphenidate in attention deficit disorder. *J. Child Psychol. Psychiat., 29,* 453–475.

Doyal, L. E., & Morton, W. A. (1984). The clinical usefulness of lithium as a antidepressant. *Hosp. Clin. Psychiat., 35*(7), 685–691.

Doyle, A. C. (1938). The sign of the four. In *The Complete Sherlock Holmes.* New York: Garden City.

Drake R., Gates, C., & Cotton, P. G. (1984). Suicide among schizophrenics: Who is at risk? *J. Nerv. Ment. Dis., 172*(10), 813–817.

Drake, R., Gates, C., & Cotton, P. G. (1986). Suicide among schizophrenics: A comparison of attempters and completed suicides. *Brit. J. Psychiat., 149,* 784–787.

Dubovsky, S. L. (1985). The psychophysiology of health, illness, and stress. In R. C. Simons (Ed.), *Understanding human behavior in health and illness* (3rd ed.). Baltimore: Williams & Wilkins.

Dubovsky, S. L. (1990). Generalized anxiety disorder: New concepts and psychopharmacologic therapies. 142nd Annual Meeting of the American Psychiatric Assoc. (1989, San Francisco, CA). *J. Clin. Psychiat., 51*(Suppl.), 3–10.

Duggan, J. P., & Booth, D. A. (1986). Obesity, overeating, and rapid gastric emptying in rats with ventromedial hypothalamic lesions. *Science, 231*(4738), 609–611.

Dunbar, F. (1948). *Synopsis of psychosomatic diagnosis and treatment.* St. Louis: Mosby.

Dunbar, F. (1954). *Emotions and bodily changes: A survey of literature on psychosomatic interrelationships, 1910–1953* (4th ed.). New York: Columbia Univ.

Dunner, D. L. & Hall, K. S. (1980). Social adjustment and psychological precipitants in mania. In R. H. Belmaker & H. M. van Praag (Eds.), *Mania: An evolving concept.* New York: Spectrum.

DuPont, R. L. (1971). Profile of a heroin-addiction epidemic. *New Engl. J. Med., 285*(6), 320–324.

Durham, R. C., & Turvey, A. A. (1987). Cognitive therapy vs. behaviour therapy in the treatment of chronic general anxiety. *Behav. Res. Ther., 25*(3), 229–234.

Durkheim, E. (1951). *Le suicide* (J. A. Spaulding & G. Simpson, Trans.). Glencoe, IL: Free. (Original work published in 1897. Paris: Librarie Felix Alcan)

Dweck, C. S. (1976). Children's interpretation of evaluative feedback: The effect of social cues on learned helplessness. *Merrill Palmer Quart., 22*(2), 105–109.

Dwyer, J., & Mayer, J. (1968–69). Psychological effects of variations in physical appearance during adolescence. *Adolescence, 3*(12), 353–380.

Dykeman, B. F. (1984). Adolescent suicide: Recognition and intervention. *Coll. Stud. J., 18*(4), 364–368.

Dykens, E. M., & Gerrard, M. (1986). Psychological profiles of purging bulimics, repeat dieters, and controls. *J. Cons. Clin. Psychol., 54*(3), 283–288.

Easterlin, R. (1987, May). Cited in A. Rosenfeld & E. Stark. The prime of our lives. *Psych. Today,* 62–72.

Eaves, L., & Schultz, S. C. et al. (1988). Genetics, immunology, and virology. *Schizo. Bull., 14*(3), 365–382.

Eckert, E. D., Goldberg, S. C., Halmi, K. A., Casper, R. C., & Davis, J. M. (1982). Depression in anorexia nervosa. *Psychol. Med., 12,* 115–122.

Eddy, D. M., Wolpert, R. L., & Rosenberg, M. L. (1987). Estimating the effectiveness of interventions to prevent youth suicides. Invitational conference on applications of analytic methods to mental health: Practice, policy, research. *Medical Care, 25*(12) 57–65.

Edelstein, B. A. (1989). Generalization: Terminological, methodological and conceptual issues. *Behav. Ther., 20*(3), 311–324.

Edgerton, R. B. (1979). *Mental retardation.* Cambridge, MA: Harvard.

Edgerton, R. B., & Bercovici, S. (1976). The cloak of competence: Years later. *Amer. J. Ment. Def., 80,* 485–497.

Edinberg, M. A., Karoly, P., & Gleser, G. C. (1977). Assessing assertion in the elderly: An application of the behavioral-analytic model of competence. *J. Clin. Psychol., 33,* 869–874.

Edman, G., & Asberg, M. (1986). Skin conductance habituation and cerebrospinal fluid 5-hydroxyindoleacetic acid in suicidal patients. *Arch. Gen. Psychiat., 43*(6), 586–592.

Edmands, M. S. (1986). Overcoming eating disorders. *J. Psychosoc. Nursing & Ment. Hlth. Services, 24,* 19–25.

Edwards, C. C. (1973). What you can do to combat high blood pressure. *Family Health, 5*(11), 24–26.

Egeland, B. (1991, Feb.). *American Association for the Advancement of Science.* Presentation.

Egeland, J. A. et al. (1984). Amish study: V. Lithium sodium countertransport and catechol methyltransference in pedigrees of bipolar probands.

Egeland, J. A., Gerhard, D. S., Pauls, D. L., Sussex, J. N. et al. (1987). Bipolar affective disorders linked to DNA markers on chromosome 11.

Eichman, W. J. (1972). Minnesota Multiphasic Personality Inventory: Computerized scoring and interpreting services. In O. K. Buros (Ed.), *The 7th mental measurements yearbook* (Vol. 1). Highland Park, NJ: Gryphon.

Eidelson, J. I. (1985). Cognitive group therapy for depression: Why and what. *Inter. J. Ment. Hlth., 13,* 54–66.

Eisenberg, L. (1958). School phobia: A study in the communication of anxiety. *Amer. J. Psychiat., 114,* 712–718.

Eisenthal, S., Koopman, C., & Lazare, A. (1983). Process analysis of two dimensions of the negotiated approach in relation to satisfaction in the initial interview. *J. Nerv. Ment. Dis., 171,* 49–54.

Eitenger, L. (1963). *Concentration camp survivors in Norway and Israel.* New York: Humanities.

Elder, J. P., Edelstein, B. A., & Fremouw, W. J. (1981). Client by treatment interactions in response acquisition and cognitive restructuring approaches. *Cog. Ther. Res., 5*(2), 203–210.

Elkin, I., Parloff, M. B., Hadley, S. W., & Autry, J. H. (1985). NIMH treatment of Depression Collaborative Research Program: Background and research plan. *Arch. Gen. Psychiat., 42*(3), 305–316.

Elkin, I., Shea, M. T., Imber, S., Pilkonis, P., Sotsky, S., Glass, D.,

Watkins, J., Leber, W., & Collins, J. (1986). *NIMH Treatment of Depression Collaborative Research Program: Initial outcome findings.* Paper presented to the American Assoc. for the Advancement of Science.

Elkin, I., Shea, M. T., Watkins, J. T., Imber, S. D. et al. (1989). National Institute of Mental Health Treatment of Depression Collaborative Research Program: General effectiveness of treatments. *Arch. Gen. Psychiat., 46*(11), 971–982.

Elkins, R. L. (1980). Covert sensitization treatment of alcoholism: Contributions of successful conditioning to subsequent abstinence maintenance. *Addict. Behav., 5*, 67–89.

Ellenberger, H. F. (1970). *The discovery of the unconscious.* New York: Basic.

Ellenberger, H. F. (1972). The story of "Anna O.": A critical review with new data. *J. History of the Behav. Sci., 8*, 267–279.

Elliott, S. N. et al. (1985). Three year stability of WISC R IQs for handicapped children from three racial/ethnic groups. *J. Psychoeduc. Assess., 3*(3), 233–244.

Ellis, A. (1962). *Reason and emotion in psychotherapy.* Secaucus, NJ: Lyle Stuart.

Ellis, A. (1973). *Humanistic psychotherapy: The rational-emotive approach.* New York: McGraw-Hill.

Ellis, A. (1976). Rational emotive therapy. In V. Binder, A. Binder, & B. Rimland (Eds.), *Modern therapies.* Englewood Cliffs, NJ: Prentice-Hall.

Ellis, A. (1976). RET abolishes most of the human ego. *Psychother. Ther. Res. Prac., 13*, 343–348.

Ellis, A. (1976). The rational-emotive view. *J. Contemp. Psychother., 8*(1), 20–28.

Ellis, A. (1977). The basic clinical theory of rational-emotive therapy. In A. Ellis & R. Grieger (Eds.), *Handbook of rational-emotive therapy.* New York: Springer.

Ellis, A. (1979). A note on the treatment of agoraphobics with cognitive modification versus prolonged exposure in vivo. *Behav. Res. Ther., 17*, 162–164.

Ellis, A. (1979). The issue of force and energy in behavioral change. *J. Contemp. Psychother., 10*(2), 83–97.

Ellis, A. (1979). The theory of rational-emotive therapy. In A. Ellis & J. M. Whitely (Eds.), *Theoretical and empirical foundations of rational-emotive therapy.* Monterey, CA: Brooks/Cole.

Ellis, A. (1984). Rational-emotive therapy. In R. J. Corsini (Ed.), *Current psychotherapies* (3rd ed.). Itasca, IL: Peacock.

Ellis, A. (1987). The evolution of rational emotive therapy (RET) and cognitive behavior therapy (BET). In J. K. Zeig (Ed.), *The evolution of psychotherapy.* New York: Brunner/Mazel.

Ellis, T. E., & Ratliff, K. G. (1986). Cognitive characteristics of suicidal and nonsuicidal psychiatric inpatients. *Cog. Ther. Res., 10*(6), 625–634.

Ellison, G. D., & Bresler, D. E. (1974). Tests of emotional behavior in rats following depletion of norepinephrine, of serotonin, or of both. *Psychopharmocology, 34*(4), 275–280.

Ellison, R. J., & Cancellaro, L. A. (1978). A study in the management of anxiety with lorazepam. *J. Clin. Pharm., 18*(4), 210–219.

Elmhirst, S. I. (1984). A psychoanalytic approach to anxiety in childhood. In V. P. Varma (Ed.), *Anxiety in children.* London: Croom Helm.

Emmelkamp, P. M. G. (1974). Self-observations vs. flooding in the treatment of agoraphobia. *Behav. Res. Ther., 12*, 229.

Emmelkamp, P. M. G. (1980). Agoraphobics' interpersonal problems: Their role in the effects of exposure in vivo therapy. *Arch. Gen. Psychiat., 37*(11), 1303–1306.

Emmelkamp, P. M. G. (1982). Exposure in vivo treatments. In A. Goldstein & D. Chambless (Eds.), *Agoraphobia: Multiple perspectives on theory and treatment.* New York: Wiley.

Emmelkamp, P. M. G. (1982). *Phobic and obsessive-compulsive disorders.* New York: Plenum.

Emmelkamp, P. M. G., & Kuipers, A. C. M. (1985). Group therapy of anxiety disorders. In D. Upper & S. M. Ross (Eds.), *Handbook of behavioral group therapy.* New York: Plenum.

Emmelkamp, P. M. G., & Mersch, P. P. (1982). Cognition and exposure in vivo in the treatment of agoraphobia: Short-term and delayed effects. *Cog. Ther. Res., 6*(1), 77–90.

Emmelkamp, P. M. G., & Rabbie, D. M. (1983, July). *Four-year follow-up of OCD after psychological treatment.* Paper to WPA, Vienna, Austria.

Emmelkamp, P. M. G., Mersch, P. P., Vissia, E., & Van der Helm, M. (1985). Social phobia: A comparative evaluation of cognitive and behavioral interventions. *Behav. Res. Ther., 23*(3), 365–369.

Emmelkamp, P. M. G., Van der Helm, M., Van Zanten, B. L., & Plochg, I. (1980). Treatment of obsessive-compulsive patients: The contribution of self-instructional training to the effectiveness of exposure. *Behav. Res. Ther., 18*(1), 61–66.

Emmelkamp, P. M. G., Visser, S., Hoekstra, R. J. (1988). Cognitive therapy vs. exposure in vivo in the treatment of obsessive-compulsives. *Cog. Ther. Res., 12*(1), 103–114.

Emrick, C. D., & Hansen, J. (1983). Assertions regarding effectiveness of treatment for alcoholism: Fact or fantasy? *Amer. Psychol., 38*, 1078–1088.

Endicott, J., & Spitzer, R. L. (1978). A diagnostic interview: The schedule for affective disorders and schizophrenia. *Arch. Gen. Psychiat., 35*, 837–844.

Endler, N. S. (1982). *Holiday of darkness.* New York: Wiley.

Engel, G. L. (1983). The biopsychosicial model and family medicine. *J. Fam. Prac., 16*(2), 409–413.

Ennis, B. J., & Emery, R. D. (1978). *The rights of patients* (ACLU Handbook Series). New York: Avon.

Enright, A. B., Butterfield, P., & Berkowitz, B. (1985). Self-help and support groups in the management of eating disorders. In D. M. Garner & P. E. Garfinkel (Eds.), *Handbook of psychotherapy for anorexia nervosa and bulimia.* New York: Guilford.

Enright, S. J. (1989). Paedophilia: A cognitive/behavioural treatment approach in a single case. *Brit. J. Psychiat., 155*, 399–401.

Epstein, L. H. (1976). Psychophysiological measurement in assessment. In M. Hersen & A. S. Bellack (Eds.), *Behavioral assessment: A practical handbook.* Oxford: Pergamon.

Epstein, S. Hypnotherapeutic control of exhibitionism: A brief communication. *Inter. J. Clin. Exp. Hyp., 31*(2), 63–66.

Erber, R. (1990, Aug.). American Psychological Association Presentation.

Erdberg, P. (1990). Rorschach assessment. In G. Goldstein & M. Hersen (Eds.), *Handbook of psychological assessment* (2nd ed.). New York: Pergamon.

Erdelyi, M. H. (1985). *Psychoanalysis: Freud's cognitive psychology.* New York: Freeman.

Eriksen, C. W., & Kuethe, J. L. (1956). Avoidance conditioning of verbal behavior without awareness: A paradigm of repression. *J. Abnorm. Soc. Psychol., 53*, 203–209.

Erikson, E. (1963). *Childhood and society.* New York: Norton.

Erikson, E. (1982). *The life cycle completed.* New York: Norton.

Erikson, K. T. (1976). *Everything in its path: Destruction of community in the Buffalo Creek flood.* New York: Simon & Schuster.

Erlich, J., & Reisman, D. (1961). Age and authority in the interview. *Public Opinion Quart., 25*, 39–56.

Ernst, K. (1985). Die psychische Behandlung Schizophreniekranker in der Klinik [The psychiatric treatment of hospitalized schizophrenics]. *Schweizer, Archiv fur Neurologie, Neurochirurgie und Psychiatrie, 136*(1), 67–74.

Eser, A. (1981). "Sanctity" and "quality" of life in a historical comparative view. In S. E. Wallace & A. Eser (Eds.), *Suicide and euthanasia: The rights of personhood.* Knoxville, TN: Univ. Tennessee.

Essman, W. B. (1986). Effect of electroconvulsive shock on serotonin activity. In S. Malitz & H. A. Sackeim (Eds.), *Electroconvulsive therapy: Clinical and basic research issues.* New York: Ann. NY Acad. Sci.

Etzioni, A. (1973, Apr.) Methadone: Best hope for now. *Smithsonian, 48*, 67–74.

Evans, F. J. (1968). Recent trends in experimental hypnotic behavioral science. *Behav. Sci., 13*, 477–487.

Evans, J. A., & Hamerton, J. L. (1985). Chromosomol anomalies. In A. M. Clarke, A. D. B. Clarke, & J. M. Berg (Eds.), *Mental deficiency: The changing outlook* (4th ed.). London: Methuen.

Everly, G. S. (1987). The principle of personologic primacy and personologic psychotherapy. In C. Green (Ed.), *Proceedings of the Conference on the Millon Inventories.* Minnetonka, MN: NCS.

Everly, G. S. (1988). *The biological basis of personality: The contribution of paleocortical anatomy and physiology.* Paper presented at the First International Congress on Disorders of Personality. Copenhagen, Denmark.

Exner, J. E. (1973). The self-focus sentence completion: A study of egocentricity. *J. Pers. Assess., 37*, 437–455.

Exner, J. E. (1978). *The Rorschach: A comprehensive system. Vol. 2: Current research and advanced interpretation.* New York: Wiley.

Exner, J. E. (1986). *The Rorschach: A comprehensive system. Vol. 1: Basic foundations* (2nd ed.). New York: Wiley.

Exner, J. E. (1987). Computer assistance in Rorschach interpretation. In J. N. Butcher (Ed.), *Computerized psychological assessment: A practitioner's guide.* Lincoln, NE: Univ. Nebraska.

Exner, J. E., Jr. (1976). Projective techniques. In I. B. Weiner (Ed.), *Clinical methods in psychology.* New York: Wiley.

Extein, I., Gold, M. S., & Pottash, A. L. (1984). Psychopharmacologic treatment of depression. *Psychiat. Clin. No. Amer., 7*(3), 503–517.

Eysenck, H. J. (1952). The effects of psychotherapy: an evaluation. *J. Cons. Psychol, 16,* 319–354.

Eysenck, H. J. (1959). Learning theory and behaviour therapy. *J. Ment. Sci., 105,* 61–75.

Eysenck, H. J. (1965). The effects of psychotherapy. *Inter. J. Psychiat., 1,* 99–178.

Eysenck, H. J. (1980). *The effects of psychotherapy.* New York: Inter. Sci.

Eysenck, H. J. (Ed.) (1960). *Behavior therapy and the neuroses: Readings in modern methods of treatment derived from learning theory.* New York: Pergamon.

Eysenck, H. J., Wakefield, J. A., & Friedman, A. F. (1983). Diagnosis and clinical assessment: The DSM III. *Annu. Rev. Psychol., 34,* 167–193.

Fairbank, J. A., Langley, K., Jarvie, G. J., & Keane, T. M. (1981). A selected bibliography on post-traumatic stress disorders in Vietnam veterans. *Prof. Psychol., 12*(5), 578–586.

Fairburn, C. G. (1981). A cognitive behavioral approach to the management of bulimia. *Psychol. Med., 11,* 707–711.

Fairburn, C. G. (1985). Cognitive-behavioural treatment for bulimia. In D. M. Garner & P. E. Garfinkel (Eds.), *Handbook of psychotherapy for anorexia nervosa and bulimia.* New York: Guilford.

Fairburn, C. G. (1985). The management of bulimia nervosa. *J. Psychiat. Res., 19*(2–3), 465–472.

Fairburn, C. G., Cooper, P. J., Kirk, J., & O'Connor, M. (1985). The significance of the neurotic symptoms of bulimia nervosa. *J. Psychiat. Res., 19*(2–3), 135–140.

Fairburn, C. G., Cooper, Z., & Cooper, P. J. (1987). The clinical features and maintenance of bulimia nervosa. In K. D. Brownell & J. P. Foreyt (Eds.), *Handbook of eating disorders.* New York: Basic.

Fairburn, C. G., Kirk, J., O'Connor, M., & Cooper, P. J. (1986). A comparison of two psychological treatments for bulimia nervosa. *Behav. Res. Ther., 24,* 629–643.

Fairweather, G. W., Danders, D. H., Maynard, H., & Cressler, D. L. (1969). *Community life for the mentally ill: An alternative to institutional care.* Chicago: Aldine.

Fallon, E. R., & Liberman, R. P. (1983). Interactions between drug and psychosocial therapy in schizophrenia. *Schiz. Bull., 9*(4), 543–554.

Falloon, I. R. H. (Ed.). (1988). Handbook of behavioral therapy. New York: Guilford.

Falloon, I. R. H., & Liberman, R. P. (1986). Behavioral family interventions in the management of chronic schizophrenia. In W. R. McFarlane (Ed.), *Family therapy in schizophrenia.* New York: Guilford.

Falloon, I. R. H., Boyd, J. L., & McGill, C. W. (1984). *Family care for schizophrenia: A problem-solving approach to mental illness.* New York: Guilford.

Falloon, I. R. H., Lindley, P., McDonald, R., & Marks, I. M. (1977). Social skills training of out-patient groups: A controlled study of rehearsal and homework. *Brit. J. Psychiat., 131,* 599–609.

Faraone, S. V., Kremen, W. S., & Tsuang, M. T. Genetic transmission of major affective disorders: Quantitative models and linkage analyses. *Psychol. Bull., 108*(1), 109–127.

Farberow, N. L. (1974). *Suicide.* Morristown, NJ: General Learning.

Farberow, N. L., & Litman, R. E. (1970). A comprehensive suicide prevention program. Los Angeles: Suicide Prevention Center of Los Angeles. Unpublished final report.

Farina, A. (1976), *Abnormal psychology.* Englewood Cliffs, NJ: Prentice-Hall.

Fava, M., Herzog, D. B., Hamburg, P., Riess, H. et al. (1990). Long-term use of fluoxetine in bulimia nervosa: A retrospective study. *Ann. Clin. Psychiat., 2*(1), 53–56.

Fawcett, J. A., & Bunney, W. E., Jr. (1967). Pituitary adrenal function and depression: An outline for research. *Arch. Gen. Psychiat., 16*(5), 517–535.

Fawcett, J., Scheftner, W., Clark, D., Hedeker, D. et al. (1987). Clinical predictors of suicide in patients with major affective disorders: A controlled prospective study. *Amer. J. Psychiat., 144*(1), 35–40.

Feighner, J. P. (1984). Trazodone in major affective disorders. *Psychopathology, 17*(Suppl. 2), 15–23.

Feingold, B. (1975). *Why your child is hyperactive.* New York: Random House.

Feldman, G. M. (1976). The effect of biofeedback training on respiratory resistance of asthmatic children. *Psychosom. Med., 38*(1), 27–34.

Fenichel, O. (1945). *The psychoanalytic theory of neurosis.* New York: Norton.

Ferguson, H. B., Rapoport, J. L., & Weingartner, H. (1981). Food dyes and impairment of performance in hyperactive children. *Science, 211*(4480) 410–411.

Fernandez, G. A., & Nygard, S. (1990). Impact of involuntary outpatient commitment on the revolving door syndrome in North Carolina. *Hosp. Comm. Psychiat., 41*(9), 1001–1004.

Ferster, C. B. (1961). Positive reinforcement and behavior deficits of autistic children. *Child. Dev., 32,* 437.

Ferster, C. B. (1966). Animal behavior and mental illness. *Psych. Rec., 16,* 345–356.

Ferster, C. B. (1973). A functional analysis of depression. *Amer. Psychol., 28,* 857–870.

Ferster, C. B. (1974). Behavioral approaches to depression. In R. J. Friedman & M. M. Katz (Eds.), *The psychology of depression: Contemporary theory and research.* New York: Wiley.

Ferster, C. B., & DeMyer, M. K. (1961). The development of performances in autistic children in an automatically controlled environment. *J. Chronic Dis., 13,* 312–345.

Feuerstein, M., & Adams, H. E. (1977). Cephalic vasomotor feedback in the modification of migraine headache. *Biofeed. Self-Reg., 2*(3), 241–254.

Fichtner, C. G., Kuhlman, D. T., Gruenfeld, M. J., & Hughes, J. R. (1990). Decreased episodic violence and increased control of dissociation in a carbamazepine-treated case of multiple personality. *Bio. Psychiat., 27*(9), 1045–1052.

Fiedler, C. R., & Antonak, R. F. (1991). Advocacy. In J. L. Matson & J. A. Mulick (Eds.), *Handbook of mental retardation.* New York: Pergamon.

Field, T. M. (1977). Effects of early separation, interactive deficit, and experimental manipulations on infant-mother face-to-face interaction. *Child. Dev., 48*(3), 763–771.

Fiester, S. J. (1986). Psychotherapeutic managment of gastrointestinal disorders. In A. J. Frances & R. E. Hales (Eds.), *Psychiatric update—American Psychiatric Association annual review* (Vol. 5). Washington, DC: American Psychiatric.

Fieve, R. R. (1975). *Moodswing.* New York: Morrow.

Fieve, R. R., Dunner, D. L. & Elston, R. (1984). Search for biological/genetic markers in a long-term epidemiological and morbid risk study of affective disorders. Symposium held at the Institute of Pharmacological Research. "Maria negri": Biological markers in mental disorders. *J. Psychiat. Res., 18*(4), 425–445.

Fieve, R. R., Kumbaraci, T., & Dunner, D. L. (1976). Lithium prophylaxis of depression in bipolar I, bipolar II, and unipolar patients. *Amer. J. Psychiat., 133*(8), 925–929.

Fieve, R. R., Platman, S. R., & Plutchik, R. R. (1968). The use of lithium in affective disorders: I. Acute endogenious depression. *Amer. J. Psychiat., 125*(4), 487–491.

Figley, C. R. (1978). Symptoms of delayed combat stress among a college sample of Vietnam veterans. *Military Med., 143*(2), 107–110.

Figley, C. R., & Leventman, S. (1990). Introduction: Estrangement and victimization. In C. R. Figley & S. Leventman (Eds.), *Strangers at home: Vietnam veterans since the war.* New York: Praeger.

Fink, M. (1974). Clinical progress in convulsive therapy. In M. Fink, S. Kety, J. McGaugh, & T. A. Williams (Eds.), *Psychobiology of convulsive therapy.* Washington, DC: Winston.

Fink, M. (1978). Efficacy and safety of induced seizures (EST) in man. *Comprehen. Psychiat., 19,* 1–18.

Fink, M. (1978). Is ECT a useful therapy in schizophrenia? In J. P. Brady & H. K. H. Brodie (Eds.), *Controversy in psychiatry.* Philadelphia: Saunders.

Fink, M. (1979). A history of convulsive therapy. *Psychiat. J. Univ. Ottawa, 4*(1), 105–110.

Fink, M. (1979). *Convulsive therapy: Theory and practice.* New York: Raven.

Fink, M. (1987). Convulsive therapy in affective disorder: A decade of understanding and acceptance. In H. Y. Meltzer (Ed.), *Psychopharmacology: The third generation of progress.* New York: Raven.

Fink, M. (1988). Convulsive therapy: A manual of practice. In A. J.

Frances & R. Hales (Eds.), *Rev. of Psychiat.* (Vol. 7). Washington, DC: American Psychiatric.

Finkel, N. J. (1988). *Insanity on trial.* New York: Plenum.

Finkel, S. (1991). Group psychotherapy in later life. In W. A. Myers (Ed.), *New techniques in the psychotherapy of older patients.* Washington, DC: American Psychiatric.

Finkelhor, D., Gelles, R. Hotaling, G., & Straus, M. (Eds.). (1983). *The dark side of families.* Beverly Hills, CA: Sage.

Fischer, K. W., & Lazerson, A. (1984). *Human development.* New York: Freeman.

Fischer, R., & Landon, G. M. (1977). On the arousal state-dependent recall of the "subconscious" experience: Statebound-ness. *Brit. J. Psychiat., 120*(555), 159–172.

Fischman, J. (1987). Getting tough. *Psych. Today, 21*(12), 26–28.

Fish, J. (1973). *Placebo therapy.* San Francisco: Jossey-Bass.

Fishbain, D. A. (1989). Buspirone and transvestic fetishism. *J. Clin. Psychiat., 50*(11), 436–437.

Fisher, J. E., & Carstensen, L. L. (1990). Behavior management of the dementias. *Clin. Psychol. Rev., 10,* 611–629.

Fisher, S. (1973). *The female orgasm.* New York: Basic.

Fisher, S., & Greenberg, R. P. (1977). Stomach symptoms and up-down metaphors and gradients. *Psychosom. Med., 39*(2), 93–101.

Fisher, S., & Greenberg, R. P. (Eds.). (1978). *The scientific evaluation of Freud's theories and therapy.* New York: Basic.

Fisher, V. (1980). *Myths and realities: A study of attitudes toward Vietnam veterans.* Washington, DC: GPO.

Flament, M. F. et al. (1985). Clominpramine treatment of childhood obsessive-compulsive disorder: A double-blind controlled study. *Arch. Gen. Psychiat., 429*(10), 977–983.

Flanagan, T., & Jamieson (Eds.). (1988). *Sourcebook on criminal justice statistics–1987.* Washington, DC: U.S. Bureau of Justice Statistics.

Fleer, J., & Pasewark, R. A. (1982). Prior public health agency contacts of individuals committing suicide. *Psych. Rep., 50*(3, Pt. 2), 1319–1324.

Fletcher, J. (1981). In defense of suicide. In S. E. Wallace & A. Eser (Eds.), *Suicide and euthanasia: The rights of personhood.* Knoxville, TN: Univ. Tennessee.

Floyd, F. J., O'Farrell, T. J., & Goldberg, M. (1987). Comparison of marital observational measures: The Marital Interaction Coding System and the Communications Skills Test. *J. Cons. Clin. Psychol., 55*(3), 2200.

Foa, E. B., & Kozak, M. J. (1985). Treatment of anxiety disorders: Implications for psychopathology. In A. H. Tuma & J. D. Maser (Eds.), *Anxiety and anxiety disorders.* Hillsdale, NJ: Erlbaum.

Foa, E. B., & Kozak, M. J. (1986). Emotional processing of fear: Exposure to corrective information. *Psychol. Bull., 99*(1), 20–35.

Foa, E. B. et al. (1984). Deliberate exposure and blocking of obsessive-compulsive rituals: Immediate and long-term effects. *Behav. Ther., 15*(5), 450–472.

Foa, E. B., Jameson, J. S., Turner, R. M., & Payne, L. L. (1980). Massed vs. spaced exposure sessions in the treatment of agoraphobia. *Behav. Res. Ther., 18*(4), 333–338.

Foa, E. B., Steketee, G. & Grason, J. B. (1985). Imaginal and in vivo exposure: A comparison with obsessive-compulsive checkers. *Behav. Ther., 16*(3), 292–302.

Foa, E. B., Steketee, G., & Milby, J. B. (1980). Differential effects of exposure and response prevention in obsessive-compulsive washers. *J. Cons. Clin. Psychol., 48*(1), 71–79.

Foa, E. B., Steketee, G., & Young, M. C. (1984). Agoraphobia: Phenomenological aspects, associated characteristics, and theoretical considerations. *Clin. Psychol. Rev., 4*(4), 431–457.

Foa, E. B., Steketee, G., Kozak, M., & Dugger, D. (1987). Effects of imipramine on depression and obsessive-compulsive symptoms. *Psychiat. Res., 21*(2), 123–136.

Foa, E. B., Steketee, G. S. & Milby, J. B. (1980). Exposure vs. response prevention in obsessive-compulsive washers. *J. Cons. Clin. Psychol., 48,* 419–420.

Foa, E. B., Steketee, G., Turner, R. M., & Fischer, S. C. (1980). Effects of imaginal exposure to feared disasters in obsessive-compulsive checkers. *Behav. Res. Ther., 18*(5), 449–455.

Fogel, B. S. (1986). ECT versus tricyclic antidepressants. *Amer. J. Psychiat., 143*(1), 121.

Foley, V. (1989). Family therapy. In R. J. Corsini & D. Wedding (Eds.), *Current psychotherapies* (4th ed.). Itasca, IL: Peacock.

Folkman, S., Lazarus, R. S., Pimley, S., & Novacek, J. (1987). Age differences in stress and coping processes. *Psychol. & Aging, 2,* 171–184.

Folstein, M., Folstein, S., & McHugh, P. (1975). Mini-mental state: A practical method for grading the cognitive state of patients for the clinician. *J. Psychiat. Res., 12,* 189–198.

Folstein, S., & Rutter, M. (1977). Genetic influences in infantile autism. *Nature, 265,* 726–728.

Fontaine, R., & Young, T. (1984). Differential efficacy of unilateral and bilateral ECT. *Amer. J. Psychiat., 141*(8), 1013–1014.

Fontana, A. F. (1966). Familial etiology of schizophrenia: Is a scientific methodology possible? *Psychol. Bull., 66*(3), 214–227.

Foster, S. L., & Cone, J. D. (1986). Design and use of direct observation. In A. R. Ciminero, K. S. Calhoun, & H. E. Adams (Eds.), *Handbook of behavioral assessment* (2nd ed.). New York: Wiley.

Foucault, M. (1965). *Madness and civilization.* New York: American Library.

Foulds, G. A. (1960). Psychotic depression and age. *J. Ment. Sci., 106,* 1394–1397.

Foxx, R. M., & Faw, G. D. (1990). Long-term follow-up of echolalia and question answering. *J. Appl. Behav. Anal., 23*(3), 387–396.

Foxx, R. M., McMorrow, M. J., Davis, L. A., & Bittle, R. G. (1988). Replacing a chronic schizophrenic man's delusional speech with stimulus appropriate response. *J. Behav. Ther. Exp. Psychiat., 19*(1), 43–50.

Foy, E., & Harlow, A. (1956). *Clowning through life.* New York: Dalton. (Original work published, 1928.)

Foy, E. W., Eisler, R. M., & Pinkston, S. (1975). Modeled assertion in a case of explosive rages. *J. Behav. Anal., 10,* 61–74.

Framo, J. L. (1975). Personal reflections of a family therapist. *J. Marriage Fam. Couns., 1*(1), 15–28.

Frances, R. J., & Franklin, J. E. (1988). Alcohol and other psychoactive substance use disorders. In J. A. Talbott, R. E. Hales, & S. C. Yudofsky (Eds.), *Textbook of psychiatry.* Washington, DC: American Psychiatric.

Francis, L. P. (1980). Assisting suicide: A problem for the criminal law. In M. P. Battin & D. J. Mayo (Eds.), *Suicide: The philosophical issues.* New York: St. Martin's.

Frank, E., Anderson, C., & Rubinstein, D. (1978). Frequency of sexual dysfunction in "normal" couples. *New Engl. J. Med., 299*(3), 111–115.

Frank, J. D. (1973). *Persuasion and healing* (Rev. ed.). Baltimore: Johns Hopkins.

Frank, J. D. (1981, Aug. 24). Therapeutic components shared by all psychotherapies. Master lecture, American Psychological Association. Los Angeles.

Frank, J. D. (1981). Reply to Telch. *J. Cons. Clin. Psychol., 49,* 476–477.

Frank, J. D. (1982). *Therapeutic components shared by all psychotherapies.* In J. H. Harvey & M. M. Parks (Eds.), *Psychotherapy research and behavior change.* Washington, DC: American Psychology Assoc.

Frank, J. D., Hoehn-Saric, R., Imber, S. D., Liberman, B. L., & Stone, A. R. (1978). *Effective ingredients of successful psychotherapy.* New York: Brunner/Mazel.

Frankel, A. S. (1988). The private psychiatric hospital as a crucible for innovative models of professional practice. *Psychotherapy, 25*(3), 429–433.

Frankel, F. H. (1984). The use of electroconvulsive therapy in suicidal patients. *Amer. J. of Psychother., 38*(3), 384–391.

Frankl, V. E. (1963). *Man's search for meaning.* New York: Washington Square.

Frankl, V. E. (1965). *The doctor and the soul* (2nd ed.). New York: Knopf.

Frankl, V. E., (1975). Paradoxical intention and dereflection. *Psychother. Theory, Res. Prac., 12*(3), 226–237.

Franklin, J. A. (1985). *Agoraphobia: Its nature, aetiology, maintenance and treatment.* Unpublished manuscript.

Franks, C. M. (1984). Behavior therapy with children and adolescents. *Annual Rev. Behav. Ther. Theory Prac., 9,* 259–308.

Franks, C. M. (1984). Behavior therapy: An overview. *Annu. Rev. Behav. Ther. Theory Prac., 9,* 1–38.

Franks, C. M. Wilson, C. T., Kendall, P. C., & Foreyt, J. P. (Eds.). (1990). *Review of behavior therapy* (Vol. 12). New York: Guilford.

Frederick, C. J. (1969). Suicide notes: A survey and evaluation. *Bull. Suicidology, 8,* 17–26.

Frederick, C. J. (1985). An introduction and overview of youth suicide. In M. L. Peck, N. L. Farberow, & R. E. Litman (Eds.), *Youth suicide.* New York: Springer.

Fredrickson, M., & Ohman, A. (1979). Heart-rate and electrodermal orienting responses to visual stimuli differing in complexity. *Psychophysiology, 20*(1), 37–41.

Freedman, M., & Rosenman, R. (1964). *Type A behavior and your heart.* New York: Knopf.

Freedman, S., Hurley, J. (1980). Perceptions of helpfulness and behavior in groups. *Group, 4,* 51–58.

Freeland, M., & Schendler, C. E. (1983). National health expenditure growth in the 1980s. *Health Care Financing Rev., 4*(3).

Fremouw, W. J., & Zitter, R. E. (1978). A comparison of skills training and cognitive restructuring-relaxation for the treatment of speech anxiety. *Behav. Ther., 9*(2), 248–259.

French, O. (1987). More on multiple personality disorder. *Amer. J. Psychiat., 144*(1), 123–124.

Freud, S. (1900). *The interpretation of dreams.* J. Strachey (Ed. and Trans.) New York: Wiley.

Freud, S. (1924). The loss of reality in neurosis and psychosis. *Collected papers, 2,* 277–282.

Freud, S. (1955). *Notes upon a case of obsessional neurosis.* London: Hogarth.

Freud, S. (1956). A case of paranoia running counter to the psychoanalytical theory of the disease. *Collected papers* (Vol. 2). London: Hogarth.

Freud, S. (1956). Analysis of a phobia in a five-year-old boy. *Collected works of Sigmund Freud* (Vol. 10). London: Hogarth.

Freud, S. (1957). *Mourning and melancholia* (Vol. 14). London: Hogarth.

Freud, S. (1963). *Introductory lectures on psychoanalysis.* London: Hogarth.

Freud, S. (1963). Three essays on sexuality (1905). In J. Strachey (Ed.), *The standard edition of the complete psychological works of Sigmund Freud* (Vol. 3). London: Hogarth.

Freud, S. (1970). On the general effect of cocaine. *Drug Dep., 5,* 17.

Frick, R., & Bogart, L. (1982). Transference and countertransference in group therapy in Vietnam veterans. *Bull. Menninger Clin., 46*(5), 429–444.

Friedberg, J. (1975, August). Electroshock therapy: Let's stop blasting the brain. *Psych. Today,* 18–23, 98–99.

Friedberg, J. (1977). Shock treatment, brain damage, and memory loss: a neurologic perspective. *Amer. J. Psychiat., 134,* 1010–1014.

Friedman, A. F., Webb, J. T., & Lewak, R. (1989). *Psychological assessment with the MMPI.* Hillsdale, NJ: Erlbaum.

Friedman, E., & Wilcox, P. J. (1942). Electrostimulated convulsive doses in intact humans by means of unidirectional currents. *J. Nerv. Ment. Dis., 96,* 56–63.

Friedman, H. S., & Booth-Kewley, S. (1987). Personality, Type A behavior, and coronary heart disease: The role of emotional expression. *J. Pers. Soc. Psychol., 53*(4), 783–792.

Friedman, H. S., & Booth-Kewley, S. (1987). The "disease-prone personality." *Amer. Psychol., 42,* 534–555.

Friedman, M., & Rosenman, R. (1959). Association of specific overt behavior pattern with blood and cardiovascular findings. *JAMA, 169,* 1286.

Friedman, M., & Ulmer, D. (1984). *Treating Type A Behavior—and your heart.* New York: Knopf.

Friedman, M., Thoresen, C. E., Gill, J. J., Powell, L. H., Ulmer, D., Thompson, L., Price, V. A., Rabin, D. D., Breall, W. S., Dixon, T., Levy, R., & Bourg, E. (1984). Alteration of type A behavior and reduction in cardiac recurrences in postmyocardial infarction patients. *Amer. Heart J., 108*(2).

Friedman, P. (1976). Overview of the institutional labor problem: The nature and extent of institutional labor in the United States. In M. Kindred, J. Cohen, D. Penrod, & T. Shaffer (Eds.), *The mentally retarded citizen and the law: President's committee on mental retardation.* New York: Free.

Friedmann, E. et al. (1983). Social interaction and blood pressure: Influence of animal companions. *J. Nerv. Ment. Dis., 171*(8), 461–465.

Friman, P. C., & Warzk, W. J. (1990). Nocturnal enuresis: A prevalent, persistent, yet curable parasomnia. *Pediatrician, 17*(1), 38–45.

Frisch, M. B., Elliott, C. H., Atsaides, J. P. et al. (1982). Social skills and stress management to enhance patients' interpersonal competencies. *Psychother. Theory Res. Prac., 19,* 349–358.

Frith, C. D. (1979). Consciousness, information processing and schizophrenia. *Brit. J. Psychiat., 134,* 225–235.

Fromm-Reichmann, F. (1943). Psychotherapy of schizophrenia. *Amer. J. Psychiat., 111,* 410–419.

Fromm-Reichman, F. (1948). Notes on the development of treatment of schizophrenia by psychoanalytic psychotherapy. *Psychiat., 11,* 263–273.

Fromm-Reichmann, F. (1950). *Principles of intensive psychotherapy.* Chicago: Univ. Chicago.

Frosch, W. A., Robbins, E. S., & Stern, M. (1965). Untoward reactions to lysergic acid diethylamide (LSD) resulting in hospitalization. *New Engl. J. Med., 273,* 1235–1239.

Fry, P. S. (1986). *Depression, stress, and adaptations in the elderly.* Rockville, MD: Aspen.

Fryer, D. (1988). The experience of unemployment in social context. In S. Fisher & J. Reason (Eds.), *Handbook of life stress, cognition and health.* Chichester: Wiley.

Futch, E. J., Lisman, S. A., & Geller, M. I. (1984). An analysis of alcohol portrayal on prime-time television. *Inter. J. Addic., 19*(4), 403–410.

Fyer, A. J. et al. (1984). Sodium lactate infusion, panic attacks and ionized calcium. *Bio. Psychiat., 19*(10), 1437–1447.

Fyer, A. J., Liebowitz, M. R., Gorman, J. M., Campeas, R. B. et al. (1988). Effects of clonidine on alprazolam discontinuation in panic patients: A pilot study. *J. Clin. Psychopharm., 8*(4), 270–274.

Gabrielli, W. F., & Plomin, R. (1985). Drinking behavior in the Colorado adoptee and twin sample. *Quart. J. Stud. Alcohol., 46*(1), 24–31.

Galanter, M. (1990). Cults and zealous self-help movements: A psychiatric perspective. *Amer. J. Psychiat., 147*(5), 543–551.

Galanter, M., Talbott, D., Gallegos, K., & Rubenstone, E. (1990). Combined Alcoholics Anonymous and professional care for addicted physicians. *Amer. J. Psychiat., 147*(1), 64–68.

Gallagher, D. (1986). The Beck Depression Inventory and older adults: Review of its development and utility. *Clin. Gerontologist, 5,* 149–163.

Gallagher, D., Wrabetz, A., Lovett, S., DelMaestro, S., & Rose, J. (1986). Depression and other negative affects in family caregivers. In E. Light & B. D. Lebowitz (Eds.), *Alzheimer's Disease treatment and family stress: Directions for research.* (DHHS Publication No. ADM 89-1569). Washington, DC: GPO.

Gallagher-Thompson, D., Hanley-Peterson, P., & Thompson, L. W. (1989). Maintenance of gains versus relapse following brief psychotherapy for depression. *J. Cons. Clin. Psychol., 58,* 371–374.

Gallagher-Thompson, D., Lovett, S., & Rose, J. (1991). Psychotherapeutic interventions for stressed family caregivers. In W. A. Myers (Ed.), *New techniques in the psychotherapy of older patients.* Washington, DC: Amer. Psychiatric.

Gallistel, C. R., Shizgal, P., & Yeomans, J. S. (1981). A portrait of the substrate for self-stimulation. *Psych. Rev., 88*(3), 228–273.

Gandour, M. J. (1984). Bulimia: Clinical description, assessment etiology and treatment. *Inter. J. Eat. Dis., 3,* 3–38.

Ganley, A. (1981). *A participant and trainer's manual for working with men who batter.* Washington, DC: Center for Women Policy Studies.

Gantz, F., Gallagher-Thompson, D., & Rodman, J. (1991). Cognitive-behavioral facilitation of inhibited grief. In A. Freeman & F. Dattilio (Eds.), *Casebook of cognitive-behavior therapy.* New York: Plenum.

GAP (Group for the Advancement of Psychiatry). (1946, Nov. 8). *9.*

GAP (Group for the Advancement of Psychiatry). (1947, Jan. 22). *18.*

Gardner, R. (1984, Jul. 12). Full moon lunacy: Fact or fiction. *Trenton Times,* p. B1.

Gardner, R. M., Morrell, J., Urrutia, R., & Espinoza, T. (1989). Judgments of body size following significant weight loss. *J. Soc. Behav. Pers., 4*(5), 603–613.

Garfield, S. L., & Bergin, A. E. (Eds.). (1986). *Handbook of psychotherapy and behavior change* (3rd ed.). New York: Wiley.

Garfield, S. L., & Kurtz, R. (1976). Clinical psychologists in the 1970s. *Amer. Psychol., 31*(1), 1–19.

Garfield, S. L., & Kurtz, R. (1977). A study of eclectic views. *J. Cons. Clin. Psychol, 45,* 78–83.

Garfinkel, B. D., Froese, A., & Hood, J. (1982). Suicide attempts in children and adolescents. *Amer. J. Psychiat., 139*(10), 1257–1261.

Garfinkel, P. E. (1985). The treatment of anorexia nervosa in Toronto. *J. Psychiat. Res., 19*(2–3), 405–411.

Garfinkel, P. E., & Garner, D. M. (1982). *Anorexia nervosa: A multidimensional perspective.* New York: Brunner/Mazel.

Garfinkel, P. E. et al. (1978). Body awareness in anorexia nervosa: Disturbances in body image and satiety. *Psychosom. Med., 40*(6), 487–498.

Garfinkel, P. E., Moldofsky, H., & Garner, D. M. (1977). The outcome of anorexia nervosa: Significance of clinical features, body image and behavior modification. In R. A. Vigersky (Ed.), *Anorexia Nervosa*. New York: Raven.

Garner, D. M. (1985). Individual psychotherapy for anorexia nervosa. *J. Psychiat. Res., 19*(2–3), 423–433.

Garner, D. M., & Bemis, K. M. (1982). A cognitive-behavioral approach to anorexia nervosa. *Cog. Ther. Res., 6*(2), 123–150.

Garner, D. M., & Fairburn, C. G. (1988). Relationship between anorexia nervosa and bulimia nervosa: Diagnostic implications. In D. M. Garner & P. E. Garfinkel (Eds.), *Diagnostic issues in anorexia nervosa and bulimia nervosa*. New York: Brunner/Mazel.

Garner, D. M., & Garfinkel, P. E. (1978). Sociocultural factors in anorexia nervosa. *Lancet, 2,* 674.

Garner, D. M., & Garfinkel, P. E. (1979). The Eating Attitudes Test: An index of the symptoms of anorexia nervosa. *Psychol. Med., 9,* 273–279.

Garner, D. M., & Garfinkel, P. E. (1980). Sociocultural factors in the development of anorexia nervosa. *Psychol. Med., 10,* 647–656.

Garner, D. M., & Garfinkel, P. E. (1981). Body image in anorexia nervosa: Measurement, theory and clinical implications. *Inter. J. Psychiat. Med., 11,* 263–284.

Garner, D. M., & Wooley, S. C. (1991). Confronting the failure of behavioral and dietary treatments for obesity. *Clin. Psychol. Rev.*

Garner, D. M., Fairburn, C. G., & Davis, R. (1987). Cognitive-behavioral treatment of bulimia nervosa: A critical appraisal. *Behav. Mod., 11*(4), 398–431.

Garner, D. M., Garfinkel, P. E., & Moldofsky, H. (1978). Perceptual experiences in anorexia nervosa and obesity. *Canadian Psychiatr. Assoc. J., 23*(4), 249–263.

Garner, D. M., Garfinkel, P. E., & O'Shaughnessy, M. (1985). The validity of the distinction between bulimia with and without anorexia nervosa. *Amer. J. Psych., 142,* 581–587.

Garner, D. M., Garfinkel, P. E., Schwartz, D., & Thompson, M. (1980). Cultural expectations of thinness in women. *Psych. Rep., 47,* 483–491.

Garner, D. M., Garfinkel, P. E., Stancer, H. C., & Moldofsky, H. (1976). Body image disturbances in anorexia nervosa and obesity. *Psychosom. Med., 38,* 327–336.

Garner, D. M., Olmsted, M. P., Polivy, J. (1983). The eating disorders inventory: A measure of cognitive-behavioral dimensions of anorexia nervosa and bulimia. In P. L. Darby et al. (Eds.), *Anorexia nervosa: Recent developments in research*. New York: Liss.

Garrison, E. G. (1987). Psychological maltreatment of children: An emerging focus for inquiry and concern. *Amer. Psychol., 42*(2), 157–159.

Garrow, J. S., Crisp, A. H., Jordon, H. A., Meyer, J. E., Russell, G. F. M., Silverstone, T., Stunkard, A. J., & Van Itallie, T. B. (1975). Pathology of eating, group report. In T. Silverstone (Ed.), *Life sciences research report 2*. Berlin: Abakon-Verlagsgesellschaft.

Garver, D. L., & Davis, J. M. (1979). Biogenic amine hypotheses of affective disorders. *Life Sciences, 24*(5), 383–394.

Garver, R. B., Fuselier, G. D., & Booth, T. B. (1981). The hypnotic treatment of amnesia in an Air Force basic trainee. *Amer. J. Clin. Hyp., 24*(1), 3–6.

Garvey, M. J., Mungas, D., & Tollefson, G. D. (1984). Hypersomnia in major depressive disorders. *J. Affect. Dis., 6*(3–4), 283–286.

Gatchel, R. J., & Baum, A. (1983). *An introduction to health psychology*. New York: Random House.

Gatchel, R. J., Paulus, P. D., & Maples, C. W. (1975). Learned helplessness and self-reported affect. *J. Abnorm. Psychol., 84*(8), 732–734.

Gatz, M., & Pearson, C. G. (1988). Ageism-revised and the provision of psychological services. *Amer. Psychol., 43,* 184–188.

Gawin, F. H., & Kleber, H. D. (1986). Abstinence symptomatology and psychiatric diagnosis in cocaine abuse: Clinical observations. *Arch. Gen. Psychiat., 43*(2), 107–113.

Gebhard, P. H. (1965). Situational factors affecting human sexual behavior. In F. Beach (Ed.), *Sex and behavior*. New York: Wiley.

Gebhard, P. H. (1969). Fetishism and sadomasochism. *Scientif. Psychoanal., 15,* 71–80.

Gebhard, P. H., Gagnon, J. H., Pomeroy, W. B., & Christenson, C. V. (1965). *Sex offenders: An analysis of types*. New York: Harper & Row.

Geer, J. H. (1965). The development of a scale to measure fear. *Behav. Res. Ther., 3,* 45–53.

Geer, J. H. (1976). Genital measures: Comments on their role in understanding human sexuality. *J. Sex Marital Ther., 2*(3), 165–172.

Geer, J. H. (1977). Sexual functioning: Some data and speculations on psychophysiological assessment. In J. D. Cone & R. P. Hawkins

(Eds.), *Behavioral assessment: New directions in clinical psychology.* New York: Brunner/Mazel.

Geer, J. H., & Maisel, E. (1972). Evaluating the effects of the prediction-control confound. *J. Pers. Soc. Psychol., 23*(3), 314–319.

Gelberg, L., Linn, L. S., & Leake, B. D. (1988). Mental health, alcohol and drug use, and criminal history among homeless adults. *Amer. J. Psychiat., 145*(2).

Gelenberg, A. J. et al. (1980). Tyrosine for the treatment of depression. *Amer. J. Psychiat., 137*(5), 622–623.

Gelenberg, A. J., Kane, J. M., Keller, M. B., Lavori, P., Rosenbaum, J. F., Cole, K., & Lavelle, J. (1989, Nov. 30). Comparison of standard and low serum levels of lithium for maintenance treatment of bipolar disorder. *New Engl. J. Med., 321*(22), 1489–1493.

Gelfand, D. M., Jenson, W. R., & Drew, C. J. (1982). *Understanding child behavior disorders*. New York: Holt, Rinehart & Winston.

Gelles, R. J., & Straus, M. A. (1987). Is violence toward children increasing? A comparison of 1975 and 1985 national survey rates. *J. Interpersonal Violence, 2,* 212–222.

Gelman, D. (1983, Nov. 7). A great emptiness. *Newsweek,* 120–126.

Gentry, W. D., & Matarazzo, J. D. (1981). Medical psychology: Three decades of growth and development. In L. A. Bradley & C. K. Prokop (Eds.), *Medical psychology: A new perspective*. New York: Academic.

George, F. R. (1990). Genetic approaches to studying drug abuse: Correlates of drug self-administration. National Institute on Alcohol Abuse and Alcoholism Neuroscience and Behavioral Research Branch Workshop on the Neurochemical Bases on Alcohol-Related Behavior. *Alcohol, 7*(3), 207–211.

Georgotas, A., & McCue, R. E. (1986). Benefits and limitations of major pharmacological treatment for depression. *Amer. J. Psychother., 40*(3), 370–376.

Gershon, L., & Shaw, F. H. (1961). Psychiatric sequelae of chronic exposure to organophosphorous insecticides. *Lancet, 1,* 1371–1374.

Gernsbacher, L. M. (1985). *The suicide syndrome*. New York: Human Sciences.

Gheorghiu, V. A., & Orleanu, P. (1982). Dental implant under hypnosis. *Amer. J. Clin. Hyp., 25*(1), 68–70.

Ghosh, A., & Marks, I. M. (1987). Self-treatment of agoraphobia by exposure. *Behav. Ther., 18*(1), 3–16.

Gil, D. (1970). *Violence against children*. Cambridge, MA: Harvard Univ.

Gilbert, J. G., & Lombardi, D. N. (1967). Personality characteristics of young male narcotic addicts. *J. Cons. Psychol., 31*(5), 536–538.

Giles, T. R., Young, R. R., & Young, D. E. (1985). Behavioral treatment of severe bulimia. *Behav. Ther., 16*(4), 393–405.

Gillberg, C., & Schaumann, H. (1982). *J. Autism Devel. Dis., 12,* 223–228.

Gillberg, C., Ehlers, S., Schaumann, H., Jakobsson, G. et al. (1990). Autism under age 3 years: A clinical study of 28 cases referred for autistic symptoms in infancy. *J. Child Psychol. Psychiat. Allied Disc., 31*(6), 921–934.

Gillin, J. C., Sitaram, N., Wehr, T. A. et al. (1984). Sleep and affective illness. In R. M. Post & J. C. Ballenger (Eds.). *Neurobiology of mood disorders*. Baltimore: Williams & Wilkins.

Ginsberg, B. G. (1984). Beyond behavior modification: Client-centered play therapy with the retarded. *Acad. Psychol. Bull., 6*(3), 321–334.

Gittelman, R., & Klein, D. F. (1971). Controlled imipramine treatment of school phobia. *Arch. Gen. Psychiat., 25,* 204–207.

Gittelman, R. & Klein, D. F. (1973). School phobia: Diagnostic considerations in the light of imipramine effects. *J. Nerv. Ment. Dis., 156,* 199–215.

Gittelman, R., & Klein, D. F. (1985). Childhood separation anxiety and adult agoraphobia. In A. H. Tuma & J. Maser (Eds.), *Anxiety and the anxiety disorders*. Hillsdale, NJ: Erlbaum.

Glass, C. R., Gottman, H. M., & Shmurak, S. H. (1976). Response-acquisition and self-statement modification for dating-skills training. *J. Cons. Clin. Psychol., 23,* 520–526.

Glass, D. C., & Singer, J. E. (1973). Experimental studies of uncontrollable and unpredictable noise. *Represent. Res. Soc. Psychol., 4*(1), 165–183.

Glaubman, H., Mikulincer, M., Porat, A., Wasserman, O. et al. (1990). Sleep of chronic post-traumatic stress patients. *J. Traumatic Stress, 3*(2), 255–263.

Glenner, G. G. (1985). On causative theories in Alzheimer's Disease. *Human Pathology, 16,* 433–435.

Gleser, G. C., Green, B. L., & Winget, C. (1981). *Prolonged psycho-*

*logical effects of disaster: A study of Buffalo Creek.* New York: Academic.

Glogower, F. D., Fremouw, W. J., & McCroskey, J. C. (1978). A component analysis of cognitive restructuring. *Cog. Ther. Res., 2*(3), 209–223.

Glynn, S. M. (1990). Token economy approaches for psychiatric patients: Progress and pitfalls of chronic psychiatric illness. *Behav. Mod., 14*(4), 383–407.

Gold, M. S. (1986). *The facts about drugs and alcohol.* New York: Bantam.

Gold, M. S. (1987). *The good news about depression: Cures and treatments in the new age of psychiatry.* New York: Villard.

Goldberg, J., True, W. R., & Henderson, W. G. (1990). A twin study of the effects of the Vietnam conflict on alcohol drinking patterns. *Amer. J. Pub. Hlth., 80*(5), 570–574.

Goldberg, T. E., Gold, J. M., & Braff, D. L. (1991). Neuropsychological functioning and time-linked information processing in schizophrenia. In A. Tasman & S. M. Goldfinger (Eds.), *American Psychiatric Press review of psychiatry* (Vol. 10). Washington, DC: American Psychiatric.

Goldbloom, D. S., Hicks, L. K., & Garfinkel, P. E. (1990). Platelet serotonin uptake in bulimia nervosa. *Bio. Psychiat., 28*(7), 644–647.

Golden, C. J. (1978). *Diagnosis and rehabilitation in clinical neuropsychology.* Springfield, IL: Thomas.

Golden, M. (1964). Some effects of combining psychological tests on clinical inferences. *J. Cons. Clin. Psychol., 28*, 440–446.

Golden, R. N., & Gilmore, J. H. (1990). Serotonin and mood disorders. *Psychiat. Ann., 20*(10), 580–588.

Golden, W. L., Geller, E., & Hendricks, C. (1981). A coping-skills approach to flooding therapy in the treatment of test anxiety. *Rational Living, 16*(2), 17–22.

Goldfarb, W. (1967). Factors in the development of schizophrenic children. In J. Romano (Ed.), *The origins of schizophrenia.* Amsterdam: Excerpta Medica.

Goldfried, M. R. (1980). Toward the delineation of therapeutic change principles. *Amer. Psychol., 35*(11), 991–999.

Goldfried, M. R. & Davison, G. C. (1976). *Clinical behavior therapy.* New York: Holt, Rinehart & Winston.

Goldfried, M. R., & Goldfried, A. P. (1977). Importance of hierarchy content in the self-control of anxiety. *J. Cons. Clin. Psychol., 45*(1), 124–134.

Goldman, D. (1949). Brief stimulus electric shock therapy. *J. Nerv. Ment. Dis., 110*, 36–45.

Goldman, H. H. et al. (1980). Community mental health centers and the treatment of severe mental disorders. *Amer. J. Psychiat., 137*(1), 83–86.

Goldney, R. D., Positano, S., Spence, N. D., & Rosenman, S. J. (1985). Suicide in association with psychiatric hospitalization. *Austral. New Zeal. J. Psychiat., 19*(2), 177–183.

Goldney, R. D., Spence, N. D., & Moffitt, P. F. (1987). The aftermath of suicide: Attitudes of those bereaved by suicide, of social workers, and of a community sample. *J. Comm. Psychol., 15*(2), 141–148.

Goldstein, A. (1976). Heroin addiction. *Arch. Gen. Psychiat., 33*, 353–358.

Goldstein, A. (1976). Opioids peptides (endorphins) in pituitary and brain. *Science, 193*, 1081–1086.

Goldstein, A. J., & Chambless, D. L. (1978). A reanalysis of agoraphobia. *Behav. Ther., 9*(1), 47–59.

Goldstein, G. (1990). Comprehensive Neuropsychological Assessment Batteries. In G. Goldstein & M. Hersen (Eds.), *Handbook of psychological assessment* (2nd ed.). New York: Pergamon.

Goldstein, G., & Hersen, M. (1990). Historical Perspectives. In G. Goldstein & M. Hersen (Eds.), *Handbook of psychological assessment* (2nd ed.). New York: Pergamon.

Goldstein, H. (1975). *Social learning curriculum: Teacher's guide.* Columbus, OH: Merrill.

Goldstein, M. J. (1981). Family factors associated with schizophrenia and anorexia nervosa. *J. Youth Adol., 10*(5), 385–405.

Goldstein, M. J. (1985). Family factors that antedate the onset of schizophrenia and related disorders: The results of a fifteen-year prospective longitudinal study. *Acta Psychiatr. Scandin. Supplementum, 319*(71), 7–18.

Goldstein, M. J., (1991). Psychosocial (nonpharmacologic) treatments for schizophrenia. In A. Tasman & S. M. Goldfinger (Eds.), *American Psychiatric Press review of psychiatry* (Vol. 10). Washington, DC: American Psychiatric.

Goldstein, M. J. (Ed.) *New developments in interventions with families of schizophrenics.* San Francisco: Jossey-Bass.

Goldstein, M. J., & Palmer, J. O. (1975). *The experience of anxiety: A casebook* (2nd ed.). New York: Oxford Univ.

Goldstein, M. Z. (1987). Treatment of families of schizophrenic patients: Theory, practice, and research. *Inter. J. Fam. Psychiat., 8*(2), 99–115.

Gomes-Schwartz, B. (1978). Effective ingredients in psychotherapy: Prediction of outcome from process variables. *J. Con. Clin. Psychol., 46*(5), 1023–1035.

Gomes-Schwartz, B. (1979). The modification of schizophrenic behavior. *Behav. Mod., 3*(4), 439–468.

Gonzales, L. R., Lewinsohn, P. M., & Clarke, G. N. (1985). Longitudinal follow-up of unipolar depressives: An investigation of predictors of relapse. *J. Consult. Clin. Psychol., 53*(4), 461–469.

Gonzales, S., Kolvin, I., Garside, R. F., & Leitch, I. M. (1979). Characteristics of parents of handicapped children: I. Preliminary findings. In B. P. Cantwell et al. (Ed.).

Good, B., & Kleinman, A. (1985). Culture and anxiety: Cross-cultural evidence for the patterning of anxiety disorders. In A. H. Tuma & J. Maser (Eds.), *Anxiety and the anxiety disorders.* Hillsdale, NJ: Erlbaum.

Goodman, R. (1990). Technical note: Are perinatal complications causes or consequences of autism? *J. Child Psychol. Psychiat. Allied Disc., 31*(5), 809–812.

Goodman, R., & Ashby, L. (1990). Delayed visual maturation and autism. *Dev. Med. & Child Neurol., 32*(9), 814–819.

Goodman, W. K., & McDougle, C. J. (1990). Serotonin reuptake inhibitors in the treatment of obsessive-compulsive disorder. *Ann. Clin. Psychiat., 2*(3), 173–181.

Goodman, W. K., McDougle, C. J., Price, L. H., Riddle, M. A. et al. (1990). Beyond the serotonin hypothesis: A role for dopamine in some forms of obsessive compulsive disorder? *J. Clin. Psychiat., 51*(Suppl.), 36–43.

Goodman, W. K., Price, L. H., Delgado, P. L., Palumbo, J. et al. (1990). Specificity of serotonin reuptake inhibitors in the treatment of obsessive-compulsive disorder: Comparison of fluvoxamine and desipramine. *Arch. Gen. Psychiat., 47*(6), 577–585.

Goodwin, D., Guze, S. & Robins, E. (1969). Follow-up studies in obsessional neurosis. *Arch. Gen. Psychiat., 20*, 182–187.

Goodwin, D. W. (1976). Adoption studies of alcoholism. *J. Operational Psychiat., 7*(1), 54–63.

Goodwin, D. W. (1976). *Is alcoholism hereditary?* New York: Oxford Univ.

Goodwin, D. W. (1979). Alcoholism and heredity: A review and hypothesis. *Arch. Gen. Psychiat., 36*(1), 57–61.

Goodwin, D. W. (1984). Studies of familial alcoholism: A review. *J. Clin. Psychiat., 45*(12, Sect. 2), 14–17.

Goodwin, D. W. (1986). Genetic factors in the development of alcoholism. *Psychiat. Clin. of N. Amer., 9*, 427–433.

Goodwin, D. W., Schulsinger, F., Hermansen, L., Guze, S. B., & Winokur, G. A. (1973). Alcohol problems in adoptees raised apart from alcoholic biological parents. *Arch. Gen. Psychiat., 128*, 239–243.

Goodwin, F. K., & Ebert, M. E. (1973). Lithium in mania: Clinical trials and controlled studies. In S. Gershon & B. Shopsin (Eds.), *Lithium: Its role in psychiatric research and treatment.* New York: Plenum.

Goodwin, F. K., & Jamison, K. R. (1984). The natural course of manic-depressive illness. In R. M. Post & J. C. Ballenger (Eds.), *Neurobiology of mood disorders.* Baltimore: Williams & Wilkins.

Goodwin, F. K., & Jamison, K. R. (1990). *Manic-depressive illness.* New York: Oxford Univ.

Goodwin, F. K., Murphy, D. L., & Bunney, W. F., Jr. (1969). Lithium carbonate treatment in depression and mania: A longitudinal double-blind study. *Arch. Gen. Psychiat., 21*, 486–496.

Goodwin, F. K., Murphy, D. L., & Dunner, D. L. (1972). Lithium response in unipolar versus bipolar depression. *Amer. J. Psychiat., 129*(1), 44–47.

Goodwin, F. K., Wirz-Justice, A., & Wehr, T. A. (1982). Evidence that pathophysiology of depression and the mechanism of action of antidepressant drugs both involve alterations in circadian rhythms. In E. Costa & G. Racagni (Eds.), *Typical and atypical antidepressants: Clinical practice.* New York: Raven.

Goodwin, J. (1980). The etiology of combat-related post-traumatic stress disorders. In T. Williams (Ed.), *Post-traumatic stress disorders of the Vietnam veteran: Observations and recommendations for the psy-*

*chological treatment of the veteran and his family*. Cincinnati: Disabled American Veterans.

Goodwin, R. A., & Mickalide, A. D. (1985). Parent-to parent support in anorexia nervosa and bulimia. *Children's Hlth. Care, 14*(1), 32–37.

Goorney, A. B., & O'Connor, P. J. (1971). Anxiety associated with flying: A survey of military aircrew psychiatric casualties. *Brit. J. Psychiat., 119*, 159–166.

Gordon, S. B., & Davidson, N. (1981). Behavioral parent training. In A. S. Gurman & D. P. Kniskern, *Handbook of family therapy*. New York: Brunner/Mazel.

Gorman, J. M., Battista, D., Goetz, R. R., Dillon, D. J. et al. (1989). A comparison of sodium bicarbonate and sodium lactate infusion in the induction of panic attacks. *Arch. Gen. Psychiat., 46*(2), 145–150.

Gorman, J. M., Fryer, A. F., Gliklich, J., King, R., & Klein, D. F. (1981). Mitral valve prolapse and panic disorder: Effect of imipramine. In D. F. Klein & J. G. Rabkin (Eds.), *Anxiety: New research and changing concepts*. New York: Raven.

Gorman, J. M., Liebowitz, M. R., Fyer, A. J., & Stein, J. (1989). A neuroanatomical hypothesis for panic disorder. *Amer. J. Psychiat., 146*(2), 148–161.

Gorman, J. M., Shear, M. K., Devereux, R. B., King, R., & Klein, D. F. (1986). Prevalence of mitral valve prolapse in panic disorder: Effect of echocardiographic criteria. *Psychosom. Med., 48*, 167–171.

Goshen, C. E. (1967). *Documentary history of psychiatry: A source book on historical principles*. New York: Philosophy Library.

Gotlib, I. H, & Robinson, L. A. (1982). Responses to depressed individuals: Discrepancies between self-report and observer-related behavior. *J. Abnorm. Behav., 91*(4), 231–240.

Gottesman, I. I. (1989). Vital statistics, demography, and schizophrenia: Editors introduction. *Schizo. Bull., 15*(1).

Gottesman, I. I. (1991). *Schizophrenia genesis*. New York: Freeman.

Gottesman, I. I., McGuffin, P., & Farmer, A. E. (1987). Clinical genetics as clues to the "real" genetics of schizophrenia: A decade of modest gains while playing for time. *Schizo. Bull., 13*(1), 23–47.

Gottesman, I. L., & Shields, J. (1982). The epigenetic puzzle. New York: Cambridge Univ.

Gottheil, E. (1987). Drug use, misuse, and abuse by the elderly. *Med. Aspects of Human Sexuality, 21*(3), 29–37.

Gottlieb, J. (1981). Mainstreaming: Fulfilling the promise? *Amer. J. Ment. Def., 86*(2), 115–126.

Gottlieb, J., & Budoff, M. (1973). Social acceptability of retarded children in nongraded schools differing in architecture. *Amer. J. Ment. Def., 78*, 15–19.

Gottlieb, J., Alter, M., & Gottlieb, B. W. (1991). Litigation involving people with mental retardation. In J. L. Matson & J. A. Mulick (Eds.), *Handbook of mental retardation*. New York: Pergamon.

Gottschalk, E. C. (1981, Apr. 3). While more firms try jury consultants, debate grows over how much they help. *Wall St. J.*

Gould, L. C. et al. (1977). Sequential patterns of multiple-drug use among high school students. *Arch. Gen. Psychiat., 34*(2), 216–222.

Gould, R. L. (1978). *Transformations: Growth and change in adult life*. New York: Simon & Schuster.

Gove, W. R. (1982). The current status of the labeling theory of mental illness. In W. R. Gove (Ed.), *Deviance and mental illness*. Beverly Hills, CA: Sage.

Gove, W. R., & Tudor, J. F. (1973). Adult sex roles and mental illness. *Amer. J. Sociol., 78*, 812–835.

Gowers, S., Kadambari, S. R., & Crisp, A. H. (1985). Family structure and order of patients with anorexia nervosa. Conference on Anorexia Nervosa and Related Disorders (1984, Swansea, Wales). *J. Psychiat. Res., 19*(2–3), 247–251.

Goyer, P. F., & Eddleman, H. C. (1984). Same-sex rape of nonincarcerated men. *J. Psychoanal. Anthropol., 141*(4), 576–579.

Graber, B., & Kline-Graber, G. (1979). Female orgasm: Role of the pubococcygeous muscle. *J. Clin. Psychiat., 40*, 348–351.

Grabowski, J., & Thompson, T. (1977). Development and maintenance of a behavior modification program for behaviorally retarded institutionalized men. In T. Thompson & J. Grabowski (Eds.), *Behavior modification of the mentally retarded* (2nd ed.). New York: Oxford Univ.

Graham, D. T., Kabler, J. D., & Graham, F. K. (1962). Physiological response to the suggestion of attitudes specific for hives and hypertension. *Psychosom. Med., 24*(2), 159–169.

Graham, J. R. (1987). *The MMPI: A practical guide* (2nd ed.). New York: Oxford Univ.

Graham, J. R., & Lilly, R. S. (1984). *Psychological testing*. Englewood Cliffs, NJ: Prentice-Hall.

Grant, C. L., & Fodor, I. G. (1986). Adolescent attitudes toward body and anorexic behavior. *Adolescence, 21*(82), 269–281.

Gray, H. (1959). *Anatomy of the human body* (27th ed.). Philadelphia: Lea & Febiger.

Gray, J. J., & Hoage, C. M. (1990). Bulimia nervosa: Group behavior therapy with exposure plus response prevention. *Psych. Rep., 66*(2), 667–674.

Graziano, A. M., & Mooney, K. C. (1980). Family self-control instruction for children's nighttime fear reduction. *J. Cons. Clin. Psychol., 48*, 206–213.

Green, B. L., Grace, M. C., Lindy, J. D., Gleser, G. C. et al. (1990). Risk factors for PTSD and other diagnoses in a general sample of Vietnam veterans. *Amer. J. Psychiat., 147*(6), 729–733.

Greenberg, D., & Marks, I. (1982). Behavioral therapy of uncommon referrals. *Brit. J. Psychiat., 141*, 148–153.

Greenberg, L. T. (1987). The dangerous patient and psychiatric liability. *Trtmnt. Trends, 2*(1).

Greenblatt, M. (1978). Psychopolitics. New York: Grune & Stratton.

Greenblatt, M. (1984). ECT: Please, no more regulations! *Amer. J. Psychiat., 14*(11), 1409–1410.

Greist, J. H., & Klein, M. H. (1980). Computer programs for patients, clinicians, and researchers in psychiatry. In J. B. Sidowski, J. H. Johnson, & T. A. Williams (Eds.), *Technology in mental health care delivery systems*. Norwood, NJ: Ablex.

Grencheff, T. (1975). A comparative study of the rehabilitation of multiple handicapped mentally retarded with and without parental training. In D. A. Primrose (Ed.), *Proceedings of the Third Congress of the International Association for the Scientific Study of Mental Deficiency*. Warsaw, Poland: Polish Medical Publishers.

Griest, D. L., & Wells, K. C. (1983). Behavioral family therapy with conduct disorders in children. *Behav. Ther., 14*, 37–53.

Griez, E., & van den Hout, M. A. (1983). Treatment of photophobia by exposure to $CO_2$ induced anxiety symptoms. *J. Nerv. Ment. Dis., 171*, 506–508.

Griffith, J. J., Mednick, S. A., Schulsinger, F., & Diderichsen, B. (1980). Verbal associative disturbances in children at high risk for schizophrenia. *J. Abnorm. Psychol., 89*, 125–131.

Grigg, J. R. (1988). Imitative suicides in an active duty military population. *Military Med., 153*(2), 79–81.

Grimshaw, L. (1964). Obsessional disorder and neurological illness. *J. Neurol. Neurosurg. Psychiat., 27*, 229–231.

Grinc, G. A. (1982). A cognitive-behavioral approach to the treatment of chronic vomiting. *J. Behav. Med., 5*, 135–141.

Grinker, R. R., & Spiegel, J. P. (1945). *Men under stress*. Philadelphia: Blakiston.

Grinspoon, L., & Bakalar, J. B. (1986). Can drugs be used to enhance the psychotherapeutic process? *Amer. J. Psychother., 40*(3), 393–404.

Grinspoon, L. et al. (Eds.). (1986). Paraphilias. *Harvard Med. School Ment. Hlth. Newsletter, 3*(6), 1–5.

Grinspoon, L. et al. (Eds.). (1986, Oct.) Mental retardation. Part. I. *Ment. Hlth. Letter, 3*(4).

Grinspoon, L., Ewalt, J. R., & Shader, R. I. *Schizophrenia: Pharmacotherapy and psychotherapy*. Baltimore: Williams & Wilkins.

Grinspoon, L., Ewalt, J. R., & Shader, R. I. (1968). Psychotherapy and pharmacotherapy and chronic schizophrenia. *Amer. J. Psychiat., 124*, 1645–1652.

Grisez, G., & Boyle, J. M., Jr. (1979). *Life and death with liberty and justice: A contribution to the euthanasia debate*. Notre Dame, IN: Univ. Notre Dame.

Grob, G. N. (1966). *State and the mentally ill: A history of Worcester State Hospital in Massachusetts, 1830–1920*. Chapel Hill, NC: Univ. Chapel Hill.

Grof, P., Angst, J., Karasek, M., & Keitner, G. (1979). Patient selection for long-term lithium treatment in clinical practice. *Arch. Gen. Psychiat., 36*(8), 894–897.

Grossman, L. S., & Wasyliw, O. (1988, Mar. 20). Cited in A. H. Rosenfeld. "Insanity rules." *Psych. Today*.

Grossman, S. P. (1986). The role of glucose, insulin and glucagon in the regulation of food intake and body weight. *Neurosci. & Biobehav. Rev., 10*(3), 295–315.

Grossman, S. P. (1990). Brain mechanisms concerned with food intake and body-weight regulation. In M. M. Fichter (Ed.), *Bulimia nervosa: Basic research, diagnosis and therapy*. Chichester: Wiley.

Groth, A. N., & Birnbaum, H. J. (1978). Adult sexual orientation and attraction to under-age persons. *Arch. Sex. Behav., 7*, 175–181.

Gruenberg, E. M. (1980). *Mental disorders.* In J. M. Last (Ed.), *Maxcy-Rosenau public health and preventive medicine* (11th ed.). New York: Appleton-Century-Crofts.

Grunebaum, H. (1985). Helpful and harmful psychotherapy. *Harvard Med. School Ment. Hlth. Newsletter, 1,* 5–6.

Grunhaus, L., Gloger, S., & Weisstub, E. (1981). Panic attacks: A review of treatments and pathogenesis. *J. Nerv. Ment. Dis., 169,* 608–613.

Gumaer, J. (1990). Multimodal counseling of childhood encopresis: A case example. *School Counselor, 38*(1), 58–64.

Gunby, P. (1981). Many cancer patients receiving THC as antiemetic. *Med. News, 245*(15), 1515.

Gupta, R. (1988). Alternative patterns of seasonal affective disorder: Three case reports from North India. *Amer. J. Psychiat., 145*(4), 515–516.

Gurling, H. M., Sherrington, R. P., Brynjolfsson, J., Read, T. et al. (1989). Recent and future molecular genetic research into schizophrenia. *Schizo. Bull., 15*(3), 373–382.

Gurman, A. (1985). On saving marriages. *Fam. Ther. Networker, 9*(2), 17–18.

Gurman, A. S., & Kniskern, D. P. (1978). Behavioral marriage therapy: II. Empirical perspective. *Family Process, 17,* 129–148.

Gurman, A. S., Kniskern, D. P., & Pinsof, W. M. (1986). Research on the process and outcome of marital and family therapy. In S. L. Garfield and A. E. Bergin, (Eds.), *Handbook of psychotherapy and behavior change: An evaluative analysis.* (3rd ed.). New York: Wiley.

Gwirtsman, H. E., Guze, B. H., Yager, J., & Gainsley, B. (1990). Fluoxetine treatment of anorexia nervosa: An open clinical trial. *J. Clin. Psychiat., 51*(9), 378–382.

Hadley, S. W., & Strupp, H. H. (1976). Contemporary views of negative effects in psychotherapy: An integrated account. *Arch. Gen. Psychiat., 33*(1), 1291–1302.

Haefely, W. (1983). The biological basis of benzodiazepine actions. *J. Psychoact. Drugs, 15*(1–2), 1–32.

Haefely, W. (1985). Biochemistry of anxiety. *Ann. Acad. Med. of Singapore, 14,* 81–83.

Haefely, W., Pieri, L., Pole, P., & Schaffner, R. (1975). Possible involvement of GABA in the central action of benzodiazepines. In E. Costa & P. Greengard (Eds.), *Mechanisms of action of benzodiazepines.* New York: Raven.

Hafner, H., & van der Heiden, W. (1988). The mental health care system in transition: A study in organization, effectiveness, and costs of complementary care for schizophrenic patients. In C. N. Stefanis & A. D. Rabavilis (Eds.), *Schizophrenia: Recent biosocial developments.* New York: Human Sciences.

Hagman, J. O., Buchsbaum, M. S., Wu, J. C., Rao, S. J. et al. Comparison of regional brain metabolism in bulimia nervosa and affective disorder assessed with positron emission tomography. *J. Affect. Dis., 19*(3), 153–162.

Hale, C. A., & Borkowski, J. G. (1991). Attention, memory and cognition. In J. L. Matson & J. A. Mulick (Eds.), *Handbook of mental retardation.* New York: Pergamon.

Hale, W. D., & Strickland, B. R. (1976). Induction of mood states and their effect on cognitive and social behaviors. *J. Cons. Clin. Psychol., 44*(1), 155.

Haley, J. (1959). An interactional description of schizophrenia. *Psychiat., 22,* 321–332.

Hall, L. (with L. Cohn). (1980). *Eat without fear.* Santa Barbara, CA: Gurze.

Hall, R. C., Hoffman, R. S., Beresford, T. P., Wooley, B. et al. (1989). Physical illness encountered in patients with eating disorders. *Psychosomatics, 30*(2), 174–191.

Hallam, R. S. (1985). Anxiety and the brain: A reply to Gray. *Bull. Brit. Psychol. Society, 38,* 217–219.

Hallam, R. S., & Rachman, S. (1976). Current status of aversion therapy. In M. Hersen, R. Eisler, & P. Miller (Eds.), *Progress in behavior modification* (Vol. 2). New York: Academic.

Halmi, K. A. (1985). Behavioral management for anorexia nervosa. In D. M. Garner & P. E. Garfinkel (Eds.), *Handbook of psychotherapy for anorexia nervosa and bulimia.* New York: Guilford.

Halmi, K. A. (1985). Classification of the eating disorders. *J. Psychiat. Res., 19*(2–3), 113–119.

Halmi, K. A., Brodland, G. & Loney, J. (1973). Prognosis in anorexia nervosa. *Ann. Internal Med., 78,* 907–909.

Halstead, W. C. (1947). *Brain and intelligence: A quantitative study of the frontal lobes.* Chicago: Univ. Chicago.

Hamilton, M. (1986). Electroconvulsive shock on serotonin activity.

In S. Malitz & H. A. Sackeim (Eds.), *Electroconvulsive therapy: Clinical and basic research issues.* New York: Ann. NY Acad. Sci.

Hamilton, M. (1988). Assessment of depression and mania. In A. Georgotas & R. Cancro (Eds.), *Depression and mania.* New York: Elsevier.

Hammen, C. L., & Glass, D. R. (1975). Expression, activity, and evaluation of reinforcement. *J. Abnorm. Psychol., 84*(6), 718–721.

Hammen, C. L., & Krantz, S. (1976). Effect of success and failure on depressive cognitions. *J. Aborm. Psychol., 85*(8), 577–588.

Hammer, E. (1981). Projective drawings. In A. I. Rabin (Ed.), *Assessment with projective techniques.* New York: Springer.

Hammond, K. R., & Summers, D. A. (1965). A cognitive dependence on linear and non-linear cues. *Psych. Rev., 72,* 215–224.

Hand, I., & Lamontagne, Y. (1974). Paradoxical intention and behavioral techniques in short-term psychotherapy. *Canad. Psychiat. Assoc. J., 19*(5), 501–507.

Hand, I., Lamontagne, Y., & Marks, I. M. (1974). Group exposure (flooding) in vivo for agoraphobics. *Brit. J. Psychiat., 124,* 588–602.

Handelsman, L. (1991). Drug and alcohol dependency. In K. Davis, H. Klar, & J. J. Coyle (Eds.), *Foundations of psychiatry.* Philadelphia: Saunders.

Hanson, J. W., Myrianthropoulos, N. C., Harvey, M. A., & Smith, D. W. (1976). Risks to the offspring of women treated with hydantoin anticonvulsants, with emphasis on the fetal hydantoin syndrome. *J. Pediat., 89,* 662–668.

Harburg, E. et al. (1973). Socio-ecological stress, suppressed hostility, skin color, and black-white male blood pressure: Detroit. *Psychosom. Med., 35*(4), 276–296.

Harding, C. M., & Strauss, J. S. (1984). How serious is schizophrenia? Comments on prognosis. *Bio. Psychiat., 19*(12), 1596–1600.

Hardt, J. V., & Kamiya, J. (1978). Anxiety change through electroencephalographic alpha feedback seen only in high anxiety subjects. *Science, 201*(4350), 79–81.

Hardy, G. E., & Cotterill, J. A. (1982). A study of depression and obsessionality in dysmorphophobic and psoriatic patients. *Brit. J. Psychiat., 140,* 19–22.

Hare, R. D., & Schalling, D. (Eds.) *Psychopathic behavior: Approaches to research.* New York: Wiley.

Hargreaves, I. R. (1985). Attributional style and depression. *Brit. J. Psychol., 24*(1), 85–86.

Harlow, H. F., & Harlow, M. K. (1965). The affectional systems. In A. Schrier, H. Harlow, & F. Stollnitz (Eds.), *Behavior of nonhuman primates* (Vol. 2). New York: Academic.

Harlow, L. L., Newcomb, M. D., & Bentler, P. M. (1986). Depression, self-derogation, substance use, and suicide ideation: Lack of purpose in life as a mediational factor. *J. Clin. Psychol., 42*(1), 5–21.

Haroutunian, V. (1991). Gross anatomy of the brain. In K. Davis, H. Klar, & J. T. Coyle (Eds.), *Foundations of psychiatry.* Philadelphia: Saunders.

Harrell, R. F., Woodyard, E., & Gates, A. I. (1955). *The effects of mothers' diet on the intelligence of the offspring.* New York: Columbia Univ.

Harris, A., Ayers, T., & Leek, M. R. (1985). Auditory span of apprehension deficits in schizophrenia. *J. Nerv. Ment. Dis., 173*(11), 650–657.

Harris, B. (1979). Whatever happened to Little Albert? *Amer. Psychol., 34,* 151–160.

Harris, B., Young, J., & Hughes, B. (1984). Appetite and weight change in patients presenting with depressive illness. *J. Affect. Dis., 6*(3–4), 331–339.

Harris, F. C., & Lahey, B. B. (1982). Subject reactivity in direct observation assessment: A review and critical analysis. *Clin. Psychol. Rev., 2,* 523–538.

Harris, S. L., & Ersner-Hershfield, R. (1978). Behavioral suppression of seriously disruptive behavior in psychotic and retarded patients: A review of punishment and its alternatives. *Psychol. Bull., 85,* 1352–1375.

Harris, S. L., & Milch, R. E. (1981). Training parents as behavior modifiers for their autistic children. *Clin. Psychol. Rev., 1,* 49–63.

Harrow, M. et al. (1988). A longitudinal study of thought disorder in manic patients. *Arch. Gen. Psychiat., 43*(8), 781–785.

Harrow, M., Grinker, R. R., Silverstein, M. L., & Holzman, P. S. (1978). Is modern-day schizophrenic outcome still negative? *Amer. J. Psychiat., 135*(10), 1156–1162.

Hart, K. J., & Ollendick, T. H. (1985). Prevalence of bulimia in working and university women. *Amer. J. Psychiat., 142*(7), 851–854.

Hart, S. N., & Brassard, M. R. (1987). A major threat to children's mental health: Psychological maltreatment. *Amer. Psychol., 42*(2), 160–165.

Hart, S. N., Germain, R., & Brassard, M. R. (1987). The challenge: To better understand and combat the psychological maltreatment of children and youth. In M. R. Brassard, R. Germain, & S. N. Hart (Eds.), *Psychological maltreatment of children and youth.* New York: Pergamon.

Hartley, D., Roback, H. B., & Abramawitz, S. I. (1976). Deterioration effects in encounter groups. *Amer. Psychol., 31,* 247–255.

Harvey, P. D., Earle-Boyer, E. A., & Levinson, J. C. (1988). Cognitive deficits and thought disorder: A retest study. *Schizo. Bull., 14*(1), 57–66.

Harvey, P. D., Keefe, R. S., & Moskowitz, J. (1990). Attentional markers of vulnerability to schizophrenia: Performance of medicated and unmedicated patients and normals. *Psychiat. Res., 33*(2), 178–188.

Hasin, D., Endicott, J., & Lewis, C. (1985). Alcohol and drug abuse in patients with affective syndromes. *Comprehen. Psychiat., 26,* 283–295.

Hathaway, S. R., & Meehl, P. E. (1951). *An atlas for the clinical use of the MMPI.* Minneapolis: Univ. Minnesota.

Hauser, S. L., DeLong, G. R., & Rosman, N. P. (1975). Pneumoencephalographic findings in the infantile autism syndrome: A correlation with temporal lobe disease. *Brain, 98,* 667–688.

Havens, L. L. (1974). The existential use of the self. *Amer. J. Psychiat., 131*(1), 1–10.

Hawkins, W. L., French, L. C., Crawford, B. D., & Enzle, M. C. (1988). Depressed affect and time perception. *J. Abnorm. Psychol., 97*(3), 275–280.

Hawton, K. (1982). Attempted suicide in children and adolescents. *J. Child Psychol. Psychiat., 23*(4), 497–503.

Hawton, K., Cole, D., O'Grady, J., & Osborn, M. (1982). Motivational aspects of deliberate self-poisoning in adolescents. *Brit. J. Psychiat., 141,* 286–291.

Hay, G. G. (1983). Feigned psychosis: A review of the simulation of mental illness. *Brit. J. Psychiat., 143,* 810.

Hay, L. R., Hay, W. R., & Angle, H. V. (1977). The reactivity of self-recording: A case report of a drug abuser. *Behav. Ther., 8*(5), 1004–1007.

Hay, W. M., Hay, L. R., & Nelson, R. Q. (1977). The adaptation of covert modeling procedures to the treatment of chronic alcoholism and obsessive compulsive behavior: Two case reports. *Behav. Ther., 8*(1), 70–76.

Hayes, B. J., & Marshall, W. L. (1984). Generalization of treatment effects in training public speakers. *Behav. Res. Ther., 22,* 519–533.

Haynes, S. G., & Feinleib, M. (1980). Women, work and coronary heart disease: Prospective findings from the Framingham heart study. *Amer. J. Pub. Hlth., 70*(2).

Haynes, S. G., Feinleib, M., & Kannel, W. B. (1980). The relationship of psychosocial factors to coronary heart disease in the Framingham study: III. Eight-year incidence of coronary heart disease. *Amer. J. Epidemiol., 111,* 37–58.

Haynes, S. N. (1990). Behavioral assessment of adults. In G. Goldstein & M. Hersen (Eds.), *Handbook of psychological assessment* (2nd ed.). New York: Pergamon.

Hayward, M. D., & Taylor, J. E. (1965). A schizophrenic patient describes the action of intensive psychotherapy. *Psychiat. Quart., 30.*

Haywood, H. C., Meyers, C. E., & Switzky, H. N. (1982). Mental retardation. *Annu. Rev. Psychol., 33,* 309–342.

Healy, D., & Leonard, B. E. (1987). Monoamine transport in depression: Kinetics and dynamics. *J. Affect. Dis., 12*(2), 91–103.

Healy, D., & Waterhouse, J. M. (1990). The circadian system and affective disorders: Clocks or rhythms? *Chronobio. Inter., 7*(1), 5–10.

Healy, D., & Williams, J. M. (1988). Dysrhythmia, dysphoria, and depression: The interaction of learned helplessness and circadian dysrhythmia in the pathogenesis of depression. *Psychol. Bull., 103*(2), 163–178.

Healy, D., O'Halloran, A., Carney, P. A., & Leonard, B. C. (1986). Variations in platelet 5-hydroxytryptamine in control and depressed populations. *J. Affect. Res., 20*(4), 345–353.

Heather, N., & Robertson, I. (1983). What we would most like to know: Why is abstinence necessary for the recovery of some problem drinkers? *Brit. J. Addic., 78*(2), 139–144.

Heather, N., Rollnick, S., & Winton, M. (1983). A comparison of objective and subjective measures of alcohol dependence as predictors of relapse following treatment. *Brit. J. Clin. Psychol., 22*(1), 11–17.

Heather, N., Winton, M., & Rollnick, S. (1982). An empirical test of "a cultural delusion of alcoholics." *Psych. Rep., 50*(2), 379–382.

Heaton, R. K., Baade, L. E., & Johnson, K. L. (1978). Neuropsychological test results associated with psychiatric disorders in adults. *Psychol. Bull., 85,* 141–162.

Heber, F. R. (1979). Research in the prevention of sociocultural retardation through early prevention. *Mental retardation, the child and his surroundings.* Washington, DC: International Union of Child Welfare.

Heflinger, C. A., Cook, V. J., & Thackrey, M. (1987). Identification of mental retardation by the System of Multicultural Pluralistic Assessment: Nondiscriminatory or nonexistent? *J. School Psychol., 25*(2), 177–183.

Heilbrum, K. S. (1980). Silverman's subliminal psychodynamic activation. A failure to replicate. *J. Abnorm. Psychol., 89*(4), 560–566.

Heilbrun, A. B., & Witt, N. (1990). Distorted body image as a risk factor in anorexia nervosa: Replication and clarification. *Psych. Rep., 66*(2), 407–416.

Heilbrun, A. B., Blum, N., & Haas, M. (1983). Cognitive vulnerability to auditory hallucination: Preferred imagery mode and spatial location of sounds. *Brit. J. Psychiat., 143,* 294–298.

Heilmen, J. R., & LoPiccolo, J. (1988). *Becoming orgasmic: A personal and sexual growth program for women.* New York: Prentice-Hall.

Heimen, J. R., Gladue, B. A., Roberts, C. W., & LoPiccolo, J. (1986). Historical and current factors discriminating sexually functional from sexually dysfunctional married couples. *J. of Marital Fam. Ther., 12*(2), 163–174.

Heimen, J. R., LoPiccolo, L., & LoPiccolo, J. (1981). Treatment of sexual dysfunction. In A. S. Gurman & D. P. Kniskern (Eds.), *Handbook of family therapy.* New York: Brunner/Mazel.

Heinrichs, D. W., & Carpenter, W. T., Jr. (1983). The coordination of family therapy with other treatment modalities for schizophrenia. In W. McFarlane (Ed.), *Family therapy in schizophrenia.* New York: Guilford.

Heller, K., & Monahan, J. (1977). *Psychology and community change.* Homewood, IL: Dorsey.

Hembree, W. C., Nahas, G. G., & Huang, H. F. S. (1979). Changes in human spermatozoa associated with high dose marihuana-smoking. In G. G. Nahas & W. D. M. Paton (Eds.), *Marihuana: Biological effects.* Elmsford, NY: Pergamon.

Henderson, S., Duncan-Jones, P., McAuley, H., & Ritchie, K. (1978). *Brit. J. Psychiat., 132,* 74–86.

Henderson, S. et al. (1978). Social bonds in the epidemiology of neurosis: A preliminary communication. *Brit. J. Psychiat., 132,* 403–400.

Hendin, H. (1987). Youth suicide: A psychosocial perspective. *Suic. Life Threat. Behav., 17*(2), 151–165.

Henig, R. M. (1988). *The myth of senility.* Washington, DC: American Assoc. of Retired Persons, and Glenview, IL: Scott, Foresman.

Henry, G. M. Weingarten, H., & Murphy, D. L. (1973). Influence of affective states and psychoactive drugs on verbal learning and memory. *Amer. J. Psychiat., 130,* 966–971.

Herbert, M. (1984). Psychological treatment of childhood neuroses. In V. P. Varma (Ed.), *Anxiety in children.* London: Croom Helm.

Herek, G. M., & Glunt, E. K. (1988). An epidemic of stigma: Public reactions to AIDS. *Amer. Psychol., 43*(11), 886–891.

Hermelin, B. (1976). Coding and the sense modalities. In L. Wing (Ed.), *Early childhood autism.* Oxford: Pergamon.

Herrenkohl, R. C., Herrenkohl, E. C., & Egolf, B. P. (1983). Circumstances surrounding the occurrence of child maltreatment. *J. Cons. Clin. Psychol., 51,* 424–431.

Hersen, M. (1976). Token economies in institutional settings. *J. Nerv. Ment. Dis., 162*(3), 206–211.

Hersen, M., & Barlow, D. H. (1976). *Single-case experimental designs: Strategies for studying behavior change.* New York: Pergamon.

Hersen, M., & Detre, T. (1980). The behavioral psychotherapy of anorexia nervosa. In T. B. Karasu & L. Bellak (Eds.), *Specialized techniques in individual psychotherapy.* New York: Brunner/Mazel.

Hersen, M., Bellack, A. S., Himmelhoch, J. M., & Thase, M. E. (1984). Effects of social skill training, amitriptyline, and psychotherapy in unipolar depressed women. *Behav. Ther., 15,* 21–40.

Herz, M. I., Endicott, J., & Spitzer, R. L. (1975). Brief hospitalization of patients with families: Initial results. *Amer. J. Psychiat., 132*(4), 413–418.

Herz, M. I., Endicott, J., & Spitzer, R. L. (1977). Brief hospitalization: A two-year follow-up. *Amer. J. Psychiat., 134*(5), 502–507.

Herz, M. I. et al. (1971). Day vs. inpatient hospitalization: A controlled study. *Amer. J. Psychiat., 127*(4), 1371–1381.

Herzog, A. (1984). On multiple personality: Comments on diagnosis, etiology, and treatment. *Inter. J. Clin. Exp. Hyp., 32*(2), 210–221.

Herzog, D. B. (1982). Bulimia: The secretive syndrome. *Psychosomatics, 23*(5), 481–487.

Herzog, D. B., Keller, M. B., Lavori, P. W., Bradburn, I. S., & Ott, I. L. (1990). Course and outcome of bulimia nervosa. In M. M. Fichter (Ed.), *Bulimia nervosa: Basic research, diagnosis and therapy.* Chichester: Wiley.

Herzog, D. B. Norman, D. K., Gordon, C., & Pepose, M. (1984). Sexual conflict and eating disorders in 27 males. *Amer. J. Psychiat., 141,* 989–990.

Heshe, J., & Roeder, E. (1976). Electroconvulsive therapy in Denmark. *Brit. J. Psychiat., 128,* 241–245.

Heston, L. L., & White, J. A. (1983). *Dementia.* New York: Freeman.

Heston, L. L., Mastri, A. R., Anderson, V. E., & White, J. (1981). Dementia of the Alzheimer type: Clinical genetics natural history and associated condition. *Arch. Gen. Psychiat., 38,* 1085–1090.

Hewitt, P. S., & Howe, N. (1988). Future of generational politics. *Generations, 12*(3), 10–13.

Hibbert, G. A. (1984). Ideational components of anxiety: Their origin and content. *Brit. J. Psychiat., 144,* 618–624.

Hicks. (1985). In R. P. Kluft (Ed.), *Childhood antecedents of multiple personality.* Washington, DC: American Psychiatric.

Higgins, R. L, & Marlatt, G. A. (1975). Fear of interpersonal evaluation as a determinant of alcohol consumpton in male social drinkers. *J. Abnorm. Psychol., 84*(6), 644–651.

Higgins, R. L., & Marlatt, G. A. (1973). Effects of anxiety arousal on the consumption of alcohol by alcoholics and social drinkers. *J. Cons. Clin. Psychol., 41*(3), 426–433.

Hilgard, E. R. (1977). Controversies over consciousness and the rise of cognitive psychology. *Austral. Psychol., 12*(1), 7–26.

Hilgard, E. R. (1977). Psychology's influence on educational practices: A puzzling history. *Education, 97*(3), 203–219.

Hilgard, E. R. (1986). *Divided consciousness: Multiple controls in human thought and action* (Rev. ed.). New York: Wiley.

Hilgard, E. R. (1986). From the social gospel to the psychology of social issues: A reminiscence. *J. Soc. Issues, 42*(1), 107–110.

Hilgard, E. R. (1987). Research advances in hypnosis: Issues and methods. *Inter. J. Clin. Exper. Hyp., 35,* 248–264.

Hillbom, E. (1960). After-effects of brain injuries. *Acta Psychiatr. Neurol. Scandin., 142*(Suppl.), 35, 125.

Hillyer, J. (1926). *Reluctantly told.* New York: Macmillan.

Himle, J. A., Himle, D. P., & Thyer, B. A. (1989). Irrational beliefs and anxiety disorders. *J. Rational, Emotive & Cog. Behav. Ther., 7*(3), 155–165.

Hinshaw, S. P., & Erhardt, D. (1991). Attention-deficit hyperactivity disorder. In P. C. Kendall (Ed.), *Child and adolescent therapy: Cognitive-behavioral procedures.* New York: Guilford.

Hinshaw, S. P., Buhrmester, D., & Heller, T. (1989). Anger control in response to verbal provocation: Effects of stimulant medication for boys with ADHD. *J. Abnorm. Child Psychol., 17,* 393–407.

Hiroto, D. S. (1974). Locus of control and learned helplessness. *J. Exp. Psychol., 102*(2), 187–193.

Hiroto, D. S., & Seligman, M. E. (1975). Generality of learned helplessness in man. *J. Pers. Soc. Psychol., 31*(2), 311–327.

Hirsch, B. J. (1979). Psychological dimensions of social networks: A multimethod analysis. *Amer. J. Community Psychol., 7*(3), 263–277.

Hirsch, S., & Leff, J. (1975). Abnormalities in parents of schizophrenics. Oxford: Oxford Univ.

Hirsch, S. R. (1979, Feb.) Do parents cause schizophrenia? *TINS,* 49–52.

Hirschfeld, R. M., & Davidson, L. (1988). Clinical risk factors for suicide. [Special Issue]. *Psychiat. Ann., 18*(11), 628–635.

Hirschfeld, R. M., & Goodwin, F. K. (1988). Mood disorders. In J. A. Talbott, R. E. Hales, & S. C. Yudofsky (Eds.), *The American Psychiatric Press textbook of psychiatry.* Washington, DC: American Psychiatric.

Hite, S. (1970). *The Hite report: A nationwide study of female sexuality.* New York: Dell.

Hobson, J. A., & McCarley, R. W. (1977). The brain as a dream state generator: An activation-synthesis hypothesis of the dream process. *Amer. J. Psychiat., 134*(12), 1335–1348.

Hodgkinson, S., Mullan, M. J., & Gurling, H. M. (1990). The role of genetic actors in the etiology of the affective disorders. [Special Issue]. *Behav. Genetics, 20*(2), 235–250.

Hodgkinson, S., Sherrington, R. Gurling, H., Marchbanks, R.,

Reeders, S., Mallet, J., McInnis, M., Petursson, H., & Brynjolfsson, J. (1987). Molecular genetic evidence for heterogeneity in manic depression. *Nature, 325,* 805–806.

Hodgson, R., & Rankin, H. (1982). Cue exposure and relapse prevention. In W. Hay & P. Nathan (Eds.), *Clinical case studies in the behavioral treatment of alcoholism.* New York: Plenum.

Hodgson, R. J., & Rachman, S. (1972). The effects of contamination and washing in obsessional patients. *Behav. Res. Ther., 10,* 111–117.

Hoebel, B. G., & Teitelbaum, P. (1966). Weight regulation in normal and hypothalamic hyperphagic rats. *J. Compar. Physiol. Psychol., 61*(2), 189–193.

Hoffman, J. W. et al. (1982). Reduced sympathetic nervous system responsivity associated with the relaxation response. *Science, 215*(4529), 190–192.

Hoffman, R. S. (1980). The itemized statement in clinical psychiatry: A new concept in billing. *J. Irreproducible Results, 26*(3), 7–8.

Hogan, R. A. (1968). The implosive technique. *Behav. Res. Ther., 6,* 423–431.

Hogarty, G. E. (1971). The plight of schizophrenics in modern treatment programs. *Hosp. Comm. Psychiat., 22*(7), 197–203.

Hogarty, G. E., & Goldberg, I. C. (1973). Drugs and social therapy in the aftercare of schizophrenic patients. *Arch. Gen. Psychiat., 28,* 54–64.

Hogarty, G. E. et al. (1974). Drug and sociotherapy in the aftercare of schizophrenic patients: II. Two-year relapse rates. *Arch. Gen. Psychiat., 31*(5), 609–618.

Hogarty, G. E. et al. (1974). Drug and sociotherapy in the aftercare of schizophrenic patients: III. Adjustment of non-relapsed patients. *Arch. Gen. Psychiat., 31*(5), 609–618.

Hogarty, G. E. et al. (1986). Family psychoeducation, social skills training, and maintenance chemotherapy in the aftercare treatment of schizophrenia: I. One-year effects of a controlled study on relapse and expressed emotion. *Arch. Gen. Psychiat., 43*(7), 633–642.

Hoge, M. A., Farrell, S. P., Munchel, M. E., & Strauss, J. S. (1988). Therapeutic factors in partial hospitalization. *Psychiatry 51*(2), 199–210.

Hogg, B., Jackson, H. J., Rudd, R. P., & Edwards, J. (1990). Diagnosing personality disorders in recent-onset schizophrenia. *J. Nerv. Ment. Dis., 178*(3), 194–199.

Hokin-Neaverson, M., Spiegel, D. A., & Lewis, W. C. (1974). Deficiency of erythrocyte sodium pump activity in bipolar manic-depressive psychosis. *Life Sciences, 15,* 1739–1748.

Holden, R. R., Mendonca, J. D., & Mazmanian, D. (1985) . Relation of response set to observed suicide intent. *Canad. J. Behav. Sci., 17*(4), 359–368.

Holinger, P. C. (1988). A prediction model of suicide among youth. *J. Nerv. Ment. Dis., 176*(5), 275–279.

Holinger, P. C., & Offer, D. (1991) Sociodemographic, epidemiologic, and individual attributes. In L. Davidson & M. Linnoila (Eds.), *Risk factors for youth suicide.* New York: Hemisphere.

Holinger, P. C., Offer, D., & Ostrov, E. (1987). Suicide and homicide in the United States: An epidemiologic study of violent death, population changes, and the potential for prediciton. *Amer. J. Psychiat., 144*(2), 215–218.

Hollander, E., Liebowitz, M. R., & Gorman, J. M., (1988). Anxiety disorders. In J. A. Talbott, R. E. Hales, & S. C. Yudofsky (Eds.), *Textbook of psychiatry.* Washington, DC: American Psychiatric.

Hollingshead, A. B., & Redlich, F. C. (1958). *Social class and mental illness: A community study.* New York: Wiley.

Hollister, L. E. (1977). Valium: A discussion of current issues. *Psychosomatics, 18*(1), 44–58.

Hollister, L. E. (1982). Plasma concentrations of tricyclic antidepressants in clinical practice. *J. Clin. Psychiat., 43*(2), 66–69.

Hollister, L. E. (1986) Pharmacotherapeutic considering in anxiety disorders. Annual Meeting of the American Academy of Clinical Psychiatrists (1985, San Francisco, CA). *J. Clin. Psychiat., 47*(Suppl.), 33–36.

Hollister, L. E. (1990). Treatment outcome: A neglected area of drug abuse research. [Special Issue]. *Drug Alc. Dep., 25*(2), 175–177.

Hollister, L. E., & Csernansky, J. G. (1990). *Clinical pharmacology of psychotherapeutic drugs* (3rd ed.) New York: Churchill-Livingstone.

Hollister, L. E., Davis, K. L., & Berger, P. A. (1980). Subtypes of depression based on excretion of MHPH and response to nortriptyline. *Arch. Gen. Psychiat., 37*(10), 1107–1110.

Hollon, S. D., & Beck, A. T. (1979). Cognitive therapy of depression.

In P. E. Kendall & S. D. Hollon (Eds.), *Cognitive behavioral interventions: Theory, research, procedures.* New York: Academic.

Hollon, S. D., & Kendall, P. C. (1980). Cognitive self statements in depression: Development of an automatic thoughts questionnaire. *Cog. Ther. Res., 4*(4), 383–395.

Hollon, S. D., & Najavits, L. (1988). Review of empirical studies on cognitive therapy. In A. J. Frances & R. E. Hales (Eds.), *American Psychiatric Press review of psychiatry* (Vol. 7). Washington, DC: American Psychiatric.

Hollon, S. D., DeRubeis, R. J., Evans, M. D., Tuason, V. B., Wiemer, M. J., & Garvey, M. (1986). *Cognitive therapy, pharmacotherapy, and combined cognitive therapy-pharmacotherapy in the treatment of depression; Vol. 1. Differential outcome.* Unpublished manuscript. Minneapolis-St. Paul: Univ. Minnesota and St. Paul-Ramsey Medical Center.

Hollon, S. D., Evans, M. D., & De Rubeis, R. J. (1985). Preventing relapse following treatment for depression: The cognitive-pharmacotherapy project. In N. Schneiderman & T. Fields (Eds.), *Stress and coping* (Vol. 2). Hillsdale, NJ: Erlbaum.

Hollon, S. D., Kendall, P. C., & Lumry, A. (1986). Specificity of depressotypic cognitions in clinical depression. *J. Abnorm. Psychol., 95*(1), 52–59.

Holmes, C. B. (1988). Comment on "Religiosity and U.S. suicide rates, 1972–1978." *J. Clin. Psychol., 41*(4), 580.

Holmes, T. H., & Masuda, M. (1974). Life change and illness susceptibility. In B. S. Dohrenwend & B. P. Dohrenwend (Eds.), *Stressful life events: Their nature and effects.* New York: Wiley.

Holmes, T. H., & Rahe, R. H. (1967). The social readjustment rating scale. *J. Psychosom. Res., 11*, 213–218.

Holroyd, J. C., & Brodsky, A. M. (1977). Psychologists' attitudes and practices regarding erotic and nonerotic physical contact with patients. *Amer. Psychol., 32*, 843–849.

Holroyd, K., Andrasik, F., & Noble, J. A. (1980). A comparison of EMG biofeedback and a credible pseudotherapy in treating tension headache. *J. Behav. Med., 3*, 29–39.

Holzman, P. S., & Matthysse, S. (1990). The genetics of schizophrenia: A review. *Psychol. Science, 1*(5), 279–286.

Hong, L. K. (1984). Survival of the fastest: On the origin of premature ejaculation. *J. Sex Res., 20*, 109–122.

Hood, L. E., Weissman, I. L., & Wood, W. B. (1978). *Immunology.* Menlo Park, CA: Benjamin-Cummings.

Hoogduin, C. A., de Haan, E., & Terluin, B. (1985). Somatische aandoeningen bij opgenomen psychiatriche patienten [Somatic illness in psychiatric inpatients]. *Tijdschrift voor Psychiatrie, 27*(2), 105–114.

Hoogduin, C. A. L. (1985). Mislukking en success bij de ambulante behandeling van dwangneurose. Doctoral dissertation, University of Leiden, Netherlands.

Hoogduin, K. (1985). Interactionale aspecten bij de behandeling van dwang [Interactional aspects of the treatment of compulsion]. *Gedragstherapie, 18*(4), 305–313.

Hooker, W. D., & Jones, R. T. (1987). Increased susceptibility to memory intrusions and the Stroop interference effect during acute marijuana intoxication. *Psychopharmacology, 91*(1), 20–24.

Hopson, J. L. (1986). The unraveling of insomnia. *Anthropol. Educ. Quart., 20*(6), 42–49.

Horn, J. C., & Meer, J. (1987, May). The vintage years. *Psych. Today,* 76–77, 80–84, 88–90.

Horn, J. M., Loehlin, J. C., & Willerman, L. (1979). *Behav. Genetics, 9*(3) 177–207.

Horney, K. (1937). *The neurotic personality of our time.* New York: Norton.

Horowitz, M., & Kaltreider, N. (1979). Brief therapy of the stress response syndrome. *Psychiat. Clin. N. Amer., 2*, 365–377.

Horowitz, M. J. (1976). *Stress response syndromes.* New York: Aronson.

Horton, D. (1943). The functions of alcohol in primitive societies: A cross-cultural study. *Quart. J. Stud. Alcohol., 4*, 199–320.

House, J. S., Landis, K. R., & Umberson, D. (1988). Social relationships and health. *Science, 241*, (4865), 540–545.

Houts, A. C., & Abramson, H. (1990). Assessment and treatment for functional childhood enuresis and encopresis. In S. B. Morgan & T. M. Okwumabaua (Eds.), *Child and adolescent disorders.* Hillsdale, NJ: Erlbaum.

Howard, K. I., Kopta, S. M., Krause, M. S., & Orlinsky, D. E. (1986). The dose-effect relationship in psychotherapy. *Amer. Psychol., 41*, 159–164.

Hoy, E., Weiss, G., Minde, K., & Cohen, N. (1978). The hyperactive child at adolescence: Cognitive, emotional, and social functioning. *J. Abnorm. Child. Psychol., 8*(3), 311–324.

Hsu, L. G. (1987). Treatment of anorexia nervosa: Dr. Hsu replies. *Amer. J. Psychiat., 144*(2), 260–261.

Hsu, L. K. G. (1980). Outcome of anorexia nervosa: A review of literature (1954–1978). *Arch. Gen. Psychiat., 37*, 1041–1046.

Hsu, L. K. G. (1986). The treatment of anorexia nervosa. *Amer. J. Psychiat., 143*(5), 573–581.

Hsu, L. K. G., & Holder, D. (1986). Bulimia nervosa: Treatment and short-term outcome. *Psychol. Med., 16*, 65.

Hudgens, R. W. (1985). Anorexia not the same as depression. *Amer. J. Psychiat., 142*(10), 1230.

Hudson, J. I., & Pope, H. G. (1990). Psychopharmacological treatment of bulimia. In M. M. Fichter (Ed.), *Bulimia nervosa: Basic research, diagnosis and therapy.* Chichester: Wiley.

Hudson, J. I., Pope, H. G., & Jonas, J. M. (1985). Antidepressant treatment of bulimia. *Adv. Behav. Res. Ther., 7*(3), 173–179.

Hughes, C. W. et al. (1984). Cerebral blood flow and cerebrovascular permeability in an inescapable shock (learned helplessness) animal model of depression. *Pharm., Biochem. Behav., 21*(6), 891–894.

Hullin, R. P., MacDonald, R., & Allsopp, M. N. (1972). Prophylactic lithium in recurrent affective disorders. *Lancet, 1*, 1044.

Humphry, D., & Wickett, A. (1986). *The right to die: Understanding euthanasia.* New York: Harper & Row.

Hunt, M. (1974). *Sexual behavior in the 1970s.* Chicago: Playboy.

Hunter, R., & MacAlpine, I. (1963). *Three hundred years of psychiatry.* Oxford: Oxford Univ.

Hurley, A. D., & Hurley, F. L. (1986). Counseling and psychotherapy with mentally retarded clients: I. The initial interview. *Psych. Aspects of Ment. Retardation Rev., 5*(5), 22–26.

Hurwitz, T. D. (1974). Electroconvulsive therapy: A review. *Comprehen. Psychiat., 15*(4), 303–314.

Hutchings, D. F., Denney, D. R., Basgall, J., & Houston, B. K. (1980). Anxiety management and applied relaxation in reducing general anxiety. *Behav. Res. Ther., 18*(3), 181–190.

Hutchinson, R. L., & Little, T. J. (1985). A study of alcohol and drug usage by nine- through thirteen-year-old children in Central Indiana. *J. Alcohol & Drug Educ., 30*(3), 83–87.

Hutt, S. J., Hutt, C., Lee, D., & Ounstead, C. (1964). Arousal and childhood autism. *Nature, 204*, 908.

Hyde, J. S. (1990). *Understanding human sexuality* (4th ed.). New York: McGraw-Hill.

Hynd, G. W., Semrud-Clikeman, M., Lorys, A. R., Novey, E. S. et al. (1990). Brain morphology in developmental dyslexia and attention deficit disorder/hyperactivity. *Arch. Neurol., 47*(8), 919–926.

Ingham, J. G. (1963). Cross-masking in neurotic patients. *Brit. J. Soc. Clin. Psychol., 4*(2), 131–140.

Ingham, J. G. (1965). A method for observing symptoms and attitudes. *Brit. J. Soc. Clin. Psychol., 4*(2), 1131–1140.

Inkeles, A. *Exploring individual modernity.* (1983). New York: Columbia Univ.

Insel, T. R. et al. (1983). Neurological and neuropsychological studies of patients with obsessive-compulsive disorder. *Bio. Psychiat., 18*(7), 741–751.

Insel, T. R. et al. (1983). Parents of patients with obsessive-compulsive disorder. *Psychol. Med., 13*(4), 807–811.

Insel, T. R., Ninan, P. T., Aloi, J., Jimerson, D., Skolnick, P., & Paul, S. M. (1984). Benzodiazepine receptors and anxiety in non-human primates. *Arch. Gen. Psychiat., 41*, 741–750.

Institute of Medicine, Division of Mental Health and Behavioral Medicine (authored by a committee under Meyer, R. E., Murray, R. F. et al). (1989). *Prevention and treatment of alcohol problems: Research opportunities (Report of a study).* Washington, DC: National Academy.

Irving, L. M. (1990). Mirror images: Effects of the standard of beauty on the self- and body-esteem of women exhibiting varying levels of bulimic symptoms. *J. Soc. Clin. Psychol., 9*(2), 230–242.

Israely, Y. (1985). The moral development of mentally retarded children: Review of the literature. *J. Moral Educ., 14*(1), 33–42.

Ito, J. R., Donovan, D. M., & Hall, J. J. (1988). Relapse prevention in alcohol aftercare: Effects on drinking outcome, change process, and aftercare attendance. *Brit. J. Addic., 83*(2), 171–181.

Iversen, L. L. (1965). *Adv. Drug Res., 2*, 5–23.

Iversen, L. L. (1975). Dopamine receptors in the brain. *Science, 188*, 1084–1089.

Izard, C. E. (1977). *Human emotions.* New York: Plenum.

Jablensky, A. (1988). Methodological issues in psychiatric classification. *Brit. J. Psychiat., 152*(1, Suppl.), 15–20.

Jackson, J. S. (Ed.). (1988). *The Black American elderly: Research on physical and psychosocial health.* New York: Springer.

Jacobs, G. A., Quevillon, R. P., & Stricherz, M. (1990). Lessons from the aftermath of Flight 232: Practical considerations for the mental health profession's response to air disasters. *Amer. Psychologist, 45*(12), 1329–1335.

Jacobson, E. (1971). *Depression.* New York: International Univ.

Jacobson, E. (1975). The psychoanalytic treatment of depressive patients. In E. J. Anthony & T. Benedek (Eds.), *Depression and human existence.* Boston: Little, Brown.

Jacobson, J. W., & Schwarz, A. A. (1991). Evaluating living situations of people with development disabilities. In J. L. Matson & J. A. Mulick (Eds.), *Handbook of mental retardation.* New York: Pergamon.

Jacobson, N. S. (1977). Problem-solving and contingency contracting in the treatment of marital discord. *J. Cons. Clin. Psychol., 45,* 92–100.

Jacobson, N. S. (1977). Training couples to solve their marital problems: A behavioral approach to relationship discord: I. Problem-solving skills. *Inter. J. Fam. Couns., 5*(1), 22–31.

Jacobson, N. S. (1977). Training couples to solve their marital problems: A behavioral approach to relationship discord: II. Intervention strategies. *Inter. J. Fam. Couns., 5*(2), 20–28.

Jacobson, N. S. (1978). A review of the research on the effectiveness of marital therapy. In T. J. Paolino & B. S. McCrady (Eds.), *Marriage and marital therapy: Psychoanalytic, behavioral, and systems theory perspectives.* New York: Brunner/Mazel.

Jacobson, N. S. (1978). Specific and nonspecific factors in the effectiveness of a behavioral approach to the treatment of marital discord. *J. Cons. Clin. Psychol., 46,* 442–452.

Jacobson, N. S. (1989). The maintenance of treatment gains following social learning-based marital therapy. *Behav. Ther., 20*(3), 325–336.

Jacobson, N. S., & Margolin, G. (1979). *Marital therapy: Strategies based on social learning and behavior exchange principles.* New York: Brunner/Mazel.

Jacobson, N. S., Berley, R., Newport, K., Elwood, R., & Phelps, C. (in press). Failure in behavioral marital therapy. In S. Colman (Ed.), *Failure in family therapy,* New York: Guilford.

Jacobson, N. S. et al. (1984). Variability in outcome and clinical significance of behavioral marital therapy: A reanalysis of outcome data. *J. Couns. Clin. Psychol., 52*(4), 497–504.

Jaffe, J. H. (1985). Drug addiction and drug abuse. In Goodman & Gilman (Eds.), *The pharmacological basis of therapeutic behavior.* New York: Macmillan.

Jaffe, J. H. (1989). Drug dependence: Opiods, nonnarcotics, nicotine (tobacco), and caffeine. In H. I. Kaplan & B. Sadock (Eds.), *Comprehensive textbook of psychiatry V,* (Vol. 1). Baltimore: Williams & Wilkins.

James, A. L., & Barry, R. (1980). A review of psychophysiology in child onset psychosis. *Schizo. Bull., 6,* 506–525.

James, W. (1890). *Principles of psychology* (Vol. 1). New York: Holt, Rinehart & Winston.

Jamison, K. R., Gerner, R. H., & Goodwin, F. K. (1979). Patient and physician attitudes toward lithium: Relationship to compliance. *Arch. Gen. Psychiat., 36,* 866–869.

Janicak, P. G., & Davis, J. M. (1986). ECT versus tricyclic antidepressants: Drs. Janicak and Davis reply. *Amer. J. Psychiat., 143*(1), 121–122.

Janicak, P. G., Davis, J. M., Gibbons, R. D. et al. (1985). Efficacy of ECT: A meta-analysis. *Amer. J. Psychiat., 132,* 297–302.

Jannoun, L., McDowell, I., & Catalan, J. (1981). Behavioral treatment of anxiety is general practice. *Practitioner, 225,* 58–62.

Jannoun, L., Oppenheimer, C., & Gelder, M. (1982). A self-help treatment program for anxiety state patients. *Behav. Ther., 13*(1), 103–111.

Janowsky, D. S., & Davis, J. M. (1976). Methylphanidate, dextroamphetamine, and levamfetamine: Effects on schizophrenic symptoms. *Arch. Gen. Psychiat., 33*(3), 304–308.

Janowsky, D. S. & Risch, S. C. (1984). Adrenergic cholingergic balance and affective disorders: A review of clinical evidence and therapeutic implications. 51st Annual Meeting of the National Assoc. of Private Psychiatric Hospitals. *Psychiat. Hospital, 15*(4), 163–171.

Jansson, L., & Ost, L. G. (1982). Behavioral treatments for agoraphobia: An evaluative review. *Clin. Psychol. Rev., 2,* 311–337.

Jansson, L., Jerremalm, A., & Ost, L. G. (1986). Follow-up of agoraphobic patients treated with exposure in vivo or applied relaxation. *Brit. J. Psychiat., 149,* 486–490.

Jarvik, M. E., & Schneider, N. G. (1984). Degree of addiction and effectiveness of nicotine gum therapy for smoking. *Amer. J. Psychiat., 141,* 790–791.

Jay, S. M., Elliot, C. H., Katz, E., & Siegel, S. E. (1987). Cognitive-behavioral and pharmacologic interventions for children's distress during painful medical procedures. *J. Cons. Clin. Psychol., 55,* 860–865.

Jefferson, J. W., & Greist, J. H. (1989). Lithium therapy. In H. I. Kaplan & B. J. Sadock (Eds.), *Comprehensive textbook of psychiatry V.* Baltimore: Williams & Wilkins.

Jefferson, L. (1948). *These are my sisters.* Tulsa, OK: Vickers.

Jemmott, J. B. (1985). Psychoneuroimmunology: The new frontier. *Amer. Behav. Scientist, 28*(4), 497–509.

Jemmott, J. B. (1987). Social motives and susceptibility to disease: Stalking individual differences in health risks. *J. Pers., 55*(2), 267–298.

Jemmott, J. B., III, & Locke, S. E. (1984). Psychosocial factors, immunologic medication, and human susceptibility to infectious diseases: How much do we know? *Psychol. Bull., 95,* 78–108.

Jenike, M. A. (1985). Monoamine oxidase inhibitors as treatment for depressed patients with primary degenerative dementia. *Amer. J. Clin. Psychiat., 142*(6), 763–764.

Jenike, M. A. (1987). Affective illness in elderly patients (Pt. 2). *Psychiat. Times, 4*(3).

Jenkins, R. L. (1968). The varieties of children's behavioral problems and family dynamics. *Amer. J. Psychiat., 124*(10), 1440–1445.

Jessor, R. (1976). Predicting time of onset of marijuana use: A developmental study of high school youth. *J. Cons. Clin. Psychol., 44*(1), 125–134.

Jimerson, D. C. (1984). Neurotransmitter hypotheses of depression: Research update. *Psychiat. Clin. N. Amer., 7*(3), 563–573.

Jimerson, D. C., Lesem, M. D., Kaye, W. H., Hegg, A. P. et al. (1990). Eating disorders and depression: Is there a serotonin connection? *Bio. Psychiat., 28*(5), 443–454.

Joasoo, A., & McKenzie, J. (1976). Stress and the immune response in rats. *Inter. Arch. Allergy & Appl. Immun., 50,* 659–663.

Johnson, C., & Flach, A. (1985). Family characteristics of 105 patients with bulimia. *Amer. J. Psychiat., 142*(11), 1321–1324.

Johnson, C., & Maddi, K. L. (1986). The etiology of bulimia: Bio-psycho-social perspectives. *Ann. Adol. Psychiat., 13,* 253–273.

Johnson, C., Lewis, C., & Hagman, J. (1984). The syndrome of bulimia. *Psychiat. Clin. N. Amer., 7,* 247–274.

Johnson, C., Stuckey, M., & Mitchell, J. E. (1985). Psychopharmacology of anorexia nervosa and bulimia. In J. E. Mitchell (Ed.), *Anorexia nervosa and bulimia: Diagnosis and treatment.* Minneapolis: Univ. Minnesota.

Johnson, D. L. (1989). Schizophrenia as a brain disease: Implications for psychologists and families. *Amer. Psychol., 44*(3), 553–555.

Johnson, F. A. (1991). Psychotherapy of the elderly anxious patient. In C. Salzman & B. D. Lebowitz (Eds.), *Anxiety in the elderly.* New York: Springer.

Johnson, F. S., Hunt, G. E., Duggin, G. G., Horvath, J. S., & Tiller, D. J. (1984). Renal function and lithium treatment: Initial and follow-up tests in manic-depressive patients. *J. Affect. Dis., 6,* 249–263.

Johnson, G. T., & Leeman, M. M. (1977). Analysis of familial factors in bipolar affective illness. *Arch. Gen. Psychiat., 34*(9), 1074–1083.

Johnson, W. R. (1981). Basic interviewing skills. In C. E. Walker (Ed.), *Clinical practice of psychology.* New York: Pergamon.

Johnston, D. G., Troyer, I. E., & Whitsett, S. F. (1988). Clomipramine treatment of agoraphobic women: An eight-week controlled trial. *Arch Gen. Psychiat., 45*(5), 453–459.

Johnston, L. D. (1985). The etiology and prevention of substance use: What can we learn from recent historical changes? *National Institute Drug Abuse Research Monograph Series, 56,* 155–177.

Johnston, L. D. et al. (1991, Jan.). *Survey report.* National Institute on Drug Abuse.

Johnston, L. D., Bachman, J. G., & O'Malley, P. M. (1982). *Student drug use, attitudes and beliefs.* Washington, DC: National Institute on Drug Abuse.

Jones, B. M., & Parsons, O. A. (1971). Impaired abstracting ability in chronic alcoholics. *Arch. Gen. Psychiat., 24,* 71–75.

Jones, D., Fox, M. M., Babigian, H. M. et al. (1980). Epidemiology of anorexia nervosa in Monroe County, NY, 1960–1976. *Psychosom. Med., 42,* 551–558.

Jones, D. M. (1985). Bulimia: A false self-identity. *Clin. Soc. Work J., 13*(4), 305–316.

Jones, K. L., & Smith, D. W. (1973). Recognition of the fetal alcohol syndrome in early infancy. *Lancet, 2,* 999–1101.

Jones, K. L., & Smith, D. W. (1975). The fetal alcohol syndrome. *Teratology, 12,* 1–10.

Jones, M. C. (1924). The elimination of children's fears. *J. Exp. Psychol., 7,* 382–390.

Jones, M. C. (1968). Personality correlates and antecedants of drinking patterns in males. *J. Cons. Clin. Psychol., 32,* 2–12.

Jones, R. T. (1977). Human effects. In R. C. Peterson (Ed.), *Marijuana research findings: 1976.* NIDA Research Monograph 14. Washington, DC: GPO.

Joseph, E. (1991). Psychodynamic personality theory. In K. Davis, H. Klar, & J. J. Coyle (Eds.), *Foundations of psychiatry.* Philadelphia: Saunders.

Jourard, S. M. (1971). *Self-disclosure.* New York: Wiley.

Joyce, C. (1988). Assault on the brain. *Psych. Today, 22*(3), 38–39, 42–44.

Julien, R. M. (1985). *A primer of drug action* (4th ed.). New York: Freeman.

Jung, C. G. (1964). *The development of personality. Collected works* (Vol. 17). Princeton, NJ: Princeton Univ.

Jungman, J. (1985). De l'agir du toxicomane a l'agir du therapeute [From the drug addict's acting out to the therapist's action]. *Information Psychiatrique, 61*(3), 383–388.

Kadushin, C. (1969). *Why people go to psychiatrists.* New York: Atherton.

Kahn, A. (1982). The moment of truth: Psychotherapy with the suicidal patient. In E. Bassuk, S. G. Schoonover, & A. D. Gill, *Lifelines.* New York: Plenum.

Kahn, R. J., & Lipman, R. (1987). Efficacy of imipramine and chloradiazepoxide in depressive and anxiety disorders questions. *Arch. Gen. Psychiat., 44*(1), 97–98.

Kahneman, D., & Tversky, A. (1973). On the psychology of prediction. *Psych. Rev., 80*(4), 237–251.

Kahneman, D., Slovic, P., & Tversky, A. (Eds.). (1982). *Judgment under uncertainty: Heuristics and biases.* Cambridge: Cambridge Univ.

Kalinowsky, L. B. (1980). Convulsive therapies. In H. I. Kaplan, A. M. Freedman, & B. J. Sadock (Eds.), *Comprehensive textbook of psychiatry* (Vol. 3). Baltimore: Williams & Wilkins.

Kallman, W. M., & Feuerstein, M. J. (1986). Psychophysiological procedures. In A. R. Ciminero, K. S. Calhoun, & H. E. Adams, (Eds.), *Handbook of behavioral assessment* (2nd ed.). New York: Wiley.

Kane, J., Honigfeld, G., Singer, J., Meltzer, H. et al. (1988). Clozapine for the treatment-resistent schizophrenic: A double-blind comparison with chlorpromazine. *Arch. Gen. Psychiat., 45*(9), 789–796.

Kane, J. M. (1986). Somatic therapy. In A. J. Frances & R. E. Hales (Eds.), *Psychiatric update — American Psychiatric Association annual review* (Vol. 5). Washington, DC: American Psychiatric.

Kane, J. M. (1987). Treatment of schizophrenia. *Schizo. Bull., 13*(1), 133–156.

Kane, J. M. (1990). Treatment programme and long-term outcome in chronic schizophrenia. International Symposium: Development of a new antipsychotic: Remoxipride (1989, Monte Carlo, Monaco). *Acta Psychiatr. Scandin., 82*(385, Suppl.), 151–157.

Kane, J. M., Woerner, M., Lieberman, J., & Rabiner, C. J. (1984). Studies on the long-term treatment of schizophrenia. *Psychiat. Hosp., 15*(4), 179–183.

Kane, M. T., & Kendall, P. C. (1989). *Anxiety disorders in children: A multiple-baseline evaluation of a cognitive-behavioral treatment.*

Kanfer, F. H., & Philips, J. S. (1970). *Learning foundations of behavior therapy.* New York: Wiley.

Kanner, A. D., Coyne, J. C., Schaefer, C., & R. S. Lazarus. (1981). Comparison of two modes of stress measurement: Daily hassles and uplifts versus major life events. *J. Behav. Med., 4,* 1–39.

Kanner, L. (1943). Autistic disturbances of affective contact. *Nerv. Child. 2,* 217.

Kanner, L. (1954). To what extent is early infantile autism determined by constitutional inadequacies? *Proceedings of the Association for Research in Nervous and Mental Diseases, 33,* 378–385.

Kanof, P. (1991). Neurotransmitter receptor function. In K. Davis,

H. Klar, & J. T. Coyle (Eds.), *Foundations of psychiatry.* Philadelphia: Saunders.

Kanter, N. J., & Goldfried, M. R. (1979). Rational restructuring vs. self-control desensitization for interpersonal anxiety. *Behav. Ther., 10,* 472–490.

Kantor, J. S., Zitrin, C. M., & Zeldis, S. M. (1980). Mitral valve prolapse syndrome in agoraphobic patients. *Amer. J. Psychiat., 137,* 467–469.

Kaplan, H. I., & Sadock, B. J. (1989). Typical signs and symptoms of psychiatric illness. In H. I. Kaplan & B. J. Sadock (Eds.), *Comprehensive textbook of psychiatry* (Vol. 1, 5th ed.). Baltimore: Williams & Wilkins.

Kaplan, H. S. (1974). *The new sex therapy: Active treatment of sexual dysfunction.* New York: Brunner/Mazel.

Kaplan, H. S. (1977). Hypoactive sexual desire. *J. Sex & Marital Ther., 3,* 3–9.

Kaplan, H. S. (1979). *Disorders of sexual desire.* New York: Brunner/Mazel.

Kaplan, N. M. (1980). The control of hypertension: A therapeutic breakthrough. *Amer. Scientist, 68*(5), 537–545.

Kaplan, R. L., & Sadock, B. J. (1989). Psychiatric report. In H. I. Kaplan & B. J. Sadock (Eds.), *Comprehensive textbook of psychiatry* (Vol. 1, 5th ed.). Baltimore: Williams & Wilkins.

Kaplan, R. M., McCordick, S. M., & Twitchell, M. (1979). Is it the cognitive or the behavioral component which makes cognitive-behavior modification effective in test anxiety? *J. Couns. Psychol., 26*(5), 371–377.

Kaplan, W. (1984). *The relationship between depression and anti-social behavior among a court-referred adolescent population.* Presented to the American Academy of Child Psychiatry, Toronto.

Karoly, P., & Rosenthal, M. (1977). Training parents in behavior modification: Effects on perceptions of family interaction and deviant child behavior. *Behav. Ther., 8*(3), 406–410.

Karon, B. P. (1985). Omission in review of treatment interactions. *Schizo. Bull., 11*(1), 16–17.

Karon, B. P. (1988). Cited in T. De Angelis, "Resistance to therapy seen in therapists, too." *APA Monitor,* 21.

Kashani, J. H., Husain, A., Shekim, W., Hodges, K., Cytryn, L., & McKnew, D. (1981). Current perspectives on childhood depression: An overview. *Amer. J. Psychiat., 138,* 143–153.

Kasl, S. V., & Cobb, S. (1970). Blood pressure changes in men undergoing job loss: A preliminary report. *Psychosom. Med., 32*(1), 19–38.

Kastenbaum, R. (1988). In moderation: How some older people find pleasure and meaning in alcoholic beverages. *Generations, 12*(4), 68–73.

Katz, A. H., & Bender, E. I. (1976). Self-help groups in western society: History and prospects. *J. Appl. Behav. Sci., 12*(3), 265–282.

Katz, J. L. (1986). Long-distance running, anorexia nervosa, and bulimia: A report of two cases. *Comprehen. Psychiat., 27*(1), 74–78.

Katz, R. J., & DeVeaugh-Geiss, J. (1990). The antiobsessional effects of clomipramine do not require concomitant affective disorder. *Psychiat. Res., 31*(2), 121–129.

Katzman, R. (1981, June). Early detection of senile dementia. *Hosp. Practitioner,* 61–76.

Kaufman, I., Frank, T., Heims, L., Herrick, J., Reiser, D., & Willer, L. (1960). Treatment implications of a new classification of parents of schizophrenic children. *Amer. J. Psychiat., 116,* 920–924.

Kaufmann, C. L., & Roth, L. H. (1981). Psychiatric evaluation of patient decision-making: Informed consent to ECT. *Soc. Psychiat., 16*(1), 11–19.

Kay, D. W. K., Fahy, T., & Garside, R. F. (1970). A seven-month double-blind trial of amitriptyline and diazepam in ECT-treated depressed patients. *Brit. J. Psychiat., 117,* 667–671.

Kay, S. R., & Singh, M. M. (1989). The positive-negative distinction in drug-free schizophrenic patients: Stability, response to neuroleptics, and prognostic significance. *Arch. Gen. Psychiat., 46*(8), 711–718.

Kaye, W. H. (1985). Eating disorders: Too little or too much. *Bio. Psychiat., 20*(3), 233–234.

Kazdin, A. E. (1975). *Behavior modification in applied settings.* Homewood, IL: Dorsey.

Kazdin, A. E. (1975). Covert modelling, imagery assessment, and assertive behavior. *J. Cons. Clin. Psychol., 43,* 716–724.

Kazdin, A. E. (1977). Artifact, bias, and complexity of assessment: The ABCs of reliability. *J. Appl. Behav. Anal., 10,* 141–150.

Kazdin, A. E. (1977). The influence of behavior preceding reinforced response on behavior change in the classroom. *J. Appl. Behav. Anal.,* 10(2), 299–310.

Kazdin, A. E. (1978). Behavior therapy: Evolution and expansion. *Couns. Psychol.,* 7(3), 34–37.

Kazdin, A. E. (1978). *History of behavior modification.* Baltimore: Univ. Park.

Kazdin, A. E. (1979). Advances in child behavior therapy. *Amer. Psychol.,* 34, 981–987.

Kazdin, A. E. (1979). Nonspecific treatment factors in psychotherapy outcome research. *J. Cons. Clin. Psychol.,* 47(4), 725–733.

Kazdin, A. E. (1986). Comparative outcome studies of psychotherapy: Methodological issues and strategies [Special Issue]. *J. Cons. Clin. Psychol.,* 54(1), 95–105.

Kazdin, A. E. (1989). Childhood depression. In E. J. Mash & R. Barkley (Eds.), *Treatment of childhood disorders.* New York: Guilford.

Kazdin, A. E., & Wilcoxon, L. A. (1976). Systematic desensitization and nonspecific treatment effects: A methodological evaluation. *Psychol. Bull.,* 83(5), 729–758.

Keane, T. M., & Kaloupek, D. G. (1982). Imaginal flooding in the treatment of a post-traumatic stress disorder. *J. Cons. Clin. Psychol.,* 50(1), 138–140.

Kebabian, J. W., & Calne, D. B. (1979). Multiple receptors for dopamine. *Nature, 277,* 93–96.

Keen, E. (1970). *Three faces of being: Toward an existential clinical psychology.* By the Meredith Corp. Reprinted by permission of Irvington Publishers.

Kegel, A. (1952). Sexual functions of the pubococcygeus muscle. *Western J. Surgical Obstetrics & Gynecology, 60,* 521–524.

Keller, M. B., Shapiro, R. W., Lavori, P. W., & Wolfe, N. (1982). Relapse in major depressive disorder. *Arch. Gen. Psychiat., 39,* 911–915.

Keller, R., & Shaywitz, B. A. (1986). Amnesia or fugue state: A diagnostic dilemma. *J. Dev. Behav. Pediatrics,* 7(8), 131–132.

Keller, S. E., Weiss, J., Schleifer, S. J., Miller, N. E., & Stein, M. (1981). Suppression of immunity by stress: Effect of a graded series of stressors on lymphocyte stimulation in the rat. *Psychosom. Med., 43,* 91.

Kelley, R. L., & Kodman, F. (1987). A more unified view of the Multiple Personality Disorder. *Soc. Behav. Pers.,* 15(2), 165–167.

Kelly, J. B. (1982). Divorce: An adult perspective. In B. B. Wolman (Ed.), *Handbook of developmental psychology.* Englewood Cliffs, NJ: Prentice-Hall.

Kelsoe, J. R., Ginns, E. I., Egeland, J. A., Garhard, D. S. et al. (1988). Re-evaluation of the linkage relationship between chromosome 11p loci and the gene for bipolar affective disorder in the Old Order Amish. *Nature, 342*(6247), 238–243.

Kendall, P. C. (1989). Maintenance and generalization of behavior change: Comments, considerations, and the "no-cure" criticism. *Behav. Ther., 20,* 499–508.

Kendall, P. C. (Ed.). (1990). *Child and adolescent therapy: Cognitive-behavioral procedures.* New York: Guilford.

Kendall, P. C., & Braswell, L. (Eds.). (1985). *Cognitive-behavioral therapy for impulsive children.* New York: Guilford.

Kendall, P. C., & Hollon, S. D. (1989). Anxious self talk: Development of the anxious self statements questionnaire (ASSQ). *Cog. Ther. Res.,* 13(1), 81–93.

Kendall, P. C. & Hollon, S. D. (Eds.). (1981). *Assessment strategies for cognitive-behavior interventions.* New York: Academic.

Kendall, P. C., & Watson, D. (Eds.). (1989). *Anxiety and depression: Distinctive overlapping features.* San Diego: Academic.

Kendall, P. C., Chansky, T. E., Freidman, M., Kim, R., Kortlander, E., Sessa, F. M., & Siquelard, L. (1991). Treating anxiety disorders in children and adolescents. In P. C. Kendall (Ed.), *Child and adolescent therapy: Cognitive-behavioral procedures.* New York: Guilford.

Kendall, P. C., Howard, B. L., & Hays, R. C. (1989). Self-referrent speech and psychopathology: The balance of positive and negative thinking. *Cog. Ther. Res.,* 13(6) 583–598.

Kendall, P. C., Kane, M., Howard, B., & Siqueland, L. (1989). *Cognitive-behavioral therapy for anxious children: Treatment manual.* Philadelphia: Temple Univ.

Kendler, K. S. (1983). Computer analysed EEG findings in children of schizophrenic parents ("high risk" children): Commentary. *Integ. Psychiat.,* 1(3), 82–83.

Kendler, K. S., Heath, A., Martin, N. C., & Eaves, L. J. (1986). Symptoms of anxiety and depression in a volunteer twin popula-

tion: The antiologic role of genetic and environmental factors. *Arch. Gen. Psychiat.,* 43(3), 213–221.

Kendler, K. S., Masterson, C. C., & Davis, K. L. (1985). Psychiatric illness in first-degree relatives of patients with paranoid psychosis, schizophrenia and medical illness. *Brit. J. Psychiat., 147,* 524–531.

Kennedy, J. L., Giuffra, L. A., Moises, H. W. et al. (1988). Evidence against linkage of schizophrenia to markers on chromosome 5 in a northern Swedish pedigree. *Nature, 336,* 167–168.

Kent, R. N., & Foster, S. L. (1977). Direct observational procedures: Methodological issues in applied settings. In A. Ciminero, K. S. Calhoun, & H. E. Adams (Eds.), *Handbook of behavioral assessment.* New York: Wiley.

Kent, R. N., O'Leary, K. D., Diament, C., & Dietz, A. (1974). Expectation biases in observational evaluation of therapeutic change. *J. Cons. Clin. Psychol.,* 42(6), 774–780.

Kety, S. (1974). Biochemical and neurochemical effects of electro-convulsive shock. In M. Fink, S. Kety, J. McGaugh et al. (Eds.), *Psychobiology of convulsive therapy.* Washington, DC: Winston & Sons.

Kety, S. S. (1974). From rationalization to reason. *Amer. J. Psychiat.,* 131(9), 957–963.

Kety, S. S. (1988). Schizophrenic illness in the families of schizophrenic adoptees: Findings from the Danish national sample. *Schizo. Bull.,* 14(2), 217–222.

Kety, S. S., Rosenthal, D., Wender, P. H. et al. (1968). The types and prevalence of mental illness in the biological and adoptive families of schizophrenics. *J. Psychiat. Res., 6,* 345–362.

Kety, S. S., Rosenthal, D., Wender, P. H. et al. (1971). Mental illness in the biological and adoptive families of adopted schizophrenics. *Amer. J. Psychiat., 138,* 302–306.

Kety, S. S., Rosenthal, D., Wender, P. H. et al. (1975). Mental illness in the biological and adoptive families of adopted individuals who became shcizophrenic: A preliminary report based on psychiatric interviews. In R. R. Fieve, D. Rosenthal, & H. Brill (Eds.), *Genetic research in psychiatry.* Baltimore: Johns Hopkins Univ.

Keuthen, N. (1980). *Subjective probability estimation and somatic structures in phobic individuals.* Unpublished manuscript. State University of New York at Stony Brook.

Keys, A., Brozek, J., Henschel, A., Mickelson, O., & Taylor, H. L. (1950). *The biology of human starvation.* Minneapolis: Univ. Minnesota.

Khantzian, E. J. (1985). The self-medication hypothesis of addictive disorders: Focus on heroin and cocaine dependence. *Amer. J. Psychiat.,* 142(11), 1259–1264.

Kidd, J. W. (1970). The "adultated" mentally retarded. Education and training of the mentally retarded. *Education & Training of the Mentally Retarded, 5,* 71–72.

Kiecolt-Glaser, J. K., & Glaser, R. (1988). Psychological influences on immunity: Implications for AIDS. *Amer. Psychol.,* 43(11), 892–898.

Kiecolt-Glaser, J. K., Garner, W., Speicher, C., Penn, G. M., Holliday, J., & Glaser, R. (1984). Psychosocial modifiers of immuno-competence in medical students. *Psychosom. Med. 46,* 7–14

Kiecolt-Glaser, J. K., Glaser, R., Shuttleworth, E. C., Dyer, C. S., Ogrocki, B. S., & Speicher, C. E. (1987). Chronic stress and immunity in family caregivers of Alzheimer's Disease victims. *Psychosom. Med., 49,* 523–535.

Kiecolt-Glaser, J. K., Ricker, D., Messick, G., Speicher, C. E., Garner, W., & Glaser, R. (1984). Urinary cortisol, cellular immunocompetency and loneliness in psychiatric patients. *Psychosom. Med., 46,* 15–24.

Kienhorst, C. W. M., Wolters, W. H. G., Diekstra, R. F. W., & Otte, E. (1987). A study of the frequency of suicidal behaviour in children aged 5 to 14. *J. Child Psychol. Psychiat.,* 28(1), 151–165.

Kiernan, C. (1981). Behavior modification and the development of communication. In P. J. Mittler & J. M. deJong (Eds.), *Frontiers of knowledge in mental retardation: Vol. 1. Social, educational and behavioral aspects.* Baltimore: Univ. Park.

Kihlstrom, J. F. (1978). Context and cognition in posthypnotic amnesia. *Inter. J. Clin. Exp. Hyp.,* 26(4), 246–267.

Kihlstrom, J. F. (1980). Posthypnotic amnesia for recently learned material: Interactions with "episodic" and "semantic" memory. *Cog. Psychol.,* 12(2), 227–251.

Kilcourse, J., Gallagher-Thompson, D., Thompson, L. W., & Sheikh, J. (1991). The relationship between anxiety and depression in other adults. *J. Geriatric Psych.*

Killilea, M. (1976). Mutual help organizations: Interpretations in the literature. In G. Caplan & M. Killilea (Eds.), *Support systems and mutual help: Multidisciplinary explorations.* New York: Grune & Stratton.

Kilmann, P. R., & Sotile, W. M. (1976). The marathon encounter group: A review of the outcome of literature. *Psychol. Bull., 83*(5), 827–850.

Kilmann, P. R., Sabalis, R. F., Gearing, M. L., Bukstel, L. H., & Scovern, A. W. (1982). The treatment of sexual paraphilias: A review of outcome research. *J. Sex Res., 18,* 193–252.

Kilmann, P. R., Wagner, M. K., & Sotile, W. M. (1977). The differential impact of self-monitoring on smoking behavior: An exploratory study. *J. Clin. Psychol., 33*(3), 912–914.

Kiloh, L. G. (1982). Electroconvulsive therapy. In E. S. Paykel (Ed.), *Handbook of affective disorders.* New York: Guilford.

Kilpatrick, D. G., Best, C. L., Veronen, L. J., Amick, A. E., Vileponteaux, L. A., & Ruff, G. A. (1985). Mental health correlates of criminal victiminization: A random community survey. *J. Cons. Clin. Psychol., 53,* 866–873.

Kilpatrick, D. G., Saunders, B. E., Veronen, L. J., Best, C. L., & Von, J. M. (1987). Criminal victimization: Lifetime prevalence, reporting to police, and psychological impact. *Crime & Delinquency, 33,* 479–489.

Kilpatrick, D. G., Sutker, P. B., Best, C. L., & Allain, A. N. (1981). Effects of a rape experience: A longitudinal study. *J. Soc. Issues, 37*(4), 105–122.

Kimmel, D. C. (1988). Ageism, psychology, and public policy. *Amer. Psychol., 43*(3), 175–178.

Kimmel, E., & Kimmel, H. D. (1963). A replication of operant conditioning of the GSR. *J. Exp. Psychol., 65*(2), 212–213.

Kimzey, S. L. (1975). The effects of extended spaceflight on hematologic and immunologic systems. *J. Amer. Med. Women's Assoc., 30*(5), 218–232.

Kimzey, S. L., Johnson, P. C., Ritzman, S. E., & Mengel, C. E. (1976, Apr.). Hematology and immunology studies: The second manned Skylab mission. *Aviation, Space, & Environmental Medicine,* 383–390.

Kincel, R. L. (1981). Suicide and its archetypal themes in Rorschach record study of a male attempter. *Brit. J. Projective Psychol. & Pers. Study, 26*(2), 3–11.

King, C. A., & Young, R. D. (1981). Peer popularity and peer communication patterns: Hyperactive vs. active but normal boys. *J. Abnorm. Child Psychol., 9*(4), 465–482.

King, L. W., Liberman, R. P., & Roberts, J. (1974). *An evaluation of personal effectiveness training (assertive training): A behavior group therapy.* Paper presented at 31st Annual conference of American Group Psychotherapy Association, New York.

King, R. D., & Raynes, N. V. (1967). *Some determinants of patterns of residual care.* First Congress of the International Association for the Scientific Study of Mental Deficiency.

Kinsey, A. C., Pomeroy, W. B., & Martin, C. E. (1948). *Sexual behavior in the human male.* Philadelphia: Saunders.

Kinsey, A. C., Pomeroy, W. B., Martin, C. E., & Gebhard, P. H. (1953). *Sexual behavior in the human female.* Philadelphia: Saunders.

Kinston, W., & Rosser, R. (1974). Disaster: Effects of mental and physical state. *J. Psychosom. Res., 18,* 437–456.

Kipnis, D. (1987). Psychology and behavioral technology. *Amer. Psychol., 42*(1), 30–36.

Kipper, D. A. (1977). Behavior therapy for fears brought on by war experiences. *J. Cons. Clin. Psychol., 45*(2), 216–221.

Kirk, S. A., & Therrien, M. E. (1975). Community mental health myths and the fate of former hospitalized patients. *Psychiatry, 38*(3), 209–217.

Kirkland, K., & Hollandsworth, J. G. (1980). Effective test taking: Skills-acquisition versus anxiety-reduction techniques. *J. Cons. Clin. Psychol., 48*(4), 431–439.

Kirsling, R. A. (1986). Review of suicide among elderly persons. *Psych. Rep., 59*(2, Pt. 1), 359–366.

Klaber, M. M. (1969). The retarded and institutions for the retarded. In S. B. Saranson & J. Doris (Eds.), *Psychological problems in mental deficiency.* New York: Harper & Row.

Kleber, H. D., & Gawin, F. H. (1987). "Cocaine withdrawal": In reply. *Arch. Gen. Psychiat., 44*(3), 298.

Kleber, H. D., & Gawin, F. H. (1987). "The physiology of cocaine craving and 'crashing' ": In reply. *Arch. Gen. Psychiat., 44*(3), 299–300.

Kleber, H. D. et al. (1985). Clonidine in outpatient detoxification from methadone maintenance. *Arch. Gen. Psychiat., 42*(4), 391–394.

Klein, D. F. (1964). Delineation of two drug-responsive anxiety syndromes. *Psychopharmacologia, 5,* 397–408.

Klein, D. F. (1981). Anxiety reconceptualized. In D. F. Klein & J. Rabkin (Eds.), *Anxiety: New research and changing concepts.* New York: Raven.

Klein, D. F., & Fink, M. (1962). Psychiatric reaction patterns to imipramine. *Amer. J. Psychiat., 119,* 432–438.

Klein, D. F., & Gorman, J. M. (1987). A model of panic and agoraphobic development. Symposium: Panic disorder (1986, Gothenburg, Sweden). *Acta Psychiatr. Scandin., 76*(335, Suppl.), 87–95.

Klein, D. F., Zitrin, C. M., Woerner, M. G., & Ross, D. C. (1983). Treatment of phobias: II. Behavior therapy and supportive psychotherapy. *Arch. Gen. Psychiat., 40,* 139–145.

Kleinman, I., Schacter, D., & Koritar, E. (1989). Informed consent and tardive dyskinesia. *Amer. J. Psychiat., 146*(7), 902–904.

Kleinman, J. E., Casanova, M. F., & Jaskiw, G. E. (1988). The neuropathology of schizophrenia. *Schizo. Bull., 14*(2).

Kleinmuntz, B. (1963). MMPI decision rules for the identification of college maladjustment: A digital computer approach. *Psychological Monographs, 77*(14, Whole No. 477).

Kleinmuntz, B. (1967). *Personality measurement: An introduction.* Homewood, IL: Dorsey.

Kleinmuntz, B. (1972). *Computers in personality assessment,* Morristown, NJ: General Learning.

Kleinmuntz, B. (1972). Minnesota Multiphasic Personality Inventory: Computerized scoring and interpreting services. In O. K. Buros (Ed.), *The 7th mental measurements yearbook* (Vol. 1). Highland Park, NJ: Gryphon.

Kleinmuntz, B., & Szucko, J. J. (1984). Lie detection in ancient and modern times: A call for contemporary scientific study. *Amer. Psychol., 39*(7), 766–776.

Klemmack, D. L., & Roff, L. L. (1984). Fear of personal aging and subjective well-being in later life. *J. Gerontology, 39*(6), 756–758.

Klerman, G. L. (1978). Long-term treatment of affective disorders. In M. Lipton, A. DiMascio, & K. F. Killam (Eds.), *Psychopharmacology: A generation of progress.* New York: Raven.

Klerman, G. L. (1981). The spectrum of mania. *Comprehen. Psychiat., 22,* 11–20.

Klerman, G. L. (1984). Characterologic manifestations of affective disorders: Toward a new conceptualization: Commentary. *Integr. Psychiat., 2*(3), 94–96.

Klerman, G. L. (1984). History and development of modern concepts of affective illness. In R. M. Post & J. C. Ballenger (Eds.), *Neurobiology of affective disorders.* Baltimore: Williams & Wilkins.

Klerman, G. L. (1986). Drugs and psychotherapy. In S. L. Garfield & A. E. Bergin (Eds.), *Handbook of psychotherapy and behavior change: An evaluation analysis* (3rd ed.). New York: Wiley.

Klerman, G. L. (1987). Cognitive dysfunction, vulnerability, and integrating theories of depression. *Integ. Psychiat., 5*(1), 32–35.

Klerman, G. L. (1987). The classification of bipolar disorders. *Psychiat. Ann., 17*(1), 13–17.

Klerman, G. L. (1988). Overview of the cross-national collaborative panic study. *Arch. Gen. Psychiat., 45*(5), 407–412.

Klerman, G. L., Weissman, M., Rounsaville, B., Chevron, E. (1984). *Interpersonal psychotherapy of depression.* New York: Basic.

Kline, N. S. (1958). Clinical experience with iproniazid (Marsilid). *J. Clin. Exp. Psychopath., 19*(1, Suppl.), 72–78.

Klineberg, O. (1963). Negro-white differences in intelligence test performance: A new look at an old problem. *Amer. Psychol., 18*(4), 198–203.

Klinefelter, D. S. (1984). The morality of suicide. *Soundings, 67*(3), 345–346.

Klopfer, B., & Davidson, H. (1962). *The Rorschach technique.* New York: Harcourt, Brace.

Kluft, R. P. (1982). Varieties of hypnotic interventions in the treatment of multiple personality. *Amer. J. Clin. Hyp., 24,* 230–240.

Kluft, R. P. (1983). Hypnotherapeutic crisis intervention in multiple personality. *Amer. J. Clin. Hyp., 26*(2), 73–83.

Kluft, R. P. (1984). Treatment of multiple personality disorder: A study of 33 cases. *Psychiat. Clin. N. Amer., 7*(1), 9–29.

Kluft, R. P. (1985). Hypnotherapy of childhood multiple personality disorder. *Amer. J. Clin. Hyp., 27*(4), 201–210.

Kluft, R. P. (Ed.). (1985). *Childhood antecedents of multiple personality.* Washington, DC: American Psychiatric.

Kluft, R. P. (1987). An update on multiple personality disorder. *J. Hosp. Comm. Psychiat., 38*(4), 363–373.

Kluft, R. P. (1987). The simulation and dissimulation of multiple personality disorder. *Amer. J. Clin. Hyp., 30*(2), 104–118.

Kluft, R. P. (1988). The dissociative disorders. In J. Talbott, R. Hales, & S. Yudofsky (Eds.), *Textbook of psychiatry.*

Kluft, R. P. (1991). Multiple personality disorder. In A. Tasman & S. M. Goldfinger (Eds.), *American Psychiatric Press review of psychiatry* (Vol. 10). Washington, DC: American Psychiatric.

Knesper, D. J., Pagnucco, D. J. (1987). Estimated distribution of effort by providers of mental health services to U.S. adults in 1982 and 1983. *Amer. J. Psychiat., 144*(7), 883–888.

Knesper, D. J., Pagnucco, D. J., & Wheeler, J. R. (1985). Similarities and differences across mental health services providers and practice settings in the United States. *Amer. Psychol., 40*(12), 1352–1369.

Knesper, D. J., Wheeler, J. R., & Pagnucco, D. J. (1985). Mental health services providers' distribution across counties in the United States. *Amer. Psychol., 39*(12), 1424–1434.

Knight, J. G. (1985). Possible autoimmune mechanisms in schizophrenia. *Interg. Psychiat., 3*(2), 134–138.

Knobel, D. (1983). Encounter resistance and logotherapy: Application of logotherapy to the psychotherapy of schizophrenia and borderline conditions. *Israel J. Psychiat. & Related Sci., 20*(4), 337–345.

Kobasa, S. C. (1979). Stressful life events, personality, and health: An inquiry into hardiness. *J. Pers. Soc. Psychol., 37*(1), 1–11.

Kobasa, S. C., Hiller, R. R. J., & Maddi, S. R. (1979). Who stays healthy under stress? *J. Occupational Med., 21,* 595–598.

Kobasa, S. C., Maddi, S. R., & Kahn, S. (1982). Hardiness and health: A prospective study. *J. Pers. Soc. Psychol., 42*(1), 168–177.

Koch, R., & Dobson, J. C. (1971). *The mentally retarded child and his family: A multidisciplinary handbook.* New York: Brunner/Mazel.

Koegel, R. L., & Covert, A. (1972). The relationship of self-stimulation to learning in autistic children. *J. Appl. Behav. Anal., 5,* 381–387.

Koegel, R. L., & Rincover, A. (1977). Research on the difference between generalization and maintenance in extra-therapy responding. *J. Appl. Behav. Anal., 10*(1), 1–12.

Koegel, R. L., Firestone, P. B., Kramme, K. W., & Dunlap, G. (1974). Increasing spontaneous play by suppressing self-stimulation in autistic children. *J. Appl. Behav. Anal., 7,* 521–528.

Kog, E., Vertommen, H., & Degroote, T. (1985). Family interaction research in anorexia nervosa: The use and misuse of a self-report questionnaire. *Inter. J. Fam. Psychiat., 6*(3), 227–243.

Kohn, P. M., Annis, H. M., Lei, H., & Chan, D. W. (1985). Further tests of a metamodel of youthful marijuana use. *Pers. & Individual Differences, 6*(6), 753–763.

Kolb, L. C. (1956). Psychotherapeutic evolution and its implications. *Psychiat. Quart., 30,* 1–19.

Kolb, L. C. (1983). Return of the repressed: Delayed stress reaction to war. *J. Amer. Acad. Psychoanal., 11*(4), 531–545.

Kolb, L. C., Burris, B. C., & Griffiths, S. (1984). Propranolol and clonidine and the treatment of post traumatic stress disorders of war. In B. A. van der Kolk (Ed.), *Post-Traumatic Stress Disorder: Psychological and Biological Sequelae.* Washington, DC: American Psychiatric.

Kolodny, R. C., Masters, W. H., Kolodner, R. M., & Toro, G. (1974). Depression of plasma testosterone levels after chronic intensive marihuana use. *New Engl. J. Med., 290*(16), 444.

Kolodny, R., Masters, W., & Johnson, J. (1979). *Textbook of sexual medicine.* Boston: Little, Brown.

Kondziela, J. R. (1984). Extreme lithium intoxication without severe symptoms. *Hosp. Comm. Psychiat., 35*(7), 727–728.

Konig, P., & Godfrey, S. (1973). Prevalence of exercise-induced bronchial liability in families of children with asthma. *Arch. Diseases of Childhood, 48,* 518.

Konopka, G. (1983). Adolescent suicide. *Exceptional Children, 49*(5), 390–394.

Kootz, J. P., Marinelli, B., & Cohen, D. J. (1982). Modulation of response to environmental stimulation in autistic children. *J. Autism Dev. Dis., 12,* 185–193.

Kopelman, M. D. (1987). Amnesia: Organic and psychogenic. *Brit. J. Psychiat., 150,* 428–442.

Koppitz, E. (1965). *The Bender-Gestalt test for young children.* New York: Grune & Stratton.

Koran, L. M. (1986). Inpatient care of patients with concomitant medical and psychiatric disorders. In A. J. Frances & R. E. Hales (Eds.), *Psychiatric Update — American Psychiatric Association annual review* (Vol. 5). Washington, DC: American Psychiatric.

Korchin, S. J. (1976). *Modern clinical psychology: Principles of intervention in the clinic and community.* New York: Basic.

Korchin, S. J., & Sands, S. H. (1983). Principles common to all psychotherapies. In C. E. Walker et al. (Eds.), *The handbook of clinical psychology.* Homewood, IL: Dow Jones-Irwin.

Kornhuber, J., Kim, J., Kornhuber, M. E., & Kornhuber, H. H. (1984). The cortico-nigral projection: Reduced glutamate content in the substantia nigra following frontal cortex ablation in the rat. *Brain Res., 322*(1), 124–126.

Korsten, M. A. et al. (1975). High blood acetaldehyde levels after ethanol administration. *New Engl. J. Med., 292*(8), 385–389.

Kosky, R. J. (1989). Should sex offenders be treated? *Austral. New Zeal. J. Psychiat., 23*(2), 176–180.

Koss, M. (1990, Aug.). *Testimony.* Senate Judiciary Committee.

Koss, M., & Harvey, M. (1987). *The rape victim.* Lexington, MA: Stephen Green.

Koss, M. P. (1990). The women's mental health research agenda: Violence against women. *Amer. Psychol., 45*(3), 374–380.

Koss, M. P., Dinero, T. E., Seibel, C., & Cox, S. (1988). Stranger and acquaintance rape: Are there differences in the victim's experience? *Psychol. Women Quart., 12,* 1–23.

Koss, M. P., Gidycz, C. A., & Wisniewski, N. (1987). The scope of rape: Incidence and prevalence of sexual aggression and victimization in a national sample of higher education students. *J. Cons. Clin. Psychol., 55,* 162–170.

Kosten, T. R., Rounsaville, B. J., Babor, T. F., Spitzer, R. L. et al. (1987). The dependence syndrome across different psychoactive substances: Revised DSM-III. *National Institute on Drug Abuse: Research Monograph Series, 76,* 255–258.

Kosterlitz, H. W., & Hughes, J. (1975). Some thoughts on the significance of enkephalin, the endogenous ligand. *Life Sciences, 17*(1), 91–96.

Kostlan, A. (1954). A method for the empirical study of psychodiagnosis. *J. Cons. Psychol., 18,* 83–88.

Kovacs, M., & Beck, A. T. (1977). An empirical clinical approach towards a definition of childhood depression. In J. G. Schulterbrandt & A. Raskin (Eds.), *Depression in children.* New York: Raven.

Kovacs, M., Rush, A. J., Beck, A. T., & Hollon, S. D. (1981). Depressed outpatients treated with cognitive therapy or pharmacotherapy: A one-year follow-up. *Arch. Gen. Psychiat., 38*(1), 33–39.

Koyama, T., Lowy, M. T., & Meltzer, H. Y. (1987). 5-hydroxytryptophan induced cortisol response and SCF 5 HIAA in depressed patients. *Amer. J. Psychiat., 144*(3), 334–337.

Kozak, M. J., Foa, E. B., & Steketee, G. (1988). Process and outcome of exposure treatment with obsessive-compulsives: Psychophysiological indicators of emotional processing. *Behav. Ther. 19*(2), 157–169.

Kozak, M. J., Rossi, M., McCarthy, P. R., & Foa, E. B. (1989). Effects of imipramine on the autonomic responses of obsessive-compulsives to auditory tones. *Bio. Psychiat., 26*(7), 707–716.

Krafft-Ebing, R. V. (1975). *Psychopathia sexualis.* New York: Putnam. (Original work published in 1886)

Kramer, M. (1983). *The continuing challenge: The rising prevalence of mental disorder associated chronic diseases and disabling conditions.* American Public Health Association Meeting: 25 years of mental health in public health and challenges for the future. *Amer. J. Soc. Psychiat., 3*(4), 13–24.

Krantz, D. S., & Glass, D. C. (1984). Personality, behavior, patterns, and physical illness: Conceptual and methodological issues. In W. D. Gentry (Ed.), *Handbook of behavioral medicine.* New York: Guilford.

Kratochwill, T. R., Mott, S. E., & Dodson, C. L. (1984). Case study and single-case research in clinical and applied psychology. In A. S. Bellack & M. Hersen (Eds.), *Research methods in clinical psychology.* New York: Pergamon.

Krauthammer, C., & Klerman, G. L. (1979). The epidemiology of mania. In B. Shopsin (Ed.), *Manic illness.* New York: Raven.

Kreisman, D., Blumenthal, R., Borenstein, M., Woerner, M. et al. (1988). *Family attitudes and patient social adjustment in a longitudinal study of outpatient schizophrenics receiving low-dose neuroleptics: The family's view.* Meeting of the Society for Life History Research on Psychopathology (1984, Baltimore, Maryland). *Psychiatry, 51*(1), 3–13.

Kriechman, A. M. (1987). Siblings with somatoform disorders in childhood and adolescence. *J. Amer. Acad. Child Adol. Psychiat., 26*(2), 226–231.

Kringlen, E. (1965). Obsessional neurosis: A long-term follow-up *Brit. J. Psychiat., 111,* 709–722.

Kripke, D. F., & Robinson, D. (1985). Ten years with a lithium group. *McLean Hosp. J., 10*, 1–11.

Kripke, D. T. (1985). Therapeutic effects of bright light in depressed patients. *Ann. NY Acad. Sci., 453*, 270–281.

Kron, L., Katz, J. L., Gorzynski, & Weiner, H. (1978). Hyperactivity in anorexia nervosa: A fundamental clinical feature. *Comprehen. Psychiat., 19*(5), 433–440.

Kuhn, R. (1958). The treatment of depressive states with G-22355 (imipramine hydrochloride). *Amer. J. Psychiat., 115*, 459–464.

Kuhn, T. S. (1962). *The structure of scientific revolutions.* Chicago: Univ. Chicago.

Kulick, A. R. Pope, H. G., & Keck, P. E. (1990). Lycanthropy and self identification. *J. Nerv. Ment. Dis., 178*(2), 134–137.

Kushner, H. L. (1985). Women and suicide and historical perspective. *Signs, 10*(3), 537–552.

Labouvie, E. W., & McGee, C. R. (1986). Relation of personality to alcohol and drug use in adolescence. *J. Cons. Clin. Psychol., 54*(3), 289–293.

Lacey, J. H. (1983). Bulimia nervosa, binge eating, and psychogenic vomiting: A controlled treatment study and long term outcome. *Brit. Med. J., 286*, 1609–1613.

Lacey, J. I. (1967). Somatic response patterning and stress: Some revisions of the activation theory. In N. H. Appley & R. Turnbull (Eds.), *Psychological stress: Issues in research.* New York: Appleton-Century-Crofts.

Lachman, S. J., (1972). *Psychosomatic disorders: A behavioristic interpretation.* New York: Wiley.

Lahey, B., Stempiake, M., Robinson, E., & Tyroler, M. (1978). Hyperactivity and learning disabilities. *J. Abnorm. Psychol., 87*, 333–340.

Laing, R. D. (1964). *The divided self* (2nd ed.). London: Pelican.

Laing, R. D. (1967). *The politics of experience.* New York: Pantheon.

Lam, R. W., Berkowitz, A. L., Berga, S. L., Clark, C. M. et al. (1990). Melatonin suppression in bipolar and unipolar mood disorders. *Psychiat. Res., 33*(2), 129–134.

Lamb, H. R. (1979). Roots of neglect of the long-term mentally ill. *Psychiatry, 42*(3), 201–207.

Lamb, H. R. (1979). The new asylums in the community. *Arch. Gen. Psychiat., 36*(2), 129–134.

Lamb, H. R. (1982). *Treating the long-term mentally ill.* San Francisco: Jossey-Bass.

Lamb, H. R. (1988). When the chronically mentally ill need acute hospitalization: Maximizing its benefits. *Psychiat. Ann., 18*(7), 426–430.

Lamb, H. R., & Goertzel, V. (1977). The long-term patient in the era of community treatment. *Arch. Gen. Psychiat., 34*(6), 679–682.

Lamb, H. R., Hoffman, F., Hoffman, A., & Oliphant, E. (1976). No place for schizophrenics: The unwelcome consumer speaks out. *Psychiat. Ann., 6*(12), 688–692.

Lambert, M. J., Shapiro, D. A., & Bergin, A. E. (1986). The effectiveness of psychotherapy. In S. L. Garfield & A. E. Bergin (Eds.), *Handbook of psychotherapy and behavior change* (3rd ed.). New York: Wiley.

Lampley, D. A., & Rust, J. O. (1986). Validation of the Kaufman Battery for Children with a sample of preschool children. *Psychol. in Schools, 23*(2), 131–137.

Lancaster, N. P., Steinhart, R. R., & Frost, I. (1958). Unilateral electroconvulsive therapy. *J. Ment. Sci., 104*, 221–227.

Landau, J., & Paulson, T. (1977). Cope: A wilderness workshop in AT. In R. E. Alberti (Ed.), *Assertiveness: Innovation application, issues.* San Luis Obispo, CA: Impact.

Landesman-Dwyer, S. (1981). Living in the community. *Amer. J. Ment. Def., 86*(3), 223–234.

Lang, A. R. (1983). Addictive personality: A viable construct? In P. K. Levison, D. R. Gerstein, & D. R. Maloff (Eds.), *Commonalities in substance abuse and habitual behavior.* Lexington, MA: Lexington.

Lang, P. J. (1985). The cognitive psychophysiology of emotion: Fear and anxiety. In A. H. Tuma & J. D. Maser (Eds.), *Anxiety and anxiety disorders.* Hillsdale, NJ: Erlbaum.

Lang, P. J., & Lazovik, A. D. (1963). Experimental desensitization of a phobia. *J. Abnorm. Soc. Psychol., 66*, 519–525.

Lang, P. J., Melamed, B. G., & Hart, J. D. (1970). A psychophysiological analysis of fear modification using an automated desensitization procedure. *J. Abnorm. Psychol., 76*, 220–234.

Langer, E. J. (1983). *The psychology of control.* Beverly Hills, CA: Sage.

Lanyon, R. I. (1984). Personality assessment. *Annu. Rev. Psychol., 35*, 667–701.

Lapouse, R., & Monk, M. A. (1959). Fears and worries in a representative sample of children. *Amer. J. Orthopsychiat., 29*, 803–818.

Lapouse, R., & Monk, M. A. (1964). Behavior deviations in a representative sample of children. *Amer. J. Orthopsychiat., 29*, 803–818.

Laraia, M. T., Stuart, G. W., & Best, C. L. (1989). Behavioral treatment of panic-related disorders: A review. *Arch. Psychiat. Nursing, 3*(3), 125–133.

Larmore, K., Ludwig, A. M., & Cain, R. L. (1977). Multiple personality: An objective case study. *Brit. J. Psychiat., 131*, 35–40.

Last, J. M., & Bruhn, A. R. (1985). Distinguishing child diagnostic types with early memories. *J. Pers. Assess., 49*(2), 187–192.

Latimer, P. R. (1983). Antidepressants and behavior therapy in agoraphobia and obsessive-compulsive disorders: A commentary. *J. Behav. Ther. Exp. Psychiat., 14*(1), 25–27.

Laube, J. J. (1990). Why group therapy for bulimia? *Inter. J. Group Psychother., 40*(2), 169–1987.

Lawrence, G. H. (1986). Using computers for the treatment of psychological problems. *Computers in Human Behav., 2*(1), 43–62.

Lazarus, A. A. (1965). The treatment of a sexually inadequate man. In L. P. Ullman & L. Krasner (Eds.), *Case studies in behavior modification.* New York: Holt, Rinehart, & Winston.

Lazarus, A. A. (1971). *Behavior therapy and beyond.* New York: McGraw-Hill.

Lazarus, A. A. (1987). The need for technical eclecticism: Science, breadth, depth, and specificity. In J. K. Zeig (Ed.), *The evolution of psychotherapy.* New York: Brunner/Mazel.

Lazarus, A. A. (1989). In R. J. Corsini & D. Wedding (Eds.), *Current psychotherapies* (4th ed.). Itasca, IL: Peacock.

Lazarus, R. S., & Cohen, J. B. (1977). Environmental stress. In I. Altman & J. F. Wohlwill (Eds.), *Human behavior and the environment: Current theory and research.* New York: Plenum.

Lazarus, R. S., & DeLongis, A. (1983). Psychological stress and coping in aging. *Amer. Psychol., 38*, 245–254.

Lazarus, R. S., & Folkman, S. (1984). *Stress, appraisal, and coping.* New York: Springer.

Leboyer, M., & Plaisant, O. (1984). Depression serotoninergique. Hypothèse ou realité? *Encephale, 9*(4), 317–330.

Leboyer, M., Babron, M. C., & Clerget-Darpoux, F. (1990). Sampling strategy in linkage studies of affective disorders. *Psychol. Med., 20*(3), 573–579.

Lee, D. E. (1985). Alternative self-destruction. *Percep. & Motor Skills, 61*(3, Part 2), 1065–1066.

Lee, E. S. (1951). Negro intelligence and selective migration: A Philadelphia test of the Klineberg hypothesis. *Amer. Sociol. Rev., 16*, 227–233.

Leenaars, A. A. (1989). *Suicide notes: Predictive clues and patterns.* New York: Human Sciences.

Leenaars, A. A., & Laster, D. (1990). What characteristics of suicide notes are salient for people to allow perception of a suicide note as genuine? *Death Studies, 14*(1), 25–30.

Leff, J., & Vaughn, C. (1980). The interaction of life events and relatives' expressed emotion in schizophrenia and depressive neurosis. *Brit. J. Psychiat., 130*, 140–153.

Leff, J., Berkowitz, R., Shavit, N., Strachan, A. et al. (1989). A trial of family therapy vs. a relatives group for schizophrenia. *Brit. J. Psychiat., 154*, 58–66.

Leff, J. P., & Vaughn, C. (1976, Nov.). Schizophrenia and family life. *Psychol. Today*, 13–18.

Leger, J. M. et al. (1979). Results of an inquiry on 50 school phobic children, their parents, and teachers. *Annales Medico Psychologiques, 137*(6–7), 568–578.

Leger, L. A. (1979). An outcome measure for thought-stopping examined in three case studies. *J. Behav. Ther. Exp. Psychiat., 10*(2), 115–120.

Leighton, A. H., Lambo, T. A., Hughes, C. C., Leighton, D. C., Murphy, J. M., & Macklin, D. B. (1963). *Psychiatric disorder among the Yoruba: A report from the Cornell-Aro mental health project in the western region, Nigeria.* Ithaca, NY: Cornell Univ.

Leitenberg, H., & Callahan, E. J. (1973). Reinforced practice and reduction of different kinds of fears in adults and children. *Behav. Res. Ther., 11*(1), 19–30.

Leitenberg, H., Agras, W. S., & Thompson, L. E. (1968). A sequential analysis of the effect of selective positive reinforcement in modifying anorexia nervosa. *Behav. Res. Ther., 6*(2), 211–218.

Leland, H. (1991). Adaptive behavior scales. In J. L. Matson & J. A. Mulick (Eds.), *Handbook of mental retardation.* New York: Pergamon.

Leon, G. R. (1977). *Case histories of deviant behavior* (2nd ed.). Boston: Allyn & Bacon.

Leon, G. R. (1984). *Case histories of deviant behavior* (3rd ed.). Boston: Allyn & Bacon.

Leon, R. L., Bowden, C. L., & Faber, R. A. (1989). The psychiatric interview, history, and mental status examination. In H. I. Kaplan & B. J. Sadock (Eds.), *Comprehensive textbook of psychiatry* (Vol. 1, 5th ed.). Baltimore: Williams & Wilkins.

Lerner, H. D. (1986). Current developments in the psychoanalytic psychotherapy of anorexia nervosa and bulimia nervosa. *Clin. Psychologist, 39*(2), 39–43.

Lerner, H. D., & Lerner, P. M. (Eds.). (1988). *Primitive mental states and the Rorschach.* Madison: Inter. Univ.

Leroux, J. A. (1986). Suicidal behavior and gifted adolescents. *Roeper Rev., 9*(2), 77–79.

LeSage, J., & Zwygart-Stauffacher, M. (1988). Detection of medication misuse in elders. *Generations, 12*(4), 32–36.

Lesser, I. M. (1988). The relationship between panic disorder and depression [Special Issue]. *J. Anx. Dis. 2*(1), 3–15.

Lesser, I. M., Rubin, R. T., Pecknold, J. C., Rifkin, A. et al. (1988). Secondary depression in panic disorder and agoraphobia: I. Frequency, severity, and response to treatment. *Arch. Gen. Psychiat., 45*(5), 437–443.

Lester, D. (1972). Myth of suicide prevention. *Comprehen. Psychiat., 13*(6) 555–560.

Lester, D. (1974). The effects of suicide prevention centers on suicide rates in the United States. *Pub. Hlth. Rep., 89,* 37–39.

Lester, D. (1985). Accidental deaths as disguised suicides. *Psych. Rep., 56*(2), 626.

Lester, D. (1985). The quality of life in modern America and suicide and homicide rates. *J. Soc. Psychol., 125*(6), 779–780.

Lester, D. (1986). Genetics, twin studies, and suicide. *Suic. Life-Threat. Behav., 16*(2) 274–285.

LeUnes, A. D., Nation, J. R., & Turley, N. M. (1980). Male-female performance in learned helplessness. *J. Psychol.,* 104, 255–258.

Levin, S. (1968). Some suggestions for treating the depressed patient. In W. Gaylin (Ed.), *The meaning of despair.* New York: Aronson.

Levine, M. D. (1975). Children with encopresis: A descriptive analysis. *Pediatrics,* 56, 412–416.

Levine, M. D. (1982). Encopresis: Its potentiation, evaluation, and alleviation. *Pediat. Clin. N. Amer., 29,* 315–330.

Levine, M. D. (1987). *How schools can help combat student eating disorders: Anorexia nervosa and bulimia.* Washington, DC: National Education Assoc.

Levine, M. D. (1988). *Introduction to eating disorders: What the educator, health, and mental health professional need to know.* Presentation at the Seventh National Conference on Eating Disorders of the National Anorexic Aid Society. Columbus, OH.

Levin, W. C. (1988, March). Age stereotyping: College student evaluations. *Res. on Aging,* 134–148.

Levinson, D. J. (1977). The mid-life transition. *Psychiatry, 40,* 99–112.

Levinson, D. J. (1977). Toward a conception of adult life course. In N. Smelser & E. H. Erikson (Eds.), *Themes of love and work in adulthood.* Cambridge, MA: Harvard Univ.

Levinson, D. J. (1984). The career is in the life structure, the life structure is in the career: An adult development perspective. In M. B. Arthur, L. Bailyn, D. J. Levinson, & H. Shepard, *Working with careers.* New York: Columbia Univ. School of Business.

Levinson, D. J. (1986). Conception of adult development. *Amer. Psychol., 41*(1), 3–13.

Levis, D. J., & Carrera, R. N. (1967). Effects of 10 hours of implosive therapy in the treatment of outpatients: A preliminary report. *J. Abnorm. Psychol.,* 72, 504–508.

Levitan, H. L. (1979). The role of dreams in the construction of psychoneurotic symptoms. *Amer. J. Psychoanal., 39*(3), 211–223.

Levitan, H. L. (1981). Implications of certain dreams reported by patients in a bulimic phase of anorexia nervosa. *Canad. J. Psychiat., 26*(4), 228–231.

Levitt, A. J., Joffe, R. T., Ennis, J., MacDonald, C. et al. (1990). The prevalence of cyclothymia in borderline personality disorder. *J. Clin. Psychiat., 51*(8), 335–339.

Levitt, E. E. (1989). *The clinical application of MMPI Special Scales.* Hillsdale, NJ: Erlbaum.

Levor, R. M., Cohen, M. J., Naliboff, B. D., & McArthur, D. (1986). Psychosocial precursors and correlates of migraine headache. *J. Cons. Clin. Psychol.,* 54, 347–353.

Levy, L. (1976). Self-help groups: Types and psychological processes. *J. Appl. Behav. Sci., 12,* 310–323.

Levy, N. B. (1985). Conversion disorder. In R. C. Simons (Ed.), *Understanding human behavior in health and illness* (3rd ed.). Baltimore: Williams & Wilkins.

Levy, N. B. (1985). The psychophysiological disorders: An overview. In R. C. Simons (Ed.), *Understanding human behavior in health and illness* (3rd ed.). Baltimore: Williams & Wilkins.

Lewin, B. D. (1950). *The psychoanalysis of elation.* New York: Norton.

Lewinsohn, P. M. (1974). A behavioral approach to depression. In R. J. Friedman & M. M. Katz (Eds.), *The psychology of depression: Contemporary theory and research.* New York: Wiley.

Lewinsohn, P. M. (1974). Clinical and theoretical aspects of depression. In K. S. Calhoun, H. E. Adams, & K. M. Mitchell (Eds.), *Innovative treatment methods of psychopathology.* New York: Wiley.

Lewinsohn, P. M. (1975). Engagement in pleasant activities and depression level. *J. Abnorm. Psychol., 84,* 644–654.

Lewinsohn, P. M. (1975). The use of activity schedules in the treatment of depressed individuals. In C. E. Thoresen & J. D. Krumboltz (Eds.), *Counseling methods.* New York: Holt, Rinehart & Winston.

Lewinsohn, P. M. (1988). A prospective study of risk factors for unipolar depression. *J. Abnorm. Psychol., 97*(3), 251–284.

Lewinsohn, P. M., & Amenson, C. S. (1978). Some relations between pleasant and unpleasant mood-related events and depression. *J. Abnorm. Psychol., 87*(6), 644–654.

Lewinsohn, P. M., & Arconad, M. (1981). Behavioral treatment of depression: A social learning approach. In J. F. Clarkin & H. I. Glazer (Eds.), *Depression: Behavioral and directive intervention strategies.* New York: Garland STPM.

Lewinsohn, P. M., & Graf, M. (1973). Pleasant activities and depression. *J. Cons. Clin. Psychol., 41*(2), 261–268.

Lewinsohn, P. M., & Shaffer, M. (1971). The use of home observations as an integral part of the treatment of depression: Preliminary report and case studies. *J. Cons. Clin. Psychol., 37,* 87–94.

Lewinsohn, P. M., Antonuccio, D. O., Steinmetz, J. L., & Teri, L. (1984). *The coping with depression course.* Eugene, OR: Castalia.

Lewinsohn, P. M., Biglan, A., & Zeiss, A. M. (1976). Behavioral treatment of depression. In P. O. Davidson (Ed.), *The behavioral management of anxiety, depression and pain.* New York: Brunner/Mazel.

Lewinsohn, P. M., Rohde, P., Teri, L., & Tilson, M. (1990, April). *Presentation.* Western Psychological Assoc.

Lewinsohn, P. M., Steinmetz, J. L., Larson, D. W., & Franklin, J. (1981). Depression related cognitions: Antecedent or consequence? *J. Abnorm. Psychol., 90*(3), 213–219.

Lewinsohn, P. M., Sullivan, J. M., & Grosscup, S. J. (1982). Behavioral therapy: Clinical applications. In A. T. Rush (Ed.), *Short-term psychotherapies for the depressed patient.* New York: Guilford.

Lewinsohn, P. M., Weinstein, M. S., & Alper, T. (1970). A behaviorally oriented approach to the group treatment of depressed persons: A methodological approach. *J. Clin. Psychol.,* 26, 525–532.

Lewinsohn, P. M., Weinstein, M. S., & Shaw, D. (1969). Depression: A clinical-research approach. In R. D. Rubin & C. M. Franks (Eds.), *Advances in behavior therapy.* New York: Academic.

Lewinsohn, P. M., Youngren, M. A., & Grosscup, S. J. (1979). Reinforcement and depression. In R. A. Depue (Ed.), *The psychobiology of the depressive disorders.* New York: Academic.

Lewis, H. L., & MacGuire, M. P. (1985). Review of a group for parents of anorexics. Conference on Anorexia Nervosa and Related Disorders (1984, Swansea, Wales). *J. Psychiat. Res., 19*(2–3), 453–458.

Lewis, M. J. (1990). Alcohol: Mechanisms of addiction and reinforcement. *Adv. Alcohol & Substance Abuse, 9*(1–2), 47–66.

Lewis, N. D. C., & Yarnell, H. (1951). Pathological firesetting (pyromania). *Nervous Mental Disorder Monographs, 82*(8).

Lewison, V. R. (1985). The compatibility of the disease concept with a psychodynamic approach in the treatment of alcoholism. *Alcoholism Treatment Quart., 2*(1), 7–24.

Lewy, A. J. (1990). The circadian system and affective disorders: Clocks or rhythms? Chronobiologic disorders, social cues and the light-dark cycle. *Chronobio. Inter., 7*(1), 15–21. (Reply to D. Healy and J. M. Waterhouse).

Lewy, A. J., Sack, R. L., Miller, L. S., & Hoban, T. M. (1987). Antidepressant and circadian phase-shifting effects of light. *Science,* 235, 352–354.

Lewy, A. J., Wehr, T. A., Goodwin, F. K., Newsome, D. A., &

Markey, S. P. (1980). Light suppresses melatonin secretion in humans. *Science, 210,* 1267–1269.

Lezak, M. (1976). *Neuropsychological assessment* (1st ed.). New York: Oxford Univ.

Libb, J. W., Stankovic, S., Freeman, A., Sokol, R. et al. (1990). Personality disorders among depressed outpatients as identified by the MCMI. *J. Clin. Psychol., 46*(3), 277–284.

Liberman, R. P. (1982). Assessment of social skills. *Schizo. Bull., 8*(1), 82–84.

Liberman, R. P., & Eckman, T. (1981). Behavior therapy vs. insight-oriented therapy for repeated suicide attempters. *Arch. Gen. Psychiat., 38*(10), 1126–1130.

Liberman, R. P., & Raskin, D. E. (1971). Depression: A behavioral formulation. *Arch. Gen. Psychiat., 24,* 515–523.

Liberson, W. T. (1945). Time factors in electric convulsive therapy. *Yale J. Bio. Med., 17,* 571–578.

Libet, J., & Lewinsohn, P. M. (1973). The concept of social skill with special references to the behavior of depressed persons. *J. Consult. Clin. Psychol., 40,* 304–312.

Libet, J., Lewinsohn, P. M., & Javorek, F. (1973). *The construct of social skill: An empirical study of several measures on temporal stability, internal structure, validity, and situational generalizability.* Mimeographed. Univ. Oregon.

Lichtenstein, E. (1980). *Psychotherapy: Approaches and applications.* Monterey, CA: Brooks/ Cole.

Lickey, M. E., & Gordon, B. (1991). *Medicine and mental illness.* New York: Freeman.

Liddle, P. F., & Barnes, T. R. (1988). The subjective experience of deficits in schizophrenia. *Comprehen. Psychiat., 29*(2), 157–184.

Lidz, T. (1963). *The family and human adaptation.* New York: International Univ.

Lidz, T. (1973). *The origin and treatment of schizophrenic disorders.* New York: Basic.

Lidz, T., & Fleck, S. (1964). *Family studies and a theory of schizophrenia.* Unpublished manuscript.

Lidz, T., Cornelison, A., & Fleck, S. (1965). *Schizophrenia and the family.* New York: International Univ.

Lidz, T., Cornelison, A., Fleck, S., & Terry, D. (1957). The intra-familial environment of the schizophrenic patient: II. Marital schism and marital skew. *Amer. J. Psychiat., 114,* 241–248.

Lidz, T., Cornelison, A. R., Singer, M. T., Schafer, S., & Fleck, S. (1965). In T. Lidz, S. Fleck, & A. R. Cornelison (Eds.), *Schizophrenia and the family.* New York: International Univ.

Lieberman, J. A. et al. (1983). Dexamethasone suppression tests in patients with panic disorder. *Amer. J. Psychiat., 140*(7), 917–919.

Lieberman, L. M. (1982). The nightmare of scheduling. *J. Learn. Dis., 15*(1), 57–58.

Lieberman, M. (1975). Some limits to research on T groups. *J. Appl. Behav. Sci., 11*(2), 241–249.

Lieberman, M. A., & Gardner, J. R. (1976). Institutional alternatives to psychotherapy: A study of growth center users. *Arch. Gen. Psychiat., 33*(2), 157–162.

Lieberman, M. A., Yalom, I. D., & Miles, M. B. (1973). *Encounter groups: First facts.* New York: Basic.

Liebowitz, M. R., Fyer, A. J., Gorman, J. M., Dillon, D., Davies, S., Stein, J. M., Cohen, B. S., & Klein, D. F. (1985). Specificity of lactate infusions in social phobia versus panic disorders. *Amer. J. Psychiat., 142,* 947–950.

Liebowitz, M. R., Gorman, J. M., Fyer, A. J., Levitt, M., Dillon, D., Levy, G., Appleby, I. L., Anderson, S., Palij, M., Davies, S. O., & Klein, D. F. (1985). Lactate provocation of panic attacks: II. *Arch. Gen. Psychiat., 42,* 709–719.

Liebowitz, M. R., Quitkin, F. M., Stewart, J. W. et al. (1983). Phenelzine vs. imipramine in atypical depression: A preliminary report. *Arch. Gen. Psychiat., 41,* 669–677.

Liem, J. H. (1980). Family studies of schizophrenia: An update and commentary. *Schizo. Bull., 6,* 429–455.

Lifton, R. J. (1973). *Home from the war: Vietnam veterans, neither victims nor executioners.* New York: Simon & Schuster.

Lindeman, J. E., & Matarazzo, J. D. (1990). Assessment of adult intelligence. In G. Goldstein & M. Hersen (Eds.), *Handbook of psychological assessment* (2nd ed.). New York: Pergamon.

Lindesmith, A. R. (1968). *Addiction and opiates.* Chicago: Aldine.

Lindholm, C., & Lindholm C. (1981, Jul.). World's strangest mental illnesses. *Science Digest.*

Lindsay, W. R., Gamsu, C. V., McLaughlin, E., Hood, E. M. et al. (1987). A controlled trial of treatments for generalized anxiety. *Brit. J. Clin. Psychol., 26*(1), 3–15.

Lindsley, D. B. (1954). Psychology. In E. A. Spiegel, "Progress in neurology and psychiatry." *Psychol. Abstracts, 29,* 391–411.

Lindstrom, L. H. (1988). The effect of long-term treatment with clozapine in schizophrenia: A retrospective study in 96 patients treated with clozapine for up to 13 years. *Acta Psychiatr. Scandin., 77*(5), 524–529.

Linehan, M. M., & Nielsen, S. L. (1981). Assessment of suicide ideation and parasuicide: Hopelessness and social desirability. *J. Cons. Clin. Psychol., 49*(5), 773–775.

Linehan, M. M. et al. (1979). Group versus individual assertion training. *J. Cons. Clin. Psychol., 47*(5), 1000–1002.

Linehan, M. M., Goldfried, M. R., & Goldfried, A. P. (1979). Assertion therapy: Skill training or cognitive restructuring. *Behav. Ther., 10*(3), 372–388.

Lingswiler, V. M., Crowther, J. H., & Stephens, N. A. (1989). Affective and cognitive antecedents to eating episodes in bulimia and binge eating. *Inter. J. Eat. Dis., 8*(5), 533–539.

Linkowski, P., de Maertelaer, V., & Mendlewicz, J. (1985). Suicidal behaviour in major depressive illness. *Acta Psychiatr. Scandin., 72*(3), 233–238.

Linsky, A. S., Strauss, M. A., & Colby, J. P. (1985). Stressful events, stressful conditions and alcohol problems in the United States: A partial test of Bales's theory. *J. Studies on Alcohol, 46*(1), 72–80.

Linton, M. (1979, Jul.). I remember it well. *Psych. Today.*

Linz, T. D., Hooper, S. R., Hynd, G. W., Isaac, W. et al. (1990). Frontal lobe functioning in conduct disordered juveniles: Preliminary findings. *Arch. Clin. Neuropsychol., 5*(4), 411–416.

Lipman, R. S. et al. (1986). Imipramine and chlordiazepoxide in depressive and anxiety disorders: I. Efficacy in depressed outpatients. *Arch. Gen. Psychiat., 43*(1), 68–77.

Lipowski, Z. J. (1980). *Delirium: Acute brain failure in man.* Springfield, IL: Thomas.

Lipowski, Z. J. (1987). Somatization: Medicine's unsolved problem. *Psychosomatics, 28*(6), 294–297.

Lipsky, M. J., Kassinove, H., & Miller, N. J. (1980). Effects of rational-emotive therapy, rational role reversal, and rational-emotive imagery on the emotional adjustment of community mental health center patients. *J. Cons. Clin. Psychol., 48*(3), 366–374.

Lipton, A. A., & Simon, F. S. (1985). Psychiatric diagnosis in a state hospital: Manhattan State revisited. *Hosp. Comm. Psychiat., 36*(4), 368–373.

Lipton, H. L. (1988). A prescription for change. *Generations, 12*(4), 74–79.

Little, K. B., & Schneidman, E. S. (1959). Congruences among interpretations of psychological test and amamnestic data. *Psychology Monographs, 73*(476).

Lloyd, C. (1980). Life events and depressive disorder reviewed: II. Events as precipitating factors. *Arch. Gen. Psychiat., 37*(5), 540–541.

Locke, B. Z., & Regier, D. A. (1985). *Prevalence of selected mental disorders.* Washington, DC: GPO.

Loeb, A., Beck, A. T., & Diggory, J. (1971). Differential effects of success and failure on depressed and nondepressed patients. *J. Ner. Ment. Dis., 152*(2), 106–114.

Loewenstein, R. J. (1991). Psychogenic amnesia and psychogenic fugue: A comprehensive review. In A. Tasman & S. M. Goldfinger (Eds.), *American Psychiatric Press review of psychiatry* (Vol. 10). Washington, DC: American Psychiatric.

Loge, D. V., Staton, R. D., & Beatty, W. W. (1990). Performance of children with ADHD on tests sensitive to frontal lobe dysfunction. *J. Amer. Acad. Child Adol. Psychiat., 23*(4), 540–545.

Logue, A. W. (1991). *The psychology of eating and drinking.* New York: Freeman.

Loney, J. (1981). Hyperkinesis comes of age: What do we know and where do we go? *Annu. Progress in Child Psychiat. Dev.,* 598–616.

Long, G. C., & Cordle, C. J. (1982). Psychological treatment of binge eating and self-induced vomiting. *Brit. J. Med. Psychol., 55,* 139–145.

Long, J. V. (1984). Natural history of male psychological health: XI, Escape from the underclass. *Amer. J. Psychiat., 141*(3), 346.

Loomer, H. P., Saunders, J. C., & Kline, N. E. (1958). A clinical and phamacodynamic evaluation of iproniazid as a psychic energizer. *Amer. Psychiat. Assoc. Res. Rep., 8,* 129.

Lopez, F. C., Campbell, V. L., & Watkins, C. E. (1986). Depression psychological separation, and college adjustment: An investigation for sex difference. *J. Counseling Psychol., 33*(1), 52–56.

LoPiccolo, J. (1985). Advances in diagnosis and treatment of male sexual dysfunction. *J. Sex Marital Ther., 11*(4), 215–232.

LoPiccolo, J. (1990). Treatment of sexual dysfunction. In A. S. Bellak, M. Hersen, & A. E. Kazdin (Eds.), *Inter. handbook of behavior modification and therapy* (2nd ed.). New York: Plenum.

LoPiccolo, J. (1991). Post-modern sex therapy for erectile failure. In R. C. Rosen & S. R. Leiblum (Eds.), *Erectile failure: diagnosis and treatment.* New York: Guilford.

LoPiccolo, J., & Friedman, J. R. (1988). Broad spectrum treatment of low sexual desire: Integration of cognitive, behavioral, and systemic treatment. In S. Leiblum & R. Rosen (Eds.), *Sexual desire disorders.* New York: Guilford.

LoPiccolo, J., & Stock, W. E. (1987). Sexual function, dysfunction, and counseling in gynecological practice. In Z. Rosenwaks, F. Benjamin, & M. L. Stone (Eds.), *Gynecology.* New York: Macmillan.

LoPiccolo, J., Heiman, J. R., Hogan, D. R., & Roberts, C. W. (1985). Effectiveness of single therapists versus co-therapy teams in sex therapy. *J. Cons. Clin. Psychol., 53*(3), 287–294.

Lorand, S. (1950). *Clinical studies in psychoanalysis.* New York: International Univ.

Lorand, S. (1968). Dynamics and therapy of depressive states. In W. Gaylin (Ed.), *The meaning of despair.* New York: Aronson.

Lorand, S. (1980). *Contemporary psychotherapies.* Chicago: Rand McNally.

Loranger, A., Oldham, J., Russakoff, L. M., & Susman, V. (1987). Structured interviews and borderline personality disorder. *Arch. Gen. Psychiat., 41*, 565–568.

Lorr, M., & Wunderlich, R. A. (1988). Self-esteem and negative affect. *J. Clin. Psychol., 44*(1), 36–39.

Losonczy, M. F. et al. (1986). Correlates of lateral ventricular size in chronic schizophrenia: I. Behavioral and treatment response measures. *Amer. J. Psychiat., 143*(8), 976–981.

Lovaas, O. I., & Simmons, J. Q. (1969). Manipulation of self-destruction in three retarded children. *J. Appl. Behav. Anal., 2*, 143–157.

Lovaas, O. I., Koegal, R., Simmons, J. Q., & Long, S. S. (1973). Some generalization and follow-up measures on autistic children in behavior therapy. *J. Appl. Behav. Anal., 6*, 131.

Lovaas, O. I., Schreibman, L., & Koegel, R. L. (1974). A behavior modification approach to the treatment of autistic children. *J. Autism Child. Schizo., 4*, 111–129.

Lovaas, O. I., Schreibman, L., Koegel, R. L., & Rehm, R. (1971). Selective responding by autistic children to multiple sensory input. *J. Abnorm. Psychol., 77*, 211–222.

Love, S. R., Matson, J. L., & West, D. (1990). Mothers as effective therapists for autistic children's phobias. *J. Appl. Behav. Anal., 23*(3), 379–385.

Lovejoy, M. (1982). Expectations and the recovery process. *Schizo. Bull., 8*(4), 605–609.

Lovett, S., & Gallagher, D. (1988). Psychoeducational interventions for family caregivers: Preliminary efficacy data. *Behav. Ther., 19*, 321–330.

Lubasch, A. H. (1982, Sep. 14). Court is told to hold a trial in the death of a drug test subject. *New York Times,* p. 7.

Lubetsky, M. J. (1986). The psychiatrist's role in the assessment and treatment of the mentally retarded child. *Child Psychiat. Human Dev., 16*(4), 261–273.

Lubin, B. (1983). Group therapy. In I. B. Weiner (Ed.), *Clinical methods in psychology* (2d ed.). New York: Wiley.

Luborsky, L. (1973). Forgetting and remembering (momentary forgetting) during psychotherapy. In M. Mayman (Ed.), *Psychoanalytic research and psychological issues* (Monograph 30). New York: International Univ.

Luborsky, L. (1984). *Principles of psychoanalytic psychotherapy: A manual for supportive expressive treatment.* New York: Basic.

Luborsky, L., & Singer, B. (1975). Comparative studies of psychotherapies: Is it true that "everyone has won and all must have prizes"? *Arch. Gen. Psychiat., 32*(8), 995–1008.

Luborsky, L., & Spence, D. P. (1978). Quantitative research on psychoanalytic therapy. In S. L. Garfield & A. E. Bergin (Eds.), *Handbook of psychotherapy and behavior change: An empirical analysis* (2nd ed.). New York: Wiley.

Ludwig, A. M., Brandsma, J. M., & Wilbur, C. B. (1972). The objective study of a multiple personality: Or are four heads better than one. *Arch. Gen. Psychiat., 26*, 298–310.

Luka, L. P., Agras, W. S., & Schneider, J. A. (1986). Thirty month follow-up of cognitive-behavioral group therapy for bulimia. *Brit. J. Psychiat., 148*, 614–615.

Lykken, D. T. (1957). A study of anxiety in the sociopathic personality. *J. Abnorm. Soc. Psychol., 55*, 6–10.

Lynn, R. (1982). National differences in anxiety and extroversion. *Progess in Exp. Pers. Res., 11*, 213–258.

Lynn, S. J., & Frauman, D. C. (1985). Group psychotherapy. In S. J. Lynn & J. P. Garske (Eds.), *Contemporary psychotherapies: Models and methods.* Columbus, OH: Merrill.

Lynn, S. J., & Rhue, J. W. (1988). Fantasy proneness: Hypnosis, developmental antecedents, and psychopathology. *Amer. Psychol., 43*(1), 35–44.

Lyon, L. S. (1985). Facilitating telephone number recall in a case of psychogenic amnesia. *J. Behav. Ther. Exp. Psychiat., 16*(2), 147–149.

Maas, J. W. (1975). Biogenic amines and depression: Biochemical and pharmacological separation of two types of depression. *Arch. Gen. Psychiat., 32*(11), 1357–1361.

Mace, N., & Rabins, P. (1991). *The 36-hour day* (2nd ed.). Baltimore: Johns Hopkins Univ.

MacFarlane, J. W., Allen, L., & Honzik, M. P. (1954). *A developmental study of the behavior problems of normal children between 21 months and 14 years.* Berkeley & Los Angeles: Univ. California.

MacHovek, F. J. (1981). Hypnosis to facilitate recall in psychogenic amnesia and fugue states: Treatment variables. *Amer. J. Clin. Hyp., 24*(1), 7–13.

Machover, K. (1949). *Personality projection in the drawing of the human figure.* Springfield, IL: Thomas.

Mackay, A. V. (1980). Positive and negative schizophrenic symptoms and the role of dopamine: I. *Brit. J. Psychiat., 137*, 379–386.

Mackenzie, T. B., & Popkin, M. K. (1987). Suicide in the medical patient. *Inter. J. Psychiat. in Med., 17*(1), 3–22.

MacLane, M. (1902). *The story of Mary MacLane.* New York: Stone.

MacLeod, C., Mathews, A., & Tata, P. (1986). Attentional bias in emotional disorders. *J. Abnorm. Psychol., 95*, 15–20.

MacPhillamy, D. J., & Lewinsohn, P. M. (1974). Depression as a function of levels of desired and obtained pleasure. *J. Abnorm. Psychol., 83*(6), 651–657.

Madden, D. J., Lion, J. R., & Penna, M. W. (1976). Assaults on psychiatrists by their patients. *Amer. J. Psychiat., 133*, 422–425.

Maddi, S. R. (1990). Issues and interventions in stress mastery. In H. S. Friedman (Ed.), *Personality and disease.* New York: Wiley.

Maddox, G. L. (1988). Aging, drinking and alcohol abuse. *Generations, 12*(4), 14–16.

Madianos, M. G., & Economou, M. (1988). Negative symptoms in schizophrenia: The effect of long-term, community-based psychiatric intervention [Special Issue]. *Inter. J. Ment. Hlth., 17*(1), 22–34.

Maher, B. (1966). *Principles of psychopathology.* New York: McGraw-Hill.

Maher, B. A. (1974). Delusional thinking and perceptual disorder. *Jour. Individual Psychol., 30*(1), 98–113.

Maher, W. B., & Maher, B. A. (1982). The ship of fools. *Amer. Psychol., 37*(7), 756–761.

Maher, W. B., & Maher, B. A. (1985). Psychopathology: I. From ancient times to the eighteenth century. In G. A. Kimble & K. Schlesinger (Eds.), *Topics in the history of psychology* (Vol. 2). Hillsdale, NJ: Erlbaum.

Mahler, M. (1965). On early infantile psychosis: The symbiotic and autistic syndromes. *J. Amer. Acad. Child Psychiat., 4*, 554–568.

Mahoney, G., Glover, A., & Finger, I. (1981). Relationship between language and sensorimotor development of Down syndrome and nonretarded children. *Amer. J. Ment. Def., 86*(1), 21–27.

Mahoney, M. J. (1977). Some applied issues in self-monitoring. In J. D. Cone & R. P. Hawkins (Eds.), *Behavioral assessment: New directions in clinical psychology.* New York: Brunner/Mazel.

Maier, S. F. (1984). Learned helplessness and animal models of depression. *Progress in Neuropsychopharm. & Bio. Psychiat., 8*(3), 435–440.

Malan, D. H. (1963). *A study of brief psychotherapy.* Springfield, IL: Thomas.

Malan, D. H. (1980). *Toward the validation of dynamic psychotherapy.* New York: Plenum.

Malcolm, A. H. (1990, Jun. 9). Giving death a hand. *New York Times,* A6.

Maletzky, B. M. (1974). "Assisted" covert sensitization in the treatment of exhibitionism. *J. Cons. Clin. Psychol., 42*(1), 34–40.

Maletzky, B. M. (1974). Behavior recording as treatment: A brief note. *Behav. Ther., 5*(1), 107–111.

Maletzky, B. M. (1977). Booster sessions in aversion therapy: The permanency of treatment. *Behav. Ther.*, 8(3), 400–463.

Maletzky, B. M. (1980). Assisted covert sensitization. In D. J. Cox & R. J. Daitzman (Eds.), *Exhibitionism: Description, assessment, and treatment.* New York: Garland STPM.

Malinow, K. L. (1981). Passive-aggressive personality disorder. In J. R. Lion (Ed.), *Personality disorders.* Baltimore: Williams & Wilkins.

Maltz, W., & Holman, B. (1987). *Incest and sexuality: A guide to understanding and healing.* Lexington, KY: Lexington.

Manderscheid, R. W., & Sonnenschein, M. A. (Eds.). (1990). *Mental Health, United States, 1990.* Rockville, MD: U.S. Dept. Health and Human Services.

Manrique-Solana, R. (1988). Communication disturbances in parents of schizophrenics. *Acta Psychiatr. Scandin.*, 77(4), 427–434.

Manschreck, T. C. et al. (1985). Deficient motor synchrony in schizophrenic disorders: Clinical correlates. *Bio. Psychiat.*, 20(9), 990–1002.

Margo, A., Hemsley, D. R., & Slade, P. D. (1981). The effects of varying auditory input on schizophrenic hallucinations. *Brit. J. Psychiat.*, 139, 122–127.

Margo, J. L. (1985). Anorexia nervosa in adolescents. *Brit. J. Med. Psychol.*, 58(2), 193–195.

Margolin, G., & Weinstein, C. D. (1983). The role of affect in behavioral marital therapy. In M. L. Aronson & L. R. Wolbery (Eds.), *Group and family therapy 1982: An overview.* New York: Brunner/Mazel.

Marks, I. M. (1969). *Fears and phobias.* New York: Academic.

Marks, I. M. (1977). Phobias and obsessions: Clinical phenomena in search of a laboratory model. In J. Maser & M. Seligman (Eds.), *Psychopathology: Experimental models.* San Francisco: Freeman.

Marks, I. M. (1981). *Cure and care of neuroses.* New York: Wiley.

Marks, I. M. (1981). Review of behavioral psychotherapy: I. Obsessive-compulsive disorders. *Amer. J. Psychiat.*, 138(5), 584–592.

Marks, I. M. (1981). Behavioral psychotherapy: Sexual disorders. *Amer. J. Psychiat.*, 138(5), 750–756.

Marks, I. M. (1985). Behavioral treatment of social phobia. *Psychopharm. Bull.*, 21, 615–618.

Marks, I. M. (1987). Comment on S. Lloyd Williams' "On anxiety and phobia." *J. Anx. Dis.*, 1(2), 181–196.

Marks, I. M. (1987). *Fears, phobias and rituals: Panic, anxiety and their disorders.* New York: Oxford.

Marks, I. M. (1989). Behavioural psychotherapy for generalized anxiety disorder [Special Issue]. *Inter. Rev. Psychiat.*, 1(3), 235–244.

Marks, I. M., & Gelder, M. G. (1965). A controlled retrospective study of behavior therapy in phobic patients. *Brit. J. Psychiat.*, 123, 571–573.

Marks, I. M., & Gelder, M. G. (1967). Transvestism and fetishism: Clinical and psychological changes during faradic aversion. *Brit. J. Psychiat.*, 113, 711–730.

Marks, I. M., & Herst, E. R. (1970). A survey of 1200 agoraphobics in Britain. *Soc. Psychiat.*, 5, 16–24.

Marks, I. M. et al. (1986). *Behavioral psychotherapy: Pocketbook of clinical management.* John Wright, Bristol.

Marks, I. M., Hodgson, R., & Rachman, S. (1975). Treatment of chronic OCD 2 years after in vivo exposure. *Brit. J. Psychiat.*, 127, 349–364.

Marks, I. M., Stern, R. S., Mawson, D., Cobb, J., & McDonald, R. (1980). Clomipramine and exposure for obsessive-compulsive rituals: I. *Brit. J. Psychiat.*, 36, 1–25.

Marks, J. (1988). Techniques of benzodiazepine withdrawal in clinical practice: A consensus workshop report. *Med. Toxicol. & Adverse Drug Exp.*, 3(4), 324–333.

Marlatt, G. A. (1976). Alcohol, stress, and cognitive control. In G. Sarason & C. D. Spielberger (Eds.), *Stress and anxiety* (Vol. 3). New York: Hemisphere.

Marlatt, G. A. (1977). Behavioral assessment of social drinking and alcoholism. In G. A. Marlatt & P. E. Natha (Eds.), *Behavioral approaches to alcoholism.* New Brunswick, NJ: Rutgers Center for Alcohol Studies.

Marlatt, G. A. (1983). The controlled-drinking controversy: A commentary. *Amer. Psychol.*, 38(10), 1097–1110.

Marlatt, G. A. (1985). Controlled drinking: The controversy rages on. *Amer. Psychol.*, 40(3), 374–375.

Marlatt, G. A., & Gordon, J. (Eds.). (1980). Determinants of relapse: Implications for the maintenance of behavior change. In P. Davidson & S. Davidson (Eds.), *Behavioral medicine.* New York: Brunner/Mazel.

Marlatt, G. A., & Gordon, J. R. (1985). *Relapse prevention: Maintenance strategies in the treatment of addictive behaviors.* New York: Guilford.

Marlatt, G. A., Kosturn, C. F., & Lang, A. R. (1975). Provocation to anger and opportunity for retaliation as determinants of alcohol consumption in social drinkers. *J. Abnorm. Psychol.*, 84(6), 652–659.

Marlett, N. J. (1979). Normalization, integration and socialization. In J. P. Das & D. Baine (Eds.), *Mental retardation for special educators.* Springfield, IL: Thomas.

Marmor, J. (1987). The psychotherapeutic process: Common denominators in diverse approaches. In J. K. Zeig (Ed.), *The evolution of psychotherapy.* New York: Brunner/Mazel.

Marquies, J. N., & Morgan, W. G. (1969). *A guidebook for systematic desensitization.* Palo Alto, CA: Veterans Admin. Hospital.

Marshall, W. L. (1979). Satiation therapy: A procedure for reducing deviant sexual arousal. *J. Appl. Behav. Annal.*, 12, 10–22.

Marshall, W. L., & Lippens, K. (1977). The clinical value of boredom: A procedure for reducing innappropriate sexual interests. *J. Nerv. Ment. Dis.*, 165, 283–287.

Marston, W. M. (1917). Systolic blood pressure changes in deception. *J. Exp. Physiol.*, 2, 117–163.

Martin, D. (1972). *Learning-based client-centered therapy.* Monterey, CA: Brooks/Cole.

Martin, F. E. (1985). The treatment and outcome of anorexia nervosa in adolescents: A prospective study and five year follow-up. *J. Psychiat. Res.*, 19(2–3), 509–514.

Martin, F. E. (1990). The relevance of a systemic model for the study and treatment of anorexia nervosa in adolescents [Special Issue]. *Canad. J. Psychiat.*, 35(6), 496–500.

Martin, G., & Pear, J. (1988). *Behavior modification* (3rd ed.). Englewood Cliffs, NJ: Prentice-Hall.

Martin, J. E. (1985). Anorexia nervosa: A review of the theoretical perspectives and treatment approaches. *Brit. J. Occupational Ther.*, 48(8), 236–240.

Martin, R. M. (1980). Suicide and false desires. In M. P. Battin & D. J. Mayo (Eds.), *Suicide: The philosophical issues.* New York: St. Martin's.

Martin, W. T. (1984). Religiosity and U.S. suicide rates, 1972–1978. *J. Clin. Psychol.*, 40(5), 1166–1169.

Maslow, A. H. (1967). Neurosis as a failure of personal growth. *Humanitas*, 3, 153–170.

Mason, J. W. (1968a). A review of psychoendocrine research on the pituitary-adrenal cortical system. *Psychosom. Med.*, 30, 576–607.

Masters, W. H., & Johnson, V. E. (1966). *Human sexual response.* Boston: Little, Brown.

Masters, W. H., & Johnson, V. E. (1970). *Human sexual inadequacy.* Boston: Little, Brown.

Matarazzo, J. D. (1972). *Wechsler's measurement and appraisal of adult intelligence* (5th ed.). Baltimore: Williams & Wilkins.

Mathews, A. (1984). Anxiety and its management. In R. N. Gaind, F. I. Fawzy, B. L. Hudson, & R. O. Pasnau (Eds.), *Current themes in psychiatry* (Vol. 3). New York: Spectrum.

Mathews, A. (1985). Anxiety states: a cognitive-behavioural approach. In B. P. Bradley & C. T. Thompson (Eds.), *Psychological applications in psychiatry.* Chichester: Wiley.

Mathews, A., & MacLeod, C. (1986). Discrimination of threat cues without awareness in anxiety states. *J. Abnorm. Psychol.*, 95, 131–138.

Matson, J. L., & Gorman-Smith, D. (1986). A review of treatment research for aggressive and disruptive behavior in the mentally retarded. *Appl. Res. in Ment. Retardation*, 7(1), 95–103.

Matsuyama, S. S., Jarvik, L. F., & Kumar, V. (1985). Dementia: Genetics. In T. Arie (Ed.), *Recent advances in psychogeriatrics.* London: Churchill-Livingstone.

Matuzas, W., & Glass, R. M. (1983). Treatment of agoraphobia and panic attacks. *Arch. Gen. Psych.*, 40(2), 220–222.

Maurer, D. W., & Vogel, V. H. (1973). *Narcotics and narcotic addiction.* Springfield, IL: Thomas.

Maurer, R. G., & Damasio, A. R. (1982). Childhood autism from the point of view of behavioral neurology. *J. Autism Dev. Dis.*, 12, 195–205.

Mavissakalian, M. (1983). Self-directed in vivo exposure practice in behavioral and pharmacological treatments of agoraphobia. *Behav. Ther.*, 14(4), 506–519.

Mavissakalian, M. (1990). Sequential combination of imipramine and self-directed exposure in the treatment of panic disorder with agoraphobia. *J. Clin. Psychiat.*, 51(5), 184–188.

Mavissakalian, M., & Michelson, L. (1983). Tricyclic antidepressants in obsessive-compulsive disorder: Antiobsessional or antidepressant agents? *J. Nerv. Ment. Dis., 171*(5), 301–306.

Mavissakalian, M., & Michelson, L. (1986). Agoraphobia: Relative and combined effectiveness of therapist-assisted in vivo exposure and imipramine. *J. Clin. Psychiat., 47*(3), 117–122.

Mavissakalian, M., & Michelson, L. (1986). Two-year follow-up of exposure and imipramine treatment of agoraphobia. *Amer. J. Psychiat., 143*(9), 1106–1112.

Mavissakalian, M. R., Jones, B. A., & Olson, S. C. (1990). Absence of placebo response in obsessive-compulsive disorder. *J. Nerv. Ment. Dis., 178*(4), 268–270.

Mavissakalian, M. R., Jones, B. A., Olson, S., & Perel, J. M. (1990). Clomipramine in obsessive-compulsive disorder: Clinical response and plasma levels. *J. Clin. Psychopharm., 10*(4), 261–268.

May, J. R. (1977). A psychophysiological study of self and externally regulated phobic thoughts. *Behav. Ther., 8*, 849–861.

May, P. R. A. (1968). *Treatment of schizophrenia*. New York: Science House.

May, P. R. A., & Simpson, G. M. (1980). Schizophrenia: Evaluation of treatment methods. In H. I. Kaplan, A. M. Freedman, & B. J. Sadock (Eds.), *Comprehensive textbook of psychiatry* (Vol. 3). Baltimore: Williams & Wilkins.

May, P. R. A., & Tuma, A. H. (1964). Choice of criteria for the assessment of treatment outcome. *J. Psychiat. Res., 2*(3), 16–527.

May, P. R. A., Tuma, A. H., & Dixon, W. J. (1981). Schizophrenia: A follow-up study of the results of five forms of treatment. *Arch. Gen. Psychiat., 38*, 776–784.

May, R. (1961). *Existential psychology*. New York: Random House.

May, R. (1987). Therapy in our day. In J. K. Zeig (Ed.), *The evolution of psychotherapy*. New York: Brunner/Mazel.

May, R., & Yalom, I. (1989). Existential psychotherapy. In R. J. Corsini & D. Wedding (Eds.), *Current psychotherapies*. Itasca, IL: Peacock.

May, R., Angel, E., & Ellenberger, H. F. (1958). *Existence: A new dimension in psychiatry and psychology*. New York: Basic.

Mays, D. T., & Franks, C. M. (1985). *Negative outcome in psychotherapy and what to do about it*. New York: Springer.

McAdoo, W. G., & DeMyer, M. K. (1978). Research related to family factors in autism. *J. Pediat. Psychol., 2*, 162–166.

McCabe, P. M., & Schneiderman, N. (1985). Psychophysiologic reactions to stress. In N. Schneiderman & J. T. Tapp (Eds.), *Behavioral medicine: The biopsychosocial approach*. Hillsdale, NJ: Erlbaum.

McCarthy, M. (1990). The thin ideal, depression and eating disorders in women. *Behav. Res. Ther., 28*(3), 205–215.

McCarthy, P. R., Katz, I. R., & Foa, E. B. (1991). Cognitive-behavioral treatment of anxiety in the elderly: A proposed model. In C. Salzman & B. D. Leibowitz (Eds.), *Anxiety in the elderly*. New York: Springer.

McClearn, G. E., & Rodgers, D. A. (1961). Genetic factors in alcohol preference of laboratory mice. *J. Compar. Physiol. Psychol., 54*, 116–119.

McClelland, D. C. (1979). Inhibited power motivation and high blood pressure in men. *J. Abnorm. Psychol., 88*(2), 182–190.

McClelland, D. C. (1985). The social mandate of health psychology. *Amer. Behav. Scientist, 28*(4), 451–467.

McClelland, D. C., & Jemmott, J. B. (1980). Power motivation, stress and physical illness. *J. Human Stress, 6*(4), 6–15.

McClelland, D. C., & Kirshnit, C. (1988). The effect of motivational arousal through films on salivary immunoglobulin. *Amer. Psychology & Health, 2*, 31–52.

McClelland, D. C., Floor, E., Davidson, R. J., & Saron, C. (1980). Stressed power motivation, sympathetic activation, immune function, and illness. *J. Human Stress, 6*(2), 11–19.

McConaghy, N. (1971). Aversive therapy of homosexuality: Measures of efficacy. *Amer. J. Psychiat., 127*, 141–144.

McCord, W., & McCord, J. (1960). *Origins of alcoholism*. Stanford, CA: Stanford Univ.

McCord, W., McCord, J., & Gudeman, J. (1959). Some current theories of alcoholism. *Quart. J. Stud. Alcohol., 20*, 727–749.

McCoy, S. A. (1976). Clinical judgments of normal childhood behavior. *J. Cons. Clin. Psychol., 44*(5), 710–714.

McCrae, R. R. (1982). Age differences in the use of coping mechanisms. *J. Gerontology, 37*, 454–460.

McFarlane, W. R. (Ed.). (1983). *Family therapy in schizophrenia*. New York: Guilford.

McFarlane, W. R., & Beels, C. C. (1986). Family research in schizo-
phrenia: A review and integration for clinicians. In W. R. McFarlane (Ed.), *Family therapy in schizophrenia*. New York: Guilford.

McGhie, A. (1961). Disorders of attention and perception in early schizophrenia. *Brit. J. Med. Psychol., 34*, 103–116.

McGlashan, T. H. (1988). A selective review of recent North American long-term followup studies of schizophrenia. *Schizo. Bull., 14*(4), 515–542.

McGlashan, T. H. (1988). Adolescent versus adult onset of mania. *Amer. J. Psychiat., 145*(2), 221–223.

McGlothlin, W. H., Anglin, M. D., & Wilson, B. D. (1978). Narcotic addiction and crime. *Criminology: An Interdisciplinary J., 16*(3), 293–315.

McGrath, P. J., Cooper, T. B., Quitkin, F. M., & Klein, D. F. (1988). Effects of imipramine and phenelzine on plasma PEA levels. *Psychiat. Res., 26*(2), 239.

McGuire, D. (1982). The problem of children's suicide: Ages 5–14. *Inter. J. Offend. Ther. Compar. Crimin., 26*(1), 10–17.

McIntosh, J. L. (1985). Suicide among the elderly: Levels and trends. *Am. J. Orthopsychiat., 55*(2), 289–298.

McIntosh, J. L. (1987). Suicide: Training and education needs with an emphasis on the elderly. *Gerontol. & Geriatric Educ., 7*(3–4), 125–139.

McIntosh, J. L. (1991). Epidemiology of suicide in the U.S. In A. A. Leenaars (Ed.), *Life span perspectives of suicide*. New York: Plenum.

McIntosh, J. L., Hubbard, R. W., & Santos, J. F. (1985). Suicide facts and myths: A study of prevalence. *Death Studies, 9*(3–4), 267–281.

McIntyre, I. M., Johns, M., Norman, T. R., & Armstrong, S. M. (1990). A portable light source for bright light treatment. *Sleep, 13*(3), 272–275.

McKeon, J., McGuffin, P., & Robinson, P. (1984). Obsessive-compulsive neurosis following head injury: A report of four cases. *Brit. J. Psychiat., 144*, 190–192.

McLean, P. D., & Hakstian, A. R. (1979). Clinical depression: Comparative efficacy of outpatient treatments. *J. Cons. Clin. Psychol., 47*(5), 818–836.

McMahon, R. J., & Wells, K. C. (1989). Conduct disorders. In E. J. Mash & R. Barkley (Eds.), *Treatment of childhood disorders*. New York: Guilford.

McNally, R. J. (1986). Behavioral treatment of a choking phobia. *J. Behav. Ther. Exp. Psychiat., 17*(3), 185–188.

McNally, R. J. (1986). Pavlovian conditioning and preparedness: Effects of initial fear level. *Behav. Res. Ther., 24*(1), 27–33.

McNally, R. J. (1986). Preparedness and phobias: A review. *Psychol. Bull., 101*, 283–303.

McNally, R. J., & Foa, E. B. (1986). Preparedness and resistance to extinction to fear-relevant stimuli: A failure to replicate. *Behav. Res. Ther., 24*(5), 529–535.

McNeal, E. T., & Cimbolic, P. (1986). Antidepresants and biochemical theories of depression. *Psychol. Bull., 99*(3), 361–374.

McNees, M. P., Hannah, J. T., Schnelle, J. F., & Bratton, K. M. (1977). The effects of aftercare programs on institutional recidivism. *J. Comm. Psychol., 5*(2), 128–133.

McNeil, E. B. (1967). *The quiet furies*. Englewood Cliffs, NJ: Prentice-Hall.

McPherson, F. M., Brougham, L., & McLaren, S. (1980). Maintenance of improvement in agoraphobic patients treated by behavioral methods — a four-year follow-up. *Behav. Res. Ther., 18*, 913–925.

McShane, W., & Redoutey, L. J. (1987). *Community hospitals and community mental health agencies: Partners in service delivery*. Annual Meeting of the Association of Mental Health Administrators (1986, San Francisco, California). *J. Ment. Hlth. Admin., 14*(2), 1–6.

Mead, M. (1949). *Male and female: A study of the sexes in a changing world*. New York: Dell.

Mednick, S. A. (1970). Breakdown in individuals at high risk for schizophrenia: Possible predispositional perinatal factors. *Ment. Hyg., 54*, 50–63.

Mednick, S. A. (1971). Birth defects and schizophrenia. *Psych. Today, 4*, 48–50.

Meehl, P. E. (1951). *Research results for counselers*. St. Paul, MN: State Dept. Education.

Meehl, P. E. (1954). *Clinical versus statistical prediction: A theoretical analysis and a review of the evidence*. Minneapolis: Univ. of Minnesota.

Meehl, P. E., & Dahlstrom, W. G. (1960). Objective configural rules for discriminating psychotic from neurotic MMPI profiles. *J. Cons. Clin. Psychol., 24,* 375–387.

Meer, J. (1985). Turbulent teens: The stress factors. *Psych. Today, 19*(5), 15–16.

Megargee, E. I. (1966). Undercontrolled and overcontrolled personality types in extreme antisocial aggression. *Psychol. Monographs, 80*(611), 3.

Megargee, E. I. (1977). New classification system for criminal offenders. *Criminal Justice & Behav., 4,* 1–116.

Megargee, E. I. (1986). A psychometric study of incarcerated presidential threateners. *Criminal Justice & Behav., 13,* 243–260.

Mehrabian, A. (1972). *Nonverbal communication.* Chicago: Aldine-Atherton.

Meichenbaum, D. H. (1971). Examination of model characteristics in reducing avoidance behavior. *J. Pers. Soc. Psychol., 17,* 298–307.

Meichenbaum, D. H. (1972). Cognitive modification of test-anxious college students. *J. Cons. Clin. Psychol., 39,* 370–380.

Meichenbaum, D. H. (1972). Examination of model characteristics in reducing avoidance behavior. *J. Behav. Ther. Exp. Psychiat., 3,* 225–227.

Meichenbaum, D. H. (1974). *Cognitive behavior modification.* Morristown, NJ: General Learning.

Meichenbaum, D. H. (1974). Self instruction methods. In F. H. Kanfer & A. P. Goldstein (Eds.), *Helping people change.* New York: Pergamon.

Meichenbaum, D. H. (1975). A self-instructional approach to stress management: A proposal for stress innoculation training. In I. Sarason & C. D. Spielberger (Eds.), *Stress and anxiety* (Vol. 2). New York: Wiley.

Meichenbaum, D. H. (1975). Enhancing creativity by modifying what subjects say to themselves. *Amer. Educ. Res. J., 12*(2), 129–145.

Meichenbaum, D. H. (1975). Theoretical and treatment implications of development research on verbal control of behavior. *Canad. Psychol. Rev., 16*(1), 22–27.

Meichenbaum, D. H. (1975). Toward a cognitive of self control. In G. Schwartz & D. Shapiro (Eds.), *Consciousness and self regulation: Advances in research.* New York: Plenum.

Meichenbaum, D. H. (1976). A cognitive-behavior modification approach to assessment. In M. Hersen & A. S. Bellack (Eds.), *Behavioral assessment: A practical handbook.* New York: Pergamon.

Meichenbaum, D. H. (1977). *Cognitive-behavior modification: An integrative approach.* New York: Plenum.

Meichenbaum, D. H. (1977). Dr. Ellis, please stand up. *Couns. Psychologist, 7*(1), 43–44.

Meichenbaum, D. H. (1986). Metacognitive methods of instruction: Current status and future prospects. *Special Services in the Schools, 3*(1–2), 23–32.

Meichenbaum, D. H., & Cameron, R. (1983). Stress innoculation training: Toward a general paradigm for training coping skills. In D. Meichenbaum & M. E. Jarenko (Eds.), *Stress reduction and prevention.* New York: Plenum.

Meichenbaum, D., Henshaw, D., & Himel, N. (1982). Coping with stress as a problem-solving process. *Series in Clin. & Comm. Psychol. Achievement, Stress, & Anx.,* 127–142.

Meketon, M. J. (1983). Indian mental health: An orientation. *Amer. J. Orthopsychiat., 53*(1), 110–115.

Melcher, J. (1988). Keeping our elderly out of institutions by putting them back in their homes. *Amer. Psychol., 43*(8), 643–647.

Meltzer, H. Y. (1987). Biological studies in schizophrenia. *Schizo. Bull., 13*(1), 77–111.

Meltzoff, J., & Blumenthal, R. L. (1966). *The day treatment center: Principles, application and evaluation.* Springfield, IL: Thomas.

Meltzoff, J., & Kornreich, M. (1970). *Research in psychotherapy.* New York: Atherton.

Melville, J. (1978). *Phobias and obsessions.* New York: Penguin.

Mendels, J. (1970). *Concepts of depression.* New York: Wiley.

Mendels, J., & Frazer, A. (1974). Brain biogenic amine depletion and mood. *Arch. Gen. Psychiat., 30*(4), 447–451.

Menke, J. A., McClead, R. E., & Hansen, N. B. (1991). Perspectives on perinatal complications associated with mental retardation. In J. L. Matson & J. A. Mulick (Eds.), *Handbook of mental retardation.* New York: Pergamon.

Menninger, K. (1938). *Man against himself.* New York: Harcourt.

Mercer, J. R. (1973). *Labeling the mentally retarded.* Berkeley, CA: Univ. California.

Merikangas, K. R., & Weissman, N. M. (1986). Epidemiology of DSM-III Axis II personality disorders. In A. J. Frances & R. E.

Hales (Eds.), *Psychiatry update* (Vol. 5). Washington, DC: American Psychiatric.

Merskey, H. (1986). Classification of chronic pain: Descriptions of chronic pain syndromes and definitions of pain terms. *Pain, 3,* 226.

Meyer, J. E. (1984). Die Therapie der Schizophrenie in Klinik und Praxis [Inpatient and outpatient treatment of schizophrenia]. *Nervenarzt, 55*(5), 221–229.

Meyer, R. E., Murray, R. F., Jr., Thomas, F. B. et al. (1989). *Prevention and treatment of alcohol problems: Research opportunities.* Washington, DC: National Academy.

Meyer, V., Levy, T., & Schnurer, A. A. (1974). Behavioral treatment of OCD. In H. R. Beech (Ed.), *Obsessional states.* London: Methuen.

Mezzich, J. E., Coffman, G. A., & Goodpastor, S. M. (1982). A format for DSM III diagnostic formulation: Experience with 1,111 consecutive patients. *Amer. J. Psychiat., 139*(5), 591–596.

Michter, M. (1990). Psychological therapies in bulimia nervosa. In M. M. Fichter (Ed.), *Bulimia nervosa: Basic research, diagnosis and therapy.* Chichester: Wiley.

Miesel, A. (1989). *The right to die.* New York: Wiley.

Miklich, D. R., Rewey, H. H., Weiss, J. H., & Kolton, S. (1973). A preliminary investigation of psychophysiological responses to stress among different subgroups of asthmatic children. *J. Psychosom. Res., 17,* 1–8.

Miklowitz, D. J., & Goldstein, M. J. (1990). Behavioral family treatment for patients with bipolar affective disorder [Special Issue]. *Behav. Mod., 14*(4), 457–489.

Miklowitz, D. J., Goldstein, M. J., Nuechterlein, K. H., Synder, K. S. et al. (1988). Family factors and the course of bipolar affective disorder. *Arch. Gen. Psychiat., 45*(3), 225–231.

Milan, M. J., & Emrick, H. M. (1981). Endorphinergic systems and the response to stress. *Psychother. Psychosom., 36*(1), 43–56.

Miles, C. P. (1977). Conditions predisposing to suicide: A review. *J. Nerv. Ment. Dis., 164*(4), 231–246.

Millar, J. D. (1984). The NIOSH-suggested list of the ten leading work-related diseases and injuries. *J. Occupational Med., 26,* 340–341.

Millar, J. D. (1990). Mental health and the workplace: An interchangeable partnership. *Amer. Psychol., 45*(10), 1165–1166.

Miller, D., & Carlton, B. S. (1985). The etiology and treatment of anorexia nervosa. *Adol. Psychiat., 12,* 219–232.

Miller, G. E., & Prinz, R. J. (1990). Enhancement of social learning family interventions for childhood conduct disorder. *Psychol. Bull., 108*(2), 291–307.

Miller, N. E. (1948). Studies of fear as an acquirable drive. I. Fear as motivation and fear-reduction as reinforcement in the learning of new responses. *J. Exp. Psychol., 38,* 89–101.

Miller, N. S., & Giannini, A. J. (1990). The disease model of addiction: A biopsychiatrist's view. *J. Psychoact. Drugs, 22*(1), 83–85.

Miller, N. S., & Gold, M. S. (1990). Benzodiazepines: Tolerance, dependence, abuse, and addiction. *J. Psychoact. Drugs, 22*(1), 23–33.

Miller, N. S., Klahr, A. L., Gold, M. S., Sweeney, K. et al. (1990). The prevalence of marijuana (cannabis) use and dependence in cocaine dependence. *N.Y. St. J. Med., 90*(10), 491–492.

Miller, P. M. (1978). Alternative skills in training in alcoholism treatment. In P. E. Nathan, G. A. Marlatt, & T. Loberg (Eds.), *Experimental and behavioral approaches to alcoholism.* New York: Plenum.

Miller, P. M., Ingham, J. G., & Davidson, S. (1976). Life events, symptoms, and social support. *J. Psychiat. Res., 20*(6), 514–522.

Miller, W. R. (1977). Behavioral self-control training in the treatment of problem drinkers. In R. B. Stuart (Ed.), *Behavioral self-management: Strategies, techniques and outcomes.* New York: Brunner/Mazel.

Miller, W. R. (1982). Treating problem drinkers: What works? *Behav. Ther., 5,* 15–18.

Miller, W. R. (1983). Controlled drinking. *Quart. J. Stud. Alcohol., 44,* 68–83.

Miller, W. R., & Dougher, M. J. (1984). *Covert sensitization: Alternative treatment approaches for alcoholics.* Paper presented at the Second Congress of the International Society for Biomedical Research on Alcoholism, Santa Fe.

Miller, W. R., & Hester, R. K. (1980). Treating the problem drinker: Modern approaches. In W. R. Miller (Ed.), *The addictive behaviors: Treatment of alcoholism, drug abuse, smoking, and obesity.* Elmsford, NY: Pergamon.

Miller, W. R., & Hester, R. K. (1986). Inpatient alcoholism treatment: Who benefits? *Amer. Psychol., 41,* 794–805.

Miller, W. R., & Seligman, M. E. (1975). Depression and learned helplessness in man. *J. Abnorm. Psychol., 84*(3), 228–238.

Millon, T. (1969). *Modern psychopathology: A biosocial approach to maladaptive learning and functioning.* Philadelphia: Saunders.

Millon, T. (1981). *Disorders of personality.* New York: Wiley.

Millon, T. (1988). Personologic psychotherapy. *Psychotherapy, 25,* 209–219.

Millon, T. (1990). *Toward a new personology.* New York: Wiley.

Millon, T., & Everly, G. S. (1985). *Personality and its disorders.* New York: Wiley.

Mills, M. C. (1985). Intervention strategies in a suicidal case. *Psych. Rep., 56*(3), 718.

Mineka, S. (1985). Animal models of anxiety-based disorders: Their usefulness and limitations. In A. H. Tuma & J. Maser (Eds.), *Anxiety and the anxiety disorders.* Hillsdale, NJ: Erlbaum.

Mineka, S., & Hendersen, R. (1985). Controllability and predictability in acquired motivation. *Annu. Rev. Psychol., 36,* 495–530.

Mineka, S., Davidson, M., Cook, M., & Keir, R. (1984). Observational conditioning of snake fear in rhesus monkeys. *J. Abnorm. Psychol.*

Mineo, B. A., & Cavalier, A. R. (1985). From idea to implementation: Cognitive software for students with learning disabilities. *J. Learn. Dis., 18*(10), 613–618.

Minuchin, S. (1970). The use of an ecological framework in the treatment of a child. In J. Anthony & C. Koupernik (Eds.), *The child in his family.* New York: Wiley.

Minuchin, S. (1974). *Families and family therapy.* Cambridge, MA: Harvard Univ.

Minuchin, S. (1987). My many voices. In J. K. Zeig (Ed.), *The evolution of psychotherapy.* New York: Brunner/Mazel.

Minuchin, S., & Fishman, H. (1981). *Family therapy techniques.* Cambridge, MA: Harvard Univ.

Minuchin, S., Rosman, B. L., & Baker, L. (1978). *Psychosomatic families: Anorexia nervosa in context.* Cambridge, MA: Harvard Univ.

Miranda, J., & Persons, J. D. (1988). Dysfunctional attitudes are mood state dependent. Meetings of the Assoc. for Advancement of Behavior Therapy. *J. Abnorm. Psychol., 97*(1), 76–79.

Mirkin, M. P. (1985). The Peter Pan syndrome: Inpatient treatment of adolescent anorexia nervosa. *Inter. J. Fam. Ther., 7*(3), 205–216.

Mirsky, I. A. (1958). Physiologic, psychologic, and social determinants of the etiology of duodenal ulcer. *Amer. J. Digestional Diseases, 3,* 285–314.

Mirsky, I. A., Miller, R. E., & Murphy, J. V. (1958). The communication of affect in rhesus monkeys. *J. Amer. Psychoanal. Assoc., 6,* 433–441.

Mischel, W. (1968). *Personality and assessment.* New York: Wiley.

Mishler, E., & Waxler, N. (1968). *Interaction in families: An experimental study of family process and schizophrenia.* New York: Wiley.

Mitchell, J. E., & Pyle, R. L. (1985). Characteristics of bulimia. In J. E. Mitchell (Ed.), *Anorexia nervosa and bulimia: Diagnosis and treatment.* Minneapolis: Univ. Minnesota.

Mitchell, J. E., & Pyle, R. L., & Eckert, E. D. (1981). The bulimic syndrome in normal weight individuals: A review. *Inter. J. Eat. Dis., 1,* 61–73.

Mitchell, J. E., Hatsukami, D., Goff, G., Pyle, R. L., Eckert, E. D., & Davis, L. E. (1985). Intensive outpatient group treatment for bulimia. In D. M. Garner & P. E. Garfinkel (Eds.), *Handbook of psychotherapy for anorexia nervosa and bulimia.* New York: Guilford.

Mitchell, J. E., Hatsukami, D., Pyle, R. L., & Eckert, E. D. (1986). The bulimia syndrome: Course of the illness and associated problems. *Comprehen. Psychiat., 27*(2), 165–170.

Mitchell, J. E., Pyle, R. L., & Eckert, E. D. (1981). Frequency and duration of binge-eating episodes in patients with bulimia. *Amer. J. Psychiat., 138*(6), 835–836.

Mitchell, J. E., Pyle, R. L., Eckert, E. D., Hatsukami, D., & Lentz, R. (1983). Electrolyte and other physiological abnormalities in patients with bulimia. *Psychol. Med., 13,* 273–278.

Mitchell, J. E., Pyle, R. L., Eckert, E. D., Hatsukami, D. et al. (1990). Bulimia nervosa in overweight individuals. *J. Nerv. Ment. Dis., 178*(5), 324–327.

Mohler, H., & Okada, T. (1977). Benzodiazepine receptor: Demonstration in the central nervous system. *Science, 198*(4319), 849–851.

Mohr, D. C., & Buetler, L. E. (1990). Erectile dysfunction: A review

of diagnostic and treatment procedures. *Clin. Psychology Rev., 10*(1), 123–150.

Mohr, J. W., Turner, R. E., & Jerry, M. B. (1964). *Pedophilia and exhibitionism.* Toronto: Univ. Toronto.

Monahan, J. (1978). Prediction research and the emergency commitment of dangerous mentally ill persons: A reconsideration. *Amer. J. Psychiat., 135,* 198–201.

Monahan, J. (1981). *The clinical prediction of violent behavior.* Washington, DC: GPO.

Monahan, J. (1984). The prediction of violent behavior: Toward a second generation of theory and policy. *Amer. J. Psychiat., 141,* 10–15.

Monahan, J., & Davis, S. K. (1983). Mentally disordered sex offenders. In J. Monahan & H. J. Steadman (Eds.), *Mentally disordered offenders.* New York: Plenum.

Monjan, A. A., & Collector, M. I. (1977). Stress-induced modulation of the immune response. *Science, 197,* 307–308.

Montagu, J. D., & Coles, E. M. (1966). Mechanism and measurement of the galvanic skin response. *Psychol. Bull., 65,* 261–279.

Montgomery, S. A. (1989). The efficacy of fluoxetine as an antidepressant in the short and long term. *Inter. Clin. Psychopharm., 4*(Suppl. 1), 113–119.

Montgomery, S. A., Dufour, H., Brion S., Gailledreau, J. et al. (1988). The prophylactic efficacy of fluoxetine in unipolar depression. *Brit. J. Psychiat., 153*(3, Suppl.), 69–76.

Moody, H. (1969). Psychedelic drugs and religious experience. In R. E. Hicks & P. J. Fink (Eds.), *Psychedelic drugs.* New York: Grune & Stratton.

Moore, N. (1965). Behavior therapy in bronchial asthma: A controlled study. *J. Psychosom. Res., 9,* 257–276.

Moore, T. W., & Paolillo, J. C. (1984). Depression: Influence of hopelessness, locus of control, hostility and length of treatment. *Psych. Rep., 54*(3), 875–881.

Moos, R. H. (1988). Psychosocial factors in the workplace. In S. Fisher & J. Reason, *Handbook of life stress, cognition and health.* Chichester: Wiley.

Moos, R. H., & Finney, J. W. (1983). The expanding scope of alcoholism treatment evaluation. *Amer. Psychol., 38*(10), 1036–1044.

Morgan, A. H., & Hilgard, E. R. (1973). Age differences in susceptibility to hypnosis. *Inter. J. Clin. Exp. Hyp., 21,* 78–85.

Morgan, C. D., & Murray, H. A. (1935). A method of investigating fantasies: The Thematic Apperception Test. *Arch. Neurol. Psychiat., 34,* 289–306.

Morgan, H. G., & Russell, G. F. M. (1975). Value of family background and clinical features as predictors of long-term outcome in anorexia nervosa: Four-year follow-up of 41 patients. *Psychol. Med., 5,* 355–371.

Morley, S. (1989). Single case research. In G. Parry & N. W. Fraser (Eds.), *Behavioural and mental health research: A handbook of skills and methods.* Hove, UK: Erlbaum.

Morokoff, P. J. (1978). Determinants of female orgasm. In J. LoPiccolo & L. LoPiccolo (Eds.), *Handbook of sex therapy.* New York: Plenum.

Morokoff, P. J. (1988). Sexuality in premenopausal and postmenopausal women. *Psychol. of Women Quart., 12,* 489–511.

Morris, G. (1983). Acquittal by reason of insanity: Developments in the law. In J Monahan & H. J. Steadman (Eds.), *Mentally disordered offenders.* New York: Plenum.

Morris, J. B., & Beck, A. T. (1974). The efficacy of antidepressant drugs: A review of research (1958–1972). *Arch. Gen. Psychiat., 30*(5), 667–674.

Morris, R. J., & Kratochwill, T. R. (1983). *The practice of child therapy.* New York: Pergamon.

Morris, R. J., & Kratochwill, T. R. (1983). *Treating children's fears and phobias: A behavioral approach.* New York: Pergamon.

Morrison, J. R. (1980). Childhood hyperactivity in an adult psychiatric population: Social factors. *J. Clin. Psychiat., 41*(2), 40–43.

Morrison, R. L., & Bellack, A. S. (1987). Social functioning of schizophrenic patients: Clinical and research issues. *Schizo. Bull., 13*(4), 715–725.

Morrow-Bradley, C., & Elliot, R. (1986). Utilization of psychotherapy research by practicing psychotherapists. *Amer. Psychol., 41*(2), 188–197.

Morse, S. J. (1982). A preference for liberty: The case against involuntary commitment of the mentally disordered. *Calif. Law Rev., 70,* 55–106.

Motley, M. T. (1988). Taking the terror out of talk. *Psych. Today, 22*(1), 46–49.

Motto, J. (1980). The right to suicide: A psychiatrist's view. In M. P. Battin & D. J. Mayo (Eds.), *Suicide: The philosophical issues.* New York: St. Martin's.

Mowrer, O. H. (1939). A stimulus-response analysis of anxiety and its role as a reinforcing agent. *Psychol. Rev., 46,* 553–566.

Mowrer, O. H. (1939). An experimentally produced "social problem" in rats [Film]. Bethlehem, PA: Psychological Cinema Register, Lehigh Univ.

Mowrer, O. H. (1947). On the dual nature of learning: A reinterpretation of "conditioning" and "problem-solving." *Harvard Educ. Rev., 17,* 102–148.

Mowrer, O. H., & Mowrer, W. M. (1938). Enuresis: A method for its study and treatment. *Amer. J. Orthopsychiat., 8,* 436–459.

Muehlenhard, C. L., & Linton, M. A. (1987). Date rape and sexual aggression in dating situations: Incidence and risk factors. *J. Couns. Psychol., 34*(2), 186–196.

Mueser, K. T., Bellack, A. S., & Brady, E. U. (1990). Hallucinations in schizophrenia. *Acta Psychiatr. Scandin., 82*(1), 29–36.

Muller, P. (1983). Was sollen wir Schizophrenen raten: Medikamentose Langzeitpropylaxe oder Intervallbehandlung? [What advice should be given to schizophrenic patients—long-term maintenance on neuroleptics or treatment at intervals?]. *Nervenarzt, 54*(9), 477–485.

Mumby, J., & Johnson, D. W. (1980). Agoraphobia: The long-term follow-up of behavioral treatment. *Brit. J. Psychiat., 137,* 417–418.

Munjack, D. J. (1979). The onset of driving phobias. *J. Behav. Ther. Exp. Psychiat., 17,* 489–493.

Munsinger, H. (1975). The adopted child's IQ: A critical review. *Psychol. Bull., 82,* 623–659.

Murphy, G. E. et al. (1979). Suicide and alcoholism: Interpersonal loss confirmed as a predictor. *Arch. Gen. Psychiat., 36*(1), 65–69.

Murphy, G. E., Simons, A. D., Wetzel, R. D. et al. (1984). Cognitive therapy and pharmacotherapy singly and together, in the treatment of depression. *Arch. Gen. Psychiat., 41,* 33–41.

Murphy, J. (1976). Psychiatric labeling in cross-cultural perspective. *Science, 191,* 1019–1028.

Murphy, J. B., & Lipshultz, L. I. (1988). Infertility in the paraplegic male. In E. A. Tanagho, T. F .Lue, & R. D. McClure (Eds.), *Contemporary management of impotence and infertility.* Baltimore: Williams & Wilkins.

Murphy, J. M. (1976, March). Psychiatric labeling in cross-cultural perspective: Similar kinds of disturbed behavior appear to be labeled abnormal in diverse cultures. *Science, 101*(4231), 1019–1028.

Murphy, J. W., & Pardeck, J. T. (1986). Computerized clinical practice: Promises and shortcomings. *Psych. Rep., 59*(3), 1099–1113.

Murphy, M., & Deutsch, S. I. (1991). Neurophysiological and neurochemical basis of behavior. In K. Davis, H. Klar, & J. T. Coyle (Eds.), *Foundations of psychiatry.* Philadelphia: Saunders.

Murray, E., & Foote, F. (1979). The origins of fear of snakes. *Behav. Res. Ther., 17,* 489–493.

Murray, H. A. (1938). *Explorations in personality.* Fairlawn, NJ: Oxford Univ.

Murray, J. B. (1982). What is meditation? Does it help? *Genetic Psychol. Monographs, 106*(1), 85–115.

Murray, J. B. (1986). Psychological aspects of anorexia nervosa. *Genetic, Social & Genetic Psychology Monographs, 112*(1), 5–40.

Mutter, C. B. (1980). *A hypno-therapeutic approach to exhibitionism: Outpatient therapeutic strategy.* Paper presented at the Annual Meeting of the American Society of Clinical Hypnosis. Minneapolis, MN.

Muuss, R. E. (1986). Adolescent eating disorder: Bulimia. *Adolescence, 21*(82), 257–267.

Myers, D., & Grant, G. (1972). A study of depersonalization in students. *Brit. J. Psychiat., 121,* 59–65.

Myers, J. K. et al. (1984). Six month prevalence of psychiatric disorder in three communities: 1980 to 1982. (1984). *Arch. Gen. Psychiat., 41*(10), 959–967.

Myers, K. M., Burke, P., & McCauley, E. (1985). Suicidal behavior by hospitalized preadolescent children on a psychiatric unit. *J. Amer. Acad. Child Psychiat., 24*(4), 474–480.

Nace, E., Orne, M. T., & Hammer, A. G. (1974). Posthypnotic amnesia as an active psychic process: The reversibility of amnesia. *Arch. Gen. Psychiat., 31*(2), 257–260.

Naka, K. et al. (1985). Yuta (shaman) and community health on Okinawa. *Inter. J. Soc. Psychiat., 31*(4), 267–274.

Nathan, P. E., & Harris, S. L. (1980). *Psychopathology and society* (2nd ed.). New York: McGraw-Hill.

Nathan, P. E., & O'Brien, J. S. (1971). An experimental analysis of the behavior of alcoholics and nonalcoholics during prolonged periods of experimental drinking: A necessary precursor of behavior therapy? *Behav. Ther., 2,* 455–476.

Nathan, P. E., Titler, N. A., Lowenstein, L. W., Solomon, P., & Rossi, A. M. (1970). Behavioral analysis of chronic alcoholism. *Arch. Gen. Psychiat., 22,* 419–430.

National Inst. for Occupational Safety & Health. (1985). Proposed national strategies for the prevention of leading work-related diseases and injuries. (Pt. 1, NTIS No. PB87-114740). Cincinnati: Assoc. of Schools of Public Health/NIOSH.

National Inst. for Occupational Safety & Health. (1988). Proposed national strategies for the prevention of leading work-related diseases and injuries. (Pt. 2, NTIS No. PB89-130348). Cincinnati: Assoc. of Schools of Public Health/NIOSH.

National Institute on Drug Abuse. (1985). *National household survey on drugs.* Washington, DC: Author.

National Institute on Drug Abuse. (1986). *Annual data, from drug abuse warning network.* Washington, DC: Author.

National Institute on Drug Abuse. (1986). *National high school senior survey.* Washington, DC: Author.

National Institute on Drug Abuse. (1987). *Second triennial report to Congress on drug abuse and drug abuse research.* Washington, DC: Author.

Naylor, G. J., Dick, D. A., Dick, E. G., Moody, J. P. (1974). Lithium therapy and erythrocyte membrane cation carrier. *Psychopharmacology, 37*(1), 81–86.

Neiger, B. L., & Hopkins, R. W. (1988). Adolescent suicide: Character traits of high-risk teenagers. *Adolescence, 23*(90), 469–475.

Neisser, U. (1985, Sep.). Voices, glances, flashbacks. *Psych. Today,* 48–53.

Nelson, R. O., & Barlow, D. H. (1981). Behavioral assessment: Basic and initial procedures. In D. H. Barlow (Ed.), *Behavioral assessment of adult disorders.* New York: Guilford.

Nelson, R. O., Hay, L. R., Hay, W. M., & Carstens, C. B. (1977). The reactivity and accuracy of teachers' self monitoring of positive and negative classroom verbalizations. *Behav. Ther., 8*(5), 972–985.

Nemiah, J. C. (1975). Obsessive-compulsive neurosis. In A. M. Freedman & H. I. Kaplan (Eds.), *A comprehensive textbook of psychiatry.* Baltimore: Williams & Williams.

Nemiah, J. C. (1989). Dissociative disorders (hysterical neuroses, dissociative type). In H. I. Kaplan & B. J. Sadock (Eds.), *Comprehensive textbook of psychiatry* (Vol. 1, 5th ed.). Baltimore: Williams & Wilkins.

Nemiah, J. C. (1989). The varieties of human experience. 1988 Annual Meeting of the American Psychiatric Assoc. *Brit. J. Psychiat., 154,* 459–466.

Neugarten, B. L. (1968). Adult personality: Toward a psychology of the life cycle. In B. L. Neugarten (Ed.), *Middle age and aging: Reader in social psychology.* Chicago: Univ. Chicago.

Neugebauer, R. (1978). Treatment of the mentally ill in medieval and early modern England: A reappraisal. *J. History of Behav. Sci., 14,* 158–169.

Neugebauer, R. (1979). Medieval and early modern theories of mental illness. *Arch. Gen. Psychiat., 36,* 477–483.

Neuringer, C. (1974). Self and other appraisals by suicidal psychosomatic and normal hospital patients. *J. Clin. Cons. Psychol., 42,* 306.

Neuringer, C. (1976). Current developments in the study of suicidal thinking. In E. S. Schneidman (Ed.), *Suicidology: Contemporary developments.* New York: Grune & Stratton.

Neville, D., & Barnes, S. (1985). The suicidal phone call. *J. Psychol. Nursing Ment. Hlth. Services, 23*(8), 14–18.

Newberger, E. H. (1983). The helping hand strikes again: Unintended consequences of child abuse reporting. *J. Clin. Child. Psychol., 12,* 307–311.

Newman, J. P., & Kosson, D. S. (1986). Passive avoidance learning in psychopathic and nonpsychopathic offenders. *J. Abnorm. Psychol., 95,* 257–263.

Newman, J. P., Patterson, C. M., & Kosson, D. S. (1987). Response perseveration in psychopaths. *J. Abnorm. Psychol., 96,* 145–149.

Nezu, A. M. (1986). Efficacy of a social problem-solving therapy approach for unipolar depression. *J. Cons. Clin. Psychol., 54,* 196–202.

Nielsen, S. (1990). Epidemiology of anorexia nervosa in Denmark from 1973 to 1987: A nationwide register study of psychiatric admission. *Acta Psychiatr. Scandin., 81*(6), 507–514.

Nihira, K., Foster, R., Shellhaas, M., & Leland, H. (1974). *AAMD Adaptive Behavior Scale, 1974 Revision.* Washington, DC: American Assoc. on Mental Deficiency.

Nijinsky, V. (1936). *The diary of Vaslav Nijinksy.* New York: Simon & Schuster.

Nisbett, R. E., & Ross, L. (1980). *Human inference: Strategies and shortcomings.* Englewood Cliffs, NJ: Prentice-Hall.

Nolen-Hoeksema, S. (1987). Sex differences in unipolar depression: Evidence and theory. *Psychol. Bull., 101*(2), 259–282.

Noonan, J. R. (1971). An obsessive-compulsive reaction treated by induced anxiety. *Amer. J. Psychother., 25*(2), 293–299.

Norcross, J. C. (1986). Special section: Training integrative/eclectic psychotherapists. *Inter. J. Eclectic Psychother., 5*(1), 71–94.

Norcross, J. C. (Ed.). (1986). *Handbook of eclectic psychotherapy.* New York: Brunner/Mazel.

Norcross, J. C., & Prochaska, J. O. (1984). Where do behavior (and other) therapists take their troubles? II. *Behav. Therapist, 7*(2), 26–27.

Norcross, J. C. et al. (1987). *Presentation.* Eastern Psychological Assoc.

Norman, D. K., & Herzog, D. B. (1986). A three-year outcome study in normal-weight bulimia: Assessment of psychosocial functioning and eating attitudes. *Psychiat. Res., 19,* 199.

Norton, G. R., Dorward, J., & Cox, B. J. (1986). Factors associated with panic attacks in non-clinical subjects. *Behav. Ther., 17,* 239–252.

Norton, G. R., Harrison, B., Hauch, J. et al. (1985). Characteristics of people with infrequent panic attacks. *J. Abnorm. Psychol., 94,* 216–221.

Novaco, R. W. (1975). Anger control: The development and evaluation of an experimental treatment. Lexington, MA: Heath.

Novaco, R. W. (1976). The functions and regulation of the arousal of anger. *Amer. J. Psychiat., 133*(10), 1124–1128.

Novaco, R. W. (1976). Treatment of chronic anger through cognitive and relaxation controls. *J. Cons. Clin. Psychol., 44*(4), 681.

Novaco, R. W. (1977). A stress innoculation approach to anger management in the training of law enforcement officers. *Amer. J. Comm. Psychol., 5*(3), 327–346.

Novaco, R. W. (1977). Stress innoculation: A cognitive therapy for anger and its application to a case of depression. *J. Cons. Clin. Psychol., 45*(4), 600–608.

Noyes, R., & Dempsey, G. M. (1974). Lithium treatment of depression. *Dis. Nerv. Sys., 35* (12), 573–576.

Noyes, R., & Kletti, R. (1977). Depersonalization in response to life-threatening danger. *Comprehen. Psychiat., 18*(4), 375–384.

Noyes, R., Anderson, D. J., Clancy, J., Crowe, R. R., Slyman, D. J., Ghoneim, M. M., & Hinrichs, J. V. (1984). Diazepam and propanolol in panic disorder and agoraphobia. *Arch. Gen. Psychiat., 41,* 287–292.

Noyes, R., Chaudry, D. R., & Domingo, D. V. (1986). Pharmacologic treatment of phobic disorders. *J. Clin. Psychiat., 47*(9), 445–452.

Noyes, R. et al. (1986). Relationship between panic disorder and agoraphobia: A family study. *Arch. Gen. Psychiat., 43*(3), 227–232.

Noyes, R., Jr., Clancy, J., Crowe, R., Hoenk, P. R., & Slymen, D. J. (1978). The familial prevalence of anxiety neurosis. *Arch. Gen. Psychiat., 35,* 1057–1059.

Noyes, R., Reich, J., Clancy, J., & O'Gorman, T. W. (1986). Reduction in hypochondriasis with treatment of panic disorder. *Brit. J. Psychiat., 149,* 631–635.

Nunes, J. S., & Marks, I. M. (1975). Feedback of true heart rate during exposure in vivo. *Arch. Gen. Psychiat., 32*(7), 933–936.

Nunes, J. S., & Marks, I. M. (1976). Feedback of true heart rate during exposure in vivo: Partial replication with methodological improvement. *Arch. Gen. Psychiat., 33*(11), 1346–1350.

Nutzinger, D. O., & Zwaan, M. (1990). Behavioural treatment of bulimia (nervosa). In M. M. Fichter (Ed.), *Bulimia nervosa: Basic research, diagnosis and therapy.* Chichester: Wiley.

O'Banion, K., & Arkowitz, H. (1977). Social anxiety and selective memory for affective information about the self. *Soc. Behav. Pers., 5*(2), 321–328.

O'Brien, C. P., & Woody, G. (1989). Evaluation of psychotherapy. In H. I. Kaplan & B. J. Sadock (Eds.), *Comprehensive textbook of psychiatry* (5th ed.). Baltimore: Williams & Wilkins.

O'Connell, D. S. (1983). The placebo effect and psychotherapy. *Psychother. Theory Res. Prac., 20*(3), 337–345.

O'Connell, R. A., Mayo, J. A., Eng, L. K., Jones, J. S., & Gabel, R. H. (1985). Social support and long-term lithium outcome. *Br. J. Psychiat., 147,* 272–275.

O'Connor, D. (1979, Oct. ). Good girls and orgasm. *Newsweek.*

O'Dell, S. L. (1974). Training parents in behavior modification: A review. *Psychol. Bull., 81,* 418–433.

O'Dell, S. L. (1985). Progress in parent training. In M. Hersen, R. M. Eisler, & P. M. Miller (Eds.), *Progress in behavior modification* (Vol. 9). New York: Academic.

O'Keefe, E. J., & Castaldo, C. (1985). Multimodal therapy for anorexia nervosa: An holistic approach to treatment. *Psychother. Priv. Prac., 3*(2), 19–29.

O'Leary, K. D., & Wilson, G. T. (1987). *Behavior therapy: Application and outcome* (2nd ed.). Englewood Cliffs, NJ: Prentice-Hall.

O'Neil, M. K., Lancee, W. J., & Freeman, S. J. (1986). Psychological factors and depressive symptoms. *J. Nerv. Ment. Dis., 174*(1), 15–23.

O'Rourke, G. C. (1990). The HIV-positive intravenous drug abuser. Special Issue: HIV infection and AIDS. *Amer. J. Occupational Ther., 44*(3), 280–283.

O'Shea, B., Falvey, J., Matthews, G., & Murphy, P. (1989). Capgras syndrome: A non-specific, often organic phenomenon. *Irish J. Psychiat., 10*(1), 13–16.

Oei, T. P., Lim, B., & Hennessy, B. (1990). Psychological dysfunction in battle: Combat stress reactions and posttraumatic stress disorder. *Clin. Psychol. Rev., 10*(3), 355–388.

Offer, D., Ostrov, E., & Howard, K. I. (1981). The mental health professional's concept of the normal adolescent. *Arch. Gen. Psychiat., 38*(2), 140–152.

Ogletree, S. M., Williams, S. W., Raffeld, P., Mason, B. et al. (1990). Female attractiveness and eating disorders: Do children's television commercials play a role? *Sex Roles, 22*(11–12), 791–797.

Ohman, A. (1987). Evolution, learning and phobias. In D. Magnusson & A. Ohman (Eds.), *Psychopathology.* New York: Academic.

Ohman, A., Erixon, G., & Lofberg, I. (1975). Phobias and preparedness: Phobic versus neutral pictures as continued stimuli for human autonomic responses. *J. Abnorm. Psychol., 84,* 41–45.

Oke, A. F., Adams, R. N., Winblad, B., & von Knorring, L. (1988). Elevated dopamine/norapinephrine ratios in thalami of schizophrenic brains. *Bio. Psychiat., 24*(1), 78–82.

Okin, R. L., & Borus, J. F. (1989). Primary, secondary and tertiary prevention of mental disorders. In H. I. Kaplan & B. J. Sadock (Eds.), *Comprehensive textbook of psychiatry* (5th ed.). Baltimore: Williams & Wilkins.

Olds, M. E., & Fobes, J. L. (1981). The central basis of motivation: Intracranial self-stimulation studies. *Annu. Rev. Psychol., 32,* 523–574.

Olmos de Paz, T. (1990). Working-through and insight in child psychoanalysis. *Melanie Klein & Object Relations, 8*(1), 99–112.

Oppenheim, R. C. (1976). Reactions to "Employing electric shock with autistic children." *J. Autism Child. Schizo., 6,* 291–292.

Orr, S. P., Claiborn, J. M., Altman, B., Forgue, D. F. et al. (1990). Psychometric profile of posttraumatic stress disorder, anxious, and healthy Vietnam veterans: Correlations with psychophysiologic responses. *J. Cons. Clin. Psychol., 58*(3), 329–335.

Osgood, M. J. (1985). *Suicide in the elderly: A practitioner's guide to diagnosis and mental health intervention.* Rockville, MD: Aspen.

Osgood, M. J. (1987). Suicide and the elderly. *Generations, 11*(3), 47–51.

Ost, L. G., Jerremalm, A., & Johansson, J. (1981). Individual response patterns in clinical patients. *Behav. Res. Ther., 19,* 439–447.

Osterweis, M. (1988). Perceptions not yet matched by research [Special Issue]. *J. Palliative Care, 4*(12), 78–80.

Osterweis, M., & Townsend, J. (1988). Understanding bereavement reactions in adults and children: A booklet for lay people. Rockville, MD: U. S. Dept. Health and Human Services.

Otto, R. K. (1989). Bias and expert testimony of mental health professionals in adversarial proceedings: A preliminary investigation. *Behav. Sci. Law, 7*(2), 267–273.

Ottosson, J. O. (1960). Experimental studies of the mode of action of electroconvulsive therapy. *Acta Psychiatr. Neurol. Scandin., 35*(145), 141.

Ottosson, J. O. (1985). Use and misuse of electroconvulsive treatment. *Bio. Psychiat., 20*(9), 933–946.

Overholser, J. C. (1990). Retest reliability of the Millon Clinical Multiaxial Inventory. *J. Pers. Assess., 55*(1–2), 202–208.

Overton, D. (1964). State-dependent or "dissociated" learning produced with pentobarbital. *J. Compar. Physiol. Psychol., 57,* 3–12.

Overton, D. (1966). State-dependent learning produced by depressant and atropine-like drugs. *Psychopharmacologia, 10,* 6–31.

Owen, F., Crow, T. J., & Poulter, M. (1987). Central dopaminergic mechanisms in schizophrenia. *Acta Psychiatrica Belgica, 87*(5), 552–565.

Owen, F., Crow, T. J., Poulter, M. et al. (1978). Increased dopamine receptor sensitivity in schizophrenia. *Lancet, 2,* 223–226.

Owens, R. G., Slade, P. D., & Fielding, D. M. (1989). Patient series and quasi-experimental designs. In G. Parry & N. W. Fraser (Eds.), *Behavioural and mental health research: A handbook of skills and methods.* Hove, UK: Erlbaum.

Pagel, M. D., Becker, J., & Coppel, D. B. (1985). Loss of control, self-blame, and depression: An investigation of spouse caregivers of Alzheimer's disease patients. *J. Abnorm. Psychol., 94*(2), 169–182.

Pagelow, M. D. (1984). *Family violence.* New York: CBS Education.

Palazzoli, M. S. (1974). *Self-starvation: From the intrapsychic to the transpersonal approach to anorexia nervosa.* London, England: Chaucer.

Palazzoli, M. S. (1985). Anorexia nervosa: A syndrome of the affluent society. *J. Strategic & Systemic Ther. 4*(3), 12–16.

Palmblad, J., Cantell, K., Strander, H., Froberg, J., Karlsson, C., Levi, L., Grnstrom, M., & Unger, P. (1976). Stressor exposure and immunological response in man: Interferon-producing capacity and phagocytosis. *J. Psychosom. Res., 20,* 193–199.

Papp, L. A., Goetz, R., Cole, R., Klein, D. F. et al. (1989). Hypersensitivity to carbon dioxide in panic disorder. *Amer. J. Psychiat., 146*(6), 779–781.

Papp, L. A., Martinez, J. M., Klein, D. F., Ross, D. et al. (1989). Arterial blood gas changes in panic disorder and lactate-induced panic. *Psychiat. Res., 28*(2), 171–180.

Pare, C. M. B. (1985). The present status of monoamine oxidase inhibitors. *Brit. J. Psychiat., 146,* 576–584.

Pare, W. (1964). The effect of chronic environmental stress on stomach ulceration, adrenal function, and consummatory behavior in the rat. *J. Psychol., 57,* 143–151.

Parker, G., Johnston, P., & Hayward, L. (1988). Parental "expressed emotion" as a predictor of schizophrenic relapse. *Arch. Gen. Psychiat., 45*(9), 800–813.

Parker, L., & Whitehead, W. (1982). Treatment of urinary and fecal incontinence in children. In D. Russo & W. Varni (Eds.), *Behavioral pediatrics: Research and practice.* New York: Plenum.

Parnas, J. et al. (1982). Behavioral precursors of schizophrenia spectrum: A prospective study. *Arch. Gen. Psychiat., 39*(6), 858–884.

Pascal, G. R., & Suttell, B. J. (1951). *The Bender-Gestalt Test: Quantification and validity for adults.* New York: Grune & Stratton.

Pasewark, R. A., & Pasewark, M. D. (1978). The insanity plea in New York State, 1965–76. *New York State Bar J., 51,* 186–189, 217–225.

Pasewark, R. A., & Pasewark, M. D. (1982). The insanity plea: much ado about little. In B. L. Bloom & S. J. Asher (Eds.), *Psychiatric patient rights and patient advocacy: Issues and evidence.* New York: Human Sciences.

Patel, C. H. (1977). Biofeedback-aided relaxation in the management of hypertension. *Biofeed. Self-Reg., 2,* 1–141.

Patelow, M. D. (1981). *Woman-battering: Victims and their experience.* Beverly Hills, CA: Sage.

Patterson, G. R. (1974). Interventions for boys with conduct problems: Multiple settings, treatments, and criteria. *J. Cons. Clin. Psychol., 42,* 471–481.

Patterson, G. R. (1977). Naturalistic observation in clinical assessment. *J. Abnorm. Child Psychol., 5*(3), 309–322.

Patton, G. C., Johnson-Sabine, E., Wood, K., Mann, A. H. et al. (1990). Abnormal eating attitudes in London schoolgirls: A prospective epidemiological study: Outcome at twelve month follow-up. *Psychol. Med., 20*(2), 383–394.

Paul, G. L. (1966). *Insight vs. desensitization in psychotherapy: An experiment in anxiety reduction.* Stanford: Stanford Univ.

Paul, G. L., & Lentz, R. (1977). *Psychosocial treatment of the chronic mental patient.* Cambridge, MA: Harvard Univ.

Paul, S. M. (1988). Anxiety and depression: A common neurobiological substrate? Symposia: Consequences of anxiety. *J. Clin. Psychiat., 49*(Suppl.), 13–18.

Paurohit, N., Dowd, E. T., & Cottingham, H. F. (1982). The role of verbal and nonverbal cues in the formation of first impressions of black and white counselors. *J. Couns. Psychol., 4,* 371–378.

Pavlov, I. P. (1928). *Lectures on conditioned reflexes.* London: Lawrence & Wishart.

Paykel, E. S. (1983). Methodological aspects of life events research. *J. Psychosomatic Res., 27*(5), 341–352.

Paykel, E. S. (Ed.). (1982). *Handbook of affective disorders.* New York: Guilford.

Paykel, E. S., & Hollyman, J. A. (1984). Life events and depression: A psychiatric view. *Trends in Neurosci., 7*(12), 478–481.

Paykel, E. S. et al. (1969). Life events and depression: A controlled study. *Arch. Gen. Psychiat., 21*(6), 753–760.

Paykel, E. S., Rao, B. M., & Taylor, C. N. (1984). Life stress and symptom pattern in outpatient depression. *Psychol. Medicine, 14*(3), 559–568.

Payne, A. F. (1928). *Sentence completion.* New York. New York Guidance Clinics.

Payte, T. J. (1989). Combined treatment modalities: The need for innovative approaches. Third National Forum on AIDS and Chemical Dependency of the American Society of Addiction Medicine. *J. Psychoact. Drugs, 21*(4), 431–434.

Peachey, J. E., & Franklin, T. (1985). Methadone treatment of opiate dependence in Canada. *Brit. J. Addic., 80*(3), 291–299.

Pearce, J. (1977). Depressive disorder in childhood. *J. Child Psychol. Psychiat., 18*(1), 78–82.

Pearlson, G. D. et al. (1984). Lateral ventricular enlargement associated with persistent unemployment and negative symptoms in both schizophrenia and bipolar disorder. *Psychiat. Res., 12*(1), 1–9.

Peck, M. (1982). Youth suicide. *Death Educ., 6*(1), 27–47.

Pemberton, B. A., & Benady, D. R. (1973). Consciously rejected children. *Brit. J. Psychiat., 123*(578), 575–578.

Pendery, M. L., Maltzman, I. M., & West, L. J. (1982). Controlled drinking by alcoholics? New findings and a reevaluation of a major affirmative study. *Science, 217*(4555), 169–175.

Pennebaker, J. W., Colder, M., & Sharp, L. K. (1990. Accelerating the coping process. *J. Pers. Soc. Psychol., 58*(3), 528–537.

Pepper, B., & Ryglewicz, H. (Eds.). (1982) *New directions for mental health services: The young adult chronic patient* (no. 14). San Francisco: Jossey-Bass.

Perls, F. S. (1969). *Gestalt therapy verbatim.* Moab, UT: Real People.

Perls, F. S. (1971). Four lectures. In J. Fagan & I. L. Shepherd (Eds.), *Gestalt therapy now.* New York: Harper & Row.

Perls, F. S. (1973). *The Gestalt approach.* Palo Alto: Science Behav.

Perris, C. (1988). Decentralization, sectorization, and the development of alternatives to institutional care in a northern county in Sweden. In C. N. Stefanis & A. D. Rabavilis (Eds.), *Schizophrenia: Recent biosocial developments.* New York: Human Sci.

Perry, P., & Tsuang, M. T. (1979). Treatment of unipolar depression following electroconvulsive therapy: Relapse rate comparison between lithium and tricyclic therapies following ECT. *J. Affect. Dis., 1,* 123–129.

Perse, T. (1988). Obsessive-compulsive disorder: A treatment review. *J. Clin. Psychiat., 49*(2), 48–55.

Perske, R. (1972). The dignity of risk and the mentally retarded. *Ment. Retardation, 10,* 24–27.

Persons, J. B. (1991). Psychotherapy outcome studies do not accurately represent current models of psychotherapy: A proposed remedy. *Amer. Psychol., 46*(2), 99–106.

Pery, J. C., & Jacobs, D. (1982). Overview: Clinical applications of the amytal interview in psychiatric emergency settings. *Amer. J. Psychiat., 139*(5), 552–559.

Peters, R. (1981). Suicidal behavior among Native Americans: An annotated bibliography. *White Cloud J., 2*(3), 9–20.

Petersen, D. (1988). Substance abuse, criminal behavior, and older people. *Generations, 12*(4), 63–67.

Peterson, D. R. (1968). *The clinical study of social behavior.* New York: Appleton-Century-Crofts.

Peterson, R. A. (1978). Rorschach. In O. K. Buros (Ed.), *Eighth mental measurements yearbook.* Highland Park, NJ: Gryphon.

Petrie, E. C., Faustman, W. O., Moses, J. A., Lombrozo, L. et al. (1990). Correlates of rapid neuroleptic response in male patients with schizophrenia. *Psychiat. Res., 33*(2), 171–177.

Pettinati, H. M., & Rosenberg, J. (1984). Memory self-ratings before and after anticonvulsive therapy: Depression versus ECT-induced. *Bio. Psychiat., 19,* 539–548.

Pfeffer, C. R. (1984). Suicidal impulses of normal children. *Inter. J. Fam. Psychiat., 5*(2), 139–150.

Pfeffer, C. R. (1986). *The suicidal child.* New York: Guilford.

Pfeffer, C. R. (1988). Risk factors associated with youth suicide: A clinical perspective. *Psychiat. Ann., 18*(11), 652–656.

Pfeffer, C. R. (1989). Assessment of suicidal children and adolescents. *Psychiat. Clin. N. Amer., 12*(4), 861–872.

Pfeffer, C. R. (1990). Clinical perspectives on treatment of suicidal behavior among children and adolescents. *Psychiat. Ann., 20*(3), 143–150.

Pfeifer, M. P., & Snodgrass, G. L. (1990). The continued use of retractable invalid scientific literature. *JAMA, 263*(10), 1420–1427.

Phares, E. J. (1979). *Clinical psychology: Concepts, methods, and profession.* Homewood, IL: Dorsey.

Phelan, J. (1976). *Howard Hughes: The hidden years.* New York: Random House.

Phillip, A. E., & McCulloch, J. W. (1966). The use of social indices in psychiatric epidemiology. *Brit. J. Preventive Soc. Med., 20,* 122–126.

Phillips, A. M., Martin, D., & Martin, M. (1987). Counseling families with an alcoholic parent. *Family Therapy, 14*(1), 9–16.

Phillips, D. P. (1974). The influence of suggestion on suicide: Substantive and theoretical implications of the Werther effect. *Amer. Sociol. Rev., 39,* 340–354.

Phillips, D. P. (1983). The impact of mass media violence on U.S. homicides. *Amer. Sociological Rev., 48,* 560–568.

Phillips, D. P., & Carstensen, L. L. (1987). "Television and suicide": Reply. *New Engl. J. Med., 316*(14), 877–878.

Philpott, R. M. (1991). Affective disorder and illness in old age. *Inter. Clin. Psychopharm., 5*(3), 7–20.

Pierloot, R. A., & Houben, M. E. (1978). Estimation of body dimensions in anorexia nervosa. *Psychol. Med., 8,* 317–324.

Pierloot, R., Wellens, W., & Houben, M. (1975). Elements of resistance to a combined medical and psychotherapeutic program in anorexia nervosa. *Psychother. Psychosom., 26,* 101–117.

Pietrofesa, J. J. (1990). The mental health counselor and "duty to warn." *J. Ment. Hlth. Couns., 12*(2), 129–137.

Pietromonaco, P. R., & Markus, H. (1985). The nature of negative thoughts in depression. *J. Pers. Soc. Psychol., 48*(3), 799–807.

Pillemer, K., & Finkelhor, D. (1988). The prevalence of elder abuse: A random sample survey. *Gerontologist, 28,* 51–57.

Pine, C. J. (1981). Suicide in American Indian and Alaskan native tradition. *White Cloud J., 2*(3), 3–8.

Pinel, P. A. (1962). A treatise on insanity. *History of medicine series* (Vol. 14). (Originally published, 1806)

Pithers, W. D. (1990). Relapse prevention with sexual aggressors. In W. L. Marshall, D. R. Laws, & H. E. Barbaree (Eds.), *Handbook of sexual assault.* New York: Plenum.

Pithers, W. D., & Cumming, G. F. (1989). Can relapses be prevented? Initial outcome data for the Vermont Treatment Program for Sexual Aggressors. In D. R. Laws (Ed.), *Relapse prevention with sex offenders.* New York: Guilford.

Pitts, F. N., Schuller, A. B., Rich, C. L., & Pitts, A. T. (1979). Suicide among U.S. women physicians, 1967–1882. *Amer. J. Psychiat., 136*(5), 694–696.

Platt, S. D. (1984). Unemployment and suicidal behavior: A review of the literature. *Soc. Sci. Med., 19*(2), 93–115.

Plotkin, R. (1983). *Cognitive mediation in disciplinary action among mothes who have abused or neglected their children: Dispositional and environmental factors.* Unpublished doctoral dissertation. Univ. Rochester.

Plotkin, W. B., & Rice, K. M. (1981). Biofeedback as a placebo: Anxiety reduction facilitated by training in either suppression or enhancement of alpha brainwaves. *J. Cons. Clin. Psychol., 49*(4), 590–596.

Pogue-Geile, M. F. (1989). The prognostic significance of negative symptoms in schizophrenia. Symposium: Negative symptoms in schizophrenia (1987, London, England). *Brit. J. Psychiat., 155*(7, Suppl.), 123–127.

Poland, R. E., Rubin, R. T., Lesser, I. M., & Lane, L. et al. (1987). Neuroendocrine aspects of primary endogenous depression: II. Serum dexamethasone concentrations and hypothalamic-pituitary-adrenal cortical activity as determinants of the dexamethasone suppression test response. *Arch. Gen. Psychiat., 44*(9), 790–795.

Pollard, C. A., & Henderson, J. G. (1988). Four types of social phobia in a community sample. *J. Nerv. Ment. Dis., 176*(7), 440–445.

Pollitt, J. (1957). Natural history. *J. Ment. Sci., 106,* 93–113.

Polster, M. (1987). Gestalt therapy: evolution and application. In J. K. Zeig (Ed.), *The evolution of psychotherapy.* New York: Brunner/Mazel.

Pomara, N., Deptula, D., Singh, R., & Monroy, C. (1991). Cognitive toxicity of benzodiazepines in the elderly. In C. Salzman & B. D. Lebowitz (Eds.), *Anxiety in the elderly.* New York: Springer.

Pomerleau, O. F., & Pomerleau, C. S. (1984). Neuroregulators and the reinforcement of smoking: Towards a biobehavioral explanation. *Neurosci. Biobehav., Rev., 8*(4), 503–513.

Pope, H. G., & Hudson, J. I. (1982). Treatment of bulimia with antidepressants. *Psychopharmacology, 78,* 167–179.

Pope, H. G., & Hudson, J. I. (1984). *New hope for binge eaters: Advances in the understanding and treatment of bulimia.* New York: Harper & Row.

Pope, H. G., & Hudson, J. I. (1986). Antidepressant drug therapy of bulimia: Current status. *J. Clin. Psychiat., 47,* 339–345.

Pope, H. G., & Hudson, J. I. (1988). Is bulimia nervosa a heterogeneous disorder? Lessons from the history of medicine. *Inter. J. Eat. Dis., 7,* 155–166.

Pope, H. G., Herridge, P. L., Hudson, J. I., & Fontaine, R. (1986). Treatment of bulimia with nomifensine. *J. Clin. Psychiat., 143,* 371–373.

Pope, H. G., Hudson, J. I., & Jonas, J. M. (1983). Antidepressant treatment of bulimia: Preliminary experience and practical recommendations. *J. Psychiat., 140,* 554–558.

Pope, H. G., Hudson, J. I., & Jonas, J. M. (1983). Bulimia treated with imipramine: A placebo-controlled, double-blind study. *Amer. J. Psychiat., 140*(5), 554–558.

Pope, K. S. (1990). Ethical and malpractice issues in hospital practice. *Amer. Psychol., 45*(4), 1066–1070.

Pope, K. S. (1990). Therapist-patient sex as sex abuse: Six scientific, professional and practical dilemmas in addressing victimization and rehabilitation. *Profess. Psych., 21,* 227–239.

Pope, K. S. (1990). Therapist-patient sexual involvement: A review of the research. *Clin. Psychol. Rev., 10,* 477–490.

Pope, K. S., & Bouhoutsos, J. (1986). *Sexual intimacy between therapists and patients.* New York: Praeger.

Pope, K. S., & Vetter, V. A. (1991). Prior therapist-patient sexual involvement among patients seen by psychologists. *Psychotherapy.*

Pope, K. S., Tabachnick, B. G., & Keith-Spiegel, P. (1986). Sexual attraction to clients: The human therapist and the (sometimes) inhuman training system. *Amer. Psychol., 41*(2), 147–158.

Pope, K. S., Tabachnick, B. G., & Keith-Spiegel, P. (1987). Ethics of practice: The beliefs and behaviors of psychologists as therapists. *Amer. Psychol., 42*(11), 993–1166.

Popper, C. W. (1988). Disorders usually first evident in infancy, childhood, or adolescence. In J. Talbott, R. S. Hales, & S. C. Yudofsky (Eds.), *Textbook of psychiatry.* American Psychiatric.

Posner, M. I., Early, T. S., Raiman, E., Pardo, P. J. et al. (1988). Asymmetries in hemispheric control of attention in schizophrenia. *Arch. Gen. Psychiat., 45*(9), 814–821.

Post, F. (1966). *Persistent persecutory states of the elderly.* Elmsford, NY: Pergamon Press.

Post, F. (1978). The functional psychosis. In A. D. Isaacs & F. Post (Eds.), *Studies in geriatric psychiatry.* Chichester, England: Wiley.

Post, F. (1980). Paranoid, schizophrenia-like, and schisophrenic states in the aged. In J. E. Birren & R. B. Sloane (Eds.), *Handbook of mental health and aging.* Englewood Cliffs, NJ: Prentice-Hall.

Post, G., & Crowther, J. H. (1985). Variables that discriminate bulimic from nonbulimic adolescent females. *J. Youth & Adol., 14*(2), 85–98.

Post, R. M. et al. (1978). Cerebrospinal fluid norepinephrine in affective illness. *Amer. J. Psychiat., 135*(8), 907–912.

Powell, G. E., & Lindsay, S. J. E. (1987). An introduction to treatment. In G. E. Powell & S. J. E. Lindsay (Eds.), *A handbook of clinical adult psychology.* Aldershot, England: Gower.

Prange, A. J. et al. (1970). Enhancement of imipramine by thyroid stimulating hormone: Clinical and theoretical implications. *Amer. J. Psychiat., 127*(2), 191–199.

Prange, A. J. et al. (1970). Use of a thyroid hormone to accelerate the action of imipramine. *Psychosomatics, 11*(5), 442–444.

Prange, A. J. et al. (1974). L tryptophan in mania: Contribution to a permissive hypothesis of affective disorders.

President's Committee on Mental Retardation. (1980, Dec.). *Report to the president, Mental Retardation: Prevention strategies that work.* Washington, DC: Office of Human Development Service.

Price, J. (1988). How to stabilize families: A therapist's guide to maintaining the status quo. *J. Strategic & Systemic Ther., 7*(4), 21–27.

Price, K. P. (1972). Predictable and unpredictable shock: Their pathological effects on restrained and unrestrained rats. *Psych. Rep., 30,* 419–426.

Price, L. H. (1990). Serotonin reuptake inhibitors in depression and anxiety: An overview. *Ann. Clin. Psychiat., 2*(3), 165–172.

Price, R. W., Brew, B., Sidtis, J., Rosenblum, M., Scheck, A. C., & Cleary, P. (1988). The brain in AIDS: Central nervous system HIV-1 infection and AIDS dementia complex. *Science, 239,* 586–592.

Priebe, S., & Wildgrube, C. (1990). Expressed emotion and lithium prophylaxis. *Brit. J. Psychiat., 157,* 624.

Prien, R. F. (1984). Five-center study clarifies use of lithium, imipramine for recurrent affective disorders. *Hosp. Comm. Psychiat., 35*(11), 1097–1098.

Prien, R. F., & Kupfer, D. J. (1986). Continuation drug therapy for major depressive episodes: How long should it be maintained? *Amer. J. Psychiat., 143*(1), 18–23.

Prien, R. F., Balter, M. B., & Caffey, E. M. (1978). Hospital surveys of prescribing practices with psychotherapeutic drugs. *Arch. Gen. Psychiat., 35*(10), 1271–1275.

Prien, R. F. et al. (1984). Drug therapy in the prevention of recurrences in unipolar and bipolar affective disorders: Report of the NIMH Collaborative Study Group comparing lithium carbonate, imipramine, and a lithium carbonate-imipramine combination. *Arch. Gen. Psychiat., 41*(11), 1096–1104.

Prince, M. (1906). *The dissociation of a personality.* New York: Longmans, Green.

Prior, M. R., & Chen, C. S. (1975). Learning set acquisition in autistic children. *J. Abnorm. Psychol., 84,* 701–708.

Pritchard, C. (1988). Suicide, unemployment and gender in the British Isles and ECC (1974–1985). *Soc. Psychiat. & Epidemiol., 23*(2), 85–89.

Probsting, E., & Till, W. (1985). Suizidalität und Arbeitslosigkeit [Suicidality and unemployment]. *Crisis, 6*(1), 19–35.

Prochaska, J. O. (1984). *Systems of psychotherapy.* Chicago: Dorsey.

Prudo, R., Brown, G. W., Harris, T., & Dowland, J. (1981). Psychiatric disorder in a rural and an urban population: II. Sensitivity to loss. *Psychol. Med., 11*(3), 801–810.

Prusoff, B. A., Weissman, M. M., Klerman, G. L., & Rounsaville, B. J. (1980). Research diagnostic criteria subtypes of depression: Their role as predictors of differential response to psychotherapy and drug treatment. *Arch. Gen. Psychiat., 37*(7), 796–801.

Pueschel, S. M., & Goldstein, A. (1991). Genetic counseling. In J. L. Matson & J. A. Mulick (Eds.), *Handbook of mental retardation.* New York: Pergamon.

Pueschel, S. M., & Thuline, H. C. (1991). Chromosome disorders. In J. L. Matson & J. A. Mulick (Eds.), *Handbook of mental retardation.* New York: Pergamon.

Puig-Antich, J., & Weston, B. (1983). The diagnosis and treatment of major depressive disorder in childhood. *Annu. Rev. Med., 34,* 231–245.

Puig-Antich, J., Perel, J., Lupatkin, W., Chambers, W. J., Tabrizi, M. A., King, J., Davies, M., Johnson, R., & Stiller, R. (1987). Imipramine in prepubertal major depressive disorders. *Arch. Gen. Psychiat, 44,* 81–89.

Pulver, A. E., Carpenter, W. T., Adler, L., & McGrath, J. (1988). Accuracy of the diagnoses of affective disorders and schizophrenia in public hospitals. *Amer. J. Psychiat., 145*(2), 218–220.

Purcell, K., Brady, K., Chai, H., Muser, J., Molk, L., Gordon, N., & Means, J. (1969). The effect on asthma in children of experimental separation from the family. *Psychsom. Med., 31,* 144–164.

Pusakulich, R. L., Nielson, H. C. (1976). Cue use in state-dependent learning. *Physiological Psychol., 4*(4), 421–428.

Putnam, F. W. (1984). The psychophysiologic investigation of multiple personality disorder. *Psychiat. Clin. N. Amer., 7,* 31–40.

Putnam, F. W. (1985). Multiple personality disorder. *Med. Aspects Human Sexuality, 19*(6), 59–74.

Putnam, F. W. (1988). The switch process in multiple personality disorder and other state-change disorders. *Dissociation., 1,* 24–32.

Putnam, F. W. (1991). Dissociative phenomena. In A. Tasman & S. M. Goldfinger (Eds.), *American Psychiatric Press review of psychiatry* (Vol. 10). Washington, DC: American Psychiatric.

Putnam, F. W., Guroff, J. J., Silberman, E. K., Barban, L. et al. (1986). The clinical phenomenology of multiple personality disorder: Review of 100 recent cases. *J. Clin. Psych., 47*(6), 285–293.

Putnam, F. W., Jr. (1985). Dissociation as a response to extreme trauma. In R. P. Kluft, *Childhood antecedents of multiple personality.* Washington, DC: American Psychiatric.

Putnam, F. W., Zahn, T. P., & Post, R. M. (1990). Differential autonomic nervous system activity in multiple personality disorder. *Psychiat. Res., 31*(3), 251–260.

Pyle, R. L., Mitchell, J. E., & Eckert, E. D. (1981). Bulimia: A report of 34 cases. *J. Clin. Psychiat., 42*(2), 60–64.

Pyle, R. L., Mitchell, J. E., Eckert, E. D., Hatsukami, D. et al. (1990). Maintenance treatment and 6-month outcome for bulimic patients who respond to initial treatment. *Amer. J. Psychiat., 147*(7), 871–875.

Quay, H. C. (1965). Psychopathic personality as pathologic stimulation seeking. *Amer. J. Psychiat., 122*(2), 180–183.

Quinlan, J., Quinlan, J., & Batelle, P. (1977). *Karen Ann: The Quinlans tell their story.* New York: Doubleday.

Quinsey, V. L., & Earls, G. M. (1990). The modificator of sexual preferences. In W. L. Marshall, D. R. Laws, & H. E. Barbaree (Eds.), *Handbook of sexual assault.* New York: Plenum.

Quitkin, F. M., Kane, J., Rifkin, A. et al. (1981). Prophylactic lithium with and without imipramine for bipolar I patients. *Arch. Gen. Psychiat., 38,* 902–907.

Rabins, P. V., Fitting, M. D., Eastham, J., & Zabora, J. (1990). Emotional adaptation over time in caregivers for chronically ill elderly people. *Age & Ageing, 19,* 185–190.

Rabkin, J. G. (1979). Criminal behavior of discharged mental patients: A critical appraisal of the research. *Psychol. Bull., 86,* 1–27.

Rachlin, S., Halpern, A. L., & Portnow, S. L. (1984). The volitional rule, personality disorders and the insanity defense. *Psychiat. Ann., 14,* 139–147.

Rachman, S. (1966). Sexual fetishism: An experimental analog. *Psych. Rec., 18,* 25–27.

Rachman, S. (1971). *The effects of psychotherapy.* Oxford: Pergamon.

Rachman, S. (1976). Observational learning and therapeutic modeling. In M. Feldman & A. Broadhurst (Eds.), *Theoretical and experimental bases of behaviour therapy.* Chichester: Wiley.

Rachman, S. (1976). Obsessional-compulsive checking. *Behav. Res. Ther., 14*(4), 269–277.

Rachman, S. (1976). The modifications of obsessions: A new formulation. *Behav. Res. Ther., 14*(6), 437–443.

Rachman, S. (1979). The concept of required helpfulness. *Behav. Res. Ther., 17*(1), 1–6.

Rachman, S. (1979). The return of fear. *Behav. Res. Ther., 17*(2), 164–166.

Rachman, S. (1985). A note on the conditioning theory of fear acquisition. *Behav. Ther., 16*(4), 426–428.

Rachman, S. (1985). Obsessional-compulsive disorders. In B. P. Bradley & C. T. Thompson (Eds.), *Psychological applications in psychiatry.* Chichester: Wiley.

Rachman, S. (1985). The treatment of anxiety disorders: A critique of the implications for psychopathology. In A. Tuma and J. Maser (Eds.), *Anxiety and the anxiety disorders.* Hillsdale, NJ: Erlbaum.

Rachman, S., & Hodgson, R. (1980). *Obsessions and compulsions.* Englewood Cliffs, NJ: Prentice-Hall.

Rachman, S., & Hodgson, R. J. (1968). Experimentally-induced "sexual fetishism": Replication and development. *Psych. Rec., 18*(1), 25–27.

Rachman, S., & Hodgson, R. J. (1974). Synchrony and desynchrony in fear and avoidance. *Behav. Res. Ther., 12,* 311–318.

Rachman, S., & Wilson, G. T. (1980). *The effects of psychological therapy, second edition.* Oxford: Pergamon.

Rachman, S. et al. (1979). The behavioral treatment of obsessional-compulsive disorders, with and without clomipramine. *Behav. Res. Ther., 17*(5), 467–478.

Rachman, S., Hodgson, R., & Marks, I. M. (1971). Treatment of chronic obsessive-compulsive neurosis. *Behav. Res. Ther., 9*(3), 237–247.

Rachman, S., Hodgson, R., & Marks, I. M. (1973). Treatment of OCD by modelling and flooding in vivo. *Behav. Res. Ther., 1,* 463–471.

Rachman, S. J. (1990). *Fear and courage* (2nd ed.). New York: Freeman.

Rachman, S. J., & Wilson, G. T. (1979). *The effects of psychotherapy.* Oxford: Pergamon.

Rachman, S. J., Hodgson, R., & Marzillier, J. (1970). Treatment of an obsessional-compulsive disorder by modelling. *Behav. Res. Ther., 8,* 385–392.

Rada, R. T. (1976). Alcoholism and the child molester. *Ann. NY Acad. Sci., 273,* 492–496.

Radtke, B. H. L., Planas, M., & Spanos, N. P. (1980). Suggested amnesia, verbal inhibition, and disorganized recall for a long word list. *Canad. J. Behav. Sci., 12*(1), 87–97.

Ragin, A. B., Pogue-Geile, M. F., & Oltmanns, T. F. (1989). Poverty of speech in schizophrenia and depression during inpatient and post-hospital periods. *Brit. J. Psychiat., 154,* 52–57.

Rahe, R. H. (1968). Life-change measurement as a predictor of illness. *Proceedings of the Royal Society of Medicine, 61,* 1124–1126.

Ralston, P. A. (1991). Senior centers and minority elders: A critical review. *Gerontologist, 31,* 325–331.

Rao, A. V. (1980). Suicide in India. In N. Farberow (Ed.), *Suicide in different cultures.* Baltimore: Univ. Park.

Rapee, R. (1986). Differential response to hyperventilation in panic disorder and generalized anxiety disorders. *J. Abnorm. Psychol., 95,* 24–28.

Raphling, D. L. (1989). Fetishism in a woman. *J. Amer. Psychoanal. Assoc., 37*(2), 465–491.

Rappaport, A. F., & Harrell, J. (1972). A behavioral exchange model for marital counseling. *Family Coordinator, 22,* 203–212.

Raskin, A. (1974). Age-sex differences in response to antidepressant drugs. *J. Nerv. Ment. Dis., 159*(2), 120–130.

Raskin, A. (1982). Assessment of psychopathology by the nurse or psychiatric aide. In E. I. Burdock, A. Sudilovsky, & S. Gershon (Eds.), *The behavioral assessment of psychiatric patients: Quantitative techniques for evaluation.* New York: Marcel Dekker.

Raskin, D. C. (1982). The scientific basis of polygraph techniques and their uses in the judicial process. In A. Trankell (Ed.), *Reconstructing the past: The role of psychologists in criminal trials.* Stockholm: Norstedt & Soners.

Raskin, M., Bali, L. R., & Peeke, H. V. (1980). Muscle biofeedback and transcendental meditation: A controlled evaluation of efficacy in the treatment of chronic anxiety. *Arch. Gen. Psychiat., 37*(1), 93–97.

Raskin, M., Peeke, H. V. S., Dickman, W., & Pinkster, H. (1982). Panic and generalized anxiety disorders: Developmental antecedents and precipitants. *Arch. Gen. Psychiat., 39,* 687–689.

Raskin, N. H. (1975). Alcoholism or acetaldehydism. *New Engl. J. Med., 292*(8), 422–423.

Raskin, N. J., & Rogers, C. R. (1989). *Person-centered therapy.* In R. J. Corsini & D. Wedding (Eds.), *Current psychotherapies.* Itasca, IL: Peacock.

Rassaby, E. R., & Paykel, E. S. (1979). Factor patterns in depression: A replication study. *J. Affect. Dis., 1*(3), 187–194.

Ray, O. S. (1983). *Drugs, society, and human behavior* (3rd ed.). St. Louis: Mosby.

Reda, M. A., Carpiniello, B., Secchiaroli, L., & Blanco, S. (1985). Thinking, depression, and antidepressants: Modified and unmodified depressive beliefs during treatment with amitriptyline. *Cog. Ther. Res., 9*(2), 135–143.

Redefer, L. A., & Goodman, J. F. (1989). Pet-facilitated therapy with autistic children. *J. Autism Dev. Dis., 19*(3), 461–467.

Redmond, D. E. (1985). Neurochemical basis for anxiety and anxiety disorders: Evidence from drugs which decrease human fear or anxiety. In A. H. Tuma & J. Maser (Eds.), *Anxiety and the anxiety disorders.* Hillsdale, NJ: Erlbaum.

Redmond, D. E., Jr. (1977). Alterations in the function of the nucleus locus coeruleus: A possible model for studies of anxiety. In I. Hanin & E. Usdin (Eds.), *Animal models in psychiatry and neurology.* New York: Pergamon.

Redmond, D. E., Jr. (1979). New and old evidence for the involvement of a brain norepinephrine system in anxiety. In W. E. Fann, I. Karacan, A. D. Pokorny, & R. L. Williams (Eds.), *Phenomenology and treatment of anxiety.* New York: Spectrum.

Redmond, D. E., Jr. (1981). Clonidine and the primate locus coeruleus: Evidence suggesting anxiolytic and anti-withdrawal effects. In H. Lal & S. Fielding, *Psychopharmacology of clonidine.* New York: Alan R. Liss.

Redmond, D. E., Jr., & Huang, Y. H. (1979). Current concepts. II; New evidence for a locus coeruleus-norepinephrine connection with anxiety. *Life Sciences, 25,* 2149–2162.

Rees, L. (1964). The importance of psychological, allergic and infective factors in childhood asthma. *J. Psychosom. Res., 7*(4), 253–262.

Reese, R. M., & Serna, L. (1986). Planning for generalization and maintenance in parent training: Parents need I.E.P.s too. *Ment. Retardation, 24*(2), 87–92.

Regier, D. A., Boyd J. H., Burke J. D., Rae, D. S., Myers J. K., Kramer, M., Robins, L. N., George, L. K., Karno, M., & Locke, B. Z. (1988). One-month prevalence of mental disorders in the U.S.: Based on five epidemiologic catchment area (ECA) sites. *Arch. Gen. Psychiat., 45,* 977.

Reid, M. K., & Borkowski, J. G. (1987). Casual attributions of hyperactive children: Implications for teaching strategies and self control. *J. Educ. Psychol., 79,* 296–307.

Reiderer, P., Sofic, E., Konradi, C., Kornhuber, J., Beckmann, H., Dietl, M., Moll, G., & Hebenstreitt, G. (1989). The role of dopamine in the control of neurobiological functions. In E. Fluckiger, E. E. Muller, & M. O. Thorner (Eds.), *Basic and clinical aspects of neuroscience: Vol. 3. The role of brain dopamine.* Berlin: Spriner Sandoz Advanced Texts.

Reifler, B. V., Larson, E., Teri, L., & Poulson, M. (1986). Dementia of the Alzheimer's type and depression. *J. Amer. Geriat. Soc., 34,* 855–859.

Reifman, A., & Wyatt, R. J. (1980). Lithium: A brake in the rising cost of mental illness. *Arch. Gen. Psychiat., 37,* 385–388.

Reik, T. (1989). The characteristics of masochism. *Amer. Imago, 46*(2–3), 161–195.

Reisinger, J. J., & Ora, J. P. (1977). Parent child clinic and home interaction during toddler management training. *Behav. Ther., 8*(5), 771–786.

Reisman, J. M. (1971). The definition of psychotherapy. *Ment. Hyg., 55*(3), 413–417.

Reiss, S. (1985). The mentally retarded, emotionally disturbed adult. In M. Sigman (Ed.), *Children with emotional disorders and developmental disabilities.* New York: Grune & Stratton.

Reiss, S., & Benson, B. A. (1985). Psychosocial correlates of depression in mentally retarded adults: I. Minimal social support and stigmatization, *89*(4), 331–337.

Reiss, S., Levitan, G. W., & McNally, R. J. (1982). Emotionally disturbed mentally retarded people: An underserved population. *Amer. Psychol., 37*(4), 361–367.

Reiss, S., Peterson, R. A., Gursky, D. M., & McNally, R. J. (1986). Anxiety sensitivity, anxiety frequency and the predictions of fearfulness. *Behav. Res. Ther., 24*(1), 1–8.

Reitan, R. M. (1966). A research program on the psychologial effects of brain lesions in human beings. In N. R. Ellis (Ed.), *International review of research in mental retardation.* New York: Academic.

Reitan, R. M., & Wolfson, D. (1985). *The Halstead-Reitan Neuropsychological Test Battery: Theory and clinical interpretation.* Tucson, AZ: Neuropsychology.

Renneberg, B., Goldstein, A. J., Phillips, D., & Chambless, D. L. (1990). Intensive behavioral group treatment of avoidant personality disorder. *Behav. Ther., 21*(3), 363–377.

*Report of the President's Commission on Mental Health.* (1978). Washington, DC: GPO.

Repp, A. C., Barton, L. E., & Brulle, A. R. (1986). Assessing a least restrictive educational environment transfer through social comparison. *Educ. & Training of the Ment. Retarded, 21*(1), 54–61.

Rescorla, R. A. (1988). Pavlovian conditioning: It's not what you think. *Amer. Psychol., 43,* 151–160.

Resick, P. A., Forehand, R., & McWhorter, A. Q. (1976). The effect of parental treatment with one child on an untreated sibling. *Behav. Ther., 7*(4), 544–548.

Resnick, A., & Lettieri, D. (Eds.). (1974). *The prediction of suicide.* Maryland: Charles.

Resnick, S. M., Gur, R. E., Alavi, A., Gur, R. C. et al. (1988). Positron emission tomography and subcortical glucose metabolism in schizophrenia. *Psychiat. Res., 24*(1), 1–11.

Restack, R. M. (1979). The sex-change conspiracy. *Psych. Today, 20,* 20–25.

Reynolds, L. (1990). Drug-free after 30 years of dependence. *Aging, 361,* 26–27.

Reynolds, W. M., & Coats, K. I. (1986). A comparison of cognitive-behavioral therapy and relaxation training for the treatment of depression in adolescents. *J. Cons. Clin. Psychol., 54,* 653–660.

Rhine, M. W., & Thompson, T. L. (1985). Hypochondriasis. In R. C. Simons (Ed.), *Understanding human behavior in health and illness* (3rd ed.). Baltimore: Williams & Wilkins.

Rice, K. M., & Blanchard, E. B. (1982). Biofeedback in the treatment of anxiety disorder. *Clin. Psychol. Rev., 2,* 557–577.

Rich, C. L., Young, D., & Fowler, R. C. (1986). San Diego suicide study: I. Young vs. old subjects. *Arch. Gen. Psychiat., 43*(6), 577–582.

Richards, C., & Lee, K. (1972). Social habilitation of the retarded. *Soc. Casework, 53,* 30.

Richings, J. C., Khara, G. S., & McDowell, M. (1986). Suicide in young doctors. *Brit. J. Psychiat., 149,* 475–478.

Rickels, K. (1978). Use of antianxiety agents in anxious outpatients. *Psychopharmacology, 58*(1), 1–17.

Rickels, K. (1983). Benzodiazepines in emotional disorders. *J. Psychoac. Drugs, 15*(1–2), 49–54.

Rickels, K. (1983). Nonbenzodiazepine anxiolytics: Clinical usefulness. *J. Clin. Psychiat., 44*(11, Sect. 2), 38–43.

Rickels, K. (1987). Antianxiety therapy: Potential value of long-term treatment. *J. Clin. Psychiat., 48* (Suppl.), 7–11.

Rickels, K., Chung, H. R., Csanalosi, I. B., Hurowitz, A. M. et al. (1987). Alprazolam, diazepam, imipramine, and placebo in outpatients with major depression. *Arch. Gen. Psychiat., 44*(10), 862–866.

Rickels, K. et al. (1978). Diazepam and halazepam in anxiety: Some prognostic indicators. *Inter. Pharmacopsychiat., 13*(2), 118–125.

Rickels, K. et al. (1978). Loxapine in neurotix anxiety: A controlled trial. *Current Therapeutic Res., 23*(1, Pt. 2), 111–120.

Rickels, K. et al. (1983). A controlled clinical trial of alprazolzam for the treatment of anxiety. *Amer. J. Psychiat., 140*(1), 82–85.

Rimm, D. C., & Litvak, S. B. (1969). Self-verbalization and emotional arousal. *J. Abnorm. Psychol., 74*(2), 181–187.

Rimm, D. C., & Masters, J. C. (1979). *Behavior therapy: Techniques and empirical findings* (2nd ed.). New York: Academic.

Ringuette, E., & Kennedy, T. (1966). *J. Abnorm. Psychol., 71,* 136–141.

Rioux, D., & Van Meter, W. (1990). The ABCs of awareness: A multimodal approach to relapse prevention and intervention — the College Hill Medical Center program. *J. Substance Abuse Treatment, 7*(1), 61–63.

Risch, S. C., Janowsky, D. S., & Gillin, J. C. (1983). Muscarinic supersensitivity of anterior pituitary ACTH and B endorphin release in major depressive illness. *Peptides, 4*(5), 788–792.

Ritchie, G. G. (1968). The use of hypnosis in a case of exhibitionism. *Psychother. Theory Res. Prac., 5,* 40–43.

Rizzuto, A. (1985). Eating and monsters: A psychodynamic view of bulimarexia. In S. W. Emmett (Ed.), *Theory and treatment of anorexia nervosa and bulimia: Biomedical, sociocultural, and psychological perspectives.* New York: Brunner/Mazel.

Robbin, A. A. (1958). A controlled study of the effects of leucotomy. *J. Neurol. Neurosurg. Psychiat., 21,* 262–269.

Robbin, A. A. (1959). The value of leucotomy in relation to diagnosis. *J. Neurol. Neurosurg. Psychiat., 22,* 132–136.

Robbins, D. R., & Alessi, N. C. (1985). Depressive symptoms and suicidal behavior in adolescents. *Amer. J. Psychiat., 142*(5), 588–592.

Roberts, M. W., & Tylenda, C. A. (1989). Dental aspects of anorexia and bulimia nervosa. *Pediatrician, 16*(3–4), 178–184.

Roberts, R. R., Jr., & Renzaglia, G. A. (1965). The influence of tape recording on counseling. *J. Couns. Psychol., 12,* 10–16.

Roberts, W. (1960). Normal and abnormal depersonalization. *J. Ment. Sci., 106,* 478–493.

Robertson, M. (1987). Molecular genetics of the mind. *Nature, 325*(6107), 755.

Robins, L. N., & Kulbok, P. (1988). Epidemiological studies in suicide. *Psychiat. Ann., 18*(1), 619–627.

Robins, L. N., & Przybeck, T. R. (1985). Age of onset of drug use as a factor in drug and other disorders. *National Institute on Drug Abuse: Research Monograph Series, 56,* 178–192.

Robins, L. N. et al. (1984). Lifetime prevalence of specific psychiatric disorders in three sites. *Arch. Gen. Psychiat., 41*(10), 948–958.

Robins, L. N., Helzer, J. E., Croughan, J., & Ratcliff, K. S. (1981). National Institute Mental Health Diagnostic Interview Schedule. Its history, characteristics, and validity. *Arch. Gen. Psychiat., 10,* 41–61.

Robinson, J. C., & Lewinsohn, P. M. (1973). Behavior modification of speech characteristics in a chronically depressed man. *Behav. Ther., 4,* 150–152.

Robinson, N. M., & Robinson, H. B. (1970). *The mentally retarded child: A psychological approach.* New York: Wiley.

Robinson, P., & Andersen, A. E. (1985). Anorexia nervosa in American Blacks. *J. Psychiat. Res., 19*(2–3), 183–188.

Robinson, P. H., Checkley, S. A., & Russell, G. F. (1985). Suppression of eating by fenfluramine in patients with bulimia nervosa. *Brit. J. Psychiat., 146,* 169–176.

Robitscher, J., & Haynes, A. K. (1982). In defense of the insanity defense. *Emory Law J., 31,* 9–60.

Rodolfa, E. R. (1982). Self-help groups: A referral resource for professional therapists. *Profess. Psychol., 13*(3), 345–353.

Roesler, & Greenfield (Eds.). (1962). *Physiological correlation of psychological disorder.* Madison, WI: Univ. Wisconsin.

Rogers, C. (1961). *On becoming a person.* Boston: Houghton Mifflin.

Rogers, C., & Dymond, R. (1954). *Psychotherapy and personality change.* Chicago: Univ. Chicago.

Rogers, C. R. (1951). *Client-centered therapy.* Boston: Houghton Mifflin.

Rogers, C. R. (1959). A theory of therapy personality, and interpersonal relationships as developed in the client-centered framework. In S. Koch (Ed.), *Psychology: A study of a science* (Vol. 3). New York: McGraw-Hill.

Rogers, C. R. (1970). *Carl Rogers on encounter groups.* New York: Harper & Row.

Rogers, C. R. (1987). Rogers, Kohut, and Erickson: A personal perspective on some similarities and differences. In J. K. Zeig (Ed.), *The evolution of psychotherapy.* New York: Brunner/Mazel.

Rogers, C. R. (Ed.). (1967). *The therapeutic relationship and its impact: A study of psychotherapy with schizophrenics.* Madison, WI: Univ. Wisconsin.

Rogers, C. R., & Sanford, R. C. (1989). Client-centered psychotherapy. In H. I. Kaplan & B. J. Sadock (Eds.), *Comprehensive textbook of psychiatry* (Vol. 1, 5th ed.). Baltimore: Williams & Wilkins.

Rogers, J. A., & Centifanti, J. B. (1988). Madness, myths, and reality: Response to Roberta Rose. *Schizo. Bull., 14*(1), 7–15.

Rohsenow, D. J., Smith, R. E., & Johnson, S. (1985). Stress management training as a prevention program for heavy social drinkers: Cognition, affect, drinking, and individual differences. *Addic. Behav., 10*(1), 45–54.

Roll, M., & Theorell, T. (1987). Acute chest pain without obvious organic cause before age 40: Personality and recent life events. *J. Psychosom. Res., 31*(2), 215–221.

Rollin, H. R. (1980). *Coping with schizophrenia.* London: Burnett.

Roose, S. S. (1991). Diagnosis and pharmacological treatment of depression in older patients. In W. A. Mayers (Ed.), *New techniques in the psychotherapy of older patients.* Washington, DC: American Psychiatric.

Root, M. P. (1990). Disordered eating in women of color [Special Issue]. *Sex Roles, 22*(7–8), 525–536.

Roper, G., Rachman, S., & Hodgson, R. (1973). An experiment on obsessional checking. *Behav. Res. Ther., 11,* 271–277.

Roper, P. D. (1967). The use of hypnosis in exhibitionism. In J. Lassner (Ed.), *Hypnosis and psychosomatic medicine.* New York: Springer-Verlag.

Rose, R. M. (1980). Endocrine responses to stressful psychological events. *The Psychiat. Clin. N. Amer., 3,* 251–276.

Rosen, G. M. (1987). Self-help treatment books and the commercialization of psychotherapy. *Amer. Psychol., 42*(1), 46–51.

Rosen, J. C., & Leitenberg, H. (1982). Bulimia nervosa: Treatment with exposure and response prevention. *Behav. Ther., 13*(1), 117–124.

Rosen, J. C., & Leitenberg, H. (1985). Exposure plus response prevention treatment of bulimia. In D. M. Garner & P. E. Garfinkel (Eds.), *Handbook of psychotherapy for anorexia nervosa and bulimia.* New York: Guilford.

Rosen, R. C., & Kopel, S. A. (1977). Penile plethysmography and biofeedback in the treatment of a transvestite exhibitionist. *J. Cons. Clin. Psychol., 45*(5), 908–916.

Rosen, R. C., & Kopel, S. A. (1978). Role of penile tumescence measurement in the behavioral treatment of sexual deviation: Issues of validity. *J. Cons. Clin. Psychol., 48*(8), 1519–1521.

Rosen, W. G. (1991). Higher cortical processes. In K. Davis, H. Klar, & J. T. Coyle (Eds.), *Foundations of psychiatry.* Philadelphia: Saunders.

Rosenbaum, M. (1980). The role of the term schizophrenia in the decline of diagnoses of multiple personality. *Arch. Gen. Psychiat., 37*(12), 1383–1385.

Rosenberg, J. B. (1983). Structural family therapy. In B. B. Wolman & G. Stricker (Eds.), *Handbook of family and marital therapy.* New York: Plenum.

Rosenblatt, W. H., Hutchins, K., & Sinnamon, H. M. (1979). Pimozide's effects of ICSS depend on the interaction of reward and effort. *Soc. Neurosci. Abstr., 5,* 350.

Rosenfeld, L., & Prupas, M. (1984). *Left alive.* Springfield, IL: Thomas.

Rosenhan, D. L. (1973). On being sane in insane places. *Science, 179*(4070), 250–258.

Rosenkrantz, A. L. (1978). A note on adolescent suicide: Incidence, dynamics and some suggestions for treatment. *Adolescence, 13*(50), 208–214.

Rosenn, D. W. (1982). Suicidal behavior in children and adolescents.

In E. Bassuk, S. G. Schoonover, & A. D. Gill, *Lifelines.* New York: Plenum.

Rosenstein, M. J., Milazzo-Sayre, L. J., & Manderscheid, R. W. (1989). Care of persons with schizophrenia: A statistical profile. *Schizo. Bull., 15*(1), 45–58.

Rosenstein, M. J., Milazzo-Sayre, L. J., & Manderscheid, R. W. (1990). Characteristics of persons using specialty inpatient, outpatient, and partial care programs in 1986. In R. W. Manderscheid & M. A. Sonnenschein (Eds.), *Mental Health, United States, 1990.* DHHS Pub. No. (ADM)90-1708. Washington DC: GPO.

Rosensock, H. A. (1985). Depression, suicidal ideation and suicide attempts in 900 adolescents: An analysis. *Crisis, 6*(2), 89–105.

Rosenthal, D. (1971). A program of research on heredity in schizophrenia. *Behav. Sci., 16*(3), 191–201.

Rosenthal, D. (1971). *Genetics of psychopathology.* New York: McGraw-Hill.

Rosenthal, D. (Ed.). (1963). *The Genain quadruplets.* New York: Basic.

Rosenthal, D., Wender, P., Kety, S., Welner, J., & Schulsinger, F. (1971). The adopted-away offspring of schizophrenics. *Amer. J. Psychiat., 128,* 307–311.

Rosenthal, N. E., & Blehar, M. C. (Eds.) (1989). *Seasonal affective disorders and phototherapy.* New York: Guilford.

Rosenthal, N. E., Sack, D. A., Skwerer, R. G., Jacobsen, F. M., & Wehr, T. A. (1989). Phototherapy for seasonal affective disorder. In N. E. Rosenthal & M. C. Blehar (Eds.), *Seasonal affective disorders and phototherapy.*

Rosenthal, R. (1963). *Experimental modeling effects as determinants of subject's responses.* New York: Appleton-Century-Crofts.

Rosenthal, R. (1966). *Experimenter effects in behavioral research.* New York: Appleton-Century-Crofts.

Rosenthal, R., & Rubin, D. B. (1978). Interpersonal expectancy effects: The first 345 students. *Behavioral & Brain Sciences, 1*(3), 377–415.

Rosenthal, T., & Bandura, A. (1978). Psychological logical modeling: Theory and practice. In S. L. Garfield & A. E. Bergin (Eds.), *Handbook of psychotherapy and behavior change.* New York: Wiley.

Rosenzweig, M. R., & Leiman, A. L. (1989). *Physiological psychology.* New York: Random House.

Rosenzweig, S. (1943). An experimental study of repression with special reference to need-persistive and ego-defensive reactions to frustration. *J. Exp. Psychol., 32,* 64–74.

Rosenzweig, S. (1987). Sally Beauchamp's career: A psychoarchaeological key to Morton Prince's classic case of multiple personality. *Genetic, Social, & General Psychology Monographs, 113*(1), 5–60.

Rosenzweig, S. (1988). The identity and idiodynamics of the multiple personality "Sally Beauchamp": A confirmatory supplement. *Amer. Psychol., 43*(1), 45–48.

Ross, A. O. (1981). *Child behavior therapy: Principles, procedures and empirical basis.* New York: Wiley.

Ross, C. A. (1990). Twelve cognitive errors about multiple personality disorder. *Amer. J. Psychother., 44*(3), 348–356.

Ross, C. A., & Gahan, P. (1988). Techniques in the treatment of multiple personality disorder. *Amer. J. Psychother., 42*(1), 40–52.

Ross, C. A., & Norton, G. R. (1989). Differences between men and women with multiple personality disorder. *Hosp. & Commun. Psychiat., 40*(2), 186–188.

Ross, C. A., Miller, S. D., Reagor, P., & Bjornson, L. et al. (1990). Structured interview data on 102 cases of multiple personality disorder from four centers. *Amer. J. Psychiat., 147*(5), 596–601.

Ross, C. A., Norton, G. R., & Wozney, K. (1989). Multiple personality disorder: An analysis of 236 cases. *Canad. J. Psychiat., 34*(5), 413–418.

Ross, C. P. (1980). Mobilizing schools for suicide prevention. *Suic. Life-Threat. Behav., 10*(4), 239–243.

Ross, D. M., & Ross, S. A. (1976). *Hyperactivity: Research, theory, and action.* New York: Wiley.

Ross, D. M., & Ross, S. A. (1982). *Hyperactivity: Current issues, research and theory* (2nd ed.). New York: Wiley.

Ross, S. B. (1983). The therapeutic use of animals with the handicapped. *Inter. Child Welfare Rev., 56,* 26–39.

Ross, S. M., Gottfredson, D. K., Christensen, P., & Weaver, R. (1986). Cognitive self statements in depression: Findings across clinical populations. *Cog. Ther. Res., 10*(2), 159–165.

Rothberg, A. (1990). Adolescence and eating disorders: The obsessive-compulsive syndrome. *Psychiatr. Clin. N. Amer., 13*(3), 469–488.

Rothenberg, A. (1986). Eating disorder as a modern obsessive-compulsive syndrome. *Psychiatry, 49*(1), 45–53.

Rotherman, M. J. (1987). Evaluation of imminent danger for suicide among youth. Annual Meeting of the American Orthopsychiatric Assoc. *Amer. J. Orthopsychiat., 57*(1), 102–110.

Rothman, D. (1985). ECT: The historical, social and professional sources of the controversy. In *NIH Consensus Development Conference: Electroconvulsive therapy.* Bethesda, MD: NIH & NIMH.

Rounsaville, B. J., Chevron, E. S., & Weissman, M. M. (1984). Specification of techniques in interpersonal psychotherapy. In J. B. W. Williams & R. L. Spitzer (Eds.), *Psychotherapy research: Where are we and where should we go?* New York: Guilford.

Rowe, D. (1978). *The experience of depression.* Chichester: Wiley.

Rowe, J. W., & Kahn, R. L. (1987). Human aging: Useful and successful. *Science, 237,* 143–149.

Rowland, C. V. (1970). Anorexia nervosa: A survey of the literature and review of 30 cases. *Inter. Psychiat. Clinics, 7*(1), 37–137.

Roy, A. (1982). Suicide in chronic schizophrenics. *Brit. J. Psychiat., 141,* 171–177.

Roy, A. (1985). Early parental separation and adult depression. *Arch. Gen. Psychiat., 42,* 987–991.

Roy, A. (1985). Suicide in doctors [Special Issue]. *Psychiat. Clin. N. Amer., 8*(2), 377–387.

Roy, A., & Linnoila, M. (1986). Alcoholism and suicide. *Suic. & Life-Threat. Behav., 16*(2), 244–273.

Roy, A., Schreiber, J., Mazonson, A., & Pickar, D. (1986). Suicidal behavior in chronic schizophrenic patients: A follow-up study. *Canad. J. Psychiat., 31*(8), 737–740.

Roy-Byrne, P., Lee-Benner, K., & Yager, J. (1984). Group therapy for bulimia: A year's experience. *Inter. J. of Eat. Dis., 3*(2), 97–116.

Roy-Byrne, P. P., Geraci, M., & Linde, T. W. (1986). Life events and the onset of panic disorder. *Amer. J. Psychiat., 143,* 1424–1427.

Rozin, P., & Fallon, A. (1988). Body image, attitudes to weight, and misperception of figure preference of the opposite sex: A comparison of men and women in two generations. *J. Abnorm. Psychol., 97*(3), 343–345.

Ruderman, A. J. (1986). Dietary restraint: A theoretical and empirical review. *Psychol. Bull., 99*(2), 247–262.

Rudestam, K. E. (1990). Survivors of suicide. In D. Lester (Ed.), *Current concepts of suicide.* Philadelphia: Charles.

Ruedrich, S. L., Chu, C., & Wadle, C. V. (1985). The amytal interview in the treatment of psychogenic amnesia [Special Issue]. *Hosp. Comm. Psychiat., 36*(10), 1045–1046.

Runck, B. (1983). Research is changing views on obsessive-compulsive disorder. *Hosp. Comm. Psychiat., 34*(7), 597–598.

Rund, B. R. (1988). Cognitive disturbances in schizophrenics: What are they, and what is their origin? *Acta Psychiatr. Scandin., 77*(2), 113–123.

Rupert, P. A., & Holmes, D. S. (1978). Effects of multiple sessions of true and placebo heart rate biofeedback training on the heart rates and anxiety levels of anxious patients during and following treatment. *Psychophysiology, 15*(6), 582–590.

Rupert, P. A., & Schroeder, D. J. (1983). Effects of bidirectional heart rate biofeedback training on the heart rates and anxiety levels of anxious psychiatric patients. *Amer. J. Clin. Biofeed., 6*(1), 6–13.

Rusak, B., & Zucker, I. (1975). Biological rhythms and animal behavior. *Ann. Rev. Psychol., 26,* 137–171.

Rush, A. J. (1979). Cognitive therapy for depression. *Austral. New Zeal. J. Psychiat., 13*(1), 13–16.

Rush, A. J. (1981). Group versus individual cognitive therapy: A pilot study. *Cog. Ther. Res., 5,* 95–103.

Rush, A. J. (1984). Cognitive therapy. In L. Grinspoon (Ed.), *Psychiatry update* (Vol. 3). Washington, DC: American Psychiatric.

Rush, A. J. (1990). Problems associated with the diagnosis of depression. *J. Clin. Psychiat., 51*(6, Suppl.), 15–22.

Rush, A. J., Beck, A. T., Kovacs, J. M., & Hollon, S. D. (1977). Comparative efficacy of cognitive therapy and pharmacotherapy in outpatient depressives. *Cog. Ther. Res., 1,* 17–37.

Rush, A. J., Hollon, S. D., Beck, A. T., & Kovacs, M. (1978). Depression: Must pharmacology fail for cognitive therapy to succeed? *Cog. Ther. Res., 2*(2), 199–206.

Rush, A. J., Weissenburger, J., & Eaves, G. (1986). Do thinking patterns predict depressive symptoms? *Cog. Ther. Res., 10*(2), 225–235.

Russell, G. (1979). Bulimia nervosa: An ominous variant of anorexia nervosa. *Psychol. Med., 9*(3), 429–448.

Russell, G. (1981). The current treatment of anorexia nervosa. *Brit. J. Psychiat., 138,* 164–166.

Rutner, I. T., & Bugle, C. (1969). An experimental procedure for the modification of psychotic behavior. *J. Cons. Clin. Psychol., 33,* 651–653.

Rutter, M. (1966). Prognosis: Psychotic children in adolescence and early adult life. In J. K. Wing (Ed.), *Childhood autism: Clinical, educational, and social aspects.* Elmsford, NY: Pergamon.

Rutter, M. (1968). Concepts of autism: A review of research. *J. Child Psychol. Psychiat., 9,* 1–25.

Rutter, M. (1971). The description and classification of infantile autism. In D. Churchill, D. Alpern, & M. DeMeyer, *Infantile autism.* Springfield, IL: Thomas.

Rutter, M., & Bartak, L. (1973). Special educational treatment of autistic children: A comparative study: I. Follow-up findings and implications for services. *J. Child Psychol. Psychiat., 14,* 241–270.

Rutter, M., & Giller, H. (1983). *Juvenile delinquency: Trends and perspectives.* New York: Guilford.

Ryan, R. (1981, Apr. 3). Study shows wide abuse of elderly. *Philadelphia Inquirer.*

Rybarczyk, B., Gallagher-Thompson, D., Rodman, J., Zeiss, A. M., Gantz, F., & Yesavage, J. (1991). Applying cognitive-behavioral psychotherapy to the chronically ill elderly: Treatment issues and case illustrations. *Inter. Psychogeriatrics.*

Sabelli, H. C. et al. (1986). Clinical studies on the phenylethylamine hypothesis of affective disorder: Urine and blood phenylacetic acid and phenylalanine dietary supplements. *J. Clin. Psychiat., 47*(2), 66–70.

Sachar, E. J., Hellman L., Roffwag, H. P., Halpern, H. P., Fukushima, D. K., & Gallagher, T. F. (1973). Disrupted 24-hour patterns of cortisol secretion in psychotic depression. *Arch. Gen. Psychiat., 28,* 19–24.

Sachs, G. S., & Gelenberg, A. J. (1988). Adverse effects of electroconvulsive therapy. In A. J. Frances & R. E. Hales (Eds.), *American Psychiatric Press review of psychiatry* (Vol. 7). Washington, DC: American Psychiatric.

Sachs, J. S. (1983). Negative factors in brief psychotherapy: An empirical assessment. *J. Cons. Clin. Psychol., 51*(4), 557–564.

Sachs, R. G. (1986). The adjunctive role of social support systems. In B. G. Braun (Ed.), *The treatment of multiple personality disorder.* Washington, DC: American Psychiatric.

Sackeim, H. A. (1986). The efficacy of electroconvulsive therapy. *Ann. NY Acad. Sci., 462,* 70–75.

Sackeim, H. A. (1988). Mechanisms of action of electroconvulsive therapy. In A. J. Frances & R. E. Hales (Eds.), *American Psychiatric Press review of psychiatry* (Vol. 7). Washington, DC: American Psychiatric.

Sacks, O. (1991, Feb. 13). Forsaking the mentally ill [Editorial]. *The New York Times.*

Sadock, B. J. (1989). Group psychotherapy, combined individual and group psychotherapy, and psychodrama. In H. I. Kaplan & B. J. Sadock (Eds.), *Comprehensive textbook of psychiatry* (Vol. 1, 5th ed.). Baltimore: Williams & Wilkins.

Sadock, V. A. (1989). Rape, spouse abuse, and incest. In H. I. Kaplan & B. J. Sadock (Eds.), *Comprehensive textbook of psychiatry* (Vol. 1, 5th ed.). Baltimore: Williams & Wilkins.

Safer, D. J., & Krager, J. M. (1984). Trends in medication therapy for hyperactivity: National and international perspectives. In K. D. Gadow (Ed.), *Advances in learning and behavioral disabilities* (Vol. 3). Greenwich, CT: JAI.

Sagawa, K., Kawakatsu, S., Shibuya, I., Oiji, A. et al. (1990). Correlation of regional cerebral blood flow with performance on neuropsychological tests in schizophrenic patients. *Schizo. Res., 3*(4), 241–246.

Sakel, M. (1938). The pharmacological shock treatment of schizophrenia. *Nerv. Ment. Dis. Monograph Series, 62,* 136.

Sales, E., Baum, M., & Shore, B. (1984). Victim readjustment following assault. *J. Soc. Issues, 40*(1), 117–136.

Salkovskis, P. M. (1986). The cognitive revolution: New way forward, backward somersault or full circle? [Special Issue]. *Behav. Psychother., 14,* 278–282.

Salkovskis, P. M. (1988). Phenomenology, assessment, and the cognitive model of panic. In S. Rachman & J. D. Maser (Eds.), *Panic: Psychological perspectives.* Hillsdale, NJ: Erlbaum.

Salkovskis, P. M., Clark, D. M., & Jones, D. R. O. (1986). A psychosomatic mechanism in anxiety attacks: The role of hyperventilation in social anxiety and cardiac neurosis. In H. Lacey & J. Sturgeon (Eds.), *Proceedings of the 15th European Conference in Psychosomatic Medicine.* London: Libbey.

Salkovskis, P. M., Jones, D. R., & Clark, D. M. (1986). Respiratory control in the treatment of panic attacks: Replication and extension with concurrent measurement of behaviour and pCO-sub-2. *Brit. J. Psychiat., 148,* 526–532.

Salkovskis, P. M., Warwick, H. M., Clark, D. M., & Wessels, D. J. (1986). A demonstration of acute hyperventilation during naturally occurring panic attacks. *Behav. Res. Ther., 24*(1), 91–94.

Sallas, A. A. (1985). Treatment of eating disorders: Winning the war without having to do battle. *J. Psychiat. Res., 19*(2–3), 445–448.

Salzman, L. (1968). *The obsessive personality.* New York: Science House.

Salzman, L. (1980). *Psychotherapy of the obsessive personality.* New York: Aronson.

Salzman, L. (1985). Psychotherapeutic management of obsessive-compulsive patients. *Amer. J. Psychother., 39*(3), 323–330.

Salzman, L., & Thaler, F. H. (1981). Obsessive-compulsive disorders: A review of the literature. *Amer. J. Psychiat., 138*(3), 286–296.

Samelson, F. (1980). J. B. Watson's Little Albert, Cyril Burt's twins, and the need for a critical science. *Amer. Psychol., 35,* 619–625.

Sanders, D. (1985). *The woman book on sex and love.* London: Joseph.

Sanders, D. (1987). *The woman report on men.* London: Sphere.

Sanderson, R. E., Campbell, D., & Laverty, S. G. (1963). An investigation of a new aversive conditioning treatment for alcoholism. *Quart. J. Stud. Alcohol., 24,* 261–275.

Sandler, M. (1990). Monoamine oxidase inhibitors in depression: History and mythology. *J. Psychopharm., 4*(3), 136–139.

Sandoval, J., Davis, J. M., & Wilson, M. P. (1987). An overview of the school-based prevention of adolescent suicide. *Special Services in the Schools, 3*(3–4), 103–120.

Sanford, R. C. (1987). An inquiry into the evolution of the client-centered approach to psychotherapy. In J. K. Zeig (Ed.), *The evolution of psychotherapy.* New York: Brunner/Mazel.

Saposneck, D. T., & Watson, L. S. (1974). The elimination of the self-destructive behavior of a psychotic child: A case study. *Behav. Ther., 5,* 79–89.

Sarbin, T. R., & Coe, W. C. (1979). Hypnosis and psychopathology: replacing old myths with fresh metaphors. *J. Abnorm. Psychol., 88*(5), 506–526.

Sarbin, T. R., Taft, R., & Bailey, D. E. (1960). *Clinical inference and cognitive theory.* New York: Holt, Rinehart & Winston.

Sargent, J., Liebman, R., & Silver, M. (1985). Family therapy for anorexia nervosa. In D. M. Garner & P. E. Garfinkel (Eds.), *Handbook of psychotherapy for anorexia nervosa and bulimia.* New York: Guilford.

Sargent, W., & Slater, E. (1941). Amnesic syndromes in war. *Proceedings of the Royal Society of Medicine, 34,* 757–764.

Satir, V. (1964). *Conjoint family therapy: A guide to therapy and technique.* Palo Alto, CA: Science & Behavior.

Satir, V. M. (1987). Going behind the obvious: The psychotherapeutic journey. In J. K. Zeig (Ed.), *The evolution of psychotherapy.* New York: Brunner/Mazel.

Satterfield, J., Canwell, D., Lesser, L., & Podosin, R. (1972). Physiological studies of the hyperactive child. *Amer. J. Psychiat., 128,* 1418–1428.

Satz, P., & Baraff, A. (1962). Changes in relation between self-concepts and ideal self-concepts of psychotics consequent upon therapy. *J. Gen. Psychol., 67,* 191–198.

Saunders, D. G. (1982). Counseling the violent husband. In P. A. Keller & L. G. Ritt (Eds.), *Innovations in clinical practice: A source book* (Vol. 1). Sarasota, FL: Professional Resource Exchange.

Saunders, R. (1985). Bulimia: An expanded definition. *Soc. Casework, 66*(10), 603–610.

Saxe, L., Cross, T. P., & Silverman, N. (1988). Children's mental health: The gap between what we know and what we do. *Amer. Psychol., 43*(10), 800–807.

Saxe, L., Cross, T. P., Silverman, N., & Batchelor, W. F. (Dougherty, D.). (1987). *Children's mental health: Problems and services.* Durham, NC: Duke Univ.

Saxe, L., Dougherty, D., & Cross, T. P. (1985). The validity of polygraph testing: Scientific analysis and public controversy. *Amer. Psychol., 40*(3), 355–366.

Sayers, J. (1988). Anorexia, psychoanalysis, and feminism: Fantasy and reality. *J. Adolescence, 11*(4), 361–371.

Scarr, S., & Weinberg, R. A. (1977). Intellectual similarities within families of both adopted and biological children. *Intelligence, 1*(2), 170–191.

Schacter, D. (1989). Autobiographical memory in a case of multiple personality disorder. *J. Abnorm. Psychol., 98*(4), 508–514.

Schad-Somers, S. P. (1990). *On the mood swings: The psychobiology of elation and depression.* New York: Plenum.

Schaefer, C. E. (1978). *Childhood encopresis and causes and therapy.* New York: Van Nostrand Reinhold.

Schaefer, H. H., & Martin, P. L. (1975). *Behavior therapy* (2nd ed.). New York: McGraw-Hill.

Schalock, R. L., Harper, R. S., & Carver, O. (1981). Independent living placement: Five years later. *Amer. J. Ment. Def., 86*(2), 170–177.

Schandler, S. L., & Grings, W. W. (1976). An examination of methods for producing relaxation during short-term laboratory sessions. *Behav. Res. Ther., 14*(6), 419–426.

Scharfetter, C. (1985). Psychopathologie und Genetik der Schizophrenie. *Schweizer Archiv fur Neurologie, Neurochirurgie und Psychiatrie, 136*(1), 29–36.

Schatzberg, A. T. et al. (1982). Toward a biochemical classification of depressive disorders: V. Heterogeneity of unipolar depressions. *Amer. J. Psychiat., 130*(4), 471–475.

Scheff, T. J. (1966). *Being mentally ill: A sociological theory.* Chicago: Aldine.

Scheff, T. J. (1975). *Labeling madness.* Englewood Cliffs, NJ: Prentice-Hall.

Scheier, M. F., & Carver, C. S. (1985). Optimism, coping, and health: Assessment and implications of generalized outcome expectancies. *Hlth. Psychol., 4*(3), 219–247.

Schiavi, R. C. (1990). Chronic alcoholism and male sexual dysfunction. *J. Sex Marital Ther., 16*(1), 23–33.

Schiele, B. C., & Brozek, J. (1948). Experimental neurosis resulting from semistarvation in man. *Psychosom. Med., 10,* 31–50.

Schilder, P. (1938). The organic background of obsessions and compulsions. *Amer. J. Psychiat., 94,* 1397–1414.

Schildkraut, J. J. (1965). The catecholamine hypothesis of affective disorders: A review of supporting evidence. *Amer. J. Psychiat., 122*(5), 509–522.

Schlichter, K. J., & Horan, J. J. (1981). Effects of stress innoculation on the anger and aggression management skills of institutionalized juvenile delinquents. *Cog. Ther. Res., 5*(4), 359–365.

Schmauk, F. J. (1970). Punishment, arousal, and avoidance learning in sociopaths. *J. Abnorm. Psychol. 76*(3, Pt. 1), 325–335.

Schoenberg, B., Kokmen, E., & Okazaki, H. (1987). Alzheimer's disease and other dementing illnesses in a defined United States population: Incidence rates and clinical features. *Ann. Neurol., 22,* 724–729.

Schoenman, T. J. (1984). The mentally ill witch in textbooks of abnormal psychology: Current status and implications of a fallacy. *Profess. Psychiat., 15,* 299–314.

Schonfeld, L., & Dupree, L. (1990). Older problem drinkers—long-term and late-life onset abusers: What triggers their drinking? *Aging, 361,* 3–11.

Schopler, E. (1976). Toward reducing behavior problems in autistic childhood. *J. Autism Child. Schizo., 6,* 1–13.

Schopler, E. (1981). Autism in adolescence and adulthood. *Proceeding of the 1981 International Conference on Autism,* 16–21.

Schopler, E., & Hennike, J. M. (1990). Past and present trends in residential treatment [Special Issue]. *J. Autism Dev. Dis., 20*(3), 291–298.

Schou, M., Juel-Nielson, N., Stromgren, E., & Voldby, H. (1954). The treatment of manic psychoses by administration of lithium salts. *J. Neurol. Neurosurg. Psychiat., 17,* 250–260.

Schover, L. R., & Jensen, S. B. (1988). *Sexuality and chronic illness.* New York: Guilford.

Schover, L. R., Friedman, J., Weiler, S., Heiman, J. R., & LoPiccolo, J. (1982). A multi-axial diagnostic system for sexual dysfunctions: An alternative to DSM-111. *Arch. Gen. Psychiat., 39,* 443–449.

Schreiber, F. R. (1973). *Sybil.* Chicago: Regnery.

Schreibman, L. (1975). Effects of within-stimulus and extra-stimulus prompting on discrimination learning in autistic children. *J. Appl. Behav. Anal., 8,* 91–112.

Schulsinger, F. (1980). *Bio. Psychopath., 31,* 583–600.

Schultz, R., Braun, B. G., & Kluft, R. P. (1989). Multiple personality disorder: Phenomenology of selected variables in comparison to major depression. *Dissociation, 2,* 45–51.

Schulz, R., & Ewen, R. B. (1988). *Adult development and aging.* New York: Macmillan.

Schutz, W. C. (1967). *Joy.* New York: Grove.

Schwartz, D. M., & Thompson, M. G. (1981). Do anorectics get

well? Current research and future needs. *Amer. J. Psychiat., 138*(3), 319–323.

Schwartz, G. (1977). College students as contingency managers for adolescents in a program to develop reading skills. *J. Appl. Behav. Anal., 10,* 645–655.

Schwartz, G. E. (1977). Psychosomatic disorders and biofeedback: A psychobiological model of disregulation. In *Psychopathology experimental models.* New York: Freeman.

Schwartz, G. E. (1977). Psychosomatic disorders and biofeedback: A psychobiological model of disregulation. In J. D. Maser and M. E. P. Seligman (Eds.), *Psychopathology: Experimental models.* San Francisco: Freeman.

Schwartz, G. E. (1982). Testing the biopsychosocial model: The ultimate challenge facing behavioral medicine? *J. Cons. Clin. Psychol., 50*(6), 1040–1053.

Schwartz, R. C., Barrett, M. J., & Saba, G. (1985). Family therapy for bulimia. In D. M. Garner & P. E. Garfinkel (Eds.), *Handbook of psychotherapy for anorexia nervosa and bulimia.* New York: Guilford.

Schwartz, S. (1978). Do schizophrenics give rare word associations? *Schizo. Bull., 4*(2), 248–251.

Schwartz, S., & Johnson, J. J. (1985). *Psychopathology of childhood.* New York: Pergamon.

Scola, P. S. (1991). Classification and social status. In J. L. Matson & J. A. Mulick (Eds.), *Handbook of mental retardation.* New York: Pergamon.

Scott, J. (1990, Jul. 25). Vertigo, not madness, may have tormented Van Gogh. *Los Angeles Times,* p. A14.

Scottish Schizophrenia Research Group. (1988). The Scottish first episode schizophrenia study: V. One-year follow-up. *Brit. J. Psychiat., 152,* 470–476.

Seay, B. M., Hansen, H. F., & Harlow, H. F. (1962). Mother-infant separation in monkeys. *J. Child. Psychol. Psychiat., 3,* 123–132.

Seay, B. M., Hansen, E. W., & Harlow, H. F. (1965). Maternal separation in the rhesus monkey. *J. Nerv. Ment. Dis., 140,* 434–441.

Sechrest, L. (1984). Reliability and validity. In A. S. Bellack & M. Hersen (Eds.), *Research methods in clinical psychology.* New York: Pergamon.

Secunda, S., Katz, M. M., & Freidman, R. (1973). *The depressive disorders in 1973.* National Institute Mental Health. Washington, DC: GPO.

Sedvall, G. (1990). Monoamines and schizophrenia. International Symposium: Development of a new antipsychotic: Remoxipride. *Acta Psychiatr. Scandin., 82*(358, Suppl.), 7–13.

Sedvall, G. (1990). PET imaging of dopamine receptors in human basal ganglia: Relevance to mental illness. *Trends in Neurosci., 13*(7), 302–308.

Seeman, P., Lee, T., Chau Wong, M., & Wong, K. (1976). Antipsychotic drug doses and neuroleptic/dopamine receptors. *Nature, 281*(5582), 717–718.

Segraves, R. T. (1988). Drugs and desire. In R. C. Rosen & S. R. Leiblum (Eds.), *Sexual desire disorders.* New York: Guilford.

Segraves, R. T. (1988). Hormones and libido. In R. C. Rosen & S. R. Lieblum (Eds.), *Sexual desire disorders.* New York: Guilford.

Seidman, L. J. (1990). The neuropsychology of schizophrenia: A neurodevelopmental and case study approach. *J. Neuropsychiat. & Clin. Neurosci., 2*(3), 301–312.

Seitz, P. F. D., & Melholm, H. B. (1947). Relation of mental imagery to hallucinations. *Arch. Neurol. Psychiat., 57,* 469–480.

Seligman, M. E. P. (1968). Chronic fear produced by unpredictable electric shock. *J. Compar. Physiol. Psychol., 66,* 402–411.

Seligman, M. E. P. (1971). Phobias and preparedness. *Behav. Ther., 2,* 307–320.

Seligman, M. E. P. (1973). Fall into helplessness. *Psych. Today, 7*(1), 43–48.

Seligman, M. E. P. (1974). Submissive death: Giving up on life. *Psych. Today, 7*(12), 80–85.

Seligman, M. E. P. (1975). *Helplessness.* San Francisco: Freeman.

Seligman, M. E. P., & Binik, Y. (1977). Safety signal hypothesis. In H. Davis & H. Hurwitz (Eds.), *Operant-Pavlovian interactions.* Hillsdale, NJ: Erlbaum.

Seligman, M. E. P., & Hager, J. (Eds.). (1972). *Biological boundaries of learning.* New York: Appleton-Century-Crofts.

Seligman, M. E. P., & Maier, S. F. (1967). Failure to escape traumatic shock. *J. Exp. Psychol., 74*(1), 1–9.

Seligman, M. E. P., Abramson, L., Sammel, A., & VonBeyer, C., (1979). Depressive attributional style. *J. Abnorm. Psychol., 88.*

Seligman, M. E. P., Abramson, L., Sammel, A., & von Baayar, C.

(1984). Depressive attributional style. *Southern Psychol., 2*(1), 18–22.

Seligman, M. E. P., Castellon, C., Cacciola, J., Schulman, P. et al. (1988). Explanatory style change during cognitive therapy for unipolar depression. *J. Abnorm. Psychol., 97*(1), 13–18.

Seligman, M. E. P., Maier, S. F., & Geer, J. H. (1968). Alleviation of learned helplessness in the dog. *J. Abnorm. Psychol., 73*(3, Pt. 1), 256–262.

Seligman, M. E. P., Maier, S. F., & Solomon, R. L. (1971). Unpredictable and uncontrollable aversive events. In F. R. Brush (Ed.), *Aversive conditioning in learning.* New York: Academic.

Seligman, M. E. P., Rossellini, R. A., & Kozak, M. J. (1975). Learned helplessness in the rat: Time course, immunization, and reversibility. *J. Compar. Physiol. Psychol., 88*(2), 542–547.

Selling, L. S. (1940). *Men against madness.* New York: Greenberg.

Selmi, P. M. (1983). *Computer-assisted cognitive-behavior therapy in the treatment of depression.* Unpublished doctoral dissertation. Illinois Institute of Technology. Chicago.

Seltz, P. F. D., & Melholm, H. B. (1947). Relation of mental imagery to hallucinations. *Arch. Neurol. Psychiat., 57,* 469–480.

Selye, H. (1974). *Stress without distress.* Philadelphia: Lippincott.

Selye, H. (1976). *Stress in health and disease.* Woburn, MA: Butterworth.

Semans, J. H. (1956). Premature ejaculation: A new approach. *Southern Med. J., 49,* 353–357.

Senate Judiciary Committee. (1991, Mar.). *Report on rape.* Washington, DC: GPO.

Senter, N. W., Winslade, W. J., Liston, E. H. et al. (1984). *Electroconvulsive therapy.* Bethesda, MD: NIH and NIMH.

Serban, G., & Gidynski, C. B. (1975). Differentiating criteria for acute chronic distinction in schizophrenia. *Arch. Gen. Psychiat., 32*(6), 705–712.

Servan-Schreiber, D. (1986). Artificial intelligence and psychiatry. *J. Nerv. Ment. Dis., 174*(4), 191–202.

Shaffer, D., & Gould, M. (1986). *A study of completed and attempted suicide in adolescents.* Presented to the National Conference on Youth Suicide. Oakland, CA.

Shaffer, J., Barclay, A., & Redman, S. (1989). Strategic therapy as a treatment approach in transvestism. *Psychother. Priv. Prac., 7*(2), 91–102.

Shaffer, M., & Lewinsohn, P. M. (1971). *Interpersonal behaviors in the home of depressed versus nondepressed psychiatric and normal controls: A test of several hypotheses.* Paper presented at Western Psychological Association. Univ. Oregon.

Shaffi, M., Carrigan, S., Whittinghill, J. R., & Derrick, A. (1985). Psychological autopsy of completed suicide in children and adolescents. *Amer. J. Psychiat., 142*(9), 1061–1064.

Shamoian, C. (1991). What is anxiety in the elderly? In C. Salzman & B. D. Lebowitz (Eds.), *Anxiety in the elderly.* New York: Springer.

Shannon, P. (1984, Aug. 10). For the mentally ill, warehouses are home. Crowded conditions and poverty transform living into a nightmare. *Miami Herald.*

Shapiro, A. K., & Morris, L. A. (1978). The placebo effect in medical and psychological therapies. In S. L. Garfield & A. E. Bergin (Eds.), *Handbook of psychotherapy and behavior change* (2nd ed.). New York: Wiley.

Shapiro, D. A. (1982). Overview: Clinical and physiological comparison of meditation with other self-control strategies. *Amer. J. Psychiat., 139*(3), 267–274.

Shapiro, D. A. (1989). Outcome research. In G. Parry & N. W. Fraser (Eds.), *Behavioural and mental health research: A handbook of skills and methods.* Hove, UK: Erlbaum.

Shapiro, D. A., & Shapiro, D. (1983). Comparative therapy outcome research: Methodological implications of meta-analysis. *J. Cons. Clin. Psychol., 51,* 42–53.

Shapiro, M. B. (1975). The single variable approach to assessing the intensity of feelings of depression. *Eur. J. Behav. Anal. Mod., 2,* 62–70.

Shapiro, S., Skinner, E. A., Kessler, L. G., Von Korff, M., German, P. S., Tischler, G. L., Leaf, P. J., Benham, L., Cottler, L., & Regier, D. A. (1984). Utilization of health and mental health services. *Arch. Gen. Psychiat., 41,* 971–978.

Shavit, Y., & Martin, F. C. (1987). Opiates, stress, and immunity: Animal studies. *Ann. Behav. Med., 9*(2), 11–15.

Shaw, B. F. (1976). A systematic investigation of two psychological treatments of depression. *Dissertation Abstracts Inter., 36*(8-B), 4179–4180.

Shaw, B. F. (1977). Comparison of cognitive therapy and behavior therapy in the treatment of depression. *J. Clin. Psychol. 45,* 543–551.

Shaw, B. F. (1984). Specification of the training and evaluation of cognitive therapists for outcome studies. In J. B. W. Williams & R. L. Spitzer (Eds.), *Psychotherapy research: Where are we and where should we go?* New York: Guilford.

Shaw, D. M. (1966). Mineral metabolism, mania, and melancholia. *Brit. Med. J., 2,* 262–267.

Shea, S. (1988). *Interviewing: The art of understanding.* Philadelphia: Saunders.

Shea, S. C. (1990). Contemporary psychiatric interviewing: Integration of DSM-III-R, psychodynamic concerns and mental status. In G. Goldstein & M. Hersen (Eds.), *Handbook of psychological assessment* (2nd ed.). New York: Pergamon.

Shear, M. K. (1988). Cognitive and biological models of panic: Toward an integration. In S. Rachman & J. Maser (Eds.), *Panic: Psychological perspectives.* Hillsdale, NJ: Erlbaum.

Shear, M. K., & Fyer, M. R. (1988). Biological and psychopathologic findings in panic disorder. In A. J. Frances & R. E. Hales (Eds.), *American Psychiatric Press review of psychiatry* (Vol. 7). Washington, DC: American Psychiatric.

Shedler, J., & Block, J. (1990). Adolescent drug use and psychological health: A longitudinal inquiry. *Amer. Psychol., 45*(5), 612–630.

Shelton, R. C., & Weinberger, D. R. (1986). X-ray computerized tomography studies in schizophrenia: a review and synthesis. In H. A. Nasrallah & D. R. Weinberger (Eds.), *Handbook of schizophrenia: Vol. 1. The neurology of schizophrenia.* Amsterdam: Elsevier.

Sheppard, M. A., Wright, D., & Goodstadt, M. S. (1985). Peer pressure and drug use: Exploding the myth. *Adolescence, 20*(80), 949–958.

Sheras, P., & Worchel, S. (1979). *Clinical psychology: A social psychological approach.* New York: Van Nostrand.

Sherer, M. (1985). Depression and suicidal ideation in college students. *Psych. Rep., 57*(3, Pt. 2), 1061–1062.

Sherfey, M. J. (1973). *The nature and evolution of female sexuality.* New York: Vintage.

Sherlock, R. (1983). Suicide and public policy: A critique of the "New Consensus." *J. Bioethics, 4,* 58–70.

Sherman, R., & Thompson, R. (1990). *Bulimia: A guide for family and friends.* Lexington, MA: Lexington.

Sherrington, C. S. (1906). *Integrative action of the nervous system.* New Haven, CT: Yale Univ.

Sherrington, R., Brynjolfsson, J., Petursson, H. et al. Localization of a susceptibility locus for schizophrenia on chromosome 5. *Nature, 336,* 164–167.

Shevitz, S. A. (1976). Psychosurgery: Some current observations. *Amer. J. Psychiat., 133*(3), 266–270.

Shneidman, E. S. (1963). Orientations toward death: Subintentioned death and indirect suicide. In R. W. White (Ed.), *The study of lives.* New York: Atherton.

Shneidman, E. S. (1973). Suicide notes reconsidered. *Psychiatry, 36,* 379–394.

Shneidman, E. S. (1981). Suicide. *Suic. Life-Threat. Behav., 11*(4), 198–220.

Shneidman, E. S. (1987, Mar.). At the point of no return. *Psychol. Today.*

Shneidman, E. S., & Farberow, N. (1968). The Suicide Prevention Center of Los Angeles. In H. L. P. Resnick (Ed.), *Suicidal behaviors: Diagnosis and management.* Boston: Little, Brown.

Shneidman, E. S., & Farberow, N. L. (1970). Attempted and completed suicide. In E. S. Shneidman, N. L. Farberow, & R. E. Litman (Eds.), *The psychology of suicide.* New York: Science House.

Shneidman, E. S., Farberow, N. L., & Litman, R. E. (1983). *The psychology of suicide.* New York: Aronson.

Shopsin, B. (1979). Part 1. Mania: Clinical aspects, rating scales and incidence of manic-depressive illness. In B. Shopsin (Ed.), *Manic illness.* New York: Raven.

Shore, J. H. (1975). American Indian suicide: Fact and fantasy. *Psychiat., 38*(1), 86–91.

Shuller, D. Y., & McNamara, J. R. (1976). Expectancy factors in behavioral observation. *Behav. Ther., 7*(4), 519–527.

Shuller, D. Y., & McNamara, J. R. (1980). The use of information derived from norms and from a credible source to counter expectancy effects in behavioral assessment. *Behav. Assess. 2,* 183–196.

Siegal, S. (1979). The role of conditioning in drug tolerance and addiction. In J. D. Keehn (Ed.), *Psychopathology in animals: Research and treatment implications.* New York: Academic.

Siegel, K. (1988). Rational suicide. In S. Lesse (Ed.), *What we know about suicidal behavior and how to treat it.* Northvale, NJ: Aronson.

Siever, L. J., & Uhde, T. W. (1984). New studies and perspectives on the noradrenergic receptor system in depression: Effects of the alpha-2 adrenergic agonist clonidine. *Bio. Psychiat., 19,* 131–156.

Siever, L. J., Davis, K. L., & Gorman, L. K. (1991). Pathogenesis of mood disorders. In K. Davis, H. Klar, & J. T. Coyle, *Foundations of psychiatry.* Philadelphia: Saunders.

Siever, L. J., Keefe, R., Bernstein, D. P., Coccaro, E. F. et al. (1990). Eye tracking impairment in clinically identified patients with schizotypal personality disorder. *Amer. J. Psychiat., 147*(6), 740–745.

Sifneos, P. E. (1979). The difficulties in teaching "psychosomatic medicine." *Psychother. Psychosom., 32*(1–4), 218–222.

Sifneos, P. E. (1980). Ongoing outcome research on short-term dynamic psychotherapy. *Psychother. Psychosom., 33*(4), 233–241.

Sifneos, P. E. (1984). The current status of individual short-term, dynamic psychotherapy and its future. *Amer. J. Psychother., 38*(4).

Sifneos, P. E. (1987). *Short term dynamic psychotherapy evaluation and technique* (2nd ed.). New York: Plenum.

Sigal, J. J., Silver, D., Rakoff, V., & Ellin, B. (1973). Some second-generation effects of survival of the Nazi persecution. *Amer. J. Orthopsychiat., 43*(3), 320–327.

Sigerist, H. E. (1943). *Civilization and disease.* Ithaca, NY: Cornell Univ.

Silberman, E. K. et al. (1985). Dissociative states in multiple personality disorder: A quantitative study. *Psychiat. Res., 15*(4), 253–260.

Silver, J. M., & Yudofsky, S. C. (1988). Psychopharmacology and electroconvulsive therapy. In J. A. Talbott, R. E. Hales, & S. C. Yudofsky (Eds.), *The American Psychiatric Press textbook of psychiatry.* Washington, DC: American Psychiatric.

Silverstone, P. H. (1990). Low self-esteem in eating disordered patients in the absence of depression. *Psych. Rep., 67*(1), 276–278.

Silverton, L., & Mednick, S. (1984). Class drift and schizophrenia. *Acta Psychiatr. Scandin., 70*(4), 304–308.

Simatov, R., Goodman, R., Aposhian, D., & Snyder, S. H. (1976). *Brain Res., 111*(1), 204–211.

Simon, M. J. (1985). The effect of manipulated expectancies on posthypnotic amnesia. *Inter. J. Clin. Exp. Hyp., 33*(1), 40–51.

Simon, R. (1987, January). Interview in Turkington, C., Treatment of depressed elderly could prevent silent suicides. *APA Monitor,* p. 13.

Simons, A. D., Levine, J. L., Lustman, P. J., & Murphy, G. E. (1984). Patient attrition in a comparative outcome study of depression: A follow-up report. *J. Affect. Dis., 6*(2), 163–173.

Simons, A. D., Murphy, G. E., Levine, J. L., & Wetzel, R. D. (1986). Cognitive therapy and pharmacotherapy for depression: Sustained improvement over one year. *Arch. Gen. Psychiat., 43*(1), 43–48.

Simons, L. S. (1989). Privatization and the mental health system: A private sector view. *Amer. Psychol., 44*(8), 1138–1141.

Simons, R. C. (1981). Contemporary problems of psychoanalytic technique. *J. Amer. Psychoanal. Assoc., 29*(3), 643–658.

Simpson, C. J., Hyde, C. E., & Faragher, E. B. (1989). The chronically mentally ill in community facilities: A study of quality of life. *Brit. J. Psychiat., 154,* 77–82.

Simpson, G. M., Pi, E. H., & White, K. (1983). Plasma drug levels and clinical response to antidepressants. *J. Clin. Psychiat., 44*(5, Sect. 2), 27–34.

Simpson, R. O., & Halpin, G. (1986). Agreement between parents and teachers in using the Revised Behavior Problem Checklist to identify deviant behavior in children. *Behav. Dis., 12*(1), 54–58.

Sines, J. O. (1966). Actuarial methods in personality assessment. In B. A. Maher (Ed.), *Progress in experimental personality research* (Vol. 3). New York: Academic.

Sines, L. K. (1959). The relative contribution of four kinds of data to accuracy in personality assessment. *J. Cons. Psychol., 23,* 483–495.

Sintchak, G., & Geer, J. (1975). A vaginal plethysmograph system. *Psychophysiology, 12,* 113–115.

Sizemore, C. C., & Huber, R. J. (1988). The twenty-two faces of Eve. *Individ. Psychol. J. Adlerian Theory Res. Prac., 44*(1), 53–62.

Sjostrom, R. (1973). 5-Hydroxyindole acetic acid and homovanillic acid in cerebrospinal fluid in manic-depressive psychosis and the effect of probenecid treatment. *Eur. J. Clin. Pharmacol., 6,* 75–80.

Skeels, H. M. (1966). Adult status of children with contrasting early life experiences: A follow-up study. *Monographs of the Society for Research in Child Development, 31*(105).

Skeels, H. M., & Dye, H. B. (1939). A study of the effects of differ-

ential stimulation on mentally retarded children. *Proceeding of the Amer. Assoc. of Mental Deficiency, 44,* 114–136.

Skinner, B. F. (1948). Superstition in the Pigeon. *J. Exp. Psychol., 38,* 168–172.

Skinner, B. F. (1948). *Walden two.* New York: Macmillan.

Skinner, H. A. (1984). Correlational methods in clinical research. In A. S. Bellack & M. Hersen (Eds.), *Research methods in clinical psychology.* New York: Pergamon.

Skinner, H. A., & Allen, B. A. (1982). Alcohol dependence syndrome: Measurement and validation. *J. Abnorm. Psychol., 91*(3), 199–209.

Skinner, H. A., & Sheu, W. (1982). Reliability of alcohol use indices: The Lifetime Drinking History and the MAST. *J. Stud. on Alcohol, 43*(11), 1157–1170.

Skodak, M., & Skeels, H. M. A final follow-up of one hundred adopted children. *J. Genetic Psychol., 75,* 85–125.

Skoff, B. F., Mirsky, A. F., & Turner, D. (1980). Prolonged brain-stem transmission time in autism. *Psychiat. Res., 2,* 157–166.

Slade, P. (1985). A review of body-image studies in anorexia nervosa and bulimia nervosa. *J. Psychiat. Res., 19*(2–3), 255–265.

Slater, E., & Shields, J. (1969). Genetical aspects of anxiety. Special Publication No. 3. M. H. Lader (Ed.). *Brit. J. Psychiat., 62–71.*

Sllison, R. B., (1978). On discovering multiplicity. *Svensk Tidskrift Hyp., 3,* 9–16.

Sloane, R. B., Staples, F. R., Cristol, A. H., Yorkson, N. J., & Whipple, K. (1975). *Psychotherapy versus behavior therapy.* Cambridge, MA: Harvard Univ.

Small, J. G., Small, I. F., Milstein, V., Kellams, J. J., & Klapper, M. H. (1985). Manic symptoms: An indication for bilateral ECT. *Bio. Psychiat., 20,* 125–134.

Smith, A. C. (1982). *Schizophrenia and madness.* London: Allen & Unwin.

Smith, D. (1982). Trends in counseling and psychotherapy. *Amer. Psychol., 37*(7), 802–809.

Smith, D. W., & Wilson, A. A. (1973). *The child with Down's syndrome (mongolism).* Philadelphia: Saunders.

Smith, I. L. (1983). Use of simulation in credentialing programs. *Profess. Practicing Psychol., 4,* 21–50.

Smith, J. M., & Baldessarini, R. J. (1980). Changes in prevalence, severity, and recovery in tardive dyskinesia with age. *Arch. Gen. Psychiat., 37*(12), 1368–1373.

Smith, M. L., & Glass, G. V. (1977). Meta-analysis of psychotherapy outcome studies. *Amer. Psychol., 32*(9), 752–760.

Smith, M. L., Glass, G. V., & Miller, T. I. (1980). *The benefits of psychotherapy.* Baltimore: Johns Hopkins Univ.

Smith, P. B. (1975). Are there adverse effects of sensitivity training? *J. Humanistic Psychol., 15*(2), 29–47.

Smith, R. M. (1974). *Clinical teaching: Methods of teaching for the retarded.* New York: McGraw-Hill.

Smith, T. C., & Smith, B. L. (1986). The relationship between the WISC-R and WRAT-R for a sample of rural referred children. *Psychol. Schools, 23*(3), 252–254.

Smoller, J. W. (1986). The etiology and treatment of childhood. In G. C. Ellenbogen (Ed.), *Oral sadism and the vegetarian personality.* New York: Brunner/Mazel.

Smyer, M. A. (1989). Nursing homes as a setting for psychological practice: Public policy perspectives. *Amer. Psychol., 44*(10), 1307–1314.

Snow, E. (1976, Dec.). In the snow. *Texas Monthly Magazine.*

Snyder, C. R. (1955). Studies of drinking in Jewish culture. IV. Culture and sobriety. A study of drinking patterns and sociocultural factors related to sobriety among Jews. *Quart. J. Stud. Alcohol., 16,* 263–289, 700–742.

Snyder, S. (1986). *Drugs and the brain.* New York: Scientific American Library.

Snyder, S. (1991). Drugs, neurotransmitters, and the brain. In P. Corsi (Ed.), *The enchanted loom: Chapters in the history of neuroscience.* New York: Oxford Univ.

Snyder, S. H. (1976). Dopamine and schizophrenia. *Psychiat. Ann., 8*(1), 53–84.

Snyder, S. H. (1976). The dopamine hypotheses of schizophrenia: Focus on the dopamine receptor. *Amer. J. Psychiat., 133*(2), 197–202.

Snyder, S. H. (1977, Mar.). Opiate receptors and internal opiates, *Scientific Amer., 44–56.*

Snyder, S. H. (1977). Opiate receptors in the brain. *New Engl. J. Med., 296,* 266–271.

Snyder, S. H. (1980). *Biological aspects of mental disorder.* New York: Oxford Univ.

Snyder, S. H. (1981). Opiate and benzodiazepine receptors. *Psychosomatics, 22*(11), 986–989.

Snyder, S. H. (1984). Cholinergic mechanisms in affective disorders. *New Engl. J. Med., 311*(4), 254–255.

Snyder, S. H., Creese, I., & Burt, D. R., (1975). The brain's dopamine receptor: Labeling with (sup 311) dopamine and (sup 311) haloperidol. *Psychopharma. Communications, 1*(8), 663–673.

Snyder, W. V. (1947). *Casebook of non-directive counseling,* Boston: Houghton Mifflin.

Sobell, L. C., Sobell, M. B., & Coleman, R. F. (1982). Alcohol-induced dysfluency in nonalcoholics. *Folia Phoniatrica, 34*(6), 316–323.

Sobell, M. B., & Sobell, L. C. (1973). Alcoholics treated by individualized behavior therapy: One year treatment outcome. *Behav. Res. Ther., 11*(4), 599–618.

Sobell, M. B., & Sobell, L. C. (1973). Individualized behavior therapy for alcoholics. *Behav. Ther., 4*(1), 49–72.

Sobell, M. B., & Sobell, L. C. (1976). Second year treatment outcome of alcoholics treated by individualized behavior therapy: Results. *Behav. Res. Ther., 14*(3), 195–215.

Sobell, M. B., & Sobell, L. C. (1984). The aftermath of heresy: A response to Pendery et al.'s (1982) critique of "Individualized Behavior Therapy for Alcoholics." *Behav. Res. Ther., 22*(4), 413–440.

Sobell, M. B., & Sobell, L. C. (1984). Under the microscope yet again: A commentary on Walker and Roach's critique of the Dickens Committee's enquiry into our research. *Brit. J. Addic., 79*(2), 157–168.

Sokol-Kessler, L., & Beck, A. T. (1987). *Cognitive treatment of panic disorders.* Paper presented at the 140th Annual Meeting of the American Psychiatric Assoc. Chicago.

Solomon, G. F. (1969). Stress and antibody response in rats. *Inter. Arch. Allergy & Applied Immun., 35,* 97–104.

Solomon, M., & Murphy, G. (1984). Cohort studies of suicide. In H. Sudak, A. Ford, & N. Rushforth (Eds.), *Suicide in the young.* London: PSG.

Solomon, R. L., Kamin, L. J., & Wynne, L. C. (1953). Traumatic avoidance learning: The outcomes of several extinction procedures with dogs. *J. Abnorm. Soc. Psychol., 48,* 291–302.

Solyom, L., Freeman, R. J., & Miles, J. E. (1982). A comparative psychometric study of anorexia nervosa and obsessive neurosis. *Canad. J. Psychiat., 27*(4), 282–286.

Solyom, L., Ledwidge, B., & Solyom, C. (1986). Delineating social phobia. *Brit. J. Psychiat., 149,* 464–470.

Somasundaram, O., Papakumari, M. (1981). A study on Down's anomaly. *Child Psychol. Quart., 14*(3), 85–94.

Sorokin, J. E., Giordani, B., Mohs, R. C., Losonczy, M. F. et al. (1988). Memory impairment in schizophrenic patients with tardive dyskinesia. *Bio. Psychiat., 23*(2), 129–135.

Sours, J. A. (1980). *Starving to death in a sea of objects: The anorexia nervosa syndrome.* New York: Aronson.

Southam, M. A., Agras, W. S., Taylor, C. B., & Kraemer, H. C. (1982). Relaxation training: Blood pressure lowering during the working day. *Arch. Gen. Psychiat., 39*(6), 715–717.

Spanos, N. P. (1982). Hypnotic behavior: A cognitive, social psychological perspective. *Res. Communications in Psychol., Psychiat. & Behav., 7*(2), 199–213.

Spanos, N. P. (1983). The Carleton University Responsiveness to Suggestion Scale: Stability, reliability, and relationships with expectance and "hypnotic experiences." *Psychological Reports, 53*(2), 555–563.

Spanos, N. P. (1984). Imagery, hypnosis and hypnotizability. In A. S. Bellack & M. Hersen (Eds.), *Research methods in clinical psychology.* New York: Pergamon.

Spanos, N. P. (1986). Hypnosis and the modification of hypnotic susceptibility: A social psychological perspective. In P. L. N. Naish (Ed.), *What is hypnosis?* Philadelphia: Open Univ.

Spanos, N. P. (1986). Hypnotic behavior: A social psychological interpretation of amnesia, analgesia, and "trance logic." *Behav. Brain Sci., 9*(3), 449–467.

Spanos, N. P. (1986). More on the social psychology of hypnotic responding. *Behav. Brain Sci., 9*(3), 489–502.

Spanos, N. P. (1990). More on compliance and the Carleton Skill Training Program. *Brit. J. Exp. Clin. Hyp., 7*(3), 165–170

Spanos, N. P. (1991). Imagery, hypnosis and hypnotizability. In R. G. Kunzendorf (Ed.), *Proceedings from American Assoc. for the Study of Mental Imagery 11th Annual Conference (Washington, DC, 1989).* New York: Plenum.

Spanos, N. P., & Bodorik, H. L. (1977). Suggested amnesia and disorganized recall in hypnotic and task-motivated subjects. *J. Abnorm. Psychol., 86*(3), 295–305.

Spanos, N. P., & D'Eon, J. L. (1980). Hypnotic amnesia, disorganized recall, and inattention. *J. Abnorm. Psychol., 89*(6), 744–750.

Spanos, N. P. et al. (1980). Effects of social psychological variables on hypnotic amnesia. *J. Pers. Soc. Psychol., 38*(4), 737–750.

Spanos, N. P., Ham, M. W., & Barber, T. X. (1973). Suggested ("hypnotic") visual hallucinations: Experimental and phenomenological data. *J. Abnorm. Psychol., 81,* 96–106.

Spanos, N. P., Radtke-Bodorick, H. L., & Shabinsky, M. A. (1980). Amnesia, subjective organization and learning of a list of unrelated words in hypnotic and task-motivated subjects. *Inter. J. Clin. Exper. Hyp., 28*(2), 126–139.

Spear, N. E. (1973). Retrieval of memory in animals. *Psych. Rev., 80,* 163–194.

Spiegel, R. (1965). Communication with depressive patients. *Contemp. Psychoanal., 2,* 30–35.

Spielberger, C. (1985). Anxiety, cognition, and affect: A state-trait perspective. In A. H. Tuma & J. Maser (Eds.), *Anxiety and the anxiety disorders.* Hillsdale, NJ: Erlbaum.

Spielberger, C. D. (1972). Anxiety as an emotional state. In C. D. Spielberger (Ed.), *Anxiety: Current trends in theory and research* (Vol. 1). New York: Academic.

Spielberger, C. D. (1972). Conceptual and methodological issues in anxiety research. In C. D. Spielberger (Ed.), *Anxiety: Current trends in theory and research* (Vol. 2). New York: Academic.

Spiess, W. F., Geer, J. H., & O'Donohue, W. T. (1984). Premature ejaculation: Investigation of factors in ejaculatory latency. *J. Abnorm. Psychol., 93*(2), 242–245.

Spitzer, R. L., & Fliess, J. L. (1974). A reanalysis of the reliability of psychiatric diagnosis. *Brit. J. Psychiat., 125,* 341–347.

Spitzer, R. L., Skodol, A., Gibbon, M., & Williams, J. B. W. (1981). *DSMIII case book* (1st ed.). Washington, DC: American Psychiatric.

Spotts, J. V., & Shontz, F. C. (1983). Psychopathology and chronic drug use: A methodological paradigm. *Inter. J. Addic., 18*(5), 633–680.

Squire, L. R. (1977). ECT and memory loss. *Amer. J. Psychiat., 134,* 997–1001.

Squire, L. R., & Slater, P. C. (1978). Bilateral and unilateral ECT: Effects on verbal and nonverbal memory. *Amer. J. Psychiat., 135*(11), 1316–1320.

Squire, L. R., & Slater, P. C. (1983). Electroconvulsive therapy and complaints of memory dysfunction: A prospective three-year follow-up study. *Brit. J. Psychiat., 142,* 1–8.

Squire, L. R., Slater, P. C., & Miller, P. L. (1981). Retrograde amnesia and bilateral electroconvulsive therapy. *Arch. Gen. Psychiat., 38,* 89–95.

Squires, R. F., & Braestrup, C. (1977). Benzodiazepine receptors in rat brain. *Nature, 266*(5604), 732–734.

Stack, S. (1981). Comparative analysis of immigration and suicide. *Psych. Rep., 49*(2), 509–510.

Stack, S. (1982). Suicide in Detroit 1975: Changes and continuities. *Suic. & Life-Threat. Behav., 12*(2), 67–83.

Stack, S. (1987). Celebrities and suicide: A taxonomy and analysis, 1948–1983. *Amer. Sociological Rev., 52,* 401–412.

Stahl, S. M. (1984). Regulation of neurotransmitter receptors by desipramine and other antidepressant drugs: The neurotransmitter receptor hypothesis of antidepressant action. *J. Clin. Psychiat., 45*(10, Sect. 2), 37–44.

Stampfl, T. G. (1975). Implosive therapy: Staring down your nightmares. *Psych. Today, 8*(9), 66–68; 72–73.

Stampfl, T. G., & Levis, D. J. (1967a). Essentials of implosive therapy: A learning theory-based psychodynamic behavioral therapy. *J. Abnorm. Psychol., 72,* 496–503.

Stanley, E. J., & Barter, J. T. (1970). Adolescent suicidal behavior. *Amer. J. Orthopsychiat., 40,* 87–96.

Starcevic, V. (1988). Diagnosis of hypochondriasis: A promenade through the psychiatric nosology. *Amer. J. Psychother., 42*(2), 197–211.

Stark, K. D., Rose, L. W., & Livingstone, R. (1991). Treatment of depression during childhood and adolescence: Cognitive-behavioral procedures for the individual and family. In P. C. Kendall (Ed.), *Child and adolescent therapy: Cognitive-behavioral procedures.* New York: Guilford.

Stark, T., & Blum, R., (1986). Psychosomatic illness in childhood and adolescence; Clinical considerations. *Clin. Pediat.*, *25*(11), 549–554.

Starker, S. (1988). Psychologists and self-help books: Attitudes and prescriptive practices of clinicians. *Amer. J. Psychother.*, *42*(30), 448–455.

Stattin, H., & Magnusson, D. (1980). Stability of perceptions of own reactions across a variety of anxiety-provoking situations. *Percept. & Motor Skills*, *51*, 959–967.

Steadman, H., Monahan, J., Hartstone, E., Davis, S., & Robbins, P. (1982). Mentally disordered offenders: A national survey of patients and facilities. *Law & Human Behav.*, *6*, 31–38.

Steadman, H. J. (1980). Insanity acquittals in New York State, 1965–1978. *Amer. J. Psychiat.*, *137*, 321–326.

Steele, B. F. (1985). The psychological aspects of pain. In R. C. Simons (Ed.), *Understanding human behavior in health and illness* (3rd ed.). Baltimore: Williams & Wilkins.

Steele, C. M., & Josephs, R. A. (1990). Alcohol myopia: Its prized and dangerous effects. *Amer. Psychol.*, *45*(8), 921–933.

Steer, R. A., Emergy, D. G., & Beck, A. T. (1980). Correlates of self-reported and clinically assessed depression in male heroin addicts. *J. Clin. Psychol.*, *36*(3), 798–800.

Steere, J., Butler, G., & Cooper, J. (1990). The anxiety symptoms and bulimia nervosa: A comparative study. *Inter. J. Eat. Dis.*, *9*(3), 293–301.

Steffenburg, S., Gillberg, C., Wellgren, L., Andersson, L. et al. (1989). *J. Child. Psychol. Psychiat.*, *30*(3), 405–416.

Steiger, H., Goldstein, C., Mongrain, M., & Van der Feen, J. (1990). Description of eating-disordered, psychiatric, and normal women along cognitive and psychodynamic dimensions. *Inter. J. Eat. Dis.*, *9*(2), 129–140.

Stein, Z., Susser, M., Saenger, G., & Marolla, F. (1972). Nutrition and mental performance. *Science*, *178*, 708–713.

Steinberg, J. A. (1986). Clinical interventions with women experiencing the impostor phenomenon. *Women & Therapy*, *5*(4), 19–26.

Steinberg, M. (1991). The spectrum of depersonalization: Assessment and treatment. In A. Tasman & S. M. Goldfinger (Eds.), *American psychiatric review of psychiatry* (Vol. 10). Washington, DC: Amer. Psychiat.

Steinglass, P., Tislenko, L., & Reiss, D. (1985). Stability/instability in the alcoholic marriage: The interrelationships between course of alcoholism, family process, and marital outcome. *Family Process*, *24*(3), 365–376.

Steinmark, S. W., & Borkovec, T. D. (1974). Active and placebo treatment effects on moderate insomnia under counterdemand and positive demand instructions. *J. Abnorm. Psychol.*, *83*, 157–163.

Steketee, G., & Foa, E. B. (1987). Rape victims: Post-traumatic stress responses and their treatment. *J. Anx. Dis.*, *1*, 69–86.

Stellar, E. (1954). The physiology of motivation. *Psychol. Rev.*, *61*, 5–22.

Stengel, E. (1964). *Suicide and attempted suicide*. Baltimore: Penguin.

Stengel, E. (1974). *Suicide and attempted suicide* (2nd ed.). New York: Aronson.

Stephens, J. H., & Kamp, M. (1962). On some aspects of hysteria: A clinical study. *J. Nerv. Ment. Dis.*, *134*(4), 305–315.

Stephenson, W. (1953). *The study of behavior*. Chicago: Univ. Chicago.

Stern, R., & Marks, I. (1973). Brief and prolonged flooding. *Arch. Gen. Psychiat.*, *28*, 270–276.

Stern, R. S., & Cobb, J. P. (1978). Phenomenology of obsessive-compulsive neurosis. *Brit. J. Psychiat.*, *12*, 233–239.

Stewart, J., de Wit, H., & Eikelboom, R. (1984). Role of unconditioned and conditioned drug effects in the self-administration of opiates and stimulants. *Psych. Rev.*, *91*(2), 251–268.

Stewart, R. B., Springer, P. K., & Adams, J. E. (1980). Drug-related admissions to an inpatient psychiatric unit. *Amer. J. Psychiat.*, *137*(9), 1093–1095.

Stillion, J. M. (1984). Perspectives on the sex differential in death. *Death Educ.*, *8*(4), 237–258.

Stokes, T. E., & Osnes, P. G. (1989). An operant pursuit of generalization. *Behav. Ther.*, *20*(3), 337–355.

Stoller, F. H. (1968). Accelerated interaction: A time limited approach based on the brief intensive group. *Inter. J. Group Psychother.*, *18*, 220–235.

Stone, A. A. (1975). *Mental health and law: A system in transition*. Rockville, MD: National Institute of Mental Health.

Stonehill, E., & Crisp, A. H. (1977). Psychoneurotic characteristics

of patients with anorexia nervosa before and after treatment and at follow-up 4 to 7 years later. *J. Psychosom. Res.*, *21*, 189–193.

Stotland, E., & Blumenthal, A. L. (1964). The reduction of anxiety as a result of the expectation of making a choice. *Canad. Rev. Psychol.*, *18*(2), 139–145.

Stoudemire, A. et al. (1985). Masked depression in a combined medical psychiatric unit. *Psychosomatics*, *26*(3), 221–228.

Straus, M. A., Gelles, R. J., & Steinmetz, S. (1980). *Behind closed doors: Violence in the American family*. New York: Anchor/Doubleday.

Strauss, J. S. (1979). Social and cultural influences on psychopathology. *Annu. Rev. Psychol.*, *30*, 397–415.

Strickland, B. R., Hale, W. D., & Anderson, L. K. (1975). Effect of induced mood states on activity and self-reported affect. *J. Cons. Clin. Psychol.*, *43*(4), 587.

Striegel-Moore, R. H., Silberstein, L. R., & Rodin, J. (1986). Toward an understanding of risk factors for bulimia. *Amer. Psychol.*, *41*(3), 246–263.

Strober, M. (1981). The relation of personality characteristics to body image disturbances in juvenile anorexia nervosa: A multivariate analysis. *Psychosom. Med.*, *43*(4), 323–330.

Strober, M. (1981). The significance of bulimia in juvenile anorexia nervosa: An exploration of possible etiological factors. *Inter. J. Eat. Dis.*, *1*, 28–43.

Strober M. (1983, May). *Familial depression in anorexia nervosa*. Paper presented at the meeting of the American Psychiatric Assoc. New York.

Strober, M., & Bowen, E. (1986). Hospital management of the adolescent with anorexia nervosa. *Clin. Psychol.*, *39*(2), 46–48.

Strober, M., & Katz, J. L. (1987). Do eating disorders and affective disorders share a common etiology? A dissenting opinion. *Int. J. Eat. Dis.*, *6*(2), 171–180.

Strober, M., & Yager, J. (1985). A developmental perspective on the treatment of anorexia nervosa in adolescents. In D. M. Garner & P. E. Garfinkel (Eds.), *Handbook of psychotherapy for anorexia nervosa and bulimia*. New York: Guilford.

Strupp, H. H. (1989). Psychotherapy: Can the practitioner learn from the researcher? *Amer. Psychol.*, *44*, 717–724.

Strupp, H. H., & Binder, J. (1984). *Psychotherapy in a new key: Time-limited dynamic psychotherapy*. New York: Basic.

Strupp, H. H., Fox, R. A., & Lessler, K. J. (1969). *Patients view their psychotherapy*. Baltimore: Johns Hopkins Univ.

Stuart, R. B. (1969). Operant interpersonal treatment for marital discord. *J. Cons. Clin. Psychol.*, *33*, 675–682.

Stuart, R. B. (1975). Behavioral remedies for marital ills: A guide to the use of operant-interpersonal techniques. In A. S. Gurman & D. G. Rice (Eds.), *Couples in conflict: New directions in marital therapy*. New York: Aronson.

Stuart, R. B. (1980). *Helping couples change: A social learning approach to marital therapy*. New York: Guilford.

Sturgeon, V., & Taylor, J. (1980). Report of a five-year follow-up study of mentally disordered sex offenders released from Atascadero State Hosptial in 1973. *Criminal Justice J. Western State Univ., San Diego*, *4*, 31–64.

Suddath, R. L., Christison, G. W., & Torrey, E. F. (1990). Anatomical abnormalities in the brains of monozygotic twins discordant for schizophrenia. *New England J. of Medicine*, *322*(12), 789–794.

Suematsu, H., Ishikawa, H., Kuboki, T., & Ito, T. (1985). Statistical studies on anorexia nervosa in Japan: Detailed clinical data on 1,011 patients. *Psychother. & Psychosom.*, *43*(2), 96–103.

Suematsu, H., Kuboki, T., & Itoh, T. (1985). Statistical studies on the prognosis of anorexia nervosa. *Psychother. & Psychosom.*, *43*(2), 104–112.

Suinn, R., & Richardson, F. (1971). Anxiety management training. A nonspecific behavior therapy program for anxiety control. *Behav. Ther.*, *2*, 498–510.

Sullivan, A. (1980). A constitutional right to suicide. In M. P. Batin & D. J. Mayo (Eds.), *Suicide: The philosophical issues*. New York: St. Martin's.

Sullivan, H. S. (1953). *The interpersonal theory of psychiatry*. New York: Norton.

Sullivan, H. S. (1954). *The psychiatric interview*. New York: Norton.

Sullivan, H. S. (1962). *Schizophrenia as a human process*. New York: Norton.

Suls, J., & Rittenhouse, J. D. (1990). Models of linkages between personality and disease. In H. S. Friedman (Ed.), *Personality and disease*. New York: Wiley.

Sulser, F. (1983). Mode of action of antidepressant drugs. *J. Clin. Psychiat.*, 44(5, Sect 2), 14–20.

Sulser, F., Vetulani, J., & Mobley, P. L. (1978). Mode of action of antidepressant drugs. *Biomed. Pharmacol.*, 27(3), 257–261.

Sundberg, N. D. (1977). *Assessment of persons*. Englewood Cliffs, NJ: Prentice-Hall.

Sundberg, N. D., Tyler, L. E., & Taplin, J. R. (1973). *Clinical psychology: Expanding horizons* (2nd ed.). Englewood cliffs, NJ: Prentice-Hall.

Suomi, S. J. (1976). Factors affecting responses to social separation in rhesus monkeys. In G. Serban & A. Kling (Eds.), *Animal models in human psychobiology*. New York: Plenum.

Suomi, S. J., & Harlow, H. F. (1975). Effects of differential removal from group on social development of rhesus monkeys. *J. Child Psychol. Psychiat.*, 16, 149–158.

Suomi, S. J., & Harlow, H. F. (1977). Production and alleviation of depressive behaviors in monkeys. In J. D. Maser & M. E. P. Seligman (Eds.), *Psychopathology: Exzperimental models*. New York: Freeman.

Suomi, S. J., Harlow, H. F., & Domek, C. J. (1970). *J. Abnorm. Psychol.*, 76, 161–172.

Suomi, S. J. (1976). Factors affecting responses to social separation in rhesus monkeys. In G. Serban & A. Kling (Eds.), *Animal models in human psychology*. New York: Plenum.

Surtees, P. C., & Ingham, J. C. (1980). Life stress and depressive outcome: Application of a dissipation model to life events. *Soc. Psychiat.*, 15(1), 21–31.

Surwit, R. S. (1982). Behavioral treatment of Raynaud's syndrome in peripheral vascular disease. *J. Cons. Clin. Psychol.*, 50(6), 922–932.

Surwit, R. S., Shapiro, D., & Good, M. I. (1978). Comparison of cardiovascular biofeedback, neuromuscular feedback, and meditation in the treatment of borderline hypertension. *J. Cons. Clin. Psychol.*, 46, 252–256.

Suter, S. (1986). *Health psychophysiology: Mind-body interactions in wellness and illness*. Hillsdale, NJ: Erlbaum.

Swartz, L. (1985). Anorexia nervosa as a culture-bound syndrome. *Soc. Sci. Med.*, 20(7), 725–730.

Swedo, S. E., Leonard, H. L., Rapoport, J. L., Lenane, M. C. et al. (1989). A double-blind comparison of clomipramine and desipramine in the treatment of trichotillomanio (hair pulling). *N. Engl. J. Med.*, 321(8), 497–501.

Swedo, S. E., Rapoport, J. L., Leonard, H. L., Lenane, M. C. et al. (1989). Obsessive-compulsive disorder in children and adolescents: Clinical phenomenology of 70 consecutive cases. *Arch. Gen. Psychiat.*, 46(4), 335–341.

Swedo, S. E., Shapiro, M. B., Grady, C. L., Cheslow, D. L. et al. (1989). Cerebral glucose metabolism in childhood-onset obsessive-compulsive disorder. *Arch. Gen. Psychiat.*, 46(6), 518–523.

Sweeney, P. D., Anderson, K., & Bailey, S. (1986). Attributional style in depression: A meta analytic review. *J. Pers. Soc. Psychol.*, 50(5), 974–991.

Swift, W. J., Ritholz, M., Kalin, N. H., & Kaslow, N. (1987). A follow-up study of thirty hospitalized bulimics. *Psychosom. Med.*, 49, 45.

Szasz, T. S. (1961). *The myth of mental illness: Foundations of a theory of personal conduct*. New York: Hoeber-Harper.

Szasz, T. S. (1963). *Law, liberty, and psychiatry*. Englewood Cliffs, NJ: Prentice-Hall.

Szasz, T. S. (1963). *The manufacture of madness*. New York: Harper & Row.

Szasz, T. S. (1977). *Psychiatric slavery*. New York: Free.

Szasz, T. S. (1987). Justifying coercion through theology and therapy. In J. K. Zeig (Ed.), *The evolution of psychotherapy*. New York: Brunner/Mazel.

Tallman, J. F. (1978). Research project. In S. Snyder, (1986). *Drugs and the brain*. New York: Scientific American Library.

Tallman, J. F. et al. (1980). Receptors for the age of anxiety: Pharmacology of the benzodiazepine. *Science*, 207, 274.

Tanagho, E. A., Lue, T. F., & McClure, R. D. (1988). *Contemporary management of impotence and infertility*. Baltimore: Williams & Wilkins.

Tancer, M. E., Brown, T. M., Evans, D. L., Ekstrom, D. et al. (1990). Impaired effortful cognition in depression. *Psychiat. Res.*, 31(2), 161–168.

Tanguay, P. E., & Edwards, R. M. (1982). Electrophysical studies of autism: The whisper of the bang. *J. Autism Dev. Dis.*, 12, 177–183.

Tanzi, R. C., St. George Hyslop, P. H., & Gusella, J. T. (1989). Molecular genetic approaches to Alzheimer's disease. *Trends Neurosci.*, 12(4), 152–158.

Tashkin, D. P., Calvarese, B., & Simmons, M. (1978). Respiratory status of 75 chronic marijuana smokers: Comparison with matched controls. Abstract in *Amer. Rev. Respiratory Dis.*, 117, 261.

Taska, R., & Brodie, H. K. (1983). New trends in the diagnosis and treatment of depression. *J. Clin. Psychiat.*, 44(5, Sect 2), 11–13.

Taube, C. A. (1990). Funding and expenditures for mental illness. In R. W. Manderscheid & M. A. Sonnenschein (Eds.), *Mental Health, U.S., 1990*. DHHS #(ADM) 90-1708. Washington, DC: GPO.

Taylor, C. B., Farquhar, J. W., Nelson, E., & Agras, S. (1977). Relaxation therapy and high blood pressure. *Arch. Gen. Psychiat.*, 34, 339–342.

Taylor, C. B., Hayward, C., King, R., Ehlers, A. et al. (1990). Cardiovascular and symptomatic reduction effects of alprazolam and imipramine in patients with panic disorder: Results of a double-blind, placebo-controlled trial. *J. Clin. Psychopharm.*, 10(2), 112–118.

Taylor, E. A., & Stansfeld, S. A. (1984). Children who poison themselves. *Brit. J. Psychiat.*, 145, 127–135.

Taylor, F., & Marshall, W. (1977). Experimental analysis of cognitive-behavioral therapy for depression. *Cog. Ther. Res.*, 1, 59–72.

Taylor, I. L. (1985). The reactive effect of self-monitoring of target activities in agoraphobics: A pilot study. *Scandin. J. Behav. Ther.*, 14(1), 17–22.

Taylor, J. R., & Carroll, J. L. (1987). Current issues in electroconvulsive therapy. *Psych. Rep.*, 60(3, Pt. 1).

Taylor, R. (1975). Electroconvulsive treatment (ECT): The control of therapeutic power. *Exchange*.

Teasdale, J. D. (1985). Psychological treatments for depression: How do they work? *Behav. Res. Ther.*, 23(2), 157–165.

Tellegen, A. (1985). Structures of mood and personality and their relevance to assessing anxiety, with an emphasis on self-report. In A. H. Tuma & J. Maser (Eds.), *Anxiety and the anxiety disorders*. Hillsdale, NJ: Erlbaum.

Telner, J. I., & Singhal, R. L. (1984). Psychiatric progress: The learned helplessness model of depression. *J. Psychiat. Res.*, 18(3), 207–215.

Telner, J. I., Lapierre, Y. D., Horn, E., & Browne, M. (1988). Rapid reduction of mania by means of reserpine therapy. *Amer. J. Psychiat.*, 143(8), 1058.

Temerlin, M. K. (1968). Suggestion effects in psychatric diagnosis. *J. Nerv. Ment. Dis.*, 147, 349–353.

Temerlin, M. K. (1970). Diagnostic bias in community mental health. *Comm. Ment. Hlth. J.*, 6, 110–117.

Tennant, C. (1988). Psychological causes of duodenal ulcer. *Austral. N. Zeal. J. Psychiat.*, 22(2), 195–202.

Teri, L. (1982). The use of the Beck depression inventory for adolescents. *J. Abnorm. Child Psychol.*, 10(2), 277–284.

Teri, L., & Lewinsohn, P. M. (1985). Group intervention for unipolar depression. *Behav. Ther.*, 8, 109–123.

Teri, L., & Lewinsohn, P. M. (1986). Individual and group treatment of unipolar depression: Comparison of treatment outcome and identification of predictors of successful treatment outcome. *Behav. Ther.*, 17(3), 215–228.

Teri, L., & Logsdon, R. (1991). Identifying pleasant activities for Alzheimer's disease patients: The pleasant events schedule-AD. *Gerontologist*, 31, 124–127.

Teri, L., & Reifler, B. V. (1987). Depression and dementia. In L. Carstensen & B. Edelstein (Eds.), *Handbook of clinical gerontology*. New York: Pergamon.

Terr, L. (1988). What happens to early memories of trauma? A study of twenty children under age five at the time of documented traumatic events. Annual Meeting of the American Psychiatry Association. *J. Amer. Academy Child Adol. Psychiat.*, 27(1), 96–104.

Test, M. A., & Stein, L. I. (1978). Community treatment of the chronic patient. *Schizo. Bull.*, 4(3), 350–364.

Theander, S. (1970). Anorexia nervosa. *Acta Psychiatr. Scandin.*, (Suppl.), 1–194.

Thigpen, C. H., & Cleckley, H. M. (1957). *The three faces of Eve*. New York: McGraw-Hill.

Thomas, A., Chess, S. Birch, H. G., Hertzig, M., & Korn, S. (1963). *Behavioral individuality in early childhood*. New York: New York Univ.

Thomas, C. S. (1984). Dysmorphophobia: A question of definition. *Brit. J. Psychiat.*, 144, 513–516.

Thomas, C. S. (1986). Cognitive therapy of obsessive-compulsive disorder: Treating treatment failures: Comment. *Behav. Psychother., 14*(1), 90.

Thompson, L., Davies, R., Gallagher, D., & Krantz, S. (1986). Cognitive therapy with older adults. *Clin. Gerontologist, 5,* 245–279.

Thompson, L., Gallagher, D., & Breckenridge, J. S. (1987). Comparative effectiveness of psychotherapies for depressed elders. *J. Cons. Clin. Psychol., 55,* 385–390.

Thompson, L., Gallagher, D., Nies, G., & Epstein, D. (1983). Evaluation of the effectiveness of professionals and nonprofessionals as instructors of "Coping with Depression" classes for elders. *Gerontologist, 23,* 390–396.

Thompson, M. S., & Conrad, P. L. (1977). Multifaceted behavioral treatment of drug dependence: A case study. *Behav. Ther., 8*(4), 731–737.

Thompson, T. L., Scully, J. H., & Thompson, W. L. (1985). The "difficult" mental patient, and the importance of consultation-liaison psychiatry. In R. C. Simons (Ed.), *Understanding human behavior in health and illness* (3rd ed.). Baltimore: Williams & Wilkins.

Thorpe, G. L., Freedman, E. G., & Lazar, J. D. (1985). Assertiveness training and exposure in vivo for agoraphobics. *Behav. Psychother., 13*(2), 132–141.

Tice, D. (1990, Aug.). *Presentation.* Washington, DC: American Psychological Assoc.

Tillich, P. (1952, Dec.). Anxiety, Religion, and medicine. *Pastoral Psychol., 3,* 11–17.

Tirelli, L. C. (1967). Some observations on the relationship between language and verbal thought in a psychotic adolescent. *J. Child Psychother., 15*(1), 113–125.

Tishler, C. L., McKenry, P. C., & Morgan, K. C. (1981). Adolescent suicide attempts: Some significant factors. *Suic. Life-Threat. Behav., 11*(2), 86–92.

Tizard, J., & Grad, J. C. (1961). *The mentally handicapped and their families: A social survey.* London: Oxford Univ.

Tkachyk, M. E., Spanos, N. P., & Bertrand, L. D. (1985). Variables affecting subjective organization during posthypnotic amnesia. *J. Res. in Pers., 19*(1), 95–108.

Todd, T. C., & Stanton, M. D. (1983). Research on marital and family therapy: Answers, issues, and recommendations for the future. In B. B. Wolman & G. Stricker (Eds.), *Handbook of family and marital therapy.* New York: Plenum.

Tolstrup, K. et al. (1985). Long-term outcome of 151 cases of anorexia nervosa: The Copenhagen Anorexia Nervosa Follow-Up Study. *Acta Psychiatr. Scandin., 71*(4), 380–387.

Torrey, E. F. (1983). *Surviving schizophrenia: A family manual.* New York: Harper & Row.

Torrey, E. F. (1988). *Nowhere to go: The tragic odyssey of the homeless mentally ill.* New York: Harper & Row.

Torrey, E. F., Albrecht, P., & Behr, D. E. (1985). Permeability of the blood-brain barrier in psychiatric patients. *Amer. J. Psychiat., 142*(5), 657–658.

Torrey, E. F., Wolfe, S. M., & Flynn, L. M. (1988). *Care of the seriously mentally ill: A rating of state programs* (2nd ed.). Washington, DC: Public Citizen Health Research Group and National Alliance for the Mentally Ill.

Tosteson, D. C. (1981, Apr.). Lithium and mania. *Scientific Amer.*

Townsend, R. E., House, J. F., & Addario, D. (1975). A comparison of biofeedback: Mediated relaxation and group therapy in the treatment of chronic anxiety. *Amer. J. Psychiat., 132*(6), 598–601.

Trimble, M. R. (1985). Cerebral function, blood flow, and metabolism: A new vista in psychiatric research: Commentary. *Integ. Psychiat., 3*(4), 297–298.

Tross, S., & Hirsch, D. A. (1988). Psychological distress and neuropsychological complications of HIV infection and AIDS. *Amer. Psychol., 43*(11), 929–934.

Trotter, R. J. (1985, Nov.). Geschwind's syndrome: Van Gogh's malady. *Psych. Today,* 46.

Trovato, F. (1986). Suicide and ethnic factors in Canada. *Inter. J. Soc. Psychiat., 32*(3), 55–64.

Trowell, I. (1979). In L. D. Hankoff & B. Einsidler (Eds.), *Suicide: Theory and clinical aspects.* Littleton, MA: PSG.

Trower, P., Yardley, K., Bryant, B. M., & Shaw, P. (1978). The treatment of social failure: A comparison of anxiety-reduction and skills-acquisition procedures on two social problems. *Behav. Mod., 2*(1), 41–60.

Truax, C. B. (1963). Effective ingredients in psychotherapy: An approach to unraveling the patient-therapist interaction. *J. Couns. Psychol., 10,* 256–263.

Truax, C., Wargo, P., & Silber, L. (1966). Effects of group psychotherapy with high accurate empathy and nonpossessive warmth upon institutionalized female delinquents. *J. Abnorm. Psychol., 71,* 267–274.

Trujillo, K. A., & Akil, H. (1991). The NMDA receptor antagonist MK-801 increases morphine catalepsy and lethality. *Pharm. Biochem. Behav., 38*(3), 673–675.

Tryon, G. (1987). *Prof. Psychol., 17,* 357–363.

Tsai, L., Stewart, M., Faust, M., & Shook, S. (1982). Social class distribution of fathers of children enrolled in an Iowa autism program. *J. Autism Dev. Dis., 12,* 211–221.

Tsuang, M. T. (1978). Suicide in schizophrenia, manics, depressives, and surgical controls: A comparison with general population suicide mortality. *Arch. Gen. Psychiat., 35*(2), 153–155.

Tsuang, M. T., Powlar, R. C., Cadorat, R. J., & Monnally, E. (1974). Schizophrenia among first degree relatives of paranoid and nonparanoid schizoprenics. *Comprehen. Psychiat., 15*(4), 295–302.

Tsuang, M. T., Woolson, R. F., & Fleming, J. A. (1979). Long-term outcome of major psychoses: I. Schizophrenia and effective disorders compared with psychiatrically symptom-free surgical conditions. *Arch. Gen. Psychiat., 36*(12), 1295–1301.

Tucker, J. A., Vuchinich, R. E., & Schonhaut, S. J. (1987). Effects of alcohol on recall of social interactions. *Cog. Ther. Res., 11*(2), 273–283.

Tulkin, S. R. (1968). Race, class, and family and school achievement. *J. Pers. Soc. Psychol., 9,* 31–37.

Tulving, E., & Watkins, O. C. (1977). Recognition of failure of words with a single meaning. *Memory Cog., 5*(5), 513–522.

Tunnell, G. B. (1977). Three dimensions of naturalness: An expanded definition of field research. *Psychol. Bull., 84*(3) 426–437.

Tunstall, C. D., Ginsberg, D., & Hall, S. M. (1985). Quitting smoking. *Inter. J. Addict., 20,* 1089–1112.

Turek, I. S., & Hanlon, T. P. (1977). The effectiveness and safety of electroconvulsive therapy (ECT). *J. Nerv. Ment. Dis., 164,* 419–31.

Turk, D. (1975). *Cognitive control of pain: A skills training approach for the treatment of pain.* Unpublished master's thesis, Univ. Waterloo.

Turk, D. (1976). *An expanded skills training approach for the treatment of experimentally induced pain.* Unpublished doctoral dissertation, U. of Waterloo.

Turkewitz, H., & O'Leary, K. D. (1981). A comparative outcome study of behavioral marital therapy and communication therapy. *J. Marital Fam. Ther., 7,* 159–170.

Turkington, C. (1987). Treatment of depressed elderly could prevent "silent suicides." *APA Monitor, 18,*(1), p. 13.

Turner, I. F., & Small, J. D. (1985). Similarities and differences in behavior between mentally handicapped and normal preschool children during play. *Child. Care Hlth. Dev., 11*(6), 391–401.

Turner, S. M., Beidel, D. C., & Jacob, R. G. (1988). Assessment of panic. In S. Rachman & J. Maser (Eds.), *Panic: Psychological perspectives.* Hillsdale, NJ: Erlbaum.

Turner, S. M., Beidel, D. C., & Nathan, R. S. (1985). Biological factors in obsessive-compulsive disorders. *Psychol. Bull., 97,* 430–450.

Turner, S. M., Hersen, M., & Bellack, A. S. (1977). Effects of social disruption, stimulus interference, and aversive conditioning on auditory hallucinations. *Behav. Mod., 1*(2), 249–258.

Twain, M. (1985). *The adventures of Huckleberry Finn.*

Tyor, P. L., & Bell, L. V. (1984). *Caring for the retarded in America: A history.* Westport, CT: Greenwood.

U.S. Bureau of the Census. (1988). *Statistical abstract of the United States* (108th ed.). Washington, DC: GPO.

Uhde, T. W. et al. (1984). Fear and anxiety: Relationship to noradrenergic function. 14th Collegium Internationale Neuro-Psychopharmacologicum Congress (Florence, Italy). *Psychopathology, 17*(3, Suppl.), 8–23.

Uhde, T. W. et al. (1984). The sleep of patients with panic disorder: A preliminary report. *Psychiat. Res., 12*(3), 251–259.

Uhde, T. W. et al. (1985). Longitudinal course of panic disorder: Clinical and biological considerations [Special Issue]. *Progress in Neuro-Psychopharm. & Bio. Psychiat., 9*(1), 39–51.

Uhde, T. W., Roy-Byrne, P. P., Vittone, B. J., Boulenger, J. P., & Post, R. M. (1985). Phenomenology and neurobiology of panic disorder. In A. H. Tuma & J. D. Maser (Eds.), *Anxiety and the anxiety disorder.* Hillsdale, NJ: Erlbaum.

Uhde, T. W., Siever, L. J., & Post, R. M. (1984). Clonidine: Acute challenge and clinical trial paradigms for the investigation and treatment of anxiety disorders, affective illness and pain syndromes. In R. M. Post & J. C. Ballenger (Eds.), *Neurobiology of mood disorders.* Baltimore: Williams & Wilkins.

Uhde, T. W., Siever, L. J., Post, R. M., Jimerson, D. C., Boulenger, J. P., & Buchsbaum, M. S. (1982). The relationship of plasma-free MHPG to anxiety and psychophysical pain in normal volunteers. *Psychopharma. Bull., 18,* 129–132.

Uhde, T. W., Vittone, B. J., & Post, R. M. (1984). Glucose tolerance testing in panic disorder. *Amer. J. Psychiat., 14*(11), 1461–1463.

Uhlenhuth, E. H., Balter, M. B., Mellinger, G. D., Cisin, I. H., & Clinthorne, J. (1983). Symptom checklist syndromes in the general population: Correlations with psychotherapeutic drug use. *Arch. Gen. Psychiat., 40,* 1167–1173.

Ullmann, L. P., & Krasner, L. (1975). *A psychological approach to abnormal behavior* (2nd ed.). Englewood Cliffs, NJ: Prentice-Hall.

Ullmann, W. R. (1974). Susceptibility to persuasive communication following change produced by counterattitudinal encoding and decoding. *Dissertation Abstracts Int., 34*(11-A), 511.

Upper, D., & Ross, S. M. (Eds.) (1980). *Behavioral group therapy 1980: An annual review.* Champaign, IL: Research.

Ursano, R. J., Boydstun, J. A., & Wheatley, R. D. (1981). Psychiatric illness in U. S. Air Force Vietnam Prisoners of war: A five-year follow-up. *Amer. J. Psychiat., 138*(3), 310–314.

Vadher, A., & Ndetei, D. M. (1981). Life events and depression in a Kenyan setting. *Brit. J. Psychiat., 130,* 134–137.

Vaillant, G. E. (1977). *Adaptions to life.* Boston: Little, Brown.

Vaillant, G. E. (1983). Natural history of male alcoholism: V. Is alcoholism the cart or the horse to sociopathy? *Brit. J. Addic., 78*(3), 317–326.

Vaillant, G. E., & Milofsky, E. S. (1982). Natural history of male alcoholism: IV. Paths to recovery. *Arch. Gen. Psychiat., 39,* 127–133.

Vaillant, G. E., & Milofsky, E. S. (1982). The etiology of alcoholism: A prospective viewpoint. *Amer. Psychol., 37,* 494–503.

Vaisanen, E., & Jalkanen, E., (1987). A double-blind study of alprazolam and oxazepam in the treatment of anxiety. *Acta Psychiatr. Scandin., 75*(5), 536–541.

Valenstein, E. S. (1973). *Brain Stimulation and motivation: Research and commentary.* Glenview, IL: Foresman.

Valle, R. (1989). Cultural and ethnic issues in Alzheimer's disease family research. In E. Light and B. D. Lebowitz (Eds.), *Alzheimer's Disease treatment and family stress: Directions for research.* (DHHS Pub. #ADM 89-1569). Washington, DC: GPO.

Van Dam, F. S., Honnebier, W. J., Van Zalinge, E. A., & Barendragt, J. T. (1976). Sexual arousal measured by photoplethysmography. *Behav. Engineering, 3*(4), 97–101.

Van den Berg, J. H. (1971). What is psychotherapy? *Humanitas, 7*(3), 321–370.

Van der Kolk, B. (1987). *Psychological Trauma.* Washington, DC: American Psychiatric.

Van Praag, H. M. (1977). The significance of dopamine for the mode of action of neuroleptics and the pathogenesis of schizophrenia. *Brit. J. Psychiat., 132,* 593–597.

Van Praag, H. M. (1978). *Psychotropic drugs: A guide for practitioners.* New York: Brunner/Mazel.

Van Praag, H. M. (1984). Precursors on serotonin, dopamine, and norepinephrine in the treatment of depression. *Adv. Bio. Psychiat., 14,* 54–68.

Van-Bourgondien, M. E., & Schopler, E. (1990). Critical issues in the residential care of people with autism. *J. Autism Dev. Dis., 20*(3), 391–399.

Vandereycken, W., & Meermann, R. (1984). *Anorexia nervosa: A clinician's guide to treatment.* New York: de Gruyter.

Varis, K. (1987). Psychosomatic factors in gastrointestinal disorders. *Ann. Clin. Res., 19*(2), 135–142.

Vaughn, C. E., & Leff, J. P. (1976). The influence of family and social factors on the course of psychiatric illness: A comparison of schizophrenic and depressed neurotic patients. *Brit. J. Psychiat., 129,* 125–137.

Vaughn, C. E., & Leff, J. P. (1976). The measurement of expressed emotion in the families of psychiatric patients. *Brit. J. Soc. Clin. Psychol., 15*(2), 157–165.

Vazquez-Barquero, J. L., Munoz, P. E., & Madoz, J. V. (1982). The influence of the process of urbanization on the prevalence of neurosis: A community survey. *Acta Psychiatr. Scandin., 65*(3), 161–170.

Velton, E. C., Jr. (1967). The induction of elation and depression through the reading of structured sets of mood-statements. *Dissertation Abstracts, 28*(4-B), 1700–1701.

Venkatest, A., Pauls, O. L., & Crowe, R. (1980). Mitral valve prolapse in anxiety neurosis (panic disorder). *Amer. Heart J., 100,* 302–305, 365.

Vernon, P. E. (1979). *Intelligence: Heredity and environment.* San Francisco: Freeman.

Vessey, S. H. (1964). Effects of grouping on levels of circulating antibodies in mice. *Proceedings of the Society of Exp. Bio. & Med., 115,* 252–255.

Vetter, H. J. (1969). *Language behavior and psychopathology.* Chicago: Rand McNally.

Victor, M., & Wolfe, S. M. (1973). Causation and treatment of the alcohol withdrawal syndrome. In G. Bourne & R. Fox (Eds.), *Alcoholism: Progress in research and treatment.* New York: Academic.

Vieth, R. (1982). Depression in the elderly: Pharmacological considerations in treatment. *J. Amer. Geriatric Society, 30,* 581–586.

Vitalino, P., Maiuro, R., Ochs, H., & Russo, J. (1989). A model of burden in caregivers DAT patients. In E. Light & B. D. Lebowitz (Ed.), *Alzheimer's Disease treatment and family stress: Directions for research.* DHHS Pub. #ADM89-1569. Washington, DC: GPO.

Volkmar, F. R., Shakir, S. A., Bacon, S., & Pfefferbaum, A. (1981). Group therapy in the management of manic-depressive illness. *Amer. J. Psychother., 35,* 226–234.

Volkow, N. D., & Swann, A. C. (1990). *Cocaine in the brain.* New Brunswick, NJ: Rutgers Univ.

Von Korff, M., Nestadt, G., Romanoski, A. et al. (1985). Prevalence of treated and untreated DSM-III schizophrenia. *J. Nerv. Ment. Dis., 173,* 577–581.

Von Zerssen, D. et al. (1985). Are biological rhythms disturbed in depression? *Acta Psychiatrica Belgica, 85*(5), 824–825.

Von Zerssen, D. et al. (1985). Circadian rhythms in endogenous depression. *Psychiat. Res., 16*(1), 51–83.

Vrasti, R., Lazarescu, M. Zegrea, D., Nussbaum, L. et al. (1988). Personalitiatea in tulburarile afective bipolare. Studiu cu ajutorul inventarelor de personalitate. *Neurologie, Psihiatrie, Neurochirurgie, 33*(3), 231–238.

Vrendenbury, K., Krames, L., & Flett, G. L. (1985). Reexamining the Beck Depression Inventory: The long and short of it. *Psych. Rep., 56,* 903–906.

Wachtel, P. (1987). *Action and insight.* New York: Guilford.

Waddel, M. T., Barlow, D. H., & O'Brien, G. T. (1984). A preliminary investigation of cognitive and relaxation treatment of panic disorder: Effects on intense anxiety vs. "background" anxiety. *Behav. Res. Ther., 22*(4), 393–402.

Wadden, T. A., & Anderton, C. H. (1982). The clinical use of hypnosis. *Psychol. Bull., 91*(2), 215–243.

Wadden, T. A., Stunkard, A. J., & Liebschutz, J. (1988). Three-year follow-up of the treatment of obesity by very low calorie diet, behavior therapy, and their combination. *J. Cons. Clin. Psychol., 56*(6), 925–928.

Wade, T. C., & Baker, T. B. (1977). Opinions and use of psychological tests: A survey of clinical psychologists. *Amer. Psychol., 32*(10), 874–882.

Wade, T. C., Baker, T. B., & Hartmann, D. P. (1979). Behavior therapists' self-reported views and practices. *Behav. Ther., 2*(1), 3–6.

Wagman, M. (1980). PLATO DCS: An interactive computer system for personal counseling. *J. Couns. Psychol., 27*(1), 16–30.

Walburg, J. A. (1985). Verslaving en behandeling [Addiction and treatment]. *Gedragstherapie, 18*(1), 7–17.

Waldinger, R. (1986). Intensive psychodynamic psychotherapy with borderline patients. *Amer. J. Psychiat., 144,* 267–274.

Walk, D. (1967). Suicide and community care. *Brit. J. Psychiat., 13,* 1381–1391.

Walker, E., & Young, T. D., (1986). *A killing cure.* New York: Henry Holt.

Walker, L. E. (1979). *The battered woman.* New York: Harper & Row.

Walker, L. E. (1984). Battered women, psychology, and public policy. *Amer. Psychol., 39*(10), 1178–1182.

Walker, L. E. (1984). *The battered woman syndrome.* New York: Springer.

Wall, A. J. (1990). Group homes in North Carolina for children and adults with autism. *J. Autism Dev. Dis., 20*(3), 353–366.

Wallace, S. E. (1981). The right to live and the right to die. In S. E. Wallace & A. Eser (Eds.), *Suicide and euthanasia: The rights of personhood.* Knoxville, TN: Univ. Tennessee.

Waller, G., Calam, R., & Slade, P. (1989). Eating disorders and family interaction. *Brit. J. Clin. Psychol., 28*(3), 285–286.

Wallerstein, R. S. (Ed.) (1957). *Hospital treatment of alcoholism: A comparative, experimental study.* New York: Basic.

Walsh, B. T. et al. (1982). Treatment of bulimia with monoamine oxidase inhibitors. *Amer. J. Psychiat., 139*(12), 1629–1630.

Walsh, D. H. (1974). Interactive effects of alpha feedback and instructional set on subjective state. *Psychophysiology, 11*, 428–435.

Walters, A. S., Barrett, R. P., & Feinstein, C. (1990). Social relatedness and autism: Current research, issues, directions. *Res. Dev. Dis., 11*(3), 303–326.

Walton, D., & Mather, M. D. (1963). The application of learning principles to the treatment of obsessive-compulsive states in the acute and chronic phases of illness. *Behav. Res. Ther., 1*, 163–174.

Waltzer, H. (1984). Suicide risk in young schizophrenics. *Gen. Hosp. Psychiat., 65*(3), 219–225.

Wanck, B. (1984). Two decades of involuntary hospitalization legislation. *Amer. J. Psychiat., 41*, 33–38.

Ward, D. A. (1985). Conceptions of the nature and treatment of alcoholism. *J. Drug Issues, 15*(1), 3–16.

Ware, J. E. et al. (1984). Health and the use of outpatient mental health services. *Amer. Psychol., 39*(10), 1090–1100.

Waring, M., & Ricks, D. (1965). Family patterns of children who become adult schizophrenics. *J. Nerv. Ment. Dis., 140*(5), 512.

Warnes, H. (1972). The traumatic syndrome. *Canad. Psychiat. Assoc. J., 17*(5), 391–396.

Warren, R., McLellarn, R. W., & Ponzoha, C. (1988). Rational-emotive therapy vs. general cognitive-behavior therapy in the treatment of low self-esteem and related emotional disturbances. *Cog. Ther. Res., 12*(1), 21–37.

Wartenberg, A. A., Nirenberg, T. D., Liepman, M. R., Silvia, L. Y. et al. (1990). Detoxification of alcoholics: Improving care by symptom-triggered sedation. *Alcoholism: Clin. Exp. Res., 14*(1), 71–75.

Washton, A. M., & Stone-Washton, N. (1990). Abstinence and relapse in outpatient cocaine addicts. *J. Psychoact. Drugs, 22*(2), 135–147.

Wasserman, I. M. (1984). Imitation and suicide: A reexamination of the Werther Effect. *Amer. Sociological Rev., 49*, 427–436.

Waters, L. (1990). Reinforcing the empty fortress: An examination of recent research into the treatment of autism. *Educ. Studies, 16*(1), 3–16.

Watson, C. G. (1987). Recidivism in "controlled drinker" alcoholics: A longitudinal study. *J. Clin. Psychol., 43*(3), 404–412.

Watson, C. G., & Buranen, C. (1979). The frequencies of conversion reaction symptoms. *J. Abnorm. Psychol., 88*(2), 209–211.

Watson, D. L., & Tharp, R. B. (1981). Self-directed behavior: Self-modification for personal adjustment. Monterey, CA: Brooks/Cole.

Watson, J. B., & Rayner, R. (1920). Conditioned emotional reaction. *J. Exp. Psychol., 3*, 1–14.

Watson, J. P., Gaind, R., & Marks, I. M. (1972). Physiological habituation to continuous phobic stimulation. *Behav. Res. Ther., 10*, 269–278.

Watson, J. P., Gaind, R., & Marks, I. M. (1971). Prolonged exposure: A rapid treatment for phobias. *Brit. Med. J., 1*(5739), 13–15.

Waxer, P. (1974). Nonverbal cues for depression. *J. Abnorm. Psychol., 83*(3), 319–322.

Weakland, J. (1960). The double-bind hypothesis of schizophrenia and three-party interaction. In D. Jackson (Ed.), *The etiology of schizophrenia.* New York: Basic.

Wechsler, H., Grosser, G. H., & Greenblatt, M. (1965). Research evaluating antidepressant medications on hospitalized mental patients: A survey of published reports during a five year period. *J. Nerv. Ment. Dis., 141*, 231–239.

Wechsler, J. A. (1972). *In a darkness.* New York: Norton.

Wegner, D. M. (1989). Do alcoholics know what they're doing? Identifications of the act of drinking. *Basic & Appl. Soc. Psychol., 10*(3), 197–210.

Wegner, D. M. (1989, June). Try not to think of a white bear. . . . *Psych. Today.*

Wehr, T. A., & Goodwin, F. K. (1981). Biological rhythms and psy-

chiatry. In S. Arieti & H. K. H. Brodie (Eds.), *American handbook of psychiatry* (Vol. 7), New York: Basic.

Wehr, T. A., Giesen, H., Schulz, P. M., Joseph-Vanderpool, J. R., Kasper, S., Kelly, K. A., & Rosenthal, N. E. (1989). Summer depression: Description of the syndrome and comparison with winter depression. In N. E. Rosenthal & M. C. Blehar (Eds.), *Seasonal affective disorders and phototherapy.* New York: Guilford.

Wehr, T. A. Reply to D. Healy & J. M. Waterhouse. (1990). The circadian system and affective disorders: Clocks or rhythms? *Chronobiology-Inter., 7*(1), 11–14.

Wehr, T. A., Sack, D. A., Rosenthal, N. C., & Cowdry, R. W. (1988). Rapid cycling affective disorder: Contributing factors and treatment response in 51 patients. *Amer. J. Psychiat., 145*(2), 179–184.

Weidlich, J. (1982). Taking it to the streets: Berkeley voters shock psychiatrists with ECT ban. *Issues in Radical Ther., 10*(3), 40–42.

Weidman, A. A. (1985). Engaging the families or substance abusing adolescents in family therapy. *J. Substance Abuse Treatment, 2*(2), 97–105.

Weinberg, J., & Levine, S. (1980). Psychobiology of coping in animals: The effects of predictability. In S. Levine & H. Ursin (Eds.), *Coping and health.* New York: Plenum.

Weinberg, J. R. (1977). Toward classifying psychoactive chemical use. *Amer. J. Drug & Alcohol Abuse, 4*(1), 77–90.

Weinberger, D. R. (1983). "Imaging of the brain: Aiding the search for physical correlates of mental illness": Comment. *Integ. Psychiat., 1*(4), 146.

Weinberger, D. R. et al. (1982). Computed tomography in schizophreniform disorder and other acute psychiatric disorders. *Arch. Gen. Psychiat., 30*(7), 770–783.

Weinberger, D. R., & Kleinman, J. E. (1986). Observations of the brain in schizophrenia. In A. J. Frances & R. E. Hales (Eds.), *Psychiatry update* (Vol. 5). Washington, DC: American Psychiatric.

Weinberger, D. R., Wagner, R. L., & Wyatt, R. J. (1983). Neuropathological studies of schizophrenia: A selective review. *Schizo. Bull., 9*, 193–212.

Weiner, E. A., & Stewart, B. J. (1984). *Assessing individuals.* Boston: Little, Brown.

Weiner, H. (1977). *Psychobiology and human disease.* New York: Elsevier.

Weiner, H. (1985). The psychobiology and pathophysiology of anxiety and fear. In A. H. Tuma & J. Maser (Eds.), *Anxiety and the anxiety disorders.* Hillsdale, NJ: Erlbaum.

Weiner, H., Thaler, M., Reiser, M. F., & Mirsky, I. A. (1957). Etiology of duodenal ulcer: I. Relation of specific psychological characteristics to rate of gastric secretion (serum pepsinogen). *Psychosom. Med., 19*, 1–10.

Weiner, H., Thaler, M., Reiser, M. F., & Mirsky, I. A. (1957). Etiology of duodenal ulcer. *Psychosom. Med., 19*, 1–10.

Weiner, I. W. (1969). The effectiveness of suicide prevention programs. *Ment. Hyg., 53*, 357–373.

Weiner, R. D. (1979). The psychiatric use of electrically induced seizures. *Amer. J. Psychiat., 136*(12), 1507–1517.

Weiner, R. D. (1984). Does electroconvulsive therapy cause brain damage? *Behav. Brain Sci., 7*, 1–54.

Weiner, R. D., & Coffey, C. E. (1988). Indications for use of electroconvulsive therapy. In A. J. Frances & R. E. Hales (Eds.), *American Psychiatric Press review of psychiatry* (Vol. 7). Washington, DC: American Psychiatric.

Weingartner, H., & Silberman, E. (1984). Cognitive changes in depression. In R. M. Post & J. C. Ballenger (Eds.), *Neurobiology of mood disorders:* Baltimore, Williams & Wilkins.

Weisheit, R. A. (1990). Domestic marijuana growers: Mainstreaming deviance. *Deviant Behav., 11*(2), 107–129.

Weiss, J. M. (1968). Effects of coping responses on stress. *J. Compar. Physiol. Psychol., 65*, 251–260.

Weiss, J. M. (1977). Ulcers. In J. D. Maser & M. E. P. Seligman (Eds.), *Psychopathology: Experimental models.* San Francisco: Freeman.

Weiss, J. M., Glazer, H. I., & Pohorecky, L. A. (1974). Neurotransmitters and helplessness: A chemical bridge to depression? *Psych. Today, 8*(7), 58–62.

Weiss, J. M., Glazer, H. I., & Pohorecky, L. A. (1976). Coping behavior and neurochemical changes: An alternative explanation for the original "learned helplessness" experiments. In G. Serban & A. Kling (Eds.), *Animal models of human psychobiology.* New York: Plenum.

Weiss, J. M., Stone, E. A., & Harrell, N. (1970). Coping behavior and brain norepinephrine level in rats. *J. Compar. Physiol. Psychol., 72,* 153–160.

Weiss, R. L., Hops, H., & Patterson, G. R. (1973). A framework for conceptualizing marital conflict, a technology for altering it, some data for evaluating it. In L. A. Hamerlynck, L. C. Handy & E. J. Mash (Eds.), *Behavior change: Methodology, concepts, and practice.* Champaign, IL: Research.

Weiss, T., & Engel, B. (1971). Operant conditioning of heart rate in patients with premature ventricular contractions. *Psychosom. Med., 3,* 1–25.

Weissman, A. N., & Beck, A. T. (1978). *Development and validation of the dysfunctional attitude scale* Paper presented at the 12th Annual Convention of the Assoc. for Advancement of Behavior Therapy. Chicago.

Weissman, M., & Klerman, G. L. (1977). Sex differences and the epidemiology of depression. *Arch. Gen. Psychiat., 34,* 98–111.

Weissman, M., & Klerman, G. L. (1985). Gender and depression. *Trends in Neurosci., 8*(9), 416–420.

Weissman, M. M. (1979). The psychological treatment of depression: Evidence for the efficacy of psychotherapy alone, in comparison with, and in combination with pharmacotherapy. *Arch. Gen. Psychiat., 36*(11), 1261–1269.

Weissman, M. M. (1987). Epidemiology of depression: Frequency, risk groups, and risk factors. In *Perspectives on depressive disorders.* Rockville, MD: National Institute of Mental Health.

Weissman, M. M. (1988). The epidemiology of panic disorder. In A. J. Frances & R. E. Hales (Eds.), *American Psychiatric Press review of psychiatry* (Vol. 7). Washington, DC: American Psychiatric.

Weissman, M. M. et al. (1979). The efficacy of drugs and psychotherapy in the treatment of acute depressive episodes. *Amer. J. Psychiat., 136*(4-B), 555–558.

Weissman, M. M. et al. (1981). Depressed outpatients: Results one year after treatment with drugs and/or interpersonal psychotherapy. *Arch. Gen. Psychiat., 38,* 51–55.

Weissman, M. M. et al. (1982). Short-term interpersonal psychotherapy (IPT) for depression: Description and efficacy. In J. C. Anchin & D. J. Kiesler (Eds.), *Handbook of interpersonal psychotherapy.* New York: Pergamon.

Weissman, M. M. et al. (1984). Depression and anxiety disorders in parents and children: Results from the Yale family study. *Arch. Gen. Psychiat., 41*(9), 845–852.

Weissman, M. M. et al. (1984). Onset of major depression in early adulthood: increased familial loading and specificity. *Arch. Gen. Psychiat., 41*(12), 1130–1143.

Weissman, M. M., & Boyd, J. H. (1984). The epidemiology of mental disorders. In R. M. Post & J. C. Ballenger (Eds.), *Neurobiology of mood disorders.* Baltimore: Williams & Wilkins.

Weissman, M. M., & Klerman, G. L. (1977). The chronic depressive in the community: Under-recognized and poorly treated. *Compr. Psychiat., 18,* 523–531.

Weissman, M. M., & Klerman, G. L. (1985). Gender and depression. *Trends in Neurosci., 8*(9), 416–420.

Weissman, M. M., & Myers, J. K. (1978). Affective disorders in a U.S. urban community: The use of Research Diagnostic Criteria in an epidemiological survey. *Arch. Gen. Psychiat., 35*(11), 1304–1311.

Weissman, M. M., Fox, K., & Klerman, G. L. (1973). Hostility and depression associated with suicide attempts. *Amer. J. Psychiat., 130*(4), 450–455.

Weissman, M. M., Myers, J. K., & Harding, P. S. (1978). Psychiatric disorders in a U. S. urban community. *Amer. J. Psychiat., 135,* 459–462.

Weissman, M. M., Myers, J. K., & Thompson, W. D. (1981). Depression and its treatment in a U. S. urban community—1975–1976. *Arch. Gen. Psychiat., 38*(4), 417–421.

Weissman, M. M., Rounsaville, B. J., & Chevron, E. (1982). Training psychotherapists to participate in psychotherapy outcome studies: Identifying and dealing with the research requirements. *Amer. J. Psychiat., 139,* 1442–1446.

Weizenbaum, J. (1966). ELIZA: A computer program for the study of natural language communication between man and machine. *Commun. Assoc. Comput. Machinery, 9,* 36–45.

Wells, K. C. (1985). Behavioral family therapy. In A. S. Bellack & M. Hersen (Eds.), *Dictionary of behavior therapy techniques.* New York: Pergamon.

Wells, K. C., Hersen, M., Bellack, A. S., & Himmelhoch, J. (1979). Social skills training in unipolar nonpsychotic depression. *Amer. J. Psychiat., 136*(10), 1331–1332.

Wells, M. E., & Hinkle, J. S. (1990). Elimination of childhood encopresis: A family systems approach. *J. Ment. Hlth. Couns., 12*(4), 520–526.

Welner, J. (1987). Efficacy of imipramine and chlordiazepoxide in depressive and anxiety disorders questioned. *Arch. Gen. Psychiat., 44*(1), 97.

Wender, P. H., Kety, S. S., Rosenthal, D., Schulsinger, F., Ortmann, J., & Lunde, I. (1986). Psychiatric disorders in the biological and adoptive families of adopted and individuals with affective disorders. *Arch. Gen. Psychiat., 43,* 923–929.

Wenzlaff, R. M., & Grozier, S. A. (1988). Depression and the magnification of failure. *J. Abnorm. Psychol., 97*(1), 90–93.

Werner, P. D., Rose, T. L., & Yesavage, J. A. (1983). Reliability, accuracy, and decision-making strategy in clinical predictions of imminent dangerousness. *J. Consult. Clin. Psychol., 51,* 815–825.

Werner, W. E., Schauble, P. G., & Knudson, M. S. (1982). An argument for revival of hypnosis in obstetrics. *Amer. J. Clin. Hyp., 24*(3), 149–171.

Wesson, D. R., & Smith, D. E. (1977). *Barbiturates: Their use, misuse, and abuse.* New York: Human Sciences.

Wettstein, R. M. (1987). Psychiatry and the law. In J. A. Talbott, R. E. Hales & S. C. Yudofsky (Eds.), *American Psychiatric Press textbook of psychiatry.* Washington, DC: American Psychiatric.

Wetzel, R. D. (1975). Self-concept and suicide intent. *Psych. Rep., 36,* 279–282.

Wetzel, R. D. (1976). Hopelessness, depression and suicidal intent. *Arch. Gen. Psychiat., 33,* 1069–1073.

Wexler, D. B. (1976). *Criminal commitments and dangerous mental patients: Legal issues of confinement, treatment, and release.* DHEW Pub. No. (ADM) 76-28650, Rockville, MD.

Wexler, D. B. (1983). The structure of civil commitment. *Law & Human Behav., 7,* 1–18.

Whitaker, C. A. (1987). The dynamics of the American family as deduced from 20 years of family therapy: The family unconscious. In J. K. Zeig (Ed.), *The evolution of psychotherapy.* New York: Brunner/Mazel.

Whitaker, J. H., Rueda, R. S., & Prieto, A. G. (1985). Cognitive performance as a function of bilingualism in students with mental retardation. *Ment. Retardation, 23*(6), 302–307.

White, G. D. (1977). The effects of observer presence on the activity level of families. *J. Appl. Behav. Anal., 10*(4), 734.

White, H. C. (1974). Self-poisoning in adolescents. *Brit. J. Psychiat., 124,* 24–35.

White, J. H., Hornsby, L. C., Boyleston, W. H., & Gordon, R. (1972). The treatment of Little Fritz: A modern-day little Hans. *Inter. J. Child Psychother., 1*(4), 7–23.

White, K., & Simpson, G. (1981). Combined MAOI-tricyclic antidepressant treatment: A reevaluation. *J. Clin. Psychopharm., 1,* 264–282.

White, L. (1964). Organic factors and psychophysiology in childhood schizophrenia. *Psychol. Bull., 81,* 238–255.

Whitehorn, J. C., & Betz, B. J. (1975). *Effective psychotherapy with the schizophrenic patient.* New York: Aronson.

Whiteside, M. (1983, Sep. 12). A bedeviling new hysteria. *Newsweek.*

Whiting, J. W. et al. (1966). *Six cultures series: I. Field guide for a study of socialization.* New York: Wiley.

Whitlock, F. A. (1967). The aetiology of hysteria. *Acta Psychiatr. Scandin., 43*(2), 144–162.

Whitlock, F. A. (1977). Psychiatric epidemiology: Its uses and limitations. *Austral. New Zeal. J. Psychiat., 11*(1), 9–18.

Whitman, T. L. (1972). Aversive control of smoking behavior in a group context. *Behav., Res. Ther., 10,* 97–104.

Widiger, T. A., Frances, A. Spitzer, R. L., & Williams, J. B. W. (1988). The DSM-III personality disorders: An overview. *Amer. J. Psychiat., 145,* 786–795.

Widom, C. S. (1991, Feb.). *Presentation.* American Assoc. for the Advancement of Science.

Wiens, A. N. (1990). Structured clinical interviews for adults. In G. Goldstein & M. Hersen (Eds.), *Handbook of psychological assessment* (2nd ed.). New York: Pergamon.

Wiens, A. N., & Menustik, C. E. (1983). Treatment outcome and patient characteristics in an aversion therapy program for alcoholism. *Amer. Psychol., 38*(10), 1089–1096.

Wiggins, J. S. (1973). *Personality and prediction: Principles of personality assessment.* Reading, MA: Addison-Wesley.

Wikler, A. (1973). Dynamics of drug dependence: Implications of a conditioning theory for research and treatment. *Arch. Gen. Psychiat., 28*(5), 611–616.

Wikler, A. (1980). *Opioid dependence: Mechanisms and treatment.* New York: Plenum.

Wilbur, C. B. (1984). Treatment of multiple personality. *Psychiat. Ann., 14,* 27–31.

Wilcox, J. A. (1990). Fluoxetine and bulimia. *J. Psychoact. Drugs, 22*(1), 81–82.

Will, O. A., Jr. (1961). Paranoid development and the concept of self: Psychotherapeutic intervention. *Psychiatry, 24*(2), 16–530.

Willenbring, M., & Spring, W. (1988). Evaluating alcohol use in elders. *Generations, 12*(4), 27–31.

Willerman, L. (1979). Effects of families on intellectual development. *Amer. Psychol., 34*(10), 923–929.

Williams, E. L., & Manaster, G. J. (1990). Restricter anorexia, bulimic anorexia, and bulimic women's early recollection and Thematic Apperception Test response. *Individ. Psychol. J. Adlerian Theory Res. Prac., 46*(1), 93–107.

Williams, J. M., Petersen, R. G., Shea, P. A., Schmedtje, J. F., Bauer, D. C., & Felten, D. (1981). Sympathetic innervation of murine thymus and spleen: Evidence for a functional link between the nervous and immune systems. *Brain Res. Bull., 6,* 83–94.

Williams, P. (1977). EEG alpha feedback: A comparison of two control groups. *Psychosom. Med., 39*(1), 44–47.

Williams, R. B., Jr. (1977). Headache. In R. B. Williams, Jr. & W. D. Gentry (Eds.), *Behavioral approaches to medical treatment.* Cambridge, MA: Ballinger.

Willner, P. (1984). Cognitive functioning in depression: A review of theory and research. *Psychol. Med., 14*(4), 807–823.

Wilner, A., Reich, T., Robins, I., Fishman, R., & van Doren, T. (1976). Obsessive-compulsive neurosis. *Comprehen. Psychiat., 17,* 527–539.

Wilson, C. P., Hogan, C. C., & Mintz, L. L. (Eds.), (1983). *Fear of being fat: The treatment of anorexia nervosa and bulimia.* New York: Aronson.

Wilson, G. (1989). Treatment outcome in bulimia. [Special Issue]. *Adv. Behav. Res. Ther., 11*(3), 161–174.

Wilson, G. T. (1978). Alcoholism and aversino therapy: Issues, ethics, and evidence. In G. A. Marlatt & P. E. Nathan (Eds.), *Behavioral approaches to alcoholism.* New Brunswick, NJ: Rutgers Center for Alcohol Studies.

Wilson, G. T. (1978). On the much discussed nature of the term "Behavior Therapy." *Behav. Ther., 9,* 89–98.

Wilson, G. T. (1987). Chemical aversion conditioning as a treatment for alcoholism: A re-analysis. *Behav. Res. Ther., 25,* 503–516.

Wilson, G. T. (1990). Clinical issues and strategies in the practice of behavior therapy. In C. M. Franks, G. T. Wilson, P. C. Kendall, & J. P. Foreyt, (Eds.), *Review of behavior therapy* (Vol. 12). New York: Guilford.

Wilson, G. T., & O'Leary, K. D. (1980). *Principles of behavior therapy.* Englewood Cliffs, NJ: Prentice-Hall.

Wilson, G. T., Rossiter, E., Kleifield, E. I., & Lindholm, L. (1986). Cognitive-behavioral treatment of bulimia nervosa: A controlled evaluation. *Behav. Res. Ther., 24*(3), 277–288.

Wilson, J. P. (1980). Conflict, stress, and growth: The effects of war on psychosocial development among Vietnam veterans. In C. R. Figley & S. Leventman (Eds.), *Strangers at home.* New York: Praeger.

Wilson, P. H. (1989). Cognitive-behaviour therapy for depression: Empirical findings and methodological issues in the evaluation of outcome. *Behav. Change, 6*(2), 85–95.

Wilson, P. H., Goldin, J. C., & Charbonneau-Powis, M. (1983). Comparative efficacy of behavioral and cognitive treatments of depression. *Cog. Ther. Res., 7*(2), 111–124.

Wilson, S., & Wilson, K. (1985). Close encounters in general practice: Experiences of a psychotherapy liaison team. *Brit. J. Psychiat., 146,* 277–281.

Wilson, T. A. (1989). Behavior therapy. In R. J. Corsini & D. Wedding (Eds.), *Current psychotherapies.* Itasca, IL: Peacock.

Wilson, W. H., Diamond, R. J., & Factor, R. M. (1990). Group treatment for individuals with schizophrenia. *Comm. Ment. Hlth. J., 26*(4), 361–372.

Wincze, J. P., & Lange, J. D. (1981). Assessment of sexual behavior. In D. H. Barlow (Ed.), *Behavioral assessment of adult disorders.* New York: Guilford.

Winfree, A. T. (1987). *The timing of biological clocks.* New York: Scientific American.

Wing, J. K. (1988). Coping with schizophrenia at home. In C. N. Stefanis & A. D. Rabavilas (Eds.), *Schizophrenia: Recent biosocial development.* New York: Human Sciences.

Wing, L. (1976). *Early childhood autism.* Oxford: Pergamon.

Wing, L. (1981). Social and interpersonal needs of autistic adolescents and adults. *Proceedings of the 1981 International Conference on Autism,* 294–312.

Wing, L., & Wing, J. K. (1971). Multiple impairments in early childhood autism. *J. Autism Child. Schizo., 1,* 256–266.

Winick, B. J. (1983). Incompetency to stand trial: Developments in the law. In J. Monahan & H. J. Steadman (Eds.), *Mentally disordered offenders.* New York: Plenum.

Winick, M., Meyeryk, K., & Harris, R. C. (1975). Malnutrition and environmental enrichment by early adoption. *Science,* 1173–1175.

Winograd, C. H. (1988). The physician and the Alzheimer patient. In L. F. Jarvik & C. H. Winograd (Eds.), *Treatment for the Alzheimer patient: The long haul.* New York: Springer.

Winokur, A. et al. (1980). Withdrawal reaction from long-term low-dosage administration of diazepam: A double-blind placebo-controlled case study. *Arch. Gen. Psych., 37*(1), 101–105.

Winokur, G., Clayton, P. J., & Reich, T. (1969). *Manic depressive illness.* St. Louis: Mosby.

Winslade, W. (1983). *The insanity plea.* New York: Scribner.

Winslade, W. J. (1988). Electroconvulsive therapy: Legal regulations and ethical concerns. In A. J. Frances & R. E. Hales (Eds.), *American Psychiatric Press review of psychiatry* (Vol. 7). Washington, DC: American Psychiatric.

Winslade, W. J., Liston, E. H., Ross, J. W. et al. (1984). Medical, judicial, and statutory regulation of ECT in the United States. *Amer. J. Psychiat., 141,* 1349–1355.

Winson, J. (1990, Nov.). The meaning of dreams. *Scientific Amer.,* 86–96.

Wirz-Justice, A., Bucheli, C., Graw, P., Kielholz, P., Fisch, H. U., & Woggon, B. (1986). Light treatment of seasonal affective disorder in Switzerland. *Acta Psychiatr. Scand., 74,* 193–204.

Wise, T. N. (1985). Fetishism—etiology and treatment: A review from multiple perspectives. *Comprehen. Psychiat., 26,* 249–257.

Witkin, M. J., Atay, J. E., Fell, A. S., & Manderscheid, R. W. (1990). Specialty mental health system characteristics. In R. W. Manderscheid & M. A. Sonnenschein (Eds.), *Mental health, United States* (DHHS Pub. No. ADM 90-1708). Washington, DC: GPO.

Wixted, J. T., Morrison, R. L. & Bellack, A. S. (1988). Social skills training in the treatment of negative symptoms [Special Issue]. *Inter. J. Ment. Hlth., 17*(1), 3–21.

Woggon, B. (1985). Schwierigkeiten bei der Neuroleptika-Behandlung schizophrener Patienten [Difficulties in treating schizophrenics with neuroleptics]. *Schweizer, Archiv fur Neurologie, Neurochirurgie und Psychiatric, 136*(1), 55–59.

Wolberg, L. R. (1967). *The technique of psychotherapy.* New York: Grune & Stratton.

Wolberg, L. R. (1987). The evolution of psychotherapy: Future trends. In J. K. Zeig (Ed.), *The evolution of psychotherapy.* New York: Brunner/Mazel.

Wold, P. N. (1984). Family attitudes toward weight in bulimia and in affective disorder: A pilot study. First International Conference on Eating Disorders (1984), New York). *Psychiat. J. Univ. Ottawa, 10*(3), 162–164.

Wolf, S., & Wolff, H. G. (1947). *Human gastric functions.* New York: Oxford Univ.

Wolf, S. & Wolff, H. G. (1948). Life situations, emotions and gastric function: A summary. *Amer. Practitioner, 3,* 1–14.

Wolfe, D. A., Kaufman, D., Aragona, J., & Sandler, J. (1981). *The child management program for abusive parents.* Winter Park, FL: Anna.

Wolfe, J. K. L., & Fodor, I. G. (1977). Modifying assertive behavior in women: Comparison of three approaches. *Behav. Ther., 8,* 567–574.

Wolfe, S., Fugate, L., Hulstrand, E., & Kamimoto, L. E. (1988). *Worst pills, best pills.* Public Citizen Health Research Group.

Wolman, B. B., & Stricker, G. (Eds.). (1990). *Depressive disorders: Facts, theories & treatment methods.* New York: Wiley.

Wolpe, J. (1958). *Psychotherapy by reciprocal inhibition.* Stanford, CA: Stanford Univ.

Wolpe, J. (1969). *The practice of behavior therapy.* Oxford: Pergamon.

Wolpe, J. (1973). *The practice of behavior therapy* (2nd ed.). Oxford: Pergamon.

Wolpe, J. (1976). Behavior therapy and its malcontents: I. Denial of its bases and psychodynamic fusionism. *J. Behav. Ther. Exp. Psychiat., 7*(1), 1–5.

Wolpe, J. (1976). Behavior therapy and its malcontents: II. Multimodal eclecticism, cognitive exclusivism and "exposure" empiricism. *J. Behav. Ther. Exp. Psychiat.*, 7(2), 109–116.

Wolpe, J. (1981). Reciprocal inhibition and therapeutic change. *J. Behav. Ther. Exp. Psychiat.*, 12(3), 185–188.

Wolpe, J. (1987). The promotion of scientific psychotherapy: A long voyage. In J. K. Zeig (Ed.), *The evolution of psychotherapy*. New York: Brunner/Mazel.

Wolpe, J., & Lang, P. (1964). A fear-survey schedule for use in behaviour therapy. *Behav. Res. Ther.*, 2, 27–34.

Wolpe, J. *The case of Mrs. Schmidt* [Transcript and record]. Nashville, TN: Counselor Recording and Tests.

Wong, B. (1979). The role of theory in learning disabilities research: An analysis of the problem. *J. Learn. Dis.*, 12, 19–29.

Woodruff, R. A., Goodwin, D. W., & Guze, S. B. (1973). *Psychiatric diagnosis*. New York: Oxford Univ.

Woodruff, R. A., Guze, S. B., & Clayton, P. J. (1971). The medical and psychiatric implications of antisocial personality (sociopathy). *Dis. Nerv. Sys.*, 32(10), 712–714.

Woods, J. H., Katz, J. L., & Winger, G. (1988). Use and abuse of benzodiazepines: Issues relevant to prescribing. *JAMA*, 260(23), 3476–3479.

Woods, S. W., & Charney, D. S. (1988). Applications of the pharmacologic challenge strategy in panic disorders research [Special Issue]. *J. Anx. Dis.*, 2(1), 31–49.

Woodside, M. R., & Legg, B. H. (1990). Patient advocacy: A mental health perspective. *J. Ment. Hlth. Couns.*, 12(1), 38–50.

Woody, G., Luborsky, L., McLellan, A. T., & O'Brien, C. P. (1988). Psychotherapy for substance abuse. 50th Annual Scientific Meeting of the Committee on Problems of Drug Dependence. *National Institute on Drug Abuse Research Monograph Series*, 90, 162–167.

Woody, G., McLellan, A. T., Luborsky, L., & O'Brien, C. P. (1986). Psychotherapy for substance abuse. *Psychiat. Clin. No., Amer.*, 9(3), 547–562.

Wooley, S., & Wooley, O. W. (1982). The Beverly Hills eating disorder: The mass marketing of anorexia nervosa. *Inter. J. Eat. Dis.*, 1, 57–69.

Wooley, S. C., & Wooley, O. W. (1985). Intensive outpatient and residential treatment for bulimia. In D. M. Garner & P. E. Garfinkel (Eds.), *Handbook of psychotherapy for anorexia nervosa and bulimia*. New York: Guilford.

Woolfolk, R. L., Carr-Kaffashan, L., McNulty, T. F., & Lehrer, P. M. (1976). Meditation training as a treatment for insomnia. *Behav. Ther.* 7(3), 359–365.

Wright, L. (1988). The Type A behavior pattern and coronary artery disease: Quest for the active ingredients and the elusive mechanism. *Amer. Psychol.*, 43(1), 2–14.

Wright, L. S. (1985). High school polydrug users and abusers. *Adolescence*, 20(80), 852–861.

Wright, L. S. (1985). Suicidal thoughts and their relationship to family stress and personal problems among high school seniors and college undergraduates. *Aolescence*, 20(79), 575–580.

Wulsin, L., Bachop, M., & Hoffman, D. (1988). Group therapy in manic-depressive illness. *Amer. J. Psychother.*, 42, 263–271.

Wurtman, J. J., & Wurtman, R. J. (1982). Studies on the appetite for carbohydrates in rats and humans. *J. Psychiat. Res.*, 17(2) 213–221.

Wurtman, J. J. et al. (1981). Carbohydrate craving in obese people: Suppression by treatments affecting serotenergic transmission. *Inter. J. Eat. Dis.*, 1(1), 2–15.

Wyler, A. R., Lockard, J. S., Ward, A., & Finch, C. A. (1976–1977). Conditioned EEG desynchronization and seizure occurrence in patients. *Biofeed. & Self-Control*, 503–512.

Wynne, L. C. (1981). Current concepts in family relationships of schizophrenics. *J. Ment. Dis.*, 169, 82–89.

Wynne, L. C., Ryckoff, I. M., Day, J. & Hirsch, S. I. (1958). Pseudomutuality in the family relations of schizophrenics. *Psychiatry, 21*, 205–220.

Yabe, K., Tsukahar, R., Mita, K., & Aoki, H. (1985). Developmental trends of jumping reaction time by means of EMG in mentally retarded children. *J. Ment. Def. Res.*, 29(2) 137–145.

Yager, J. (1982). Family in the pathogenesis of anorexia nervosa. *Psychosom. Med.*, 44, 43–60.

Yager, J. (1985). The outpatient treatment of bulimia. *Bull. Menninger Clin.*, 49(3), 203–226.

Yalom, I. D. (1985). *The theory and practice of group psychotherapy* (3rd ed.). New York: Basic.

Yap, P. M. (1951). Mental diseases peculiar to certain cultures: a survey of comparative psychiatry. *J. Ment. Sci.*, 97, 313–327.

Yaryura-Tobias, J. A. (1977). Obsessive-compulsive disorders: A serotonergic hypothesis. *J. Orthomol. Psychiat.*, 6(4), 317–326.

Yates, A. (1989). Current perspectives of the eating disorders: I. History, psychological and biological aspects. *J. Amer. Acad. Child Adol. Psychiat.*, 28(6), 813–828.

Yates, A., Leehey, K., & Shisslak, C. M. (1983). Running—An analogue of anorexia? *New Engl. J. Med.*, 308, 251–255.

Yesavage, J., Brink, T. L., Rose, T. L., Lum, O., Huang, V., Adey, M. & Leirer, V. (1983). Development and validation of a geriatric depression sceening scale: A preliminary report. *J. Psychiat. Res.*, 17, 37–49.

Yontef, G. M., & Simkin, J. F. (1989). Gestalt therapy. In R. J. Corsini & D. Wedding (Eds.), *Current psychotherapies*. Itasca, IL: Peacock.

Yost, E., Beutler, L., Corbishley, A. M., & Allender, J. (1986). *Group cognitive therapy: A treatment approach for depressed older adults*. New York: Pergamon.

Young, J. G., Kavanagh, M. E., Anderson, G. M., Shaywitz, B. A., & Cohen, D. J. (1982). Clinical neurochemistry of autism and associated disorders. *J. Autism Dev. Dis.*, 12, 147–165.

Young, T. J. (1987). PCP use among adolescents. *Child Study J.*, 17(1), 55–66.

Youngren, M. A., & Lewinsohn, P. M. (1980). *J. Abnorm. Psychol.*, 89(3), 333–341.

Zahn, T. P. (1977). Autonomic nervous system characteristics possibly related to a genetic predisposition to schizophrenia. *Schizo. Bull.*, 3(1), 49–60.

Zarit, S. H., Orr, N., & Zarit, J. M. (1985). *The hidden victims of Alzheimer's disease: Families under stress*. New York: New York Univ.

Zarr, M. L. (1984). Computer-mediated psychotherapy: Toward patient-selection guidelines. *Amer. J. Psychother.*, 38(1), 47–62.

Zax, M., & Cowen, E. L. (1969). Research on early detection and prevention of emotional dysfunction in young school children. In C. D. Speilberger (Ed.), *Current topics in clinical and community psychology* (Vol. 1). New York: Academic.

Zax, M., & Cowen, E. L. (1976). *Abnormal psychology: Changing conceptions*. New York: Holt, Rinehart & Winston.

Zeiss, A. M., Lewinsohn, P. M., & Munoz, R. F. (1979). Nonspecific improvement effects in depression using interpersonal skills training, pleasant activity schedules, and cognitive training. *J. Cons. Clin. Psychol.*, 47, 427–439.

Zeiss, A. M., Rosen, G. M., & Zeiss, R. A. (1977). Orgasm during intercourse: A treatment strategy for women. *J. Cons. Clin. Psychol.*, 45, 891–895.

Zeller, C. L. (1982). Treatment of ego deficits in anorexia nervosa. *Amer. J. Orthopsychiat.*, 52(2), 356–359.

Zellner, D. A., Harner, D. E., & Adler, R. L. (1989). Effects of eating abnormalities and gender on perceptions of desirable body shape. *J. Abnorm. Psychol.*, 98(1), 93–96.

Zetin, M. (1990). Obsessive-compulsive disorder. *Stress Med.*, 6(4), 311–321.

Ziegler, D. K., & Paul, N. (1954). Hysteria. *Diseases Nerv. Sys.*, 15, 30.

Ziegler, F. J., & Imboden, J. B. (1962). Contemporary conversion reactions: II. A conceptual model. *Arch. Gen. Psychiat.*, 6(4), 279–287.

Zigler, E., & Muenchow, S. (1979). Mainstreaming: The proof is in the implementation. *Amer. Psychol.*, 34, 993–996.

Zilbergeld, B. (1978). *Male sexuality*. Boston: Little, Brown.

Zilboorg, G., & Henry, G. W. (1941). *A history of medical psychology*. New York: Norton.

Zimbardo, P. G., Andersen, S. M., & Kabat, L. G. (1981, June). Induced hearing deficit generates experimental paranoia. *Science*.

Zimberg, S. (1978). Treatment of the elderly alcoholic in the community and in an institutional setting. *Addict. Dis.*, 3, 417–427.

Zimmer, B., & Gershon, S. (1991). The ideal late life anxiolytic. In C. Salzman & B. D. Lebowitz (Eds.), *Anxiety in the elderly*. New York: Springer.

Zisook, S. (1985). A clinical overview of monoamine oxidase inhibitors. *Psychosomatics*, 26, 240–246.

Zitrin, C. M. (1983). Differential treatment of phobias: Use of imipramine for panic attacks. *J. Behav. Ther. Exp. Psychiat.*, 14(1), 11–18.

Zitrin, C. M., Klein, D. F., & Woerner, M. G. (1978). Behavior therapy, supportive psychotherapy, imipramine, and phobias. *Arch. Gen. Psychiat.*, 35(3), 307–316.

## R-60     References

Zitrin, C. M., Klein, D. F., & Woerner, M. G. (1980). Treatment of agoraphobia with group exposure in vivo and imipramine. *Arch. Gen. Psychiat., 37*(1), 63–72.

Zitrin, C. M., Klein, D. F., Woerner, M. G., & Ross, D. C. (1983). Treatment of phobias: I. Comparison of imipramine hydrochloride and placebo. *Arch. Gen. Psychiat., 40*(2), 125–138.

Zitrin, C. M., Woerner, M. & Klein, D. F. (1981). Differentiation of panic anxiety from anticipatory anxiety. In D. F. Klein & J. Rabkin (Eds.), *Anxiety: New research and changing concepts.* New York: Raven.

Zohar, J., Insel, T. R., Zohar-Kadouch, R. C., Hill, J. L. et al. Serotonergic responsivity in obsessive-compulsive disorder: Effects of chronic clomipramine treatment. *Arch. Gen. Psychiat., 45*(2), 167–172.

Zoller, A. F. (1950). An experimental analogue of repression. I. Historical summary. *Psychol. Bull., 47,* 39–51.

Zonana, H. V., Wells, J. A., Getz, M. A., & Buchanan, J. A. (1990). The NGRI Registry: Initial analyses of data collected on Connecticut insanity acquitees: I. *Bull. Amer. Acad. Psychiat. Law, 18*(2), 115–128.

Zuckerman, D. M., Prusoff, B. A., Weissman, M., & Padian, N. (1980). Personality as a predictor of psychotherapy and pharmacotherapy outcome for depressed outpatients. *J. Cons. Clin. Psychol., 48*(6), 730–735.

Zuckerman, M. (1978). Sensation seeking and psychopathy. In R. D. Hare & D. Schalling (Eds.), *Psychopathic behavior: Approaches to research.* New York: Wiley.

# SOURCES OF ILLUSTRATIONS

**Chapter 1, opposite 1:** George Cruikshank, *The Blue Devils,* William H. Helfand Collection, Philadelphia Museum of Art; **4(t):** Korbal Collection/Superstock; **4(b):** Carol Beckwith; **5(b):** Catherine Allemand/Gamma-Liaison; **7:** Thomas Szasz; **8(t):** Travis Amos; **9:** John W. Verano; **10(t):** Girolamo Di Benvenuto, *St. Catherine Exorcising a Possessed Woman* (15th c.), Denver Art Museum, Kress Collection; **10(b):** National Library of Medicine; **11:** Zentralbibliothek, Zurich; **12:** Bettmann Archives; **14:** National Library of Medicine; **15(t):** NYPL Rare Book Room; **15(b):** Sir John Soanne's Museum, London; **16(l):** Wellcome Institute Library, London; **16(r):** Bettmann Archives; **17(t):** *Pinel Has the Irons Removed from the Insane,* Academie de Medicine, Paris, Giraudon Art Resource; **18(l):** Charles Wilson Peale, Independence National Historical Park Collection; **18(r):** The Library Company of Philadelphia; **19:** National Library of Medicine; **20:** Jerry Cooke/Photo Researchers; **21:** Wellcome Institute Library, London; **22(t):** Bettmann Archives; **22(b):** Mary Evans Picture Library/Sigmund Freud Copyrights; **24:** Dan McCoy/Rainbow; **Chapter 2, 28:** Henry Alken, *Calves' Heads and Brains,* Ars Medica, Philadelphia Museum of Art, Smith Kline Beckman Corporation Fund; **33(t):** Centre National de Recherches Iconographiques; **33(b):** From Zola-Morgan et al., 1986; **35:** Hank Morgan/Rainbow; **36:** Moira Lerner; **40:** Susan Lapides/Design Conceptions © 1984; **41:** Catherine Karnow/Woodfin Camp & Associates; **43:** Bettmann Archives; **44(tr):** Archives of the Institute for Psychoanalysis; **44(r):** Harvard University Office of News and Public Affairs; **44(c):** National Library of Medicine; **44(bl):** Karsh/Woodfin Camp & Associates; **45(c):** Association for the Advancement of Psychoanalysis of the Karen Horney Psychoanalytic Institute and Center; **45(bl):** Bettmann Archives; **46:** Austrian Press and Information Service; **49(t):** Ken Heyman/Black Star; **49(b):** The National Broadcasting Company, Inc.; **50:** Albert Bandura; **52:** Leif Skoogfors/Woodfin Camp & Associates; **54:** Joel Gordon; **55:** Bettmann Archives; **60:** Peter Turnley/Black Star; **61:** Jim Hubbard; **Chapter 3, 66:** Ed Pritchard/Tony Stone Worldwide; **71:** Edna Morlok; **72:** Edna Morlok; **75:** Rob Nelson/Picture Group; **79:** Walter Reed Army Institute of Research; **83:** AP/Wide World; **84:** Rhoda M. Karp; **Chapter 4, 90:** Franz Bühler, *Fabulous Animals,* Prinzhorn Collection, Heidelberg; **99:** Hans Huber Medical Publisher, Berne; **100(l):** Sing-Si Schwartz/B.D. Picture Service; **100(r):** Reprinted by permission of the publishers from Henry A. Murray, *Thematic Apperception Test,* Cambridge, Mass.: Harvard University Press, © 1943 by the President and Fellows of Harvard College, © 1971 by Henry A. Murray; **102:** Rick Friedman/Black Star; **110:** Dan McCoy/Rainbow; **112:** G E Medical Systems; **113(tr):** NIH; **113(br):** Dan McCoy/Rainbow; **114:** Travis Amos; **119:** National Library of Medicine; **120:** Fogg Art Museum, Harvard University; **126:** © 1984 by Doug Milman and Gerald Mayerhofer, *Are You Normal,* New York: Quill; **Chapter 5, 130:** Edvard Munch, *Evening (Melancholia),* 1896, Prints and Photographs, NYPL, Astor, Lenox, and Tilden Foundations; **132:** Jim Wilson/Woodfin Camp & Associates; **135:** Robert Maass/Photoreporters; **137:** © 1987 Matt Groening, Life in Hell Cartoon Co.; **138:** Ursula Edelmann, Frankfurt; **139:** Mary Evans Picture Library/Sigmund Freud Copyrights; **142:** Jimi Lott, Spokane (Wash.) *Review & Chronicle;* **145:** Lief Skoogfors/Woodfin Camp & Associates; **146:** János Kalmár; **147:** Joseph Wolpe; **150:** Joel Gordon; **152:** Richard Bergh, *Hypnotic Seance,* 1887, Nationmuseum, Stockholm; **157(t):** James D. Wilson; **157(b):** Bettmann Archives; **161:** Ralph Crane, *Life,* © 1968 Time Warner Inc.; **162:** Marc Geller; **163:** Ruth Westheimer; **166(l):** Salvador Minuchin; **166(r):** Avanta Network; **167:** Liz Mangelsdorf/*San Francisco Examiner;* **170:** Joel Gordon; **172:** Arnold Lazarus; **Chapter 6, 176:** George Scholz, *Nightly Noise,* 1919, The Fishmann Collection; **180(t):** MOMA Film Stills Archive; **180(b):** Kobal Collection/Superstock; **181:** Tom Sanders/Photri; **185:** George Tooker, *The Subway,* 1950, Whitney Museum of American Art, Juliana Force Purchase 50.23; **190:** MOMA Film Stills Archive; **192:** Mary Evans Picture Library/Sigmund Freud Copyrights; **195:** MOMA Film Stills Archive; **196:** Ferdinand Hamburger, Jr., Archives of The Johns Hopkins University; **201:** Julie Newdol, Computer Graphics Laboratory, UCSF, © Regents, University of California; **203:** Nick Didlick/Reuters — Bettmann Archives; **212:** Smithsonian Institution/National Air and Space Museum; **216(t):** Larry Burrows, *Life,* © Time Warner Inc.; **216(b):** Christopher Morris/Black Star; **219:** Michael Schumann/SABA; **Chapter 7, 222:** Pierre Boulat/Woodfin Camp & Associates; **227:** USAir; **230:** Michael Melford; **231:** Andrew Sacks/Black Star; **240:** Gary Larson, Universal Press Syndicate; **241:** Michael Maloney/*San Francisco Chronicle;* **242:** Dan McCoy/Rainbow; **243:** Julie Newdol, Computer Graphics Laboratory, UCSF, © Regents, University of California; **250:** National Archives; **251:** Alain Keler/Sygma; **253:** J. P. Laffont/Sygma; **Chapter 8, 256:** Vincent van Gogh, *At Eternity's Gate,* 1890, Rijksmuseum Kröller-Müller Otterlo; **258:** George P. A. Healy, 1887, The National Portrait Gallery, Smithsonian Institution; **260:** Edvard Munch, *Melancholia, Laura,* 1899, Oslo kommunes kunstsamlinger Munch-Museet; **263(t):** Manfred Kreiner/Black Star; **263(b):** Gary Guisinger; **267:** Homer Sykes/Woodfin Camp & Associates; **268:** AP/Wide World Photos; **270:** Harlow Primate Laboratory, University of Wisconsin; **281:** Julie Newdol, Computer Graphics Laboratory, UCSF, © Regents, University of California; **282:** The Dorothea Lange Collection, Oakland Museum; **287:** Frank O'Brian/*Boston Globe;* **289:** A. Knudsen/Sygma; **291:** Lilly Library; **Chapter 9, 296:** Paul Klee, *Voice from the Ether,* 1939, Victoria and Albert Museum/Art Resource; **298:** Chuck Fishman/Woodfin Camp & Associates; **306:** Phil Huber/Black Star; **310:** Will McIntyre/Photo Researchers; **317:** Travis Amos; **318:** Gerd Ludwig/Woodfin Camp & Associates; **320:** Roger Allen Grigg; **Chapter 10, 326:** Frida Kahlo, *The Suicide of Dorothy Hale,* 1938–1939. Phoenix Art Museum, gift of anonymous donor; **333:** Karsh/Woodfin Camp & Associates; **334:** Travis Amos; **337:** Joel Gordon; **338:** Steve Nickerson/Black Star; **343:** AP/Wide World Photos; **346:** John Kaplan/Media Alliance; **349:** H. Yamaguchi/Gamma-Liaison; **351:** A. Tannenbaum/Sygma; **357:** Edward Abbott; **Chapter 11, 362:**

# NAME INDEX

# SUBJECT INDEX

# DSM IV: A PREVIEW OF CHANGES AND OPTIONS

**DSM-IV**, the American Psychiatric Association's latest revision of the *Diagnostic and Statistical Manual of Mental Disorders,* is scheduled for publication in 1993. The task force preparing the new edition has published a **DSM-IV Options Book (1991)** in which it has summarized the changes that it is considering (*not* recommending) and has made this available to clinicians around the world. Final decisions about these changes will be based on the criticisms and suggestions of clinicians, as well as on the results of further research and analyses.

The following are some of the more prominent changes under consideration. They include a number of new categories that do not appear in DSM-III-R, as well as changes in names, deletions, and changes in organization and criteria. Although not all these proposed changes will ultimately be incorporated into DSM-IV, they are encapsulated here to give you an idea of some of the current lines of thinking in a field that is continually evolving to adapt to new information and meet new needs.

## NEW CATEGORIES UNDER CONSIDERATION

**Feeding Disorder of Infancy or Early Childhood** A feeding disturbance in the very young marked by a persistent failure to eat adequately and a failure to gain weight over the course of a month or more.

**Voice Disorder** An abnormality of vocal pitch, loudness, quality, tone, or resonance that seriously interferes with educational or occupational achievement, or with social communication.

**Postpsychotic Depression of Schizophrenia** A major depressive episode that occurs during the residual phase of **schizophrenia** or **schizophreniform disorder.** An alternative label might be **postschizophrenic depression.**

**Secondary Catatonic Disorder** A catatonic pattern that is related to a *medical condition* rather than to schizophrenia.

**Bipolar II Disorder** A bipolar pattern consisting of major *depressive* episodes and *hypomanic* episodes. An alternative label might be **major depressive disorder with hypomanic episodes.**

**Mixed Anxiety-Depressive Disorder** A disorder marked by a mixture of anxiety and depressive symptoms that collectively cause significant impairment or distress. The symptoms do not meet the full requirements of either an **anxiety** or **mood disorder.**

**Factitious Disorder by Proxy** A disorder in which an individual (usually a parent) artificially creates physical symptoms in another person (usually a child) for the purpose of indirectly assuming the sick role.

**Trance and Possession Disorder** A dissociative pattern in which a person experiences either a *trance* (a temporary alteration in state of consciousness) or *possession* (a conviction that one has been taken over by a spirit) that causes significant impairment or distress.

**Binge Eating Disorder** An eating disorder marked by repeated binges, but without the compensatory behaviors, or purges, that characterize **bulimia nervosa.**

**Late Luteal Phase Dysphoric Disorder (LLPDD)** A pattern in which, over the course of at least one year, a woman experiences disabling symptoms in the week before menses, including at least five symptoms such as marked affective lability, anger, tension, depressed mood, decreased interest in activities, lethargy and fatigue, difficulty concentrating, appetite changes, sleep changes, and subjective sense of being overwhelmed. The disorder causes marked impairment and is significantly more severe and less common than **premenstrual syndrome (PMS).**

**Personality Change Disorder** A persistent personality disturbance that represents a *change* from an individual's previous personality characteristics and includes the development of personality features not previously seen. The personality change is enduring, inflexible, and maladaptive, and causes significant impairment or distress. It may result from a catastrophic experience, another mental disorder, or a medical condition.

## CATEGORY NAME CHANGES UNDER CONSIDERATION

**Learning Disorders**
may replace **Academic skills disorders**

**Phonological Disorder**
may replace **Articulation disorder**

**Substance-Related Disorders**
may replace **Psychoactive substance use disorder**

**Acute Psychotic Disorder**
may replace **Brief reactive psychosis**

**Major Depressive Disorder**
may replace **Major depression**

**Specific Phobia**
may replace **Simple phobia**

**Pain Disorder**
may replace **Somatoform pain disorder**

**Dissociative Amnesia**
may replace **Psychogenic amnesia**

**Dissociative Fugue**
may replace **Psychogenic fugue**

**Nightmare Disorder**
may replace **Dream anxiety disorder**

## CATEGORY DELETIONS UNDER CONSIDERATION

**Avoidant Disorder of Childhood**
may become a particular kind of **social phobia**

**Overanxious Disorder of Childhood**
may become a particular kind of **generalized anxiety disorder**

**Cluttering**
may become a particular kind of **expressive and receptive language disorder**

## ORGANIZATIONAL OR CRITERION CHANGES UNDER CONSIDERATION

**Disorders Usually First Diagnosed During Infancy, Childhood, or Adolescence**

• Three types of **attention-deficit hyperactivity disorder** may be distinguished—*inattentive* vs. *hyperactive* vs. *impulsive*—and a related category, **attention deficit disorder without hyperactivity,** may be added.